HANDBOOK OF DESIGN, MANUFACTURING AND AUTOMATION

HANDBOOK OF DESIGN, MANUFACTURING AND AUTOMATION

Edited by
RICHARD C. DORF
University of California Davis
Davis, California

and

ANDREW KUSIAK
The University of Iowa
Iowa City, Iowa

A Wiley-Interscience Publication
JOHN WILEY & SONS, INC.
New York • Chichester • Brisbane • Toronto • Singapore

Library of Congress Cataloging in Publication Data:

Handbook of design, manufacturing and automation / editors, Richard C.
    Dorf and Andrew Kusiak.
        p.   cm.
    Includes index.
    ISBN 0-471-55218-6
    1. Manufacturing processes—Automation.   I. Dorf. Richard C.
II. Kusiak, Andrew.
TS183.H65   1994
670.42'7—dc20   94-7901

Printed in the United States of America

10 9 8 7 6 5 4 3 2 1

This book has been dedicated to the founders of modern engineering design and manufacturing:

Professor Moshe M. Barash, Purdue University,
Dr. Eugene M. Merchant, Institute of Advanced Manufacturing Sciences,
Cincinnati, Ohio
Professor S.-M. (Sam) Wu (deceased), University of Michigan

EDITORIAL BOARD

CONTRIBUTORS

Sadashiv Adiga
Department of Industrial Engineering
  and Operations Research
University of California
Berkeley, California

M. (Appa) Anjanappa
Department of Mechanical
  Engineering
University of Maryland
Baltimore, Maryland

Ronald Askin
Systems and Industrial Engineering
University of Arizona
Tucson, Arizona

Adedji B. Badiru
School of Industrial Engineering
University of Oklahoma
Norman, Oklahoma

Atul Bajpai
Advanced AI & Engineering Systems
General Motors Technical Center
Warren, Michigan

Stephen Becker
Department of Process Automation
  Techniques
Technical University of
  Hamburg-Harburg
Hamburg, Germany

David Belson
Department of Industrial and System
  Engineering
University of California
Los Angeles, California

Bopaya Bidana
Department of Industrial Engineering
University of Pittsburgh
Pittsburgh, Pennsylvania

Richard Billo
Department of Industrial Engineering
University of Pittsburgh
Pittsburgh, Pennsylvania

Lisa J. Burnell
Industrial Engineering and Computer
  Science Departments
University of Texas
Arlington, Texas

Amiya Chakravarty
Seinsheimer Professor of Operations
  Management
Tulane University
New Orleans, Louisiana

Jen-Ming Chen
Department of Information
  Management
The National Cheng University
Chung-Li, Taiwan

Karthikeyan Chithayil
The Pennsylvania State University
University Park, Pennsylvania

Deborah F. Cook
Management Science Department
Virginia Tech
Blacksburg, Virginia

Paul H. Cohen
The Pennsylvania State University
University Park, Pennsylvania

Sanchoy K. Das
Division of Industrial and
  Management Engineering
New Jersey Institute of Technology
Newark, New Jersey

Warren R. DeVries
Department of Mechanical
  Engineering
Rensselaer Polytechnic Institute
Troy, New York

Kevin J. Dooley
Department of Mechanical
  Engineering
University of Minnesota
Minneapolis, Minnesota

D. Dubois
LAAS
Toulouse, France

Yoram Eden
School of Business Administration
Tel Aviv University
Tel Aviv, Israel

D. R. Falkenburg
Department of Industrial and
  Manufacturing Engineering
Wayne State University
Detroit, Michigan

Craig Friedrich
Institute for Manufacturing
Louisiana Tech University
Ruston, Louisiana

L. F. Gelders
Katholieke Universiteit Leuven
Leuven-Heverlee, Belgium

Donald Gerwin
School of Business, Faculty of Social
  Sciences
Carleton University
Ottawa, Ontario, Canada

Mikell P. Groover
Department of Industrial Engineering
Lehigh University
Bethlehem, Pennsylvania

Yehonathan Hazony
College of Engineering
Boston University
Boston, Massachusetts

G. G. Hegde
Joseph M. Katz Graduate School of
  Business
University of Pittsburgh
Pittsburgh, Pennsylvania

Katsundo Hitomi
Kyoto University
Kyoto, Japan

Cheng Hsu
Department of Decision Sciences and
  Engineering Systems
Rensselaer Polytechnic Institute
Troy, New York

J. Jara-Almonte
Institute for Micromanufacturing
Louisiana Tech University
Ruston, Louisiana

Mark Klein
Boeing Computer Services
Bellevue, Washington

Sounder R. T. Kumara
The Pennsylvania State University
University Park, Pennsylvania

Thomas R. Kurfess
Department of Mechanical
  Engineering
Carnegie Mellon University
Pittsburgh, Pennsylvania

Andrew Kusiak
Industrial Engineering, College of
  Engineering
University of Iowa
Iowa City, Iowa

John E. Lenz
CMS Research
Oshkosh, Wisconsin

Robert Lumia
Robot Systems Division
National Institute of Standards and
  Technology
Gaithersburg, Maryland

Charles J. Malmborg
Department of Decision Sciences and
  Engineering
Rensselaer Polytechnic Institute
Troy, New York

Ronald J. Monassa
General Motors Advanced
  Engineering
Warren, Michigan

Virginia Miller
Boeing Aerospace and Defense
Irving, Texas

Bijayananda Naik
School of Business
University of South Dakota
Vermillion, South Dakota

Vivek Narayanan
Department of Industrial Engineering
University of Pittsburgh
Pittsburgh, Pennsylvania

Shimon Y. Nof
School of Industrial Engineering
Purdue University
West Lafayette, Indiana

Ralf Parr
Department of Process Automation
  Techniques
Technical University of
  Hamburg-Harburg
Hamburg, Germany

J. C. Pascal
LAAS
Toulouse, France

L. Pintelon
Katholieke Universiteit Leuven
Leuven-Heverlee, Belgium

John W. Priest
Industrial Engineering and Computer
  Science Departments
University of Texas
Arlington, Texas

James M. Pruett
Department of Quantitative Business
  Analysis
Louisiana State University
Baton Rouge, Louisiana

Venkat N. Rajan
School of Industrial Engineering
Purdue University
West Lafayette, Indiana

K. P. Rajurkar
Nontraditional Manufacturing
  Research Center
University of Nebraska
Lincoln, Nebraska

Shivakumar Raman
School of Industrial Engineering
University of Oklahoma
Norman, Oklahoma

Stephen Raper
Department of Engineering
  Management
University of Missouri
Rolla, Missouri

Boaz Ronen
School of Business Administration
Tel Aviv University
Tel Aviv, Israel

Jose M. Sanchez
Centro de Inteligencia Artificial
Instituto Technologico y de Estudios
  Superiores de Monterey
Monterey, Mexico

Subhash Sarin
Department of Industrial and Systems
  Engineering
Virginia Polytechnic Institute and
  State University
Blacksburg, Virginia

Hassan M. Selim
Department of Management
  Information Systems
University of Arizona
Tucson, Arizona

Yung C. Shin
Mechanical Engineering
Purdue University
West Lafayette, Indiana

Nanua Singh
Department of Industrial and
  Manufacturing Engineering
Wayne State University
Detroit, Michigan

Manbir Sodhi
Department of Industrial and
  Manufacturing Engineering
University of Rhode Island
Kingston, Rhode Island

Stephen L. Starling
Department of Computer Science and
  Business
University of Pittsburgh
Pittsburgh, Pennsylvania

Ming-Reng Sung
Deceased

Kwei Tang
Department of Quantitative Business
   Analysis
College of Business Administration
Louisiana State University
Baton Rouge, Louisiana

Asoo J. Vakharia
Department of Management
   Information Systems
University of Arizona
Tucson, Arizona

Robert Valette
LAAS
Toulouse, France

Dharmaraj Veeramani
Department of Industrial Engineering
University of Wisconsin
Madison, Wisconsin

Jose A. Ventura
Department of Industrial and
   Management Systems Engineering
Penn State University
University Park, Pennsylvania

Francois Vernadat
INRIA
Metz, France

H.P. Ben Wang
Department of Industrial Engineering
FAMU/FSU College of Engineering
Tallahassee, Florida

Y. Wang
Department of Mechanical
   Engineering
University of Maryland
Baltimore, Maryland

R. O. Warrington
Institute for Micromanufacturing
Louisiana Tech University
Ruston, Louisiana

Tohru Watanabe
Department of Computer Science and
   Systems Engineering
Ritsumeikan University
Kyoto, Japan

A. Dale Whittaker
Agricultural Engineering Department
Texas A&M University
College Station, Texas

Sencer Yeralan
Industrial and Systems Engineering
University of Florida
Gainesville, Florida

R. I. M. Young
Department of Manufacturing
   Engineering
Loughborough University of
   Technology
Loughborough Leicestershire
U.K.

Chun Zhang
Department of Industrial Engineering
FAMU/FSU College of Engineering
Tallahassee, Florida

Hongchao Zhang
Department of Industrial Engineering
University of Texas
Lubbock, Texas

Albert Y. Zomaya
Department of Electrical and
   Electronic Engineering
University of Western Australia
Australia

PREFACE

The *Handbook of Design, Manufacturing and Automation* is concerned with the organization and transformation of resources into useful products and goods. Manufacturing of quality goods is a primary concern of all competitive firms operating today in the global economy. The goal of this *Handbook* is to provide up-to-date, cogent answers to the myriad problems arising in design, operations, and management of products and manufacturing systems.

For this *Handbook*, we have secured contributions from leading practitioners and researchers. This balance of articles explains the issues and clearly exposes the reader to potential approaches as well as offers new insights to the seasoned engineer.

The *Handbook* consists of 49 articles prepared by 76 authors. The topics covered range from organizing concurrent engineering teams, design, fixtures, packaging, control, planning, costs, robotics, and inspection to simulation, scheduling, information systems, and automation, among others.

The *Handbook* was devised and planned so that the reader, using the table of contents and the index, will be able to locate references to a topic of concern and easily access information referring to a problem at hand.

We are particularly pleased to thank Prof. George A. Bekey, Prof. Umberto Cugini, Prof. Allan Desrochers, Dr. Barry B. Flachsbart, Dr. Philip H. Francis, Prof. William A. Gruver, Prof. Thom J. Hodgson, John Lenz, Larry G. McMullen, Dr. Kiyoshi Niwa, Dr. H. Van Dyke Parunak, Herman M. Reininga, Prof. Urlich Rembold, Prof. Nam Suh, Prof. Tohru Watanabe, Prof. Ming-Tzong Wang, Prof. J. J. Warnecke, and Prof. H. P. Wiendahl who served on the Editorial Board. Their advice was valuable and their support appreciated.

We also wish to express our thanks to Frank Cerra and Michalina Bickford of John Wiley & Sons, Inc. who served as Editor and Production Manager, respectively.

Davis, California   RICHARD C. DORF
Iowa City, Iowa   ANDREW KUSIAK
August 1994

CONTENTS

HANDBOOK OF DESIGN, MANUFACTURING AND AUTOMATION

SECTION I
AUTOMATION

CHAPTER 1
Automation

MIKELL P. GROOVER
Lehigh University

Automation is a technology in which a process or procedure is accomplished by means of programmed instructions usually combined with automatic feedback control to ensure the proper execution of the instructions. Although automation can be used in a wide variety of application areas, the term is most closely associated with manufacturing. In fact, the origination of the term is attributed to Del Harder, an engineering manager at Ford Motor Co. around 1946, who coined it to describe the use of automatic devices and controls in mechanized production lines. Table 1.1 presents a list of typical applications of automation in manufacturing and nonmanufacturing areas. Attention in this chapter will be directed toward automation technology as it is applied to manufacturing operations.

1.1 COMPONENTS OF AN AUTOMATED SYSTEM

Based on the above definition of automation, three basic components of an automated system can be identified: (*1*) power to accomplish the process, (*2*) machine programming, and (*3*) feedback controls. The arrangement of these building blocks of automation is shown schematically in Figure 1.1. All systems that qualify as being automated must include these components, with the exception of certain systems that operate by means of open-loop control rather than feedback (closed-loop) control.

Power to Accomplish the Process

An automated system performs some action to accomplish its function, and the action requires power. Most power sources used in automated manufacturing systems are based on electrical energy. Use of electric power has the following benefits in the operation of an automated system: (*1*) it can be readily converted to other forms of power—mechanical, hydraulic, pneumatic; (*2*) low level electric power can be used for signal transmission, information processing, and data storage; and (*3*) electrical energy can be conveniently stored in long-life batteries.

The actions performed by an automated system can be divided into two categories: processing and movement or positioning. These categories are especially appropriate in a manufacturing system, in which processing refers to the operation performed on the work part (e.g., machining, forming, molding); and movement or positioning refers to the transport and placement of the part before, during, and after the manufacturing process. These actions require power. Table 1.2 indicates the various power and energy requirements in selected manufacturing processes.

Machine Programming

The actions performed by an automated system are determined by a program of instructions. The program operates the system without human intervention, although the automated process or procedure may involve human interaction (e.g., an automated teller machine). The instructions contained in the program specify the details of each action that must be accomplished, the

3

TABLE 1.1. Applications of Automation

Manufacturing Applications

Automated guided vehicles, conveyors, and other automated material handling systems
Automated storage–retrieval systems
Automatic assembly machines
Computer numerical control
Industrial robots
Process control using computers or programmable logic controllers
Transfer lines

Nonmanufacturing Applications (selected examples)

Air transportation: automatic pilots, airline reservation systems
Banking: automatic teller machines, check sorting machines
Communications: automatic telephone switching systems
Consumer products: automobile engine control, controls for household appliances
Military: guided missles, automatic gun aiming systems
Postal service: automatic mail sorting machines
Rail transportation: urban mass transit systems
Retail: bar code (Universal Product Code) and inventory record systems

---

sequence in which the actions must be performed, and variations in the sequence that may be required depending on circumstances.

In the simplest automated systems, the machine actions comprise a well-defined work cycle that is repeated continuously with little or no deviation from cycle to cycle. Many mass production operations fall into this category; examples include automatic screw machine cycles, stamping press operations, plastic molding, and die casting. These processes date back many decades, and the equipment has traditionally been controlled by hardware components such as cams, electromechanical relays, and limit switches. In addition to controlling the equipment, these components and their arrangement served as the program of instructions that regulated the sequence of actions in the work cycle.

Although these devices are often quite adequate for the modest control action requirements of these programs, modern controllers are based on microcomputers. The program of instructions for computer-controlled production equipment has included a variety of media over the years, such as punched paper tape (still used for numerically controlled machine tools), magnetic tape, diskettes, computer memory, and other modern storage technologies.

Computer control provides the opportunity for additional functions to be incorporated in the operation, beyond simply regulating the machine cycle. Some of the additional functions include (*1*) improving and upgrading the control software, including the addition of control

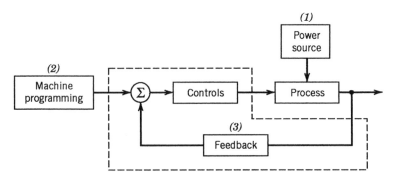

Figure 1.1. Components of an automated system. (*1*) Power to accomplish the process, (*2*) machine programming, and (*3*) feedback controls.

TABLE 1.2. Examples of Power and Energy Requirements in Selected Manufacturing Processes

Casting: Heat energy is used to heat and melt the metal preparatory to pouring into a mold cavity where solidification and cooling occur.

Heat Treating: Energy is applied to heat the work part to effect desirable microstructural changes in the metal. Heat treatments are also performed on ceramics.

Machining: Power to accomplish the relative speed and feed motions between the cutting tool and the work part, and to overcome the shear strength of the work material in forming the chip.

Metal Forming: These operations include forging, extrusion, rolling, and wire drawing, in which various powered tools are used to overcome the flow strength (yield strength) of the metal to effect shape change.

Molding: Heat and mechanical energy is applied to polymers (thermoplastic, thermosetting plastics, and rubbers) to transform them into a highly plastic consistency for molding. The applied heat also cures the thermosets and rubbers.

Sheet Metalworking: Operations include cutting, bending and forming, and drawing of sheet metal stock. In cutting, power is used to exceed the shear strength of the metal. In bending, forming, and drawing, shape change is effected by applying power to exceed the flow strength of the metal.

Sintering of Ceramics and Powdered Metals: Heat energy is applied (below the melting point) to cause local fusion of the ceramic or metallic particles into a solid form.

functions not foreseen during initial equipment design; (2) safety monitoring; (3) monitoring of process data such as equipment performance and product quality; (4) diagnostic routines for maintenance and to expedite repairs when equipment breakdowns occur; and (5) a convenient human–machine interface. Modern computer-controlled programmable machines also are capable of higher level functions, such as decision making and process optimization.

The decision-making capability of the system is included in the program in the form of instructions that execute different actions depending on conditions and circumstances. Under one set of conditions, the system responds one way, but under a different set of conditions, it responds in another way. Many of the decisions are routine. A typical case is a manufacturing system designed to process more than one part or product style, and the system must be programmed to execute the appropriate processing steps for each style. Robotic spot welding lines in automobile final assembly plants are often designed with this capability. The robots are programmed to perform alternative welding cycles for two or three different body styles, e.g., two- and four-door sedans and station wagons. As a car body enters a given workstation, sensors detect which body style it has, and the robots perform the proper series of spot welds for that style.

Decision making also allows an automated system to cope with unanticipated events in the work cycle, such as a broken tool or a part not positioned correctly in a fixture or other malfunction in the process. Many decision-making situations rely on the ability of the system to use sensors to monitor the process and sense the environment. The sensors indicate the presence of the unexpected event, and the program commands the system to deal with the event in an appropriate manner. This type of decision-making capability is often called error detection and recovery.

Process optimization is another aspect of programming in the operation and control of a production process. Optimization is applicable in situations where there is (1) a well-defined economic performance criterion, such as product cost, production rate, or process yield, and (2) the relationships between the process variables and the performance criterion are known. In these cases, the control program is designed to make adjustments in the process variables that tend to drive the process toward an optimal state.

Feedback Controls

Feedback controls are widely used in automated systems to ensure that the programmed commands have been properly executed. A feedback control system consists of five basic components (Figure 1.2): (1) input signal, (2) process, (3) output, (4) feedback sensing elements, and (5) controller and actuators. The input signal represents the desired value of the process output.

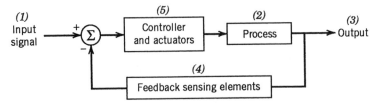

Figure 1.2. Diagram of a feedback control system.

The output is some variable that is being measured and compared with the input. The output value is a function of the process. Sensing elements close the loop between output and input. Finally, the controller and actuators compare the output with the desired input and make adjustments in the process to reduce the difference between them.

An important example of feedback control in manufacturing is a positioning system. A typical purpose of the positioning system in production operations is to move a work part to a desired location relative to a tool or work head. Examples of positioning systems include numerical control machine tools, spot welding robots, electronic component insertion machines, and coordinate measuring machines. In operation, a programmed instruction directs the positioning system to move the worktable to a certain location defined by coordinate values in an axis system (e.g., x and y values in a Cartesian coordinate system). For an x–y positioning table, two feedback control systems are required, one for each axis. A common actuator for each axis in such a system consists of a leadscrew driven by an electric motor; rotation of the leadscrew is converted into translation of the table (Figure 1.3). The controller receives the coordinate value (e.g., x-value) as its input from the program and transmits a signal to the motor to drive the leadscrew. As the table moves closer to the desired location, the difference between actual x-position and input x-value is reduced. The actual position is sensed by a feedback sensor, commonly an optical encoder. In the ideal, the controller drives the motor until the actual table position is equal to the desired input position.

As the example of the positioning system indicates, the process input is determined by the control program in an automated system. The program consists of a sequence of steps, each step in turn being sent as an input to the controller and actuator of the system. As each step is executed, the next step is then transmitted. In this step-by-step manner, the program is executed.

Open-loop versus Closed-loop Systems

Some automated systems operate without feedback control, or some of the processing steps accomplished by the system operate without feedback control. This type of operation is called an open-loop system (Figure 1.4) as distinguished from a closed-loop system, which includes feedback. Open-loop systems are appropriate in applications with the following characteristics: (1) the actions accomplished by the system are simple, such as binary actions like turning on a motor or energizing a solenoid; (2) the reliability of the actuating function is high; (3) the reaction forces opposing the actuation are minimal; and (4) there are no external sources of variability acting on the system that affect the control function. If these characteristics are not present, then a control system that includes feedback sensing of the output variable is probably necessary.

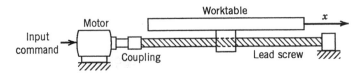

Figure 1.3. Operation of a positioning system. The diagram shows the configuration of one axis of the system.

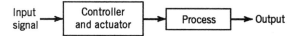

Figure 1.4. Open-loop system in which the programmed commands are executed without feedback sensing.

To illustrate the open-loop case, consider a positioning system that operates without feedback control. An open-loop positioning system might consist of a stepper motor whose output shaft is attached to a leadscrew that moves a worktable. The diagram for this system would be similar to the previous closed-loop positioning mechanism, except that no feedback sensor is present. The controller receives a program instruction that defines the desired position. A sequence of pulses is transmitted to the stepper motor, which drives the leadscrew to rotate a precisely metered fraction of a turn for each pulse received. Thus each pulse moves the worktable a known linear distance. The table is moved to the desired final position by computing the exact number of pulses required and then sending those pulses to the motor. Operating in the proper application, whose characteristics match the preceding list, an open-loop positioning system is highly reliable.

1.2 HISTORICAL DEVELOPMENT OF AUTOMATION

The history of automation has been a long evolutionary process, consisting of the development and refinement of the basic building blocks and highlighted by periodic discoveries and inventions. The history can be divided into two periods: before 1945 and after 1945 (or the end of World War II).

Early Development

The earlier period is represented by the slow development of basic devices such as the wheel, pulley, lever, screw, and gear and their application in assemblies such as waterwheels, windmills, and steam engines. These assemblies provided power sources to operate machinery. The Watt steam engine introduced an important feature in the machine design: the flying-ball governor. The governor consisted of a ball on the end of a hinged lever that was attached to a rotating shaft and that controlled a throttle valve. As the rotating speed of the shaft increased, centrifugal force caused the ball to move outward, forcing the lever to reduce the valve opening and slowing the motor speed. The flying-ball governor stands as an important early example of feedback control—one of the building blocks of automation.

Another development of significant note in the history of automation was the Jacquard loom, invented around 1800. This was a machine for weaving cloth from yarn whose operation was determined by metal plates containing holes. The hole pattern in a given plate controlled the shuttle motions, which in turn controlled the weaving pattern of the cloth produced. Different hole patterns produced different cloth patterns. Thus the Jacquard loom was the forerunner of the programmable machine.

By the early 1800s, the basic building blocks of automation (power source, feedback control, and programmable machines) had been developed, although the components were rudimentary and they had not been adequately assembled into working systems. It took many refinements and inventions to set the stage for the modern automation age. The development of electric power, a mathematical theory of servomechanisms, and mechanized machines for mass production (e.g., transfer lines) whose programs were fixed by their hardware configuration all had occurred by the end of World War II.

Modern Development

The modern era since 1945 has witnessed the development of a number of technologies that have contributed significantly to automation. These technologies include the digital computer, integrated circuits leading to microprocessors and other small electronic components, mass

TABLE 1.3.   Historical Developments and Milestones in Automation

Date	Development
Ancient times	Wheel, lever, pulley, cutting implements; assemblies such as water-wheels, carts
Middle ages	Windmill, mechanical clock
1765	Watt's steam engine
1801	Jacquard's loom
1876	First player piano—a programmable machine
1913	Moving assembly line for the Ford Model T
1924	Mechanized transfer line for machining automobile engine components in England
1946	Harder coins the term *automation*
1946	First electronic digital computer (ENIAC)
1952	Numerical control (NC) machine tool developed at MIT; credit for the NC concept is given to J. Parsons and F. Stulen
1954	First industrial robot designed in the United States; patent issued in 1961 for "programmed article transfer," developed by G. Devol
1960	Solid-state integrated circuit developed by J. Kilby of Texas Instruments, Inc.
1961	First Unimate robot based on Devol's design installed to unload parts in a die-casting operation
1961	Development automatically programmed tooling (APT), a programming language for NC machine tools
1967	First flexible manufacturing system (FMS) installed at Ingersoll-Rand plant in the United States.
1971	Microprocessor developed at Texas Instruments, Inc.
1973	Computer language for programming industrial robots developed at Stanford Research Institute
1979	The VAL language for robot programming, based on the 1973 development study introduced commercially by Unimation, Inc.
1980	Personal computer using microprocessor introduced by Apple Computer
1990	Memory chips with megabyte capacity developed

data storage techniques, new sensor technologies such as lasers, and new software for machine programming. Table 1.3 dates many of the important milestones in the development of early and modern automation technology.

1.3   PRODUCTION AUTOMATION

Automation is a widely used term in manufacturing. In this context, automation can be defined as a technology concerned with the application of mechanical, electronic, and computer-based systems to operate and control production. Examples of this technology include

- Automatic machine tools to process parts.
- Automated transfer lines and similar sequential production systems.
- Automatic assembly machines.
- Industrial robots.
- Automatic material handling and storage systems.
- Automated inspection systems for quality control.
- Feedback control and computer process control.
- Computer systems that automate procedures for planning, data collection, and decision making to support manufacturing activities.

Automated production systems can be classified into two basic categories: fixed automation and programmable automation.

Fixed Automation

Fixed automation is what Harder was referring to when he coined the word *automation*. Fixed automation refers to production systems in which the sequence of processing or assembly operations is fixed by the equipment configuration and cannot be readily changed without altering the equipment. Although each operation in the sequence is usually simple, the integration and coordination of many simple operations into a single system makes fixed automation complex. Typical features of fixed automation include (*1*) high initial investment for custom-engineered equipment, (*2*) high production rates, (*3*) application to products in which high quantities are to be produced, and (*4*) relative inflexibility in accommodating product changes.

Fixed automation is economically justifiable for products with high demand rates. The high initial investment in the equipment can be divided over a large number of units, perhaps millions, thus making the unit cost low compared with alternative methods of production. Examples of fixed automation include transfer lines for machining, dial indexing machines, and automated assembly machines. Much of the technology in fixed automation was developed in the automobile industry; the transfer line (dating to about 1920) is an example.

Programmable Automation

For programmable automation, the equipment is designed in such a way that the sequence of production operations is controlled by a program, i.e., a set of coded instructions that can be read and interpreted by the system. Thus the operation sequence can be readily changed to permit different product configurations to be produced on the same equipment. Some of the features that characterize programmable automation include (*1*) high investment in general-purpose programmable equipment, (*2*) lower production rates than fixed automation, (*3*) flexibility to deal with changes in product configuration, and (*4*) suited to low and/or medium production of similar products or parts (e.g., part families). Examples of programmable automation include numerically controlled machine tools, industrial robots, and programmable logic controllers.

Programmable production systems are often used to produce parts or products in batches. They are especially appropriate when repeat orders for batches of the same product are expected. To produce each batch of a new product, the system must be programmed with the set of machine instructions that correspond to that product. The physical setup of the equipment must also be changed: special fixtures must be attached to the machine, and the appropriate tools must be loaded. This changeover procedure can be time-consuming. As a result, the usual production cycle for a given batch includes (*1*) a period during which the setup and reprogramming is accomplished and (*2*) a period in which the batch is processed. The setup–reprogramming period constitutes nonproductive time of the automated system.

The economics of programmable automation require that as the setup–reprogramming time increases, the production batch size must be made larger so as to spread the cost of lost production time over a larger number of units. Conversely, if setup and reprogramming time can be reduced to zero, the batch size can be reduced to one. This is the theoretical basis for flexible automation, an extension of programmable automation. A flexible automated system is one that is capable of producing a variety of products (or parts) with minimal lost time for changeovers from one product to the next. The time to reprogram the system and alter the physical setup is minimal and results in virtually no lost production time. Consequently, the system is capable of producing various combinations and schedules of products in a continuous flow, rather than batch production with interruptions between batches. The features of flexible automation are (*1*) high investment for a custom-engineered system, (*2*) continuous production of mixtures of products, (*3*) ability to change product mix to accommodate changes in demand rates for the different products made, (*4*) medium production rates, and (*5*) flexibility to deal with product design variations.

Flexible automated production systems operate in practice by one or more of the following approaches: (*1*) using part family concepts, by which the parts made on the system are limited in variety; (*2*) reprogramming the system in advance and/or off-line, so that reprogramming does not interrupt production; (*3*) downloading existing programs to the system to produce previously made parts for which programs are already prepared; (*4*) using quick-change fixtures so that physical setup time is minimized; (*5*) using a family of fixtures that have been designed for a limited number of part styles; and (*6*) equipping the system with a large number of quick-change tools that include the variety of processing operations needed to produce the part family. For these approaches to be successful, the variation in the part styles produced on a flexible automated production system is usually more limited than a batch-type programmable automation system. Examples of flexible automation are the flexible manufacturing systems for performing machining operations that date back to the late 1960s.

1.4   REASONS FOR AUTOMATING

Companies undertake projects in production automation for various reasons, including the following:

1. *Increase in Productivity.* Automation of an operation usually increases production rate and output per labor hour.

2. *Reduction of Labor Cost.* As labor cost increases, economics tends to force a substitution of automated equipment for labor. Because production rate is usually increased and labor cost is reduced by use of automated equipment, the unit cost of product is reduced.

3. *Labor Shortages.* In many industrialized nations, there is a labor shortage (e.g., Japan and Germany), forcing these countries to increase production by seeking alternatives to the use of labor. Automation is such an alternative.

4. *Trend of Labor Toward the Service Sector.* In the United States, labor shortages have not been a problem as in other industrialized countries. However, in the United States, there is a general trend toward employment in the service sector and lower employment levels in manufacturing. The growth of government employment as well as insurance, personal services, entertainment, legal, sales, etc. has resulted in a largely service economy in the United States. One of the reasons is that people tend to view factory work as demeaning and undesirable. Implementation of automation in manufacturing has contributed to this trend.

5. *Safety.* Automation of a production operation tends to remove the human from direct participation in the operation. This improves safety in potentially dangerous production situations. The Occupational Safety and Health Agency (OSHA) has motivated the automation of unsafe jobs.

6. *High Cost of Materials.* Higher levels of efficiency in processing of raw materials requires tighter controls in manufacturing, which can often be achieved through automation.

7. *Improved Quality.* Automated production usually achieves greater consistency in processing. Consistency is one measure of product quality. Automobile companies have achieved significant gains in product quality through the automation of certain critical assembly processes such as robotic spot welding of car bodies.

8. *Reduction of Manufacturing Lead Time.* Manufacturing lead time is the time between customer order and delivery of the finished product. Automation usually means less time to produce the product, leading to greater customer satisfaction and a competitive advantage in manufacturing.

9. *Reduction of Work-in-Process.* Work-in-process is product in the factory either being processed or between processing operations. It is inventory that represents an investment cost to the manufacturer that cannot be recovered until the product is shipped. Automation tends to reduce work-in-process by reducing the time the product spends in the factory. Reducing manufacturing lead time reduces work-in-process.

10. *Increase in Flexibility.* The increase of flexibility is of growing concern to manufacturers: flexibility to change quickly over from one product to another and flexibility to accommodate new products. With programmable automation, these flexibilities can be achieved.

11. *High Cost of Not Automating.* There is a competitive advantage in automating a manufacturing plant. The advantage often shows up in sometimes intangible ways, such as improved quality, higher sales, better labor relations, and better company image. Companies that do not automate often find themselves at a competitive disadvantage with their customers, their employees, and the general public.

TABLE 1.4. Automation Strategies

Strategy	Result of Implementation
Specialization of operations	Reduced operation cycle time; increased production rate, capacity
Combined operations	Reduced number of operations, handling, nonoperation time; increased production rate, capacity
Simultaneous operations	Reduced operation cycle time, number of operations, handling, nonoperation time; increased production rate, capacity
Integration of operations	Reduced number of operations, handling, nonoperation time; increased production rate, capacity
Increased flexibility	Reduced setup time, manufacturing lead time, work-in-process; increased use
Automated material handling and storage	Reduced nonoperation time, manufacturing lead time, work-in-process
Automated inspection	Reduced scrap rate
Process control and optimization	Reduced operation time, scrap rate; increased production rate, capacity
Plant operations control	Reduced nonoperation time manufacturing lead time; increased use, capacity
Computer integrated manufacturing (CIM)	Reduce manufacturing lead time, design time, production planning time; increased use, capacity

1.5 AUTOMATION STRATEGIES

A number of fundamental strategies exist for improving productivity in manufacturing operations. These strategies often involve the use of automation technology and are, therefore, called automation strategies. Table 1.4 summarizes the 10 strategies, indicating the likely effects of each strategy on operating factors such as cycle time, nonproductive time, manufacturing lead time, and other production parameters. The 10 strategies are explained below.

Specialization of Operations

Specialization of operations is analogous to "labor specialization" or "division of labor" which is used to improve labor productivity. As applied in automation, the principle involves the use of special-purpose equipment designed to perform one operation with maximum efficiency. Examples include automatic screw machines, tube-seam welding machines, and other special high production machines.

Combined Operations

Production usually consists of a sequence of processing steps. Complex parts may require many individual operations during their fabrication, each operation requiring a different machine. The objective in combining operations is to reduce the number of separate production machines through which the part must be processed. This is implemented by combining more than one operation at a given machine, thereby reducing the number of machines needed to complete the part. Because each machine usually requires a changeover of fixtures and tooling from the previous job, setup time can be reduced by combining operations. In addition, material handling and nonoperation time can also be reduced. A numerical control machining center is a good example of combined operations, because several machining steps are combined in one setup.

Simultaneous Operations

The strategy of combined operations can be extended by not only performing multiple processing operations at the same workstation but also performing the operations simultaneously. In effect, two or more processing (or assembly) steps are carried out at the same time on the part, thereby reducing total cycle time at the machine. A good example of simultaneous operations is the use of multiple-spindle drills that perform a large number of hole-drilling operations simultaneously.

Integration of Operations

A related but alternative strategy is to connect multiple workstations together into a single integrated system, using automated part transfer devices to move parts between stations. The system can be viewed as a single machine, and thus the number of separate machines through which the product must be scheduled is reduced. However, because the system consists of multiple workstations, each capable of processing a separate workpart, several parts can be processed simultaneously. This results in a high production rate, the rate being limited by the slowest workstation in the sequence. Systems of this type are sometimes referred to as a serial production system. Examples of these production systems include transfer lines, dial indexing machines, and automatic assembly machines.

Increased Flexibility

While most of the strategies described above are intended principally for high production, there is a need to automate job shop and medium volume production by increasing the flexibility of the processing equipment. Increased flexibility can be achieved in several ways, according to the flexible automation concepts discussed earlier. Primary objectives are to reduce setup time and machine programming time. Achieving these objectives reduces nonproductive time, manufacturing lead time, and work-in-process. Flexible manufacturing systems (FMSs) and flexible manufacturing cells (FMCs), usually designed to accomplish machining on part families, illustrate this strategy.

Automated Material Handling and Storage

Opportunities exist to reduce nonproductive time by using automated material handling and storage systems. Mechanized or automated part handling systems are employed in transfer lines, flexible manufacturing cells, and similar production systems. The obvious advantage is reduction in labor cost. Other benefits include reduced work-in-process and shorter manufacturing lead times. Examples of automated material handling systems include mechanized and automated conveyor systems and automated guided vehicle systems.

Automated storage systems also can be used to reduce labor, work-in-process, and manufacturing lead times. The tremendous advantage of an automated storage system is that it provides control over the inventory stored in it. Raw materials, parts, tools and fixtures, and finished products can be put into storage and retrieved rapidly and accurately. Lost materials are minimized. Examples of automated storage systems include automated storage–retrieval systems and carousels.

Automated Inspection

Inspection procedures are traditionally accomplished by manual methods after the part has been processed, which means that the quality level has already been established by the time the part is inspected. Manual inspection is a time-consuming activity, and inspection costs can be significant. Automating the inspection function can result in substantial labor savings. Including automated inspection into the manufacturing process allows the process to be corrected as the product is being made. This reduces scrap and improves the overall quality level of the product.

Process Control and Optimization

Control is one of the fundamental building blocks of automation. Process control includes various control schemes and optimization strategies designed to operate the individual manufacturing processes and equipment so as to achieve certain objectives related to the specific process. Common objectives in process control and optimization, sometimes called objective functions in the language of control theory, include (*1*) minimum product cost, (*2*) maximum production rate, (*3*) maximum yield, and (*4*) various objectives that attempt to minimize variations in process and product parameters. The last objective might be considered a quality improvement goal. Thus benefits that one hopes to derive by this automation strategy include reduced cycle times and costs and improved product quality.

Plant Operations Control

The previous strategy is concerned with controlling individual manufacturing processes. Plant operations control is concerned with controlling the entire factory. In pursuing this strategy, one attempts to manage and coordinate the aggregate plant operations more efficiently. Areas that lie within the scope of aggregate plant operations include process planning, production scheduling, shop floor control, and quality control; these areas are discussed elsewhere in the handbook. Implementation of the plant operations control strategy usually requires use of local area networks in the factory.

Computer Integrated Manufacturing

Computer technology has had a dramatic effect on the development of automation. Virtually all production systems installed today use computer systems. The term *computer integrated manufacturing* (CIM) denotes the use of computers to design the products, plan the production, control the operations, and accomplish many of the business-related functions in a manufacturing firm. Computer integrated manufacturing suggests a bringing together of the various diverse functions of manufacturing by means of computer systems. It is in the data processing and information flow within a firm that this integration primarily occurs. The control of production equipment by computers facilitates integration in a CIM system.

Implementing CIM involves taking the previous strategy of plant operations control one step further by connecting the factory operations with the engineering and business functions of the firm. This requires extensive use of the computer and associated databases, and it also requires a high level of local and long-distance computer networking in the company.

1.6 EXAMPLES OF AUTOMATED PRODUCTION SYSTEMS

Most manufacturing operations can be automated. Given the large number of manufacturing processes and assembly operations used in industry (the number is in the thousands) and the many possible ways in which any given operation can be automated, the variety of automated systems would seem to be unlimited. However, although the number of specific automation solutions may be limitless, they can be classified into a limited number of categories. In this section, some of the principal categories and examples of automation in manufacturing are described.

Automated Production Lines

An automated production line is a production system consisting of a series of automated workstations connected by an automatic parts transfer mechanism (Figure 1.5). A raw work part begins at one end of the line and passes through each station, where an operation is accomplished. The stations perform processing or assembly operations such as machining, pressworking, and spot welding. Automated production lines represent an evolution of the early manual assembly lines used in the automotive industry. Examples include transfer lines (associated primarily with machining), dial indexing machines, integrated sheet metal press lines, and certain automated assembly machines.

Automated production lines illustrate several automation strategies, including specialization of operations and integration of operations. Transfer lines and similar systems are often cited as examples of fixed automation, although modern automated lines are controlled by computers and/or programmable logic controllers. Although their control system is programmable, the

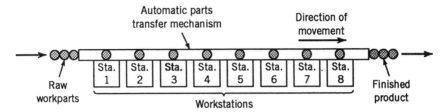

Figure 1.5. Schematic diagram of an eight-station automated production line.

configuration of the production hardware limits these systems in adapting to changes in product configuration. They are, therefore, best suited to high production.

One of the biggest problems in managing an automated production line is system reliability. When one component in the system malfunctions (e.g., one workstation fails), it often means that the entire line must be shut down to make repairs. As the equipment becomes increasingly complex (as the number of stations on the line is increased), the reliability decreases. This translates into more frequent malfunctions and a higher proportion of downtime during operation. Various means are available to reduce the effect of these problems, such as the use of computer monitoring and diagnostic systems, scheduling cutting tool changes instead of waiting for each individual tool to fail, and using storage buffers between stations along the line to allow sections of the line to operate independently.

Position and Motion Control Systems

Many manufacturing operations require the positioning of a work head or tool relative to a work part to accomplish a process. In some cases, the positioning is required before the process is performed. For example, in a drilling operation, the part must be moved to the proper location, and then the hole is drilled at that location. This type of positioning is often called point-to-point control. In other applications, the tool is moved while the process is being carried out. Milling is an example of this. The work part is fed past a rapidly rotating cutting tool, which removes material from the part to achieve the desired geometry. This type of motion control is called continuous path control. In drilling, milling, and other machining operations, position and motion control systems of the type described here are called numerical control (NC) systems. NC is a form of programmable automation in which a machine tool is controlled by a program consisting of properly coded numeric symbols (hence the name numerical control).

The initial applications of numerical control were in metal machining, the first NC machine tool dating from 1952. However, position control and motion control is a central feature of many processing and assembly operations. The applications can be divided into two categories: (*1*) machine tool applications and (*2*) nonmachine tool applications.

Machine Tool Applications

In the machine tool category, NC is widely used for machining and other metalworking processes. In these applications, NC is used to control the position of a tool relative to a work part. Without NC, a human worker would manually have to position the part and the tool. Some of the principal machine tool applications of numerical control are described below.

- *Machining Centers*. These machines are NC machine tools with additional automatic features beyond conventional position and motion control. Some of the additional features (Figure 1.6) include automatic tool changing, automatic work part positioning to present more than one surface to the cutting tool, and automatic pallet shuttles to change work parts. The machining center concept has been adapted to turning machines, resulting in highly automated turning centers with automatic features similar to machining centers.

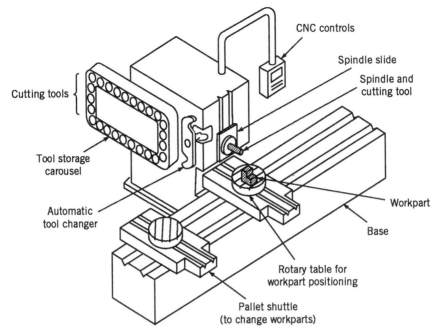

Figure 1.6. A NC machining center, showing the important features: (*1*) automatic tool changer, (*2*) automatic part positioning, and (*3*) automatic pallet shuttles to change workparts.

- *Grinding Machines.* NC can be used to control the grinding of parts with irregular geometries (e.g., nonflat, noncylindrical).
- *Pressworking Machines.* NC presses equipped with multiple punch and die sets are capable of punching holes of different size and shape on flat sheet stock. Special NC presses can also perform bending operations and laser cutting.
- *NC Tube-bending Machines.* These machines can be programmed to bend tube stock to specified angles under numerical control.
- *Flame-cutting Processes.* These processes include flame cutting, laser cutting, electron-beam cutting, and plasma-arc cutting. They share a common feature in that they all cut a narrow kerf in metal sheet or plate stock by melting the metal to separate the parts. The cutting path is controlled by NC.
- *Wire EDM.* Wire EDM is a form of electric discharge machining in which a thin wire is the electrode used to cut a thin kerf in a metal plate, in some respects similar to the way an electric bandsaw works. The cutting path is guided by NC. The process can produce parts with complex two-dimensional outlines.

Nonmachine Tool Applications

This category includes operations such as assembly and inspection. The list includes

- *Welding Machines.* Spot welding and continuous arc welding are automated by NC. Spot welding is programmed as a point-to-point operation, whereas arc welding is a continuous path operation.
- *Component Insertion Machines.* These machines are used extensively in electronics to insert components into printed circuit boards (PCBs) to form an electronic assembly. The NC program defines the *x–y* positions on the PCB where components are to be placed.

• *Coordinate Measuring Machines.* A coordinate measuring machine (CMM) is an inspection machine possessing a contact probe that can be moved to measure $x-y-z$ locations on the surface of a work part. CMMs can be programmed to move the probe from one location to the next, recording the coordinates of the contact position, and automatically inspecting the part.

Benefits usually cited for numerical control in these applications include (*1*) reduced nonproductive time, (*2*) less time to complete a production order, (*3*) simpler fixtures, (*4*) greater flexibility to alter the production schedule and deal with engineering changes, (*5*) better accuracy, and (*6*) reduced human error.

Industrial Robotics

An industrial robot can be defined as a general-purpose programmable machine possessing certain anthropomorphic characteristics. The anthropomorphic characteristic that is common to virtually all industrial robots is a manipulator arm, consisting of multiple joints that allow it to be moved to various positions and orientations within the robot's work envelope. At the end of the arm is attached a special tool called an end effector. This is a custom-engineered gripper or tool designed for the particular task that the robot is to perform. Thus the end effector is the special tooling that allows the general-purpose robot to perform a particular application. Depending on the type of end effector, the robot can be programmed to perform any of various industrial applications, including material handling, machine loading and unloading, spot welding and continuous arc welding, spray painting, and assembly. This handbook includes a chapter devoted specifically to the topic of industrial robotics.

Industrial robots might be included within the scope of the previous position and motion control systems, because their applications always involve movement of a manipulator to perform some task. However, the capabilities of robotics technology far surpasses position and motion control defined in the preceding category. These capabilities include interfacing with other equipment such as NC machine tools for loading and unloading applications, employing sophisticated sensor systems such as machine vision, interfacing with human workers, and decision making.

Process Control

One of the fundamental building blocks of automation is feedback control. In general use, process control refers to the control of a continuous or semicontinuous process, using feedback measurement loops to implement a given control strategy. The control strategy usually involves an attempt to optimize some performance characteristic of the process, such as cost or quality. In some cases, performance is defined as minimizing the variations about some specified set point for the process.

Process control is most often associated with the processing industries, such as chemical processing, petroleum refineries, and similar operations in which product demand is high and production involves use of a continuous process. Process control also is widely used in semicontinuous processes, including some chemical processes, steel-making and other basic metals processing, and other operations in which the product is made in batches rather than continuously. In modern process control applications, the digital computer is used to implement the appropriate control strategy, both for the continuous and semicontinuous cases. With the availability of ultra–high speed computers and high frequency sensors and data collection systems, process control is being applied to processes with ever-shorter operation cycle times such as those used in discrete parts manufacturing.

Flexible Manufacturing Systems and Cells

Flexible manufacturing systems (FMSs) and flexible manufacturing cells (FMCs) represent a highly automated form of production system. They consist of a group of processing workstations interconnected by means of an automated material handling system, all operating under computer control, and designed to process a variety of work part configurations. The worksta-

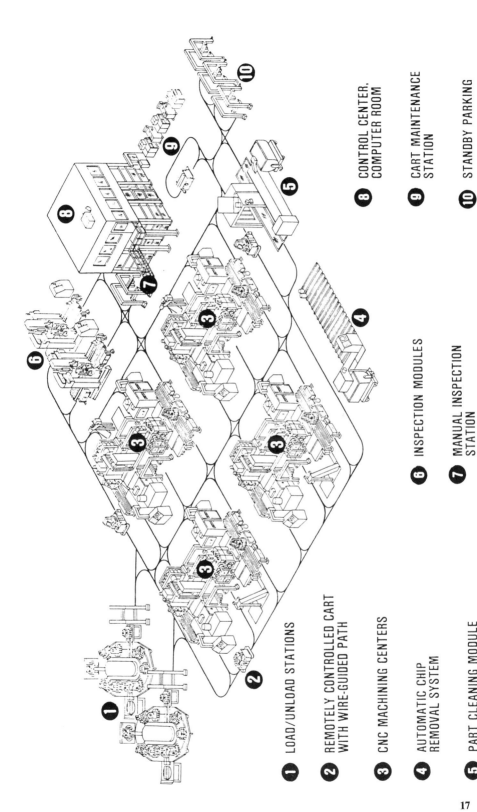

1 LOAD/UNLOAD STATIONS

2 REMOTELY CONTROLLED CART WITH WIRE-GUIDED PATH

3 CNC MACHINING CENTERS

4 AUTOMATIC CHIP REMOVAL SYSTEM

5 PART CLEANING MODULE

6 INSPECTION MODULES

7 MANUAL INSPECTION STATION

8 CONTROL CENTER, COMPUTER ROOM

9 CART MAINTENANCE STATION

10 STANDBY PARKING

Figure 1.7. A flexible manufacturing system for machining. Courtesy of Cincinnati Milacron.

tions are usually NC machines, and the material handling systems sometimes include industrial robots; thus flexible manufacturing systems and cells are integrated systems that are made up of lower level automated production systems. The difference between a FMS and a FMC is sometimes defined in terms of the number of workstations (machine tools) included: a FMS includes four or more machines, while a FMC contains three or fewer. However, this is not a universally accepted dividing line.

The most common application of this technology is in machining. An example of a machining-type flexible manufacturing system is illustrated in Figure 1.7. There are hundreds of installed FMSs and FMCs throughout the world that perform machining operations. FMS–FMC technology embraces the principles of flexible automation; i.e., it is an extension of programmable automation in which setup time and programming time are minimized, precluding the need to produce parts in batches. Parts of differing configurations can be mixed on the same production system. As demand for different products changes, the system can be readily rescheduled without significant disruptions and delays.

1.7   ECONOMIC AND SOCIAL ISSUES IN AUTOMATION

The trend toward automation seems unavoidable in modern industrialized nations. There are several economic and social factors tending to promote the development of automated factories in the future, including (1) the desire of companies and nations to remain competitive in manufacturing, (2) the desire to improve productivity, (3) the desire to increase machine use, (4) the high cost of work-in-process inventory, (5) the desire to reduce manufacturing lead time, (6) the desire to be responsive to customer demands, (7) the need to conserve raw materials and energy, (8) the trend in the labor force to seek employment in the service sector, and (9) the concern for worker safety. There are several economic and social issues that must be addressed by individual companies and by society in general as the trend toward automation in manufacturing continues.

Types of Work in the Automated Factory

The nature of work in a factory dominated by automation is different from that in a plant employing largely direct labor in its manufacturing operations. Although automation implies operating equipment without the direct participation of labor, people are still needed to perform certain tasks in the plant. The types of work in a highly automated plant are discussed below.

Equipment Maintenance

When production depends on automated machinery, reliability and maintenance of the machines becomes critically important. In a highly integrated factory, breakdown of one key machine can stop production in the entire plant. Skilled, highly trained technicians are needed to maintain and repair the equipment in a highly automated factory.

Computer Programming

Plant computer systems and computer-controlled machines must be programmed, product and process data must be entered, and so on. Although much of the routine part programming will be automated and algorithms augmented by artificial intelligence and expert systems will be used, there will still be a need for personnel skilled in computer programming. It is unlikely that the company's information system and database will remain fixed for any length of time. There will be a continual need to update programs, bring new software on-line, and enter new data in the system in the future automated factory.

Engineering Project Work

The future automated factory is likely never to be finished. New production technologies and computer systems will be developed, and there will be a need to incorporate these technologies in factory operations to remain competitive. Skilled engineers and technicians will find many employment opportunities in the automated factory of the future.

Plant Supervision

A limited staff of professional managers and engineers must be responsible for managing plant operations. It is likely that the technical skills of managers will increase in importance due to the increased technological sophistication of the systems in the plant and the limited number of specialized technical personnel available. This would represent a shift from today's factory management where emphasis is placed on personnel management.

Factory Interface

There will be certain positions in which humans will still be required to interface with the outside world. Human workers will be needed at loading and unloading docks, office staff will be needed to support the factory, and perhaps a receptionist will be needed in the front lobby.

Plant Security

Most of the security functions in an automated future factory will be accomplished by robotic systems and sophisticated sensors. A limited staff of human security guards will be needed to manage the security operations.

Impact on Labor

The future automated factory will have a reduced number of workers and little or no direct labor participation in production. Automation means substitution of machines for human workers. The implications for direct labor in factory operations are clear: unskilled workers will not be needed to tend production machines and perform manual labor tasks. As automation is implemented, a shift from direct labor jobs to indirect labor jobs will occur. Direct labor work tends to be well defined, manual, and repetitive. The skill level required is generally low. Indirect factory labor work is sometimes manual but not as well defined and not as repetitive. Many of the jobs for indirect labor require skill and training. As discussed above, the positions include maintenance, computer programming, engineering (especially in fields such as electrical and electronics, industrial, manufacturing, and mechanical engineering), and technical supervision.

The shift from direct to indirect labor in future factories will adversely affect labor unions, unless they can recruit in employment categories in which they have traditionally not been successful. Skilled professional and semiprofessional technical workers often identify themselves with management—indeed, management positions are often filled from their ranks—and they have not been fruitful fields for recruitment by labor unions. Growing membership among these workers represents a difficult challenge for labor unions.

Because there are differences in skill requirements between current direct labor jobs and future indirect labor positions, some workers who qualify for jobs in today's conventional factories will not qualify for indirect labor positions in future automated factories. Some of the unskilled workers can be retrained, but others will be unemployable. This kind of job displacement is no doubt a negative aspect of automation. However, if companies do not automate their factories for the future, there is likely to be no future for these companies. The resulting impact on labor in this case will be far more negative.

Retraining and Education

As the world moves toward a more technological society, technical education assumes greater importance. There are two aspects of the technical educational issue that need to be addressed: educating young people still in school and retraining workers who are displaced by automation. If the United States is to remain economically competitive, it is imperative that its young people are trained in sufficient numbers to design, build, and operate the automated production systems that will be used in the factories of the future. For workers currently in the workforce who are displaced by automation technologies, some difficult questions arise concerning the retraining of these workers. First, who should pay the high cost of technical retraining? Should the company that is introducing automation pay the expense? The labor unions? Or should government (which means the taxpayers)? Second, what are the obligations of the worker who is retrained? If the company pays for retraining, is the worker obligated to remain with that company? If employment opportunities in the local community are scarce, must the worker move to another geographical area to seek employment? This may not appeal to a worker who has roots in the local community. Third, with the increasing complexity of technology, how much retraining can the displaced worker absorb? A 50-year-old worker laid off from the local steel mill who graduated from a vocational high school more than 30 years ago may find it difficult to learn computer programming, the technical principles of a machine vision system, or other sophisticated programmable machine.

Finally, two questions that relate to both the education of young people and the retraining of existing workers are (*1*) How does society retrain the teachers who will retrain the workforce? and (*2*) How will the educational laboratories continually modernize the equipment to accomplish the retraining? Some of the technologies in which training is required are still emerging, and there are few teachers who have been exposed to and educated in these technologies. How does society retrain the teachers presently instructing in the fading technologies so that they can retrain the workers in the emerging technologies? These are difficult questions for which there are no easy answers.

BIBLIOGRAPHY

C.R. ASFAHL, *Robots and Manufacturing Automation*, John Wiley & Sons, Inc., New York, 1992.

A. ASHBURN, "People and Automation," *Am. Mach. Automated Manufac.*, Vol. 130, No. 6, 97–112 (June 1986), Special Rep. 787.

R.U. AYRES, *Computer Integrated Manufacturing, Vol. I: Revolution in Progress*, Chapman and Hall, London, 1991.

C. EMERSON, "Detroit-Style Automation," *Am. Mach. Automated Manufact.*, Vol. 131, No. 7, 81–92 (July 1987), Special Rep. 796.

M.P. GROOVER, *Automation, Production Systems, and Computer Integrated Manufacturing*, Prentice-Hall, Inc., Englewood Cliffs, N.J., 1987.

M.P. GROOVER, J.E. HUGHES, JR., and N.G. ODREY, "Productivity Benefits of Automation Should Offset Work Force Dislocation Problems," *Indust. Eng.*, 50–59 (Apr. 1984).

M.P. GROOVER, M. WEISS, R.N. NAGEL, and N.G. ODREY, *Industrial Robotics: Technology, Programming, and Applications*, McGraw-Hill Book Co., Inc., New York, 1986.

D.W. PESSEN, *Industrial Automation*, John Wiley & Sons, Inc., New York, 1989.

DEFINITIONS

Automation. A technology in which a process is accomplished by programmed instructions, usually combined with automatic feedback to ensure proper execution of the instructions.

Computer integrated manufacturing (CIM). Extensive use of computer systems to design the products, plan the production, control the operations, and accomplish many of the business-related functions in a manufacturing firm.

Feedback control. A means of controlling a process in which the value of the output is measured and compared with the desired input value; any difference is used to drive the output into agreement with the input.

Fixed automation. An automated production system in which the sequence of processing is fixed by the equipment configuration.

Flexible automation. An extension of programmable automation in which a variety of parts can be processed without significant changeover time for reprogramming and changing the physical setup.

Flexible manufacturing system (FMS). A highly automated form of production system, consisting of multiple processing stations (e.g., NC machines) interconnected by an automated material handling system and controlled by a computer system; the FMS is designed to process a variety of work part configurations.

Industrial robot. A programmable machine possessing certain anthropomorphic characteristics, most notably a multiple jointed arm whose motions can be controlled to perform various industrial tasks.

Numerical control (NC). A form of programmable automation in which equipment (usually a machine tool) is controlled by means of numerical data; the central operating feature of NC involves control of the relative position of a tool and workpart.

Programmable automation. An automated production system in which the processing sequence is controlled by a program of instructions that can be read and interpreted by the equipment.

SECTION II
ENGINEERING DESIGN

CHAPTER 2
Concurrent Engineering

DAVID BELSON
University of Southern California

2.1 AN OVERVIEW OF CONCURRENT ENGINEERING

Concurrent engineering (CE) is the development of products by integrating design with other tasks such as the planning of manufacturing, quality, and marketing. Products are developed more quickly and often at a lower cost with higher quality by simultaneously completing these tasks along with the use of modern design tools. This approach addresses issues pertaining to the entire life cycle of a product. In addition to the basic functionality of a product, the product's manufacturability, serviceability, and even recyclability are addressed. Such a broad view requires input from a wide variety of skills, which often require new tools so they can be dealt with on a simultaneous basis.

Concurrent engineering's primary feature is to use a team approach to the creation or improvement of new products. Various discipline, such as marketing, quality assurance, and finance participate as a group that completes the product development process by doing tasks in parallel rather than sequentially. CE typically includes the use of computer tools such as computer-aided design (CAD), shared databases, and standards to facilitate communications. The availability of a common language, in the form of a standardized description of the components of a product, is often critical to concurrent engineering's success.

In terms of the typical manufacturing organization's culture, in the past each function developed its own terminology, or language, and each group believed that the other disciplines were somehow alien. An us-verses-them attitude too often existed. With concurrent engineering, these attitudes are broken down and replaced by all members working as a team for a common goal. Philosophies that emphasize the importance of customer service are often conducive to formulating a common approach.

Each discipline that is part of the CE team requires computer software to do analysis and to keep track of its product-related data. Moreover, the computers used by each discipline must be able to communicate with each other to exchange necessary information. Therefore, data standards are an important issue in concurrent engineering; a common language must be spoken by all participants and the participants' computers.

Concurrent engineering can be broadly defined, and it is frequently categorized under several different names, including simultaneous engineering and integrated product development. Integrated product development has been used in many military projects. In some cases, CE is merely labeled by the particular feature of CE used, such as multidisciplinary teams (MDT) or design-for-manufacturability (DFM).

2.2 HISTORICAL BACKGROUND

As the U.S. auto industry saw its market share decreasing in the 1980s, the Ford Motor Co. initiated a team approach to the development of the Ford Taurus. Similarly, other companies used CE ideas to deliver a better product, at less cost in a shorter time. John Deere used it to cut 30% off development costs, AT&T used it to halve development time on a new electronic switching system, and Cadillac used it to improve quality. However, the design and manufacturing of a complex product such as a car or an airplane involves more than just gathering together a team of people. Much of CE is possible only because of new technology available at a reasonable cost.

A critical element in the successful development of new products is the use of new tools. Manufacturing automation and design automation have become more accessible. The specific tools vary with the job. Computers are generally on the desks of the person designing the product and the person planning how to make the product, and computers operate the equipment making the product. However, these tools cannot be effective unless they are able to communicate with each other. Integration of technology has meant that standardized interfaces exist and standard data descriptions are agreed on. Computers must talk a common language or translators between computers must be available. The topic of communication between different computer types (platforms) is important to CE. CE requires the integration of groups of people as well as the integration of computers and related technology.

The U.S. federal government implemented an initiative originally called computer-aided logistic support (CALS) that involves data standards to support CE and organizational changes in the government's purchasing to create the savings expected from CE. Similarly, a number of other countries have instituted CE and data standards organizations to further the implementation of CE. CALS goals will be met over several decades. Standards are set for digital communication between contractors and subcontractors as well as with the government. In conjunction with this program, the National Institute of Standards and Technology (NIST) established standards for conformance. Associations are organized in specific industries to facilitate electronic data interchange (EDI). Also, CE-related programs have been initiated by the U.S. Department of Commerce and other agencies. Many government requests for proposals (RFP) for major manufactured products such as aircraft, satellites, and ships require that bidders give evidence that they will be using CE.

Although new technology speeds the design and planning tasks, it also presents problems. Organizations implementing new tools such as CAD or computer-aided engineering (CAE) have found the tools difficult to learn and use. New technology often causes job responsibilities to change and may eliminate certain positions, although it may add new ones. Overcoming such problems may require new training, incentives, and participation by the affected employees. Many organizations have found that increasing participation by employees in important decisions is a valuable asset. Empowering the employee often creates a more motivated employee who makes a greater contribution to the organization's objectives. Moreover, the idea of the boss–employee relationship has been found to be less productive than a teamwork approach (1). Concurrent engineering is in concert with this participatory concept.

Although automation and computer technology present implementation problems, they also present opportunities for improved communications. Just as the telephone changed communications between people, computers present a new dimension. Computerized mail, for example, makes efficient communications between individuals and groups possible. Electronic meetings of teams can be held without everyone being in the same room or even working at the same time. EDI computer software is helping to move documents among people so that paperwork is avoided. Images of paperwork, such as drawings, purchase orders, and specifications, can be quickly transferred between computers rather than the slower movement of physical paper documents. In the past, much of the delays in converting a product idea into a delivered product were caused by "waiting for the paperwork."

2.3   THE MOTOVATION FOR CONCURRENT ENGINEERING

To be a world-class competitor a company must bring its high quality products quickly to market (2). In the late 1980s, the Japanese were able to create a new automobile in roughly half the time taken by American companies. The reason for the long delay in the American case was the typical procedure by which new products were developed. Engineers first design a product and only once that is complete do later tasks such as manufacturing engineering and marketing begin. Having engineers first finish their design and then "throw it over the wall" to manufacturing was the common U.S. practice.

In contrast, CE emphasizes teamwork by which several people from different disciplines work together while they simultaneously complete the development of a new product. Such parallel completion of tasks should be executed quicker than when doing the tasks sequentially. This may sound relatively easy, but it turns out that a number of technologies are necessary and considerable cultural change must take place in an organization for CE to succeed. Many different disciplines are involved in product development. For example, new products require the planning or assembly procedures; inspection; maintenance; marketing; input from vendors,

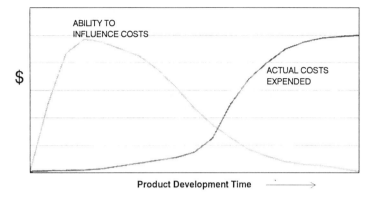

ABILITY TO
INFLUENCE COSTS

ACTUAL COSTS
EXPENDED

$

Product Development Time ⎯⎯⎯⎯⟶

Figure 2.1. The timing of costs during product development.

customers, finance, accounting, and other disciplines; and the engineering design of the physical geometry of the product.

Concurrent engineering is a popular and frequently discussed way for manufacturing to improve competitiveness and for the government, specifically the U.S. Department of Defense, to purchase better products for less cost. An Institute for Defense Analysis report (3) defined concurrent engineering as "a systematic approach to the integrated, concurrent design of products and their related processes, including manufacture and support. This approach is intended to cause the developers, from the onset, to consider all elements of the product life cycle from conception through disposal, including quality, cost, schedule, and user requirements." Concurrent engineering is simply designing a product, its size, shape, materials, etc., and at the same time designing the manufacturing processes and related support that will be needed once the product is delivered.

Much of the motivation for concurrent engineering is based on the economic leverage of addressing all aspects of the design of a product as early as possible. Many industries have documented the fact that while the out-of-pocket costs for product development are small during the early stages, the impact on final costs is large (Figure 2.1). If the quality of work done during the early stages is improved, there will be a large effect on later stages once actual manufacturing has commenced.

2.4 THE FEATURES OF CONCURRENT ENGINEERING

Concurrent engineering does not occur in a single form. Its features vary from industry to industry, from organization to organization, and from product to product. Sometimes a particular product requires a unique CE plan. The specific features of CE vary with the implementation but generally include a combination of the following ingredients.

Multidisciplinary Teams

Groups representing two or more functional areas are gathered to develop a product consisting of people from various disciplines. Many such teams may be necessary. The particular membership of the team depends on the product involved and the overall organization. Generally, the team at least includes engineering design and manufacturing engineering. It may include many other disciplines such as finance, marketing, research and development (R&D), logistics, purchasing, and quality control. Customers and vendors are sometimes included. There may be a hierarchy of teams, with individual teams concerned with one part of a product (such as the door of a car) or with a system (such as the hydraulic system of an airplane). A team leader is needed, but equality and participation of all members are absolutely necessary.

The hierarchy of teams may be for the development of a part of a product. Integration or overall teams (teams of teams) may be formed that consist of representatives of subteams or new sets of members, representing necessary functions concerned with the overall product. For a large and complex product, there may be several levels of teams. Team networks may be created to focus on certain operational issues.

Tools

Electronic tools exist to support the work done by product design engineers and to communicate their output in the form of computer-generated images rather than as paper drawings. These CAD tools have proven efficient in communicating designs to members of the CE multidisciplinary teams. The existence of such computer software has facilitated the development of CE. The details of a product's design, such as its geometry, materials, and costs, are often kept in electronic form. The effectiveness of CE is helped by making design-related databases available to all disciplines and all parts of the organization involved with the product. However, such sharing requires data standards so that all involved understand the data. By agreeing on uniform descriptions of products and parts of products, communication is much easier. These standards can address the geometry of a part as well as the operating and maintenance data about a product. Furthermore, the software must be friendly, or easily useable, by all the various disciplines. Due to the long tradition of separateness of disciplines, many parts of the organization have difficulty in understanding the computer systems and terminology of other areas.

Much of the progress in facilitating electronic communications of design data have been via organizations set up for such purposes. Published standards such as the Product Data Exchange Standard (PDES) and the earlier International Graphical Exchange Standard (IGES) are examples of efforts to create widely accepted product descriptions. Included are descriptions of the product beyond the geometry, e.g., materials, production processes, and product usage. These extensive standards are largely created by volunteer groups, consisting of representatives form a variety of organizations and countries.

Communication and Design

Schemes have been developed to aid design engineers and ensure that their products will not cause problems and undue costs for subsequent tasks such as manufacturing and testing. For example, rules to facilitate manufacture of parts called design-for-manufacture (DFM) are provided to design engineers. These rules warn the designer to avoid configurations that machine tools will find difficult or costly. In a sense, DFM provides the time and cost for manufacturing a product while it is being designed rather than waiting for the industrial engineer to do such estimates after the design is complete. Also, design-for-assembly (DFA) and design-for-inspection (DFI) rules are available to help avoid problems on those areas. In addition, CAD systems can incorporate these "design-for-X" (DFX) rules so that the engineer respects these rules while the geometry of a part is determined. Thus some of the aspects of CE are initiated by the computer.

Computer support, such as CAD, facilitates the work of engineering design, but tools such as computer-aided process planning (CAPP) are helpful for manufacturing. This determines what machines (lathes, drills, welding, etc.) are needed and how and when they are to be used. With CAPP, manufacturing can respond quickly to changes just as engineering design can with its CAD system.

Facilities

Certainly the work space for the CE team must be conducive to the type of work to be done. This involves the availability of tools as well as the organization of work space. Because CE involves frequent interaction of groups, adequate meeting space must be provided. Conference rooms often are used, but because the team of people must occupy them for a significant time, the rooms must be comfortable for the long term. Group meeting space may become the home workstation for team members. This space should allow ease of discussion, including accoutrements such as blackboards (or white boards), computer displays, and teleconferencing capabilities. Convenient access to product mock-up space may be beneficial. For one auto company, a car can be driven throughout its new design offices. A small shop to construct prototypes may be needed.

At the start, many CE teams are located in a single new facility or location. But it is important to consider the necessity of consolidating the entire team in a single location. This may be costly in terms of moving people and equipment. A large project team may be impractical for a single building. Nevertheless, colocation of all members will ensure the highest level of interaction. One must trade-off the intangible benefits of greater face-to-face contact with the real dollar cost of moving people and construction.

Culture, Organization Structures, and Change

Multidisciplinary teamwork, employee participation, and the simultaneous execution of tasks may be quite new for many organizations. Such changes require a different culture from the existing one. Acceptance of change is necessary if CE is to be effective. Many CE implementers have reported that their organization's willingness to change was the most critical ingredient for success in CE. An attitude of skepticism or defense of traditional methods is probably fatal. The necessary open attitude toward change must be achieved before technology can have a useful impact. This means that teams must share a vision, values, discipline, accountability, and incentives so that they can make use of the technology and organizational resources available to them.

The typical pyramid structure of the manufacturing organization is sometimes in conflict with the multidisciplinary team approach to CE. The functional divisions must be willing to forgo some of their prerogatives to empower the decision making of the newly created design teams. This may mean that certain managers must relinquish their authority. Such changes can jeopardize middle management jobs and eliminate certain overhead functions. The organization benefits from the cost reduction, but the threat to jobs naturally engenders opposition.

Manufacturing of products is far from being a simple task—companies are producing a constantly changing mix of increasingly complex products. Global competition results in even shorter product life cycles. Market conditions and requirements change every day. To compete effectively, manufacturing must be responsive to customers. Many manufacturing concepts are complementary to CE; computer-integrated manufacturing (CIM) addresses computer linking, while CE addresses people and group integration. All are necessary.

CE also must address the subdisciplines that plan, control, and execute manufacturing. Material and production plans are at the beginning. The next steps are to control the manufacturing process through priority planning, schedule release, and detailed allocation of resources. The execution of the plan, the physical delivery of components and/or materials, the assembly or fabrication, and the packaging of semifinished or finished goods complete the production process. With CE, the design engineers focus more on the mechanics of parts fabrication than without CE, but there still is the issue of assembly. Assembly and fabrication of parts are important but often ignored during product design. Manufacturing must assemble the product and execute additional process steps such as packout, storage, and shipping.

Quality Methods

Quality and product maintainability are also objectives of CE. Quality can be better addressed if it is considered at the start of the design process rather than as an inspection task once the product is complete. The simultaneous nature of CE permits quality to be designed into the product from the start. In terms of maintenance and service of products, these issues are also better addressed at the start of design. Simplifying maintenance should be considered by the CE team. In many sophisticated products, the documentation needed for maintenance becomes overwhelming large but the CE team can work to reduce it and to convert documentation to a more convenient electronic form.

Most practitioners of CE have found that in addition to traditional inspection and statistical measures to police quality—such as statistical quality control (SQC)—quality from the customer's viewpoint must be considered. Quality must mean that a product has been responsive to the needs of the customer. The concept of the voice of the customer and techniques to relate customer interests to product features are an important directive to the CE team. Quality function deployment (QFD) is a technique to organize such matters in a structured way (4, 5).

QFD develops matrices that start with customer interests and then relate them to product attributes. These attributes are then related to product parts and processes. The design of the matrix is done in a graphic way so as to focus attention of the important relationships as well as the interrelationships. The interrelationships may mean that improvement in one aspect of a product may degrade a product in another aspect, e.g., improvement in an automobile's gas mileage may decrease its ability to accelerate. However, by relating both aspects to the customers' interests, the product team will be in a better position to make such trade-offs.

Another approach to achieving a quality product is to design a product in terms of various parameters (dimensions, materials, etc.) and how they appear to deliver the requirements of the customer. Experimenting with various alternatives can provide data indicating the best settings of key parameters. The Taguchi (6) technique helps define an efficient way to conduct such experiments and to incorporate them in a product's final design.

Accounting and Metrics

Accounting for costs is an important ingredient in the CE team's decision making. It needs to know the cost impact of its decision. The effect of dealing with total product costs by all functions is one of the primary benefits of concurrent engineering. All functions, such as design and manufacturing must consider the impact of their decisions. Traditionally, each function looked at costs from its own provincial viewpoint. For example, manufacturing would worry about the costs of making a product and not sufficiently consider the impact on performance, which is the focus of design engineers, and marketability. Conversely engineering and marketing would focus on their priorities.

Cost accounting data form the historical basis for an organization's understanding of its costs. One form of accounting called activity-based accounting (ABC) has been particularly useful in identifying costs for use in CE. ABC measures costs in terms of what costs are caused by each activity, such as drilling a hole or completing a piece of paperwork. The more common form of accounting, financial accounting, is concerned with allocating costs to departments, placing a value on inventory, and determining taxes. That type of accounting is often not useful for CE purposes.

Future expected costs as well as actual costs are important to the design team. Accounting data can be applied to mathematical models that predict future costs and analyze alternate plans. Optimal plans can be estimated, and the models can be used to decide on a mixture of manufacturing processes. Such models, when provided to the CE team, can be used to create more efficient plans. The CE team has the responsibility to ensure that these cost models are accurate and are properly interpreted.

Lessons Learned

The CE team tries to avoid mistakes of the past and needs to know the lessons learned from previous efforts. Ideally, such information would be available in a computerized on-line service that would warn designers of certain problems when making design choices. The availability of lessons learned is a benefit to both design and manufacturing. Too often such lessons remain only with an individual. Some companies have incorporated this knowledge in their CAD systems with a certain amount of expert system attributes.

Capturing lessons learned is not a simple task. Often this involves identifying what design aspects cause manufacturing problems as well as what designs are particularly easy and cost effective. These may be unique to the particular facility or general to the industry. Some software capture this information and communicate it to the designer. The information may be quite specific or it may be generalized into the form of a manufacturability index number.

Participation

Employee participation within CE should result in better understanding and communication. For example, the manufacturing department is sometimes seen by the overall organization as a cost generator and not an income producer, in contrast to other departments. A successful CE team spirit will mean that everyone is recognized for his or her role in increasing revenue and decreasing costs.

Few well-defined CE procedures exist to make participation happen, particularly those that are agreed on as applicable at more than one company. It is desirable for organizations to decide that CE should not be highly structured or follow precise guidelines. CE is a basic philosophy that allows for flexibility and freedom for the teams involved. Flexibility can empower the team and encourage participation. There is a wide variety of interpretations of CE. Much of this diversity is a result of varied settings. A large organization producing a complex product, such as aircraft or automobiles, implements a different CE than a small company producing a relatively simple electronic component. The large organization will have a wider variety of disciplines and participating departments.

Several methods exist for enhancing participation and the creative potential of a group. For example, one method is the nominal group technique (NGT). In this method, each team member first writes down as many ideas as he or she can on a piece of paper. Then each individual in turn presents one idea. These are listed on a blackboard or flip chart by the team leader. After all ideas are listed, the group begins a discussion of the ideas with a focus on clarification to avoid duplication but not criticism of the ideas. Finally, the ideas are prioritized, or the best idea is selected by a mathematical voting process. Other team methods such as the Delphi method are available in literature on decision analysis and industrial psychology. These methods emphasize contributions from all team members and use their expertise and experience. The idea of CE and team design is not to make everyone a generalist. The real power of a team approach is in continued technical skills and specialization of team members used on a group basis.

2.5 ECONOMICS

CE provides important savings, which result from a number of factors. Many industries have found that the cost to make a change is related to when the change must be made. The later the change is made the more costly it will be (Figure 2.2). When the design of a product is merely preliminary ideas or sketches, changes are relatively easy. However, when the product is designed in detail, when production facilities have been built, or when production has already begun, the cost of a change is large. With CE the need for changes are more often found in the early stages of the product development process because all the disciplines are addressed earlier. Manufacturing, marketing, support, and others are at the design table and have an early opportunity to impact the design.

It has been found that many tasks previously done one after the other can be completed in

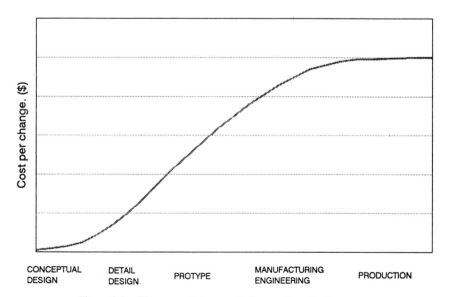

Figure 2.2. The cost of changes during product development.

parallel. Not all product development tasks lend themselves to simultaneous completion but many do. In some cases, the individual tasks when done simultaneously take longer, but cost savings are still realized. The reduction in costs does not come from the reduction in people, but from a shift in people more to the front-end processes where the reduction in cost will come through reduction in rework, less scrap, fewer engineering change orders (ECOs), and less warranty and support costs.

With CE, the timing of costs often changes. Considering downstream requirements such as manufacturing early in the product development cycle will result in lower total costs but increased activity early in development. Accelerated design and development efforts mean increased labor in the early stages. This means that increased costs must be budgeted for early phases of product development, although these will be offset by later savings. When disciplines work as part of a team rather than in separate organizations, people often do a better job of communicating. So-called stove pipe organizations separate people, making it difficult for employees to understand the needs and problems of others. The disciplines in stove pipe organizations often mistrust each other, have different terminology, and must redo others' work. The added communication time and redundant efforts are costly.

Concurrent engineering also affects scheduling and systems such as materials requirements planning (MRP). CE should result in shorter lead times, which increase the need for reliable scheduling. CE can also create more rapid changes at an earlier stage than before, which an MRP system and other automated manufacturing planning systems can use by getting the right information to the right place at the right time. An inaccurate or slow MRP system probably is made worse by CE.

2.6 IMPLEMENTATION

Converting the product development process to one employing concurrent engineering can be done on a comprehensive basis, or implementation can be phased in product by product. Some organizations have implemented CE only in certain functional areas; however, this is in conflict with the basic idea of CE. Most organizations have found that a change to CE requires careful study and planning and often a gradual change to the new approach. Training is a particularly big factor in the chances of a successful change. Engineers and operations staff play a key role in CE, but these people often have little training in organizational change and group motovation. Training in such issues must take place; otherwise there will be a focus only on mechanical issues, such as computer software or data standards, and not on the human requirements.

The first step is to evaluate where changes must take place. Perhaps many of the necessary features of CE are already in place; therefore, a review of current practices is warranted. Several concurrent engineering checklists have been published to help in this evaluation (e.g., CALS/ISG publications and ref. 7). These reviews generally include an examination of the following:

1. *Organization*. The extent to which design teams are capable and are used.
2. *Communications Infrastructure*. The ability to access and manipulate product data as well as to manage the product development project.
3. *Requirements*. Accessibility of product data, standards, documentation, and validation information.
4. *Product Development*. The ongoing review of design matters such as component libraries, manufacturability information, and supplier data.

After the review of current practices and a determination of necessary changes, the following tasks are generally required:

1. *A Detailed Plan*. Steps necessary to complete the changes must be scheduled and budgeted and responsibilities must be defined.
2. *Training*. Teamwork, use of new computer tools, and other CE features require training. Merely assembling a group of people in a room does not ensure teamwork. Team leaders must be trained; skills must be learned. Sometimes such training can be conducted by employees with experience with previous CE implementations.

3. *Purchase of Tools.* Necessary new systems, such as shared product databases, communication systems, and other facilities, must be purchased. Related training in the use of tools must also take place.

4. *Senior Management Directives.* Radical change will not take place unless the staff believes that management is truly behind the idea. Support must be made explicit.

5. *Facilitators.* People with experience in concurrent engineering and design management can sit in on CE team meetings and advise team leaders. The lessons learned from other CE implementations can be used and passed on by such individuals.

6. *Changes to Budgeting.* Because work is done by teams that are not part of the traditional departmental hierarchy, budgeting practices must be revised.

7. *Evaluation Measures.* The effectiveness of change should be measured so that the extent, or lack, of success can be determined. Measures should be defined at the start and reported regularly. In the spirit of teamwork, team members should be informed of their results. Some organizations have incorporated measures of success into employee incentives.

2.7 RESEARCH IN CE

CE presents a number of opportunities for scientific research. For example, the current literature does not provide much help in how to prioritize the list of CE's features or how to select the optimal subset of CE features for a specific situation. No comprehensive model yet exists to explain the interrelationships between the components of CE. For example, when creating multidisciplinary teams, it is not known how important it is to colocate team members or what specific aspects of a shared database among disciplines are particularly beneficial to the multidisciplinary team. It is apparent that the mix of CE features used varies widely from organization to organization and varies from product to product. The mix of CE features appears to impact the net results; in fact, there seems to be some synergy between features such that the net benefit is not proportional to the number of features used. One feature when combined with another may greatly increase net benefits. A significant portion of the research in CE has been at the Concurrent Engineering Research Center (CERC) at the University of West Virginia. The center's work, funded by the U.S. Department of Defense, has resulted in many conferences, publications, and demonstrations of projects that use new computer software and organizational approaches.

GLOSSARY

Automated design tools. Systems to enable the use of computers by designers of products. These include software to do the design tasks of drafting and engineering analysis.

CALS. Computer-aided logistic support is a U.S. government initiative to eliminate paper and improve efficiency through the use of digital techniques and other methods such as concurrent engineering.

Colocation. When the work spaces of the members of a multidisciplinary design team are in the same physical space, which facilitates interaction between team members.

Integrated product development. The organization of product development with joint participation of all functional groups. Generally synonymous with the term *concurrent engineering.*

Multidisciplinary team. A group consisting of people from various disciplines. The particular makeup of the team depends on the specific product to be developed and the organization.

Over the wall. The tendency of design groups to toss the plans for new products developed "over the wall" to manufacturing without ensuring that the products can be manufactured. In other words, no feedback occurs from subsequent groups.

Quality function deployment. A technique to relate customer requirements to engineering characteristics, such as the physical design of a product by the use of a matrix-like diagram

Simultaneous engineering. To do several product development tasks at the same time, instead of sequentially. An example would be to plan the manufacturing processes in parallel with the physical product being designed. In some cases, simultaneous engineering is used synonymously with the term *concurrent engineering.*

BIBLIOGRAPHY

1. C.M. SAVAGE, *5th Generation Management,* Digital Press, New York, 1990.
2. R.J. SCHONBERGER, *World Class Manufacturing,* The Free Press, New York, 1986.
3. R.I. WINNER et al., *The Role of Concurrent Engineering in Weapons Systems Acquisition,* Institute for Defense Analysis, Alexandria, Va., 1988, Rep. No. R-338.
4. Y. AKAO, "Quality Function Deployment," *Quality Prog.* (Oct. 1983).
5. D. CLAUSING, "The House of Quality," *Harvard Bus. Rev.* (1986).
6. G. TAGUCHI, *Introduction to Quality Engineering,* UNIPUB-Kraus International Publications, White Plains, N.Y., 1986.
7. D.E. CARTER and B.S. BAKER, *Concurrent Engineering: The Product Development Environment for the 1990s,* Mentor Graphics, Portland, Ore., 1991.

Suggested Readings

W. BENNIS and B. NANUS, *Leaders,* Harper & Row, New York, 1985.

G. BOOTHROYD and P. DEWHURST, *Product Design for Assembly,* Boothroyd and Dewhurst, Inc., Wakefield, R.I., 1987

W.E. DEMMING, *Out of the Crisis,* MIT Center for Advanced Engineering, Cambridge, Mass., 1986.

D. HALL, "Concurrent Engineering (CE)," *CALS J.,* 96 (1992).

J.R. HAUSER and D. CLAUSING, "The House of Quality," *Harvard Bus. Rev.* (3), 63–73 (1988).

R.H. HAYES, S.C. WHEELRIGHT, and K.B. CLARK, *Dynamic Manufacturing,* The Free Press, New York, 1988.

J.M. JURAN, *Juran on Planning for Quality,* The Free Press, New York, 1988.

A. KUSIAK, *Concurrent Engineering: Automation, Tools, and Techniques,* John Wiley & Sons, Inc., New York, 1993.

NEVINS and WHITNEY, *Concurrent Design of Products and Processes,* McGraw-Hill Book Co., Inc., New York, 1989.

M. SCHRAGE, *Shared Minds: The New Technologies of Collaboration,* Random House, New York, 1990.

S.G. SHINA, *Concurrent Engineering and Design for Manufactured Products,* Van Nostrand Reinhold Co., Inc., New York, 1991.

J.P. WOMACK, D.T. JONES, and D. ROOS, *The Machine That Changed the World,* Rawson Associates, New York, 1990.

CHAPTER 3

Concurrent Engineering: Issues, Models, and Solution Approaches

Andrew Kusiak
University of Iowa

3.1 INTRODUCTION

Products and components are frequently designed without considering constraints imposed by a manufacturing system. With the introduction of concurrent engineering, design and manufacturing engineering are viewed as an integrated area. Perhaps the first and the most visible relationship between design and manufacturing has been manifested by the design-for-automated assembly (see, e.g., ref. 1). Most of the literature on design-for-manufacturing does not consider constraints related to manufacturing systems but rather deals with manufacturing processes. Although the area of design-for-manufacturing processes is still evolving and remains an important effort within concurrent engineering, there is a need to look at other aspects of manufacturing.

An aspect of manufacturing that offers a high potential for improvement of productivity is concerned with design-for-manufacturing operations. In fact, the cost of operating a manufacturing system can be significantly reduced if enough consideration is given to design of products and components. Improvements in design processes should be accompanied by effective design of manufacturing systems.

3.2 LITERATURE REVIEW

The literature concerned with concurrent engineering is rather extensive; however, the author is not aware of any references discussing to a meaningful extent the research outlined in this chapter. Numerous references either mention the topics of this proposal or are indirectly related to this proposal. Some of the representative papers are reviewed next.

Corbet (2) summarized the main issues involved in design for economic manufacturing as follows: establish the specification and target cost; identify the likely high cost areas; supply cost target information to design, manufacturing, and purchasing; prepare preliminary design, with inputs from manufacturing engineering; supply target cost to appropriate manufacturing and purchasing areas; and continue development, ensuring that costs incurred by modifications do not increase the target costs.

Stoll (3) identified the following two major goals of concurrent design: parallel development of the product and the manufacturing process, and evaluation of multiple product and process design alternatives. He defined concurrent design as a five-step process:

Step 1: Definition of functional requirements and constraints of the design problem and development of manufacturability design goals.
Step 2: Optimization of current product design methods using the principles of design-for-manufacturing and methodologies such as parts reduction assessment and robustness assessment.
Step 3: Identification of innovative new product and process concepts that are easy to manufacture.

Step 4: Evaluation, combination, and refinement of the results of step 3 into one of more "best" concepts.

Step 5: Selection of one or more best designs from the list preferred concepts developed in step 4.

A concurrent design process is supported by a number of different methodologies and tools that include design axioms, design-for-manufacturing guidelines, manufacturing process design rules, group technology, failure mode and effects analysis, and value analysis.

Foreman (4) identified four principal categories of tools that make a concurrent design process work: total quality control (Taguchi method, quality function deployment, process control planning), computer integrated manufacturing (simulation and analysis, electronic data interchange, networks and data communications, group technology, value engineering, solid modeling), just-in-time productivity improvement (design-for-manufacturing, including assembly, synchronous manufacturing, continuous improvement programs), and human systems (project management, communications, problem solving).

El-Gizaway and Hwang (5) developed a strategy for concurrent product and process design for aerospace components. This strategy involves the following activities: development of an initial design concept, definition of product constraints, knowledge-based manufacturability analysis, tentative process selection, product redesign for manufacture, and modular modeling of products and processes. The product design is evaluated with respect to productivity and cost objectives.

Cutkosky and Tenenbaum (6) described a methodology for concurrent product and process design and its implementation in a computational framework. The methodology assumes simultaneous design of a part or assembly and the process for producing it. The computational framework actually resembles a concurrent engineering term. It consists of a number of knowledge sources (human experts and expert systems) for simultaneous execution of various life-cycle activities of the product.

Assemblability is one of the most important life-cycle values of a product. The most popular approaches for design-for-assembly are the Hitachi assemblability evaluation method (7) and the design-for-assembly (1). The assemblability evaluation method (AEM) was developed to improve the design quality for better assembly. The AEM identifies weak points in the design by assessing the difficulty of assembly operations (through an assemblability evaluation score) and calculating the estimated assembly cost. The complete assembly operation of a design is a combination of elementary operations that are represented by symbols. There are about 20 elementary assembly operations, each assigned a penalty score that is a function of the penalty scores of all the elementary assembly operations involved. The estimated assembly cost is evaluated to verify the improvement of the design quality.

Design-for-assembly (DFA) is a method for quantitative assembly evaluation. The method involves two major steps: determine whether a part can be eliminated from the design to minimize the number of parts, and estimate the handling and assembly costs for each part to determine whether proposed design changes save in assembly cost. The handling and assembly costs are based on the type of the assembly process used—manual, robotic, or high speed automatic.

Brown et al. (8) proposed an integrated approach to quality engineering in support of design-for-manufacturing. The approach is based on the use of QFD for specification of customer attributes, product features and functions, component characteristics, process characteristics, and production operations. The QFD cascade allows for carrying new, difficult-to-meet, and important requirements from one stage to the next with more detailed investigation performed at each subsequent stage.

Rehg et al. (9) described a concurrent design system that integrates various life-cycle values of a product into the design process. The system framework consists of three types of design knowledge sources: design agents, or program modules for performing design activities; design critics, who analyze an evolving design from different aspects; and design translators, who are responsible for mapping one design representation into another.

Ishii et al. (10) proposed a general framework for the development of knowledge-based systems that allows for applying the concurrent design approach in the area of mechanical design. The underlying concept of this framework is called design compatibility analysis. The concept allows for analysis of the compatibility of a proposed design with design requirements and constraints and analysis of the proposed design elements' compatibility within the system. It also provides a justification for the results of the compatibility analysis and suggests design improvements.

Development of a prototype system for concurrent design based on the principle of cooperative work of specialists was described in Altenhof et al. (11). The system, which allows for incorporation of reliability, maintainability, and supportability requirements in a concurrent design process, consists of five elements: a human element (an individual or a team of experts that interacts with the system through a user interface), a CAD–CAE system for design of products, an estimator–predictor element (which receives the design feature and determines values of design-dependent parameters), an evaluator element (for evaluation of the current state of the product design), and a database of economic and physical factors.

A computer-aided environment for concurrent design was presented by Subramanyan and Lu (12). The environment, based on the model-based reasoning concept, provides capabilities for feature-based product modeling, manufacturability facility modeling, process design, and manufacturability analysis. Thompson and Lu (13) developed a methodology for representing and implementing the design rationale as a concept that enables concurrent execution of product and process design activities. The concept is illustrated by designing a prototype computer-based environment for concurrent design. The design rationale is represented in terms of design plans for future product and process activities and design constraints detected during the design process. The design rationale supports the four most important concepts in the system framework: product specifications, product designs, process designs, and manufacturing resources.

Molloy et al. (14) presented a rule-based approach for representation of design-for-assembly knowledge. The feature-based part representation is used for DFA analysis at the part level, ensuring that the part is easily handled and oriented, and at the product level for generation of the assembly sequence. The assembly sequence is determined by generating its disassembly sequence. The disassembly sequence is generated by identification of movable directions of each part.

Knight and Kim (15) described a system for assisting human experts in specific domains in performing concurrent design. The system applies the QFD method for product and process design. Four basic modules of the system perform the concept selection, component design, manufacturing process selection, and process parameter selection activities. Each of these activities is divided into three phases: specification of the problem, generation of possible solutions, and selection of the best alternative. The most recent coverage of many topics in concurrent engineering is presented in refs. 16 and 17.

3.3 CONCURRENCY ANALYSIS

Consider the design process of an electronic product that involves thousands of activities (the example is taken from an industrial company). The entire design process is divided into seven phases. Phase 3, product definition–requirements allocation, is used to illustrate the concepts presented in this chapter. The design activities involved in phase 3 are represented as the process graph shown in Figure 3.1. The shaded nodes in Figure 3.1 are the review activities. The matrix representation of the design process is shown in Figure 3.2. Applying the concurrency algorithm to the matrix in Figure 3.2, the matrix in Figure 3.3 is obtained.

Six groups of activities are identified: G-1 = {1, 2, 3, 4, C1, 14, 20, 25}; G-2 = {6, C2, 15, 28, 31}; G-3 = {7, 13, 22, 30}; G-4 = {16, 17, 29}; G-5 = {C3, 21, 32}; and G-6 = {23}. C1 = {12, 24}, C2 = {8, 5, 9, 10, 11, 26}, and C3 = {18, 19, 27} and are coupled activities. It is observed that the dependencies among groups of activities are indicated by elements outside the block diagonal matrices. For example, activities 2 and 4 in group G-1 should precede activities 6 and 9 in group G-2, respectively. Similarly, activities 12 and 24 in group G-1 have to precede activities 15, 28, and 31 in group G-2. One has to complete the activities 2, 4, 12, and 24 as soon as possible to begin the downstream activities in G-2. The groups of activities identified can be performed in parallel, if their predecessors have been completed.

The six groups of activities are represented as a process tree (Figure 3.4). A link between any two groups (levels) represents dependency between the corresponding groups. It is important to show activities in the upper level that impact the lower-level activities. For example, there are some dependencies between level 1 (G-1) and level 2 (G-2) activities. To begin the activities in level 2, activities 2, 4, 3, 13, 12 and 24 in level 1 have to be completed, because they impact the level 2 activities. A manager should monitor these activities to avoid delay in information transfer to the lower-level activities. Note that the temporal relationship among groups of activities leads to the Gantt chart in Figure 3.5. Some activities begin when their predecessors at the upper-level have been completed.

A dependency path is defined as the maximum length chain of activities in the process tree.

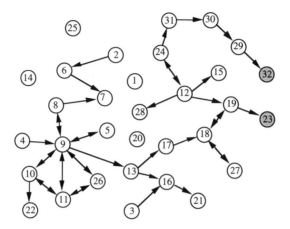

Figure 3.1. The process graph of phase 3.

According to this description, it is observed that the dependency path is 4–C2–13–17–C3–23. A project manager should focus on monitoring activities along the dependency path.

Concurrency analysis detects potential activities that can be performed in parallel. One may attempt to remove or redefine the dependency among groups of activities to increase the degree of concurrency. For example, if the dependency between activities 2 and 6 in Figure 3.3 is

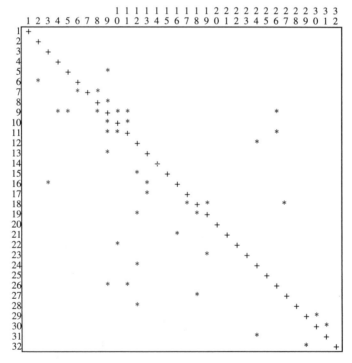

Figure 3.2. The activity–activity incidence matrix corresponding to the process graph in Figure 3.4.

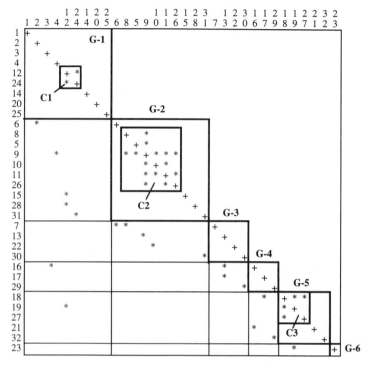

Figure 3.3. The transgularized activity–activity incidence matrix corresponding to the matrix in Figure 3.2.

removed, activity 6 can be performed in the first level. The concurrency of the design process increases. Note that the temporal relationship between groups of activities indicate that the groups overlap.

The benefits of the concurrency analysis are as follows (18):

- Potential groups of activities that can be performed in parallel are determined.
- A critical dependency path is determined without considering the time aspect.

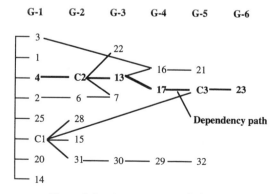

Figure 3.4. A process tree of phase 3.

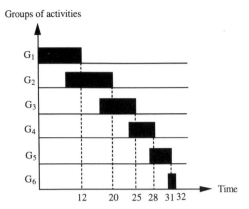

Figure 3.5. Gantt chart of the design process.

• The duration of product development time may be reduced, due to the increased degree of concurrency of the design process.

3.4 THE VALVE DESIGN PROBLEM

In this section, the concept of design negotiation is illustrated with the example of a poppet relief valve (19). Figure 3.6 shows the schematic of a poppet relief valve, which includes a poppet valve, poppet valve stem, and helical compression spring enclosed in a pipe (20). The poppet relief valve allows flow of the fluid from the inlet to the outlet when the pressure of the fluid exceeds a certain threshold pressure called the "cracking" pressure. If the pressure is greater than the cracking pressure, the fluid opens the poppet valve and holds it in equilibrium against a helical compression spring. If the pressure is below the cracking pressure, the poppet valve is held against a seal, thereby cutting off fluid flow from the inlet to outlet.

The goal of the design of a relief valve is to optimize the flow. This overall goal is expressed in terms of three subgoals: minimizing flow area, minimizing valve size, and minimizing the volume of spring. Three subgoals are assigned to three design agents (DAs), respectively: valve DA, enclosure DA, and spring DA (Figure 3.7). The valve DA is responsible for determining the configuration of valve with optimal flow based on the valve requirements. After completing the configuration design, the valve DA passes some parameters to the spring DA and the enclosure DA. The spring DA must design a spring to determine the cracking pressure, the distance the poppet will move, and the stability of the seal in the closed position. The size and the thickness of stem and enclosure are determined by enclosure DA. Note that valve DA dominates the entire design process, because it makes design decisions first and transfers the required infor-

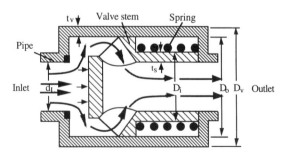

Figure 3.6. Schematic of a poppet relief valve.

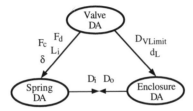

Figure 3.7. Collaboration among valve DA, spring DA, and enclosure DA.

mation to the agents in a downstream design process. In collaborative design, all agents are assumed to be benevolent, i.e., they assist each other to reach a compromise solution.

The variables and goals for each design agent are defined as follows:

Valve DA:
    Decision variables: d_L, C_v, C_f, K, L_i
    Aspiration levels: $D_{v\text{Limit}}$, $L_{i\text{Limit}}$
    Intermediate variables: d_o, F_c, d_{eo}, d, F_d
    Goal: $L_i \leq L_{i\text{Limit}}$, $D_v \leq D_{v\text{Limit}}$

Enclosure DA:
    Decision variables: D_V, S_p, A_1, A_2, t_s
    Aspiration level: $A_{1\text{Limit}}$, $A_{2\text{Limit}}$
    Intermediate variables: t_v, D_i, D_o
    Performance variable: D_V
    Goal: $D_V \leq D_{V\text{Limit}}$

Spring DA:
    Decision variables: D, d, G, r_{s1}, r_{s2}
    Aspiration levels: $r_{s1\text{Limit}}$, $r_{s2\text{Limit}}$, $V_{H\text{Limit}}$, $B_{S\text{Limit1}}$, $B_{S\text{Limit2}}$, $V_{S\text{Limit}}$
    Intermediate variables: K, C_s, K_s, S_s, N, L_s, L_f, D_o, D_i, C_{11}, C_{12}
    Performance variables: V_S, B_s
    Goal: $V_S \leq V_{S\text{Limit}}$, $B_S \leq B_{S\text{Limit}}$

Note that D_v is determined by the enclosure DA, and it is passed back to the valve agent who determines only an upper-bound of D_v. The aspiration level is defined as an acceptable range of a variable. It is assumed that each agent has its aspiration level that secures its interest.

The constraints and design variables are listed in ref. 20. The goal of each agent provides only a guidance for design. Decisions made in the upstream design process have impact on the decisions in the downstream design process. For example, the decisions made by valve DA impact the decisions made by the spring DA and enclosure DA.

3.5 DESIGN-FOR-RELIABILITY

Manufacturing engineers should design manufacturing systems that are highly reliable. The performance of a manufacturing system should not deviate from its nominal value. One way to increase the reliability of a manufacturing system is by providing duplicate manufacturing capabilities, not necessarily the duplicate machine tools. To design a reliable system, various design options need to be carefully evaluated before the final design decision is reached.

To illustrate the reliability issue in design of manufacturing systems, assume that the following processes must be performed in a manufacturing cell (MC).

   1. Milling (M)
   2. Drilling (D)
   3. Turning (T)

Due to the nature of the process plans for the parts designed, the machines must be arranged in a series: {milling machine, drilling machine, turning machine}. It has been estimated that to meet

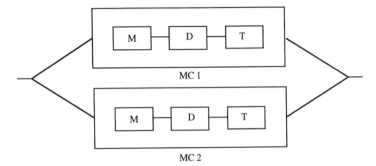

Figure 3.8. Design 1: each of the two manufacturing cells contains a series of three machines.

the product demand, at least two copies of each machine must be purchased. A question arises of how to arrange machines on the manufacturing floor.

The following designs are considered:

1. Place one of each milling machine, drilling machine, and turning machine in series in one manufacturing cell and provide two of such cells (Figure 3.8).
2. Place two machines of each kind in parallel and form a series combination of these parallel units (Figure 3.9)

Assume that the probability that the machines {M, D, T} will function without failure is {0.9, 0.95, 0.8}, respectively. The two design options can be evaluated on the basis of the reliability theory.

Design 1:
  It is required that at least one of the two manufacturing cells functions.
  P{at least one of the two cells functions}
  $= 1 - $ P{neither of the two cells functions}
  $= 1 - [(1 - r(\mathbf{p}))(1 - r(\mathbf{p}'))]$
  where p_i (p_i') is the probability that machine number i, which belongs to machine cell MC 1, (MC 2) functions
  P{at least one of the two cells functions}
  $= 1 - [(1 - (0.9 \cdot 0.95 \cdot 0.8))(1 - 0.9 \cdot 0.95 \cdot 0.8))]$
  $= 0.90$

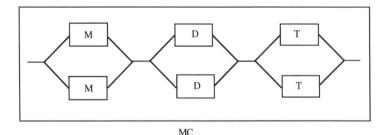

Figure 3.9. Design 2: arrange two machines of each kind in parallel and form a series of these parallel machines.

Design 2:
It is required that at least one of the two machines of each type functions.
P{the machine cell functions}
$$= r[1 - (1 - \mathbf{p})(1 - \mathbf{p}')]$$
$$= (1 - (0.1)(0.1))(1 - (0.05)(0.05))(1 - (0.2)(0.2))$$
$$= (0.99)(0.9975)(0.96)$$
$$= 0.948$$

From the calculations above, it is clear that replicating machines leads to a system with higher reliability than replicating cells. The design of a manufacturing system presented in Figure 3.9 is more reliable than the design in Figure 3.8.

3.6 DESIGN-FOR-RECONFIGURABILITY, -REPEATABILITY, AND -FLEXIBILITY

The ability of a manufacturing system to be reconfigured as the production mix changes is closely related to the type of manufacturing resources (hardware and software) selected and the arrangement of hardware on a manufacturing floor. To design a manufacturing system that can be reconfigured to meet the changing production demand, one must understand the relationship between the structure of products and the structure of a manufacturing system.

The reconfiguration of a manufacturing system may involve relatively minor changes to the system such as, for example, reassigning of operators, retooling of machines, or rearrangement of machine tools. To avoid frequent rearrangement of machine tools (which are expensive, especially in metal-cutting and mechanical assembly processes), manufacturing systems must be designed to allow for reconfiguration at minimum cost and physical movement of equipment. Also, the reconfigured system when brought back to its original configuration should ensure repeatability of production, i.e., manufacture products or components that meet all specifications regarding quality, standards, and so on.

One way to come up with a reconfigurable system is to design a core manufacturing facility that would be stable in time. Such a facility should be supported by machine tools, stations, and other resources that could be easily rearranged. As an example, consider the manufacturing system shown in Figure 3.10. A number of products are manufactured in the core manufacturing facility jointly with the supporting machine tools. The supporting machine tools can be arranged in 8 possible positions (see Figure 3.10). The layouts of the manufacturing floor for product 1 and product 2 are shown in Figure 3.11a. Machines 1, 2, 3, 4, and 5 are used. The manufacturing floor needs to be reconfigured when the product mix is changed to product 3, product 4, and product 5. The machines required for manufacturing the new product mix are machines 1, 6, and 7. The suitable positions for these machines are found according to a number of criteria.

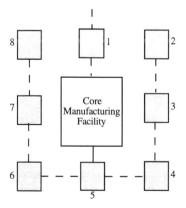

Figure 3.10. The core manufacturing facility with eight possible positions for supporting machines.

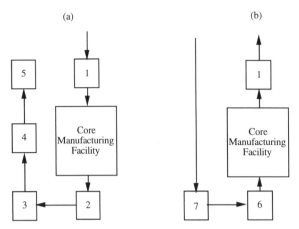

Figure 3.11. (a) Machine layout for products 1 and 2. (b) Machine layout after reconfiguration.

The layout after reconfiguration is shown in Figure 3.11b. The direction of flow of material is also changed in the new layout.

The reconfiguration involves assigning machines required for the new product mix to the eight available locations with certain constraints. The machines and locations can be represented as vertices of a bipartite graph, and the problem of assigning machines to these locations can be represented as a bipartite matching problem. Edges are drawn from a machine vertex incident onto the feasible location vertices (Figure 3.12). The feasible location for each machine can be determined based on the material handling system used. The weight assigned to each of the edges drawn between machine vertex and the location vertex is determined based on the cost of material movement. The solution of the matching problem provides the minimum cost assignment of machines to the locations.

The approach described above provides only a conceptual framework for dealing with design of products and components for reconfigurability and repeatability. Industrial scenarios of this problem involve a number of qualitative constraints that must be considered jointly with

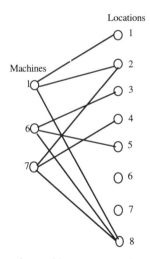

Figure 3.12. The reconfiguration problem represented as a bipartite matching problem.

a number of quantitative constraints. An artificial intelligence approach can be used to handle the qualitative constraints (see, e.g., ref. 21).

3.7 DESIGN-FOR-PRODUCTIVITY, -SCHEDULING, -SETUP REDUCTION, AND -INVENTORY MANAGEMENT

Products and parts have traditionally been designed without consideration of the operations aspects of their manufacture. Designs of manufacturing systems are frequently driven by savings of the capital investment without giving consideration to the long-term savings from operating those systems. Planning, scheduling, inventory management, setup reduction, and other operational issues of manufacturing have become important design considerations with the advances in concurrent engineering. It appears that many operational difficulties can be eliminated by proper design of products and manufacturing systems, rather than by development of costly and complex software for making operational decisions. One must remember that design has a great impact on the product life-cycle cost; however, the design cost is only a fraction of the product life-cycle cost. The short-term savings from the investment in the manufacturing resources should not overshadow the long-term savings from operating manufacturing systems. The impact of design decisions on the operating cost of manufacturing systems might be difficult or even impossible to reverse without costly redesigns.

3.8 DESIGN-FOR-PRODUCTIVITY

To discuss the impact of design decisions on operational issues, such as the setup cost, material handling cost, and throughput rate, one must understand the relationship between the structure of products and the structure of a manufacturing system. This relationship is discussed next.

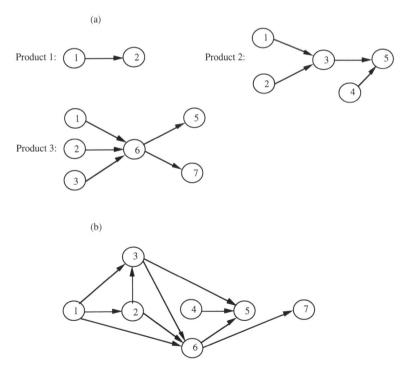

Figure 3.13. (a) Directed graph G_p for each product p = 1, 2, 3, 4. (b) The superimposed graph G.

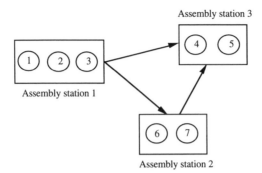

Figure 3.14.   A design of assembly system generated from graph G in Figure 13b.

Consider the design of a product (assembly) with a number of assembly operations. For each product, a production volume has been determined. Based on the type of operations and the relationship among them, an assembly system is designed. It is important to estimate early in the design process the impact of the structure of products on the structure of an assembly system.

Modifying the structure of a product being designed, one can generate a desired design of an assembly system. In turn, the extent to which the structure of products should be modified is determined by the analysis of the structure of an assembly system. Consider the following example.

Four products with the assembly structure shown in Figure 3.13a have been designed. The structure of a product $p = 1, 2, 3, 4$ is represented by a directed graph G_p. Each node in the directed graph G_p represents an assembly operation required by product p and an edge represents the precedence relationship between two assembly operations. Because the four products are to be assembled in the same assembly system, the graphs in Figure 3.13a can be combined into a superimposed graph G (Figure 3.13b). Based the superimposed graph G in Figure 3.13b, a design of the assembly system in Figure 14 is obtained. Assume that the assembly system in Figure 3.14 is balanced, i.e., the capacity constraint at each assembly station is not exceeded.

Analyzing the design in Figure 3.14 and the product structures in Figure 3.13a, one can see that the design of assembly system in Figure 3.14 can be improved by modifying the structure of

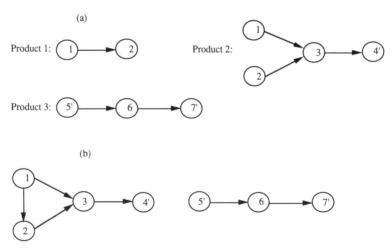

Figure 3.15.   **(a)** Modified product design. **(b)** Modified superimposed graph G'.

Assembly station 1

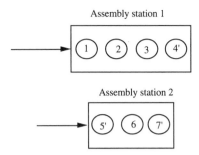

Assembly station 2

Figure 3.16. The modified design of the assembly system.

some products. Assume that the structure of product 2 can be modified by eliminating operations 4 and 5 and incorporating an operation 4', and the structure of product 3 can be modified by eliminating operations 1, 2 and 3, and adding operation 5' and 7'. The modified product designs and the corresponding superimposed graph G' are shown in Figure 3.15.

The modified design of the assembly system is shown in Figure 3.16. Because the flow between assembly stations 1, 2, and 3 has been eliminated, the new assembly system includes two stations with some duplicate operations. The operational characteristics of the new system (Figure 3.16) such as the setup cost, material handling cost, throughput rate, and reliability are far superior than the design in Figure 3.14. Of course, the above discussed considerations apply to processes other than assembly, such as machining any fabrication.

3.9 DESIGN-FOR-SCHEDULING

To illustrate the impact of design decisions on one of many operational aspects, an example of a design rule aimed at improving schedulability of components is formulated. Design Rule 1: assign parts (products) to the existing machining (assembly) cells. A manufacturing system may consist of a number of group-technology cells. In the case in which enough production capacity is available, parts should be designed to fit the machine cells (Figure 3.17).

Cellular scheduling applies to physical as well as logical (virtual) machine cells (for discussion of cellular manufacturing see ref. 22). The physical cells are obtained by locating machines in the adjacent locations, while the logical cells are visible to the information system only and they are created without physical rearrangement of machines (stations). Details of design for scheduling are discussed in ref. 23.

3.10 CONCLUSIONS

In this chapter, concurrent engineering was viewed from the manufacturing systems perspective. The following issues were discussed:

1. Modeling the design process.
2. Rules for design-for-reliability, reconfigurability, repeatability, and flexibility of manufacturing systems.

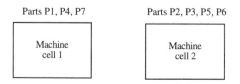

Figure 3.17. A cellular manufacturing system.

3. Rules for design-for-productivity, design-for-scheduling, design-for-setup reduction, and design-for-inventory reduction as well as rules considering other operational issues of manufacturing systems.

Acknowledgments

The research presented in this chapter has been partially supported by the research contract DAAE07-93-CR080 from the U.S. Army Tank Automotive Command and contracts from four industrial sponsors. Four doctoral students U. Belhe, W. He, R. Vojosevic, and J. Wang have contributed to some of the ideas presented.

BIBLIOGRAPHY

1. G. BOOTHROYD, C. POLI, and L.E. MURCH, *Automatic Assembly*, Marcel Dekker, Inc., New York, 1982.
2. J. CORBET, "Design for Economic Manufacture," *Ann.* **35**(1), 93–97 (1986).
3. H.W. STOLL, "Simultaneous Engineering in the Conceptual Design Phase" in *Simultaneous Engineering*, Society of Manufacturing Engineering, Dearborn, Mich., 1990, pp. 165–171.
4. J.W. FOREMAN, "Gaining Competitive Advantage by Using Simultaneous Engineering to Integrate Your Engineering, Design, and Manufacturing Resources" in *Simultaneous Engineering*, Society of Manufacturing Engineers, Dearborn, Mich., 1990, pp. 92–105.
5. A.S. EL-GIZAWAY and J.-Y. HWANG, *A Strategy for Concurrent Design of Aerospace Components*, paper presented at the Winter Annual Meeting of the ASME, San Francisco, Calif., Dec. 1989.
6. M.R. CUTKOSKY and J.M. TENENBAUM, "A Methodology and Computational Framework for Concurrent Product and Process Design," *Mech. Machine Theory* **25**(3), 365–381 (1990).
7. S. MIYAKAWA, T. OHASHI, S. INOSHITA, and T. SHIGEMURA, *The Hitachi Assemblability Method and Its Applications*, paper presented at the Second International Conference on Product Design for Assembly, 1986.
8. A.D. BROWN, P.R. HALE, and J. PARNABY, "An Integrated Approach to Quality Engineering in Support of Design for Manufacture" in J. Corbet, M. Dooner, J. Malleka, and C. Pym, eds. *Design for Manufacture: Strategies, Principles and Techniques*, Addison-Wesley Publishing Co., Inc., Reading, Mass., 1991, pp. 146–162.
9. J. REHG, A. ELFES, S. TELUKDAR, R. WOODBURY, M. EISENBERGER, and R. EDHAL, "CASE: Computer-Aided Simultaneous Engineering" in J.S. Gero, ed., *Artificial Intelligence in Engineering*, Elsevier, New York, 1988, pp. 339–360.
10. K. ISHI, "Modeling of Concurrent Engineering" in A. Kusiak, ed., *Concurrent Engineering: Automation, Tools, and Techniques*, John Wiley & Sons, Inc., New York, 1993, pp. 19–39.
11. J.L. ALTENHOF, W.J. FABRYCKY, M.-F. FENG, and R.G. MITCHINER, "Concurrent Mechanical System Design: A Computer-Aided Design Demonstration" in E.J. Haug ed., *Proceedings of the First Annual Symposium on Mechanical System Design in a Concurrent Engineering*, The University of Iowa, Iowa City, 1989, pp. 497–512.
12. S. SUBRAMANYAN and S.C.-Y LU, *Computer-Aided Simultaneous Engineering for Components Manufactured in Small and Medium Lot Sizes*, paper presented at the Winter Annual Meeting of the ASME, San Francisco, Calif., Dec. 1989.
13. J.B. THOMPSON and S.C.-Y. LU, *Representing and Using Design Rationale in Concurrent Product and Process Design*, paper presented at the Winter Annual Meeting of the SME, San Francisco, Calif., Dec. 1989.
14. E. MOLLOY, H. TANG, and J. BROWNE. "Design for Assembly within Concurrent Engineering," *Ann. CIRP* **40**(1), 107–110 (1991).
15. T.P. KNIGHT and S.T. KIM, "A Knowledge System for Integrated Product Design." *J. Intel. Manufact.* **2**(1), 17–25 (1991).
16. A. KUSIAK, ed., *Intelligent Design and Manufacturing*, John Wiley & Sons, Inc., New York, 1992.

17. A. KUSIAK, ed., *Concurrent Engineering: Automation, Tools, and Techniques,* John Wiley & Sons, Inc., New York, 1993.

18. A. KUSIAK and J. WANG, "Efficient Organizing of Design Activities," *Int. J. Prod. Res.* **31**(4), 753–769 (1993).

19. J.L. LYONS, *Lyons' Valve Designer's Handbook,* Van Nostrand Reinhold Co., Inc., New York, 1982.

20. S.M. KANNAPAN and K.M. MARSHEK, "An Approach to Parametric Machine Design and Negotiation in Concurrent Engineering" in A. Kusiak, ed., *Concurrent Engineering: Automation, Tools, and Techniques,* John Wiley & Sons, Inc., New York, 1993, pp. 509–533.

21. K.I. KAMEYAMA, "Real-Time Constraint Checking in the Design Process" in A. Kusiak, ed., *Concurrent Engineering: Automation, Tools, and Techniques,* John Wiley & Sons, Inc., New York, 1993, pp. 111–130.

22. A. KUSIAK, *Intelligent Manufacturing Systems,* Prentice-Hall, Inc., Englewood Cliffs, N.J., 1990.

23. A. KUSIAK and W. HE, "Design of Components for Schedulability," *Eur. J. Operation. Res.,* in press (1994).

CHAPTER 4

Design Decision Analysis and Expert Systems in Concurrent Engineering

JOSÉ M. SÁNCHEZ
Instituto Tecnologico y de Estudios
Superiores de Monterey

JOHN W. PRIEST and LISA J. BURNELL
Automation and Robotic Research
Institute

4.1 INTRODUCTION

In the book *In Search for Excellence* (1) numerous references are made to the fact that it is still possible to finish projects under budget and on time. One of the instances singled out repeatedly is the success of the "skunk works" at Lockheed. An analysis of that approach reveals many factors that contributed to its success. Some of those were the reliance on the best technical expertise available and off-the-shelf solutions. The question is, can such efforts succeed today when systems are so much more complex and when technology changes so rapidly? An understanding of the decision analysis process in concurrent engineering environments is one part of this solution.

Concurrent engineering (CE) is the simultaneous, interactive, and interdisciplinary involvement of design, manufacturing, and field-support engineers to reduce development cycle time while ensuring design performance, high quality and reliable products, and support responsiveness. The key to successful concurrent engineering deployment is the front end, or early involvement of these interdisciplinary functions to improve quality, reduce cost, and shorten design cycle time. Producibility, reliability, and quality start with the design, at the beginning of the industrial process, and must be pursued continuously throughout the development, test, and manufacture of the product (2). This process is not a series of discrete events but requires a high degree of coordination of engineering disciplines, which are interdependent and interrelated within the total design element. CE breaks down the traditional functional barriers by integrating team members across different business entities within an organization. Each team member is involved in all aspects of product development from the very beginning, and each member has a respected voice in this development process.

A regular characteristic of an engineering team approach is that different groups of engineers might be knowledgeable in a particular subject and may work on a project with their own agenda. Thus several potential conflicts may appear that are unrecognized until product manufacturing or product use begins. Undesirable effects such as a high number of engineering change notices (ECNs) or long product development cycles can be caused by this lack of communication and coordination. To reduce or even eliminate these problems, the development and deployment of an effective CE approach requires the following:

- Flexible multiattribute decision models to represent the process by which a product development team could simultaneously accomplish design debate, negotiation, and conflict resolution.
- Knowledge representation schemata and tools to support and implement them, providing the integration requirements imposed by a CE context.

51

- Tools that facilitate the simultaneous communication of several engineering and nonengineering disciplines.
- Quantitative and qualitative tools that measure the impact of decisions on product cost, performance, reliability, etc. Assessment tools could be used to provide an engineering team with the capability to judge the relative merits of various design attributes and to evaluate alternatives with respect to life cycle implications.

Recently, the benefits of combining decision analysis with expert systems have been recognized. A number of works have been published in the last few years suggesting possible techniques for improving the state of decision analysis systems by merging them with expert systems (3–8). Intelligent decision support systems (IDSSs) are a combination of standard decision analysis methods and artificial intelligence (AI) techniques that can provide powerful tools to a product development group. This chapter describes the general characteristics of the decision-making process in concurrent engineering scenarios. It also presents considerations for applying artificial intelligence techniques and design decision analysis as viable mechanisms for developing a concurrent engineering decision support system.

4.2   CONCURRENT ENGINEERING

Historically, company departments have been isolated functionally from one another, with product development design and manufacturing progressing in a sequential manner (Figure 4.1). Instead of designing and engineering the product in a functional and manufacturable configuration at the very outset of product inception, improvements were made at a later date in the form of ECNs, resulting in an almost endless cycle of nonvalue added labor. This traditional design approach has generated friction among the different project participants. Each functional area worked under a fixed schedule, fixed budget, and unique objectives and measures. If process engineering requests that design engineering make a component design change that would simplify the assembly process, a typical response might be "We're out of time and out of money." This mentality is commonly referred to as the "throw-it-over-the-wall" approach to conducting business.

The term *concurrent engineering* or *simultaneous engineering* (SE) is the watch word for the world-class manufacturing companies in the commercial as well as government and defense industries. This is noted in an Institute for Defense Analysis (IDA) report (9), in which CE is defined as "a systematic approach to the integrated, concurrent design of products and their related processes, including manufacture and support. This approach is intended to cause the developers, from the outset, to consider all elements of the product life cycle from conception through disposal, including quality, cost, schedule, and user requirements."

Benefits are realized quickly by using CE concepts in the form of reducing direct labor costs, life cycle time, inventory, scrap, rework, and engineering changes. More intangible benefits include part number reductions, process simplification, and process step reduction (10). CE has also proved to be a valuable tool for maintaining competitiveness in today's ever-changing and expanding world market. For example, the Japanese are already leaders in implementing CE design. Japanese companies require half the time that U.S. companies do to deliver major products, such as aircraft and automobiles (11). This success is attributable to the fact that CE contributed significantly to the reduction in the product development cycle.

Establishing a CE program is not without drawbacks. It requires acceptance by the employees but, more so, the total commitment and backing by management. CE requires a great deal of planning and a good communication–data transfer framework that must be firmly established within the organization. For example, computer hardware and software tools and local area networks must be compatible with one another. Acquiring new or additional computing and data-processing tools must be researched thoroughly to maintain this continuity. These are by no means the exclusive limitations to this approach. Furthermore, work teams are not always the ideal way to organize work for every type of operation. If an organization's product or service requires a significant labor component, it likely would benefit from the work team approach. The question to consider is whether an increase in human efficiency will generate an increase in productivity. In a process chemical plant, for example, "where two workers with very specialized skills watch over 4 million dollars worth of equipment, improving the productivity of those two enormously is going to have a negligible overall impact" (12).

The key to implementing a successful CE program is involving all departments within the corporation in a team approach, starting at concept design. In addition to internal company

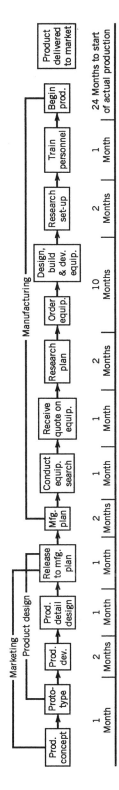

Figure 4.1. Product development process.

53

considerations, building a mutual partnership based on trust and integrity with external suppliers and vendors also contributes to a systematic approach for CE.

4.3   DESIGN DECISION ANALYSIS FOR CONCURRENT ENGINEERING

Design decision analysis (DDA) can be considered as the process by which a product development team contemplates and evaluates a choice of actions in an uncertain and multiattribute design environment. Although the process may help to generate new design alternatives, an analysis is typically performed on a prespecified set of alternative designs. The goal of DDA is to recommend a given design or to show that all currently considered designs are below overall expectations. Some of the many design elements and analyses involved are shown in Figure 4.2. A balance between performance, technical risk, cost, schedule, producibility, reliability, and other attributes should be established. All trade-off studies need to address the possible impacts of design decisions on all aspects at the appropriate level of detail. To be most effective, design decision analysis must be an integral, timely part of the detailed design process. To that end, a DDA for concurrent engineering must be defined based on a multiattribute decision structure that includes a clear set of guidelines for goal definition, identification and analysis of design criteria, weighting evaluation criteria, alternative identification and assessment, sensitivity analysis, and alternative selection.

Goal Definition

The first step in any trade-off analysis must be the definition of the goal to be achieved. Goals identify important product and life-cycle issues that must be considered during the concurrent development of a product. As an example, a system's goal can be identified with one of the following categories (13):

Goal	*Focus*
Develop a product in the shortest period of time	Development cycle time
Select a product design based on the capability of the product to meet customer's requirements	Product performance issues
Select products for which design attributes increase the system's capability to accommodate easily design changes	Design flexibility
Select product designs that lead to a minimum cost	Product cost

Identifying the design goals in the very beginning of a design decision analysis for concurrent engineering will allow more options to be considered, thus increasing the likelihood that the best selection will be made.

Identification and Analysis of Design Criteria

Evaluation attributes or criteria are management and engineering design's measures (i.e., minimize total assembly time) used to evaluate the degree to which a design alternative can achieve a goal. Product evaluation criteria must be those that are quantifiable and relevant to achieving a preestablished design goal. In a CE environment these criteria represent the agreement of the CE development team and depend on management policies and the manufacturing environment. Although the number of issues related with the product development life cycle can be extensive, the following two criteria are given as examples.

- *Design Producibility.* Level in which a product can be easily manufactured with the available technology, on time, and at the minimum cost.
- *Technical Risk.* The acceptable level of risk that a company is willing to take when developing a new product.

The validity of a selected design criteria should be appreciated based on its contribution to a system's goal, its facility to be independently handled at several levels of product detail, the possibility to be measured or estimated with reasonable effort, and its capability to be used to differentiate solutions without bias between alternatives.

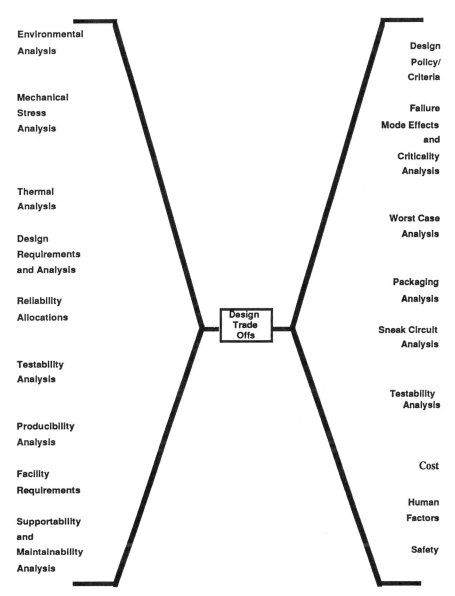

Figure 4.2. Relationship of design elements in trade-off studies.

Weighting Evaluation Criteria

Each criterion needs a weighting factor to determine the relative importance in the final value of a potential design alternative. One common method used in weighting decision criteria is a pairwise comparison (14), by which all criteria are compared with each other two at a time. For each comparison, the criterion judged more important in differentiating the alternative, receives a score of 1, while the other receives a score of 0. Once all comparisons are made, weights are assigned using the following formula (14):

TABLE 4.1. Relative Weights for a Pairwise Comparison

Criteria	Decisions 1	2	3	N^a	Weight
Technical risk	1	1		3	0.50
Producibility	0		1	2	0.33
Cost		0	0	1	0.17
Totals				6	*1.00*

$^a N$ = the number of 1's + 1.

weight = (number of 1's + 1)/(total decisions + number of criteria)

For example, the relative weights assigned to three product design criteria (technical risk, producibility, and cost) using a pairwise comparison are shown in Table 4.1. Other weight elicitation methods, such as hypothetical trade-offs or conjoint measurement, could also be used. To make trade-offs, the expert must know the range of values each criterion can take on. Because the decision model is to be used on a class of designs, as opposed to a one-time analysis of a single design, the possible individual criterion values are defined over the range from minimum, or worst, acceptable to maximum, or best, plausible.

By using a multiattribute analysis, objective and subjective selection criteria are incorporated to provide a single numerical value that represents the relative worth of each alternative. This approach overcomes the inherent burden of highly mathematical models and the weakness of most qualitative analysis.

Alternative Identification and Assessment

After establishing a baseline for design requirements and goals, the next step in the concurrent decision-making process is the identification, analysis, and evaluation of design alternatives. Product size, complexity, the constraints on the product design, and the needed manufacturing technology are among the factors that ensure that every specified alternative is sufficiently distinct to allow differentiation.

A utility function can be used to describe a relationship between a set of states of same dimension of value (e.g., cost, quality, process tolerances, schedule, and reliability) and the degree of utility corresponding to that state. Thus the value or utility of each alternative can be calculated as a measure of preference for various values of a variable, measuring the relative strength of desirability that the decision maker has for those values. Suppose $\{a_1, a_2, \ldots, a_m\}$ are the available alternatives (i.e., designs) in a decision problem, $\{X_1, X_2, \ldots, X_N\}$ is a set of attributes or criteria, and x_n denotes a specific level of X_n. Then if the axioms of decision theory are to be obeyed, the alternative a_m should be selected that maximizes the expected utility

$$E[u \mid a_m] = \int_{X_1} \cdots \int_{X_N} u(x_1, x_2, \ldots, x_N) f_M(x_1, x_2, \ldots, x_N) \, dx_1, dx_2 \ldots dx_N$$

where f_m is the probability density function over $\{X_1, X_2, \ldots, X_N\}$, given that a_m is selected, and u is a utility function. Utility will then represent the preference that the CE team has adopted for a particular parameter (3). For each alternative, the steps involved are

1. Because of the inherent difficulty in assessing an n-dimensional utility function, attempts are generally made to structure a CE model such that utility functions can be defined for individual attributes (15). If certain preferential and independence conditions hold, then $u(x_1, x_2, \ldots, x_n)$ has the form of an additive utility function:

$$u(x) = \sum_{n=1}^{N} k_n u_n(x_n) f_n(x_n), \quad 0 \leq u_n(x_n) \leq 100$$

where $u_n(x_n)$ is a utility function over a single attribute x_n; $f_n(x_n)$ is a probability density function over x, and k_n are scaling constants (weights), which sum to 1. For example, for

Observed utility weight & performance value

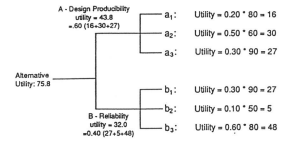

A = Design producibility = f (a_1 , a_2 , a_3); B = reliability = f (b_1 , b_2 , b_3)

a_1 =	Tooling Requirements	b_1 =	Warranty cost as a percent of selling cost
a_2 =	Auto-insertable components usage	b_2 =	Average repair time
a_3 =	Components spacing & orientation	b_3 =	Failure rate

Figure 4.3. Alternative evaluation process.

alternative A at criterion i, let u = utility, k = criterion weight, and x = performance value, then

$$u_i(a) = k_i x_i(a)$$

2. For all other criteria, the alternative's utility is the product of a criterion's weight and the sum of alternative values for all that criterion's subcriteria. The utility value at criterion j with n subcriteria (i = 1 to n) for alternative A is given by

$$u_j(a) = k_j \sum k_i x_i(a)$$

The example in Figure 4.3 shows a design alternative that is evaluated based on a combined effect of design producibility and reliability.

Sensitivity Analysis

Sensitivity analysis is recommended to refine a concurrently developed design model. It can help validate the model and identify model improvement possibilities. In a sensitivity analysis, uncertain quantities in the model, such as new assessment criteria, weights, or utility function definitions are varied to determine their impact on the final result. This is often called what-if analysis. Model reduction possibilities may also become apparent by considering the global weights of each criterion. This is a measure of the impact an individual criterion has on the final result. Thus a criterion that has an insignificant effect on the final analysis can be eliminated to reduce the design model complexity.

Alternative Selection

A CE approach for selecting a preferred alternative could be based on the maximization of expected utility (MEU) principle. Maximum expected utility is the philosophical belief and primary axiom that underlines decision theory and can be summarized as follows: given a set of preferences expressed as a utility function, beliefs expressed as probability distributions, and a set of decision alternatives, a decision-making team should choose that course of action that maximizes utility. Where probability theory provides a framework for coherent assignment of beliefs with incomplete information, utility theory introduces a set of principles for consistency among preferences and decisions. MEU is highly defensible and broad in scope. However, it is specifically designed to deal with preference and uncertainty (16). The result of the decision analysis is a single numeric value that identifies the best alternative as the one with the highest score.

4.4 MULTIATTRIBUTE DECISION STRUCTURE

Concurrent decision making is an increasingly complex problem, especially in areas such as strategic planning and product development. Such decision analysis requires a series of decision scenarios that, although repetitive, might need meaningful attention on the unique aspects of each specific situation. In different manufacturing firms, for example, product development decisions require attention not only to the unique characteristics of the field but also to the unique preferences of company.

An analysis of the concurrent engineering design problem itself reveals the significance of the decisions involved in product development. That is, to produce good designs, good decisions should be made. Thus it can be concluded that an effective support for concurrent engineering environments must support all the decision aspects of the product development life cycle. This leads to the suggestion that a multiattribute decision structure should be used to develop a concurrent engineering approach. An example of a viable multiattribute decision framework is shown in Figure 4.4.

A decision analysis using a multiattribute decision approach allows the CE team to contemplate a choice of action in a multiattribute environment. They clarify choices by using systematic deductive analysis and help to establish a basic framework for debate, negotiation, and conflict resolution. Although a multiattribute model for CE is a valid approach, a disadvantage

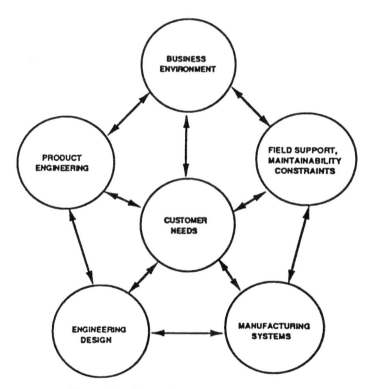

Figure 4.4.   CE multiattribute decision framework.

of the method is that it creates only a model of the real world; therefore, it is subjected to several limitations:

- The validity of the results is limited by the quality of available data.
- The choice of alternatives, selection criteria, and weighting factors can bias the results.
- The number of alternatives and criteria that can be evaluated is limited by the ability to analyze concurrently multiple options.

It also is important to recognize that a multiattribute concurrent decision analysis is not usually intended to be completely descriptive or autonomous. It is difficult to be descriptive, because most people do not express their ideas systematically, and the analysis is usually not autonomous, because of the unique aspects of the decision and preferences of the decision maker.

4.5 COMPUTING TECHNOLOGIES

Computer-aided tools are available today to assist engineers with the search for optimal solutions of some factors (e.g., structural analysis, design for assembly, circuit time analysis, etc.). In addition, computerized prototypes that are based on expert systems have been designed to capture expert knowledge and deliver it to those less experienced in that particular field. With the recent advances in computing technologies, information-processing theories, and engineering techniques, it may be feasible to develop an integrated concurrent design system that satisfies the needs of a specific domain. Enabling technologies may include those for enhanced information sharing–comparing, automated management of requirements and constraints, and integration of dissimilar computer equipment. Computing technologies such as artificial intelligence, local area networks (LAN), and simulation are emerging as important components of design systems. A CE system built from these technologies can have the capabilities for syntheses and extensive analysis of product and processes design, for the graphical depiction of the product and processes, for the real-time monitoring and controlling of a part production, and for the creation of the physical product.

Expert Systems

Decisions are becoming increasingly complex, especially in such areas as strategic planning, manufacturing management, and engineering design. These areas present decision problems that require special consideration to the unique aspects of every specific situation. To address design decision problems such as design decision complexity, debate, negotiation, and conflict resolution, several researchers in the area of product development are looking to the methods and tools of AI. The hope is that this technology will provide the needed leverage. Although a great deal of progress has been made in applying expert systems techniques in areas such as design for producibility (15, 17), computer aided process planning (18, 19), and intelligent decision support systems (3), the published results have made limited use of knowledge representation or new knowledge-based programming tools. A predominant approach seems to be one of recording if–then rule structures generally, with an attendant loss of efficiency and flexibility.

As artificial intelligence becomes more and more popular as a tool for supporting the baseline of a decision-making process, it becomes increasingly clear that AI techniques can be used to provide support for managing the multiattribute decision analysis of concurrent engineering environments. An approach using AI techniques with great potential for CE is an intelligent decision support system.

Intelligent Decision Support Systems

A new approach to CE and design can be adopted by combining decision theory and expert systems. As a result, a system can be developed that is based on a strong theoretical foundation yet is easy to use. Such a system would have the ability to integrate effectively diverse and conflicting objectives to determine the relative desirability of a product design.

IDSS is a software tool useful in making decisions involving, for example, product design alternatives, technological risk evaluation, and manufacturing strategic planning. An IDSS stores not only data but also decision-making models built from a set of rules and guidelines needed for making structured or unstructured decisions. While structured decisions are those for which we can provide the information requirements in advance, because we can predict they will happen, unstructured decisions cannot be predicted. This results in a difficulty to define what information will be needed to assist the decision-making process. An IDSS can be of great support in dealing with unstructured decisions.

Critical to any intelligent decision support system is its capability to store complex decision models (knowledge) and its capability to retrieve those models easily. The ability to implement efficiently such a knowledge of addressable characteristic has immediate applications in CE environments. An approach to represent complex decision models and conflict-resolution schemata is a neural net. Neural nets have great potential in CE, for which many objectives could be pursued in parallel, using high computation rates. Instead of solving a problem following a serial approach, a neural net model could explore many competing design criteria simultaneously, using parallel nets conformed of several decision models connected by links with variable weights. Thus AI, neural nets, and DSS could be keys for solving current design decision analysis problems of CE scenarios.

Local Area Networks

One of the desirable characteristics in a CE environment is the ability simultaneously to share data or information (inline or offline) among the members of a product development team. This capability can be provided by using a LAN. The purpose of a local area network is to distribute computer systems to place processing power where it is needed in a factory. In this scenario, the term *distributed* is the opposite of using a host-type architecture, in which a centralized computer system supports the entire spectrum of manufacturing functions. Incorporating LAN technology in CE systems, however, requires additional research work on communicating product design data, defining exchange formats and interface standards for communicating data, implementing plantwide computer control, using engineering databases for decision making, and using browsing techniques for continuous product design reviews.

Simulation

Modeling and simulation are engineering tools for evaluating and optimizing engineering design and products. Simulation allows engineers to do trade-off studies before the product is built, so that the design can be optimized. Simulation also can be used to increase the understanding of how the product interfaces with the environment. This understanding gives the designer a better appreciation of the benefits, costs, and attributes of each design requirement.

There are several reasons for using simulation in concurrent engineering environments. First, for developing a new product there might not be another convenient approach. If a mathematical model is rapidly available or if a mathematical solution is obvious, this option will probably take less effort and will have a lower cost. Simulation can be seen as an alternative when analytical solutions are not easily available. Although simulation is a viable tool for CE, the biggest challenge for its use is to develop a simulation model with effective communication between the various disciplines involved in CE.

4.6   THE CEPCB SYSTEM

The concurrent engineering for printed circuit board assembly (CEPCB) system has been developed by CIM Systems, Inc., as a proof of concept prototype that can assist a company's CE methodology for developing printed circuit boards (20). Although the long-term objective of this effort is to build a fully integrated CE decision support system, the research effort has been concentrated on:

- A selected group of printed circuit board designs with a defined size limit.
- A limited number of through-hole components.
- An identifiable group of assembly processes suitable for PCBs with defined capabilities and ranges of application.

- An identifiable group of machine types with defined assembly capabilities.
- A methodology that identifies potential producibility problems on a feature-by-feature basis, scores these evaluations, and ranks them with a global design producibility index (DPI) technique.

A series of PCB development methodologies can be established to meet a CE scenario or to meet the unique goals of a particular group of users. However, there are some basic issues that can apply to any CE approach that was considered as a goal for this project (21):

- Identify cannot-build situations.
- Identify areas of technical risk.
- Optimize the product through design parameter trade-off studies.
- Compare competing design alternatives.

Implementing such a dynamic product development initiative requires a heuristic decision-based approach that combines computer power with the reasoning of an engineering team.

System Conceptual Design

CEPCB is an intelligent decision support system based on a concurrent multiattribute trade-off analysis methodology. Its purpose is to assist a concurrent engineering team in selecting the best available option in environments involving multiple, conflicting objectives. The goal of the project is to develop a software system that allows all the disciplines contributing to the product development to share complex design and manufacturing information needed in the concurrent engineering process. The domain for this cooperative effort is targeted for PCB assembly and is shown conceptually.

The tool's primary value is that it integrates knowledge from traditionally separated department and organizations in a concise form and content. Its multifaceted database of knowledge crosses all the boundaries relevant to the production of PCBs, from conceptual design to final testing. The system then applies its knowledge to derive producibility metrics and to support CE in the following categories: electrical and electronic issues; standards, board layout, and manufacturing capabilities; part selection and control, quality, and reliability; and maintainability, cost, and technical risk. The principal software modules of the system are shown in Figure 4.5.

Considerable information about components for a PCB is made available by CAD. The system has a CAD interface module that is capable of reading a bill of materials (BOM) directly from a supported CAD system. Each component on the BOM is checked against the "corporate" component database to warn the designer of any nonstandard components as well as nonrecommended components. Then the CEPCB system analyzes the components for assemblablity based on the capabilities of the manufacturing facility under consideration. An example of manufacturing rules and parameters is shown in Table 4.2.

The CEPCB system was developed on a Sun SPARC station, running Sun OS 4.1, with C^{++} (version 2.0) as the programming language. The user interface is based on the Open Look standard from AT&T and uses the point-and-click concept, with the combination of window, button, and menu from command selection and options.

By testing the CEPCB system with several PCB design assemblies, it was found that the system can evaluate different product development environments with slightly different parameters. The research also showed that a multiple knowledge base approach is appropriate for CE. By accounting for the many interrelated factors that have an impact on PCB product development, the system provides an unbiased assessment of potential design alternatives and helps to solve design conflicts on the spot. Finally, the use of the system by industry experts will provide historical information that should lead to further modifications and improvements.

4.7   SUMMARY

Formally established procedures to handle the design decision analysis can help eliminate expensive design requirements that would be expensive to produce. Unfortunately, only a small number of computerized DSS exist today that can be applied to the CE field. The use of artificial

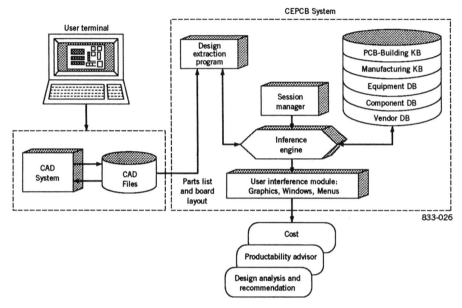

Figure 4.5. CEPCB system architecture.

TABLE 4.2. Sample of PCB Assembly Rules and Criteria

Rules	Board 1	P.I.[a]	Ratio	Normal P.I.	Board 2	P.I.	Ratio	Normal P.I.
PCB hole < min	N	+5		+5	N	+5		+5
PCB length > X	N				N			
PCB width > Y	N				N			
Are any two sides ⊥ or ‖	Y	+1		+1	Y	+1		+1
PCB hole pattern standardized	Y	+2		+2	Y	+2		+2
1/4 inch free space around board	Y	+1		+1	N	−1	.166	−.166
PCB double sided	N				N			
PCB multilayered	Y	−2			Y	−2		
PCB thermal plane	N				N			
PCB overall thickness < X	Y	+2			Y	+2		
Board totals				+9				+7.83

[a] P.I. = producibility index.

intelligence methodologies will, however, be a critical component in future intelligent decision support systems. This chapter has reviewed several computing technologies that can be applied toward that end as well as a CE approach for design decision analysis.

BIBLIOGRAPHY

1. T. PETERS and R.H. WATESMAN, *In Search for Excellence,* Warnel Books Co., New York, 1989.
2. J.W. PRIEST, *Engineering Design for Producibility and Reliability.* Marcel Dekker, Inc., New York, 1988.
3. L.J. BURNELL, J.W. PRIEST, and K. BRIGGS, "An Intelligent Decision Theoretic Approach to Producibility Optimization in Conceptual Design," *J. Intel. Manufact.* **2,** 189–196 (1991).
4. G.I. DOUKIDIS, F. LAND, and G. MILLER, *Knowledge Based Management Support Systems,* Ellis Horwood Ltd., Chichester, UK, 1989.
5. S. HOLTZMAN, *Intelligent Decision Systems,* Addison-Wesley Publishing Co., Inc., Reading, Mass., 1989.
6. D. SAMSON, *Managerial Decision Analysis,* Richard D. Irwin, Inc., Homewood, Ill., 1988.
7. Y. SAWARAGI, K. INOUE, and H. NAKAYAMA, eds, *Toward Iterating and Intelligent Decision Support Systems, Vol. 2, Proceedings, Kyota, Japan, 1986,* Springer-Verlag, New York, 1987.
8. E. TURBAN, *Decision Support and Expert Systems,* Macmillan Publishing, New York, 1988.
9. R.I. WINNER, J.P. PENNELL, H.E. BERTRAND, and M.M.G. SLUSARCZUK, *The Role of Concurrent Engineering in Weapons System Acquisition,* Institute for Defence Analysis, Detroit, Mich., 1988, Rep. R-338.
10. L. GOULD, "Competitive Advantage Begins with Concurrent Engineering," *Manag. Automation,* 31 (Nov. 1990).
11. S. EVANCZUK, "Concurrent Engineering the New Looks of Design," *High Perform. Syst.,* 16–17 (Apr. 1990).
12. C. LEE, "Beyond Teamwork," *Training,* 31 (June 1990).
13. D.G. REINERTSEN, "Whodunit? The Search for the New-Product Killers," *Elect. Bus.* (July 1983).
14. L.M. DONNELL and J.W. ULVILA, *Decision Analysis of Advanced Scout Helicopter Candidates,* Defense Technical Information Center, Alexandria, Va., February 1980, Final Tech. Rep. PR80-1-307.
15. J.W. PRIEST and L.J. BURNELL, "Case Studies of an Intelligent Decision Theoretic Approach for Production Development," J. Multi-Crit. Decision Anal., in press.
16. R.L. KEENEY and H. RAIFFA, *Decisions with Multiple Objectives: Preferences and Value Tradeoffs,* John Wiley & Sons, Inc., New York, 1976.
17. J.M. SÁNCHEZ and J.W. PRIEST, "Knowledge Based Producibility Decisionmaker," in *Proceedings of the Second International Symposium on Artificial Intelligence,* AAAI/ITESM, Monterey, NL., México, October 1989.
18. H.P. WANG and R.A. WYSK, *Turbo-CAPP: A Knowledge-based Computer Aided Process Planning System,* paper presented at the 19th CIRP Seminar on Manufacturing Systems.
19. R.A. WYSK, *Automated Process Planning and Selection Program: APPAS,* unpublished Ph.D. thesis, Purdue University, Lafeyette, Ind., 1977.
20. P. PIUMSOMBOON and J.M. SÁNCHEZ, *Concurrent Engineering System for Printed Circuit Board Assemblies (CEPCB),* CIM Systems, Inc., Richardson, Tex., Nov. 1991, Phase I, Final Rep. SBIR AF91-126.
21. J.M. SÁNCHEZ and J.W. PRIEST, "Knowledge Based Producibility Assessment System for Printed Circuit Boards," in *Proceedings of the Manufacturing International '92,* Vol. 1, ASME, Atlanta, Ga., March 1990, pp. 73–76.

CHAPTER 5

Integrated Support for Process, Conflict, and Rationale Management in Cooperative Design

MARK KLEIN
Boeing Computer Services

5.1 WHY WE NEED COORDINATION TECHNOLOGY

Increasingly, complex artifacts are designed* in large manufacturing concerns by complex processes distributed across time, participants, and functional perspectives. The design of a commercial jet, for example, requires the integrated contribution of thousands of individuals spread over several continents and a span of decades. Effective coordination is critical to the success of this cooperative process because the distributed activities are typically highly interdependent, e.g., due to shared resources, input–output relationships and so on. The sheer complexity of these interdependencies, however, has come to overwhelm traditional manual organizational schemes and paper-based coordination techniques, resulting in huge unnecessary rework costs, slowed schedules, and reduced product quality. As a result, while individual productivity may be high, failures of existing coordination support practices and technologies have severe impacts on the bottom line.

But what actually do we mean by coordination? Support for cooperative design can be viewed as being divided into three layers, each built on top of the ones beneath it (Figure 5.1).

But what actually do we mean by coordination? Support for cooperative design can be viewed as being divided into three layers, each built on top of the ones beneath it (Figure 5.1).

- *Communication*. Allowing participants in the design process to share information (this involves networking infrastructures).
- *Collaboration*. Allowing participants collaboratively to update some shared design description (this involves support for teleconferencing, etc.)
- *Coordination*. Ensuring the collaborative actions of multiple participants working on a shared design are coordinated to achieve the desired result as efficiently as possible.

This chapter focuses on the topmost layer, with the understanding that significant challenges exist in providing mature effective technology for the supporting layers. In the conclusion to this chapter the requirements presented by integrated coordination technology for the underlying collaboration and communication layers are discussed.

Each of the three kinds of distribution in cooperative design have been addressed to date by three distinct coordination support technologies (Figure 5.2).

- *Distribution across participants* requires support for the sequencing of tasks and flow of information among participants; this is addressed by process management (i.e., workflow, planning–scheduling) technologies.

---

* In this chapter, the word *design* is taken to describe all aspects of an artifact's description, including the requirements, geometric definition, materials, manufacturing plan, and supporting documentation. *Collaborative* design thus refers to collaboration both between disciplines at a given stage (e.g., between various systems and structure groups in design engineering) as well as between stages over the product life cycle (e.g., between design and manufacturing engineering).

Figure 5.1. Layers of support for cooperative design.

- *Distribution across perspectives* arises because the participants involved work on different interacting aspects of the design and/or have different often-incompatible goals; consistency among their design actions can be maintained with the support of conflict management (i.e., constraint or dependency management) technologies.
- *Distribution across time* arises because the nature and rationale for design decisions made at an earlier stage often need to be available later on, e.g., to support product changes as well as the design of other similar products; this is addressed by memory management (i.e., rationale capture, organizational memory) technologies.

Each of these technologies face different challenges that have limited its effectiveness in different ways. The central thesis of this chapter is that truly effective coordination in cooperative design requires an integrated approach wherein dependencies across all the dimensions of design distribution are modeled and managed in a single computational framework. This integrated approach synergistically combines the strengths and avoids the weaknesses of the contributing coordination support technologies. This chapter reviews the state of the art of existing coordination technologies, identifies their current limitations, and presents an implemented model of integrated cooperative design coordination called iDCSS. The chapter concludes with a discussion of directions for future work.

5.2 CURRENT COORDINATION SUPPORT TECHNOLOGY

This section reviews the state of the art of the three types of coordination technology currently available for cooperative design support. For each technology, the coordination problem addressed, the current state of the art, and the technical challenges that must be met to provide improved support given current limitations will be considered.

Process Management

Problem Addressed

The distribution of cooperative design across multiple participants requires that we be able to control the flow of tasks and information among them, i.e., be able to define and perform effective business processes. Generally, such processes are documented in difficult-to-access

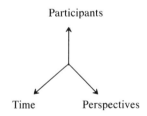

Figure 5.2. Types of distribution in cooperative design.

Manual	Ad-hoc	Structured conversations	Workflow interpreters

Degree of Structure Imposed By Process Management Tool

Figure 5.3. Types of process management systems.

and quickly obsolete paper documents if they are formally modeled at all. As a result, it can be time-consuming to train new people in how one's business works, valuable expertise about effective business processes can be lost as employees become unavailable, and existing processes can become increasingly ineffective in the absence of a good global understanding of what they actually are. The execution of business processes, in addition, is typically manual and paper based. Bottlenecks (e.g., due to uneven workload distribution), long flow times (e.g., due to slow work package distribution), and errors (e.g., because the preferred process was not followed) can occur all too often. There also is little information available on the state of the work flowing through a business process, making tracking of work items and the analysis of business process effectiveness a time-consuming and error-prone task.

State of the Art

A wide range of process management technologies have become available to address these concerns. These technologies can be placed on a continuum according to the extent to which they impose limits on how a business process can be performed (Figure 5.3). Manual systems impose essentially no constraints on how a process is performed, allowing work packages, for example, to be lost, be routed to obsolete mail addresses, and so on. Ad hoc systems, typically based on electronic mail, depend on process participants to decide to whom a work package should go next but ensure that the work package is routed correctly once this decision is made. They also typically provide some degree of tracking. Structured conversation systems such as those based on the contract net (1) or speech act (2) approach provide a system-imposed protocol that structures how tasks can be distributed. These typically allow one to track entire "conversations" (series of task assignment negotiations and progress updates) as a unit.

Workflow systems interpret a process model produced by a process capture tool.* Processes are modeled as sequences of tasks, each assigned to a given individual or group, interspersed with decision points; these tools typically provide a graphical display of the process like that shown in Figure 5.4. Once the process has been modeled in this way, participants in a given process simply perform their individual tasks and rely on the workflow system to understand the process and ensure it is followed and tracked correctly.

Challenges

The key limitation of current process management technology is that the process execution structure it enforces is related indirectly at best to the underlying realities that shape these processes. Processes arise when a given task is too large to be performed effectively by a single

---

* Such tools usually allow a human user to define a business process using text-based or drawing tools, but in some cases they can provide automated process definition (i.e., planning) support, wherein a process model is derived from a description of the requirements it must satisfy.

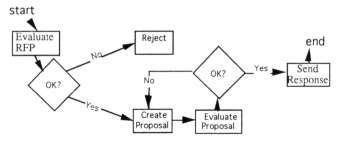

Figure 5.4. Graphical process model.

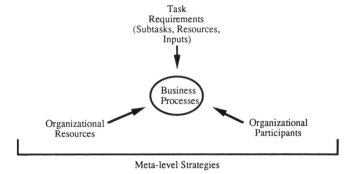

Figure 5.5. The factors that shape processes.

individual and thus must be decomposed (often recursively) into subtasks that taken together achieve the top-level goal. These tasks have interdependencies that may require some serialization in task execution. Some tasks, for example, may require as input the outputs produced by other tasks. Tasks that both use some limited organizational resource (e.g., a piece of equipment) may be serialized to avoid contention for that resource. Tasks can be merged if it turns out that one task, perhaps expanded slightly in scope, can achieve the requirements for two or more tasks more efficiently. New tasks may be generated dynamically to resolve conflicts between design actions taken by participants performing different tasks in the process. Finally, tasks will be assigned to individuals or groups based on how skills and responsibilities are distributed throughout the organization. Because there are often many different alternatives available for how we do any of these things, processes are shaped by (implicit or explicit) metalevel control strategies* that determine which options will be selected (Figure 5.5).

How well do current process management technologies account for the constraints that shape processes? They fail in two ways. Most process management technologies (i.e., the manual, ad hoc, and structured conversation approaches) include no model of any of the above-described constraints and thus offer no way of ensuring that the constraints are enforced. They include, for example, no model of how tasks should be sequences, what resources are available to perform them and so on. We have to rely on the human participants to make the correct decisions, but it is the very difficulty of making and enforcing these decisions in complex processes that led to the development of process management technology in the first place.

Workflow systems, by contrast, are capable of enforcing constraints on the detailed nature of a process. We can specify precisely what tasks will be done in what sequence by whom and using what resources. The problem with this approach is that any given process model represents a "frozen" or "compiled" picture of what an appropriate process was for a set of task, resource, and organizational constraints and policies that applied at some time in the past. This model can become inefficient or even harmful should these change, i.e., should an *exception* occur. We can consider an exception to be any departure from an "ideal" process that perfectly uses the current organizational resources, satisfies all extant policies, and encounters no problems during process execution. Exceptions can thus include any significant change in resources, organizational structure, company policy, task requirements, or task priority. They can also include incorrectly performed tasks, missed due dates, resource contentions between two or more distinct processes, opportunities to merge tasks between different processes, conflicts between actions taken in different process steps, and so on. Process models typically compile in conditional branches to deal with common anticipated exceptions. If unanticipated exceptions occur, however, which they do frequently in modern organizations, we are faced with "patching" the compiled process model without any computer support to ensure that we are not violating the relevant organizational constraints and policies. As a result, even organizations that make extensive use of workflow technology can find it difficult to respond quickly and appropriately to changes in their requirements, policies, and resources. More effective support

---

* Examples of metalevel policies for task assignment are support cross-training by routing tasks to people who need experience with that kind of task" and "maximize throughput by routing tasks to acknowledged experts."

for process management in cooperative design, then, requires that we have a rich model of the task, resource, and organizational constraints as well as policies that apply for a given organization and be able dynamically to define the most effective process as exceptions occur.

Conflict Management

Problem Addressed

Cooperative design is distributed across multiple functional perspectives addressing interrelated aspects of a single design. When many perspectives are involved, maintaining consistency (i.e., avoiding conflicts) among these distributed design activities becomes a significant challenge with major potential impacts on product cost, quality, and timeliness. The design of an airplane, for example, involves groups dedicated to many different structures (e.g., wings, doors, and struts), systems (e.g., fuel, electrical, and hydraulic), analysis disciplines (e.g., noise propagation and stress analysis), and manufacturing functions (e.g., major assembly planning, detailed part planning, and tool design). The functions–groups working on these different perspectives are highly interdependent. For example, a change in the geometry of a wheel-well structure requires corresponding changes in the routing of the hydraulic lines, because they are typically attached to major structural members. Changes in the hydraulic line routing necessitates in turn changes in the electrical line routing because of safety-related requirements concerning the physical separation between hydraulic and electrical systems. If the hydraulics group is not made aware of the relevant structural changes in a timely manner, it will waste valuable time designing hydraulic structures based on an obsolete view of the structural members and be forced to rework the design once the conflict is finally discovered. This problem is exacerbated by the ripple effect of such changes: the electrical group and all those groups affected by its design decisions will be forced to abandon and rework the results of their efforts. Because maintaining scheduled commitments is often a priority in large manufacturing concerns, the group doing the rework may have to resort to short flow-time solutions that typically cost much more and may offer reduced product quality.

Current conflict management approaches in large manufacturing concerns are almost entirely manual. Functional groups within a given life-cycle stage typically maintain consistency by the use of predefined interface conventions (e.g., hydraulic lines are always routed before electrical lines) as well as by more-or-less formal communication techniques such as cross-functional meetings and coordination memos that inform all potentially affected groups of a change made to some portion of the design. Consistency across life-cycle stages (e.g., between design engineering and manufacturing engineering) is maintained by the use of design-for-X (e.g., design for manufacturability) rules, concurrent engineering team meetings, and "liaison" organizations that communicate conflicts detected by later life-cycle perspectives (e.g., manufacturing) to earlier stages (e.g., design engineering) and request changes to resolve the conflicts.

Such manual approaches to conflict management have become increasingly costly and ineffective as the sheer scale of cooperative design activities have grown. Predefined design-for-X and interface rules can be needlessly restrictive and lead to nonoptimal designs. Engineers typically find themselves inundated with high volumes of coordination memos and cross-functional team meetings, many of which turn out to be irrelevant to their particular job. Errors of omission can occur, wherein a conflict may not be detected and addressed until, for example, the product is actually being assembled. Once a conflict has been detected, it may take weeks for a change request to propagate back to the responsible design group and result in the appropriate design modification. All of this conflict management activity is mediated by large liaison and change management organizations that tie up significant amounts of human and other resources.

State of the Art

Conflict management technology is emerging to address these issues by providing computer-supported propagation of the consequences of design decisions. This involves notifying affected perspectives of (proposed or actual) design decisions and their potential impact. This can include simply defining the constraints some design decision places on another (so the affected designers can proactively avoid conflicts) as well as indicating when a design change made elsewhere conflicts with design decisions one has already made. Systems based on least-com-

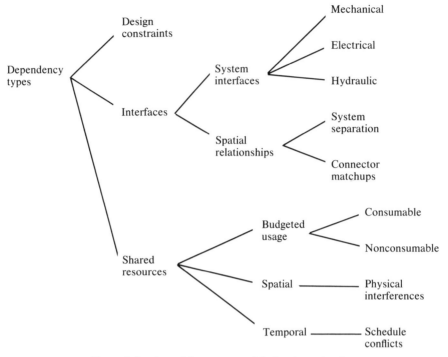

Figure 5.6.   A partial taxonomy of design dependencies.

mitment design approaches (3) allow preliminary information about design decision impacts to be received even before a detailed design has been completed by another perspective.

There are relatively few kinds of design interdependencies. A partial taxonomy is shown in Figure 5.6. Design decisions can be interdependent because they share a limited resource (e.g., a power supply or available RAM), because they affect components connected by some kind of interface (e.g., connected components in a hydraulic or electrical system), or because they are explicitly constrained to be so by the designer (e.g., the volume and density of a part specified to have a given weight). Different technologies are available to support impact detection for each kind of dependency. Geometric conflict detection technology (i.e., checking for physical interference between adjoining parts) is widely available, as are systems for detecting temporal conflicts (e.g., scheduling conflicts) and resource budget violations for most kinds of resources.* Spatial relationship constraint violation detection (e.g., for checking if two connectors match up properly or that fuel and electrical systems are separated sufficiently to meet safety requirements) is also becoming available, based on geometric feature detection technology. System interface and design constraint dependencies can be propagated using a constraint propagation infrastructure. A number of constraint propagation systems are available, including commercial products such as PECOS and research systems (4–6).

Support for conflict resolution is an area of active study in research settings (17–15), but technology for this purpose is currently unavailable in commercial settings. This technology relies, in general, on the fact that there are relatively few abstract classes of conflict and

---

* Resource limit violation is detected differently, depending on the kind of resource involved. For example, overuse of a monetary budget can be found simply by summing individual expenditures and comparing them with the budget. Detecting space overuse is somewhat more complicated, even in the two-dimensional case (i.e., checking for adequate floor space); equipment whose total area does not exceed the available floor space may not fit in a given area due to the particular shapes of the equipment involved. A functional resource that is not used up over time but can only support a finite number of simultaneous users (e.g., a computer terminal) has resource overuse detected in yet a third way.

associated general strategies for resolving them. Conflict resolution can then be achieved by heuristically classifying the conflict (16) and then instantiating an associated strategy to generate a suggested conflict resolution approach (17).

Challenges

Determining the cross-perspective impact of design decisions requires design representation standards capable of representing design information throughout the product life cycle, including requirements, functional architecture, product geometry, and manufacturing plans. These standards must support high level features (including components, their functions, and resource uses) and abstract descriptions to allow least-commitment design. Existing standards do not provide adequate coverage or expressiveness yet.

Many kinds of design impacts can be inferred using basic physical principles. For example, we can use Ohm's law to infer how a change in the voltage at one end of a resistor will affect the voltage at the other. In many cases, however, the interrelationships between design decisions will be idiosyncratic to a design and must be expressed explicitly by the designers. For this purpose, the design representation language must be able to represent decision interrelationships. Interfaces to computer-aided engineering (CAE) tools* need to be extended to allow one to describe in this language the interdependencies between design decisions captured using different systems. Currently, such systems stand alone, making it impossible to describe, for example, how some part geometry motivated a particular manufacturing plan decision.

Another key challenge is improving the scalability of the design decision impact assessment process; untrammeled dependency propagation can quickly become computationally intractable and overwhelm designers with floods of information on the impact of multitudes of design changes made elsewhere. Abstract or qualitative representations of design decisions and dependencies are needed to allow meaningful, if approximate, assessments of design decision impacts at significantly reduced computational cost. We also need to be able to specify context-sensitive policies concerning what kind of dependency impact detection should be done when.

Finally, better support needs to be provided for computer-supported conflict resolution. The first step in resolving a conflict is typically to understand how it occurred and why. Current conflict management technology records what other design decisions impinged on this one but does not keep track of the intent or history (e.g., rejected options) behind the decisions. We need to be able to access a rich representation of the rationale behind conflicting design decisions. In addition, the resolution of a conflict is typically reached through a multistep process (e.g., negotiation over resource assignments) involving the people who produced the conflicting design decisions. These processes need to be integrated into a general and robust process management approach.

Memory Management

Problem Addressed

The distribution of cooperative design across time implies the need to remember the reasoning underlying design decisions made throughout the product life cycle. When an artifact is designed, the typical output includes blueprints, CAD files, manufacturing plans, and other documents describing the final result of a long series of deliberations and trade-offs. The underlying history, intent, and logical support (i.e., the rationale) for the decisions captured therein, however, are usually lost or are represented at best as a scattered collection of paper documents, project and personal notebook entries, and the recollections of the product's designers. This design rationale information can be difficult to access by humans and is represented such that computers can provide little support for managing and using it.

The potential benefits of more effectively capturing such rationale are manifold. The reasoning behind decisions becomes available for all team members to critique and augment (18). Participants affected by design changes can be identified readily (19). Existing designs that addressed similar requirements can be retrieved, understood, and modified to meet current needs (20). As noted above, the causes and potential resolutions for conflicts between designers can be identified (17). Design decisions can be easily documented for new team members, new designers, and new product users (21).

---

* Computer aided engineering tools include CAD (computer-aided design), CAM (computer-aided manufacturing), and CAPP (computer-aided process planning) systems.

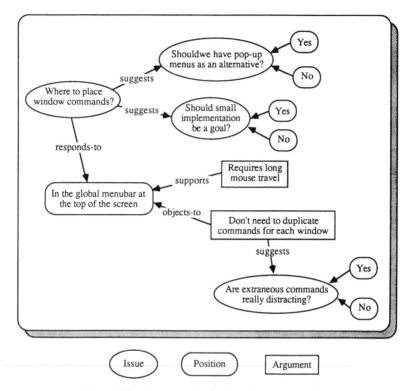

Figure 5.7.   An example of rationale representation.

State of the Art

Many decision rationale capture approaches have been developed (e.g., refs. 18, 19, 22–24). Although the details differ, all represent rationale as graph structures, in which nodes represent entities such as issues and criteria and links between nodes represent relationships between the connected entities (Figure 5.7). Existing rationale languages differ in the kinds of entities that are used and in how they can be interrelated. While they may differ in expressiveness, they overlap substantially, sometimes simply using different terminology for entity and relationship types with substantially the same semantics.

These approaches typically capture the rationale for decision making in general but not design in particular; in design settings they add, in effect, another document to the set produced by existing design tools (Figure 5.8). While one system that integrates design and rationale representation does exist (24), it uses a domain-specific design representation (for kitchen design) not easily generalized to other domains.

Challenges

Existing rationale capture languages face limited expressiveness and, therefore, limited computational usefulness due to lack of integration with generic design representations. Because the associated decision rationale capture tools are not integrated with design tools, they face the potential for inconsistency between the rationale and design descriptions, spotty capture of design rationale, and the tendency to waste time on issues that later prove unimportant (24). What we really need are systems that allow cooperative design participants to conveniently describe the dependencies between decisions captured by existing design tools (Figure 5.9). The rationale for a product geometry decision, after all, consists of such things as the requirements it attempts to satisfy and the other geometry decisions on which it logically depends. A manufac-

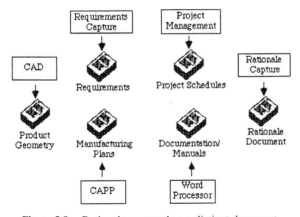

Figure 5.8.   Rationale captured as a distinct document.

turing plan decision, similarly, is justified by supporting decisions such as project schedules and product geometry.

Existing rationale language technology has been used mainly to capture the pros and cons concerning alternative solutions to a given problem, but not design intent, the relationships between design decisions, or their history, all of which, of course, can be extremely important. Rationale capture can be burdensome, especially given that the person who benefits is generally different from the person required to describe it. This is exacerbated by the fact that it is often unclear where and in how much detail rationale should be described, because the person who enters the rationale is unlikely to know how it will be used or even by whom. We should be able to describe preferred rationale capture processes to delimit what and how detailed rationale should be captured. If possible, these preferred processes should provide default rationale templates that can be quickly customized to describe the rationale for a given decision.

5.3   iDCSS: AN INTEGRATED APPROACH TO COOPERATIVE DESIGN COORDINATION

Coordination support technology has evolved to support effective coordination in the face of dependencies between different aspects of cooperative design. Each of the different technologies focus on one set of dependency type but fail to account for others; this is the source of many of their individual limitations. Described below is an integrated approach that attempts to model and account for all the kinds of dependencies that occur in cooperative design and as a result synergistically combines the strengths and avoids the weaknesses of the contributing

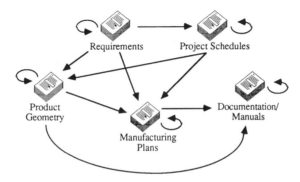

Figure 5.9.   Rationale as decision interdependences.

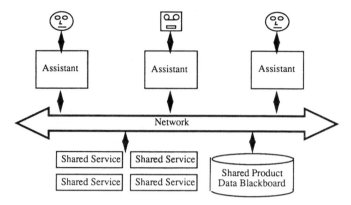

Figure 5.10.   The iDCSS architecture.

technologies. A preliminary implementation of this approach has been created called iDCSS for integrated design collaboration support system (pronounced *IDEX*). iDCSS is the latest result of 5 yr of work, including studies of cooperative design (25) as well as several previous systems such as the DCSS conflict management system (17), the DRCS design rationale capture system (26), and a prototype workflow system.* The sections below consider iDCSS's architecture, its underlying design model, and how it supports the three kinds of cooperative design coordination identified above.

Architecture

iDCSS has a distributed client–server architecture (Figure 5.10). Shared product data and services are made available by servers to all clients via a network. Clients are design agent–assistant pairs in which agents can be either human or machine based and assistants are computer programs that help coordinate the design activities of their associated agents. Human designers work in front of dedicated workstations executing their assistant, whereas machine-based design agents are independent processes communicating with distinct assistant processes. The code currently runs on networked Symbolics Lisp machines and is written in Common Lisp.

Design Model

iDCSS is based on a model of cooperative design derived from classical systems engineering work (28) as well as AI models of artifact design (11, 29–33) and planning (3, 34). These models have been applied successfully to a wide variety of domains, including electrical, electronic, hydraulic, and mechanical systems as well as software.

   In this model, physical artifacts are viewed as collections of modules, which can represent entire systems, subsystems, or their components, each with characteristic attributes and whose interfaces (with their own attributes) are connected by typed connections. Artifact designs are refined using an iterative least-commitment synthesize-and-evaluate process. An artifact description starts as one or more abstract modules, representing the desired artifact, with specifications represented as desired values on module attributes. This is refined into a more detailed description by constraining the value of module attributes, connecting module interfaces (to represent module interactions), decomposing modules into submodules, and specializing modules by refining their class (Figure 5.11). Plans are viewed as (perhaps partially) ordered collections of tasks and are also defined in an iterative least-commitment manner.

---

* Many of the process management ideas in this chapter were developed for the TCAPS workflow management system described in ref. 27.

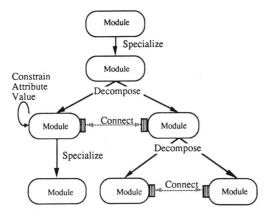

Figure 5.11. The design refinement process.

In parallel with the iterative refinement of the design description is evaluation of the design with respect to how well it achieves the design specifications. Based on this analysis, we may choose to select one design option over another or to modify a given option to address an identified deficiency. The stages of specification identification, design option definition, evaluation, and selection–modification can be interleaved arbitrarily and thus often occur in an iterative fashion throughout the design process.

Designers, in addition to reasoning about the design itself (i.e., at the domain level), also reason about the *process* they use to define the design (at the *meta*level) (35). A designer may have a plan, for example, for how the design itself will be created. If several design options are available, a designer may reflect on which option to select. If a conflict between two or more design goals and actions occurs, a fix for the conflict needs to be found. The design-reasoning process is generally goal driven, in the sense that actions are taken as part of strategies intended to achieve goals such as meeting a specification, refining a design option, making a control choice, and resolving a design conflict.

Process Management

From the perspective of a designer, the design process starts when a goal shows up in his or her to do list; at the very beginning of the product life cycle, it will be the goal to design a product that meets a given set of requirements (Figure 5.12). The local queue lists goals assigned to this designer specifically, whereas the group queue lists goals that can be performed by any of a group of people that includes the current designer. In the latter case, the designer must volunteer to take on that goal, at which point it moves off of all the group queues and onto the designer's private queue. Both domain-level goals (e.g., to find the voltage for a power supply) and meta level goals (e.g., to decide which of several alternative solutions to select for a given goal) appear on this to do list.

To start performing the task specified by the entry in the to do list, the designer double-clicks on the goal to create a "task performance plan" with an associated window as shown in Figure 5.13. A task performance plan collects all the information, tools, and subprocesses needed by a designer to achieve a given goal. Using the associated task performance window, a designer can bring up views allowing one to look at and update different subsets of the complete set of product data from different perspectives. Every icon in Figure 13 represents one view. A view can correspond to a CAE application and may display product requirements, geometry, manufacturing plans, design process plans, supporting design documentation, or even the rationale (underlying argument structure) for a given design decision. In the following example, views display the design version history, related functional components, attributes, and manufacturing plan for a component (Figure 5.14).

The rationale for any design decision can be captured using the iDCSS rationale language. This is a typed link language designed to match the iDCSS design model and built from previous

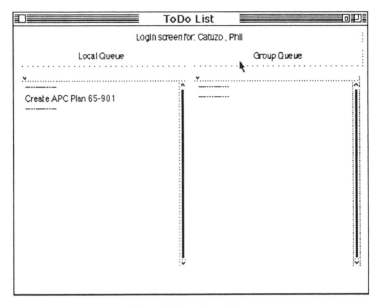

Figure 5.12. A to do list.

work in decision rationale capture (18, 19, 22, 23). In this language, design rationale is represented as sets of claims. Any claim can serve as part of the rationale for another claim, so we
can make claims about the design, claims describing the rationale for design decisions, claims
describing why we should believe this rationale (or not), and so on. The iDCSS rationale
language is summarized in Figure 5.15. The items in Roman type represent types of design
decisions, whereas the arrows labeled in italic type represent allowable kinds of typed links
between them, pointing from the sources to the targets.

A designer can build up a rationale description using a simple extension of the user interface
provided for describing the designs themselves. The menus brought up by selecting an assertion
with the pointing device include context-sensitive lists of the types of links allowable starting
from that assertion. To create a link, one simply selects the link type and the assertion that is the
target of the link. The net result of describing design rationale in this way is a graph of decisions
interrelated by typed rationale links. A detailed description of the iDCSS rationale language and
user interface scheme is given in ref. 36.

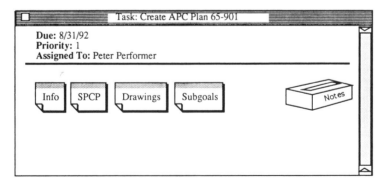

Figure 5.13. A task performance window for a goal.

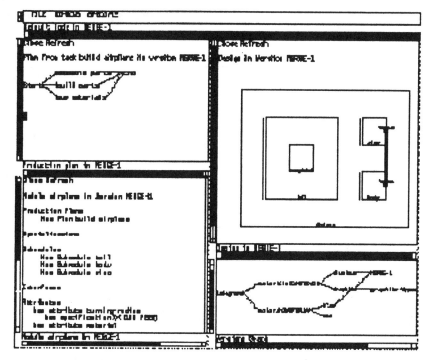

Figure 5.14. Task window with several open views.

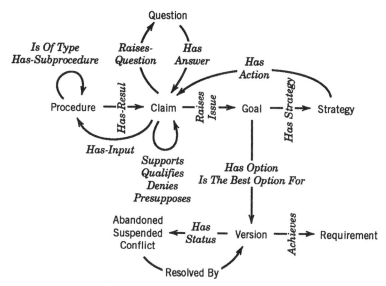

Figure 5.15. iDCSS rationale language.

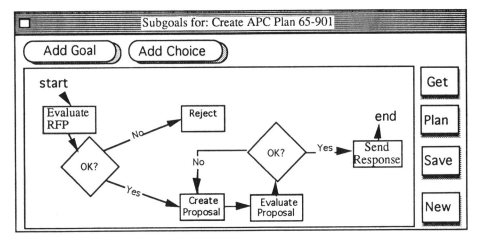

Figure 5.16. The subgoals view for a task performance plan.

A designer will often need to create subgoals to handle different tasks whose results are needed to achieve the current goal. The subgoals for a task performance plan appear in the "subgoals" view for that plan's window (Figure 5.16). The preferred process for performing subgoals can be defined graphically or by using an automated planning tool that defines a process based on the subgoal requirements, organizational resources, and current policies.

By default, subgoals are assigned to the person who generated them and appear in his or her to do list nested under their parent goal. A designer may need to assign these goals to someone else, e.g., because they require specialized expertise or the designer is simply too busy. To decide who the task should be assigned to the user defines task assignment constraints (in terms of desired skills, experience, organizational position, post, etc.) and allows the system to identify the one or more candidates who meet these job descriptions. iDCSS uses an organizational model for this purpose; this model stores the organization chart, the members, managers, support people, and other resources for each organizational unit as well as the job descriptions that each person can fulfill. An organization model can be displayed and edited using the view shown in Figure 5.17. Job descriptions for an individual are viewed and updated using the view in Figure 5.18.

The rationale behind task assignment and sequencing decisions can be captured, just like all other design decisions in iDCSS, using the link language. One can justify assigning a task to a given individual, for example, by a link to a job description for that individual in the organization model that shows he or she has the necessary skills. Similarly, one can justify serializing two tasks by a link from the resource conflict that is shown to result if the two tasks are performed simultaneously.

A user's assistant can store predefined task performance plans for accomplishing different goals; these can be retrieved by the assistant and provided as starting points that the users may then modify to provide the desired task performance environment. This can be used to represent the company's preferred processes for achieving given goals; the preferred task performance window is then automatically opened when the designer opens the task for the first time. These predefined windows can be defined manually or may be "learned" by recording a task performance plan that a user defined for that goal in the past and then storing it as a reusable case. Precompiled task performance plans, however defined, should record the rationale underlying the decisions they store just as user-defined windows do, so we can replan appropriately when exceptions occur.

The iDCSS process management approach is derived directly from existing approaches but adds a critical feature. One can record the dependencies underlying process decisions so that if these decisions change (i.e., an exception occurs) the affected processes can be identified and modified appropriately. In this way, the brittleness of conventional process management approaches can be avoided.

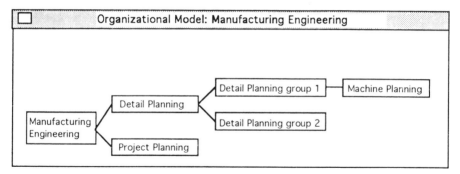

Figure 5.17. The organization model view.

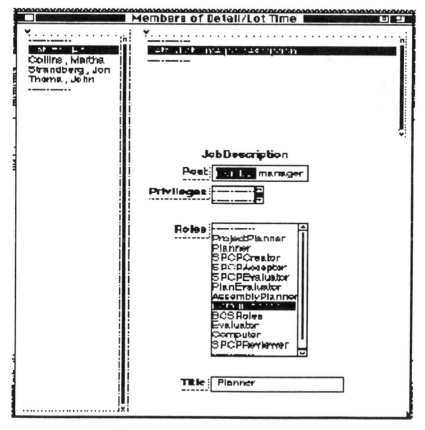

Figure 5.18. The job description view.

Conflict Management

When design decisions (made about product or plans) interact in some way, the influence of one design decision on another and whether a conflict has resulted can be detected using the impact detection service. This service can be applied equally well to product or process descriptions. If the service is applied to design process plans, for example, it helps ensure that the multiple subprocesses making up the global design process can be performed without exceeding the organizations' resources. If the service is applied to product decisions, it helps ensure that the design decisions made by different designers are consistent. When a conflict is detected, the metalevel goal of resolving that conflict is asserted, supported (using the link language) by the facts used by the conflict detection procedure to infer the existence of the conflict. This goal appears on the user's to do list just like any other goal. A user may manually define a resolution for that conflict, using the standard task performance plan window, or else can call on the conflict resolution service to define one or more suggested task performance plans for resolving the conflict.

The integrated iDCSS model offers some important advantages over existing conflict management technology. It provides the beginnings of a least-commitment, high level feature full product life-cycle representation so we can maintain consistency across a greater range of the product design life cycle. A uniform and expressive link language–user interface allows the user to define the rationale for any design decision in terms of any other design decision. This can be used by the impact detection service to propagate design decision impacts and also by the conflict resolution service to help understand the cause and possible resolutions for a conflict. Preferred design processes that specify when and how the impact detection service should be triggered can be defined using task performance plans; this allows us to control the impact detection cost–benefit ratio. Finally, task performance plans provide a mechanism for representing and executing conflict resolution strategies.

Memory Management

iDCSS includes a robust memory management approach as an integral part of its operation. The reasons underlying product and process design decisions are captured in one uniform formalism that combines the argumentation and intent information of conventional rationale languages, the decision dependencies represented in conflict management technology, and the history captured by process management technology. This provides greater expressiveness and, therefore, allows greater computational support than conventional nonintegrated approaches. The iDCSS approach also is more natural than previous approaches, because rationale can be attached directly to the design decision it refers to rather than to a piece of text that acts as a proxy. This prevents inconsistency between the rationale and design and avoids the tendency faced in conventional rationale systems to waste time on irrelevant issues. Conflict detection helps focus rationale capture; it allows us to concentrate on the rationale underlying controversial decisions rather than straightforward ones. Finally, we can use preferred processes defined in task performance plans to describe to what extent the rationale behind given design decisions need to be described; this allows us to focus rationale capture efforts on those design aspects thought most critical. The task performance plans can even specify default rationale templates (link language network fragments) that the user is asked to fill in for a given design goal, thus further reducing the rationale capture burden in routine design settings.

5.4 CONCLUSIONS

The iDCSS system integrates technologies for coordinating cooperative design over agents, perspectives, and time in a way that combines the strengths and avoids the weaknesses of the component technologies. Figure 5.19 is a summary of this synergism. Process management technology provides processes to control impact detection, implement conflict resolution plans, delimit rationale capture, and represent decision history. Conflict management ensures consistency among design processes and provides the design dependency component of the iDCSS rationale language. Finally, the memory management component provides rationale to support conflict management and intelligent process replanning in the face of exceptions. The power of this approach comes from representing all design dependencies in a single uniform way and from leveraging a small set of generic coordination services (for impact detection, rationale

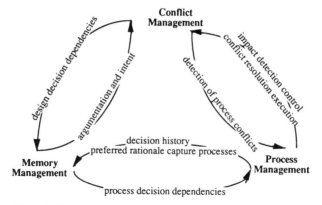

Figure 5.19.   Synergism among iDCSS component technologies.

capture, process definition, and execution as well as conflict resolution) that use this dependency information.

While this integrated approach does appear to offer significant advantages over current nonintegrated coordination technologies, clearly many challenges remain. Effective design coordination requires a communication infrastructure that provides sufficiently expressive and inclusive data standards (e.g., extending and integrating existing standards like PDES/STEP and IDEF) as well as highly scalable network access to shared heterogeneous data and services (e.g., based on semantic database integration services such as CARNOT). Scalable and effective technology for supporting collaborative editing of shared product data sets is needed and must address such issues as control of chalk passing, versioning, and release authority control. The existing coordination support services must be improved (e.g., conflict management technology must produce more robust generic knowledge bases of impact propagation, conflict classification, and conflict resolution expertise) and new services must be added (e.g., a task merge service that uncovers opportunities to define merged tasks more efficiently than their predecessors or a retrieval service that can fetch previous relevant design experience). Finally, existing CAE applications must be enhanced so they can take effective advantage of these coordination services. This requires the ability to describe design decisions using high level features and to express design dependency links across applications as well as making these applications workflow enabled so they can take advantage of process management technology functionality.

Acknowledgments

The author would like to thank his colleagues Roland Faragher-Horwell, Art Murphy, Steve Poltrock, Kish Sharma, and Debra Zarley for their substantial contributions to the ideas underlying this chapter, especially in the area of process management.

BIBLIOGRAPHY

1. R.G. SMITH, "The Contract Net Protocol: High-Level Communication and Control in a Distributed Problem Solver," *IEEE Trans. Comput.* **C29**(12), 1104–1113 (Dec. 1980).
2. T. WINOGRAD, "A Language/Action Perspective on the Design of Cooperative Work," *Proc. CSCW 86*, 1986, pp. 203–220.
3. M.J. STEFIK, "Planning with Constraints (Molgen: Part 1 & 2)," *Artif. Intel.* **16**(2), 111–170 (1981).
4. S.C.Y. LU, "Integrated and Cooperative Knowledge Processing Technology for Concurrent Engineering" in S.C.Y. Lu, ed., *Knowledge-Based Engineering Systems Research Laboratory Annual Report,* University of Illinois, 1991.

5. K. SMITH, H. KARANDIKAR, J. RINDERLE, D. NAVINCHANDRA, and S. REDDY, "Representing and Managing Constraints for Computer-Based Cooperative Product Development." in *Third Annual Symposium on Concurrent Engineering*, June 1991, pp. 475–490.

6. J. BOWEN and D. BAHLER, "Constraint-Based Software for Concurrent Engineering," *IEEE Comput.* **26**(1), 66–68 (Jan. 1993).

7. G.J. SUSSMAN and G.L. STEELE, "Constraints—A Language for Expressing Almost-Hierarchical Descriptions," *Artif. Intel.* **14**, 1–40 (1980).

8. M.S. FOX and S.F. SMITH, "Isis—A Knowledge-Based System for Factory Scheduling," *Expert Sys.* (July 1984).

9. Y. DESCOTTE and J.C. LATOMBE, "Making Compromises among Antagonist Constraints in a Planner," *Artif. Intel.* **27**, 183–217 (1985).

10. D.C. BROWN, *Failure Handling in a Design Expert System*, Butterworth & Co. (Publishers) Ltd., Kent, UK, 1985.

11. S. MARCUS, J. STOUT, and J. MCDERMOTT, "VT: An Expert Elevator Designer," *Artif. Intel. Mag.* **8**(4), 39–58 (Winter 1987).

12. I. GOLDSTEIN, "Bargaining between Goals," *IJCAI*, 175–180 (1975).

13. C. HEWITT, "Offices Are Open Systems," *ACM Trans. Office Info. Syst.* **4**(3), 271–287 (1986).

14. R. WILENSKY, *Planning and Understanding*, Addison-Wesley Publishing Co., Inc., Reading, Mass., 1983.

15. S. LANDER and V.R. LESSER, *Negotiation to Resolve Conflicts among Design Experts*, Tech. Report, Department of Computer and Information Science, Aug. 1988.

16. W.J. CLANCEY, "Classification Problem Solving," *AAAI*, 49–55 (1984).

17. M. KLEIN, "Supporting Conflict Resolution in Cooperative Design Systems," *IEEE Sys. Man Cybernet.* **21**(6) (Dec. 1991).

18. J. LEE and K.Y. LAI, "What's in Design Rationale?" *Hum.-Comput. Interaction* **6**(3–4), 251–280 (1991).

19. A. MACLEAN, R. YOUNG, V. BELLOTTI, and T. MORAN, "Questions, Options and Criteria: Elements of a Design Rationale for User Interfaces," *J. Hum. Comput. Interaction* **6**(3–4), 201–250 (1991).

20. J. MOSTOW and M. BARLEY, "Automated Reuse of Design Plans," *Proc. ICED*, IEEE, 632–647 (Aug. 1987).

21. R. BALZER, "Capturing the Design Process in the Machine," in *Rutgers Workshop on Knowledge-Based Design Aids*, 1984.

22. K.C.B. YAKEMOVIC and E.J. CONKLIN, "Report on a Development Project Use of an Issue-Based Information System," *CSCW 90 Proc.*, 105–118 (1990).

23. R. MCCALL, *PHIBIS: Procedurally Hierarchical Issue-Based Information Systems*, paper presented at the Conference on Planning and Design in Architecture, ASME, Boston, 1987.

24. G. FISCHER, A.C. LEMKE, R. MCCALL, and A.I. MORCH, "Making Argumentation Serve Design," *J. Hum. Comput. Interaction* **6**(3–4), 393–419 (1991).

25. M. KLEIN and S.C.Y. LU, "Conflict Resolution in Cooperative Design," *Int. J. Artif. Intel. Eng.* **4**(4), 168–180 (1990).

26. M. KLEIN, "Capturing Design Rationale in Concurrent Engineering Teams," *IEEE Comput.* (Jan. 1993).

27. R. FARAGHER-HORWELL, M. KLEIN, and D. ZARLEY, "Overview and Functional Specifications for TCAPS Task Coordination and Planning System: A Computer-Supported Workflow Management System," Boeing Co., Bellvue, Wash., Dec. 1992, Boeing Computer Services Tech. Report BCS-G2010-130.

28. B.S. BLANCHARD and W.J. FABRYCKY, *Systems Engineering and Analysis*, Prentice-Hall, Inc., Englewood Cliffs, NJ, 1981.

29. J. MCDERMOTT, "R1: A Rule-Based configurer of Computer Systems," *Artif. Intel.* **19**, 39–88 (1982).

30. D.C. BROWN, "Capturing Mechanical Design Knowledge," *Am. Soc. Mech. Eng. CIME* (Feb. 1985).

31. S. MITTAL and A. ARAYA, "A Knowledge-Based Framework for Design," *Am. Assoc. Artif. Intel.,* 856–865 (1986).

32. C. TONG, "AI in Engineering Design," *Artif. Intel. Eng.* **2**(3), 130–166 (1987).

33. M. KLEIN and S.C.Y. LU, "Insights into Cooperative Group Design: Experience with the LAN Designer System," In G. Rzevski and R.A. Adey, eds., *Proceedings of the Sixth International Conference on Applications of Artificial Intelligence in Engineering (AIENG '91)*, University of Oxford, Oxford, UK, July 1991, pp. 143–162.

34. D. CHAPMAN, "Nonlinear Planning: A Rigorous Reconstruction," *IJCAI-85* **2**, 1022–1024 (1985).

35. R. WILENSKY, "Meta-Planning," *AAAI,* 334–336 (1980).

36. M. KLEIN, "DRCS: An Integrated System for Capture of Designs and Their Rationale," in *Proceedings of Second International Conference on Artificial Intelligence in Design,* Carnegie Mellon University, Pittsburgh, 1992.

CHAPTER 6

Organization of Teams in Concurrent Engineering*

RONALD G. ASKIN
University of Arizona

MANBIR SODHI
University of Rhode Island

6.1 INTRODUCTION

Definition and Objective of Concurrent Engineering

A number of factors have forced manufacturing companies to rethink how they do business. Firms that dominated their industry in the 1960s and 1970s have seen global competition erode their markets. The rapid pace of technological innovation, proliferation of component suppliers, and customer demands for product customization have opened the way for small, specialty firms to carve out niche markets. Many industries have witnessed a shift from mass production with an emphasis on incremental reductions in variable production costs to flexible manufacturing and rapid introduction of new product models. Concurrent engineering (CE) offers a strategic approach to product development that enables the firm to compete successfully in regard to length of the development cycle and appropriateness of the product for the intended market. CE began to develop in the late 1970s as U.S. manufacturing firms began studying the product design and development procedures of foreign competitors. A review of the history of concurrent engineering has been published (1).

Concurrent engineering may be described as the empowerment of multidisciplinary teams to design a product simultaneously, its manufacturing processes and tooling, test procedures and equipment, and support activities, using open interchange of information and application of trade-off analyses to obtain optimal results over the product life cycle. The objective of CE is to break down the barriers within the traditional design and manufacturing organization and to develop and deliver rapidly products that satisfy, and even delight, customers. Typically, marketing, design, test, manufacturing, service, and purchasing representatives are included on design teams. The teams are empowered and charged with the task of developing a product. The design process is driven by customer input. Emphasis is on collaboration with both the customer and other internal functions. Instead of the test, manufacturing, and reliability engineers being called in after the fact simply to indicate whether the design is good or bad, these individuals participate in the design process, indicating what aspects of any contemplated design will cause problems and working to find alternatives that are also acceptable from design and marketing perspectives.

It has been widely observed that the cost of engineering changes to correct design errors increases exponentially with the time to detection. Early decisions often dictate the majority of development and manufacturing costs, thus it is crucial that initial decisions on technology, processes, and materials, be made carefully. The cost of a required change for enhancing product performance, quality, or safety may be minimal during the product conceptualization phase, bothersome in both time and expense if caught during design review, but burdensome if required after prototype construction and testing, and bankrupting if found after full-scale

* This work was supported in part by the National Science Foundation under grant no. DDM 9006710

production and product delivery. Carter and Baker (1) note that on the average there are three prototype turns for an application specific integrated circuit. Such failures are wasteful and time-consuming. With short product life cycles, these failures may result in a product never getting to market as competitors capture the market first and the firm is forced to leap-frog the competition or concede the product line. The objective of concurrent engineering is to avoid design review failures by involving all relevant disciplines and concentrating on product life-cycle factors throughout the design process.

CE uses multidisciplinary teams with frequent communication and integrated information systems to facilitate product development. It can be helpful to have team members come together to review designs periodically or at specific milestones in the design process, but it is often preferable to have an integrated team that continuously monitors the design process and detects and corrects any problems as they arise.

Concurrent engineering thus produces better designs in less time. Beyond improving the quality of products and reliability of the design process, concurrent design reduces development makespan by its very nature. Consider a simple model of the design process. Product development requires the following basic tasks.

1. Conceptual design.
2. Conceptual design review.
3. Component design.
4. Component design review.
5. Test system development.
6. Manufacturing process and tooling design.
7. Environmental analysis review.

Due to information requirements, each task may require all or part of certain other tasks to be completed before the task begins. Figure 6.1a indicates the development cycle with traditional sequential design activities, and Figure 6.1b shows the advantage of concurrent design. An additional advantage of integrated CE, not reflected in the figures, is the reduction in repeated loops through these steps, resulting from design review failures. As shown in Figure 6.2, the use of design teams with information exchange and group decision making reduces the number of design changes needed and moves the design changes earlier in the process. This substantially reduces costs and development cycle time by avoiding wasted effort.

CE can be used for small product modification projects involving only a few individuals, each with multiple responsibilities, or large-scale programs, involving many participants in each discipline. For simplicity of presentation, we will make the assumption that the size of the project is such that an individual is responsible for work in each discipline: marketing, design, test, manufacturing, and purchasing. However, the concepts are equally valid, and readily extendable, to the case of larger projects with hierarchical team structures. In that event, there may be an interdisciplinary team of managers overseeing a number of interdisciplinary teams each with responsibility for a component of the overall system. Each member on these teams may represent a team within their own discipline working on their aspect of the component.

6.2 THE USE OF TEAMS

The use of teams is a key aspect of CE. Crucial to the success of CE is the existence of teams containing expertise in all areas relevant to product development. The teams must be composed of motivated individuals who possess good communication skills, training in group decision processes, and continuous access to current design information. The team should be empowered to make decisions and be led by a skilled facilitator with adequate authority.

Team Formation

Team formation is the first critical step toward achieving breakthrough success with concurrent engineering. Important team characteristics are the following.

1. The team must include a member of all disciplines responsible for product development and manufacture. This includes all disciplines potentially affected by team decision.

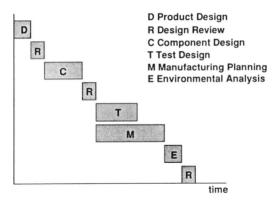

a: Sequential "Over The Wall" Design

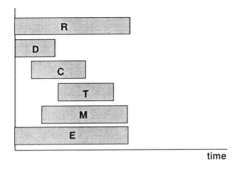

b: Concurrent Engineering Team Schedule

Figure 6.1.   Sequential versus concurrent project duration.

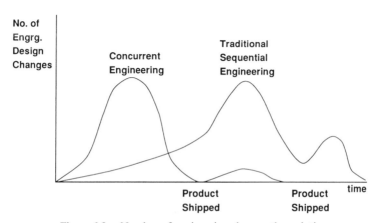

Figure 6.2.   Number of engineering changes through time.

Failure to meet this requirement jeopardizes the feasibility of resultant design and risks construction of roadblocks by disenfranchised groups. A 1990 study of the electronics industry found that the typical component design team in the United States consisted of 8 members, whereas the average size in Japan was 18. Results from organizational behavior research indicate that the more open ended the problem and the greater the amount of synthesis required, the more members the team should contain.

2. Team members must be capable of compromise and willing to accept decision by consensus. Members should be free thinking and motivated to solve problems instead of promoting traditional, parochial perspectives.

3. Team members should share a broad view and be dedicated to the success of the firm instead of being narrowly defined by the historical practice in their discipline.

4. Team members should have a knowledge background that allows them to understand the technical issues involved in the other disciplines represented on the team. Although they need not be technical experts in all areas, they should understand the terminology, technology, and key issues.

5. Team members should identify strongly with the team, and it may be preferable to have their primary allegiance to the team and not the discipline that they represent. However, it is just as important not to have any dominant voices that can dictate all decisions. Assuming deadlines will be met out of necessity and rational people will compromise in the face of these impending deadlines, equally vociferous voices each protecting their own disciplinary interests will often lead to suboptimal but workable solutions. A single dominant person, however, can lead to designs that fail to meet many criteria, e.g., a design that uses state-of-the-art technology but that cannot be readily produced or maintained or for which problems such as heat dissipation or corrosion limit reliability.

Co-location, the physical assignment of team members to a common work area is important for smooth team functioning. Experience indicates that the frequency of communication between workers depends on their proximity. Humans cannot be expected to interact as often if they are spatially separated. If space cannot be found for co-location, electronic mail capability should be provided to encourage frequent communication. As E-mail tends to be informal, it maintains some of the social aspects of interpersonal communication that tend to be lost in the exchange of physical documents. These social aspects are important for building a team identification among members.

Team Training

Teams are typically formed to handle tasks too large or demanding for a single individual (2). Because the effectiveness of a team is a function of the ability of its members to work together, it is necessary to identify factors determining the quality of team performance and training strategies to ensure team effectiveness.

Various models of group processes have been developed. Hackman (3) proposed a model conceptualizing group processes in an organizational environment, and some variables influencing team performance and training have been identified. These include the capability of team members to work together over time, the satisfaction of member needs, the acceptability of task outcomes by those individuals demanding or receiving them, the level of effort exerted by team members, the amount of knowledge and skill team members can apply to the task, and the resources such as tools, equipment, space, and staff allocated to the team. Hackman argues that the organizational environment of a team has a significant influence on its effectiveness. An implication of this is that teams should be trained in settings similar to the actual performance environment.

An interesting study of eight teams in disparate settings (4) provides evidence of the dynamic nature of team performance strategies. Based on detailed records of team meetings, Gersick (4) found that each team defined a method of performing its task in the first meeting. However, without exception, midway through the predetermined time given to each team to complete the task, each team modified the original strategy for completing the task. This modified strategy was followed until the task was completed. This indicates that team performance results from a dynamic exchange of information and resources among team members and that teams modify performance strategies at certain points in their life cycle.

A team evolution and maturation (TEAM) model (5) synthesizes the two findings of Gersick's study. This model is shown in Figure 6.3 (2). It predicts the stages that teams go through

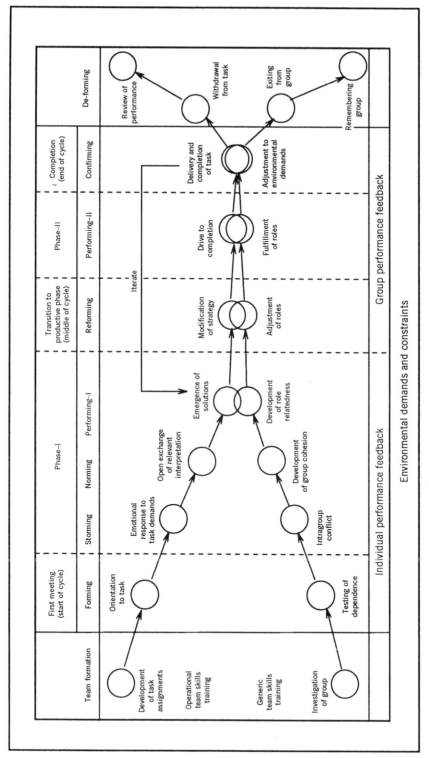

Figure 6.3. The team evolution and maturation model (adapted from ref. 2).

before, during, and after the performance of a task. It suggests that teams evolve through a series of developmental stages. The starting point and exact trajectory followed varies from team to team, depending on member experiences, individual skill requirements, task requirements, and the environmental context. It also hypothesizes that the satisfactory performance of a team is contingent on the successful resolution of two tracks. These tracks are operational team skills and general team skills training. Operational team skills are skills needed to perform the task at hand, while general team skills relate to behavioral and attitudinal responses needed by members to function effectively as a team. The convergence of these two tracks symbolizes the belief that teams experience a merging of task and teamwork skills after a period of intragroup conflict.

In addition to the models mentioned above, task-oriented models of team performance emphasize the relationship of team performance and task complexity and organization. Task complexity relates to the level of skill required to perform the subtasks. Task organization refers to the interdependencies that exist between subtasks of a team—many interrelated tasks imply a high level of team organization. Because many metrics can be defined for team tasks, it is advised that multiple measures be used to analyze team assignments (2). Task-oriented models of team performance imply task complexity and organization can be used not only to determine the optimal work and communication structures but also to guide individual and team training skills. For tasks with low levels of organization (i.e., few interdependencies exist among subtasks), the emphasis may be placed on individual performance and training. However, for tasks with high organization, effort should be devoted to developing team skills. In the literature, task-oriented models have performed impressively for predicting team performance.

Based on the models presented above, an integrated framework for team performance and training has been presented (2) (Figure 6.4). This framework shows that in general team performance is the outcome of dynamic processes governing the evolution of coordination and communication patterns in teams. The influence of organizational, task, individual, and team characteristics is also shown. Training should be used to influence these processes and their relation to team performance.

The expected performance of a team has historically been considered a function of the average skill level of the team members; however, this is not true for all tasks. Some studies show that the relationship between average skill level and overall team performance can be low. It has been suggested that this small relationship is the result of process loss. Process loss occurs whenever team members' efforts are spent in team coordination. Thus team performance may not necessarily improve by improving the skill levels of individual members.

Providing team members with information about the nature of other members' subtasks improves the quality of team performance. Training for coordination should help team members to identify their task interdependencies and should emphasize the undesirable consequences of failure to coordinate the team efforts correctly.

When individual and team training skills are combined, a decision on the optimal mix of the two has to be made. In addition, the sequence in which each should be presented must be decided. The relative level of each type of training depends on the task complexity and structure. Based on models outlined here, it follows that team training should be sequenced so that team members are allowed to master individual skills before team training skills are taught. This strategy is supported by numerous reports on its effectiveness. The training environment must replicate the actual working environment. If task conditions are stressful, then the training environment should be stressful as well. This fidelity to working conditions also is useful because it helps to identify tasks that may degrade under stressful conditions.

One of the most important factors in training is the feedback provided to the team members. Feedback may relate to individual performance or to team performance as a whole. Providing only team feedback does not recognize the contribution of individual members to the overall effort. Providing individual feedback alone does not foster team coordination skills. It has been suggested that individual feedback should be given during the initial phases of the task so as to develop individual skills, whereas team feedback should be provided in the later stages of training. Studies show that team performance improves most on that aspect of performance about which feedback is provided. This reinforces the need to maintain several metrics of team performance so that the team can be effective in all areas required. The timeliness of feedback is also important. Delays lessen the impact of feedback.

In the context of concurrent engineering, teams shall usually be composed of members of different departments of the organization. To be effective, team members must possess a variety of skills.

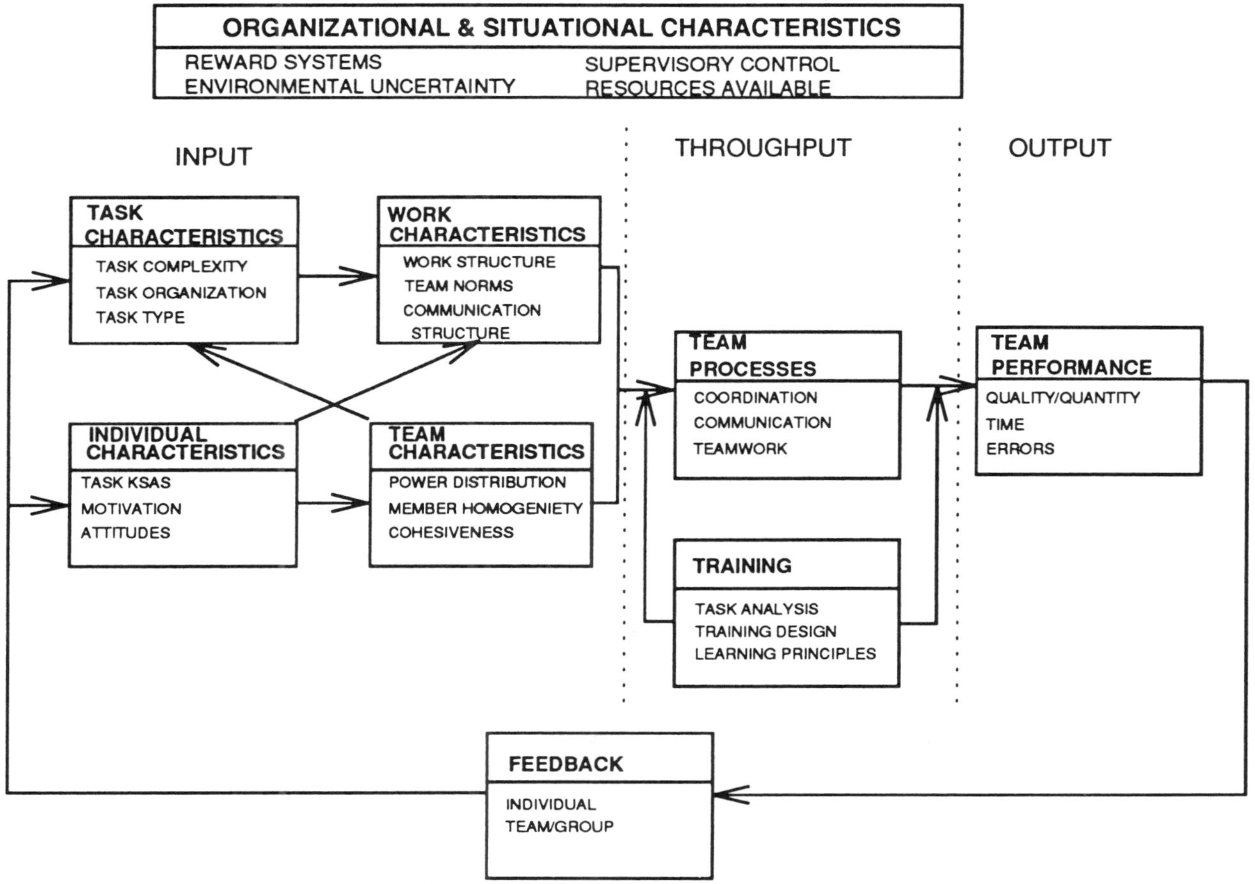

Figure 6.4. Integrated model of team performance and training (adapted from ref. 2).

1. Members must be facile with information access and exchange. CE relies on the timely exchange and use of information. Members must be able to query the integrated database to keep current on design parameter specifications.

2. Members should be able competently to represent their discipline. At a minimum, they must know all issues that could create problems and be able to identify the expert in their discipline and have access to that individual as needed.

3. Members should have a basic understanding of other disciplines represented on the team. In particular, team members should be conversant in the important issues in those disciplines and understand the terminology. Otherwise, miscommunication occurs and frustration develops.

4. Members should be given training in group-decision processes and optimal trade-off analysis. Brainstorming and affinity diagrams are useful tools for the conceptual design phase. Likewise, the ability to think about trade-offs between design options and criteria across the entire product life cycle is important. Ideally, the members should be provided with methodologies for optimizing multiobjective decision problems.

5. Members should be taught tolerance of the peculiarities of other disciplines. Manufacturing engineers are charged with constantly producing physical products on schedule. Accordingly, they spend much of their time concentrating on standardizing and executing the details of scheduling, maintenance, and production control to produce parts that have already been well defined. Traditionally, they seldom have time for conceptualizing major process changes. Design engineers, on the other hand, have relatively long-term deadlines and sketchy input instructions. They tend to be creative, conceptual thinkers but are less concerned with the details. Teams should consider such differences as an asset, because both types of skills are important.

Individual training aimed at reinforcing these skills should be an on-going effort within each department. While team training should also be imparted periodically to personnel, when a team is assembled for a particular project, an evaluation of the individual skill level of each member with respect to the project should be made, and if needed, individual training be given. The entire team should then be coached on team coordination skills, even if some of the team members have received similar training before. This will seed the communal focus on which the performance of the team will ultimately depend.

Team Leadership and Meeting Management

A properly formed and trained team, with access to relevant information, has the opportunity for success. The operation of the team will determine if the CE effort succeeds. Team operation is the responsibility of the team leader. The leader may be a member with a discipline responsibility or a manager at the next level. In either case, the leader should have the following traits and responsibilities.

1. The major objective of the leader is to see that the development process proceeds in a timely fashion and all problems are solved. Issues affecting multiple members and disciplines should be resolved by consensus.

2. It is the responsibility of the team leader to garner the necessary resources: human, hardware, and software. It is the leader's responsibility to provide access to an integrated database and monitor the updating of that database by each team member. The leader should ensure that the team's success does not depend on other groups or events. If the team is to be held responsible for the outcome of its work, it should have the ability to effect its success or failure. The team should be given access to any computer software analysis packages needed to ensure the feasibility of its decisions. If clerical support is needed for generating reports, then adequate staff should be dedicated to the team. Moreover, it is helpful if the team can be kept intact for the project's duration. Substituting a team member from one discipline partway through the development process will slow up all members due to the necessity to educate the new member and establish new interpersonal relationships.

3. The leader must act as a cheerleader to motivate members and obtain their buy-in to the team. It can be helpful to have senior management address the team and participate in

occasional updates to convince team members of the visibility and strategic importance of their work.

4. The leader should believe in empowering members to make decisions, but must also be able and willing to settle disputes.

5. The team leader participates strongly in defining the problems to be addressed by the team. It is the leader's responsibility to ensure that the problems addressed by the team fit with the corporate strategy. Thus the leader maintains contact with upper management and serves as the conduit for relevant strategic information to the team members.

6. The team leader oversees the assignment of tasks to team members. Once the problem definitions and task assignments are agreed to, it is normally best if the leader allows the members to find the solution and convince others of its appropriateness. The leader should supervise to ensure that members are communicating between themselves and with the information system. By staying current with the reported status of each team task, the leader can ensure that the project is progressing on a reasonable schedule and all members have the same information.

7. The team leader sets the agenda for each meeting. The agenda should match the team's progress relative to its project schedule and consider current decisions that impede progress along the critical path of the product development project.

8. Following each meeting, the leader is responsible for seeing that information concerning progress is distributed. This includes distributing meeting minutes to team members and updating the information system.

9. The leader also is responsible for providing an institutional memory to prevent past mistakes from being repeated.

10. The leader should recognize that all individuals are different. Constructive effort and demonstration of team spirit by members should be rewarded as well as individual accomplishment.

The first stage in team operation is to foster communication between team members. This task is not always easily accomplished. Members often come with strong allegiances to their discipline (design, test, or manufacturing for instance), prejudices about the other disciplines, a discipline-oriented mind-set and vocabulary, and a natural resistance to changing the historical mode of over-the-wall product development. The first step, therefore, is to become acquainted with one another as individuals and to accept the importance of the other individuals and the necessity of their contribution. It must be emphasized that the best designed product is worthless unless there is a customer who wants its functions and features and it can be manufactured and delivered within an acceptable time frame and price schedule.

A common vocabulary must be developed. This is best accomplished through quantification of all customer requirements. The process begins by eliciting information from customers on the functions desired and acceptable price. This information must then be translated into the internal vocabulary of the firm. Representatives from the various disciplines in the firm must agree on the meaning of the internal words. Then, these internally described requirements are converted into quantitative specifications such as 10 amps $\pm$ 0.1, 1000 hours between failures, or 0 to 60 in 8.0 s. The house of quality (6) approach has become a popular format for conducting the product conceptualization phase. A basic form is shown in Figure 6.5. Customers provide the "Whats" requirements for the product and the relative importance of each. The team then brainstorms the set of "Hows" possible for meeting the requirements. The Hows are quantified into engineering units such as psi or amps, cost–difficulty factors are added, the relative importance of the Hows for meeting the Whats is determined, and a benchmarking evaluation of existing company product performance versus the competition is performed. At this point, judgments can be made about proper target values for each How. This step should conclude with an agreement on the objective of the team. It may be to deliver to the customer in four months an acceptable prototype that could be manufactured at a rate of 200 per day at a cost of $2 each. After completing the house, the engineering characteristics (or Hows) become the Whats for the next level of the design process. The process is repeated until all design and manufacturing details are specified.

It is crucial that buy-in for the outcome of the group-planning process is obtained from all team members. If one team member is interested in the "perfect design," one that does everything and another is only interested in getting an acceptable prototype out the door, then dissatisfaction and conflict will inevitably develop. As a team develops a common, shared

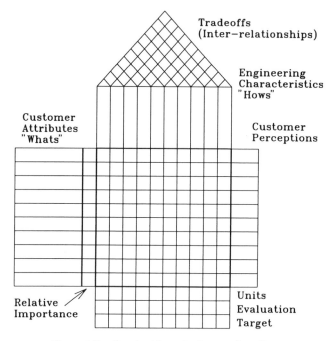

Figure 6.5.   Standard form for house of quality.

vision and familiarity among team members increases, it is possible to go beyond communication to collaboration. When collaborating, team members work together constructively toward a
common goal. The readily adapt their work to suit the needs of other team members, and they
identify with the team as much as with their discipline. Team members are learning, and a
synthesis takes place wherein idea sharing leads to improved designs not just mutually acceptable designs.

The culmination of the product conceptualization phase includes a set of performance
criteria and characteristics for the product. The team must then decide who has responsibility
for each of the criteria and characteristics. For each criteria or feature, a test procedure must be
identified for ensuring achievement of that target. The product may also be broken down into
components at this stage and the team must agree that these components can be integrated to
meet overall product objectives. It is also advantageous at this point to brainstorm potential
problems and conflicts between criteria and component integration. This serves as the initial
check for design for manufacturability and design for testability.

Organizational roadblocks can impede CE. Supervisors must support product development
teams and allow team members to devote their time and effort to team projects. Obviously, the
attitude take by the permanent supervisor is critical. While turf battles are inevitable, and the
team members will have a natural inclination and responsibility to support the interests of their
discipline, the supervisor should make it clear that the objective is for the team to develop a
solution that is optimal for the overall firm, subject to the technical constraints imposed by the
state of the art in each discipline. The team should not become a battleground for interdiscipline
squabbling and positioning within the company. It is desirable for the team to develop its own
esprit de corps. As discussed earlier, co-location for the duration of the project is advisable to
foster group identification as well as to facilitate communication. Acceptance of peers and
respect for one's contribution are basic tenets of the human hierarchy of needs. Once the
individual becomes part of the team, his or her motivation is affected by the attitude of other
team members toward the individual.

Computer Support for Teams

The principal benefit of team formation is the synergy obtained by organizing workers in a peer group. This synergy results from the exchange of ideas and the sharing of the expertise of individual team members by the entire team. However, teams may be composed of members dispersed in different locations. This dispersion mandates the implementation of efficient procedures for sharing and timely disbursement of information to all team members. Even in a small organization where all team members are co-located, scheduling conflicts can impose the same requirements on information sharing and distribution.

Exchange of ideas is usually accomplished through meetings. However, the proliferation of computers has extended the traditional concept of face-to-face meetings. Today, meetings can be of the following types:

1. Traditional (face-to-face) meetings.
2. Teleconferencing (voice) meetings.
3. Videoconferencing (voice and picture) meetings.
4. Computer network conferencing (text and graphics) meetings.

Traditional meetings have the advantage of allowing rapid exchange and discussion of ideas. However, such meetings can be dominated by personalities rather than issues and may need to be controlled to maintain the focus. Teleconferencing is usually less formal than other meeting methods. Its principal advantage is that transmission time is cheap and available on demand. However, the lack of formality makes this a less attractive means of communication. Videoconferencing has not gained widespread popularity as a means of exchanging ideas, primarily because of the special equipment usually needed. Also, transmission may not be available on demand. Another often quoted reason for the lack of popularity of videoconferencing is the attitudinal problem of (non)users—there is usually a reluctance to conduct a spirited discussion with a camera.

Computer network conferencing is fast becoming a preferred means of meeting, mainly due to the increasing availability of hardware and software needed for the task. Computer networks within organizations are now commonplace, and with the implementation of the proposed electronic super highways, rapid transfer of large files and messages around the world will be routine. It is estimated that more than 60% of all PCs are currently linked together, and this figure is expected to increase as the decade progresses.

Sophisticated software support for team use of computers is also emerging. A new term, *groupware,* has been coined for this class of software. A formal definition of groupware is any information system designed to enable groups to work together electronically (7). Stevenson (8) classifies the tasks performed by groupware into the following two categories:

Information Sharing. Tools devoted to the free exchange of information fall under this heading. They provide efficient mechanisms for accessing and moving data.
Information Management. Tools in this category are concerned with the organization and facilitation of work processes rather than communication of information. Attention is focused on where, why, and how the work gets done. In addition, functions such as the status of projects, creation of new tasks, and location of files and messages are the responsibility of tasks in this category.

Tasks related to information sharing include messaging (or E-mail), file transport, group faxing, WAN (wide area network) connections, workgroup scheduling, BBS-style discussion, real-time chat, structured meeting support, decision support, shared contact database, shared information database, and collaborative documents. Tasks related to information management include access control (security), data search and retrieval, archiving, forms routing and tracking, task routing and tracking, and forms and report creation (5). Software packages currently available with some of all these features include CM/1, Lotus Notes, Beyond Inc., Digital Team Links, and Futurus Team.

On a more sophisticated note, group decision process rooms are now available. These rooms allow each team member to interact through computer terminals. Software generally allows users to conduct several conversations simultaneously, adding their input to each issue as appropriate. Members can vote electronically and have results automatically tabulated and displayed for discussion.

Software for the use of group decision support that resides on a single computer operated by an individual team member also has been included among the computer support requirements of teams (9). Examples of this type of software include Boothroyd and Dewhurst's design-for-assembly (DFA) and design-for manufacture (DFM) software, which quantifies design factors so as to aid the group in design activities by forcing it to reach a consensus on the measurement ratings used to assess a design alternative's ease of assembly or manufacture. However, such software tools must support the team interaction and not replace team members. One of the requirements of software used in a group setting is speed: the key to consistent measurements made by a group is rapid iteration (9). Used properly, the group process of using the computer tool should be as valuable as the analytical results derived from its use (10).

Advantages and Disadvantages of Groupware

The following benefits of groupware are listed in ref. 11.

> Cutting down on face-to-face meetings frequency.
> Reducing meeting time
> Curtailing missed communication.
> Reducing physical transfer of information.
> Eliminating time lost to interruptions.
> Enabling quick decision making.
> Speeding organizational learning.
> Increasing flow of information.

Among the disadvantages of groupware are the following.

> *Information Overload.* Because it is easy to transmit and exchange information, excessive information flow can occur.
> *Forced Structure.* The use of common tools forces a structure that may or may not be conducive for all team activities. Not all packages provide adequate support for all tasks, and the management should evaluate the needs of the team and find the best tools for those particular needs. Too structured meetings can lead to a stifling of creativity.
> *Groupthink.* A risk associated with group-based decision-making processes is that individual viewpoints can be buried even when they are correct (7).

In conclusion, team performance can be greatly enhanced by provision of appropriate computer support. Among the tools gaining popularity are computer network-based systems and groupware software tools.

Information Systems

We have already alluded to the importance of integrated information systems. Converting from a sequential to concurrent development mode places new demands on the information system. Whereas previously it may have been acceptable to only ensure validity and completeness of documentation at the point the design was handed over the wall, concurrent development requires real-time updating the task status and design decisions.

The information system should support a reporting system that routinely informs all team members as decisions are made or parameters are specified. In this manner, all participants have access to the latest version of the major design decisions. The information system should also be open to inquiry regarding details for all decisions. For instance, upon changing a geometric dimension or tolerance for a part, the purchasing or manufacturing representative on the team should be able to review that change for cost and feasibility. Upon changing a design specification for component location on a printed-circuit board, before the board designer invests considerable time in board layout, the manufacturing engineer should be able to confirm that component spacing is acceptable for assembly and the test engineer should be able to confirm that test hookups will be possible; heat dissipation problems also could be considered. The design knowledge base must be open to interrogation of design details by all team members. Ideally, the design database should include tools for generating reports on the history of design

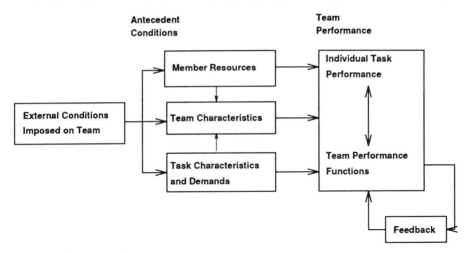

Figure 6.6. Conceptual model of team performance (adapted from ref. 2).

changes, a justification or explanation of the trade-offs that led to that change or specification, a record of design problems and solution approaches tried, and automatic highlighting of potential problems caused by each design decision. This latter feature can be based on historical records; a detailed model of purchasing, manufacturing, and test capabilities; or internal design rules. The set of quantified product performance objectives should be included in the knowledge base and the information system should continuously track the status of the current product design relative to those objectives.

The information system should support hierarchical reporting as well as vertical. At each level, participants must be able to check how their design decisions mesh with higher level goals. Managers must be able to track the performance of each subtask and ensure compatibility with other ongoing activities. Additional advantages accrue from the development of the integrated design knowledge base. Because many problems are multidisciplinary, team members may be able to contribute to solving problems faced by other members. The member with the solution may be aware of the existence of a problem only through examination of the knowledge base.

Team Performance Evaluation

Team performance is a result of individual and collective efforts of team members. The overall performance of a team can suffer not only because of unsatisfactory performance of team members but also because the team fails to coordinate. To be able to judge the performance of a team, it is necessary to understand how humans function together effectively.

A conceptual model for team performance is shown in Figure 6.6 (12). In this representation, external conditions include the time allocated to perform the task, job-operating procedures, power, and authority allocation. Member resources include individual skills and motivation, attitude, personalities, and traits of team members. Task characteristics relate to individual and synchronized activities necessary for effective team performance. Team characteristics include group cohesion, group size and structure, and team leadership. Feedback relates to the type and timeliness of information relating to team performance provided by either internal procedures or external judges.

A taxonomy for team performance is shown below (13). This taxonomy is based on studies on team performance (14, 15). Shiflett validated the performance by observing combat teams and combat support teams in the army, while Cooper used the taxonomy to evaluate command and control (C^2) teams of the air force for managing combat missions and coordinating responses in crisis situations. This classification can be used not only to set standards for judging the performance of concurrent engineering teams, but for team activities as well.

Taxonomy for Team Performance

1. Orientation functions
   a. Information exchange regarding member resources and constraints
   b. Information exchange regarding team tasks, goals, and mission
   c. Information exchange regarding environmental characteristics and constraints
   d. Priority assignment among tasks
2. Resource distribution functions
   a. Matching member resources to task requirements
   b. Load balancing
3. Timing functions (activity pacing)
   a. General activity pacing
   b. Individual activity pacing
4. Response coordination functions
   a. Response sequencing
   b. Time and position coordination of responses
5. Motivational functions
   a. Development of team performance norms
   b. Generating acceptance of team performance norms
   c. Establishing team-level performance–rewards linkages
   d. Reinforcement of task orientation.
   e. Balancing of team orientation with individual competition
   f. Resolution of performance-relevant conflicts
6. Systems monitoring functions
   a. General activity monitoring
   b. Individual activity monitoring
   c. Adjustment of team and member activities in response to errors and omissions

Cooper also included a category on procedure maintenance relating to the ability of the team to adhere to set procedures for responding to situations. However, this category is meaningful in military organizations and may not usually be applicable in concurrent engineering related teams.

It is possible to assign different weights to the categories of this taxonomy to generate different schemes for assessing the performance of teams. Obviously, any such scheme should place significant emphasis on the team's ability to complete satisfactorily the task for which it was assembled.

Member Motivation and Reward Structure

Teams are more likely to be successful when the team members have a personal stake in the team outcome. Thus it is important to hold all team members responsible for the outcome of the team effort. Irregardless of whether team members still reside officially according to the firm's organizational chart in their professional discipline group, their performance evaluation and compensation should be tied to their contribution to the team and the overall success of the team.

To support the evaluation of the team, accounting systems should be set up to track product life cycle costs. Small increases in design effort may pay off many times over the product development, manufacture, and service life. However, if design cost is budgeted, tracked, and used for control purposes, emphasis will be on releasing the design as soon as possible without adequate evaluation and optimization.

Productivity measurement must be modified as well. The objective is to create a design of a successful product in a short time frame. Thus time to market and market share captured are the relevant measures. Poor productivity measures can lead to the wrong behavior. If a design or layout engineer is measured based on the number of layouts drawn, the motivation is to stay in isolation in his or her workstation and draw the part in a personally pleasing and simple manner. After all, the engineer believes (minor) changes can always be made later, and that new drawings will increase productivity. The system encourages designers to do it over instead of doing it right.

TABLE 6.1. Human Resource Classes for Product Design

1. Customer
2. Design engineer
3. Marketing representative
4. Manufacturing manager
5. Production engineer
6. Process engineer
7. Product engineer
8. Probe test engineer
9. Electrical test engineer
10. Packaging engineer
11. CAD technician

6.3 EXPERIMENTAL EVALUATION

To examine the effect of teams on project length, an experimental simulation study was conducted. A representative list of human resources (potential team members) for the design of semiconductor devices is given in Table 6.1. These classes, along with the parameter values used below were generated following discussion with several firms in this industry. The hypothesis guiding the study was that the CE team concept may reduce product development cycle time by dedicating human resources to the project and by reducing the probability of design failures as the design is passed on and tested at the next stage. Figure 6.7 gives an overview of the principal steps in the design process.

The general problem of completing a number of product development projects falls into the class of multiple project, constrained resource, scheduling problems. Each project has a set of activities. Each activity requires a certain commitment of resources for completion. Generally, activity times and the set of activities are assumed to be known. Solution procedures for single projects are reviewed and compared in ref. 16. We are interested, however, in the situation in which multiple projects are being planned, and these projects come into existence dynamically over time. Literature in this area is sparse, but one study (17) concluded that due dates can be accurately estimated by fitting a new project into an existing schedule upon its arrival and adding an expected delay factor. Our actual situation also is characterized by random activity times (at least for some activities). Moreover, design review failures may cause cycling through the activity network, and thus branching is probabilistic. Other issues must also be considered in project management. Workers may be dedicated to a single project at a time or allowed to work part time on several projects. Single-project dedication will probably result in idle time while waiting for supporting activities; however, if effort is split among too many projects or activities, the worker will become less efficient because he or she may forget the details of specific projects and because of the unavoidable changeover time in switching between projects. Project durations will also increase due to parallel processing. In larger projects, several technicians may be allowed to work simultaneously on different aspects of an activity. Situations of this type can often be handled by dividing activities into subactivities, each of which requires a single unit of resource during its performance.

Algorithms for Labor Assignment and Team Formation

We will now consider several approaches for allocating workers to projects. To test the usefulness of teams, we must specify precisely how teams are to be formed and the alternative policy if teams are not used. We will contrast the use of teams with a general labor pool policy. We assume each activity requires a nonnegative time commitment from each resource. Limits may exist on the number of units of each resource that can be applied at one time. We let M be the number of resource classes. Before presenting these policies formally, we need the following additional notation:

Θ_k equals $(1_k, \ldots, N_k)$, the set of activities required for project k
R_j the number of resources of type j available, $j = 1, \ldots, M$

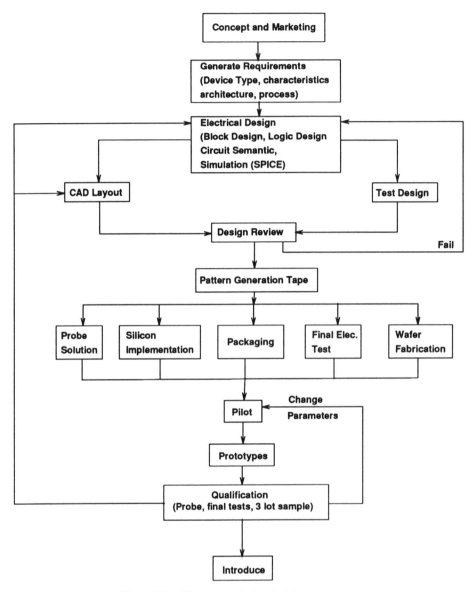

Figure 6.7. Major steps in the decision process.

s_k time project k will be available to begin design
t_{ijk} total time of resource j needed to complete activity i of project k
n_{ijk} maximum number of resource j that can be constructively assigned to activity ik at any time
r_{ijk} proportion of time an assigned resource j is devoted to activity ik during processing, $0 \leq r_{ijk} \leq 1$
c_{ik} completion time of activity ik

The n_{ijk} values indicate whether a activity can be shared among resources of the same type. For instance, in large projects, managers may be able to split the entire design into pieces and assign each piece individually. In smaller projects, this may just lead to waste and duplication, thus we would restrict $n_{ijk} = 1$. Values of $r_{ijk} < 1$ indicate that the activity is intermittent. For instance, the CAD technician and design engineer may iteratively pass the design back and forth during development. While the CAD technician is working on the layout, the design engineer may be able to work on another project and vice versa.

Our objective is to reduce throughput time for design projects given resource limits. Accordingly, we will use the objectives of minimizing makespan and mean flow time. Let $C_k = \max_{i \in \Theta_k} c_{ik}$ be the completion time of project k. Then, makespan is given by

$$C_{\max} = \max_k C_k$$

the earliest time at which all projects are completed. Mean flow time for all projects is given by

$$\overline{F} = \frac{\sum_{k=1}^{K} (C_k - s_k)}{K}$$

Our objective is to minimize makespan and mean flow time. Accordingly, scheduling will be based on first-in-system–first-served (FISFS) and shortest-processing-time (SPT) rules. FISFS is used for ordering projects, and SPT for ordering activities within projects. A resource is said to be *free* if it is not assigned to any activity. An activity is *available* if all of its predecessors for the same project are completed and a positive amount of at least one resource required by the activity is free. $IP\{ik\}$ is the set of immediate predecessor activities for ik. We let A be the set of activities available to be started at any point in time. Variables X_{ijkt} indicate the amount of resource j assigned to activity ik at time t. The completion time of activity ik is then given by

$$c_{ik} = \max_j \min\{\tau : \int_0^\tau r_{ijk} X_{ijkt} dt = t_{ijk}\}$$

Task ik is available at time t if the following two conditions are met:

$$\max_{s \in IP\{ik\}}\{c_s\} \le t$$

and there exists some resource j, with $t'_{ijkt} > 0$ and

$$\sum_{ik} X_{ijkt} < R_j$$

where t'_{ijkt} is the unfulfilled portion of t_{ijk} at time t. We can compute

$$t'_{ijkt} = t_{ijk} - \int_0^t r_{ijk} X_{ijk\tau} d\tau$$

We now describe scheduling policies for the use of labor pools and design teams. Our scheduling heuristics perform as deterministic stimulations. We move forward in time, always assigning as much resource as is free, up to the limit n_{ijk}, to the available activities. Tasks are ordered by FISFS, with ties being broken by SPT. We begin with two alternative scheduling policies for allocating human resources from labor pools.

Labor Pool Heuristic I

Step 0: Initialize. $\tau = 0$. Task $ik \in A$ if $s_k = 0$, and $IP\{ik\} = \phi$. $R'_j = R_j$ for all j.
Step 1: Select task. If all projects are complete, stop. If A empty, go to 3. Otherwise, from A, select the activity with minimum s_k and then minimum t_{ijk}. Call this activity $i'k'$. If no such activity exists, update τ until A is nonempty.
Step 2: Allocate resources. Set $X_{i'jk'\tau} = \min\{R'_j, n_{i'jk'}\}$ for all j with $t_{i'jk'} > 0$. Set $R'_j = R'_j - r_{i'jk'}X_{i'jk'\tau}$. Remove $i'k'$ from A and go to 1.
Step 3: Update. Advance τ until an active activity is completed or a new project is available. Update $t'_{ijk\tau}$, R'_j, and A. Go to 1.

Labor Pool Heuristic II

The first labor pool heuristic allocated as much effort as possible to the earliest arriving project and shortest-time activities. Alternatively, resources could be shared among all available activities. This forms the essence of the second labor pool heuristic.

All steps are as in labor poor heuristic I except allocating resources.

Step 2: Allocate resources. For available activities ik, set $X_{ijk\tau} = R_j/r_{ijk}a_j$, where a_j is the number of available activities with $t'_{ijk\tau} > 0$. If, for any ik, $X_{ijk\tau} > n_{ijk}$, set $X_{ijk\tau} = n_{ijk}$ and proportionally allocate remaining resource.

Design Team Heuristic

Next, consider the use of teams. Each team will contain a lead design engineer, process engineer, test engineer, and technician. Remaining labor classes may be included in teams, treated as pools or assumed to be infinite. In the case that r_{ijk} values are small, we will allow up to U projects to be assigned to a team at any time. We will assign projects and schedule activities as follows:

$Y_{kl\tau}$ equals 1 if team l is assigned to project k at time τ and 0 otherwise
N_l the number of projects currently assigned to team l
$N_{jl\tau}$ the number of projects assigned to team l at time τ for which there exists an available activity ik with $t'_{ijk\tau} > 0$
Z_{jl} number of class j resources in team l, normally 1

The labor scheduling heuristic is then

Step 0: Initialize. $\tau = 0$. $N_l = 0$ for all l. $k \in A$, if $s_k = 0$. All $Y_{kl0} = 0$.
Step 1: Assign projects. If A nonempty, select $k' \in A$ such that $s_{k'} = \min_{k \in A}\{s_k\}$. If there exists l such that $N_l < U$, then set $Y_{l'k\tau} = 1$ where $l' = \text{argmin}\{N_l\}$. Set $N_{l'} = N_{l'} + 1$. Remove k from A. If A nonempty, go to 1; otherwise 2.
Step 2: Update. Advance τ until an active project is complete or a new project arrives. Time is updated from activity completion to activity completion. At each step update $t'_{ijk\tau}$ as above, where

$$X_{ijk\tau} = \min\left\{ \frac{Z_{jl(k)}}{r_{ijk}N_{jl(k)\tau}}, n_{ijk} \right\} \; if \; Y_{lk\tau} = 1$$

and any residual resource is allocated proportionally.

The allocation rule in step 2 assumes shared processing similar to labor pool heuristic II. A FISFS–SPT rule also could be used.

Experimental Conditions

An experimental study was performed to determine if design review failures significantly affect performance measures. If this is the case, then teams offer potential advantages when competing on time-to-market. Using the project steps of Figure 6.7, five sets of projects were generated randomly; labor requirements were guided by the mean values shown in Table 6.2 for each labor class and activity. Each set contained 100 projects. Standard deviations were set at 10% of mean time. Workers were assigned to a project full time with, at most, one worker per class on any project (i.e., $n_{ijk} = r_{ijk} = 1$). The system assumed 10 project engineers and five of each of the other classes. Designs were allowed to fail at review and qualification stages with 0%, 10%, 25%, or 50% probability.

Figures 6.8 and 6.9 present makespan and mean flow time results for labor pool heuristic I. As we might suspect for makespan, the number of projects to which a worker could be simultaneously assigned had little effect. The interesting phenomenon is that the effect of the design failure probability is highly significant. The qualification failure probability had little impact until it was raised to 50%. This finding suggests that it might be reasonable to use teams early on in the conceptual development, but less is gained by maintaining the team past the design review

TABLE 6.2. Mean Project Task Times in Man-Years

Activity	Labor Class									
	2	3	4	5	6	7	8	9	10	11
Concept	0.1	0.2								
General requests	0.2		0.05	0.1	0.1	0.1				
Electrical design	0.3									
CAD layout	0.1									0.1
Test design							0.05	0.05		
Design review	0.03			0.03		0.03				0.03
Pattern general tape			0.02							
Probe							0.06			
Silicon implant			0.02				0.06			
Packaging									0.1	
Final electrical test								0.06		
Wafer fabrication			0.02			0.1				
Pilot			0.02	0.02	0.02	0.02				
Prototype	0.1		0.02	0.02	0.02	0.02				
Qualification	0.1		0.02	0.02	0.02	0.02	0.02	0.02	0.02	
Introduce		0.02	0.02							

stage. Similar results are shown in Figure 9 except that for mean flow time it is clearly preferable to assign workers to a single project. By assigning workers to a single project, that project progresses at a faster rate and we obtain a steady rate of project completions. In general, results of labor pool heuristic II were similar to heuristic I. As one would expect, for the same reason that a single project per worker was preferred, mean flow times were slightly higher for heuristic II.

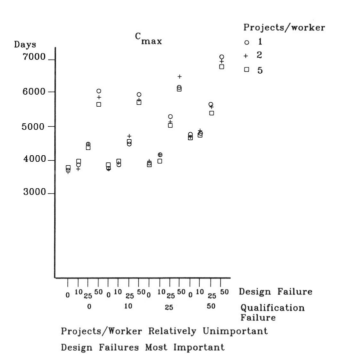

Figure 6.8. Variation of make span versus design and qualification failures.

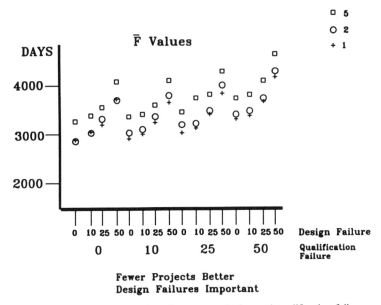

Figure 6.9. Variation of mean flow time versus design and qualification failures.

6.4 SUMMARY

We have seen that the use of teams is an important component of concurrent engineering. By providing teams with the proper physical, information, and human resources, product development projects can be conducted faster and yield better results. The extent of the improvement depends on the willingness of upper management to lead the team effort and institute the required organizational changes, such as giving team leaders the authority to evaluate workers; providing space, technical tools, and support staff to teams; and empowering teams to make decisions. The greater the level of design project failures with the old approach, the greater the opportunity for improvement with team-oriented concurrent engineering.

BIBLIOGRAPHY

1. D.E. CARTER and B.S. BAKER, *Concurrent Engineering: The Product Development Environment for the 1990s,* Addison-Wesley Publishing Co., Inc., Reading, Mass., 1992.
2. E. SALAS, T.L. DICKINSON, S.A. CONVERSE, and S.I. TANNENBAUM, "Towards and Understanding of Team Performance and Training" in *Teams, Their Training and Performance,* ed. R.W. Swezey and E. Salas, Ablex Publishing Corp., Norwood, N.J., 1992, chap. 1, pp. 3–29.
3. J.R. HACKMAN, *A Normative Model of Work Team Effective,* Yale University, New Haven, Conn., 1983, Tech. Rep. 2.
4. C.J.G. GERSICK, "Time and Transition in Work Teams: Towards a New Model of Group Development," *Acad. Manage. Rev.* **31,** 274–309 (1988).
5. B.B. MORGAN, JR., A.S. GLICKMAN, E.A. WOODARD, A.S. BLAIWES, and E. SALAS, *Measurement of Team Behaviors in a Team Environment,* Naval Training Center, 1986, Tech. Rep. NTSC TR 86 014.
6. J.R. HAUSER and D. CLAUSING, "The House of Quality," *Harvard Bus. Rev.,* 66, 63–73 (1988).

7. R. JOHANSEN, *Groupware: Computer Support for Business Teams,* Free Press, New York, 1988.

8. T. STEVENSON, "Groupware: Are We Ready?" *PC Mag.* **12**(11), 267–299 (1993).

9. D.A. DIEROLF and K.J. RITCHER, *Concurrent Engineering Teams,* Institute for Defense Analysis, Alexandria, VA, 1990, Tech. Rep. IDA P-2516.

10. W. CRALLEY, D.A. DIEROLF, and K.J. RITCHER, *Computer Support for Conducting Supportability Trade-offs in a Team Setting,* Institute for Defense Analysis, Alexandria, VA, 1990, Tech. Rep. IDA P-2313.

11. S. OPPER and H. FERSKO-WEISS, *Technology for Teams: Enhancing productivity in Networked Organizations,* Van Nostrand Reinhold, Co., Inc., New York, 1992.

12. V.F. NIVEA, E.A. FLEISHMAN, and A. REICK, *Team Dimensions: Their Identity, Their Measurement and Their Relationships,* Response Analysis Corp. 1978, Tech. Rep. DAHC19-78-C-0001.

13. E. SALAS, T.L. DICKINSON, S.A. CONVERSE, and S.I. TANNENBAUM, "Towards a Taxonomy of Team Performance Functions" in *Teams, Their Training and Performance,* ed. R.W. Swezey and E. Salas, Ablex Publishing Corp. Norwood, NJ, 1992, chap. 2, pp. 31–56.

14. S.C. SHIFLETT, S.J. PRICE, and F.M. SCHEMMER, *The Definition and Measurement of Team Functions,* 1982, Tech. Rep. MD:ARRO.

15. M. COOPER, S.C. SHIFLETT, A.L. KOROTKIN, and E.A. FLEISHMAN, *Command and Control Teams: Techniques for Assessing Team Performance,* 1984, Tech. Rep. MD:ARRO.

16. J.H. PATTERSON, "A Comparison of Exact Approaches for Solving the Multiple Constrained Resource, Project Scheduling Problem," *Manage. Sci.* **30**(7), 854–867 (1984).

17. J. DUMONT and V.A. MABERT, "Evaluating Project Scheduling and Due Date Assignment Procedures: An Experimental Analysis," *Manage. Sci.* **34**(1), 101–118 (1988).

CHAPTER 7

CAD Software

VIRGINIA MILLER
Boeing Aerospace and Defense

7.1 CAD PACKAGES REVIEWED

Introduction

Two- and three-dimensional (2D, 3D) software design packages are available on a personal computer (PC) and mainframe or network platforms with as many options as the imagination allows. The more power or functions the system offers, the longer the time required to learn the system. The 2D packages perform simple spatial functions such as scaling, while the 3D packages also do solid modeling, wire framing, and analysis of component material properties. As there are many packages to choose from and many special operations performed, a description and discussion of five packages follow.

Common CAD Screen Layouts

The display screens of the packages typically have features such as on the screen status line, function–procedure prompts, and pull-down menus both on screen and accessed from sidebar menus. Error reporting ranges from limited messages of the MicroStation to the more complex error checking of Mentor to print, plot, and save.

Common Command Structures

Input commands are entered by function keys, mouse, and keyboard in all cases and by a pointer–digitize tablet (an icon-driven graphic command) with AutoCAD and MicroStation. All have sidebar command menus. AutoCAD and I/EMS are right sided, whereas Mentor and CATIA have theirs on the left side. Additional pull-down menus are available from the sidebar and are accessed with a mouse.

MicroStation, I/EMS, and AutoCAD have an additional feature that allows one drawing to be imported into another via XREF and Fence. AutoCAD, I/EMS, and CATIA approximately evaluate material properties, such as Possion's ratio, center of gravity, and the bulk and elastic modulus, and all have the ability to do thermal finite element analysis (FEA).

Some common features are basic geometric shapes and text creation, shape modification, dimensioning, tolerancing, and mapping part attributes to parts. The different design command names and functions will be given for each package. Isometric projection and wire-frame geometry are available in I/EMS, AutoCAD, CATIA, and in the 3D programs of MicroStation and Mentor.

7.2 AUTOCAD

Description

AutoCAD is a PC-based, 2D and 3D mechanical design and drafting package. Geometric shapes and figures are created and modified for engineering drawing. A reduced instruction set processor (RISC), with a limited number of instructions, is built into the processor, reducing the response time to run some applications on the AutoCAD development system (ADS). Cross-hairs and a mouse are used to locate geometric shapes within the work area. A $X-Y$ construction plane is used for the 2D mode that uses a three-point origin placed by the user, known as the user coordinate system (UCS) (1).

Command Structure

To support many applications, AutoCAD has an open architecture for easy customization of menus. The main menu is the screen menu, which includes the drawing editor, configuration, plot, file utility, and operating parameters menus. A dialogue box appears when selected items are chosen from the pull-down menus to assist the user. The following are examples of screen editor commands.

1. Set-up types of measurements or limits to the drawing area.
2. Blocks allows drawings to be grouped for insertion in other parts of the drawing.
3. Dim adds dimensions, and tolerances changes the drawing size.
4. Display commands refresh, redraw, or automatically redraw the screen and changes the viewing area.
5. Draw creates and modifies geometric shapes and adds text.
6. Edit allows modification of the actual drawing geometry using trim, move, rotate, and extend commands.
7. Inquiry shows the location of a point or angle, evaluates areas, and gives database information.
8. Layer changes the visibility, color, and line type of a layer.
9. Settings controls the grid spacing, axis, size of the target box, and color.

Other special menus are the utility or directory files, 3D for 3D drawings, and autoshade to show shading or a shadowing from a chosen line of light.

Discussion

The AutoCAD commands are path dependent, e.g., the undo command will remove the screen image and any previous drawing layers up to an earlier drawing level. Other features are AutoLISP and ADS. AutoLISP is an AutoCAD program that enhances the AutoCAD drawing and editing commands. For example, reference coordinates can be created and 2D spirals, holes, or slots in a 3D surface can be programmed and saved. AutoLISP is an interpretive system, with instructions being read, interpreted, validated, and then executed in sequence.

Description of ADS

ADS is an AutoCAD development system using a C language base interface into the core and an independent C compiler. The AutoCAD core holds the basic instruction set of the AutoCAD platform, maintains the database, and allows access to the data, using AutoCAD geometry commands, functions, and C options. Limited animation is available.

Solid modeling and wire frames are created using simple Boolean rules to add or subtract geometric shapes to a drawing shape, e.g., a pipe is created by using two cylinders to obtain an inside and outside diameter, (ID, OD). These types of 2D forms are used to generate solids or extruded solids of revolution.

7.3 MICROSTATION 32

Description

MicroStation 32 (version 3.2) is a 2D mechanical drafting package with 3D wire-frame capability (2). The 2D package is quick and easy to use with no shape or drawing distortion. The in–out logic is in a noun–verb format.

Version 4.0 has a graphical user interface; movable and resizable views; movable command windows with pull-down menus; and enhanced 3D capability for 3D modeling, dimensioning, and global modifications.

Display Screen

The display screen has an additional control called a tool palette and numbered–names view screens. Dialogue and setting boxes are accessed from the pull-down menu. The setting boxes change how a design is displayed, placed, scaled, and dimensioned.

An element selection is accessed from the tool palette and allows manipulation of geometric shapes. These elements are isolated on the display screen using a "fence," or a line encircling the element to allow one element at a time to be modified or all elements moved. The work area is a view window that shows a partial or whole design and can be rotated, numbered, and saved for reuse.

Command Structure

The icon tablet holds the design menu of common geometric shapes of arcs, parabolas, circles, lines, etc. Dimensioning menus control scale and radial, linear angular, and dimensioning characteristics. Drawing manipulation menus change coordinates, dynamics, views, rotation, and depth and allows elements to be copied, deleted, undone, redone, and colored. Additional menus allow the attributes of text, level, scale, etc. to be changed.

Construct menus are unique to MicroStation and allow creation of lines, tangents, bisectors, parallel lines, and extension. Analytic operations find and scale distances between points and areas (unlike AutoCAD), while environmental parameters of inches, decimals, millimeters etc. are set by default or entered into a seed file for scaling and dimensioning.

Discussion

Other special features of MicroStation 32 are the reference and 3D projection menus. The fence feature, mentioned earlier, acts to exclude elements either inside or overlapping the fence boundary. Elements overlapping the fence can be clipped to modify only the design elements inside. The elements inside the fence can be moved, copied, and deleted and the weight, color, and style can be changed.

A reference file can be imported into the design file for viewing and construction, without needing additional memory. Elements inside the reference file cannot be changed but can be added to the design file. In addition, the file is used to create a drawing larger than the memory capacity of the system. More than one file can be in a drawing, and it is displayed without any intelligence.

7.4 I/EMS

Description

The I/EMS is a 3D stand-alone or mainframe workstation for mechanical design (3, 4). Workstations can be added as needed.

Command Structure

I/EMS allows a top-down or bottom-up drawing. In the top-down design approach, all subelements of the design are within one model. This design file becomes a first definition or predefinition of the design.

The file structure holds four file types: layout model, atomic, reference assembly, and the drawing sheet. The layout model file is a set of the solid elements created in the design file. These file elements include the fit check of the end of assembly and the operating environment of the assembly. The atomic model is the file location of a component or part solid. These part–

components views are used to create the assembly and held in the reference assembly file. The drawing sheet file is the address of the visible and hidden edges of a model, or reference assembly files, and holds the dimensions and geometric tolerances for a formal released drawing.

Product data management (PDM) is the product data management base in I/EMS. When a part is finished, a check categorizes the part in the catalog of attribute fields.

Discussion

The design starts with a layout of a conceptual model of parts, profiles, and axis of rotation such as a mechanical design block as a switch or hardware buildups. Dimensions and tolerances are not added at this level.

I/EMS has a unique feature of associative geometry and point. For example, when a design element, a length of line, is placed in association with a graphic element, the line will change as the graphic element is manipulated. An important concern in using I/EMS is understanding how a design is globally modified. The form or shape used to format the design is the set of geometric approximations used for global modifications. Designs formatted as a wire frame, solid, and B-spline all have different approximating equations. This feature can then affect the form, fit, or function of the end product. In addition, I/EMS can be used to create models for numerical-controlled (NC) data and model postprocessing data.

7.5   CATIA

Description

Computer-Graphics Aided Three-Dimensional Interactive Application (CATIA) is a mechanical design package for creating 2D and 3D designs. CATIA can show depth perception between design elements and analyze kinematic information. CATIA is a one database system that allows a warm start or work to be done at the last immediate level (4).

Command Structure

Besides the common input commands, a special file menu includes the following:

1. File, to change from one design model to another.
2. Read, to retrieve a stored file.
3. Delete, deletes a design from a current field.
4. Create, creates a new design from an empty file.

A four-button graphics pointer with locating cross-hairs allows item selection and movement to and around the display screen. Special modify commands are erase and limit. Erase removes design elements just created, and limiting features include trim, corner, chamfer, and modify.

Discussion

Along with the common input commands, dials are used to zoom, change, and rotate the geometry of the screen image, while cursor buttons select, move, and access window commands (5). A lighted program function keyboard (LPFK) allows for up to 32 separate functions. An onscreen prompt reminds the designer of the current screen status, and a toggle is available for quick input changes.

Designs are created using common geometric forms of point, line, curve, etc. as well as the erase functions. The point function is defined as a point or a location in space, and the line function uses vectors to creates lines. Such options are parallel, horizontal, vertical, angle, and tangent show position and orientation of the line relative to an axis, and a curve command creates circles, ellipses, and curves. Examples of the modify command are erase and limit. The erase command removes the design elements just created. Other commands allow the design form to be trimmed, cornered, and chamfered and change the graphics capabilities of line texture and color.

7.6 MENTOR

Description

Mentor is an electrical systems design package, including hardware, schematic capture, PC layout, documentation, and limited 3D design (6). This application is used on Apollo and Sun platforms.

The Mentor Package Station has a shared database for the electrical designs in the Board Station and 3D design. The Board Station consists of software packages connected by the Board Station database. The packages in order used are Librarian, Package, Layout, and Fablink. The Board Station and the Package Station databases are accessed through PCB Portal.

PCB Portal is a bidirectional porting system to access and exchange Package Station files and the Board Station designs held in the small parts library. The Package, or 3D design, Station includes PCB Portal, 3D Design/Autotherm, and the Package Station database. Features include wire-frame modeling, shape rotation, relative distance between elements, basic and cutaway views, specific global updates such as between part geometry and footprint, and mechanical drafting. The 3D platform is now supported by SDRC, a solid-based design and drafting of mechanical parts; a dimension-driven package for solids modeling, and production drafting.

Command Structure and Discussion

Another support package is DOC, document preparation package automatically creates the design documentation of design descriptions, manuals, and other support documentation. Texts are developed and edited using data from the Package Station database. The operations of these programs overlap.

NETED is a packaging program used to create electrical schematics and hold the schematic rules, the logic defining the electrical limits of the circuit. The schematics can be created in both a top-down and bottom-down rule format. A functional block diagram (a global logic command) such as the schematic logic used to turn on a light is a top-down approach. This is a generic level without the component value rating, number of ohms, or capacitance. From this block, the lower-level block logic commands are created, such as turn on a blue or red light. NETED is a path-dependent program with as detailed a level of schematic as needed. The schematics are limited by the sheet size. Multiple sheets show the lower schematic level of one functional block. A multipage connect is used to carry over the net intelligence from one sheet to the next. NETED routes between two components but does not recognize higher levels of electrical knowledge required. For example, when a point trace (circuit connection between two points) is not electrically connected or there are dangling traces or nets, an error message is sent but the program continues. In addition, NETED will not know what components should be connected together but that two components can be. Mentor does not allow movement between programs when there are error messages. Netnames are the names given nets, vertices, connections, and the updated parts evaluated between the Librarian and the schematic blocks of NETED.

Librarian creates a part matrix independent of NETED. Part geometries, electrical footprints, part attributes, board outline, and process information are included within the part matrix. A part number, logic symbols, and pin numbers can be assigned to parts at this time. Examples of components attributes added are types such as resistors, capacitors, transistors, and nan gates and are named, e.g., RLRXXX versus RWRXXX for a resistor. Other types of text are added as bonding or other manufacturing processes. Part geometries are mapped to the schematic symbol, a pin number is given to a specific part footprint, and the outline of the printed circuit board (PCB) is defined.

SYMED is a shell that can be accessed within NETED and is used to add schematic symbols not in Librarian. The schematic rules check for duplication of reference designators, expected connections, and shorts. Shorts are allowed.

Packaging merges the schematic intelligence created in NETED with the information in Librarian. Rules are checked at this level for misconnected and unconnected netnames and pin assignments versus netname.

Layout locates components on the PCB, and routes traces or components can be auto-placed. When the parts are placed, a back annotate command fixes the coordinate locations of the parts on the PCB and imports this information back into the Layout program. An autorouting command checks for the shortest path connections between traces but cannot identify rule exceptions. One exception would be when the wave solder process requires a larger distance between surface mount pads than the electrical requirement of shortest distance between pads. The alternative is to route by hand. Each layer of the PCB is routed separately and a window shows the current layer and checks that the routing is correct. The concern about routing between layers is the creation of a via which takes place on the PCB, reducing room for other components. Mentor also allows for blind and tented vias.

When the layers have been routed, the back annotate command saves these component positions to an ascii file. The internal rules send an error message if the traces are interfering with a part, through hole, and via. Simple spatial relationships between components are checked.

Fablink is the drawing package that creates Artwork, picture sheets, drill and trim data, PCB fabrication files, the Gerber information, and other information needed for production.

7.7 SPATIAL KNOWLEDGE NEEDED FOR CAD DESIGN

The design begins with an idea or a mental picture. In industry, this picture will become the product. This design must be communicated to many people in the design and manufacturing process, and a common format is required to present this design idea so everyone understands the information needed to complete their part of the product cycle. A CAD package is one vehicle to standardize the design style.

To create the design using CAD, a designer needs to see the completed design, imagine what the individual parts look like, visualize the design in action or literally "see what one thinks" in one's mind's eye. This type of spatial visualization is the equivalent of verbal reasoning. What the mind's eye sees is the space between two design elements and their orientation, shape, weight, and position. What the mind is doing is called spatial understanding.

Spatial understanding begins with seeing lines and planes in the form of squares and geometric shapes and how these shapes appear from different positions and angles. To develop this understanding, the designer must understand the drawing format of the lines, 2D–3D shapes and their relative positions, views and how to extract information from these views (spatial reasoning) using spatial imagination or the ability to see the end product.

7.8 SPATIAL UNDERSTANDING OF CAD DESIGNS

Drawing Presentation

Spatial understanding begins with seeing how the individual design elements contribute to the whole design. The design format (style of the design communication) consists of lines, planes, the edges formed at the intersection of planes (a line), and the intersection of two lines (a point). A point is a reference location for position and direction between other design points and shapes. The perspective of a shape can distort the dimensional perception of the object.

In Figure 7.1, the 2D shapes become a line showing height or width in the side and top views. The circle in the top and side views is a line equal to the diameter, while the diamond becomes a line equal to its width in the top view and its height in the side view. The 3D cube is a square in any view (7).

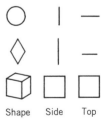

Figure 7.1. Orientation views.

Shape   Side   Top

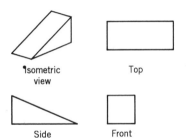

Figure 7.2. Relative views.

The complete design process is a visual thought processes that begins with sight. Sight provides a sense of shape and contour; touch, a sense of volume, weight, and texture. These attributes determined by sight are part of the perception of an object. Sight and touch establish a relationship between the 2D and 3D shapes, and the process of visual matching has begun.

In 3D, the position and form of a design element requires all three views to show a completed shape (Figure 7.2). A triangular prism is seen in a 3D view, but while the top view shows a rectangular surface, this is foreshortened to a square in the front view. The side view is a triangle giving the width and height. The 2D view does not accurately represent the 3D object.

Relative position and orientation are given by three views of front, side, and bottom; and the complete design information is given in the six views of top and rear for width, left side, front, right side, and bottom side for depth (8) (Figure 7.3).

The entire design gives redundant information but does not add to the 3D understanding of the design. Depending on the design complexity, all views may be needed to see the whole perspective (Figure 7.4). Position and orientation provide the design element with a sense of its relationship in a space. The edges and vertices create the sense of volume.

Drafting conventions commonly use three planar projections of the top, side, and front to give the entire design shape. The choice of views must show a clear and complete description of the design. Depth is lost in an orthogonal projection, as the view is flattened. The perception of depth disappears when a 2D, planar surface is the only available view (9). Without spatial visualization, it is almost impossible to see an entire design. In Figure 7.4, the two ends of the cover are curved in the isometric view and flattened in the planar views.

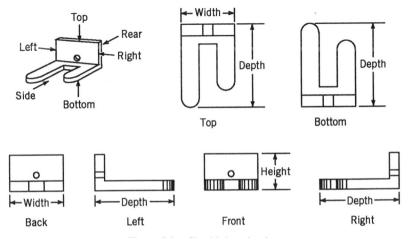

Figure 7.3. Six third-angle views.

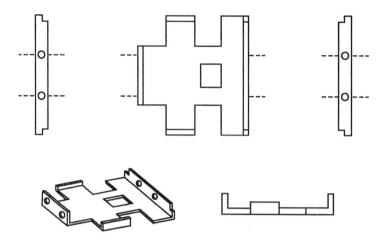

Figure 7.4. Third-angle view of cover.

Orthogonal Views

In 3D orthogonal projection, a sense of position and direction is directed to a specific plane. When the three mutually normal planes are defined as x, y, and z, the following information holds true. The front view is the first view, while the other five views are seen by rotating the side of the object toward the viewers' eyes in 90° increments. The top, front, and bottom views are on the vertical plane, while the back, left, front, and right side views are aligned horizontally (8) (Table 7.1). All views and attributes are seen in Figure 7.3.

Limitations of the 2D design occur when design points coincide. Surfaces can hide other internal design features. For example, a design with a hardware buildup or a bonding process can hide neighboring design elements.

Representation of hidden lines and features in a CAD package can further limit the design perspective. A numerical procedure is used to obtain converging lines and can eliminate the design points and vertices needed for clarity. Additional programming is required to evaluate which points should be eliminated.

Using the three or six orthogonal views, all the spatial information is available but not the complete picture given in an isometric view. The entire design is easily seen but not the relative distances and positions of the internal design elements. These are found by measurement rather than sight. Orthogonal views best represent groups of surfaces and edges but not complex assemblies. The design does not look like the object. The 2D shapes are visually continuous but not physically continuous (9).

Third- and First-Angle Views

In the United states, designs are drawn using the third-angle projected views. In third-angle views, projections are made to the front, right side, and top planes from a design placed in a hinged glass box. In the top plane, the hinge is along the edge closest to the observer, and in the

TABLE 7.1. Orthogonal Views

View	Visible Plane	Missing Plane	Attributes
Front	y, x	z	Height, width
Side	y, z	x	Height, depth
Top	x, z	y	Width, depth

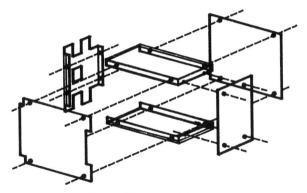

Figure 7.5.   Isometric view.

right plane, the hinged edge is along the right side of the front plane. The views relate to the planes of the box as it is unhinged. All views are shown in Figure 7.2. In other countries, first-angle views are used. In first-angle views, the front, top, and right-side views are projected onto the back, bottom, and left sides, respectively. The observer looks at the box as in third-angle views but the line of sight is through the nearest, third-angle plane onto the next plane. For example, the right-side view is projected to the left-side plane and the top view, onto the bottom plane (10). The arrangement of the third-angle views is top, front, and right side, while in first-angle views, it is right, front, and top.

Pictorial Drawing (Isometric Projection)

Multiview drawings are used to show correctly complex design shapes with exterior views. Several faces of the design are shown at the same time, representing what the viewer actually sees. Viewers without technical training can understand the drawing (9). Several faces of the drawing are seen as they appear at successive stages of the design.

The four types of projection used are

1. *Multiview.* The observer looks directly at an object projected onto a plane and the line of sight is normal to the plane.
2. *Oblique.* The observer is at infinity and the line of sight is oblique to the plane.
3. *Perspective.* The observer is at a finite distance and the lines of sight converge at the observer's eye.
4. *Axonometric projection.* Similar to multiview, but the object is projected with more than one face (8).

Isometric View

Isometric projection is a type of axonometric projection in which the edges or axes of the design object make equal angles (120°) with the projection plane. All edges are foreshortened equally (Figure 7.5). More than one face of the design is shown as well as how each design element relates to the others. A clear picture of the assembly buildup is seen.

7.9   SPATIAL REASONING

Geometric Relationships

The spatial relationships between design elements and the complete design can be interpreted as attributes of relative position, orientation, and volume. This information is found in the views;

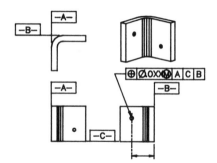

Figure 7.6. GD&T design tolerancing.

the depth and width from a top view, width and height from the front, and height and depth from the right. The views are then merged into a 3D picture. Because we live and breathe and see in 3D, it is difficult to interpolate from 2D or from the common three design views.

The spatial positions and orientation of the design elements are found by induction using the information presented in the three views. The designer should be able mentally to visualize a complete design, rotate it, and place it in its operating environment. The spatial understanding to see and move a design in space includes an awareness of the space occupied by the design elements, fit between the design elements, and the entire design environment.

These internal relationships between the elements of the design are controlled by using geometrical design and tolerancing (GD&T) dimensioning techniques.

Position and Tolerances

Geometric dimensioning and tolerancing techniques set the acceptable range of design and material variations for interchangeable parts and standardize the design intent. Tolerancing controls variations of specific dimensions on different parts and ensures fit between parts made in widely separated locations. The other alternative is tight dimensioning, an expensive and prohibitive approach to obtaining fit. The exactness (tightness) of the dimensions depends on the degree of accuracy required. Tolerancing controls the dimension variation by setting the maximum and minimum variations between key features, a design attribute (height, width, etc.) to be dimensionally controlled. Geometric tolerancing controls location, position, shape, and shape variations between mating parts relative to a datum. Datum dimensions fix the position of a design element in 2D or 3D space. Six points are used to locate an object in 3D space, whereas three points fix the design with respect to a fixed plane. Two other points will fix the object's position with respect to a second plane, and an additional point, with respect to a third plane. These three planes form the data identified by letters of the alphabet in a box (A, B, C). All data are positioned at 90° with respect to each other. In a Cartesian coordinate system, these data are in the x, y, and z planes.

Key features or characteristic are limited using geometric symbols. MMC in a circle is a maximum material callout and controls such surface variation. MMC sets the upper limit that gives a part the maximum amount of material (11), while the least material condition (LMC) limits a part to the least amount of material. Other feature limits are of location, shape, or form. Position, concentricity, and symmetry are tolerances of location; straightness, flatness, roundness, parallelism, squareness, and profile are of shape.

The design in Figure 7.6 is a heat sink. To dissipate the heat, a continuous metal contact between mating parts is required. GD&T controls the key features of hole location relative to the mating hole and the amount of material, using the maximum material limit (11).

Spatial Reasoning

To develop a design that operates as required and is producible, the designer must be able to account for how and why the design elements move during processing and how they react in the operating environment. The capability of spatial visualization alleviates the possibility of fit

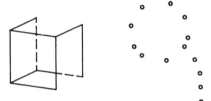

Figure 7.7.   Whole pattern completion.

interferences before building the part. This prevents parts that cannot be built with current tools or will not fit in the end product.

Spatial visualization consists of spatial perception, reasoning, and synthesis. Spatial perception is the beginning of shape recognition, pattern matching, and rotation. Spatial reasoning uses the perceptions and develops relationships such as the spatial relationships between objects in space, static and dynamic reasoning or pattern projection, analogy and deduction, and dynamic reasoning (12).

Spatial pattern matching begins with the recognition of common features or a whole pattern approach. It is a natural tendency to take a design, picture, or feature and find the familiar features and imagining other views or combinations. The design or design element is examined for pattern differences from a known pattern or for pattern similarities. Common pattern features are those of shape, texture, color, and line. A computer performs pattern matching using a point-by-point search-and-match routine. The designer can identify features from the whole shape or by similarities between groups of features. The latter is the beginning of part standardization. The whole pattern approach is used in the child's game of connect the dots (Figure 7.7).

Dynamic Reasoning

When the shape or design form is established, a designer must be able visually to manipulate the shape and see the different views in different orientations. In Figure 7.8, none of the blocks has the same configuration as another. Rotate each set of blocks to see if there are any similarities of features or orientation. Blocks A and B have the same number of blocks at each end, while C has four and two. When B's blocks are rotated 90° counterclockwise, they match A. C's blocks will not match block configuration of A or B without changing the position of a column of blocks.

The spatial reasoning becomes more difficult when the object is first visualized in the mind and then manipulated. One of a pair of dice is used for this exercise. To begin, visualize the five visible faces of the die. The five views are front, one dot; right side, two dots; back, six dots; left side, five dots, and top, three dots. Rotate the die 90° clockwise. Imagine the front view. Rotate the die again 90° and imagine the front view. Finally rotate the die in its present position, 90° up and out of the page. Imagine the number of dots on the front face. The die faces as rotated are five, six and four dots.

The spatial information required is a recall of a known picture: the die. The spatial reasoning requires rotation of a metal deduction to find a view not mentioned but available from the

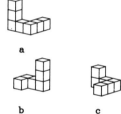

a

b   c   Figure 7.8.   Visual deduction.

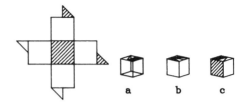

Figure 7.9. Dynamic spatial reasoning.

information. The designer is developing the spatial ability to picture and foresee an object in one view while keeping the original view in mind.

Most designs are a part of a larger structure or environment. Movement of the design is now related to that of a mating part or a reaction to an environmental condition. Any design rotation is now two phased. First, the design is rotated or moves about its own axis or center of gravity and, second, about an axis relative to the environment. The designer needs the ability to foresee relative movement between moving parts and forces acting on the parts. This type of spatial understanding is dynamic reasoning or the ability to visualize movement of shapes or objects along a path. The entire shape is mentally pictured and then the image is manipulated.

In Figure 7.9, a box is pictured unfolded. Two faces are shaded for reference. Choose the configuration of the box when built up. The correct box is the first one.

Other types of spatial reasoning are analogy and induction. Analogy is recognition of a pattern or relationship between objects. The designer begins with recognizing similar features and associates them with a larger pattern. The visual reasoning goes from the specific to the general. Visual deduction is the process of reasoning from an abstract or general concept to the concrete or specific visual image. Figure 7.10 is a variation of the child's game, tower of Hanoi. Five numbered disks are on a peg, ranging from the disk with largest diameter on the bottom to smallest diameter on the top. The rules of the game are (1) a larger disk cannot be placed on a smaller disk, (2) no two even or two odd disks can be together, and (3) no more than two disks can be moved at one time. The object of the game is to move the five disks to another peg so they are in the smallest to the largest diameter.

7.10 SPATIAL IMAGINATION

Spatial Effects of the Manufacturing Processes

The electrical or mechanical design will go through a series of manufacturing processes during the production cycle. Some of these processes occur during assembly buildup and some to accommodate other processes. Manufacturing processes can add weight to a product (such as in painting and bonding) or volume (such as a hardware and wire buildup) or can cause an interference in fit due to successive operations (such as adding insulation or sleeving). The processes are affected by the design materials, the position or orientation of following subassemblies, and the cumulative effects of these characteristics on the completed product.

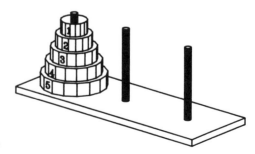

Figure 7.10. Tower of Hanoi variation.

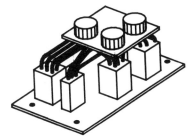

Figure 7.11. Wire bundle buildup.

Physical reactions occur between incompatible materials or from other chemicals used on the completed product. Chemical cleaning can corrode or deteriorate solder joints or the plastic cover of a part. Part position and orientation can be changed from adding insulating sleeves for abrasion protection, wire buildup between connectors and switches, and painting or plating, which adds volume to the design and takes up space. Designs do not usually account for secondary operations that add volume and interfere with fit.

Component knowledge can be used to anticipate cumulative process effects on a design. For example, a printed circuit board can warp and twist within acceptable limits and still prevent production of a reliable product. In one case, a connector was placed on a printed circuit board within the warp area. This caused the metal leads of the connector to touch the metal case and short out the card.

The operation of the product can cause heat or humidity that must be accounted for in the design. Electrical components can degrade or have premature failure when subject to extreme conditions.

Process attributes are not in most CAD software and must be supplied by the designer. The designer must be able to anticipate process effects on the design and the cumulative effects of pressure, liquid, or heat.

Spatial Synthesis

Synthesis is the ability to combine the part, process, and design information to create a functioning, reliable product. Spatial understanding of the design format begins the design process but it is only the beginning. Good designs can lead to failure if not combined with the intuitive and manufacturing process knowledge. A number of flawed product designs have been created using CAD packages and assuming that relevant product and process information was included (13).

For example, the *Challenger* operating performance had not been modeled for extreme cold conditions and the Hubble telescope lens was inaccurately ground and the compensating computer program was based on outdated star charts. Design failures usually result from faulty judgment rather than faulty calculations.

The designer begins with an idea and must be able logically to foresee the progression of the idea through to the finished product. Some of the information is implicit in the material, size, shape (part attributes), or orientation of the part. Process effects on the design is implied by the known effects on similar products and must be found by inference. When the designer is unable to foresee the cumulative effects of the design elements on the whole design, cost, rework and liability increase.

Figure 7.11 is an example of inadequate spatial reasoning of a design. The circular connectors located in the top plate are connected to the rectangular switches in the bottom plate by hand-routed wires. The released design presents the top and bottom plates and the corresponding location of connectors and switches in the traditional third-angle views. The wiring is given in a 2D format, and each end of the connections is labeled by a symbol such as J1, J1 or S1, S2. There is no isometric layout showing how the wires are routed between the connectors and the switches. When the wire is hand routed and a protective sleeving installed over the wire, the wire diameter is increased, decreasing the available room for subsequent wires. Other process changes include additional time to sleeve over 20 wires, a larger wire diameter that does not fit in the allotted space, stressed wires at the point of insertion into the connector, and no room allotted for use of tools to install switch hardware. Spatial perception and reasoning was not used to foresee how the design elements affected each other.

Design failure occurs when the theory behind the design is inadequately applied. The first design of the courtyard walkway supports in the Kansas City Hyatt was one long steel rod supported from the ceiling. The design was changed to two steel support rods, placed side by side, extending through the walkway above it. The amount of weight-bearing load that could be supported on the walkways was reduced. The weight limit was exceeded by people walking and dancing on the walkway during a dance, causing the catastrophic failure of the rods.

7.11 RECOMMENDATIONS

A successful design is a combination of an understanding of the physical limits of the design and the CAD package used. The packages are simulations that either simplify the physical reality or use a set of rules not usually noticed by the designer. The successful designer must then be able to evaluate the CAD results, add process information, and use spatial imagination to design for the product life cycle. The CAD package used is a matter of preference, but the intuitive knowledge of the designer is required.

BIBLIOGRAPHY

1. R. LEIGH, *Autocad; A Concise Guide to Commands and Features,* Ventana Press, Chapel Hill, N.C., 1989.

2. *MicroStation 32, User's Guide,* Version 4.0, Document No. DGA0341410, Bentley Systems, Inc. and Intergraph Corp., Huntsville, Ala., 1991.

3. P. BALLARD, *CAS EMS User's Guide,* The boeing Co., Seattle, 1992.

4. *Intergraph/Engineering Modeling System (I/EMS) Operator Training Guide—Basics,* No. DMA1036A0, Intergraph Corp., Huntsville, Ala., 1992.

5. *CATIA, Basic Wireframe, Course Number 6C-61361 Manual,* The Boeing Co., Seattle, 1991.

6. *Getting Started with Engineering Packaging Manual,* Mentor Graphics Corp., Beaverton, Ore., 1989.

7. W. WONG, *Principles of Three-Dimensional Design,* Van Nostrand Reinhold Co., Inc., New York, 1973.

8. F. GIESECKE and CO-WORKERS, eds., *Engineering Graphics,* 3rd ed., Macmillan Publishing Co., Inc., New York, 1981.

9. H. SEDWICK, "The Geometry of Spatial Layout in Pictorial Representation" in M. Hagen and co-workers, eds., *The Perception of Pictures,* Vol. 1, Academic Press, New York, 1980.

10. M. SPOTTS, *Dimensioning and Tolerancing for Quantity Production,* Prentice-Hall, Inc., Englewood Cliffs, N.J., 1983.

11. American National Standard Engineering Drawings and Related Documentation Practices, *Dimensioning and Tolerancing,* ANSI Y14.5M, ASME, New York, 1982.

12. R. McKIM, *Experiences in Visual Thinking,* Brooks/Cole Publishing Co., Monterey, Calif., 1972.

13. E. FERGUSON, "How Engineers Lose Touch," *Am. Heritage Invention Technol.* **8**(3), 16–24 (1993).

DEFINITIONS

CAD Package. A software program capable of performing drafting, design, and analysis operations.

Dynamic Reasoning. The ability to picture mentally an object and manipulate that object in space.

First-Angle View. Right-side, front, and top views of an object projected on to a second hinged plane. These views are used in countries other than the United States.

Isometric View. View of an object placed, so all lines projected are of equal length.

Orthogonal View. Commonly used views of top, front, and right side of an object, showing the length, depth, and height.

Spatial Understanding. The ability to see spatial relationships between design elements and foresee effects of processes and environment on the design.

Third-Angle View. Top, front, and right-side views of an object projected onto a hinged plane. These views are used in the United States.

CHAPTER 8
Design for Manufacturing

YEHONATHAN HAZONY
Boston University

8.1 INTRODUCTION

The last decade and a half has seen extensive penetration of *computer-aided technologies* into the design and manufacturing activities of industry. This progress, which started with simple computer-aided drafting systems, has lead to various levels of sophistication and automation of design-to-manufacture systems. These developments were driven by several forces:

- The need for large improvements in industrial productivity as a prerequisite to industrial competitiveness.
- The dramatic changes in the design, cost and availability of new computer and communication hardware, which could be applied to improve manufacturing productivity.
- The relatively slow but yet continuous development of new application-software systems, which are prerequisite for accomplishing the goal of industrial productivity.

The hardware/software products available today to meet the needs of industry vary extensively in concept, in capabilities, and in costs. The introduction of the new technology may fail because of mismatch between expectations and the actual capabilities of a particular product, rather than because of failure of the technology. Unfortunately, it often takes several years and large investments to recognize such a failure.

This chapter describes current capabilities as well as future directions of the evolving technology. It exposes the reader to basic underlying concepts, terminology, capabilities, and cost considerations. Such knowledge is needed to minimize the risk of failure due to false expectations, bad choice of product, underinvestment in human resources, and other hidden costs.

8.2 SOME BASIC CONCEPTS

This section discusses the definitions of some of the common concepts and acronyms used in the context of this technology.

Computer-Aided Drafting (CAD)

Computer-aided drafting is aimed at enhancing the productivity of the drafting component of the traditional concept-to-product cycle. A good system will enhance rather than restrict the flexibility and freedom of the draft-person, as compared with what is provided by the pencil, paper, and drafting board. However, in traditional industrial settings, this flexibility is constrained by requirements imposed by the engineering design, on one end, and industrial practices on the other end. These constraints are traditionally imposed by rule books and human supervisory structure. A computer system which attempts to capture these two aspects of the *drafting paradigm,* will be classified as a more advanced system.

Computer-Aided Design (CAD)

Computer-aided design systems aim at the needs of the engineering-design function, rather than the drafting function of the industrial enterprise. The distinction is based on the traditional paradigm where the drafting function provides support for the design function. Another distinction is based on the role played by engineering analysis. Traditionally, there is an overlap between design and drafting concerning the analysis component of the process. While some analysis, like surface–volume–mass calculations, falls in the domain of the drafting function, more sophisticated analysis, e.g., final-element analysis (FEA), is clearly within the domain of the design function. A computer-aided design system is expected to incorporate a more extensive set of analytical tools, responding to the needs of both the design and drafting functions.

Advanced systems for computer-aided design systems build upon the extensive use of solid modeling (1) to subsume the role played by the drafting function. Furthermore, such systems lead towards the full integration of the entire design-to-manufacture (DTM) process. This trend is driven by such concepts as

- the paperless factory.
- rule-based design.
- feature-based design.
- parametric design.
- customized design.

The Paperless Factory

Traditionally, the engineering and drafting functions are addressed by separate departments, where engineering designs are passed to drafting departments for the detailing process and the production of engineering drawings. However, one aspect of the introduction of this new technology is the move towards paperless industry, which transforms the DTM process to depend more on "computerized-databases" and less on engineering (paper) drawings. Furthermore, the concept of paperless factory extends all the way to the manufacturing function, and with help from some other concepts it facilitates the full integration of the design-to-manufacturing process (2).

Rule-Based Design

The concept of rule-based systems for computer-aided design plays a prominent role in the design of VLSI and computer systems. This development was dictated by the enormous amount of details entailed in the realization of VLSI and computer-systems design. This level of details would be mind boggling if it is to be totally handled by a human organization without the computer. The rules captured and utilized in such computer-aided design systems may be classified as error-prevention rules, and data-expansion rules. Both classes of rules, which are traditionally associated with the drafting department, have been for the most part taken over by the CAD systems for VLSI design. A similar process may eventually prevail for all other CAD systems. A rule based approach to CAD has been demonstrated in research environment, (2, 3) and is being advertized by some commercial software systems.

The concept of design by rules may be extended to include,

- functionality rules.
- geometric rules.
- manufacture rules.
- assembly rules.
- costing rules, etc.

Feature-Based Design

The concept of feature-based design was advanced as an attempt to simplify mechanical-process design as an extension of CAD (4–7). In this approach, a mechanical design consists of a collection of standard geometric features, accompanied by standard processes to create these features. The list of such features includes prismatic shapes, cylinders, cones, slots, holes, rounds, fillets, etc. The potential of this approach was found to be limited since in many situations it is difficult, if not impossible, to describe a mechanical design in terms of a limited set of standard geometric features.

Parametric Design

The need for parametric design emerged once it became apparent that the impact of conventional CAD systems on industrial productivity is limited. This limitation is due to the fact that early CAD systems where developed following the drafting paradigm, where the draft-person is responsible for all the details embedded in a paper drawing. The drafting paradigm does not protect the design from inevitable human errors. Consequently, engineering changes introduced during the life-cycle of a product often require the laborious redesign of the product or component, even in areas which should not be directly affected by the design change.

Parametric design attempts to overcome these limitations, and thus, obtain a significant-additional improvement in industrial productivity. Parametric design may be viewed as an extension of feature-based design, such that not only the different features are parametrized but also the geometric inter-relationships between features are expressed parametricly. In principle, if all geometries are expressed through parametric relationships than any design change can invoke an automatic reconstruction of the design, based on the parametric structure and design rules.

Customized Design Systems

Many mechanical designs cannot be described in terms of parametrized relationships between a standard set of geometric features. Such designs are generated using traditional methods of descriptive geometry aided by the drafting board or a computer-aided drafting system. However, it is possible to capture and quantify the parametric relationships governing such designs and embed them in a customized design system. The purpose of such an implementation is to simplify similar followup designs and to respond to subsequent engineering changes during the life cycle of the corresponding product. A prerequisite to such an approach is that the costs of developing a customized system is substantially less than the realized cost savings. Advanced platforms for software-system development are available today that make it possible to build such systems at the typical cost of one to two person-years of effort (8).

Computer-Aided Manufacture (CAM)

The introduction of "numerical control" (NC) to the operation of production machines precedes the introduction of modern CAD systems. The evolution of this technology lead to "computerized-numerical-control" (CNC) and "distributed-numerical-control" (DNC). In CNC mode a production machine, e.g., lathe or milling machine, is controlled by a simple computer, driven by an NC program (code). In DNC mode the NC-controller is fed its programs through a communication line from a remote computer.

The initial direction of development of systems for computer-aided manufacture (CAM) was aimed at producing the voluminous NC code required to produce a part using numerically controlled machines. More advanced systems attempt to assist the task of process design and implementation of engineering changes, in addition to the tedious process of generating the prerequisite NC code. CAM systems have traditionally evolved independently of their CAD counterparts. This independence proved to present a formidable barrier to the further improvement of manufacturing productivity. The term "CAD-CAM integration" was introduced to describe the need to overcome these barriers.

Computer-Integrated Manufacture (CIM)

The term computer-integrated manufacturing (CIM) was introduced to represent an overall unified computer system which provides the vehicle to achieve manufacturing productivity (2). A full CIM system would provide a centralized control of the manufacturing environment, addressing two main requirements: vertical integration, and horizontal integration.

The term *vertical integration* describes the capability of the computer system to integrate the full process from design conception to part manufacture. The concept that the full DTM process is implemented in one hardware/software system preempts the generation of barriers between the different functions of the process, and thus eliminates the need to overcome them later on.

The term *horizontal integration* describes a hardware/software network solution, encompassing all the functionalities exercised on the manufacturing floor. Such a capability would control and optimize the flow of material, process, programs, and products through the manufacturing floor. The inclusion of the flow of programs in this list is aimed at achieving flexible automation.

Manufacturing Automation

Hard Automation

The most extensive automation was achieved in the past in the form of large-scale transfer lines, as exemplified by the automotive and food industries. Such transfer lines are characterized as "hard automation" because they are commonly dedicated to one product. Historically, the automation of such transfer lines has been implemented via dedicated hardware. Initially this dedicated (hard) automation was implemented through mechanical and electro–mechanical hardware. With the advent of computer technology more of the automation functions were implemented by electronic and computer-based controllers. However, a computerized transfer line which is driven by software but dedicated to a single product would still be considered as hard automation.

Soft Automation

Flexible automation utilizes computers to control the flow of material, process, software, and products across the manufacturing floor physically. The flow of software is included in the list (and in the system design and implementation) to ensure that programs and schedules may be dynamically changed to meet the requirements of changing products or product mix. Another prerequisite to the implementation of soft automation is in the choice of machinery, transfer mechanisms, and connectivity between production centers. Early implementations manifest themselves as Flexible-Manufacturing Centers (FMC), or Flexible-Manufacturing Systems (FMS), which describe the flexible automation of individual production centers as *islands of automation*. More ambitious undertaking of flexible automation deal with complete production lines and are represented by Flexible Transfer Lines. The advances in flexible automation further emphasize the need to break the barriers between CAD and CAM, to facilitate fast flow of NC programs representing new products or engineering changes.

Rapid-Response Manufacturing (RRM)

The term *rapid-response manufacturing* (RRM) has been coined to describe a system that reduces substantially the art-to-part turnaround time. It intends to provide a broader scope than the often-used term of *rapid prototyping*. The approach to RRM may be through the introduction of new and more rapid manufacturing technology (9), and/or through the achievement of high design productivity, through the introduction of design automation. *Seamless design-to-manufacture* (SDTM) offers the methodology for achieving design productivity through design automation (10).

8.3   DESIGN-TO-MANUFACTURE

Early in the separate evolution of CAD and CAM it was recognized that a significant improvement in productivity could be attained if the two separate processes of part design and process design could be integrated. The idea of a combined design team simultaneously considering the functional, structural, and manufacturing implications of part design required in many places breaking traditional–organizational barriers. However, once these barriers started to fall it turned out that the barriers to "CAD/CAM integration" were more substantial. These barriers proved to be to a large extent due to technical rather than organizational problems. The recognition of the technical nature of the problems opens the door to technical solutions which can eventually lead to the desired goals of productivity. The nature of the difficulties as well an approach to their solutions are discussed below.

CAD/CAM Barriers

The major barrier to streamlining CAD/CAM operations stems from the historical approach to integration which was based on the computer-aided drafting paradigm. This approach substantially improved the interfaces between the workstation and the designer for the purpose of a very efficient approach to drafting. This CAD paradigm requires an extensive human involvement in creating all the details of a design. In this mode, the responsibility for detailing, dimensioning, tolerancing, and rule-checking is left in the hands of the computer-assisted draftsperson. Because of these human functions, it was quickly apparent that adding hardware and software interfaces between existing CAD and CAM systems was not sufficient. This approach only served to improve the quality of the interface between the design and manufacture functions, but not remove the barrier altogether.

Any instance of a computer–person interface, as good as the implementation might be, creates an ample opportunity for the introduction of human errors. Providing such an interactive interface to facilitate the transfer of data between inconsistent CAD and CAM systems, just elevated the quality of this function to that of all other human interfaces within the CAD/CAM sequence. This did not address the problems caused by such human involvement, and the possibility that such an involvement might be entirely unnecessary.

Integrated CAD/CAM

The evolution of CAD/CAM interfaces suffered from basic flaws in the original design of such systems, which were not designed to be parametric and rule driven. Consequently, the interface between them was developed to handle only format conversions and the transfer of detailed design data. Such interfaces could not maintain parametric relationships and or the constructive elements of rule-based design and data expansion. Unfortunately, it is impossible to incorporate these features as an afterthought, neither to the CAD/CAM components nor to the interface between them.

These two elements, parametric design and rule-based design, are at the foundation of advanced CAD–CAM systems. By the nature of commercial enterprizes, the internal details of commercial systems are considered proprietary, and the thrust of R&D and future plans are secret. Consequently, it is impossible to pass judgment on how far they will progress in the direction of improved design and manufacture productivity. Their ultimate success will depend on factors which do not necessarily reflect on the potential of the technology. The achievable goals of this technology will be discussed in the context of a system for "Seamless Design-to-Manufacture (SDTM)," which was implemented in an open academic research environment (10). The SDTM system was developed to explore and demonstrate new productivity limits of the technology.

Seamless Design-to-Manufacture (SDTM)

The term "seamless" is introduced to signify the elimination of all the intermediate human interfaces, characteristic to conventional CAD/CAM systems. These interfaces are regarded as "seams", associated with extensive, time consuming and error-prone human interactions. The SDTM system includes an interactive front-end consisting of a set of tools for conceptual design. These tools include facilities for rule-based parametric design for both part and process. Such capabilities are required if the interactive-conceptual design is to drive the entire design-to-manufacture cycle in a fully automated way. To accomplish such a high level of design automation, the part geometry as well as the manufacturing process have to be fully parametrized. In addition, the appropriate design and process rules have to be captured, quantified, and embedded in the design.

The approach of computer-assisted conceptual design, combined with parametric and rule-based design, provide a level of design automation which represents a break-through in productivity. In situations where all stages between conceptual design and prototype production are automated, the turnaround time depends essentially on the conceptualization ability of the design team. The rest of the cycle time depends on the power of the computer used and on the highly optimized production (facilitated by the system) on the available DNC-controlled production center. This can lead to a turnaround time of the order of 24 hours for engineering changes of very complex parts. The various elements which are prerequisite to the implementation of an SDTM system are outlined below.

Conceptual Part and Process Design

A system for conceptual part design is based on the traditional paradigm separating design from drafting. In this paradigm a design engineer sketches an idea (on paper or a CAD screen) and then annotates the sketch with a set of critical parameters accompanied by some rules. This annotated sketch is then transmitted to the drafting department for detailing, dimensioning, tolerancing, and rule checking. An SDTM system builds upon the data and rules captured in the sketch, and additional sets of data and rules embedded in the system and representing past experience. It uses these data, parameters and rules, to produce the rest of the information required to generate the manufacturing process automatically and drive the appropriate machining centers (2, 3, 10, 11). The implementation of SDTM systems is based on the premise that the stage of conceptual design must include all the new ideas, parameters, geometric relationships and rules which fully define a new design. All the rest of the design-to-manufacture cycle can be automatically driven by a *complete* set of new and historical (legacy) rules.

Parametric vs Traditional Design

In traditional design, the sketch produced by the design engineer is detailed and dimensioned by the drafting department. The expanded details and associated dimensions are captured as annotations on the paper-drawing, or the CAD screen. However, during the process of generating these annotations the draft-person has to go through a complete evaluation of the (parametric) relationships between all components of the design. Unfortunately, the results of such analysis are captured in the form of annotation data rather than parametric design data. In parametric design the sequence is reversed, i.e., the designer starts with establishing all the parametric relationships between components of the design and the appropriate CAD system embeds them in an internal geometric model. The geometric model consists of a parametric-mathematical representation of the design geometry.

These two design paradigms require two different mind sets of the designer, which may interfere with the design process. However, an advanced CAD/CAM system may bridge between the two modes. It can permit the designer (who so chooses) to enter the sketch in the traditional drafting mode, followed by automatic conversion of the geometric representation to a parametric one once the detailing and dimensioning stages are complete. The parametric representation is indispensable if the system is to be augmented to incorporate design by rules.

Design and Process Rules

A parametric representation of the part geometry and process-design geometry permits the automatic regeneration of the design following a change of one or more design parameters. However, an arbitrary change of a design parameter may produce a new design which is out of the universe of acceptable and feasible designs. To prevent such occurrences, the SDTM employs the method of *rule-based* design. When a parametric change is introduced through the interactive-conceptual part and process design interface, the system checks the consequences of the change against a library of legacy rules. If a rule is violated, the design change is rejected and the designer is informed about the violated rule(s). When a problem is encountered in which the violated rule was not previously recognized, the SDTM system should provide a mechanism to add a new rule to the library of legacy rules.

Computer Analysis

Complex designs often call for extensive computer analysis. Examples for such analysis would include:

- Surface-volume analysis.
- Structural analysis.
- Structural-dynamical analysis.

- Aerodynamical analysis.
- Fluid-dynamical analysis.
- Acoustical analysis.
- Process analysis, etc.

Each of these analysis is based on a computerized implementation of a mathematical–geometric model, which might be simple or complicated to create. If multiple types of analysis are called for, each may require its own model for the digital computations. These models can be generally generated automatically based on the existence of a parametric representation of the design, and rule-based geometry generators. The philosophy underlying SDTM leads itself naturally to the incorporation of "computer-aided analysis." The facts that different models have to be generated for different purposes, require the ability to include and invoke different classes of rules. Furthermore, it becomes advantageous to include analytical-model design into the inter-active conceptual design front-end of SDTM. It is important to recognize that arbitrary design of secondary geometric features may add unjustifiable manufacturing and/or analytical cost. Early involvement of the manufacture and analysis specialists in the conceptual design may offer substantial time and cost savings.

Geometric Modeling

All three major components of the SDTM, part-geometry design, process design, and analysis, are based on the use of geometric modeling. Even the simplest computer-aided drafting system creates a geometric model of the design. However, such a system may capture some of the model data in the form of drawing annotation. In such a case the corresponding geometric model is based on the involvement of human perception in the completion and interpretation of the design data. The move towards higher level of design automation requires a complete computerized model, supported by a corresponding computer-modeling capability. Such a modeling capability will be called upon to generate the very large number of different detailed geometries required by the various stages of the design-to-manufacture cycle. To be able to accomplish this level of automation in model generation, a high degree of modeling and data integrity has to be enforced by the respective system (12). Such a requirement cannot be enforced in retrospect on existing design systems, but has to be included in the foundations of the system during original system design and implementation.

Instrumented Testing and Design Productivity

A very important consequence of comprehensive design automation, offered by the SDTM approach, is that it can produce an order of magnitude reduction of the art-to-part cycle time. This facilitates rapid prototyping of actual parts made of the material specified by the design. This rapid prototyping process creates the opportunity to run instrumented-laboratory testing on the actual parts. Including physical-instrumented testing as an integral component of the iterative design process could have a substantial impact on design quality, and thus on productivity.

8.4 GEOMETRIC MODELING IN CAD/CAM TECHNOLOGY

All versions of CAD and CAD/CAM systems involve geometric modeling in various degrees, and therefore vary in the amount of human involvement required by the process. The more advanced is the system, the more significant is the role of geometric modeling, and the less human involvement is called for. Furthermore, the reduced human involvement is associated with a higher level of productivity. The relationship between geometric modelling and productivity is outlined below, following the broad classification in terms of conventional, advanced, and post CAD/CAM systems.

Conventional CAD/CAM Systems

Conventional CAD/CAM system have proven themselves in many industrial settings of small and large companies. They have introduced significant improvements of productivity and often proven to fit the specific needs of these companies at that time. The traditional drafting approach to mechanical design is based on the use of tools of descriptive geometry to describe three-dimensional designs. Such tools are based on the use of sets of two-dimensional cross sections of the design to define a three dimensional object fully. A large amount of details and dimensioning data is captured in the form of textual annotations on the corresponding drawings. Conventional CAD/CAM systems evolved as three independent components, the interactive-drafting front-end, interactive process design, and a post processor for NC-code generation.

Such systems depend heavily on the involvement of an experienced draftsperson in the design process. By the time the tool trajectories are generated with sufficient accuracy and reliability to pass the scrutiny of the rule checking by the post processor, a pretty good understanding of part and process geometry was generated and distributed among the various professionals involved in the process.

For the iterative design-to-manufacture cycle to conclude successfully, an extensive amount of model building and rule checking is required. However, this is conducted mostly by the human operator(s), with relatively little assistance from the CAD/CAM system. Unfortunately, this knowledge is not captured in a form that could be used by the computer to automate this effort when the design process is repeated next time. The need for more advanced systems, which build upon such information, arises when further productivity improvements are called for.

Advanced CAD/CAM Systems

Advanced CAD/CAM systems are generally attempting to capture all the design knowledge referred to above in the form of computer-driven parametric and rule based design. To accomplish that, it is necessary to resequence the design process and introduce parametric-geometric relationships in the conceptual-design stage, rather than later during detailing, dimensioning, and process design stages. Such a resequencing will introduce the advantages of a computerized rule-based approach, namely,

- The rules are applied up-front in the early design stage rather than at later design stages, or when a "post processor" is called upon to verify manufacturability rules prior to generating the final NC-code, and
- A significant amount of the design and process geometry are automatically generated via the application of design rules coupled with parametric-design representations.

Parametric and rule-based systems constitute a different approach to geometry representation, than what is manifested in traditional design, and thus require a different set of geometry-generation tools. The geometry is represented by a *computerized-geometric model,* which is built with the help of a computerized *geometric modeler.* The significant role played by automatic geometry generation dictates rigorous *data-integrity* requirements from the underlying *graphical-data-base.* The existence of a computerized-geometric model, generated by a geometric modeler, is what differentiate between conventional and advanced CAD/CAM systems. However, different advanced systems vary in the extent that they utilize tools of geometric modeling to generate derived geometries and automate the design-to-manufacture cycle.

Geometric Models and Graphical Databases

A computerized geometric model includes a graphical database and algorithms, which provide a complete description of the geometry of a part or product. Such a model provides also, through a related set of tools (algorithms), all the relevant derived information called for by the complete design process. The graphical database consists of a collection of data items, including scalers, vectors, matrices, and items of higher structural complexity. These combine with the relevant algorithms to generate the required information. The model describing the part and manufacturing process employed in metal cutting by a machining center is outlined below. In order to facilitate the automatic generation of manufacturing process and final NC-code, the model, and associated graphic-database have to include information on,

- Part geometry
- Stock geometry
- Tool geometry

- Data and rules for fixture geometry generation
- Data and rules for tool-protection zones
- Machine tool capability and tooling data
- Data and rules for process geometry generation (including process orientation, depth of cut, etc.)
- Data and rules for tool trajectory generation (including machine instructions, feed and speed, etc.)
- Data and rules for analytical model generation, etc.

The high level of automation called for in the derivation of these data creates the requirement for rigorous data integrity. Such data integrity has to be maintained in all stages of the design-to-manufacture cycle. The consequence of lack of data and model integrity is that the design falls apart following some of the geometric or analytical operations applied to the model. This requirement made it practically impossible to upgrade existing conventional systems to include the capabilities offered by parametric and rule-based design. The list of data items and rules given above serve to illustrate the range of capabilities possible in an advanced CAD/CAM system. However, when evaluating such systems it is important to note that different systems offer strength in different aspects of the overall design-to-manufacture cycle, but not necessarily at all aspects of the process. Some of the new systems are more effective on the rule-based side of the process while other may have the advantage on the side of parametric design. Furthermore, contemporary parametric and/or rule-based systems are typically stronger on the CAD side of the process than on the CAM side of it, and are not yet mature enough to cover the list given above fully.

The Geometric Modeler

The term geometric modeler is used here to include all components of the system which participate in the generation of the required geometry. In the context of the present discussion, a comprehensive geometric modeler will include,

- Part-geometry generators: standard components, and non-standard components.
- Constructive geometry operations: union, subtraction, and intersection.
- Process geometry generators: skin generation (for processing), slicing, shadowing, tool-protection zone generation, tool trajectory creation, and 5-axis interpolation, etc.
- Analytic model generators: skin generation (for analysis), etc.

Part Geometry Generators. The list of standard geometry components includes prismatic shapes, cylinders, cones, spheres etc. The list of nonstandard components includes components generated by a parametric representation based on a specific mathematical equation, and components constructed by a collection of standard surface patches, i.e., nonuniform rational B-splines (NRBS).

Constructive-Solid Geometry (CSG). Given a set of geometric components, an object can be created through the standard set of geometric (boolean) operations, namely, union, subtraction, and intersection. Such operations are fully consistent with parametric and rule-based design, since all components and their geometric relations to each other may be fully parameterized. The rule-based approach can prevent unacceptable geometries from being created. An example for an unacceptable geometry could be a case where the change of various parameters produces a geometry consisting of two or more disjoint components.

Process-Geometry Generators. Examples include: *Skin generation.* The metal-cutting operation includes a least three steps: roughing, semifinish, and finish. The last step requires a very fine representation of the "skin" of the part for tool-path generation.

Slicing. The first step in the metal cutting process, the roughing cycle, is often implemented by removing excess material in sequential parallel layers. These layers can be generated applying a "slicing" algorithm to the combined-geometric model of the stock, fixtures, and part. Each slice contains a set of closed contours, representing the three components of the model.

Shadowing. The tool trajectories corresponding to a roughing cycle using a given tool orientation, have to comply with the process rule stating that undercutting is to be avoided. To accomplish that the boundaries controlling the roughing cycle at a given layer are derived from

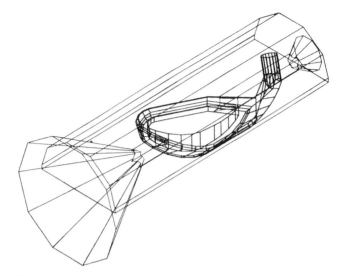

Figure 8.1. The combined geometric model of the part, stock and fixtures, at the end of the first step of the rough-milling cycle of a golf club head.

the shadow cast by the part of the object behind the tip of the cutting tool. This corresponds to the shadow of the part of the object protruding from the layers cut previously. The process modeler, which is part of the geometric modeler, has to include the shadowing function if the tool path generation is to be automated.

Tool trajectory creation. The tool trajectory of the roughing cycle in a particular process layer has to remove all the excess material bounded by the stock, part and fixtures. The tool trajectories are generated and sequenced following a set of process rules, which also provide for the definition of varying feed rates. These tool trajectories could be derived automatically based on the available boundary contours and a set of process rules (11–13).

5-Axis interpolation. Some elements of the metal-cutting process of complex surfaces require the simultaneous 5-axis control of the tool-tip location and the tool orientation. There exists geometric coupling between the linear coordinates used to define the tool-tip location and the cylindrical (or spherical) coordinates used to define the tool orientation. This creates the need for a 5-axis interpolation algorithm to guarantee that the tool tip (or side of the tool) does follow the desired 3-d surface (12). The geometric modeler has to generate these trajectories based on surface definition and some geometric rules in order to automatically generate the required NC-code. This 5-axis interpolation algorithm serves to illustrate that process-dependent algorithms have to become part of the geometric modeler.

Geometric Modeling for SDTM

Seamless-design-to-manufacture encompasses all the advantages of parametric and rule-based design, based on the use of geometric modeling as outlined above. The geometric modeling capability of an SDTM system has to produce all the geometric data required for part design, process design, and analysis. The volume of graphical data required for a full implementation of automatic process generation and automatic NC-code generation far exceeds the data corresponding to part geometry and part analysis.

For this process to proceed in a fully automated way, SDTM has to rely on a rule-based parametric geometric modeler. In addition, such a system has to be able to address designs which are not described in terms of constructive-solid modeling, i.e., are not based on a standard set of primitive-geometric shapes. Present generation of advanced CAD/CAM systems do not attain this level of completeness. Consequently, a contemporary realization of

Figure 8.2. The geometric model of a 5-blade marine propulsor. For simplicity, only cylindrical projections of the parametrically generated air-foils are shown.

SDTM has to be capable of customization for a particular class of designs. Such customization builds upon the ability to construct specific geometry generators, which may or may not depend on the classical components of constructive-solid geometry. Two such cases are cited below.

Figure 8.1 shows a geometric model for an intermediate process step in the design-to-manufacture of a golf-club head. The model generated by a customized SDTM system represents the combined geometry of part, stock and fixtures after the first step in the rough-milling cycle. The golf-club head was milled out of a cylindrical stock, which was reduced by the rough milling of excess material at the bottom of the club. The automatic process generator recognizes the difference between part, stock, and fixture geometries. Consequently, the part and fixture geometries remain untouched while the stock geometry is being modified by the process. After the first step of rough-milling the A-axis was rotated by 180 degrees, preparing for the next rough-milling step. Note that the fixture geometry includes two bar stubs merged with two conical tool-protection zones, designed to protect the A-axis chuck and the tailstock. In order to prevent interference with the milling of the back pocket of the golf-club head, the fixture components should not protrude into the golf-club head. To this end the bar stubs where generated by geometric subtraction of the club head from a single bar prior the generation of the back pocket.

The design of a golf club demonstrates a part geometry which does not lead naturally to a parametric description in terms of a standard set of geometry primitives. This SDTM is using tools of constructive-solid geometry, based on the use of a parametric definition of prismatic shapes, a conic-round generator, and a pocket generator. Design parametrization made it possible to automate process and NC-code generation fully, resulting in an art-to-part turn around of under 72 hours.

Figure 8.2 shows a design of a marine propulser. This design was produced using a customized geometry generator, based on the mathematical description of a propulser blade. The parametric description of this design is based on a cylindrical projection of the parametrized-mathematical shape of an airfoil. This cylindrical characteristic of the design is reflected in the figure. The parametrized-geometry generator made it possible to implement a fully automated process design and NC-code generation. The blade was explicitly defined for 10 radial stations

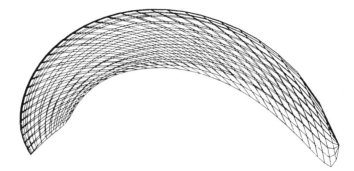

Figure 8.3. The geometric model of the "skin" of a blade, used by the tool-trajectory genera-tor. The tool trajectories are generated as strings of linear intersections of the quadrilateral surface elements.

through a parameter table. The larger number of intermediate airfoils, called for by the manufac-turing process, was generated through interpolation in parametric space. The art-to-part turn around time achieved in this demonstration was under 72 hours.

Figure 8.3 illustrates the skin created for a single blade for the purpose of tool-trajectory generation as part of the roughing and semi-finish cycles. The skin represents the surface of the blade in terms of a set of quadrilateral, three-dimensional surface elements. These surface elements are described as "rolled surfaces," which correspond to the way machining trajecto-ries are generated. The finish cycle requires a different approach to skin generation.

Figure 8.4 depicts the tool trajectories generated for one layer cut during the semi-finish cycle. The cross-section of the blade (solid areas) consists of two polygons, a thick one on the left close to the root, and a very thin one on the right close to the tip of the blade. The shadows of the sections cut in previous layers are also shown. These are introduced to prevent undercut-ting. The excess material left due to shadowing is removed in a later process step. Also shown are cross-sections of the stock, fixtures, and tool-protection zones. This step includes a "con-sumable-fixture," which is a structural-support beam to be removed during a later step in the semi-finish cycle.

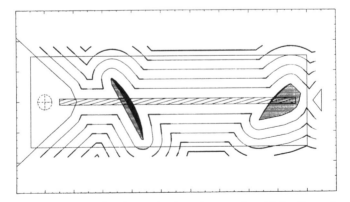

Figure 8.4. Tool trajectories for the production of a propulsor blade. Shown is one rough milling layer. Shadows of previously cut layers and cross-sections of the blade, stock, fixtures, and tool protection cones are included. Varying line thicknesses correspond to varying feed rates.

8.5 OPPORTUNITIES BEYOND CAD/CAM

The development of commercial CAD/CAM systems is generally driven by perceived-market demand, rather than by technological advances. The customized approach makes it possible to implement and demonstrate the SDTM methodology without waiting for commercial CAD/CAM systems to advance and provide comparable capabilities. Because of the proprietary nature of industrial research, published explorations into future extensions of the technology come generally out of the academic environment. Implementations of customized systems can incorporate some of the new developments, e.g., in the areas of computer-aided-tolerancing (4, 6, 14), automatic process design, (2, 3, 10–13, 15) automatic fixture design (12, 16–18), parallel machining (19), and concurrent processing (20). A sequence of such successive implementations can eventually evolve into a comprehensive general-purpose system.

Historically, the main contribution of CAD and CAM to increased productivity was due to the advent of interactive computing in general, and interactive-computer graphics in particular. Interactive interfaces were introduced to improve the productivity of the professionals involved in all aspects of the design-to-manufacture cycle. In contrast, a full implementation of SDTM introduces interactive interfaces for conceptual design for all aspects of part design, process design, and analysis. Conceptual design is building upon the advantages of parametric and rule-based design. SDTM eliminates most of the human interactions which are the focus of traditional CAD/CAM, and constitute an inevitable source for the introduction of human errors. Due to these distinctions SDTM may be classified as a post-CAD/CAM technology.

Productivity Considerations

The extent of a company's investment and risk-taking in pursuing improved productivity depends on considerations of competitiveness as much as it depends on availability of advanced technology and adequate human resources. The fact that appropriate technology is out there, in itself, would not be as compeling as the fact that the competition is already taking advantage of such a technology. However, such an approach contains the risk that a company is surpassed in the productivity race in spite of substantial investments and advances in DTM automation technology. This would occur when the competition moves to a higher level of technology, producing further productivity gains. Consequently, the choice of adequate technology is risky, and has to be made with the full knowledge of the technology advantages available to the competition.

Presently, the SDTM approach outlines an ultimate goal in productivity achievement. Such a goal can help formulate a strategy which can avoid dead-ended, costly investments in productivity. Further consideration has to be given to emerging facilitating technologies which may have a profound impact on the realization of high productivity goals. Relevant advancements in facilitating technologies are outlined below.

Hardware: Engineering Workstations

Traditional geometric modelers were incessant consumers of computer cycles. The extension of the functionality of such modelers, to include the automatic generation of process geometry and NC-code, produces an even larger demand for computer cycles. However, this ceased to present a problem in view of recent fast developments in the design and power of engineering workstations. Consequently, the costs of computer hardware adequate for the implementation of advanced SDTM systems can be far below the cost of the respective machining centers.

Software-Development Platforms

Evolution in software-development technology lags substantially behind developments in computer hardware. Advances in high-level software-development systems are repeatedly side-tracked by efforts to impose premature standardization of engineering-software methodology. Such attempts were made in the past to impose languages such as Fortran, Basic, Pascal, Lisp, etc. as the required software-development environment for engineering applications. This criticism also applies today to the thrust towards C and C++ type languages. The SDTM demonstrations cited above were implemented using a platform for graphical and parametric programming based on a graphical extension of the APL2 language (8). These implementations consumed typically one person-year effort each. They demonstrate the cost effectiveness that could be achieved in the future using advanced high-level software-development platforms.

Alternative Technologies

It is important to mention several new process technologies offering advantages in the domain of rapid prototyping and rapid response manufacture. These techniques build on new process technologies in addition to advances in design automation. Examples are the methods of stereo-lithography, laminated-object manufacturing (LOM) and selective-laser sintering (SLS) (9). These methods offer fast manufacturing with select materials, and they typically generate a three-dimensional *model* of the part, rather than a physical prototype. SDTM offers a similar concept-to-part turnaround time, producing prototypes made out of the actual material required, which can be tested in the appropriate mechanical and thermal environment. The rapid availability of real prototypes facilitates the introduction of instrumented testing into the iterative design cycle, with the large potential impact on product quality.

Customized *vs* Generic Approach

The SDTM case studies cited above have been implemented as customized systems. The availability of a high-productivity application-development platform played a key role in the implementation of these demonstrations. In contrast, commercial ÇAD/CAM systems adopt a generic approach to system design. This preference is driven primarily by market considerations, where a broad enough market is sought in order to cover the large development cost of traditional generic systems. An advanced software-development methodology can reduce the implementation cost of customized systems to a point where the cost-recovery issue has to be reconsidered.

8.6 CONCLUSIONS

The customized approach to SDTM has been demonstrated to provide a breakthrough in productivity in several case studies. Software-productivity tools make it possible to implement customized systems at costs which can be justified in terms of one problem at a time. However, a choice between the customized and generic approaches depends to a large extent on human-resource considerations. The customized approach to SDTM requires a different set of skills than the straight forward utilization of generic CAD/CAM systems. Furthermore, the move from traditional design practices towards the approach of rule-driven parametric design signifies a design-culture change, which may be as profound as the change between the traditional paper-based design and CAD/CAM.

It is important to note that in the traditional-design paradigm, all the parametric-geometric relationships and the relevant design and manufacture rules are eventually sorted out by the time the design-to-manufacture cycle is complete. However, all these relationships and rules are not captured in the computer system and thus cannot be used to automate process design and NC-code generation. In contrast, an SDTM system includes facilities and mechanisms to capture all this information for the purpose of automation. Once engineers are equipped with the mathematical skills required by rule-driven parametric design, it becomes natural to change the sequencing of the design process. Consequently, design parameters and design rules are applied upfront rather than at the detailing, dimensioning, and verification stages. This change in the design paradigm is prerequisite to the achievement of a high level of automation of the design-to-manufacture cycle.

The cost involved in affecting such cultural changes has to be weighed in the balance against the potential for productivity improvements offered by SDTM. In many situations, the choice has to be made between losing a manufacturing industry to competition or re-educating the management and engineering workforce to bring them up to a new technology. The customized approach of SDTM offers a gradual transition mechanism in the form of limited case studies. However, such an approach is bound to fail if the teams involved are not subjected to an appropriate retraining program.

BIBLIOGRAPHY

1. H.B. VOLCKER and V.A. HUNT, "The Role of Solid Modeling in Machine-Process Modeling and NC Verification," *Proceedings of the 1981 International Congress of the Society of Automotive Engineers,* Detroit Mich., Feb. 1981.

2. Y. HAZONY, "Towards the Factory of the Future," *Perspectives in Computing* (IBM), **3**(4), 4–11 (Dec. 1983); (also "Special Report", *ibid,* pp. 40–41); "Towards CAD-CAM Integration," *SME Report* MS84-196, 1984.

3. K. PREISS and E. KAPLANSKY, "Automatic Part Programming for CNC Milling by Artificial Intelligence Techniques," *Journal of Manufacturing Systems* **4**(1), 51–63 (1985).

4. A.A.G. REQUICHA, "Representation of Geometric Features, Tolerances, and Attributes in Solid Modelers Based on Constructive Geometry," *IEEE Journal of Robotics and Automation,* **RA-2,** 156–166 (1986).

5. X. DONG and M. WOZNY, "FRAPES, A Frame-based Feature Extraction System," *Proceedings of the 1988 International Conference on Computer Integrated Manufacturing,* The Rensselaer Polytechnic Institute, Troy, N.Y., The Computer Society of the IEEE, The Computer Society Press, 1988, pp. 296–305.

6. J.F. JACKOBSON, G.M. RADACK, and F.L. MERAT, "Incorporating Knowledge of Geometric Dimensioning and Tolerancing into a Feature-Based CAD System," *Proceedings of the Second International Conference on Computer Integrated Manufacturing,* Rensselaer Polytechnic Institute, Troy N.Y., IEEE Computer Society Press, 1990, pp. 152–159.

7. H. SAKURAI and D.C. GOSSARD, "Recognizing Shape Features in Solid Models," *IEEE Computer Graphics and Applications,* **10**(5), 22–32 (1990).

8. Y. HAZONY and L. ZEIDNER, "Customized Systems for Engineering Applications," *IBM Systems Journal* **31**(1), 94–113 (1992).

9. S. ASHLEY, "Rapid Prototyping Systems," *Mechanical Engineering,* 34–43 (April 1991).

10. L. ZEIDNER and Y. HAZONY, "Seamless Design-to-Manufacture (SDTM)," *Journal of Manufacturing Systems,* **11**(4), 269–284 (1992).

11. L.E. ZEIDNER, "Automatic Process Generation and the SURROUND Problem: Solution and Applications," *Manufacturing Review,* **4**(1), 53–60 (1991).

12. Y. HAZONY, "Design for Manufacture: A Geometric Modeler for Geometric Integrity," *Manufacturing Review* **4**(1), 33–43 (1991).

13. T.R. KRAMER, "Pocket Milling with Tool Engagement Detection," *Journal of Manufacturing Systems* **11**(2) (1992).

14. J.U. TURNER, "New Methods for Tolerance Analysis in Solid Modeling," *Proceedings of the 1988 International Conference on Computer Integrated Manufacturing,* Rensselaer Politechnic Institute, Troy N.Y., IEEE Computer Society Press, 1988, pp. 306–314.

15. A.A.G. REQUICHA and J. VANDENBRANDE, "Automatic Process Planning and Part Programming," *Artificial Intelligence: Implications for CIM,* 301–326 (1988).

16. Y.C. CHOU and M.M. BARASH, "Computerized Fixture Design for Solid Models of Workpieces," *Proceedings of the Symposium on Integrated and Intelligent Manufacturing,* ASME Annual Meeting , ASME, N.Y., 1986, pp. 131–141.

17. H. SAKURAI, "Automatic Setup Planning and Fixture Design for Machining," *Journal of Manufacturing Systems,* **11**(1), 30–37 (1992).

18. C.H. CHANG, "Computer Assisted Fixture Planning for Machining Process," *Manufacturing Review,* **5**(1), 15–28 (1992).

19. J.B. LEVIN and D. DUTTA, "Computer Aided Process Planning for Parallel Machines," *Journal of Manufacturing Systems,* **11**(2), 79–92 (1992).

20. L.E. ZEIDNER, "Surver Networks: Software Integration Tools For CIM," *Proceedings of the International Conference on Computer Integrated Manufacturing (CIMIC),* Rensselaer Polytechnic Institute, Troy N.Y., IEEE Computer Society Press, pp. 226–235, RPI, 1988.

CHAPTER 9
Design for Automated Manufacturing

M. ANJANAPPA and Y. WANG
University of Maryland

9.1 INTRODUCTION

The development of a mechanical product consists of a large number of distinct processes or stages. Product design is the first step of the activity that transforms a concept into its functional and physical realization. The product development then proceeds with manufacturing processes, which usually include planning, machining, inspection, and assembly. One of the most important considerations during development is the manufacturability while maintaining quality. Thousands of decisions about geometry, material, and processes are routinely taken; many times with little or no information about their effects beyond design. These various facets of design and manufacturing, individually and collectively, have significant effects on the product development time and cost incurred. More important, there are complex interactions between them, and decisions made concerning one aspect may impact others. Particularly, decisions made in the product design stage can either ease or increase the downstream manufacturing and assembly requirements significantly.

To reduce product development time and cost, while retaining high quality, a variety of industries all over the world are increasingly deploying various automation technologies. These technologies can be broadly classified as follows:

- Computer-aided design (CAD).
    - Computer-aided drafting.
    - Computer-aided engineering (CAE).
- Computer-aided manufacturing (CAM).
    - Computer numerical controlled (CNC) machine tools.
    - Computer controlled robots.
    - Flexible manufacturing systems (FMS).
    - Automated material handling systems.
- Computer-aided manufacturing tools.
    - Computer integrated manufacturing (CIM).
    - Artificial intelligence (AI) technology–based packages
    - Computer-aided process planning (CAPP)
    - Material resource planning (MRP)

The emergence of the automated design and manufacturing systems led to the realization that major change in the design process as traditionally practiced is needed. Product design and implementation of manufacturing technologies to produce the product cannot be treated separated if the promised increases in flexibility and productivity of the automated manufacturing system are to be fully achieved. It is essential that product functional requirements and the ease of manufacturing are simultaneously considered in the early stage of the product development. The concept of integration of automated design and manufacturing functions has been developed into a new technology: design for automated manufacturing. This new concept of integrating design with manufacturing systems yields significant advantages such as reduced market lead time, increased product quality, and reduced life-cycle cost (1, 2).

Design for automated manufacturing is a computer-aided engineering tool that gives the designer access to various aspects of manufacturing process through a series of individual modules that provide graphical displays and expert advice of manufacturing information. Its aim is to link the current computer automated design and manufacturing functions, to incorporate manufacturing considerations into the design process, and to define design alternatives that help facilitate improvement of the total productivity performance of the design and manufacturing system as a whole.

The scope of these individual modules depends on whether the product under consideration is a component or a system. The latter can introduce a level of complexity that is several orders of magnitude larger than that of a component. Even for a component, it is appropriate to speak initially about a class of components aggregated using a group technology approach. In its broadest sense, design for automated manufacturing is concerned with comprehending relationships between the functional requirements of a product and its manufacturing requirements and using the knowledge to maximize the total production performance in terms of quality, cost, and productivity.

In this chapter, we limit our discussions to prismatic components that can be manufactured with a machining cell. The major aspects of manufacturing are machining, assembly, and inspection, and the concerns of productivity performance are limited to cost. In other words, we consider the "design-to-component manufacture cycle" as a building block of the "concept to product life cycle." The chapter is organized as follows: in section 2 the design process of mechanical components is described. Overall configuration of a design for automated manufacturing system is outlined in section 3, followed by detailed descriptions of the major modules of the system.

9.2   CONCEPT TO PRODUCT LIFE CYCLE

Product Design

Engineering design consists of many stages, each of which uses (perhaps large and widely varying) chunks of knowledge. Ullman and Dietterich (3) note a typical definition of design to be "the creative decision-making process for specifying or creating physical devices to fulfill a stated need."

A product design typically consists of identification, defination, synthesis, analysis, optimization, and presentation iterative structures. The problem identification phase of design may result from higher order task decomposition, and typically this knowledge takes form as a request for proposals. The definition of the design is the stage during which the design engineer translates the identified need into engineering requirements, primarily by mapping qualitative needs into quantitative specifications. The synthesis phase is the least understood phase, during which a design engineer generates ideas (as many as possible) for satisfying the definition of the problem. In the analysis phase, several analytic techniques are applied to potential designs. The results of analysis are processed through the optimization phase to modify and improve the design. The presentation phase is the complement of the identification phase in which the designer receives feedback of the product's performance. This feedback, when corrections are in order, consists effectively of a new problem identification.

Design-to-Component Manufacturing Cycle

The design-to-component manufacturing cycle is identical to the product design process except that here we deal with a single component at a time. This consists of a series of sequential steps as shown in Figure 9.1. A typical design of a component uses the supplied specific requirements (functional, aesthetic, and cost) along with general information (physical science and empirical) to identify, define, and synthesize a preliminary design. This design is analyzed and optimized in an iterative manner. The successful preliminary design is presented for detailed design and drafting, which is then fed to the process planning. Here the manufacturing process of the component is produced along with materials and tools–fixture requirements. Manufacturing of the component is then achieved and processed through finishing operation, if found necessary, before being sent to quality control. One of the several prevalent methods (100% inspection, SPC, etc.) of quality assurance is conducted. The acceptable part then goes to shipping–distribution. Unacceptable components are fed back to process planning and design for further action. Although not discussed here, the issues of timing, scheduling, and database handling are important elements of automation.

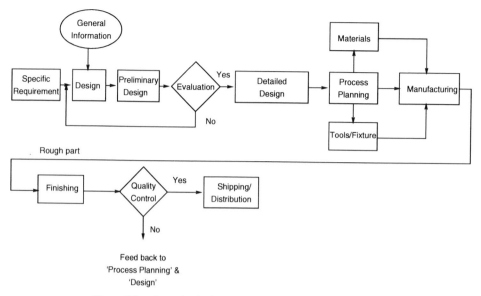

Figure 9.1. Steps in design to component manufacturing cycle.

The cycle has the following five important, often overlapping phases: design, interfacing, process planning, machining, and quality assurance. Each of the phases raises specific issues for design for automated manufacturing, which are discussed below.

Design

The particular part must satisfy design axioms of independent functional specification and minimum information content. Important issues addressed include reasoning by analogy, innovation via heuristics, algorithmic computation, quality versus cost, range of design and scale, manufacturability, and maintenance of an iterative design environment, preferably with a feature-based CAD system.

Interfacing

The interfacing phase primarily deals with the need for a standard approach to communication, i.e., the ability to translate within the design to manufacture path. Important issues include data representation using initial graphics exchange specification (IGES) and product data exchange specification (PDES), and appropriate languages for different functions (AutoLisp or Prolog for planning, Basic or C for design, etc.).

Process Planning

One of the most important issues is that of geometrical representation and feature extraction from the finalized design. Other issues for purposes of planning the machining process are qualitative versus heuristic rule, spatial and temporal reasoning, interference avoidance, intelligent fixturing, maintenance of accuracy, hard physics versus soft expert advice, and manufacturing system dynamics.

Machining

Although the machine tool performance is given, it is necessary to define those attributes that will satisfy the other three functions described above. This often includes machining accuracy, available speeds–feeds, and the internal language of the machine controller and, more important, the ability to interface with it.

Quality Assurance

Quality assurance is increasingly considered a key element for competing in the manufacturing of discrete components. Some of the issues that must be addressed include statistical process control (SPC), in-process inspection, off-line inspection, standards of communication such as dimensional measuring interface specification (DMIS), and automated inspection data analyzer.

9.3 SYSTEM CONFIGURATION FOR DESIGN FOR AUTOMATED MANUFACTURING

The initial design process usually consists of the development of a set of functional specifications. These specifications often comprise a combination of materials, loads and deflection, constraints on connectivity, volume and weight limitations, tolerances and surface finishes, environmental considerations, etc. In addition, budgetary and time constraints for the entire process may be stated, as may be the allowable cost of the component.

The design engineer often times strives to satisfy the functional specifications with the assistance of commercially available software tools such as finite element and optimization programs. In addition, a system configured for design for automated manufacturing must also provide the designer with the necessary computer-aided tools to control, modify, and otherwise influence the manufacturing process by which the component is to be produced. With these real-time interactive tools, the designer can optimize the component geometry, material, and processes to minimize the cost while maintaining functional and quality requirements.

As discussed in the earlier, there are numerous individual tools (that provide graphic display and expert advise) that are being used in a variety of industries. A typical configuration of a design for automated manufacturing system is shown in Figure 9.2.

The system is a shell in which the user designs a component using modules such as CAD, intelligent feature extractor, manufacturability analyzer, CAE tools, and quality control analyzer. The designer, using a design knowledge capture module, can also document the explanatory knowledge (reasoning, thought process behind a design decision, etc.) that will be useful in an automated manufacturing environment. Heuristic and intelligence are introduced into many of the modules.

The process of design for automated manufacturing begins with the designer providing design input via a CAD environment. This design input is quantified by the design based on the specific requirements (functional, aesthetic, and cost) along with the general information (scientific, physical, and empirical). Several alternate approaches are available for component design in a design-for-manufacturing environment. In the first approach, a commercial wire-frame–based CAD system can be used to create the design database, which is then translated through IGES, to create a neutral format design file. This file then becomes the input to the intelligent feature extractor whose output is a machinable component feature file.

As an alternative approach, the component can be designed using a feature-based CAD system. The system uses as its building block a host of primitive machinable features. This approach creates the machinable feature file directly. This approach to component design replaces the dual activities of wire-frame–based CAD followed by feature extraction. The advantage of feature-based design is that the higher level semantic information supplied by the designer is not lost in the conversion of the drawing to lower level geometry data. However, there are certain disadvantages. For example, some of the flexibility inherent to generic wire-frame–based CAD tools may not be available. Although, the feature-based design systems are gaining more acceptance, the need for the feature-extraction process will also continue.

As a third alternative, solid modeler-based CAD systems provide the designer with a much higher level of interaction capability. The designer will be able to specify a hole as simply a hole rather than series of instructions needed by other CAD systems. More important, solid modeler-based CAD designs lend themselves easily for downstream analysis with various CAE tools.

The output from each of the three approaches, at a minimum, consists of all the necessary design data about each feature of the component, along with the tolerance and material information. In the earlier versions, the tolerance and material information are entered manually by the designer and appended to the output file of the CAD systems.

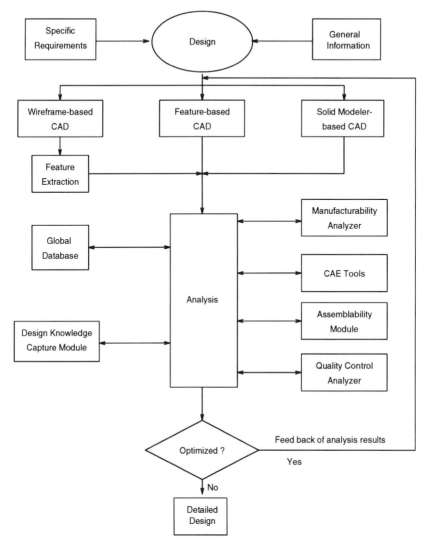

Figure 9.2. Typical configuration of design for automated manufacturing.

With the completion of the preliminary design of the component, the design now enters the analysis stage, in which the design is evaluated for automated manufacturing with the objective of minimizing the cost while retaining the functionality and high quality of the component. This is achieved by evaluating the preliminary design with the aid of the various tools as shown in Figure 9.2.

At first, the preliminary design is evaluated for its functional satisfaction using CAE tools. Some of the most common analyses done include load-deflection, constraints on connectivity, volume–weight constraints, and environmental considerations. In addition, overall cost and time may have to be satisfied.

Once it is found satisfactory, the manufacturability analyzer will be used to identify manufacturing and cost parameters using a global database as the source of available resources. Interactive modification may be done, if found necessary. Similarly, the assemblability module will evaluate the preliminary design for ease of assemblability and the quality control module will check for ease of inspection and determine if automated inspection with the available tools is feasible. If the design is modified based on any of the analyses, the modified design may have to be reevaluated for its functional requirements using CAE tools.

Finally, the design knowledge capture module is used interactively, by the designer, to capture the explanatory knowledge, which (typically known only to the designer but never documented) explains the thought process behind the various design decisions. This explanatory knowledge, not available in a typical design file, is most useful for designing components for a complex system and systems with long service life. This approach makes the design for automated manufacturing more rewarding.

If these analyses provide the optimum design, the next stage, detailed design is entered. If, however, the analyses indicate suboptimal design, the designer can redesign the component using the analysis results and recommendations. In the rest of the chapter, detailed discussions of each of these analysis tools are provided.

9.4 MANUFACTURABILITY ANALYZER

Decisions made during the design stage commits major resources for the remainder of the manufacturing cycle. These initial design decisions can be changed (if found necessary) with access to a suitable manufacturability analyzer. This provides the least effort before finalizing the design, resulting in a significantly reduced cycle time and reduced product cost.

The objective of a typical manufacturability analyzer is to identify manufacturing and cost parameters and then to eliminate design errors and features that are difficult to machine. With access to a global database of available cutting tools, material, and fixtures, the manufacturability analyzer can decompose the design feature by feature, interface with the user about areas of concern or difficulties, and offer information on correction. The manufacturability analyzer will reject any design that cannot be manufactured with existing system hardware before the process planning begins.

Table 9.1 shows a manufacturability parameter matrix for a general automated manufacturing system, for example, a flexible manufacturing cell (FMC) (4). The columns of the table show the characteristics of the machined part and the X's show how the manufacturability parameters depend on the machined part. For example, as per requirement 1, the available stock sizes must meet the design requirement for the part to be manufacturable in the FMC. It is necessary to know the part's outer dimensions and material so there are X's in the weight and outer size and material columns. When determining whether a design is machinable, some parameters may be considered immediately, whereas others need not be considered until after the process plan is completed. For example, the parameters of requirement 1 (drawing limits) do not depend on the machining process, whereas the parameters of requirement 3 and 4 (frequency and cost) depend on the process plan. The goal of the manufacturability module is to let the designer know, immediately, whether his or her design is manufacturable within the given manufacturing facility. It will also suggest ways in which the part may be made more producible. The following sections discuss how the necessary parameters are considered in the manufacturability analysis.

Intelligent Evaluation of Manufacturing Cost

Cook (5) notes that "producing satisfactory parts at the lowest possible cost can be called as the first law of production." A manufacturability analysis must consider all the parameters listed in Table 9.1 to minimize the cost of a part. The cost of manufacturing a part is discussed widely in literature (6). For example, the total cost of manufacturing a part can be written as

$$C_{TOT} = C_{MC} + C_{MAT} + C_T \tag{1}$$

where C_{MC} is the machining cost, C_{MAT} is the material cost, and C_T is the tool cost incurred per part. The machining cost can be further divided into machine cost and labor cost for actual cutting time and noncutting time as well.

The standard time for cutting, setting, material handling, and other shop-related activities are increasingly made available as part of the global database. Most of these standards are based on machining handbooks, such as the *American Machinist Cost Estimator Guide*, supple-

TABLE 9.1. Manufacturability Parameters for an Automated Manufacturing System

| A Design Is Manufacturable in an FMC if It Can Be Made | Information Needed to Check the Manufacturability | | | | |
	Tolerance Bending Finish	Contours Shapes Radii	Tool Interference	Weight and Outer Size	Material
Can the design use FMC's					
stock sizes?				X	X
cutting tools?	X	X	X		X
fixtures?	X	X	X	X	X
software?		X			
machines?	X	X	X	X	X
robot?				X	
material handling system?				X	
What is the					
raw material supply?				X	X
cycle time?	X	X	X	X	X
tool wear?	X	X			X
cell availability?					
yield?	X	X			X
handling time?				X	
What are the costs due to					
raw material?				X	
cycle time?	X	X	X	X	X
tool wear?	X	X			X
yield rate?	X	X			X
handling?				X	
pallet storage?				X	
others?					

mented with some basic AI techniques. These rule-based techniques provide the flexibility necessary to estimate accurately nonstandard operations. The required knowledge base is assembled through a historical study of the shop estimates.

Equation 1 is useful for minimization of the cost with respect to any of the parameters such as material cost, cutting speed, and tool life. Implicit in the estimation is the effect of tolerance on the cost of production, which must be specified by the designer. As a rule of thumb, tolerances should be applied to permit the greatest speed and economy of manufacturing of a part, consistent with functional requirements. Considering only the tolerance, manufacturing cost can be written as

$$C = \sum_{i=1}^{n} \frac{k_i}{t_i^2} \tag{2}$$

where, t_i is the tolerance of a critical dimension, n is the number of critical dimensions, and k_i is the constant corresponding to the generation of the ith dimension, which depends on the person and machine used. The cost increases parabolically with the decrease in tolerance. Many authors have documented this phenomenon. For example, Phillip (7) provides a detailed and comprehensive presentation. However, in this chapter, the information is presented in a different perspective—normal machining accuracy versus controlled machining accuracy. For machining operations in an automated manufacturing environment a nominal accuracy for normal machining is usually chosen to be different from the nominal accuracy for controlled machining. Hence, a design for automated manufacturing system should alert the designer if the tolerances are too tight and cannot be made in normal operating conditions but require a slower and more controlled machining, thus increasing the cost of machining.

For example, if it is a drilling operation, the surface finish of the hole may vary from 1.6 to 6.35 μm (63 to 250 microinches) (according to ANSI surface roughness), depending on the

TABLE 9.2. Achievable Tolerances and Surface Finishing in Automated Manufacturing Environment (Developed by ANSI)

	Tolerances and Surface Finishing			
	Normal		Controlled	
Operation	Tolerance (mm)	surface (μm)	Tolerance (mm)	Surface (μm)
End milling	0.40	6.3	0.10	1.6
Surface milling	0.40	6.3	0.25	3.2
Drilling	0.40	6.3	0.10	1.6
Reaming	0.12	1.6	0.02	0.8
Grinding	0.025	1.6	0.008	0.2

condition of drill bit. If the surface finish requirement is, say 1.6 μm (63 microinch), the machinist can look over the drill bits in the magazine and choose one that is in better condition. However, in an automated manufacturing environment, the CNC machine will choose the first available drill bit without knowing its condition. Hence, the automated manufacturability analyzer will choose 6.3 μm as the achievable surface finish in a normal drilling condition and a surface finish of 1.6 μm under a controlled drilling condition. Table 9.2 shows typical values for various machining operations.

As an alternative, several cost evaluators have used a machining index as a parameter to quantify the relative difficulty of machining (7). The machining index typically addresses the following issues:

- Complexity of geometry.
- Required surface finish.
- Required dimensional and form tolerances.
- Type of material.

For example, a normal end milling operation requiring a surface finish of 6.3 μm is considered to have a machining index of 0, whereas a controlled end milling operation (i.e., with sharp tool and slow feed rates) that can generate a surface finish of 1.6 μm may have a machining index of 1.

Feature-Based Evaluation of Manufacturability

Following the criterion of the overall cost of the part production, as discussed earlier, manufacturability of each feature will be checked. Typically, the analyzer accesses the manufacturing facility global database (describing all the machining capabilities and limitations) to perform the manufacturability analysis in two stages: (1) selection of multiple materials–machines–tools–fixtures and (2) the optimum material–machine–tool–fixture for each feature (4, 8).

Selection of Multiple Materials–Machines–Tools–Fixtures

In this stage, the manufacturability of each feature is checked, and a list of possible materials–machines–tools–fixtures is generated without considering the tolerance requirements. All analyzers, at the least, consider the following issues:

- *Material.* Stock size, availability, excessive machining.
- *Machines.* Limits of movements, accuracy.
- *Tools.* Shape, size, geometry.
- *Fixture.* Availability, accuracy.

If no stock material of the correct type and size is found, the design is terminated. If material is found, the analyzer warns the user for any possible excessive machining. It then searches for

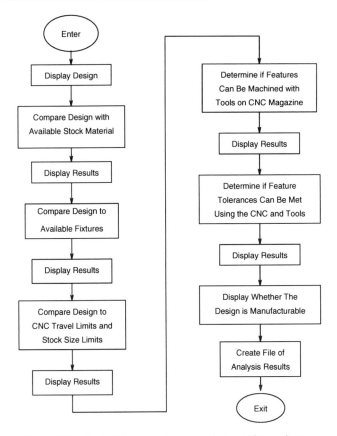

Figure 9.3. Control flow chart of manufacturability analyzer.

available fixtures and machining centers that can handle the dimensions of the raw material and allow the spindle travel necessarily for machining. If fixture or machine is determined inadequate, the design is not manufacturable. Finally, the design is analyzed to determine if the available cutting tools are capable of machining the part with considerations given to dimensions, radii sizes, and whether the feature bottom is round, conical, or flat. Recommendations are made to change the corner radii if it differs from the tool radius that has been selected. For each feature, a list of usable material, machines, tools, and fixtures is made. If there is one or more combinations available for machining each feature, the design is manufacturable.

Optimum Material–Machine–Tool–Fixture

This stage considers form, profile, orientation, location, and runout as given in ANSI Y14.5. With access to the file generated above, the analyzer looks at each feature and searches for the combination of machine–tool–fixture that is capable of holding the requested tolerances. Both normal and controlled machining conditions are considered to determine the capability. If no combination in the list is capable of holding the tolerances, the feature cannot be machined correctly, and the design is considered unmanufacturable.

Figure 9.3 shows the flow chart of a typical analyzer. The analyzer generates a file listing the selected stock, machine tool, fixture, all features and cutting tools capable of machining them under normal conditions. In addition, a separate list of the features with tight tolerances requiring specific tools and their recommended cutting speeds, feeds, and depths is generated; these features require controlled machining. If the design is not manufacturable, information concerning the cause and possible solutions is included.

9.5   AUTOMATED QUALITY ASSURANCE

The manufacture of precision machined parts usually involves a series of complicated processes. Depending on the nature of the process, there is a good probability that some errors will occur. Hence, in the discrete part manufacturing industry, first piece inspection, using coordinate measurement machines (CMM), is practiced widely. If the first piece inspection fails, it is necessary to identify the source of error and then take corrective action. If corrective action is not economical, then the part must be redesigned and new process plans prepared to overcome the known source of error.

In either case, the inspection data must be analyzed by a panel of experts to identify the most probable error source. This is usually a time-consuming and expensive procedure. Hence, an important capability of an automated manufacturing system is its ability to extract qualitative information from the inspection data and to present this information to the designer and process planner, instantaneously, so that corrective measures can be taken. This may require the redesign of the part. Hence, presenting the relevant information to the designer and process planner in an automated fashion can make the practice of design for automated manufacturing feasible in terms of time and cost incurred.

First Article Inspection

A typical first article inspection in an automated manufacturing environment would involve the following:

1. Inspecting the part using a CMM.
2. Determining the errors by comparing measured values to the upper and lower design dimensional limits.
3. Analyzing the inspection data to determine the most probable source of error (if any).
4. Recommending corrective action to the designer and process planner.

Task 1 can be easily automated with the introduction of neutral-language formats, such as initial graphics exchange specification (IGES), product data exchange specification (PDES), and dimensional measuring interface specification (DMIS). Task 2 requires a specific algoirthm to evaluate the measurement data and to determine dimensional and form errors. Different algorithms may yield different results (9). Tasks 3 and 4 are complex in nature and require a heuristic approach to organize and analyze the data (10). An algorithm-based inspection data analyzer (10) is one method used to achieve this.

Inspection Data Analyzer

To serve the environment of a design for automated manufacturing, an inspection data analyzer is usually based on the features. Normally, both dimensional and form tolerances of a set of features are analyzed. For example, an inspection data analyzer used in a design-to-component manufacturing cycle of prismatic parts can analyze all the primitive features needed to represent parts made on a vertical CNC milling machine. This includes, at a minimum, slots, pockets, holes, and overall boundary features.

Error Sources

Error sources, in general, can be broadly classified as deterministic and random in nature. Random error sources, primarily due to the process dynamics, are typically accepted as is and considered as a limiting factor for a given machine or process. The deterministic error sources are numerous and can be eliminated if they can be identified. The most probable error sources for each of the primitive features encountered in a prismatic part can be classified as shown in Table 9.3.

TABLE 9.3. Error Sources for a Machined Prismatic Part

	Tool Errors					Machine Errors							Miscellaneous Errors					
						Positioning Errors					Thermal Deformation	Workpiece Deflection	Incorrect Setup			Stock Error		
	Tool Size Incorrect	Tool Size	Tool Wear	Tool Runout	Tool Deflection	Servo Lag	Out of Calibration	x-y Positioning	Square-ness	Spindle Tram	Thermal Deformation	Workpiece Deflection	Part within Fixture	Fixture within Table	Incorrect Stock Size	Length Incorrect	Width Incorrect	Thickness Incorrect
Boundary																		
Width	X		X	X	X		X		X			X	X	X	X		X	
Length	X	X	X	X	X		X		X			X	X	X	X	X		
Thickness	X	X	X	X			⟩		X				X	X				X
Slot																		
Width	X	X	X	X	X							X	X	X				
Location								X	X									
Depth										X								
Pocket																		
Width	X	X	X	X								X	X				X	
Length	X		X		X			X	X			X						
Location					X				X				X	X		X	X	
Depth										X	X							X
Hole																		
Size	X	X	X	X									X	X		X	X	X
x location	X	X	X					X			X		X	X		X		
y location	X							X			X		X	X			X	

149

Each row in Table 9.3 represents one of the dimension–form errors measured on a prismatic part. Each column in the table represents all the error sources. An X in any column indicates that the dimension–form error measured might have been caused by that particular error source. For example, there are 11 X marks in the boundary width dimension row. This indicates that if an error exist in this dimension, it might have been caused by any one or combination of 11 error sources.

Incorrect tool size and type are due to incorrect tool selection even before machining is done. Similarly, the tool can be worn or show runout before machining. Tool wear, tool runout, and deflection also can occur during the machining cycle. This may be the direct result of improper machine feeds and speeds, depth of cut, tool shank size, and material.

Machine errors, are typically classified as position errors and thermal deformation errors. Both are repetitive in nature, except that the thermal deformation is, in addition, a function of time. Position errors (such as servo lag, out of calibration, x–y positioning, squareness, and spindle tram) are caused by usage over a period of time and are repetitive. Position errors are present in a brand-new machine, but they are within specifications considered to be the limitations of the machine.

Miscellaneous errors are grouped together. These include workpiece deflection due to cutting force and incorrect fixture–workpiece orientation. Finally, the stock size boundary errors, such as incorrect length, width, and thickness, can cause errors in various dimensions.

Method of Analysis

The logic used in an inspection data analyzer is patterned after steps that would be taken by a panel of experts trying to determine why a part has been machined incorrectly. In the algorithm-based inspection data analyzer reported in ref. 10, a total of six algorithms are used to analyze the inspection data for errors in prismatic parts. They are

1. Boundary size analysis.
2. Slot and pocket edge analysis.
3. x and y hole location analysis.
4. Hole diameter analysis.
5. Combined tool error analysis.
6. Combined machine and fixture analysis.

The first four analyses determine the most likely source of error that was based on solely dimensional and database analyses. Questions arise when one considers that there may be multiple error sources present or that the initial error determination may be incorrect when reviewing all data from the other routines. The last two analyses, therefore, address the coupling effects. The output from such an inspection data analyzer is now available to the designer, quickly and with little expense, and can be of immense assistance while redesigning in an automated manufacturing environment.

9.6 DESIGN KNOWLEDGE CAPTURE

In the design for automated manufacturing environment, changes in the preliminary design must be made as requested by the manufacturability analyzer. Manufacturability may be satisfied with minor modifications, but in many cases it may require a significant overhaul of the design. In this case, the designer needs not only the definitive knowledge that describes the current design but also the explanatory knowledge that explains how the design decisions were made.

Traditionally, the knowledge captured in the form of various documentation falls under the category of definitive knowledge, the portion of the designer's knowledge that is needed to manufacture the design. However, a designer's knowledge includes more than definitive information, it also includes some explanatory information targeted at the analyses he or she conducted and the decisions he or she made (11). The lack of knowledge retention in available mechanisms becomes more critical when the original designer is no longer available. The existence of a comprehensive design knowledge capture (DKC) system within the design for automated manufacturing environment has considerable economic and strategic importance.

Although no commercial DKC systems are reported, there are systems that take a step toward DKC. The ICAD system developed by ICAD Inc., is an example of a parametric design

TABLE 9.4. Design Knowledge Types

Design Phase	Traditional Definitive Knowledge	Explanatory Knowledge
Identification	Overall objective	Same
	Task requirements	
Definition	State of the art	Experience
	Specification	Heuristics
	Standards	Intuition
	Task decomposition	Rule of thumb
Synthesis	Geometric data	Highly qualitative?
	Types of material	
	Manufacturing specification	
	Selection of parts	
Analysis	Analytical results	Choice of analysis
	Finite element analysis	Interpretation of results
	Basic design rules	Heuristics
	Scientific	
	Empirical	
Optimization	Alternative designs	Same
	Cost estimates	
	Size limits	
Presentation	Acceptability norms	Same

system. It considers any design to be a hierarchical arrangement of subdesigns, the way engineers think in terms of function, relationships, and properties. ICAD captures design intent within the design definitions, not within specific parts. Another example is the knowledge-based system approach taken to develop a DKC system (12). This is a frame-based DKC system. Although each DKC system may follow a different approach, a typical KBS system will have the following two basic components:

1. Identifying the type, quantity, and the acquisition method of knowledge.
2. Obtaining a knowledge representation scheme.

Knowledge Type and Acquisition Method

The determination of what design knowledge to capture must be preceded by an understanding of knowledge needs. The definitive design knowledge, such as part drawings, provides all the necessary information required to manufacture the part. This is well documented, and all existing mechanisms provide this capability. In general, the explanatory knowledge must include information on the procedures used for defining and decomposing a design task, analysis performed, evaluation methods selected, and rationale for all of the above. Table 9.4 shows the design knowledge types needed to explain the what (definitive knowledge) and why (explanatory knowledge) of a design that embodies the comprehensive engineering design knowledge.

Knowledge acquisition is the process by which facts, rules, patterns, heuristics, and operations used by humans to solve problems in a particular domain are elicited. There are two main approaches for eliciting knowledge: protocol and interactive methods. Protocol methods require defining a priori what knowledge should be captured. This can lead to inaccurate and incomplete knowledge bases due to improper protocol definition. Nonetheless, and although this is a time-consuming process, it is the most commonly used method. Interactive methods employ mechanisms that attempt to make knowledge determinations on the fly, by communicating with the designer.

Knowledge Representation Scheme

The knowledge representation scheme is not universal because the design knowledge is large, difficult to model, and not constant. Many techniques have been developed, and in general, they

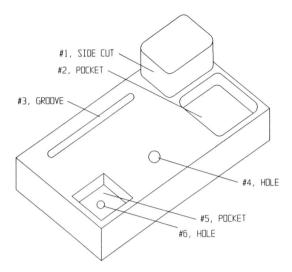

Figure 9.4. An example part.

fall into three categories: functions, production rules, and semantic networks. For example, the DKC system reported in ref. 12 uses semantic networks to represent knowledge through use of graphic structures. While different semantic networks emphasize different relationships between chunks of knowledge, they all use a graph structure with nodes, representing concepts, connected by links, representing semantic relationships between the concepts (13).

Typically, frames describe a class of objects and particular instances of classes of objects. The descriptions are contained within a slot-and-filler structure within a frame. Each frame may have several slots, which represent attributes of the particular object, and each slot may be filled with a value; frames may be linked hierarchically and enable an inheritance mechanism. For example, in engineering design, each piece of a design may have its own mechanical drawing stored in computerized form. Now it would be useful to have each part represented as a frame, each with a slot representing the drawing. One way to implement this would be to specify explicitly the appropriate drawing as the value of the drawing slot of the corresponding frame.

An implementation of the frame based system, Forms, is an enhanced version of experimental representation language. A form (which is a frame in the Forms package) consists of five fields. The first field, Name, specifies the name of the form, and the second, Type, specifies whether the form describes a class of objects or a specific object. Parent, the third field, specifies the name of the immediate parent of the form. Note that the tree structure limits this field to a single value. The highest level form will have a Parent value of 0. The fourth field, Instance, gives a list of the names of all forms that have declared this form as the immediate parent. And the last field, With, gives a list of all the slots, aspects, and values. Each slot–aspect–value set is a list of the form (slot aspect value), so the With field is a list of these lists.

TABLE 9.5. Tolerance Table for Each Feature[a]

Feature Number	Profile (mm)	Surface Finish (μm)	Flatness and Circularity (mm)
1	0.762	2.54	0.381
2	0.762	7.62	0.381
3	0.762	7.62	0.381
4	0.038	7.62	0.152
5	0.203	7.62	0.381
6	0.381	7.62	0.152

[a] Output from the tolerance input program. Design name: dfam. From ref. 4.

TABLE 9.6. Results of the Manufacturability Analyzer[a]

Analysis	Result	Selection	Remarks
Stock analysis	Successful	Stock #2	But it requires facing off 24 mm (0.95 in.), which is excessive machining. A better stock size could be selected if the total design height were less than 75 mm (2.95 in.).
Fixture analysis	Successful	Fixture #1	But it requires the part to be held along the broad side
Machine analysis	Successful	Machine #1	
Tool analysis	Unsuccessful		⟨*feature # {tools selected}*⟩ ⟨1{504,505,506,513,515}⟩ ⟨2{see note}⟩ ⟨3{516}⟩ ⟨4{502,507,508}⟩ ⟨5{see note}⟩ ⟨6{502,507,508}}⟩ *Note:* #2(pocket): tools found, but interfere with feature #1; #5(pocket): no tools to make sharp corners.
Tolerance analysis	Unsuccessful		⟨*feature # {machining processes, tool types, tool ID's, speeds (m/ sec), feeds (m/tooth/rev), axial depth of cut (mm), radial depth of cut (mm)}*⟩ ⟨1{none: surface finish and flatness cannot be met}⟩ ⟨2{no tolerance analysis}⟩ ⟨3{normal}⟩ ⟨4{controlled, drill & reamer, 508&518,1.27&1.524, 0.00018&0.00028}⟩ ⟨5{no tolerance analysis}⟩ ⟨6{normal}⟩

[a] Data from the design-for-manufacturability analyzer. Design name: dfam. From ref. 4.

This is an active research-and-development topic, and many more interesting, economically feasible, design knowledge capture systems can be expected in the near future.

9.7 AN EXAMPLE

The example is illustrated by using the manufacturability analyzer developed at the University of Maryland (4). The analyzer, written in C, resides on a Sun workstation interfaced to a vertical machining center-based FMC. This FMC is capable of machining a part with prismatic features only.

As an example, consider a case in which the designer has designed the part as shown in Figure 9.4, using a CAD package (Cadkey in this case). The design file is then processed through the IGES translator and then through a feature extractor to generate a feature file. At this stage the designer enters tolerances for each feature, which become the input for the manufacturability analyzer. Table 9.5 shows the tolerance chain for the example part.

Table 9.6 shows a summary of results obtained for the example part when the analyzer finished the check of manufacturability. The stock analysis was successful in selecting stock #2, Aluminum block $152.4 \times 101.6 \times 101.6$ mm^3 ($6 \times 4 \times 4$ in.^{3}). However, 24 mm (0.95 in.) of material must be removed from the top. This excessive machining could be avoided if the design could be changed to accommodate next size stock. Similarly, the fixture analysis was successful and fixture #1 was selected. It, however, required holding the piece along the broad side. In the next analysis, the analyzer was able to select machine #1 to create the part.

The program now searches the global database to determine if each of the features can be machined with available tools. In this particular case, the search was unsuccessful. Feature #2, a rectangular pocket, cannot be machined because the tool collet interferes with feature #1. Also, feature #5 failed because no tools were found to get the sharp corners.

Although the part was found not manufacturable, the tolerance analysis was performed to see what other problems may exist. Feature #1, the side cut, cannot be held to the requested surface finish or flatness. No tolerance analysis was performed on features #2 and #5 because no tool was selected. Feature #4 requires controlled machining. The redesign and analysis must be performed iteratively, until it is found to be manufacturable.

9.8 SUMMARY

In a design for automated manufacturing environment, the design engineer becomes involved in the manufacturing process of the component being developed. The designer is aided by several analysis tools or modules that can identify the design constituents that influence manufacturing processes and cost. Manufacturability of each geometric feature of the component is checked for the available manufacturing capabilities. The designer is shown with a wide range spectrum of possible problems within the design. Furthermore, because the analysis tools reject designs for problems ranging from stock selection to surface finish, the designer will be encouraged to consider those issues from the beginning of the product development cycle. A method for representing the elusive explanatory knowledge in addition to the traditional definitive knowledge was discussed. The design knowledge capture system, built on top of a frame system for knowledge representation, is a valuable tool to be integrated in the system of design for automated manufacturing.

Acknowledgments

The authors would like to acknowledge the contribution of D.K. Anand, J.A. Kirk, J. Dickstein, J. Herndon, and M.J. Courtright to this work.

BIBLIOGRAPHY

1. H.W. STOLL, "Design for Manufacturing: An Overview," *Appl. Mech. Rev.* **39**(9), 1356–1364 (1986).
2. Z. DONG, "Design for Automated Manufacturing" In A. Kusiak, ed., *Concurrent Engineering: Automation, Tools, and Techniques,* John Wiley & Sons, Inc., New York, 1993, pp. 207–233.
3. D.G. ULLMAN and T.A. DIETTERICH, "Mechanical design methodology: Implications on future development of computer aided design and knowledge based systems," *Eng. With Comput.* **2**, 21–29 (1987).
4. M. ANJANAPPA et al., "Manufacturability Analysis for a Flexible Manufacturing Cell," *J. Mech. Design ASME Trans.* **113**, 372–378 (1991).
5. N. COOK, *Manufacturing Analysis.* Addison-Wesley Publishing Co., Inc., Reading, Mass., 1966.
6. G.E. DIETER, *Engineering Design: A Materials and Processing Approach.* McGraw-Hill Book Co., Inc., New York, 1983.
7. F.O. PHILLIP, *Cost Estimating,* 2nd ed., Prentice-Hall, Inc., Englewood Cliffs, N.J., 1984.
8. M. ANJANAPPA et al., "Automated Rapid Prototyping with Heuristics and Intelligence: Part 1," *Int. J. Comput. Integrated Manufac.* **4**(4), 29–231 (1991).
9. Y. WANG, "Minimum Zone Evaluation of Form Tolerances," *Manufac. Rev.* **5**(3), 213–220 (1992).
10. M. ANJANAPPA et al., "Automated Inspection Data Analyzer for Closed Loop Manufacturing" in *Proceedings of Manufacturing International—1990,* pp. 55–62.
11. D.B. WECHSLER and K.B. CROUSE, *An Approach to Design Knowledge Capture for the Space Station.* NASA, Houston, 1985, Space Station Tech. Rep. TR-N85-12597.
12. J.A. HERNDON et al., "Frame-Based Implementation of a Design Knowledge-Capture Scheme," *Knowledge-Based Sys* **4**(1), 35–51 (1991).
13. C. GARG-JANARDAN and G. SALVENDY, "A Conceptual Frame Work for Knowledge Elicitation," *Int. J. Man-Machine studies* **26**(4), 521–531 (1987).

CHAPTER 10

Tolerancing for Design and Manufacturing

CHUN ZHANG and H.-P. BEN WANG
The University of Iowa

10.1 INTRODUCTION

Basic Concepts

Tolerances

Tolerance is one of the most important parameters in product and process design, and tolerancing clearly plays a key role in design and manufacturing. Tolerance is defined as the maximum deviation from a nominal specification within which the part is acceptable for its intended purpose. A tolerance is usually expressed as lower and upper deviations from the nominal value.

Manufacturing involves applying a series of operations to components (parts, subassemblies, etc.). These operations are intended to ensure specific geometry on workpieces. Dimensions in engineering drawings specify ideal geometry: size, location, and shape. Because variations exist in both processes and materials, the manufacturing process creates a part that has an approximate geometry of the ideal. Tolerances are introduced to specify and control the variations. With the advent of assembly lines, it became critical to manufacture interchangeable parts. The use of replacement parts for maintenance operations also requires the interchangeability of parts. Tolerances are used to ensure that parts have this property.

Design and Manufacturing Tolerances

Two types of tolerances are often used: design tolerances and manufacturing tolerances. Design tolerances are related to the operational requirements of a mechanical assembly or of a component; whereas manufacturing tolerances are mainly devised for a process plan for fabricating a part (1). Manufacturing tolerances must ensure the realization of design tolerances. For example, three manufacturing processes are used to make a $20^{+0.01}$-mm hole. The processes include drilling, boring, and grinding. Assume the following dimensions and tolerances must be maintained in these processes: $21.5^{+0.2}$, $20.5^{+0.05}$, and $20^{+0.01}$. Then $20^{+0.01}$ is called the design dimension and tolerance for the hole. The manufacturing (machining) dimensions and tolerances for the drilling, boring, and grinding processes are $21.5^{+0.2}$, $20^{+0.05}$, and $20^{+0.01}$, respectively.

Tolerance Analysis and Synthesis

There are two kinds of tolerancing exercises performed in product and process design: tolerance analysis and tolerance synthesis. Tolerance analysis involves identification of related tolerances in a design, and calculation of the stackup of these related tolerances. The process of tolerance accumulation is modeled, and the resultant tolerance is verified. If design requirements are not met, tolerance values are adjusted and the stackup recalculated. Tolerance synthesis, on the other hand, is the process of allocating tolerance values associated with design requirements in terms of functionality or assemblability among identified related design (or manufacturing) tolerances. It is a process of distributing tolerance values among a number of related dimensions.

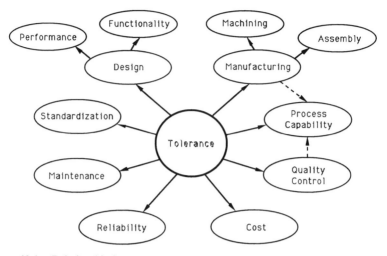

Figure 10.1. Relationship between tolerance and other design–manufacturing activities.

Worst-Case and Statistical Tolerancing

A tolerancing problem can be solved based on either a worst-case approach or a statistical approach. In the worst-case approach, the extreme values of tolerances are considered. Complete interchangeability is ensured for all in-tolerance parts. Because the machining of parts is performed on different machine tools, or on the same machine tools but at different points in time, the dimensions on the parts are independent stochastic variables. Thus statistical tolerance calculation is valid. In the statistical approach, tolerance calculations are performed based on the fact that actual part dimensions are randomly distributed about their nominal values. While allowing larger tolerances to be used in design and manufacturing, statistical tolerancing leads to lower manufacturing costs. However, scraps will be produced as the result of the statistical method. The worst-case tolerance synthesis applies to single piece or small-lot production for critical applications, e.g., aerospace aircraft; whereas the statistical method makes much more sense for mass production.

Impact of Tolerances in Design and Manufacturing

Both design and process engineers are concerned about the effects of tolerances. Designers usually specify tight tolerances to ensure the performance and functionality of the design. Process engineers prefer loose tolerances, which make parts easier and less expensive to produce. Therefore, tolerance specifications become a critical link between design and manufacturing. Good tolerance design ensures quality products at low cost. Figure 10.1 shows the relationship between tolerance and other design–manufacturing activities. As can be seen from the figure, tolerance design has a far-reaching influence that touches nearly every aspect of design and manufacturing.

10.2   TOLERANCE ANALYSIS

Tolerance Stackup

The basis for rational tolerance specification is to develop an analytical model to evaluate the accumulation of tolerances in a mechanical assembly or accumulation of machining tolerances in component manufacturing. In assembly applications, critical clearances or fits of an assembly are usually controlled by the stackup of several component tolerances. Similarly, in machining applications, a blueprint tolerance may be affected by a set of related machining tolerances. In both cases, the problem of tolerance stackup exists. A tolerance stackup problem can be analyzed by either a worst-case or a statistical approach. They are described in the following sections.

Tolerance Stackup Analysis: A Worst-case Model

Dimension chain analysis is an effective tool for tolerance stackup analysis. A dimension chain is a set of interrelated dimensions that form a closed loop. This chain of dimensions refers to a single part or a group of parts. Dimension chains can be classified, based on their form, into the following four categories (2):

1. *Linear Parallel Dimension Chains.* The dimension chains that comprise linear dimensions and parallel links on the same plane.
2. *Linear Nonparallel Dimension chains.* The dimension chains that comprise linear dimensions and nonparallel links on the same plane.
3. *Angular Dimension Chains.* The dimension chains with angular dimensions.
4. *Space Dimension Chains.* The dimension chains in space in which some dimensions do not lie on the same plane.

The first class of dimension chains is the simplest and most commonly used. The discussion here will focus on the analysis of this type of dimension chain. The following are the symbols and terminology for dimension chain analysis:

Resultant link (X_R)	The dimension that is indirectly obtained by other dimensions in a dimension chain
Component link (X_i)	Individual dimensions in a dimension chain other than the resultant link. Here, X_i represents the nominal value of dimension i
Increasing link	The component link that can cause the resultant link to enlarge when it is increased itself
Decreasing link	The component link that can cause the resultant link to shrink when it is increased itself
X_R	Nominal dimension of the resultant link
Δ_{LR}, Δ_{UR}	Lower and upper deviation of the resultant link
δ_R	Tolerance of the resultant link ($\delta_R = \Delta_{UR} - \Delta_{LR}$)
X_{Rmax}, X_{Rmin}	Maximum and minimum dimensions of the resultant link
XI_i	Nominal dimension of increasing link i
$\Delta_{LI_i}, \Delta_{UI_i}$	Lower and upper deviation of XI_i
δI_i	Tolerance of increasing link i ($\delta I_i = \Delta_{UI_i} - \Delta_{LI_i}$)
XI_{imax}, XI_{imin}	Maximum and minimum dimensions of increasing link i
XD_i	Nominal dimension of decreasing link i
$\Delta_{LD_i}, \Delta_{UD_i}$	Lower and upper deviation of XD_i
δD_i	Tolerance of increasing link i ($\delta \Delta_i = \Delta_{UD_i} - \Delta_{LD_i}$)
XD_{imax}, XD_{imin}	Maximum and minimum dimensions of decreasing link i
δ_i	Tolerance of component link i

The following equations can be used to perform the worst-case tolerance calculation in a dimension chain:

$$X_R = \sum XI_i - \sum XD_i$$
$$X_{Rmax} = \sum XI_{imax} - \sum XD_{imin}$$
$$X_{Rmin} = \sum XI_{imin} - \sum XD_{imax}$$
$$\Delta_{LR} = \sum \Delta_{LI_i} - \sum \Delta_{UD_i}$$
$$\Delta_{UR} = \sum \Delta_{UI_i} - \sum \Delta_{LD_i}$$

or

$$\delta_R = X_{Rmax} - X_{Rmin} = \sum \delta I_i + \sum \delta D_i = \sum \delta_i$$

Figure 10.2 shows a dimension chain. In this example, an assembly with three components is considered. In the assembly, two blocks (components 2 and 3) are mounted on the left and right

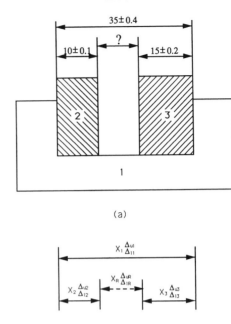

Component links: X_1, X_2, X_3
Concluding link: X_R

Figure 10.2. An example of a dimension chain.

(b)

sides of the slot on the component 1. The drawing of the assembly is given in Figure 10.2a, and the dimension chain is illustrated in Figure 10.2b. The gap between blocks 2 and 3 is the resultant link.

Based on the definitions given above, increasing and decreasing links can be identified. Among the three component links, X_1 is found to be an increasing link and X_2 and X_3 are decreasing links. Using the equations for dimension chain analysis, the dimension and tolerance on the resultant link for the example can be calculated as follows:

$$X_R = \sum XI_i - \sum XD_i = 35 - (10 + 15) = 10 \text{ mm}$$
$$\Delta_{LR} = \sum \Delta_{LI_i} - \sum \Delta_{UD_i} = -0.4 - (0.1 + 0.2) = -0.7 \text{ mm}$$
$$\Delta_{UR} = \sum \Delta_{UI_i} - \sum \Delta_{LD_i} = 0.4 - (-0.1 - 0.2) = 0.7 \text{ mm}$$

or

$$\delta_R = \sum \delta_i = \pm 0.4 \pm 0.1 \pm 0.2 = \pm 0.7$$

Therefore, the dimension and tolerance on the resultant link is 10 ($\pm$0.7) mm. The dimension chain analysis can be used for either assembly or machining dimension and tolerance analysis. The applications of dimension chain analysis to both design (assembly) and manufacturing (machining) tolerancing are given below.

Tolerance Stackup Analysis: A Statistical Method

In the worst-case tolerance stackup analysis, the extreme conditions of manufacturing errors are considered. This approach is mathematically simple but may lead to unnecessarily tight tolerances, which increase manufacturing costs. Because the dimensional variations of machined parts (other than single-piece production) naturally follow a statistical distribution, the chance of a part being machined at the extreme dimension is usually negligibly small. Thus statistical tolerancing method makes much more sense as far as economical factor is concerned.

In statistical tolerance analysis, each individual dimension in a dimension chain may be described as an independent random variable. The distribution of the dimensions depends on the manufacturing process used to produce it. A commonly used distribution for machined part dimensions is the normal distribution. Based on this assumption, the tolerance stackup can be expressed as follows:

$$\delta_R = (\delta_1^2 + \delta_2^2 + \cdots + \delta_n^2)^{1/2} = \left(\sum \delta_i^2\right)^{1/2}$$

This model is often called the root sum square (RSS) model, because the component tolerances add as the root sum squared. It can be seen from the above equation that compared with the worst-case approach the statistical approach results in larger component tolerances for a given resultant tolerance and thus requires lower manufacturing costs.

The above statistical tolerancing formulation is developed based on the normal distribution assumption. However, in real production, this assumption may not always be valid. The distribution may be flatter or skewed due to setup errors or tool wear. Some modifications to the RSS approach have been introduced to handle the asymmetric or nonrandom distributions. Bender (3) and Gladman (4) proposed correction factor methods; whereas Greenwood and Chase (5) introduced a unified tolerance analysis method based on the estimated mean shift model. Bjorke (6) developed the TOLTECH system, based on a β distribution assumption, to overcome some of the difficulties associated with the normal distribution approximation. Another class of statistical tolerancing method is Monte Carlo simulation (7). This approach predicts accurate results. However, it is computation intensive.

10.3 COST-TOLERANCE MODEL

For mechanical parts, the manufacturing error on a dimension primarily depends on the following factors:

Accuracy of machine tool.

Accuracy of fixture.

Accuracy of tool.

Setup error.

Deformation of the machining system (including machine tool, fixture, tool, and workpiece) under external forces.

Thermal deformation of the machining system.

Measurement error.

Impurity of material.

These errors can be grouped into two categories: deterministic and random. For example, the manufacturing error on the diameter of a reamed hole due to the inaccuracy of the reamer diameter is a deterministic error. The manufacturing error caused by the variation of material hardness is a random error. The total manufacturing error on the dimension of a part feature is the combined effect of the above-mentioned errors. These errors are mainly related to the inaccuracies of machine tool, fixture, tool, setup, gage, and material. In addition, the operator skill level is a factor that affects manufacturing error. In a manufacturing firm, there usually exist a number of alternate combinations of machine tools and auxiliary equipment for a manufacturing process. Each combination is associated with a manufacturing precision level and cost. A higher precision level (tighter tolerance) usually requires a higher manufacturing cost, due to the need for a more accurate machine tool, fixture, tool, setup and more skillful operators. The precision of the process varies, depending on the accuracy of resources (including equipment, material, and operator). Therefore, for a specific manufacturing process, there is a monotonic decreasing relationship between manufacturing cost and precision in a certain range.

Several models were reported to describe this cost tolerance relationship, such as Sutherland function, reciprocal function, reciprocal square function, and exponential function (8).

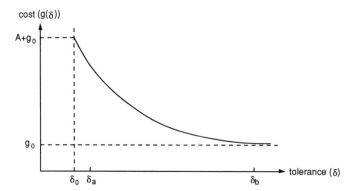

Figure 10.3. A manufacturing process cost-tolerance curve.

Among them, the exponential function is found to be relatively simple and accurate (9). The following is the mathematical representation of the exponential cost-tolerance function (10). A graphical representation is shown in Figure 10.3.

$$g(\delta) = Ae^{-B(\delta-\delta_0)} + g_0$$

$$\delta_1 < \delta < \delta_u$$

In this model, A, δ_0, and g_0 determine the position of the cost-tolerance curve, while B controls the curvature of it. These parameters can be derived using a curve-fitting approach based on experimental data. δ_1 and δ_u define the lower and upper bounds of the region, respectively, in which the tolerance is economically achievable. For different manufacturing processes, these parameters are usually different.

10.4 TOLERANCE SYNTHESIS

Design (Assembly) Tolerance Synthesis

Design (assembly) tolerancing is to allocate design tolerances on individual components that ensure the critical clearance or fit in an assembly. A number of design tolerance allocation approaches have been used in practice or have been proposed in the literature. They are described as follows.

Equal Tolerances Method

The equal tolerance method allocates the same tolerances on all components: for worst case,

$$\delta_i = \frac{\delta_R}{n}$$

and for RSS,

$$\delta_i = \frac{\delta_R}{\sqrt{n}}$$

where δ_i is the tolerance on component i, δ_R is the resultant tolerance (on a critical clearance or fit), and n is the number of components involved. This approach will not provide good results, because it does not consider the difference in the manufacturing of individual components. However, this approach requires only simple calculations.

Equal Precision Method

In manufacturing practice, the complexity of machining different dimensions are not the same. It is more appropriate to allocate component tolerances based on their nominal dimensions. The following is the equal precision method: for worst case,

$$\delta_R = \sum \delta_i \quad \text{and} \quad \frac{\delta_i}{C_i} = \text{constant}$$

and for RSS,

$$\delta_R = \sqrt{\sum \delta_i^2} \quad \text{and} \quad \frac{\delta_i}{C_i} = \text{constant}$$

where C_i is the tolerance factor for component i and can be determined as follows (11):

$$C_i = 0.45 \sqrt[3]{D_i} + 0.001 \times D_i$$

where D_i is the dimension of component i.

Minimum Cost Method

In the above two approaches, tolerance allocation are performed by rule of thumb. They are neither optimization nor cost-driven methods. Because design tolerancing has a great impact on product quality and cost, much attention has been given to optimal design tolerance allocation. Many analytical models have been introduced for optimization of design tolerancing. A basic formulation is given below:

$$\min G = \min \left(\sum_{i=1}^{n} g_i(\delta_i) \right)$$

subject to: for worst case,

$$\sum \delta_i \leq \delta_R$$

and for RSS,

$$\sqrt{\sum \delta_i^2} \leq \delta_R$$

$$\delta_{il} < \delta_i < \delta_{iu}$$

where, G, total manufacturing cost; $g_i(d_i)$, manufacturing cost of producing tolerance δ_i on component i; δ_R, the resultant tolerance; δ_{il}, δ_{iu}, lower and upper bounds of tolerance δ_i; and n, number of components. This optimization model can be solved by using the Lagrange multiplier method (12). However, when more than one resultant tolerance is imposed, this solution procedure is invalid. Some optimization algorithms were introduced to solve this class of problems (e.g., 13–16). In recent years, several more comprehensive models and solution procedures have been introduced for optimal design tolerancing. Chase et al. (17) introduced a procedure for not only finding out the least-cost set of tolerances, but also selecting the least-cost process from a set of alternative processes for each dimension for an assembly. Three solution algorithms were employed to solve this problem. Lee and Woo (18) proposed a mathematical model for the optimal design tolerancing problems with linear or nonlinear tolerance stackups. In their work, the tolerancing problem was formulated as a probabilistic optimization model and was further simplified into a deterministic nonlinear programming problem. An algorithm was also developed and was proven to converge to the global optimum. Zhang and Wang (19) used a simulated annealing algorithm to solve the design tolerancing problem involving alternative process selection. Based on the authors' observations, the simulated annealing was found to be an effective and robust solution algorithm for optimal design tolerancing problems. The optimal design tolerancing has long been studied for its importance to product quality and costs. More research efforts are still needed for developing analytical models and solution procedures for complex assembly models and the integration of design tolerancing and manufacturing tolerancing, which will make a unique contribution to concurrent engineering (CE).

Manufacturing (Machining) Tolerance Allocation

Manufacturing tolerance allocation is to determine properly the manufacturing tolerances in intermediate manufacturing processes for a part fabrication. A mechanical part usually has a number of dimensions and thus the machining of the part is for the realization of those dimensions. In manufacturing practice, a dimension is usually obtained by performing several manufacturing processes. The number of processes depends on the complexity of geometry and the tolerance–surface finish requirements on the dimension and its related surfaces. The relationships between machining dimensions involved in a part fabrication are often complex, especially when a large number of operations are used to make the part. Tolerancing charting has been used to establish the relationships among the machining dimensions. It provides the process engineer with an effective tool for machining dimension and tolerance analysis.

This section is designed to walk the engineer systematically through the basic steps of tolerance charting. The symbols used in this section are defined below:

L_i — Nominal value of machining dimension i
L_{XY} — Nominal distance between part (or workpiece) surfaces X and Y
Z_i — Nominal value of the stock removal for machining dimension i
D_{LZ_i} — Lower deviation of the stock removal for machining dimension i
D_{UZ_i} — Upper deviation of the stock removal for machining dimension i

Figure 10.4a shows the drawing of a bushing, and Figure 10.4b indicates the process routing of producing the bushing. The boldface lines in the figure show the surfaces being cut in that operation. This example is used to illustrate the procedure of the application of the tolerance chart.

Preparation of a Tolerance Chart

Step 1. Draw in a half view of the part at the top of the chart. Number each vertical surface (Figure 10.5).
Step 2. Draw vertical dimensioning lines from each numbered surface of the part to the bottom of the chart.
Step 3. Write blueprint dimensions between these surfaces above the sketch. Number these blueprint dimensions and establish a dimension table on the right-hand side of the sketch. Create columns for:
  1. Blueprint dimension number.
  2. Basic dimension.
  3. Deviations.
  4. Component links affecting the resultant dimension.
Step 4. Establish tables under the sketch. On the left, establish columns for:
  1. Operation number.
  2. Name of operation.
  3. Surface being machined.
  On the right, establish columns for:
  1. Machining dimension.
  2. Deviations of machining dimension.
  3. Stock removal.
  4. Variation of stock removal.
  5. Component links affecting stock removal.
  Operation numbers are listed in a reversed sequence. If more than one surface is machined in the same operation, the surfaces are also listed in a reversed sequence relative to the sequence of machining.
Step 5. Drawing machining dimension lines underneath the part sketch. A machining dimension line has an arrow at one end and a dot at the other. The arrow points at and touches the surface being cut. The dot is an implied datum. Number the machining dimension lines from the top to the bottom.

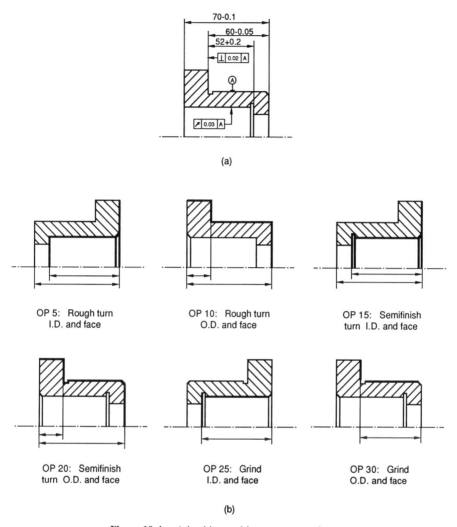

(a)

(b)

Figure 10.4.   A bushing and its process routing.

To make the chart easy to read, dimension lines for stock removals are not shown on the chart. For the same surface machined in different operations, the arrows on the machining dimension lines are directed to the same vertical dimension line. Dimension 1 in OP 30 and Dimension 3 in OP 20, dimension 4 in OP 20 and Dimension 8 in OP 10 are such examples. After these five steps, the basic frame of a tolerance chart is constructed. Figure 10.5 shows the failure of the tolerance chart for the bushing machining.

Calculation of Machining Dimensions and Tolerances Using a Tolerance Chart

After the tolerance chart is prepared, machining dimensions and tolerances can be calculated. The procedure of calculations is given below.

Step 1. Fill in blueprint dimensions and tolerances in the design dimension table.
Step 2. Identify dimension chains for blueprint dimensions and fill in the component links by which the blueprint dimensions are ensured.

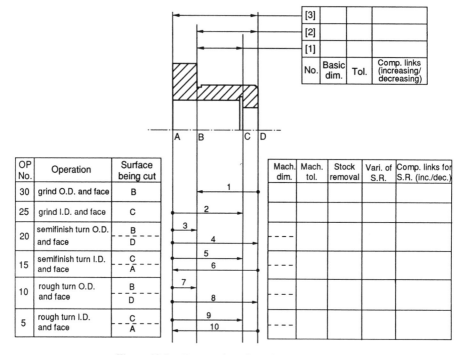

Figure 10.5. Preparation of a tolerance chart.

A blueprint dimension may be indirectly obtained through a set of related machining dimensions. In this case, a dimension chain is formed. In the dimension chain, the blueprint dimension is the resultant link and those machining dimensions are component links. They are identified in the following approach:

1. Starting from both ends of a blueprint dimension, draw vertical tracing lines downward.
2. When a dot representing the datum of a machining dimension is encountered, continue going downward. When an arrow, which represents a surface being machined, if encountered, turn and go along the dimension line.
3. Continue the procedure until the two tracing lines meet at a certain dot. All the machining dimensions that either one of the two tracing lines has passed through, are component links of the blueprint dimension.

Figure 10.6 shows the procedure of identifying the dimension chain for blueprint dimension [1]. In the figure, two vertical tracing lines are drawn from both ends (surfaces B and C) of blueprint dimension [1] ($52^{+0.2}$), the tracing line from surface B meets the arrow of machining dimension 1, and turns in the direction of the dimension. After reaching the dot of the dimension, the tracing line goes downward to the arrow of machining dimension 4 and turns in the direction of the dimension. On the other side, the tracing line from surface C encounters the arrow of machining dimension 2, then goes along the dimension to the dot. After that, the tracing line goes downward and meets the tracing line from surface B at the dot of machining dimension 4. Therefore, the component links of blueprint dimension [1] include machining dimensions 1, 2, and 4. Similarly, machining dimension 1 and machining dimension 4 are found to be the component links of blueprint dimensions [2] and [3], respectively.

When there is only one component link for a blueprint dimension, the blueprint dimension is directly ensured by only that machining dimension. Otherwise, if a blueprint dimension has more than one component link, the dimension is indirectly obtained and further calculation is

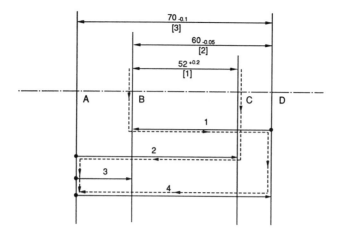

Figure 10.6. An example of a blueprint dimension chain.

required for finding out its dimension and tolerance. As discussed above, a component link may be of either an increasing link or a decreasing one, depending on its relationship with the resultant link. The increasing and decreasing component links can be identified by using the rule given in section 2 and can be used to justify the component links for machining the dimension chain. For example, in blueprint dimension chain [1], machining dimensions 1 and 2 are increasing links, whereas machining dimension 4 is a decreasing link.

Step 3. Calculate basic dimensions between part surfaces.

Some of the basic dimensions between part surfaces are given in the part drawing. However, machining dimensions are not necessarily all identical to the blueprint dimensions. Therefore, to determine nominal values of machining dimensions, basic dimensions between each pair of part surfaces on the part drawing should be calculated.

Taking the bushing as an example, the given blueprint dimensions are as follows:

$$L_{AD} = 70 \text{ mm}, \ L_{BD} = 60 \text{ mm}, \ L_{BC} = 52 \text{ mm}$$

Other basic dimensions can be calculated as follows:

$$L_{AB} = L_{AD} - L_{BD} = 70 - 60 = 10 \text{ mm}$$
$$L_{AC} = L_{AB} + L_{BC} = 10 + 52 = 62 \text{ mm}$$
$$L_{CD} = L_{BD} - L_{BC} = 60 - 52 = 8 \text{ mm}$$

Step 4. Determine tolerances on machining dimensions.

The tolerance on a machining dimension can be determined as follows:

1. If a machining dimension is the only one determining the result of a blueprint dimension, the tolerance on the blueprint dimension is taken as the tolerance of the machining dimension. For example, the tolerance on machining dimension 1 is assigned to −0.05 according to blueprint dimension [2].

2. If a machining dimension is related to the attainment of more than one blueprint dimension, its tolerance is determined based on the blueprint dimension with the tightest tolerance.

3. If a blue print dimension is ensured by more than one machining dimension, its tolerance will be distributed among those machining dimensions. For example, the tolerance on

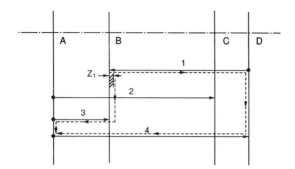

Figure 10.7. An example of a stock-removal dimension chain.

blueprint dimension [1] $(+0.2)$ can be distributed to tolerances on machining dimensions 1, 2, and 4 as -0.05, $+0.05$, and -0.1, respectively.

4. If a machining dimension is not related to the attainment of any blueprint dimensions, its tolerance can be determined based on the process accuracy. For example, based on the accuracy of the semifinish turning process, the tolerance on machining dimension 3 can be assigned to -0.09. The accuracy data for commonly used manufacturing processes are usually found in manufacturing textbooks and handbooks.

Step 5. Identify dimension chains for stock removals and calculate the variations of stock removals.

Due to the tolerances on machining dimensions in the previous and current operations, the actual stock removals may vary within a certain range. To ensure sufficient stock removal for each operation, the variation of the stock removal should be examined. A stock-removal dimension chain can be used to identify the related machining dimensions (component links) and calculation of the variation of the stock removal. In the chain, the stock removal is treated as the resultant link. The identification of a stock-removal dimension chain can be performed using the following approach.

1. Starting from the arrow of the machining dimension where the stock removal is being machined, draw tracing lines along two routes. The first is drawn along the machining dimension and the second downward.
2. In both routes, when an arrow is encountered, the tracing line turns in the direction of the machining dimension; when a dot is encountered, the tracing line goes downward. These two routes will finally meet at a dot of a certain machining dimension. All machining dimensions passed through by either of the two routes are component links of the stock removal.

Figure 10.7 shows an example of a stock-removal dimension chain. In this example, the stock removal on machining dimension 1 is the resultant link. By using the above tracing approach, machining dimensions 1 (increasing link), 3 (increasing link), and 4 (decreasing link) are found to be the component links for the stock removal. The variation of a stock removal can be calculated based on its dimension chain. In the example shown in Figure 10.7, the upper and lower deviations of stock removal Z_1 are calculated below:

$$\Delta_{UZ_1} = (0 + 0) - (-0.1) = +0.1 \text{ mm}$$
$$\Delta_{LZ_1} = (-0.05 - 0.09) - 0 = -0.14 \text{ mm}.$$

Step 6. Determine the nominal values of stock removals.

The nominal values of stock removals for various manufacturing processes can be determined from data in manufacturing handbooks or based on experience. For our example, the stock removals for finish and semifinish processes (Z_1 to Z_6) are assigned to 0.3, 0.3, 0.6, 1.0, 1.0, and 1.0 mm, respectively. After the assignment of the stock removal values, they should be checked against their nominal values for variations. If the minimum value of a stock removal is too small, its nominal value can be increased accordingly. When the variation of a stock removal is too large, the tolerances of related machining dimensions can be reduced, if little difficulty occurs in these operations. Stock removals in roughing operations are determined by subtracting the sum of stock removals in semifinish and finish operations from the total stock removal of the blank. In the bushing example, the stock removals for roughing operations (Z_7 to Z_{10}) are assigned to 2.5 mm each. After nominal values of all stock removals are determined, put them in the table.

Step 7. Determine the nominal machining dimensions.

The machining dimensions by which the blueprint dimensions are directly ensured should be determined first. The nominal values of these machining dimensions should be the same as those of the respective blueprint dimensions. For example, the machining dimensions 1 and 4 directly ensure the blueprint dimensions [2] and [3]. Therefore, their nominal values are assigned to 60 and 70 mm, respectively.

Next, the machining dimensions that indirectly ensure blueprint dimensions are determined. Necessary calculations are required for these machining dimensions. For example, blueprint dimension 1 ($52^{+0.2}$) is indirectly ensured by machining dimensions 1, 2, and 4. Because the dimensions and tolerances of machining dimensions 1 and 4 and the tolerance of machining dimensions 2 have already been determined, the nominal value of machining dimension 2 can be determined through dimension chain calculation. From equations given in section 2, we have

$$(52 + 0.2) = (60 + L_2 + 0.05) - (70 - 0.1)$$

$$L_2 = 62.05 \text{ mm}$$

After the nominal values of all machining dimensions related to the attainment of blueprint dimensions are determined, the nominal values of the distances between each pair of workpiece surfaces in the intermediate manufacturing operations can be calculated. The results are $L_{BD} = 60$ mm; $L_{AC} = 62.05$ mm; $L_{AD} = 70$ mm; $L_{BC} = 52.05$ mm; $L_{AB} = 10$ mm; and $L_{CD} = 7.95$ mm.

The nominal values of the machining dimensions that are not related to the attainment of blueprint dimensions are determined by adding (or subtracting) nominal machining stock removals to (or from) the corresponding nominal distances between workpiece surfaces. For the bushing example, the nominal values of machining dimensions 3 and 5 to 10 are calculated below:

$$L_3 = L_{AB} + Z_1 = 10 + 0.3 = 10.3 \text{ mm}$$

$$L_5 = L_{AC} - Z_2 = 62.05 - 0.3 = 61.75 \text{ mm}$$

$$L_6 = L_{AD} + Z_4 = 70 + 1 = 71 \text{ mm}$$

$$L_7 = L_{AB} + Z_6 + Z_3 + Z_1 = 10 + 1 + 0.6 + 0.3 = 11.9 \text{ mm}$$

$$L_8 = L_{AD} + Z_6 + Z_4 = 70 + 1 + 1 = 72 \text{ mm}$$

$$L_9 = L_{AC} + Z_6 - Z_5 - Z_2 = 62.05 + 1 - 1 - 0.3 = 61.75 \text{ mm}$$

$$L_{10} = L_{AD} + Z_8 + Z_6 + Z_4 = 70 + 2.5 + 1 + 1 = 74.5 \text{ mm}$$

After these seven steps, a complete tolerance chart of the bushing fabrication can be obtained as shown in Figure 10.8. This chart can be used as a record of machining dimensioning and tolerancing. The data of machining dimensions and tolerances can be used in detailed process planning.

It can be seen from the above description that the preparation of a tolerance chart is a tedious and time-consuming task. Research work has been conducted to apply computers to the tolerance chart generation. Ahluwalia and Karolin (20) developed a computer-aided tolerance control system (CATC) based on the tolerance chart technique. This system employed a microcomputer to go through the steps of generating a tolerance chart. Computer graphics were used to display part drawings and tolerance charts. Li and Zhang (21) introduced an approach to applying the tolerance chart to computer-aided process planning (CAPP) systems for precision

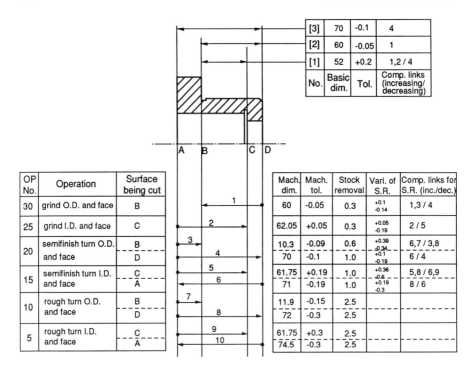

No.	Basic dim.	Tol.	Comp. links (increasing/decreasing)
[3]	70	-0.1	4
[2]	60	-0.05	1
[1]	52	+0.2	1,2 / 4

OP No.	Operation	Surface being cut	Mach. dim.	Mach. tol.	Stock removal	Vari. of S.R.	Comp. links for S.R. (inc./dec.)
30	grind O.D. and face	B	60	-0.05	0.3	+0.1 / -0.14	1,3 / 4
25	grind I.D. and face	C	62.05	+0.05	0.3	+0.05 / -0.19	2 / 5
20	semifinish turn O.D. and face	B / D	10.3 / 70	-0.09 / -0.1	0.6 / 1.0	+0.39 / -0.34 ; +0.1 / -0.19	6,7 / 3,8 ; 6 / 4
15	semifinish turn I.D. and face	C / A	61.75 / 71	+0.19 / -0.19	1.0 / 1.0	+0.36 / -0.6 ; +0.19 / -0.3	5,8 / 6,9 ; 8 / 6
10	rough turn O.D. and face	B / D	11.9 / 72	-0.15 / -0.3	2.5 / 2.5		
5	rough turn I.D. and face	C / A	61.75 / 74.5	+0.3 / -0.3	2.5 / 2.5		

Figure 10.8.   Completed tolerance chart of the bushing machining.

manufacturing. In this work, machining dimension and stock removal chains were automatically identified using a graphical algorithm. The machining dimensions and tolerances were allocated, followed by a feasibility examination. In recent years, optimization of manufacturing tolerances has been given more and more attention. Irani et al. (22) introduced an optimization approach to tolerance charts. In their approach, a special tracing algorithm was used to identify tolerance chains. Optimal tolerance allocation among individual cuts was achieved through a linear goal programming model instead of existing heuristic methods. Considering the real conditions of manufacturing, Fainguelernt and Weill (23) developed a model for manufacturing tolerance optimization. The objective of this model was to allocate machining tolerances as large as possible subject to the constraints of the limiting design tolerances. In this model, the main factors influencing tolerance were considered such as machining errors, setup errors, workpiece positioning errors, and tool wears. Manufacturing tolerance optimization is one of the most important research areas in manufacturing. More research efforts are needed to integrate manufacturing tolerancing, quality control, and other related issues.

10.5 SUMMARY

Tolerance is one of the most important parameters in design and manufacturing. Interest in tolerance analysis is rapidly increasing in industry due to the quest for high quality products at low cost. In this chapter, the most important issues in design and manufacturing tolerancing were described. The taxonomies of tolerance and tolerancing were introduced, followed by the discussion of tolerance analysis and tolerance synthesis of design (assembly) and manufacturing (machining). The analytical models were presented for those tolerancing topics with illustrative examples. A brief review of the research work conducted on each topic was given at the end of each section. This chapter provides a basic introduction to design and manufacturing tolerancing.

BIBLIOGRAPHY

1. M.M. SFANTSIKOPOULOS, "A Cost-Tolerance Analysis Approach for Design and Manufacturing," *Int. J. Adv. Manufact. Tech.* **5,** 126–134 (1990).
2. H.P. WANG and J.K. LI, *Computer-Aided Process Planning,* Elsevier, Science Publishing Co., Inc., New York, 1991.
3. A. BENDER, "Statistical Tolerancing as It Relates to Quality Control and the Designer," 1968. SAE Paper No. 680490, New York.
4. C.A. GLADMAN, "Techniques for Applying Probability to Tolerancing of Machined Dimensions," 1959, CSIRO Tech. Paper 11, Melbourne.
5. W.H. GREENWOOD and K.W. CHASE, "A New Tolerance Method for Designers and Manufacturers," *Trans. ASME, J. Eng. Industry* **109,** 112–116 (1987).
6. O. BJORKE, *Computer-Aided Tolerancing,* 2nd ed., ASME Press, New York, 1989.
7. E.A. LEHTIHET and B.A. DINDELLI, "TOLCON, Microcomputer-Based Module for Simulation of Tolerances," *Manufact. Rev. ASME* **2**(3), 179–187 (1989).
8. Z. WU, W.H. ElMARAGHY, and H.A. ElMARAGHY, "Evaluation of Cost-Tolerance Algorithms for Design Tolerance Analysis and Synthesis," *Manufact. Rev. ASME* **1**(3), 168–179 (1988).
9. P.F. OSTWALD and M.O. BLAKE, "Estimating Cost Associated with Dimensional Tolerance," *Manufact. Rev. ASME* **2**(4), 277–282 (1989).
10. Z. DONG and A. SOOM, "Automatic Optimal Tolerance Design for Related Dimension Chains," *Manufact. Rev. ASME* **3**(4), 262–271 (1990).
11. X.Y. WANG, Z.X. JI, R.T. WANG, and J.M. ZHANG, *Principles of Process Planning,* Beijing Institute of Technology Publisher, Beijing, 1990.
12. K.W. CHASE and W.H. GREENWOOD, "Design Issues in Mechanical Tolerance Analysis," *Manufact. Rev. ASME* **1**(1), 50–59 (1988).
13. W. MICHAEL and J.N. SIDDALL, "The Optimization Problem with Optimal Tolerance Assignment and Full Acceptance," *Trans. ASME J. Mech. Design* **103,** 842–848 (1981).
14. D.B. PARKINSON, "Assessment and Optimization of Dimensional Tolerances," *Comput. Aided Design* **17,** 191–199 (1985).
15. M.F. SPOTTS, "Allocation of Tolerances to Minimize Cost of Assembly," *Trans. ASME J. Eng. Industry* **95,** 762–764 (1973).
16. F.H. SPECKHART, "Calculation of Tolerance Based on a Minimum Cost Approach," *Trans. ASME J. Eng. Industry* **94,** 447–453 (1972).
17. K.W. CHASE, W.H. GREENWOOD, B.G. LOOSLI, and H.F. HAUGLUND, "Least Cost Tolerance Allocation for Mechanical Assemblies with Automated Process Selection," *Manufact. Rev. ASME* **3**(1), 49–59 (1990).
18. W. LEE and T.C. WOO, "Tolerance: Their Analysis and Synthesis," *Trans. ASME J. Eng. Industry* **112,** 113–121 (1990).
19. C. ZHANG and H.P. WANG, "The Discrete Tolerance Optimization Problem," *Manufact. Rev. ASME,* **6**(1), 59–70 (1993).
20. R.S. AHLUWALIA and A.V. KAROLIN, "CATC—A Computer Aided Tolerance Control System," *J. Manufact. Sys.* **3**(2), 153–160 (1986).
21. J. LI and C. ZHANG, "Operational Dimensions and Tolerances Calculation in CAPP Systems for Precision Manufacturing," *Ann. CIRP* **38**(1), 403–406 (1989).
22. S.A. IRANI, R.O. MITTAL, and E.A. LEHTIHET, "Tolerance Chart Optimization," *Int. J. Prod. Res.* **27**(9), 1531–1552 (1989).
23. D. FAINGUELERNT and R. WEILL, "Computer-Aided Tolerancing and Dimensioning in Process Planning," *Ann. CIRP* **35**(1), 381–386 (1986).

CHAPTER 11
Fixture Design Principles for Machining Systems

ROLAND J. MENASSA
General Motors Advanced Engineering

WARREN R. DEVRIES
Rensselaer Polytechnic Institute

11.1 INTRODUCTION

Long- and short-term market demand shifts are two dominating factors that have forced major manufacturers to adopt flexible manufacturing systems. Major technologic innovations can cause long-term market shifts, and dynamic world events lead to short-term swings. Both are difficult to forecast. Traditionally, manufacturers have dealt with these market uncertainties by tooling their manufacturing facilities with dedicated systems that are capable of handling high market demands. This approach, however, leads to underutilization of manufacturing systems, capital, and human resources. In addition, introducing new products with systems dedicated to manufacture a single part is at a high price in terms of time and capital. While capital is expensive, time is of the essence when markets are changing.

Manufacturing systems that can quickly adapt to the introduction of new products became the logical alternative to cope with market demand uncertainties. Three major physical elements that make up these manufacturing systems for mechanical parts are

- Workstations, e.g., a robot in assembly, a coordinate measuring machine in inspection, or a drilling station in machining.
- Material handling systems to move workpieces between workstations, e.g., free transfer systems in machining.
- Workholding and tooling, e.g., pallets that are used in all aspects of manufacturing or programmable clamps and vises.

Technologic advances in the first two elements (e.g., head-indexing and head-changing machining workstations or shuttle systems and automated guided vehicles for handling materials and workpieces) are in workstation and material handling flexibility. Workholding, however, remains a weak link in achieving full system flexibility, because it is extremely sensitive to product design and manufacturing methods. Pallets, while they offer workholding flexibility, are difficult to justify from a business standpoint because of their maintenance cost and the long design lead time that may be equivalent to that for dedicated fixturing. Therefore, flexibility and reduced lead time in workholding is not necessarily achieved with complicated and costly designs, but by simultaneously or concurrently being able to design fixtures early in the planning stages of new products using computer-aided design (CAD) models rather than prototypes.

If we consider where fixture design traditionally is done, it may vary with the frequency of product design changes. For example, major machine tool builders that specialize in systems for engines usually supply their own fixtures for parts that have not had radical design changes for many years. These fixture designs are only slight modifications of previous designs that are probably quite close to "optimal" based on experience and redesign. On the other hand, components that have constant design changes, like small housings and pumps, or that change because of new process technologies, like thin castings for transmission cases, usually require new fixture design. Often this part of the process design is farmed out to firms that specialize in fixture design. These specialty firms rely on the experience of their tool designers to be competitive and successful. If the part or process is significantly different from the experience base of the craftsworkers, experiments with prototype parts are used in place of analysis to validate the designs. This, when compared with the advances in product design analysis, makes fixture design a bottleneck from a fast-to-market viewpoint. For systems with a goal of a lot size of one, fixture design is also a key issue. Without adaptable fixturing, many of the advantages of flexible automation cannot be fully realized. However, if good fixture design practice is not used in flexible or computer-integrated manufacturing systems, fixtures that are more flexible in their applications may be less rigid mechanically and not produce high quality parts.

As a result, the need in fixture design is not just for innovative hardware concepts, but also for formal design principles, analysis, and synthesis techniques to reduce this lead time for both high and low volume quality manufacture. This chapter concentrates on fixture design for machining and the techniques that have been developed to aid in the design process. The topics addressed are

- Fixture definition driven by the manufacturing application, the annual part throughput, and the part geometry.
- Fixture locating principles as they pertain to prismatic, rotational, and irregular parts and the different fixturing elements and fixture functions.
- Descriptions of approaches to fixture design that take into account part stability, locating, and clamping.
- Presentation of practical design considerations that address unique fixturing requirements and experience-based rules.

These topics, covered either as rules or as software tools, provide ways to use practical knowledge early in process planning and design. This reduces lead time and allows fixture designs and configurations to be developed before prototype parts are available.

11.2 DESIGN CRITERIA AND FIXTURING FUNCTIONS

Some of the considerations in fixture design are illustrated in Figure 11.1. Major inputs are the workpiece geometry and tolerances, the process plan, and the features that must be produced in a fixturing setup. Constraints that a fixture designer must deal with are features already designed into a part for locating or supporting, and selecting from available elements to locate and support a part. Much of this chapter concentrates on the methods and means to design a fixture. In almost all cases, the design criteria include

- Accurate positioning of a workpiece.
- Minimizing workpiece deflection, because fixtures are used to enhance the accuracy and repeatability of workpieces.
- Fixture rigidity, as one of the ways to minimize workpiece deflections.
- Protection of critical surfaces from scratches and marking.
- Stability or insensitivity of the fixture design to slight variations from loads and geometries of the workpieces.
- Accessibility for loading and machining, i.e., to put quickly and with minimal skill a workpiece in a fixture and to machine all surfaces with the fewest fixturing setups, which is of great importance in flexible manufacturing systems that are robot or machine loaded.

These are a few of the design criteria. As Figure 11.1 shows, the methods, inputs and constraints are aimed at selecting the fixturing elements, positioning them, and predicting whether the forces and clamping sequence will produce a part that meets the product design specifications.

Fixturing Functions

A fixture is a device used for positioning and holding a workpiece in a specified three-dimensional space. While fixtures differ in design and intended application, the hardware elements are

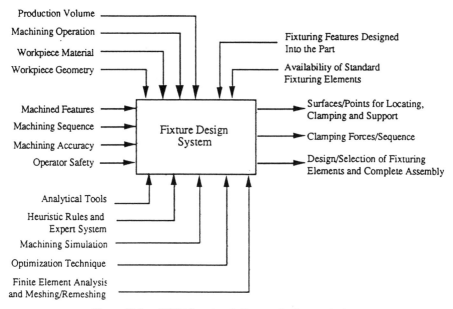

Figure 11.1. IDEF functional diagram for fixture design.

functionally divided into categories for supporting, locating, and clamping. There are several fixturing elements designed to meet each one of the three functions of a fixture. The bottom tier of Figure 11.2 gives examples of fixture elements used to achieve the locating, holding, and clamping functions of a fixture.

Classification of Fixtures

Fixturing hardware can be classified in several ways as Figure 11.3 illustrates: (*1*) the fixture may travel or remain with the workstation, (*2*) the fixture may be reused and may conform to workpieces with complex geometry; and (*3*) the fixture may vary with specific applications.

Mobility of the Fixture

A pallet is a traveling fixture that is transferred, manually or automatically, from one workstation to another while the part is permanently held against the fixture. Many flexible machining systems use this approach, but as was pointed out earlier, these pallets can be expensive to

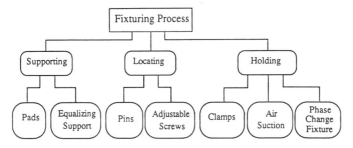

Figure 11.2. Ways to perform basic fixturing functions.

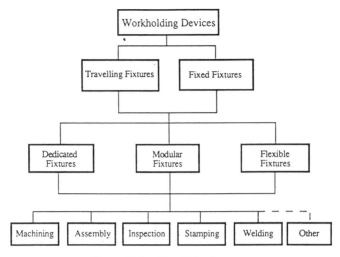

Figure 11.3. Classifying fixtures.

design and keep in service once they are designed. If the part is transferred manually or automatically from one workstation to another, but the fixture is permanently mounted on the workstation table, this is called a fixed fixture. This is usually the approach with manual machining and a number of transfer line systems.

Reusability and Adaptability

In addition to their mobility, fixtures can be classified based on their adaptability to different parts. While the design goal is the ability to conform to any geometry and be able to handle lot sizes from one to several million units, the three classifications discussed below are more common.

Dedicated fixtures are designed to accommodate a single part without any mechanical provisions for adjustments. These fixtures are typically built for high volume production systems and are intended for automatic part loading and unloading. Fixturing elements are assembled using dowels or key ways and are bolted down to a base. These fixtures are overdesigned to withstand the harsh demands of high volume automated production.

Modular fixtures can perhaps be viewed as the most conventional of the three classifications. Modular fixtures are used in the low volume job shop and the prototype environments often encountered in research and development. A modular fixture consists of a set of standard components that can be assembled like building blocks. Unlike dedicated fixtures, modular fixtures are capable of handling a wide variety of part sizes and shapes. These building blocks are often assembled either on bases that can be located with dowel pins on a machine-tool table or on a "tombstone" for a horizontal machine tool. The components of such fixtures include bases, locating points, clamping devices, and support structures. These components can be located using bases that have either a series of evenly spaced precision holes or evenly spaced T slots. Companies such as Bluco Technique, Carr Lane, and Jergens are large producers of modular fixturing components. Although most modular fixtures are assembled manually, much research has gone into the automatic assembly of fixtures by robots using electromagnetic base plates or special kinematic locks to hold down the fixturing components after final positioning.

Flexible fixtures are often designed using the group technology idea of a family of parts; the fixture is designed to accommodate part geometries that belong to this group technology family. Fixture layout adjustments are handled through automatic mechanical provisions. (This automation usually means driven under program control, by which fixturing components are positioned or activated by computer commands without human intervention.) Flexible fixtures are usually built with tight tolerances so that fixturing layout changes will still maintain tolerances without requiring validation, even for small batch sizes. Flexible fixtures are typically built for

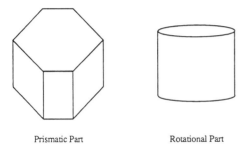

Prismatic Part   Rotational Part

Figure 11.4. Schematic of a prismatic and rotational part.

low to medium volume production systems and are intended for automatic part loading and unloading. Flexible fixtures are sometimes used with high volume production systems because of anticipated and periodic product changes. Fixture layout adjustments in these situations are made manually. Flexible fixtures are designed to be rugged and robust, much like dedicated fixtures, to withstand mechanical wear of moving fixturing elements.

Some fixtures today also include sensors to provide intelligence from the fixture to the workstation to enable accurate workpiece location by an operating device (e.g., machine tool or robot). These sensors may be built in (switches or pressure transducers) or external to the system (laser equipment) to detect shifts in the part during processing. The intelligence in such a fixture enables some error recovery or adaptive response to these occurrences. Research examples of these concepts can be found in refs. 1 and 2.

Phase change fixturing is aimed at providing a simple, quick way to hold and locate complex part geometries (cf. ref. 3). A workpiece is held by immersing it in the fixture medium that is in a liquid or semiliquid phase or pseudo-phase of a fluidized bed of pellets. When the liquid or fluidized bed behaves as a solid, it holds the workpiece. An important benefit of this technology is the ability of the fixture to conform to almost any part geometry, thus providing uniform support for complex part geometries. The limitation of this approach is the fixture's holding force.

Fixtures Based on Application

Fixtures, particularly dedicated ones, have traditionally been classified by application, as the bottom tier of Figure 11.3 illustrates. This chapter considers machining applications almost exclusively, even though the ideal fixture would satisfy all applications, a goal that has not been achieved yet. But it should serve as a reminder that when it is possible to use the same fixture, or at least the same fixture design methodology, much time, effort, and cost can be saved by trying to develop a unified approach to these important manufacturing design problems.

Fixturing Hardware Selection

Part geometry plays a principal role in selecting the type of fixture to be used. The two major classifications considered here are shown in Figure 11.4.

- *Prismatic.* A solid having polygonal bases that are parallel and congruent and sides that are parallelograms.
- *Rotational.* A solid generated by a straight line moving parallel to itself and describing with its ends any fixed curve.

There are variations and exceptions to these definitions, e.g., irregular-shaped parts may have both straight and circular side surfaces. In such cases, expert judgment is used to classify parts based on intended functionality and basic part structure. Two classifications under which irregular parts are classified are shown in Figure 11.5.

- *Irregular Prismatic.* A solid having parallel bases and sides that are either parallelograms or contours.

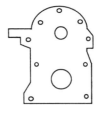

Figure 11.5. Schematic of irregular parts.   Irregular Prismatic Part   Irregular Rotational Part

- *Irregular Rotational.* A solid generated by a straight line moving parallel to itself and describing with its ends contours and straight lines.

Types of Machining Fixtures

As Figure 11.4 showed, fixtures have a variety of classifications but are identified by type within each classification and manufacturing process. In the case of machining fixtures there are at least four classifications.

Plate fixtures have a flat base plate and the main fixture reference surface is parallel to the mounting surface, i.e., machine's worktable. Plate fixtures (Figure 11.6) are typically used with vertical-spindle workstations and can accommodate both prismatic and rotational parts.

Tombstone or angled-plate fixtures have a reference surface that is normal to the mounting surface. These fixtures (Figure 11.7) are typically used with horizontal spindle workstations and can accommodate both prismatic and rotational parts.

Vise jaw fixtures have one stationary jaw for part locating and a movable jaw for part clamping. These fixtures (Figure 11.8), are typically used with vertical spindle workstations but are occasionally used with horizontal spindle workstations by mounting the vise on a tombstone fixture. Like the previous classifications, vises can accommodate both prismatic and rotational parts.

Chucks use radially adjustable jaws to establish axis of rotation (Figure 11.9). These fixtures are typically used with turning centers or horizontal spindle workstations, but occasionally are used with vertical spindle workstations. Three-jawed chucks, the motions of which are coordinated, can be used for axi-symmetric parts. A four-jawed chuck with independent jaws is used for parts that are not axi-symmetric but need a surface of revolution, a bored hole, to be generated. Mounting a workpiece on a four-jawed chuck requires more skill and effort than a three-jawed chuck, because the axis of rotation of the machined feature and the axis of rotation of the fixture have to be adjusted until they coincide.

All four fixture types can be mounted on an indexing table with a single or multiple axis of orientation so that as many features on the part can be machined in one fixture. This will eliminate feature-to-feature tolerance variations as a result of refixturing.

Locating Principles and Fixturing Elements for Machining

The important aspect of fixturing is the process of locating and supporting a part in three-dimensional space. As Figure 11.10 shows, a part, prismatic or rotational, has 12 degrees of freedom, six of which are translational ($\pm X$, $\pm Y$, $\pm Z$), and six of which are rotational ($\pm \alpha$, $\pm \beta$,

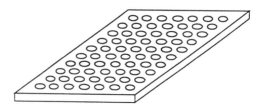

Figure 11.6. Plate fixture.

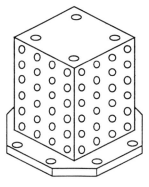

Figure 11.7. Tombstone or angled-plate fixture.

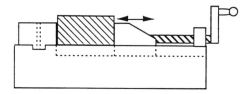

Figure 11.8. Vise jaw fixture.

Pie-Chuck **Figure 11.9.** Chuck fixture.

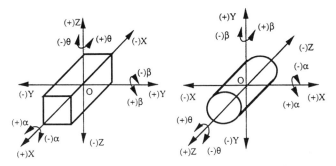

Figure 11.10. Degrees of freedom for a prismatic and cylindrical part.

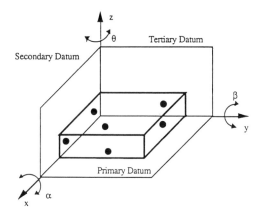

Figure 11.11. Reference data, using the 3–2–1 principle.

$\pm\theta$). Workholding principles have been devised for prismatic and rotational parts to confine all the important degrees of freedom, so that during machining the part will not shift or rotate along or around any axis of motion. (This excludes rotation about a spindle axis for a rotational part.) This is done by selecting and positioning supports and locators to arrest this motion passively and by clamping to arrest the remaining degrees of freedom.

Prismatic Parts

The 3–2–1 locating principle is the process of supporting against the primary plane and locating along the secondary and tertiary plane when fixturing a prismatic part. It is assumed that one of the parallel surfaces is used to locate the three supports in the primary reference plane. Although the primary datum restricts certain degrees of freedom, $(-Z, \pm\alpha, \pm\beta)$, its main purpose is to support the weight of the part and to resist the gravitational force and the normal forces applied to the primary reference plane; thus the word *supporting*. Side surfaces that are candidates for locating purposes are chosen to position the part in relationship to the set of three mutually perpendicular planes jointly called a datum reference frame (Figure 11.11). The secondary and tertiary data restrict the remaining degrees of freedom $(-X, -Y, \pm\theta)$, except for the translation along the positive $+X$, $+Y$, and $+Z$ axes, which are arrested by holding. Locators along the secondary and tertiary data are used for both locating and taking up clamping or machining loads.

Locating a prismatic workpiece against side locators, as described with the 3–2–1 principle for prismatic parts, offers a great degree of part positioning repeatability. However, this method of locating in most cases is not suitable for high volume automated part loading and unloading

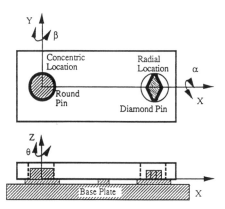

Figure 11.12. Radial and concentric locating for prismatic parts.

because of the two extra motions that are required to crowd the part against the secondary and tertiary reference planes. Complicated fixturing mechanisms are typically expensive, difficult to maintain, and a source of equipment downtime. In such a case, two precision holes are machined into the part and are referenced by two locating pins: a diamond for radial location and a round pin for concentric location (Figure 11.12). The diamond pin is relieved on two sides to provide a positive stop in one direction so that the tertiary plane is established with the round pin only. The secondary plane of reference is established with both the round and diamond pin.

Concentric and radial locating system arrests 11 degrees of freedom. The secondary and tertiary planes, formed by the two pins, will restrict motion along four translational directions ($\pm X$, $\pm Y$) and around four rotational directions ($\pm \alpha$, $\pm \beta$). The primary plane will restrict one translational axis ($-Z$) and two rotational axes ($\pm \theta$). Clamping will then arrest the remaining single degree of freedom along the translational axis ($+Z$). Concentric and radial locating is preferred over 3–2–1 locating for prismatic parts for ease of part loading and unloading and for its economical advantage. However, part clamping heavily relies on friction, because the pins are typically small in diameter and used only for locating purposes. Thin castings can easily distort under these conditions.

Rotational Parts

Fixturing rotational parts is accomplished by supporting and locating against two planes that pass through two parallel lines and that are perpendicular to each other (Figure 11.13). Both planes will restrict motion along two translational axes ($-Y$, $-Z$) and around four rotational axes ($\pm \beta$, $\pm \theta$). In practice, V blocks are used to locate rotational workpieces. The part is then bumped against the tertiary plane, which passes through a locator and is perpendicular to the first two planes of reference. The tertiary plane will arrest the translational motion along the $-X$ axis. This method of locating arrests seven degrees of freedom only, and the part can rotate around $\pm \alpha$ and can move along the $+X$, $+Y$, and $+Z$ axes. Although the remaining motions are arrested by holding, this locating scheme does not provide accurate angular location around the $\pm \alpha$ axis of rotation.

Concentric and radial locating schemes are two principles most often used in combination to provide true positioning. While concentric location uses a circular surface for locating, radial locating can use either a circular or a planar surface. Concentric location can use either an internal or an external diameter. The two locating schemes are illustrated in Figure 11.14.

The locating principle for rotational parts when applied to pure cylindrical workpieces does not provide radial location and must rely on friction to arrest part rotation. Radial location becomes important when drilling holes on a bolt circle like that shown in Figure 11.14. A fair percentage of rotational parts in practice have noncylindrical features. These flat features become data and help establish radial location. Figure 11.14 illustrates two locating principle cases that apply for irregular rotational parts.

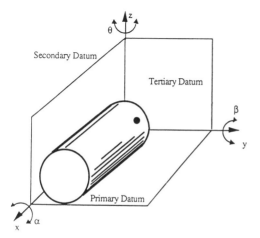

Figure 11.13. Locating principle for rotational parts.

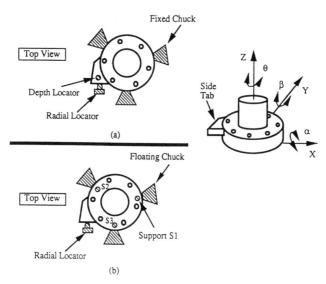

Figure 11.14. Radial and concentric locating for rotational parts.

Case 1. In Figure 11.14a, the part is located concentrically on the reference surface formed by the outside diameter with a three-jaw chuck. This establishes the axis of rotation and restricts four translational axis of motion ($\pm X$, $\pm Y$) and four rotational degrees of freedom ($\pm \alpha$, $\pm \beta$). In this case, the tab has two locating functions: it restricts motion along the $-Z$ axis by a locator positioned on the bottom side and restricts rotation around the $+\theta$ axis of rotation by a radial locator placed against the side surface. The remaining two degrees of freedom are restricted by applying the holding pressure through the jaw. If forces parallel to the axis of rotation are not large, this is a satisfactory method.

Case 2. If the axial forces are large, as they might be in a facing operation, Figure 11.14b shows how the part can be located and supported. The part rests on three supports to establish the primary plane. This will restrict motion along the $-Z$ axis and rotation around the $\pm \alpha$ and $\pm \beta$ axis. The radial locator is positioned against the side surface to arrest the $+\theta$ axis of rotation as shown in Figure 11.14b. A locator against the bottom surface of the tab is not needed in this case, because that plane of reference is established by the supports. The remaining degrees of freedom are arrested by using a floating chuck that does not disturb previously established reference planes.

There are certain situations in which the locating pins are used for a rotational part. In that case the radial and concentric locating principle for prismatic parts applies.

Fixture Elements

Locating, supporting and clamping elements are the three main components that make up a fixture. The tooling industry offers a great selection for each fixturing element, and the selections vary from simple and basic to intelligent and elegant. Production volume, part life cycle, and stiffness have an impact on the selection of these components. Although the selection is diverse, this chapter presents the most common fixturing elements.

Locators

Locators are fixturing elements used to provide stops along the part surfaces as defined by the X and Y plane of reference (see Figure 11.10). Locators are designed in many different shapes and types, depending on their specific purpose, and fall under three categories.

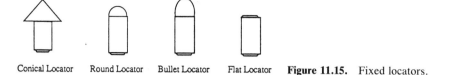

Conical Locator   Round Locator   Bullet Locator   Flat Locator   **Figure 11.15.**   Fixed locators.

Fixed or hard locators are used to counteract machining and clamping forces that develop in the primary reference plane when a workpiece is positioned against the locators that define the secondary and tertiary data in the 3–2–1 locating principle. Fixed locators also interact with the primary datum for rotational parts described by the radial and concentric locating principle. They are widely used in cases for which no adjustments are required. Figure 11.15 illustrates four basic designs.

Soft or spring loaded locators are used to soft clamp vertically fixtured parts as illustrated in Figure 11.16. They are typically used with manually loaded tombstones to provide temporary holding pressure before hard clamping.

Adjustable locators are used to facilitate the locating of irregular or as-cast surfaces. Adjustable locators are also known as redundant locators and are used in addition to the minimum required number of locators along the secondary and tertiary data. Adjustable locators (Figure 11.17) are used with thin parts that are subject to excessive deflections.

Swivel or self-adjustable locators are used to accommodate surface variations with rough castings or to locate against slight angular surfaces. The design consists of a ball in a socket with a flat surface on the ball (Figure 11.18).

Supports

Supports are fixturing elements used to provide a vertical stop and are used to counteract gravitational loads and machining thrust forces. Both adjustable and self-adjusting supports can be used for the same purpose. In most cases, the hardware is interchangeable with adjustable locators. The differences in support hardware design are the surfaces against which these fixturing elements interact. In most cases, the hardware is primarily a function of the surface that must be supported.

Fixed–Hard Supports are in general flat surfaces that are either machined into the fixture or are bolted down to the fixture (Figure 11.19). Equalizing supports are used in cases in which three supports fail to provide a stable primary location. Four pads are used in situations in which two of them are integrated into one piece and pivot around one point only. Equalizing supports are illustrated in Figure 11.20.

Clamps

Clamps are fixturing elements used to arrest the remaining degrees of freedom in a workpiece. Clamps are used to counteract machining loads either by direct opposition (action–reaction) or through frictional forces. Clamps can be applied against the top or side surfaces of a part and are actuated manually or automatically.

Bolt clamps are the simplest form of clamping, used to simulate functional part loads during machining so that tolerances are met when the part is loading in service. Cam clamps (Figure 11.21) make use of a lever arm and eccentric cam to hold the part. Eccentric cam clamps allow high pressure to be exerted and are used for fast clamping.

Wedge clamps generate holding forces by driving the clamp detail against an inclined flat or conical surface called the wedge. Figure 11.22 illustrates a flat wedge.

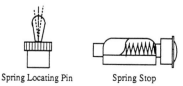

Spring Locating Pin   Spring Stop   **Figure 11.16.**   Soft locators.

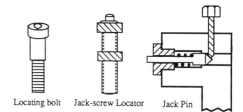

Figure 11.17.   Adjustable locators.

Locating bolt   Jack-screw Locator   Jack Pin

Figure 11.18.   Self-adjusting locators.   Swivel Locator

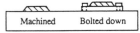

Figure 11.19.   Fixed supports.

Machined   Bolted down

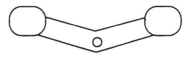

Figure 11.20.   Equalizing supports.

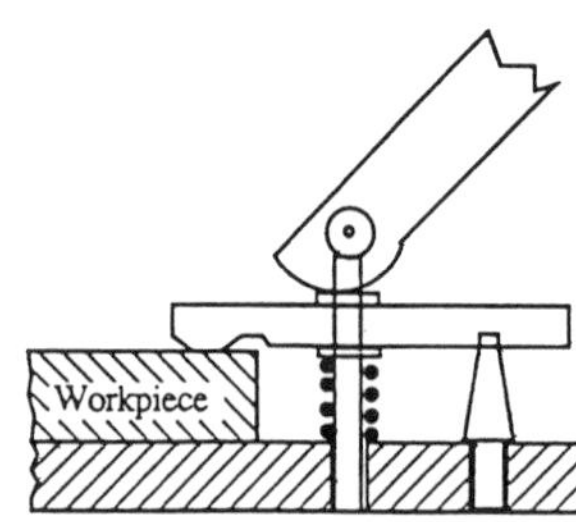

Figure 11.21.   Cam clamps.

Workpiece

Figure 11.22.   Wedge clamps.

Workpiece

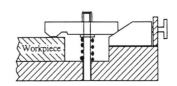

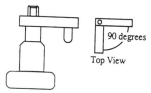

Figure 11.23. Swing clamps.

Swing clamps are widely used in automated applications. These clamps are usually hydrauli-cally operated so that upon activation or deactivation of the clamp, the holding bar swings inward or outward by 90° to clamp or release the part. Swing clamps (Figure 11.23) allow continuous contour-milling by swinging away from the part to clear the cutter path.

Toggle clamps rely on a self-locking mechanism to achieve a desired clamp path and can achieve a wide range of holding forces. They are also used in applications in which fast part loading and unloading is desired. Most existing designs are based on path or motion generator mechanisms. Figure 11.24 illustrates a side toggle clamp.

11.3 APPROACHES TO FIXTURE DESIGN

Planning Requirements

A tool designer's first step in designing a fixture is acquiring all part-related information before committing to hard line designs. These requirements are established by planning, product, and manufacturing engineers.

Part Life and Volume. Yearly part production volumes and overall life cycle are parame-ters determined early on in the planning stages that impact the workholder configuration. Figure 11.25 illustrates that the selection of a fixturing system is, in general, based on the interaction of volume and life.

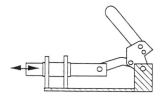

Figure 11.24. Toggle clamps.

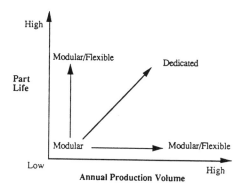

Figure 11.25. Planning parameters impact on fixture design.

Product Parameters

Part Geometry. Part size and shape help the tool designer establish part classification, e.g., prismatic or rotational, which in turn defines the appropriate locating principle and candidate reference data. The overall size of the fixture and fixturing elements also are determined by knowing the geometry of the part.

Part Material. The magnitude of the resulting machining forces are directly related to the material being cut. Machining softer parts, like aluminum, generates smaller cutting forces, and therefore, the fixturing design requirements are relaxed.

Part Machining Accuracy. Geometric dimensioning and tolerancing drives fixturing design. In general, a reference datum like a hole or a surface is established from which all features are dimensioned. Part functionality in some instances dictates that certain features are to be dimensioned to other features, and in these situations the part is refixtured to a new reference datum. Knowing where this manufacturing datum will be is important for design engineers.

Machined Features. Similarly, for tooling and manufacturing, the choice and number of reference data required depend on the spatial location of part features to be machined. Machining tolerances are best controlled when all the features are machined with a single fixturing setup. In practice, most parts require more than one fixturing setup, and the best workholding scenario, based on a careful feature review, is one that minimizes the number of fixturing layouts.

Manufacturing Parameters

Machining Operations. Machining operations like drilling and milling are characterized by cutting force magnitudes and directions. Cutting force magnitudes drive the design and size of the fixturing elements, while cutting force directions drive the layout of the fixturing elements.

Machining Sequence. Machining operations are performed in a predetermined sequence to achieve the required machining quality. The sequence of operations in turn dictates the number of fixturing setups. An optimal workholding scenario is one that minimizes the number of fixturing setups while maintaining part quality. Planning, product, and manufacturing parameters are preliminary requirements that must be considered simultaneously to achieve required part quality.

Design Requirements

This section concentrates on fixture design based on the number of part fixturing setups, while assuming all other preliminary requirements are satisfied. Because most parts, in practice, are neither pure prismatic nor pure rotational, fixturing design requirements are addressed using irregularly shaped parts. The following design requirements apply for parts that can be finish machined in one fixturing setup. The reference data are established from as-cast surfaces.

Irregular Prismatic Parts. The 3–2–1 locating principle is widely applied for positioning both irregular and pure prismatic parts and is used when tight machining tolerances and part positioning repeatability are required.

Irregular Rotational Parts. Irregular and pure rotational parts are positioned using cases 1 and 2 of the concentric and radial locating principle. Two guidelines are identified based on part functionality:

- *Guideline 1.1.* Case 1 is applied, as shown in Figure 11.14a, if the Z axis of rotation is functionally independent of the tertiary plane defined by the X and Y axes. The part is fixtured using a fixed-chuck configuration, a depth locator, and a radial locator.
- *Guideline 1.2.* Case 2 is applied, as shown in Figure 11.14b, if the axis of rotation is functionally dependent (i.e., must be perpendicular to the mounting surface) on the tertiary plane (e.g., middle bore as a bearing surface). The part must establish its primary

surface by resting on three supports and uses a floating chuck and one radial locator as shown in Figure 11.14b.

Parts that are manufactured in medium to high volume production systems or that require machining on all surfaces in low volume production systems are refixtured several times before producing a finish machined product. Because as-cast surface data are limited to one fixturing setup, additional reference data are machined into the part.

Irregular Prismatic Parts. The first fixturing setup uses the 3–2–1 locating principle, because surfaces are readily available on rough castings. Two guidelines are

- *Guideline 2.1.* If a product design requires tight machining tolerances, the part is first located against as-cast surfaces using the 3–2–1 locating principle to generate a second set of finished surfaces. The part is then refixtured by locating against the new machined surfaces using the same locating principle. Although part positioning repeatability is ensured, the 3–2–1 locating principle incurs a higher fixturing cost for automatic loading conditions, because additional mechanisms are required for proper part positioning.
- *Guideline 2.2.* If a product design requires nominal machining tolerances, the part is first located against as cast surfaces using the 3–2–1 locating principle. Two locating dowel holes are machined into the part to establish the secondary and tertiary planes of reference and support pads are machined to establish the primary plane of reference. An inherent locating tolerance is caused by the hole clearance required to insert the locating pins into the locating holes, as shown in Figure 11.12. Subsequent refixturing uses the dowel holes.

The exception to machining additional reference data when parts are refixtured is when the remaining machining operations are surface-generating operations (e.g., milling). In such a case, secondary and tertiary locations are not critical.

Irregular Rotational Parts. The concentric and radial locating principle is as basic to rotational parts as the 3–2–1 locating principle is to prismatic parts. In the first fixturing setup shown in Figure 11.26b, surface XY is machined to establish a second depth surface and the main bore is machined to establish a second concentric locating datum. Depending on the capability of the turning station, all holes on surface XY could be drilled in the same setup to help establish radial location as well. Using Figure 11.26 as an example, two locating setups are identified, depending on feature functionality.

Noncritical Feature Functionality. The second fixturing step shown in Figure 11.26c and d, uses a single locator to establish depth from the XY machined surface. The part is either concentrically located around the outside diameter with a fixed chuck and radially located using the outer tab (Figure 11.26c) or concentrically located around the inside diameter with a fixed concentric expanding locator and radially located using a diamond pin and one of the holes (Figure 11.26d).

Critical Feature Functionality. The third fixturing setup shown in Figure 11.22e and f, uses three supports to establish depth from the XY machined surface. The part is either concentrically located around the outside diameter with a floating chuck and radially located using an outer tab (Figure 11.26e) or concentrically located around the inside diameter with a floating concentric expanding locator and radially located using a diamond pin and one of the holes (Figure 11.26f).

Reference Datum Selection

3–2–1 Locating Principle

Secondary and Tertiary Reference Data. The selection of the secondary and tertiary reference surfaces is based on part geometry and on the machining load directions that are applied when the fixture is used. By considering the loads in laying out the fixture, the forces can be used to assist in holding the workpiece in the fixture, thus minimizing the number of locating points and the deflections caused by clamping. Two guidelines are

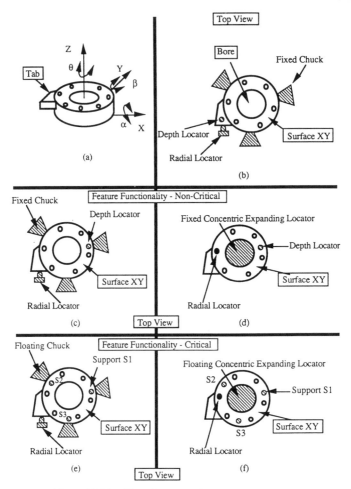

Figure 11.26. Fixturing setup for rotational parts.

- *Guideline 3.1: Sides Intersected by Forces.* Candidate data are sides that are intersected by the machining forces. Referring to Figure 11.27 as an example both the left and bottom side will be intersected by the force vector as the cutter traverses the part. Candidate edges are then identified along candidate sides against which locators can be positioned.

- *Guideline 3.2: Secondary Datum Is Longest.* Guideline 3.1 identifies the longest edge as the secondary datum, which will have two locators, and by default, the remaining reference is the tertiary datum with a single locator. Referring to Figure 11.27 the left side (length L) is longer than the bottom side (length l), and therefore, it becomes the secondary datum while the bottom side is designated as the tertiary datum.

Concentric and Radial for Prismatic Parts:

Secondary and Tertiary Reference Data. The two dowel holes establish both the secondary and tertiary reference data. The axes of the dowel holes must be orthogonal to the primary reference plane defined by the supports S_1, S_2, and S_3. In general, the two dowel holes are functional and are used to align the part during assembly. A rule for selecting the position of dowel holes is

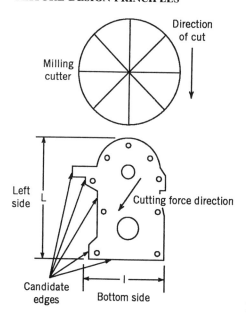

Figure 11.27. Selection of secondary and tertiary d:

- *Guideline 3.3: Position of Dowel Holes.* To maximize part stability, the two dowel holes are to be machined as far apart as possible and diagonal to each other (Figure 11.28).

Concentric and Radial for Rotational Parts:

Radial Reference Datum. The radial reference datum is established from tabs attached to the outside circumference of a rotational part. The edge selection is such that the radial locator opposes the direction of cutting forces (Figure 11.29). The primary reference datum for all three locating principles is common and is by default the datum that the part rests on.

Locator Positioning against Reference Data

Once the reference data are identified, proper locator positions are determined to provide the greatest part stability (see, e.g., ref. 4).

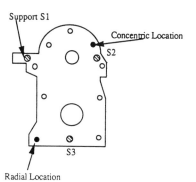

Figure 11.28. Position of dowel holes.

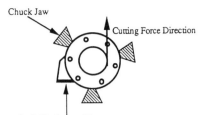

Figure 11.29. Selection of radial reference datum.

3–2–1 Locating Principle

Secondary and Tertiary Reference data. A single guideline is identified for each of the reference data:

- *Guideline 3.4: Secondary Datum.* The two locators placed against the secondary datum are to be positioned as far apart as possible (Figure 11.30).
- *Guideline 3.5: Tertiary Datum.* The single locator placed against the tertiary datum is to be positioned as far away from the secondary datum as possible (Figure 11.30).

Both guidelines are designed to maximize part stability such that any machining load or moment will not cause the part to shift or rotate under cutting conditions.

Concentric and Radial Locating

The radial locator (Figure 11.31) is positioned as far away from the center of rotation as possible along the radial reference datum to minimize the load on the locator while maximizing the moment that can be resisted.

Support Positioning against Primary Reference Datums

Unlike the secondary and tertiary data, there is no unique solution to positioning the supports against the primary datum, because it depends primarily on part stiffness. The general guideline to achieve part stability is to position the supports such that the triangle formed contains the part center of gravity as shown in Figure 11.32.

11.4 PRACTICAL DESIGN CONSIDERATIONS

Practical design considerations must be taken into account when applying basic fixture design techniques to avoid costly fixture retools. Part stiffness and machining forces should be considered during fixture design to achieve proper support positioning and clamping loads prediction.

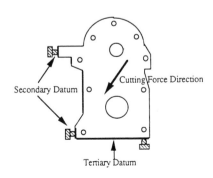

Figure 11.30. Locator positions against secondary and tertiary data.

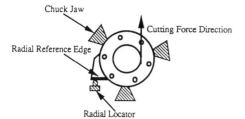

Figure 11.31.   Locator position against radial datum.

Most of the practical design problems can be analyzed using statics, dynamics, and a full knowledge of machining. But at initial design stages, many times the information available is incomplete so the analysis methods cannot be used. Then it is useful to have some general design rules that are based on these principles of mechanics. Some of the guidelines include the following.

- *Guideline 4.1.* Although a part must not move, excessive holding pressures and inappropriate clamp locations are two leading causes of distortions when a part is removed from a fixture. To avoid this problem when using a top holding clamp, pressure points should be applied directly above the supports, and in a side-holding approach, pressure points should be applied against solid locators.
- *Guideline 4.2.* Even if a fixture design allows both a roughing and finishing cut to be made in one fixturing setup, clamps are often released between roughing and finishing cuts. This is because part stiffness changes as material is removed, which can lead to residual stresses; removing clamps relieves these stresses, minimizing finished workpiece distortions.
- *Guideline 4.3.* Rotational parts with a large length-to-diameter ratio require two chucks to avoid whipping due to both spindle runout effect and part tip deflection under its own weight. Two chucks are used, one fixed to establish part position and one floating to support the part. Chip and coolant buildup over time are detrimental to floating chuck performance.
- *Guideline 4.4.* Irregular rotational parts, although they offer radial reference data, must be dynamically balanced while fixtured.
- *Guideline 4.5.* Thin rotational parts that are made of soft materials, like aluminum, and that are fixtured using chucks are easily distorted. Once unclamped, the part exhibits the lobing effect, e.g., three lobes for a three-jawed chuck. Part lobing is eliminated by increasing the number of jaws per chuck or by using a mandrel to increase rigidity.
- *Guideline 4.6.* More than three supports are needed for large parts that will distort under their own weight or thin prismatic parts that easily deflect under cutting loads. One way to accomplish this is with supports that are spring loaded and mechanically locked or that are

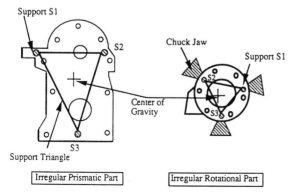

Figure 11.32.   Support positions against primary datum.

hydraulically activated by pressure-sensing devices. When this approach is used, the three primary fixed supports still establish that datum, but the additional active supports compensate for distortion.

- *Guideline 4.7.* Dowel holes, lugs, pads, and tabs are typical features used to establish reference data. These features should be designed into the part as value-added features that are used as part of the final assembly. Nonvalue added datum features, however, should not be machined off, because they should be used as final assembly or inspection data.

- *Guideline 4.8.* Because chips and dirt can easily collect on flat surfaces or rough surfaces, it is better to have point contact than a large distributed contact area. Resting parts against flat surfaces or concentrically locating a rotational part with collets are two examples of full-surface contact.

- *Guideline 4.9.* Machined chips buildup is one of the leading factors to part positioning misalignment and to extended fixture repair time. Design chip-shedding features (e.g., sloped surfaces) into the primary reference so that chips can be flushed away with minimal efforts.

- *Guideline 4.10.* Parts for product validation need to be machined using production-intent fixtures that can replicate fixturing setup, fixture element stiffness, and clamping pressures to predict accurately production tolerances and to avoid slow system ramp up.

11.5 CONCLUSIONS AND FUTURE DIRECTIONS

Designing fixtures for workholding is still largely experience based and is carried out by tool designers. However, to capture this knowledge and begin to design tooling early, which is the philosophy of simultaneous engineering, requires more formal design and optimization methods. Computer-aided fixture design tools typically solve specific types of problems in fixture design or emphasize specific design criteria. Consequently, efforts to address the issues involved in incorporating these criteria, while making design analyses fast, is important so that engineers will use these concurrent engineering design tools. Some of the issues that still need to be addressed are

- *Limited Geometric Coverage.* Many existing fixture design systems work only with simple geometry and are not able to handle 3-D curved surfaces common on many real parts.
- *Lack of Integration.* Many fixture design systems are capable of solving specific fixture design problems but cannot be used to provide a complete solution to fixture design. Also, many systems are not coupled with an advanced solid modeling system and thus do not have the kind of geometric modeling and manipulation capability needed for fixture design.

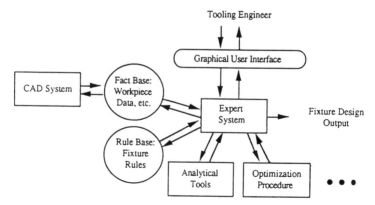

Figure 11.33. Schematic of a fixture design system.

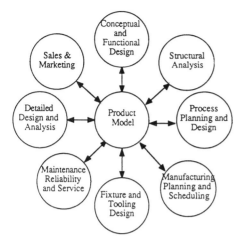

Figure 11.34. Tooling design as a component of concurrent engineering.

- *Inefficiency of Analytical Procedures.* Some algorithms used for fixture design are computationally intensive. Optimization procedures and finite element analysis are such examples.

These issues have limited the acceptance of fixture design systems in industry and will have to be resolved before computer-aided fixture design tools become practical and effective engineering solutions in today's industry.

The fixture design paradigm shown in Figure 11.33 can lead to a number of specific configurations for a computer-aided fixture design system. In this system, the fact base contains the descriptions of a part, the initial workpiece, and machined features that can be generated from a CAD system. The fact base also contains manufacturing related data such as machining sequence and machine tool descriptions from a computer-aided process planning system. Some of the fixture design rules covered in this chapter are stored in the rule base of the system for the initial fixture synthesis. Then various analytical procedures can be called on by the system to perform kinematic analysis, force analysis, deformation analysis, accessibility analysis, etc. The tooling engineer will be able to interact with the system through the graphical user interface to direct the operation of the system when necessary.

Within the framework of concurrent or simultaneous engineering, the proposed fixture design system will be most effective in reducing lead time when it is used early in the development of a product. As illustrated in Figure 11.34, the issue of tooling design can be considered simultaneously with the product design process and many other life-cycle issues: manufacturing planning, assembly, maintenance, environmental impact, and marketing. Although not addressed in this chapter, an important area of research is the development of methodologies to evaluate a tooling design cost–complexity analysis of a product at early stages of design. Such capabilities will allow fixture complexity early in the product development cycle, thus avoiding problems that may arise later on. As a result, further reduction in the time and cost of product development can be achieved.

BIBLIOGRAPHY

1. J.L. COLBERT, R.J. MENASSA, and W.R. DeVRIES, *A Modular Fixture for Prismatic Parts in an FMS,* paper presented at the 14th NAMRC, 1986.

2. B. BENHABIB, K.C. CHAN, and M.Q. DAI, "A Modular Programmable Fixturing System," *ASME Trans. J. Eng. Industry* **113**(1), 93–100 (1991).

3. M.V. GHANDI and B.S. THOMPSON, "Phase Change Fixturing for Flexible Manufacturing Systems," *J. Manufact. Sys.* **4**(1), 29–39 (1985).

4. R.J. MENASSA and W.R. DeVRIES, "Locating Point Synthesis in Fixture Design," *Ann. CIRP* **38**(1), 165–170 (1989).

Suggested Readings

A. ALLCOCK, "Case for Modular Fixtures," *Mach. Prod. Eng.* **147**(3759), 64–65 (1989).

H. ASADA and A.B. BY, *Implementing Automatic Setup Change via Robots to Achieve Adaptable Assembly,* paper presented at the IEEE Control Conference, 1984.

H. ASADA and A. BY, "Kinematic Analysis of Workpart Fixturing for Flexible Assembly with Automatically Reconfigurable Fixtures," *IEEE J. Robot. Automat.* **RA-1**(2) (1985).

B. BIDANDA and P.H. COHEN, *Development of a Computer Aided Fixture Selection System for Concentric, Rotational Parts,* paper presented at the ASME annual winter meeting, 1990.

Bluco Technik, *Modular Fixturing System,* Bluco Technik, 1992.

J. BOERMA and H. KALS, "FIXES, a System for Automatic Selection of Set-Ups and Design of Fixtures," *Ann. CIRP* **37**(1), 443–446 (1988).

W.E. BOYES, ed., *Jigs and Fixtures,* 2nd ed., SME, Dearborn, Mich., 1982.

Y.C. CHOU and M.M. BARASH, *Computerized Fixture Design from Solid Models of Workpieces,* paper presented at ASME annual winter meeting, 1986.

Y.C. CHOU, V. CHANDU, and M.M. BARASH, "A Mathematical Approach to Automatic Configuration of Machining Fixtures: Analysis and Synthesis," *ASME Trans. J. Eng. Industry,* Vol. 111, No. 4, pp. 299–306, 1989.

P.H. COHEN and R.O. MITTAL, *A Methodology for Fixturing and Machining of Prismatic Components,* paper presented at the 15th NSF Conference on Production Research and Technology, 1989.

M. DAIMON, T. YOSHIDA, N. KOJIMA, H. YAMAMOTO, and T. HOSHI, "Study for Designing Fixtures Considering Dynamics of Thin Walled Plate and Box Like Workpieces," *Ann. CIRP* **34**(1), 319–322 (1985).

W.R. DeVRIES, *Analysis of Material Removal Processes,* Springer-Verlag, New York, 1992.

X. DONG, W.R. DeVRIES, and M.J. WOZNY, "Feature-Based Reasoning in Fixture Design," *Ann. CIRP* **40**(1), 111–114 (1991).

J. ENGLERT and P.K. WRIGHT, "Principles for Part Set-Up and Workholding in Automated Manufacturing," *J. of Manufact. Sys.* **7**(2), 147–161 (1988).

FixturePro 2.0 Tooling Component Database for Computer Aided Fixture Design Jergens, Inc., Cleveland, Ohio, 1989.

A. FRIEDMANN, *The Modular Fixturing System, A Profitable Investment,* paper presented at the International Conference on Manufacturing, 1984.

M.V. GANDHI and B.S. THOMPSON, "Automated Design of Modular Fixtures for Flexible Manufacturing Systems," *J. Manufact. Sys.* **5**(4), 471–474 (1986).

T. HORIE, "Adaptability of a Modular Fixturing System to Factory Automation," *Bull. Jpn. Soc. Prec. Eng.* **22**(1), 1–5 (1988).

W. JIANG, Z. WANG, and Y. CAI, "Computer-Aided Group Fixture Design," *Ann. CIRP* **37**(1), 145–148 (1988).

H.S. LEE and M.R. CUTKOSKY, "Fixture Planning with Friction," *ASME Trans. Eng. Industry* **113,** 320–327 (1991).

J.D. LEE and L.S. HAYNES, *Finite Element Analysis of Flexible Fixturing System,* paper presented at the Japan–USA Symposium on Flexible Automation, 1986.

G. LEWIS, *Modular Fixturing Systems,* paper presented at the 2nd International Conference on Flexible Manufacturing Systems, 1983.

M. MANI and W.R.D. WILSON, *Automated Design of Workholding Fixtures Using Kinematic Constraint Synthesis,* paper presented at the 13th NAMRC, 1988.

A. MARKUS, Z. MARKUSZ, J. FARKAS, and J. FILEMON, "Fixture Design Using Prolog: An Expert System," *Robot. Comput. Integrated Manufact.* **1**(2), 167–172 (1984).

Mecatool, *Pallet Clamping System,* Mecatool, 1992.

R.J. MENASSA, *Synthesis, Analysis and Optimization of Fixtures for Prismatic Parts,* Ph.D. dissertation, Rensselaer Polytechnic Institute, Troy, N.Y., 1989.

R.J. MENASSA and W.R. DeVRIES, "A Design Synthesis and Optimization Method for Fixtures with Compliant Elements" in P.H. Cohen and S.B. Joshi, eds., *Advances in*

Integrated Product Design and Manufacturing, ASME, New York, 1990, pp. 203–218, Publication No. G00569.

R.J. MENASSA and W.R. DeVRIES, "Optimization Methods Applied to Selecting Support Positions in Fixture Design," *ASME Trans. J. Eng. Industry* **113**(4), 412–418 (1991).

Mitee-Bite Products, *Omni-Lock Pallet Changer,* Mitee-Bite Products Co., 1992.

D.T. PHAM and A.D. LOZARO, "Finite Element Study of a Workpiece in a Machining Fixture," *Math. Comput. Model.* **14,** 1024–1028 (1990).

QU-CO, *Modular Fixturing System Catalog,* QU-CO, 1992.

H. SAKURAI and D.C. GOSSARD, *Geometric Modeling in Setup Planning and Fixture Design* paper presented at the IFIP WG 5.2 Workshop on Geometric Modeling in Computer-Aided Design, 1990.

A. SLOCUM, *Development of a Flexible Automated Fixturing System,* paper presented at the SME Conference on Advanced Machining Technology for Cells and FMS, 1986.

M. YEONG, An Efficient Numerical Algorithm Applied to Fixture Design Optimization, M.Eng Thesis, Rensselaer Polytechnic Institute, Troy, N.Y., 1990.

K. YOUCEF-TOUMI and J.H. BUITRAGO, "Design and Implementation of Robot Operated Adaptable and Modular Fixtures," *Robot. Comput. Integrated Manufact.* **5**(4), 343–356 (1989).

SECTION III

MANUFACTURING PROCESSES AND TOOLS

CHAPTER 12
Manufacturing Processes

SHIVAKUMAR RAMAN
University of Oklahoma

12.1 CASTING AND FOUNDRY PROCESSES

Casting is one of the oldest processes known to humankind. In the process of casting, liquid metal is poured into a mold cavity and is solidified in that cavity to shape and size a part as per specifications. Thus casting is characterized as a solidification process involving a phase change (from liquid to solid). Several variables affect the solidification process, including the temperature and fluidity of the material being poured, the thermal properties of the casting and mold cavity, the shape and size of the mold, and the liquid delivery channels. Based on the mold material alone, casting is classified into permanent mold casting and expendable mold casting. The expendable mold casting processes involve the destruction of the mold to remove the solidified casting, while the permanent method reuses the same mold for making several castings. Examples of expendable mold casting are sand casting, shell molding, plaster and ceramic mold casting, and investment casting. Typical permanent mold casting methods include pressure casting and die casting. Depending on the classification, several properties of the mold materials become important to casting. In sand casting, properties such as collapsibility and permeability become important.

Solidification

Pure metals exhibit a characteristic melting point and change from solid to liquid at that temperature. Alloys, on the other hand, exhibit a freezing range during which the material is in a semisolid, semiliquid state. A liquidus temperature marks the beginning of freezing above which the material is fully in liquid phase. The solidus temperature indicates the full formation of the solid phase and the end of freezing. Because many applications involve the use of alloys rather than pure metals, the knowledge of phase diagrams and cooling curves of the alloy system is critical in determining the casting temperatures.

The casting solidification takes place in three stages: liquid contraction, liquid to solid phase change, and cooling of solid casting from solidus to room temperature. There is generally shrinkage associated with each of these stages during cooling. Proper shrinkage calculations must be made to prevent defects in casting such as tearing and porosity.

The solidification time in a casting process is largely influenced by the thickness-to-surface area ratio or the volume-to-surface area ratio. The larger the surface area and/or lower the volume, the smaller the solidification time and the faster the cooling. Thus a thick plate may exhibit slower cooling than a thin plate, other conditions and materials remaining the same.

Mold Cavity

In sand casting and most typical casting processes, a casting flask is used to house and support the mold cavity. The mold cavity may be constructed in one or two halves. The latter type is more typical in the casting of difficult shapes. The top half (Figure 12.1) is called the cope and the bottom the drag. Gates and runners are used to deliver liquid to the mold cavity from a pouring basin. The gating system design is critical in casting, because the premature solidifica-

197

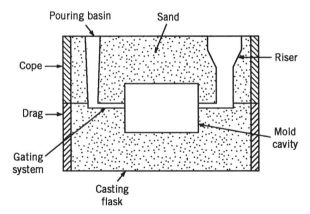

Figure 12.1. A typical casting flask used in sand casting.

tion of the metal in the gates will not allow liquid metal to be delivered to the mold cavity. Risers are also provided to ensure adequate supply of liquid metal to the mold cavity. Vents are provided to allow the unwanted gases to escape.

Design Considerations and Casting Defects

Consideration of casting defects is critical in mold design and material selection. To a large extent, casting and mold design is an experience-based discipline with little, if any, closed-form models. Violent pouring, turbulent flow of liquid, energy losses due to collision with sharp corners in the mold, and entrapping of gases must all be avoided. Porosity is a defect that may be caused by shrinkage or gases. Gases get entrapped during pouring and must be allowed to escape from the mold cavity. Better still, pouring in an inert atmosphere may reduce the chances of gas entrapment. Shrinkage porosity is more difficult to control, and a proper consideration of mold parameters, casting metal, and shape and size attributes is necessary. Tearing may arise at the joints between thin ribs and the rest of the casting. Warping may occur during solidification of large plates.

In sand casting, a common defect is a wash, which is caused by a destroyed mold during pouring. In large castings, multiple gates delivering liquid to the cavity are not uncommon. In such cases, the two streams of liquid may not fuse together causing a cold shut. Liquid in a particular part of the cavity might prematurely solidify preventing liquid flow into the further parts causing a misrun. Scabs, scars, and blisters are also common surface defects caused by escaping gases.

Adequate allowances for shrinkage must be provided during the design and reflected in the pattern construction. Draft allowance (a small angle provided on the pattern) must be given to facilitate easy removal of casting from the mold cavity. A machining allowance is usually provided to allow for finishing after casting when dimensional control is critical. Sharp corners must be avoided to prevent energy losses, abrupt changes (transitions) in cross-section between adjacent sections in a part must be avoided to prevent shrinkage cavities at intersections, and casting thin sections must be avoided.

Casting Materials

One of the most commonly cast materials is cast iron, due to its lower melting point than iron and steel as well as other excellent properties. Cast iron castings are used in diverse applications such as engine cylinders and machine tool beds. Steel may also be cast for special applications. Nonferrous metals such as copper and its alloys and aluminum and its alloys are easily cast due to their low melting points, whereas the casting of high melting point materials such as titanium alloys and metals such as tungsten and molybdenum is complex. Typically, low melting point metals may be die cast and high melting point metals are easier to sand cast.

Sand Casting

In sand casting, typically a wood or metal pattern is used to construct the mold cavity. Patterns may be constructed in single piece, split piece, or match plate configurations. The pattern is placed in the flask and covered and compacted with the sand mixture (sand, water, and/or other binders). The pattern is removed from the flask, and the gating system is cut in the mold for fluid delivery. Provisions for internal cavities are made using cores. Cores may be constructed with sand and held in place in the mold cavity using core prints or chaplets. The liquid metal is poured into the cavity and allowed to solidify. Upon cooling, the casting is removed from the cavity by breaking the mold. Multiple cavities may be incorporated in the same flask to accommodate for several castings, thereby increasing the production rate. Sand used for making the mold cavity may be moist during pouring, in which case it is called green sand. Skin-dried sands may be used for better control of dimensional properties at the loss of some collapsibility.

Other Expendable Mold Casting Processes

Plaster and ceramic molds may also be used in place of sand to create mold cavities. Shell molding is a procedure whereby a coated pattern is placed in a chamber and sand particles are bombarded on the pattern. The thin, uniform sand layer on top of the pattern is separated from the pattern by a parting agent and used as the mold cavity for casting. A lost foam process uses polystyrene patterns that evaporate on contact with liquid metal in the mold cavity, thus replacing the space occupied by the pattern with the liquid metal.

Investment casting is gaining much importance in the near net shape manufacturing circles, as high dimensional control is achieved during casting. In investment casting, wax patterns are prepared and a refractory slurry is used to cover the patterns. The wax is eventually melted out and cavities for casting are created. These cavities are filled with liquid metal, solidified, and broken to obtain high quality castings. More than one casting may be made at one time.

Die Casting

Die casting uses a nonexpendable die cavity instead of a sand mold to prepare castings. The die material is usually a die or mold steel. Pressurized liquid metal is pumped into the die cavity with a piston mechanism, using either a cold chamber or hot chamber. The metal is held under pressure until solidification. The casting is removed from the die after solidification. Better dimensional control is usually achieved with die casting than with sand casting. Smaller parts are cast using die casting. Die wear may result, impairing quality of parts and must be controlled.

Other Casting Processes

Low pressure casting or pressure casting does not require high pressures as used in die casting. Centrifugal casting is used to produce symmetrical cross-sections. The liquid is poured into a rotating cavity and liquid metal is thrown outward due to the centrifugal forces. Centrifuging is a variation of this process, by which a rotating delivery channel delivers liquid to cavities located at its periphery. Squeeze casting is typically a combination of forming and casting processes, by which a liquid is squeezed during solidification with a punch.

12.2 FORMING AND WORKING

Forming is a process that involves the application of pressures and temperatures to change the shape and size of an object in solid phase. Thus no solidification is required such as in casting. Most general forming or working operations may be classified into hot working, warm working, and cold working. Hot working is done at high temperatures reaching above recrystallization and at low pressures, and cold working is performed close to room temperature and at high pressures. Generally, the hot working range of temperatures are above 60% of the melting point of the metal, the cold working temperatures are less than 30% of the melting point, and warm working temperatures lie in between these ranges. Hot working is associated with scales, poor surface quality, and poor dimensional control, whereas good dimensional and surface integrity may be achieved with cold forming. In some near net shape processes, a cold forging operation may be the last process used before the part is put to its use.

The strength and other mechanical properties of the material being formed directly affect is working. A hard and brittle material is seldom formable, and a soft and ductile material is easily formed. Many materials undergo significant softening at high temperatures and become more ductile rendering them easier to form.

In terms of material fabrication, several forming processes exist. These include rolling, forging, extrusion, and sheet metal operations. These processes invariably subject the material to three-dimensional stress states, the calculation of which is important in shape formation.

Rolling

In the most general configuration for rolling, a set of cylindrical rollers is used to reduce the thickness (or cross-section) of a plate or sheet. The length of the rolled sheet increases if the width or thickness of the rolls is large. If width is comparable in magnitude with the thickness, the width also increases, causing spreading.

The rollers or rolls are rotating in opposite directions pulling the materials in and reducing its thickness (Figure 12.2). Rolling is considered to be a semicontinuous process rather than a discrete manufacturing process.

Typically, the velocity of the rolls is higher than the sheet speed at entry and lower than the sheet speed at exit. In ideal situations, a neutral or no-slip point can be assumed midway in the contact between roll and sheet where the velocity of roll and sheet are equal. Friction is required to draw the sheet through the gap; however, large amounts of friction consume more power.

The angle subtended by the arc of contact between the roll and workpiece is called the roll angle. The maximum possible draft is the maximum reduction of thickness possible in a single pass, which depends on the roll radius and the coefficient of friction. Large diameter rolls and large reductions per single pass tend to deform the bulk of the material, whereas smaller radii tend to deform only the surface layers. Thus rolling may be used for surface hardening of sheet metals.

High pressures are applied by the strip on the rolls during rolling, causing flattening of rolls. Furthermore, the elastic deformation of the rolls leaves a crown on the center of the sheet. To avoid this, the rolls are made barrel shaped to have a camber. Thermal camber may also arise in hot rolling, causing a reverse effect on the strip. If rolling variables are not properly controlled,

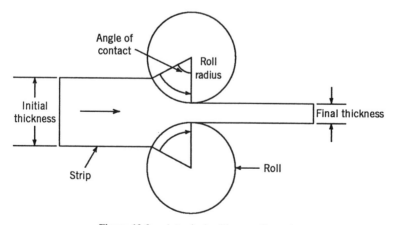

Figure 12.2.   A typical rolling configuration.

the strip tends to become wavy, torn, or defective. Because rolling is a preparatory operation to many sheet metal operations, rolling variables must be well controlled to yield good-quality sheet.

Rolling is typically performed in rolling mills. The rolling mills may be two-high, three-high, or cluster mills. While two-high is the most common configuration, three-high mills are used for large thickness reductions. Cluster mills use a small roll to contact the work, while larger rolls support the small rolls. The smaller rolls reduce the friction and power consumption, and the large rolls prevent deformation on the small rolls. Tandem configurations are used for continuous cross-section reduction whereby the roll gap progressively tightens (with different sets of rolls placed in tandem).

Ring rolling is procedure of reducing the cross-section of a ring, thereby expanding its diameter. Shape rolling uses shaped rolls to make the material conform to a definite geometry. Thus varied cross-sections are possible to make I-sections, C-sections, etc. Thread rolling is an alternative to thread cutting on a lathe. Two threaded rolls or two flat dies are made to roll over a round bar to obtain threads on the bar.

Forging

Forging operations have existed for several centuries. A part is typically forged into its desired shape and size by application of high compressive loads. Two common types of forging configurations are open die type and closed die type. In open die forging, a part is held in an anvil and repeatedly hammered or pressed. This process is usually not a precision process, and the achievable tolerances are limited. Sharp corners may be removed using open die forging. Typical applications include the preparation of bars of various symmetric cross-sections.

Closed die or impression die forging uses a die cavity to achieve the desired size and shape rather than an open anvil. Depending on the contours of the part to be produced, several preforging operations may be desired. These include fullering, edging, and blocking. The edging operation draws metal into an area, whereas the fullering operation draws metal away from an area.

Coining is a special type of closed die forging utilizing extremely large pressures to obtain the intricate details needed to create the required impressions. Heading operations are used, for creating heads on bolts by increasing the cross-section at the specified end. In swaging, radial forces are utilized to change the cross-section of parts.

Both hammers and presses are used for forging. The hammers apply impact loading, while the presses allow for gradual loading. Different types of power sources may be used for the actuation of forging machines: gravity drop, hydraulic, pneumatic, and electromechanical. Forging dies are usually made of tool and die steels and typical materials forged include carbon and alloy steels, aluminum alloys, magnesium alloys, and copper alloys.

Extrusion

Extrusion is a widely employed process for making door and window railings, door knobs, tubes, and several symmetric and nonsymmetric industrial parts. Extrusion involves the pushing of a metal through a die to change its cross-section (Figure 3). Forward extrusion (Figure 12.3a) is the most common configuration, and a load is applied on the part with a plunger in the

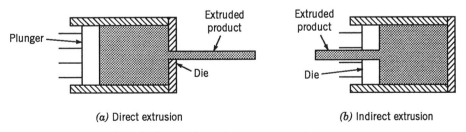

(a) Direct extrusion   (b) Indirect extrusion

Figure 12.3. A schematic of two types of extrusion.

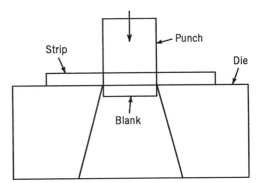

Figure 12.4. A simple schematic of shearing operations.

same direction as the part is exiting the die. Forward extrusion is analogous to the pressing of toothpaste out of a tube. Indirect extrusion (Figure 12.3b) applies a load opposite to the direction of the extruded part. Hydrostatic extrusion uses a fluid between the plunger and the part to reduce friction. The transmission of the load is hence achieved using an incompressible fluid medium. The drawing process is similar in many respects to extrusion, and is achieved by pulling a part through a die cavity to change its cross-section.

Several parameters affect the extrusion and the extruded product, including the die angle, properties of the part being extruded, the original and final cross-sections of the part, and the friction between the extrusion cylinder and the part. The die angle is critical because the metal can form a dead zone during extrusion and prevent the rest of the metal behind it from getting extruded. The dead zone also influences the finish of the extruded product.

The metal flow in extrusion is critical and in many ways analogous to the flow of fluid in a channel. The grains of an extruded product are preferentially oriented and hence anisotropic. A pipe defect is common in extrusion, whereby oxides and impurities tend to collect toward the center due to improper metal flow. Internal and surface cracks may also develop during extrusion. Lubrication is important for reducing friction.

Sheet Metal Operations

Sheet metal operations are routine to the production of several consumer items. The most important applications of sheet metal forming are the automobile body, cooking utensils, bent pipes, etc. The sheet metals are obtained by successive rolling of plates. These sheets are then cut to desired shapes using shearing operations. The shearing operations use a shear blade, similar to common scissors, and a shear press (Figure 12.4). When the removed blank is the workpiece for a subsequent operation, the process is called blanking. If the hole on the sheet is the desired workpiece for subsequent processing, the process is called punching. Punching is an alternative to drilling a hole in the sheet. The clearance between the die and punch is critical in determining the part quality of the sheared product. The shearing presses may be simple, progressive, or compound, depending on the number of operations they are required to perform.

The sheared sheet is usually subjected to one or more operations before the part is put to use. Bending, as the name suggests, allows for bending of the sheet to various shapes and sizes. Bending is usually accomplished with a press brake. The minimum bend radius of different materials is different and must be considered before undertaking a bending operation.

Deep drawing is an operation for making cups. A press is used with sufficient clearance between a die and punch. The part is held in the die with work holders and is pulled into the die by the action of the punch. Complex stress states are introduced at the various parts of the cup, and proper control is required to avoid wrinkles and ensure quality of parts.

In one common type of a spinning operation, a sheet is pressed against a rotating form die and shaped accordingly. Complex contours may hence be formed with relative ease. Stretch forming is done with a form die to stretch a part at various places. Explosive forming is performed for the rapid production of complex contours. This process is usually done underneath water; and an explosive charge is detonated, transmitting a shock wave to the sheet. This shock wave makes the sheet conform to the die cavity.

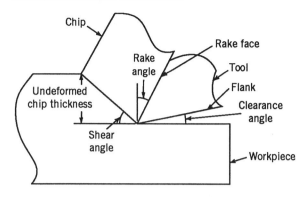

Figure 12.5. A schematic of orthogonal cutting.

12.3   MATERIAL REMOVAL PROCESSES

Material removal or machining processes use a cutting tool (Figure 12.5) to remove layers of material from a workpiece in the form of chips to shape and size an object. The cutting tool may employ a single cutting edge or multiple edges. A cutting tool resembles a wedge with complex angles. The face of the cutting tool supports the chip, a flank is perpendicular to the face and a rake angle is given to the face to achieve positive cutting action.

Machining is a unique process that involves high strains, strain rates, and localized deformation that are not typical of common material testing procedures. Machining may be considered expensive in some cases due to the large wastage of material, and inevitable in others for which demanding specifications require high tolerance and surface control. There are several types of machining operations for producing different ranges of shapes and dimensions such as turning for producing external cylinders; boring for producing internal cylinders; drilling for producing holes; and facing, milling, planing, and shaping for producing flat shapes.

Chips in Machining

The type of chip formed during machining may be continuous, discontinuous, segmented, or continuous with a built-up edge. Continuous chips are the most common, while cutting ductile materials and discontinuous chips are common in brittle material machining. Continuous chips may be difficult to break and can cause problems by tangling with the tool post and other parts of the machine tool. Chip breakers are hence employed to break the chips. Segmented chips are common during the machining of titanium, whereas machining cast iron yields discontinuous chips. In general, a built-up edge is formed at low speeds while cutting alloys. The built-up edge involves a gradual deposition of work material on the tool, its buildup and work hardening, and a subsequent shearing from the tool to be carried away by the flowing chip. Built-up edge leads to poor finish and may cause early wear on the tool.

Orthogonal Cutting

The work and tool materials, the cutting tool geometry, the cutting speeds, feeds, and depths of cut are typically presettable cutting inputs, while cutting forces and power, chip type, surface finish, cutting temperatures, and tool wear are output variables of the cutting process. The interaction between the input and output variables is important in determining the machinability (ability to machine) and in designing the cut.

An orthogonal model of cutting (two dimensional) may be assumed to derive appropriate relationships between the input and output variables, although an oblique model of cutting (three dimensional) may be more complete. Figure 12.5 shows the tool–chip–work system used by most orthogonal cutting models. Because this interface is critical in determining the machining efficiency, this has been studied extensively over the years. This inset is common to most machining operations and used as such in our discussions.

The shear zone causes separation between the chip and work and consumes energy. At high cutting speeds this zone may be approximated by a plane called the shear plane. The shear plane is inclined to the direction of the cutting velocity by an angle Φ, the shear angle. The chip so formed moves over the rake face of the cutting tool generating frictional work. Friction may also arise at the tool (flank) and work interface in actual cutting, but it is assumed to be negligible in most work. The sum of work done in shear and friction approximately equals the work input into the process. The determination of the work rate in these zones requires the knowledge of velocities and forces in these zones.

Cutting during continuous chip formation was analyzed using mechanics equations by Merchant during the mid-1940s. Merchant assumed an orthogonal cut and a sharp tool to derive force relationships at the shear plane and rake face (tool–chip interface). A velocity triangle was used to determine the components of velocities in the shear and friction zones. The chip thickness ratio, or the ratio of the undeformed chip thickness to the deformed (actual) chip thickness, may be used to evaluate the shear angle for a given rake angle of the tool. Minimum energy models and upper bound approaches have also been used in the past to theoretically derive relationships for the shear angle.

Tool Wear and Tool Life

Machining involves the gradual action of a tool on a workpiece, and the tool is subject to friction, high stresses, and high temperatures. The combination of these variables affects the life of the tool and impairs its cutting efficiency. Tool life is defined as the active life of the tool when it is cutting satisfactorily. Tool life may be defined in terms of the actual time to failure, the volume of material cut before failure, or the number of components produced before failure. The tool life may be brought to an end through gradual mechanisms such as wear or by sudden mechanisms such as fracture and chipping.

Wear in cutting tools may occur due to plastic deformation by shear or compression, diffusion, attrition, adhesion, abrasion, or other mechanisms. Determination of the exact mechanism causing wear is difficult and depends on the tool–work pairing. The tool commonly wears in the face (crater wear), flank (flank wear or wear land), or nose. Wear in cutting tools is generally accelerated by increasing cutting speeds. The temperatures rise rapidly at high speeds, causing rapid wear. This was observed as early as the first decade of this century by Taylor who formulated a tool life equation that related tool life and the cutting speed. This relation has since been modified to incorporate the effect of other cutting variables such as feeds, depths of cut, etc. Tool wear monitoring and adaptive control systems are being developed by several researchers for sensing and evaluating the condition of the cutting tool during machining. This is because the tool wear can cause the tools to produce inferior quality parts that no longer meet specifications. The automatic sensing and monitoring is all the more desired in the modern automated machine shop.

Cutting Tool Developments

Tool materials must possess sufficient strength to withstand the stresses generated in machining. High hardness is desired for wear resistance, and good toughness is desired to withstand mechanical and thermal shocks and cyclic loads. The most important property, however, is the retention of hardness and strength at the elevated temperatures commonly encountered during machining. Tool materials must also present themselves chemically immune to the work material during deformation and high temperatures.

The development of cutting tool materials has constantly strove to keep a balance among the above-mentioned properties. Carbon tool steels and cast cobalt alloys are seldom used today. High speed steels and carbides are more common. Carbides can retain their hardness at elevated temperatures better than high speed steels; however, they are lower in toughness. Ceramics, cubic boron nitrides (CBN) and diamonds can be used at higher speeds than carbides for machining most materials. Diamond tools are good for machining aluminum with long tool life but degrade while machining steel at high cutting speeds due to chemical reactions. Tough substrates are also coated with hard wear–resistant coatings, using chemical or physical vapor deposition. It has been reported that the tool life of coated tools is significantly better than that of uncoated tools.

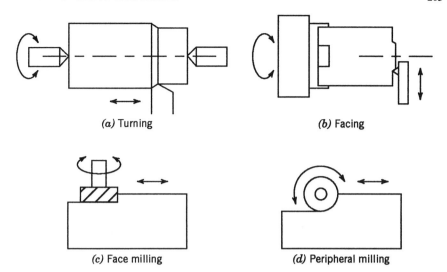

(a) Turning   (b) Facing

(c) Face milling   (d) Peripheral milling

Figure 12.6.   Typical machining operations.

Lathe Operations

In turning (Figure 12.6a), the workpiece is held between centers or in a chuck (and supported at the tail stock by a live or dead center) and rotated, and a single-point cutting tool moves axially to remove material. Turning is usually performed in a lathe. Desired cutting speeds and feeds may be set using gears and other transmission mechanisms. Facing (Figure 12.6b) is performed on a lathe by moving the tool radially toward the center from the periphery. A facing operation allows for the determination of a datum and is usually performed before turning. Centering operations uses a centering tool (that resembles a drill) and is performed to create a bearing surface for supporting the bar at the tailstock (for long bars). Other operations performed in a lathe include grooving, form turning, taper turning, step turning, chamfering, knurling, parting, and cutoff. Single and multiple spindle automats (with fixed configurations), production machinery such as turret and capstan lathes, and numerically controlled (NC) machine tools are also used for advanced functions and specialized applications.

Operations for Producing Complex Shapes

Common milling operations may be classified into face milling and peripheral milling (Figure 12.6c and d). In face milling, the face of a multipoint cutter is used to create a flat surface on a milling machine. In peripheral milling, the periphery of a cylindrical multitooth cutter is used to create flat surfaces. The cutter generally rotates in the milling machine and the workpiece (held in a table) is translated. Depending on the shape and size of the part being machined, different types of workholding devices and fixtures are used to locate and clamp the workpiece. End milling is popular in pocket machining. Slots and keyways are also easily cut with a milling machine. Milling operations are also used to create complex profiles and surfaces, using copy milling attachments and specialized software (with computer numerical control (CNC) machines). Shaping and planing operations use a translating single-point cutting tool to create a flat surface. In shaping, the work is stationary and the tool is translating, whereas in planing, the workpiece is moving and the tool is stationary. Gear shaping and gear hobbing are employed to cut gears.

Hole-Making Operations

Drilling is a hole-making operation that uses a two- (or multiple-) flute cutter. The cutter has two active cutting edges and a lip. The flutes run helically through the axis of the cutter and provide for easy chip clearance. Although drilling may be performed in a lathe, drilling machines are also widely employed. Drill jigs may be used that not only locate the work but also guide the tool. Drill jigs are commonly used for drilling holes along a pitch circle diameter (as present in several flange components). A boring operation serves to enlarge a previously drilled hole using a single point cutter and is a precision operation capable of producing fine internal surfaces. Boring may be performed in lathes or boring machines. Reaming is also a hole-finishing operation that uses a multipoint cutter. Counterboring and countersinking are done to create bearing surfaces for bolt and screw heads. Spot facing generates a flat surface perpendicular to a previously drilled hole axis.

Finish Operations

Grinding operations use finely ground abrasive particles bonded by a resin material on wheels for finishing workpieces. The cutting action of each individual grain is similar in most ways to the action of a single-point cutting tool. The material removal rate is typically small, and surface roughnesses generated are fine. Higher accuracy processes such as honing, lapping, and polishing use finer abrasive powders and rotational configuratons for fine finishing. Recently, ultraprecision machining (UPM) is gaining better acceptance in consumer industry. In UPM, the cutting tool is a single-point diamond mounted on an extremely rigid machine tool structure capable of removing material at subatomic (nanometric) levels. The mechanics at subatomic depths of cut are under research at the present time.

12.4 JOINING PROCESSES

Common joining processes are welding, mechanical fastening, and adhesive bonding. Each of these processes have different application environments. Only welding processes are discussed in this chapter. Welding is most commonly a solidification type process used to join similar or dissimilar materials. Welding processes may be classified according to the energy used to achieve fusion between the members.

Arc Welding

Arc welding (Figure 12.7a) uses the heat generated between two electrodes to heat and melt the metals to be joined or filler materials. Solidification of the molten metal in a prepared joint completes the weld. The electrodes may be consumable as in shielded metal arc welding (SMAW) and gas metal arc welding (GMAW) or nonconsumable as in gas tungsten arc welding (GTAW).

In SMAW or stick welding, a stick electrode is used as the filler material. A flux usually covers the electrode and provides a protective atmosphere during welding. The flux also serves to remove impurities from the molten metal. An arc is struck between the filler electrode and the work (electrode), which melts the consumable filler. The gap distance is maintained by adjusting the position of the filler electrode. Most processes of this kind are manual and are generally used in repair and maintenance.

In GMAW, previously known as metal inert gas (MIG) welding, a continuously fed (through a gun) coated filler is used as one electrode and the workpart is the other electrode. An inert gas is also supplied through the gun that provides a protective atmosphere during welding. The arc gap can be maintained constant manually or by using automatic means. Three types of metal transfer are common: spray, globular, and short-circuiting. The weld variables are different in each of these transfer modes.

In GTAW, previously referred to as tungsten insert gas welding, a nonconsumable electrode is used to strike the arc and the filler is provided externally. An inert atmosphere is still maintained to prevent contamination of the weld. In submerged arc welding (SAW), the welding is done submerged under flux. Long seams may be drawn using this process, and the process can also be easily automated.

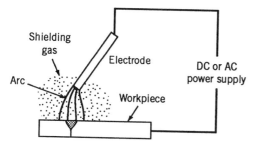

(a) A schematic of arc welding processes

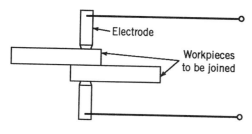

(b) A schematic of resistance spot welding

Figure 12.7. Two common types of welding.

Other Welding Processes

Resistance welding (Figure 12.7b) uses the electrical resistance of the gap between two electrodes to cause localized heating. In resistance spot welding, two overlapped parts are placed between the two electrodes. Four sets of resistances exist: the resistances of the plates, the resistances of the electrodes, the resistances of the air gap between the electrodes and the plates, and the resistance of the air gap between the plates. The heat in the latter must be maximized to cause fusion between the plates. This resistance principle may also be used to achieve seam welds.

In one type of friction welding (a solid-state welding process) a bar is rotated at high speeds and brought to rest by placing its abutting end against another stationary bar. The heat generated due to friction causes localized bonding between the abutting ends. In thermit welding, the chemical reaction between certain metal oxides and reducing agents is used to generate the necessary heat for welding. Focused high energy beams are used in laser beam and electron beam welding.

Gas combustion heating is the other predominant mode of heating for welding. The combustion is usually achieved using a mixture of oxygen and acetylene. Acetylene serves to ignite and oxygen serves to retain the flame. The relative percentages of oxygen and acetylene in the mixture are varied to achieve different types of flames. An oxidizing flame consists of excess oxygen, the carburizing (reducing) flame consists of excess acetylene, and a neutral flame consists of equal amounts of oxygen and acetylene. The level of heat varies with the type of flame.

Brazing and Soldering

Brazing and soldering may be used when high temperatures of welding are not permitted or when dissimilar materials are to be joined. The capillary action of the molten metal into the joint achieves the joining. The two processes are differentiated based on the differences in temperatures of the weld metal. Many filler materials used for soldering have melting points close to room temperature. Soldering is commonly employed in electronic part joining.

Weld Joints

Different types and configurations of joints may be used for welding, depending on the application. Most commonly, the butt joint is used to weld along abutting edges, whereas a lap joint is used on overlapped plates. T joints, and corner joints, may also be used for other applications. The single V-groove and the single square-groove joints apply the weld beads only on one side of joint, whereas the double-V-butt configuration applies the weld on both sides. Joint preparation for welding is extremely important for joint strength. Defects in welding such as blow holes can also reduce the joint strength.

12.5 POWDER METALLURGY

In recent years, powder metallurgy has become an important type of manufacturing process for accurate production of parts of hard materials and complex profiles. One type of the process involves three main stages: powder production, blending, compaction, and sintering. Isostatic compaction may also be used to substitute for compaction and sintering. Fine metal powders of hard materials such as tungsten carbide are mixed with a binder and thoroughly mixed and blended to achieve uniform properties. The mixture is poured into a die and compacted to avoid porosity and other defects. The part is heated or sintered to achieve complete fusion between the particles. Usually, some finishing is done after the part has undergone sintering. Carbide cutting tool inserts, gears, etc. are usually made using this process.

12.6 ASSEMBLY PROCESSES

Assembly is generally not discussed as a traditional manufacturing process and does not undergo the typical deformations and solidification associated with other processes discussed thus far. However, in the modern shop most parts require at least one type of assembly or other. Joining processes are important in the context of assembly. Mechanical fastening with screws and bolts, adhesive bonding, and riveting are common in the industrial workplace. Assembly is done for several reasons:

A part may be too difficult to fabricate in one piece, keeping in mind the capability and economics of existing manufacturing processes.

A relative motion between the various parts of a component may be desired during service.

Ease of disassembly and cleaning may be important to the functioning of the part.

Assembly is a process of providing some connection between two or more components to make a functional work part. Many common consumer products such as wristwatches, automobiles, and chairs are assemblies of several parts. A passenger airplane is an assembly of more than 10,000 parts. Assembly can be achieved manually or using automated machines. Assembly stations and transfer lines in an automotive factory use combinations of hardware and software to enable assembly. Production of all parts belonging to an assembly may be impossible in a single shop and several subcontracts are required to make several subassemblies. The translation of specifications of the assembly into the specifications of each individual part comprising the assembly is an extremely difficult aspect of design. The design of specifications for each individual part requires a careful consideration of economics, tolerances, functionality, location of component, fit or contact type, transmission of load, stresses, and deformations imposed by the assembly on the various parts, etc. The sequence of assembly is also important and requires careful planning.

12.7 ECONOMICS, ACCURACY, AND AUTOMATION

Several candidate processes exist for the production of a part to meet certain specifications, and a single part may require more than one process to fabricate it completely. The cost of a manufacturing process plays an important role in its selection. In general, the cost of manufacturing increases with the accuracy requirements. High tolerance and surface finish specifications demand higher costs of production, whereas poor finish and tolerances may no longer meet functionality demands.

Sand casting processes are considered to be economical when large quantities of production justify the initial investments. However, these processes do not have the ability to produce high tolerance and surface finish on the parts. In situations in which such accuracy requirements are placed, it is necessary to follow the casting with a postfinishing operation. In contrast, die casting may be used for producing parts near its net shape, without any requirements for postfinishing. The dies and equipment are significantly capital intensive, and maintenance (e.g., against die wear) is also critical.

Hot working processes are not too different from sand casting procedures in terms of the accuracy that they can produce, whereas cold working procedures may be used as commercial alternatives to machining. Machining is considered expensive due to the large material wastage. Machining also requires significant skill and labor, much of which, however, is now automated.

Automated machining setups have certainly helped to reduce the setup times of machining operations, in spite of high initial investments; the operator monotony is reduced, better consistency is achieved, and labor shortages are compensated for. The NC machine uses numerals and letters to provide programmable flexibility to existing machines to meet the demands of batch production. Computer-controlled machining centers have progressed significantly over the years, enabling the fast and accurate production of complex parts.

Joining processes are economical where assemblies are needed. However, proper principles of design for assembly must be followed. Thus the number of components in an assembly must be optimized to balance functionality and ease of assembly.

BIBLIOGRAPHY

Suggested Readings

E.J.A. ARMAREGO and R.H. BROWN, *The Machining of Metals,* Prentice-Hall, Inc., Englewood Cliffs, N.J., 1969.

E.P. DEGARMO, J.T. BLACK, and R. KOHSER, *Materials and Processes in Manufacturing,* 7th ed., Macmillan Publishing Co., New York, 1988.

S. KALPAKJIAN, *Manufacturing Engineering and Technology,* 2nd ed., Addison-Wesley Publishing Co., Inc., Reading, Mass., 1992.

Machining Data Handbook, Vols. 1 and 2, 3rd. ed., Machining Data Center, Metcut Research Associates, Cincinnati, Ohio, 1980.

H.W. POLLACK, *Tool Design,* 2nd ed., Prentice-Hall, Inc., Englewood Cliffs, N.J., 1988.

Tool and Manufacturing Engineers Handbook, Vols. 1–5, 4th ed., Society of Manufacturing Engineers, Dearborn, Mich., 1984.

E.M. TRENT, *Metal Cutting,* 2nd ed., Butterworth London, 1984.

CHAPTER 13

Nontraditional Manufacturing Processes

K.P. RAJURKAR
University of Nebraska at Lincoln

13.1 INTRODUCTION

The development of present and future manufacturing technology must meet the following major conditions imposed by customer requirements:

1. Rising overhead, capital equipment, and labor costs dictate that production operations be automated wherever possible.
2. The vastly superior properties of innovative materials such as superalloys, composites, and ceramics require new manufacturing techniques; these materials simply cannot be processed with traditional machining methods.
3. The soaring costs of the disposal of industrial waste and increasingly stringent environmental regulations necessitate the development of environmentally self-contained processes that generate a nontoxic wastestream.

Many advanced materials cannot be machined by traditional means, or at best they are machined with excessive tool wear and at high costs. In addition, the complexity and surface quality of machined parts, tools, and dies have dramatically increased. The traditional machining techniques cannot be used to machine and polish many part geometries such as deep internal cavities, miniaturized microelectronics, and fine features. Traditional machining processes (such as turning, milling, drilling, grinding, etc.) rely on direct mechanical contact between the tool and workpiece, and this fundamental physical requirement inherently limits the processes. Traditional methods also cause undesired changes in the properties of a workpiece, such as residual, mechanical, and thermal stresses, which require additional processes to be eliminated. Many new workpiece materials are either harder than conventional cutting tools or cannot withstand the high cutting forces involved in traditional machining. There is an acute need to develop new manufacturing methods and improve existing techniques that are capable of economically machining advanced materials such as superalloys, ceramics, plastics, and fiber-reinforced composites. Nontraditional manufacturing (NTM) processes can machine precision components from these sophisticated materials. NTM processes offer the advantages of a reduced number of machining steps and a higher product quality (1). NTM can also exist within the realm of automated production. Economic considerations require that technologies such as FMS, computer integrated manufacturing systems (CIMS), computer-aided engineering (CAE), computer numerical control (CNC), robotics, machine vision, and artificial intelligence be employed not only on the shop floor but throughout all facets of the corporate structure. Computer-aided design (CAD) may require a physical model in hours rather than months; stereolithography makes this possible. Fortunately, many NTM processes are especially well suited to on-line monitoring and adaptive control and thus can easily be interfaced with a manufacturer's database. The machining of sandwiched titanium honeycomb structural material used in the aerospace industry, the finishing of airfoil surfaces of gas turbine impellers, the drilling of 1000 holes of 0.635-mm diameter in a 0.635-mm-thick aluminum oxide substrate, the manufacturing of aircraft engine turbine blades, the drilling of small but uniform holes in precision injector nozzles required in the automotive and aircraft industries, and the making of dies and molds of hardened materials are some of the applications of these NTM processes.

NTM processes may be broadly categorized in two ways: processes in which there is a nontraditional mechanism of interaction between the tool and workpiece and processes in which nontraditional media are used to transfer of energy from the tool to the workpiece. Nontraditional interaction mechanisms include chemical, electrochemical, thermal, and mechanical with high impact velocity. Nontraditional media include solids, abrasives, aqueous and nonaqueous liquids, gas, plasma, ions, electrons, and photons. NTM processes are also often characterized by a high energy density in the machining region. In electrochemical machining (ECM), current densities range from 0.1 to 10 A/mm^2. High power thermal interactions range from 10^5 to 10^7 W/mm^2 in electrical discharge machining (EDM), and the mechanical interactions present in water-jet machining (WJM) result in dynamic pressures from 20 to 50 kg/mm^2 (2). Also, in NTM processes, the energy can be transferred in discrete pulses or continuously, and the energy at a given time can be applied to a localized portion of the workpiece or over a broad machining area (3). This chapter briefly reviews the state of the art of NTM processes. The focus is on the process mechanism, equipment, capabilities, applications, limitations, and research and development issues.

13.2   ELECTRICAL DISCHARGE MACHINING

EDM is among the earliest of NTM processes, having had its inception 50 years ago in a simple die-sinking application. The two principal types of EDM are die-sinking EDM and wire EDM (WEDM). Die-sinking EDM is traditionally performed vertically, but it may also be conducted horizontally. Die-sinking EDM has been greatly refined since the 1940s with the advent of transistorized pulse generators, planetary and orbital motion techniques, CNC, and adaptive control. Orbital motion was introduced to EDM during the early 1970s. Orbital motion is composed of simultaneous electrode movement along the vertical axis with a lateral movement out of the workpiece center. Thus the electrode center describes a horizontal circular orbit. This orbit is characterized by the eccentricity and the angular speed of the translation. The former is controlled by the servo system just like the vertical feed, while the angular speed of the translation can be chosen freely. WEDM is a special form of EDM in which the electrode is a continuously moving conductive wire. Five-axis CNC WEDM is now routinely employed in complex three-dimensional contour machining jobs (1). Another application of electrical discharge machining is electrical discharge grinding (EDG), which is used for precision machining of electrically conductive workpieces. A rotating, electrically conductive grinding wheel is used as the "electrode" or cutting tool in EDG. The EDM state-of-the-art practice achieved significant technological breakthroughs during the late 1980s owing to two major advances: improvement in the performance of the EDM process and advancements in the level of automation for EDM. The EDM process has been improved by reduced damage from arcing, lowered tool wear ratio, and less frequent wire rupture in WEDM. The level of automation has increased through on-line adaptive control strategies.

Process Mechanism

EDM is a thermoelectric process that erodes material from the workpiece by a series of discrete sparks between a work and tool electrode immersed in a liquid dielectric medium. These electric discharges melt and vaporize minute amounts of the work material, which are then ejected and flushed away by the dielectric. A wire EDM generates spark discharges between a small wire electrode (usually smaller than 0.5 mm diameter) and a workpiece, with deionized water as the dielectric medium, and erodes the workpiece to produce complex two- and three-dimensional shapes according to a numerically controlled (NC) path. The essential components of die-sinking and wire EDM are shown in Figures 13.1 and 13.2, respectively.

The mechanism of the spark generation and subsequent work and tool material erosion is complex and far from completely understood. However, the most agreed on process mechanism for EDM may be divided into four stages. When a voltage is applied through a dielectric medium across the gap between the tool and workpiece, an electric field builds along the path of least resistance. This causes a breakdown of the dielectric and initiates the flow of current. In the second stage, electrons and ions migrate toward the cathode and anode at high current density, forming a column of vapor and initiating the melting of the workpiece. When a voltage

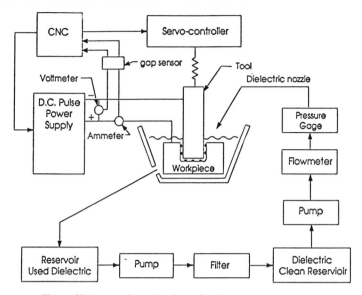

Figure 13.1. A schematic view of a die-sinking EDM system.

is no longer applied to the gap, the column collapses and a portion of molten metal is ejected from the workpiece and a crater is formed. Finally, debris that remains on the workpiece is flushed away with the dielectric, and the machining cycle is repeated with the application of a subsequent pulse.

Process Parameters

EDM process performance is influenced by a large number of parameters and their interactions. In die-sinking EDM, the erosion rate, tool wear, and resulting surface integrity and geometry depend on pulse characteristics (such as current, voltage, on-time, off-time, polarity, and pulse

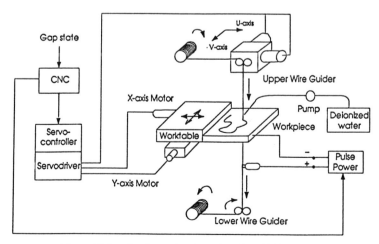

Figure 13.2. A schematic view of a wire-EDM system.

shape), work and tool material properties, dielectric flushing conditions (such as flow rate, pressure, direction of flow, and amount of debris contamination), dielectric properties (such as type, dielectric strength, and viscosity), electrode geometry and working depth, and machine characteristics (such as servo control parameters, stiffness, and accuracy). Besides these parameters, wire EDM performance also is influenced by the wire material characteristics (diameter, tensile strength, electrical properties, coatings, etc.), wire tension, wire feed rate, and wire guides and alignment.

The erosion rate is a function of electric discharge energy coupled with electrical and thermal conductivity and melting temperature of work material. For a given material, the erosion rates are affected mainly by pulse parameters such as discharge current, discharge time, and pulse on-time. For the same peak current, an increase in the pulse on-time will initially result in higher erosion rate. However, for a large on-time with a constant duty factor (i.e., the off-time being the same as the on-time), the erosion rate will eventually start decreasing after reaching an optimal value. The erosion rate also increases with an increase in peak current. In general, the power of the spark and frequency defined by the number of pulses per second determine the process performance. The low frequency and high power combination results in high metal removal with rough surface finish and low tool wear. The high frequency and low power combination, on the other hand, leads to low metal removal with fine surface finish and appreciable tool wear. The cutting speed in WEDM, often measured by the cutting area per unit time, is affected by pulse power characteristics, cutting area (determined by workpiece thickness and wire diameter), the dielectric and its flushing condition, workpiece and wire materials, and wire tension. An increase in the thickness of workpiece and wire diameter increase the cutting speed. However, the cutting speed decreases if the workpiece is too thick to allow proper dielectric flushing. Different wire materials may significantly affect the cutting speed. For instance, brass wire may have 30% cutting speed increase in machining steel compared with bronze wire under similar conditions.

Special coating or additives have been used in newly developed wires to increase the cutting speed. A dielectric (usually deionized water) with high resistivity is required for cutting carbides or aluminum alloys, whereas a dielectric with low resistivity may be better for machining steels with high cutting speed. Some organic additives in the dielectric water also improve the cutting speed. Within a considerable range, an increase in wire tension significantly increases the cutting speed. The higher tension decreases the wire vibration amplitude and hence decreases the cut width, so that the speed is higher for the same discharge energy. In general, an increase in the discharge frequency and discharge current increases the cutting speed.

The surface roughness is mainly determined by the discharge energy. When deionized water is used, a weak electrolytic polishing effect results in a slight decrease in the surface roughness in cutting steel or copper materials but leads to a small increase in the surface roughness in cutting some carbides due to the selective electrolytic dissolution. An increase in the cutting speed is usually accompanied by a decrease in the surface smoothness. The surface layer in WEDM with deionized water has the same kind of recasting layer and heat-affected zone as obtained in the die-sinking EDM using an oil-based dielectric. The WEDM-generated surface layer does not have the carbon usually found in the die-sinking EDM-generated surface layer due to the decomposition of the oil-based dielectric. The dimensional accuracy in WEDM depends mainly on the mechanical accuracy of the machine and the variation of the cut width distribution. State-of-the-art WEDM machines feature positional accuracy to ± 0.0762 mm or smaller. The variation in the cut width, however, is not easy to control. It is affected by pulse parameters, feed rate, wire vibration and tension, resistivity of the dielectric, and changes in workpiece residual stress.

Equipment and Machining Parameters

More than 15 manufacturers make EDM in various configurations, including simple manually operated vertical machines, horizontal machines, CNC EDM with orbital features, and CNC machining centers. The type of EDM machines depends on the field of application and the size range of tooling processed in that field. Many characteristics of EDM are unique and dictated by the process as well as the requirements of the workpiece. These machines are like all machine tools in that rigidity and accuracy must be built in. Proper installation, use, and maintenance must be practiced. All EDM systems include the machine (frame, ram, worktable, tool and workpiece holders, and clamping devices), pulse-power supply, tool electrode, dielectric system, and servo control system (see Figure 13.1).

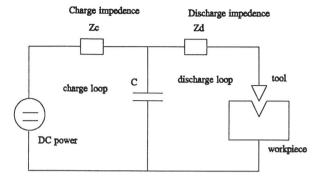

Figure 13.3. A schematic diagram of an EDM relaxation power.

EDM Power System

AN EDM power system transforms the utility AC power into pulsed DC power with 30 to 300 V and several milliamperes of peak current. There are different types of power systems in use now. The simplest power system is the relaxation power (Figure 13.3), which consists of a charge loop and a discharge loop. When the DC voltage is applied on the capacitor C through the charge impeder Z_c, the voltage across the gap between the workpiece and the tool will build up until the dielectric in the gap is broken down. During the breakdown, electric spark erosion occurs, and the capacitor charges rapidly through the discharge impeder Z_d, leading to a sharp decrease in the voltage across the gap. The extinction of the sparks is followed by a recuperation of the gap state. In practice, the impeders Z_c and Z_d can be resistors (R), inductors (L), diodes (D), or their combinations and are correspondingly called RC, RLC, RLCD, and RLCL circuits. When this type of power supply is used, the discharge depends on the gap size and the gap physical state, which leads to difficulties in controlling the pulse energy, frequency, and pulse shapes. The main merits of this type of power supply is that it is cheap to build and smooth surfaces can be obtained with proper operation. It is used mainly in some fine finish machining or fine hole drilling. Another principal type of power supply is independent power (Figure 13.4).

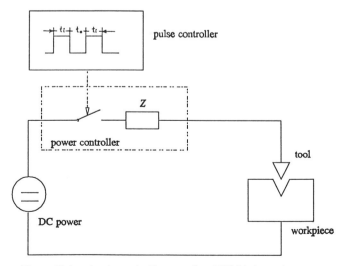

Figure 13.4. A schematic diagram of an EDM independent power.

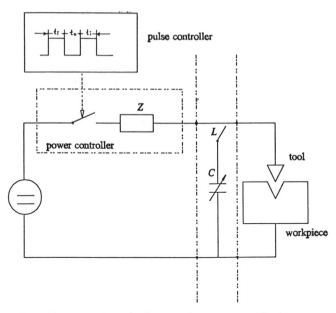

Figure 13.5. A schematic diagram of an EDM combination power.

It consists of a DC power source, a pulse controller, and a power controller. The pulse controller sets a time (or frequency) basis and controls the on and off states of the power controller. The power controller, which consists of an electronic switch circuit and a current-limiting circuit, delivers the pulse to the gap with the required power. When this type of power supply is used, the voltage pulses are independent of the gap size and the gap state. Some EDM machines are equipped with power supplies that are a combination of the relaxation and independent power supplies. They are designed for improving surface roughness. The scheme of these power supplies is illustrated in Figure 13.5. In these power supplies, the power controller in the independent power supplies can effectively control the discharge time of the capacitor in the relaxation circuit, which in turn controls the discharge frequency (usually increases the frequency). The discharge energy is determined by both the capacitance of the capacitor and its voltage, while the voltage is controlled by the transistor. Other types of EDM power supplies may be found in use, including voltage pulses with different shapes or current pulses with controlled front slopes for different machining requirements.

Tool Materials

The basic requirements for a tool material are high electrical conductivity, high melting point, and high thermal conductivity. These properties not only serve the purpose as a tool electrode but also give the tool a spark-resisting capability. The tool materials should also be easy to machine and be inexpensive. The most frequently used materials are graphite and bronze for machining steels and copper tungsten for machining carbides. Other tool materials include brass and tungsten. All materials are available in different grades or alloys that can be used for specific needs. Graphite has high melting point and fairly high thermal conductivity. It is easy to mold into complicated shapes by different means such as conventional cutting processes or ultrasonic machining. The particle size can be as large as 0.20 mm for rough machining or as small as 0.013 mm for fine detail forming and smooth surface finishing. Bronze works well as a tool material. It is often used when a smooth surface is required. Compacted bronze electrodes are used for high production applications. Brass has shown good performance in machining some titanium alloys; however, it has high rate of tool wear. Copper tungsten is used for producing fine details, smooth surfaces, and high precision EDM work. Its most prominent feature is its ability to minimize the tool wear, because of its strong spark-resisting capability. Silver tungsten works as well as copper tungsten, and the corner wear of this material in EDM operation is better than copper tungsten. Copper graphite is an alloy of the copper with graphite that is often used in EDM of carbides.

Dielectric Fluids

The main functions of the dielectric fluid are to insulate the gap before high energy is accumulated, to concentrate the discharge energy to a tiny area, to recover the gap condition after the discharge, and to flush away the discharge products. The two most commonly used dielectric fluids are petroleum-based hydrocarbon mineral oils and deionized water. The oils should have high flash points and proper viscosities. High insulation, high density, and high viscosity oils have the positive effects of concentrating the discharge channels and the discharge energy, but they may have difficulty flushing away the discharge products. For common EDM operations, kerosene is widely used with different additives, such as those for inhibiting gas bubble formation or deodoring. Silicone fluids and mixtures of these fluids with petroleum oils have given excellent results in certain applications. For instance, higher removal rates, less tool wear, and better surface finishes have been obtained in machining titanium alloys. Other dielectric fluids with varying degrees of success include some polar compounds such as aqueous solutions of ethylene glycol, water-in-emulsions, and distilled water.

Dielectric flushing is important in EDM operations. Different flushing methods can be used, depending on the tool and workpiece shapes, the machining areas, and tolerance requirements. The commonly used methods are immersion flushing (the sparking area is submerged under the dielectric fluid), spray or jet flushing (a spray nozzle or several nozzles are aimed at the sparking area), and the combined use of the immersion and spray flushing. Other methods include the forced flow of dielectric fluid to the machining area through a channel (or several channels) made in the tool or in the workpiece. The immersion flushing and spray flushing (or the combined flushing) are easy to use and do not require specially made holes or channels in the workpiece or in the tool. For deep cavity sinking or hole drilling, when needed, holes or channels must be made in the tool or in the workpiece to deliver dielectric fluid to the entire machining area with required pressures, flow direction, and flow rates (1).

Servo Control

The servo control is used to keep the interelectrode gap within a small range of variations around a desired setting during machining. The gap size control is vital in EDM machining. A large gap leads to an open circuit without discharge, while too small a gap leads to arcing or short-circuiting. Typical values of the gap can be 0.010 to 0.050 mm, although gaps as small as several micrometers or as large as several hundred micrometers can be found, depending on the voltage, current, and dielectric media. To maintain a proper gap size the tool feed rate should equal the material removal rate in the feed direction. It is often not easy to implement, because the removal rate is often not constant and varies with the change in the gap condition, e.g., a change in machining area or flushing condition. Therefore, a constant tool feed cannot be used. Instead, a servo controller is used to change the tool feed rate according to the gap conditions. A servo controller takes the gap signals (e.g., the average voltage) as the measure of the gap size and compares them with the servo reference signal (e.g., the servo reference voltage). If the sensing signals indicate the gap is too large for normal sparks, the tool feed rate will increase with a controlled pace, or if the gap sensing signals detect arcing or short-circuiting, the servo controller will react by reversing the feed direction to let the dielectric fluid flush the gap clear and then resume the machining. More sophisticated gap-monitoring systems under development tend to use more detected parameters to identify different gap states (4, 5). On-line adjustment of the servo reference voltage also may be required for the system to adapt to the change of the gap condition, but it is usually not easy to conduct the adjustment. The other important aspect of EDM servo systems is the servo mechanism, which should offer a wide range of controlled feed rates, fast response, high stability, antidisturbance ability, no overshoot, sufficient load capacity, and adequate feed distance. The following lists show the important input and output parameters with their general ranges. For die-sinking EDM:

Input Parameters	Range
Voltage	40–400 V (DC)
Gap between electrode and workpiece	0.0127–0.0508 mm
Current density	10^3–10^4 A/mm^2
Discharge time	10^{-7}–10^{-3} s
Polarity	Plus to minus or minus to plus

Output	Range
Volumetric metal removal rate	$0.000273–0.0273$ mm^3/sec
Surface finish	$0.178–0.254$ μm
Maximum aspect ratios for drilling small holes	$100:1$
Accuracy	±0.0254 to 0.127 mm

For WEDM:

Input Parameters	Range
Current	$0.5–128$ A
Pulse duration	$0.4–3200$ μsec
Frequency of pulses	$1–250$ kHz
Capacitance	$0.0–3.3$ μF
Wire speed	$0.2–15$ m/min
Wire tension	$0.5–2$ kg

Output	Range
Linear-cutting rate	$0.635–1.905$ mm/s in 25.4-mm-thick steel
Surface finish	$0.127–0.254$ μm
Accuracy	±0.00254 mm over 152.4 mm

Applications, Process Capabilities, and Limitations

Because the EDM process uses high energy electric-thermal erosion (instead of mechanical cutting forces) to remove material, it is capable of machining mechanically difficult-to-cut materials such as hardened steels, carbides, high strength alloys, and even the ultrahard conductive materials like polycrystalline diamond and some ceramics. Also, EDM is effective in machining brittle but electrically conductive materials or shaping low rigid structures, because the tool does not contact the workpiece and no substantial mechanical force is exerted on the workpiece. Because the tools are made of soft materials, they can be easily made into complicated shapes. EDM can machine complicated shapes with prefabricated tools. The process is particularly well suited to sinking cavities and drilling irregularly shaped holes. Another important feature of EDM is that it can be fully automated. The only limit in machinability is the electrical conductivity of the workpiece material. The conductivity of 0.1 (ohm cm)$^{-1}$ is considered as the minimum value for EDM to be effective (6, 7). The other problems in EDM include tool wear and the irregularity of the tool wear as well as limitations of EDM to machine sharp corners because of the existence of the gap between the tool and the workpiece. A recently developed EDM process called micro-EDM expands the EDM capability to a new perspective in EDM fine part fabrication (8). This process can achieve a surface roughness of 0.1 μm R_{max} and a high accuracy (roundness can be as small as 0.1 μm, and the straightness of some fine parts can be as small as 0.5 μm) through the control of small discharge energy and the new method of fine tool fabrication. Microholes with diameters as small as 0.015 mm can be drilled with this technique.

The surface layers of workpieces machined by EDM will be altered metallurgically and chemically after going through the extremely high energy thermal process (up to $12,000°C$) accompanied by the dielectric cooling process. The layer usually differs significantly from the base material in the metallurgical structures due to recasting, and it also contains gas holes, tool material particles, and other impurities from the dielectric (such as carbon). The thickness of the layer may vary from 0.01 to 0.4 mm, depending largely on the workpiece materials and the discharge energy involved. This layer consists of three sublayers: the recast layer or white layer (0.01 to 0.04 mm) on the top of surface of the workpiece, the heat-affected layer (<0.25 mm) formed by heat and cooling (as well as the diffusion from the recast layer), and the conversion (or transformed) layer where a change in grain structure from the base structure is apparent. Among the three sublayers, the heat-affected one may have severe metallurgical damage (such as boundary cracking) because of the thermal stress. Microcracking is another major surface defect due to the high stress of the sudden recasting process. The microcracks may adversely affect the material fatigue strength and thermal strength, though they may be as fine as several hundredths of a micrometer. The generation of these microcracks depends on many factors, such as the workpiece material properties (e.g., brittleness) and the discharge energy. Carbides and metallic ceramics, for example, are more susceptible than steels to microcracks.

Recent Research Activities and Future Trends

In recent years, improving of the machining capabilities for advanced materials, increasing the technological performance, and enhancing the automatic operation level seem to be the main directions of research activities targeted to meet the current and future needs in manufacturing industries. A brief description of some research activities is given below.

Machining Advanced Materials

The requirement and importance of advanced and superhard materials such as engineering ceramics in industries are drastically increasing. EDM is one of the best options for processing some electrically conductive ceramics. These materials have high strength and thermal resistance features. Conventional EDM yields relatively lower material removal rates. A comprehensive investigation of the machinability of different kinds of oxide and silicon-type ceramics is reported in ref. 7. The correlations among the electrical conductivity, cutting rate, surface roughness, and control parameters of pulse generators for different ceramics have been determined. This research reveals that when machining a silicon (Si3N4 + TiN) ceramic, the material removal rate can reach 0.1167 mm^3/sec with a peak current of 20 A and on-time of 15 μs. The tool wear ratio can be less than 20% when the on-time is larger than 30 μs and the peak current is 20 A. A fracture analysis of surfaces generated by EDM of ceramic components shows that the parameters achieved with this technique have more information about the profile than parameters obtained with conventional methods (9). The machinability of these advanced materials depends on their electrical conductivity and thermal behavior. Attempts to understand the material-removal mechanism based on thermal analysis are continuing, as is the development of advanced EDM pulse power supplies that will machine the modern materials more efficiently.

Mirror Surface Machining

Unlike the electrochemical machining (ECM) process, it is relatively difficult to achieve a highly smooth surface with EDM. Present EDM technologies are able to generate a mirrorlike surface only within 1,000 mm^2 (10). A new EDM die-sinking method reported in ref. 11 produces a mirrorlike surface ($Ra < 0.1$ μm) in an area as large as 50,000 mm^2. This EDM system uses silicon as the electrode material and a silicon powder suspension in the dielectric fluid.

Ultrasonic-assisted EDM

Ultrasonic vibrations of the tool electrode in EDM have been found to improve the overall performance of the process. The high frequency pumping action of the vibrating electrode surface accelerates the dielectric circulation, which results in almost 80% saving in machining time during finishing stages. The pressure change caused by ultrasonic vibrations results in more effective discharges, which causes more material erosion and less surface damage (12).

Control and Automation

Fully automatic and unattended machining operations are the main developing trends of EDM equipment for use in CIM environments in future manufacturing industries. Fully automatic EDM operations should provide satisfactory productivity, and the processes should be reliable, i.e., without any arcing damage (in die sinking) or wire rupture (in wire cutting). Extensive efforts are being directed toward developing monitoring and control systems to avoid arcing in die-sinking EDM and wire breakage in wire-EDM (13). The technological parameters should be generated automatically according to the instantaneous machining conditions as well as the machine part requirements. All operations of EDM equipment should be handled by the mainframe computer in CIM systems (14).

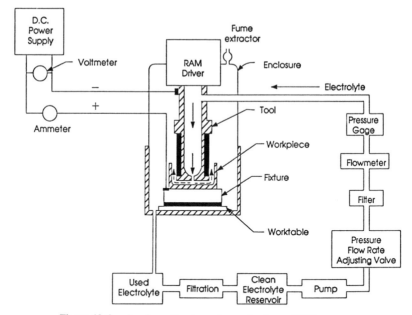

Figure 13.6.   A schematic view of a vertical ram ECM system.

13.3   ELECTROCHEMICAL MACHINING

Although ECM is a relatively new process, the underlying principle is not new. In the 19th century, Michael Faraday (1791–1867) was the first to study electrolysis. Since that time, it has become common knowledge that when a DC power supply is applied to two electrically conductive materials that are submerged in an electrolyte, material from the positive pole (anode) is deposited onto the negative pole (cathode). Although this action of electroplating has been used for many years for adding metals to the surface of parts, the reverse application of removing material found its application about 35 years ago.

Process Mechanism

ECM is an electrochemical anodic dissolution process in which a direct current with high amperage and low voltage is passed between a workpiece (the anode) and a preshaped tool (the cathode). At the anodic workpiece surface, metal is dissolved into metallic ions by the deplating reaction, and thus the tool shape is copied into the workpiece. The electrolyte is forced to flow through the interelectrode gap to remove the metal ions and the heat generated by the deplating action. The tool is fed toward the workpiece while maintaining a small gap. A schematic of a cavity-sinking–type ECM is shown in Figure 13.6.

Process Parameters

The parameters that influence ECM can be classified into four categories: electrical parameters (such as current, current density, and voltage), electrolyte parameters (such as electrolyte velocity, pressure, ingredient, temperature, and concentration), tool parameters (such tool feed rate), and workpiece parameters (such as contour gradient, radii, flow path, and flow cross-section). These factors and their relationships are shown in Figure 13.7. Because of the complex interactions between the metal removal and the machining parameters, it has been difficult to quantify exactly the relationship between them. However, for a simple machining process

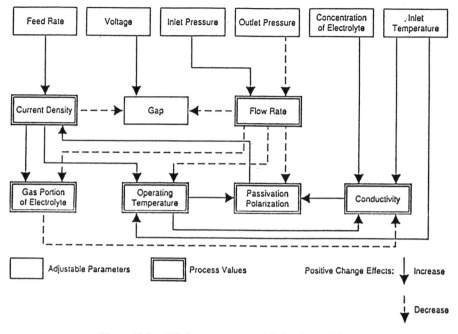

Figure 13.7. ECM parameters and their effects (16).

involving parallel plane electrodes with no change in electrolyte conductivity (Figure 13.8), the anodic metal removal can be determined using Faraday's law:

$$m = \frac{AIt}{zF}$$

where m is the mass of metal electrochemically machined by passing current I amperes for time t, in seconds; A is the atomic weight of the dissolving ions, z is their valency, and F is Faraday's constant ($F = 96,500$ C). The quantity A/zF is known as the anodic electrochemical equivalent.

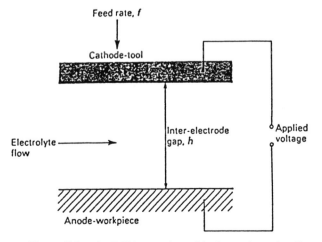

Figure 13.8. An ECM operation with planar electrodes (2).

When a constant feed is given to the tool at a rate of f, the rate of change in gap width h relative to the tool surface is given by

$$\frac{dh}{dt} = \frac{AJ}{zF\rho_a} - f$$

where J is the current density and ρ_a is the density of the workpiece material. From Ohm's law, the current density J is given by $J = (\kappa_e V/h)$, where κ_e is the electrolyte conductivity and V is the voltage across the gap. Hence, the basic equation for the gap change rate becomes

$$\frac{dh}{dt} = \frac{A\kappa_e V}{zF\rho_a h} - f$$

When $dh/dt = 0$, the machine is said to be in the equilibrium state, i.e., the tool feed rate equals the workpiece metal removal rate. From this basic equation, the corresponding equilibrium gap size is

$$h_e = \frac{A\kappa_e V}{zF\rho_a f}$$

The equilibrium gap is one of the decisive factors affecting the shaping accuracy of the workpiece. When the feed rate $f = 0$, the gap change is a function of time and is given by

$$h^2 = h^2(0) + \frac{2A\kappa_e Vt}{zF\rho_a}$$

where $h(0)$ is the initial gap size at time $t = 0$. This method of ECM is often used for etching or deburring when a shallow pattern is machined or surface irregularities are removed quickly without the need for tool feed.

The electrolyte selection plays an important role in ECM dimension control. The most important feature of the electrolyte in this regard is the relationship between the current efficiency and the current density. Figure 13.9 shows a typical example (2). In this case, the sodium nitrate solution is preferable, because the local metal removal rate is high at the small gap locations where both the current density and the current efficiency are high, whereas the local removal rate is low at the large gap locations where both the current density and current efficiency are low. This results in the gap distribution tending toward uniformity. Ideally, the cutoff current density should be as large as possible (so that the overcut due to any stray current

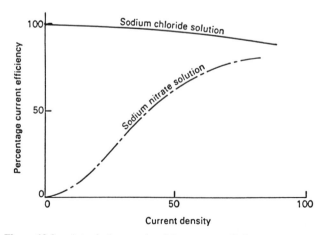

Figure 13.9. A typical example of the current efficiency change (2).

can be reduced), and the slope of the current efficiency curve should be as steep as possible (so that a small gap difference, and hence a small current difference, in different locations would lead to a significant difference in the metal removal rates in those locations). The current efficiency in ECM depends on the anodic material and the electrolyte. Recent work also shows that when pulsed voltage is applied instead of the commonly used continuous voltage, proper use of pulse parameters (e.g., pulse on-times) can significantly improve the current efficiency. The following list gives general ranges of the ECM operation parameters:

Input Parameters	Range
Voltage	8–30 V (DC)
Current	50–40,000 A
Current density	10–300 A/cm^2
Tool feed rate	0.2–15 mm/min
Equilibrium gap	0.1–0.5 mm
Electrolyte temperature	25–65°C
Electrolyte pressure	65 kPa to 3.0 MPa

The following list gives the typical ranges of output parameters for ECM (15, 16):

Output Parameters	Range
Surface roughness (Ra)	0.25–0.75 μm
Tolerance	±0.05 to ±0.012 mm
Machining rate	0.5–10 mm/min

ECM Equipment

As shown in Figure 13.6, the ECM operation requires

1. A high current, low voltage DC electric power system with sufficient amperage and adjustable voltage.
2. A tool feed system that feeds the tool into the workpiece while maintaining a proper gap between the tool and the workpiece.
3. An electrolyte system that supplies the gap with pressurized, flowing electrolyte with filtration and controlled temperature.
4. A cathode tool prepared with an approximate mirror image of the shape to be machined into the workpiece.

Some of the state-of-the-art machines are also equipped with sophisticated spark and short-circuit protectors and process control systems.

ECM Machines

ECM machines are available in different sizes, configurations (vertical, horizontal, or combined configurations) and current capacities (50 to 40,000 A), depending on the application. Methods of loading, setup, tooling, and control vary from machine to machine. Several unique aspects of ECM have necessitated the development of some new concepts in machine tool design. These concepts include coping with the rigors of machining in a saline environment, handling high electric currents, and developing a ram driver that moves extremely slowly and accurately and is free from stick-slip against high forces. ECM machinery operates at rather substantial electrolyte pressures, commonly in the order of 1380 kPa (17).

Electrolytes

The main functions of the electrolyte in ECM are to carry electric current, to remove the debris of the electrochemical reactions from the gap, to carry away heat generated by the machining process, and to maintain a constant temperature in the machining region. The primary requirements of a electrolyte can be listed as follows:

1. The anions in the electrolyte solution should be able to let the anode dissolve uniformly at a high speed. The anions should not react with the anodic metal to generate a passive film on the anodic surface. In practice, electrolytes containing anions of Cl^-, SO_4^{2-}, NO_3^-, ClO_3^-, and OH^- are often used.

2. The cations in the electrolyte solution should not deposit on the cathode surface, so that the cathode shape remains unchanged. To satisfy this requirement, electrolytes with alkaline metallic cations, such as potassium and sodium, are used. Electrolytes containing Cu^{2+}, Zn^{2+}, Fe^{2+}, and Al^{3+}, which are of high standard electrode potentials, should be avoided.

3. The electrolyte should have a high electrical conductivity and low viscosity to reduce the power loss due to electrolyte resistance and heat generation and to ensure good flow conditions in the extremely narrow interelectrode gap.

4. The electrolyte should be safe, nontoxic, and less erosive to machine. Neutral salts are preferred. Acid electrolytes are used only for small hole drilling when the reaction products need to be dissolved into the electrolyte.

5. The electrolyte should be able to maintain its stable features, such as its ingredients and pH value, during the machining period, and its conductivity and viscosity should have small temperature coefficients.

6. The electrolyte should be cheap and easily available.

Industrial ECM operations usually involve electrolytes that are a mixture of different electrolytes to meet multiple requirements. The electrolytes are usually chosen considering the workpiece material, the desired dimensional tolerance, the surface finish requirements, and the desired productivity. Electrolytes used in ECM are classified into several categories: aqueous or nonaqueous, organic or nonorganic (based on solvent types), acid, alkaline or neutral, mixed or nonmixed (based on number of ingredients), and passivating or activating (based on their effects on the anodic surface).

Tool Electrodes

The design, fabrication, and testing of tool electrodes are the important tasks in any industrial ECM operation.

Tool Material. An ECM tool material should be a good electrical and thermal conductor, easily machinable, resistant to sparking and chemical erosion, and strong enough to withstand electrolyte pressure. The most commonly used materials are copper, brass, stainless steel, and titanium. Copper tungsten is also often used for its spark-resisting quality.

Tool Structure and Electrolyte Flow Design. The uniformity of electrolyte flow over the machining region is of utmost importance for an ECM operation. The electrolyte flow design basically involves selecting the electrolyte flow method. Three types of flow are usually employed (2): forward flow, reverse flow, and side flow. The selection of the flow method is based on the workpiece shape to be machined. The forward flow and the reverse flow methods are usually used for drilling holes or for sinking cavities with depths, whereas the side flow method is often used for noncavity shaping (such as the shaping of turbine blades). The forward flow of the electrolyte needs simple tool structures and fixtures to implement, but it may lead to poor flow conditions. The reverse flow of the electrolyte can reduce the occurrence of cavities and the variation of the electrolyte pressure and velocity. The basic requirement is that the electrolyte should flow uniformly through the entire machining area.

Tool Shape Design. The dimensional accuracy of the workpiece surface machined by ECM depends on the distribution of the gap between the tool surface and the workpiece surface. When complex shapes are involved, this gap is not uniformly distributed. Therefore, the tool surface shape is often not the perfect mirror image of the workpiece. Because it is difficult to determine the gap distribution analytically, approximation methods are often used along with trial-and-error during actual machining. One example of approximation used is the $\cos \theta$ method (18), which is based on the following equation to estimate the gap distribution:

$$h = h_e/\cos \theta \ (\theta < 60°)$$

where θ is the angle between the tool feed direction and the workpiece's normal direction at the location under calculation and h is the gap at this location. Many computational techniques (including finite element and boundary element methods) have been developed to solve the tool design and workpiece shape prediction problems.

ECM Applications, Capabilities, and Limitations

ECM is an electrochemical process and does not involve substantial mechanical or thermal forces. ECM is capable of machining any electrically conductive metallic material, and the process is generally unaffected by the hardness and the strength of the materials. It can be used for machining high strength, high temperature alloys (such as titanium alloys); hardened steels; and even carbides. As ECM is a non–chip-forming process, no cutting forces are involved, and hence, ECM can be used to machine parts with low rigidity such as parts with thin walls. ECM can be used to machine complex contours; irregular shapes; slots; and small, deep, or noncircular holes.

Because of the high costs of equipment investment, tooling, setup, and maintenance, electrochemical machining is most often applied when shaped cavities are machined into alloys that are difficult to shape by conventional methods. The traditional applications of ECM process are the shaping of turbine blades, blade disks, engine castings, gun barrel rifles, forge dies and molds, noncircular holes, etc. Other applications of ECM include electrochemical deburring, electrochemical housing, and electrochemical turning. However, ECM can only be used for machining electrically conductive materials. Usually, sharp corners or clear cuts cannot be obtained by ECM. There are also certain limitations on the attainable dimensional accuracy and the surface finish, depending on the complexity of the shape, workpiece material, and electrolyte. One of the major disadvantages of the ECM process is the generation of huge quantities of sludge and spent electrolyte. These wastes need significant processing before they can be safely disposed. The cost of landfilling increases over the years, adding to the cost of ECM.

Research Issues

The ECM process is complex, involving many physical parameters and their interactions. Many attempts have been made to model the process, develop an accurate tool design procedure, and develop process monitoring and controlling systems (15). However, the change in the electrolyte conductivity, current efficiency, and overpotentials are difficult to model and control. Many issues such as tool design for complicated shapes and local gap monitoring and control need to be addressed. These have been some of the research areas in ECM development. Attempts at improving the dimensional accuracy of ECM include ECM with pulsed currents, ECM with gas-mixed electrolytes, ECM with small gaps, and ECM using passivating electrolytes (15). Because of the hazardous wastes generated by ECM, some research has also been carried out on the recycling of the wastestream.

13.4 ABRASIVE FLOW MACHINING

Abrasive flow machining (AFM) is a nontraditional finishing process that is used to deburr, polish, or radius surfaces and edges by flowing a semisolid abrasive medium over these areas. The process has a wide range of applications from critical aerospace and medical components to high production volumes of parts such as dies and fuel injector nozzles. AFM can reach even the most inaccessible areas, processing multiple holes, slots, or edges in one operation. Since the initial development and use of the process in the mid-1960s, the process has gained widespread acceptance in the modern manufacturing industry (19).

Process Mechanism

Abrasive flow machining operates by flowing a viscoelastic, abrasive-laden putty through or across the workspace. The abrasive-laden compound is forced through a restrictive passage formed by a work part–tooling combination. This causes the viscosity of the medium temporarily to rise. The abrasive grains are held tightly in place at this point and the medium becomes a deformable grinding stone. The medium uniformly abrades the passage walls. Medium viscosity will return to normal after it passes through the restricted area. Metal removal will be highest in the area with the greatest restriction (1, 19).

Process Parameters and Capabilities

The process parameters that have the largest impact on AFM results are the number of cycles, extrusion pressure, grit composition and type, and fixture design (1, 19, 20). The amount of stock removal per surface from AFM is around 1.2 to 1.5 times R_{max}, the maximum peak-to-valley roughness height. AFM can produce surface finishes around 2 μin. (0.05 μm) R_a. Because it removes material uniformly, it cannot fix surface defects or correct taper problems. AFM can deburr holes as small as 0.008 in. (0.2 mm) and radius edges from 0.001 to 0.060 in. (0.025 to 1.5 mm). Tolerance can be held to ±0.0002 in. (5 μm).

AFM Equipment

The major components of AFM equipment are the machine, the tooling, and the medium. A standard abrasive flow machine consists of two vertically opposed medium cylinders. The lower cylinder is filled with a given volume of the medium. The workpiece and fixtures are hydraulically clamped between the medium cylinders. The putty is then extruded through the workpiece and tooling plates and into the upper cylinder. This constitutes one upstroke. The action is then reversed as the putty is forced down through the part and into the lower cylinder. This completes one AFM cycle (1, 19).

AFM tooling acts to hold the part, direct the flow of abrasives, and help form restrictive passages. The highest metal removal will occur in the area with the greatest media flow restriction. The choice of a suitable media viscosity is important to the process. A stiff base will give nearly pure extrusion while a less viscous base will cause greater radii at the passage openings (19).

Abrasive flow compounds are made by mixing the abrasive grains with a flowable semisolid plastic carrier called the medium base. The medium base consists of a rubberlike polymer and a lubricating diluent. Different mixes of these two ingredients allow a wide range of medium viscosities. The compounds are specified by viscosity, abrasive size, type, and quantity (21). The main abrasives used in AFM are aluminum oxide, silicon carbide, boron carbide, and diamonds. Diamonds are used to machine hard materials such as tungsten carbide. Aluminum oxide performs well in a variety of applications and is relatively inexpensive. Silicon carbide provides high metal removal and is probably the most common abrasive used. Boron carbide is limited to use on hard materials due to its high cost (1).

Applications

It was previously stated that the process was initially developed for critical deburring of aircraft valve bodies and spools. The applications for this intriguing process have grown enormously due to its flexibility, consistency, and competitive cost. Specific examples include the blending of radii on large jet engine compressor disks (20). Also, fuel injector bodies are deburred and polished in an automated AFM system at production rates of 30,000 parts per day (19).

The extrusion die application is an excellent example of AFM actually increasing product performance. The AFM process leaves a fine directional finish that is parallel to the material flow through the die, thus improving die performance (22, 23). The AFM process also is being used to port intake manifolds and cylinder heads. Besides polishing, AFM provides a larger cross-sectional area and greater airflow capacity, which increase horsepower potential. Tests with intake manifold runners on stock Chevrolet and Ford 5.0 L parts showed that AFM increased the flow of all runners and provided far less runner-to-runner variation. AFM also removed the sharp edges and casting imperfections that create unwanted restrictions. Besides the automobile after-market industry, manufacturers and users of jet ski products are improving performance with the AFM process (24).

Research Issues

The relationship between abrasive concentration, grain size, and medium viscosity and AFM process performance was studied (25). The influence of these parameters on metal removal, surface roughness, and edge radius size was reported. A rheological evaluation of the medium viscosity (MV) polyborosiloxane medium without abrasive addition was reported (26). The relationship between wall shear stress and shear rate for the MV media was determined by capillary rheometry. The material was found to have a pseudoplastic nature. The material flowed more readily in restrictions as the coefficient of viscosity was lowered, because of the increased shear rate. At the same time, the wall shear stress was higher. Proper AFM operation may depend on these properties. Other tests showed a time-dependent rheotropic behavior for the MV polyborosiloxane. In addition, simple barrel compression tests confirmed that the MV polyborosiloxane has a degree of compressibility (around 2% compression at 16,000 KPa) (26). The effect of media viscosity and extrusion pressure on metal removal and surface roughness was studied (27) scanning electron microscope (SEM) photographs showed that the major improvement in surface finish takes place within the first few cycles. Current research is aimed at understanding the process mechanism and at the development of an on-line monitoring and control system.

13.5 ABRASIVE FLUID JET MACHINING

Abrasive fluid jet machining (AFJM), including abrasive jet machining (AJM) and abrasive water jet machining (AWJM), is one of the newest nontraditional manufacturing processes. It makes use of the erosive action of an abrasive-laden fluid (water or gas) jet for cutting and drilling operations. Among the processes in AFJM, AWJM is the fastest developed process. It is considered to be an update to WJM and AJM and is introduced in detail in this section.

Process Mechanism of AWJM

AWJM combines the principles of AJM and water jet machining (WJM). In AWJM, material is removed from the workpiece when a high velocity fine-abrasive water jet impinges on its surface. Abrasive water jets (AWJs) are formed by mixing abrasive particles with a stream of water to form a highly focused jet, traveling at speeds of 600 to 800 m/s. AWJs are formed in the nozzle system as shown in Figure 13.10, in which pressurized water is forced through a sapphire orifice to form a coherent water jet with high velocity. The water jet and a stream of solid abrasives are introduced into a mixing and accelerating tube constructed of hard material. The initially coherent water jet breaks into droplets that accelerate the solid particles. As a result of the momentum transfer between the water and abrasives through the nozzle, a high velocity, abrasive-laden water jet is formed. The cutting process using the jets is a controlled depth penetration of the material. The material removal is the result of erosion, shearing, and failure under localized stress fields. The removal rate depends on the specific properties of the material being machined and the parameters of the process (28, 29).

Process Parameters

The parameters involved in the AWJM can be classified as follows (30):

1. *Hydraulic Parameters.* Water jet pressures (up to 400 MPa), jet orifice (0.075 to 0.635 mm), jet hydraulic power (typically 40 Kw), water flow rate (typically 0.1 to 0.2 L/s)

2. *Abrasive Parameters.* Abrasive flow rate (up to 10 g/s), abrasive particle mesh size (60 to 150), abrasive material (e.g., garnet, aluminum oxide, or silicon carbide).

3. *Mixing Parameters.* Mixing tube length and mixing tube diameter.

4. *Traverse Parameters.* Traverse speed, number of passes, standoff distance, and jet angle.

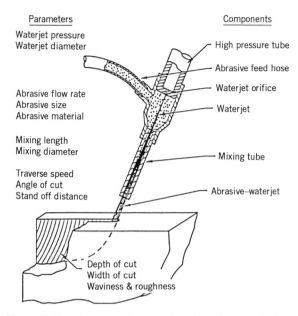

Figure 13.10. A schematic view of an AWJM system (30).

The depth of cut increases with the increase in water jet pressure but decreases with traverse speed as well as with standoff distance. AWJ-machined surfaces may undergo external surface texture effects or internal effects on the integrity of the material. Studies have shown that AWJ-machined surfaces are generally rough but are free from any mechanical, thermal, and metallurgical effects. Surface waviness is a jet-related phenomenon similar to laser-, plasma-, and water-jet–produced surfaces. The variations in the dynamic parameters (pressure, abrasive flow rate, and traverse rate) affect the uniformity of the waviness. The traverse rate has been found to be the most significant of these parameters. Surface roughness significantly depends on the particle size.

Proper selection of AWJ parameters is essential for the elimination of burrs, delaminations, and cracks. For instance, burr formation is sensitive to the particle size, delamination is sensitive to the abrasive–water flow rate, crack formation depends on the pressure, microcracking is sensitive to the particle size, and the geometry of kerf taper and wall straightness depend on the machinability of the material and depth of cut.

Equipment

The basic components of an AWJM system include a water jet and an abrasive jet nozzle, a pump system, an AWJ feed system, and control and monitoring units. The abrasive jet nozzle provides efficient mixing of the abrasive and the water jet as well as the high velocity of the mixed jet. Different nozzle types are used (1, 31), including single water jets, multiple water jets, and annular water jet. The most commonly employed system in industry is the single water jet systems. Multiple water jets are applied in special situations when wide kerfs are required. The AWJM nozzles are generally made of either tungsten carbide or sapphire. The function of the pumping system in AWJM is to produce the high velocity water jet that will ultimately transfer its momentum to the abrasives. High pressure pumps (typically intensifier types) are capable of continuously pumping water at pressures of up to 400 MPa. Medium-pressure pumps, with pressure ranges of up to 170 MPa, are usually of the intensifier or crankshaft type (30). Typical water flow rates and power levels used in AWJ machining applications are 0.1 L/sec and 40 kW, respectively. For uniform machining action to occur, the abrasive flow system must deliver a precisely controlled flow of abrasive particles to the abrasive jet nozzle. The abrasive delivery system consists of a storage hopper, a flow control valve, and a feed tube. An abrasive feed rate of up to 10 g/s is typical in high-pressure AWJM applications. For most applications, the hopper is located within 10 m of the machining nozzle for a consistent flow of abrasives. The water jet used for this process is essentially the same as that used for water jet machining. A water jet that has a velocity of approximately 900 m/s is produced when highly pressurized water is passed through a 0.075- to 0.635-mm-diameter nozzle. For extended life times, the nozzle is fabricated of sapphire, and can be expected to last 250 to 500 h. In addition to the basic components that comprise an AWJM system, several other components are required. As with the WJM, industrial users of AWJM must use a catcher in their operations to minimize noise and to contain the jet after it exits the workpiece.

Applications, Process Capabilities, and Limitations

AWJM is effective in slitting, drilling, contour cutting (turning and milling), etching, cleaning, deburring, and polishing of a variety of nonmetallic and metallic materials such as wood, paper, asbestos, plastics, rubber, nylon, Fiberglas, germanium, silicon, high strength steels, and alloys. Compared with conventional cutting and piercing methods, AWJM uses low cutting forces (though harder materials require higher operating pressures), and the operation is virtually vibration free (28, 29). Brittle nonmetallic materials, such as acrylic, graphite, and silica glass, can easily be cut by AWJM without damage. Also, abrasive jet operations do not produce heat-affected zones in the material. A promising AWJM application that has been investigated is cutting the sandwiched honeycomb structural material currently used in the aerospace industry. The edges of structural aluminum plates have been successfully bevel cut in preparation for subsequent welding operations. The AWJM process is also capable of being used as a cleaning tool. A robotic AWJM system is reportedly used to clean and descale large castings. The contour cutting by AWJM gives its capability of trepanning and cavity sinking. Milling with the AWJ process involves the production of cavities with controlled depths, using multipass and nonthrough cutting. AWJM operations can be automated with numerical control and robotic technology. The limitations of the process include stray cutting and surface waviness, high equipment costs, hazard from the rebounding abrasives, high level of noise, and low nozzle life.

Research Issues

The rapid wear of AWJ nozzles (from a maximum of 4 h to as little as 5 min) substantially lowers the productivity. The degree of automation and productivity of AWJ can be improved if on-line sensing of nozzle wear replaces visual inspection. Recent research is focused on acoustic, optical, electrical, and mechanical methods of sensing nozzle wear. Sophisticated robotic–AWJ combined systems will be a continuous growth area for this technology. In the future, the integration of accurate AWJ sensor technology and computer-aided manufacturing (CAM) will allow true on-line control of this process (32).

13.6 LASER BEAM MACHINING

Laser is an acronym for light amplification by stimulated emission of radiation. A laser beam is a monochromatic (single wavelength) and highly collimated (with small divergence angles of 10^{-2} to 10^{-4} rad) energy source with a focused power density. When focused and concentrated over a small diameter spot with a high power density, laser beams can be used to cut, drill, shape, weld, and heat treat materials.

Process Mechanism

Electrons can jump to orbits away from the nucleus (i.e., to higher energy levels). This excited atom spontaneously emits the absorbed energy as the electron drops back to a lower energy orbit. If an additional quantum of energy is absorbed by the electron while the atom is in the excited state, two quanta of energy are radiated with the same wavelength as that of the stimulating energy. This is the physical phenomenon of the main principle of the laser-generating mechanism. The power density of a laser beam can be increased by focusing for material processing applications. The beam power density and the interaction time between the laser beam and the workpiece determine the resulting action of the laser beam (such as weld, cut, or heat treat). For instance, a highly defocused beam of power densities 1.5×10^2 to 1.5×10^4 W/ cm^2 (10^3 to 10^5 W/in.^{2}) is used for rapid heating of a surface without melting. Power densities of 1.5×10^4 to 1.5×10^5 W/cm^2 (10^5 to 10^6 W/in.^{2}) are generally applied for melting, welding, or cladding applications. Cutting and drilling require power densities higher than 1.5×10^6 to 1.5×10^8 W/cm^2 (10^7 to 10^9 W/in.^{2}) (1).

Process Parameters

The selection of the type of laser for a particular application depends on the beam's power, wavelength, temporal mode, spatial mode, and focal spot size. Output power is the basic characteristic of a laser. Using an underpowered laser system will result in increased processing time or an inability to perform the desired machining operations, while using an overpowered laser system will cause excessive expenses. In general, CO_2 lasers give the highest continuous beam power, while Nd : YAG lasers provide the highest peak power for pulsed operation. The amount of laser power required is determined by examining the optical and thermal properties of the workpiece material or group of materials to be machined.

The laser's optical properties affect machining performance. Among the optical properties, the absorptivity of the optical material has the most significant influence on laser power outputs. The absorptivity of materials depends highly on the wavelength of incident light, and thus certain lasers are more suitable for processing certain classes of materials. For example, some metals (such as aluminum and copper) show low absorptivity at a wavelength of 10.6 μm, which is the characteristic wavelength for CO_2 lasers. Therefore, to machine these materials effectively, either a high power laser or one with a different wavelength must be used. These materials, however, can be machined more effectively by using a Nd : YAG laser with a 1.06 μm wavelength, as the copper and aluminum absorptivity values are much higher for this wavelength. The value of the absorptivity depends on the wavelength of the beam impinging on the surface, surface roughness, temperature, phase of the material, and the use of surface coatings. Estimation of power requirements can be performed using models for the specific laser machining process that relate the material properties, operating parameters, and material removal characteristics (33).

Lasers can operate in either a continuous wave (CW) mode or a pulsed beam mode. In the continuous wave mode, the laser beam is emitted without interruption. In the pulsed beam mode, the laser beam is emitted periodically. CW operation offers the advantage of smooth machined surfaces. However, the surface quality improvement is at the expense of the high electrical power input required to maintain a continuous beam.

The beam profile can be characterized by its transverse electromagnetic mode (TEM) (34). TEM modes are generally denoted in the form of TEM_{nm}. The subscripts n and m represents the number of nodes in directions orthogonal to the beam propagation, such as TEM_{00} or TEM_{01} (Figure 13.11). TEM_{00} has a Gaussian spatial distribution and is usually considered the best mode for laser machining because the phase front is uniform and there is a smooth dropoff of irradiance from the beam center. In materials processing, irradiance (power per unit area) of the laser beam at the material surface is of prime importance (35). Irradiance great enough to melt or vaporize any material can be generated by focusing a laser beam. The maximum irradiance is obtained at the focal point of a lens, where the beam is at its smallest diameter; the location of this minimum diameter is called the focal spot. Irradiance values of billions of watts per square centimeter can be obtained at the focal spot. Due to high temperatures reached at the erosion front, the material near it undergoes phase transformation, resulting in the creation of a heat-affected zone. While the laser beam energy is not sufficient to melt the material in the heat-affected zone, it is high enough to heat treat the material to a harder state. The results presented in ref. 36 show that the heat-affected zone increases with workpiece thickness and decreases with feed rate. The width of the heat-affected zone on the beam entry side was also found to be less than on the exit side. The change in microhardness of the kerf edges was greater on the exit side, but the microhardness was normal at a distance of less than 0.1 mm from the edge of the kerf. Because the laser beam energy is concentrated into a small spot, the phase transformation effect is highly localized and the heat-affected zone is small.

The laser cutting efficiency for other metals such as aluminum and copper depends on surface finish as well as the workpiece thickness. Because these materials are highly reflective,

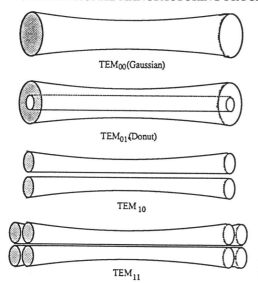

TEM$_{00}$(Gaussian)

TEM$_{01}$(Donut)

TEM$_{10}$

TEM$_{11}$

Figure 13.11. An example of a transverse electromagnetic mode (33).

sheets with smooth untreated surfaces cannot be easily cut with a laser. The cutting efficiency can be improved by either creating a rough surface to absorb both incident and reflected laser beam energy or by using an absorbent coating to engage the incoming laser beam.

Equipment

A LBM system consists of four major subsystems (Figure 13.12): laser beam generation, beam delivery, workpiece positioning, and auxiliary devices. Beam generation is accomplished within the laser device. Lasers used for LBM must be of high power, reliable, and relatively low in acquisition cost. The most commonly used lasers are CO_2 and Nd : YAG. The beam delivery system consists of optical components that direct the laser beam onto the workpiece surface. The important components in the beam delivery system are beam polarizers, mirrors and beam splitters, focusing lenses and fiber optic couplings. Auxiliary components, including gas jet nozzles and safety equipment, are used in support of the laser machining process. The function of the workpiece positioning system is to control the movement between the laser beam and the workpiece. Two types of systems are often used. With the first type of system, the laser beam is fixed but the workpiece performs the required movement by using a numerical control unit. This

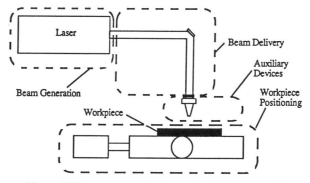

Figure 13.12. A schematic view of an LBM system (33).

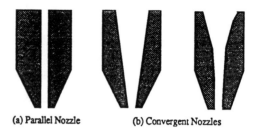

Figure 13.13. Coaxial nozzles used in LBM: **(a)** parallel and **(b)** convergent nozzles (33).

(a) Parallel Nozzle   (b) Convergent Nozzles

type of system allows a high degree of accuracy and high scanning velocities. For large workpieces, however, the laser beam is moved. A combination of workpiece and laser beam positioning can also be used in a coordinated fashion to machine intricate contours on parts.

A number of laser systems have been developed with multiaxis robotics manipulation of beam position. This is useful to perform welding, cutting, and drilling operations. The advantage in using a multiaxis numerical control system is the reduced space requirement for machining large workpieces. The disadvantage of the multiaxis system is that the accuracy of positioning and velocity are limited when machining workpieces with complicated geometries. An effective laser machining requires maximum expulsion of the molten material that is formed at the erosion front. For this purpose, a laser head is used to enclose the focusing laser beam and direct the coaxial gas jet toward the erosion front. The driving force for material expulsion is created by a pressure gradient at the erosion front, resulting from the use of a coaxial or off-axial gas jet. In laser cutting, a coaxial jet is used to create a large pressure difference between the top and bottom of the kerf. This pressure difference forms a downward driving force, which expels molten material through the bottom of the kerf. In laser grooving, an off-axial jet is used to create a pressure gradient along the erosion front (with high pressure at the bottom and low pressure at the top). This pressure gradient results in an upward driving force, which expels molten material from the top of the groove. Therefore, in laser grooving, off-axial jets are more effective than coaxial jets in providing a driving force for molten material expulsion. Most current laser systems use a coaxial nozzle with a parallel or convergent flow passage (Figure 13.13) (33).

Recent experimental studies in nozzle design have used convergent–divergent and ring nozzles to improve laser cutting. As convergent–divergent nozzle is used in conjunction with a supersonic jet to produce a more favorable shock structure for through-cutting (Figure 13.14a). Convergent–divergent nozzles minimize the sharp corners encountered on convergent jets, resulting in less divergence of the exiting gas. A ring nozzle allows the simultaneous flow of two gases through separate circular and annular sections (Figure 13.14b). The gas jet parameters found significantly to affect the pressure gradient include the reservoir pressure, nozzle–workpiece distance, jet targeting point, and jet attack angle. A high reservoir pressure results in a large pressure difference between the bottom and top of the erosion front. The nozzle–workpiece distance affects the jet diameter at the kerf inlet. In general, small nozzle–workpiece

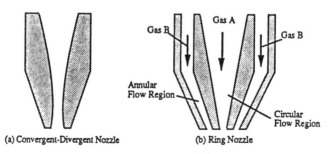

(a) Convergent-Divergent Nozzle   (b) Ring Nozzle

Figure 13.14.   **(a)** Convergent–divergent and **(b)** ring nozzles used in LBM (33).

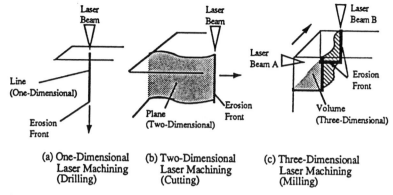

Figure 13.15.   Schematic of one-, two-, and three-dimensional laser machining (33).

distances and large jet attack angles are the principal jet characteristics that produce a large pressure gradient at the erosion front.

Lasers pose a safety hazard due to the high energy densities present in the beam, specular reflections, and the fumes that may be emitted by the workpiece during processing. All industrial lasers are classified as class IV lasers (37) (hazardous to view under direct or diffusely scattered conditions and fire hazard). The following precautions should be taken in a production environment:

The beam delivery system should totally enclose the laser beam.

The workpiece, laser head, and positioning stages should be enclosed to prevent the escape of stray beams.

Applications, Capabilities, and Limitations

LBM is capable of machining metals, ceramics, plastics, composites, wood, glass, and rubber. Laser drilling has been used in industry for producing holes in turbine blades, combustion chambers, and aerosol nozzles, among other applications. Laser cutting is used to produce intricate two-dimensional shapes in workpieces made out of materials such as sheet metal and paper up to 15 mm thick with high cutting speeds. Laser scribing has been used to create channels in ceramic substrates for cooling and identification labels in finished parts. Research efforts are made on three-dimensional laser machining to implement turning, milling, and threading operations (33). Figure 13.15 illustrates different operations by LBM (33).

With the development of miniaturization of electronic components in recent years, an emerging field for laser machining is the area of micromachining. Typical micromachining processes produce kerfs with depth and width less than 100 μm. Although CO_2 and Nd : YAG lasers are both used in micromachining, pulsed Nd : YAG lasers are more common due to their high energy densities and small focused spot (to 2 μm diameter in some applications) (38).

LBM is a viable process to mechanical material removal methods in many industrial applications, particularly in the processing of difficult-to-machine materials such as hardened metals, ceramics, and composites. The unique characteristics of LBM determine its machining capability. As a thermal process, the effectiveness of LBM depends on the thermal properties and, to a certain extent, the optical properties rather than the mechanical properties of the material to be machined. Therefore, materials that have low thermal diffusivity and conductivity are particularly well suited for laser machining. Laser machining is a noncontact process and no cutting forces are generated by the laser. As a result, it does not cause tool wear and mechanically induced workpiece surface damage. When combined with a multiaxis workpiece positioning system or robot, the LBM can be used for drilling, cutting, grooving, welding, and heat-treating processes on a single machine. This flexibility eliminates the transportation necessary for processing parts with a set of specialized machines. LBM's capability also includes its potential to perform multidimensional cutting.

The main issues in any laser machining process are material removal rate, dimensional accuracy, and surface quality. The material removal rate is governed in each case by the propagation speed of the erosion front. Dimensional accuracy is determined particularly by the hole taper for laser drilling, the kerf geometry for laser cutting, and the groove shape for three-dimensional machining. Surface quality for all laser machining processes is related to factors such as surface roughness, dross formation, and the heat-affected zone.

The capabilities and limitations of LBM drilling can be summarized as follows:

1. Higher accuracies and smaller dimensions can be achieved with laser drilling than with conventional drilling methods. Depending on the focusing lens used, hole diameters between 0.001 and 0.050 in. (0.018 and 1.3 mm) are achievable.

2. High drilling rates can be achieved in a production environment by using a pulsed beam source. By coordinating workpiece motions with the pulse period, drilling rates above 100 holes/s can be achieved.

3. The laser allows holes to be drilled at high angles of incidence to the surface (up to 80°). Shallow angle drilling is difficult to achieve mechanically due to tool directions.

4. Holes with stepped diameters cannot be drilled using a laser.

5. Due to instabilities in the laser drilling process, depth control in blind hole drilling is difficult.

6. For deep holes, the effects of beam divergence may become unacceptable.

Large-diameter holes (diameters above 0.050 in. or 1.3 mm) can be produced by a trepanning method, in which the beam is scanned in a circular trajectory to obtain the final geometry. The trepanning method is actually a circular through-cutting technique, with the machining speed determined by a scanning velocity of the beam.

The capabilities and limitations of two-dimensional laser cutting can be summarized as follows:

1. For most industrial materials with workpiece thicknesses up to 10 mm, laser cutting produces a significantly higher material removal rate than mechanical cutting or shearing.

2. Laser cutting produces kerf widths that are narrower than those achievable with mechanical cutting. This results in less material wasted during cutting operations.

3. When coupled with a multiaxis position control system for the workpiece or beam, shapes can also be cut from curved workpieces. Conventional mechanical methods can cut only flat workpieces effectively. Lasers can be applied to trimming operations to remove flash and burrs from curved parts.

4. For cutting of fibrous material such as wood, paper, or composites, the laser beam vaporizes the volume of material to be removed, thereby eliminating the residue and debris that remain after mechanical cutting. This reduces the need for solid waste collection and disposal and reduces the health hazard in the work environment.

5. Laser cutting effectiveness declines as the workpiece thickness increases. Workpieces greater than 15 mm in thickness generally cannot be cut effectively by modern industrial lasers.

6. Laser cutting produces a tapered kerf shape, compared with the straight vertical kerf walls achievable by conventional methods. The kerf taper is a result of the divergence of the laser beam and becomes more pronounced as the workpiece thickness increases. The kerf taper can be reduced by adjusting the focal point of the laser beam to the interior of the workpiece instead of at the workpiece surface.

Three-dimensional laser machining, laser grooving, and laser scribing have the following advantages over conventional techniques (33):

1. Three-dimensional laser machining can perform turning, threading, and milling operations on materials that are difficult to machine mechanically due to high hardness, brittleness, and abrasiveness.

2. Lasers can be used to scribe or mark permanent identification patterns on metallic or ceramic parts. Laser-marked IDs can withstand greater amounts of wear than those marked with other methods.

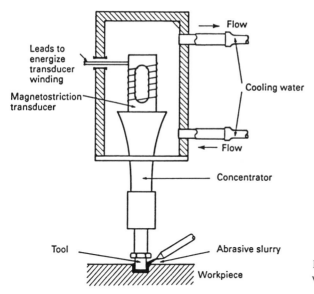

Figure 13.16. A schematic view of an USM system (2).

3. Because lasers can be focused to a small spot, they are ideal for micromachining applications to repair defective integrated circuit components that would otherwise be scrapped.

Research Issues

The main research in LBM is concentrated on three-dimensional machining. Research also is attempting to use optic fibers to transport high power laser beams in the factory. Simultaneous use of more than one laser beam is also of immense interest for researchers.

13.7 ULTRASONIC MACHINING

Ultrasonic machining (USM) was developed primarily because of the need to machine hard, brittle materials effectively. USM is a process in which material is removed from the workpiece surface by the cutting action of an abrasive slurry driven by a vibrating tool at a high frequency (above 20 Khz) (1, 2, 17). Ultrasonic machining process is able to machine effectively all materials harder than 40 HRC, although USM is applicable to nearly any material, whether conductive or nonconductive, metallic, ceramic, or composite.

Process Mechanism

In the USM process, the mechanical ultrasonic vibration, which is generated by the conversion of high frequency electrical signals to high frequency linear mechanical motion by a transducer, is transmitted to the tool through a tool holder (Figure 13.16). The tool is shaped in the exact configuration to be reproduced into the workpiece. The tool vibrates with an amplitude less than 0.1 mm. For efficient material removal to take place, the tool and tool holder must be designed with due consideration of mass, shape, and mechanical properties so that resonance can be achieved within the frequency range of the USM machine. The gap between the vibrating tool and workpiece is filled with an abrasive slurry of water and small abrasive particles.

The material removal due to USM is complex and not fully understood. The generally agreed on mechanisms responsible for material removal in ultrasonic machining are listed below (39).

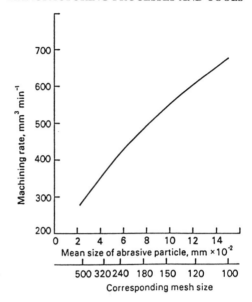

Figure 13.17. Change of MRR with grit size in USM (2).

1. Direct impact of the abrasive particles on the workpiece by the tool results in material removal and particle crushing. This is possible when the abrasive particle sizes are larger than the working gap.
2. Impact of the free-moving abrasive particles with a certain velocity on the workpiece is possible when the size of the particles is smaller than the working gap.
3. Erosion of the work surface occurs due to cavitation effects of the abrasive slurry. It has been reported that among the above-mentioned mechanisms, the first two are primarily responsible for major stock removal (40, 41). As material is removed, a counterbalanced gravity feed, or servo motor–driven feed mechanism, continuously advances the tool into the newly formed cavity, maintaining a constant gap between the tool and workpiece.

Although the volumetric material removal rates of USM are relatively low, the process remains economically competitive because of its ability to generate complex cavities or multiple holes in workpiece materials with a single tool pass, especially in drilling and shaping hard or fragile materials. In addition, due to the absence of direct contact between tool and workpiece, USM is a valuable process for avoiding in-process breakage of fragile workpieces.

Process Parameters

The major USM process variable affecting removal rate, accuracy, and surface finish are the tool vibration amplitude and frequency, abrasive size, and tool tip force. The amplitude of tool vibration has a significant effect on the removal rates. With an increase in the amplitude, the removal rate generally increases linearly. Grit size and amplitude of tool vibration have a similar and closely related effect on material removal rates (MRR). As shown in Figure 13.17, the MRR rises with grit size until the grit size becomes comparable with the vibration amplitude. Machining rates have been found to increase with the increase of concentration of abrasive up to concentrations of 40% by volume. The distribution of the slurry over the machining zone is also found to affect machining rates. The improved flow of slurry results in enhanced machining rates. Figure 13.18 shows a rise in machining rate with the static load of the tool on the workpiece during USM. The tool tip forces are usually less than 50 N, but forces as high as 500 N are possible. In most USM operations, the frequency of vibration is set between 10 and 40 Khz, with the most common frequency being 20 Khz. In most cases, the frequency is not considered in USM because the user rarely varies the frequency over a wide range. Standard

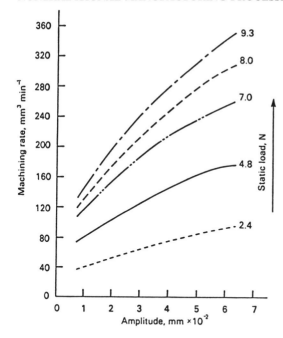

Figure 13.18. Change of MRR with the static tool load (2).

equipment offers a narrow range of frequency adjustment. The effect of frequency on MRR appears to be more pronounced in the machining of brittle materials than in the machining of ductile materials. A higher frequency of vibration often increases the machining rates. The abrasive particle size affects the surface finish of the workpiece. The surface finish improves with a decrease in grain size of the abrasives. The amplitude of vibration has a smaller effect on roughness. As the amplitude is increased, the surface roughness increases, because individual grains are pressed further into the workpiece surface. In USM, the surface finish depends on the workpiece materials and grain sizes (Figure 13.19) (2). The viscosity of the liquid carrier for the abrasive also affects surface finishes.

Equipment

All USM machines share common subsystems regardless of the physical size or power. The most important of these subsystems are the power supply, transducer, tool holder, and abrasive material. The power supply for USM is a high power, harmonic-wave generator. It converts low frequency (60 Hz) electrical power into high frequency (approximately 20 kHz) electrical power. This electrical power is then supplied to the transducer to create the mechanical vibration. Two types of transducers are often used in USM systems: piezoelectric and magnetostrictive. Piezoelectric transducers exhibit an extremely high electromechanical conversion efficiency (up to 96%), which eliminates the need for water cooling of the transducer. This type of transducer is available with power capacities up to 900 W. Magnetostrictive transducers are usually constructed from a laminated stack of nickel or alloy sheets that, when influenced by a strong magnetic field, have a change in their length. Magnetostrictive transducers offer higher power capacity but have low electromechanical conversion efficiencies (20 to 35%), and water cooling is necessary. The function of the tool holder is to connect the tool to the transducer and hence to transmit the sonic energy to the tool. The most commonly used materials to construct tool holders are monel, titanium, and stainless steel, which are of good acoustic properties and highly resistant to fatigue cracking. Tool holders are often available in two configurations: nonamplifying and amplifying. Nonamplifying tool holders are cylindrical and result in the same stroke amplitude at the output end as at the input end. Amplifying tool holders have a modified cross-section and are designed to increase the amplitude of the tool stroke as much as 600%.

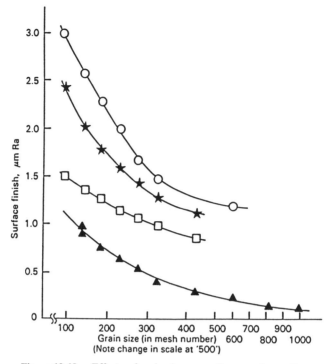

Figure 13.19.   Effects of grain size on surface roughness (2).

Because of the gain in tool stroke, amplifying tool holders are able to remove material up to 10 times faster than the nonamplifying types.

To minimize tool wear, tools should be made of relatively ductile materials such as stainless steel, brass, and mild steel. The harder the tool material, the faster its wear rate. Depending on the abrasive, the workpiece material, and the tool material, workpiece–tool wear ratios can range from 1:1 to 100:1. Several abrasives are available in various particle (grit) sizes for USM, including diamond (HK = 6500 to 7000), cubic boron nitride (CBN; HK = 4700), boron carbide (B_4C; HK = 2800), silicon carbide (SiC; HK = 2480 to 2500), and aluminum oxide (Al_2O_3; HK = 2000 to 2100). Boron carbide is the most widely used abrasive in USM operations. It is often used for processing such materials as tungsten carbide, metals, high density ceramics, minerals, and semiprecious and precious stones. Silicon carbide is used primarily for low density ceramics, glass, silicon, germanium, and mineral stones. Aluminum oxide is used for glass, low density sintered or hard-powder compounds. The abrasive grain size influences the removal rate and surface finish. Abrasives for USM are generally available in grain sizes ranging from 10 to 140 μm (mesh numbers 800 to 240). Smaller grain sizes produce finer finishes but reduce the machining rate. The abrasive material is mixed with water to form the slurry. The most common abrasive concentration is 50% by weight; however, this can vary from 30% to 60%. Thinner mixtures are used to promote flow efficiency when drilling deep holes or when forming complex cavities. The main parameters and outputs for USM can be listed as follows:

Parameter	Range
Power supply frequency	20 kHz
Abrasive hardness	2000–7000 HK
Tolerance	±0.025 to ±0.007 mm
Aspect ratio	40:1
Penetration rate	0.025–25 mm/min

Applications and Process Capabilities

Ultrasonic machining is effective for precision machining of hard or brittle materials. USM is limited by the softness of the material. Workpiece materials softer than 40 HRC result in prohibitively long cycles. The best machining rates can be obtained on materials harder than 60 HRC.

Some of the successful ultrasonic machining applications involve drilling holes or machining cavities in ceramic materials. Special USM tools are often used to produce simultaneously a multitude of holes in different patterns. These gang-drilling techniques significantly increase productivity without compromising quality. A novel use for ultrasonic machining has been the multistep process for fabricating silicon nitride (Si_3N_4) turbine blades. The first step in manufacturing the blades uses a shaped tool to trepan ultrasonically the blade blank from a billet of Si_3N_4. A second shaped tool is then used to generate the rough airfoil shape by trepanning in a direction 90° to the initial cut and to a specific depth. After the cut is completed, a diamond-slicing wheel is used to cut in from the sides to intersect with the bottom of the trepan cut.

A variation of USM known as rotary ultrasonic machining (RUM), involves the use of rotating diamond-plated tools for drilling, milling, and threading operations. The RUM tool is vibrated axially at a frequency of approximately 20 kHz, which acts to reduce friction between the tool and workpiece material and to eliminate loading of the diamond abrasive. The amplitude of the ultrasonic vibrations is less than that used for USM, typically less than 0.025 mm. The most popular use of RUM is for drilling high aspect ratio holes in hard, brittle materials. Current capabilities include hole diameters from 0.5 to 40 mm at depths up to 300 mm. Aspect ratio up to 200% can be achieved using roughing and finishing passes. Milling by RUM is accomplished with diamond-plated cutting tools used in the same manner as conventional end mills. Because of the rapid material removal rate and low cutting forces in exceptionally hard materials, RUM milling is finding many new applications. By rotating both the tool and workpiece, internal and external threading operations can be achieved. Although the initial cost of RUM equipment is higher than conventional drilling, milling, and thread-grinding equipment, this difference is quickly offset by the savings realized from the extended tool life, increased productivity, and reduced workpiece breakage.

One of the advantages of USM is that the machining is burrless and distortionless. The machining does not have any thermal effect. Cavity sinking by USM is achieved in a single pass. The limitations of USM include tool wear during machining due to the impact of abrasive grit. The tool must be changed frequently. Frequent tune-ups are also necessary to keep the system running at the high frequency. The slurry transportation system design also limits the depth of holes produced by USM. The tool design, to a certain extent, is still a trial-and-error procedure.

Research Issues

The research in USM process continues to be focused on understanding the process mechanism, parametric relationship, and integration with other processes such as EDM (42, 43). Recent efforts have also been directed toward finding RUM process relationships (44, 45).

BIBLIOGRAPHY

1. G.F. BENEDICT, *Nontraditional Manufacturing Processes*, Marcel Dekker, Inc., New York, 1987.
2. J.A. McGEOUGH, *Advanced Methods of Machining*, Chapman and Hall, London, 1988.
3. K.P. RAJURKAR et al., "The Role of Nontraditional Manufacturing Processes in Future Manufacturing Industries" in *Proceedings of Manufacturing International '92*, ASME, Dallas, Texas, 1992, pp. 23–37.
4. W.M. WANG and K.P. RAJURKAR, "Improvement in EDM Tool Wear Ratio and Material Removal Rate with Modified R.F. Control Unit," in *Transactions of the North American Manufacturing Research Institute of SME*, Dearborn Mich., 1990 Vol. 18, pp. 244–249.
5. K.P. RAJURKAR and W.M. WANG, "Real Time Stochastic Model and Control of EDM," *Ann. CIRP* **39**(1), 187–190 (1990).
6. R. SNOEYS, "Non-Conventional Machining Techniques, The State of the Art" in K.P. Rajurkar, eds., *Advances in Nontraditional Machining, PED* **22**, 1–22 (1986).

7. W. KONIG, D.F. DAUW, G. LEVY, and U. PANTEN, "EDM-Future Steps Towards the Machining of Ceramics," *Ann. CIRP* **37**(2), 623–631 (1988).

8. H. LI, *Micro-EDM,* paper presented at the EDM conference on SME, Grand Rapids, Mich., 1991.

9. D.F. DAUW, C.A. BROWN, J.P. van GRIETHUYSEN, and J.F.L.M. ALVERT, "Surface Topography Investigations by Fractal Analysis of Spark-Eroded, Electrically Conductive Ceramics," *Ann. CIRP* **39**(1), 161–165 (1991).

10. N. SAITO, "Recent Electrical Discharge Machining (E.D.M.): Techniques in Japan," *Bull. Jpn. Soc. Precision Eng.* **18**(2), 110–116 (1984).

11. N. MOHRI, N. SAITO, and M. HIGASHI, "A New Process of Finish Machining on Free Surface by EDM Methods," *Ann. CIRP* **40**(1), 207–210 (1991).

12. D. KREMET, J.L. LEBRUN, B. JOSARI, and A. MOISAN, "Effects of Ultrasonic Vibrations on the Performances in EDM," *Ann. CIRP* **38**(1), 199–202 (1989).

13. J.P. KRUTH, *Automatic Control in Electro Physical and Chemical Machining,* paper presented at the 10th International Symposium of Electromachining (ISEM-X), Magdeburg, Germany, 1992.

14. M.F. DeVRIES, N.A. DUFFIE, J.P. KRUTH, and D.F. DAUW, "Integration of EDM within a CIM Environment," *Ann. CIRP* **39**(2), 665–672 (1990).

15. K.P. RAJURKAR, C.W. WALTON, and T.A. KOTTWITZ, "State-of-the-Art Assessment of the Electrochemical Machining Process" in *Report to the National Center for Manufacturing Sciences,* 1990, pp. 98–105.

16. D.G. RISKO, *Electrochemical Machining,* paper presented at the SME Non-Traditional Machining Conference, Orlando, Fla., 1989.

17. T.J. DROZDA and C. WICKS, *Tool and Manufacturing Engineers Handbook,* Vol. 1, SME, Dearborn, Mich., 1983.

18. J.A. McGEOUGH, *Principles of Electrochemical Machining,* Chapman and Hall, London, 1974.

19. L.J. RHOADES, "Abrasive Flow Machining," SME, 1989, Tech. Paper No. MR89-145.

20. W.B. PERRY, "Abrasive Flow Machining," *Abrasive Eng. Soc. Mag.,* (Sept.–Oct.) (1982).

21. J. STACKHOUSE, "Abrasive Flow Machining" in *Proceedings of the 4th Biennial International Manufacturing Technology Conference,* National Machine Tool Builders Association, McLean, Va., 1988, pp. 57–70.

22. T. KOHUT, *Surface Finishing with Abrasive Flow Machining* in *Proceedings of the Fourth International Aluminum Extrusion Technology Seminar,* Vol. 2, The Aluminum Association, Washington, D.C., 1988.

23. T. KOHUT, "Automatic Die Polishing" in *Extrusion Productivity Through Automation,* Vol. 1, The Aluminum Association, Washington D.C., 1984, pp. 193–202.

24. D. EMANUAL, "Power Putty," *Hot Rod* (Sept.) 48–51 (1991).

25. K. PRZYLEN, "Abrasive Flow Machining—A Process for Surface Finishing and Deburring of Workpieces with a Complicated Shape by Means of an Abrasive Laden Medium" in K.P. Rajurkar, ed., *Advances in Non-Traditional Machining, PED* **22**, 101–110 (1968).

26. A.J. FLETCHER, J.B. HULL, J. MACKIE, and S.A. TRENGOVE, "Computer Modelling of the Abrasive Flow Machining Process" in *Proceedings of the International Conference on Surface Engineering: Current Trends and Future Prospects, Toronto, Ontario, Canada, June 1990,* pp. 592–601.

27. R.E. WILLIAMS and K.P. RAJURKAR, "Metal Removal and Surface Finish Characteristics in Abrasive Flow Machining" in R.J. Stango and P.R. Fitzpatrick, eds., *Mechanics of Deburring and Surface Finishing Processes, ASME, PED* **38**, 93–106 (1989).

28. U.S. Pat. 4,648,215. M. Hashish, M. Kirby, and Y.H. Pao.

29. G.P. TILLY and W. SAGE, "The Interaction of Particle and Material Behavior in Erosion Process," *Wear* **16**, 447–465 (1970).

30. M. HASHISH, "Advanced Machining with Abrasive Waterjets—Theory and Applications," in *Proceedings of the Nontraditional Machining Symposium, Orlando, 1989,* pp. 1–44.

31. M. HASHISH, *Steel Cutting with Abrasive Waterjets,* paper presented at the 6th International Symposium on Jet Cutting Technology, BHRA, UK, April 1992.

32. M. HASHISH, *Current Capabilities for Precision Machining with Abrasive-Waterjets* paper presented at the Nontraditional Machining Symposium, Orlando, Fla., 1991.

33. G. CHRYSSOLOURIS, *Laser Machining–Theory and Practice,* Springer-Verlag, New York, 1991.

34. Y. ARATA, H. MARUO, I. MIYAMOTO, and S. TAKEUCHI, *Improvement of Cut Quality in Laser-Gas-Cutting Stainless Steel,* paper presented at the First International Laser Processing Conference, 1981.

35. S. COPLEY, *Laser Machining Ceramics,* paper presented at the First International Laser Processing Conference, 1981.

36. V.P. BABENKO and V.P. TYCHINSKII, "Gas-Jet Laser Cutting [Review]," Sov. J. Quantum Elec. **2**(5), 399–410 (1973).

37. J.T. LUXON and D.E. PARKER, *Industrial Lasers and Their Applications,* Prentice-Hall, Inc., Englewood Cliffs, N.J., 1985, pp. 200–242.

38. K.R. BUBE, A.Z. MILLER, A. HOWE, and B. ANTONI, "Influence of Laser-Trim Configuration on Stability of Small Thick-Film Resistors" in *Lasers in Modern Industry,* Society of Manufacturing Engineers, Dearborn, Mich., 1979, pp. 245–250.

39. V. SOUNDARARAJAN and V. RADHAKRISHNAN, "An Experimental Investigation on the Basic Mechanism Involved in Ultrasonic Machining," *Int. J. Machine Tool Des. Res.* **26**(3), 307–321 (1986).

40. M.C. SHAW, "Ultrasonic Grinding," *Microtechnik* **10**(6), 257–260 (1956).

41. V.F. KAZANTSEV, "Ultrasonic Cutting" in *Physical Principles of Ultrasonic Technology,* Vol. 1, Plenum Press, New York, pp. 3–37.

42. G.S. KANITH, A. NANDY, and K. SINGH, "On the Mechanics of Material Removal in Ultrasonic Machining," *Int. J. MTDR* **19**, 33–41 (1979).

43. D. KREMER et al., "Ultrasonic Machining Improves EDM Technology, Electromachining in J.R. Crookall, ed., *Proceedings of the 7th International Symposium 12–14 Apr. 1983,* Brimingham, UK, pp. 67–76.

44. D. PRABHAKAR, P.M. FERREIRA, and M. HASELKORN, "An Experimental Investigation of Material Removal Rates in Rotary Ultrasonic Machining" in *Transactions of the North American Manufacturing Research Institute of SME,* Dearborn, Mich., 1992, Vol. 20, pp. 211–218.

45. C. CRUZ and K.P. RAJURKAR, "Study of Rotary Ultrasonic Machining of Al_2O_3 and PSZ," *Proceedings of the Symposium on Machining of Composite Materials II (ASM),* Pittsburgh, Pa., Oct. 1993.

CHAPTER 14
Machine Tools

Yung C. Shin
School of Mechanical Engineering
Purdue University

14.1 INTRODUCTION

Machine tools are the machinery used to process metals and nonmetallic materials to get desired shapes or properties in manufacturing industries. Therefore, they constitute the core of manufacturing systems. The modern form of machine tools was first introduced during the industrial revolution in the 18th century with the birth of steam engines. Those steam engine–powered machine tools opened the era of automation along with the use of jigs and fixtures. Particularly, the continual development of new tool materials since the early 20th century has been the major driving force in advancing the technology of machine tools. More rigid and higher speed machine tools have been required to use fully the capability of new tool materials. It is not uncommon to see machining operations of cast iron with cutting speeds exceeding 3000 fpm in the automotive industry today.

The way of automation using machine tools changed significantly as the demands of market shifted from inflexible automation for mass production to flexible automation for batch production. The introduction of numerically controlled (NC) machine tools made it possible to perform a variety of jobs on a single machine. Since its inception, the use of NC machine tools has shown a rapid growth. Currently, more than 75% of the money spent to purchase new machine tools goes to computer numerically controlled (CNC) machine tools.

Accuracy of CNC machine tools has improved significantly. Accuracy better than 0.0002 to 0.0003 in. is commonly achieved on production CNC machining centers at present. This improved accuracy is attributed to construction of more rigid and precision mechanical components, use of computer controlled compensation of positional errors, and adoption of more advanced microprocessors to generate required trajectory commands. In modern CNC machining centers, many in-process sensors are used to feedback various operating conditions to the controllers. In some cases, machine controllers can make adjustments automatically to improve accuracy or performance.

Similar progress has been made in forming machine tools. For instance, precise control of a forming process is achieved by continuous monitoring of pressure or temperature and controlling the ram velocity to improve the properties of a part being formed. Various machine tools for nontraditional processes have also been developed. Electrodischarge machines (EDM) are used to erode the work material by discharging electric sparks between the tool and workpiece. Both spark voltage and feed must be controlled. Laser cutting machines can cut various difficult-to-cut materials by focusing high energy light beams onto a small area and thereby vaporizing the material.

In general, most machine tools require precise motion control with feedback of various sensor signals. Manufacturing processes are typically stochastic, time varying, or uncertain due to the variation of material property, temperature, and environmental conditions. Therefore, true automation of machine tools would require intelligent process condition monitoring, diagnostics, and intelligent control. Detailed treatment of these subjects is beyond the scope of this book. This chapter describes some of the important basic attributes of modern machine tools.

Figure 14.1. Optical encoder.

14.2 SENSORS AND ACTUATORS FOR MACHINE TOOLS

In any motion control system, sensors and actuators largely affect the performance of the system. Machine tools must provide precise positioning or motion often in a synchronized fashion along a desired trajectory. Hence, proper selection and use of sensors and actuators is very important. Some commonly used sensors and actuators are discussed next.

Sensors

In general, there are two types of sensors: digital and analogue. Digital sensors generate outputs that can be directly fed into a digital computer. Digital signals are more immune to noise and do not require A/D converters. However, resolution can be limited by the physical construction of sensors. Typical digital sensors are optical encoders, photodiode arrays for vision systems, and laser interferometers. On the other hand, analogue sensors produce a voltage proportional to the measured variable. Therefore, signals must be converted into a digital form by using an A/D converter.

The direct variables typically measured in machine tool control are position, velocity, load, torque, power, temperature, pressure, strain, etc., although not all of them are required to be measured. The major characteristics one must consider in choosing sensors are the dynamic bandwidth, range, resolution, and sensitivity. For instance, a capacitance sensor might give a good resolution, but might have a limited operating range in distance.

Positional sensors are the most commonly used type for machine tool control, because positioning of moving parts is the primary function of them. The positional sensors are used to measure either linear or angular displacement. Encoders and resolvers are by far most commonly used. An encoder consists of a thin disk with many transparent and opaque slots, a light source and photo detectors. As the disk rotates with a shaft, the light beam penetrates through the transparent slot or gets blocked by an opaque area, as shown in Figure 14.1. Photodetectors receive the light beams and produce a voltage. Therefore, as the shaft rotates, a pulse train is generated and the number of pulses counted determines the position.

Resolvers and synchros are, on the other hand, analogue devices. A resolver consists of a stator coil, to which an AC current is supplied, and a rotor coil, where an alternating current is induced, as shown in Figure 14.2. The amplitude of the induced current changes as the rotational angle increases. If an alternating voltage, V_s, is applied to the stator coil by

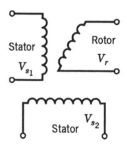

Figure 14.2. Rotary resolver.

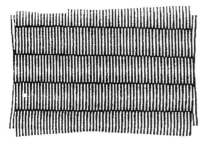 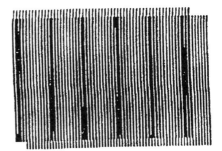

Figure 14.3. Moire fringe patterns in optical gratings.

$$V_{S_1} = V \sin \omega t$$
$$V_{S_2} = V \cos \omega t \tag{1}$$

then induced voltage in the rotor becomes

$$V_r = V_{S_1} \cos \theta - V_{S_2} \sin \theta$$
$$= V \sin (\omega t - \theta) \tag{2}$$

where θ is the rotational angle of the rotor with respect to the stator and ω is the frequency of the alternating current.

The synchros differ from resolvers in the number of stator windings. The stator of a synchro has three windings (Y connection) 120° apart, while a resolver uses two windings for the rotor, which are 90° apart. The induced voltage in the rotor caused by two perpendicular stator coils shows the same phase shift as the angular position with respect to the stator winding. Linear resolvers work in a similar fashion to rotary resolvers. The principal difference is that windings are made on a linear scale so that linear position can be directly measured.

Moire fringe gratings use two sets of finely graded glass scales. One set of grating is oriented slightly angled against the other set to form fringes as shown in Figure 14.3. As one set of grating glides against the other, the fringe patterns move along in a greatly amplified fashion. The magnification depends on the distance between the grades on the grating and the angle of alignment. The pitch of the fringes can be interpolated to obtain improved resolution. This type of sensor is used for very high precision machines and are known to be one of the most accurate technique for measuring displacement.

Other position sensors include potentiometers, linear variable differential transformers (LVDT), capacitance probes, proximeters, and laser interferometers. Laser interferometers can provide excellent resolution as well as a long measurement range. The latest laser interferometers use double-frequency lasers. A portion of the beam is reflected through a fixed mirror, while the other beam travels through air and gets reflected by a mirror mounted on the moving object. Due to the Doffler effect, there is a slight variation in the frequency of the reflected beam from the moving mirror, and thus fringe patterns are formed. The fringes can be used to detect the change in frequency, which is proportional to the velocity of the object. This principle is schematically shown in Figure 14.4. Despite the high accuracy, the high cost limits the use of laser interferometers to large machines or high precision machine tools.

Velocity sensors are necessary for the velocity control loop in machine tools. Tachometers are the most commonly used velocity sensors. Tachometers are similar to small DC motors in structure and consist of a permanent magnet stator and a wound armature. As the armature rotates through the magnetic field generated by the stator, a voltage is induced in the armature coil proportionally to the rotational speed. Typical output of a tachometer shows an AC ripple superimposed on the DC output. A tachometer with low ripple amplitude should be considered in designing a control system. If necessary, this ripple effect can be eliminated by using a low pass filter.

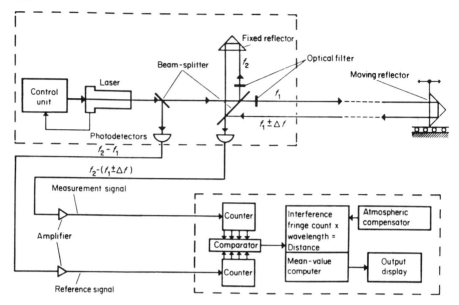

Figure 14.4.   Principles of a double-frequency laser.

In-process Monitoring

To realize automated operation of CNC machine tools, many process conditions must be monitored and diagnosed, and a suitable control action must be taken. Desirable process conditions to be monitored would entail tool wear, took breakage, surface roughness, part accuracy, vibration, chip break, etc. Many of these process conditions are not directly measurable during the process, and hence indirect sensing techniques must be adopted.

Monitoring of tool wear has been attempted with many different techniques, including force, acoustic emission, vibration, temperature, optical, and motor power. Among these techniques, those based on the measurement of cutting force and acoustic emission are most promising. Currently, commercial tool wear monitoring systems based on these two techniques are available. The major shortcoming of these techniques at present is the lack of robustness in the sense that monitored signals are sensitive to the variation of cutting condition and hence must be calibrated for each specific condition.

Inferencing tool wear by measuring the geometry change using a gap detection sensor has been tried for turning processes. This technique is relatively easy to implement and less sensitive to the cutting condition change. However, separating machine tool positioning error and deflection becomes a problem. Workpiece geometry can be measured by using various optical, pneumatic, mechanical and ultrasonic methods. Optical techniques can provide accurate measurements and appear to be attractive for high precision machines. However, the alignment of optics is usually difficult and they are limited to the measurement of dry and clean surfaces. Mechanical types such as friction rollers are less accurate, but more robust.

Monitoring of vibration levels is usually achieved by using an accelerometer or a velocity pickup. Chatter can be detected by either monitoring vibration amplitudes or cutting forces. Excessive vibration can degrade workpiece quality and can cause tool breakage or machine damage. Surface roughness is an important attribute of workpiece quality. Unfortunately, profileometers cannot be used for in-process measurements. Optical techniques have been proposed by a number of researchers, but there is no commercially available system for in-process monitoring. Ultrasonic techniques have shown a high potential for such applications.

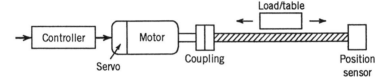

Figure 14.5.   Schematic diagram for a feed drive.

Actuators

There are two types of actuators used for machine tools: electric and hydraulic motors. Electric motors provide a wide range of speeds and torques with relatively small size, and hence are suitable for small- to medium-size machines. On the other hand, hydraulic motors are mainly used for heavy-duty machines that require high torque or force. Control of hydraulic motors is, however, more difficult due to nonlinear characteristics of various components in the hydraulic system. These actuators are used to construct feed drives and, therefore, are required to have good velocity controllability. A typical feed drive is schematically shown in Figure 14.5. A signal from the controller is amplified and supplied to the motor. The motor produces a torque to rotate the shaft through a coupler, while linear motors drive the table directly. The position or velocity signal measured by an encoder, a resolver, or a tachometer is fed back to the controller so that closed-loop control of the feed drive can be achieved.

Electric motors can be categorized into DC motors, stepping motors, and AC motors. DC motors have low moment of inertia and provide high acceleration torque. Excellent speed controllability over a wide range also makes them suitable for various control schemes. DC motors are widely used for spindles and feed drives. Typical DC motors consist of a rotor called armature, a stator, and a commutator with brushes. When a DC voltage is supplied to the armature, a torque is generated due to the magnetic field generated by the stator coil. This principle is schematically shown in Figure 14.6. The electrical equation for the armature is

$$V_A = R_A \cdot I_A + V_b + L_A \frac{dI_A}{dt} \tag{3}$$

where V_A is the supplied voltage to the armature, R_A is the resistance in the armature winding, L_A is the leakage inductance in the armature winding, and V_b is the back-induced emf. The back-induced emf is a function of rotational speed and is given by

$$V_b = K_b \cdot \omega(t) \tag{4}$$

where K_b is called voltage constant. The torque developed by the motor is used to drive the inertia and is represented by

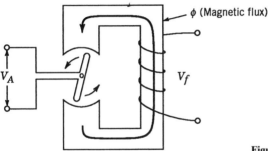

Figure 14.6.   Principle of a D-C motor.

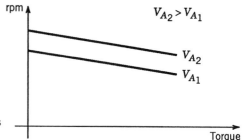

Figure 14.7. Steady-state characteristics of D-C motors.

$$T_m = K_T \cdot I_A(t)$$

$$= J \frac{d\omega(t)}{dt} + T_L + b\omega(t) \tag{5}$$

where J is the moment of inertia of the rotor and shaft, T_L is the external torque, and b is the damping coefficient. The steady state characteristics of DC motors are shown in Figure 14.7.

DC motors vary in construction and design. Wound-field DC motors have both armature and stator windings (coils). Permanent magnet direct-drive motors are constructed with a permanent magnet and stator and are often called torque motors. Brushless DC motors use a permanent magnet rotor with alternating current supplied to the stator coil, thereby eliminating the problem of the brush wear, and thus they resemble some AC motors.

AC motors can overcome the disadvantage stemming from slip rings and brushes used in DC motors and provide high efficiency, speeds, and constant torque. However, due to the difficulty in controlling speed, earlier applications of AC motors were limited to constant speed drives such as the spindle motor of manual machines, for which discrete speed selection was possible by using gears or pulleys. Recently, with the development of more sophisticated controllers, AC motors have become more popular for variable speed control applications.

AC motors consist of a rotor and a stator with separate windings. The magnetic flux in the stator alternated by an AC supply generates a rotating field that induces a voltage with a resultant current in the stator windings and, consequently, produces a torque. Therefore, this type of AC motor is called an induction or asynchronous motor. On the other hand, the rotor windings can be supplied with DC or replaced with permanent magnets. This type is called a synchronous AC motor and is similar to a brushless DC motor.

Stepping motors have little significant in modern machine tools. In principle, the speed of a stepping motor is controlled by a number of pulses generated per second. The rotor can be either a permanent magnet or a three-phase winding. Most stepping motors are used with open-loop control, although closed-loop control is possible. Due to the low cost and easiness of operation, stepping motors are used in small nonprecision machine tools or in peripheral devices such as tool indexing mechanism.

14.3 MACHINE TOOL ACCURACY

Accuracy of processed parts largely depends on the accuracy of the machine tool used. Therefore, recent years have seen a major thrust to improve the accuracy of machine tools. For instance, in machining, the accuracy of the machine tool has improved 10-fold for every 20 yr (1). Currently, machining accuracy of 5 to 10 μm from regular machine tools and 0.1 μm from precision machine tools is commonly achieved. The major improvement of accuracy is attributed to the use of computer numerical control, improved design and construction of machine base structure, precision drive mechanism, precision sensors, and feedback control to compensate for errors.

Many numerically controlled machine tools do not operate within the prescribed accuracy. This stems from the fact that the actual accuracy of machine tools varies widely, depending on setup, installation, operating environment, operator, and operating history. Therefore, it is

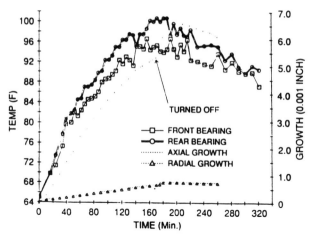

Figure 14.8. Thermal growth of a spindle. From ref. 2.

important to understand various possible sources of errors and to make a proper adjustment or compensate for the errors.

There are several factors that contribute to the inaccuracy of machine tools:

- Machine tool positional errors.
- Environmental temperature change.
- Deflection or distortion caused by clamping or process forces.
- Spindle out of roundness.
- Spindle thermal growth.
- Vibration.
- Operating condition.

The sources of these errors must be properly identified and characterized. Depending on the nature of these errors, they can be categorized into (*1*) quasi-static errors such as geometric errors, deflection, or thermally induced errors; (*2*) dynamic errors such as spindle out-of-roundness, vibration, or kinematic error; and (*3*) workpiece and tooling errors.

Thermal errors are often the most significant errors (*2*). If not properly compensated for, they can exceed several times the desired accuracy of a machine tool. These errors can result from the environmental temperature change or internal heat generation during operation, such as that from bearings. A typical thermal growth of a spindle is shown in Figure 14.8. To minimize these errors, a symmetric structure is desirable, and thermal isolation can be used. Also, thermal deformation can be precalculated or measured and compensated for by monitoring the temperature gradient.

Geometric errors arise due to imperfect geometry of various axes and can contribute significantly to the inaccuracy of a finished part. These errors can be further divided into positional error and angular error. To compensate for these errors, error components of each axis are usually measured by a laser interferometer, and the total error is predicted by using a kinematic transformation (*2, 3*). During movement, the positioning errors of a machine axis over repeated cycles exhibit apparent random characteristics due to many unknown sources of errors. More specifically, machine tool motion errors can be decomposed into deterministic (repeatable) and stochastic (nonrepeatable) parts as shown in Figure 14.9. Positional accuracy is the worst possible error and is typically defined as

$$\varepsilon = \max\{|\mu + 3\sigma|, |\mu - 3\sigma|\} \tag{6}$$

where μ is the mean positional accuracy and σ is the variance of random part. The error

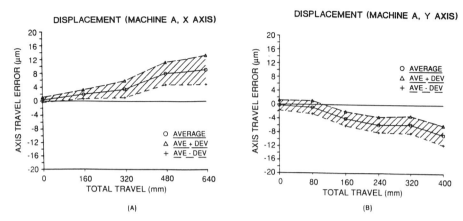

Figure 14.9. Positional errors of machine tool axis motion. From ref. 2.

compensation technique can only eliminate the mean positional errors but will not reduce the total error to zero. The stochastic part also is used to define the repeatability of a machine (4).

Slideways and bearings are critical components that affect the positional accuracy. Important considerations to be made in selecting slideways and bearings are stiffness, damping capability, accuracy, and wear resistance. Typical slideways for machine tools are constructed with hydrostatic, hydrodynamic, aerostatic, aerodynamic, or rolling bearings.

Spindles are one of the most important components of machine tools, because the error caused by a spindle directly affects the part accuracy. Spindle out of roundness and static and dynamic stiffness must be carefully considered. Both spindle out of roundness and stiffness vary with rotational speed (2, 5). Therefore, it is important to understand these characteristics as a function of rotational speed. The definition and test procedure for the spindle out of roundness are described in the ANSI/ASME standard B89.3.4.M, *Axes of Rotation*.

14.4 COMPUTER NUMERICAL CONTROL

Numerical control (NC) opened the era for flexible automation using machine tools. Use of computer programming provides the flexibility to switch from one job to another without modifying the hardware. In numerically controlled machines, the commands to control the movement of machine axes and the sequence of operation are generated by the computer, based on user-specified instructions, called the part program. In general, CNC (or NC) can interpret at least a portion of the data and perform interpolation, thereby minimizing the required user input. In addition, computer control in NC machines minimizes the dependence on operator skills and improves productivity. Therefore, in modern machine tools, NC is an indispensable technology.

The idea of controlling machine tools by a program was first conceived by John Parson in 1948. In 1951, a contract was awarded to MIT, which built and demonstrated a prototype machine in the following year by using the first digital computer to process information. Furthermore, the automatically programmed tools (APT) language was introduced as a programming tool by MIT in 1956. In the early days, punched tapes were used to read information into the controller; however, these have become obsolete with the introduction of CNC based on microprocessors and magnetic media. CNC machines comprise three major components: part program, machine control unit (MCU), and processing equipment. Part programs generated by users are interpreted by MCU, which generates commands to various actuators. Part programs generated by using high level languages such as APT must be first translated into machine-readable codes. CNC machine-readable functions are defined in ISO and EIA standards and are known as G and M functions, which are interpreted in the same way by most CNCs.

Programming directly with G and M codes is called manual programming. Manual programming is time-consuming and is prone to human errors. Therefore, many advanced programming

TABLE 14.1.   Examples of G and M Functions

Code	Function
G00	Point to point positioning
G01	Linear interpolation
G02	Circular interpolation (CW)
G03	Circular interpolation (CCW)
G17	xy plane for interpolation
G90	Absolute dimension programming
G91	Incremental dimension programming
M06	Tool change
M03	Clockwise spindle rotation
M08	Coolant start
M09	Coolant stop

tools have been developed to eliminate the need to use manual programming. However, it is still desirable for operators to become familiar with manual part programming to modify effectively the program at the machine level. Some examples of G and M codes are shown in Table 14.1.

Today, many computer-aided design (CAD) and computer-aided manufacturing (CAM) software packages provide automated part programming. Users need to specify only the geometry of a part, cutting tools, and cutting conditions to be used. Tool paths can be automatically generated and converted into a machine-readable program through postprocessing. Automated part programming allows one to generate part programs quickly from design drawings and is becoming a critical part in computer-integrated manufacturing.

A coordinate system must be defined in CNC machines for programming. Typically, the z axis is defined to coincide with the axis of rotation of a spindle and remaining translational axes are defined perpendicularly to the z axis. When a CNC machine has rotational axes, they are called a, b, and c axes and defined following the right-hand rule as shown in Figure 14.10. The fixed zero (home) position is typically located in the lower left corner of the table. On the other hand, the floating zero is an arbitrary point in the work envelope set by the operator. Basic length unit (BLU) determines the resolution of positioning and depends on the total travel length of an axis and the size of the word used in the microprocessor. For example, if 16-bit words are used in the microprocessor for the total travel length of 500 mm, then BLU becomes

$$\text{BLU} = \frac{500}{2^{16} - 1} = 0.00763 \text{ mm}$$

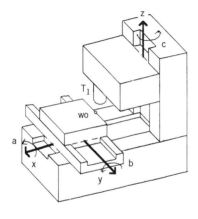

Figure 14.10.   Axis definition of machine tools.

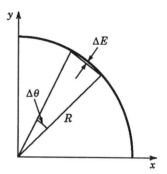

Figure 14.11. Contour error in circular interpolation.

whereas an 8-bit microprocessor will yield

$$BLU = \frac{500}{2^8 - 1} = 1.96 \text{ mm.}$$

Therefore, it is important to choose a CNC that will give adequate resolution.

One of the basic functions of CNC is interpolation. In point-to-point (PTP) interpolation, only the beginning and ending points are specified. The axis of a machine will travel at the maximum velocity possible. A good example of the use of this interpolation is positioning of x and y axes in drilling machines. This is the simplest type of interpolation. Straight-line interpolation is used to move the axes at a constant velocity, as required in milling or turning operations. Linear interpolation can be done either along any particular axis direction or in a diagonal direction. The latter requires coordination of motions in multiple axes. Contouring involves combination of movements in multiple directions. This can be done by breaking a curve into many small segments and connecting them by a series of straight lines. Due to this straight-line approximation, there exists inherent contouring error. The number of linear segments and the interpolation technique determine the error. For example, the contour error ΔE in circular interpolation is given by

$$\Delta E = R \left(1 - \cos \frac{\Delta \theta}{2} \right) \tag{7}$$

where R is the radius of an arc and $\Delta \theta$ is the incremental angle used. In most CNC machines, the error due to interpolation is small (Figure 14.11).

14.5 PROGRAMMABLE LOGIC CONTROL

Programmable logic controllers (PLC) are indispensable in CNC machines. While a CNC processor interprets the user instructions (i.e., executes part programs, performs interpolation, and generates all the necessary motion control commands), PLC performs error checking, interfaces with all the peripheral devices, and provides logic control. Therefore, PLC is an integral part of CNC controllers. A schematic diagram of a typical PLC is shown in Figure 14.12. PLC replaces the traditional electromechanical relay devices with programming. Relay switches, which were predominantly used in the early days, require rewiring when manufacturing jobs or sequences are changed. In addition, they are susceptible to mechanical failures. On the other hand, PLC provides flexibility to switch from one operation to another through the change of programs. There are several unique characteristics of PLCs to be noted.

PLCs have input and output modules that can be interfaced with multiple sensors and actuators. The input and output (I/O) ports are available in either digital or analogue form. Digital I/O ports can be used to process binary information individually or more complex numbers as a group. Analogue I/O ports are typically used for PID controls. PLCs perform deterministic scanning in the sense that the instructions stored in memory are scanned cyclically at a fixed time interval. PLC memory has a hierarchical structure, with each level given

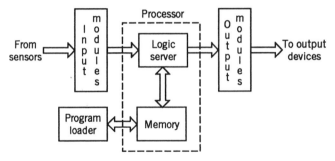

Figure 14.12. Schematic diagram of a programmable logic controller.

different priorities. The tasks that are most critical, such as machine emergency stop due to failure, are stored in the memory with the highest priority, whereas non–time-critical tasks, such as graphical display, are stored in the memory with the lowest priority. Due to deterministic scanning, the programs with the highest priority are scanned and executed for every scanning cycle whether or not the tasks with lower priorities are completed, thereby ensuring a safe operation of machine tools. The executive program of many PLCs performs diagnostic checks before each scanning. If a fault condition arises, it sets all the outputs to safe states and waits for fault to clear. This feature can be a critical advantage of using PLCs over other controllers for expensive machine tools.

The PLC of a CNC machine continually communicates with CNC while the part program is being executed. For example, the PLC obtains instructions such as tool change and coolant on and off from the memory-exchange area of CNC and sends out signals to appropriate output devices and receives signals from the sensors monitoring process conditions. Programming languages for PLCs are ladder diagrams; statement lists (STL); high level languages such as PASCAL, BASIC, and C; and GRAFCET. Statement lists are mnemonic codes for various Boolean operations and similar to assembly languages. Most PLCs used for CNC machine tools are programmed by using STL. The disadvantage of this language is that it is difficult to debug a large program or understand the flow. Ladder diagrams are a popular means of programming PLCs. Due to its graphical representation, it is easier for users to understand the logical flow.

14.6 MACHINE TOOL CONTROL

To achieve high precision required for modern machine tools, accurate servo control of axes is required. Positional errors in each axis can result in geometric error of the part. Therefore, it is important to minimize the positional error of each axis. If more than one axis is moving at the same time, their motions must be synchronized. Force control is sometimes desired to maximize the metal removal rate or to prevent tool breakage or bearing failure. Force control is typically achieved by regulating the speed of a drive. Chatter or vibration control is used to maintain an acceptable level of vibration. This can be done by suppressing vibration with an active controller or using a passive device. Some of these control schemes are introduced in this section.

Feedback Control

A schematic diagram of a typical position control loop of a feed drive with a DC motor is shown in Figure 14.13. Modern CNC machine tools use two feedback loops: one for the position loop and the other for the velocity loop. Typically, the position loop is controlled by a proportional (P) controller, while the inner velocity loop is controlled by either a proportional or proportional–integral (PI) controller.

The dynamics of the DC servo motor and leadscrew is typically approximated by a first-order model. Assuming that a proportional controller (K_ω) is used for the velocity loop for

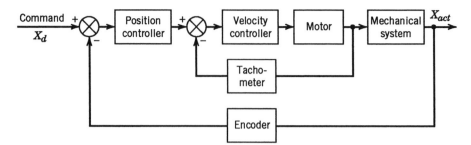

Figure 14.13. Schematic diagram of a position control loop of a feed drive.

simplicity, the entire system shown in Figure 14.12 can be modeled as shown in Figure 14.14. The angular velocity, $\omega(s)$, of the shaft is represented by

$$\omega(s) = \frac{K_m}{1 + \tau_m s} u(s) \tag{8}$$

where K_m is the feed dynamics gain and τ_m is the time constant for the feed dynamics. Let us assume that gains of the encoder and tachometer are denoted by K_e and K_T and the gear ratio from the motor to the table velocity is denoted by K_g. Then the transfer function of the inner velocity loop is given by

$$\frac{\omega(s)}{v(s)} = \frac{\dfrac{K\omega K_m}{1 + K_T K_\omega K_m}}{1 + \dfrac{\tau_m}{1 + K_T K_\omega K_m} s} \tag{9}$$

Now, let us consider some characteristics of the inner velocity control loop. The static gain of the velocity loop is

$$G_v(0) = \frac{K_\omega K_m}{1 + K_T K_\omega K_m} \tag{10}$$

For sufficiently large gains, the static gain reduces to

$$G_v(0) \approx \frac{1}{K_T} \tag{11}$$

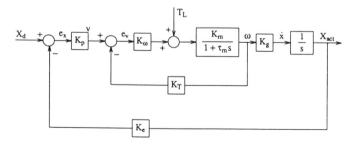

Figure 14.14. Control loops for a feed drive with a D-C motor.

i.e., it is inversely proportional only to the tachometer gain K_T. In addition, the time constant of the velocity loop is represented by

$$\tau_v = \frac{\tau_m}{1 + K_T K_\omega K_m} \tag{12}$$

Therefore, it can be seen that the velocity control loop shortens the time constant of the mechanical system substantially, because $K_T K_\omega K_m$ is usually much larger than unity.

The overall transfer function of the positional loop is given by

$$\frac{X_{\text{act}}(s)}{X_d(s)} = \frac{K_p K_\omega K_m K_g / \tau_m}{s^2 + (1 + K_T K_\omega K_m)/\tau_m \cdot s + K_p K_\omega K_m K_g K_e / \tau_m} \tag{13}$$

Therefore, the natural frequency of the entire system is

$$\omega_n = (K_p K_\omega K_m K_g K_e / \tau_m)^{1/2} \tag{14}$$

and the damping ratio is

$$\zeta = \frac{(1 + K_T K\omega K_m)/\tau_m}{2[K_p K_\omega K_g K_e / \tau_m]^{1/2}}$$

$$\approx \frac{K_T}{2} \left[\frac{K_\omega K_m}{K_p K_g K_e K \tau_m} \right]^{1/2} \tag{15}$$

If there is no velocity feedback loop, then the damping ratio is given by

$$\zeta = \frac{1}{2[K_p K_\omega K_m K_g K_e \tau_m]^{1/2}} \tag{16}$$

Therefore, the velocity loop increases the damping ratio of the overall system without affecting the natural frequency.

The time response of a feed drive system for a step input can be written in the form of

$$x(t) = A \left\{ 1 - \exp\left(-\zeta \omega_n t\right)/(1 - \zeta^2)^{1/2} \cdot \sin\left[\omega_d t + \tan^{-1}\frac{(1 - \zeta^2)^{1/2}}{\zeta}\right] \right\} \tag{17}$$

where $\omega_d = \omega_n (1 - \zeta^2)^{1/2}$ is the damped natural frequency and A is the magnitude of the step input. The step responses of a second-order system with various damping ratios are shown in Figure 14.15. To obtain a desired response, proper controller parameters must be chosen. If the system parameters are not completely known, one can use the well-known Ziegler-Nichols (6) tuning procedure to design the controllers.

Contouring Errors

In the operation of most machine tools, complicated trajectories or velocity profiles are often required. Therefore, the controller designed to satisfy the specifications for a step input will yield positional errors when input profiles are more complicated. Let's consider a response for the system described in the previous section for a ramp input. If we assume that the input is given by

$$X_{\text{com}} = \alpha \cdot t \tag{18}$$

then the response is represented by

$$x(t) = \alpha \left\{ t + \left[\exp\left(-\zeta \omega_n t / \omega_d\right) \right] \sin\left(\omega_d t + 2\phi\right) - \frac{2\zeta}{\omega_n} \right\} \tag{19}$$

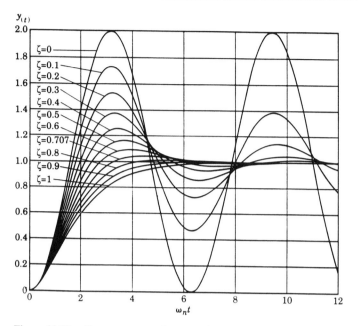

Figure 14.15. Step responses of a second-order system. From ref. 6.

where $\phi = \tan^{-1} \dfrac{(1 - \zeta^2)^{1/2}}{\zeta}$. The steady-state position is given by

$$x_{ss} = \alpha \left(t - \frac{2\zeta}{\omega_n} \right) \tag{20}$$

thus yielding positional error

$$e_{x,ss} = \alpha \frac{2\zeta}{\omega_n} \tag{21}$$

$$= \frac{\alpha(1 + K_T K_\omega K_m)}{K_p K_\omega K_m K_g K_e}$$

Therefore, the actual response for a ramp input will show a finite amount of error, which is proportional to the speed, as shown in Figure 14.16.

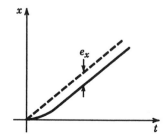

Figure 14.16. Response of a machine tool axis for a ramp input.

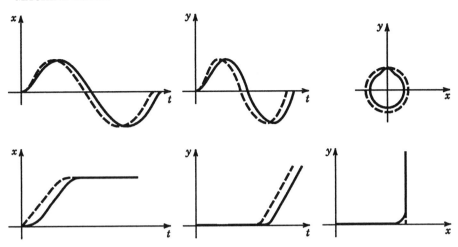

Figure 14.17. Examples of profile errors.

For single axis motion, this velocity lag would cause no problem, because it does not affect the accuracy of profile. However, when multiple axes are used, the velocity lags would result in profile errors. Some examples of these errors are shown in Figure 14.17. These errors can be somewhat minimized by tuning the so-called velocity amplification factor, K_v, defined by

$$K_{v_x} = \frac{\dot{x}}{e_x} \tag{22}$$

$$= \frac{K_p K_\omega K_m K_g}{(1 + K_T K_\omega K_m) + \tau_m s}$$

Hence, the positional error depends on the velocity amplification factor:

$$e_x = \frac{\dot{x}}{K_{v_x}} \tag{23}$$

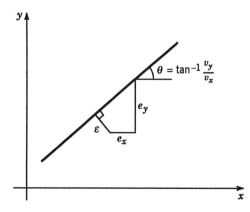

Figure 14.18. Geometric error caused by simultaneous motion.

Let us consider a two-axis system that will make a linear trajectory. The x and y positions in steady state are given by

$$x(t) = v_x \cdot t - e_x \tag{24}$$
$$y(t) = v_y \cdot t - e_y$$

The geometric error produced by simultaneous motions is shown in Figure 14.18 and can be represented by

$$\varepsilon = e_y \cos \theta - e_x \sin \theta \tag{25}$$
$$= \frac{e_y v_x - e_x v_y}{v}$$

Using equation 23, equation 25 can be rewritten as

$$\varepsilon = \frac{v_x v_y}{v} \cdot \frac{K_{vx} - K_{vy}}{K_{vx} + K_{vy}} \tag{26}$$

Therefore, it is clear that matched gains or high gains will reduce the geometric error.

However, if the slope of the line becomes different or a curved trajectory is needed, profile errors are unavoidable. To further reduce these errors, more advanced control schemes must be used. In recent years, various techniques have been proposed such as cross-coupling, feed-forward, and adaptive controllers. However, these subjects are beyond the scope of this chapter. Users must select an appropriate controller based on the performance requirements.

BIBLIOGRAPHY

1. N. TANIGUCHI, "Current Status and Future Trends of Ultraprecision Machining Processes," *Metalworking*, 34–47 (1982).
2. Y.C. SHIN, H. CHIN, and M.J. BRINK, "Characterization of CNC Machining Centers," *J. Manufact. Sys.* **10**, 407–421 (1992).
3. P.M. FERREIRA and C.R. LIU, "A Method for Estimating and Compensating Quasistatic Errors of Machine Tools," *ASME J. Eng. Industry* 149–159 (1993).
4. Y.C. SHIN and Y. WEI, "A Statistical Analysis of Positional Errors of a Multiaxis Machine Tools," *Precision Eng.* **14**, 139–146 (1992).
5. Y.C. SHIN, "Bearing Nonlinearity and Stability Analysis in High Speed Machining," *ASME J. Eng. Industry*, **114**, 23–30 (1992).
6. G.F. FRANKLIN, J.D. POWELL, and A. EMANI-NAEMI, *Feedback Control of Dynamic Systems*, 2nd ed., Addison-Wesley Publishing Co., Inc., Reading, Mass., 1991.

CHAPTER 15
Robotics

Shimon Y. Nof and Venkat N. Rajan
Purdue University

15.1 INTRODUCTION

Industrial robotics is the science of designing, building, and applying industrial robots. This chapter will review briefly what industrial robots are and explain a number of industrial engineering (IE) techniques that have been developed and applied in recent years for planning various applications of robots in industry. The objective is to provide tools for the study of relevant aspects of robots in working environments for the purpose of optimizing overall performance of the work system. Specifically, robot work should be optimized to (*1*) minimize the time per unit of work produced; (*2*) minimize the amount of effort and energy expanded by operators; (*3*) minimize the amount of waste, scrap, and rework; (*4*) maximize quality of work produced; and (*5*) maximize safety.

What are robots? In the late 1970s the Robotic Industries Association (RIA; formerly the Robot Institute of America) defined a robot as "a manipulator, designed to move material, parts, tools or specialized devices through variable programmed motions for the performance of a variety of tasks." Although this definition does not directly include pick-and-place arms as robots, teleoperators and remotely controlled devices are often referred to also as robots. The International Standards Organization (ISO) has a more lengthy definition of an industrial robot:

> A machine formed by a mechanism including several degrees of freedom, often having the appearance of one or several arms ending in a wrist capable of holding a tool or a workpiece or an inspection device. In particular, its control unit must use a memorizing device and sometimes it can use sensing or adaptation appliances taking into account environment and circumstances. These multipurpose machines are generally designed to carry out a repetitive function and can be adapted to other functions.

The RIA and ISO definitions both stress the multifunctional and programmable capabilities and, therefore, exclude special-purpose "hard automation" tools and equipment typically found in high volume production. Also excluded are manual remote manipulators, which are extensions of human hands for use in, for example, sterile, hot, or radioactive environments.

In Japan, the Japanese Industrial Robot Association (JIRA) classifies industrial robots by the method of input information and the method of teaching:

1. *Manual Manipulators.* Manipulators directly activated by the operator.
2. *Fixed-sequence Robot.* Robot that once programmed for a given sequence of operations is not easily changed.
3. *Variable-sequence Robot.* Robot that can be programmed for a given sequence of operations and can easily be changed or reprogrammed.
4. *Playback Robot.* Robot that "memorizes" work sequences taught by a human being who physically leads the device through the intended work pattern; the robot can then create this sequence repetitively from memory.
5. *Numerically Controlled (NC) Robot.* Robot that operates from and is controlled by digital data, as in the form of punched tape, cards, or digital switches; operates like a NC machine.
6. *Intelligent Robot.* Robot that uses sensory perception to evaluate its environment and make decisions and proceeds to operate accordingly.

In essence, the industrial engineer will seek the most effective industrial robot or other equipment solution for the application at hand; therefore, the definition may be less relevant than understanding the robotic technology.

The long history of automation and mechanization as well as the science fiction background leading to industrial robotics are well documented. The first patent for a 1954 robot design was issued in the UK (in 1957) to the British inventor Cyril W. Kenward. Earlier in the United States, around 1946, George C. Devol invented and in 1952 patented a magnetic recording device to control a machine. In 1954 Devol invented the Programmed Article Transfer, which was patented in 1961. Devol's inventions were harnessed by Joseph F. Engelberger who built the first working industrial robot in 1959. The first successful robot installation was in 1961 for tending a die casting machine at a General Motors plant.

Whether or not robotics should have become a successful innovation was analyzed by Engelberger (1). He cited three essential technologies that became available after World War II and were crucial to the development of industrial robots: servo mechanism theory, digital computation, and solid-state electronics, which made it all economically feasible. On the other hand, Engelberger suggested that prerequisite conditions for successful use of industrial robots are (1) there must be a perceived need and (2) appropriate technology and competent practitioners must be available. In this chapter, a number of useful techniques to measure, plan, and evaluate the effectiveness of robots in industry are described.

A pioneering mobile robot called Shakey was developed at Stanford Research Institute from 1967 to 1969. It was a wheel-based robot with two servo controlled drive wheels and one free caster, and its main objective was to serve as a test bed for artificial intelligence (AI) research. Although mobile robots have great potential for industrial application, the leading user of mobile robots to date has been the nuclear industry. Early computer vision systems began to appear in the 1950s, but their development for robot applications started in the mid-1960s in several AI labs, including MIT, Stanford, and SRI. By the 1980s, a good number of companies had developed commercial vision systems for industrial applications.

To complete this brief historical background, let us consider robot programming languages. The first commercially available industrial robot system developed in the late 1950s by Devol and Engelberger included a teaching-by-showing method of programming that is still widely used today. WAVE, the original robot programming language developed at Stanford AI labs in 1970–1974, resembled more a machine language and was combined with a vision system. However, the first commercial robot programming language, VAL, was released by Unimation for their PUMA robots in 1979 and was an extension of BASIC.

The first-generation of robot systems was defined for the various robots with limited computer power. Their main intelligent functions include programming by showing a sequence of manipulation steps by a human operator using a teach box. Without any sensors, these robots require a prearranged and relatively fixed factory environment and, therefore, have limited use.

The second-generation of robot systems was enhanced by the addition of a computer processor. A major step in industrial robotics development was the integration of a computer with the industrial robot mechanism (2). This has provided real-time calculation of trajectory to smooth the motions of the end effector and integration of some simple force and proximity sensors to obtain external signals. The main applications of second-generation robots include spot and arc welding, spray painting, and some assembly.

Third-generation robot systems incorporate multiple computer processors and multiple arms that can operate asynchronously to perform several functions. Distributed hierarchical computer organization is preferred, because it can coordinate motions and interface with external sensors, other machines, and other robots and can communicate with other computers. These robots can already exhibit intelligent behavior, including knowledge-based control and learning abilities. Their main advantage for industrial application is and will be in their ability to integrate flexibly and quickly to unstructured factory environments.

Japan ranks as the world's top robot-producing and -using country, with more than 40% of the world's industrial robot installations. The reasons for this penetration are sociological and technological factors that are unique to Japan: industrial robots brought productivity and quality gains in Japanese industry, coupled with improvements of the work environment. These have perpetuated the social demand for more robots as well as increased the expectation from this technology.

The relatively short history of industrial robots, about 40 yr, has been full of ingenious innovations. It is anticipated that with the current explosion of AI research and development efforts the next 40 yr will be just as exciting. The interested reader is referred to refs. 1 and 3 for further historical insights.

15.2 INDUSTRIAL ROBOT TECHNOLOGY OVERVIEW

Types of Robots

Industrial robots are available in a variety of arm configurations, power sources, control systems, and industrial uses. The most common general characteristics of industrial robots are

  Arm configuration.
  Number of axes (commonly referred to as degrees of freedom).
  Load-carrying capability (payload).
  Work envelope.
  Control system (which defines the level of intelligence).
  Power source.
  Speed of movement.
  Repeatability and accuracy.
  Reliability.

Figure 15.1 shows the four most common fixed-pedestal, stationary robot arm configurations. Each is shown as a three-axis structure; typical robots have from four to six axes, with the one to three axes added in the end-of-arm tooling (also referred to as end effectors). Figure 15.1a shows the cartesian, or rectilinear, arm configuration. A useful variation is the gantry structure, for which the arm hands down from a rectangular frame and can move in x, y, z cartesian space. The cartesian robot arm configuration has three linear and no rotational axes. It is suited for operations that require essentially up-and-down motions, as in palletizing or machine tending, or in assembly operations, for which precise positioning is required. Figure 15.1b illustrates the cylindrical arm, consisting of two linear and one rotational axis. These robots are often found in simple palletizing and material-handling operations that require up–down and turnaround motions.

  Figure 15.1c shows a spherical arm. This was actually the first industrial robot type selected by Unimation in the early 1960s for its Unimate 2000. It has one linear and two rotational axes. It is found in numerous industrial applications such as machine loading, palletizing, painting, and spot welding. Figure 15.1d illustrates the vertically articulated robot arm, also called revolute, jointed, or anthropomorphic. It has three rotational axes and has no linear axes. Like the spherical robot, the articulated robot requires servo control to coordinate its axes. This robot geometry has the advantage that it provides the largest working volume or envelope per area of floor space required. The alternative, horizontally articulated selective compliance assembly robotic arm (SCARA), is suited for rapid small-parts insertion tasks.

  In addition to stationary robots, there is a strong trend to develop robots designed especially for mobility. A simple form of mobility can be provided by mounting a robot on a rail. There are basically two variations of the mobile robot: The multilegged and the wheel- or tread-driven robots. Multilegged robots, of which the six-legged is the most popular configuration, has been applied for off-road applications in construction and military tasks. Such devices offer superior mobility for unstructured areas but have problems of robustness, stability, and control of leg motions. Omnidirectional wheel-based robots are becoming more common. Their simpler mechanical configuration and control systems provide better performance than the multilegged robots, but they are suited for the more structured industrial environment. They will provide robot service particularly for maintenance and irregular handling of tools or materials (Figure 15.2). The four common robot installations in industrial applications are shown in Figure 15.3, and they include the floor-mounted robot, the machine-console manipulator, the mobile robot, and the gantry or overhead robot.

Major Robot Components

Manipulator

A manipulator usually consists of an open chain of links and segments, jointed or sliding relative to one another for grasping and moving objects, usually in several degrees of freedom. It can be remotely controlled by a human (manual manipulator) or a computer (programmable manipulator). Guidelines for the selection of manipulator arms are summarized in Table 15.1.

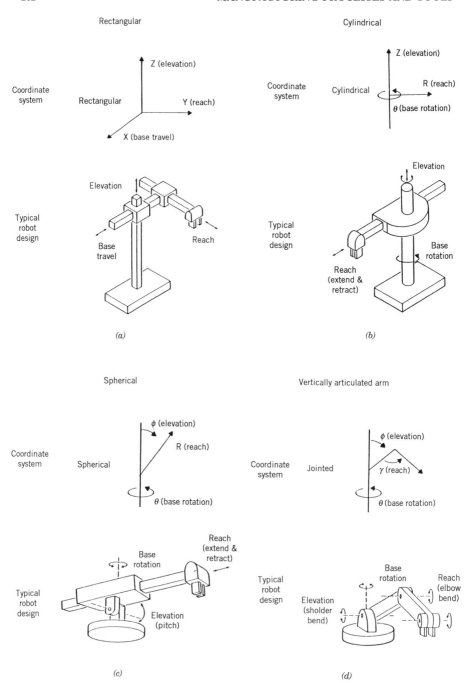

Figure 15.1. Basic robot configurations.

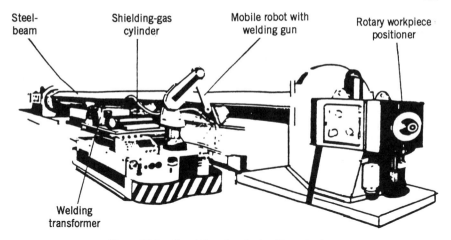

Steel-beam   Shielding-gas cylinder   Mobile robot with welding gun   Rotary workpiece positioner

Welding transformer

Figure 15.2. Omnidirectional wheel-based robot.

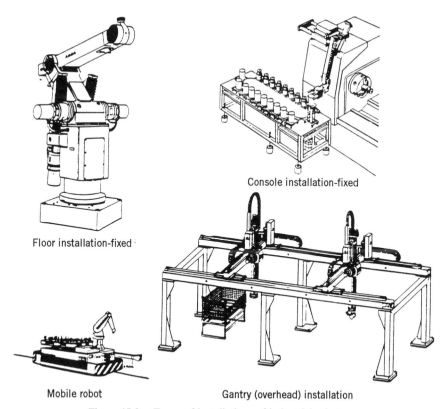

Floor installation-fixed

Console installation-fixed

Mobile robot

Gantry (overhead) installation

Figure 15.3. Types of installations of industrial robots.

TABLE 15.1. Functional Relationship between Task, Number of Programmable Axes, and Robot Control as a Function of Arm Arrangement[a,b]

Task / Kinematic chain		3T		2T 1R		1T 2R		1T 2R		3R		>3 axes >3R	
Movement A and B	Orientation to Surface	Number of Programmable Axes											
		PTP	CP	PTP	CP	PTP	CP	PTP	CP	PTP	CP	PTP	CP
A and B (movement I)	None —	1		1		2	2	1	2		2		2
	dx	2		2		3	3	2	3		3		3
	dx dy	3		3		4	4	3	4		4		4
	dx dy dz	4		4		5	5	4	5		5		5
A and B (movement II)	None	(2)	2			3	2	3	2		3		3
	dx	(3)	3			4	3	4	3		4		4
	dx, dy	(4)	4			5	4	5	4		5		5
	dx, dy, dz	(5)	5			6	5	6	5		6		6
A (movement III)	None		3		3		3		3		3		3
	dx		4		4		4		4		4		4
	dx, dy		5		5		5		5		5		5
	dx, dy, dz		6		6		6		6		6		6

[a] From ref. 4.
[b] ▦ not necessary; ( ) possible under certain circumstances; ▨ no solution/without practical value.

Power Supply

There are three main power sources used for industrial robot systems: pneumatic, hydraulic, and electric. Some robots are powered by a combination of electric and one other power source. Pneumatic power, although inexpensive, is mostly used for simpler robots because of its inherent problems, such as noise, leakage, and compressibility. Hydraulic power is also noisy and subject to leakage but is relatively common in industry because of the high torque and power and its excellent ability to respond swiftly to motion commands. It is particularly suited for large and heavy part or tool handling such as in welding, material handling, machine tending, and some assembly as well as for smooth, complex trajectories such as in painting and finishing. Electric power provides the cleanest and quietest actuation and is preferred because it is self-contained (no pumps or compressors are needed). On the other hand, it may present electric hazards in highly flammable or explosive environments.

Control System

The control system implements in the robot the designed-control scheme, including sensors, manual input and mode selection elements, interlocking and decision-making circuitry, and output elements to the operating mechanism. It provides the "brains" of the robot and distinguishes it from fixed ("hard") automation. The robot control system includes its programming

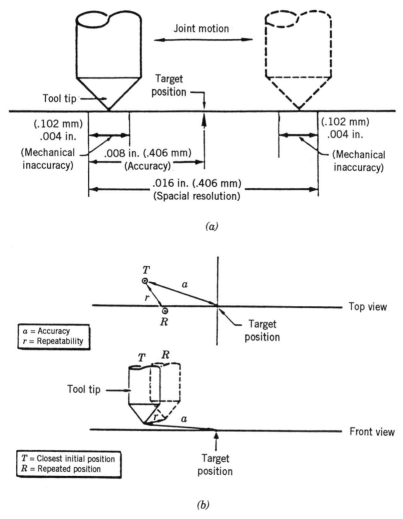

Figure 15.4. (*a*) Robot's accuracy–resolution relationship. (*b*) Robot's accuracy–repeatability relationship. Repeatability shown here as better than accuracy.

method by teaching, using a teach box; by showing, actually leading the robot manipulator through the desired motions; or by programming. The control system also determines two major performance measures of the robot: its accuracy and repeatability. The first implies the precision with which the robot can reach a programmed position or orientation. The second implies the tolerance range over which a programmed motion can be repeated several or many times. While the accuracy of robots is difficult to establish in a standard way, repeatability has been standardized. Typically, industrial robots will have a repeatability better than ±0.01 in., and more precise robots will be within ±0.003 in. (Figure 15.4).

Tooling and End Effectors

Tooling and end effectors are the robot hands that link the manipulator to the part or tool being manipulated. Examples include grippers, paint spraying nozzles, welding guns, vacuum cups, and gauging instruments. A checklist of factors for selecting grippers is summarized in Table 15.2.

15.3 APPLICATIONS IN INDUSTRY

Current and emerging robot applications in industry can be categorized based on the complexity and requirements of the job. They range from simple, low technology pick-and-place and palletizing operations through medium technology painting, some assembly and welding operations to high technology precision assembly, inspection, and multirobot operations.

TABLE 15.2. Checklist of Factors in the Selection and Design of Grippers[a]

Factor	Consideration
Part to be handled	Weight and size
	Shape
	Changes in shape during processing
	Tolerances on the part size
	Surface condition, protection of delicate surfaces
Actuation method	Mechanical grasping
	Vacuum cup
	Magnet
	Other methods (adhesives, scoops, etc.)
Power and signal transmission	Pneumatic
	Electrical
	Hydraulic
	Mechanical
Gripper force	Weight of the object
(mechanical gripper)	Method of holding (physical constriction or friction)
	Coefficient of friction between fingers and object
	Speed and acceleration during motion cycle
Positioning problems	Length of fingers
	Inherent accuracy and repeatability of robot
	Tolerances on the part size
Service conditions	Number of actuations during lifetime of gripper
	Replaceability of wear components (fingers)
	Maintenance and serviceability
Operating environment	Heat and temperature
	Humidity, moisture, dirt, chemicals
Temperature protection	Heat shields
	Long fingers
	Forced cooling (compressed air, water cooling, etc.)
	Use of heat-resistant materials
Fabrication materials	Strength, rigidity, durability
	Fatigue strength
	Cost and ease of fabrication
	Friction properties for finger surfaces
	Compatibility with operating environment
Other considerations	Use of interchangeable fingers
	Design standards
	Mounting connections and interfacing with robot
	Risk of product design changes and their effect on the gripper design
	Lead time for design and fabrication
	Spare parts, maintenance, and service
	Tryout of the gripper in production

[a] From ref. 5.

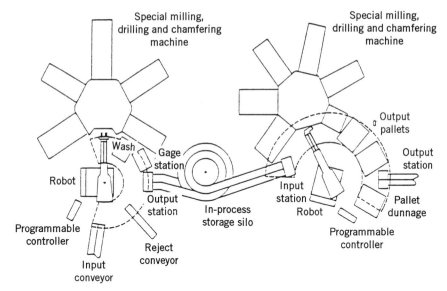

Figure 15.5. Flexible machine tool cell. Courtesy of UAS Universal Automation Co.

Pick-and-place, Machine-tending, and Palletizing Operations

The earliest applications of robots were in machine loading–unloading, pick-and-place, material transfer, sorting, and palletizing operations. Such robots typically were not servo controlled and worked with pneumatic or hydraulic power. The load-carrying requirements were high, working in dirty or hazardous factory environments. Replacing unskilled human labor often in hazardous jobs, these robots had to be robust and low in initial and maintenance costs. Figure 15.5 depicts such an industrial application.

Painting, Finishing, and Welding Operations

The next level in the sophistication of industrial robot applications was in spray painting, finishing operations, and spot and arc welding (Figure 15.6). These applications complemented or replaced certain skilled human labor. Often the justification was by eliminating dangerous environmental exposures. These applications often require tracking complex trajectories such as painting surface contours, hence servo controlled articulated or spherical robot structures were used. Lead-through teach modes became common, and sometimes sophisticated sensors are employed to maintain process consistency (e.g., monitoring the weld weave in seam welding operations). Experience has shown that when properly selected and implemented, these robotic applications usually lead to reduced overall manufacturing costs and improved product quality compared with manual method.

Assembly Operations

The most advanced level of technology employing third-generation industrial robots is found in assembly. System repeatability is of utmost importance. End-of-arm tooling must be compliant, i.e., have both force and displacement control to adjust part insertions, which require that the robot actually "feel" its way along. This technology usually requires a measure of artificial intelligence. Assembly robots generally are electronically driven and operate in clean environ-

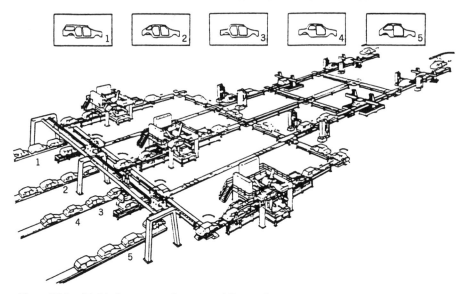

Figure 15.6. Multirobot system for spot welding. A five-model final assembly line with three conformation and tack welding stations (each with six robots) followed by two robotic finishing lines is shown. A total of 400 spot welds are made on each car at a production rate of 150 cars/h. Courtesy of Sciacky Corp., France.

ments. Assembly robots are expected to exceed lower technology applications. Figure 15.7 shows robotic assembly operations.

Other Applications

Other typical applications of robots include inspection, quality control, and repair; processing such as laser and water jet cutting and drilling, riveting, and clean-room operations; and applications in the wood, pharmaceutical, paper, and food-processing industries. As industrial robot technology and robot intelligence improve even further, additional applications may be justified effectively.

15.4 JUSTIFICATION CONSIDERATIONS IN APPLYING INDUSTRIAL ROBOTS

While engineering economy techniques are useful for justification of capital investment or equipment replacement, there are specific economic considerations related to industrial robots. The following considerations are based on surveys and case studies (6).

Hazardous Environment Operations

A variety of applications involve human activity under hazardous conditions. Such applications provide a primary motivation for the use of robots instead of humans to improve working conditions.

Die Casting. Eliminate hand degating and handling of gates, storage of parts and trimmings, material handling.

Forging. Eliminate human operation in hot, dirty, noxious environments.

Injection Molding. Eliminate human operation in hot, noxious environments, and ensure compliance with OSHA regulations involving dies.

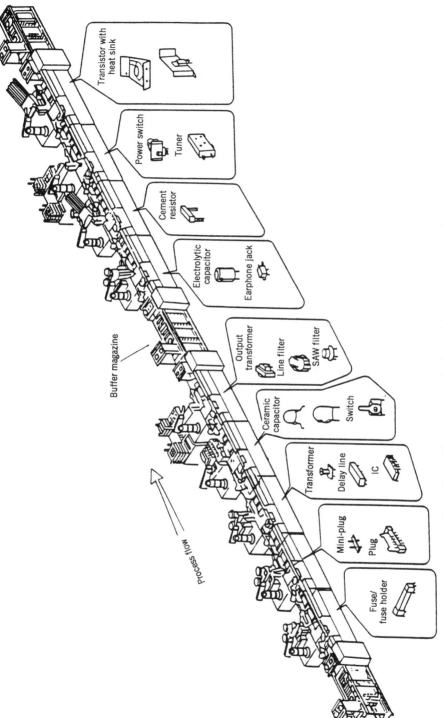

Figure 15.7. Robotic assembly line for electronic components.

Stamping. Eliminate hand-in-die hazard.

Machine Loading. Eliminate human operation in environments with cutting oil fumes, chips, and noise.

Material Handling. Eliminate tedious and heavy tasks.

Welding. Eliminate handling of heavy weld guns, heat exposure, and eyesight damage.

Finishing and Painting. Eliminate paint spray hazard and exposure to flammable paint material.

Improved Quality

Use of robots can improve quality of a process due to higher accuracy and repeatability or by performing the process under conditions that lead to higher quality but are not conducive for human operation.

Diet Casting. Reduced scrap due to consistent cycle times, less damage from dies and tie bars, better quality on long and flat parts by controlling quench sequence.

Investment Casting. Uniform shell and better castings, consistent timing, draining, faster spinning.

Forging. Hot trim instead of cold trim improves part quality, consistent part placement, properly timed operations.

Die Forging. Consistent lubrication.

Injection Molding. No damage or contamination; stable cycle times, especially on more than one unit.

Welding. Consistent arc welding, reduction of weld spots in spot welding due to consistency.

Finishing and Painting. Consistent film build and coverage.

Assembly. No missing parts, no misassembled parts, no visibly defective parts used.

Inspection. Consistent results due to reduced reading and recording errors.

Reduced Cost

Costs can be reduced due to savings in labor cost and reduced use of some process and safety equipment.

Die Casting. Eliminate labor cost; reduced remelt cost; avoid cost of safety equipment, as much as $20,000/machine; typical payout period is from 9 months to 2.5 yr, depending on heads, shifts, etc.

Investment Casting. Labor savings.

Forging. Labor savings, no relief required.

Injection Molding. Labor savings.

Stamping. Labor savings, particularly with large parts.

Machine Loading. Labor savings; reduce in-process handling by arranging machines in "cell"; however, relocation of machines may be a major expense.

Material Handling. Labor savings; savings due to elimination of hoists and other mechanical aids for handling heavy parts; may require part orientation, which may be costly.

Welding. Labor savings on multiple-shift operations; savings in energy consumption and electrode–weld tip replacement due to consistent spot welding; can reduce administrative and training costs for replacement of welders in arc welding operations where labor turnover tends to be high; may require precise fixturing, indexing, or line tracking ability that add to costs.

Finishing and Painting. Material savings; overspray, trigger control, and removing humans from the booth reduces costs by reducing makeup air requirements and allows concentration of solvents for paint recovery or emissions control; labor savings.

Assembly. Labor savings, requires capital expenditures to avoid obsolescence.

Inspection. Visual inspection can often be combined with handling–transfer operation for savings, avoid cost of expensive custom-made gauging devices.

Improved Performance

Robots can perform tedious, repetitive tasks at greater speeds and with continuous operation.

Die Casting. Faster production rate, runthrough breaks, and lunch; more parts/day; run multiple machines served by single robot.

Investment Casting. Faster than humans; can handle heavier trees, e.g., wax cluster with 100 turbine blades in same time as 50-blade cluster, whereas a human could not handle a 100-blade tree.

Forging. Higher production, especially on heavy parts for which a human requires help of a second human and/or hoist.

Injection Molding. Faster production on large parts, especially on large machines or on molds with more than two cavities; completion of secondary operations such as trimming, palletizing, and packing during machine cycle.

Stamping. Reduced changeover time for different parts compared with usual press automation; avoid purchase of safety equipment required with manual press operations, but could lead to expensive interlocks. A recent installation, e.g., had two lines of three presses, two robots per line transferring parts from press 1 to press 2 and from 2 to 3, a third line with two presses and one robot—five robots in all at about $35,000 each, interlocks between robots and presses cost about $100,000, which is about 45% of total installation cost.

Machine Loading. Ability to handle heavy parts.

Material Handling. More uniform packing, higher density, ability to handle heavy parts, faster than people on long reach, no walking.

Finishing and Painting. Better overspray, trigger control, less booth cleanup from reduced overspray.

Assembly. Higher productivity, especially in systems with robots and people; if robots are set up to pace operations, can often combine assembly and test or in-process inspection with 100% assurance of test performance, people tend to skip such steps because it is not obvious when not performed.

Inspection. Higher productivity due to higher speeds, can provide 100% inspection on operations for which sampling was formerly done, can inspect moving parts.

15.5 PLANNING ROBOT WORK IN INDUSTRY

For given job requirements a general ergonomics procedure entails the analysis and evaluation of whether a human or a robot should be employed for the job. If a robot is employed, the best combination of robot models and work method, implying also the best workplace, should be selected. In integrated human and robot systems the best combination must be designed. The subsequent sections cover the ergonomics techniques that are useful for robot job design in practice. The topics covered are

Analysis of work characteristics.

Work methods analysis.

Performance measurement.

Integrated human and robot ergonomics.

Analysis of Work Characteristics

To implement effectively an ergonomic procedure, a general list of considerations in planning robot work can be prepared. In addition to such a general analysis, it is also necessary to know the detailed characteristics and skills of today's industrial robots as well as those of humans. A series of the robot–human charts can serve this purpose well.

The Robot–Human Charts

Robot–human charts, originally prepared by Nof, Knight, and Salvendy (7), are developed with two functions in mind, namely (*1*) to aid engineers in determining whether a robot can perform a job and (*2*) to serve as a guideline and reference for robot specifications. Table 15.3 presents the robot–human charts for comparison of physical skills of humans and robots. The robot–human charts can also be useful in job design of combined systems, which integrate both robots and human operators. They contain three principal types of work characteristics.

1. Physical skills and characteristics, including manipulation, body dimensions, strength and power, consistency, overload, underload performance, and environmental con-

TABLE 15.3. Robot–Human Charts: Comparison of Robot and Human Physical Skills and Characteristics[a]

Characteristics	Robot	Human
	Manipulation	

Body	a. One of four types:
	  1. Uni- or multiprismatic
	  2. Uni- or multirevolute
	  3. Combined revolute–prismatic
	  4. Mobile
	b. Typical maximum movement and velocity capabilities:
	Right-left traverse
	  5–18 m at 500–1200 mm/s
	Out-in traverse
	  3–15 m
	  500–1200 mm/s
		a. A mobile carrier (feet) combined with 3 df wrist like (roll, pitch, yaw) capability at waist
		
		b. Examples of waist movement:[b]
		Roll: ≈180°
		Pitch: ≈150°
		Yaw: ≈90°

Arm	a. One of four primary types:
	  1. Rectangular
	  2. Cylindrical
	  3. Spherical
	  4. Articulated
	b. One or more arms, with incremental usefulness per each additional arm
	c. Typical maximum movement and velocity capabilities:
	Out-in traverse
	  300–3000 mm
	  100–4500 mm/s
	Right-left traverse
	  100–6000 mm
	  100–1500 mm/s
	Up-down traverse
	  50–4800 mm
	  50–5000 mm/s
	Right-left rotation
	  50–380°[c]
	  5–240°/s
	Up-down rotation
	  25–330°
	  10–170°/s
		a. Articulated arm composed of shoulder and elbow revolute joints
		
		b. Two arms, cannot operate independently (at least not totally)
		
		c. Examples of typical movement and velocity parameters:
		Maximum velocity: 1500 mm/s in linear movement.
		Average standing lateral reach: 625 mm
		Right–left traverse range: 432–876 mm
		
		Up-down traverse range: 1016–1828 mm
		
		Right-left rotation (horizontal arm) range: 165–225
		Average up-down rotation: 249

TABLE 15.3. (*Continued*)

Characteristics	Robot	Human

Wrist	a. One of three types:
	  1. Prismatic
	  2. Revolute
	  3. Combined prismatic/
	    revolute
	    Commonly, wrists have
	    1–3 rotational df: roll,
	    pitch, yaw, however, an
	    example of right–left and
	    up–down traverse was
	    observed
		a. Consists of three rotational
		  degrees of freedom: roll,
		  pitch, yaw.

	b. Typical maximum move-
	  ment and velocity capabili-
	  ties:
	  Roll
	    100–575°^{d}
	    35–600°/s
	  Pitch
	    40–360°
	    30–320°/s
	  Yaw
	    100–530°
	    30–300°/s
	  *Right-left traverse (uncom-
	  mon)*
	    1000 mm
	    4800 mm/s
	  *Up-down traverse (uncom-
	  mon)*
	    150 mm
	    400 mm/s
		b. Examples of movement
		  capabilities
		  Roll: ≈180°
		  Pitch: ≈180°
		  Yaw: ≈90°

End effector	a. The robot is affixed with
	  either a hand or a tool at the
	  end of the wrist. The end
	  effector can be complex
	  enough to be considered a
	  small manipulator in itself
		a. Consists of essentially four
		  degrees of freedom in an
		  articulated configuration.
		  Five fingers per arm each
		  have three pitch revolute
		  and one yaw revolute joints

	b. Can be designed to various
	  dimensions
		b. Typical hand dimensions:
		  Length: 163–208 mm
		  Breadth: 68–97 mm (at
		  thumb)
		  Depth: 20–33 mm (at meta-
		  carpal)

Body dimensions	a. Main body:
	  Height: 0.10–2.0 m
	  Length (arm) 0.2–2.0 m
	  Width: 0.1–1.5 m
	  Weight: 5–8000 kg
	b. Floor area required: from
	  none for ceiling-mounted
	  models to several square
	  meters for large models
		a. Main body (typical adult):
		  Height: 1.5–1.9 m
		  Length (arm): 754–947 mm
		  Width: 478–579 mm
		  Weight: 45–100 kg
		b. Typically about 1 m² work-
		  ing radius

Strength and power	a. 0.1–1000 kg of useful load
	  during operation at normal
	  speed:
	  reduced at above normal
	  speeds
		a. Maximum arm load: <30 kg;
		  varies drastically with type
		  of movement, direction of
		  load, etc.

TABLE 15.3. *(Continued)*

Characteristics	Robot	Human
	b. Power relative to useful load	b. Power: 2 hp $\simeq$ 10 s 0.5 hp $\simeq$ 120 s 0.2 hp $\simeq$ continuous 5 kc/min Subject to fatigue: may differ between static and dynamic conditions
Consistency	Absolute consistency if no malfunctions	a. Low b. May improve with practice and redundant knowledge of results c. Subject to fatigue: physiological and psychological d. May require external monitoring of performance
Overload–underload performance	a. Constant performance up to a designed limit, and then a drastic failure b. No underload effects on performance	a. Performance declines smoothly under a failure · b. Boredom under local effects is significant
Environmental constraints	a. Ambient temperature from $-10°$ to 60°C b. Relative humidity up to 90% c. Can be fitted to hostile environments	a. Ambient temperature range 15–30°C b. Humidity effects are weak c. Sensitive to various noxious stimuli and toxins, altitude, and air flow

[a] From ref. 7.
[b] Where possible 5th and 95th percentile figures (8) are used to represent minimum and maximum values. Otherwise, a general average value is given.
[c] A continuous right–left rotation is available.
[d] A continuous roll movement is available.

straints. Table 15.3 provides details of this category. Typical ranges of maximum motion capabilities (TRMM) are given for several categories of body movement and speed and arm and wrist motions. To clarify the meaning of TRMM, consider the following example. For robot arm right–left traverse, the table lists a maximum movement range of 100 to 6000 mm at a maximum velocity range of 100 to 1500 mm/s. This means, that for the surveyed population of robot models, it was found that a maximum arm right–left linear motion is typically between 100 mm (for some models) and up to 6000 mm (for some other models). The maximum velocity values for right–left travel were found to be from 100 up to 1500 mm/s.

2. Mental and communicative characteristics. The robot–human charts contain mental and communicative system attributes for robots and humans, as provided in ref. 7.

3. Energy considerations. A comparison of representative values of energy-related characteristics, such as power requirements, and energy efficiency for robots and humans is given in ref. 7.

Certain significant features that distinguish robots and human operators (7), such as the following, can effectively be used to select jobs that robots can do well.

1. The more similar two jobs are, the easier it is to transfer either robot or human from one job to the other. For humans, such transfer is almost entirely a question of learning or retraining. For robots, however, as job similarity decreases, robot reconfiguration and reprogramming (retraining) become necessary for economical interjob transfer.

2. Humans possess a set of basic skills and experience accumulated over the years and, therefore, may require less detail in their job description. Today's robots, on the other hand, perform each new task essentially from scratch and require a high degree of detail for every micromotion and microactivity.

3. Robots do not have any significant individual differences within a given model. Thus an optimized job method may have more generality with robot operators than with human operators.

Robot sensing, manipulative, and decision-making abilities can be designed for a given specialized task to a much greater degree than can a human's abilities. Of course, this specialization may entail the cost of decreased transferability from one task to another.

Robots are unaffected by social and psychological effects (such as boredom) that often impose constraints on the engineer attempting to design a job for a human operator.

Job Selection for Robots

In planning work in industry two decisions must be made.

1. *Selection.* Who should perform a given task or set of tasks—a human operator or a robot?

2. *Specification.* What are the specifications of the job and the skills? If a robot was indicated in the first decision, complete robot specifications are also sought.

Usually three cases can be identified:

1. A human operator must perform the job because the task is too complex to be performed economically by any available robot.

2. A robot must perform the job because of safety reasons, space limitation, or special accuracy requirements.

3. A robot can replace a human operator on an existing job, and the shift to robot operation could result in improvements such as higher consistency, better quality, lower costs, and so forth. Labor shortages in certain types of jobs may also result in robot assignments.

In the first two cases, the selection is clear. In the third case, the main concern is whether a robot can at all perform a given task. The robot–human charts provide a means of identifying job activities that can or cannot be done by robots or humans. Another approach for assessing different dimensions in the problem is a systematic comparison between robot time and motion (RTM) task method elements for a robot, and methods time measurement (MTM) elements for a human operator. Additional information for this decision can be obtained from a database of robot work abilities.

Robot Anatomy and Distribution of Work Abilities

A thorough examination of industrial robots and their controls (9) provides an anatomy of the basic structure and controls of robots and reveals their resulting limitations, particularly in the area of sensor ability and task interactions. To determine the current abilities of industrial robots, literature describing numerous models was summarized and analyzed in two forms (10, 11): characteristic frequency distributions and motion–velocity graphs. Such a survey can provide the job analyst with detailed and specific work ability to determine if a robot can perform a job and which robot is preferred.

Planning Work Methods and Processes

A good work method determines how well limited resources, such as time, energy, and materials, are being used and has a major influence on the quality of the product or output. A strategy for designing new methods or for improving existing methods is composed of seven steps (12):

1. Determine the purpose of the method.
2. Conceptualize ideal methods.

3. Identify constraints and regularity.

4. Outline several practical methods, using principles such as those in Table 15.4.

5. Select the best method outline by evaluating the alternatives and using criteria such as hazard elimination, economics, and control.

6. Formulate the details of the selected method outline.

7. Analyze the proposed method for further improvement.

Work methods must be documented for records, ongoing improvement, time study, and training. Several tools are available for methods documentation as well as for gathering and analyzing information about work methods (13), e.g., process charts, workplace charts, multiple activity charts, and product flow sequence charts.

Motion Study

Work performance is usually accomplished by a combination of motions, and this is certainly true for robot work. The effectiveness of the movement can be measured in terms of time and accuracy. Motion study applies various techniques to examine thoroughly all of the motions that comprise a work method. Based on this examination, alternative methods can be evaluated, compared, and improved. One of the most useful practices in motion study is the use of video cameras. While the various charts identified earlier are commonly used in motion study, the use of videotape or film has several advantages: it provides data acquisition and records facts that are unobtainable by other means, it can provide quick study results, it allows individual analysis of simultaneous activities, it allows detailed analysis away from the actual work area, and it provides a permanent record for future reference and training. One disadvantage, however, is that this technique can be applied only if there is access to an existing system.

Job and Skills Analysis

Job and skills analysis methods have been used for cost-reduction programs in human–human and conventional human–machine work environments and for the effective selection and training of personnel. The job analysis focuses on what to do, while the skills analysis focuses on the "how." The method, as it has been traditionally applied for human work, includes three major stages:

1. Examine the task to be analyzed to understand what and how the operator must do the job. If it is not possible to observe an existing task, assess how the task would be performed.

TABLE 15.4.   Principles for Methods Design[a]

1. Design only to accomplish necessary purposes in the most ideal way.
2. Consider all system elements and dimensions.
3. Design for regularity before considering exceptions.
4. Focus on what should be, rather than on what is.
5. Consider layout and equipment design.
6. Eliminate or minimize all motions.
7. Consider best operator's position:
   Keep people's back straight and their hands close to their body.
   Keep robots close to points of operation to minimize motion distance.
8. Handle objects and record information only if needed, and then only once.
9. Minimize use of all resources: time, energy, materials, money.
10. Follow motion economy principles.

[a] Revised from ref. 12.

2. Using Table 15.5*a*, document the what and the how of task performance.
3. From the documentation in Table 15.5, examine in a systematic way the possibilities of performing the task in different ways, including the following guidelines that are relevant for human operators:
   a. Use of kinesthetic (sense of direction) instead of visual senses.
   b. Reduction of factors complicating the task performance ("noise").
   c. Reduction or use of perceptual load associated with task performance.
   d. Use of principles of motion economy and workplace design to simplify the task.
   e. Resequence, eliminate, or combine elements.

Alternative ways are compared by the time it takes to perform them, complexity, quality, error probability, cost, safety, training and skill requirements, and so forth. Based on such analysis, the best method to perform a task can be selected and implemented.

The features that distinguish robot and human operators, as discussed previously, necessitate modification of the original human job and skills analysis method (7). As before, a task is broken down to elements that are specified with their time and requirements. However, the columns are modified as shown in Table 15.5*b*.

Limbs Column. The human left hand, right hand column is replaced by a limbs column, because the robot may be designed to have any number and variety of limbs (e.g., arms, grippers, special tool hands, etc.).

Memory and Program Column. A column for memory and decision details is added for the analysis of robot performance. These details will determine what type of computer memory

TABLE 15.5. Job and Skills Analysis[a]

a. Human Performance

Element	Time	Left Hand, Right Hand	Vision	Other Senses	Comments
An operationally definable task component that has a clear beginning and end points (e.g., moving an item from point A to point B)	Time to perform the given element	Describes which part of the element is performed by which hand (Separate columns are used for left hand, right hand)	Indicates the extent to which vision is used for the performance of the element (e.g., confirm by vision the current position of an object)	Indicates the extent to which other senses such as touch, kinethesis, hearing, etc. are used for the performance of the element	Components of the element where some special precaution has to be exercised (e.g., in joining two parts, the holes in component A must match the holes in Component B)

b. Robot Performance

Element	Time	Senses	Limbs	Memory and Program	Comments
As above except each element is a detailed micromotion	Time to perform the given element	Each of the major robot senses, namely, vision, touch, force compliance, is treated in the same manner that vision is treated above (a separate column can be used for each)	Each of the robot limbs is treated individually (in separate columns) as left–right human arms are treated above	Specific memory requirements needed for the element such as word length, storage capacity, etc; program required includes reference information and logic for decision making in the element	Comments about special requirements such as engineering tolerances, electricity, air pressure, and other utilities

[a] From ref. 7.

and processing capability is needed, if at all. Humans have their own memory, but decisions that are self-explanatory and often trivial for humans must be completely specified for robots. Robots may be designed, as explained earlier, with no programmability (i.e., with a fixed sequence), a variable sequence that is fixed differently from time to time, or with computer and feedback mechanisms that control the robot operations. The cost of a robot increases, of course, with the degree of programmability and sophistication of computer control: higher levels of robot control require additional investment in hardware. Furthermore, limited controllers may be based on pneumatic control that requires relatively simply human skills to resequence. More complex operations may require computer control with associated system software and control programmers. Therefore, a work method that permits a fixed sequence will need a simple, cheaper robot and be preferred to one that needs periodic resequencing or complex programming.

Comment Column. The comment column is for details about additional requirements such as position tolerances and utilities. Special precautions that are typical in the human-oriented analysis are probably not necessary here because they should appear in written decision logic information.

As indicated previously, robots possess no basic knowledge or experience and, therefore, necessitate much detail in the task specifications. Thus elements will most commonly specify micromotions, with their time measured in seconds (or minute/100). Once a task is specified, its analysis basically follows the three stages described in the human-oriented method: (*1*) examine task elements, (*2*) document the what and how of all elements, and (*3*) systematically examine and evaluate alternative ways. However, because it is possible to select a robot and design its capabilities to best suit the task requirements, the performance evaluation in the last stage should be expanded as follows.

From the documentation in Table 15.5*b*, examine systematically, using robot motion economy principles, the possibilities of performing the task in different ways and of using different robots.

Motion Economy Principles

Principles of motion economy were proposed first by Frank Gilbreth in 1923 and later formalized and expanded by Barnes (14) and others. The purpose of these principles is to guide the development, troubleshooting, and improvement of work methods and workplaces, with special attention to human operators. Some of the principles, however, can be adopted or adapted for robot work, while some are not useful for robot work. Following is a list of important principles for human operators, and their relevance to robot work.

Principles Related to Operator

1. *Hands and arms should follow smooth, continuous motion patterns.* This principle may be useful for robot work when process quality considerations require it (e.g., in painting to eliminate jerky strokes). See principle 2 under "Principles Concerning Robots."

2. *Human hands should move simultaneously and symmetrically, beginning and ending their motions together.* This principle is irrelevant for robots because coordinated robot arms can operate well under distributed computer controls.

3. *Minimize motion distance, within practical limits.* To reduce motion time and improve accuracy by not operating overextended limbs. Relevant for both humans and robots.

4. *Both hands should be used for productive work.* This principle is irrelevant for robots because the number of arms can be chosen to maximize utilization.

5. *Work requiring the use of eyes should be limited to the field of normal vision.* Directly relevant to robots whenever vision is required.

6. *Actions should be distributed and assigned to body muscles according to their abilities.* This principle is only partially useful for robots—the robot work abilities should be specified according to the precise task requirements.

7. *Muscular force required for motions should be minimized.* On the one hand, body momentum should be used to advantage; on the other hand, momentum should be minimized to reduce the force required to overcome it (e.g., it is better to slide parts than to carry them).

Principles Related to the Work Environment

1. *Workplace should be designed for motion economy* (i.e., tools, parts and materials should be placed in fixed, reachable positions, and in the sequence in which they are used by a robot). In addition, the height of a work surface should be designed within the robot work envelope.

2. *Tools and equipment should be designed and selected with ergonomics guidelines.* This principle is concerned with the dimension and shape of items handled by end-of-arm tooling, with safety and effectiveness in mind.

3. *Materials handling equipment should be selected to minimize handling time and weight.* For instance, parts should be brought as close as possible to the point of use; fixed items position and orientation simplify pickup and delivery.

Principles Concerning Time Conservation

1. *All hesitations, temporary delays or stops should be questioned.* Regular, unavoidable delays should be used to schedule additional work. For instance, in a foundry, delays caused by metal cooling-off period can be used by robots for gate removal; in machine tending, when one machine is performing a process the robot can load–unload another machine.

2. *The number of motions should be minimized.* Elimination and combination of work elements are the two most common methods to achieve this goal.

3. *Working on more than one part at a time should be attempted.* This principle can be generalized to multiarm robots. Again, the number of robot arms or hands can be chosen for the most effective work method.

Principles Concerning Robots. These new principles are based mainly on the fact that robot work abilities can be designed and optimized to best fit the task objectives.

1. *Reduce the robot's structural complexity* (i.e., minimize the number of arms and arm joints that are determined by the number of hand orientations; reduce the robot dimensions that are determined by the distance the robot has to reach; reduce the load that the robot has to carry). These will result in a requirement for a cheaper robot, lower energy consumption, simpler maintenance, smaller work space.

2. *Simplify the necessary motion path.* Point-to-point motion requires simpler control of positioning and velocity compared with continuous path motion.

3. *Minimize the number of sensors,* because each sensor adds to installation and operating costs by additional hardware, information processing, and repairs. Use of robot with no senses is preferred to one sense, one sense is preferred to two, and so on.

4. *Use local feedback if at all necessary, instead of nonlocal feedback:* for example, use of aligning pins for compliance provides quick local feedback. Use of touch or force sensors requires wiring and processing by a control system. Local feedback may add operations and may increase the overall process time, but usually needs no wiring and no information processing.

5. *Use touch or force sensors, if at all necessary, instead of vision systems,* because the cost of the latter is significantly higher and requires more complex computer support. However, when vision is necessary as part of an operation, attempt to minimize the number of lenses that are required, as this will simplify information processing requirements and shorten the visual sensing time.

6. *Take advantage of robot abilities that have already been determined as required* to reduce the cost and time of the job method. In other words, if a sensor or a computer must be provided for a certain task function, use it to improve the performance of other functions.

15.6 PERFORMANCE MEASUREMENT

Performance measurement, including work measurement, performance prediction, and performance evaluation, accompanies a work system throughout its life cycle. In the planning and design stages performance prediction is required to evaluate the technical and economic feasibility of a proposed job plan and to compare and select the best out of a set of feasible alternatives. During the development and installation stages, performance measurement provides a yardstick for progress toward effective job implementation. In the regular, ongoing operations, performance evaluation serves to set and revise work standards, troubleshoot bottlenecks and conflicts, train workers, and estimate cost and duration of new work orders. Another vital function of performance measurement at this stage is the examination of new work methods, technologies, and equipment that can be used to upgrade, expand, and modernize the existing operations on the job.

Work Measurement and Time-and-Motion Studies

Robot designers have long been concerned with planning robot motions in an optimal way (i.e., accurately follow specified trajectories while avoiding collisions and moving at the minimum amount of time) (15). For instance, early studies (16) investigated the minimum cycle time problem of a robot moving among obstacles by analyzing alternative combinations of simultaneous motions of different joints. Others (17–20) examined additional problems of motion control optimization. From a work method point of view, however, cycle times can be reduced by carefully following the motion principles described previously. For instance, Birk and Franklin (21) found that proper placement of workpieces led to improved performance. Others (22–25) performed time-and-motion studies to evaluate, select, and compare alternative robot system designs.

RTM Method

The RTM method (26–29) for predetermined robot cycle times is based on standard elements of fundamental robot work motions. RTM is analogous to the MTM technique (30, 31), which has long been in use for human work analysis. Both methods enable users to estimate the cycle time for given work methods without having to first implement the work method and measure its performance. Therefore, these methods can be highly useful for selection of equipment as well as work methods without having to purchase and commit to any equipment. MTM users, however, must consider human individual variability and allow for pacing effects. RTM, on the other hand, can rely on the consistency of robots and apply computational models based on physical parameters of each particular robot model.

The RTM methodology provides a high level, user-friendly technique with the following capabilities:

1. Systematically specifies a work method for a given robot in a simple, straightforward manner.
2. Applies computer aids to evaluate a specified method by time to perform, number of steps, positioning tolerances, and other requirements so that alternative work methods can be compared.
3. Repeats methods evaluation for alternative robot models until the best combination is established.

The RTM system is composed of three major components: RTM elements, robot performance models, and an RTM analyzer. The system has been implemented, experimented with, and applied with several robot models, including the Stanford Arm equipped with touch and force sensing, Cincinnati Milacron's T3, PUMA, Unimates, and others. Several companies have adopted and applied the RTM methodology, and there has been one development of a commercial product (ROFAC, Robot Factor) based on RTM (32).

The RTM user can apply 10 general work elements to specify any robot work, by breaking the method down to its basic steps. The RTM elements are shown in Table 15.6, and they are divided into five major groups:

RTM Group 1. Movement elements—REACH, MOVE, and ORIENT.
RTM Group 2. Sensing elements—STOP-ON-ERROR, STOP-ON-FORCE, TOUCH, and VISION.

TABLE 15.6.   RTM Symbols and Elements

Element Number		Symbol		Definition of Element	Element Parameters
1		Rn		*n-Segment reach:* Move unloaded manipulator along a path composed of *n* segments	Displacement (linear or angular) and velocity or Path geometry and velocity
2		Mn		*n-Segment move:* Move object along path composed of *n* segments	
3		ORn		*n-Segment orientation:* Move manipulator mainly to reorient	
4		SEi		*Stop on position error*	Error bound
	4.1		SE1	Bring the manipulator to rest immediately without waiting to null out joints errors	
	4.2		SE2	Bring the manipulator to rest within a specified position error tolerance	
5		SFi		*Stop on force or moment*	Force, torque, and touch values
	5.1		SF1	Stop the manipulator when force conditions are met	
	5.2		SF2	Stop the manipulator when torque conditions are met	
	5.3		SF3	Stop the manipulator when either torque or force conditions are met	
	5.4		SF4	Stop the manipulator when touch conditions are met	
6		VI		Vision operation	Time function
7		GRi		*Grasp an object*	
	7.1		GR1	Simple grasp of object by closing fingers	
	7.2		GR2	Grasp object while centering hand over it	Distance to close–open fingers
	7.3		GR3	Grasp object by closing one finger at a time	
8		RE		Release object by opening fingers	
9		T		Process time delay when the robot is part of the process	Time function
10		D		Time delay when the robot is waiting for a process completion	Time function
11		MB		Mobility elements	
	11.1		SMF	Straight movement forward	
	11.2		SMS	Straight movement sideways	
	11.3		STS	Spin turn on the spot	Parameters: velocity and path functions
	11.4		CAO	Curve with a 90° angle with change of orientation	
	11.5		DMC	Diagonal movement with a constant orientation	

RTM Group 3. Gripper or tool elements—GRASP and RELEASE.

RTM Group 4. Delay elements—PROCESS-TIME-DELAY and TIME-DELAY.

RTM Group 5. Mobility elements—straight movements, spin turn, curve, and diagonal movement.

By applying the RTM elements with the parameters shown in Table 15.6, alternative robot work methods can be analyzed, evaluated, compared, and improved.

RTM Performance Models

The two ways to approach the modeling of robot work are by (*1*) approximating empirical data gained from laboratory experiments and (*2*) engineering design of the robot operation. The first way is exemplified by the use of element tables and regression equations; the other by the use of motion control models and motion path analysis. The simplest modeling approach, which follows the original MTM approach for human work methods, applies a set of tables with estimates for each element according to particular parameters. Tables are developed based on laboratory experiments with the robot type for which data are prepared.

Table 15.7 contains time data for elements REACH (R1) or MOVE (M1), and ORIENT (OR1) for Cincinnati Milacron's T³ robot (Figure 15.8). REACH and MOVE elements for the T³ are identical, because carried weight does not affect performance time. The table approach is relatively simple, though it requires extensive laboratory experimentation to develop the table values for each robot model family. However, once tables are established for a particular robot type, they can be applied by everybody. Times for motions at distances not in the table can easily be interpolated. It is important to note that despite the relative simplicity of this approach, it was found to be quite satisfactory for its prediction purposes. In laboratory experiments variations between predictions based on the table approach and actual, measured time values of complete tasks have been within the range of about ±5 to 10%.

TABLE 15.7.   RTM Tables for Cincinnati Milacron's T³ REACH–MOVE and ORIENT

1. Reach (R1) or Move (M1)

Distance to Move (cm)	Time (s) at Velocity (cm/s)				
	5.0	12.5	25.0	50.0	100.0
1	0.4	0.4	0.4	0.4	0.4
30	6.4	2.8	1.6	1.0	0.8
100	21.3	8.7	4.5	2.4	1.4

2. ORIENT (OR1)

Angle to Move (deg)	Time (s) at Velocity (cm/s)				
	5.0	12.5	25.0	50.0	100.0
15	3.0	1.4	0.8	0.6	0.6
60	10.8	4.6	2.5	1.4	0.9
120	21.3	8.7	4.6	2.5	1.4

Regression equations developed for the RTM system relate mathematically the motion time to its major factors. Such operations were tested and have been found to yield a predictive accuracy similar to that of the table's approach (28). A different modeling approach predicts motion time according to the pattern by which the robot velocity is controlled. For the T³, like several other robot models, the velocity is controlled as shown in Figure 15.9. From kinematic relations, and experimental work for short motions, equations can be developed. Basically, motions include acceleration and deceleration segments, and if they are sufficiently long, also a slew motion (i.e., at constant velocity). Mobility elements have also been developed for RTM following the velocity control method. The predictive accuracy of this modeling approach, as found in laboratory experiments, has been in the range of −2 to +3%.

Robot motions were also modeled by specifying the complete motion path geometry. Based on robot joints and link velocities, the motion time can be computed. It should be noted, however, that the detailed input data required for the geometric specification of each motion path are usually not available during advanced work planning stages. In addition to the various motion elements, various sensor time elements have been developed (see Table 15.6, elements

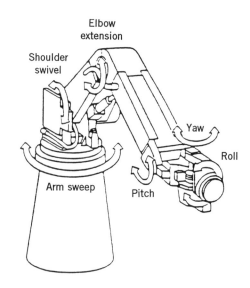

Figure 15.8. Cincinnati Milacron's T³ robot. Courtesy of Cincinnati Milacron.

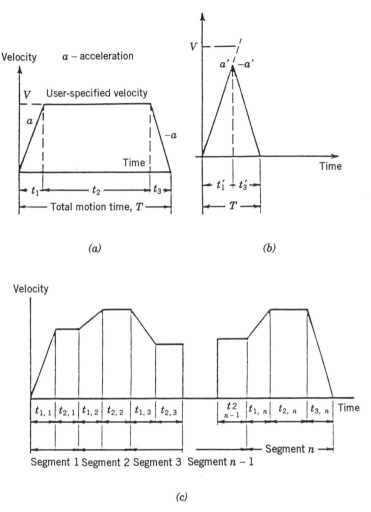

Figure 15.9. Velocity patterns. (*a*) Velocity pattern of regular one-segment T³ motions. (*b*) Velocity pattern of short one-segment T³ motions. (*c*) Velocity pattern of general multisegment T³ motions.

4, 5, and 6). The time functions for sensors depend on hardware and software characteristics of the sensors.

RTM Analyzer

The RTM analyzer has been developed (10, 28) to provide a means of systematically specifying robot work methods with direct computation of performance measures. The input to the RTM analyzer includes control data (e.g., task and subtask titles, type of robot, and type of RTM model to apply) and operation statements. The statements specify robot operations, each represented by RTM element and its parameters; and control logic that provides capabilities of REPEAT blocks, PARALLEL blocks, conditional branching, and probabilistic generation of conditions.

A simplified RTM, a subset of RTM, was also developed for point operations such as spot welding, drilling, and riveting (33). In point operations the robot carries a tool or a part during the whole operation; the same operation type is performed repeatedly along one or more paths, and the execution time of the tool at each point is well known and can be calculated rather than estimated. Taking advantage of these characteristics, the specification and computation can be simplified with little loss of accuracy.

Performance Simulators and Robot Graphic Simulators

A number of performance simulators have been developed for the analysis and evaluation of robotic work (34–36). Another type of robot performance analysis is by graphics simulation. The main objective of such simulations is to observe the geometric and spatial aspects of the robot workplace. A number of examples of simulations are available (37–39).

Another approach to simulation is physical simulation, as described by Nof et al. (41). Using a computer-controlled scale model of a robot arm, the load–unload operation on machining centers was studied. A good example of the use of simulation for robot work analysis is described by Kondoleon (25). He studied alternative configurations of robotic assembly of automobile alternators, including a single-arm programmable station with several, alternative work methods, two synchronized arms co-working on the same unit, and two arms working on different parts of the product. The objective was to increase cycle time efficiently, mainly by reducing the tool change time. An interesting alternative that was examined entailed the building of several assemblies together by specialized tooling, thus spreading the tool change time over many units. For instance, it was found by the simulation that at a higher cost of fixturing, building six units together reduced the cycle time per unit by about 40%. On the other hand, building twice as many units, 12 units together, yielded a reduction of only about 44%. These reductions held approximately the same for five alternative methods. However, the preferred method of complete assembly of units at one station (for 1, 6, or 12 at a time) required a cycle time about 20% shorter than the worst alternative considered, and about 13% shorter than the average cycle time of all five alternatives. Thus a performance simulation combining the details of work method, workplace, and control strategy can provide highly useful information to designers.

Graphic Simulators

Graphic simulators have been developed to design robotic systems and recently also to serve as part of their interactive control system. Engineers can select robots by evaluating, in simulation, alternative manipulators integrated into a work cell, considering machines in the cell, material and tool flow, and control strategies. In addition to evaluating many alternatives without physically acquiring, installing, and programming the robots, the advantages of such simulation are that new, creative design concepts can be tried, and the design or redesign efforts are performed off-line and do not disrupt the factory floor. Graphic simulators are also excellent tools for programming and debugging robot motions, including the detection and prevention of errors and safety problems. Details about organization of a robot graphic simulator (Figure 15.10) and the theory behind robot simulation, including kinematic and dynamic robot modeling, computer graphics and simulator organization can be found in refs. 41 and 42.

General robot graphic simulators include libraries of numerous robot models from various robot makers and have the capability to translate simulation programs to various robot languages. Two leading examples of such simulators are Interactive Graphics Robot Instruction Program (IGRIP) and ROBCAD, both three-dimensional graphic systems for the design, simulation, and off-line programming of robotic, or flexible automation systems (Figure 15.11). Such simulators provide, in addition to the off-line design functions listed earlier, work-cell layout and placement design, reachability studies, cycle-time estimation, maintenance of robot programs, communication with CAD systems, and monitoring of teleoperated manipulators.

15.7 ROBOT WORKPLACE DESIGN

The best workplace is the workplace that supports and enables the most effective accomplishment of the chosen work method. The layout of a workplace determines, in general, four main work characteristics:

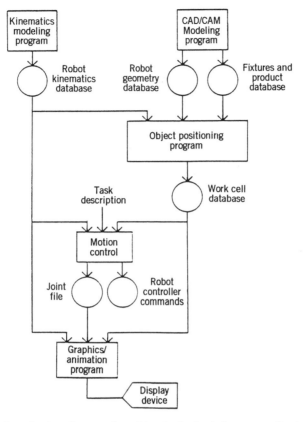

Figure 15.10. Organization of a general graphic robotic simulation system. Rectangles indicate software modules and circles indicate data (from ref. 41).

1. The distance of movements and the motions that must be carried out to fulfill the task.
2. The amount of storage space.
3. The delays caused by interference with various components operating in the workplace.
4. The feelings and attitudes of operators toward their work. The latter, obviously, is not a concern for robots.

Typical configurations of robotic workplaces are shown in Figure 15.12. General information about the design of a workplace layout can be found in work by Apple (43) and Francis and White (44). In traditional ergonomics a workplace is designed for human operators, as developed, for instance, by Bonney and Case (45). Hence, there are anthopometric, biomechanical, and other human factors considered. In analogy, in regard to robotic workplaces, robot dimension and other physical properties such as reachability, accuracy, gripper size, and orientation will determine the design of the workplace. In addition, requirements as those shown in Table 15.8 must be considered: whether tasks are variable and/or are handled by one or more robots; whether workplace resources are shared by the robots; the nature and size of components stationed in the workplace; and the characteristics of parts flow into, within, and outside of the workplace. Several researchers have studied specific layout models for robot systems (46). Because all robot operations are controlled by a computer, several robots can interact while concurrently performing a common task and even share resources (47, 48)—a difficult requirement when people must interact under a tight-sequencing control. Thus a robotic workplace can be optimized with regard to the layout and also planned for effective control of operations.

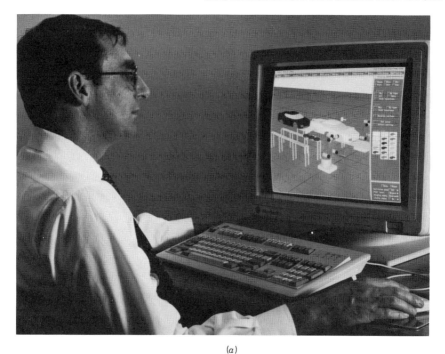

(a)

(b)

Figure 15.11. Graphic simulator of robotic and flexible production systems. Courtesy of Technomatix, Inc. (a) Interactive simulations of a robotic manufacturing cell using ROBCAD. (b) Drilling and riveting of an airframe subassembly. An external track extends the robot work envelope.

TABLE 15.8. Classification of Robotic Workplaces

Robots	Tasks	Stations Inside Workplace: Machines, Feeders, Other Equipment	Input–Output Flow
Simple robot	Single or multiple tasks Fixed or variable motion sequence	Uniform or different station area Fixed or variable equipment	Single or multiple entry, exit One or more directions of flow
Multiple robots	Single or multiple tasks per robot per team With or without task interaction	With or without equipment sharing (for multiple robots)	With or without part grouping (binning, kitting, magazining, palletizing)
Multiple robot cells	With or without cell overlap		

LAYOUT EXAMPLE #1

CONVEYOR CONFIGURATIONS

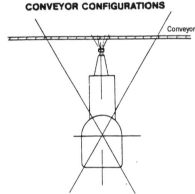

• Straight line conveyor limits access by robot, by in & out movement of robot.

LAYOUT EXAMPLE #2

CONVEYOR CONFIGURATIONS

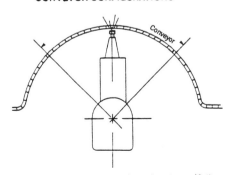

• Wrap around conveyor takes advantage of full radial motion of robot. (90 to 300 degrees.)

LAYOUT EXAMPLE #3

PUNCH PRESS SYSTEM

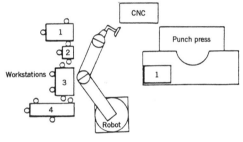

• Various sheet metal blanks stored in designated work stations.
• Robot picks part from station sequentially as long as all stations are full.
• When part is removed from station "cnc" control is notified which program to use to operate the punch press.
• All parts look same to the robot. Parts all bank off two edges when located in machine.
• Vacuum cup hand used for versatility.
• Random access programming required in robot.

Figure 15.12. Layout examples.

LAYOUT EXAMPLE #4

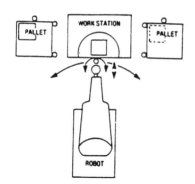

- At least 3 axes of motion required.
- Extensive axes motions complicate programming task.

LAYOUT EXAMPLE #5

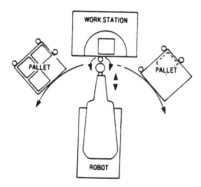

- At least 3 axes of motion required.
- Axes motions reduced somewhat, but programming still not simple.

LAYOUT EXAMPLE #6

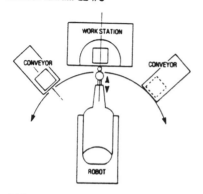

- At least two axes of motion required.
- Simplest of last three work stations to program.

LAYOUT EXAMPLE #7

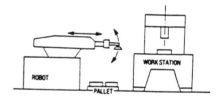

- Variation in heighth between work station and pallet will require additional robot axes as shown.
- Increases programming effort.

LAYOUT EXAMPLE #8

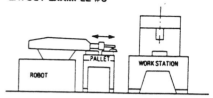

- Axes of robot motion reduced by making work station heighth and part pickup, *same!*
- Simpler programming task.

LAYOUT EXAMPLE #9

"SAFETY"

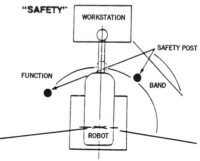

- You never trust a robot within its mechanical function parameters.
- Overpowering restriction posts or other barriers are the only acceptable protection for humans in the area.
- Interlock gates should be used to keep personnel out of robot area.
- Interlock footpads can also be used.

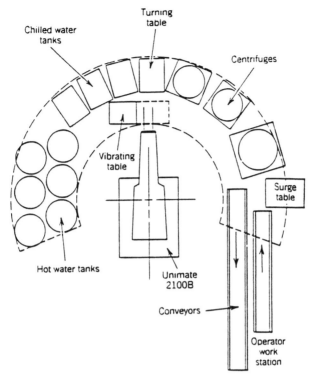

Figure 15.13. Robotic applications that integrate human operators for the operation completion. A large robot carries out the air separation from mercury in clinical thermometer manufacturing, Human role: control the flow of baskets on conveyors in/out to prevent glass breakage.

15.8   INTEGRATED HUMAN AND ROBOT ERGONOMICS

A vital area in robotic job design is the integration of humans and robots in work systems. While industry has tended to separate employees from robot activities as much as possible, mainly for safety reasons, there are several important issues to consider.

Roles of Human Operators in Robotic Systems

Except for unmanned production facilities, people will always work together with robots, with varying degrees of participation (Figure 15.13). Parsons and Kearsley (49) offer the acronym SIMBIOSIS to the roles of humans in robotic systems:

Surveillance—monitoring of robots.

Intervention—setup, startup, shutdown, programming, and correcting.

Maintenance.

Backup—substituting manual work for robotic at breakdown or changeover.

Input and Output—manual handling before and after the robotic operation.

Supervision—management, planning, and exception handling.

Inspection—quality control and assurance beyond automatic inspection.

Synergy—combination of humans and robots in operation (e.g., assembly or supervisory control of robots by humans).

In all of these roles the objective is to optimize the overall work performance. The idea is to plan a robotic system with the required degree of integration to use best the respective advantages of humans and robots working in concert. Human factors considerations in planning robot systems for these roles (49–55) include job and workplace design, work environment, training, safety, pacing, and planning of supervisory control.

Learning to Work with Robots

Both individuals and organizations using robots must learn to work effectively with the robots. Aoki (56) describes the progress of his company in using robots. Robot performance in die casting was improved over time, following the learning curve model. The workers planning and operating the robot first improved its work method and program; then they improved the program (and method) further and introduced improvements in hardware. This is basically a process of organizational learning that is based on learning by a group of individuals to better use robots. Many other companies report similar progress in adopting robot operators, similar to adopting any new technology.

In a prototype study (57), the objective was to investigate how employees, as individuals, perceive and accept a new robot, the first in their company. Workers were interviewed 2.5 months before and 2.5 months after the robot introduction. As can be expected, with time and experience workers increased their understanding about what a robot really is. However, with time, workers' beliefs about robots (e.g., the potential hazards associated with robots) became more complex and pessimistic. In addition, an increase in stress was indicated among workers interacting directly with the robot. Further research is needed on this problem; however, the researchers saw their findings as another indication that effective strategies for correct introduction of robots to the factory are vital to the success of robot implementations.

15.9 MULTIROBOT APPLICATIONS

Use of multiple robots with various levels of interactions are emerging applications in industry. Multirobot systems can mainly be classified into two groups: autonomous and cooperative. Under autonomous operation, each robot performs a prespecified set of tasks and does not interact with the other robots in the system. Such a system can be viewed as a collection of single robot work cells organized as a multiple robot system to perform a collection of tasks.

A cooperative multirobot system exploits the ability of the robots to perform tasks independently or by cooperation. Thus it provides the flexibility of single robot cells by having robots perform tasks independently along with the added dimension of task performance obtained by using the cooperative capabilities of robot sets (48, 58). A given cooperative multirobot system is capable of performing a wide variety of tasks. In addition, such systems have enhanced reliability due to the ability to perform tasks assigned to failed robots by using other single robots or cooperative robot sets with the required capabilities. Some of the types of tasks that can be performed by cooperating robot sets are shown in Figure 15.14. While autonomous multirobot systems can be used to mimic high production volume and hard automation lines with greater flexibility, cooperative multirobot systems are mainly useful for small volume, large variety part production.

Some research issues related to multirobot systems are kinematics–dynamics of cooperating robots (59, 60), motion planning and collision avoidance in shared workspaces (61), multirobot cooperation activity control (62), and cooperation requirement planning for multirobot assembly (58). Figure 15.15 shows the graphical simulation snapshot of a flexible fixturing operation based on the cooperation requirement planning system implementation (58).

15.10 SUMMARY AND FUTURE TRENDS

Techniques and knowledge developed by robot companies and researchers have been identified and described as necessary for planning effective, industrial robot work. Traditional engineering tools can be extended to develop human–robot work systems. On the other hand, new

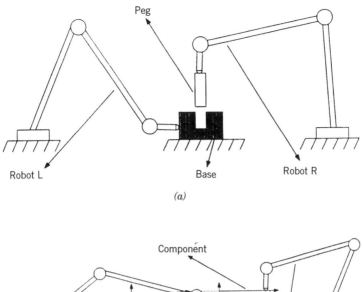

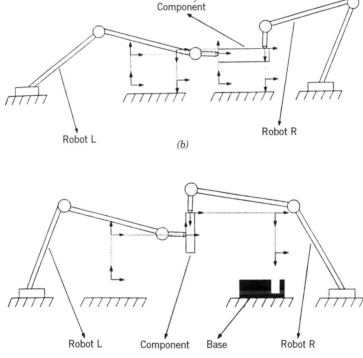

Figure 15.14. Three principal types of cooperation between robots: (*a*) flexible fixturing, (*b*) transport of an unwieldy or heavy component from one location to another by parallel cooperation, and (*c*) transport of a component from one location to another by sequential cooperation due to inaccessibility of both the initial and final locations to any single robot.

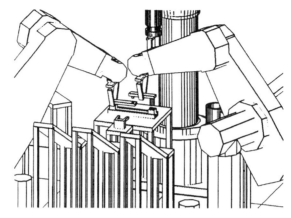

Figure 15.15. Snapshot of a flexible fixturing operation graphical simulation based on the cooperation requirement planning system implementation (58), using the ROBCAD simulator on a Silicon Graphics IRIS 4D/80GT graphics workstation.

TABLE 15.9. Emerging Capabilities and Trends of Industrial Robotics Systems

Recognition and inference of random parts position–orientation by vision

Tactile sensing used for part recognition, position–orientation inference and inspection

Computer interpretation of visual and tactile data by sensor fusion

Task level and knowledge-based programming

Multiple manipulator coordination for cooperating robots

General-purpose hands and flexible grippers

Knowledge-based trajectories and trajectory strategies generation

Natural-language communication with human operators

Mobility for wide-area tasks and factory integration

Self-diagnostic fault tracing and self-repair

Inherent safety

Neural controllers for learning and fuzzy logic controllers to enhance robot autonomy

techniques have evolved from traditional methods for the purpose of planning the work of robots themselves. Basically, robots offer a new dimension in work design by allowing design of the "operator" (i.e., the robot) itself. Table 15.9 summarizes available and emerging capabilities and trends in industrial robotics. It is expected that further research and practice will lead to the development and refinement of additional, innovative robot ergonomic techniques and knowledge.

BIBLIOGRAPHY

1. J.F. ENGLELBERGER, in S.Y. Nof, ed., *Handbook of Industrial Robotics,* John Wiley & Sons, Inc., New York, 1985, pp. 3–8.
2. M. CORWIN, "The Benefits of a Computer-Controlled Robot" in *Proceedings of the 5th International Symposium on Industrial Robotics,* SME, 1975, pp. 453–469.

3. R.C. DORF and S.Y. NOF, (eds.) "Pioneers in Robotics," "Robot Evolution," "Robot Systems, Evolution," and "Vision Systems, History" in *International Encyclopedia of Robotics, Applications and Automation,* Vols. 1–3, John Wiley & Sons, Inc., New York, 1988.

4. H.J. WARNECKE, R.D. SCHRAFT, and M.C. WANNER, "Mechanical Design of the Robot System" in S.Y. Nof ed., *Handbook of Industrial Robotics,* John Wiley & Sons, Inc., New York, 1985, pp. 44–79.

5. M.P. GROOVER, M. WEISS, R.N. NAGEL, and N.G. ODRY, *Industrial Robotics, Technology, Programming, and Applications,* McGraw-Hill Book Co., Inc., New York, 1986.

6. V.D. HUNT, *Industrial Robotics Handbook,* Industrial Press, New York, 1983.

7. S.Y. NOF, J.L. KNIGHT, and G. SALVENDY, "Effective Utilization of Industrial Robotics—A Job and Skill Analysis Approach," *AIIE Trans.* **12**(3), 216–225 (1980).

8. W.E. WOODSON, *Human Factors Design Handbook,* McGraw-Hill Book Co., Inc., New York, 1981.

9. J.Y.S. LUH, "An Anatomy of Industrial Robots and Their Controls," *IEEE Trans. Auto. Control* **28**(2), 133–153 (1983).

10. S.Y. NOF, "Robot Ergonomics: Optimizing Robot Work" in S.Y. Nof, ed., *Handbook of Industrial Robotics,* John Wiley & Sons, Inc., New York, 1985, pp. 549–604.

11. R.A. PENNINGTON, E.L. FISHER, and S.Y. NOF, "Analysis of Robot Work Characteristics," *Indust. Robot,* 166–171 (1982).

12. G. NADLER, *The Planning and Design Professions: An Operational Theory,* John Wiley & Sons, Inc., New York, 1981.

13. D.O. CLARAK, and G.C. CLOSE, "Motion Study," in G. Salvendy, ed., *The Handbook of Industrial Engineering,* 2nd ed., John Wiley & Sons, Inc., New York, 1992, Chapt. 3.2.

14. R.M. BARNES, *Motion and Time Study,* 6th ed., John Wiley & Sons, Inc., New York, 1968.

15. M. BRADY et al., eds., *Robot Motion Planning and Control,* MIT Press, Cambridge Mass., 1982.

16. D.L. PIEPER and B. ROTH, *The Kinematics of Manipulators under Computer Control,* paper presented at the 2nd International Conference on Theory of Machines and Mechanisms, Warsaw, Poland, Sept. 1969.

17. M.E. KAHN and B. ROTH, "The New-Minimum-Time Control of Open-Loop Articulated Kinematic Chain," *ASME Trans. J. Dynamic Sys. Measurement Control* **93**, 164–172 (1971).

18. J.Y.S. LUH and M.W. WALKER, "Minimum-Time along the Path for a Mechanical Arm" in *Proceedings of the 1977 IEEE Conference on Decision and Control,* 1977, pp. 775–759.

19. P.M. LYNCH, *Minimum Time, Sequential Axis Operation of a Cylindrical Two Axis Manipulator,* paper presented at the Joint Automatic Control Conference, Charlottesville, Va., 1981.

20. J.Y.S. LUH and C.S. LIN, "Optimum Path Planning for Mechanical Manipulators," *ASME Trans. J. Dynamic Sys. Measurement Control* **103**, 142–151 (1981).

21. J.R. BIRK and D.E. FRANKLIN, "Pitching Workpieces to Minimize the Cycle Time of Industrial Robots," *Indust. Robot* **1**(5), 217–222 (1974).

22. W.L. VERPLANK, *Research on Remote Manipulation of NASA Ames Research Center,* U.S. Department of Commerce, Washington, D.C., 1976, NBS Spec. Pub. No. 459.

23. J. VERTUT, *Experience and Remarks on Manipulator Evaluation,* U.S. Department of Commerce, Washington, D.C., 1976, NBS Spec. Pub. No. 459.

24. P.F. ROGERS, "Time and Motion Method for Industrial Robots," *Indust. Robot* **5**, 187–192 (1978).

25. A.S. KONDOLEON, *Cycle Time Analysis of Robot Assembly Systems,* SME, Dearborn, Mich., 1979, Paper No. MS79-286.

26. R.L. PAUL and S.Y. NOF, "Work Methods Measurement—A Comparison between Robot and Human Task Performance," *Int. J. Product. Res.* **17**(3), 277–303 (1979).

27. S.Y. NOF and R.L. PAUL, "A Method for Advanced Planning of Assembly by Robots" in *Proceedings of SME AutofactWest*, 1980, pp. 425–435.

28. S.Y. NOF and H. LECHTMAN, "Analysis of Industrial Robot Work by the RTM Method," *Indust. Eng. J.*, 1982.

29. B. REMBOLD and S.Y. NOF, "Modeling the Performance of a Mobile Robot with RTM," *Int. J. Product. Res.* **29** (1991).

30. H.B. MAYNARD, G.J. STEGEMERTEN, and J.L. SCHWAB, *Methods-Time Measurement*, McGraw-Hill Book Co., Inc., New York, 1948.

31. W. ANTIS, J.M. HONEYCUTT, and E.N. KOCK, *The Basic Motions of MTM*, 4th ed., Maynard Foundations, Pittsburgh, Pa., 1973.

32. R.L. HERSHEY, A.M. LETZT, and S.Y. NOF, "Computerized Methods for Predicting Robot Performance," *Autofact* **5**, 3.9–16 (1983).

33. H. LECHTMAN and S.Y. NOF, "Performance Time Models for Robot Point Operations," *Int. J. Product Res.* **21**(5) 659–673 (1983).

34. T. KUNO, T.F. MATSUNARI, H. MORIBE, and T. IKEDA, "Robot Performance Simulator" in *Proceedings of the 9th ISIR*, 1979, pp. 323–330.

35. D.J. MEDEIROS, R.P. SADOWSKI, D.W. STARKS, and B.S. SMITH, "A Modular Approach to Simulation of Robotic Systems," in *Proceedings of the 1980 Winter Simulations Conferences*, pp. 207–214.

36. A.P. ROBINSON and S.Y. NOF, "SINDECS-R: A Robotic Work Cell Simulator" in *Proceedings of the 1983 Winter Simulation Conference*, Arlington, Va., pp. 350–355.

37. R.D. SCHRAFT and U. SCHMIDT, *A Computer Aided Method for the Selection of an Industrial Robot Technology*, paper presented at the 3rd Annual Conference on Industrial Robot Technology, Nottingham, UK, Mar. 1976.

38. W.B. HEGINBOTHAM, M. DONNER, and K. CASE, "Robot Applications Simulation," *Indust. Robot*, 76–80 (June, 1979).

39. S. KRETCH, "Robotic Animation," *Mech. Eng.* (Aug., 1982).

40. S.Y. NOF, W.L. MEIER, and M.P. DEISENROTH, "Computerized Physical Simulators Are Developed to Solve IE Problems," *Indust. Eng.*, 70–75 (Oct., 1980).

41. C.A. KLEIN and A.A. MACIEJEWSKI, "Simulators, Graphic" in R.D. Dorf and S.Y. Nof, eds., *International Encyclopedia of Robotics and Automation*, John Wiley & Sons, Inc., New York, 1988.

42. Y.F. YONG, J.A. GLEAVE, J.L. GREEN, and M.C. BONNEY, "Off-line Programming of Robotics" in S.Y. Nof, ed., *Handbook of Industrial Robotics*, John Wiley & Sons, Inc., New York, 1985, pp. 366–380.

43. J.M. APPLE, *Plant Layout and Material Handling*, 3rd ed., John Wiley & Sons, Inc., New York, 1977.

44. R.L. FRANCIS and J.A. WHITE, *Facility Layout and Location*, Prentice-Hall, Inc. Englewood Cliffs, N.J., 1974.

45. M.C. BONNEY and K. CASE, "SAMMIE Computer Aided Work Place and Work Task Design System," *CAD/CAM*, 3–4 (Feb.–March 1978).

46. S.C. SARIN and W.E. Wilhelm, "Prototype Models for Two-Dimensional Layout Design of Robot Systems," *IIE Trans.* **16**(3) (1984).

47. V.N. RAJAN and S.Y. NOF, "A Game Theoretic Approach for Cooperation Control," *Int. J. Comput. Integrated Manufact.* **3**(1), 47–59 (1990).

48. S.Y. NOF and D. HANNA, "Operational Characteristics of Multi-Robot Systems with Cooperation," *Int. J. Product. Res.* **27**(3), 477–492 (1989).

49. H.M. PARSONS and G.P. KEARSLEY, "Robotics and Human Factors: Current Status and Future Prospects," *Hum. Factors* **24**(5), 535–552 (1982).

50. J.M. HOWARD, "Focus on the Human Factors in Applying Robotic Systems," *Robotics Today*, 32–34 (Dec., 1982).

51. D.D. LURIA, "Technology, Employment, and the Factory of the Future," *Proc. Autofact*, Detroit 18–181 (1982).

52. G. SALVENDY, "Review and Reappraisal of Human Aspects in Planning Robotic Systems," *Behav. Inform. Technol.* **2**(3), 263–287 (1983).

53. J.G. KREIFELDT, "Ergonomics, Human-Robot Interface" in R.C. Dorf and S.Y. Nof, eds., *International Encyclopedia of Robotics, Applications and Automation*, John Wiley & Sons, Inc., New York, 1988, pp. 451–462.

54. R.M. WYGANT, "Ergonomics, Robot Selection" in R.C. Dorf and S.Y. Nof, eds., *International Encyclopedia of Robotics, Applications and Automation*, John Wiley & Sons, Inc., New York, 1988, pp. 462–477.

55. M.G. HELANDER, "Ergonomics, Workplace Design" in R.C. Dorf and S.Y. Nof, eds., *International Encyclopedia of Robotics, Applications and Automation*, John Wiley & Sons, Inc., New York, 1988, pp. 477–487.

56. K. AOKI, *High-Speed and Flexible Automated Assembly Line—Why Has Automation Successfully Advanced in Japan?* paper presented at the 4th International Conference on Production Research, Tokyo, 1980.

57. L. ARGOTE, P.S. GOODMAN, and D. SCHKADE, *The Human Side of Robotics: Results from a Prototype Study on How Workers React to a Robot*, Carnegie Mellon University, Pittsburgh, Pa., 1983, Tech. Rep. CMU-RI-TR-83-11.

58. V.N. RAJAN, *Cooperation Requirement Planning for Multi-Robot Assembly Cells*, Ph.D. dissertation, Purdue University, West Lafayette, Ind., 1993.

59. G.R. PENNOCK and B.C. VIERSTRA, "The Inverse Kinematics of a Flexible Fixture" in *Proceedings of the 10th OSU Applied Mechanisms Conference, 1988*, Vol. 2, pp. 1–7.

60. G. RODRIGUEZ, "Recursive Forward Dynamics for Multiple Robot Arms Moving a Common Task Object," *IEEE Trans. Robotics Auto.* **5**(4), 510–521 (1989).

61. J.W. ROACH and M.N. BOAZ, "Coordinating the Motions of Robot Arms in Common Workspace," *IEEE J. Robotics Auto.* **RA-3**(5), 437–444 (1987).

62. O. MAIMON, *Activity Controller for a Multiple Robot Assembly Cell*, Ph.D. dissertation, Purdue University, West Lafayette, Ind., 1984.

Suggested Readings

C.R. ASFAHL, *Robots and Manufacturing Automation*, 2nd ed., John Wiley & Sons, Inc., New York, 1992.

I. ASIMOV, *Robot Visions*, Penguin Books, New York, 1991.

R.C. DORF and S.Y. NOF, eds., *International Encyclopedia of Robotics, Applications and Automation*, Vols. 1–3, John Wiley & Sons, Inc., New York, 1988.

J.F. ENGELBERGER, *Robotics in Practice, Management and Applications of Industrial Robots*. American Management Assoc., New York, 1980.

K.S. FU, R.C. GONZALES, C.S.G. LEE, *Robotics Control, Sensing Vision, and Intelligence*, McGraw-Hill Book Co., Inc., New York, 1987.

M.P. GROOVER, M. WEISS, R.N. NAGEL, and N.G. ODRY, *Industrial Robotics, Technology, Programming, and Applications*, McGraw-Hill Book Co., Inc., New York, 1986.

S.Y. NOF, *Handbook of Industrial Robotics*, John Wiley & Sons, Inc., New York, 1985.

S.Y. NOF, *Robotics and Material Flow*, Elsevier Science Publishers, Amsterdam, The Netherlands, 1986.

H.J. WARNECKE and R.D. SCHRAFT, *Industrial Robots, Application Experience*, IFS Publications, Kempston, UK, 1982.

CHAPTER 16
Machine Tool Programming— Techniques and Trends

R. I. M. YOUNG
Loughborough University of Technology

16.1 INTRODUCTION

One of the major successes in the application of computers in manufacturing industry has been in the control of machine tools. The use of computer numerically controlled (CNC) machines has improved the production capability, the quality, and the complexity of components that can be produced by machining. Machine tool programming is central to the successful use of CNC machines. This chapter introduces current programming techniques and look at trends in future integrated software support, which will advance the levels of automation that can be achieved in machine tool programming.

The first demonstration of a prototype numerically controlled (NC) milling machine was demonstrated at MIT following research in the early 1950s. Since then, the rate of progress of computing and control technologies has been a principal contributor to manufacturing effectiveness. A wide range of computer numerically controlled machine types now support today's manufacturing industry, ranging from punching, machining, and grinding machines to inspection machines and robots.

The computer numerical control of machines is performed by the provision of a set of coded numerical instructions that provide motion and position data to the machine via a controller. These three elements—machine, controller, and numerical code—form the basis of any CNC machine system, as illustrated in Figure 16.1. Although CNC systems cover a wide range of processes, this chapter concentrates on machining, as this is the process to which CNC is most commonly applied. This chapter uses machining centers as the machine type against which examples are illustrated, although the descriptions would also, in the main, be applicable to turning work. The requirements for other processes can be assumed to be similar, and the reader is referred to the "Suggested Readings" for further depth and for details on other processes. The chapter is concerned with the numerical code that must be generated to drive CNC machine tools, describing the ways in which it can be produced currently as well as addressing the trends toward higher levels of automation in future software systems.

16.2 CURRENT METHODS IN MACHINE TOOL PROGRAMMING

Machine Tool Control Requirements

A machine tool performs a number of functions that must be captured and represented by machine tool control techniques. These functions are

- To select appropriate cutting tools.
- To determine related cutting conditions.
- To drive cutting tools around the workpiece to achieve the required product dimensions.

The following subsections introduce the control requirements for these functions to be captured in a machining part program.

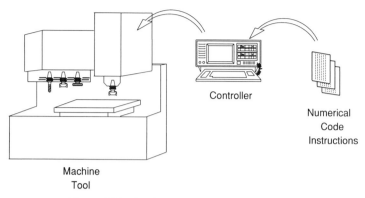

Figure 16.1.   Basic elements of a CNC system.

Selecting Cutters

With manually operated machines, the operator inserts the cutters into the machine tool spindle by hand. In CNC machining, the requirement for tool changing is automated by providing a tool magazine along with the CNC machine. The magazine is then stocked with the cutters appropriate for the work to be performed on the machine. Magazines can range in capacity from as low as six tools to as many as several hundred tools. It is then a requirement of the CNC controller to select the particular cutters from the tool magazine and place them in the machine spindle when required. The link from the part program to the machine tool magazine is achieved by numbering each of the tool pockets in the magazine. The part programmer must then know which cutter is to be placed in each of the magazine pockets. With this information he or she can call the relevant cutters as required. An illustration of a machine tool layout showing a tool magazine and machine controller is provided in Figure 16.2.

Cutting Conditions

Spindle speeds on manually operated machine tools are set and controlled on the machine by the operator, and feed rates are controlled by hand. With CNC machines, all speed and feed rate information is input to the machine controller, which then automatically controls the cutting conditions. However, as this is an aspect of cutting technology for which variation in speed and feed rate values may be needed during machining, there is typically a manual override control that will allow the operator to vary, within limits, the program settings.

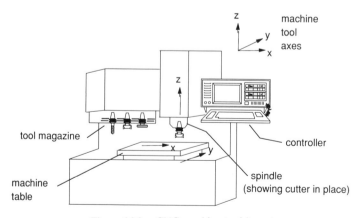

Figure 16.2.   CNC machine tool layout.

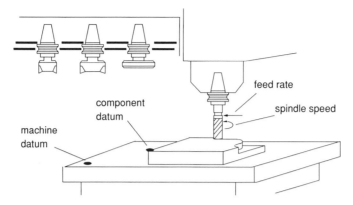

Figure 16.3. Machine reference points.

Cutter Position

To define the cutter position in CNC machining it is necessary to have a coordinate axis system and an origin that can provide a zero reference position. In machine tool control, a right-handed convention is typically used to represent the axes as shown in Figure 16.2, with the machine tool spindle running along the z axis. All coordinate positions can then be defined using this axis system and a zero point on the machine tool table. Positions can be defined either in absolute or incremental mode. Absolute coordinates are referenced to a global zero point on the machine tool table, while incremental coordinates are referenced to a temporary datum point. This datum point is defined relative to the global zero point. Figure 16.3 illustrates typical datum points on a machine and a component. Additional reference points may also exist on a fixture, which are not shown in the figure.

Cutter Offsets

To accommodate the variation in cutter diameter and length, offset values are carried in the machine tool controller for each tool in the tool magazine. The diameter and length (measured relative to the machine tool spindle) of each cutter can be measured using a tool presetter, and these values are input to the machine tool controller against the pocket in the tool magazine that will carry the cutter. Using tool length offsets means that the end point of each cutter can be used as the reference position when describing the motions that the cutters should perform (Figure 16.4). Using diameter offsets means that the profile on the component to be machined can be used to position the cutter rather than the center line of the cutter itself.

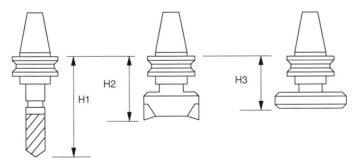

Figure 16.4. Tool length offsets.

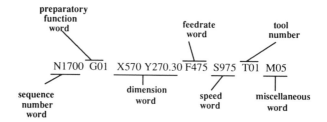

Figure 16.5. An example program block.

Cutter Motions

Cutter motions need to be performed at rapid rates when moving around the machining area and at feed rate when machining. Cutter motion from one position to another is the means by which machining is achieved, and the control over such motions is, therefore, particularly important. Motions are made up of linear moves or circular interpolations. These may be performed as moves in single axes or across combinations of axes, depending on the capability of the machine tool.

Numerical Control Codes

Instructions to the machine are supplied as an ordered set of control codes, which are executed in sequence. Each control code provides the machine with a specific instruction, and the full set of control codes must fulfill the range of possible instructions that the machine tool can perform. The control codes are grouped into lines, or blocks, of code that are then built up in sequence to form a part program, which constitutes the full set of instructions to be performed in the particular machining sequence required. An example of a program block is illustrated in Figure 16.5, and an example part program is shown in Figure 16.6, which could be used to machine the profile represented in Figure 16.7. The control codes used in part program production can be classified under the headings listed and explained below. The reader should note that while the descriptions are generally applicable, each type of machine tool controller has its own variants. Readers are, therefore, recommended to refer to the user manuals of each particular machine tool controller for a full definition of the codes available in each particular case.

Sequence Numbers (N codes)

Each line (block) in a part program must have a number. This number is preceded by the letter N and called a sequence number. It is worth noting that there is no defined convention for part names. Some controllers use names, while others use numbers. It is necessary to check with the controller manual in each particular case. It is also good practice to use sequence numbers in multiples of 5 or 10. This means that it is easy to introduce later modifications to a part program by adding intermediate lines without having to renumber the whole part program.

Preparatory (G) Codes

G codes are used to prepare the controller for the codes that are to follow. For example, G01, the linear interpolation at feed rate code, tells the controller that the spindle should be moved to the position that follows, at the defined feed rate. A range of sample G codes are illustrated in Table 16.1.

Position Codes (X, Y, and Z)

The X, Y, and Z codes inform the controller of the position to move to, using the previously described preparatory code to define the mode of movement. Positions can be defined in any combination of the three axes. When an axis value is omitted, the previous value is maintained. For example, the code N060 G00 X 10 Y 20 Z − 30, for line 60, moves the cutter at rapid rate to position (10, 20, −30). In line 70, the code N070 G01 Y 50 moves the cutter linearly, at feed rate, to position (10, 50, −30).

```
N0010(ID,PROG,)
N0020 G90
N0030 G71
N0040 G00X0.0 Y0.0 Z100.0
N0050 T01 M06
N0060 S2000 M03
N0070 G00 X-20.0 Y-20.0
N0080 Z-10.0
N0090 G03 X-12.652 Y-23.044 I7.348 J7.348 F150.0
N0100 X-2.26 Y-12.652 I0.0 J10.392
N0110 X-5.303 Y-5.303 I-10.392 J0.0
N0120 G02 X-7.5 Y0.0 I5.303 J5.303
N0130 G01 Y75.0
N0140 G02 X0.0 Y82.5 I7.5 J0.0
N0150 G01 X20.0
N0160 G02 X27.5 Y75.0 I0.0 J-7.5
N0170 G01 Y67.0
N0180 G03 X30.0 Y64.5 I2.5 J0.0
N0190 G01 X37.0
N0200 G03 X39.5 Y67.0 I0.0 J2.5
N0210 G01 Y75.0
N0220 G02 X47.0 Y82.5 I7.5 J0.0
N0230 G01 X75.0
N0240 G02 X107.5 Y50.0 I0.0 J-32.5
N0250 G01 Y0.0
N0260 G02 X100.0 Y-7.5 I-7.5 J0.0
N0270 G01 X0.0
N0280 G02 X-5.303 Y-5.303 I0.0 J7.5
N0290 G03 X-12.652 Y-2.26 I-7.349 J-7.349
N0300 X-23.044 Y-12.652 I0.0 J-10.392
N0310 X-20.0 Y-20.0 I10.392 J0.0
N0320 G00 Z2.0
N0330 M30
N9999 (END,PROG)
```

Figure 16.6. An example NC part program.

Cutter Selection (T), Speed (S), and Feed Rate (F) Codes

A *T* code identifies the next tool to be used when a tool change is called for. The number used with the *T* code identifies the tool pocket from which the next tool should be taken. The tool already in the spindle will be returned to its allocated pocket. The *S* code defines the spindle rotation speed in revolutions per minute, while the *F* code defines the feed rate of the cutter. For example the program block N050 S1500 F200 specifies a spindle speed of 1500 rpm and a feed rate of 200 mm/min in line 50 of a part program.

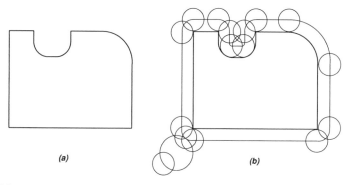

(a)   (b)

Figure 16.7. **(a)** An example profile to be machined. **(b)** The example profile showing the cutter path.

TABLE 16.1. Sample *G* Codes

G Code	Function
G00	Position (rapid rate)
G01	Linear interpolation (cutting feed rate)
G02	Circular interpolation (counterclockwise)
G03	Circular interpolation (clockwise)
G09	Stop
G21	Input in millimeters
G28	Return to reference point
G40	Cutter compensation cancel
G41	Cutter compensation left
G42	Cutter compensation right
G43	Tool length compensation plus direction
G44	Tool length compensation minus direction
G49	Tool length compensation cancel
G53	Cancel fixture offset
G56	Set fixture offset
G65	Macro call
G80	Canned cycle cancel
G83	Peck drill cycle
G84	Tapping cycle
G90	Absolute command
G91	Incremental command
G92	Program absolute zero point

*Miscellaneous (*M*) Codes*

A number of miscellaneous commands are defined using *M* codes. A range of these are described in Table 16.2. Examples of commonly used miscellaneous codes are M03 to start a clockwise rotation of the machine tool spindle, M06 for an automatic tool change, and M30 to end the program and reset.

Manual Data Input

The most basic way to construct a part program using numerical control codes is to use manual data input (MDI). Using this method, the operator works at the machine tool controller and simply inputs the NC code statements, line by line, to the controller. As can be imagined, this

TABLE 16.2. Sample *M* Codes

M Code	Function
M00	Program stop
M02	Program reset
M03	Spindle forward
M04	Spindle reverse
M05	Spindle stop
M06	Auto tool change
M08	Coolant on
M09	Coolant off
M13	Spindle forward and coolant on
M30	Program reset and rewind
M98	Subprogram call
M99	Subprogram end

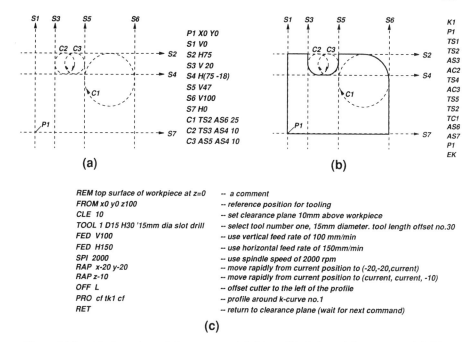

Figure 16.8. (a) An unbounded geometry definition. (b) A bounded geometry definition. (c) Tooling commands to machine the profile.

method is highly error prone when it is necessary to input large amounts of data for a new part program. However, it is a useful technique when minor modifications to existing part programs are required.

Part Programming Languages

Producing part programs manually is a long, tedious, and error-prone task, especially for complex machining. A part programming language simplifies the production of part programs. Such languages provide the part programmer with the means to define the geometric shapes around which cutters should be driven and the tooling commands that define which cutters should be used and their associated data such as speed and feed rate information.

Languages to support NC code production were first developed in the late 1950s and early 1960s. Automatically programmed tools (APT), the first of these tools, were developed at MIT in the 1950s, while extended subset of APT (EXAPT) was developed in Germany in the 1960s. There are now many part programming systems available based on similar languages. These provide the user with a ready means to define the geometry to be machined and a set of tooling-related commands. The tooling commands enable the user to specify cutters and the cutting conditions to be used and to link the cutters to the geometry to be machined.

To illustrate the use of a part programming language consider the simple profile shown in Figure 16.7a and the required tool path shown in Figure 16.7b. An example of a part programming language, to define this profile and generate machining commands is illustrated in Figure 16.8. Figure 16.8a shows how an unbounded geometry representation of the profile to be machined can be defined in terms of points (P codes), lines (S codes) and circles (C codes). Lines and circles are defined as having a direction; positive upward and from left to right for lines, positive clockwise for circles. Figure 16.8b shows how this geometry can be bounded to provide a boundary around which a cutter can be driven. Here the points, lines, and circles are "joined" together into a K curve. As can be seen in the figure, the K curve starts and ends at a point and follows around the lines and circles in the required order to define the boundary. Each line segment name is preceded by the letter T or A. These letters stand for tangential and antitangential and are used to indicate the direction of the K curve relative to the line segment. Tangential is used if the K curve is in the same direction as the line, whereas antitangential represents the opposite. Figure 16.8c illustrates a set of tooling commands that can be used to select a cutter, its cutting conditions, and then to profile the selected geometry.

Once the machining that is to be performed has been defined using the part program language statements, the completed part program must be converted to NC code. The NC code produced must be appropriate for the machine tool controller that is to be used on the machine that will manufacture the part. This is achieved by defining conversion routines, called postprocessors, for each different type of machine tool controller. The part program language statements are passed through the postprocessor to generate the NC part program.

CAM Systems

Producing NC code using part programming languages and postprocessors is significantly easier than manual production. These tools form the base from which computer-aided manufacturing (CAM) systems have been developed. CAM systems add the graphical capability of computers to visualize the geometry of the part that has been defined. They also enable the part program to be simulated, using the same graphical capability, thereby enabling the programmer to test the likely results of the program before ever approaching a machine tool.

A simulated tool path around the example profile discussed above is illustrated in Figure 16.7b. Although the example used here is simple, CAM systems can be used to generate NC part programs for complex geometric shapes. They can be used to support multiple-axis machining systems and may offer separate modules to support a number of processes. These may range from milling and turning, to punching and wire erosion, to more complex multispindle turning centers. In addition to part programming, related modules to support the part programmer may be offered in these systems such as tooling databases or direct numerical control (DNC) support. DNC provides direct access to the machine tool controller such that part programs can be passed, as required, to the controller from a separate computing system on which the CAM system is based.

CAD–CAM Systems

Although CAM systems provide substantial benefits over manual NC code production, they are still time-consuming and require the user to define the geometry of the components to be machined. This geometry is often already available in a two- or three-dimensional computer-aided design (CAD) package. Linking CAD and CAM systems (CAD–CAM) currently provides the most effective way to generate NC code from existing computer-based design drawings. This enables the geometry definition in the CAD system to be used in the CAM system, thereby overcoming the need to duplicate the geometry definition phase. To do this, the geometry from the CAD system is passed into the CAM system and then converted into the form required by the CAM system. An example of this can be seen in Figure 16.9, in which a golf club is modeled using a CAD system and the same data are used to generate machining paths for its manufacture.

Geometric representations that are used to support NC code generation fall into three categories: two-dimensional (2D) systems, three-dimensional (3D) surface modeling systems, and 3D solid modeling systems. All three are currently used in commercial systems, although the 2D system is the most common and provides straightforward solutions to a wide range of code generation problems. Surface model based systems provide a successful route to the representation of complex surface geometry, such as is found in automotive body panels, aerospace components, and many plastic products. CAM systems linked to surface modelers provide the capability to manufacture such complex surfaces with much greater accuracy and consistency than could previously have been envisaged. Solid modelers cannot capture the same surface complexity as surface models; however, they do offer a complete and unambiguous representation of the objects being modeled (1). As such they provide the greatest potential to support algorithmic solutions to problems for which higher levels of automation are sought. They are used for collision checking and NC verification and are a prime mover in a wide range of research aiming to increase the levels of automation in part program generation.

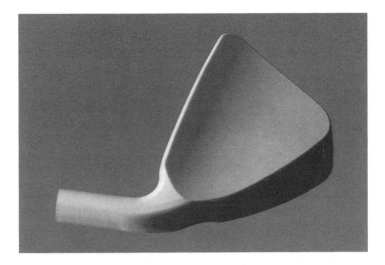

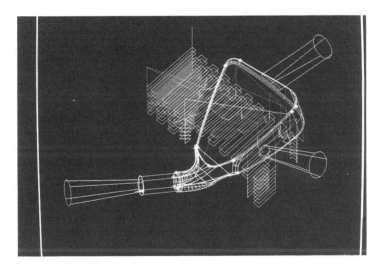

Figure 16.9. An example surface CAD model and related tool paths.

In addition to providing input geometry to CAM, some CAD–CAM systems offer additional functionality, which is possible when the CAD and CAM information can be combined. Some CAD–CAM systems based on three-dimensional solid models offer collision-checking algorithms. These systems allow the user to represent the geometry of the component to be machined, the fixtures, the cutters, and the machine tool. The motion of the cutter can then be checked to ensure that no collisions will take place. Further functionality can be offered by NC verification systems. These systems take as input the NC code. This is then interpreted to produce geometric images of the material being removed from the workpiece, providing a 3D visual verification of the cutter paths.

Using geometry from a CAD system requires that the CAM system is aware of the data structures that define the geometry. This can either be achieved by sharing common data structures or by defining a separate data standard that both systems can use for data interchange. The former technique is appropriate when both the CAD and CAM systems are developed by the same company. The latter technique is necessary to provide a level of compatibility between software products from different companies.

Ensuring that geometry definitions can be interpreted by different software tools is a problem that is common to many design and manufacturing applications. This has led to a range of standards that have come about both through the International Standards Organization with the initial graphics exchange specification (IGES) (2) and through the use of de facto standards such as DFX. DFX is a geometry definition file generated by Autocad. The popularity of this program has led many related suppliers to develop their products to work with DFX files to ensure compatibility.

16.3   TOWARD AUTOMATION OF MACHINE TOOL PROGRAMMING

There are two principal problem areas that must be understood and overcome before substantial advances in the levels of automation of machine tool programming can be achieved. These key areas are

1. To improve the functionality of part programming systems.
2. To understand the information structures that support part programming systems such that new integrated and extensible systems can be developed.

Trends toward information support and functional improvements are discussed, respectively, in the following sections.

Integrated Systems

Compatibility of data between applications that are to be linked together is a critical aspect of ensuring that data transfer is successful. The simple linking of CAD geometry to tool path generation, as was described above, has been achieved by using standard data exchange methods. However, identifying an appropriate standard has not been a straightforward business. The IGES standard has been evolving since 1980 (3). The problem of identifying appropriate data structures that can be used to link applications increases significantly in complexity as we look forward to the automation of machine tool programming. This is because there is a need not only to link two applications (CAD and tool path generation) through a common geometry definition but to link many other applications covering the range of functions that a part programmer performs. Furthermore, there is a need to cover the range of information, beyond geometry, that a part programmer uses.

Typically, the technique used to add new functionality to a system has been to write interfaces to link the new software to any other program with which it should communicate (Figure 16.10a). As systems grow, this approach leads to many problems, not least of which is ensuring that the data that are used by each application is compatible. As software systems move toward providing higher levels of automation, they must be extensible, based on a common underlying data structure that can provide the data input required for each new function and accept the results of each new function (Figure 16.10b). Providing a common base of data with which functions can interact in this way offers an integrated, extensible approach (4). As a new function is added, only two interfaces need be written: one to extract data from the database and one to send the results of the function back to the database. An experimental code generation system based on this data model concept is reported in ref. 5. This uses a product data model as its central database, capturing product data such as geometry, dimensions and tolerances, features, and process-planning instructions. It shows how a number of part programming related functions can be supported and integrated through this product-modeling environment. The identification of data structures that should be used to represent product data, covering the full life cycle of a product, is a major area of current research and one in which data standards are progressively being defined through the Standard for the Exchange of Product Data (STEP), a committee of the International Standards Organization (6).

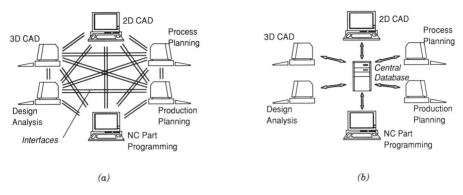

Figure 16.10. (a) System interfacing. (b) System integration.

Advanced Functionality for Part Programming Systems

If higher levels of automation are to be achieved in generating NC code, there is a need to understand the functions that part programmers perform and how software packages can best capture these processes. Apart from generating tool paths, part programmers are concerned with different levels of planning the machining process. At the lowest level, cutter speeds and feed rates must be selected. At a slightly higher level, the operations to be performed in each setup must be identified and cutters to perform the machining must be selected. These cutters must also be allocated to appropriate tool magazine pockets, and cutter offset values must be defined. At the highest level of machine-specific planning, the setup sequence to be used must be chosen as well as the fixtures to be used. At this level, there is effectively an overlap between the functions to be performed to support process planning and the functions to support part program generation. Which category these functions are classified with is of no particular significance as long as their existence is accepted as a prerequisite for fully automated part program generation. A view of the functions required to support automated part program generation is illustrated in Figure 16.11 while a more detailed description of their interactions can be found in ref. 7.

Each of the functional areas described above have been the subject of research either individually or in combination. Research generally addresses either rotational component or prismatic component machining. The following discussion provides the reader with a view of some of the principal aspects of research in these areas.

Cutter Path Generation

Algorithms for cutter path generation are generally well developed. The main area for further progress related directly to cutter path generation is concerned with the machining of sculptured surfaces using surface-modeling technology. Here the problem is to achieve greater accuracy in surface machining, overcome problems of gouging, and bring the machined surface within the surface tolerance. This can be attributed to the position and orientation of the cutter relative to the surface being machined, and research is being pursued to extend the algorithms currently available to overcome these problems (8).

Cutter Speed and Feed Rate Selection

Selecting cutting data such as speed and feed rate information can be achieved either through the use of look-up tables or through the use of equations relating to the required tool life of the cutter. Metcut's "Machinability Data Handbook" provides an example of the look-up approach, initially provided in reference books but now available in database form (9). These data provide the programmer with valuable guidance as to the cutting data to use and are currently the most useful support tool for cutting data selection. However, the data provided do need to

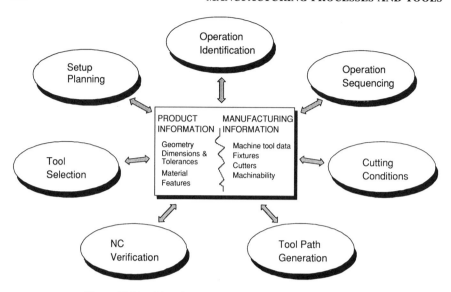

Figure 16.11.   Functions to support part program generation.

be interpreted and modified by the programmer to suit the specific cutting situation, and therefore, they cannot provide fully automated support for NC code generation.

The use of tool life equations, based on the research of Taylor has the potential, in theory, to provide a fully automated solution and flexible solution. This is illustrated by the work of Hinduja et al. (10), who identify cutting conditions for turned components based on different tool life criteria. However, before equations to represent the machining process can be used with confidence, the effects on machining conditions of the materials being machined, the cutter materials and geometry, the machining geometry, and the machine tools themselves must be understood and captured in appropriate process models. A considerable research effort has been spent in this area, but with only limited success in well-specified machining situations (11). The problem of achieving consistently good results from cutting data has led to a high level of interest in the use of sensor monitoring of machining conditions. The addition of closed-loop feedback and control of cutting conditions on the machine during cutting provides the best chance of success in generating and controlling cutting conditions automatically.

Operation and Tool Selection

Operation and tool selection research can be viewed as having two principal themes. The first being to capture the technological information required to identify operations and select cutters. The second being to identify the geometric data that will define operation and cutter constraints. A range of research has addressed the technological aspects of the problem. These in general identify the types of operation that need to be performed (such as facing, end milling, slotting, drilling, etc.) and then link these to the types of cutter that can be used to produce the operation. The field of possible cutters that can be used is then narrowed by applying constraints such as tip geometry (12), production time, and cost (13). The sequence of operations may also influence the selection of the best cutter. Limiting the number of tools needed in the tool magazine as well as the number of tool changes are also important factors in selecting the best tool set to be used.

The geometric influence on part program generation is perhaps the one of most overall significance and complexity. The automatic identification of simple shapes such as holes, slots, and pockets, and their links to tooling, has been possible for some years now. An example of such work can be found in ref. 14. The problems that have yet to be successfully resolved are concerned with the common situations in which there are a number of interacting shapes on a component that must be identified and decomposed into machining operations and an appropriate machining sequence (15). Interactions that must be recognized include overlapping features, features that sit directly under each other, and feature interactions that produce thin wall problems. Some progress has been made. Feature precedence can be identified (16) and geometric queries can be defined to identify simple feature interactions (17). The most significant problem lies in determining how to break down complex geometry into a set of overlapping machining operations. Although a range of feature recognition research has been finding solutions to this problem, none can yet tackle a realistic set of components.

Setup Planning

Most research advancing the levels of automation that can be achieved in part program production has been constrained to consider problems for which the setups to be used have already been defined. However, some researchers have considered how setup planning can be supported by computer systems. The technological aspects of setup planning that have been addressed have led researchers into considering appropriate techniques on which to base fixture design and selection. These include consideration of the 3–2–1 locating principle (18), the clamping forces that fixtures must apply (19), and the analysis of tolerance relationships (20).

Geometric evaluations of CAD models hold the same problems of feature identification for setup planning as were discussed in the previous section. Again, some progress has been made with comparative checks being made between alternative fixturing strategies (17) and the identification of required setup directions (21). The need to evaluate tolerance relationships as well as geometry increases significantly the complexity of developing automated solutions to setup planning, as does the interaction with fixture design problems. Linking representations of tolerance data to geometric representations also is still at an early stage of development. It is, therefore, likely to be some time before adequate solutions to automated setup planning are available.

The Interpretation of Geometric Information

It is generally accepted that if automated systems are to be successful they must be based on a complete, and unambiguous, geometric representation. This cannot be provided by 2D or surface modelers but can be provided by solid modelers (1). This has led to a wide range of research that has pursued the interpretation of solid model geometry into a form that is useful to support part programming functions. This interpretation of geometry into meaningful forms for different software applications is addressed under the "features technology" banner.

Features technology falls into two principal categories: feature recognition, which aims to assess a geometric model to identify features, and feature-based design systems, for which the user is constrained to build a model using predefined features. Predefined features capture the required interpretation of the geometric shape before it is applied to the component design. This means that when the manufacturing methods for a shape is well understood (e.g., holes), the process information can be captured and associated with the shape. However, this approach is limited in its applicability (22). Although it may support geometric analysis techniques in providing higher levels of automation to part programming systems, it will not provide an independent, broad-based solution to geometric interpretation for other than overly simplistic components.

Feature recognition, on the other hand, has much greater potential to provide higher levels of automation. However, feature recognition is a complex problem that is only now beginning to progress beyond the identification of simplistic shapes. The geometric analysis techniques that are being developed have the potential to offer different interpretations of data, dependent on the viewpoint of the particular application. This is essential if useful results are to be achieved as the significance of a shape depends on the manufacturing viewpoint being taken. For example, features for fixturing are different from features for datum setting, and these are different from features for machining, etc. Also the geometric analysis techniques used in feature recognition have the potential to be used to identify the feature overlap and feature proximity problems described in previous sections.

A Summary of Trends Toward Automation

Current part programming systems support cutter path generation based principally on user interaction with geometric representations of the parts to be machined. The highest level of part programmer support comes from CAD–CAM systems for which the geometric information for part programming can be converted from the CAD geometry. CAD–CAM systems can be found that are based on 2D geometry, surface modeling, and solid modeling. Additions to basic tool path generation are available in the form of collision checking and NC verification.

In the short term, future improved functionality of tool path generation for complex machining is likely, e.g., improved generation of machining paths for sculptured surfaces and added functionality for complex multitooling situations such as multiaxis lathes with live tooling. The addition of feedback control from the machine should also offer greater control over cutting conditions. In the longer term, integrated systems should provide extensible systems, giving high data integrity and hence confidence to system users and developers. The most substantial moves toward higher levels of automation will come as the functions that part programmers currently perform manually are captured in software programs. A prerequisite for this will be to develop an understanding of how product data—including geometric, dimension, and tolerance data—represented in CAD systems can be interpreted to provide the range of information required by a part programmer.

In the foreseeable future the most appropriate developments will provide part programmers with a high degree of flexibility and supporting information on which they can base their decisions. Full automation is unlikely to be successful, except in the simplest of machining situations.

BIBLIOGRAPHY

1. M. MANTYLA, *An Introduction to Solid Modelling*, Computer Science Press, Rockville, Md. 1988.

2. B. SMITH and J. WELLINGTON, *Initial Graphics Exchange Specification Version 5.0*, U.S. Department of Commerce, National Bureau of Standards, Gaithersburg, Md. 1990.

3. R.J. Mayer, "IGES: One Answer to the Problems of CAD Database Exchange," BYTE, **12**(6), 209–214 (1987).

4. A. MCKAY and M.S. BLOOR, "The Role of Product Models in Effective CADCAM" in *Proceedings of the IMechE European Conference on Effective CADCAM '91*, MEP, Suffolk, England. 1991, pp. 113–119.

5. R.I.M. YOUNG and R. BELL, "Machine Planning in a Product Model Environment," *Int. J. Product. Res.* **30**(1), 2487–2513 (1992).

6. PDES/STEP, *Product Data Exchange Specification* (first working draft), National Institute of Standards and Technology, National Engineering Laboratory, Gaithesburg, MD. 1988, NISTIR 884004.

7. R.I.M. YOUNG and R. BELL, "Machine Planning: Its Role in the Generation of Manufacturing Code from Solid Model Descriptions," *Int. J. Product. Res.* **27**(5), 847–867 (1989).

8. C.G. JENSEN and D.C. ANDERSON, "Accurate Tool Placement and Orientation for Finish Surface Machining," *Concurr. Eng. PED.* **59**, 127–145 (1992).

9. *Cutdata*, Metcut Research Associates, Cincinnati, Ohio, 1985.

10. S. HINDUJA, D.J. PETTY, M. TESTER, and G. BARROW, "Calculation of Optimum Cutting Conditions for Turning Operations," *Proc. Inst. Mech. Eng.* **203**, 81–92, (1985).

11. J.F. KAHLES, "Machinability Data Requirements for Advanced Machining Systems," *Ann. CIRP* **36**(2), 523–529 (1987).

12. R. MELKOTE and D.L. TAYLOR, *An Implementation of Rule Based Selection of Milling Cutters, Feed Rates and Spindle Speeds*, paper presented at the ASME International Conference on Computers in Engineering, 1988.

13. S.S. CHEN, S. HINDUJA, and G. BARROW, "Automatic Tool Selection for Rough Turning Operations," *Int. J. Mach. Tools Manufact.* vol. 29, no. 4, 1989.

14. B.K. CHOI, M.M. BARASH, and D.C. ANDERSON, "Automatic Recognition of Machined Surfaces from a 3D Solid Model," *Comput. Aided Des.* **16**(2), 81–86 (1984).

15. J.C.H. CHUNG, R.L. COOK, D. PATEL, and M.K. SIMMONS, "Feature Based Geometry Construction for Geometric Reasoning" in *Proceedings of Computers in Engineering Conference*, ASME, New York, 1988, pp. 497–504.

16. S. JOSHI, N.N. VISSA, and T.C. CHANG, "Expert Process Planning System with Solid Model Interface," *Int. J. Product. Res.* **26**(5), 863–885 (1988).

17. R.I.M. YOUNG and R. BELL, "Fixturing Strategies and Geometric Queries in Set-up Planning," *Int. J. Product. Res.* **29**(3), 537–550 (1991).

18. R.J. MENASSA and W.R. DEVRIES, "Locating Point Synthesis in Fixture Design," *Ann. CIRP* **38**(1), 165–169 (1989).

19. M.R. CUTKOSKY and S.H. LEE, *Fixture Planning with Friction for Concurrent Product/Process Design,* paper presented at the NFS Engineering Design Research Conference, 1989.

20. J.R. BOERMA and J.J. KALS, "Fixture Design with FIXES: The Automatic Selection of Positioning Clamping and Support Features for Prismatic Parts," *Ann. CIRP* **37**(1), 443–446 (1989).

21. J. CORNEY, D.E.R. CLARK, J.L. MURRAY, and Y. YUE, "Automatic Classification of 21/2 D Components," *Concurrent Eng. PED* **59**, 85–99 (1992).

22. R.I.M. YOUNG and R. BELL, "Design by Features: Advantages and Limitations in Machine Planning Integration," *Int. J. Comput. Integrated Manufact.* **6**(1–2), 105–112 (1993).

Suggested Readings

M.P. GROOVER and E.W. ZIMMERS, Jr, *CAD/CAM Computer Aided Design and Manufacture,* Prentice-Hall, Inc., Englewood Cliffs, N.J., 1984.

H.B. KIEF and T.F. WATERS, *Computer Numerical Control,* Macmillan, New York, 1992.

R.G. RAPELLO, *Essentials of Numerical Control,* Prentice-Hall, Inc., Englewood Cliffs, N.J., 1986.

I. ZEID, *CAD/CAM Theory and Practice,* McGraw-Hill Book Co., Inc., New York, 1991.

CHAPTER 17
Material Handling

L. F. GELDERS and L. M. A. PINTELON
Catholic University of Leuven (Belgium)

17.1 INTRODUCTION

The industrial revolution (late 18th and early 19th centuries) initiated the factory system of modern industry as we know it today. The contrast between the old domestic industry and this modern industry lies mainly in the fact that power-engine machines began to be employed to vastly increase labor and productivity per hour of the individual worker. As the factory system developed, the need for material handling equipment also arose and developed, both in manufacturing and distribution operations.

It is not easy to formulate a good definition for material handling. Defining material handling merely as "handling materials" is largely unsatisfactory because it involves moving, packaging, and storing as well as control activities. Moreover, "materials" may be anything from mail in a postal system to money in a banking system, product units in a manufacturing system, chemical liquids in a piping system, pallets in a warehouse, bulk materials in a refining site, or even people in a transportation system.

From an engineering point of view, material handling may be defined as "the art and science involved in picking the right system, composed of a series of related equipment elements or devices designed to work in concert or sequence in the movement, packaging, storage and control of materials in a process or logistics activity." Each system must be designed to serve in its specific operating environment and for specific materials. Although the possible contexts for the material handling systems vary a lot, the basic principles of sound material handling apply for each of them. It also is important to note that there is a strong interaction between material handling and other facilities design aspects such as building layout, storage methods, order picking concepts, etc. Tompkins and White (1) give a rather descriptive definition of material handling, which covers all the important objectives: "the best material handling solution from the host of alternative solutions that usually exist uses the right method to provide the right amount of the right material at the right place, at the right time, in the right sequence, in the right position and at the right cost."

It is clear that material handling does not add value to the product, but performing material handling "right" can be of considerable influence on the profitability of the manufacturing or warehousing function in question. Sule (2) mentions that material handling can account for 30% to 75% of the total cost and that efficient material handling can be primarily responsible for reducing a plant's operating cost by 15% to 30%. Material handling becomes more and more capital intensive and less and less labor intensive. The material handling industry grew from $20 billion in 1977 to $52 billion in 1990 (3).

Stating that the objective of material handling is to have the least possible handling is probably true, but it lacks some practicality. More specific objectives of a material handling system are

To increase the efficiency and effectiveness of material flow.

To increase productivity in manufacturing (plant) or in distribution (warehouse).

To increase space and equipment use.

To improve safety and working conditions.

To reduce material handling costs.

To avoid too high capital requirements.

To ensure a high level of system's flexibility, reliability, availability, and maintainability.

To improve integration between material and information flow.

To smooth the flow of materials through the logistics pipeline (from supplier to final customer).

The purpose of this chapter is to introduce some basic concepts of material handling in a manufacturing environment (Figure 17.1). It is beyond the scope of this text to give a detailed description of all possible types of material handling equipment (which would be too large a task anyway). The chapter merely wants to provide some insights in the complexity of the material handling process and to point out some tools that may be useful either in evaluating and improving an existing system or in designing a new system. Throughout the chapter sufficient attention will be paid to the interaction between material handling and other functions, e.g. order picking and storage.

17.2 BASIC PRINCIPLES OF MATERIAL HANDLING

The principal equation of material handling system design is often formulated as follows (1):

$$\text{Materials} + \text{Moves} + \text{Methods} = \text{Best System}$$

The underlying idea is that the best handling is the least handling. Therefore, the emphasis is on a critical attitude toward the whole material handling process, i.e., the "why" of material handling. Supporting questions may be the "what," "where," "when," "how," "who," and "which," aiming to establish the type of materials to be moved, their main characteristics, the quantities to be moved, the units to be handled, the sources and destinations for each move, the frequencies and speed at which the moves must be made, the methods that can be used to execute the moves, the party responsible for the handling process (physical and information flow), equipment alternatives with their specifications, etc. The Materials Handling Institute, Inc., synthesized the experiences of many practitioners into a list of 20 material handling principles. Table 17.1 is a slightly modified list. This list presents rules of thumb that may be

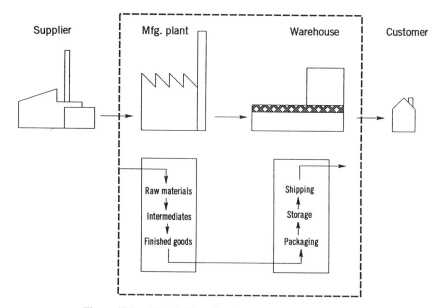

Figure 17.1. Material handling in a manufacturing context.

TABLE 17.1. Basic Material Handling Principles

1. *Planning.* Study the problem thoroughly to identify potential solutions and constraints and to establish clear objectives.
2. *Flow.* Integrate data flow with physical material flow in handling and storage.
3. *Simplification.* Try to simplify material handling by eliminating, reducing, or combining unnecessary movements and equipment.
4. *Gravity.* Use gravity to move material wherever possible, while respecting limitations concerning safety and damage.
5. *Standardization.* Standardize handling methods and equipment wherever possible.
6. *Flexibility.* Use methods and equipment that can perform a variety of tasks.
7. *Unit load.* Handle product in as large a unit load as possible.
8. *Maintenance.* Plan maintenance carefully to ensure high system reliability and availability.
9. *Obsolescence.* Make a long-range plan, taking into account equipment life cycle costs and equipment replacement.
10. *Performance.* Determine the efficiency, effectiveness, and cost of the material handling alternatives.
11. *Safety.* Provide safe material handling equipment and methods.
12. *Ecology.* Use equipment and procedures that have no negative impact on the environment.
13. *Ergonomics.* Take human capabilities and limitations into account while designing a material handling system.
14. *Computerization.* Consider computerization wherever viable for improved material and information control.
15. *Utilization.* Try to obtain a good use of the installed capacity.
16. *Automation.* Consider automation of the handling process to increase efficiency and economy.
17. *Operation.* Include operating costs (energy) in the comparison of material handling alternatives.
18. *Integration.* Integrate as much as handling and storage activities into one coordinated system, covering receiving, inspection, storage, transportation, production, packaging, warehousing, and shipping.
19. *Layout.* Keep in mind that layout and material handling are closely linked and that an interactive procedure is often needed to obtain their best coordination.
20. *Space use.* Choose the material handling equipment so that effective use is made of all (cubic) space.

helpful in remembering most of the important issues concerning material handling systems. Based on the list, many checklists have been developed and are available in the literature (2).

17.3 MATERIAL HANDLING EQUIPMENT

Classification

Many different types of material handling equipment exist and picking the right one for the application at hand is not an easy task. Fortunately, the literature provides us with many classifications and selection tables that may be useful in determining the right type of equipment. It is beyond the scope of this text to give a detailed discussion on this matter. For a more detailed description of the equipment discussed below the reader is referred to specialized literature (1, 2, 4–6). Some important issues involved in the selection procedure will be noted and a brief description of the three principal types of material handling equipment (trucks, conveyors, and cranes and hoists) will be given. Figure 17.2 shows these equipment types. Establishing whether you need a truck, a conveyor, or a crane and hoist for a given application and, in the next step, which type of this family will fit your needs best involves analysis of the materials to be moved, the nature of the moves, the method to be used, etc. Table 17.2 lists these aspects.

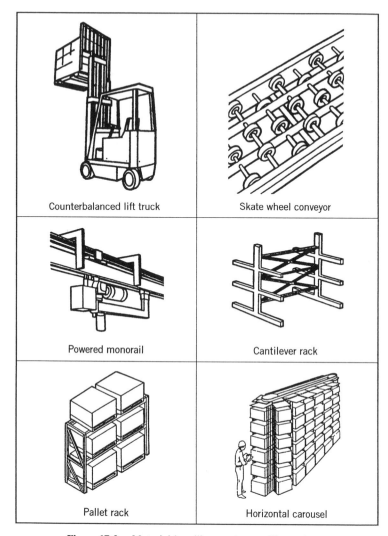

Figure 17.2. Material handling equipment illustrations.

   Applying the criteria of Table 17.2, it is possible to say that conveyors are used for moving materials (bulk or units) continuously over a fixed path. Their advantages are their high capacity, adjustable speed, and versatility (floor or overhead version). They offer the possibility for the combination of transportation with other activities like sorting and inspection and can even be used for temporary storage. Further advantages are that no straight paths or aisles are required and that they can easily be used in automated load transfer operations. Note that many suppliers offer modularly designed equipment for the most common types of conveyors used in a manufacturing environment. Disadvantages include the hindering of mobile equipment (i.e., floor conveyors may hinder the lift trucks' movements) and the fact that conveyors are fixed-path equipment, serving only a limited area. Ill-designed conveyor systems are often bottle-necks in the manufacturing (transportation) system, not in the least through the impact of conveyor breakdowns on the whole system. The best-known conveyor types are belt conveyor, slat conveyor, roller conveyor, wheel conveyor, gravity chart, trolley conveyor, and tow line conveyor. Special types of conveyors include pneumatic, magnetic, vibratory, screw, and bucket conveyors.

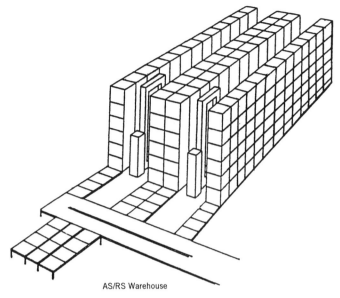

AS/RS Warehouse

Figure 17.2.   (*Continued*)

TABLE 17.2.   Choosing a Material Handling Solution

Materials to be moved:
- Type: bulk, packaged, units
- Volume and throughput: low, medium, high
- Shape: regular, irregular
- Size: small or large; uniform or nonuniform
- Weight: uniform or nonuniform
- Sturdiness: sturdy or fragile
- Hazards: safe or hazardous

Moves to be performed:
- Indoors or outdoors
- Vertical or horizontal
- Long or short haul
- Fixed or flexible routes (area)
- Straight or complex routes
- One-way or two-way routes
- Cross-traffic: none, sometimes, intense
- Speed: low or high, variable or constant
- Frequency
- Concurrent processing needs (e.g., transportation plus inspection or transportation plus sorting)

Methods to be used:
- Load support (e.g., none, pallets)
- Degree of automation required
- Floor and building characteristics
- Interfaces: load–unload, storage

Other:
- Flexibility
- Power supply
- Investment and budget issues
- Training needs
- Safety aspects
- Reliability, availability, maintainability

Industrial trucks are used for moving mixed or uniform loads intermittently over various paths with suitable surfaces. Their primary function is transferring as well as lifting and loading–unloading of materials. Their advantages include the fact that they generally do not require fixed paths and that high use rates may be achieved through their flexibility. The disadvantages are that they have only a limited capacity per trip, that (preferably straight) aisles are required, and that they do not allow combination with other operations. There are many different types of trucks, including the hand trucks like the four-wheel hand truck and pallet jack, classic counter-balanced forklift trucks (with all possible auxiliary equipment like clamps and rams), narrow-aisle order-picking trucks, straddle carriers, personnel and burden carriers, and automatic guided vehicles (AGVs).

Cranes and hoists are overhead devices used for moving varying loads intermittently between points within an area. They are fixed by supporting and guiding rails, and their primary function is transferring (and lifting). Cranes are among the oldest type of fixed-path equipment and are the backbone of overhead handling in steel mills, metal-fabricating shops, and wherever heavy loads must be moved. Other types of cranes are mounted on the wall or floor pedestal and provide a more limited range of movement, still others are mobile and portable. Hoists are a basic type of overhead lifting equipment and can be suspended from a rail, track, crane, ridge, or trolley. They may be manually, electrically, or pneumatically powered. Advantages of cranes and hoists are their minimum interference with the work on the floor (which may save valuable floor space) and the potential use for loading–unloading operations. Disadvantages include the large investments combined with the often fairly low use rate and the fact that they can serve only a limited area. Moreover, they are often limited to a straight line. Classic crane types are the well-known bridge crane, tower crane, jib crane, gantry crane, and stacker crane. An outgrowth of cranes and hoists is the automated storage–retrieval systems (AS/RS). Related to this is the currently popular miniload and storage-carousel systems used in warehouses.

Obviously, the equipment mentioned above should be combined with the right type of auxiliary equipment such as dock boards and levelers, storage equipment (e.g., pallet racks, cantilever racks, drive-in or drive-through racks, and bin racks), and packaging equipment (e.g. palletizer, shrinkwrap, or stretchwrap equipment).

Developments in Handling Equipment

The developments in material handling equipment reflect the intense economic change currently going on. Industry is looking for improved productivity, lower inventory levels, greater responsiveness to customer needs, and better control. New developments in technology as well as new combinations of established technology in material handling, advanced information handling techniques, and appropriate management techniques can all contribute to achieve these goals.

General trends in material handling are the following:

- A focus on equipment modularity and standardization:
  Movable or reconfigurable.
  Easily expandable.
  Flexible, i.e., able to handle diverse products and/or routing patterns.
  Easily integrated with other types of equipment.
- An increased emphasis on ergonomics and safety.
- An increased attention for the environment, especially concerning the choice of packaging materials.

Some examples of trends in specific equipment are given in Table 17.3.

17.4   INTEGRATED MATERIAL HANDLING

From the above discussion, it is apparent that material handling cannot be studied as an isolated logistics function. For example, there are several important interrelationships between layout and material handling; storage issues, like selectivity and density, and material handling; and order picking and material handling. Some typical illustrations of these interactions will be given here. The numbers cited are, of course, indicative and may vary with specific applications.

TABLE 17.3.   Trends for Some Material Handling Equipment

Equipment	Trend
Lift truck	Ergonomic design; exhaust emissions regulations (environment)
Storage	AS–RS; getting smaller and more standardized
Order picking	A-frames for order picking of small items
Conveyors	New developments in sorting conveyors
Overhead handling equipment	Monorails—new technology applications for carriers and drive mechanisms; cranes, hoists—very high standardization
Packaging	Environmental concern about film recycling; pallet recycling and repairability concerns
AGV	Increasing use; more nonwire guidance; new battery technology; increased standardization of equipment and software
Dock management	Further development of computer-based dock management systems

[a] LiFo = Last in, first out
FiFo = First in, first out

Figure 17.3 shows the difference between a product and process layout. In a product layout, material handling requirements are reduced and special-purpose equipment can be used. Design changes, however, will cause the layout and corresponding material handling system to become obsolete. Some computer-aided layout techniques allow a simultaneous optimization of layout and material handling equipment selection. A typical example is COFAD (7).

Table 17.4 lists minimum storage aisle widths requirements for a variety of handling vehicles. Variations within the categories are possible because of design (sitdown versus setup

Product layout (fixed product routing)

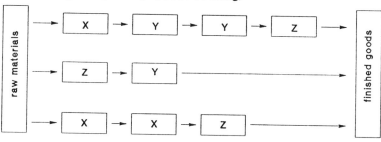

Process layout (variable product routing)

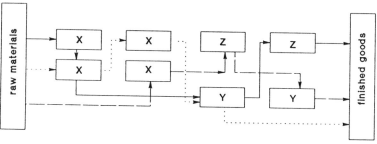

Figure 17.3.   Layout types.

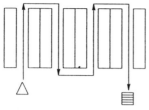

orderpicker picks complete orders;
one at the time

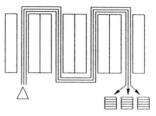

orderpicker picks complete orders;
several at the time

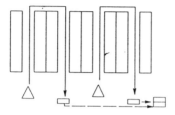

orderpicker picks part of an order;
one at the time

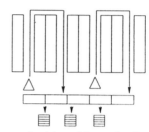

orderpicker picks parts of orders;
several at the time

Legend:

Figure 17.4. Order picking patterns.

TABLE 17.4. Storage Aisle Requirements for Different Types of Trucks

Truck	Aisle Width (feet)
Counterbalanced lift truck	10 to 15
Reach trucks	8
Straddle trucks	6.5 to 7.5
Side-loaders	5 to 7
Order pickers	4

TABLE 17.5. Trade-off between Storage Selectivity and Storage Density: Some Examples for Given Warehouse Space and Pallet Size

Storage Racks	Truck Type	Selectivity[a]	Density
One-deep pallet rack	Counterbalanced truck	100%	Low
Two-deep pallet rack	Double-reach straddle truck	LIFO (50%)	Medium
Drive-through rack	Counterbalanced truck	FIFO	High

[a] Lifo = Last in, first out
 Fifo = First in, first out

TABLE 17.6.   Order-picking Systems

Characteristic	Pick-to-Cart	Man-aboard Vehicle	Carousel
Pick rate	Low	Medium-high	Medium-high
Cost/square foot	Low	Medium	High
Picking accuracy	Medium	Medium	High
Maintenance requirements	Low	High	Medium
Reconfigurability	High	Low	Low

trucks), load capacity, and maximum lift heights. Table 17.5 shows the trade-off between storage density and storage selectivity for different combinations of storage racks and trucks. Figure 17.4 shows different potential order-picking patterns for part-to-picker systems. The choice of the pattern depends on item characteristics (weight and volume), order characteristics (number of lines), storage method characteristics (dedicated or random), etc. Table 17.6 compares some common order-picking systems. The pick-to-cart and man-aboard vehicle systems are "human-to-goods" solutions, whereas the carousel is a "goods-to-human" solution.

Considering the above interactions is important and makes the material handling system design process an iterative one. Due to the problem complexity few models have been developed for this purpose. Gray, Karmarkar, and Seidmann (8) is an exception here. The iterative process used in this chapter is schematically pictured in Figure 17.5.

It is clear also that the material handling system, as a part of the overall logistics system of the company, will also be affected by the current issues and trends in logistics, e.g., the need for smaller, more frequent and faster deliveries. The material handling equipment needs to be compatible with the emerging objectives of smoothing the flow of materials and speeding up the throughput in the logistics chain. The material handling system is also related to other business functions, e.g., marketing and advertising. A simple example can clarify this relationship. Suppose a certain item is stored and distributed on pallets containing 12 boxes each. Suppose marketing launches a promotion campaign with the slogan "Buy 12, get 2 free." Such a campaign will increase handling and orderpicking substantially, whereas a campaign slogan of "Buy 10, get 2 free" will decrease the total handling effort.

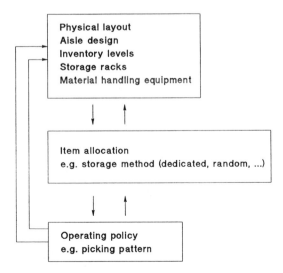

Figure 17.5.   Integrated design approach.

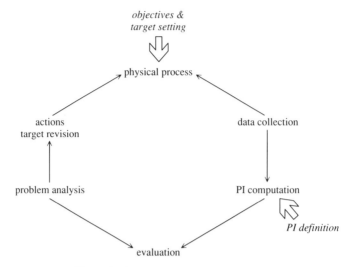

Figure 17.6. Performance indicator cycle.

17.5   ANALYZING AN EXISTING SYSTEM

Quantitative Analysis

Nowadays managers on all company levels face a wealth of information on many different subjects. This abundance of data is sometimes difficult to cope with. Often information is presented to the manager in a rather broad way and includes incorrect, outdated, and incomplete data. Apparently the last step in the information system is often omitted: The information is available but is not user friendly. An additional processing step is required to discriminate between important signals and routine information. Performance indicator (PI) systems are a means for this purpose, because they allow large amounts of data to be summarized into a few relevant key numbers. Although PIs are not fundamentally new, a recent renewed interest in this idea may be noted in many business areas, especially in logistics, of which material handling systems form an important component. Figure 17.6 illustrates the PI cycle. Note that the purpose of the PI cycle is not only to report on past performance but to anticipate problems and to try to correct them in a continuous improvement program. The target-setting process is difficult and situation dependent, e.g., the ratio of the time for material handling to the total operating time will preferably be low in a workshop but may be high in a warehouse; moreover, in the latter situation, the target depends on the degree of automation applied in the warehouse. The targets should be carefully determined to motivate people to work toward them. Setting targets too high will demotivate people (''We can never reach them anyway'') as well as setting them too low.

The PI definition process is a crucial aspect in the PI cycle. It is a time-consuming process in which PIs are suggested, analyzed critically, and redefined until there is a consensus about their usefulness. The computation and data collection methods should be carefully defined for each PI. Data integrity and timeliness are, of course, required features for the PIs.

Three basic types of PIs may be distinguished: measuring efficiency, measuring effectiveness, and measuring productivity. Efficiency ratios report on how well resources have been used. Effectiveness ratios report on how well the objective was reached, and productivity ratios relate input needed to output achieved. Figure 17.7 gives generic definitions for each of those types. When reporting on the material handling process some further general indicators may be useful to complete the performance picture (e.g., the number of products in the warehouse). Table 17.7 illustrates performance measures in each category for material handling systems. Note that although most PIs are ratios, this is not absolutely necessary.

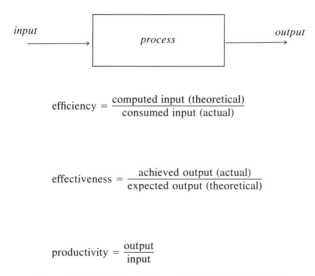

$$\text{efficiency} = \frac{\text{computed input (theoretical)}}{\text{consumed input (actual)}}$$

$$\text{effectiveness} = \frac{\text{achieved output (actual)}}{\text{expected output (theoretical)}}$$

$$\text{productivity} = \frac{\text{output}}{\text{input}}$$

Figure 17.7.   Basic performance indicator (PI) types.

Related to these PI issues is the increasingly popular competitive benchmarking technique. The main idea of competitive benchmarking is to compare one's own performance with that of the competitors to detect one's weaknesses and strengths. From there, the areas for improvement may be identified. Benchmarking in general is a technique used to establish world-class performance in certain processes (e.g., manufacturing performance). Auguston (9) described a benchmarking study concerning warehouse performance conducted in U.S. industry. The issues studied were productivity, timeliness, order-picking accuracy, order cycle time, and inventory accuracy.

TABLE 17.7.   Material Handling Performance Indicators

Performance	Example	Illustration of PI
Effectiveness	Throughput time	Order cycle time, i.e., time between material handling job request and its completion
	Accuracy–reliability	Service level, i.e., number of okay jobs per total number of jobs
	Scrap	Damage ratio, i.e., number of damaged loads per total number of loads
Efficiency	Space	Warehouse space use, i.e., storage space occupied to available storage space
	Equipment	Lift truck use, i.e., items moved per hour vs. theoretical capacity
Productivity—General	Material handling vs. context	Material handling labor ratio, i.e., material handling personnel to total operating personnel
	Material handling vs. process	Movement ratio, i.e., number of moves to number of productive operations

Qualitative Analysis

A qualitative material handling system analysis or a material handling audit may be conducted on different levels: strategic, tactical, and operational. A strategic audit will be geared toward the contribution of the material handling system in supporting the corporate goals. A typical question to be answered here is, "Does the company need its own warehouse or should it rent outside storage space?" Another strategical question deals with the level of centralization versus decentralization. Nowadays, companies want to shorten the distribution cycle between the manufacturing plant and the final customer. Therefore, in certain industries (e.g., the food industry) we see a tendency to larger distribution centers, servicing the final vendors directly (e.g., grocery stores). A tactical audit will try to answer questions concerning medium-term investment and operating costs. A typical issue addressed here is the useful economic life of the material handling equipment. An operational audit emphasizes the daily operations of the warehouse and thus concerns the flow of materials and information. It is the latter audit type that will be further discussed here.

Analyzing an existing material handling system means to determine whether the system is functioning efficiently and smoothly (without creating bottlenecks) and transporting the units when and where needed. The literature provides many handy checklists for identifying inefficiencies in the material handling system (e.g., refs. 10, 11).

One could, of course, rely on experiences and judgment and try to identify all inefficiencies in the material handling system by walking around in the plant and by observing the running of the system. This will probably take a lot of time and chances are pretty high that certain inefficiencies will be overlooked just because the observer is so used to them (the "we-did-it-like-this-for-years-so-why-change-now" phenomenon). Using a good checklist will help to avoid this while saving valuable time. By a "good" checklist we mean a checklist based on experience in many different companies and taking into account the principal areas of the material handling system. The concept of such a checklist is illustrated in Table 17.8.

Most of the questions require a yes or no answer and sometimes there is room for comments. Sometimes the checklists ask for some more detailed answers, e.g., "never–some-times–always" or "very high–high–medium–low–very low." The questions are seldom open questions, because they are difficult to process. It is clear that a certain amount of customization of a general literature checklist will always be needed for any specific situation. A careful study of the completed checklist allows one to identify the potential areas of improvement.

17.6 DESIGNING A NEW SYSTEM

Design Process

Designing a new material handling system, whether starting from zero or from an existing system that needs to be replaced, is not an easy task. Table 17.9 list the design process steps. Step A is the basic step. This step describes what the function of the material handling system will be and in which environment it will operate, e.g., warehouse or shop floor. In step B, a detailed analysis concerning the requirements for handling, storing, and controlling is made. It is important here to take into account all interrelationships with other functions (as discussed above).

The next step is a crucial one, because in step C all the alternatives that will be considered in the study are developed. The existence of a large variety of equipment with different capabilities and limitations makes this step a tough one. Equipment selection lists, both general and specific, may be helpful here. The rapidly changing technology in some areas (e.g., computer control) adds to this complexity. Also factors such as available funds, building characteristics, and management philosophy concerning automation may influence this step.

Figure 17.8 illustrates several degrees of automation and their suitability for different throughput levels. Of course, lists like the material handling principles and a concept like the material handling equation (discussed earlier) may be useful here, as they help form a basis for the critical evaluation of the system's requirements. Notice that several elements will favor more automation, while others will favor less automation. Among the elements that favor automation are centralized distribution, better space use, increasing labor cost, nonavailability of labor, improved working conditions, and smaller and therefore more handling units. One element favoring less automation is the tendency toward shrinking inventories, i.e., smaller warehouses. But the principal reason why people hold back in automation decisions is business

TABLE 17.8. Checklist for Material Handling Systems (MHS)

1. General Questions
   - Topic: global aspects of the MHS
   - Examples:
     Is the MHS flexible enough to cope with changing product volumes and mixes, throughput and service needs, technology options, customer requirements, etc?
     Is the MHS integrated with the production system? Are interfaces with other business functions working okay?
     Is standardization a main concern while investing in new equipment?
     Has the company clear objectives concerning the degree of automation to apply to the MHS?
2. Specific Questions
   - Topic: different areas of (and interfaces with) the MHS
   - Examples:
     2.1. Receiving, including dock operations and inspection
     Does the dock equipment match the types of warehouse vehicles used?
     Could doors between dock and warehouse help to reduce energy costs?
     Do quality control and inspection reports satisfy the needs of the customer, i.e., the manufacturing process?
     2.2. Storage
     Are there any unnecessary packing–unpacking operations needed due to lack of standardization or choice of the wrong unit load?
     Is the storage equipment sized correctly for the materials stored?
     Is the trade-off between storage density and selectivity optimized?
     2.3. Handling operations in the manufacturing process
     Is there any backtracking in the flow path?
     Are there any areas with traffic congestion?
     Is production work delayed owing to poorly scheduled delivery and removal of material?
     2.4. Order picking
     Are travel distances between picks minimized where possible?
     Would a part-to-picker instead of a picker-to-part system improve the picking operations?
     Are low-activity items out of the way but accessible to pickers when necessary?
     2.5. Packaging
     Are mispicked orders corrected in a timely manner?
     Is volume sufficiently high to justify addition of automatic packing equipment to replace manual operations?
     Did you make the right choice between strapping, wrapping, etc?
     2.6. Shipping
     Are receiving and shipping operations separated so that they do not interfere?
     Are the shipping operations well planned?
     Would additional equipment speed up the loading operations?
3. Information flow and data collection
   - Topic: the amount and type of data collected, the data processing and information flow accompanying the material flow
   - Examples:
     Does a computerized database of inventory information exist?
     Does each stock-keeping unit have a unique identification number?
     Is there a satisfactory performance reporting?

uncertainty, illustrated by rapidly changing product ranges and the increased difficulty to predict volumes, product mixes, etc. However, the primary benefit of automation is system discipline, resulting in increased accuracy, better ergonomics, and fewer returned shipments.

In step D in Table 17.9, the alternatives from the previous step are evaluated. Different methods may be used. Parsaei and Mital (12) give an overview of available techniques to evaluate and justify such investment projects. Note, however, that obtaining the necessary data is not always an easy task. First of all there are the single-objective methods. This category

TABLE 17.9. Steps in Designing a Material Handling System

A. Define the intended function of the material handling system.
B. Analyze the requirements for handling, storing and controlling.
C. Generate alternatives.
D. Evaluate alternatives.
E. Select preferred design.
F. Implement the selected design.

includes the classic investment criteria like payback period, net present value, internal rate of return, and profitability index. It is important here to take into account the whole expected lifetime of the equipment to obtain an as accurate as possible overview of the generated cash flows. Sometimes integer programming models are used to choose among possible projects when there is a budget constraint. Second, there are multiobjective methods such as scoring, analytical hierarchy processes, and goal programming. The third category contains the probabi-

Control	Power	Illustration
Manual	Manual	Man carries load
		Load is carried on a two-wheel hand truck
		Mechanical help, e.g. pulley, is used
Manual	Gravity	Use flow racks
Manual	External	Use walkie truck
Mechanized	External	Conveyor is started with push-button system
Semi-automated	External	Electronic control through start of program
Fully automated	External	AS/RS

(a)

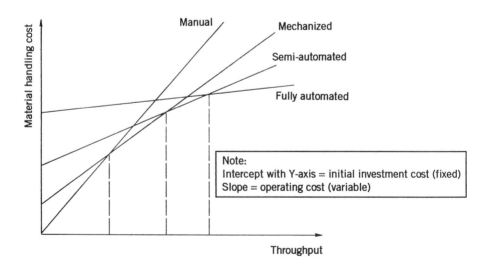

(b)

Figure 17.8. Levels of automation.

listic–stochastic methods like decision tree analysis, optimistic–pessimistic analysis, and Monte Carlo simulation. The fourth and last category contains the fairly recent fuzzy set methods.

Besides these quantifiable measures, there are also a number of intangible aspects to be taken into account, e.g., improved customer services, more predictable performance, reduced scrap, better quality of working life, and preparation for more integration. It is clear that Japanese management practice tends to give much more weight to these service-related criteria than we were used to in the Western world. Note also that system modularity is an important issue, although difficult to quantify. Modular equipment means equipment that is movable or reconfigurable, easily expandable, flexible, and easy to integrate with other equipment. The latter issue and the corresponding requirements for interfaces with other systems such as warehousing and manufacturing are important. It should be noted, too, that the classic design-to-implementation cycle may take several months (and even more than 1 yr) to implement systems designed to narrow customer requirements. The use of (semi-)standardized and modular equipment may considerably speed up the total project time and may decrease investment costs.

Automation: Theory Versus Practice

In this section some rules of thumb for automation projects are summed up. The rules are based on experiences with Belgian firms. Some case studies illustrating these rules may be found in ref. 13.

1. *Define the Strategic Competitive Objective.* Ideally, any automation begins with an explicit definition of the competitive strategy, including the effects of such factors as competitive behavior, market demands, and technological opportunities.

2. *Define Objectives for Systems Productivity, Availability, and Market Dependability.* These objectives have been identified as those cited by managers as their motives for improving material handling systems. It is necessary to approach this stage from two directions: current requirements and possible future requirements.

3. *Examine the Role of System Automation.* This stage involves defining in more detail exactly how system automation should contribute to the levels of dependability, productivity, and availability set by the company competitive strategy.

4. *Build Small Cohesive Teams in an Appropriate Environment.* Involving the right people is imperative for any type of project. Management is typically unaware of the extensive demands automation places on the organization and its support system (both human and technical). For example, new skills, planning maintenance, and integration of different levels of computers may be required.

5. *Take a Hard Look at the Current System.* Often companies go for automation without first evaluating and improving the existing material handling or storage system. Performing a material handling or warehousing audit and then examining the potential or rationalizing and simplifying the existing operations before installing advanced material handling and warehousing technologies is the cardinal principle.

6. *Examine a Feasible Range of Alternative Technologies.* The first question to be answered in the design phase is, "Which type of system can solve our problem?" Here a range of feasible alternative technologies should be considered given the endogenous and exogenous variables. The endogenous variables are the characteristics of units to be handled and stored, the nature of current material handling and warehousing operations, the current automation level, and the intention to increase this level in the future. Exogenous variables include specific manufacturing or distribution characteristics (e.g., throughput and sales) and relative competitive standing measured in terms of quality and price. An example is given in Table 17.10.

   Feasibility includes not only technical feasibility but also economical feasibility. Conceptually, the decision criterion for investing in an automated system is similar to many other investment decisions: the net benefits, tangible and intangible, should result in a positive net present value. During the screening phase a number of alternative solutions can be eliminated from further consideration. Useful techniques at this stage are queueing network models and aggregated simulation.

TABLE 17.10. Alternative Material Handling Solutions for Different Combinations of Throughput and Item Size

Throughput	Item Size		
	Small	Medium	Large (pallet)
Low	Sliding aisle shelving	Mezzanine; carousel, paternoster	Block stacking, standard, racking
Medium	High density, modular, miniload	Man-on-board, carousel	Unit load, AS/RS
Large	Miniload	Miniload, man-on-board	Unit load, AS/RS

7. *Evaluate the Detailed Physical Design.* The detailed design of the system contains the layout, the number of aisles, the exact number of handling equipment required, the type and speed of equipment, pallet positions per pickup or dropoff, and the storage method (random, class based, etc.). Other important decisions in the design of automated material handling and storage systems concern the specification of the size and location of warehouses and the size and location of load–unload stations. Several mathematical models are available to assist the designer in assessing and determining the detailed design parameters. Standard operations research and industrial engineering techniques (14) are also helpful at this stage, especially simulation tools.

8. *Use Simple and Efficient Operational Policies.* Manufacturing or distribution advantage will erode over time as other companies acquire the same technology. Therefore, a great deal of emphasis should be placed on the operating system. Operating policies can be divided into two groups: medium term and short term. The medium-term operating policies attempt to balance the use of material handling and storage system for a given demand and service level. The short-term operational policies deal with the detailed decision making required for real-time operation of the system such as batching and picking in order picking, dispatching and routing in an AGV system, and crane or aisle selection for storage and retrieval in AS/RS systems. We believe that the greater benefit of automation and its flexibility will come from designing simple and efficient operational policies.

9. *Design Modular Control Software.* The complexity of software and its interfaces with other software is a well-known problem. To facilitate later changes in the control software for modifying the operational policies or introducing and extending the system, a modular software is necessary.

10. *Define Performance Indicators.* Steady improvement or adjustment of the operational policies is required. Therefore, it is absolutely necessary to identify a number of performance measures and collect information for these measures. For example, in case of an AGV system, these indicators can be mean time between failures (MTBF), mean time to repair (MTTR), flow time ratios, response times, and demand variance over time. This information will help management to take corrective actions.

The above principles cannot, of course, provide an answer to all the detailed questions usually asked when automating material handling and warehousing systems, but they give a sensible line of action for dealing effectively with advanced automation.

17.7 CONCLUSIONS

Material handling is part of the logistics function of the firm and, therefore, affects the logistics performance. This performance should be consistent with the overall business objectives of customer service, quality, profitability, environmental issues, etc.

Automation is not an objective on itself. Often automated solutions solve only part of the problem, because sufficient attention has not been paid to the peripheral handling (on the border of the system). An appropriate level of automation will take into account both the uncertainty of the business environment and the world-class performance standards of today. In any case, careful planning is required. New tendencies include the desire of faster implementation, modular and reusable design, and systems integration.

BIBLIOGRAPHY

1. J.A. TOMPKINS and J.A. WHITE, *Facilities Planning,* John Wiley & Sons, Inc., New York, 1984.

2. D.R. SULE, *Manufacturing Facilities: Location, Planning and Design,* PWS-Kent Publishing Co., Boston, 1988.

3. *Modern Materials Handling* **46**(7), 7 (June 1991).

4. T.H. ALLEGRI, *Materials Handling: Principles and Practice,* Van Nostrand Reinhold, Co., Inc., New York, 1984.

5. G. SALVENDY, *Handbook of Industrial Engineering,* John Wiley & Sons, Inc., New York, 1992.

6. J.A. WHITE, *Production Handbook,* John Wiley & Sons, Inc., New York, 1987.

7. J.A. TOMPKINS and R. REED, "An Applied Model for the Facilities Design Problem," *Int. J. Product. Res.* **14**(5), 583–595 (1976).

8. A.E. GRAY, U.S. KARMARKAR, and A. SEIDMANN, "Design and Operation of an Order-consolidated Warehouse: Models and Applications," *Eur. J. Operations Res.,* **58**, 14–36 (1992).

9. K.A. AUGUSTON, "Warehousing/Distribution: Compare Yourself to the Best . . . and Worst," *Mod. Materials Handling,* **47**, 48–51 (May 1992).

10. W.J. RANSOM, "How Efficient Is Your Warehouse?" *Modern Materials Handling,* **42**, 1987.

11. J.A. WHITE, "The Road to World-Class Warehousing," *Mod. Materials Handling,* **47**, 6–39 (Mar. 1992).

12. H.R. PARSAEI and A. MITAL, *Economics of Advanced Manufacturing Systems,* Chapman & Hall, London, 1992.

13. L. GELDERS and J. ASHAYERI, *Lessons Learned from Automation: Theory versus Practice,* paper presented at the *10th ICAW,* Dallas, Oct. 1989.

14. J. ASHAYERI, L. GELDERS, and L. VAN WASSENHOVE, "A Microcomputer-based Optimization Model for the Design of Automated Warehouses," *Int. J. Product. Res.* **23**(4), 825–829 (1985).

GLOSSARY

Automated storage/retrieval system (AS/RS). A combination of equipment and controls that handles, stores, and retrieves materials with precision, accuracy, and speed under a defined degree of automation. Such systems range from relatively simple manually controlled order-picking machines operating in small storage structures to relatively complex, computer-controlled storage–retrieval systems that are totally integrated into the manufacturing and distribution process.

Carousel. A concept consisting of a set of horizontally revolving storage baskets or bins. The conveyor is basically a trolley conveyor with the carrier's storage baskets densely spaced around the conveyor. The drive mechanism rotates the carriers clockwise or counterclockwise to bring the appropriate basket to the picking station.

Conveyor. A horizontal, inclined, or vertical device for moving or transporting bulk materials, packages, or objects in a path predetermined by the design of the device and having fixed or selective points of loading and discharge.

Crane. A machine for lifting and/or moving a load. A hoisting mechanism is an integral part of the machine.

Order picking. The activity by which a small number of goods is extracted from a warehousing system to satisfy a number of independent customer orders.

Truck. A mobile, mostly power-driven vehicle used to carry, push, pull, lift, stack, or tier material.

Unit load. A number of items arranged such that they can be handled as a single object. This can be accomplished, e.g., by palletization or containerization.

CHAPTER 18

Understanding the Role of Packaging in Manufacturing and Manufacturing Systems

STEPHEN A. RAPER and MING-REN SUN
University of Missouri at Rolla

18.1 BACKGROUND

One of the focus areas of this handbook, manufacturing systems, receives an abundance of coverage in the available literature. Moreover, the literature is likely to keep expanding at a rapid rate due to continual theoretical breakthroughs and technological advances. One area that is not usually included in this body of literature but, as is proposed in this chapter, should be the area of packaging and packaging systems design. This chapter shows that a basic understanding of packaging is necessary to optimize manufacturing systems design.

The relationship between manufacturing and packaging can be generally shown as in Figure 18.1. This view represents the notion that an interconnected relationship exists between the manufacturing system and the packaging system and that upon manufacture of a product and a package a necessary "marriage" or bonding between the two occurs. (Of course, the need for a package is dictated by the manufacture of a product.) The strength of the relationship, or the degree of bonding, that may occur and, consequently, the degree of emphasis placed on packaging systems in a company or organization is heavily influenced by both the particular product that is manufactured and the industry category the company competes in. As an example, an industry or company that produces heavy parts such as electric motors may look at packaging only as a containment vessel, such as a corrugated box. On the other extreme, industries such as consumer foods and products, pharmaceuticals, and beer and beverages entirely depend on the package and packaging systems for the success of the product in the marketplace. In the first example, the product is dominant in the relationship and strong emphasis is placed on manufacturing systems design with packaging design merely an afterthought. The packaging system may be considered a separate entity from the manufacturing system. In the latter example, the product and the package are equally dominant in the relationship, implying that manufacturing and packaging system design are equally important or that the packaging system may be considered a subset of the manufacturing system.

An additional driver in raising the awareness of packaging in society, and further motivation for including a discussion of the subject in this handbook, is the increased emphasis on environmental awareness and solid waste. Certainly, packaging waste is a large proportion of the total solid waste within this country. The drive to reduce the amount of packaging waste that is present in landfills will ultimately affect packaging system design. This in turn will place demands and burdens on manufacturing system design. In other words, changes to the packaging system that address environmental concerns may require changes in the manufacturing systems. As an example, reducing the amount of protective packaging for a delicate electronic device, may require that the device be redesigned to be more rugged and capable of survival in harsh distribution environments.

In sum, the primary purpose of this chapter is to describe how and why packaging systems design should be included in any discussion of manufacturing systems design. This chapter seeks to inform practitioners (both academic and industrial) of the potential benefits of understanding packaging and packaging systems and how that understanding may lead to more

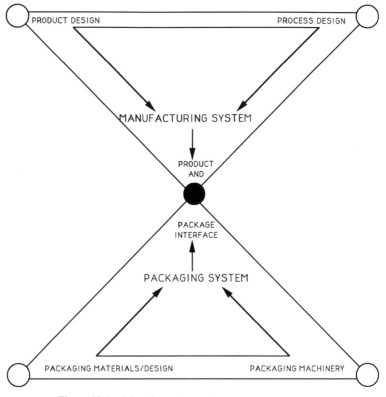

Figure 18.1.   Manufacturing and packaging interface.

effective manufacturing systems design. The majority of the chapter is intended to provide the reader with a basic understanding of packaging and how it fits within an organization. Also included in this chapter is an integrated design model proposed by Sun. This model primarily focuses on the relationship between product design and packaging design. However, when manufacturing is viewed in the broadest sense, the model could be adapted to the notion that manufacturing systems design includes product design or at least is a logical next step in the process.

18.2   PACKAGING DEFINED

It has been estimated that approximately 95% of all goods produced in the United States are packaged at one time or another. In addition, virtually all of the 0.25 million or more product-producing and distribution companies in the United States are users of packaging materials and equipment (1, 2). With those figures in mind, it would seem easy to answer the question "What is packaging?" However, it is an often asked question that is not easy to answer. Simply, packaging may be defined as that material, form, or vessel that contains a product. For instance, a corrugated box and foam cushioning that contain a computer or the aluminum can that contains a soft drink may be considered packages, or packaging.

A formal definition of packaging as proposed by the Institute of Packaging Professionals is as follows:

> *The enclosure of products, items or packages in a wrap, pouch, bag, box, cup, tray, can, tube, bottle or other container form to perform one or more of the following major functions: containment for handling, transportation and use; preservation and protection of the contents for required shelf and*

use life and sometimes protection of the external environment from any hazards of contact with contents; identification of contents, quantity, quality and manufacturer—usually by means of printing, decoration, labeling, package shape or transparency; facilitate dispensing and use. If the device or container performs one or more of these functions, it is a package (3).

As this formal definition shows, many different materials, structures, and forms may be considered as the package, or packaging.

Rather than defining packaging formally, it may be described in terms of functions or functionality. In general, the package has four primary functions: containment, protection, performance, and communication (4). The basic function of any package is to contain a product or products for purposes such as storage or transportation. The protection function is twofold in that the package must protect the product from the surrounding environment and protect the surrounding environment from the product, if necessary. For example, a package may protect a fragile electronic product from various drops and impacts, and conversely, the package may protect the surrounding environment from a hazardous or dangerous chemical product. In terms of performance, the package can be designed to be easy opening, reusable, recyclable, biodegradable, tamper evident, etc. And finally, a package must communicate what the product is, promote an image, or meet mandatory labeling or legal requirements. As was mentioned in the previous section, the package or packaging system is heavily influenced by the industry it is used in. For instance, most consumer-oriented packaging will place heavy emphasis on the performance, communication, and protection functions. Whereas packaging geared toward institutional or military markets will place heavy emphasis on protection and performance functions.

The package itself may be viewed at three different levels: as a primary, secondary, or tertiary package. By way of example, consider the packaging for soft drinks. The primary package for the soft drink is an aluminum can and easy-open lid. It is the package that is in intimate contact with the product. The secondary or unitizing package could be a paperboard container used to hold 12 individuals cans or the plastic Hi-Cone rings used to hold 6 cans. The tertiary package would then be the corrugated tray used to combine the secondary packages for subsequent palletization. In general, the secondary package is the unitizing package and the tertiary package is the shipping container (5). In some instances, one package could be a primary and tertiary container.

Note that there is growing body of literature on packaging or packaging engineering related to electronic components packaged either onto mother boards or inside electronic devices such as a computer and the packing of circuits onto chips. That literature has a narrow focus and includes many theoretical ideas and concepts. Packaging as described in this chapter is not related.

18.3   PACKAGING IN THE END-USE ORGANIZATION

This section examines how the packaging function is viewed in an organizational context and how it may impact other functional areas. Packaging has been described as "one of the most complex functions in business today" (3). It is also a function that is cross-disciplinary in nature. Typically, the package not only must fulfill the four functions mentioned above but also must maintain the quality of the product; act as a marketer; cut or at least contain costs related to the materials used in the packaging; and minimize distribution, handling, and storage costs. To accomplish effectively these and many other requirements, packaging must function in a cross-disciplinary environment. This is shown by the use of the wheel and hub in Figure 18.2.

The package interacts with many of the major functions in an organization (Figure 18.2) The package in many instances must act as a sales and marketing tool or must promote and support a marketing strategy; thus marketing will have significant input into the overall packaging strategy of a company. Engineering typically is responsible for specifying and installing packaging lines and equipment capable of efficiently and profitably running the various package types (primary, secondary, and tertiary). Operations usually desires packaging that is capable of being run and maintained without negatively impacting efficiency and productivity, which is a key issue in the development of efficient manufacturing systems. Purchasing must buy the packaging (materials and containers) pursuant to their interests (often low cost is important). Quality control and assurance are concerned that packaging will indeed maintain the quality of the product (6). Traffic, warehousing, and distribution want packaging that minimizes storage and transportation expenses while at the same time provides adequate protection against shock, vibration, and

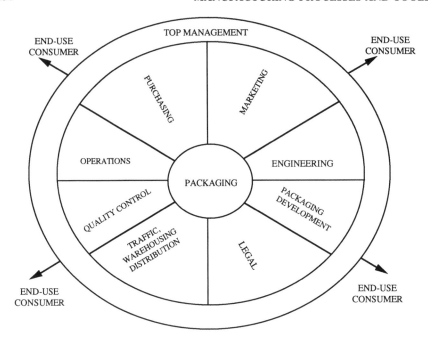

Figure 18.2.   Cross-disciplinary nature of packaging.

other typical hazards prevalent in that environment. The legal department is concerned with the plethora of laws and regulations aimed at or required of packaging at local, state, federal, and even global levels. Given the recent emphasis on environmental awareness, the importance of the legal aspects of packaging will likely increase. Packaging development and technology, if such a function exists, must coordinate between many of the above listed areas as well as solve problems related specifically to the package and packaging systems. The end user, in turn, requires packaging that is environmentally friendly and offers convenient features, for example. And, of course, management wants packaging that positively contributes to organizational objectives (6).

Although the wheel and hub shown in Figure 18.2 shows packaging at the center of the hub, one could easily develop a corresponding wheel and hub with manufacturing at the hub and packaging shown as a spoke. Again, this depends on the industry and the functions that packaging is to serve. To reemphasize, in many instances manufacturing systems and packaging systems may in fact be synergistic and Figure 18.2 could be modified to show both manufacturing and packaging at the hub.

18.4   CONFLICTING GOALS AND OBJECTIVES

All of the areas described above place many conflicting demands and requirements on packaging. For instance, operations wants packaging that runs efficiently on existing packaging equipment lines, which often implies less complex shapes and styles. Marketing, on the other hand, wants the package to act as a sales tool and, therefore, demands packaging shapes and styles that may be difficult to run efficiently on existing packaging lines and systems. In addition, purchasing may want to buy the least expensive packaging, which could lead to product and package quality problems, both within the facility and out in the field.

Many organizations do not have a formal packaging function or department, thus packaging responsibilities such as design and specification, testing, material procurement, machinery, and actual product packaging may lie in any of the above mentioned functional areas, in whole or in part. In these cases, functional biases often create problems. In addition, shortcomings in these areas can cause serious packaging problems that may impact the delivered product quality and

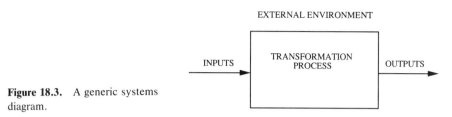

EXTERNAL ENVIRONMENT

INPUTS | TRANSFORMATION PROCESS | OUTPUTS

Figure 18.3. A generic systems diagram.

cost. In larger and more packaging-oriented industries such as consumer foods, beverages, pharmaceuticals, and even computer and electronic firms, a formally identified packaging functional area may exist. Even so, the complexities and potential problems related to packaging as noted above are still common (6, 7).

18.5 A SYSTEMS VIEW OF PACKAGING

The previous sections defined packaging and showed that within an organization is is typically an interdisciplinary function. This section describes packaging from a systems view. That is, it shows that packaging is not an independent entity in and of itself, but rather it is an integral part of a much larger integrated system.

A system can be represented in its most basic form as shown in Figure 18.3. Inputs are fed into a process where they are then transformed into an output. The surrounding external environment can directly or indirectly affect this process. The integrated system, of which packaging is an important and necessary part, follows the same basic logic and is shown in Figure 18.4.

In this view, inputs such as materials, methods, machines, labor, and capital are converted into products through the transformation process. This may also be referred to as the manufacturing subsystem. Through this process, control is maintained such that when the product leaves the manufacturing subsystem it has attained a certain level of quality. To maintain this quality level, a marriage between the product and the package then occurs in the packaging subsystem. The product and package are united or married into the primary package by a variety of packaging materials and forms using various types of packaging machinery. The primary package is subsequently unitized into the secondary package, which is placed in the tertiary package for palletization and storage in the warehouse of the production facility.

The packaged product now becomes an output and can follow two paths. In the first path, the packaged product goes through transport links and becomes an input to another transformation process, repeating the process as previously discussed. Thus the quality built into the product and maintained by the package takes on added significance. In the second path, the packaged product goes through transport links and becomes an input into a distribution subsystem. In this subsystem, breaking of bulk (depalletizing), warehousing, and further distribution occur. The packaged product (primary and secondary) again becomes an output and goes through another series of transport links before becoming an input into a retail subsystem.

In the retail subsystem, the packaged product (usually only the primary package) is stocked and made ready for purchase by a consumer. The consumer purchases the packaged product and ultimately will divorce or separate the product from the package. The package itself must either be disposed of, reused, or recycled.

A second view of this integrated system is shown in Figure 18.5. This view shows how the various subsystems are interconnected. Also included in the figure are the marketing subsystem and the external environment. Throughout this entire integrated system, the package must maintain the quality of the product in a cost-effective and efficient manner. The package must often act as a marketer, through many different channels of distribution and in a host of different wholesale and retail environments. The package must be able to protect the product through the various transport links, where hazards such as shock, vibration, and temperature extremes may damage or destroy the product. The packaging machinery component of the packaging subsystem must also be integrated efficiently and effectively into the manufacturing process that produces the product.

In this view, it is assumed that the marketing strategy of the company will influence the inner subsystems. However, marketing strategy will also be influenced by end-use customer desires.

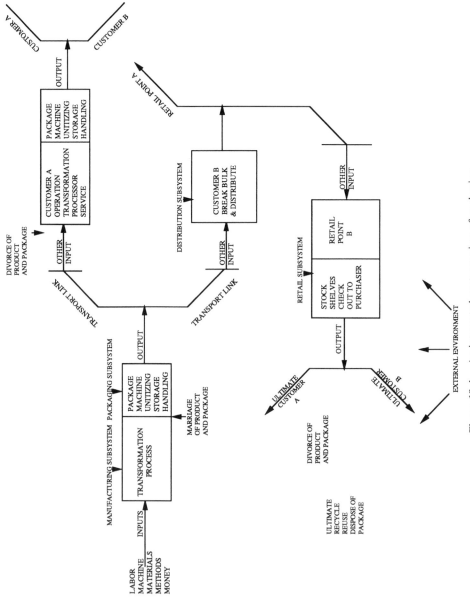

Figure 18.4. An integrated systems view of packaging.

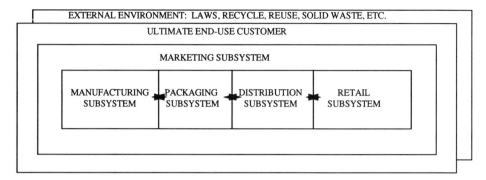

Figure 18.5. A different view of the integrated system.

The external environment represented in Figure 18.5 includes such issues as the laws and regulations aimed at packaging as well as disposing, recycling, and reusing the package after the end-use customer receives the packaged product. The integrated systems view of packaging as described above helps to establish packaging's cross-disciplinary nature. It also shows that designing packages and packaging systems is a complex task that cannot (or should not) be pursued independent of product, process, and manufacturing system design.

18.6 PACKAGING AND PRODUCT DESIGN

Product design and packaging design are two important functions in the manufacturing and distribution of goods. They are complicated tasks and involve many variables and environmental factors. Furthermore, packaging design is similar to product design in that both are creative processes that integrate many complex constraints, variables, and demands to meet the requirements of manufacturing and distribution systems and the user. Many manufacturing and distribution problems can be attributed to poor product design and packaging design processes, both of which are normally conducted in a linear fashion instead of a concurrent fashion. Conventional design and manufacturing procedures often suffer from long lead times, high cost, and low process efficiencies. They normally prescribe a sequential structure similar to that shown in Figure 18.6.

Newer integrated design strategies and techniques such as (Design for Assembly–Design for Manufacturing) and simultaneous and concurrent engineering, seek to eliminate most of the problems mentioned above by pursuing product and process design concurrently. The product, instead of the product and its packaging, is the major focal point in these design strategies. Consequently, packaging design may be done in an ad hoc manner and may not be given sufficient analytical consideration. This could possibly lead to a limited ability to increase product quality and packaging quality and also could lead to poor production efficiencies. Thus the manufacturing system that is put in place to produce the product may not be an optimum system.

In addition to the factors listed above, not including packaging design into product and process design may lead to unnecessary or excessive costs. It has been estimated that distribution costs account for 12% of sales revenue and packaging material costs account for an

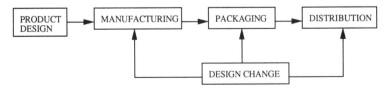

Figure 18.6. A sequential design structure.

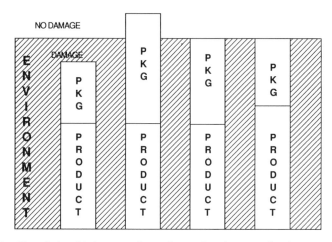

Figure 18.7.   The relationship between the product and package as related to potential damage.

additional 10% to 15%. Consequently, errors in packaging design, from a materials selection standpoint or secondary and tertiary packaging design standpoint, could lead to substantial losses in profit (8). The errors may also be negatively impacting manufacturing costs, again, by not having an optimum system designed initially.

Product damage costs in shipment and in distribution can also be significant. The losses of product or packaging damage may include claim payments, processing costs, added inventory costs, production costs, and the cost resulting from the loss of customer goodwill. It is not unusual that 5% to 15% of products that are shipped are damaged in distribution channels. But the total cost and amount of damage is not known with great certainty by industry (9).

Products and packages can be damaged in shipment as a result of a number of severe environmental effects or hazards. Typically, product damage due to handling shock is of the greatest magnitude, but vibration may cause significant damage as well. Some firms claim that there is almost no damage losses for their products in shipment. While this may be a good claim, it might also indicate overpackaging of their products. Product design and packaging design as it relates to overpackaging and underpackaging is shown in Figure 18.7.

When Figure 18.7 is applied to individual packaged products, it shows the various ways the product and package can be designed to provide adequate protection from damage in any given environment. The first column shows that the package does not afford enough protection to prevent damage to the product, resulting in product damage loss, loss of customer goodwill, etc. As a matter of note, underpackaging may be a viable option if products are transported as unit or pallet loads. In this case, the sum of the parts (unitized load) affords more protection than the individual parts (individual packages). The second column shows the case of overpackaging for which there is more than enough protection provided by the package. This situation can lead to excessive packaging costs. The third and fourth columns both show that adequate protection is provided by the package. However, the fourth column indicates a design change in the product that subsequently allows a lesser amount of packaging to provide adequate protection against damage. The implication here is that a product design change coupled with a packaging design change may in fact reduce the overall costs associated with that product and package, although this may not always be the case.

There is a growing body of literature devoted to protective product and packaging design and their interrelationship. The November 1992 issue of *Test Engineering and Management* gives a good introductory description of well-developed test procedures for cased goods and cushioned-packaging development (10). It will also enlighten the reader in regard to equipment required to perform the test procedures.

Without question, product and process design are two important functions in an organization. Packaging design is equally as important, yet still does not obtain sufficient attention in newer integrated design methodologies. This importance is particularly evident when we consider the impact of packaging on the consumer, the manufacturer, and the marketplace. The effectiveness of product and packaging design will influence the other functional efficiencies of the corporation. Marketing and sales cannot function well if products have a reputation of being damaged during shipment or are fragile, requiring special handling that usually costs more. Consumers may base their perception of the quality of a product on the appearance of its package. Failure to design the product and its package adequately can result in unnecessary expense and labor in production and unnecessary handling or materials in distribution. In addition, improper product and package design are often time-consuming and costly to modify once production and distribution has begun. The challenge then is to strive for integrated product and packaging design. This not only provides an ideal tool for design engineers to enhance their design capability but also increases the efficiency and effectiveness of manufacturing and distribution as well as reducing costs from damaged and excessive materials usage. Consumers can then enjoy better products at reduced costs, which also may have a less negative impact on the environment.

18.7 AN INTEGRATED DESIGN METHOD

The previous discussion alluded to the need for an integrated design methodology that does in fact include packaging design. An integrated product and packaging design method, proposed by Sun (11), which can enhance the design process is shown in Figure 18.8. This integrated design model depicts a process to coordinate design engineering, manufacturing engineering, packaging design, distribution, and marketing with teamwork simultaneously and at an early stage in the product research and development process. Ideally, this model can be used most effectively by a design team for which each member of the team has some knowledge of the other team member's area. Ideally, it may be desirable that each team member have expertise in other disciplines. In practice, this is difficult to achieve, due to time constraints and personnel limitations in the organization. To solve these problems, the model employs external supporting systems that include most of the current methods or computer-aided design tools. Some of those may include DFA–DFM, CAD–CAM, CAE, computer-aided packaging design, packaging and manufacturing simulation software, expert systems and neural networks, and group technology.

The integrated design model involves a focus on the simplification of the product and packaging design process and controllable variables such as form and dimension factors in the product properties and shape and size components in the package. It also requires a focus on integrating design engineering information and communication (12).

Proper use and utilization of the integrated design model provides a number of benefits as follows:

Optimizes qualitative and quantifiable design processes for the state of the art in product and packaging design.

Reduces the necessity of redesign for packaging by getting it involved early in the design process, instead of as an afterthought.

Integrates design requirements with manufacturing technology, distribution constraints, marketing needs, etc.

Centralizes cost estimation efforts.

Employs a design team technique to eliminate "design department" barriers.

In addition, the integrated design model can enhance the efficiencies and effectiveness of both product and package design (13). Proper product design can increase manufacturing competitiveness, improve product quality, reduce total manufacturing costs, lower the hidden cost of unnecessary tasks, and shorten product development and initial startup cycle times. A properly designed package can enhance a product's attractiveness to win the initial sale, while its structural and functional strengths ensure an undamaged product so that people will buy the product again. Therefore, integrating product and packaging design should result in a multitude of synergistic benefits for the overall design process.

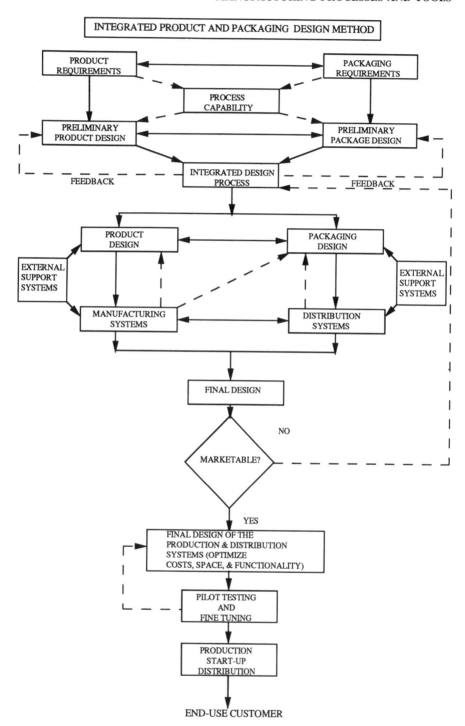

Figure 18.8. An integrated product and package design method.

18.8 THE MANUFACTURING AND PACKAGING INTERFACE

Intuitively and logically, the goal of any manufacturing system, whether it is primarily a manual or fully automated computer-integrated manufacturing system, should be to produce products in the most efficient and cost-effective manner as possible. This should be true even if the system was not developed based on an integrated approach as offered in the previous section. Also inherent in any manufacturing system should be the desire to produce the product at a certain stated level of quality. In the case of an electronic device, the requirement may be to last a certain number of hours without failure or need for repair. Or in the case of a food or beverage, the product must satisfy certain criteria such as taste and color for a certain stated shelf life.

Within the confines of the factory where the product is produced, certain quality or process control programs are in place to ensure that the desired level of quality is first achieved and then maintained. However, after the product is produced, it more than likely must be packaged for further shipment and distribution, until it arrives in the hands of the final user or consumer. Thus the marriage or bonding between the product and the package, referred to in the initial section of this chapter, now has added significance. The package or packaging system must ensure that the quality level achieved in the manufacturing system is maintained. This notion is even more compelling when it is realized that mass-distribution systems allow products to be made in one location and subsequently used by a final consumer several thousand miles away in an altogether different location.

To maintain the levels of quality in the product, the package should be designed from a systems philosophy. Earlier in this chapter the systems perspective was developed and how the packaging subsystem fits with other subsystems such as manufacturing and distribution was discussed. However, the packaging subsystem was not defined. Simply, the packaging subsystem is the combination of packaging materials or forms and packaging machinery that is developed to make sure a product maintains the quality level desired at the point or time of manufacture. Furthermore, the packaging system must protect the product throughout distribution and final disposition of the product to its ultimate end user.

The initial definition of packaging offered in this chapter—that material, form, or vessel that contains a product—in its simplest sense implies a union between the product and package with no reference to the machinery required. Much like machinery common to many manufacturing situations, packaging machinery can run from manual means to fairly complex and fully automated machinery. In the industries for which the ending of the manufacturing system and the beginning of the packaging system is hard to determine or may even overlap, the machinery can be quite sophisticated. Packaging occurs at three levels—primary, secondary, and tertiary— and the packaging machines used for each level can be quite different and may require the ability to handle different packaging materials and forms. But, ultimately a product is united with a package and the potential for adverse consequences exists. For instance, the packaging material chosen may not be suitable for the product produced or the material may not run on the machinery due to dimensional discrepancies in the material.

For its part, the materials portion of the packaging subsystem has continued to evolve at a rapid pace. A plethora of new materials and packages are introduced annually. Packaging machinery and packaging machinery systems (from filler to palletizer), on the other hand, are changing at a much slower pace. Within the last 2 to 4 yr packaging machines have just begun to take advantage of the power of Programmable Logic Controllers (PLCs), sensors for line diagnostics and control, and some automated inspection. Limited use has been made of robotics and the technologies for automatic changeover and dynamic line control of packaging machinery.

In sum, this section has shown that an interface does exist between manufacturing and packaging and that this interface can be extremely important. In addition, the interface on the packaging side is made up of not only packaging materials but also packaging machinery. Packaging machinery is increasing in sophistication, although not nearly as rapidly as machinery more common to manufacturing. The increasing complexity of both packaging materials and packaging machinery combined with increasingly complex manufacturing systems give validity to integrated design philosophies such as that proposed here. Furthermore, if the requirements placed on manufacturing and packaging systems are ignored, the potential for adverse consequences (down time, lost productivity, low efficiencies, and poor product quality) exists.

18.9 CONCLUSIONS

The primary aim of this chapter is to enlighten the reader as to the applicability, if not necessity, of including packaging and packaging systems design concepts into product, process, and manufacturing system design concepts initially rather than as an afterthought. It is clear that there is a substantial body of literature devoted specifically to manufacturing theory and concepts. Rarely will packaging receive coverage in this literature. The reasons for this omission are not entirely clear. One reason may be that packaging is not a well-understood concept. It is, after all, a broad concept that means different things to different people and different industries. Nonetheless, understanding how packaging may impact an organization in general or manufacturing systems in particular may provide benefit to those who read and use this handbook. Toward that end, this chapter provides enough information about the concept so that someone not familiar with packaging can understand what it is and how it fits in and interacts with other functional areas of an organization.

This chapter also explores the similarities between product and package design and suggests that not pursuing an integrated design philosophy may lead to inefficient and costly product and packaging design. This, in turn, can lead to less-than-optimal manufacturing systems development. An integrated design model proposed by Sun, provides a way to overcome this potential deficiency and, with modification, can be applied directly to manufacturing system design. In addition, some of the relationships between manufacturing and packaging systems are further developed and future trends in packaging machinery issues are identified.

BIBLIOGRAPHY

1. S. SACHAROW and A.L. BRODY, *Packaging: An Introduction,* Harcourt Brace Jovanovich, Duluth, Minn., 1987.
2. D.L. ABBOTT, *Packaging Perspectives.* Kendall/Hunt Publishing Co., Dubuque, Iowa, 1989.
3. Institute of Packaging Professionals, *Glossary of Packaging Terms,* Institute of Packaging Professionals, Reston, Va., 1988.
4. H.J. RAPHAEL and D.L. OLLSON, *Packaging Production Management,* AVI Publishing Co., Westport, Conn., 1976.
5. *Packaging in Perspective, A Report to the Ad Hoc Committee on Packaging,* Arthur D. Little, Inc., Cambridge, Mass. Feb. 1974.
6. S.A. RAPER, *Corporate Packaging Management: An Integrated Approach,* Ph.D. dissertation, University of Missouri at Rolla, 1989.
7. S.A. RAPER, *Packaging Management Organisations: A Case Study,* M.S. thesis, University of Missouri at Rolla, 1987.
8. *World Packaging Directory,* World Packaging Organisation, Cornhill Publications Ltd., 1988.
9. D. TWEDE, *The Process of Distribution Packaging Innovation and Its Relationship to Distribution Channel Structure,* Ph.D. dissertation, Michigan State University, Lansing, 1988.
10. *TEST Engineering and Management,* 10–17 (Oct./Nov. 1992).
11. *Fundamentals of Protective Packaging Design Seminar,* Lansmont Corp., Monterey, Calif.
12. M.-R. SUN, *Integrating Product and Packaging Design for Manufacturing and Distribution: A Survey and Cases,* Ph.D. dissertation, University of Missouri at Rolla, 1991.
13. M.-R. SUN, Y. OMURTAG, and J. SOLOMON, *Integrated Product and Packaging Design for Manufacturing and Distribution* paper presented at the 8th annual conference on University Programs in Computer Aided Engineering, Design, and Manufacturing, Ann Arbor, Mich., Aug. 1990.

SECTION IV

PRECISION ENGINEERING AND MICROMANUFACTURING

CHAPTER 19
Precision Engineering

THOMAS R. KURFESS
Carnegie Mellon University

The expansion of technology and the growth of international competition has spurred manufacturers to increase their productivity while improving their quality. In many cases quality improvement requires the enhancement of production system precision. This chapter discusses some of the basic concepts in precision engineering, including definitions, basic principles of metrology and performance, and design concepts for precision engineering.

This chapter is concerned with the design and implementation of high precision systems. It only scratches the surface of the vast and expanding field of precision engineering by addressing a few key topics that are applicable to machine tools over a broad spectrum of precision and accuracy. The first topic to be discussed is the Deterministic Theory. It provides a foundation that over the past 25 years has yielded the highest precision machine tools ever designed and realized. An example of such a machine tool is the Large Optics Diamond Turning Machine (LODTM) at the Lawrence Livermore National Laboratory, which has a resolution of 0.1 μin. (10^{-7} in). Following the brief discussion on the Deterministic Theory, this chapter presents basic definitions, a discussion of typical errors, and the development of an error budget. Finally, basic principles to reduce motion and measurement errors are discussed.

19.1 DETERMINISTIC THEORY APPLIED TO MACHINE TOOLS

The following statement is the foundation of the Deterministic Theory: *"Automatic machine tools obey cause and effect relationships that are within our ability to understand and control and that there is nothing random or probabilistic about their behavior"* (Dr. John Loxham). Typically, the term *random* implies that the causes of errors cannot be determined nor can they be addressed, and the best one can do is to quantify these errors statistically. Errors that appear to be random are *apparent* nonrepeatable errors that the design engineers have decided to quantify statistically rather than completely understand. Using statistical approaches to evaluate results is reasonable when the variables causing errors are too numerous and expensive to sort out using physics and good metrology (1). In all cases, machine tool errors that appear random are not random, rather they have not been completely addressed in a rigorous fashion.

Under the Deterministic Approach, errors are divided into two categories: repeatable, or systematic, errors, and apparent nonrepeatable errors. Systematic errors are those errors that recur as a machine executes specific motion trajectories. Typical causes of systematic errors are linear slideways not being perfectly straight or improper calibration of measurement systems. These errors repeat consistently. Typical sources of apparent nonrepeatable errors are thermal variations, variations in procedure, and backlash. Apparent non-repeatable errors mask the true accuracy of machine tools and cause them to *appear* to be random. If these errors can be eliminated or controlled, a machine tool should be capable of having repeatability that is limited only by the resolution of its sensors. Figure 19.1 presents some of the factors affecting workpiece accuracy (2).

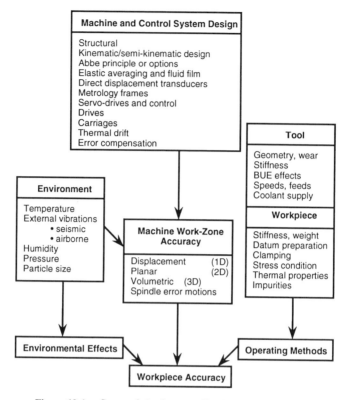

Figure 19.1.   Some of the factors affecting workpiece accuracy.

19.2   BASIC DEFINITIONS

Before one can begin discussions on precision systems and manufacturing, several definitions must be made. Strict adherence to these definitions is necessary to avoid confusion during the ensuing discussions. The following definitions are taken from ANSI B5.54-1992:

Accuracy is a quantitative measure of the degree of conformance to recognized national or international standards of measurement.

Repeatability is a measure of the ability of a machine to position a tool sequentially with respect to a workpiece under similar conditions.

Resolution is the least increment of a measuring device; the least significant bit on a digital machine.

The clearest way to define accuracy and repeatability is by visualizing a target as shown in Figure 19.2. The points on the target are the results of "shots" at the center of the bulls-eye. Accuracy is the ability to place all of the points near the center of the target. Thus, the better the accuracy, the closer the points will be to the center of the target. Repeatability is the ability to consistently cluster or group the points at the same location on the target. (Precision is often used as a synonym for repeatability; however, it is a nonpreferred, obsolete term.) Resolution may be thought of as the size of the points on the target. The smaller the points, the higher the resolution (3, 4).

Radial error motion is the error motion of a rotary axis normal to the Z reference axis and at a specified angular location (5).

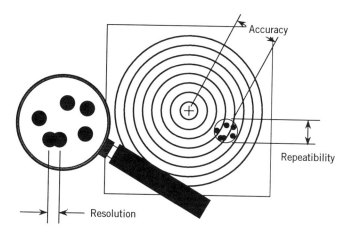

Figure 19.2. Visualization of accuracy, repeatability, and resolution.

Runout is the total displacement measured by an instrument sensing a moving surface or moved with respect to a fixed surface.

Slide straightness error is the deviation from straight line movement that an indicator positioned perpendicular to a slide direction exhibits when it is either stationary and reading against a perfect straightedge supported on the moving slide, or moved by the slide along a perfect straightedge which is stationary.

Error is defined as the difference between the actual response of a machine to a command issued according to the accepted protocol of the machine's operation and the response to that command anticipated by the protocol.

Error motion is the change in position relative to the reference coordinate axes, or the surface of a perfect workpiece with its center line coincident with the axis of rotation. Error motions are specified as to location and direction and do not include motions due to thermal drift.

Error motion measurement is a measurement record of error motion which should include all pertinent information regarding the machine, instrumentation and test conditions.

19.3 MOTION

Although machine tools are, indeed, flexible structures, this chapter will treat them as rigid with moving elements (slides and spindles) also behaving as rigid bodies. Rigid body motion is defined as the gross dynamic motions of extended bodies that undergo relatively little internal deformation. A rigid body can be considered to be a distribution of mass fixed to a rigid frame (6). This assumption is valid for average sized machine tools. As a machine tool becomes larger, its structure will experience larger deflections and it may become necessary to treat it as a flexible structure. Such deflections are ignored in this section. Also presented here is a fundamental approach to linking together the various rigid body error motions of machine tools.

Rigid Body Motion and Errors

For this discussion, the various components of a machine tool are considered rigid bodies, such as the slide and carriage system depicted in Figure 19.3. There are six degrees of freedom defined for a rigid body system: three translational degrees of freedom along the X, Y and Z axes, as well as three rotational degrees of freedom about the X, Y and Z axes. For the linear slide depicted in Figure 19.3, it is desirable to have only one degree of freedom: a single translational degree of freedom along the X axis. The other 5 degrees of freedom are treated as errors (7).

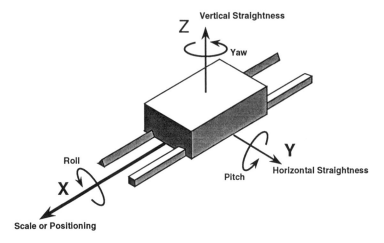

Figure 19.3.   Slide and carriage rigid body relationships.

For the translational stage shown in Figure 19.3 there are 2 straightness errors and 3 angular errors. In addition, the ability of the slide to position along its axis is measured as scale errors. These definitions are given below:

Scale Errors are the differences between the position of the read out device (scale) and that of a known reference linear scale (along the X axis).

Straightness Errors are the nonlinear movements that an indicator sees when it is either (*i*) stationary and reading against a perfect straightedge supported on a moving slide or (*ii*) moved by the slide along a perfect straightedge which is stationary (see Fig. 19.4) (5). Basically, this translates to small unwanted motion (along the Y and Z axes) perpendicular to the designed direction of motion.

Angular Errors are small unwanted rotations (about X, Y and Z axes) of a linearly moving carriage about three mutually perpendicular axes.

While slides are designed to have a single translational degree of freedom, spindles and rotary tables are designed to have a single rotational degree of freedom. Figure 19.5 depicts a single degree of freedom rotary system (a spindle) where the single degree of freedom is rotation about the Z axis. As with the translational slide, the remaining 5 degrees of freedom for the rotary system are considered to be errors (8). As shown in Figure 19.5 there are 2 radial motion (translational) errors, 1 axial motion error, and 2 tilt motion (angular) errors. A sixth error term

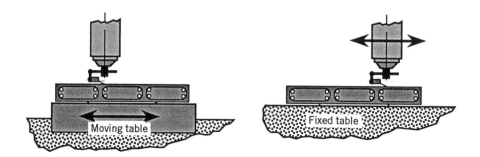

Figure 19.4.   Sideways straightness relationships.

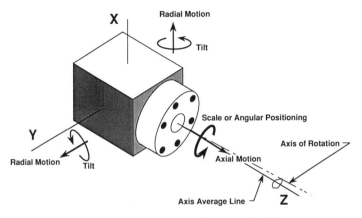

Figure 19.5. Spindle rigid body relationships.

for a spindle exists only if it has the ability to index or position angularly. The definitions below help to describe spindle error motion:

Radial Error Motion is the translational error motion in a direction normal to the Z reference axis and at a specified axial location (along the X and Y axes).

Axial Error Motion is the translational error motion collinear with the Z reference axis of an axis of rotation (about the Z axis).

Tilt Error Motion is the error motion in an angular direction relative to the Z reference axis (about the X and Y axes).

Face Motion is the rotational error motion parallel to the Z reference axis at a specified radial location (along the Z axis).

Figure 19.6 is a plan view of a spindle with a perfect part demonstrating the errors discussed for a spindle. Note that in the presence of angular motion, both the magnitude and the location must be specified when speaking of radial and face motion (9).

As previously stated, runout is defined as the *total* displacement measured by an instrument sensing against a moving surface or moved with respect to a fixed space. Thus, runout of the perfect part rotated by a spindle is the combination of the spindle error motion terms depicted in Figure 19.6 and the centering error relative to the spindle axis of rotation (9).

Most machine tools consist of a combination of spindles and linear slides. The relationships between the various axes of multi-axis machine tools must also be considered. Figure 19.7, for example, presents the error terms for positioning a machine tool (without a spindle) with *three* orthogonal linear axes. There are six error terms per axis, totaling 18 error terms for all three axes. In addition, three error terms are required to completely describe the axes relationships (e.g., squareness) for a grand total of 21 error terms for this machine tool. Figure 19.8 shows a simple lathe where two of the axes are translational and the third is the spindle rotational axis.

The following definitions are useful when addressing relationships between axes:

Squareness: a plane surface is "square" to an axis of rotation if coincident polar profile centers are obtained for an axial and face motion polar plot at different radii. For linear axes, the angular deviation from 90° measured between the best fit lines drawn through two sets of straightness data derived from two orthogonal axes in a specified work zone (expressed as small angles).

Parallelism: the lack of parallelism of two or more axes (expressed as a small angle).

For machines with fixed angles other than 90°, an additional definition is given:

Angularity is the angular error between two or more axes designed to be at fixed angles other than 90°.

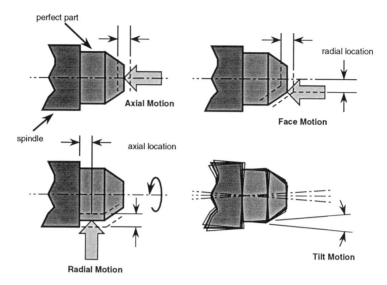

Figure 19.6. Spindle error motion.

Average Axis Line: for rotary axes it is the direction of the "best fit" straight line (axis of rotation) obtained by fitting a line through centers of the least squared circles fit to the radial motion data at various distances from the spindle face.

This is depicted in Figure 19.9. Measurement of radial motion data are discussed later in this chapter.

Similarly, linear slides must have a specific theoretical direction along which they traverse, although in reality they do not track this axis perfectly. This theoretical axial line is the slide's equivalent of the average axis line for a spindle and is termed the axis direction:

Axis Direction is the direction of any line parallel to the motion direction of a linearly moving component. The direction of a linear axis is defined by a least squares fit of a straight line to the appropriate straightness data (ANSI B5.54-1992).

The best fit is necessary since the linear motion of a slide is never perfect. Figure 19.10 presents typical data used in determining axis direction in one plane. The position indicated on the horizontal scale is location of the slide in the direction of the nominal degree of freedom. The displacement on the vertical scale is the deviation perpendicular to the nominal direction.

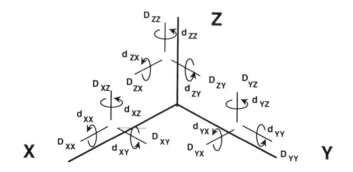

Figure 19.7. Errors terms for a machine tool with three orthogonal axes.

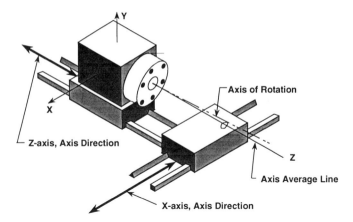

Figure 19.8. Typical machine tool with three desired degrees of freedom, the lathe.

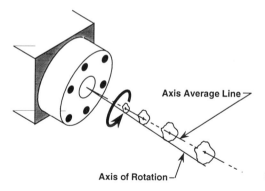

Figure 19.9. Determination of axis average line.

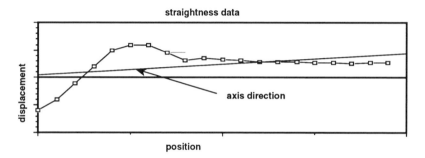

Figure 19.10. Determination of axis direction.

The axis direction is the best fit line to the straightness data points plotted in the figure. It should be noted that these data are plotted for two dimensions; however, three dimensional data may be used as well (if necessary). Measurement of straightness data is discussed later in this chapter.

Sensitive Directions

Although there are six error terms associated with an individual axis, typically there are certain error components that have a greater effect on the machine tool's accuracy than others. The directions that are most affected by particular errors are termed sensitive directions, and those directions that remain relatively unaffected are considered nonsensitive directions. Sensitivities must be well understood for proper machine tool design and proper accuracy characterization.

An excellent example demonstrating sensitive directions is the single-point lathe. Figures 19.11 and 19.12 depict a lathe and its sensitive directions. The objective of the lathe is to turn the part to a specified radius, R, using the tool. The tool is constrained to move in the X-Z plane of the spindle. It is clear that if the tool moves horizontally (due to an error) in the X-Z plane, the error will manifest itself in the part shape and be equal to the unwanted move. If the tool moves vertically, the change in the size and shape of the part is very small. Therefore, it can be said that the accuracy is *sensitive* to X and Z axis nonstraightness in the horizontal plane but nonsensitive to the X and Z nonstraightness in the vertical plane (the Y direction in Figure 19.11).

The error, S, can be approximated for motion in the vertical (nonsensitive) direction by using the equation:

$$S \approx \frac{\varepsilon^2}{8R}; \quad \varepsilon \ll R$$

Sensitive directions do not necessarily have to be fixed. In the case of the lathe described in the above example, the sensitive direction is fixed; however, other machine tools have rotating sensitive directions. Figure 19.13 depicts a lathe which has a *fixed sensitive direction* (fixed cutting tool position relative to the spindle) and a milling machine with a rotating cutting tool which has a *rotating sensitive direction*. Since the sensitive direction of the mill rotates with the boring bar it is constantly changing directions (3, 4).

Amplification of Angular Errors, The Abbe Principle

One of the most common errors in a machine's ability to position a linear slide accurately is due to the slide's measuring scales (used for position feedback) not being in line with the functional point where positioning accuracy is desired. The resulting linear error at the functional point is caused by the angular motion of the slide that occurs from nonstraightness of the guide ways. The magnitude of the error is the product of the offset distance from the measuring system to the functional point and the angular motion that the slide makes when positioning from one point to another.

This error is called Abbe Error after Dr. Ernst Abbe. Abbe (a co-founder of Zeiss Inc.) was the first person to mention this error (10). He wrote, "If errors in parallax are to be avoided, the measuring system must be placed coaxially with the axis along which the displacement is to be

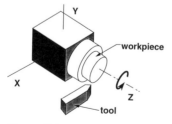

Figure 19.11.   Sketch of a lathe configuration.

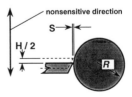

Figure 19.12.   Sensitive direction for a lathe.

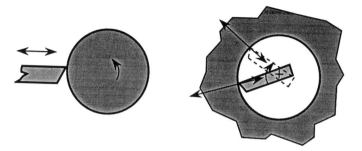

Figure 19.13.   Fixed and rotating sensitive directions.

measured on the workpiece." This statement, named "The Abbe Principle," has also been called the first principle of machine tool design and dimensional metrology. In order to cover those situations where it is not possible to design systems coaxially, a generalized Abbe Principle reads: "The displacement measuring system should be in line with the functional point whose displacement is to be measured. If this is not possible, either the slideways that transfer the displacement must be free of angular motion or angular motion data must be used to calculate the consequences of the offset" (11).

An excellent illustration of the Abbe Principle is to examine the vernier caliper and compare it to a micrometer. Both of these instruments are two point measurement instruments, that is they measure the distance between two points. Figure 19.14 shows these two instruments measuring a linear distance D. The graduations for the caliper are *not* located along the same line as the functional axis of measurement. As shown in Figure 19.14, if the caliper bar is bent, causing the slide of the caliper to move through an angle θ when measuring D, then the resulting measurement is an Abbe Error. The distance A, the distance between the measurement graduations and the point of measurement, is called the Abbe Offset.

$$E = A \sin (\theta)$$

Since the angle, θ, will be very small for most situations, the Abbe Error can be accurately approximated as the product of the Abbe Offset and the angle expressed in radians. Since most angular errors are measured in arc seconds, it is perhaps easier to remember that 1 arc second is equal to approximately 4.8 μin./in. so the calculation becomes:

Abbe Error (μin.) = [Abbe Offset (in.)] · [angular error (s)] · [4.8(μin./in.)]

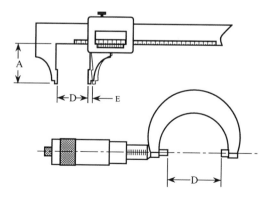

Figure 19.14.   Micrometer and caliper comparison for Abbe offsets and errors.

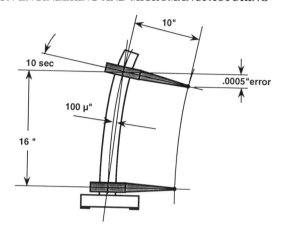

Figure 19.15. Abbe error for a
height gauge.

As a comparison, the measuring system of the micrometer is the screw and graduated drum that
are coaxially located to the distance being measured. Angular errors will have no effect on the
measured distance, since the Abbe Offset is zero. Thus, the micrometer obeys the Abbe Principle and is typically considered more accurate than the caliper.

Figure 19.15 also demonstrates the Abbe Error for a height gauge. Here the slide of the
gauge has a uniform angular motion of 10 arc seconds error (that is exaggerated in the figure).
This is the equivalent of a 100 μin. non-straightness over the length of the slide. The probe arm
of length 10 in. amplifies and transforms this angular error into a linear error in the height
measurement by the following relationship

$$E = A \sin (\theta) = [10(\text{in.})] \cdot \sin[10(\text{s})] = [10(\text{in.})] \cdot \sin[10(\text{s})] = 0.000485 \text{ in.}$$

Using the approximate relationship that 1 arc s is equal to approximately 4.8 μin./in., the error
may also be computed as

$$E = [10(\text{in.})] \cdot [10(\text{s})] \cdot [4.8(\mu\text{in.}/\text{in.})] = 480 \mu\text{in.} = 0.000480 \text{ in.}$$

Thus, an error of approximately 485 μin. is realized due to the angular motion error of the probe
arm as it traverses the length of the height gauge slide (3).

Reducing Abbe Error

There are three methods that may be used to reduce the effects of Abbe Error. The first is to
reduce the Abbe Offset as much as possible. For example, one can place measurement instrumentation coaxially with the points being measured, or place templates for tracer lathes in the
plane of the tool motion. Such modifications will eliminate Abbe Error completely.

In many cases, machine designers are forced to place measurement devices at some distance
from the functional measurement axis. The retro-fitting of machine tools with glass scales is an
excellent example. In the retro-fit case, the replacement of the wheel gages (with typical
resolutions of 0.0001 in.) on a machine tool with glass scale linear encoders that have an order of
magnitude higher resolution may cause the machine's positioning accuracy to be worse than the
original design, due to larger Abbe Offsets for the glass scales. Such a retro-fit does not obey the
Abbe Principle; however, the engineers effecting the retro-fit may not have an alternative to
increasing the Abbe Offset since it may be difficult to find a location to mount the linear scales
that is close to the working volume.

Besides reducing the Abbe Offset, designers may employ two other methods to abate the
effects of Abbe Error: (*i*) use slideways that are free of angular motion, or (*ii*) use angular
motion data to calculate the consequences of the offset (map out the Abbe Error). Although
either of these two methods may be used to correct for Abbe Error, slideways will never be
completely free of angular motion, and tighter angular motion specifications can be expensive.
Using angular motion data to correct the Abbe Errors requires more calculations in the machine

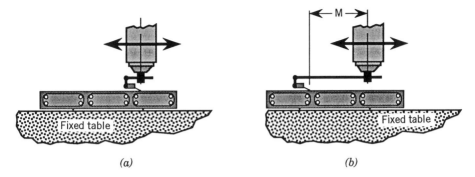

Figure 19.16. Visualization of the Bryan principle for straightness measurements.

controller. The best option is to minimize Abbe Offsets before attempting to correct for them (11).

The Bryan Principle

A corollary to the Abbe Principle addresses angular error when determining straightness. Known as the Bryan Principle, this corollary states: "The straightness measuring system should be in line with the functional point whose straightness is to be measured. If this is not possible, [two options are available] either the slideways that transfer the straightness must be free of angular motion or angular motion data must be used to calculate the consequences of the offset" (11). Either of these two options may be used to improve straightness measurements; however, they may require expensive modifications to the machine tool and its controller. As with the Abbe Principle, it is always best, if possible, to comply with the Bryan Principle and design machines with zero offsets (11). Figure 19.16 demonstrates this principle with a fixed table straightness test. The set-up presented in Figure 19.16(a) obeys the Bryan Principle since the probe tip is located in line with the spindle axis. However, Figure 19.16(b) does not obey the Bryan Principle since the probe tip is at a distance M from the spindle axis.

19.4   SOURCES OF ERROR AND ERROR BUDGETS

All machine tools will have geometric errors. This is a fact that no level of investment can eliminate. At best, the design engineer can reduce the various errors that a machine possesses. An error budget is the realization that a perfect machine without error cannot be constructed. The error budget is an attempt to separate and quantify a machine tool's errors into its basic components. The components of the error are then budgeted such that the combination of the various acceptable errors does not exceed the total desired error of the machine tool. The goal of the engineer is to design a machine tool such that the components of the error are not exceeded in the design. Often the initial error budget cannot be achieved and the errors must be redistributed until a technically feasible and economically viable design is reached.

Sources of Errors

Generally, the sources of errors may be broken into four categories: geometric errors, dynamic errors, workpiece effects and thermal errors. This section presents a brief discussion of these errors, providing some insight into their causes and possible methods to reduce their effects (4).

Geometric Errors

Geometric errors manifest themselves in both translational and rotational errors on a machine tool. Typical causes of such errors are lack of straightness in slideways, nonsquareness of axes, angular errors and static deflection of the machine tool. Angular errors are, perhaps, the least understood and most costly of the various geometric errors. They are complicated by the fact that they are typically amplified by the linear distance between the measurement device and the point of measurement (*Abbe Error*). However, with proper procedures, instrumentation, and careful metrology, these errors can be identified, predicted and held within the desired level of the error budget.

Dynamic Errors

Dynamic errors are typically caused by machine tool vibration (or chatter). They are generated by exciting resonances within the machine tool's structure. Current research is investigating the prediction of vibrations in machine tools; however, from a practical perspective, this is quite difficult. Usually, a machine tool is built and its resonant frequencies are determined experimentally. The machine's controller can then be programmed to avoid combinations of feeds and speeds that may excite its various resonances. Typically, the best one can do during the design phases of machine tools is to design a structure that is stiff, light weight and well damped.

Workpiece Effects

The workpiece can affect a machine tool's accuracy and precision in two manners: deflection during the cutting process and inertial effects due to motion. Deflection may be addressed by using proper fixturing to provide support for the part. This is a relatively simple and well understood solution.

Inertial effects of the workpiece, however, are not as simple to address. They may manifest themselves in several manners, including asymmetry about a rotating axis and overshoot on a linear slide. If the part is asymmetric and is being turned on a lathe, the asymmetry may cause periodic spindle deviations which reduce accuracy. A typical solution to these rotary problems is to balance the spindle with the workpiece mounted on it. Other inertial effects are seen as large parts are moved rapidly in high production rate machines. Because of the high velocities and large masses of the workpieces, the machine tools may overshoot their target point. Basically, the machine's brakes are not powerful enough to stop the part at the desired position without overshooting that position. Proper design of servo systems, as well as reasonable trajectories (smooth acceleration and velocity profiles), can substantially reduce inertial errors. Also, position probes used in conjunction with the machine tool can inform the controller if the workpiece is, indeed, in the proper location.

Thermal Errors

Thermal errors are probably the most significant set of factors that cause apparent non-repeatable errors in a machine tool. These errors result from fluctuating temperatures within and around the machine tool, and from non-fluctuating conditions at constant temperatures other than 20°C. Although deviations in machine tool geometry from thermal causes may be theoretically calculated, such an analysis has been quite elusive in practice. Thus, proper thermal control is required.

For typical machine tools, thermal errors may be caused by a wide variety of fluctuating heat sources: motors, people, coolant, bearings and the cutting process. Furthermore, variations in the temperature of the environment can cause substantial thermal errors. For example, temperatures in a machine shop may swing from 95°F in the summer to 65°F or cooler in the winter. For higher precision machine tools, sources such as overhead lighting and sun light may substantially contribute to thermal errors.

Thermal errors may be reduced substantially by proper procedure and design. Errors due to motors and bearings heating-up during use are reduced by warming-up the machine tool before it is used. Typically, high precision grinders are not shut down unless they are not being used for a substantial period of time. The grinding wheels for such grinders are kept spinning at their operational speed continuously, even when the machine is idle. This ensures that the grinder wheel motor, and consequently the grinding wheel, are at a constant temperature. To further eliminate thermal effects, coolant temperature as well as environmental temperature should be controlled. The target temperature for the machine tool's environment and coolant is typically 20°C (68°F) which is the national (and international) temperature at which all distance measurements are made (12).

Finally, there are several design techniques that may be employed to reduce thermal effects, such as reducing the thermal capacitance of the machine tool. This permits the entire machine tool to thermally equilibrate rapidly rather than have thermal gradients, thus reducing the amount of time required for the system to warm-up. The use of materials with similar coefficients of thermal expansion (C_{te}), or the kinematic isolation of materials with different C_{te}'s will reduce thermally induced stresses in the system. For example, glass scales having a low C_{te} are often fixed at both ends to steel machines having a higher C_{te}. When the temperature of the machine varies, the steel structure will deform more from the thermal variations than the glass scale. Since the scale is significantly less rigid than the steel structure, the scale may undergo deformation as scale and structure deform at different rates. This could generate an error in the measurement system. A solution to this problem is to fix the scale at one end, and mount the other end of the scale such that there is compliance in the scale's sensitive direction. When the two bodies change size at different rates the stresses are then mostly absorbed by the compliant mount (3, 13).

Determination and Reduction of Thermal Errors

The environment in which the machine tool operates has a significant effect on the performance of the machine tool. Typically, in high precision applications thermal effects are the largest single source of errors (14). Figure 19.17 is a block diagram depicting various sources of thermal disturbances that influence machine tools. As stated in ANSI B5.54, "Thermally caused errors due to operating a machine tool in a poor environment cannot be corrected for by rebuilding the machine tool, nor are they grounds for rejection of a machine tool during acceptance test unless the machine is specified to operate in that particular environment." Furthermore, thermal error cannot be eliminated by enhanced control algorithms or the addition of sensors. This section briefly discusses basic concepts of thermal behavior characterization, and simple methods to limit errors caused by varying thermal conditions.

To quantify the effects of thermal errors on a machine tool's performance, the Thermal Error Index (TEI) is used. The TEI is the summation, without regard to sign, of the estimates of

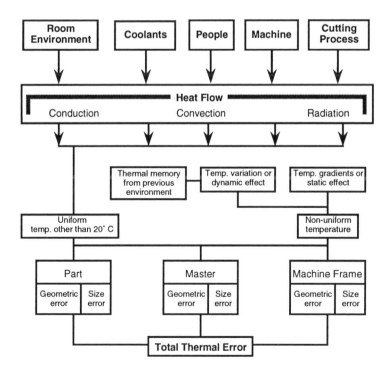

Figure 19.17. Factors thermally effecting machine tool environment.

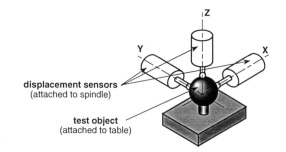

Figure 19.18.   Three axis drift test.

all thermally induced measurement errors, expressed as a percentage of the working tolerance or total permissible error. The TEI and its computation are explained thoroughly in ANSI B89.6.2-1973 (12). The computational procedures account for uncertainties in the quantification of various parameters, such as expansion coefficients and the differential expansions of various materials when machines are operated at temperatures other than 20°C. The ANSI standard B5.54-1992 provides a method of using the TEI to develop contractual agreements for the purchasing and selling of machine tools and manufactured parts. It states that calibration, part manufacture and part acceptance procedures are valid if all pertinent components of the system are at 20°C, or it can be shown that the Thermal Error Index (TEI) is a reasonable and acceptable percentage of the working tolerance.

An important value used in the computation of the TEI is the Temperature Variation Error (TVE). The TVE is the maximum possible measurement error induced solely by the deviation of the environment from average conditions. In particular this applies to repeatability, linear displacement accuracy and telescoping ball bar performance measurement results. The TVE may be determined from measurements using a standard drift test. Figure 19.18 presents a schematic for a 3-Axis drift test using three orthogonally positioned, air-bearing LVDTs (Linear Variable Differential Transformer) (5). Once the set-up in Figure 19.18 is established, the LVDT signals are sampled and recorded over a long period of time (typically 24 hours). The results are used to quantify the amount of error motion that is generated along three orthogonal directions via thermal drift over a long period in time. The error recorded in a drift test is often used to provide a bound on the repeatability of a machine tool since a machine's repeatability is limited by the amount of drift that it experiences.

There are several factors that must be considered if the machine tool and environment are to be thermally controlled. The first is the operating environment temperature of the machine. The standard temperature at which machine tools should be calibrated is 20°C (68°F). Proper temperature control of the ambient air around the machine tool is critical in high precision operations. This includes temperature control of the environment as well as providing sufficient circulation to remove any excess heat generated by the system. Even seemingly small heat sources such as lights and sun light can substantially add to thermal errors.

Control of the coolant temperature must also be exercised. Variations of coolant temperature of more than 30°F are typical in many plants depending on the time of the year and even the time of the day, in particular if a central coolant system is used. Furthermore, a constant flow rate of coolant should be supplied to the machine tool to eliminate any type of time dependent thermal gradients in the machine. In fact, some machine tools are *oil showered* specifically to engulf the machine tool in temperature controlled oil. Even the composition of the coolant is critical for temperature control. Water based coolants will evaporate, cooling the machine more than expected depending on environmental conditions. This will cause changing thermal gradients over time and yield thermal errors in the machine tool (15).

Clearly, thermal gradients will exist in a machine tool; however, it is important that these gradients remain constant with respect to time. For example, a large electric motor on a lathe will generate heat. Ideally, it is best to remove this heat. However, in reality sections of the machine tool that are nearest to the motor will have a higher temperature. Thus, from a spatial perspective, thermal gradients exist. However, as long as those gradients do not change in a temporal fashion, the machine tool's repeatability will not be significantly affected by the thermal gradients (3).

Developing an Error Budget

The error budget is based on the behavior of individual components of the machine tool as well as their interactions with other components. Since no machine is perfect, an error exists in determination of the location of the cutting tool with respect to the workpiece. This error is called the tool positioning error or TPE. The error budget is concerned with determining the effect of system variations (systematic and nonsystematic) on the TPE. The error budget should contain as many of the sources of error as possible. However, the designer should understand how each individual source of error affects the TPE. Large error components that are in highly sensitive directions (thus, contributing greatly to the TPE) should be addressed first. Other error components with lower sensitivities may be too small to be considered until larger TPE components have been reduced.

To use an error budget properly, two tasks must be undertaken: determine the sources of error within the machine tool and its environment, and determine how those sources of error combine to affect the TPE. This chapter is limited to a brief discussion on the identification and combination of errors that affect the machine tool. However, extensive research has been conducted on these issues and it is recommended that an engineer be familiar with the literature before using an error budget (4). This section is concerned with combining errors that affect a machine tool in similar fashions. That is to say, various error components can be combined to determine their overall contribution to the TPE in a particular direction, if the proper procedures are followed.

The errors discussed in the previous section may be placed into three categories when developing an error budget:

1. "**Random** which under apparently equal conditions at a given position, does not always have the same value, and can only be expressed statistically."
2. "**Systematic** which always have the same value and sign at a given position and under given circumstances. (Wherever systematic errors have been established, they may be used for correcting the value measured.)"
3. "**Hysteresis** is a systematic error (which in this instance is separated out for convenience). It is usually highly reproducible, has a sign depending on the direction of the approach, and a value partly dependent on the travel. (Hysteresis errors may be used for correcting the measured value if the direction of the approach is known and an adequate pre-travel is made.)" (10).

Systematic errors, e_{sys}, may be considered vector quantities that have both magnitude and direction. They may also be added in a vector sense. That is to say that all systematic errors of a machine tool along a particular axis may be summed together to yield the total systematic error. Because the errors do possess direction (positive or negative in a specified direction), individual errors may either increase the total system error or actually reduce the error via cancellation.

Random errors, however, must be treated via a statistical approach. The portions of an error budget that represent random errors are *always* additive. That is to say, they will always make the error larger because the sign of their direction, as well as the magnitude of the error, is a random quantity.

Root mean square (RMS) error is often used to quantify random errors where the random errors tend to average together. The combined random RMS error is computed as the geometric sum of the individual RMS errors. Thus, for N random error components, the total RMS error is given by

$$(RMS_{tot})_i = \sqrt{\left(\sum_{j=1}^{N} (RMS_j)^2 \right)}$$

where RMS_j is the jth component of random error in the ith direction. This results in a total overall error of

$$(e_{RMS})_i = \left| \sum (e_{sys})_i + \sum (e_{hyst})_i \right| + (RMS_{tot})_i$$

where $(e_{sys})_i$ and $(e_{hyst})_i$ are the systematic error and hysteresis error of the system along the ith axis. The absolute values about the systematic and hysteresis error make them positive quantities which are added to the always positive quantity of the random error. This reflects the fact that random error can only increase the total error; however, systematic errors may cancel each other.

Quite often, random errors are described in terms of a total peak-to-valley amplitude, PV. PV_j may be considered the separation of two parallel lines containing the jth error signal. PV_j is related to RMS_j by the following equation

$$PV_j = (K_j)(RMS_j)$$

where K_j is a scalar quantity that depends on the error signal's probability distribution. The values of K_j for uniform and $\pm 2\sigma$ Normal (Gaussian) distributions are 3.46 and 4, respectively. Typically, the value for the uniform distribution ($K_j = 3.46$) is used, since individual error traces are not generally Normally distributed. If there are some central tendencies for the distribution, the uniform assumption will be conservative (17). Using the relationship for PV_j given above, the total random error generated by combining N random error components in the ith direction is given by

$$(e_{PV,rand})_i = \frac{1}{2\sqrt{3}} \left[\sum_{j=1}^{N} (PV_j)^2 \right]_i$$

The total error in the ith direction for the peak-to-valley scenario is

$$(e_{PV})_i = \left| \sum (e_{sys})_i + \sum (e_{hyst})_i \right| + (e_{PV,rand})_i$$

19.5 SOME TYPICAL METHODS OF MEASURING ERRORS

There can be quite a long list of parametric error sources associated with a multi-axis machine tool and a wide variety of measurement techniques that may be used. This chapter cannot possibly discuss or even list all of the techniques; however, several of the most common and powerful techniques are discussed. This section concentrates on a few of the techniques that are used for the determination of scale errors, straightness errors, and radial motion of a spindle (or rotary table). The techniques presented are not the only techniques available to qualify machine tools; however, they are a set of powerful tools that are relatively easy to implement and quite useful.

Before the various procedures for error measurement are described, it is worthwhile to discuss the laser measurement system, one of the most versatile measurement systems available to the metrologist. The laser measurement system may be used to measure linear displacement, angular displacement, straightness, squareness and parallelism. The laser measurement system, often referred to as a laser interferometer, consists of the following components:

1. The laser head that is the laser beam's source.
2. A tripod or stand on which to mount the laser head.
3. An air sensor to measure the temperature, humidity and barometric pressure of the ambient air.
4. A material sensor to measure the temperature of the machine tool's measurement system.
5. A linear interferometer that actually performs the interference measurements.
6. A measurement corner cube (or linear retro-reflector) to reflect the laser beam off of the point being tracked.
7. A reference corner cube to split and recombine the beam generating the beam interference needed for the interferometer.

Figure 19.19 is a drawing of a laser interferometer and its components set-up for a linear displacement test.

Figure 19.20 is a schematic of the basic operational configuration of a laser measurement system. The beam originates in the laser head and is sent through the reference corner cube where it is split. Part of the beam continues to the measurement corner cube where it is reflected

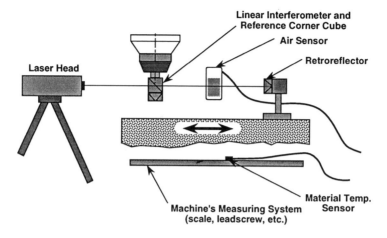

Figure 19.19.   Laser interfermometer set-up for linear displacement test.

back towards the reference corner cube. The two beams are then recombined in the reference corner cube where they may combine (interfere) in a constructive or destructive manner. The combined beam then continues to the interferometer. The interferometer measures the amount of interference between the two beams, and determines the distance traveled between the initial location of the measurement corner cube and its current position.

Laser interferometers typically use either a single or multiple frequency helium-neon gas laser. The interferometer simply counts the number of wavelengths that the slide traverses between two points. Thus, the laser interferometer can only measure relative displacements as opposed to absolute distances. It can only inform the operator as to the number of wavelengths of light between two points. The wave length of the laser is typically stabilized and known to better than 0.05 parts per million.

There are three basic guidelines in setting-up the laser measurement system:

1. Choose the correct set-up to measure the desired parameter (e.g., distance) and verify the directional signs ($\pm$) of the system.

2. Approximate the machine tool's working conditions as closely as possible. For example, make sure that the machine tool is at its operational temperature. Machine tool scales may be made of material that will change length as their temperature varies. This change in length directly affects their position output.

3. Minimize potential error sources such as environmental compensation, dead path and alignment.

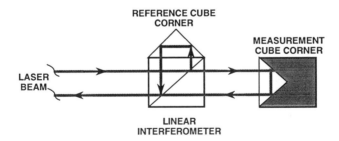

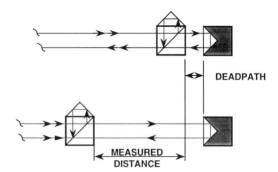

Figure 19.21. Laser interfermometer dead path.

The potential error sources from the environment are variations in air temperature, humidity and barometric pressure. These affect the velocity of light and thus the wavelength of light in the atmosphere. The wavelength of the laser light will vary one part per million for each

1°C (2°F) change in air temperature

2.5 mm (0.1 in.) Hg change in absolute barometric pressure

30% change in relative humidity

As a comparison, if the machine's scales are made of steel they will expand or contract one part per million for every 0.09°C (0.16°F). The accuracy of the laser interferometer is directly determined by how accurately the ambient conditions are known.

Typically, laser interferometers will come equipped with environmental measurement systems that are capable of tracking the temperature, barometric pressure, and humidity during a test. This information is used to electronically alter the displacement values, compensating for the change in the velocity of light in air under the measured conditions. Thus, proper compensation can eliminate most environmental effects on the system. There is, however, an area known as the dead path where compensation for the velocity of light error is not applied. The dead path, shown in Figure 19.21, is the distance between the measurement corner cube and the reference corner cube when the laser interferometer is nulled or reset. The compensation for the velocity of light error is applied only to the portion of the path where displacement is measured, as shown in Figure 19.21. To minimize the dead path error, the unused laser path must be minimized by placing the reference corner cube as close to the measurement corner cube as possible. The interferometer should then be reset, and the set of distance measurements made by moving the reference corner cube away from the measurement corner cube. Changes in the ambient environmental conditions during the measurement will only be considered for the measured distance and not for the dead path. However, if the dead path is small and the measurements are made over a short time period, the ambient conditions typically will not change enough to generate significant velocity of light errors. Dead path error may be further reduced by having a well-controlled environment.

Misalignment of the laser beam to the machine tool's linear axis of motion will result in an error between the measured distance and the actual distance. This error is typically called cosine error and is depicted in Figure 19.22. If the axis of motion is misaligned with the laser beam by an angle, θ, then the measured distance, $L_{measured}$, is related to the actual machine distance, $L_{machine}$ by the following equation:

$$L_{measured} = L_{machine} \cos{(\theta)}$$

Cosine error will always result in the measured value being less than the actual machine value when the machine and the reference are perfect ($L_{measured} < L_{machine}$).

When properly used, the laser measurement system is a powerful tool that is useful for determining many types of errors. It is very important to understand the basic theory of the laser measurement system's operation and the correct procedures before using it. If employed improperly, it can easily generate erroneous results that may not be at all obvious.

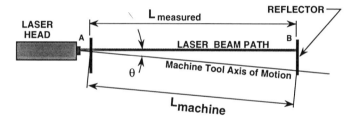

Figure 19.22. Geometry for cosine error.

Linear Displacement Errors

As previously stated, the linear displacement error is the difference between where the machine's scale indicates that a carriage is and where the carriage is actually located. To determine linear displacement error an accurate external reference device for measuring travel distance must be used. Typically, a laser measurement system is employed for this task. This section is concerned with the use of the laser measurement system to measure linear displacement.

The determination of linear displacement errors is accomplished by a simple comparison of the linear scale output to that of the laser interferometer at different locations along a particular machine tool slideway. The set-up for such a measurement is shown in Figure 19.19. The laser measurement system should be set-up in accordance with the procedures, previously outlined, minimizing errors such as dead path errors, cosine errors and environmental errors. The table of the machine tool is then moved in increments of a given amount along the length of the slideway. At each interval, the table is brought to a stop, and the distance traveled is computed from data gathered from the scales. The scale distance is compared to the distance measured using the laser interferometer. The difference between the two distances is the linear displacement error. These measurements and comparisons are repeated several times along the entire length of the slideway, mapping the scale errors for the slideway. It should be noted that the linear displacement error includes not only the machine's scale errors but the Abbe Errors due to angular motion of the carriage.

Spindle Error Motion—Donaldson Reversal

As was discussed earlier, when a spindle or rotary table rotates, it has some error motion in the radial direction termed radial motion. It is important to measure the amount of radial motion in order to characterize spindle performance and understand the amount of error contributed by the spindle or rotary table to the machine tool's total error. To measure the radial motion of a spindle or rotary table, a gauge ball is centered on the axis of rotation of the table and rotated. A probe is placed on the surface of the ball and radial deviations of the probe tip are recorded (see Figure 19.23). If the gauge ball was perfect and it was perfectly centered, the signal from the probe would be the radial motion of the table.

Unfortunately, the gauge ball is not a perfect sphere and the resulting probe signal is a combination of the radial motion of the spindle and the imperfections in the gauge ball. Donaldson developed a method for completely separating gauge ball non-roundness from spindle radial motion (18). This method has been termed Donaldson ball reversal. All that is needed for ball reversal is

1. A spindle with radial motion that is approximately an order of magnitude less than the value of roundness desired (this is a rule of thumb).
2. An accurate indicator (preferably electronic).
3. Recording media (polar chart or a computer).

The following assumptions are made:

1. The radial motion is repeatable.
2. The indicator accurately measures displacement.

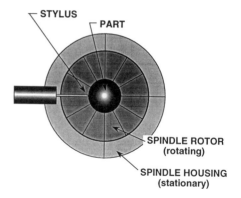

Figure 19.23. Radial motion set-up.

There are two set-ups for ball reversal that are shown in Figure 19.24. In the first set-up, the ball is mounted on the spindle with point B of the ball located at point A on the spindle. The stylus of the probe is located at point B on the ball. The spindle is then rotated 360° and the motion of the stylus is recorded. The signal from the stylus, $T_1(\theta)$ is given by the sum of the non-roundness of the gauge ball, $P(\theta)$, and the radial motion of the spindle, $S(\theta)$

$$T_1(\theta) = P(\theta) + S(\theta)$$

The spindle is then rotated back 360° and the gauge ball is relocated on the spindle such that point B is rotated 180°, and is at a position opposite to point A on the spindle. The probe is also positioned opposite point A and brought into contact with the gauge ball at point B. The spindle is once again rotated 360° and the data from the probe are recorded. The signal from the probe, $T_2(\theta)$ is

$$T_2(\theta) = P(\theta) - S(\theta)$$

From the two data sets, $T_1(\theta)$ and $T_2(\theta)$, the spindle radial motion may be computed as

$$S(\theta) = \frac{T_1(\theta) - T_2(\theta)}{2}$$

and the gauge ball non-roundness may be computed as

$$P(\theta) = \frac{T_1(\theta) + T_2(\theta)}{2}$$

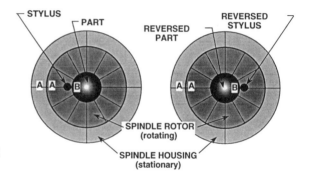

Figure 19.24. Donaldson ball reversal set-up.

This set of simple linear combinations of $T_1(\theta)$ and $T_2(\theta)$ provides information on both the ball and the spindle without using secondary or intermediate standards. The method is also independent of the errors in either the gauge ball or the spindle. Thus, it is considered a self-checking method (18).

If the spindle does not use rolling elements (e.g., an air bearing or hydrostatic bearing), then the spindle does not need to be rotated backwards 360° degrees between the two set-ups. Rotating the spindle back 360° between set-ups is necessary to ensure that all of the rolling elements exactly repeat the same motions each time the data are taken. Furthermore, if the spindle is being used as a rotary axis, then it should only be used for the 360° measured by the reversal method. If the use of a rotary table with rolling element bearings exceeds the test rotation range, then the measured radial motion of the table, $S(\theta)$, will not correctly represent the radial motion of the table outside of the original 360° range. If more rotation than 360° is necessary, then the reversal should be done for a larger range of rotation.

Straightness Errors—Straightedge Reversal

As was discussed earlier, when a machine table moves along a slideway, it experiences straightness errors along the slide perpendicular to the axis of travel. The straightness errors must be measured to determine the amounts and directions of error that the slideway nonstraightness is contributing to the overall machine tool error. To measure the nonstraightness of a slideway, a straight edge is placed on the machine table parallel to the axis direction. A probe is placed normal to the surface of the straight edge and deviations of the probe tip are recorded (see Figure 19.25). The resulting probe signal is the nonstraightness of the slideway, the nonstraightness of the straightedge, and the nonparallelism of the straightedge to the axis. (If the slideway was perfectly straight and the straight edge was also perfect, the signal from the probe would be a straight line.)

In a fashion similar to Donaldson ball reversal, a method termed straight edge reversal can be used to separate the nonstraightness of the straight edge from the nonstraightness of the slideway. All that is needed for straight edge reversal is

1. A straight edge that has a length equal to the length of the slideway to be measured.
2. An accurate indicator (preferably electronic).
3. Recording media (strip chart or a computer).

The following assumptions are made:

1. The slideway straightness error is repeatable.
2. The indicator accurately measures displacement.

There are two set-ups for straight edge reversal. The first is shown in Figure 19.25, and the second is shown in Figure 19.26. In the first set-up, the straight edge is mounted on the table

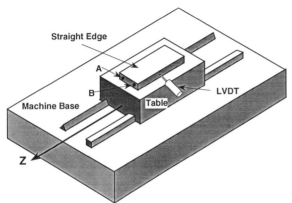

Figure 19.25. Nonstraightness measurement (first set-up).

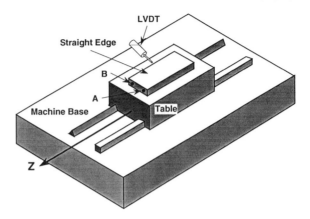

Figure 19.26. Second set-up
for straight edge reversal.

with a three point kinematic mount. Point B of the straight edge is located at the front of the table and point A at the rear of the table. The stylus of the probe is located on the side of the straight edge nearest to point B. The table is then moved along the entire length of the slideway and the motion of the stylus is recorded. The signal from the stylus, $T_1(Z)$, is given by the sum of the nonstraightness of the straight edge, $P(Z)$, and the nonstraightness of the slideway, $S(Z)$

$$T_1(Z) = P(Z) + S(Z)$$

The table is then positioned back to its original starting point and the straight edge is relocated (flipped) on the table such that point B is at the rear of the table and point A is at the front of the table as shown in Figure 19.26. The probe is also moved to the rear of the table such that it is in contact with the side of the straight edge that is nearest point B. The table is once again moved along the entire length of the slideway and the data from the probe are recorded. The signal from the probe, $T_2(Z)$, is

$$T_2(Z) = P(Z) - S(Z)$$

From the two data sets, $T_1(Z)$ and $T_2(Z)$, the slideway nonstraightness error may be computed as

$$S(Z) = \frac{T_1(Z) - T_2(Z)}{2}$$

and the straight edge nonstraightness error may be computed as

$$P(Z) = \frac{T_1(Z) + T_2(Z)}{2}$$

This set of simple linear combinations of $T_1(Z)$ and $T_2(Z)$ provides information on both the straight edge and the slideway without using secondary or intermediate standards. The method is also independent of the errors in either the straight edge or the slideway. Thus, it is considered a self-checking method (7).

Angular Motion—Electronic Differential Levels

The angular motion about axes may be determined using a variety of tools including laser measurement system, autocollimator and electronic differential levels. This section presents angular motion measurement using a set of electronic levels. This technique is simple and the levels are relatively inexpensive in comparison to a laser measurement system or autocollima-

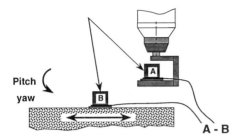

Figure 19.27. Pitch measurement set-up using electronic levels.

tor. Since electronic levels use gravity as a reference, they are limited to angular motion about axes in a horizontal plane. Thus, roll and pitch errors may be determined for axes in the horizontal plane, and pitch and yaw may be determined for vertical axes.

The electronic level is an instrument that measures small angles using the direction of gravity as a reference. A typical set-up for determining the pitch of an axis is shown in Figure 19.27. The two levels, A and B, are used differentially in one plane yielding the angular motion of one level relative to the other level. Level A is located in the tool location, and level B is located where the workpiece is mounted. These locations insure that the angular motions computed will be those that are experienced between the workpiece and the tool. To perform the measurement, the table is moved along its entire length, stopping at fixed distances along the length of the slideway. It is important that the table is brought to a complete stop at each point where the readings are taken. This permits the levels to stabilize so that accurate data can be recorded. The two levels are then read and the value from B is subtracted from A, resulting in the relative angular motion between the two levels. The table is then moved to the next location where another reading is taken. This procedure is repeated until the angular motion for the entire axis is mapped. The roll of the slide may be measured by simply rotating the two levels 90° about the vertical axis and repeating the procedure. Yaw measurement requires the use of either a laser angular interferometer or an autocollimator.

19.6 CONCLUSION

Precision engineering is a leading edge and ever advancing area. This chapter has presented some of the basic ideas, principles, and tools used to design high precision systems. There is a wide variety of other concepts available to engineers designing precision machine tools or metrology systems, and the reader is encouraged to make use of the references provided throughout this chapter. In conclusion, adherence to fundamental principles and the combination of good design, metrology and practice are necessary to realize machine tools of the highest precision.

BIBLIOGRAPHY

1. J.B. BRYAN, "The Power of Deterministic Thinking in Machine Tool Accuracy," UCRL-91531, Sept. 1984.

2. C. EVANS, *Precision Engineering: An Evolutionary View,* Cranfield Press, Bedford, United Kingdom, 1989.

3. D.L. CARTER, J.B. BRYAN, H. HAUSCHILDT, and C. CHUNG, notes from "Machine Tool Accuracy Workshop," Lawrence Livermore National Laboratory and the Society of Manufacturing Engineers in cooperation with The American Society of Mechanical Engineers, Livermore, Calif., Jan. 1993.

4. A.H. SLOCUM, *Precision Machine Design,* Prentice-Hall, Englewood Cliffs, N.J., 1992.

5. *ANSI B5.54-1991,* "Methods for Performance Evaluation of Computer Numerically-Controlled Machining Centers," American Society of Mechanical Engineers, 1991.

6. S.H. CRANDALL, D.C. KARNOPP, E.F. KURTZ, JR., and D.C. PRIDMORE-BROWN, *Dynamics of Mechanical and Electromechanical Systems,* Robert E. Krieger Publishing Company, Malabar, Fla., 1982.

7. J.B. BRYAN and D.L. CARTER, "How Straight is Straight?" *American Machinist*, 61–65 (Dec. 1989).

8. J.B. BRYAN, R.R. CLOUSER, and E. HOLLAND, "Spindle Accuracy," *American Machinist*, 149–164 (Dec. 4, 1967).

9. *ANSI B89.3.4M-1985*, "Axes of Rotation," American Society of Mechanical Engineers, 1985.

10. E. ABBE, "Measuring Instruments for Physicists," *Journal for Instrumental Information*, **10**, 446–448 (1890).

11. J.B. BRYAN, "The Abbe Principle Revisited—An Updated Interpretation," *Precision Engineering*, **1**(3), 129–132 (1989).

12. *ANSI B89.6.2-1973*, "Temperature and Humidity Environment for Dimensional Measurement," American Society of Mechanical Engineers, 1973.

13. J.B. BRYAN and E.R. MCCURE, "Heat vs Tolerances," *American Machinist*, Special Report No. 605 (June 5, 1967).

14. J.B. BRYAN, "International Status of Thermal Error Research," *Annals of the C.I.R.P.* **26**, 203–215 (1968).

15. J.B. BRYAN, D.L. CARTER, R.W. CLOUSER, and J.H. HAMILTON, "An Order of Magnitude Improvement in Thermal Stability with Use of Liquid Shower on a General Purpose Measuring Machine," *ASME Technical Paper IQ82-936*, presented at the Precision Machining Workshop, St. Paul, Minn., 1982.

16. C.I.R.P. Scientific Committee for Metrology and Interchangability's, "A Proposal for Defining and Specifying the Dimensional Uncertainty of Multiaxis Measuring Machines," *Annals of the C.I.R.P.* **27**(2), 623–630 (1978).

17. R.R. DONALDSON, "Error Budgets," *Technology of Machine Tools, a Survey of the State of the Art by the Machine Tool Task Force*, R.J. Hocken working group chairman, UCRL-52960-5, Oct. 1980.

18. R.R. DONALDSON, "A Simple Method for Separating Spindle Error from Test Ball Roundness Error," *Annals of the C.I.R.P.* **21**(1), 125–126 (1972).

TERMINOLOGY

Accuracy is formally defined as quantitative measure of the degree of conformance to recognized national or international standards of measurement.

Repeatability is formally defined as a measure of the ability of a machine to sequentially position a tool with respect to a workpiece under similar conditions.

Resolution is the least increment of a measuring device; the least significant bit on a digital machine.

Radial error motion is the error motion of rotary axis normal to the Z reference axis and at a specified angular location (see Figure 4 of ANSI B5.54).

Runout is the total displacement measured by an instrument sensing a moving surface or moved with respect to a fixed surface.

Slide straightness error is the deviation from straight line movement that an indicator positioned perpendicular to a slide direction exhibits when it is either stationary and reading against a perfect straightedge supported on the moving slide, or moved by the slide along a perfect straightedge which is stationary.

Error is defined as the difference between the actual response of a machine to a command issued according to the accepted protocol of the machine's operation and the response to that command anticipated by the protocol.

Error motion is the change in position relative to the reference coordinate axes, or the surface of a perfect workpiece with its center line coincident with the axis of rotation. Error motions are specified as to location and direction and do not include motions due to thermal drift.

Error motion measurement is a measurement record of error motion which should include all pertinent information regarding the machine, instrumentation and test conditions.

Scale errors are the differences between the position of the read out device (scale) and that of a known reference linear scale (along the X axis).

Straightness errors are the nonlinear movements that an indicator sees when it is either *i*) stationary and reading against a perfect straightedge supported on a moving slide or *ii*) moved by the slide along a perfect straightedge which is stationary (see Figure 4 of ANSI B5.54-1992). Basically, this translates to small unwanted motion (along the Y and Z axes) perpendicular to the designed direction of motion.

Angular errors are small unwanted rotations (about X, Y and Z axes) of a linearly moving carriage about three mutually perpendicular axes.

Radial error motion is the translational error motion in a direction normal to the Z reference axis and at a specified axial location (along the X and Y axes).

Axial error motion is the translational error motion collinear with the Z reference axis of an axis of rotation (about the Z axis).

Tilt error motion is the error motion in an angular direction relative to the Z reference axis (about the X and Y axes).

Face motion is the rotational error motion parallel to the Z reference axis at a specified radial location (along the Z axis).

Squareness is a plane surface is "square" to an axis of rotation if coincident polar profile centers are obtained for an axial and face motion polar plot at different radii. For linear axes, the angular deviation from 90° measured between the best fit lines drawn through two sets of straightness data derived from two orthogonal axes in a specified work zone (expressed as small angles).

Parallelism is the lack of parallelism of two or more axes (expressed as a small angle).

Angularity is the angular error between two or more axes designed to be at fixed angles other than 90°.

Average axis line for rotary axes is the direction of the "best fit" straight line (axis of rotation) obtained by fitting a line through centers of the least squared circles fit to the radial motion data at various distances from the spindle face.

Axis direction is the direction of any line parallel to the motion direction of a linearly moving component. The direction of a linear axis is defined by a least squares fit of a straight line to the appropriate straightness data (5).

Acknowledgments

The author would like to take this opportunity to thank Messrs. James B. Bryan and Donald L. Carter of the Lawrence Livermore National Laboratory (LLNL) for the many valuable discussions that we have had about a wide variety of topics related to precision engineering. This chapter is the culmination of many long discussions with these two gentlemen as well as many other engineers at LLNL, Carnegie Mellon University, other universities and numerous corporations.

CHAPTER 20

Micromanufacturing

"Smaller, lighter, and less expensive consumer products, industrial machines, instruments, . . . possibilities limited only by man's imagination."

J. Jara-Almonte, C. Friedrich, and R.O. Warrington
Institute for Micromanufacturing
Louisiana Tech University

Microelectromechanical systems (MEMS), microsystems technologies (MST) and micromanufacturing are relatively recent phrases and acronyms that have become synonymous with the design, development, and manufacture of microdevices and -systems. Micromanufacturing encompasses MEMS and MST and, in addition, includes processes related to the production and packaging of microsystems. Integration of mechanical and electrical components, including built-in computers, can be formed into systems that must be connected to the macroworld. Macro-, mini-, micro-, and nanotechnologies are all a part of MEMS and micromanufacturing. At this point in the development of the technology, it is becoming apparent that minisystems, with microcomponents, could well be the economic drivers of the technology for the foreseeable future. A few applications of these devices are shown in Figure 20.1. This chapter provides a general overview of this emerging technology. It is hoped that it will provide a sense of what MEMS is and how it might be used to enhance manufacturing.

20.1 INTRODUCTION

MEMS technologies have their roots in research activities in the early 1960s, as the first micropressure sensors were fabricated using an anisotropic etching method (1). Since then, the fabrication techniques developed in microelectronics have begun directly to impact the progress in micromechanics. During these years, pioneer research work in electrostatically driven microstructures was performed (2), which a decade later found further development in surface micromachining for sensor formation (3).

In the 1970s, numerous industrial companies were involved in the efforts to commercialize the existing microfabrication technologies for a new generation of products featuring light weight, small volume, and high efficiency. Among those pioneers, Texas Instruments succeeded in marketing microthermal printing heads for computer printers (4). At the end of the 1970s, the controlled anisotropic undercut etching technique was further developed, which resulted in microcantilever beams and similar micromechanical structures.

The continuing exploitation of LSI processing methods in the 1980s opened considerable opportunities for the further invention of unique silicon-based micromechanical devices as well as the creation of new markets (5–9). In response to the growing need for application specific integrated circuit chips (ASICs), custom design and fabrication facilities have been implemented. The concept of the IC foundry quickly found its expression as the silicon micromechanics foundry in the development and production of micromechanical structures (10). Also during this time, based on a combination of deep-etch lithography and subsequent high precision replication, a new micromachining technique, known as the LIGA process, was introduced in Germany for producing three-dimensional microstructures (11, 12). Innovative improvements and modifications to this process have subsequently been made by researchers at the

(a)

(b)

Figure 20.1. Examples of MEMS devices. (*a*) Microaccelerometer. Courtesy of Lucas NovaSensor. (*b*) Nickel microconnectors. Courtesy of Kernforschungszentrum, Karlsruhe. GmbH.

University of Wisconsin (13). Besides conventional electromagnetic actuators, various types of electrostatic motors and actuators featuring simple structures, microsize, and high force-to-volume ratios were developed worldwide (14–17). Also, different materials were investigated for possible applications in the microrobot domain, such as the shape memory alloys (SMA) (18).

Parallel to the endeavors of pushing ahead the micromanufacturing technique down to the order of submicron and nanometer scales, there have been numerous activities reported that focus on applying different micromachining technologies to fabricate end products that are mainly mini with microcomponents, such as the compact microheat exchangers produced with

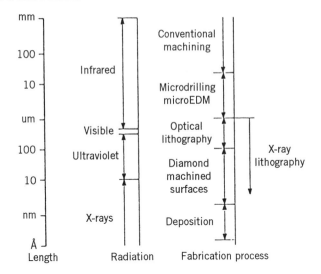

Figure 20.2. Dimensional magnitudes covered by micromanufacturing.

diamond bit cutting (19). To meet the increasing need for metrology and product inspection in the submicron and nano scale, atomic-force microscopes (20) and scanned-probe device arrays (21) are under further development. Also, micro-EDM, molding, plating, and many other new techniques are emerging to augment the microsensor and actuator fabrication (22). It is evident that micromanufacturing technologies will lead to commercialization of revolutionary devices that will dramatically change our lives in the 21st century.

Although micromanufacturing and conventional precision machining use many of the same techniques and equipment, the goals are different. Precision engineering is informally defined as the production of parts with a size-to-tolerance ratio greater than 10,000 (23). In micromanufacturing, the goal is to produce mini- and microsystems (typically 1 or less cm in size) with microcomponents (typically 1 to 100 μm in size) with sufficient tolerances to achieve functionality and repeatability. These tolerances may well be smaller than in precision engineering.

Micromanufacturing covers several orders of dimensional magnitude, as depicted in Figure 20.2, which is a comparison of this range and the electromagnetic spectrum. Note that Figure 20.2, does not show the extremes of micromanufacturing, such as x-ray lithography, which can produce submicron features with ease. The integration of components across several orders of dimensional magnitude is key to MEMS applications. Minisystems can be enhanced with microcomponents. Figure 20.3 shows an ore-grinding ball instrumented with an accelerometer, signal processing, and transmission circuitry to broadcast impact accelerations during the grinding process. The centimeter-size ball contains micro-scale sensors and circuitry, which in turn have tolerances in the nanometer range. MEMS applications require metrology over several orders of magnitude.

Metrology

A progression in micrometrology has occurred in parallel to the microminiaturization revolution. Perhaps the first improvement was the scanning electron microscope (SEM; first marketed by Cambridge, Ltd., in the 1960s). A feature smaller than the wavelength of visible light, ~0.5 μm, cannot be seen directly. However in an SEM, the wavelength of an electron accelerated to 30 keV is approximately 0.007 nm, which is a typical upper accelerating voltage, although some SEMs use 40 keV. The SEM resolution is not limited by the illuminating wavelength but rather the interaction of the electron beam and the sample. The short wavelength of an accelerated electron gives rise to extremely high lateral (X, Y directions) resolution of the sample, typically 1 nm. As the high energy electron beam is rastered across the sample, it liberates many

Figure 20.3. Cross-section of an instrumented grinding ball. Courtesy of Institute for Micromanufacturing.

subsequent electrons from the sample. The output intensity of an electron detector (many types are available) is displayed on a cathode-ray tube (CRT) to form an image.

One advantage, or disadvantage, with SEM is that the energy of the electrons results in sample penetration. Therefore, as a higher electron accelerating voltage is selected, resulting in higher lateral resolution, the image is actually of the subsurface region of the sample. The electron penetration depth is a function of the accelerating voltage and the atomic number (atomic cross-section) of the sample and is typically in the micron range. Field emission guns have been developed to provide a higher signal-to-noise ratio, which allows operation at a lower accelerating voltage, reducing sample damage from the electron beam. A field emission source provides an image brightness several orders of magnitude brighter than more conventional tungsten or lanthanum hexaboride (LaB$_6$) sources at the same accelerating voltage.

One drawback of SEM is the inability to perform out-of-plane (Z direction) metrology, except when the sample is tilted to provide a cross-sectional view. Some work has been performed using aerial photogrammetry techniques, but these do not have the required accuracy. Other work has attempted to correlate the backscatter electron signal with topography. However, backscatter electrons are generated below the sample surface, and the quantity of backscatter electrons depends on the local atomic number of the target. In many high aspect ratio micromanufactured parts with vertical relief, this form of metrology is not possible.

Two methods that provide reasonable lateral resolution (1 μm regime) along with Å-level vertical resolution are contact stylus and noncontact optical interference profilometers. Contact profilometers use a pointed (typically a tip radius of several microns or less) stylus that traverses across the sample with a selectable contact force on the order of mgr. The load is maintained by a force feedback scheme coupled with a linearly variable displacement transformer or capacitor. These profilometers are relatively slow for three-dimensional surface maps because of the need to make repeated scans. Such devices are routinely limited to a range of several hundred microns with Å-level vertical resolution and lateral resolution depending on the tip radius.

Another method for producing high vertical resolution is interference microscopy. This technology uses an interferometer with one of the light beams reflecting off of the sample surface while the reference leg is produced in the microscope objective. After the reflected and reference beams are recombined, the vertical profile of the sample is obtained by integrating the interference signal (fringes) over the detector. The lateral resolution is limited by the working magnification, the quality of the optics (diffraction limited resolution), and the pixel density of the detector. Such interferometric microscopes, while allowing Å-level vertical resolution and submicron lateral resolution, are limited by their lateral field of view and depth of focus. A dynamic focusing technique, whereby the microscope objective is piezoelectrically moved at

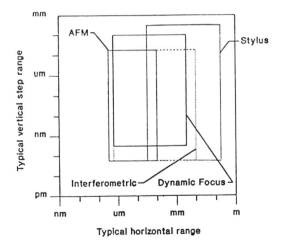

Figure 20.4. Typical ranges of MEMS metrology tools.

fixed intervals and the interference pattern is detected at each interval, allows peak-to-valley ranges from 3 Å to more than 1 mm with lateral resolution comparable with the interference microscopes. One disadvantage of the dynamic focusing technique is the need to store the detector array at each vertical scan interval, thus requiring large amounts of computer memory and a fast processor to analyze each slice in a reasonable amount of time. The typical microscope "slices" the sample every 70 nm. If only 100 μm of vertical range is to be used the resulting image requires more than 92 megabytes of storage.

The most recent breakthrough in surface micrometrology is the scanning probe microscope. Scanning probe microscopes can function in a variety of metrology modes. For surface metrology, the atomic force microscope (AFM) is widely used. This instrument uses an etched, sharp tip to probe the sample with light contact force. The point is held on a small, flexible cantilever, and a laser is reflected off of the back side of the tip and onto a sensitive differential photodetector. The geometry of the light path provides long "levers" resulting in extreme vertical sensitivity. As the tip scans the surface and deflects, the reflected laser beam provides a signal allowing piezoelectric vertical movement of the sample to maintain constant contact force (cantilever deflection). This vertical movement is mapped along with the piezoelectrically driven lateral sample movement to provide X, Y, and Z surface topography. A typical AFM has a field of view of approximately 100 μm^2 and a vertical range of perhaps 15 μm. The AFM is capable of atomic resolution under optimal conditions. Many other scanning probe technologies are available but will not be described herein. This is a rapidly changing field that holds much promise for real-time, in situ metrology of molecular-level processes.

As will be subsequently shown, work in MEMS does not necessarily require the high resolution in metrology tools as is needed in semiconductor fabrication or basic research. Because MEMS structures routinely have relatively large vertical steps in the topography, vertical range of measurement rather than resolution is more important. Imagine, for example, the difficulty in measuring the roughness of the bottom of a 75-μm deep trench when the trench is less than 5 μm wide. This represents a typical challenge in MEMS micrometrology. A comparison of typical vertical step range and horizontal range of several common tools is shown in Figure 20.4. Because the technology is advancing so rapidly, this figure should be used as only a starting point for identifying the appropriate metrology instrument.

20.2 LITHOGRAPHY

In its most general sense lithography is simply the transfer of a master pattern onto another surface. Here, the word is used in a more restrictive sense by limiting the discussion to photolithography in which the pattern transfer medium is light. Even in this restrictive use, there are many routine examples of lithography; photographs and photocopies are everyday examples of products made by lithography. One might even argue that the picture seen on a television screen

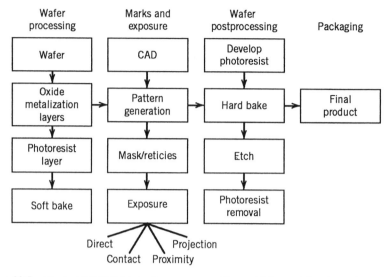

Figure 20.5. Typical MEMS fabrication sequence. For multiple mask levels, various steps in the first three columns would be repeated.

is a form of lithography, as electrons are used to excite the phosphorus on the screen. In the following discussion on lithography, the term is used only to refer to the processes used in microfabrication of circuits and MEMS devices. At the same time, the term *light* is used in reference to visible, infrared, and ultraviolet wavelengths.

Lithography in MEMS Fabrication

Lithography is just one of the many steps required to fabricate a successful MEMS application. Although lithography will not determine the success of the fabrication sequence, lithography is one of the most important steps in batch fabrication of MEMS devices. Fortunately, there is a vast amount of information available about integrated circuit lithography that can be directly applied to MEMS fabrication. However, as the MEMS technologies advance, new lithography applications developed specifically for this new technology will emerge; deep-ultraviolet and deep-x-ray lithographies, which are discussed in the next section, are examples of this.

The typical steps required to transfer a MEMS pattern onto a wafer are summarized in Figure 20.5, starting from the preprocessing of the silicon wafer through the lithography to the postprocessing and packaging steps. Details of the lithography process are shown in Figure 20.6. The following discussion will describe the sequence of events within each block and process level portrayed in Figure 20.5 and 20.6.

Wafer Preprocessing

The typical preprocessing phase depicted in Figure 20.5. consists of covering the wafer with an etch-mask layer and depositing a photoresist over this layer. A wafer is first cleaned and the surface of the Si wafer is coated with an etch-mask layer such as SiO_2 or SiN_4. (The purpose and process used for the etch-mask layer for this step is explained in the section on MEMS processes.) Then, a liquid organic photoresist is poured over the SiO_2 layer, as the wafer is spun at a few hundred rpm. The viscosity and rotational speed and angular acceleration of the wafer determine the thickness of the liquid photoresist layer. The photoresist is usually applied at a lower angular speed; then, the speed is increased to achieve the desired film characteristics. It is imperative to keep the air around the liquid photoresist as clean as possible to minimize imperfections caused by airborne particles trapped in the resist.

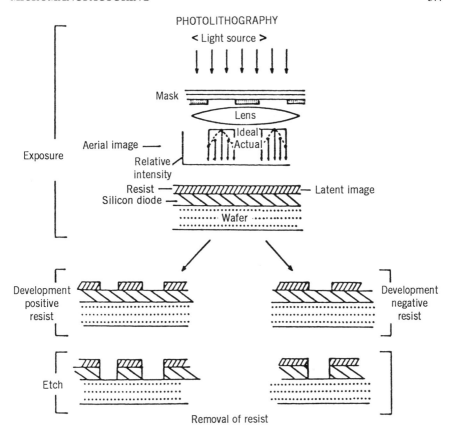

Figure 20.6. Schematic of a typical photolithographic process in MEMS.

Manufacturers provide photoresists in liquid form in a solvent base. Photoresists come in two types: positive and negative, each with its own recommended, matched developer. As its name implies, a positive photoresist will yield the positive of the mask pattern on the photoresist. That is, the developer will remove the photoresist regions that have been exposed to light, while the unexposed regions will remain on the SiO_2 layer. In contrast, a negative photoresist will provide a negative of the pattern drawn on the glass wafer by leaving behind the photoresist in the regions exposed to light, once the wafer is developed as seen in Figure 20.6.

The liquid photoresist film is solidified during a soft bake in an oven at around 100° to 200°C. The adhesion of the photoresist to the SiO_2 is partially a function of the soft bake. Insufficient soft baking results in poor adhesion, whereupon the photoresist will tend to lift off during postprocessing. Overbaking leads to brittle photoresist layers that will tend to crack during postprocessing. An adequate softbake will result in a photoresist with good adhesion to the oxide, rendering a light-sensitive, smooth layer that will react when light with a specific wavelength strikes it. Any adhesion deficiencies are easily manifested by curling and lift-off of the resist during postprocessing. Obviously, it is better to prevent any potential adhesion problems by using a *hard bake* after the soft bake to ensure dryness or by applying an adhesion promoter before applying the photoresist.

Masks and Exposure

A mask is prepared before exposing the desired pattern on the photoresist layer. The purpose of this mask is to create a desired pattern on photoresist by selectively blocking and transmitting

PROJECTION PRINTING

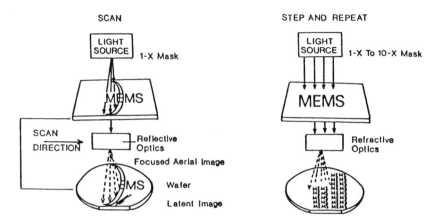

Figure 20.7. Two common projection printing techniques.

light. An optical mask (x-ray masks are different) consists of a clear glass substrate with a chrome film on one side. The desired pattern is drawn on the chrome film with a pattern generator. Light shown through the mask and lens will produce what is termed an *aerial image* over the resist and a *latent image* in the resist once it is exposed (see Figure 20.6).

During the exposure, the mask may be in contact with the wafer (contact printing) or it may be physically separated from the wafer surface (proximity printing). Although contact printing provides better resolution, proximity printing provides a longer mask life, because there is less wear and tear on the master pattern. The reason contact printing provides better resolution (or critical dimension; CD) is that whenever a sharp edge is encountered by light, edge diffraction occurs and the intensity of the incident light is smeared over the target region. The difference between the ideal and actual aerial images in Figure 20.6 shows how the light intensity diminishes gradually at the edge of the mask pattern, and as a result, the photoresist image will not be as sharp as the original pattern. An approximate equation for the theoretical resolution in proximity printing is

$$Resolution = \sqrt{\lambda[(gap) + (Photoresist\ thickness)]} \qquad (1)$$

where λ is the wavelength of the exposing radiation, and *gap* is the distance between the mask and the top of the photoresist (zero for contact printing).

Contact and proximity printing fall in a category called shadow printing. An alternate type of exposure using reflective and/or refractive optics, called projection printing, is being used extensively in the microelectronics industry. Two common ways to achieve projection printing—scanning and stepping—are shown in Figure 20.7. Both ways alleviate problems caused by having the mask and wafer close to each other; however, both systems have lower resolution capabilities due to lens imperfections and optics limitations. Resolution for a projection system can be approximated by

$$Resolution \approx \frac{K_1 \lambda}{NA} \qquad (2)$$

where *NA* is the numerical aperture of the optical system (effectively the ability of the lens to collimate light), and K_1 is a process-dependent constant that has a nominal value of 0.75 in production. As can be seen from Equations 1 and 2, resolution can be lowered by decreasing the wavelength, λ, and in the case of the projection printing, by increasing the numerical aperture of the lens. The trade-off of increasing the numerical aperture is a decrease in the depth of focus:

$$Depth\ of\ focus \approx \frac{K_2 \lambda}{(NA)^2} \qquad (3)$$

where K_2 is also a process-dependent constant with a nominal value of 0.5 in production. To produce patterns of finite thickness on the photoresist, the latent image must be in focus through the thickness of the resist. The depth of focus is the tolerance for clear latent images, although this can be somewhat compensated by resist chemistry and development.

While specially formulated photoresists have been developed to compensate for diffraction effects, resolution is typically improved by using shorter wavelength light sources. Figure 20.8 shows several exposure sources and their associated light wavelengths. A mercury arc lamp (i, g, or h lines) is the most common light source used in optical lithography, while lasers are used in ultraviolet lithography. To illustrate that resists and light sources need to be matched, the selectivity curves for a positive and negative resist used in optical lithography are also presented in Figure 20.8. Figure 20.8 also shows typical wavelengths of light that can be obtained from high energy photons and electrons. The area where $\lambda \leq 100$ nm is referred to as *radiolithography*. Light sources in this region include synchrotrons (x-rays), ion, and electron beam guns. The ion and electron beams are limited in resolution by scattering and x-ray resolution; this is discussed further below. Electron beams are used in mask making and repair. Furthermore, both ion and electron beams can be used to write directly on resist layers on wafers.

Postprocessing

The development of the resist differentiates between those areas that have received light and those that have not. This mechanism is somewhat different for negative and positive photoresists. In negative resists, the areas exposed to light form polymer chains that make those regions more impervious to the solvents in the developer. The developer attacks the unexposed areas more easily as cross-linking has not occurred in these areas. In positive photoresists, the regions exposed to light have the photoresist converted to a base-soluble carboxylic acid compound, while the unexposed areas remain the same. The carboxylic acid is removed by a reaction with a basic or alkaline developer.

The development is usually carried out in either an immersion bath or by spraying the developer onto the wafer. It is thought that spray developing yields higher contrast or differential solubility than immersion developing because fresh developer is forced to the surface of the photoresist and it allows better control of the developer chemistry in contact with the wafer. Several commercial monitoring systems are available to aid in the development control, but these can not be covered here.

Several factors have a marked effect on the quality of the development. The development time is probably the most important of these factors. Insufficient development time leads to undeveloped regions on the wafer, while excessive exposure time leads to reduced inhibitor concentration and increased dissolution rate. To complicate matters more, the ideal exposure time is a function of the photoresist film uniformity and the soft-bake parameters used. Increased soft-bake times reduce the solvent content of the resists, hardening the resist film and preventing penetration by the developer. The concentration of the developer is another factor affecting development time. The ideal development time is proportional to the concentration. The developer temperature also affects development time as the activity of the developer is a nonlinear function of temperature. The developer activity is generally greater at higher temperatures; however, the increased activity is not linear with temperature and thus should be monitored carefully. Finally, the agitation of the developer also has an effect on the quality of the development. Normally, sufficient agitation to bring fresh chemicals to the surface of the wafer is desired, but not so much that the adhesion of the resist will be compromised.

Once the photoresist is developed, it is sometimes postbaked to increase the resistance to subsequent etching process. Any remaining solvents from either resist or developer are removed in this step, leaving a harder, more impermeable film. However, in some cases this can cause some residual stress problems in the photoresist. The etch that follows transfers the photoresist pattern to the SiO_2 layer. This is accomplished using a hydrofluoric acid (HF) and ammonium fluoride (NH_4F). The ratio of HF to NH_4F varies according to process parameters. Obviously, the integrity of the photoresist during the etch will be key to having a good pattern transfer.

Other factors that have an effect on the resolution and quality of pattern transferred to the SiO_2 layer include (*1*) HF–NH_4F concentration, (*2*) time, (*3*) temperature, and (*4*) agitation. The concentration will have a direct impact on the etch rate and the undercutting of the SiO_2 layer. *Undercutting* is a phenomenon that occurs when the etch travels laterally underneath the photoresist. Etch time is always a function of the SiO_2 layer thickness; sufficient etch time is needed to etch through the layer, but overetching degrades the photoresists, degrading the quality of the SiO_2 mask. Temperature is, perhaps, the most important parameter, as the etch

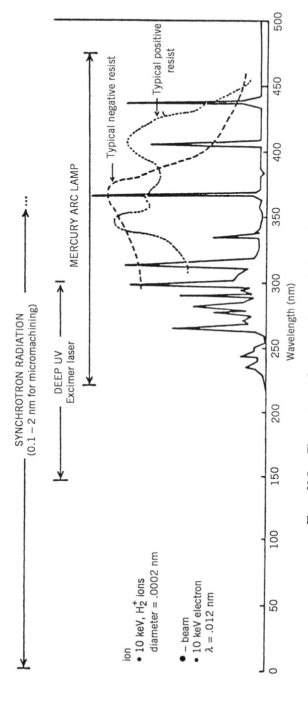

Figure 20.8. The spectrum of a mercury lamp and photoresist selectivity.

rate and thus etch time vary nonlinearly with temperature. Finally, agitation is required to bring fresh chemicals in contact with the SiO_2 layer, but too much agitation will help tend to lift off the photoresist.

In microelectronics, current efforts are aimed at reducing the minimum feature size to increase the device density on a wafer. For instance, submicron (<1 μm) feature sizes are desirable, and current research is aimed in this direction. In MEMS fabrication, the minimum feature size is normally greater than 1 μm, and current research focuses on applications that require thicker devices than those used in microelectronics. This means that materials and processes are aimed at fabricating thicker microstructures. The following section describes how certain microelectronic fabrication procedures have been adapted to the fabrication of MEMS devices.

20.3 TRADITIONAL MEMS PROCESSES

There are several ways to achieve batch fabrication of microelectromechanical systems. These processes have been traditionally classified into four distinct groups: bulk, surface, deep ultraviolet lithography (DUV), and deep x-ray lithography (LIGA). The major characteristics of each process group are presented in this section. Although each process group has its own unique set of fabrication steps and constraints, they are not mutually exclusive. That is, the processes within each group can be mixed and matched to obtain the desired final design; this will be seen in some of the examples presented below.

Bulk Micromachining

Historically, bulk micromachining was the first process group to be developed. The fundamental characteristic of this process group is the generation of the desired features by material removal, similar to carving. Starting with a bulk piece of material, usually silicon, the desired features are attained by etching away the undesired material, leaving behind the desired features. The material to be removed is exposed to etchants while the desired features are protected with etch masks (not to be confused with lithography masks). The etchants can be in a liquid state (wet etching) or a gaseous-plasma state (dry etching). Moreover, the etchants can act equally in all directions (isotropic etching) or act in a preferential direction (anisotropic etching).

Wet etching can be carried out by immersing the wafer in the etchant or by spraying the etchant onto the wafer. Isotropic wet etches are commonly carried out using a combination $HF–HNO_3$ etchant mixture. The nitric acid forms an oxide over the Si wafer, which is removed by the hydrofluoric acid. The etch rate mainly depends on the etchant concentration and to a minor extent on the dopant level of the wafer, crystal orientation, and temperature. There are numerous other mechanisms at work during the etching process that cannot be covered here. The overall effect is that $HF–HNO_3$ etches do not allow a high degree of dimensional control over their operating ranges.

Anisotropic wet etching can be achieved with the etchants described in Table 20.1. The preferential material removed occurs by the creation of a hydrous silica and the subsequent dissolution by the complex that is formed. Because single crystal silicon exhibits a diamond cubic structure, as do other semiconductors (Ge and Sn), there is a lower atom density in the $\langle 100 \rangle$ direction than in the $\langle 111 \rangle$ direction. The etch rates of the anisotropic etchants in Table 20.1 are greater along the $\langle 100 \rangle$ direction. In fact, the etches exhibit a self-stopping property on the $\langle 111 \rangle$ planes.

The cross-sections of a [100] and a [110] wafers anisotropically etched with KOH and water through a small hole in the etch mask are shown in Figure 20.9. These typical shapes are the result of the slow rate with which KOH etch attacks the $\langle 111 \rangle$ plane, as can be verified in Figure 20.10. This figure shows the etch rates (μm/h) as a function of the KOH concentration in water and the crystallographic orientation of the wafer. Typical etch rates have been included in Table 20.1 for each etchant. Note that numerous factors can affect the ideal etch rates. Some of these are highlighted here. The etch rate typically increases at higher etch temperatures. Contamination of the etchant bath decreases the etch rate. Substrate dopants affect the etch rates. In fact, heavy boron doping has been successfully used as an etch stop in bulk micromachining.

TABLE 20.1.   **Sample Etch Rates for Wet Anisotropic Etchants (Water Is the Dilutant)**

Etchant	Temperature Range (°C)	Masking Films	Complexing Agent	Sample Etch Rate (μm/h)
KOH	22–90	SiN_4, SiO_2, Cr–Au	isopropanol, n-propanol, butanol, AlOH	120 at 85°C [110] Si
EPW (ethylenedi-amine–pyrocate-chol–water)	55–118	Cr, Au, Ni, Ag, Cu, Ta	pyrazine, hydra-zine, benzo-quinone, pyridazine,	80 at 118°C [100] Si
Hydrazine (N_2H_4–H_2O)	70–120	SiO_2, SiN_4, Al		200 at 120°C [100] Si

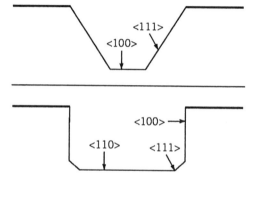

Figure 20.9.   [100] and [110] Si wafer cross-section showing the resulting etched shapes using a rectangular mask window and KOH etchant (25).

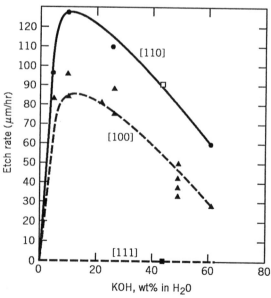

Figure 20.10.   The etch rate of KOH on different orienta-tions of Si wafers as a func-tion of KOH concentration in water (25).

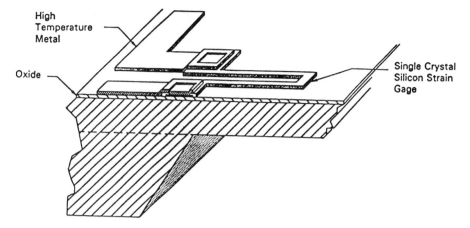

High
Temperature
Metal

Oxide

Single Crystal
Silicon Strain
Gage

Figure 20.11.   An isometric view of a pressure sensor made by wafer bonding. The dotted line shows the initial location of the hydrated surfaces.

Processes Used in Both Bulk and Surface Micromachining

Two related problems with wet etching are undercutting, sometimes called etch bias, and dissolution of the mask material during etching. Combined, these two problems make it difficult to control dimensional accuracy with wet etches, which is critical when the features are in the micron range. Dry etching provides an alternative process that renders more control over dimensional accuracy; however, this improvement comes with a higher investment in equipment. Dry etching equipment comes in a variety of configurations, which can not all be covered here. Only the two dry processes used in MEMS are covered here, plasma and ion beam etching.

In a plasma etch, an RF frequency (in the 10's of MHz range) is used to energize the etchant gas, causing it to break down into a mixture of atomic and ionized species. This mixture is guided to a wafer in a vacuum, where the species react with the exposed surface. Two common arrangements are available for plasma etches: barrel and planar. In the barrel configuration, the plasma is generated in the same chamber as the wafer, while in the planar geometry the plasma generation occurs in a separate area. While the barrel configuration can provide a higher throughput, accuracy and uniformity are usually better in the planar configuration.

The fundamental principle in ion beam etching is the removal of material by moving particles. This removal can be simply physical or a combination of physical and chemical phenomena. Anisotropy and resolution of the etch are quite good because the particle sizes are in the ion and atom range and the particles are guided unidirectionally toward the target wafer. When the chemical component is omitted by using an inert gas, only the momentum of the ions and atoms are used to etch material. This can generate high temperatures on the target surface. For this reason, in many MEMS applications reactive ion etching (RIE) is used. Not only does RIE result in a lower surface temperature but it has a high selectivity for SiO_2 over Si when CF_4–H_2 is used as the etchant gas. In fact, SiO_2-to-Si etch ratios of 35:1 can be achieved this way, allowing fairly good control over patterning of the sacrificial SiO_2 layer in surface micromachining.

Another process commonly classified under bulk micromachining is the relatively new anodic wafer bonding process, which is an additive technology. Two wafers can be joined forming a single crystal morphology. This is done by first hydrating the two wafer surfaces to be joined. This provides an OH stem to each Si atom on the wafer surfaces. The wafers are brought in contact with each other at an elevated temperature and a DC voltage is applied across the two wafers. The OH stems migrate away from the interface layer as H_2O vapor and O_2 gas, leaving behind a monolithic, single crystal morphology, without evidence of an interface layer. This technique has been commercially used to create pressure sensors with sealed vacuum cavities (Figure 20.11).

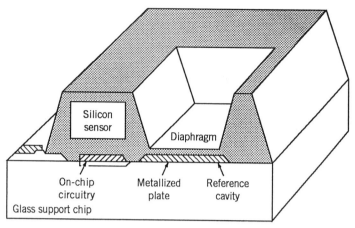

Bulk-silicon double-sided process

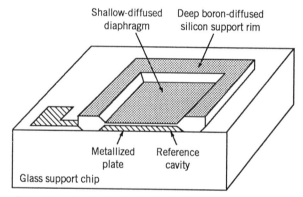

Bulk-silicon dissolved-wafer single-sided process

Figure 20.12.   Silicon membrane made by the bulk dissolved wafer process compared with a conventional micromachined micromembrane.

Another new process in the bulk micromachining repertoire is the bulk-dissolved wafer process. As the name implies, the unneeded portion of a silicon wafer is removed by dissolving it with an appropriate etch. An example and comparison of this process with more traditional micromachining is presented in Figure 20.12. A microdiaphragm is made by doping a wafer with boron, rendering the doped silicon impervious to a KOH etch. Then the wafer is bonded to the Pyrex substrate and etched in a KOH solution. Thus only the doped portions of the wafer, the microdiaphragm and supports, remain after the KOH solution dissolves the wafer.

Surface Micromachining

In surface micromachining, the desired features are generated by successively depositing material, patterning it, and removing the undesired material. The more common process for depositing material in MEMS applications is chemical vapor deposition (CVD). CVD is a gas-reaction process that allows the deposition of many types of layers. The material deposited on the wafer is a function of the chemical reaction taking place in the chamber. The more common reactions used in MEMS fabrication are summarized in Table 20.2. One commonality of the CVD process

TABLE 20.2. Common CVD Reactions used in MEMS Films

Reactants	Conditions	Resulting Film and By-products
SiH_4	H_2; 900°C	Si (poly) + 2 H_2
SiH_4	N_2; 650°C	Si (poly) + 2 H_2
$SiH_4 + O_2$	N_2, Ar; 300–500°C	$SiO_2 + H_2$
Si $(OC_2H_5)_4$	N_2, Ar; 730–750°C	SiO_2 + 2 H_2O + 4 C_2H_4
$SiX_4 + 2 H_2 + 2CO_2$	H_2; ~1200°C	SiO_2 + 4 HX + 2 CO
3 $SiH_4 + 4 NH_3$	NH_3, H_2; 750–1000°	Si_3N_4 + 24 H_2
3 $SiCl_4 + 4 NH_3$	NH_3, H_2; 750–1100°C	Si_3N_4 + 12 HCl

is the elevated temperature at which the reactions take place. This can result in significant residual stresses in deposited films, because of the different thermal expansion coefficients of the materials used in surface micromachining. This sometimes requires an annealing step after a CVD deposition or a special design to alleviate any residual stress problems. An additional concern about CVD processes is the hazardous gases most commonly used; except for argon and nitrogen, most gases are toxic, flammable, corrosive, and pyrophoric.

The main features in surface micromachined structures are made with polysilicon films. These films can be annealed to relieve internal stresses, and they can be deposited over sacrificial layers. A sacrificial layer, such as SiO_2 can be used to create overhanging or unsupported polysilicon films. This characteristic of surface micromachined structures has the advantage that it is compatible with existing IC fabrication procedures; hence the driving and feedback circuitry can be built next to the structure. The disadvantage of this technology is that the polysilicon structures tend to be thickness limited to less than 5 μm by the deposition equipment. It is possible to deposit several successive layers to increase the thickness; however, this decreases the resolution of the minimum feature possible, and it cannot compete with the next two technologies.

The order in which the layers are deposited, patterned, and removed varies with each application. Because there is no standard sequence of steps for every possible MEMS device, an example is presented below to illustrate surface micromachining fabrication. Figure 20.13 shows a pair of microgripper jaws fabricated by a combination of surface and bulk micromachining steps, which are explained below. The grippers can handle a 7-μm-diameter euglena, about a tenth of the diameter of a human hair. Figure 20.13 is a sequence of diagrams showing the cross-section of a wafer as it would appear after discrete fabrication steps. First, the wafer is doped positively (p^+) with boron to provide an etch stop. Phosphosilicate glass (PSG) is deposited over the entire substrate using a low pressure–chemical-vapor deposition (LPCVD) chamber. Then a layer of polysilicon is deposited using LPCVD as well. The desired features are patterned on the polysilicon layer and the unwanted material was removed in a CCl_4 anisotropic plasma etch. Additional PSG layers are deposited on the bottom of the cross-section to prepare the wafer for the bulk micromachining steps (to protect certain areas). Finally, the wafer is bulk micromachined in EDP and the microgripper released.

Deep Ultraviolet Lithography

In deep ultraviolet lithography (DUV), a high energy light source with wavelength in the order of 200 nm is used in conjunction with a thick resist to create deep features in the resist. Typical resists include photosensitive polyimide and polymethylmethacrylate (PMMA). An example of this procedure is shown in Figure 20.14. First, a seed layer of the platinum or titanium is deposited on a wafer substrate. Then a thick coat of the resist is deposited on the seed layer. With photosensitive resist of the appropriate viscosity, it is possible to deposit up to a 50-μm-thick resist layer. An optical mask is used in conjunction with an ultraviolet light source to expose the resist to the desired pattern. The resist is then developed, leaving behind the exposed seed layer and resist walls. The remaining resist can now be used as a mold.

The mold with the metallic seed layer can now be filled with metal by electroplating. For example, for a nickel structure, the voids in the mold can be filled by immersing the wafer and mold in a nickel sulfamate bath along with a nickel anode. A DC voltage applied across the

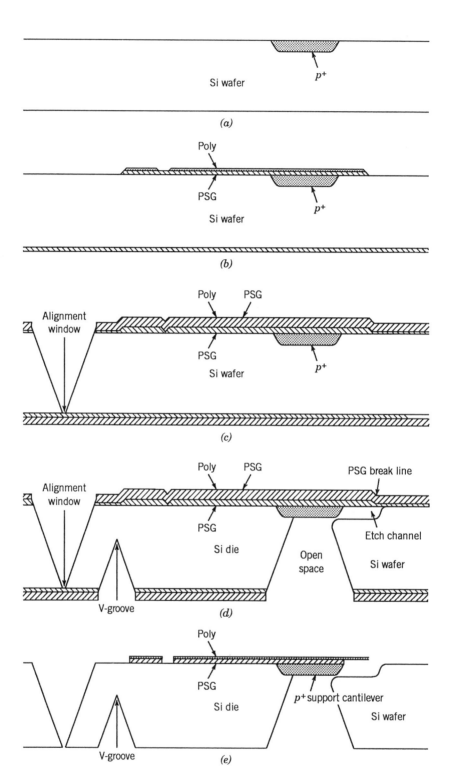

Figure 20.13. Processing sequence used to create the microgripper in Figure 20.13.

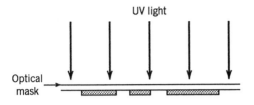

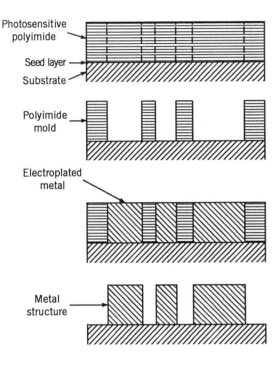

Figure 20.14. Schematic of DUV fabrication steps.

nickel anode and wafer causes nickel ions to migrate from the anode to the wafer, filling the voids with metal. The remaining resist can then be removed with an appropriate etchant, leaving the freestanding nickel microstructure. An example of a microgear and pin fabricated in the outlined manner is shown in Figure 20.15. Note that the surface texture of the electroplated structures appears rougher than the polysilicon surface.

X-ray Micromachining

Another technique for obtaining structures and devices with high aspect ratios uses the high energy and deep penetrating power of x-rays. After the far UV range (approximately 200 nm), the vacuum UV extends down to 40 nm where the soft x-ray region begins (from 20 to 100 nm most materials are opaque to radiation). One of the key considerations for using x-rays for micromachining is the type of source. Point sources, such as plasma or electron bombardment, are relatively inexpensive, have a small footprint, and are readily available. These sources have two major drawbacks: (*1*) they are not very bright (low flux) and (*2*) because the x-rays cannot be collimated, the finite source size causes penumbral blurring and beam divergence causes the geometric distortion shown in Figure 20.16. These problems are reduced with a synchrotron radiation source. The high flux radiation from the synchrotron is inherently collimated and is available throughout the soft x-ray regime from 0.1 to 40 nm. The drawbacks are the synchro-

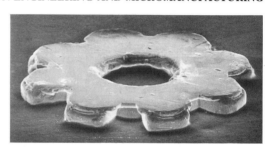

Figure 20.15. Microgear made by DUV fabrication (29). Photograph courtesy of Institute for Micromanufacturing; sample, Georgia Tech.

tron's cost (approximately $20 million in 1993 dollars for the storage ring alone), its large footprint (on the order of 29 m radius for a warm ring), and relative complexity (in this case you must be a rocket (synchrotron) scientist to run it). The synchrontron produces radiation by accelerating relativistic electrons normal to the direction of motion using bending magnets. A schematic representation of the storage ring at the Center for Advanced Microstructures and Devices (CAMD) (Louisiana State University in Baton Rouge) is shown in Figure 20.17. This figure shows the multiple beam lines, the bending magnets, the linear accelerator for the initial injection of the electrons, and the three straight sections that could be used for undulators or wigglers (i.e., beam-modification devices). The radiation can be obtained at a number of locations on the storage ring and requires a beam transport line and exposure station at the end of the beam line. The collimated horizontal fan of radiation available at the exposure station would typically be 5 × 50 mm.

The dominant process for micromachining with x-rays is the LIGA, process which was developed at the Nuclear Research Center in Karlsruhe (KfK), Germany (11, 12). The basic steps for the LIGA process are shown in Figure 20.18. The process is similar to the optical lithography processes for the exposure and development steps. As Figure 20.19 shows, there are numerous possibilities for the mass production of structures and devices using either the metal or plastic structures. Of particular interest is the ability to mass produce parts with the metal molds without reusing the radiation source. Yield from this process is probably low; however, data are not readily available.

Advantages of the LIGA-type processes include lateral dimensions less than 5 μm with structural heights on the order of 1 mm and aspect ratios greater than 200, and a flexible design

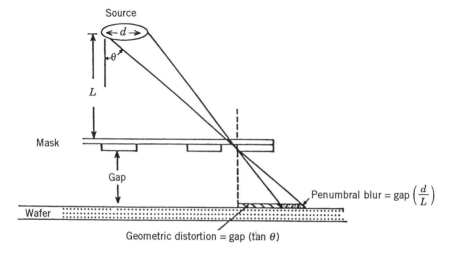

Figure 20.16. Aerial image distortions caused by the finite source size and beam divergence from point x-ray sources.

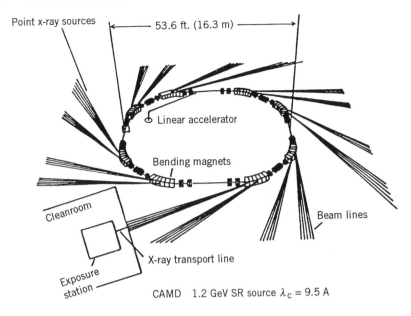

CAMD   1.2 GeV SR source λ_c = 9.5 A

Figure 20.17.   Schematic of the synchrotron (storage ring) at CAMD.

with a wide variety of materials (e.g., plastic, nickel, and ceramics). Even at the extremely high aspect ratios, good edge acuity can be obtained as is shown in Figure 20.19. The limiting factors for the resolution, accuracy, and depth for the LIGA process are the latent dose image and the dynamic behavior of the resist-developer system (24). The resist of choice for x-ray micromachining applications is PMMA; however, x-ray resist research is ongoing. The other accuracy limiting effects are the Fresnel diffraction from the soft x-rays and the high energy photoelectron effect in the resist in the harder x-ray regime. These two effects can be plotted versus the wavelength of the radiation source as shown in Figure 20.20. From this figure the nominal wavelength for x-ray micromachining is 0.2 to 0.3 nm (24).

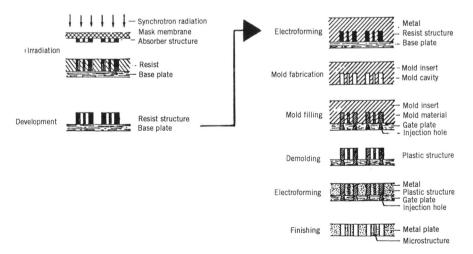

Figure 20.18.   Basic steps of the LIGA process. (Courtesy of Ref. 12.)

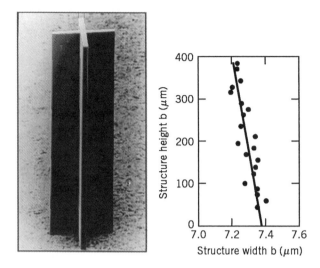

Figure 20.19. Lateral dimension deviation of a cross-bar test structure (24).

A typical x-ray exposure schematic is shown in Figure 20.21 (27). The prefilter (Kapton) lowers the absorbed energy below the damaging dose—the dose that would cause the resist, PMMA in this case, to swell and bubble—while the mask absorber (gold) reduces the dosage below the threshold dose (above which development would occur). The development dose is the dose required for sufficient exposure of the PMMA so that complete removal occurs upon development. In this case, approximately 300 μm of resist would be completely exposed in 3 hours using the storage ring at the University of Bonn.

The discussion above has presented a brief overview of x-ray micromachining, more recent developments include sacrificial layer LIGA (or SLIGA), an area the x-ray micromachining

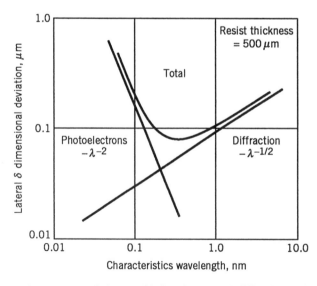

Figure 20.20. LIGA accuracy limits considering the Fresnel diffraction and photoelectron effect (24).

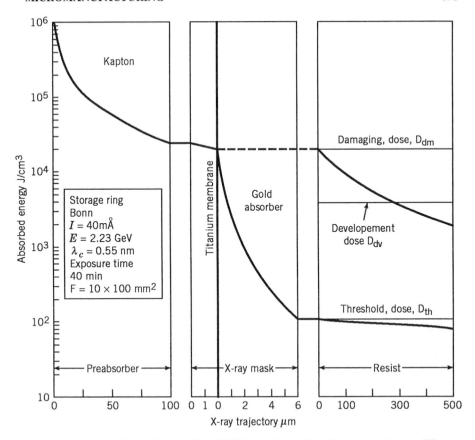

Figure 20.21. Absorbed energy in a PMMA specimen along the x-ray trajectory (27).

group at the University of Wisconsin has pioneered (13) and stepped structures using multiple x-ray exposures (26). In LIGA, continuous control of the device or structure width, with depth, has been very limited. New designs for the exposure stations will allow for tilt and rotation of the mask and wafer with respect to the synchrotron radiation source and could make the LIGA process truly three-dimensional. Interesting applications of this exciting technology are discussed in a later section.

20.4 ALTERNATIVE–COMPLIMENTARY MEMS PROCESSES

There are several micromachining technologies that complement the lithography methods. The alternative processes are more conventional machining processes that have been modified to allow small feature size and some irregular feature shapes. In all of these processes, except the energy machining processes, the bulk material removal exerts forces on the sample and the cutting tool. Because of this, the tools are delicate and much care must be taken to minimize cutting forces through proper cutting parameters and minimum vibration. The first of the alternative processes is microdiamond machining.

Microdiamond Machining

Microdiamond machining differs from more conventional diamond machining in that the tool's cutting edge features are below the 100-μm range. The goal is for small workpiece features

TABLE 20.3. Diamond Machinable and Difficult-to-Machine Materials

Machinable Crystals	Machinable Metals	Machinable Plastics	Difficult-to-Machine Metals
Silicon	Aluminum and alloys	Polymethyl-methacrylate	Nickel alloys
Germanium	Cooper and alloys	Propylene	Beryllium and alloys
Lithium niobate	Gold	Styrene	Ferrous alloys[a]
Zinc sulfide	Silver	Polycarbonate	Stainless steel[a]
Gallium arsenide	Tin	Fluoroplastics	Titanium and alloys
Cadmium telluride	Zinc, electroless nickel		Molybdeum and alloys[a]

[a] Prolonged tool life has been demonstrated when machined at liquid nitrogen temperature (30).

rather than high surface finish (i.e., optics, etc.). The properties that make diamond an excellent cutting tool (high hardness, stiffness, thermal conductivity, and sharp edge) are exploited to allow a high strength tool with a small cutting area. Because of the high stress and temperature present in the cutting zone, not all engineering materials are diamond machinable. The diamond machinabilities of some typical engineering materials are summarized in Table 20.3. A material that is not considered diamond machinable may well be cut by diamond, but it presents a severe machining environment, greatly reducing tool life.

Although diamond is available in both single crystal and polycrystalline morphologies, single crystal is preferred in microdiamond machining because of the high degree of accuracy obtained when the cutting edge is aligned with a crystallographic plane. A comparison of the mechanical and thermal properties between diamond and high speed steel is shown in Table 20.4. As can be seen, diamond is stronger, stiffer, capable of a higher operating temperature, and a better thermal conductor. High thermal conductivity is especially important when machining plastics or other low thermal conductivity materials. The heat generated in the cutting interface is more easily carried away by the diamond, thus reducing the cutting interface temperature and helping maintain dimensional accuracy and proper cutting conditions.

Because features of less than 100 μm are routinely machined, the positional accuracy and stability of the machine tool are important factors. The workpiece is usually turned by an air-bearing spindle. Air bearings have several advantages over mechanical and hydrodynamic bearings. Under normal operation, the rotor rides on a cushion of air separating it from the stator. Because there is no physical contact of the axial or thrust faces, there is no vibration from mechanical rolling elements. However, because air bearings have a one order of magnitude less stiffness than mechanical bearings, workpiece balance is important to reduce dynamic-induced vibration. An air bearing is also inherently cleaner and has much lower drag at high rotational speed than mechanical bearings. The tool positioner must also have high accuracy, resolution, and repeatability for the production of small features with reasonable tolerances. A 100-μm-size feature with a relative tolerance of 0.1%, requires tool positioning accuracy of 0.20 of a wavelength of visible light. Therefore, active positional feedback schemes are almost always used. These normally incorporate either (1) a linear or angular interferometer or (2) a linear or rotational interferometer-based optical encoder. Tool accuracy and repeatability in the nanometer range is possible. Thermal effects dominate at this level of precision.

TABLE 20.4. Mechanical Properties of Diamond and High Speed Steel[a]

Characteristic	Diamond	High Speed Steel
Elastic modulus, GPa	1000	206
Shear modulus, GPa	300	79
Critical tensile stress, GPa	4[b]	4
Room-temperature thermal conductivity W/(m · K)	1600	60
Maximum cutting temperature, °C	1600	650

[a] Refs. 31 and 32.
[b] 1600°C.

Figure 20.22.   Diamond machined micro heat exchanger plate. Courtesy of Institute for Micromanufacturing.

Applications for microdiamond machining in micromanufacturing are widespread. Examples include flow passages for microcompact heat exchangers and surface enhancement to reduce convection boundary resistance. Figure 20.22 is a portion of a single heat exchanger plate. The entire plate is 25 mm on a side and contains 50 flow passages. Each passage is 100 μm wide at the bottom and 80 μm deep. The material is high conductivity copper foil 125 μm thick. When stacked and bonded, these plates form a cross-flow heat exchanger 1 cc in volume with a weight less than 0.3 N (1 oz). Such a device has a thermal capacity of many kilowatts, depending on operating conditions. Figure 20.23 is a view of a microturbulator plate that can be used to enhance boundary layer disruption in microcompact heat exchangers. The foil may be successively cut in several directions to produce relief structures (33).

Microdiamond machining may also be used to complement lithography processes. Microdiamond machining has been demonstrated to produce trenches in PMMA with an aspect ratio of over 10 : 1 and a width of 100 μm. This provides a means for low aspect ratio structures in PMMA at a small fraction of the cost necessary in x-ray lithography.

Microdrilling

Other alternative fabrication methods are microdrilling and micromilling. Microdrilling uses micron-scale spade drill bits that are produced by grinding and lapping high speed steel or tungsten carbide. At present, twist drills of the size used (25 μm and less in diameter) are not generally available. Twist drills of this size can be made by with the ion-milling process, which will be presented below. The spade drill blank is inserted into a high concentricity, hardened steel mandrel and ground as a single unit. The mandrel is used as the spindle in the drilling operation. In the drill, the mandrel rides on flat diamond bearings in the form of a V-block. This eliminates vibration and eccentricity from mechanical bearings. Drills with an aspect ratio of 7 : 1 are common down to a diameter of 10 μm. These drills are used for hard materials such as stainless steel. Drills with higher aspect ratios are under design and production for the drilling of PMMA.

A tool geometry similar to a spade drill but with a flat end and side edges may be used for micromilling. In milling, the side forces can be destructive to the tool; therefore, the tool is

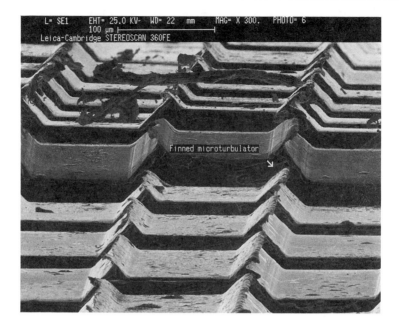

Figure 20.23. Boundary-layer microturbulators for enhanced convection. Courtesy of Institute for Micromanufacturing.

generally larger than in drilling. However, the micromills may be used to produce features with a complex geometry on the PMMA surface. In addition, they may be used to enhance the geometry near the surface of lithography-based features (such as rounded edge at the top of a trench). Although microdrilling and milling are not yet mainstream alternative processes, they hold much promise because of the flexibility of the processes and the ability to machine sidewall features. An example of microdrilling is shown in Figure 20.24.

Micro–Electrical Discharge Machining

Electrical discharge machining (EDM) is an important precision machining process in conventional manufacturing. Perhaps the only disadvantage is the requirement that the workpiece be electrically conductive. Micro-EDM uses a high frequency, low energy spark to ablate the workpiece material. The micro-EDM electrode is a small, round wire, which is held such that a gap of only several microns is maintained between the electrode and workpiece. Air is used as a dielectric fluid in the gap. Fresh dielectric is pulled into the gap because the electrode is spun at high speed (several thousand rpm). The discharge circuit consists of a capacitor, charging resistor, and direct current power supply. Discharge of the capacitor takes place when sufficient voltage is present to break down the dielectric barrier. Typical discharge is 60 to 110 V. So that a high surface finish is maintained, the discharge energy must be in the nanojoule range. This requires special care in limiting stray capacitance in the entire machine. Therefore, many of the machine components are ceramic or insulators. Micro-EDM has been used to machine micron-size holes in silicon and stainless steel (34).

Laser Ablation Micromachining

Laser ablation micromachining (LAM) is the first of two types of energy beam machining that have been adapted to micromanufacturing. LAM uses a small, low power excimer laser that has little beam divergence. By using converging optics, the focus spot size can be made quite small,

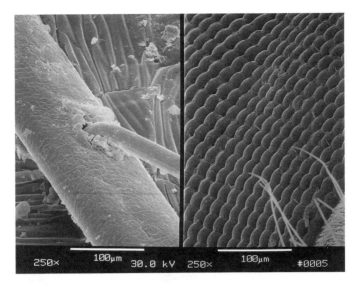

Figure 20.24. Individual lenslets of a fly's eye compared to a 25 μm diameter wire placed through a microdrilled hole in a human hair. Photograph courtesy of Institute for Micromanufacturing; sample, National Jet Co.

thus concentrating the light energy, which results in high workpiece temperature when absorbed. Typically ultraviolet (excimer) lasers are used with wavelengths in the 190- to 300-nm range. LAM can be used in two ways. The first is more similar to lithography. In projection LAM, a mask with openings of the final feature size is used. The spot size of the laser is normally about 0.5 μm because of the laser beam divergence and the diffraction limitation of the focusing optics. This small of a beam may not be practical for direct machining because of the time required to machine larger features. Therefore, a beam with a larger diameter (10 μm) can be used, which is transmitted or absorbed by the mask allowing small, complex-shaped patterns on the sample surface.

The second LAM method is direct writing of the feature shape with the laser beam. This method has longer write times than the projection LAM, but it can use a lower power laser because there is no mask absorption. A key parameter in LAM is the beam fluence on the sample. Typical fluence levels for various spot sizes and several material classifications are shown in Figure 20.25 while a typical written surface is shown in Figure 20.26.

Focused Ion Beam Machining

A second energy beam micromachining technique is focused ion beam machining (FIB). FIB typically operates like a scanning electron microscope except gallium ions are accelerated at the workpiece instead of electrons. Because of the much higher kinetic energy of the heavy ions, material may be removed from the sample. An FIB uses a pointed tungsten filament wetted with gallium. A 6-keV extraction voltage is used to liberate gallium ions, similar to a cold field emission SEM. The ions are then accelerated to 20 keV and guided to impact the substrate. The entire system is under computer control.

The desired geometry is rendered as a pixel map, then the ion beam can be directed to any pixel or series of pixels and will dwell on a pixel for a certain time, depending on the required dosage. The beam is deflected over the sample by an eight-pole electromagnet in the column. Although the current through the sample is in the nanoampere range, the target current density is on the order of 1 A/cm^2. Many materials can be FIB machined. The spot size is approximately 0.3 μm in diameter, so small features are also possible. A scanning electron micrograph of a tuning fork in tungsten is shown in Figure 20.27. For certain materials, the machining rate can

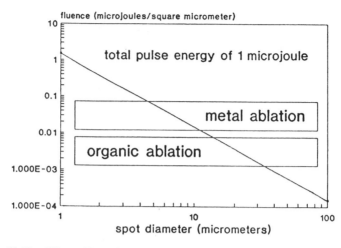

Figure 20.25.   Effect of laser fluence level on LAM. Courtesy of Potomac Photonics.

Figure 20.26.   Diamond microgear machined with KrF laser. Courtesy of Potomac Photonics.

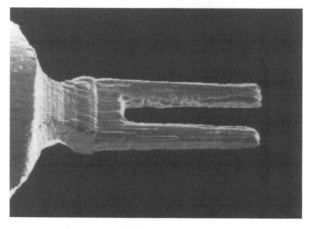

Figure 20.27.   Tungsten ''tuning fork'' made with FIB. Courtesy of Institute for Micromanufacturing.

Figure 20.28.   RIE of a diamond with a FIB. Courtesy of Institute for Micromanufacturing.

be increased by introducing a reactive gas into the sample chamber. Diamond, for example, will be machined much faster if xenon difluoride (XeF_2) is present at the diamond surface. Such a process was presented in the previous section. A micrograph of reactive ion etched diamond is shown in Figure 20.28.

20.5   APPLICATIONS

This section presents some commercial applications of the technologies described in this chapter. It is recognized that this field is new and as it matures more commercially viable applications will come to market. In fact, it is anticipated that by the time this handbook goes to print, several additional applications not covered here will be available. As mentioned in the introduction to this chapter, one of the first commercial applications of the MEMS technology was the thermal print head, initially marketed by Texas Instruments in the late 1970s. Since then, many other applications have come to market; however, no applications have stirred as much interest among both investors and researchers as microsensors, which are currently fueling the growth of companies devoted to MEMS products. The following sections will discuss some of the prominent applications of microdevices, recognizing that due to space other potential future applications cannot be fully covered here.

Pressure Sensors

Micropressure sensors are made primarily by bulk-micromachining processes and are packaged on either glass or ceramic substrates. Examples of micromachined pressure sensors before and after packaging are shown in Figure 20.29. The current applications target medical, manufacturing, and consumer product markets. In the medical arena, micropressure sensors have replaced other macroscale sensors. Traditionally, blood pressure is measured with an occlusive cuff around a limb; however, in some applications, in situ measurements are desirable. For example, in some cardiac diagnoses and monitoring situations it is necessary to take the blood pressure directly in a vein or artery. Before micropressure sensors, a fluid-filled catheter was inserted into the artery or vein and connected to a commercial pressure sensor outside the body. Now micropressure sensors can be mounted directly at the tip of the catheter to measure arterial or venous blood pressure. The measured pressure is converted to a voltage signal, which is carried out of the body to a signal processing unit. The resulting system provides true in situ measurements, reduces the amount of equipment in the operating room, and is easier to insert.

Another biomedical application for micropressure sensors is beside drip systems. Traditionally, bedside intravenous (iv) delivery systems have been used in hospitals to control a patient's fluid balance and deliver drugs. The flow rate of these systems is controlled by gravity and either a rotary valve or a clamp on the polymer delivery tubing. These old-fashioned drip systems are being replaced by a bank of infusion pumps, which are controlled by micropressure sensors. The pumps provide the motive force for delivery at a rate that is controlled by a programmable microprocessor, which in turn uses the micropressure sensor signals to determine the delivery rate. Both iv fluid and drugs can be delivered and monitored this way. The bank of micropressure sensors is disposable, to minimize the risk of infection.

Smallest
production
pressure
sensors using Silicon
Fusion Bonding for
catheter tip medical
applications (3 chips
located on the head
of a pin for size
comparison).

Pressure sensor die family
(NPD) demonstrates the size
advantage of Silicon Fusion
Bonding (three small chips
in the middle foreground) in
comparison to the more
traditional silicon-glass die
structures.

(a)   (b)

Figure 20.29. Silicon micropressure sensors before and after packaging. Courtesy of Lucas NovaSensor.

In the automotive area, micropressure sensors are used in a variety of locations, depending on the manufacturer. For instance, they have been used in intake manifolds, engine oil delivery systems, hydraulic and brake line lines, air bag canisters, and combustion chambers. There are also active programs to use micropressure sensors in other areas. For instance, Goodyear will soon be marketing a "smart" truck tire that, among many functions, will be able to measure and keep track of the inflation pressure.

In the consumer products area, pressure sensors can be found in several items. Electronic tire pressure gauges contain a micropressure sensor in the tip that delivers a voltage signal to a processor that in turn drives a liquid crystal display (LCD), showing the reading in either pounds per square inch, pascals, or atmospheres. Some digital watches have a micropressure sensor to measure barometric pressure variations to determine altitude or measure depth under water for scuba divers. Some pneumatic exercise equipment employ micropressure sensors to determine the level of effort the user is putting forth. Even the apparel industry is gearing up to use micropressure sensors. A couple of the major athletic shoe manufacturers are conducting feasibility and marketing studies for a "pump" shoe that will be able to give the wearer a readout of the air bladder pressure.

Microaccelerometers

Microaccelerometers have found a widespread use in the automotive industry. Perhaps the best known of these applications is the air bag. A successful air bag system needs to (1) constantly monitor the acceleration of the automobile, (2) determine whether the deceleration has reached a crash threshold, and (3) activate an air bag only when the threshold has been exceeded. It is well known that successful air bag deployment systems were available as far back as the mid-1960s. However, these systems were not commercially viable for two principal reasons: safety was not as important a factor in the public's mind then as it is now and acceleration sensors and control systems with sufficient sensitivity and accuracy were prohibitively priced for the consumer market. With the advent of the *self-testing,* silicon microaccelerometer, which can be batch produced for a few dollars a piece, the era of the air bag system as standard equipment has arrived.

There are other applications of microaccelerometers in the automotive area. Batch-produced microaccelerometers are used in antiskid braking systems (ABS) to determine when to take the brakeline pressure away from the driver. They are also used in both active and semiactive suspension systems to determine the acceleration variation at each wheel (for fully active suspensions), which can then be used to provide a compensating displacement of the suspension system. Microaccelerometers are used in many antitheft devices to determine when a car has been moved without consent of the owner. Finally, they are also used in large numbers in laboratory studies of crashes to determine the dynamic deformation of the car structure during impact. Note that traditional piezoelectric accelerometers are orders of magnitude more expensive, making it more difficult to justify their use in these type of applications.

Microtips

The technologies described in this chapter are being used to create microtips that can be used in two relatively new forms of scanning microscopy: AFM and STM. The first tip is made on a micromachined silicon cantilever beam using bulk and surface micromachining techniques, whereas the second microtip is made with an FIB. The micromachining techniques previously described allow the first tip to have a two-atom tip, although some researchers claim that a one-atom tip is possible. The second tip has a base approximately 4 μm in diameter and a usable tip length of more than 100 μm.

An exciting new use of microtips is the reverse process of that used in STMs. Rather than using the tip to scan the surface, the tip can be used to modify the surface. Researchers working on storage devices predict that storage densities of up to 1 Tbit/cm^2 (10^{12} bits/cm^2) may be possible using microtips and the same principles used in CD technology, exceeding magnetic storage limitations by orders of magnitude. Many other sensors and actuators fabricated by the technology described here are possible, and active research efforts around the world are being carried out to commercialize them as well as provide more new applications. Because of space restrictions it is not possible to cover applications still in the research stages here. The reader is encouraged to review the suggested readings at the end of the chapter to gain a more complete and up-to-date understanding of this young, fast-moving field.

20.6 SUMMARY

The key to future technological applications will be the ability to integrate rapidly and effectively the macro, mini, micro, and nano worlds. Basic science is driving the scale down to, and beyond, the nanodomain. These investigations are necessary to understand material properties and behavior at the fundamental level. These studies are also necessary to understand the fundamental interactions between materials and outside influences, such as electrical and magnetic fields, gravity, light, and electromechanical driving forces. Although the science learned at this level will greatly aid in the design and control of micro- and nanodevices, these devices must still adapt to, and become useful for, the macro world.

Total integration will not be possible at the process level because of the large difference in the dimensional orders of magnitude within the domain. Therefore, it is necessary to design and fabricate assist devices so that either humans or their kinematic extensions can grasp, manipulate, position, adjust, and assemble nano, micro, and mini things into useful systems that are connected to the macro world. In addition, it will be necessary to develop the speed, sensitivity, reliability, and inspection aspects of micromanufacturing so that these systems may move from the laboratory to a production environment.

Certainly, there will be many technical factors to overcome in the development of MEMS technology, and while the United States currently has the technical advantage in many areas of MEMS, this lead is quickly eroding. Funding for MEMS research in Japan and Germany can be estimated at 5 to 10 times the expenditure in the United States (approximately $20 million/yr in the United States) (35), and commitment from industry appears to be lacking. A potentially more damaging problem may be the management of the technology (36), or lack thereof in the case of the United States. The awesome display of technology management and transfer by the Japanese through the Ministry of International Trade and Technology (MITI) and the Germans through the VDI/VDE Technology Center are just two examples of their commitment to this technology. In the United States, there appears to be mounting interest in MEMS; however, each governmental agency (recently NIST, NASA, DARPA, and the U.S. Army) is doing its own technology assessment with little or no coordination or even knowledge of the others' activities.

The world market for this technology has been estimated at over 10 billion ECU (European Currency Unit, $1.25/ECU) by the year 2000 (9) with the beneficiary being almost every industry type: "We must be aware that microsystems components very seldom will be a business by themselves. The economic success will depend primarily on the advantage they bring for the customer using a system product" (9). Embedded MEMS devices and systems will certainly be important; however, economic success for this technology in this country will ultimately depend on how effectively we take this technology from the laboratory to manufacturing.

BIBLIOGRAPHY

1. O.N. TUFTE, P.W. CHAPMAN, and D. LONG, "Silicon Diffused–Element Piezoresistive Diaphragms," *J. Appl. Phys.* **33,** 3322–3329 (1962).

2. H.C. NATHANSON, W.E. NEWELL, R.A. WICKSTROM, and J.R. DAVIS, "The Resonant-Gate Transistor," *IEEE Trans. ED.* **14,** 117–133 (1967).

3. R.T. HOWE and R.S. MULLER, "Resonant-Microbridge Vapor Sensor," *IEEE Trans.* **33,** 499–506 (1986).

4. *Texas Instruments Thermal Character Print Head, EPN3620,* Texas Instruments, 1977, Bull. DL-S7712505.

5. H. FUJITA, "Trends and Outlook for Micromachining and Micromechatronics," *JEE,* special issue, part 2, 26–31 (1992).

6. K. PETERSEN, "Silicon as a Mechanical Material," *Proc. IEEE* **70**(5), 420–457 (1982).

7. R. MULLER, *From ICs to Microstructures: Materials and Technologies,* paper presented at the IEEE MEMS 87 Workshop, Hyannis Port, Mass. 1987.

8. K.D. WISE and K. NAJAFI, "Microfabrication Techniques for Integrated Sensors and Microsystems," *Science,* **254,** 1335–1341.

9. G. TSCHULENA, *Micromechanics Business Opportunities,* paper presented at the MST 92 Conference 1992.

10. K. PETERSEN, *The Silicon Micromechanics Foundry,* paper presented at the IEEE MEMS 87 Workshop, Hyannis Port, Mass., 1987.

11. E.W. BECKER, H. BETZ, W. EHRFELD, W. GLASHAUSER, A. HEUBERGER, H.J. MICHAEL, D. MÜNCHMEYER, S. PONGRATZ, and R.V. SIEMENS, "Production of Separation Nozzle Systems for Uranium Enrichment by a Combination of X-ray Lithography and Galvano-plastics, *Naturwissenschaften* **69,** 520–523 (1982).

12. W. EHRFELD, P. BLEY, F. GÖTZ, P. HAGMAN, A. MANER, J. MOHR, H.O. MOSER, D. MÜNCHMEYER, W. SCHELB D, SCHMIDT, and E.W. BECKER, *Fabrication of Microstructures Using the LIGA Process,* paper presented at the IEEE MEMS 87 Workshop Hyannis Port, Mass., 1987.

13. H. GUCKEL, K. SKROBIS, T. CHRISTENSON, J. KLEIN, S. HAN, B. CHOI, and E. LOVELL, *Fabrication of Assembled Micromechanical Components via Deep X-ray Lithography,* paper presented at the IEEE MEMS 91 Workshop, Nara, Japan, 1991.

14. S.D. SENTURIA, *Microfabricated Structures for the Measurement of Mechanical Properties and Adhesion of Thin Films,* paper presented at the 4th International Conference on Solid-State and Sensors and Actuators Transducers, Tokyo, 1987.

15. W.S. TRIMMER and K.J. GABRIEL, "Design Consideration for a Practical Electrostatic Micromotor," *Sensors Actuators* **11,** 189–206 (1987).

16. H. FUJITA and A. OMODAKA, "The Fabrication of an Electrostatic Linear Actuator by Silicon Micromachining," *IEEE Trans.* **35,** 731–734 (1988).

17. S.C. JACOBSEN, R.H. PRICE, J.E. WOOD, T. RYTTING, and M. RAFAELOF, *Wobble Motor: An Electrostatic Planetry-Armature Microactuator,* paper presented at the IEEE MEMS 89 Workshop, Salt Lake City, Utah, 1989.

18. K. KURIBAYASHI, *Milimeter Size Joint Actuator Using Shape Memory Alloy,* paper presented at the IEEE MEMS 89 Workshop, Salt Lake City, Utah, 1989.

19. C.R. FRIEDRICH AND R.O. WARRINGTON, *Machining of Metal Foils for Use in Microcompact Heat Exchangers,* paper presented at the MST 90 Conference, Berlin, Germany, 1990.

20. L.C. KONG, B.G. ORR, and K.D. WISE, *A Micromachined Silicon Scan Tip for an Atomic Force Microscope,* paper presented at the IEEE Solid-State Sensor Workshop, Hilton Head, S.C. 1990.

21. N.C. MACDONALD, *Single Crystal Silicon Nanomechanisms for Scanned-Probe Device Arrays,* paper presented at the IEEE Solid-State Sensor and Actuator Workshop, Hilton Head, S.C., 1992.

22. J. SIMON, G. ENGELMANN, O. EHRMANN, and H. REICHL, *Plating of Microstructures for Sensors,* paper presented at the MST 91 Conference, Berlin, Germany, 1991.

23. C.J. EVANS, *Precision Engineering: An Evolutionary View,* Cranfield University Press, 1989.

24. W. EHRFELD and D. MUNCHMEYER, "Three Dimensional Microfabrication Using Synchrotron Radiation," Nucl. Instru. Methods Phys. Res., **A303**, 523–531 (1991).

25. E. BASSOUS, "Anisotropic Etching of Silicon for 3-D Microstructure Fabrication—A Review," *IEEE Trans.,* 619–645.

26. M. HARMENING, W. BACHER, P. BLEY, AL EL-KHOLI, H. KALB, B. KOWANZ, W. MENZ, A. MICHEL, J. MEHR, *Molding of Three-Dimensional Microstructures by the LIGA Process,* paper presented at the IEEE MEMS 92 Workshop, Travëmunde, Germany, 1992.

27. P. BLEY, W. MENZ, W. BACHER, K. FEIT, M. HARMENING, H. HEIN, J. MOHR, W. SCHOMBURG, and W. STARK, *Applications of the LIGA Process in Fabrication of Three-Dimensional Mechanical Structures,* paper presented at the 1991 International Microprocesses Conference, Kanazawa, Japan, 1991.

28. C.J. KIM, A.P. PISANO, and R.S. MULLER, "Silicon-Processed Overhanging Microgripper," *J. Microelectromech. Sys.* **1**(1), 31–36 (1992).

29. B. FRASIER and M.G. ALLEN, *High Aspect Ratio Electroplated Microstructures Using a Photosensitive Polyimide Process,* paper presented at the IEEE MEMS 92 Workshop, Travëmunde, Germany, 1992.

30. C.J. Evans, personal communication, October 1991.

31. G.V. SAMSONOV, *Handbook of the Physicochemical Properties of the Elements,* Plenum Press, New York, 1968.

32. E.P. DEGAMO, J.T. BLACK, and R.A. KOUSER, *Materials and Processes in Manufacturing,* Mcmillan, New York, 1984.

33. C.R. FRIEDRICH, J. HE, and R.O. WARRINGTON, *Modeling and Development of a 3-D Fluid Micro Compact Heat Exchanger,* paper presented at the Athens 91 Conference, Athens, Greece, 1991.

34. T. MASAKI et al., *Micro Electro–Discharge Machining and Its Applications,* paper presented at the IEEE MEMS 90 Workshop, Napa Valley, Calif., 1990.

35. K.W. BREDLEY and R. STEEB, Rand Corp.

36. M.B. LYNCH and R.O. WARRINGTON, *Research Mix and Transfer of Technology in Micromanufacturing Research,* paper submitted to the 4th International Conference on Management of Technology.

Suggested Readings

BRODIE and MURRAY, *The Physics of Microfabrication,* Plenum Press, New York, 1987.

DANGLEMAYER, *ESD Program Management,* Van Nostrand Reinhold Co., Inc., New York, 1990.

D.J. ELLIOT, *Integrated Circuit Fabrication Technology,* 2nd ed., McGraw-Hill Book Co., Inc., New York, 1989.

Introduction to Microlithography, ACS Symposium Series, 1983.

R.C. JAEGER, *Introduction to Microelectronic Fabrication,* Vol. 5, Addison-Wesley Publishing Co., Inc., Reading, Mass.

JAIN, *Excimer Laser Lithography,* SPIE Press, 1990.

KOCH, *Handbook on Synchrotron Radiation,* Vols. 1a, 1b, and 2, Elsevier, Amsterdam, The Netherlands, 1983.

KOZICKI, Hoenig, and Robinson, *Cleanroom Practices,* Van Nostrand Reinhold Co., Inc., New York, 1991.

W.M. MOREAU, *Semiconductor Lithography—Principles, Practices and Materials,* Plenum Press, New York, 1987.

Prolith/2 User's Manual, Finle Technologies, 1992.

S.M. SZE, VLSI Technology, McGraw-Hill Book Co., Inc., New York, 1993.

WARNES, *Electronic Materials, Van Nostrand Reinhold Co., Inc., New York, 1990.*

Useful Journals and Proceedings

IEEE MEMS Workshop (annual conference proceedings)

Journal of Microelectromechanical Systems (IEEE/ASME)

Journal of Micromechanics and Microengineering (Institute of Physics)

Micro Systems Technologies (annual conference proceedings)

Nanotechnology (Institute of Physics)

Precision Engineering (Butterworth-Heinemann)

Sensors and Actuators (Elsevier Sequoia)

Solid State Sensors and Actuators (biannual conference proceedings)

Symposium on Microlithography (annual conference proceedings)

Transducers (biannual conference proceedings)

SECTION V
DESIGN OF MANUFACTURING SYSTEMS

CHAPTER 21
Analysis and Design of Manufacturing Systems

KATSUNDO HITOMI
Kyoto University

21.1 MEANINGS OF MANUFACTURING SYSTEMS

Definitions of Production and Manufacturing

Production means "to make something new" and stems from the word *producere* ("to lead forward"). From a broad viewpoint, production is a creation of utility, including tangible goods (products) and intangible services. However, in a narrow sense, production is understood to be "the transformation of raw materials into products by a series of energy applications, each of which affects well defined changes in the physical or chemical characteristics of the materials" (1). Because this definition applies only to producing tangible goods (products) such as in manufacturing and process industries, it is termed manufacturing (or manufacture).

The original meaning of *manufacturing* was "to make things by hand" (*manu factum*). However, the present meaning is much broader: the conversion of a design into a finished product. *Production* has a more narrow sense, namely, the physical act of making the product (2). In 1983, CIRP defined manufacturing as a series of interrelated activities and operations involving the design, materials selection, planning, manufacturing production, quality assurance, management and marketing of the products of the manufacturing industries. (CIRP is the International Conference on Production Engineering.)

As explained above, production creates utility or increases the measure of value of economic goods—either tangible (products) or intangible (services)—which are outputs generated by activities of conversion from inputs called factors of production (raw materials, productive labor, productive facilities, and production methods). Raw materials are converted technologically through production processes, creating tangible products (manufacturing) and intangible services. This activity can be viewed as an input–output system, as shown in Figure 21.1 (3).

Definitions of Systems

As described above, production and manufacturing make up an input–output system. The word *system* appeared in 1619, meaning "organized whole." The essential sense of this term captures its organic (or materialistic) characteristics, or the synergy effect, i.e., the total optimization is greater than the sum of the partial optimizations. This effect was suggested by Laozi, a Chinese philosopher, about 2500 yr ago; a bit later, it was noted independently by the Greek philosopher Aristotelēs.

The state that is not systemized is *chaos*. It was first recognized and mentioned by the Chinese philosopher Zhuanzi about 2400 yr ago. This word now means a mode that creates an unforeseen irregular behavior or pattern despite the deterministic character of following a certain, specific rule.

The four basic attributes that characterize the system are as follows:

1. *Assemblage.* A system consists of a plural number of distinguishable units. A unit that behaves with a strong independence in a system is called a module, or holon.

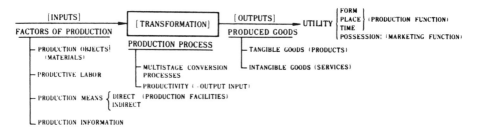

Figure 21.1. Basic meaning of production and manufacturing.

2. *Relationship*. For several units assembled together to be admissible as a system, a relationship (or an interaction) must exist among the units.

3. *Goal Seeking*. An actual system as a whole performs a certain function or aims at a single or multiple objectives.

4. *Adaptability to Environment*. A specific, factual system behaves to adapt to the changes in its surroundings, or external environment.

On the basis of the above consideration, four essential definitions of systems can now be given as follows (4):

1. *Abstract (or Basic) Definition*. Based on the first two attributes above, a system is a collection of recognizable units having relationships among the units.

2. *Structural (or Static) Definition*. Based on all four attributes, a system is a collection of recognizable units having relationships among the units, aiming at a specified single or multiple objectives subject to its external environment.

3. *Transformational (or Functional) Definition*. From the last attribute, the effects that the environment has on the system are inputs (these include unforeseen disturbances), and conversely, the effects that the system has on the environment are outputs. From this consideration, a system receives inputs from its environment, transforms them to outputs, and releases the outputs to the environment, while seeking to maximize the productivity of the transformation.

4. *Procedural (or Dynamic) Definition*. The process of transformation in the input–output system consists of a number of related stages, at each of which a specified work is carried out. By successively performing the work related to the precedence relationship of each of these stages, a function or task is completed. Thus a system is a procedure, i.e., a series of chronological, logical steps by which all repetitive tasks are performed.

Definitions of Manufacturing Systems

The phrase *manufacturing system* was employed as early as in 1815 by Owen, a utopian socialist; this term is not new. At that time it meant factory system, or a series of inventions that were created during the industrial revolution in Great Britain about 200 yr ago. Early in this century, the systems view in management and manufacturing was emphasized. Nowadays, the term *manufacturing system(s)* signifies a broad systematic view of manufacturing. It is basically recognized as a production function that converts the raw materials into the finished products, and this function is controlled by the management system that performs planning and control (5). It should be noted that from a wider viewpoint the manufacturing (production) system plays a role in constructing the international structural power together with the financial system, the security system, and the knowledge system (6).

On the basis of such concepts and views of the meanings of manufacturing and systems so far discussed, manufacturing (or production) systems can now be defined in the following three aspects (7):

1. *The Structural Aspect of Manufacturing Systems*. Based on structural (or static) definition of the system, the manufacturing system is a unified assemblage of hardware, which includes workers, production facilities (including tools, jigs, and fixtures), materials-

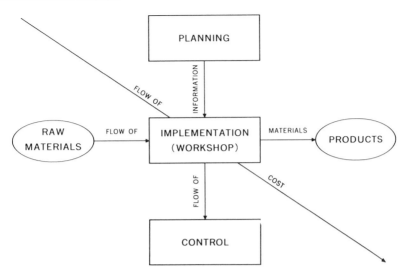

Figure 21.2. Three flows concerning manufacturing: flow of materials, flow of information, and flow of costs.

handling equipment, and other supplementary devices. Thus the structural aspect of the manufacturing system forms a static spatial structure of a plant, i.e., the plant layout. This aspect can be viewed as a production system. This phrase appeared in 1907. Since 1943 it has been also used to mean the inference mechanism operated by knowledge-based systems in the field of artificial intelligence (a different terminology should be introduced for this meaning).

2. *The Transformational Aspect of Manufacturing Systems.* Based on a transformational (or functional) definition of the system, the manufacturing system is defined as the conversion process of the factors of production, particularly the raw materials, into the finished products, aiming at a maximum productivity. This system is concerned with the flow of materials (or material flow). This is a common method of defining production systems or, in some cases, machining systems.

3. *The Procedural Aspect of Manufacturing Systems.* Based on a procedural definition of the system, the manufacturing system is the operating procedures of production. This constitutes the so-called management cycle, i.e., planning, implementation, and control. This process was recognized in Germany in the late 19th century, and Fayol established the functions of this process in 1916. Planning is selection, from among the alternatives, of the future course of action; implementation executes practical activities according to the plan (schedule); and control is measurement and correction of the performance of the activities to make sure that the management objectives and plans are being accomplished (8). Hence the manufacturing system plans and implements the productive activities to convert raw materials into products and controls this process to reduce or eliminate deviation of the actual performance from the plan. This procedure—production management—constitutes the flow of information (or information flow) for effective and economical production.

Both material and information flows pointed out in 2 and 3 above were advocated as early as 1913 by Church. In a modern factory equipped with a flexible manufacturing system (FMS) or computer-integrated manufacturing (CIM), the flow of information plays a major role and must be synchronized with the flow of materials (Figure 21.2).

Integrated Manufacturing Systems

In considering the detailed procedure of manufacturing it is practically useful to divide the procedure into the following four stages, as shown in Figure 21.3.

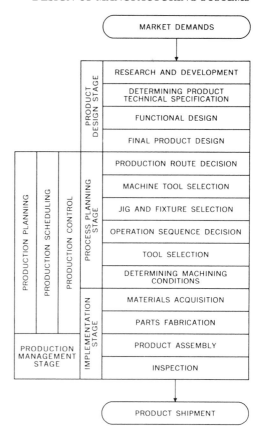

Figure 21.3. Procedure of integrated
manufacturing systems.

1. *Product Design Stage.* In this stage, the technical specifications of the products to meet
   the market needs are decided through research and development (R&D) activities, then
   the product design, including the specific functions and the ergonomic–aesthetic aspects,
   is completed for realizing the function, quality, reliability, and safety to be exhibited in
   use of products.

2. *Process Planning Stage.* To produce the products efficiently and economically, an optimal process route is decided and machines, tools, and jigs to be used are selected,
   together with optimum decisions of an operation sequence and machining conditions.

3. *Implementation Stage.* Raw materials are acquired, parts are machined, and then the
   required products are assembled and inspected. The finished products are shipped and
   distributed to the market or the customers.

4. *Production Management Stage.* The aggregate production plan and the detailed schedule for the above production processes are made, and the production control is done
   when needed.

An effective systems approach surely plays an important role in coordinating the interactions
between these four stages. This procedure is called an integrated manufacturing system (IMS).
    Recently, an IMS has also been recognized to be an *intelligent* manufacturing system, using
artificial intelligence such as expert systems and intelligent machines (9). At present, the Japanese Ministry of International Trade and Industry (MITI) plays a role in an international
cooperative IMS project, although this is not a new idea, because this phrase originally appeared in 1978.

Manufacturing Systems Engineering

It is fundamentally important for the efficient and economical execution of production activities to unify completely the material flow (manufacturing processes) and the information flow (production management). This unified and integrated approach to manufacturing discipline is called manufacturing (or production) systems engineering. This was advocated in 1975 (10). It emphasizes the following five aspects:

1. The clarification of the concepts of manufacturing systems and their basic functions and structures, including the problem of manufacturing systems design and, particularly, their material flow.

2. The optimization of manufacturing systems, focusing on optimum decision making for production.

3. The control of manufacturing systems and the automation of manufacturing, i.e., factory automation (FA) and computer-integrated manufacturing (CIM).

4. The processing of production information for manufacturing systems within a strict time frame, i.e., information flow for production management.

5. The recognition of economy for manufacturing systems, including cost management and profit planning, particularly, the flow of costs (or value) (see Figure 21.2).

Efficiency of Manufacturing Systems

Efficiency of manufacturing can be evaluated from several viewpoints.

QCD

Most often the product's value can be determined from the following three aspects: (*1*) function and quality—Q(uality), (*2*) production cost and price—C(ost), and (*3*) production quantity and time (due date)—D(elivery). Thus it is a primary objective of manufacturing to make products with a desired function fast and at a low cost.

Productivity

A measure of the effectiveness of the production process is normally termed productivity. It is abstractly defined as the ratio between input and output and is interpreted as the relationship between physical resources used in manufacturing and the units of output produced in a specified period of time. The contents and dimensions of the inputs and the outputs specify various kinds of productivity: physical productivity, for which the outputs are measured in units; value productivity, for which the outputs are measured in monetary values; and factor productivity, such as labor productivity, capital productivity, land productivity, and raw material productivity, each of which is related to each of the factors of production. Total productivity is concerned with all of the factors of production. It is an overall measure that expresses the contribution of the factors of production to efficiency attained by a manufacturing firm.

Figure 21.4 shows the international comparison of the trends of labor productivity increase in the manufacturing industry. Figure 21.5 represents the international comparison of physical productivity and added-value productivity in 1990 in the levels of the gross domestic product (GDP), the manufacturing sector per person employed and per hour, setting Japan's productivity at 100. Japan's manufacturing productivity is high in a physical sense but is especially low in added-value productivity per hour.

Yield Ratio and Efficiency Index

Table 21.1 shows Japan's industrial power in 1990. Yield ratio is the ratio of added value against output in percentage for an industrial sector; the larger this measure (maximum is 100), the more efficient that industrial sector is. Japan's manufacturing shows this measure to be 35.5%, which is the lowest among all the industrial sectors.

Efficiency index means the share of GDP over the proportion of labor force for an industrial sector. This measure indicates how efficiently an industrial sector is operating in a nation from the viewpoint of labor use. If this index holds a value above 1, that industrial sector is efficient;

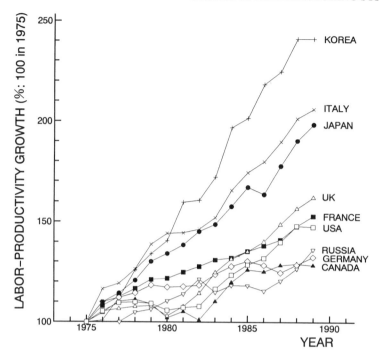

Figure 21.4. Trends of labor productivity increase in the manufacturing industry, international comparison.

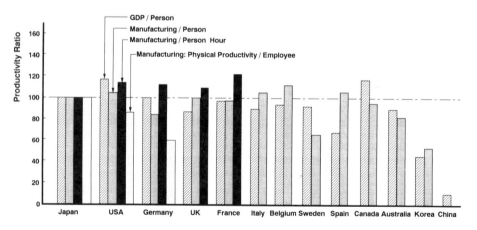

Figure 21.5. Physical productivity and added-value productivity per person employed and per hour, international comparison (Japan: 100).

TABLE 21.1. Japan's Industrial Power in 1990

Industry	Labor Force		Output			GDP			Yield Ratio Percent (B/A)	Efficiency Index (b/a)
	Million	Percent (a)	Trillion Yen (A)	Million Yen or per Capita	Percent	Trillion Yen (B)	Million Yen or per Capita	Percent (b)		
Primary	6.16	9.4	20.31	3.30	2.3	11.83	1.92	2.6	58.2	0.28
Agriculture, Forestry and Fishing	6.06	9.2	18.03	2.98	2.1	10.55	1.74	2.4	58.5	0.26
Mining	0.10	0.2	2.29	22.63	0.3	1.28	12.66	0.3	55.9	1.86
Secondary	21.73	33.1	456.33	21.00	52.1	177.06	8.15	39.5	38.8	1.19
Manufacturing	15.35	23.4	348.07	22.68	39.7	123.44	8.04	27.5	35.5	1.18
Construction	6.02	9.2	86.19	14.83	10.2	42.13	7.00	9.4	47.2	1.03
Electric, gas, and sanitary	0.37	0.6	19.07	51.81	2.2	11.49	31.22	2.6	60.3	4.58
Subtotal (goods production)	27.89	42.4	476.64	17.09	54.4	188.89	6.77	42.1	39.6	0.99
Tertiary (production)	37.83	57.6	399.98	10.57	45.6	259.49	6.86	57.9	64.9	1.01
Commerce	11.70	17.8	84.91	7.26	9.7	54.50	4.66	12.2	64.2	0.68
Others	20.70	31.5	255.33	12.34	29.1	163.94	7.92	36.6	64.2	1.16
Nonprofit	5.43	8.3	59.74	11.01	6.8	41.04	7.56	9.2	68.7	1.11
Total	65.72	100	876.62[a]	13.34[b]	100	448.38[c]	6.82[d]	100	51.1	1

[a] $6,054.4 billion.
[b] $92.1 thousand.
[c] $3,096.8 billion.
[d] $47.1 thousand.
(Note) $1 = 144.79 yen in 1990.

the larger this index, the more efficient that industrial sector is. Japan's manufacturing industry had an index of 1.18 in 1990, hence it is rather efficient. The U.S. manufacturing industry had a 1.23 (see Table 21.2), more efficient than in Japan.

Minimum Time, Minimum Cost, and Maximum Profit Rate

The following three fundamental evaluation criteria are used in manufacturing optimization.

1. *The Maximum Production Rate or Minimum Time Criterion.* This maximizes the amount of products produced in a unit time interval, hence it minimizes the production time per unit piece. It is the criterion to be adopted when an increase in physical productivity is desired, neglecting the production cost needed and/or profit obtained.
2. *The Minimum Cost Criterion.* This criterion refers to producing a product at the least cost and coincides with the maximum profit criterion, if the unit revenue is constant. It is the criterion to be adopted when there is ample time for production.

TABLE 21.2. U.S.'s Industrial Power in 1990

Industry	Labor Force		GDP			Efficiency Index (b/a)
	Million	Percent (a)	$billion	$thousand per Capita	Percent (b)	
Primary	4.09	3.5	135.2	33.1	3.5	1.02
Agriculture, Forestry and Fishing	3.36	2.9	97.1	28.9	2.5	0.89
Mining	0.73	0.6	38.1	52.2	1.0	1.61
Secondary	30.46	25.8	1,174.0	38.5	30.7	1.19
Manufacturing	21.18	18.0	846.8	40.0	22.1	1.23
Construction	7.70	6.5	234.4	30.5	6.1	0.94
Electric, gas, and sanitary	1.58	1.3	92.8	58.6	2.4	1.81
Subtotal (goods production)	34.55	29.3	1,309.2	37.9	34.2	1.17
Tertiary (service production)	83.37	70.7	2,519.9	30.2	65.8	0.93
Commerce	24.27	20.6	655.6	27.0	17.1	0.83
Others	59.10	50.1	1,864.3	31.5	48.7	0.97
Total	117.91	100	3,829.1[a]	32.5	100	1

[a] Exclusive of the Government services ($657.9 billion).

3. *The Maximum Profit Rate Criterion.* This maximizes the profit in a given time interval. It is the criterion to be recommended when there is insufficient capacity for a specific time interval.

Profit rate is calculated as follows:

$$\text{Profit rate} = (\text{Price} - \text{Production cost})/\text{Production time}$$

It is noteworthy that the optimal value under the maximum profit rate criterion exists in a range between the optimal values under the other two criteria. For example, the maximum profit rate machining speed is greater than the minimum cost machining speed and less than the minimum time machining speed.

21.2 STRUCTURE OF MANUFACTURING SYSTEMS

Plant Layout

The structure of manufacturing system—the plant layout pattern—is basically decided by the relationship between the number of products P and the production quantity Q, and classified in the following three ways.

1. *Product (or Flow-line or Production-line) Layout.* In the case of a large $Q:P$ ratio, continuous mass production is justified. Production facilities and auxiliary services are located according to the process route for producing the product, generating the linear material flow.

2. *Process (or Functional) Layout.* In the case of a small $Q:P$ ratio, or jobbing or small-lot (batch) production, machines of like types are located together as work centers in one area of the plant. In this case, the flow of materials is not smooth, resulting in low productivity.

3. *Group Technology (GT) (or Cellular) Layout.* In the case of an average $Q:P$ ratio, when a great variety of products can be grouped into several families, these families are manufactured as lots of similar parts, and machines are arranged to meet this type of production, thereby resulting in higher productivity. This is a pattern of layout between the above two patterns.

Examples of the three layout patterns are depicted in Figure 21.6. Incidentally, group technology is a technique that increases a production lot size by grouping various parts and products with similar shape, dimension, and/or process route. Production with this concept (cellular manufacturing) increases productivity (11).

To determine an optimum layout, analytical methods such as mathematical programming, graph theory, and branch-and-bound methods are useful. Practically, layout patterns depend mainly on the types of products and their quantities, as mentioned above. Layout planning is usually done in a heuristic way, and a best layout plan is selected from among several alternatives. An effective method from the practical standpoint is systematic layout planning (SLP) (12). The modified SLP pattern is depicted in Figure 21.7. In this layout process five key factors are important: product (P), quantity (Q), routing (R), supporting services (S), and time (T). The layout decision proceeds as follows: (*1*) inputting these five data, (*2*) determining the flow of materials, (*3*) investigating the activity relationships, (*4*) drawing a flow and/or activity relationship diagram, (*5*) determining space, (*6*) creating a space relationship diagram, (*7*) adjusting the diagram, (*8*) conducting an optimization analysis, and (*9*) evaluating and determining the best layout.

Computerized Plant Layout

Computerized layout algorithms are classified into the construction and the improvement types (13). The former constructs the layout by building up a solution from the beginning by successively selecting and placing activities (departments) until a satisfactory layout plan is achieved. The typical algorithm is computerized relationship layout planning (CORELAP). The second

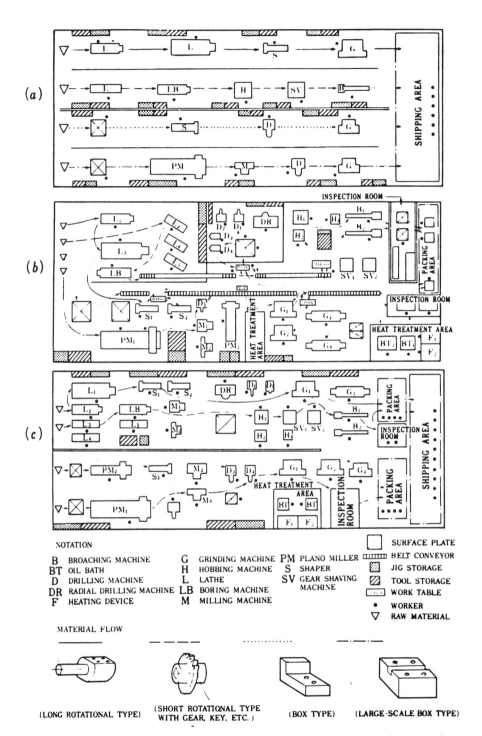

Figure 21.6. Three types of layout pattern: **(a)** product layout, **(b)** process layout, and **(c)** cellular layout.

413

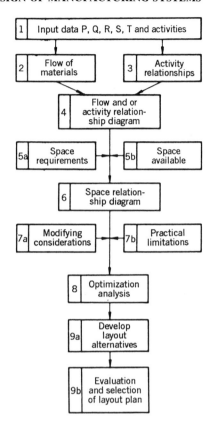

Figure 21.7. A modified SLP procedure.

type requires a complete initial (often existing) layout and exchanges locations of activities to improve the layout design. The typical algorithm of this type is the computerized relative allocation of facilities technique (CRAFT).

Installing Flexible Manufacturing Systems

To produce automatically a variety of parts and products, which is a requirement of today's manufacturing, it is necessary to combine the following four automatic activities and allocate hardware equipment with high flexibility.

1. *Fabrication.* In fabricating parts with machine tools, it is necessary to provide several dozen cutting tools to be exchanged automatically. Machining centers and turning centers can operate in this way with high flexibility. Industrial robots also have flexibility in product assembly.

2. *Setup of Workparts.* For automatic loading and unloading of parts to and from machine tools or pallets, mechanical hands or robots are available. Palletizing is also useful.

3. *Transfer of Workparts.* Mechanical hands or robots, for a short distance, and conveyors or automated guided vehicles (AGVs), for a long distance, can help transfer workparts from the warehouses to the machine tools, between the machine tools, and from the machine tools to the warehouses.

4. *Storage of Workparts.* Automated warehouses or carousels for small-scale works are used to store raw materials and final products. Occasionally, in-process works are temporarily stocked on the conveyor or pallet.

Combining the above-mentioned automated facilities with high flexibility and computer control, a flexible manufacturing system (FMS) is realized for multiproduct, small-batch production. FMS is the most advanced production method in computer-aided manufacturing and plays an important role in constructing a CIM. There are three kinds of FMSs.

1. *Flexible Machining Cell (FMC).* This is a basic configuration consisting of a machining center or a turning center and a robot or a pallet pool. A larger-scale system is constructed by combining several basic systems.

2. *Flow-type FMS.* Several machining centers and turning centers are laid out according to the work flow in a linear or loop-type configuration. This is sometimes called a flexible transfer line (FTL).

3. *Random-access–type FMS.* This type of FMS contains several machining centers and/or turning centers, conveyors or AGVs, and automated warehouses. Complicated workpieces with various shapes and operations are inserted in the system at random. Each workpiece is transferred to the appropriate machine tools, fabricated according to machining instructions, and unloaded from the machines to be transferred to the exit. Sometimes the system can store in-process workpieces and exchange jigs and fixtures automatically. The system has information-processing functions to generate, stock, transmit, and control a variety of information for multiproduct, small-batch production. In addition, it has managerial functions to generate machining schedules and perform stock and process controls.

21.3 TRANSFORMATION IN MANUFACTURING SYSTEMS

Flow of Materials in Manufacturing Systems

As mentioned earlier, the activity of manufacturing is regarded as the flow of materials. From the macroeconomic and social viewpoints this is the logistic system consisting of the material-supply system, the materials-handling system, and the physical-distribution system (Figure 21.8). The materials-supply system deals with transportation of raw materials and parts from the raw material suppliers to the manufacturer. The materials-handling system is concerned with handling and transfer of workpieces inside the factory, and the physical-distribution system transports and distributes produced goods to ultimate customers. Concerning the material flow inside a factory, the manufacturing system conducts the following three basic activities as shown in the block labeled "manufacturing system" in Figure 21.8.

Conversion

Conversion is the function of converting the form of the workpieces by the activity called operation. An operation is done at a specific workstation or work center, where machine tools, jigs, fixtures, tools, operators, etc. are suitably arranged. A product or job is normally completed through a series (or set) of operations, which constitutes a multiple-stage production

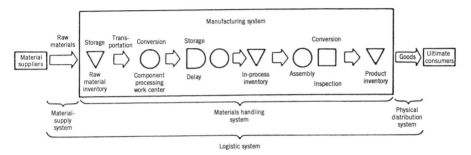

Figure 21.8. The logistic system made up of the material-supply system, the materials-handling system, and the physical distribution system.

process. Through this process, raw materials are converted into products, changing their form and structure, thereby successively increasing form utility.

Transportation (Transfer)

Transportation is the function of transferring workpieces between workstations and is often called materials handling. Although this activity generates place utility, it is not a direct operation, hence reduced materials handling increases manufacturing efficiency. The amount of materials handling in a manufacturing system is fairly large at present, i.e., the materials handling costs 30% to 75% of the total cost. Consequently, it is necessary to eliminate transportation. This can be achieved in the following ways: (*1*) Reduce the transfer distance by establishing a smooth material flow, (*2*) decrease the number of transfer activities, and (*3*) determine an optimal transfer route and speed by constructing a straight continuous route and by setting a balanced or synchronized transfer activity.

Storage (Delay)

Storage is the function of elapsed time accompanied by no change of form and place of workpiece; typical examples are the stock at the warehouse and a temporary stay between workstations. In general, associated with imbalance between the conversion and transportation functions, stagnation of material flow occurs between the time of raw material supply and the start of its use for manufacture, between two successive stages of the production processes, and the time to finish the product and to ship it to the market. These delays are called raw materials inventory, (work-)in-process inventory, and finished-product inventory, respectively. Thus inventories play essential roles as buffer stocks for a smooth, flexible material flow and generate time utility. Finished-product inventory absorbs the difference between the individual activities of production and marketing by shipping a variety of products well timed to the customers' orders and wants (just-in-time (JIT) supply) and, on the other hand, setting the manufacturing system for its stable utilization.

Another use of the storage function is the parts-oriented production system. This system actively holds and uses the parts inventory, which plays a more important role than just storage of parts. A variety of products are assembled on the receipt of orders by suitably combining those parts, resulting in much reduction of production leadtime.

Product Planning

End products to be produced by the manufacturing system are decided as a result of strategic production planning. Product planning involves conducting research and developing new material goods that meet the market needs for customer satisfaction. It is a never-ending function in the dynamic surroundings of a competitive situation, because a single product generally possesses a life cycle. As shown in Figure 21.9, the sales volume and revenue for a particular new product tend to rise in the initial period after the product's introduction. There follows a period of growth as the customers' recognition and acceptance have increased with a rapid increase of purchasing power. In the period of maturity, the sales volume still increases; however, as additional competitive products appear in the market, the profit tends to decrease as a result of the reduction of the selling price. In the saturation and decline periods, freshness of the product may be lost and the volume of sales and hence the profit decrease.

In the planning system for a new product, the market needs predominate. With the information based on the market research or data from the marketing and sales departments of the firm, the general specifications of a new product are established. When ideas of the product are proposed for the market commodity, the technical specifications can be established by the creative abilities of product R&D, thus leading to the final design. At this stage, some change of the product's general specifications previously determined may be allowed. The reason is that the design ideas for a new product are not always directly related to reality. Therefore, the decision made to bring a new product to actual production depends on whether the compromise made for practical manufacturing receives the market acceptance.

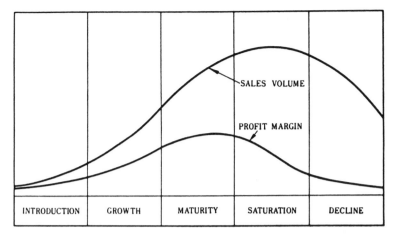

Figure 21.9.   The product life cycle.

Product Design

Following the research and development, the product design is completed, which is the final stage of product planning. The product can now perform a specified function, which is based on the technical specifications for the product. This must contain the following three phases:

1. *Functional Design.* This is the design expressing the shape and ensuring the function that the product to be manufactured must possess. Function means the functional characteristics that the product should possess while it is in operation; with this the use value is generated and the possession utility is provided to the ultimate users.

2. *Production Design (or Design for Manufacture).* This aspect of design is concerned with easy and economical production relative to the conversion of raw material into the finished product, from the viewpoints of both manufacturing technology and production process planning. The effectiveness of this design is closely related to productivity and the product cost.

3. *Industrial (or Marketing) Design.* This is the design, or styling, that is used to influence people to buy the product with its eye appeal and the design for easy use of the product by the ultimate customers, based on human engineering aspect (ergodesign). In this design stage, care should be taken to ensure that aspects of functional and production design are not ignored.

The following features must be considered in the product design.

- Effective function with simplification.
- Quality, reliability, safety, and maintainability.
- Economical production (lower in cost).
- Easy handling by users (human-engineering aspect).
- Aesthetic appearance (pleasing to look at).
- Resource-saving aspect.

There are several points in product design to be kept in mind:

1. *Life-cycle Design.* Design considering a whole life of a product including waste and recycling.

2. *Modular Design.* Design of a product by a suitable combination of standard parts, components, and subassemblies.

3. *Robust Design.* Design to be tolerant of the environmental changes, such as fail-safe design and foolproof design.

Recent trends of automated assembly are toward design of both components and products in such a way that operations—feeding, transferring, and fastening—are easily and accurately performed on the machine. The number of parts should be fewer. Parts are to be standardized and symmetrical or, if not, of a special geometrical feature (such as an additional flat, lug, notch, or groove) for easy orientation and positioning. As far as possible, separate fasteners such as screws, bolts, and rivets should be avoided for clamping. When unavoidable, simple, straight plunging motion is to be specified, rather than rotational. Products should be designed so as to be assembled step-by-step, loading parts from the top onto the dominant base component.

Computerized Product Design

Computerized product design (computer-aided design (CAD)) uses computers, graphic display, automatic drawing machines, and other peripheral devices for interactive or automatic design and drawing. For geometric modeling (pattern design), regular two-dimensional models, wireframe models, surface models, and solid models are used. The most visual solid models include (*1*) constructive solid geometry (CSG), in which primitives such as cubes, cylinders, spheres, and pyramids, are assembled by set calculation; and (*2*) boundary representation (B-reps), in which boundaries are combined together. Computer aid can also perform structural analysis by finite element methods, characteristics analysis for vibration, fluid and heat transfer, and optimization analysis using systems theory, mathematical programming techniques, and artificial intelligence (expert systems). This procedure is often called computer-aided engineering (CAE).

Process Planning

Production processes or process routes, through which raw materials are effectively converted into the planned products with a series of operations on multiple-stage workstations, are to be determined after the aggregate production planning and completion of product design. This decision making is called process planning. It depends on the kinds and quantities of products to be finished, kinds of raw materials and parts, production facilities and technology on hand, etc. Basically, the task of process planning includes the following two stages (14): process design, macroscopic decision making of an overall process route for converting the raw material into a product, and operation design, microscopic decision making of individual operations contained in the process route.

The main decision problems in process design are to analyze the work flow of converting raw material into a finished product, or flow(-line) analysis, and to select the workstation for each operation included in the work flow. These two aspects of process design are interrelated, hence must be decided simultaneously. Workstations to meet the work flow determined are selected economically by choosing an alternative with the least cost from the alternatives that combine available production facilities or machine tools together with operative labor capacity.

Because the volume of output influences the total production cost, efficient production facility must be selected according to production quantity. Figure 21.10 shows how to select an optimum machine tool according to the expected production or sales volume by means of the break-even chart and analysis.

Operation design is concerned with the detailed decisions of production implementation, i.e., the types of operations to be performed in the production process. The content of each operation is determined in connection with process design and may be broken down into several steps, such as loading the workpiece in the chuck of the machine tool, starting the machine, and unloading the workpiece from the chuck and placing it on the conveyor. The method of operation is analyzed from the viewpoints of a combination of machine elements and human elements (human–machine system), operative worker, and work simplification. Traditional industrial engineering (IE) tools are effective as visual aids.

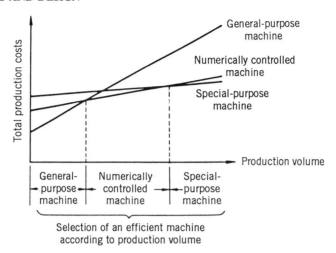

Figure 21.10. Break-even chart for selecting an efficient production facility according to production volume.

Automated Process Planning

A vast amount of knowledge and experience of manufacturing technology is needed for process planning, automated process planning—often called computer-aided process planning (CAPP). It is classified into the following two methods.

1. *Retrieval (or Variant) Method.* Technical laws concerning appropriate sequences of operations are put in a process file, from which an appropriate process route is retrieved for producing a given shape. GT is often employed in this method.
2. *Generative Method.* An optimum process route and production facility are determined automatically, based on manufacturing principles and logic with the help of artificial intelligence and expert systems (if–then or production rules).

Line Balancing

As in a progressive assembly line where successive production stages (workstations) take the form of a conveyorlike system and work is performed continuously, a balance among production stages should be kept in such a way that a smooth material flow is obtained by almost equalizing the production times at all production stages, thus minimizing idle times at the workstations. This line balancing aims at minimum cycle time, minimum number of workstations, optimal grouping of work elements, etc. A method of computerized line balancing developed is computer-assembly line balancing (CALB), which also sequences mixed models on a conveyor.

Logistics Analysis

From a wide viewpoint, the flow of materials constitutes a serial functional chain of procurement, production, distribution, inventory, and sales through which raw materials are procured from outside suppliers, processed, assembled at workshops, and stored in warehouses as inventories, and finished products are delivered to consumers as commodities through distribution channels, as represented in Figure 21.11. Transportation-type linear programming, the shortest-route analysis, graph theory, etc. are applicable to the optimal decision of this problem. Logistics management plays a role in this field.

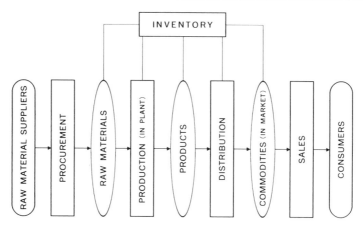

Figure 21.11. Flow of materials in the manufacturing system: procurement, production, distribution, inventory, and sales.

21.4   PROCEDURE IN MANUFACTURING SYSTEMS

Flow of Information and Production Management Systems

As previously mentioned, production management is the procedure of manufacturing systems. This consists of the following five stages, as represented in Figure 21.12 (15).

1. *Aggregate Production Planning.* This determines the kinds of product items and the quantities to be produced during the specified time periods.
2. *Production Process Planning.* This determines the production processes (or process routes) by which raw materials are effectively transformed into finished products.
3. *Production Scheduling.* This determines an actual implementation plan defining the time schedule for every job contained in the process route adopted, i.e., when, with what machine, and who does what operation?
4. *Production Implementation.* This function executes actual production operations according to the time schedule.
5. *Production Control.* Whenever the actual production progress and performances deviate from the production standards (plans and schedules) set at the planning stages 1, 2, and 3 above, such deviations are measured and modifications are appropriately made.

Stages 1, 2, and 3 constitute planning. Stage 4 is implementation, which forms the flow of materials. Stage 5 is control. In production management, the cycle of planning, implementation, and control plays a basic role in effective manufacturing activities. Stage 2 deals with basic production technology; it is named the flow of technological information. While a series of functions—stages 1, 3, and 5—is concerned with management activities; it is named the flow of managerial information.

The above five steps are operational, which means that the activities are decided and performed inside the firm. At a higher level is located the strategic planning function, which is concerned with strategic issues existing between the firm and its environment (market, competitors, society, etc.), such as long-range planning, profit planning, and pricing of the products to be sold. The strategic and operational phases are fundamental to the effective performance of the firm (16).

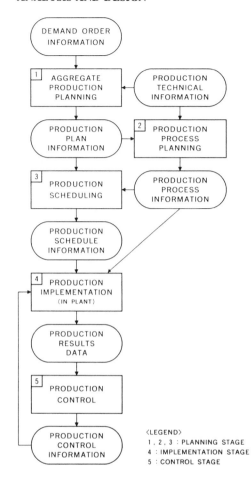

Figure 21.12. The procedural aspect of the manufacturing system: the flow of information.

Aggregate Production Planning

Optimal Product Mix

Optimal product mix determines the proper combination of the kinds of items to be produced with the existing production capacity. If there is insufficient capacity to produce the entire amount of products demanded, such a demand cannot be sufficiently fulfilled. In such a case, optimal product mix (optimal kinds of products and their production quantities) should be properly selected. Some of the policies employed to solve this problem are to maximize the total profit obtained by production under the capacity constraint and to maximize the total amount of products ordered even at the sacrifice of profit gained. Multiple-objective optimization is applied to this analysis, and the hierarchical production planning including production scheduling is also made. Group technology is also applied to production management.

Requirements Analysis

Requirements analysis determines the quantity to be produced for every product under consideration in a specific period. Quantitative techniques such as mathematical programming, especially linear programming, quadratic decision analysis, and functional analysis are useful to assist decision making for solving this problem.

Suppose we want to produce N kinds of products or parts with M kinds of production resources. Let us assume that a_{ij} units of resource i ($= 1, 2, \ldots, M$) are required to produce a unit of product j ($= 1, 2, \ldots, N$), from which c_j units of profit are gained. If only b_i units are available for resource i, determine an optimal product mix and optimal production quantities. Here the values of a_{ij}, b_i, and c_j are all constants; a_{ij} is called the technology coefficient.

To solve this product-mix and requirements problem, let the amount of product j ($= 1, 2, \ldots, N$) be x_j. By taking the total profit to be obtained as a production goal, this short-range production planning is formulated so as to maximize

$$z = \sum_{j=1}^{N} c_j x_j$$

which is the total profit gained, subject to

$$\sum_{j=1}^{N} a_{ij} x_j \le b_i \ (i = 1, 2, \ldots, M)$$

which indicate restriction of production resources, and

$$x_j \ge 0 \ (j = 1, 2, \ldots, N)$$

which are nonnegativity requirements, showing a zero or positive quantity of production. This problem is of a well-known linear programming (LP) type and determines optimal product items j^* and production quantities x_j^*, thereby producing a maximum profit z^*.

For a long-term production planning the following logical relationship always holds at each period of the time horizon:

Final inventory = Initial inventory + Production quantity − Sales quantity

MRP

MRP is an abbreviation for materials requirements planning or manufacturing resource planning. It is a systematic procedure of widely used computer-based software for production planning applied to a large job shop production in which multiple products are manufactured in lots through several processing steps (17). First, MRP establishes a master production schedule (MPS), which is an aggregate plan showing required amounts versus planning periods for multiple end items to be produced. Then, with use of a bill of materials and an inventory file, production information for dispatching multiple jobs is produced on the hierarchical multiple-stage manufacturing systems by considering the common parts and the substitution of many parts included in multiple products. Thus MRP schedules and controls a total flow of materials from the raw materials to the finished products on a time basis (usually, weekly).

The possibilities of assembling products and of machining parts are also examined in relation to the capacity of production facilities. This function is called capacity requirements planning (CRP). The general procedure of MRP is (1) calculating the requirements for products and parts, (2) making up the lot, (3) subtracting leadtimes, and (4) CRP.

Lot-size Analysis

In intermittent (or lot or batch) production, the demand rate is small compared with the possible production rate, and a product is manufactured periodically in a quantity that will just satisfy the demand for a specified period. In such a case, the production decision (economic lot size and optimal production cycle) is usually made to minimize the total production costs, which are taken as the sum of setup cost, manufacturing cost, and inventory cost. The economic lot size is

$$Q_l^* = \sqrt{2 r_c s / (1 - r_c / r_p) h}$$

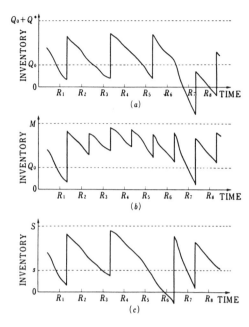

Figure 21.13. Comparison of three inventory policies, using the same demand pattern: **(a)** the fixed-order policy, **(b)** the replenishment policy, and **(c)** the (S,s) policy.

where r_p and r_c are production and consumption rates ($r_p > r_c$), h is inventory-holding cost per unit piece of product per unit time, and s is setup cost per cycle. Then, optimal production cycle time is

$$T^* = Q_1^*/r_c = \sqrt{2s/(1 - r_c/r_p)hr_c}$$

The recent tendency is to meet market needs for a variety of products; this kind of production type has also been investigated (18). Only one-piece (one-of-a-kind) production is performed practically, especially in Japan, although this type of production ascertains no optimization because a strict condition should hold for just one piece as the economic lot size.

Inventory Analysis

Inventory analysis determines the quantities and timing of each item to be ordered or to be held at the level of purchased raw materials, work-in-process, and finished products. The economic order quantity (EOQ) is determined by minimizing the sum of ordering cost and inventory-carrying cost as in the following formula:

$$Q_o^* = \sqrt{2cD/h},$$

where c is the cost of placing an order, h is the annual carrying cost per unit, and D is the annual demand in units. The fixed-order quantity system places an order of Q_o^* whenever the inventory on hand drops to a particular level, referred to as the reorder point. The replenishment system places an order amount so as to fill the replenishment level at the regular review times. The (S,s) system is more flexible, in that both reorder point and reorder quantity are varied. Comparison of these three inventory policies, using the same demand pattern, is shown in Figure 21.13.

Production Smoothing

Production smoothing evens out the level of production and adapts to fluctuation of demands that come from the market, thus resulting in high use of production facilities. Management policies for this purpose are time adaptation, inventory adaptation, intensive adaptation, quantitative adaptation, and subcontract adaptation (19).

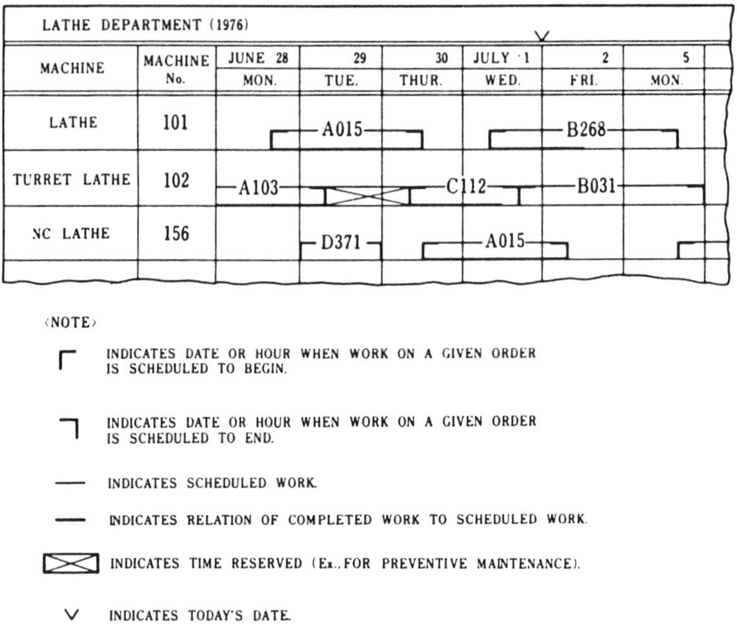

LATHE DEPARTMENT (1976)							
MACHINE	MACHINE No.	JUNE 28 MON.	29 TUE.	30 THUR.	JULY 1 WED.	2 F RI.	5 MON.
LATHE	101		⌐—A015——⌐			⌐—B268——⌐	
TURRET LATHE	102	⌐A103—⌐	⌐——✕——⌐	C|12—⌐	⌐—B031—⌐		
NC LATHE	156		⌐— D371 —⌐		⌐——A015——⌐		⌐

(NOTE)

⌐ INDICATES DATE OR HOUR WHEN WORK ON A GIVEN ORDER IS SCHEDULED TO BEGIN.

⌐ INDICATES DATE OR HOUR WHEN WORK ON A GIVEN ORDER IS SCHEDULED TO END.

—— INDICATES SCHEDULED WORK.

—— INDICATES RELATION OF COMPLETED WORK TO SCHEDULED WORK.

✕ INDICATES TIME RESERVED (Ex.. FOR PREVENTIVE MAINTENANCE).

V INDICATES TODAY'S DATE.

Figure 21.14.   The Gantt chart.

Production Scheduling

Job Sequencing

Job sequencing determines the order of processing jobs to be performed on a single machine. Attention is paid to the permutation of schedules for this problem. Several basic rules have been presented for obtaining an optimal schedule with respect to the evaluation criteria used, such as the shortest-processing-time rule for minimizing the mean flow time by sequencing the jobs in order of nondecreasing processing time and the earliest-due-date rule for minimizing the maximum lateness or tardiness by sequencing the jobs in order of nondecreasing due date (20). In addition, feasible schedules are made by dispatching the jobs with an appropriate priority (or dispatching) rule, according to a certain measure of performance. Simulation techniques are often employed to decide this rule.

Operations Scheduling

Operations scheduling determines the order and schedule (drawn as a Gantt chart, Figure 21.14) for processing several jobs on several machines, as in a machine shop. A few rules and algorithms for this purpose have been developed for flow-shop scheduling and job-shop scheduling, such as Johnson's algorithm for minimizing the makespan on two-machine flow shops, Petrov's heuristic method by applying Johnson's algorithm on multistage flow shops, the group scheduling technique for determining the optimal group and job sequences by applying GT, optimized production technology (OPT) considering the resource restricts, the graphical method for two-job job shops, Jackson's method for two-machine job shops, application of the branch-and-bound method, etc.

Project Scheduling

In long-range scheduling, as in scheduling the construction of a new factory, ship, highway, etc., short periods such as seconds or minutes are not significant in production scheduling.

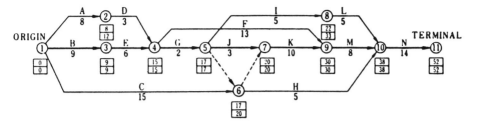

Figure 21.15. PERT network based on the basic data given in Table 21.3.

Because many and varied kinds of work elements are contained in this type of scheduling, a reasonable schedule must be made for a smooth and effective implementation of production. Typical solution techniques for solving this type of scheduling problem are called project scheduling; e.g., the program evaluation and review technique (PERT) for determining a feasible schedule by indicating the critical path (see the bold arrows in Figure 21.15, which is based on the 14 activities indicated in Table 21.3) and the critical path method (CPM) for determining the optimal schedule by considering the trade-off relation between time and cost (21).

Production Control

Control of Logistics

Control of logistics is the control function for the flow of materials. It includes the following:

1. *Purchasing Control.* Control for acquisition of production resources (factors of production).
2. *Production Control (or Process Control).* Control for time (due date) and quantities to be produced.
3. *Quality Control.* Control and assurance of the desired quality for finished products.
4. *Sales Control.* Control for performing the target of sales.
5. *Inventory Control.* Control for excess storage and shortages. This function is often grouped with production planning.

TABLE 21.3. List of Activities for Analyses by PERT

Activity Code	Activity Content	Preceded Activities	Duration (Week)
A	Demand forecast	—	8
B	Product development	—	9
C	Capital acquisition	—	15
D	Production planning	A	3
E	Product design	B	6
F	Plant planning	D, E	13
G	Profit planning	D, E	2
H	Materials acquisition	C, G	5
I	Operators acquisition	G	5
J	Production design	G	3
K	Facilities acquisition	C, J	10
L	Operators training	I	5
M	Plant layout	F, K	8
N	Manufacture	H, L, M	14

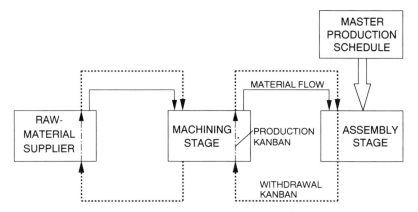

Figure 21.16.   The pull-through type production system with *kanbans* circulated.

Control of Production Resources

Control of production resources is a control function for the factors of production. It includes the following:

1. *Personnel Control.* Control for acquiring human resources and skills.
2. *Facilities Control.* Control for effective use and maintenance of production facilities.
3. *Cost Control.* Control for the cost required for production.

JIT Production

One of the topics in the field of production control is just-in-time production, which is considered as the Japanese-style manufacturing system with quality control (QC) circle activities and total quality control (TQC). This system was initiated through the effort of Toyota Automobile Industries, Ltd. in Japan and is now getting world attention (22). The principle of JIT is to make or supply the required product items in the required amounts at the required time, thereby resulting in minimum, even zero, inventory. This valuable principle, however, is not new, in that this was advocated in 1928 by Alford as the laws of production control; he even included the phrase *at low prices*. The production schedule is input only at the final stage of the manufacturing system, then the demanded items are withdrawn from the previous stages with the circulation of *kanbans* (cards), on which the items and their quantities needed are indicated (Figure 21.16). Only quantities of parts and products indicated on production *kanbans* are produced successively in the previous stages. In this sense, this production system is known as the pull-through system rather than the usual push system.

This system works effectively, in connection with employer–employee cooperation, daily workstation rotation, trained multiple-job–performing operators, and the systems adaptability to market fluctuation. These days it is pointed out that frequent transportation of parts and products required by JIT brings about air pollution.

TQC and TPM

Total quality control is a company-wide daily implementation of QC activities from top management through middle and lower management to workshop-level laborers. This activity done on the shopfloor is called QC circle, or quality circle. TQC or total quality management (TQM) is one of the management techniques that succeeded in Japan (23).

Similarly, facilities control or productive maintenance is also implemented on a company-wide basis. It is called total productive maintenance (TPM).

Computerized Production Management Systems

Computerized production management requires optimum control of production information for an integration of planning, implementation, and control. The latest information needed for this management decision at the right time at the lowest possible cost is adequately provided by means of the management information system (MIS) supported by a total-systems approach.

A typical procedure of computerized production management is communications-oriented production information and control system (COPICS), which was proposed in 1972 by IBM. This is concerned with an approach to CIM that seeks a management (planning–implementation–control) oriented system by data communication with a common database through the use of computers, display terminals, shop floor terminals, etc., in an on-line, real-time mode. It deals with establishing a production plan based on a demand forecast, implementing productive activities from the purchase of raw materials through production to the shipment of the finished products and allocating and managing production resources such as production facilities, labor force, and materials.

COPICS is composed of the following 12 interrelated modules via a system database: (1) engineering and production data control, (2) customer order servicing, (3) forecasting, (4) master production schedule planning, (5) inventory management, (6) manufacturing activity planning, (7) order release, (8) plant monitoring and control, (9) plant maintenance, (10) purchasing and receiving, (11) stores control, and (12) cost planning and control.

21.5 JUSTIFICATION OF MANUFACTURING SYSTEMS DESIGN

Flow of Costs and Value Systems for Manufacturing

Raw materials are converted into finished products, which constitutes the flow of materials, as mentioned earlier. Through this production process costs occur and are accumulated along with production activities. Cost control or cost management is concerned with this economic production mode, constituting the flow of costs. This flow of costs was recognized in 1922 as the flow of value (*Fluß der Wert*) by Nicklisch. The importance of the economic aspect in manufacturing was pointed out by Babbage in 1832 and by Towne in 1886. The flow of costs is now recognized as one of the three basic flows in the manufacturing systems discipline, along with the flow of materials and the flow of information (24). These three flows should work effectively in close cooperation for efficient and economical manufacturing (see Figure 21.2).

Product Cost Structure

Costs that occur during manufacturing are classified in the following ways: (1) material cost, which occurs through the use of materials; labor cost, which occurs by the employment of laborers; and overhead, caused by others; and (2) direct cost, which is recognized directly as a cost, and indirect cost which is not recognized directly. The combination of these two kinds of costs—the total cost—is composed of the manufacturing cost and the commercial cost. The former is made up of the direct and indirect costs, each of which contains the material cost, the labor cost, and the overhead. The latter is made up of the general administrative expense and the sales expense. Addition of an appropriate profit to the total cost creates the selling price (full-cost, or markup, pricing method). This cost structure was proposed as early as 1913 by Nicholson. The average figures in percentage of the cost components against the manufacturing cost and the total cost are indicated in (Figure 21.17) for the case of Japan's small and medium manufacturing enterprises for 1990. The total value of U.S. manufacturers' factory shipments was $2.8 trillion in 1990. The cost of materials was $1.5 trillion (53.6%); payroll, $0.5 trillion (17.9%); and profits, tax, and other items, $0.8 trillion (28.6%).

Profit Planning

Profit is calculated by the revenue (selling price) minus the total cost. To obtain a reasonable amount of profit the break-even (or cost–volume–profit) analysis is useful. In this analysis, costs are divided into the fixed cost (a), which is invariant with the production volume (x), and

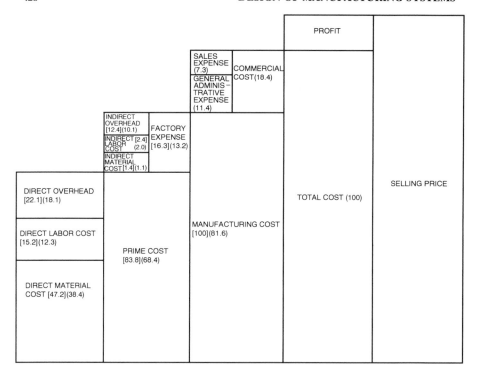

Figure 21.17. Product cost structure. Figures in brackets and in parentheses indicate the average percentage of the cost components against the manufacturing cost and the total cost, respectively, in the case of Japan's small to medium manufacturing firms in 1990.

the variable cost, which varies with x. Setting unit variable cost as b, the total cost is $a + bx$. Denoting the unit revenue as c, the total revenue is cx. The difference between the total revenue and the total cost is profit obtained by:

$$p(x) = (c - b)x - a$$

The break-even point producing zero profit is obtained by:

$$x_{BE} = a/(c - b)$$

The sales in monetary value at this point is

$$y_{BE} = a/(1 - b/c)$$

where b/c is the rate of variable cost and 1 minus b/c is the marginal rate of profit (Figure 21.18). An amount of profit P can be obtained by producing the volume x_P determined by

$$x_P = (a + P)/(c - b)$$

In 1990, the small- and medium-size enterprises in Japan showed 539.32 million yen ($3.72 million) for the average fixed cost (a), 918.72 million yen ($6.35 million) for the average variable cost (bx), and 1521.23 million yen ($10.51 million) for the total sales (cx) ($1 = 144.79 yen in 1990). Then the total profit was 63.19 million yen ($436 thousand) and $y_{BE} = 1361.68$ yen ($9.40 million). The rate of profit on sales was 4.2% and the rate of y_{BE} on sales was 89.5%.

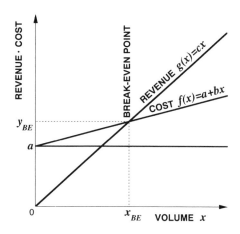

Figure 21.18. Break-even chart for profit planning.

Economic Justification of Investment

The rationale of the capital investment for production facilities is judged from the standpoint of engineering economy. Several such methods are described below.

Rate-of-return (on Investment) Method

Rate-of-return is the most commonly used method of investigating effectiveness of a capital investment by calculating anticipated annual net profit (after allowing for depreciation) expressed as a percentage of the capital invested. When there are several alternatives for investment, such as in the general- and special-purpose machine tools and automatics, we will choose an alternative with the largest rate of return on investment.

This method is a sort of discounted cash-flow method and measures the average rate of interest (or discount) r, such that the total sum of the present worth of profits P_j ($j = 1, 2, \ldots, H$) over the economic life length H in which a facility is capable of operation equals the capital invested I, according to the following formula.

$$\sum_{j=1}^{H} \frac{P_j}{(1 + r)^j} = I$$

An alternative associated with the largest r is chosen. A variation of this method is known as the new MAPI method, which deals with the economic replacement of equipment. MAPI stands for Machinery and Allied Products Institute.

Minimum-cost Method

Unit production cost is estimated for each proposal for investment and an alternative associated with the least cost is chosen. The old MAPI method is a variation of this method.

Payoff (or Pay-back) Period Method

The anticipated annual savings in direct costs, resulting from the introduction of the proposed investment, are first determined. The payoff (or pay-back) period is calculated as the number of years in which the initial cost of investment, after allowing for resale of the old equipment, is all repaid by those savings. An alternative associated with the shortest payoff period or one having the payoff period shorter than the predetermined reasonable period is considered acceptable.

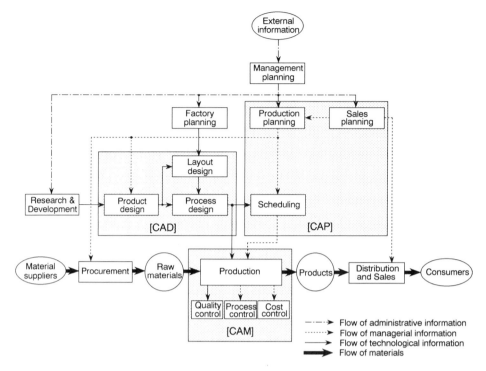

Figure 21.19. Framework of functions concerning manufacturing and computer aids: CAD, CAM, CAP, and OA.

Present-worth (or Present-value) Method

The present worth method is a sort of the discounted cash flow method. The total sum of the present value of discounted cash earning (before depreciation and after tax) S_j ($j = 1, 2, \ldots, H$) over the economic life length of a facility H is calculated as follows:

$$S = \sum_{j=1}^{H} \frac{S_j}{(1 + r)^j}$$

where r is the rate of discount. If S exceeds the capital invested, then the proposal is evaluated as acceptable.

Which method should be used depends basically on the size of the capital invested. When it is comparatively small, the minimum-cost method is sufficient, while in case of a large investment planning the rate-of-return on capital invested is evaluated for each alternative. Analytical results by other methods are also examined before a best plan is chosen.

Manufacturing Strategy: CIM

CIM is a computerized system that integrates the computer aids of the following three different functions with a common database, i.e., it has the following contents (Figure 21.19) (25):

1. Computer aid to the production function (automated flow of materials, which includes procurement, production, quality control, process control, cost control, and distribution and sales), or CAM.

2. Computer aid to the design function (automated flow of technological information, which includes research and development, product design, process design, and layout design), or CAD.

3. Computer aid to the management function (automated flow of managerial information, which includes sales planning, production planning, and production scheduling, or CAP.

Thus integration of the automated flow of materials and automated flow of information can be recognized as a concept of CIM. This is the embodiment of the concept of manufacturing systems engineering. CIM is also a realized mode of system integration (SI) with the following three features: (*1*) syncretism, integrating different fields while maintaining their autonomy; (*2*) symbiosis, obtaining symbiotic gain; and (*3*) synergy, synergistically obtaining amplification effects.

In application, CIM is perceived as the integration of three functions: production, sales, and technology. It intends to ensure reduction of the leadtime and flexible adaptation to large-variety, small-batch production through the computerized processing of the entire processes from order receipt to product shipment.

A common definition of CIM has not yet been established, but it can be understood as follows: CIM is a flexible market-adaptive strategic manufacturing system that integrates three different functions—design, production, and management—through an information network with computers. CIM was advocated in 1973 by Harrington; it is now recognized as a means of corporate strategy for manufacturing firms. The strategies of a corporate system with CIM covering three basic areas—CAM, CAD, and CAP, as previously described—together with office automation (OA) for automated administrative functions (automated flow of administrative information, which includes management planning and factory planning) is explained below (see Figure 21.19).

1. Strategy of CAM: unmanned small-lot production for a variety of products.

2. Strategy of CAD: quick design and product development.

3. Strategy of CAP: reduction of leadtime and flexible production management.

4. Strategy of OA: sales promotion, corporate automation, and global production.

Manufacturing Excellence

Flexible Production

Technology-centered full automation principally composed of highly advanced production technologies not only is insufficient in flexibility but also is confronted with a lack of innovative flexibility, greater vulnerability to failure, and above all, neglect of human skills, robbing workers of their pride and pleasure of work, in spite of an enormous amount of capital investment (3,600 billion yen, i.e., about $28 billion in 1989). Manufacturing a variety of products of super high quality with the use of high technologies but still drawing heavily on skills of workers is what flexible production or a human-centered (anthropocentric) system is all about. This mode of production pays attention to a new metaphysical "production philosotechnology" beyond the conventional subjective production skills and objective production techniques.

High Added-value Production

As shown in Table 21.1, Japan's manufacturing industry yielded 39.7% of the total output with 23.4% of the total labor population in 1990. Although the efficiency is certainly high in this respect, a more important scale, added value or GDP (which represents the total output less the total input), was only 27.5%; in this sense manufacturing cannot be said to be extremely efficient. The efficiency index defined in earlier as the GDP share over the labor force ratio in the manufacturing sector, is 1.18, the highest level among all industries. However, the manufacturing industry of the United States, which has been stagnating in recent years, shows a greater efficiency index as mentioned earlier; hence Japan's manufacturing industry is not particularly superior. It is particularly important to note that the yield ratio, the GDP share over output, as defined earlier, is 35.5% for Japan's manufacturing industry, the lowest level among all industrial sectors.

Recognizing such inefficiency of the manufacturing industry, this sector should slough off from a situation of high volume production and dumping-like sales activities, with little profits obtained. By developing highly original, high quality products with high added values, manufacturers will be able to ensure appropriate profits through better coordinated production.

Resource-saving and Environment-preserving (Green) Production

In Japan, which has built up an affluent society, 1334 million t domestic natural resources and 711 million t imported resources (about 15% of the world's annual resources distributed) were used in 1990. As a result 1246 million t of buildings, structures, and products were accumulated and 73 million t of export products were manufactured, while producing industrial wastes (19 kinds) of 222 million t and general wastes of 51 million t, totaling to 273 million t. The resources recycled amounted to 182 million t, a little more than 8% of overall resources used. Viewing the import and export of materials and products to and from Japan, the export is only 73 million t and the import is 711 million t, showing an extreme imbalance.

Recognizing the above actualities in Japan (26), design and production in the coming age should be directed to the preservation of the environment in view of the material flow (procurement to production to distribution to consumption to disposal to recycling) in the early stage of design, thereby resulting in permanently sustainable development by taking resource saving into account. The throw-away culture caused by mass production and mass consumption should be also stopped for the sake of natural resource preservation; a concept of socially appropriate production (27) for manufacturing excellence is especially needed in manufacturing systems design.

BIBLIOGRAPHY

1. S. DANØ, *Industrial Production Model,* Springer-Verlag, Vienna, 1966.
2. R.E. YOUNG and R. MAYER, "The Information Dilemma: To Conceptualize Manufacturing as Information Process," *Ind. Eng.* **16**(9) 28–34 (1984).
3. K. HITOMI, *Decision Making for Production* (in Japanese), Chuokeizai-sha, Tokyo, 1972.
4. K. HITOMI, "Concept and Design of Systems" (in Japanese) in H. Wakuta, ed., *Design of Accounting Information Systems,* Japan Management Association, Tokyo, 1971, pp. 69–101.
5. K. HITOMI, *Planning Theory for Production* (in Japanese), Yuhikaku, Tokyo, 1975.
6. S. STRANGE, *States and Markets,* Pinter Publishers, London, 1988.
7. K. HITOMI, *Manufacturing Systems Engineering—A Unified Approach to Manufacturing Technology and Production Management,* Taylor & Francis, London, 1979.
8. H. KOONTZ and C. O'DONNELL, *Management—A Systems and Contingency Analysis of Managerial Functions,* 6th ed., McGraw-Hill Book Co., Inc., New York, 1976.
9. A. KUSIAK, *Intelligent Manufacturing Systems,* Prentice-Hall, Inc., Englewood Cliffs, N.J., 1990.
10. K. HITOMI, "Manufacturing Systems Engineering: The Concept, Its Context and the State of the Art," *Int. J. Comput. Integrated Manufact.* **3**(5), 275–288 (1990).
11. I. HAM, K. HITOMI, and T. YOSHIDA, *Group Technology—Applications to Production Management,* Kluwer-Nijhoff Publishing, Boston, 1985.
12. R. MUTHER, *Systematic Layout Planning,* 2nd ed., Cahners Books, Boston, 1973.
13. R.L. FRANCIS, L.F. McGINNIS, Jr., and J.A. WHITE, *Facility Layout and Location—An Analytical Approach,* 2nd ed., Prentice-Hall, Inc., Englewood Cliffs, N.J., 1992.
14. H.L. TIMMS and M.F. POHLEN, *The Production Function in Business—Desicion Systems for Production and Operations Management,* 3rd ed., Richard D. Irwin, Homewood, Ill., 1970.
15. K. HITOMI, *Production Management Engineering* (in Japanese), Corona Publishing, Tokyo, 1978.
16. H. HUEBNER and H. HOEFER, "Strategy Oriented Production Management" in G. Doumeingts and W.A. Carter, eds., *Advances in Production Management Systems,* Elsevier, Amsterdam, The Netherlands, 1984, p. 55.

17. J. ORLICKY, *Material Requirements Planning,* McGraw-Hill Book Co., Inc., New York, 1975.

18. K. HITOMI, "Non-mass, Multi-product, Small-sized Production: The State of the Art," *Technovation* **9**(4), 357–369 (1989).

19. E. GUTENBERG, *Grundlagen der Betriebswirtschaftslehre. Bd I: Die Produktion,* Springer-Verlag, Berlin, 1955.

20. K.R. BAKER, *Introduction to Sequencing and Scheduling,* John Wiley & Sons, Inc., New York, 1974.

21. J.J. MODER, C.R. PHILLIPS, and E.W. DAVIS, *Project Management with CPM, PERT and Precedence Diagramming,* Van Nostrand Reinhold, Co., Inc., New York, 1983.

22. Y. MONDEN, *Toyota Production System,* Industrial and Management Press, Norcross, Ga., 1983.

23. Y. KOGURE, *Japan's TQC* (in Japanese), Nikkagiren Publishing, Tokyo, 1988.

24. K. HITOMI, *Introduction to Today's Advanced Manufacturing* (in Japanese), Dobunkan, Tokyo, 1994.

25. K. HITOMI, ed., *Principles of Computer-Integrated Manufacturing* (in Japanese), Kyoritsu Publishing, Tokyo, 1993.

26. K. HITOMI, "Present Trends and Issues in Japanese Manufacturing and Management," *Technovation* **12**(3), 177–189 (1992).

27. K. HITOMI, "Strategic Integrated Manufacturing Systems: The Concept and Structures," *Int. J. Product. Econ.* **25**(1–3), 5–12 (1991).

CHAPTER 22
Group Technology

Asoo J. Vakharia
The University of Arizona

Hassan M. Selim
Cairo University, Egypt

22.1 INTRODUCTION

A report on manufacturing technology from the U.S. General Accounting Office (GAO) estimates that discrete parts manufacturers contribute to more than 70% of the total income derived in the production of complex metal products and at least 50% (a figure that is anticipated to rise to 90% by 1995) of all such items are made in batches of less than 50 units. Hence improving the efficiency of these manufacturing systems has the potential for improving the international competitiveness of organizations producing such parts as well as increasing national productivity levels. To tackle this problem, the two dominant strategies that have emerged in recent years are computer-integrated manufacturing (CIM) and just-in-time–total quality control (JIT–TQC). CIM has been primarily developed in the United States and focuses on increasing efficiency through the computerization of tasks and an integration of activities through computer links and databases. JIT–TQC, on the other hand, is of Japanese origin and holds that improvements in manufacturing can be obtained through waste elimination, employee involvement and a focus on materials flow. Group technology (GT) can be regarded as an idea or philosophy that can link the CIM and JIT–TQC concepts. For example, GT can be used to rearrange existing facilities to improve the materials flow (one of the principal objectives in implementing a JIT–TQC program) and create manufacturing cells. These cells, once created, can be regarded as potential candidates for automation and implementing a CIM system.

GT is a rational method of organizational management based on the principle that similar things should be done similarly. In the context of manufacturing, these "things" include product design, process planning, fabrication, assembly, control, and even the use of a standard methodologic approach for system design. Manufacturing environments producing a medium variety and volume of parts stand to benefit the most from GT. In product design and process planning, the use of part coding systems and generic plans for composite models of part families allows rapid development of new part designs and avoids proliferation of unnecessary parts. Cellular Manufacturing (CM) provides a means for implementing GT concepts on the shop floor. Dissimilar machines are grouped together to form a cell that is dedicated to the production of one or more part families. The general concept of machine layout and part routing is illustrated in Figure 22.1. Typically, a part family is a set of parts that share manufacturing, and possibly design, characteristics. A family consists of parts that require the same machines and can ordinarily share tooling. Ideally, cells are constructed with all the machines and tooling necessary to produce an entire family of parts. Due to demand patterns and use, a cell may produce more than one family. One tenet of GT for manufacturing is to break up the shop facility into production cells (e.g., a cell may contain one machining center, on-machine inspection and monitoring devices, tool and part storage, a robot, and the associated control hardware), with each cell being dedicated to the processing of a set of part families (e.g., a part family may consist of several rotational parts requiring similar tooling, which can be completely processed on the machines included in a cell).

The differences between the job shop (or process layout) method and GT (or cellular layout) are as follows. In the functional job shop layout, all parts travel through the entire shop, and thus scheduling and materials control are difficult. Furthermore, job priorities are difficult to

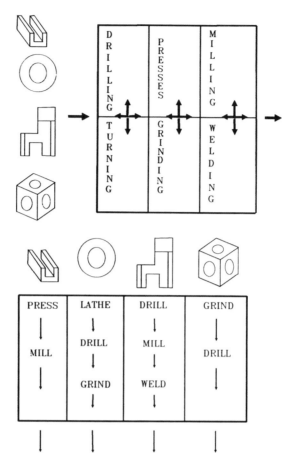

Figure 22.1. Functional versus GT layout.

set, and hence managers traditionally maintain large inventories to ensure that ample work is always available. On the other hand, a change to GT ensures that most of the parts flow through a single cell. Thus the materials flow is simplified and the scheduling task is made much easier. Workers within a cell may be cross-trained on all the machines within the group and follow a job from start to finish. Because similar parts are grouped, this leads to a reduction in the number of setups required and allows a quicker response to the changing conditions (an essential requirement to compete effectively in the dynamic world markets).

The cost savings attributable to GT have been documented by several users. For example, the range of percentage savings reported by U.S. manufacturers are (1):

- Setup costs decreased 20% to 60%.
- Labor costs decreased 15% to 25%.
- Tooling costs decreased 20% to 30%.
- Rework and scrap decreased 15% to 75%.
- Machine tools costs decreased 15% to 25%.
- Work-In-Process Inventory costs decreased 20% to 50%.

In another company where GT was implemented, the reported benefits include a 32% increase in sales, a 44% decrease in overall inventory, and an 83% decrease in the shipment of late orders.

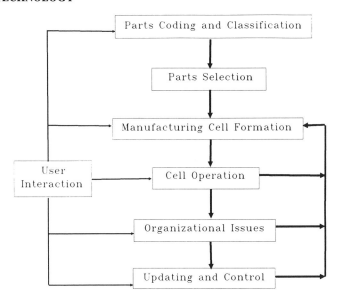

Figure 22.2.   A framework for implementing GT.

A framework for GT implementation is shown in Figure 22.2. A brief discussion about each stage in the framework follows.

1. *Parts Coding and Classification System.* Coding and classification of parts forms one of the basic tenets of implementing GT. This is due to the fact that these systems provide the benefits of reduced parts proliferation and process planning simplicity to enhance the success of GT implementations. Hence, this is often regarded as the first step of a successful long-lasting GT implementation.

2. *Part Selection.* Regardless of whether we are looking at an existing or new plant, two diametrically opposing strategies can be followed in implementing GT. One strategy is to specify a narrow set of parts for which a manufacturing cell is created. This is often referred to as the pilot cell approach. Although such an approach typically requires less time, it could lead to measurement problems in terms of the exact benefits of the partial conversion. However, this approach is followed by many organizations that either favor a wait-and-see approach or in cases where top management is not willing to favor a complete reorganization without evidence of the results.

A second strategy is to propose a complete conversion to GT. In such a case, the entire part population is analyzed and after identifying part families, the entire plant is reorganized into manufacturing cells. Although the assessment problems described earlier do not arise in this case, this approach requires a complete change in organization, operating procedures, and perhaps some additional investment in equipment.

3. *Manufacturing Cell Formation.* This step focuses the three interrelated issues: (*1*) identifying part families, (*2*) identifying manufacturing cells, and (*3*) allocation of families to cells or vice versa. In addition, it also addresses issues related to plant layout (i.e., the relative arrangement of cells in the plant) as well as within-cell equipment layout.

4. *Cell Operation.* Once a cellular layout has been identified, then specific issues related to cell operation need to be addressed. These include worker assignment, batch sizes, scheduling, and materials flow within each cell as well as overall control of the cellular system.

5. *Organizational Issues.* Based on the composition of the cells and some of the operational requirements, there will be a need to restructure the organizational setup for each cell and the plant as a whole. These issues relate to allocation of responsibility and authority within each cell as well as the complete system.

6. *Updating and Control.* Finally, issues related to monitoring cell performance and product quality within each cell need to be addressed. These need to be updated frequently to reflect the changing requirements of the cell system as well as the organization.

Each step in this implementation framework requires user interaction. The latter stages often require a feedback mechanism to establish compatibility.

22.2 CODING AND CLASSIFICATION SYSTEMS

Coding and classification of parts have several potential uses for GT-based manufacturing system. In a generic sense, a coding and classification scheme is used to record, retrieve, and sort relevant information about a set of objects. In manufacturing, part codes describe characteristics that facilitate the retrieval and identification of similar parts, and based on appropriate classification schemes, these codes can be used to identify part families. Several examples attest to the importance of using coding and classification systems in GT. For example, Tatikonda and Wemmerlöv (2) report that some reasons for implementation of a classification and coding system for GT are the following:

- Improved communications through common vocabulary.
- Increased capacity of existing equipment.
- Increased process planning productivity.
- Standardization in process plans, designs, and terminology.
- Reduced time for engineering changes.
- Reduced cost of quality.
- Increased productivity on a plantwide basis.

Selecting and Designing a Coding System for GT

Part codes can be defined as a string of numeric (or alphabetical or alphanumeric) characters that represents much of the relevant information on the materials required to manufacture the part, the characteristics of the part (size, shape, etc.), and the processing operations or machining requirements. In developing a coding system, four general principles of industrial coding have been proposed (3):

1. No code should exceed five characters without a break in the code string. COROLLARY: The shorter the code, the fewer the errors.
2. Identify codes of fixed length and pattern. COROLLARY: Varying-length codes within a given class of materials proliferate error rates and require justification in handling (right or left) to the longest code in use.
3. All-numeric codes produce fewest errors. COROLLARY: A fixed-length, all-numeric code of five or fewer digits is best.
4. Alphanumeric combination rules are acceptable if the alpha field is fixed and used to break a string of numbers. COROLLARY: Alpha and numeric codes intermixed in the same code position cause excessive transaction errors.

Other considerations that guide the selection and design of a coding system for GT are code detail and code structure. Each of these are discussed in more detail below.

Code Detail

The amount of detail maintained in the part codes is a function of several factors. The part family identification process is simplified if a code describing all the relevant details (i.e., materials, design, and processing) of every part that could be created. However, this would require a code that is inherently complex and hence impractical to use. A preferred alternative is to ensure that the coding scheme chosen helps to create families of parts for which a "composite" part can be identified.

The level of detail in the code structure required also is a function of the users of the code. For example, manufacturing engineers require information on process plans for parts, whereas design engineers need information on part features for developing new part designs. Hence, if the code is to be useful for diverse users, it would be fairly complex. However, the code design and/or selection process must also focus on integrating the trade-off between the costs of collecting the information to develop a code and the benefits of having a code structure that reflects all such information. Attributes that are dynamic such as part demands should not be included in the code structure to avoid constantly changing information. On the other hand, an indicator for a standard, high volume production item justifying specific tooling might be appropriate. In sum, the level of detail is a function of use and the cost–benefit trade-off in developing a coding system.

Code Structure

Coding is the process of assigning symbols to a set of code fields. Given the differences in symbolic representations as well as variations in symbol assignments, there are three types of code structures.

1. *Monocodes.* A monocode (or hierarchical code) is an integrated code of fewest characters that describes a population of data in a balanced, logical, and systematical order, in which each code character qualifies a succeeding code. In such a code, each digit amplifies the information in the previous digit, and hence these are referred to as hierarchical codes. Such a system provides an extremely compact code structure that contains an enormous amount of information. Furthermore, this type of coding system is effective for data retrieval based on geometric shape and size or dimensions of the part. One obvious disadvantage of this code is that the digits in a monocode cannot be interpreted by themselves but depend on the meaning contained in the preceding digit. Furthermore, such interrelationships in symbols makes this type of coding scheme difficult to construct and learn.

2. *Polycodes.* In direct contrast to monocodes, in a polycode each digit has a distinct meaning *across* all parts. Thus a 2 in the sixth field always indicates the same part attribute. Coding schemes that generate polycodes are easier to develop and apply than monocode schemes. Obviously, polycodes can be quite long. The differences between the information storage capacity of the monocodes and polycodes can be illustrated using the following example. Assume that the code is to consist of two symbols and that in each of the code fields the digits 0 through 9 are to be used. With a monocode 110 ($10^1 + 10^2$) unique characteristics can be potentially stored, whereas with a polycode only 20 ($10^1 + 10^1$) can be stored.

3. *Hybrid Codes.* Given the problems and advantages associated with both monocodes and polycodes, commercial systems incorporating features of each have been developed. Thus frequently accessed characteristics with few options are included in a polycode, while uncommon characteristics with larger variety are captured by the monocode. Hence, a hybrid (or mixed-mode) code will typically have a section that is set up as a polycode and then a section with several hierarchical digits.

Classification: The Key to Simplification

One medium through which GT can be implemented is a classification system. The objective of such a system is to organize part codes in a hierarchical structure to identify groups of similar and dissimilar parts. Classification systems in GT belong to one or more of the following five categories:

1. *Product-oriented System.* Part families are based on groups of individual products manufactured. Note that a part may belong to multiple families using such a classification scheme, because it could be used in the fabrication of a number of product groups. The use of such a system would lead to the identification of product-focused cells but would not necessarily simplify the materials flow. In addition, if the number of products being produced is fairly large, such a classification could result in identifying a large number of cells.

2. *Function-oriented System.* Creation of part families based on product and assembly names would result from the application of a functional classification scheme (gear box cells, casting cells, impeller cells, etc.). However, such a classification could lead to

extensive machine duplication within cells, and furthermore, materials flow simplification (one of the key aspects of GT) may not be achieved.

3. *Design-oriented System.* The shape and/or overall materials use drives the creation of part families using the design-oriented classification. The major use of such a classification is that it leads to reduction in part variety, because it facilitates design retrieval for new part designs. This type of classification has been used with some success for manufacturing cell formation.

4. *Process-oriented System.* This classification systems groups parts using the same sets of processes or the same set of operations. Hence this system can be used in conjunction with an appropriately devised coding scheme to identify part families. These families, in turn, can be used to identify groups of machines to create a manufacturing cell. Below, we describe methods of cell formation that have used this classification scheme to develop cell formation procedures.

5. *Design and Process–oriented System.* Commercial developers of GT software have typically developed such a classification scheme. The focus of the design-based classification scheme is to simplify the design engineering process, while process classification can lead to identifying part families and manufacturing cells. Hence such systems span the design and cell formation activities for GT implementation.

Although several classification schemes exist to develop part families in the context of GT, it appears that the design and process–oriented classification system would be preferred. The reader interested in an example of the use of such a scheme for a machine shop is referred to Ivanov (4).

Composite Parts

Classification systems result in part families with similar design and/or manufacturing attributes. The development and specification of a composite part for each part family that results is the next logical step. In essence, a composite part is a hypothetical or actual part within a family that represents the design and manufacturing attributes for each part included in the family. Typically, the equipment assignment for a manufacturing cell built around a set of part families is based on the processing requirements for the composite part. Furthermore, fixtures and tooling requirements for each piece of equipment would also be specified.

In addition to specifying the equipment, tooling, and fixture requirements for each cell, the composite part does the following.

1. Aids in the design process, because it can be used as a basis around new part designs. Note that once a composite part design is developed and stored in a computer-aided-design (CAD) database, it can be retrieved to facilitate new part designs. Furthermore, if all the design and manufacturing features of a new part are also included as features of a composite part, the new part can immediately be assigned to a cell for processing.

2. Facilitates tooling and fixture setups within a part family. Note that if equipment setups are based on a composite part, we know that these setups can be used to process at least one part in the family.

3. Helps to identify part groups, leading to a substantial reduction in the size of the grouping problem. Furthermore, groups of composite parts can ensure that setup savings can be realized by combining these parts in a single cell.

Major Coding Systems Currently Available

Several commercial and nonproprietary coding and classification systems have been developed since the inception of GT. For a selected listing of such systems and the country in which they were developed, the reader is referred to Ham, Hitomi, and Yoshida (5). Although the majority of such systems have been designed for part coding, they can also be used to code and classify other items. In recent years, the trend seems to be on the development of integrated systems that are useful not only to code and classify parts but also to develop systems that help to implement GT. Hence, some of the newer systems also include modules that focus on the facility layout, process planning, and scheduling aspects of GT. A comparison of the major features of some of the more popular systems that are currently available is shown in Askin and Vakharia (6).

In recent years, there have been a few papers that have focused explicitly on commercial systems. For example, Wemmerlöv (7) compares the cost and benefits associated with three systems, and Tatikonda and Wemmerlöv (2) report insights from studying seven companies that have implemented coding and classification systems. Examples of part codes developed using multiple systems are shown in Schlafer (8).

22.3 MANUFACTURING CELL FORMATION

Once coding, classification and selection of parts to be manufactured in a cellular manufacturing system are established, the third stage is to form the manufacturing cells. If the number, types, and capacities of production machines; the number and types of parts to be manufactured; and the routing plans and machine standards for each part are known, manufacturing cell formation approaches decide which machines and associated parts should be grouped together to form manufacturing cells. To do this, there must exist a basic relationship between a part and a set of machines. Parts are related if they are processed on the same group of machines, while machines are related if they process the same set of parts.

The manufacturing cell formation problem requires assigning workers, part types, machines, and tooling to specific cells. This problem can be formulated as a mathematical program. The formulation will be described for completeness, but the master problem is beyond current solution capabilities. We use the following notation:

Indices

g index for groups, $1, \ldots, G$
i index for operations for part j, $1, \ldots, I_j$
j index for part types, $1, \ldots, N$
k index for workers, $1, \ldots, K$
l index for operation types, $1, \ldots, L$
m index for machine types, $1, \ldots, M$

Parameters

a_{mk} binary indicator for worker k having skill to operate type m machines
A_m proportion of operator attention required while a machine of type m is operating
C_m fixed cost per period per type m machine
c_m variable cost per period to operate a machine of type m
d_j demand for part type j per period
h handling cost per intergroup move
L_j number of unit loads of part type j produced per period
U_M upper bound on number of machines allowed in a cell
R_m cost to train and maintain skill for a worker to operate a type m machine
s_l cost per period to stock tooling for operation type l
t_{ijm} unit processing time to perform operation i of part j on machine type m
T effective available time per machine per period
θ desired level of cross-training (redundancy on machine operation)

Decision Variables

W_{kg} 1 if worker k is assigned to group g; 0 otherwise
X_{ijg} 1 if operation i of part j is assigned to group g; 0 otherwise
Z_{lg} 1 if tool l is used in group g; 0 otherwise
Y_{mg} the number of machines of type m assigned to group g
T_{mg} amount of training on type m machines in group g

A mathematical program representing our planning problem is then as follows:

$$\text{Minimize } Z = \sum_{m=1}^{M} \sum_{g=1}^{G} C_m Y_{mg} + \sum_{m=1}^{M} c_m \sum_{g=1}^{G} \sum_{j=1}^{N} \sum_{i=1}^{I_j} d_j t_{ijm} X_{ijg}$$

$$+ \sum_{l=1}^{L} s_l \sum_{g=1}^{G} Z_{lg} + h \sum_{j=1}^{N} \sum_{i=1}^{I_j} \sum_{g=1}^{G} L_j v_{ijg}^{+}$$

$$+ \sum_{m=1}^{M} \sum_{g=1}^{G} R_m T_{mg}$$

subject to:

$$\sum_{g=1}^{G} X_{ijg} = 1 \qquad \qquad \forall \text{ operations } ij \qquad (2)$$

$$\sum_{i=1}^{I} \sum_{j=1}^{N} d_j t_{ijm} X_{ijg} \leq TY_{mg} \qquad \forall \text{ } m \text{ and } g \qquad (3)$$

$$\sum_{O_{ij}=l} X_{ijg} \leq LZ_{lg} \qquad \qquad \forall \text{ } i \text{ and } g \qquad (4)$$

$$X_{ijg} - X_{i-1,jg} = v_{ijg}^{+} - v_{ijg}^{-} \qquad \forall \text{ } i > 1, j \text{ and } g \qquad (5)$$

$$\sum_{m=1}^{M} Y_{mg} \leq U_M \qquad \qquad \forall \text{ } g \qquad (6)$$

$$T_{mg} + \sum_{k=1}^{K} a_{mk} W_{kg} \geq \theta Y_{mg} \qquad \forall \text{ } m \text{ and } g \qquad (7)$$

$$\sum_{g=1}^{G} W_{kg} = 1 \qquad \qquad \forall \text{ } k \qquad (8)$$

$$\sum_{k=1}^{K} W_{kg} \geq \sum_{m=1}^{M} A_m \sum_{i=1}^{I} \sum_{j=1}^{N} d_j t_{ijm} X_{ijg} \qquad \forall \text{ } g \qquad (9)$$

$$Z_{lg}, W_{kg}, X_{ijg} \varepsilon \{0, 1\}; Y_{mg} \text{ integer} \qquad (10)$$

The objective function minimizes the sum of costs for purchasing machines (fixed cost such as depreciation, opportunity cost, and time-based maintenance), variable cost of using machines, tooling cost, material handling cost, and amortized worker training cost per period. Tooling cost needs to be considered only if tools are associated with operations and tooling will be kept in each cell that performs that operation. Material handling cost assumes an incremental charge for moving a load between cells and accumulates this cost for all intercell moves. We could integrate the machine layout problem into our formulation, but because the object of cell formation is to create independent cells, this should not be necessary. After cells are formed conceptually, within-cell layout can be handled by traditional layout approaches.

Constraints 2 force each operation of each part to be assigned to a unique cell. Constraints 3 ensure that each cell has an adequate allocation of machines of each type to perform its assigned workload. The left-hand side accumulates total workload for machines of type m in the cell and the right-hand side gives the time available on these machines; each period is based on machine assignments. Constraints 4 simply serve to indicate which operations are performed in each cell. If tooling costs do not depend on this information, these constraints can be eliminated along with the Z_{lg} binary variables. Constraints 5 pick out the intercell moves. The v_{ijg}^{+} variables will be 1 if part j's ith operation is performed in a different cell from the preceding operation. If this occurs, the objective function is charged a cost h for each load of part j moved per period. If operation sequences are not fixed, this constraint set can be replaced by one that counts the number of cells to which part type j is assigned for one or more operations, and the objective can be modified accordingly. Constraints 6 limit the number of machines in each cell. Without this constraint, the optimal solution to the cell formation subproblem is to use a single cell, because the model assumes within-cell moves are free.

While the cell formation problem has been previously formulated in several forms by various researchers, we are unaware of any existing mathematical statements of the worker assignment problem. Several approaches are possible. The approach used in the formulation above resembles a covering problem given the machine assignments. Constraints 7 ensure that at least θ workers are trained with the skills to operate each machine in each cell. Values of θ greater than 1 allow for worker sharing, a key aspect of successful just-in-time systems. Cross-training to allow such flexibility is a key aspect of group operations. Constraints 7 also tie together the cell

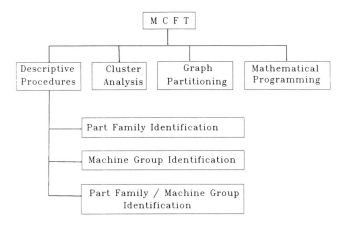

Figure 22.3.   Classification of manufacturing cell formation techniques.

formation variables with worker assignments. Constraints 8 assign each worker to exactly one group. Finally constraints 9 ensure an adequate workforce in each cell to meet total workload. It should be noted that this model does not guarantee feasibility at the operation level. To ensure that a feasible assignment of workers to machine exists, we must incorporate individual worker skills into this latter set of constraints. We could add constraints of the form

$$\sum_k w_{mkg} \geq \sum_m A_m \sum_j \sum_i d_j t_{ijm} X_{ijg} \tag{11}$$

for all m and g where the w_{mkg} variables indicate the amount of time worker k is assigned to type m machines in group g. We would also have to constrain the w_{mkg} to agree with the binary W_{kg} variables. We will attempt to avoid including these detailed constraints initially, and check to see if they need to be explicitly included after experience is gained with solution procedures.

Dynamic and stochastic versions of the problem incorporate changing and probabilistic demand, respectively. Capacity constraints could be formulated for each period of the season or the complete planning horizon. The formulation above assumes knowledge of the machine type to be used for each operation. If machines are flexible, the X_{ijg} variables can be expanded to include a machine index and the model may select machines. The t_{ijm} parameters in this case would represent conditional times.

As noted before, the formulation presented above is computationally complex and beyond current solution capabilities. Hence, researchers have developed procedures to solve subsets of this problem. Selim, Vakharia, and Askin (9) proposed a classification of the manufacturing cell formation techniques (MCFT) based on the solution methodology. The proposed classification is shown in Figure 22.3. A discussion about each solution technique follows.

Descriptive Procedures

The descriptive manufacturing cell formation procedures can be classified further into three major classes (10). The first class, part families identification (PFI), begins the cell formation process by identifying the families of parts first and then allocates machines to part families. Figure 22.4 shows the PFI steps. The second class, machine groups identification (MGI), is shown in Figure 22.5. The third class of the descriptive manufacturing cell formation procedures, part families and machine grouping (PF–MG), identifies part families and machine groups simultaneously (Fig. 22.6).

Part Families Identification

Familiarity with the parts spectrum is employed to establish criteria for bringing together groups of parts. The simplest way that part families have been identified is by part name or part

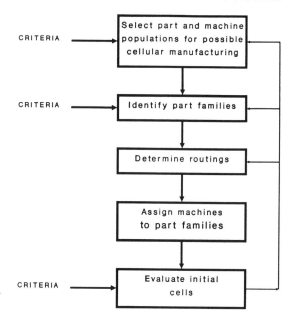

Figure 22.4. Part families identification.

function. For example, manufacturers of valves identified valve bodies, valve plugs, valve rings, and valve stems as part families for which manufacturing cells were then established. Some firms' experiences show that for certain types of manufacturing there exist "natural" families of parts that are suitable for cellular manufacturing and that can be identified by name.

Another method of PFI is to use visual examination of the part spectrum to form families of parts that look alike. One of the best known examples of this approach involves Langston Co. of Camden, New Jersey. Every seventh part on the stock list was selected and placed on a grid of 1

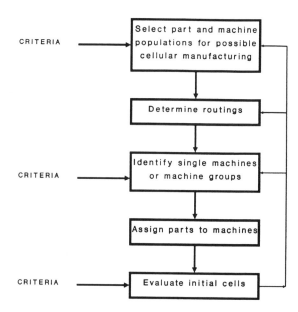

Figure 22.5. Machine groups
identification.

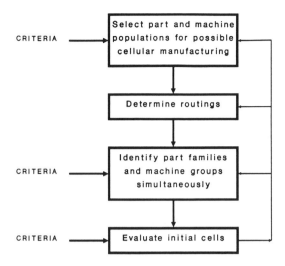

CRITERIA → Select part and machine populations for possible cellular manufacturing

Determine routings

CRITERIA → Identify part families and machine groups simultaneously

CRITERIA → Evaluate initial cells

Figure 22.6. Part families and machine group identification.

in.^{2}, which was then photographed. The pictures of 3000 selected components were visually examined and grouped into part families of like shape and size. More than 93% of the items fell into one of six families: (*1*) small cubed parts, (*2*) medium cubed parts, (*3*) small bar stock parts, (*4*) small cylindrical parts, (*5*) medium cylindrical parts, and (*6*) large cylindrical parts.

A third technique for PFI is to use a focused approach by which all of the major components of an assembled product or product group are singled out for cellular manufacturing. This strategy is common in connection with the design of flexible manufacturing systems. Coding and classification methods are then used to form part families for cellular manufacturing.

Machine Groups Identification

de Beer and de Witte (11) proposed a visual examination method that distinguishes between primary, secondary, and tertiary machines. The primary machines are one-of-a-kind and constrained to be assigned to a single machine group. Secondary machines may occur in more than one machine group. Tertiary machines may potentially appear in each machine group. A matrix is setup that considers aggregated and ordered routing information. The matrix is visually examined in an effort to identify clusters of primary machines. Similar efforts with respect to secondary and tertiary machines then follow to create machine groups and allocate parts to them.

Part Families and Machine Grouping

The production flow analysis (PFA) approach of Burbidge (12) has been widely used for PF–MG identification. PFA is a technique used to improve the material flow system of an enterprise. It is applied in four stages:

1. Factory flow analysis (FFA) studies the flow of materials between processing units, combines them to form major groups, and finds the simplest possible flow system between these units.
2. Group analysis (GA) finds the combinations of machines known as groups and the lists of parts they produce, which are known as families.
3. Line analysis (LA) studies the flow of materials between machines inside each group.
4. Tooling analysis (TA) finds tooling families of parts that use the same tooling in their setups and also finds the optimum loading sequence.

PFA analyses the information given in route cards to find the answers to the above four problems. PFA as originally presented used manual reordering of a machine-component matrix to form machine cells in its second phase (i.e., GA). The general procedure to identify cells is called nuclear synthesis. It is applied in eight main steps:

1. List all the parts made on each machine type and count their number.
2. Find a nucleus (key) machine, used to make the smallest number of parts.
3. Form a module (set) containing all parts that use this machine and all other machines used to make them.
4. Split the module if the nucleus machine is used with two or more different groups of other machines and remove for individual examination exceptional parts that require the use of machines not otherwise used in the module.
5. Repeat steps 2, 3, and 4 until all parts and machines are in modules.
6. Combine modules to form groups.
7. Eliminate exceptional parts by rerouting, changing part designs, or by subcontracting.
8. Check loads in each group imposed by a number of test programs on all machine types required in more than one group. Plan division of machines of these types between groups.

MCFT Using Cluster Analysis

Cluster analysis is composed of many diverse techniques for recognizing structure in a complex dataset. The main objective of this statistical tool is to group either entities or their attributes into clusters such that individual elements within a cluster have a high degree of "natural association" among themselves. MCFT using cluster analysis can be classified into three major categories: (*1*) array-based clustering techniques, (*2*) hierarchical clustering methods, and (*3*) nonhierarchical clustering techniques. MCFT techniques in each category are briefly discussed below.

Array Based Clustering Techniques

The processing requirements of components on machines can be represented by an incidence matrix, which is referred to as machine-component matrix (MCM). MCM has 0 and 1 entries. A 1 entry in row i and column j of the matrix indicates that component j has an operation on machine i, whereas a 0 entry indicates that it does not. Table 22.1a shows the MCM for a simple six-machine, 12-component example. The array based-MCFT tries to allocate machines to groups and components to associated families by appropriately rearranging the order of rows and columns to find a block diagonal form of the 1 entries in the MCM. Table 22.1b shows a block diagonal arrangement achieved by row and column permutations. Note that groups may not be totally independent. Methods for ordering the MCM have been developed by McCormick et al. (13), King (14), Kusiak and Chow (15) and Askin et al. (16).

TABLE 22.1. Machine Component Matrices

Table 22.1a. Unordered MCM

Machine (j)	Component (i)								
	1	2	3	4	5	6	7	8	9
1		1	1			1			1
2	1				1			1	
3	1			1			1		
4		1	1			1			1
5				1			1		
6	1				1			1	

Table 22.1b. Ordered MCM

Machine (j)	Component (i)								
	8	5	1	4	7	3	6	2	9
6	1	1	1						
2	1	1	1						
3			1	1	1				
5				1	1				
1						1	1	1	1
4						1	1	1	1

Hierarchical Clustering Techniques

Hierarchical clustering uses an alternative approach to exploiting the information in the MCM using similarity coefficients. Similarity coefficients are measures of the degree of commonality between pairs of machines or components. Large values indicate that the pair should be in the same group. Let x_i be the number of components using machine i, and x_{ij} the number of components using *both* machines i and j. The Jaccard coefficient has been used to define the similarity (ms_{ij}) between machines i and j:

$$ms_{ij} = \frac{x_{ij}}{(x_i + x_j - x_{ij})} \tag{12}$$

Values close to 1.0 indicate strong commonality between the machines, while values close to 0 indicate that the machines do not process many common parts. A part operation similarity measure (ps_{ij}) has been developed by Vakharia and Wemmerlöv (17):

$$ps_{ij} = \alpha \left(\frac{y_{ij}}{y_i}\right) + (1 - \alpha) \left(\frac{y_{ij}}{y_j}\right) \tag{13}$$

In this measure, y_i is the total number of machine types required to process part i and y_{ij} is the number of machine types required to process *both* parts i and j, $0 \le \alpha \le 1$ and $y_i \le y_j$.

Regardless of whether similarities are defined in terms of part or machine type pairs, hierarchical clustering uses this information to create machine or part clusters. Essentially, hierarchical techniques may be subdivided into agglomerative methods that proceed by a series of successive fusions of the machine types (parts) into groups (families), and divisive methods that partition the complete set of machine types (parts) successively into groups (families). All the agglomerative hierarchical techniques ultimately reduce the data to a single cluster, containing all the machines (parts), and divisive techniques will finally split the entire set of machines (parts) into groups (families), each containing a single machine (part).

Hierarchical clustering may be represented by an inverted tree structure, or dendrogram, illustrating the fusions or divisions that have been made at each successive stage of the analysis. Most of the hierarchical clustering techniques used in manufacturing cell formation are agglomerative. In a recent study, Vakharia and Wemmerlöv (17) found that the most appropriate agglomerative clustering techniques are average linkage (AL) and set merging (SM).

The result of applying the AL technique to a five-by-five machine similarity coefficient matrix is shown in Table 22.2. We begin with five clusters, one per machine. Using Table 22.2a, we combine machines C and D to form cluster CD with a similarity coefficient value of 0.75. Employing average linkage, the updated similarity coefficient matrix is shown in Table 22.2b. At the next stage, we combine machines A and E to form cluster AE with the similarity value of 0.67. Once again, the updated similarity matrix is computed using average linkage, as shown in Table 22.2c. Now we combine machine clusters AE and CD to form cluster ACDE at a similarity value of 0.33. Finally, with a similarity value of 0.07 (see Table 22.2d), we combine machine cluster ACDE with machine B to create cluster ABCDE. The procedure terminates at this point

TABLE 22.2.   Similarity Coefficient Matrices

Table 22.2a.

Machines	Machines				
	A	B	C	D	E
A	—	0.00	0.33	0.33	0.67
B		—	0.00	0.00	0.33
C			—	0.75	0.00
D				—	0.67
E					—

Table 22.2b.

Machines	Machines			
	A	B	CD	E
A	—	0.00	0.33	0.67
B		—	0.00	0.33
CD			—	0.11
E				—

Table 22.2c.

Machines	Machines		
	AE	B	CD
AE	—	0.11	0.33
B		—	0.00
CD			—

Table 22.2d.

Machines	Machines	
	ACDE	B
ACDE	—	0.07
B		—

because only one group exists. This process is schematically illustrated using a dendogram in Figure 22.7.

Nonhierarchical Techniques

Nonhierarchical clustering methods are iterative methods, and they begin with either an initial partition of the MCM or the choice of few seed points. In either case, one must decide the number of clusters in advance. In classical methods of nonhierarchical clustering, the arbitrary

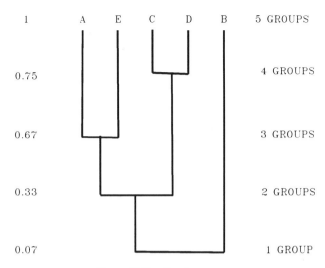

Figure 22.7. Dendrogram.

seed points chosen in the beginning are either continuously updated as and when new members join the cluster or at the end of every iteration. A distance function (usually Euclidean) is employed for computing the nearness between points in space and seed points.

Graph Partitioning Approaches

Graph theoretic approaches to manufacturing cell formation have been proposed by Rajagopalan and Batra (18) and Askin and Chiu (19). Graph theoretic models have the advantage of providing a visual interpretation of the problem. A graph $G = (N, A)$, is composed of a set of nodes N and arcs A. Each nondirected arc connects two nodes. The arc connecting nodes i and j may have an associated cost, c_{ij}. The simplest graph uses a node for each machine and arcs representing relationships between machines. Relationships are measured by intermachine similarity coefficients or actual material flows between the machines. The latter choice is preferable when an ordered production sequence is known. The flow or coefficient value is called the arc "cost." Arcs are excluded if the cost is 0, or in some cases, if below an arbitrarily selected threshold. Rajagopalan and Batra (18) propose first finding the maximal complete subgraphs or cliques of the machine-machine similarity graph. A clique is a set of nodes with an arc cost of at least threshold T between every pair of nodes in the clique. Maximal implies that no clique is contained in another clique. Cliques can be thought of as natural machine groups. Using cliques as initial cells, parts are assigned. Each cell is then treated as a node in a new graph. Arc costs represent material flow between cells. One then applies graph partitioning to this new graph to obtain final cells.

Mathematical Programming Models

Kumar et al. (20) developed a 0–1 quadratic programming with linear constraints to solve the part grouping problem. The quadratic model has been converted to two linear problems and dealt with as $k-$ decomposition problem. Kusiak (21) and Kusiak and Heragu (22) proposed a 0–1 integer programming formulation of the clustering problem, known as the p-median model. The objective of the p-median model is to maximize the total sum of similarities between parts. The number of part families and the number of parts in each family must be determined a priori (namely, p part families). Different versions of the p-median model are presented. The first version, known as the generalized p-median model, considers the process plans of the parts in permuting the columns of the machine-component matrix (i.e., each part may have more than one column with each column corresponding to a different process plan). Another version is the quadratic model, which is relaxed to get the linear p-median model. The p-median model is simple and easy to understand. The task of updating the formulation is straightforward as well. However, the size of the formulation is quite large compared with other models. Through an iterative procedure, it can be used to find the required number of part families. However, this is not an easy task and depends on users' experience, preference, and judgment. Obviously, the similarity coefficient of the objective function plays a significant role in computational efficiency.

Choobineh (23) proposes a two-stage procedure. The first stage of the procedure attempts to uncover the natural part families by using a clustering algorithm based on Jaccard's similarity coefficient. The stage of the proposed procedure is a linear integer programming model that considers the economics of production in CF. The goals of the second stage are to find the number and type of machines in each cell and assign all the part families to the cells. The objective of the model is to minimize the sum of the production costs and the costs of acquiring and maintaining the machines.

Vakharia, Askin, and Sen (24) developed a multiple objective integer mathematical model to solve the CF problem. The objectives considered in the proposed model are (*1*) minimization of the intercell material handling cost, (*2*) minimization of the investment in equipment, (*3*) maintaining acceptable equipment use levels, and (*4*) identification of a reasonable size cells. This model is one of the first models to consider multiple design objectives simultaneously in developing a cell design.

Wei and Gaither (25) presented a 0–1 integer programming model for minimizing the cost associated with intercellular transfers. Intercellular transfers occur for two reasons: (*1*) the part was an exceptional part or (*2*) the cell did not have enough capacity to process all parts assigned to it. Furthermore, limits on cell size were considered in the model. The principal limitation associated with this formulation is the occasional oversimplification. For example, parts were randomly assigned to machines when multiple machines were available. Thus two parts having identical processing requirements could potentially be assigned to two different machines.

Shafer and Rodgers (26) proposed a goal-programming model that combines the p-median formulation and the Traveling Salesman Problem. The p-median portion is used to identify the part families, and the TSP formulation is for developing a sequence for processing the parts within each family such that setup times are minimized. Because the goal programming formulations presented are difficult to solve, a two-stage heuristic is presented. Table 22.3 provides a summary and comparison of the mathematical programming formulations discussed in this section.

Current Trends

Flexibility presents a challenge to cell formation. Functional layouts (job shops) are insensitive to changes in product mix and product design that do not generally cause major disruptions. However, with cells, each product represents a greater proportion of the cell capacity, thus machines may be overloaded in one cell and idle in another. There is a need for a manufacturing cell formation method to incorporate manufacturing flexibility. In general, a GT system consists of:

- A set of part families to be processed in the system.
- A set of machines arranged in groups or cells.
- A set of means for controlling and monitoring the action of the machine cells and the movement of material.

Because these sets are constructive elements of all the GT systems, their characteristics and interconnections determine the system's attributes. It is also logically possible to derive different types of flexibility. Following this line of inquiry, we can classify flexibility in GT as within-cell flexibility, between-cell flexibility, and system flexibility.

Within-cell flexibility depends on the elements in a cell (i.e., the part families and machines allocated to the cell), and it can be operationalized as:

1. *Machine Flexibility.* The percentage of operations that each machine in a cell is capable of performing with respect to all operations that the CM system can perform.
2. *Part Operation Flexibility.* The percentage of total cells that can completely manufacture a part type allocated to a particular cell.

TABLE 22.3. Summary of Mathematical Models for CF[a]

Objective(s)	Number of Constraints	Number of Variables	Solution Technique(s)	Reference
Minimize number of exceptional parts	$P + C$	PC	K-decomp (QAP)	19
Maximize sum of similarities	P-MED $P^2 +$ $P + 1$ GN-MED $P +$ $1 + q^2$	P^2 q^2	IP code Lindo	20, 21
Minimize costs of machine duplication and cell operation	$F(1 + PC) +$ $MC + 1$	$C(F + P + M$	None	22
Minimize costs of machine duplication and materials handling	$O + C(1 +$ $M + O)$	$C(M + O)$	Zoom	23
Minimize the opportunity costs of exceptional parts	$2M + C +$ $P(C + 2)$	$P(M + 2) + MC$	Zoom	24
Minimize materials-handling costs, cell conversion costs, and total setup times	New 4 $+4F +$ $3P^2F + 3P +$ $MF(3 + P)$ Exist $M + 1$ Mix $M + 1$	$PF + 2P^2F +$ $8MF + 2PMF$ $PF + 2P^2F +$ $6MF + 2PMF$ M	None None None	25

[a] C = number of cells, O = number of operations, q = number of process plans, F = number of part families, P = number of parts, M = number of machines.

3. *Cell Process Flexibility.* Referred to as cell comprehensiveness, it is the ability of the cell to produce different part types completely with no intercell moves.

Between-cell flexibility depends on the importance of allowing intercell moves as well as within-cell flexibility. If the within-cell flexibility is high enough to process all part families without any need for intercell moves, then there is no between-cell flexibility needed for the current product families. The greater the number of exceptional parts in the GT system, the higher the between-cell flexibility should be.

System flexibility depends on product flexibility, the ability of the CM system to handle different product mixes, and volume flexibility, the responsiveness of the CM system to the changes in part production volumes.

Manufacturing cell formation methods should consider the different manufacturing flexibilities while forming part families and machine groups to assess and quantify the flexibility trade-off between process layout and cellular layout. Not that by incorporating flexibility into a GT system, a company can gain a competitive edge. For example, a cellular system with a high product flexibility is capable of producing a large variety of part types and introducing more new products to the market compared with a completely dedicated GT system.

22.4 CELL OPERATION AND CONTROL

Once manufacturing and part families have been established, the next logical step is the establishment of operation and control procedures for the system as well as for each individual cell. In this section, we briefly discuss issues relating to layout (system and individual cell), batch sizing, scheduling, and production planning and control.

Layout Issues

The layout of individual cells depends on the intercellular flow of materials between them. On the other hand, the layout of equipment within cells can be determined by the routing of parts that are to be manufactured within each cell. Thus the manner in which manufacturing cells and part families are identified has an impact on the layout problem in GT. Given this interrelationship between cell formation and (system and cell) layout, there has been some effort to integrate these two problems by researchers and practitioners. We now proceed to describe these efforts.

Cell System Layout

As noted earlier, the problem of relative layout of each cell is considerably simplified if the intercellular flow of materials between cells is minimized. This explains why the focus of most of the cell formation techniques described earlier is on the primary objective of cell independence. Hence, if it is possible to identify several cells that are completely independent (i.e., parts processed within these cells do not need to visit any other cell for processing and also no parts from other cells are processed on equipment included in these cells), then the relative layout of such cells is not a major issue.

For the remaining cells, the relative layout can be determined in several ways:

1. If there is a substantial intercellular flow between *all* these cases and it is nonunidirectional, then the relative layout of these cells can be determined using the standard quadratic assignment formulation (QAF), which attempts to minimize the distance times the materials flow between cells.

2. If, on the other hand, the materials flow between two or more cells is simply a function of the fact that parts within these cells all require a common process (e.g., heat treatment), then the relative layout of these cells could be organized as shown in Figure 22.8a.

3. A final possibility is the layout of cells using the assembly structure as shown in Figure 22.8b. In this figure, cells at the level 1 are independent (in the sense there is no materials flow between them). However, these cells fabricate parts that are needed for subassembly production in the cells at level 2. Once again, all cells at level 2 are independent but act as feeder cells for the assembly cells at level 3. This type of system layout is quite typical in the electronics industry for circuit board manufacturing.

Individual Cell Layout

Alternative equipment layouts within each cell are shown in Figure 22.9. In general, the two types of layout are the GT flow line and the GT job shop. The choice of the appropriate layout depends on the individual part routings for each cell. The GT flow line is the most efficient because it not only maintains the unidirectional flow of materials within each cell (and thus leads to throughput time reductions) but also simplifies the batch sizing and scheduling problems within each cell (discussed later). Furthermore, it facilitates the implementation of JIT manufacturing within the cell and requires the use of a simple materials handling system to transport batches between successive machines. This type of layout can also help in implementing transfer batch sizes that are small compared with the manufacturing batch sizes. To determine the relative placement of equipment within each cell to obtain a flow line layout, methods for obtaining a product line layout could be adopted.

The GT job shop layout can be implemented when the part routings within each cell are more complex. Although this layout represents the rearrangement of a large job shop to a smaller cellular job shop, it does have some benefits over the original shop. For example, the throughput time in a cellular job shop is considerably reduced compared with the original system, because parts do not need to be moved between departments. Furthermore, the complexity of the scheduling problem is lower in a cellular job shop compared with the original shop simply due to a reduction in the size of the problem. To determine the relative placement of equipment in such a shop, we could use the machine layout methods that have been developed. For example, if the size of the cell is fairly small (i.e., less than 15 machines), then the optimal layout of the equipment can be specified using the QAF. On the other hand, if there are more than 15 machines within a cell, the traditional heuristics for machine layout (such as CRAFT) could be utilized.

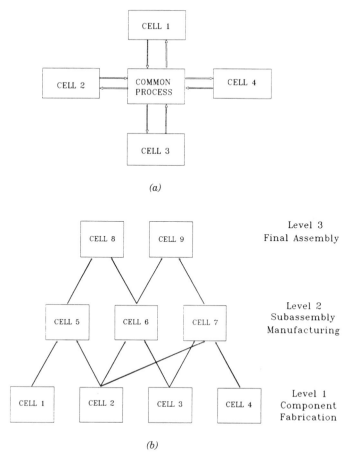

Figure 22.8. Alternative cell layouts.

Batch Sizing

Rather than focus on the specific models for batch sizing that have been developed for GT systems, our discussion focuses on the impact of certain cost and production parameters on optimal batch size determination in such systems. Note that the total manufacturing cost per part (T_c) can be compared as:

$$T_c = \frac{K_c Q_m}{R} + K_c T_h + T_p O_h + Q K_c \left(\frac{1}{2R} + T_p\right) + \frac{S_u O_h}{Q} \tag{14}$$

where K_c is $C_p I_r + C_s$ (dollars per hour); C_p, price per part in dollars; I_r, opportunity cost of capital (percent); C_s, storage costs in dollars per part per year; Q_m, minimum stock level in units; T_h, total lead time (excluding the total machining time) in hours; T_p, total machining time in hours; O_h, general overhead rate in dollars per hour; Q, batch size in units; R, usage rate of the part in units per year; and S_u, total setup time in hours. Based on this cost equation, the optimal batch size (Q_o) can be determined as:

$$Q_o = \left[\frac{2 R S_u O_h}{K_c (1 + 2 R T_p)}\right]^{1/2} \tag{15}$$

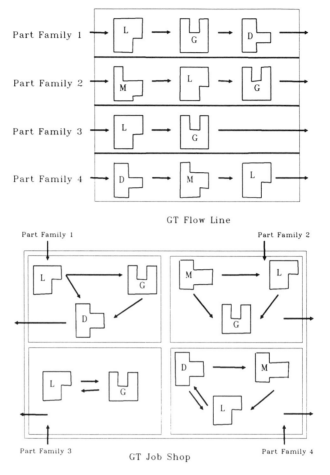

Figure 22.9.   Alternative layouts within cells.

Thus if we assume that we can stabilize the demand rates for parts manufactured in the GT cells, the optimum batch size (Q_o) is a function of:

$$Q_o = \phi \left[\frac{O_h, S_u}{T_p, K_c} \right] \qquad (16)$$

Given that D_L is a function of S_u (i.e., a portion of direct labor costs D_L are determined by the magnitude of setup times), O_h is a function of M_c (i.e., the overhead allocated to a part is determined by the magnitude of plant depreciation and investment costs M_c), K_c is a function of C_s and C_l (i.e., the total holding costs are determined by the per unit storage costs and inventory investment C_l), and C_l is a function of T_h (i.e., inventory investment is determined by the lead time) then:

$$Q_o = \phi \left[\frac{O_h, S_u, D_L, M_c}{T_p, C_s, C_l, T_h} \right] \qquad (17)$$

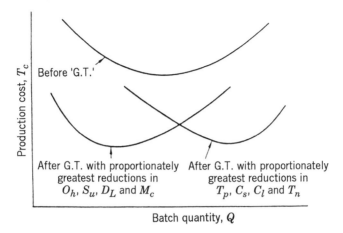

Figure 22.10. Increased and decreased batch sizes with GT.

Given equation 17, we can note that if there is an increase in O_h and a simultaneous increase in C_s, then batch sizes Q_o may not change. Hence, there is a possibility that the introduction of GT may not necessarily lead to reduction in batch sizes. In general, it can be argued that the cost parameters involved in determining T_c and hence, Q_o are reduced with a GT implementation. However, this leads to the following conclusions (Figure 22.10):

- If a company experiences proportionately greater reductions in T_p, C_s, C_l, and T_h compared with O_h, S_u, D_L, and M_c, then batch sizes would actually tend to *increase* after a GT implementation.
- If, on the other hand, the reverse occurs (i.e., a company experiences proportionately greater reductions in O_h, S_u, D_L, and M_c compared with T_p, C_s, C_l, and T_h), then batch sizes would *decrease* after a GT implementation.

Thus, the changes in batch sizes after a GT implementation depends on the proportional changes between sets of cost parameters rather than individual changes in these parameters. We now proceed to examine the potential changes in some of these cost parameters caused by a GT implementation:

1. *Overhead Costs O_h.* Typically, reductions in O_h are likely to occur because of an increased operating efficiency from GT. However, the value added from a GT implementation is greater when it is introduced in the most comprehensive manner involving *all* aspects of company operation. Thus a distinction needs to be pointed out between a company that has created a single pilot cell GT implementation against another that has carried out a more complete analysis of its part population and developed a completely integrated GT implementation. In general, the latter company is more likely to encounter significant reductions in O_h.

2. *Setup Costs S_u.* Reduction in setup costs has been touted as one of the major benefits of GT implementations. However, this cost reduction is a function of two principal factors: (1) the degree of part similarity in terms of production requirements *and* design features and (2) the scale and consistency of demand for the parts within each family. Hence S_u is likely to be significantly reduced due to GT not only when the parts within each family are highly similar but also when the demand for these parts is stable and high.

3. *Direct Labor Cost D_L.* If the cellular GT system is completely labor intensive, then it is likely that D_L may increase with GT, as workers are not multifunctional, and hence wages may need to be higher. On the other hand, reductions in D_L due to GT may take place if (1) the products are easy to manufacture (i.e., there is no need for highly skilled workers) and when the large degree of part similarity within families allows significant reductions

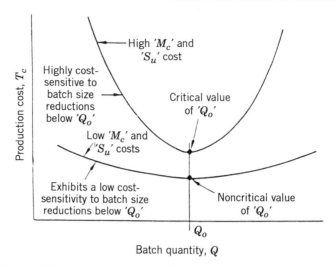

Figure 22.11. Cost-sensitivity variation for the same optimum batch size.

in setup times, and/or (2) when the implementation of GT facilitates the introduction of NC equipment that requires significantly lesser labor.

4. *Depreciation and Investment Costs M_c.* Note that if M_c and S_u are high, then the total cost curve is highly sensitive to changes in the optimal batch size Q_o. On the other hand, if a company retains a low cost plant and manages to control setup costs after implementing GT, the total cost curve is much flatter and less sensitive to adopting an alternative batch size to Q_o. This is illustrated in Figure 22.11.

This discussion has pointed out that a simple reduction in individual cost parameters due to a GT implementation does not necessarily lead to batch size reductions. On the other hand, the focus should be on the simultaneous reduction of a set of costs after a GT implementation to reduce batch sizes. This, in some sense, requires a total company approach to GT implementation.

Scheduling

Both static and dynamic scheduling methods have been applied to develop efficient schedules for manufacturing cells. Some of this work uses analytical methods for solving the static flow line cell scheduling problem. Given that this problem is computationally complex, combinatorial search-based procedures have been developed using simulated annealing and tabu search (27). Each of these methods attempts to improve the quality of any starting solution either in a random manner (i.e., simulated annealing) or by using information on prior solutions to prevent cycling (i.e., tabu search). The results indicate that for solving the static flow line cell scheduling problem, the tabu search procedure outperforms the simulated annealing procedure in terms of make span and also requires less computation time.

For a dynamic flow line cell scheduling problem, Wemmerlöv and Vakharia (28) report the results of a simulation experiment. In this case, the performance of four job-based scheduling rules (i.e., rules that ignore information on family affiliation in developing a schedule) and four family-based scheduling rules was compared under several operating scenarios (such as ratio of setup to run time, machine utilizations and number of families processed in the cell). Their results indicate that:

1. In virtually all cases, the family based scheduling rules dominated the job-based scheduling rules. Hence in developing schedules for flow line cells, the information regarding family affiliation needs to be incorporated in the scheduling method.

2. Dynamic family-based scheduling rules are preferred when few part families are processed, while the static family-based rules are a better choice when a larger number of families are processed in the cell.

3. Family-based scheduling methods provided the largest efficiencies when cell utilizations and the setup times (compared with run times) were high.

Mosier, Elvers, and Kelly (29) report the results of a simulation experiment for a job shop manufacturing cell. In this case, the major scheduling decisions are (*1*) when to switch between part families, (*2*) which part family should be chosen for processing next, and (*3*) which particular job in a family should be chosen next. To make decisions (*1*) and (*2*), the authors investigated the impact of three scheduling rules, and to make decision (*3*), the authors investigated five dynamic job rules. The results of the experiments (using different machine utilizations and total machine setup times) are

1. For decisions 1 and 2, the authors found that the selection rule WORK (i.e., the family with the largest total work content is chosen for processing) minimized mean flow time, mean lateness, and mean tardiness.

2. For decision 3, as expected, they found that once a family is chosen for processing, the jobs within the family should be processed in order of SPT to minimize mean flow time and mean lateness.

In sum, prior work on scheduling indicates that there are substantial efficiencies that can be obtained by considering family affiliations in developing scheduling procedures. However, the layout of the cell, ratio of setup to run time, average cell use, and number of part families processed in the cell all have some impact on the selection of the appropriate scheduling method.

Production Planning and Control

Production planning and control is concerned with directing–regulating the flow of materials through each manufacturing cycle. In general, the focus of the discussion in this section is on describing the period batch control (PBC) method for planning and controlling GT systems. In general, there are three major steps in implementing this method for planning and control:

1. Divide the planning horizon into cycles of equal length (assume n weeks is the length of each cycle). Based on a sales forecast, generate an end-product build schedule for a given cycle (this schedule shows timing and quantity of end products to be assembled in a cycle). Note that these end products are expected to be sold in the cycle following the completion of the assembly cycle.

2. Explode the end-product build schedule into its part requirements using a list order form (analogous to a bill of materials). All these parts will essentially be manufactured in the cycle immediately preceding the assembly cycle.

3. Parts scheduled for production in a cycle are categorized by family affiliation and lists of families to be manufactured in each cell are generated. Planned loading sequences for each cell, created to take advantage of similar setups, are used to develop sequences for parts within each cell.

The advantages of using the PBC (or single cycle, single phase) approach to production planning and control are as follows. First, there is some planning involved in developing a single cycle approach as opposed to a random ordering of parts to be manufactured. Second, if there are stable demand patterns for products, the PBC approach helps to create consistent planned loading sequences for each cell. Third, paperwork reduction and simplification of scheduling within each cell and the GT system can be realized. Finally, WIP and part inventories within the system are reduced because production is limited to requirements for meeting the end-product build schedule.

On the other hand, there are some problems associated with using PBC. The first and most obvious issue is determining the correct cycle length given that end-product demands are not necessarily stable. More recently, this problem has been addressed by Kaku and Krajewski (30). However, the issue of whether one can determine a cycle length that is constant given time-varying demand patterns remains an issue that has not been resolved. A second problem focuses on capacity imbalances in GT cells. Note that PBC simply advocates the creation of a uniform cycle but does not address the loading issue in individual cells. Even if this problem is not critical in a particular cycle, the changing load patterns across cycles, due to uneven demands, can lead to a system that suffers from overcapacity and undercapacity use. Finally, PBC makes some restrictive assumptions about the manufacturing system in terms of stable demands so that planned loading sequences can be used for a number of cycles. The unrealistic nature of such assumptions in today's market-driven environment has led to the PBC approach being implemented in few companies.

In sum, although the PBC method does provide some general guidelines for planning and control for GT systems, there are some unresolved questions in this arena. On the other hand, note that the Japanese have used cellular systems for some time. Although their planning and control methods differ, the PBC approach, by focusing on making the cycle length small, does emulate the JIT manufacturing philosophy.

22.5 IMPLEMENTATION OF GT

It is essential for the manufacturing manager to recognize the fact that when GT is introduced, there will be some major issues that need to be resolved. Typically, when GT is introduced in a plant, the existing structure, personnel, methods, and procedures will be affected. In this section, we discuss the potential ramifications of changes in the plant in several areas. First, the implementation of GT has an impact across all functional areas in a company. For example, to obtain the operating efficiencies associated with GT cells, the demand for key end products will need to be stabilized. This will probably require a closer coordination and communication between the marketing and operations functions. Although there may be some resistance by marketing and sales personnel to such requirements (i.e., stable demand forecasts), the positive impact of GT in terms of reduced cycle times leading to quicker market responsiveness should also be communicated. Regarding the accounting and financial functions, the cost-gathering system will need to be restructured and the potential use of activity-based costing systems for implementation in GT should be explored. Finally, there will also be a need for the human resource management function to change its motivational policies regarding personnel as well as foster the concept of team management within each GT cell.

Second, there needs to be substantial changes in the structural configuration of the operations function. The traditional structure of stores, production planning, manufacturing, quality control, maintenance, and engineering subfunctions in operations will undergo substantial change. In one observed implementation of GT, the company implemented seven manufacturing cells. Each cell was the complete responsibility of a cell manager who reported directly to the operations manager. Each cell manager was directly responsible for production planning and control of his or her individual cell. Furthermore, each cell had its own separate stores, manufacturing, and quality subfunctions. In addition, all the cell managers had one design and one manufacturing engineer who reported directly to them. Such a restructuring has led to the creation of a plant-within-a-plant philosophy within the company and has facilitated the implementation of control procedures.

Third, the implementation of GT will require the creation of a team atmosphere within each cell. Hence there is a need to educate and involve the workers within each cell in the implementation process. Not that one of the requirements for GT to be successful (in terms of increased throughput and increased quality) is that the workers within each cell identify with the output of the cell and also are involved in the decision-making process within each cell. A typical listing of the activities of a team of workers within each cell includes cell layout consultation; process planning; quality and process control; time standards development; equipment setup; operation and preventative maintenance; managing WIP inventory, materials handling, and flow; determining work schedules; and training and orientation activities for new members. Finally, it has been found that most successful implementations of any new technology require the initial and continued support of top management as well as a project champion. In the context of GT, this is especially true, and their importance cannot be overemphasized.

BIBLIOGRAPHY

1. U. WEMMERLÖV and N.L. HYER, "Cellular Manufacturing in the U.S. Industry: A Survey of Users," *Int. J. Product. Res.* **27**(9), 1511–1530 (1989).

2. M.V. TATIKONDA and U. WEMMERLÖV, "Adoption and Implementation of Group Technology Classification and Coding Systems: Insights from Seven Case Studies," *Int. J. Product. Res.* **30**(9), 2087–2110 (1992).

3. W.F. HYDE, *Improving Productivity by Classification, Coding and Data Base Standardization,* Marcel-Dekker, Inc., New York, 1981.

4. E.K. IVANOV, *Group Production Organization and Technology,* Business Publications Ltd; London, 1968.

5. I. HAM, K. HITOMI, and T. YOSHIDA, *Group Technology—Applications to Production Management,* Kluwer-Nijhoff Publishing, Hingham, Mass., 1985.

6. R.G. ASKIN and A.J. VAKHARIA, "Group Technology—Cell Formation and Operation" in D.I. Cleland and B. Bidanda, eds., *The Automated Factory Handbook: Technology and Management,* TAB Books, Inc., New York, 1990, pp. 317–366.

7. U. WEMMERLÖV, "Economic Justification of Group Technology Software: Documentation and Analysis of Current Practices," *J. Operations Manage.* **9**(4), 500–525 (1990).

8. G.H. SCHLAFER, "Implementing CIM," *Am. Machinist,* 152–174 (Aug. 1981).

9. H. SELIM, A.J. VAKHARIA, and R.G. ASKIN, *Mathematical Models for Cell Formation: Review and Extensions,* paper presented at the ORSA/TIMS Joint National Meeting, Nashville, 1991.

10. V. WEMMERLÖV and N.L. HYER, "Procedures for the Part Family/Machine Group Identification Problem in Cellular Manufacturing," *J. Operations Manage.* **6**(2), 125–148 (1986).

11. C. DE BEER and J. DE WITTE, "Production Flow Synthesis," *CIRP Ann.* **27,** 389–392 (1978).

12. J.L. BURBIDGE, *Production Flow Analysis,* Oxford Science Publications, Oxford, UK, 1989.

13. W.T. McCORMICK, JR., P.J. SCHWEITZER, and T.W. WHITE, "Problem Decomposition and Data Reorganization by a Clustering Technique," *Operations Res.* **20**(5), 993–1009 (1972).

14. J.R. KING, "Machine Component Groupings in Production Flow Analysis: An Approach Using a Rank Order Clustering Algorithm," *Int. J. Product. Res.* **18**(2), 213–232 (1980).

15. A. KUSIAK and W. CHOW, "Efficient Solving of the Group Technology Problem," *J. Manufact. Sys.* **6**(2), 117–124 (1987).

16. R.G. ASKIN, J.B. GOLDBERG, S.H. CRESWELL, and A.J. VAKHARIA, "A Hamiltonian Path Approach for Restructuring the Part-Machine Matrix for Cellular Manufacturing," *Int. J. Product. Res.* **29**(6), 1081–1100 (1991).

17. A.J. VAKHARIA and U. WEMMERLÖV, "Hierarchical Clustering Techniques and Dissimilarity Measures Applied to the Manufacturing Cell Formation Problem," *DSI Proc.* **3,** 1345–1347 (1992).

18. R. RAJAGOPALAN and J.L. BATRA, "Design of Cellular Production Systems: A Graph-Theoretic Approach," *Int. J. Product. Res.* **13**(6), 567–579 (1982).

19. R.G. ASKIN and S. CHIU, "A Graph Theoretic Procedure for Group Technology Configuration," *Int. J. Product. Res.* **28**(8), 1555–1572 (1990).

20. K.R. KUMAR, A. KUSIAK, and A. VANNELLI, "Grouping of Parts and Components in Flexible Manufacturing Systems," *Eur. J. Operational Res.* **24,** 387–397 (1986).

21. A. KUSIAK, "The Generalized Group Technology Concept," *Int. J. Produc. Res.* **25**(4), 561–569 (1987).

22. A. KUSIAK and S. HERAGU, "Group Technology," *Comput. Ind.* **9,** 83–91 (1987).

23. F. CHOOBINEH, "A Framework for the Design of Cellular Manufacturing Systems," *Int. J. Product. Res.* **26**(9), 1511–1522 (1988).

24. A.J. VAKHARIA, R.G. ASKIN, and S. SEN, "Cell Formation in Group Technology: A Mathematical Programming Approach," *DSI Proc.* **1,** 178–180 (1989).

25. J.C. WEI and N. GAITHER, "An Optimal Model for Cell Formation Decisions," *Decision Sci.* **21**(2), 416–433 (1990).

26. S.M. SHAFER and D.F. ROGERS, "A Goal Programming Approach to the Cell Formation Problem for Cellular Manufacturing," *J. Operations Manag.* **10**(1), 28–43 (1991).

27. J. SKORIN-KAPOV and A.J. VAKHARIA, "Scheduling a Flow-Line Manufacturing Cell: A Tabu Search Approach," *Int. J. Product. Res.,* in press.

28. U. WEMMERLÖV and A.J. VAKHARIA, "Job and Family Scheduling of a Flow-Line Manufacturing Cell: A Simulation Study," *IIE Trans.* **23**(4), 383–393 (1991).

29. C.T. MOSIER, D.A. ELVERS, and D. KELLY, "Analysis of Group Technology Scheduling Heuristics," *Int. J. Product. Res.* **22**(5), 857–875 (1984).

30. B.K. KAKU and L.J. KRAJEWSKI, *Strategic Implications of Production Planning and Control in Group Technology,* College of Business, Ohio State University, Athens, 1987, Working Paper 87-83.

CHAPTER 23

Facility Design: The Block Layout Planning Process for Manufacturing Systems

CHARLES J. MALMBORG
Rensselaer Polytechnic Institute

23.1 INTRODUCTION

Manufacturing facility design is integral to the design of the product to be manufactured, the manufacturing process, and the production plan. It is among the most fundamental steps of the manufacturing system design process and is a key determinant of the system's effectiveness. The most critical phase in the design of manufacturing facilities is block layout planning. Block layout planning refers to the allocation of space and determination of adjacency relationships of the major work centers of a facility. It establishes the primary material flow patterns and activity relationships within a facility. It results in the preliminary outline of a facility floor plan that eventually results in the detailed drawings describing the facility. In most manufacturing applications, block planning considers the flow of materials and information as well as qualitative factors defining the "closeness relationships" between work centers. The relative importance of material flow relationships versus qualitative activity relationships in a given situation is usually a function of the products to be manufactured and the processes used. Once these elements are specified, block layout planning leads to the development and evaluation of alternative facility plans. Several computerized and manual methods for block layout planning are available to practitioners. The selection of the appropriate method is determined by factors that include the problem size, the stage of the facility design process at which block planning begins, the type of manufacturing system, and the amount and form of information available to the decision maker. In this chapter, several manual and computerized methods for block layout planning are discussed. In addition, recently developed methods using a more integrated approach to the problem and incorporating a broader base of design information are described.

Overview of the Block Layout Planning Process

Traditionally, block layout planning is a two-phase sequential process involving determination of space requirements followed by determination of adjacency relationships. The determination of space requirements is itself a two-phase process by which the planner first determines working envelopes and storage requirements for individual machining centers and then groups machining centers and supporting activities into planning departments. A planning department is one contiguous element or department in the block plan that includes the grouped machining centers and support activities along with appropriate space allowances for utilities, aisles, other ancillary facilities, etc. An excellent description of how such allowances are determined is provided in ref. 1. Several criteria influence the grouping decision. These criteria span a wide range of organizational objectives and can include product family grouping, materials handling and flow relationships, supervision, process specialization, etc. A good discussion of departmental planning is provided in ref. 2.

Once departments are defined, the focus of the block planning process is on adjacency relationships. That is, the determination of where within the overall layout of the facility that each department will reside. In some cases, departmental locations are determined by functional requirements. For example, a shipping and receiving department may need access to a dock facility located on the periphery of a layout. Apart from functional requirements, the interrelationships between departments will influence the block plan. As indicated earlier, these relationships can be broadly classified as (material and information) flow relationships and (qualitative) activity relationships. There are several standard tools used in planning flow relationships. In roughly sequential order, these include (*1*) the assembly chart, which provides an overview of the flow of subcomponents of the final product; (*2*) the operation process chart, which is an augmentation of the assembly chart and includes processing information at individual work centers; and (*3*) the from–to chart, which summarizes the volume and type of material flow between work centers. An excellent discussion of these standard tools and several other tools for material flow analysis is provided in refs. 1 and 3. Ultimately, the material flow within a facility is characterized by a material flow matrix, which summarizes the volume of flow per unit time between each pairwise combination of work centers of a facility. In many cases, separate material flow matrices are defined for each unit handling load used within a facility. In addition to flow relationships captured in the material flow matrix, the information base for block layout planning includes a summary of activity relationships captured in the form of an activity relationship chart (2). In this standard block planning tool, the importance of the qualitative relationship between each pairwise combination of work centers in a facility is classified. This classification scheme is described in more detail below.

Role of Block Planning in the Facility Design Process

The importance and difficulty of the block planning process is a function of the type of manufacturing facility that is being designed. In most cases, manufacturing facilities can be classified as product layouts, group layouts, or process layouts. A product layout is typically used for flow shops, e.g., a high volume assembly process. In this situation, the layout of the facility is essentially determined by the flow pattern of the workpiece, typically resulting in strong sequential dependencies among work centers. In a product layout, the primary material flows are typically clustered along the diagonal of the material flow matrix. In this case, the role of block planning is usually limited to fitting departments efficiently into the periphery of the facility and locating support facilities. A group layout is typically used for cellular manufacturing facilities where some variation of group technology is used. Often, the strategy of a group layout is to attain the efficiencies of a product layout for much lower production volume and higher product diversity. In this case, there is only limited flow between machine cells with most flow concentrated within individual cells. In a sense, the pattern of material flow resembles that found in a flow shop. Correspondingly, the scope of block layout planning for group layouts is somewhat similar to that for product layouts. The scope of block layout planning is generally more extensive in process layouts. Process layouts are typically used in batch manufacturing (i.e., job shop), situations in which the flow path of many different products can include the entire facility. As a result, the material flow matrix for a process layout is typically more dense in that there are significant flow relationships between many pairwise combinations of areas. This makes the block planning process more complex by forcing it to incorporate more extensive flow data. Most of the techniques described in the remainder of this chapter are applicable to process layout planning.

Limitations of Traditional Block Layout Planning Methods

Most traditional approaches to block layout planning use a hierarchical approach to deal with the complexity of layout development. At the first planning level, individual space requirements for departments are determined. These space allocations are then fixed in the determination of adjacency relationships. In most cases, planning of adjacency relationships focuses only on the minimization of materials handling volume distance and/or the maximization of activity relationships. A major limitation of this approach is that it cannot address the potential dependence between space requirements and adjacency relationships. For example, if two departments have a strong material flow relationship, locating them at opposite ends of a facility may result in slow response times from the supporting materials handling system. This may cause wider fluctuations in work-in-process inventory levels that can have significant implications for storage space requirements in the individual departments. Recent work (4) attempts to address these problems through a more integrated approach to block layout planning. The approach also broadens the criteria space typically used in block layout planning to link more closely the process with product, process, and schedule design.

23.2. TRADITIONAL METHODS FOR BLOCK LAYOUT PLANNING

Traditional approaches to block layout planning include techniques focused uniquely on material flow or activity relationship planning as well as attempts to integrate simultaneously these criteria in block layout planning. In general, when problems involve 20 or fewer departments, manual methods are preferable to computerized methods. Perhaps the best known manual approach to block layout planning is described in by Muther (5). This method, known as systematic layout planning (SLP), is an integrated approach to block layout planning that considers both flow and activity relationships. The framework of SLP includes extensive tools for the measurement and documentation of material flows and a unique classification of activity relationships known as the AEIOUX scale. Within this framework, activities (departments) with the strongest relationships are classified as having an A relationship implying that closeness is *a*bsolutely necessary. Less important activity relationships are classified in decreasing order of closeness importance as *e*ssential, *i*mportant, *o*rdinary closeness is okay, *u*nimportant, and *x* for undesirable. Using this classification of activity relationships for all pairwise combinations of departments as a foundation, Muther's method combines activity relationships with data on the flow of materials to generate a relationship diagram. The relationship diagram represents the importance of departmental relationships by the thickness of lines drawn between equal-size boxes symbolizing departments. The relationship diagram is then augmented with space requirements for individual departments and converted into a space relationship diagram that scales the size of the boxes in the relationship diagram are to be consistent with space requirements. Modifying considerations and practical limitations are incorporated to obtain a series of layout alternatives that undergo systematic evaluation. Muther's method is appealing to practitioners because it provides extensive tools supporting documentation of the facility design process. It makes it easy for the block planner to organize information and document the reasoning behind each step of the block planning process. In addition, Muther (6) has written a complementary book documenting a technique for planning the design of the materials handling system supporting the block layout plan. This technique is known as systematic handling analysis and provides many of the same advantages as SLP.

Apart from Muther's method, other well-known integrated techniques for block layout planning include Nadler's (7) ideal systems approach, Apple's (1) plant layout procedure, and Reed's (8) plant layout procedure and relationship diagramming (2). The reader should consult one or more of these references for detailed information on a specific approach to block layout planning. However, to convey a flavor of these techniques, two generic block planning procedures are described below. These techniques are classified as graphical layout methods and include an activity relationship–based method known as the spiral technique and a material flow–based method known as travel charting.

The Spiral Technique

The spiral technique is a six-step, qualitative layout creation method that does not require an initial solution. As such, it is often used to construct an initial layout based on activity relationships. Often, this initial layout is subsequently used in conjunction with a material flow–based layout improvement method such as travel charting. The steps of the spiral technique are summarized below.

1. Create scaled paper cutouts for each department, including several alternative shapes for each department (e.g., squares of different sizes and rectangles with different length-to-width ratios).
2. Classify the relationship between each pairwise combination of departments in accordance with the AEIOUX rating system.
3. Place the department with the highest combined relationship with other departments in the layout center, i.e., the most A relationships with other departments using the AEIOUX hierarchy to break ties.

4. Select the unplaced department having the strongest relationship with the departments along the periphery of the partial layout. Select the best fitting feasible shape for this department and place it at the appropriate location along the partial layout periphery. Adjust the partial layout based on modifying considerations and practical limitations while taking maximum advantage of activity relationships with the department just placed.

5. Repeat step 4 until all departments have been placed in the partial layout. Adjust the final layout to attain the desired shape of the layout periphery. Substitute alternative shapes for individual departments as necessary.

6. Repeat the process to develop several layout alternatives and score each one using an appropriate model (frequency of adjacency relationships, product of user-assigned relationship weights and boundary lengths, etc.). Select the most preferred layout.

As suggested by the above steps, the spiral technique provides the user with little systematic guidance in developing layout alternatives. Nonetheless, it is a quick-and-simple technique that has proven to yield acceptable results for problems with fewer than about 20 departments. The reader should note that the use of quantitative scoring models in such cases is useful only for detecting order of magnitude differences between alternatives.

The Travel Charting Technique

Travel charting is a material flow–based, layout improvement technique that requires an initial solution to initiate. Typically, it is applied in conjunction with the spiral method, which provides the initial solution. To apply the travel charting method, the material flow matrix for a facility must first be generated from production and product-routing data. An illustration of how this is done is presented later in this chapter. The steps of the travel charting method are summarized below:

1. Generate a distance matrix for the current layout alternative. Generally, this distance matrix is constructed by computing the rectilinear or euclidean distance between the centroids of each department in the current layout. Thus the distance matrix provides the travel distance between each pairwise combination of departments in the current layout (i.e., if there are N departments, it is an N - by - N square matrix). The distance matrix may or may not be symmetric, depending on constraints that exist on travel patterns within a facility (e.g., restricted travel aisles, walls, etc.).

2. Compute the elements of the travel chart. The travel chart is a matrix of the same dimension as the material flow matrix and distance matrix. The element in each cell of the travel chart is the product of the corresponding elements of the material flow matrix (unit handling loads per unit time) and the distance matrix (distance measure). Typical units of the travel chart are unit load feet per unit time from one department to another. The sum of the elements of the travel chart is the total unit load feet for the proposed layout. This quantity is referred to as the facility materials handling volume distance. The materials handling volume distance is the fundamental material flow–based measure of effectiveness for a layout. It captures the compatibility of a product–process–production plan (as represented by the material flow matrix) and a block plan (as represented by the distance matrix).

3. Adjust the current layout to reduce materials handling volume distance based on insights provided by the travel chart. Insights provided by the travel chart include large individual elements that may suggest two departments that should be located more closely in the layout. Alternatively, excessive row and column totals might suggest departments that explain a disproportionate amount of the total volume distance and, therefore, should be located more centrally in the block plan.

Following adjustment of the block plan to achieve the minimum possible materials handling volume distance, there is typically an iterative adjustment process to obtain the best possible trade-off between activity relationships and volume distance. Computerized methods for block planning are described next. In most cases, these represent some variation of the spiral method or travel charting method applicable for larger problems.

22.3 COMPUTERIZED METHODS FOR BLOCK LAYOUT PLANNING

Among the most popular commercially available computer packages for block layout planning are ALDEP (9), CORELAP (10), CRAFT (11), COFAD (12), and PLANET (13). In this section, three representative packages are described. However, all such packages for block planning should be differentiated from drawing packages, e.g., computer-aided design (CAD) packages, which are used for creating layout representations. Typically, a drawing package will be used much later in the design process, after the final block plan is created. In fact, the block planning packages do not actually produce a block plan, but are used to develop a spatial array from which a block plan is eventually created. A common misconception among uses that leads to disappointment in the performance of block planning software is that the packages will generate something close to a block plan. In fact, there is typically a great deal of design work required in upgrading a computer-generated spatial array to a practical block layout plan.

The earliest versions of computer-aided block planning software date back to the early 1960s. Even though the algorithmic basis of most current versions of this software is not too far removed from the original versions, current packages offer many features not previously available. These include the potential to handle much larger problems (e.g., hundreds of departments), the availability of more extensive interactive features, the capacity for easier data preparation and entry, the existence of microcomputer versions, and the availability of more extensive capabilities for handling constraints. Certain features are common to all block planning software. Among these is the need for the user to define the unit area used by the model. The unit area is the dimension of the unit of space represented by one character within the spatial array output by a software package. For example, the unit area could represent a 10-by-10-foot square or a 10-by-50-foot rectangle of floor space. If the space allocated to a department is 1000 square feet and the unit area was 10-by-10 feet, it would be input as ten unit areas. The spatial array obtained from a computer package merely summarizes adjacency relationships between departments. Due to the possibility of different shapes represented by unit areas, a spatial array does not necessarily bear a strong physical resemblance to the eventual block plan that is created from it.

In the next few paragraphs, three of the most popular computer-aided block planning software packages are described. As this discussion emphasizes, individual packages may be appropriate for different stages of the block planning process. They also offer different user options for controlling the block planning process. However, it should be noted that most packages can be distinguished by three primary attributes; the departmental order of entry, the placement logic, and the scoring model. Departmental order of entry refers to the logic used for either selecting departments to place in a partial layout, or selecting departments to move within an existing layout. Placement logic refers to the rules used in determining how the relative positions of individual departments are fixed within the layout. Scoring models refer to the basis on which layout alternatives are evaluated for the purpose of generating intermediate and final layouts. In the discussion below, these attributes are the focus of the specific methods discussed. A more extensive discussion of computer-aided layout packages can be found in ref. 14.

The ALDEP Package

The automated layout design program (ALDEP) package was developed during the 1960s. It is useful for generating many alternative spatial arrays for a given problem. It is an activity relationship–based layout creation package that also requires the user to input two key control parameters known as the minimum department preference and the sweep width. The package works by selecting an initial department randomly for placement in the upper left corner of a rectangle representing the layout periphery. It lays a strip of unit areas starting at this point, and moves downward in the layout until all of the unit areas allocated to this initial department are placed. The width of this strip (in unit areas) is the sweep width designated by the user. This logic is referred to as the vertical scan technique. Once the initial department is placed in this manner, ALDEP seeks to find an unplaced department with an A relationship with the department just placed. If no such unplaced department exists, it looks for a department with an E relationship, and so on, until the next department is selected for placement. When it is selected, it is placed in the layout using the vertical scan technique until the lowest row of the spatial array is reached. At this point, the vertical scanning process works back up the spatial array, laying strips (with width equal to the sweep width) until reaching the first row. The degree to which ALDEP will look for lower order relationships with the department just placed is defined by the minimum department preference specified by the user. For example, if the user specifies a minumum department preference of E, ALDEP will stop looking for the next department to place if it cannot find an unplaced department with at least an E relationship. In such cases, it makes a random selection among the unplaced departments. Therefore, if a user specifies a high department preference, more random selections will result.

Once all departments are placed in the layout, ALDEP scores the spatial array based on the frequency of each classification of activity relationship represented by an adjacency in the spatial array. Typically, ALDEP will use different numerical weights for the AEIOUX relationships. These are used to generate numerical quantitative score for the layout. Most versions of ALDEP will refrain from printing out any spatial array that does not achieve a minimum acceptable score. Due to its use of random number seeds in generating layout alternatives, ALDEP can be used to generate a large number of spatial arrays. Therefore, even though the vertical scan method can result in nonoperational department shapes, ALDEP is quite useful in brainstorming to develop creative alternatives.

The CORELAP Package

The computerized relationship layout planning (CORELAP) package was also developed during the 1960s. Among the most popular activity relationship–based block planning software packages, it can be classified as a deterministic layout creation package. It is deterministic in the sense that for a given set of inputs, CORELAP will generate only one spatial array. Apart from assigning activity relationships, the major user control parameters for most versions of CORELAP include the length-to-width ratio of the final block plan and the weights assigned to the different classes of activity relationships. CORELAP selects the initial department to enter in the layout based on the highest total closeness rating (TCR) for each department. The TCR is obtained by computing for each department the sum of the (user-assigned) AEIOUX weights associated with the relationships to all other departments in the block plan. Once the initial department is entered in the partial layout, CORELAP computes a placement rating for each unplaced department. This is done by computing the product of the boundary length and the relationship weight that results when the department is placed to maximum (scoring) advantage along the partial layout periphery. Once the department resulting in the highest placement rating is placed in the partial layout, the process is continued until all departments are placed. In some versions of CORELAP, several alternative shapes may be considered in the placement rating calculation. In all cases, placement is restricted by the length-to-width ratio specified by the user. Tie breaking within CORELAP is based on the TCR of remaining unplaced departments. Once all departments are placed by CORELAP, the layout is scored using the sum of the products of the numerical closeness rating and length of the shortest path between boundaries for each department pair, a negatively scaled measure. Problems sometimes encountered with CORELAP include gaps in the spatial array, resulting from department placement along the partial layout periphery, and limited control options for generating alternative spatial arrays. In effect, CORELAP is a computerized version of the spiral technique.

The CRAFT Package

The computerized relative allocation of facilities technique (CRAFT) was also developed during the 1960s. This package is a material flow–based layout improvement technique that is essentially a computerized version of the travel charting technique. CRAFT requires the user to specify an initial spatial array as well as the material flow matrix. CRAFT computes the materials handling volume distance for the initial spatial array and then attempts to generate alternative arrays with lower materials handling volume distance. This is done by interchanging the locations of equisize and/or adjacent departments. Control options available to the CRAFT user include the choice of using pairwise interchanges, three-way interchanges, pairwise interchanges following by three-way interchanges, three-way interchanges followed by pairwise interchanges, or the best of three-way and pairwise interchanges. In most versions of CRAFT, each department is considered sequentially with all eligible interchanges attempted. The process continues until no interchanges can be found that result in a marginal reduction in materials handling volume distance. Often, CRAFT can result in dramatic improvements to existing layouts. Interactive, easy-to-use, PC-based versions of the package are widely available. Most versions of CRAFT allow the user to fix the locations of specific departments when desired, use dummy departments when necessary, print intermediate spatial arrays, and restrict departmental interchanges. The major problem encountered when using CRAFT is that the interchange logic can result in nonrectangular department shapes as the algorithm attempts to minimize the distances between department centroids. As a result, users often elect to use intermediate spatial arrays generated by CRAFT as the basis for developing block layout plans.

23.4 EXTENDING TRADITIONAL BLOCK LAYOUT PLANNING METHODS

As indicated earlier, a particularly important class of block layout planning problems involves job shop manufacturing facilities. In a typical job shop, material flow is supported by a fixed number of vehicles (industrial trucks, automated guided vehicles, etc.). Ideally, block layout planning for such problems should integrate the space planning and adjacency relationship planning steps to address the dynamic relationship between space requirements and adjacency relationships, which was described earlier in this chapter. This dynamic relationship is a result of the interaction of the production plan and the materials handling resources available in a system. Because slack capacity in a materials handling system can be applied to reduce storage queue fluctuations and thereby conserve storage space requirements, a more specialized layout procedure is needed. An extension of traditional block layout planning methods that addresses this relationship through integration of the departmental space planning and location steps of block layout planning is described in ref. 4. This method can be applied within an iterative, CRAFT-like block layout planning procedure. The strategy of the method is analytically to describe trade-offs in handling and storage requirements for a range of operating scenarios to support development of robust block layout alternatives. Manufacturing system operating dynamics captured in the method reflect factors that include (1) production scheduling, (2) part design and routings, (3) handling parameters (vehicle fleet size, speed, routings, dispatching rules, etc.), and (4) storage parameters. Thus the method also provides the user with a wide range of criteria (in addition to materials handling volume distance and work in process (WIP) storage space requirements) for use in iteratively developing and evaluating alternative block layout plans. The remaining paragraphs of this section describe the principal features of this method, including modeling of storage and handling trade-offs and the use of design and production data in block layout planning.

Modeling Storage and Handling Capacity Trade-offs

Design parameters influencing the relationship between handling and storage requirements in the operation of a manufacturing system include the vehicle fleet size, facility layout, and handling and storage equipment parameters. Operating parameters influencing this relationship include the production schedule, vehicle efficiency, dispatching, part and vehicle routings, and WIP storage disciplines. The model described in this section is designed to account for these factors to characterize storage and handling trade-offs. In a typical job shop system, a number of different products are manufactured with departments arranged in a process layout. Based on the routings and forecasted production levels for each product, the rate of unit load flow can be computed for each pairwise combination of departments in the facility. If we assume that unit loads throughout a system are uniform for handling purposes, (e.g., a fully palletized system), we can characterize the handling load associated with a given production schedule in the material flow matrix. The actual material flow volume distance associated with this matrix is then determined by the product routings and the block plan of the facility. Because it is necessary to measure vehicle requirements per unit time to assess materials handling performance, vehicle travel times are obtained through application of vehicle speeds and load transfer times. Given material flow rates and travel times between departments, the feasibility of material flow in a system is determined by the available materials handling and WIP storage capacities.

Handling capacity is primarily influenced by the number of vehicles available and the dispatching rules used to control them. Vehicle dispatching refers to the rules applied to determine the sequence of handling transactions served and the assignment of vehicles to transactions. WIP storage capacity is measured by the number of unit loads that can be stored and how this capacity is distributed among departments in the layout. Notation used in describing handling and storage capacity is summarized below.

W the number of departments served by the handling system
M the material flow matrix containing the elements m_{ij} for $i, j = 1, \ldots, W$, which represent the average number of (loaded vehicle) transactions per hour between departments i and j
T the travel time matrix for the materials handling system containing the elements t_{ij} for $i, j = 1, \ldots, W$, which represent the vehicle travel time between departments i and j
N the vehicle fleet size
e the proportion of each hour that vehicles are available to service transactions (i.e., vehicle efficiency)

If there are no limitations on WIP storage capacity, the minimum possible materials handling workload for a facility (as measured in required vehicle minutes per unit time) can be estimated as:

$$\phi = \left(\sum_{i=1}^{W} \sum_{j=1}^{W} m_{ij} t_{ij} + \sum_{i=1}^{W} \sum_{j=1}^{W} t_{ij} x_{ij} \right) \Big/ \left(\sum_{i=1}^{W} \sum_{j=1}^{W} m_{ij} \right) \tag{1}$$

where, following the approach in ref. 15 the x_{ij} values are obtained from the solution to the linear transportation problem given by:

$$\text{Min: } \sum_{i=1}^{W} \sum_{j=1}^{W} t_{ij} x_{ij} \tag{2}$$

subject to:

$$\sum_{j \subset P1} x_{jk} = |h_k| \; k \subset P2$$

$$\sum_{j \subset P2} x_{jk} = h_k \; k \subset P1$$

$$x_{ij} \geq 0 \; \forall_{ij}$$

In the above formulation, $P1$ and $P2$ refer to the set of departments for which the h_k values are positive and negative, respectively, with:

$$h_k = \sum_{j=1}^{W} m_{jk} - \sum_{j=1}^{W} m_{kj} \; (k = 1, \ldots, W) \tag{3}$$

The logic of the formulation for ϕ in Equation 1 is to compute the vehicle minutes of travel necessary to meet the materials handling workload, M assuming that WIP storage can be used to minimize empty travel associated with vehicle recirculation. The minimum volume of empty travel between departments is obtained from the travel minimizing assignment of net vehicle importing departments to net vehicle exporting departments. Because it assumes infinite storage capacity at each department, Equation 1 represents a lower bound on the actual material handling capacity needed to serve the material flow requirement in a system.

Storage capacity and WIP inventory are scarce resources, and it is not generally feasible to dispatch vehicles to minimize materials handling. Rather, vehicles are dispatched with transaction completions to prevent queue overflows at individual departments and provide acceptable waiting times for transaction demands. This results in more empty travel as vehicles respond to transaction requests from departments that may not have unit loads prepared to transfer to departments with pending handling transaction demands. For the extreme case of no WIP storage capacity, the number of vehicles required approaches the maximum number of simultaneously active transactions.

In practical cases, a system will use a combination of vehicle-initiated and department-initiated dispatching (16). Vehicle-initiated dispatching rules are invoked when vehicles select from an active queue of transactions (e.g., minimum outgoing remaining queue space, first come first severe (FCFS), nearest department, random department, and unit load shop arrival time). Department-initiated dispatching rules are invoked when this queue is empty, and new transactions select among idle vehicles (e.g., least utilized vehicle, longest idle vehicle, random vehicle, and nearest vehicle). Systems with more slack capacity tend to invoke department-initiated dispatching rules more often than systems with less slack capacity. The selection of a dispatching rule combination usually reflects objectives, including resource conservation, workload leveling among vehicles, and service leveling among departments.

Dispatching influences the interaction between handling and storage resources by responding to the status of WIP queues in determining the volume of vehicle resources consumed in recirculation travel. It follows that a key issue in modeling the relationship between handling and storage is the expected waiting time experienced by queued transactions. Although this varies with individual departments, an expected value for a system can be approximated for various dispatching scenarios. To obtain this value, assume a starting approximation of vehicle utilization. One possibility is to use

$$U' = \left\{ (1/2) \left[\lambda \left(3\phi - 2 \Big/ \sum_{i=1}^{W} \sum_{j=1}^{W} t_{ij} x_{ij} \right) \Big/ \sum_{i=1}^{W} \sum_{j=1}^{W} m_{ij} \right] \right\} / 60eN,$$

$$= \left\{ \left(3\phi - 2 \left(\sum_{i=1}^{W} \sum_{j=1}^{W} t_{ij} x_{ij} \right) \right) \right\} / 120eN \tag{4}$$

because

$$\lambda = \sum_{i=1}^{W} \sum_{j=1}^{W} m_{ij}$$

U' represents the average of utilization values associated with the minimum possible travel volume (from Equation 1) and the value associated with the assumption that empty travel volume exactly equals loaded travel volume.

Equation 4 can approximate the proportion of time that a system invokes department-initiated versus vehicle-initiated dispatching. For example, if a random vehicle–random department (RV–RD) dispatching rule combination is applicable, we can approximate a refined estimate of the average empty travel time per transaction using

$$\omega = U' \sum_{i=1}^{W} p_i' \left(\sum_{j=1}^{W} p_j t_{ij} \right) + (1 - U') \sum_{i=1}^{W} p_i \left(\sum_{j=1}^{W} p_j' t_{ji} \right) \tag{5}$$

where p_i approximates the probability that a free vehicle is located at department i, and p_j' estimates the probability that department j is the source of a transaction request. These probability estimates are obtained directly from M using

$$p_j = \sum_{i=1}^{W} m_{ij} \Big/ \sum_{i=1}^{W} \sum_{j=1}^{W} m_{ij} \quad (j = 1, \ldots, W) \tag{6}$$

$$p_j' = \sum_{i=1}^{W} m_{ij} \Big/ \sum_{i=1}^{W} \sum_{j=1}^{W} m_{ij} \quad (j = 1, \ldots, W) \tag{7}$$

Using ω as a starting estimate of the average empty travel time per transaction, it is possible to apply a procedure described in ref. 17 to estimate empty travel as a function of the number of vehicles. In this procedure, a queuing model is used to approximate the probability distribution of the number of transactions in process that results from the materials handling workload (λ), and the system average service rate (μ) where

$$\lambda = \sum_{i=1}^{W} \sum_{j=1}^{W} m_{ij} \text{ and } \mu = \left[\left(\left(\sum_{i=1}^{W} \sum_{j=1}^{W} m_{ij} t_{ij} \right) \Big/ \lambda \right) + \omega \right]^{-1} \tag{8}$$

With the exception of FCFS dispatching, application of queuing models in this context does not account for the specific preemption pattern that can result from a dispatching rule combination. However, empirical studies (17, 18) have shown a high degree of consistency between queuing and simulation results in estimating dispatch travel volume and the probability distribution of the number of active transactions in a closed, discrete materials handling system. Using a simple M–M–N model such as that described in ref. 19, the probability distribution of the number of active transactions can be approximated as:

$$P_0 = \left\{ \sum_{i=0}^{N-1} (\lambda/\mu)^i/i! + (\lambda/\mu)^N/(N!(1 - \lambda/\mu)) \right\}^{-1} \tag{9}$$

$$P_j = \{(\lambda/\mu)^j P_0\}/j! \ (j = 1, \ldots, N)$$

$$P_j = \{(\lambda/\mu)^j P_0\}/N! N^{j-N} \ (j = N + 1, \ldots, \infty)$$

The expected value of empty vehicle travel time as a function of N has separate components associated with vehicle- and department-initiated dispatching. For RV/RD dispatching, the component associated with vehicle initiated dispatching is simply:

$$EV_v = \left(\sum_{l=N}^{\infty} P_i \right) \sum_{i=1}^{W} p_i' \sum_{k=1}^{W} p_k t_{ik} \tag{10}$$

The component for department-initiated dispatching can be formulated as:

$$EV_D = \left\{ \sum_{l=0}^{N-1} P_l \sum_{j=1}^{W} p_j \sum_{k=1}^{W} p_k t_{kj} \left[1 - (1 - p_k)^l \right] \right\} \tag{11}$$

In Equation 11, the product term, $p_k t_{ik} [1 - (1 - p_k)^l]$, is interpreted as the joint probability of a random selection of a vehicle from department k, and the probability of a free vehicle being available at department k. The value of this probability is conditional on there being l free vehicles at the time the vehicle selection is made.

An estimate of the empty vehicle travel time based on the fleet size and dispatching rule combination, $(\tau = EV_v + EV_w)$, can be used to approximate the service level provided by the materials handling system (i.e., the expected waiting time following requests for transactions), using

$$\beta = [((\lambda/\mu))^N P_o/(N!(1 - \lambda/N\mu))]/(N\mu - \lambda) \tag{12}$$

where

$$P_0 = \left\{ \sum_{i=1}^{N-1} (\lambda/\mu)^i/i! + (\lambda/\mu)^N/N! \ (1 - \lambda/N\mu) \right\}^{-1} \tag{13}$$

with λ as defined in Equation 8 and

$$\mu = \left[\left(\left(\sum_{i=1}^{W} \sum_{j=1}^{W} m_{ij} t_{ij} \right)/\lambda \right) + \tau \right]^{-1} \tag{14}$$

When vehicle initiated dispatching is invoked, transaction waiting time consists of β, plus the time necessary for vehicles to travel from the location where the last transaction was completed to the dispatch department. When department-initiated dispatching is invoked, waiting time consists only of travel time from the current location of the vehicle to the dispatch department. For a specific department i, this time can be approximated as:

$$\mu_{Oi} = \left\{ \left(\sum_{l=N}^{\infty} P_l \right) \left(\beta + \sum_{j=1}^{W} p_j t_{ji} \right) \left(\sum_{l=0}^{N-1} P_l \sum_{j=1}^{W} p_j t_{ji} \left[1 - (1 - p_j)^l \right] \right) \right\}^{-1} \ (i = 1, \ldots, W) \tag{15}$$

where the Oi subscript denotes Equation 15 as the "service rate" for the output queue at department i, and the product term, $[1 - (1 - p_j)^l]$, is the formulation of the conditional joint probability of a free vehicle being dispatched from department j. Assuming no constraints on WIP storage and recognizing that unit loads arrive to the output queue at department i at the rate:

$$\lambda_{Oi} = \sum_{j=1}^{W} m_{ij} \quad (i = 1, \ldots, W) \tag{16}$$

the resultant probability distribution of the output queue system states at department i can be approximated by a single-channel Poisson queuing model (19) as:

$$\pi_{Oi0} = (1 - \lambda_{Oi}/\mu_{Oi}) \tag{17}$$

$$\pi_{Oiq} = (\lambda_{Oi}/\mu_{Oi})^q (1 - \lambda_{Oi}/\mu_{Oi}) (q = 1, \ldots, \infty)$$

Analagous results for the input storage queue at department i are obtained as:

$$\lambda_{Ii} = \sum_{j=1}^{W} m_{ji} \,(\mu_{Ii} = \eta_i; i = 1, \ldots, W) \tag{18}$$

$$\pi_{Ii0} = (1 - \lambda_{Ii}/\mu_{Ii}) \tag{19}$$

$$\pi_{Iiq} = (\lambda_{Ii}/\mu_{Ii})^q (1 - \lambda_{Ii}/\mu_{Ii}) (q = 1, \ldots, \infty)$$

where η_i represents the standard processing time for unit loads in the input queue at department i. The η_i terms for $i = 1, \ldots, W$ represent parameters associated with the processing function within each department. For example, if a department was a numerically controlled machining center, η_i would represent the machining cycle plus makeready time for each workpiece.

The above results are applicable when WIP storage is decentralized and input and output storage queues are dedicated. In situations in which randomized storage is used at individual departments (i.e., input and output unit loads share the same physical storage spaces), the probability distribution for the WIP storage queue at department i can be derived from the joint probabilities of the individual queue states as:

$$\pi_{iq} = \sum_{l=0}^{q} (\pi_{Il}\pi_{O(q-1)}) (q = , \ldots, \infty) \tag{20}$$

Application of the Model in Block Layout Planning

The results described in the previous section are simple approximations to the potentially complex operating dynamics of a batch manufacturing system. However, they do provide an opportunity to integrate the department space allocation and location steps in the block layout planning process to take advantage of storage and handling trade-offs. This can be done by providing the user with an opportunity to adjust the total department space allocation, or repartition a fixed set of department storage locations during the block planning process. (Alternatively, the user can adjust production levels, product routings, vehicle fleet size, vehicle routings, dispatching rules, or efficiency factors to model alternative operating scenarios.) As each scenario is created, the model provides the user with utilization measures, storage queue probability distributions, and materials handling volume distance measures that are useful in guiding the block layout planning process.

To illustrate the model, consider the problem of developing a block layout plan for a 60,000 square foot manufacturing facility with six major departments: A, milling; B, grinding; C, lathes; D, surface finishing; E, CNC machining; and F, inspection and test. Five products are to be manufactured in the facility with the product routings, demand levels (in units per hour) and processing rates summarized in Figure 23.1. For simplicity, assume that travel distances on vehicle routings are proportional to the rectilinear distance between the cartesian coordinates of

Product	Product Routing	Demand Level
1	A-B-D-F-E-F	14
2	A-C-D-B-E-B-F-B-F	10
3	F-D-B-D-C-E-F	22
4	D-C-A-E-F	17
5	C-B-E-F-D-E-F	8

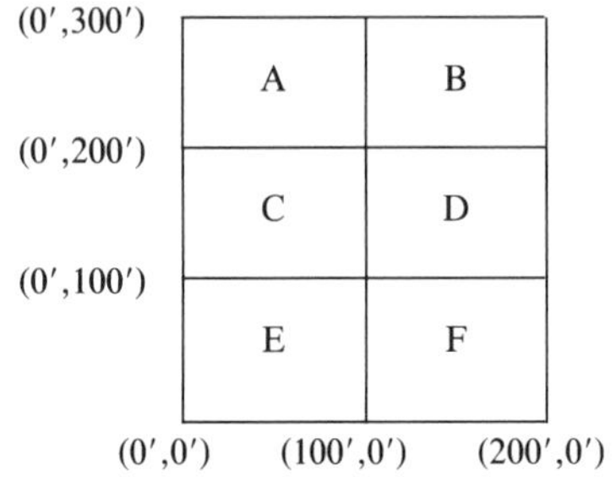

```
(0',300')  ┌──────┬──────┐
           │      │      │
           │  A   │  B   │
           │      │      │
(0',200')  ├──────┼──────┤
           │      │      │
           │  C   │  D   │
           │      │      │
(0',100')  ├──────┼──────┤
           │      │      │
           │  E   │  F   │
           │      │      │
           └──────┴──────┘
         (0',0')  (100',0')  (200',0')
```

Department	Processing Rate (η_i)	Centroid Coordinates
A	25 (unit loads/h)	(50,250)
B	100	(150,250)
C	70	(50,150)
D	150	(150,150)
E	90	(50,50)
F	120	(150,50)
Vehicle efficiency		$e = 0.9$
Vehicle speed		400 feet/min
Vehicle dispatching		RV–RW
Load transfer time		15 s
Department storage discipline		randomized

Figure 23.1. Summary of initial block layout and production scenario.

the centroids of department pairs. Vehicle efficiency is 90% (i.e., vehicles are available for serving materials handling an average of 90% of the operating period), the load transfer time for vehicles is 15 s, and vehicles travel at an average rate of 400 feet/min.

To initialize the model, a starting layout with each department having an equal space allocation is generated. This initial layout is also illustrated in Figure 23.1. It is assume that 50% of the total space within each department is dedicated to WIP storage. Therefore, in the initial layout of Figure 23.1, each department has 5,000 square feet devoted to WIP storage (i.e., about 17% of the facility total of 30,000 square feet of storage space). Arbitrarily setting the materials handling fleet size to $N = 15$, the results summarized in Table 23.1 are generated for the initial problem using the model. The results in Table 23.1 include

1. Material flow matrix for the production plan M.
2. Travel time matrix for the layout and vehicle parameters T.
3. The p_i and p_i' probability values.
4. The probability distribution of the number of handling transactions in the system.
5. The estimated empty vehicle travel time and the vehicle waiting time in the system.
6. The arrival and service rates for WIP queues at departments.
7. The state probabilities for the input and output storage queues at departments and the state probabilities for each department under the randomized storage assumption.

To evaluate the effectiveness of the current storage space allocation, a service level (de-noted δ_i) is defined with respect to the storage queue at each department. Assuming randomized

TABLE 23.1. Summary of Model Outputs from the Initial Layout

Material Flow Matrix for the Production Plan (in unit loads/h)

		A	B	C	D	E	F
	A	0	14	10	0	17	0
	B	0	0	0	36	18	20
$M =$	C	17	8	0	10	22	0
	D	0	32	39	0	8	14
	E	0	10	0	0	0	69
	F	0	10	0	30	14	0

Travel Time Matrix for the Layout and Vehicle Parameters (in min)

		A	B	C	D	E	F
	A	0.50	0.75	0.75	1.00	1.00	1.25
	B	0.75	0.50	1.00	0.75	1.25	1.00
$T =$	C	0.75	1.00	0.50	0.75	0.75	1.00
	D	1.00	0.75	0.75	0.50	1.00	0.75
	E	1.00	1.25	0.75	1.00	0.50	0.75
	F	1.25	1.00	1.00	0.75	0.75	0.50

p_i and p_i' Probability Values

Work center (i)	A	B	C	D	E	F
p_i	0.0427	0.1859	0.1231	0.1910	0.1985	0.2588
p_i'	0.1030	0.1859	0.1432	0.2337	0.1985	0.1357

Probability Distribution of the Number of Transactions in the Materials Handling System

i	0	1	2	3	4	5	6
P_i	0.0006	0.0043	0.0161	0.0400	0.0745	0.1110	0.1379
i	7	8	9	10	11	12	13
P_i	0.1468	0.1367	0.1132	0.0844	0.0572	0.0355	0.0204
i	14	15	16	17	18	19	20
P_i	0.0108	0.0054	0.0027	0.0013	0.0007	0.0003	0.0002

Vehicle Travel Time, Waiting Time, and Use

$EV_v = 0.095$ min
$EV_w = 0.5726$ min
$\beta = 0.036$ min
Volume Distance = 91,484 vehicle feet/h
Estimated Vehicle Use = 28.2%

Department Storage Queue Service and Arrival Rates

Department (i)	A	B	C	D	E	F
μ_{Oi}	80.89	88.88	95.08	106.30	95.23	106.49
λ_{Oi}	41.00	74.00	57.00	93.00	79.00	54.00
μ_{Ii}	25.00	100.00	70.00	150.00	90.00	120.00
λ_{Ii}	17.00	74.00	49.00	76.00	79.00	103.00

Department Storage Queue Probability Distributions

Department A

i	0	1	2	3	4	5	6	7
π_{Oi}	0.4931	0.2500	0.1267	0.0642	0.0325	0.0165	0.0084	0.0042
π_{Ii}	0.3200	0.2176	0.1480	0.1006	0.0684	0.0465	0.0316	0.0215
π_i	0.1578	0.1873	0.1679	0.1347	0.1020	0.0747	0.0534	0.0377
i	8	9	10	11	12	13	14	15
π_{Oi}	0.0021	0.0011	0.0006	0.0003	0.0001	0.0001	0.0000	0.0000
π_{Ii}	0.0146	0.0099	0.0068	0.0046	0.0031	0.0021	0.0014	0.0010
π_i	0.0263	0.0182	0.0126	0.0086	0.0059	0.0041	0.0028	0.0019

TABLE 23.1. *(Continued)*

Department B

i	0	1	2	3	4	5	6	7
π_{Oi}	0.1674	0.1394	0.1160	0.0966	0.0804	0.0670	0.0558	0.0464
π_{Ii}	0.2600	0.1924	0.1424	0.1054	0.0780	0.0577	0.0427	0.0316
π_i	0.0435	0.0684	0.0808	0.0849	0.0838	0.0794	0.0733	0.0663
i	8	9	10	11	12	13	14	15
π_{Oi}	0.0387	0.0322	0.0268	0.0223	0.0186	0.0155	0.0129	0.0107
π_{Ii}	0.0234	0.0173	0.0128	0.0095	0.0070	0.0052	0.0038	0.0028
π_i	0.0591	0.0521	0.0455	0.0395	0.0341	0.0292	0.0250	0.0213
i	16	17	18	19	20	21	22	23
π_{Oi}	0.0089	0.0074	0.0062	0.0052	0.0043	0.0036	0.0030	0.0025
π_{Ii}	0.0021	0.0016	0.0012	0.0009	0.0006	0.0005	0.0003	0.0003
π_i	0.0181	0.0153	0.0129	0.0109	0.0092	0.0077	0.0065	0.0054

Department C

i	0	1	2	3	4	5	6	7
π_{Oi}	0.4005	0.2401	0.1439	0.0863	0.0517	0.0310	0.0186	0.0111
π_{Ii}	0.3000	0.2100	0.1470	0.1029	0.0720	0.0504	0.0353	0.0247
π_i	0.1201	0.1561	0.1525	0.1326	0.1084	0.0852	0.0652	0.0490
i	8	9	10	11	12	13	14	15
π_{Oi}	0.0067	0.0040	0.0024	0.0014	0.0009	0.0005	0.0003	0.0002
π_{Ii}	0.0173	0.0121	0.0085	0.0059	0.0042	0.0029	0.0020	0.0014
π_i	0.0363	0.0266	0.0193	0.0140	0.0100	0.0072	0.0051	0.0036

Department D

i	0	1	2	3	4	5	6	7
π_{Oi}	0.1252	0.1095	0.0958	0.0838	0.0733	0.0641	0.0561	0.0491
π_{Ii}	0.4933	0.2500	0.1266	0.0642	0.0325	0.0165	0.0083	0.0042
π_i	0.0617	0.0853	0.0905	0.0872	0.0803	0.0723	0.0643	0.0568
i	8	9	10	11	12	13	14	15
π_{Oi}	0.0429	0.0376	0.0329	0.0288	0.0252	0.0220	0.0193	0.0168
π_{Ii}	0.0021	0.0011	0.0006	0.0003	0.0001	0.0001	0.0000	0.0000
π_i	0.0500	0.0439	0.0384	0.0377	0.0295	0.0258	0.0226	0.0197

Department E

i	0	1	2	3	4	5	6	7
π_{Oi}	0.1704	0.1414	0.1173	0.0973	0.0807	0.0670	0.0555	0.0461
π_{Ii}	0.1222	0.1073	0.0942	0.0827	0.0726	0.0637	0.0559	0.0491
π_i	0.0208	0.0356	0.0455	0.0519	0.0554	0.0568	0.0567	0.0554
i	8	9	10	11	12	13	14	15
π_{Oi}	0.0382	0.0317	0.0263	0.0218	0.0181	0.0150	0.0125	0.0103
π_{Ii}	0.0431	0.0378	0.0332	0.0291	0.0256	0.0224	0.0197	0.0173
π_i	0.0533	0.0506	0.0477	0.0445	0.0413	0.0381	0.0349	0.0319
i	16	17	18	19	20	21	22	23
π_{Oi}	0.0086	0.0071	0.0059	0.0049	0.0041	0.0034	0.0028	0.0023
π_{Ii}	0.0152	0.0133	0.0117	0.0103	0.0090	0.0079	0.0069	0.0061
π_i	0.0291	0.0264	0.0239	0.0216	0.0194	0.0175	0.0157	0.0140

Department F

i	0	1	2	3	4	5	6	7
π_{Oi}	0.4929	0.2499	0.1267	0.0643	0.0326	0.0165	0.0084	0.0042
π_{Ii}	0.1417	0.1216	0.1044	0.0896	0.0769	0.0660	0.0567	0.0486
π_i	0.0698	0.0953	0.0998	0.0948	0.0860	0.0761	0.0665	0.0577
i	8	9	10	11	12	13	14	15
π_{Oi}	0.0022	0.0011	0.0006	0.0003	0.0001	0.0001	0.0000	0.0000
π_{Ii}	0.0417	0.0358	0.0307	0.0264	0.0227	0.0194	0.0167	0.0143
π_i	0.0498	0.0429	0.0369	0.0317	0.0273	0.0234	0.0201	0.0173
i	16	17	18	19	20	21	22	23
π_{Oi}	0.0000	0.0000	0.0000	0.0000	0.0000	0.0000	0.0000	0.0000
π_{Ii}	0.0123	0.0106	0.0091	0.0078	0.0067	0.0057	0.0049	0.0042
π_i	0.0148	0.0127	0.0109	0.0094	0.0080	0.0069	0.0059	0.0051

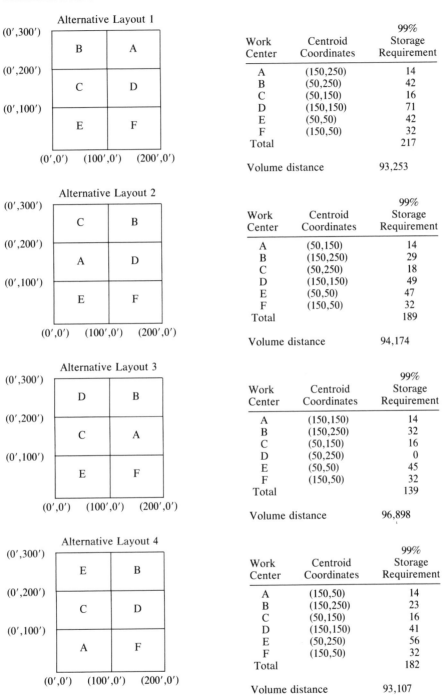

Alternative Layout 1

Work Center	Centroid Coordinates	99% Storage Requirement
A	(150,250)	14
B	(50,250)	42
C	(50,150)	16
D	(150,150)	71
E	(50,50)	42
F	(150,50)	32
Total		217

Volume distance   93,253

Alternative Layout 2

Work Center	Centroid Coordinates	99% Storage Requirement
A	(50,150)	14
B	(150,250)	29
C	(50,250)	18
D	(150,150)	49
E	(50,50)	47
F	(150,50)	32
Total		189

Volume distance   94,174

Alternative Layout 3

Work Center	Centroid Coordinates	99% Storage Requirement
A	(150,150)	14
B	(150,250)	32
C	(50,150)	16
D	(50,250)	0
E	(50,50)	45
F	(150,50)	32
Total		139

Volume distance   96,898

Alternative Layout 4

Work Center	Centroid Coordinates	99% Storage Requirement
A	(150,50)	14
B	(150,250)	23
C	(50,150)	16
D	(150,150)	41
E	(50,250)	56
F	(150,50)	32
Total		182

Volume distance   93,107

Figure 23.2. Alternative layouts used to measure the sensitivity of storage requirements to departmental location.

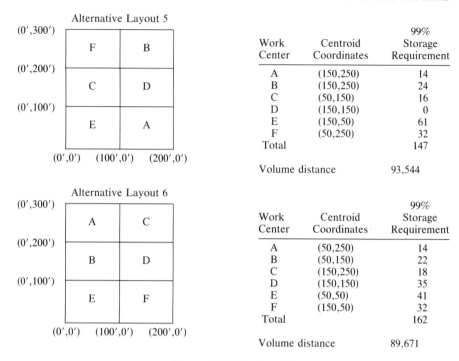

Figure 23.2 (*Continued*)

storage at each department, δ_i is used to solve for the storage requirement at department i, b_i, in unit loads using

$$\delta_i = \sum_{k=0}^{b_i} \pi_k \qquad (21)$$

Thus b_i represents the storage level at department i that is sufficient $\delta_i \times 100\%$ of the time. Assuming that $\delta_i = 0.99$ for $i = 1, \ldots, W$, the resultant storage requirements for departments A through F can be computed from Table 23.1. to yield $b_A = 14$, $b_B = 30$, $b_C = 16$, $b_D = 36$, $b_E = 44$, and $b_F = 32$ for a total storage requirement of 172 unit loads.

To determine the degree of sensitivity of storage requirements to departmental location, the series of pairwise interchanges summarized in Figure 23.2 were evaluated. Figure 23.2 also summarizes the anticipated storage requirements by department associated with each layout and the materials handling volume distance in unit load feet per hour. As Figure 23.2 suggests, storage requirements can vary significantly for alternative adjacency relationships in a layout. Using total WIP storage minimization as a criterion, alternative layout 3 (Figure 23.2) results in an approximate savings of 20% in WIP storage requirements.

Based on selection of alternative layout 3, the total WIP storage space allocation is reduced by 20%, i.e., 6,000 square feet. The remaining 24,000 square feet of storage space is then reallocated between the six departments in approximate proportion to expected requirements at the 99% service level. This results in revised layout 1 show in Figure 23.3. To improve this layout further with respect to materials handling volume distance, the series of pairwise interchanges illustrated in the remaining diagrams of Figure 23.3 were attempted. This resulted in selection of revised alternative layout 4 being selected as the preferred block layout plan. Given the volume distance minimizing layout for the current storage space allocation, the resulting storage space requirements distribution is compared with the current space allocation. As shown in Figure 23.3, individual storage space requirements in the volume distance minimizing

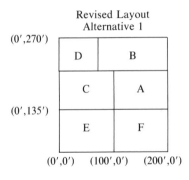

Revised Layout
Alternative 1

Work Center	Centroid Coordinates	99% Storage Requirement
A	(150,150)	14
B	(133,225)	25
C	(50,150)	16
D	(33,225)	0
E	(50,67)	41
F	(150,67)	32
Volume distance		91,635

Revised Layout
Alternative 2

Work Center	Centroid Coordinates	99% Storage Requirement
A	(50,150)	14
B	(133,225)	24
C	(150,150)	16
D	(33,225)	0
E	(50,67)	43
F	(50,67)	32
Volume distance		92,388

Revised Layout
Alternative 3

Work Center	Centroid Coordinates	99% Storage Requirement
A	(150,150)	13
B	(67,225)	25
C	(50,150)	16
D	(167,225)	0
E	(50,67)	42
F	(150,67)	32
Volume distance		92,150

Revised Layout
Alternative 4

Work Center	Centroid Coordinates	99% Storage Requirement
A	(50,150)	14
B	(67,225)	26
C	(150,150)	15
D	(167,225)	0
E	(50,67)	44
F	(150,67)	32
Volume distance		91,260

Figure 23.3. Layout alternatives following the space reallocation step.

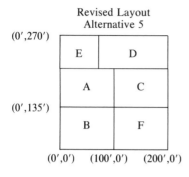

Revised Layout
Alternative 5

(0',270')		
E	D	
A	C	
(0',135')		
B	F	

(0',0')   (100',0')   (200',0')

Work Center	Centroid Coordinates	99% Storage Requirement
A	(50,150)	14
B	(50,67)	26
C	(150,150)	16
D	(167,225)	0
E	(67,225)	46
F	(150,67)	32
Volume distance		92,365

Revised Layout
Alternative 6

(0',270')		
F	D	
A	C	
(0',135')		
E	B	

(0',0')   (100',0')   (200',0')

Work Center	Centroid Coordinates	99% Storage Requirement
A	(50,150)	14
B	(150,67)	25
C	(150,150)	16
D	(167,225)	0
E	(50,67)	46
F	(67,225)	32
Volume distance		91,847

Figure 23.3   (*Continued*)

layout are within 10% of the revised storage space allocation for all departments. At this point, the storage space allocation between departments could be revised and the layout development procedure repeated. Alternatively, other parameters describing the facility could be varied before developing a block layout plan with the objective of devising a layout that is robust with respect to the plausible range of operating scenarios.

23.5 SUMMARY

The most crucial step in the design of manufacturing facilities is block layout planning. Block layout planning defines the location of individual work centers and supporting facilities within a layout, eventually leading to specification of the detailed floor plan of the facility. It is a fundamental determinant of the overall effectiveness of a manufacturing system. Effective block planning requires consideration of the design of the product to be manufactured, the processes used, and the production plan. Block layout planning considers both the flow of materials and activity relationships in defining the space requirements and adjacency relationships in a facility. This process is particularly challenging in the case of batch manufacturing systems, because a process layout typically involves heavy material flows between many pairwise combinations of departments. Several manual and computerized methods are available to support the designer in block layout planning. However, most methods assume a two-phase hierarchical process involving the space allocation to departments followed by the specification of adjacency relationships in a layout. Due to the dynamic relationship between space requirements and the location of departments in a manufacturing facility, a need exists for block planning methodologies that can simultaneously address the space allocation and adjacency relationship determination steps.

   To address this need, a heuristic, analytical model was described. The model simultaneously considers production scheduling, plant layout, WIP storage capacity, vehicle fleet size, part and vehicle routings, vehicle dispatching, and other key aspects of a manufacturing system design. Because these parameter values are rarely known with certainty during the block planning phase of facility design, sensitivity studies based on a range of prospective parameter values are crucial. The extended method of block planning described in this chapter provides an analytical method for these types of sensitivity analyses. As a result, it provides the user with the flexibility to enumerate intelligently the layout design solution space during the block layout planning process.

BIBLIOGRAPHY

1. J.M. APPLE, *Plant Layout and Material Handling,* 3rd. ed., John Wiley & Sons, Inc., New York, 1977.
2. J.A. TOMPKINS and J.A. WHITE, *Facilities Planning,* John & Wiley & Sons, Inc., New York, 1984.
3. B.W. NIEBEL, *Motion and Time Study,* 8th. ed., Irwin, Homewood, Ill., 1988.
4. C.J. MALMBORG, "A Heuristic Model for Simultaneous Storage Space Allocation and Block Layout Planning," *Int. J. Product. Res.,* in press.
5. R. MUTHER, *Systemic Layout Planning,* 2nd. ed., Cahners Books, Boston, 1973.
6. R. MUTHER, *Systemic Handling Analysis,* 2nd. ed., Cahners Books, Boston, 1973.
7. G. NADLER, "What Systems Really Are," *Mod. Materials Handling* 2(7), 41–47 (1965).
8. R. REED, *Plant Layout: Factors, Principles and Techniques,* Irwin, Homewood, Ill., 1961.
9. J.M. SEEHOF and W.O. EVANS, "Automated Layout Design Program," *J. Ind. Eng.* 18(12), 194–200 (1967).
10. R.C. LEE and J.M. MOORE, "CORELAP—Computerized Relationship Layout Planning," *J. Ind. Eng.* 18(3), 194–200 (1967).
11. G.C. ARMOUR and E.S. BUFFA, "A Heuristic Algorithm and Simulation Approach to Relative Location of Facilities," *Manage. Sci.* 9(2), 294–309 (1963).
12. J.A. TOMPKINS and R. REED, "An Applied Model for the Facilities Design Problem," *Int. J. Product. Res.* 14(5), 583–595 (1976).
13. M.P. DEISENROTH and J.M. APPLE, *A Computerized Plant Layout Analysis and Evaluation Technique (PLANET),* Institute of Industrial Engineers, Norcross, Ga., 1972, Tech. Paper 1962.
14. R.L. FRANCIS, L.F. MCGINNIS, and J.A. WHITE, *Facility Layout and Location: An Analytical Approach,* Prentice-Hall, Inc., Englewood Cliffs, N.J., 1992.
15. W.L. MAXWELL and J.A. MUCKSTADT, "Design of Automatic Guided Vehicle Systems," *IIE Trans.* 14(2), 114–124 (1982).
16. P.J. EGBELU and J.M.A. TANCHOCO, "Characterization of Automatic Guided Vehicle Dispatching Rules," *Int. J. Product. Res.* 22(3), 359–374 (1984).
17. C.J. MALMBORG and Y.C. SHEN, "Fleet Size Based Modeling of Vehicle Dispatching Effects in Discrete Materials Handling Systems," Rensselaer Polytechnic Institute, Troy, N.Y., Oct. 1991, DSES Rep. Ser.
18. C.J. MALMBORG and Y.C. SHEN, *Simulation Based Validation of Real Time Control Rules in Discrete Materials Handling Systems,* paper presented at the 1991 IEEE International Conference on Systems, Man and Cybernetics, Charlottesville, VA., Oct. 1991.
19. W.L. WINSTON, *Operations Research: Applications and Algorithms,* Duxbury, Boston, Mass., 1987.

SECTION VI

PLANNING, SCHEDULING, AND CONTROL OF MANUFACTURING SYSTEMS

CHAPTER 24
Computer Integrated Production Planning and Control

SUBHASH C. SARIN
Virginia Polytechnic Institute and State University

SANCHOY K. DAS
New Jersey Institute of Technology

2.4 INTRODUCTION

The concept of integration in manufacturing is key to designing and operating these systems to achieve high levels of productivity. It involves the coordination of design, manufacturing, and management. The concept of integrated manufacturing is not new. It is a concept that has been practiced by the designers in the past, but its value seems to have been lost in the drive for "big is better" after the 1940s. With the 1970s there was a growing realization that there was a problem with American manufacturing. Managers and researchers had become aware that manufacturing was relatively costly, inflexible, of a low quality, and of low technology content. It was during this time that the concept of integration was rediscovered as a new technology, a new weapon. In 1974, Harrington introduced this new technology as computer-integrated manufacturing (CIM).

A model of computer-integrated manufacturing and its associated technologies is given in Das and Sarin (1). It consists of three technological elements—computer-aided design (CAD), computer-aided manufacturing (CAM), and computer integrated production planning and control (CIPPC)—and a fourth element—management. There are three significant areas of integration among these four technologies: integration 1: management with CAD, CAM, and CIPPC; integration 2: CAD with CAM; and integration 3: CAM with CIPPC.

Most of the current research in manufacturing systems integration can be classified in one of the above categories. The specific technologies identified in integration 1 are manufacturing automation protocol (MAP), technical and office planning (TOP) standards, and open systems interconnection (OSI). MAP, TOP, and OSI are primarily focused on systems architecture and organization. Both MAP and TOP are expected ultimately to result in a system of standards for the entire CIM. Descriptions of MAP, TOP, and OSI are provided by Beale (2). Integrated computer-aided manufacturing (ICAM)* (1000) focuses on the architecture of the factory of the future. It presents a framework for organizing all the functions, information types, and interactions typical of a manufacturing system (3).

The planning and control of manufacturing systems involve organizing and managing the process of converting raw materials into a predesigned finished product. The subject and concept of CIPPC is relatively less developed than the more prominent elements of CAD and CAM. In reality, CIPPC is an outgrowth of CIM rather than the converse. But in the achievement of

---

* ICAM is a research program of the U.S. Air force. Started in 1978 and located at the Wright Patterson AFB, the ICAM program is the largest single program in the Department of Defense's Manufacturing Technology (ManTech) program. The annual budget for ICAM is in excess of $20 million. The objective of ICAM is to advance the state of the art of CAM in the aerospace industry. There are several research thrusts in the program, the numerical code after ICAM indicates a particular research thrust. Further information on ICAM can be obtained from ref. 3.

CIM, the component of CIPPC is expected to be most critical. DeMeyer (4), in a survey of integration issues in future manufacturing systems, found the issues relating to the planning and control function to be more frequently cited than those relating to CAD and CAM. DeMeyer attributed this to the naturally integrative nature of CIPPC and predicted it would be the pivotal element in integrated manufacturing systems.

As the degree of automation increases, the production control function becomes the key to the success of the manufacturing facility (5). Furthermore, with a concurrent increase in automation and computerization, there is an increase in the domain of the production control function. Thus the development of sophisticated and well-designed CIPPC systems must parallel the developments in CAD and CAM. In recent times, this parallel development has not occurred. The present relative weakness of technologies and concepts in the production management area is primarily due to the nature of the people who manage this function. Top management has generally given a low priority to production management, and as a result, production managers have been cautious and reactive in nature. Unless the control function is given more visibility, the developments will continue to be limited in the future (6).

Present attempts at designing CIM typically substitute for the CIPPC element by using an existing computerized production control system such as MRP-II. While some researchers claim these systems provide a natural hub for CIMS (7), others argue they will not schedule the factory of the future (8). The fact is that there has been a limited effort at developing a CIPPC system with a CIM focus. The intent of this chapter is to provide the framework for an operating CIPPC system and present relevant elements that constitute such a system.

The material presented here may be classified into three categories. First, we discuss the topic of production planning and control. Second, we examine and project what production control systems will look like in the factory of the future. Third, we discuss integrating approaches and tools in the production control area. Primarily, tools such as materials requirements planning (MRP), MRP-II, just-in-time (JIT), optimized production technology (OPT), hierarchical production planning (HPP), flexible machine system (FMS) scheduling, and synchronized manufacturing are discussed. Their applicability and integrability with CIM are evaluated. Consequently, the relevant issues and characteristics of an integrated production control system are identified. The presentation is by no means exhaustive of all methods. Capacity requirements planning, due date setting, and other modules of production control are not covered here.

24.2 PRODUCTION PLANNING AND CONTROL

The literature on production control is diverse and extensive. The subject not only concerns the problems of scheduling and material management but also overlaps into the sciences of inventory control, operations management, material handling, maintenance management, and information management. Tools and techniques vary from single-machine sequencing algorithms to large-scale MRP systems. Comprehensive treatments of the subject have been published (9–12). Collections of significant papers are also available (13–15). Several texts in the operations research area discuss typical problems in the production control area (16, 17). The subject of machine scheduling is a subset of production control. Comprehensive treatments of scheduling are available (18–22).

The trend in current-day production control is to build large-scale computer-based systems. These systems are typically based on well-known approaches such as MRP, JIT, and OPT. Several commercial packages such as MAPICS (IBM, Armonk, N.Y.), SCHEDULEX (Numetrix, Ltd., Toronto), MCS-3 (Micro Manufacturing Systems, Columbus, Ohio), Cullinet (Cullinet Software, Inc., Westwood, Mass.), AMAPS (Camsen Corp., Minneapolis), PMS (Boeing Computer Services, Seattle), Factorial (Factorial Systems, Inc., Austin, Tex.), and MAC-PAC (Arthur Anderson, Washington, D.C.) are currently available. An exhaustive list of commercially available packages is given by Koelsch (23). These packages are usually designed for specific types of manufacturing environments and are not based on a generic framework. Also, no discussion of the logic on which these packages are based exists. However, several comparative studies of specific techniques have been reported. Ritzman et al. (24) and Krajweski et al. (25) present a comparison of MRP, Kanban, and ROP based on simulation results of a manufacturing system. Gelders and Van Wassenhove (26) present a critique of MRP, JIT, and OPT in capacity-constrained situations. Seward et al. (27) compare MRP and HPP. Most of these studies conclude that there is no global best technique and success depends on selecting the right technique. Shivnan et al. (28) trace the evolution of production control approaches from economic order quantity (EOQ) to MRP to JIT and OPT. They show that this evolution describes a transitional trend from strictly limited scope quantitative models to a systems perspective.

The bulk of the comparative studies focus on the performance of these systems in a simulated environment. Few studies truly analyze the basic difference in control logic, strategic issues, decision framework, integrability, and competitiveness of these approaches. A review of control trends in manufacturing systems is provided by Gershwin et al. (29). They list the central issues in future systems to be complexity, hierarchy, discipline, capacity, uncertainty, and feedback and evaluate work in the area of production control along these issues. An exhaustive literature review of production control as applicable to the shop floor is provided by Melynk et al. (30). The nature of shop floor control changed greatly in the last 40 yr. During the 1950s and 1960s, most of the focus was on scheduling and dispatching algorithms. During the 1970s, perspectives began to broaden and the interdependence of activities within and outside the shop floor was recognized. Since the 1980s, these interdependencies are being integrated into single large-scale computerized systems.

On the subject of machine scheduling Graves (31) reports on a brief review of production scheduling theory and presents a categorization of existing research activities in relation to theory. Graves also compares scheduling theory and practice and concluded that there is anything but a one-to-one correspondence between the two. Emmons (32) lists the assumptions, objectives, and optimal policies for several job shop scheduling algorithms. Such a listing can be used by a practitioner to integrate an existing algorithm into a macrocontrol system. Eilon (33) attempts a classification for the numerous solution approaches to the production scheduling problem. The classification scheme is based on (1) the type of production and the environment in which it is carried out, (2) the objective or objectives to be attained, (3) the constraints on the systems and on the scheduler, and (4) the control or decision variables to be determined. This scheme also is applicable to the production control problem. It provides the framework for creating a library of scheduling techniques.

The subject of inventory control is closely related to production control and ideally should be an integral part of a CIPPC. Maintaining inventory is a nonvalue adding process and its reduction is one of the primary objectives of production control. There is a common misconception that certain approaches to production control, such as JIT, will result in zero inventories (34). The reality is that zero inventories are not possible, and it is only an expression referring to a situation of low inventories. A common analogy used by the Japanese to describe inventories and production problems is to liken the inventory to water in a river and production problems to rocks in the river (35). When the water (inventory) is high the rocks (problems) are covered and the waterway is clear. Reducing inventory exposes the problems and forces their detection and removal. What is often not realized is that draining the water (zero inventories) will result in no flow (production). Clearly, there will always be inventory and the study of inventory models will continue to be an important subject.

General treatments of inventory models are presented by Naddor (36) and Silver and Peterson (37). While Naddor provides a classic treatment of the various inventory models, Silver and Peterson approach inventory management as a part of the production planning and control problem. the subject of inventory modeling is one of the most developed applications of operations research. But just as in the case of production scheduling, there is a considerable gap between theory and practice. Barancsi et al. (38) identify five causes for this gap:

1. The organizational structure of companies does not allow for the creation of comprehensive models.
2. Decision makers are skeptical of theoretical models and are adverse to their application.
3. Systems designers are not aware of available models and when and how they are applicable.
4. Current computer support is oriented toward database activities and not decision making.
5. A great proportion of models were created because of the mathematical aspect of the problem without considering the possibility of application.

Barancsi et al. (38) have developed a detailed classification system of existing inventory models as a guide to their implementation by managers. Their classification scheme is based on 10 codes that represent the operating characteristics of the models. They have currently incorporated 336 models in their system and plan to expand it to more than 1000 models. Their system is computer based and is a pragmatic approach to closing the gap between theory and practice. A similar classification system is needed for machine scheduling algorithms.

The determination of lot sizes is a classic problem in both shop floor control and inventory control. Extension of the simple EOQ model to the myriad situations that characterize manufacturing gives rise to some formidable problems. Although the current focus is on minimizing setup times, lot sizing remains an important area of production control. Bahl et al. (39) provide a comprehensive survey of lot sizing approaches. They identify four types of production control scenarios:

1. Single-level unlimited resources.
2. Single-level constrained resources.
3. Multiple-level unlimited resources.
4. Multiple-level constrained resources.

In these scenarios, single-level denotes independent demand and multiple-level denotes dependent demand. Their review is categorized on the basis of these four scenarios.

The subject of production control is quite broad, and considerable work in this area is reported in the literature. Production control is what shapes the character of a plant. With the present thrust toward FMS, CIM, and the factory of the future, radical changes in the production control function are expected. In the next section, we examine some of these expected changes.

24.3   PRODUCTION CONTROL IN THE FACTORY OF THE FUTURE

In this section, we discuss production control systems for CIM and the factory of the future. The nature of this futuristic function depends on what our vision of the future factory is. Two descriptions follow.

The production planning part of the system would use product information to set up an optimized production plan for the manufacture of the product, choosing proper equipment and processes, sequence of operations, operating conditions and so on. This numerical information is in turn used to control the array of automatic machines and equipment that do the actual manufacture and assembly of the product. These machines are capable of automatically setting themselves up, handling parts, selecting tools, and carrying out automatically a variety of processes, self-optimizing, and feeding back information to the control system. This system, as it constantly receives this information of the actual performance, compares this with ideal performance planned earlier. Then, as it finds performance beginning to depart from the planned optimum, overrides the original plan, performing dynamic scheduling, adjusting operating conditions to maintain optimum minimum cost performance (40).

In the factory of the future, automated systems will facilitate production at every step, beginning with electronic receipt of the customer order. The product will be designed uniquely for the customer on a CAD system, and routing will be created on a computer-aided process planning (CAPP) system in accordance with the resource capacities and workloads. Instructions will be given to the automated storage and retrieval system (ASRS) to pick materials and tools. An automated guided vehicle (AGV) will deliver these materials to robots and direct numerical control (DNC) machines, which will perform the correct processes. The vehicle will then deliver the products to the shipping dock. Artificial Intelligence systems will tie all these systems together and make adjustments for any conflicts. Data will move from customer to supplier and through their respective facilities smoothly, without the stopping and starting that exists when people are the interface (8).

Clearly, the development of production control methodologies for these futuristic systems would require a combination of both macro- and microapproaches. Sadowski (41) describes this as the ultimate control system, and according to him, although many of the necessary capabilities do exist, such systems are a long way from being developed. Mather (8) argues that the lack of an effective control system will impede progress toward the factory of the future and stresses the need to explore this area actively. Research should strive toward incorporating certain desirable features in future production control systems. It is these features that will make it possible to manage and control the complexity and dynamism of the factory of the future.

The expression *factory of the future* is usually synonymous with an automated manufacturing facility. O'Grady (42) gives an overview of the latest developments in production control systems for automated manufacturing and characterizes these systems to have low lead times and low work-in-process (WIP) inventory levels due to two reasons. First, the time to manufacture a part on an automated machine is considerably less than that on a manual machine. The shorter production time will require a more careful monitoring of production activities. Second, the high capital investment in automated machinery will warrant a high rate of machine utilization. This will require a more integrated approach to production control and capacity balancing.

Another attribute commonly associated with the factory of the future is the aspect of flexibility. Achieving flexibility in all aspects of production operations is one of the primary goals of the future (43). Both Hayes and Wheelwright (44) and Skinner (6) describe production planning and control as critical infrastructural elements for the development of a competitive manufacturing strategy primarily because production control is the means for maximizing utilized flexibility in a system (45). Zelenovic (46) defines flexibility of a production system as "a measure of its capacity to adapt to changing environmental conditions and process requirements." Based on this definition and the concepts introduced by Buzacott (47), seven types of flexibility together define system flexibility: machine, product, process, routing, operation, volume, and expansion. The capacity of a system to display these flexibilities to a large degree depends on the production control system. Recognizing the importance of flexibility, several new flexible scheduling approaches have been developed (48). These techniques are mainly focused on FMS applications. There does not appear to be much effort to introduce flexibility into large-scale systems such as MRP as yet. One notable technique in this vein is being developed by Parunak et al. (49). They attempt to induce flexibility by moving decision making closer to the point of activity. This strategy imposes fewer constraints on the possible alternatives and reduces the reaction time in decision making.

Cellular manufacturing and group technology are also expected attributes of the factory of the future. Greene and Sadowski (50) list some of the advantages of cellular manufacturing as reduced material handling, reduced tooling, reduced setup time, reduced expediting, reduced WIP, and reduced part makespan. The attainment of these advantages again depends on the capability of the production control system. Sinha and Hollier (51) review some of the production control problems associated with cellular manufacturing. They list recommendations for the development of effective future production control.

One factor often cited as being radically different in future manufacturing systems is the objective function. The primary strategy in designing future manufacturing systems and their associated subsystems should be to enhance competitiveness. Traditionally, production control approaches have adopted a simple criterion as the objective function. Such approaches will not be suitable for future needs. Haas (52) appropriately states the need for a change in objective functions:

> *Typically, manufacturing decisions are still taken in an operational framework defined by internal performance standards—machine downtime, scrap rate, work-in-process inventories, and the like. But the real test of manufacturing decisions is their impact on the company's performance in the dog-eat-dog world of global competition. A manufacturing decision that might be downright stupid in operational terms alone may look very different when seen from strategic perspective.*

The prevalent use of *cost* and *efficiency* as objective functions for planning and control of U.S. plants played a large part in their increasing inability to succeed competitively (53). Furthermore, the corporate objective and manufacturing strategy needs to be translated into operational meanings for production control. Because strategies are typically broad based, the objective function of future production control systems can be expected to be of the multicriteria type. There are already several approaches that exhibit this attribute, including the use of goal programming approaches to the multiperiod scheduling problem (54), a multiobjective decision-making model for the aggregate production planning problem (55), a multiobjective program for selection of prospective customer orders (56), and a model that combines quality objectives with inventory objectives (1). These systems model the objective as a multidimensional vector of system characteristics. The problem in future systems will not be the ability to handle multidimensional vectors but the definition and aggregation of these vectors. The use of multicriteria objectives matrices is a possible approach.

Following the above line of discussion, a list of desirable features of future production control systems can be assimilated from a review of the literature (Table 24.1). Most of these features are briefly discussed next. The features that are directly related to integration are further discussed in the next section.

TABLE 24.1. Features of Production Control in the Factory of the Future

Integrated control of production resources
Low WIP inventory
Real-time control
Short scheduling scope
Unit inventory turns per day
Unit EOQ (batch size)
Unit key machine use
Exhibit system flexibility
Real-time simulation of decision alternatives
Integration with management and CAD–CAM
Integration with corporate objective and manufacturing strategy
Suited for cellular manufacturing and group technology
Distributed decision processing
Automated decision processing with database
Finite capacity scheduling
Distributed decision making
Short production and procurement lead times
Using multiple decision-making techniques
Incorporating artificial intelligence algorithms
Incorporating the use of statistical methods

Integrated Control of Production Resources

The execution of a production control operation usually requires a workable machine tool, the part(s) to be worked on, an operator, necessary tooling, and appropriate instructions. In addition, transportation resources are required to convey these resources to the site. Traditional approaches to production control typically control only a subset of these resources and, as a result, are often unable to meet the schedule due to constraints imposed by an unaccounted for resource. An effective technique should be able to control all required resources in an integrated fashion to ensure balanced use of resources and avoid surprises.

Low WIP Inventory

Minimization of WIP inventory has always been a major objective of production control systems, but in future systems it will be almost imperative to maintain a low WIP level. Reducing manufacturing lead time is a must to be competitive, and lead time is made up of processing time and queue time. Queue time translates into WIP inventory. The contradiction is that in assemble-to-order situations WIP translates into shorter lead times. But there are other disadvantages associated with WIP, such as inflexibility, additional space, and part deterioration. All of these must be balanced to determine the optimal WIP. In the past, the practice has been to increase WIP to cover other more fundamental problems (as the Japanese have shown). Lower WIP will put a strain on production control, and Vollmann et al. (12) make a classic statement when they say we need to "substitute information for inventory." The intent of a CIPPC system should be to use the prodigious amounts of data generated in CIMS to tackle production problems.

Real-time Control

CIM promises the ability to communicate at any time between a production controller and any other resources within its domain. This capacity will enable the production control mechanism to ensure immediate transfer of directives, based on new information, for better performance. This capacity is termed *real-time control*. There are two possible interpretations of real-time control. First, the scheduling interval is reduced to be equal to activity time so that the system schedules one activity at a time and actually schedules in real time. Second, whenever an unexpected, but relevant, event occurs in or outside the system, the controller immediately readjusts the schedule accordingly and conveys overriding directives to all resource nodes. Unexpected events would include equipment breakdowns, order changes, vendor failures, and priority changes. Real-time control also implies all future schedules are based on confirmed occurrence of past events and not on assumed occurrence.

Futuristic visions force us to achieve the first interpretation. Realistically, the second meaning is more achievable and beneficial (there is a lower bound to the optimal scheduling period). A few researchers have begun treating the subject of real-time control in the event of disruptions (57). The use of perturbation analysis approaches appear to be most promising in this area (58).

Short Scheduling Scope

The scheduling scope is the time interval after which the schedule is regenerated (also called time bucket or planning period). In current applications of MRP, the scheduling period is usually 1 week, and in applications of JIT it is usually 1 day. In the majority of other approaches, the scheduling period is usually about 1 month. In the future, scheduling periods can be expected to be in the 1 day to 1 week interval. But, in combination with real-time capabilities, the effective scheduling period will actually be less, because disruptions occurring within the period will be accounted for. In effect, we will consider a medium-scope schedule but actually implement a short-scope schedule only. The production control system will automatically release the short-term schedule sequentially and reschedule at the end of the medium-term scope.

Unit Inventory Turns per Day

Inventory turnover is defined as the ratio between the average inventory value of a company and its total production value. Shunk (59) assigns a daily turnover rate of 1 (approximately 250 annual turnover) as the goal of future production control. The best Japanese firms have as yet achieved annual inventory turns of only about 80 to 90. Inventory turns are surrogate measures for the change rate of an organization. It is a well-documented fact that the change rate of society increases with time. Achieving unit inventory turns will almost be mandatory by the end of this century.* Goldratt (60) even envisions the situation of negative inventory turns. In such a situation a company will be able to turn around inventory so rapidly that it would be paid for the finished product before having to pay for the raw material. Thus a negative inventory cost would be incurred.

Unit EOQ (Batch Size)

The EOQ is one of the earliest and most well-known results in inventory theory. It has been the basis for designing the bulk of the decision rules in inventory theory. Unfortunately, it molded managers into the EOQ paradigm who become overly concerned with its derivation rather than with the management of the factors that control it (44). The Japanese were the first to get out of the paradigm and practically created a science of reducing setup times. For instance, the time required to change over a heavy press in the hood and fender stamping department at a U.S. auto plant was about 6 h, at Volvo about 4 h, and at Toyota about 12 min (35). Viewed in isolation, setup times do not appear a strategic variable, but when translated into lower EOQs and inventory cost and greater flexibility, they result in a competitive advantage.

Lower EOQs increase the workload of a production control system because more units must be controlled. Future systems must have the capacity to track almost every part in the system. It is important to note that the production control system will strive to attain the EOQ but it cannot minimize the EOQ. Lowering the EOQ is a problem of setup costs and not of control.

---

* Inventory turns are a function of the physical size of the product being manufactured. Unit inventory turns will be expected for companies producing an average-size product (e.g., appliances and automobiles). For large products, we would expect lower inventory turns.

Unit Key Machine Use

The capital cost of automated machinery is significantly higher than that of a traditional machine. In addition, there is the cost of the associated communication and computation equipment. Justification of these costs will imply a higher machine use rate. In future systems the pressure is going to be on producing more with less. Clearly, all machines cannot have the same use rate due to the unavoidable imbalance in capacity. In any system there are certain key (bottleneck) machines whose production rate determines the production rate for the entire system. The production control system must focus on these machines first. As Goldratt (60) has so aptly stated, "an hour lost at a bottleneck is an hour lost for the total system." Future production control systems must first identify the primary key machines and then the secondary key machines and then ensure use rates of close to one for these machines.

Exhibit System Flexibility

A flexible system is created in two phases. First, it is designed to be flexible and then it is managed to exhibit that flexibility. FMS and other individual machine tools make it possible to achieve the first phase. Achieving the second phase will depend primarily on the capability of the production control system. Specifically, process flexibility, operation flexibility, routing flexibility, and volume flexibility capabilities need to be managed by the controller. The work in FMS scheduling has already made considerable progress in this direction (48, 61) and several applications are beginning to exhibit their flexibility.

Real-time Simulation of Decision Alternatives

Digital simulation is usually used in one of two modes: testing (*1*) how a proposed system will function and (2) how an existing system will function under a proposed control directive. The second of these modes is a common application in production control. The simulation model is used to estimate the operating performance of a proposed schedule. In real-time simulation, this would be done immediately before schedule release. Furthermore, simulation is an excellent tool for estimating performance variations due to changes in decision variables and system parameters. Simulation can also be used to achieve two other desired feature listed above: real-time control and short- and medium-term schedules. For instance, if a disruption occurs in the middle of the term, the controller may either reschedule the system or use simulation to adapt the decision variables accordingly. Simulation would probably be a faster and more economical alternative. The adjustments could then be implemented in the next short-term schedule.

Progress in the development of simulation tools has been phenomenal in recent years. A comprehensive treatment of simulation is provided by Shannon (62). Several languages and packages have been developed. Pritsker (63) has developed the SLAM language, which is particularly applicable to production control. SIMAN (64) is also becoming increasingly popular for simulation of material handling systems. Other example packages are GASP, GPSS, SIMON, SEE-WHY, FORSSIGHT, Q-GERT, SIMSCRIPT, and SLAM-II (65). These packages will usually require considerable effort in model building and learning. Several FMS-specific simulators, which ease the modeling effort, have been developed. The best known are GCMS, MAST, and MUSIK (65). A comparison of simulation packages is provided by Shannon and Philips (66) in which they highlight the IDSS package as being most suitable for future applications. Future production control systems must be able to build simulation models and interface with the simulator.

Integration with Management and CAD–CAM

Integration of CIPPC with CAD–CAM and management corresponds to integrations 1 and 3 in the CIM model. The link between manufacturing and production control is not unidirectional. The bulk of the decisions made by the controller affects manufacturing, and it needs feedbacks on these decisions. With increased automation, both CIPPC and CAM will be "blind" to several operating problems. The tool room, maintenance, scrap removal, material supply, and floor operators need to inform CIPPC of their suggestions and problems. Only then can continuous improvement become a reality. Unit product quality is one of the goals of the future, and quality is often determined by the production schedule. Feedback on schedule–quality issues is a must.

There have been several new developments in the area of integrating CAD and CAM (integration 2). These include the initial graphic exchange system (IGES) and product exchange system (PDES). Several other similar developments in Europe are reviewed by Kochan (67). These developments are a step toward improving communication in a manufacturing system. Production control systems must be able to interface with these systems and effectively use the available data.

Production control is a function that is primarily managerial in nature. The decisions made by it need to be integrated with accounting, marketing, forecasting, and top management. Melynk et al. (30) discuss each of these interfaces. Such integration is already practiced, but the tendency is for information to flow from management to control, and not the reverse. There is a lot of control information that can be beneficial to management.

Integration with Corporate Objectives and Manufacturing Strategy

The concept of manufacturing strategy was first introduced by Skinner (6, 68). His thesis being that manufacturing must be linked to the corporate strategy if the corporation is to remain competitive in the long run, because manufacturing is the primary value-adding function in the firm. A manufacturing strategy consists of a pattern of decisions affecting the element of manufacturing systems. Hayes and Wheelwright (44) list eight decision categories that constitute a manufacturing strategy: capacity, facilities, technology, vertical integration, work force, quality, production control, and organization. The manufacturing strategy should be translated into a relevant strategy for each of these categories. An effective production control system is not one that maximizes efficiency or minimizes cost, but one that supports the manufacturing strategy. A hierarchical structure for operationalizing the production control strategy through the system needs to be an integral part of the controller.

Suited for Cellular Manufacturing and Group Technology

The concepts of cellular manufacturing and group technology (GT) are particularly applicable in a medium-volume, mixed-product setup. The most common method for implementing these concepts is production flow analysis (PFA) (69, 70). PFA divides the manufacturing resources into part families, machine cells, and tooling groups. Scheduling in these environments requires special algorithms. Mosier et al. (71) analyze some of the existing heuristics in this area. The development of more effective techniques and their integration with large-scale controllers is needed.

Distributed Decision Processing

Technology is providing many data-processing alternatives: minis, micros, and mainframes. The processing systems vary from totally centralized to totally distributed. Distributed processing, with a high level of local intelligence, provides the data flexibility and reliability for CIM systems. Ranky (72) gives a summary of the principles of distributed processing, computer networks, and database management as applicable to CIM. In a distributed system, each node executes specific tasks, and the tools required for executing those tasks are made available to that node. Architectures such as MAP enable the distributed nodes to interact closely with each other and access the required information. In effect, the managing and computing loads are spread over all nodes, which can work in parallel to solve problems faster.

The impact of local area networks (LANs) and distributed processing on production control are beginning to be investigated. Shaw (73) describes a distributed control approach based on a network bidding scheme. In his approach, a central cell announces a required task to all feasible cells. The cells, in turn, transmit their bids for production to their central cell. When all bids are received, the central cell selects the cell with the optimal bid for production. Shaw used the augmented petri net (APN) technique to model the bidding scheme. In a simulation study, Shaw found the bidding mechanism to be significantly better than a centralized scheme. Future systems must move away from the centralized, single-model approach and focus on a distributed approach with a mechanism for connecting the nodes.

Automated Decision Processing with Database

The control of a large system requires processing large amounts of data. This processing involves data storage, retrieval, and transfer. To ensure that these activities are executed rapidly and efficiently requires a structured database. Sophisticated databases have already been developed for CAD and CAM applications. As of yet, there are no true databases for the CIPPC function. Production control typically piggybacks on the CAD, CAM, and management databases. The argument being that the information used by the controller also is used for other activities, including accounting, marketing, engineering, etc. This problem of external and internal data has led to the development of distributed databases (DDBs) that are networked together. The MAP system provided specifications and a protocol for the development of DDBs for manufacturing. Future production control systems must have their own databases and be part of the DDB system and follow MAP guidelines. Ranky (72) introduces some of the recent developments in database technology and discusses their application in CIMS.

Rolstadas presents a first cut at defining data structures for a production control databases (in ref. 74). Two basic database structures are defined: one that describes the product structure and the other that describes the resources needed to produce the product. Based on these two structures, several interactions in the control system are discussed.

Finite Capacity Scheduling

Capacity is a permanent constraint to production control. The problem of developing an optimal schedule within capacity is a difficult problem. Many of the frustrations and unreliabilities associated with production control stem from capacity constraints. Controllers are in the habit of transferring their overload problems to the shop floor by releasing an unachievable schedule. Six sins of production control have been identified:

1. Not loading to the capacity of the shop's natural bottlenecks.
2. Lack of schedule adherence and correction.
3. Not rescheduling to current priorities.
4. Increasing lead times on parts that have been late.
5. Expediting only today's shortages.
6. Pulling assembly kits too early.

Of the six sins, the first three are a direct consequence of the capacity constraint. These sins will be unacceptable in the future and must be accounted for by the controller.

The need for finite capacity scheduling has led to the development of several new approaches. Common practice is to develop a schedule and then create a corresponding capacity requirements plan. If the required capacity exceeds available capacity, then the load is trimmed and the schedule regenerated. This cycle is repeated until a feasible schedule is generated. The drawbacks in the approach are (1) the capacity requirements routines are usually rough cut and not always reliable, (2) the task of trimming the load requires an accompanying priorities scheme, and (3) the cycle involves significant amounts of computation time.

It is necessary that future systems consider schedule and capacity simultaneously. The OPT technique and FMS scheduling approaches follow this route. In the situation of tight capacity, the controller functions as a priority-preserving mechanism (26), i.e., it preserves those jobs with a higher priority assignment system. An interesting concept with reference to the relationship between capacity and other performance measures has been introduced. Analyzing production systems as networks of queues, a performance trade-off curve was developed relating capacity, lead time, and WIP. From the curves, it is possible to estimate the corresponding lead time and WIP for given capacity. Approaches similar to this for integrating capacity into the control function are needed.

We have identified here desirable features for production control systems for the factory of the future. These are neither exhaustive nor mandatory. They are in a sense a wish list, and it is unlikely any one system will incorporate all the features. It is important that the development of the features be approached in an integrated fashion. Furthermore, in designing or formulating a production control system, attempts must be made to consider these features.

24.4 INTEGRATION IN PRODUCTION CONTROL SYSTEMS

Though numerous techniques and approaches have been developed in the area of production control, there has been limited work on developing macrosystems that integrate the various activities constituting the production control function. In the absence of techniques that consider the total function, the other techniques are in reality ineffective. In this section, we present approaches that have focused on modeling the big picture of production control. To begin with, we need to clarify our understanding of production control.

There is no standard definition of production control, and the operational meaning usually depends on the particular application. Two generic definitions follow.

> *Production control is the function of management which plans, directs, and controls the materials supply and processing activities of an enterprise. Where, planning is the process of deciding what to do in the future, directing comprises the operation of issuing orders, and control can be described as the constraining of events to follow plans (10).*

> *Controls the production of the necessary products in the necessary quantities at the necessary time in every process of a factory and also among companies (35).*

Clearly, production control involves the making of certain decisions toward meeting a certain objective. It is how these decisions are made and their interrelationships considered that determines integration. One of the earliest works on integration in production control is by Holstein (75). He presented an integrated view of the whole process. This view can be interpreted as a graphical definition of a production planning and control system (Figure 24.1). Eight classes of activities are identified in this definition:

1. Forecasting future demand.
2. Order entry.
3. Long-term capacity plan.
4. Master scheduling.
5. Inventory planning and control.
6. Short-term scheduling.
7. Short-term capacity planning.
8. Dispatching, releasing, and shop floor control.

Holstein's definition identifies the major information flows that connect these activities. The majority of current production control frameworks and flow charts are variations of this basic function.

While Holstein defines integration within the controller, Harrington (76) describes production control in the context of the manufacturing function. His description is developed via the ICAM functional definition method (IDEF). Figure 24.2 describes the manufacturing function, while Figure 24.3 describes the production function. Boxes 1 to 5 in Figure 24.3 define the production control function. Thus box 3 places production control in the context of manufacturing. Both Holstein and Harrington provide detailed descriptions of the functions identified in Figures 24.1 to 24.3.

Several books and papers describe production control in general and these usually define the macroproduction control problem. But, in contrast, there is no comprehensive microscopic definition of the entire production control problem. Such a definition would list all the decisions to be made by this function. Although a macrodefinition is explanatory, it is the microscopic definition that operationalizes the function. The lack of an overall microscopic definition is a roadblock to achieving integration. A starting point in this direction is execution of an input–output analysis. Parnaby (77) reports the following inputs and outputs for the production control function:

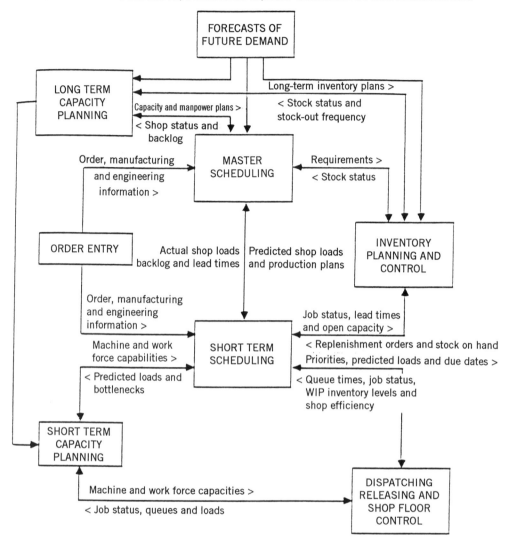

Figure 24.1. Graphical definition of a production planning and control system (75).

Inputs	*Outputs*
Knowledge of present and planned state of production process.	Raw materials ordering schedule.
Detailed product design.	Allocation of work by time to work centers.
Order quantities.	Listing of production procedures.
Materials stock levels.	Labor use plan.
Finished stock levels.	Machinery use plan.
Labor availability.	Performance checking procedures.
Resource restrictions.	Performance standards.

Notice that all the inputs are data while the outputs are primarily decisions, implying production control is primarily a decision-making system. The closest approximation to the overall micro-

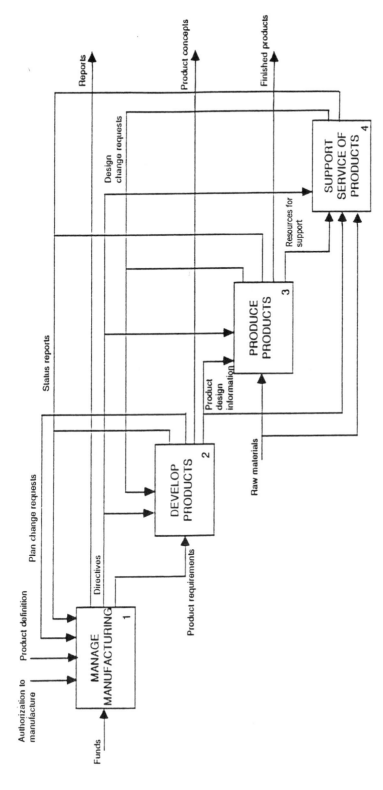

Figure 24.2. IDEF definition of the manufacturing function (76).

495

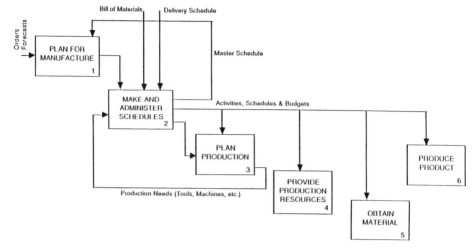

Figure 24.3. IDEF definition of product goods.

scopic definition of the production control problem is the composite function model of manufacturing developed in the ICAM program (78, 79). This function model was developed using the IDEF methodology and documents, in network fashion, all functions occurring in manufacturing and their relevant inputs and outputs. The production control function is one of several functions modeled. In the subsequent project, the ICAM program developed the composite information model of manufacturing, which documents current information flows in U.S. manufacturing (79).

Traditionally, production control modeling has focused on one or two of the functions identified by Holstein (75). Seward et al. (27) observe that in most companies these functions are executed separately and are loosely interfaced with minimal automatic data transfer. The most common interfaces are between master scheduling and short-term scheduling. The majority of the functional developments are in the areas of inventory control and shop floor control. The development models usually provide optimal solutions for their specific unit of analysis. But they are not always compatible with models that focus on larger system. In developing a subsystem model, the developer must always keep in mind the wider context of the system in which the subsystem operates. If a subsystem model is developed without relating back to the overall model from which it came, then the new model will not be easily integrated into the overall system model (78). One of the natural laws of systems integration is if a subsystem procedure is not compatible with its parent system procedure, then the subsystem procedure will be overridden no matter how optimal a solution it may provide. Traditional approaches to production control tend to be a victim of this law, and this is a primary cause of the theory-to-practice gap. The implication though is not that all research must be top down. Rather, integration should be an inherent goal in the development process, with validation checks to ensure that objectives, constraints, variables, assumptions, concepts, and relevance are consistent with the parent system. Integration is a feature of design and not of consequence and must be approached as such. The dimensions identified earlier in the integration framework may be used as a guideline for the validation process.

To achieve integration in production control, we need a decision system that operationalizes the definitions of Holstein and Harrington. There are at least four modeling approaches for developing such a system:

1. Integration through a single mathematical model.
2. Integration through a decision framework.
3. Integration through a network model.
4. Integration through a structured model.

Each of these approaches attempts to optimize the whole rather than the parts. They all involve the handling of large-scale models and are difficult to implement. The most common problems are the large data requirements, data accuracy and reliability, integration with related systems, and computer requirements.

Integration Through a Single Mathematical Model

The most obvious solution to integration is the development of a single model that represents the entire system. Assuming all decisions and their interrelationships can be quantified, a mathematical model can be designed. No such model for the entire control function exists. However, models that consider major portions of the function have been designed. The most common approach is the aggregate production planning problem (APPP), which consists of determining for each period the required labor, production rate, and inventory level. A variety of solution approaches for this problem have been presented (80). The most well known approaches are by Dzielinski and Gomory (81) and Lasdon and Terjung (82). These approaches are LP based and, in addition, use decomposition or bounding methods.

The first problem with these methods is the difficulty in solving them. The resulting LPs are very large. A problem with 1000 items and a 12-period planning horizon has 2 million variables. Second, they consider only short-term scheduling, short-term capacity planning, and shop floor control. Third, they ignore the inherent uncertainties of the shop floor. In addition to these, there are other managerial problems. However, in certain cases these approaches provide significant benefits. King and Love (83) report the implementation of the Lasdon and Terjung (82) approach to a tire company. In association with other techniques, this approach resulted in significant benefits to the company.

Integration Through a Decision Framework

One approach to solving large, complex problems is to partition them into manageable subproblems and link these subproblems to account for interrelationships. There are several strategies for this decomposition and subsequent linking. Possible strategies are hierarchy, decision scope, functional, or as needed in time. MRP, MRP-II, JIT, HPP, and OPT are production control frameworks of this type. In addition, several other frameworks of this type are reported in the literature. The frameworks are typically strong in one area and weak in others, and usually cover only a part of Figure 24.1. Almost all are computer based, but they vary in the amount of required environmental interaction. A brief review of the major approaches follows.

Materials Requirements Planning

The earliest frameworks were of the functional or decision-scope type. These frameworks were order entry and executed as many consecutive functions as possible. Some examples are the bill of materials, Gantt chart, parts explosion, and Martino's PART system (84). These early systems evolved into Orlicky's MRP system (85). MRP is designed to make purchased and in-house manufactured parts available for dispatch before they are needed by the next stage of production. MRP executes the following activities: short-term scheduling, purchase-order scheduling, part-production ordering, shipping scheduling, and short-term capacity planning (in the closed-loop version). The linking or integrating mechanism is the dependent demand concept and it results in the time-phased requirements of materials and parts, MRP does not consider the time-phased requirements of machines, labor, tools, and other resources. In reality, MRP is not a decision-support system but more of an activity-support system. Its primary purpose is to organize the complex activities occurring on the plant floor through the use of database technology. The benefits of MRP are primarily due to this organization and resulting information flow.

Due to the ease of programming the MRP logic, and its natural database structure, several software packages for MRP are currently available. But, only 9.5% are class A* users (25). Criticisms of MRP are common in the literature. Mather (8) even labels MRP's scheduling process as fundamentally illogical. The problems with MRP can be classified as relating to technical factors, process factors, and innerenvironmental factors. Some of these factors relate to the integrability of MRP, and these are of special interest here. MRP is primarily a mechanism for initiating production and assembly of parts. It is a "backward" scheduling method with a "push" type production. The state date is usually back calculated from a required delivery date on the basis of present lead times. This back calculation is made without considering resource availability. Gelders and Van Wassenhove (26) describe MRP as an infinite loader and emphasize the importance of simultaneously considering capacity and materials requirements. Another problem with MRP is its static nature. Lead times and schedules are intimately correlated, but MRP assumes that schedules depend on lead times and not the converse (28). There is no feedback mechanism in MRP, and it functions primarily as a planning methodology and not for controlling. MRP is a centralized planning system, and it attempts to integrate the plant through its centralized plan.

To account for some of the above problems, MRP was enhanced by Wright (86) to MRP-II. MRP-II includes all the functions identified by Holstein's (75) definition and also considers integrations 1 and 3. In addition to MRP, it consists of two additional subsystems. The first includes long-range planning and master scheduling; the second focuses on shop floor control. MRP-II is described as being the total management system for integrating and coordinating the activities of all functions. There is, however, only limited documentation of MRP-II available.

The majority of manufacturing is managed in a functional manner and hence is naturally inclined to the application of MRP and MRP-II. This is one of the principal reasons of the high adoption rate for these systems. Functional frameworks are the easiest to implement. Their effectiveness, though, depends on the linking mechanism and the functional decision making process.

Hierarchical Production Planning

Several frameworks for describing the structure of decision support systems have been proposed in the literature (87). The framework most commonly applied to production control is by Anthony (88), who provided a classification of managerial activity based on the purpose of the decision-making activity. Three levels of decision making are identified: strategic, tactical, and operational. Based on this framework, a problem may be hierarchically partitioned into subproblems. Each subproblem is constrained by the parameters of its lower problems and by the solution of its upper problem. Such a hierarchically integrated system for production planning was first developed by Hax and Meal (89). They divided the problem into three distinct levels of aggregation: items, families, and types. The divided problem is solved by first solving an aggregate production-planning problem and then two subsequent disaggregations. Several approaches for the disaggregation have been suggested (90). The overall approach is equivalent to solving a single problem. Graves (31) derived the Hax–Meal hierarchy as a natural decomposition of a primal optimization problem.

HPP overlaps the activities of long-term capacity planning, master scheduling, short-term scheduling, and short-term capacity planning. The integrating mechanism is the disaggregation process, which links the subproblems. HPP is a finite scheduler and focuses on the capacity constraint. It attempts to balance capacity so that demand is met. Thus it is an effective planning method in situations of seasonal demand. The major problem with HPP is that it is an integrative approach for a partial problem. HPP cannot be run alone and must be implemented in conjunction with other decision and information systems to provide it with the large amount of data required. Meal et al. (91) have proposed integrating HPP with MRP to overcome the problem. They recommend the use of MRP to generate the master schedule and HPP as the capacity planning module.

HPP is a mechanism for hierarchical integration but does not consider lateral integration. Van Dierdonck and Miller (92) define one measure of integrability as the frequency and intensity of lateral relations and communications. Lateral integration is primarily important from a control perspective. CIM will provide the capability for extensive lateral communication, and the implementation success of a CIPPC depends on its ability to exploit this capability. Gelders and Van Wassenhove (93) explore the problems created by hierarchical integration and discuss the issues of infeasibility, inconsistency, and suboptimality. They describe two case studies in which a HPP was implemented. They recommend that the decision models at each level be carefully integrated, else we may create islands of decision making. They also emphasize the need for a cross-functional management team to oversee the implementation process.

Several other hierarchical control approaches are reported. Kimemia and Gershwin (94) developed a hierarchical system for short-term scheduling and shop floor control in an FMS. Their system is designed to minimize WIP and accounts for system uncertainties. Other ap-

---

* A class A user is defined as one using a closed-loop MRP system for both priority planning and capacity planning.

proaches are based on the NBS–AMRF hierarchical control architecture for automated manufacturing. The architecture has been divided into five levels: facility, shop, cell, workstation, and equipment. Long-term decisions are made at the facility level, coordination of resources and jobs are at the shop level, the cell level schedules jobs through the cell, the workstation level sequences operations within the cell, and the equipment level controls tools and materials. Parunak et al. (49) propose a heuristic control approach based on this hierarchy. Their approach is different from the Hax–Meal approach in that machines rather than items are grouped together. Parunak et al. propose using the expert system scheduler ISIS (7) at the upper levels and other heuristics at the lower level. Their approach is still at the experimental stage, and its integrability is untested.

Hierarchical approaches are effective means of achieving integration and can be expected to be a part of a CIPPC system. But they must be combined with lateral integration approaches to be successful. Hierarchical approaches are amenable to optimization modeling and are particularly useful in decomposing larger problems. Furthermore, CIM systems are naturally inclined to hierarchical control as demonstrated at the NBS–AMRF.

Just-in-time Kanban

The concept of just-in-time manufacturing has been implemented by managers for years, one of the earliest practitioners being Henry Ford at the River Rouge plant (95). But the concept was first transformed into a science by Taiichi Ohno of the Toyota Motor Co. (96). JIT-Kanban, as it is now called, is a means not only for production control but also for factory management. Our interest here is only in the production control element. However, from an integration perspective, it is important to note that several of the attributed benefits are due to the close communication between management and shop operations.

Two distinguishing features of JIT-Kanban are gleaned from Ohno's (97) historical discourse. First, as opposed to other systems that emphasize inventory control more than shop floor control, JIT-Kanban places more emphasis on shop floor control. Ohno observes that when one is weak in shop floor control, one tends to try to cover the defect with skills in inventory control. Second, while most systems consist only of a planning and scheduling mechanism, JIT-Kanban consists of both a planning mechanism and a controlling mechanism. It is this controlling mechanism that characterizes JIT-Kanban into a ''pull'' system, as opposed to the ''push'' system. In such a system, production is initiated by demand in a successive station and not by arrival of a part. Similar to other approaches, the JIT-Kanban system has an annual production schedule, a monthly master production schedule, and a daily dispatching procedure. Relevant portions of these plans are communicated to individual workstations. In other systems the workstations execute the plan independently, but JIT-Kanban uses the kanban cards to trigger execution of the planned operations, i.e., the kanban cards (or for that matter, actual demand) are the lateral integrating mechanism.

In JIT-Kanban, the shop floor boundaries extend to suppliers and customers. Hence, lateral integration crosses the organizational boundary. Several researchers are currently investigating the dynamics of kanban (98). One of the critical factors is the number of kanban cards in the system, because the number of cards puts an upper bound on the WIP. The number of cards is typically determined by the formula:

$$n = DL(1 + l)/C$$

where n is the number of cards, D is the average demand, L is the production lead time, l is a safety factor, and C is the container size. This formula is used only in situations in which the setup time has been reduced to an almost negligible amount. In situations in which the setup time is significant, the number of kanbans is a function of the traditional economic lot size (35). The calculated number of kanbans is really only a guideline. At Toyota, supervisors may adjust the number of kanbans on a real-time basis. This enables the system to adjust to different situations.

Although the kanban cards are the primary integrating mechanism in JIT-Kanban, there are several other lessons to be learned from it. Nine such lessons have been noted, some of which are especially important from an integration perspective. First, production quality is a function of production control and must be considered during CIPPC design. Second, facilities are laid out not only to optimize production flow but also to facilitate production control. Third, production control must exploit the intelligence and decision-making capability of supervisors and line operators. JIT-Kanban systems require a considerable degree of commitment on the part of workers who make the system run. In CIM, the relative number of workers will be considerably less. Furthermore, their responsibilities will also be more as a result of increased system complexity. Under these conditions, several of the JIT-Kanban characteristics are inappropriate. Still, this approach exhibits the importance of a floor level control mechanism.

FMS Scheduling and Control

The new wave in production control is the scheduling of FMS facilities. It is also an area of extensive application of operations research methodologies. FMS scheduling tends to be closely integrated with CAM. Several fixed design attributes in traditional systems are flexible in FMSs and are modeled as control variables, thereby resulting in a dynamic system configuration. Buzacott and Yao (47) review the development of FMS analytical models. They report the bulk of the development has occurred at five sites: Purdue, MIT-Draper Labs, MIT-LIDS, Harvard, and Toronto. Other reviews of FMS control are available (48). Several FMS-specific techniques have been developed, and examples have been reported (48, 61). Control in a FMS is typically invoked directly from a computer and most techniques are mathematical programming based. In addition, the application of artificial intelligence methods is increasing. Current FMS scheduling and control approaches have achieved significant improvements in performance. Bessant and Haywood (99), in a survey of fifty FMSs, report an average decrease of 74% in lead time and 68% in WIP and a 63% increase in machine use. Each of these were listed earlier as desirable attributes of future production control. The bulk of these benefits are the result of hard integration, but in the future we can expect greater benefits from soft integration as well.

At least five frameworks for the FMS production control problem can be identified. These are listed in Table 24.2. All the frameworks may be classified as hierarchical in nature. Almost all are accompanied by prescriptive algorithms that have been programmed and tested. Apart from the framework by Hildebrandt (100), the others are considerably similar and make the same decisions in different procedures. Hildebrandt's approach is focused on FMSs in which machines are prone to failure. All the frameworks overlap short-term scheduling and capacity planning and shop floor control. One problem with these systems is that they tend to be decoupled from the plant controller, and the approach by Kimemia and Gershwin (94) even

TABLE 24.2. FMS Production Control Decision Frameworks

		Research Group		
Purdue (ref. 12)	MIT-LIDS (ref. 100)	MIT-Draper Labs (ref. 94)	Toronto (ref. 47)	Carnegie Mellon (ref. 101)
FMS production control is divided into five subproblems: 1. Part type selection 2. Machine grouping 3. Production ratio 4. Resource allocation 5. Loading	FMS production control decisions are structured in three levels: 1. Find the mix of jobs entering the system and the machine assignment for each configuration of the working–failed condition to minimize makespan 2. Find the sequence of jobs entering the system in each failure condition to maximize the average production rate 3. Find the input time for each job and the next operation for each job in each failure condition to minimize delay	FMS production control is decoupled from the plant master schedule and has a hierarchial structure: 1. Flow control: regulates the production rate of each job type 2. Routing control: determines the optimal routing of jobs 3. Sequence control: determines the sequence and time to release an external job and next operation on an internal job	FMS production control has the following basic hierarchial decision structure: 1. Prerelease planning: deciding which jobs are to be manufactured 2. Input control: determining the sequence and timing of release of jobs to the system 3. Operational control: ensuring movement between machines and deciding which is to be processed next by a machine	There are four levels in FMS production control: 1. Strategic planning 2. Capacity planning 3. Scheduling 4. Dispatching

positions incoming and outgoing buffers. Thus there is a lack of integration between the FMS and the rest of the plant. Another problem is the exponentially increasing complexity with size (number of parts and machines). One solution to these problems is to model the plant as a set of small FMS subsystems. A protocol of cooperation between the subsystems can then be implemented, as suggested by Berman and Maimon (102). Their approach focuses on the transportation and distribution of parts and resources via the material handling system, which is the integrating mechanism. The integration of their approach with the five frameworks needs to be investigated.

FMS production control frameworks provide excellent approaches for integration within the FMS. But they are not good at integrating the total plant control function. The research groups have adopted a structured approach to the problem and several of the characteristics are applicable to CIPPC design. The approaches also exhibit the capability of using mathematical models effectively and efficiently.

Optimized Production Technology

Of the five production control frameworks reviewed in this category, OPT is the newest and most controversial. Furthermore, OPT is the only framework which is a specific product (Creative Output Inc., Milford, Conn.) and not a reported knowledge concept. Though the overall structure of the methodology is known, several of the control procedures use proprietary knowledge. A brief review of the methodology is reported by Jacobs (103). The OPT technique includes a control methodology and management philosophy; users are required to implement both. In that regard, OPT achieves considerable integration 1, because management is sensitive to production control. Goldratt via his two books *The Goal* and *The Race* is now shaping the approach into a total factory management system (see ref. 60).

The foundation of the OPT approach is summarized in nine rules, which are adopted by all users. The first rule is the most important and the essence of the approach. That is, balance flow and not capacity. The approach assumes imbalanced capacity is an unavoidable characteristic and focuses instead on balancing the flow. The OPT scheduler identifies the bottleneck stations for a given order schedule. The bottleneck station and all stations downstream of it are scheduled forward. The upstream stations are scheduled backward. Thus the interfacing mechanisms are the bottleneck stations and the balanced flow the integrating mechanism. This concept is also called synchronized manufacturing (60). In such a system, the flow rate of the plant is dictated by the bottleneck stations. In contrast, in a JIT-Kanban system the flow rate is dictated by the last station.

It is not clear whether OPT covers long-range capacity planning or inventory control. It is primarily an approach for minimizing WIP at the shop floor level. The approach is highly centralized, and there is no control module because it assumes strict adherence to schedule.

Other Approaches

The above five approaches to achieving production control integration via a decision framework are the most commonly known. There are, in addition, other approaches. A hierarchical decentralized architecture for production control has been presented that proposes a tailored optimization program for each stage in the process, with constraints coming from upstream and downstream stages and the hierarchical controller. Shaw (73) reports a distributed scheduling approach designed for CIM applications. His approach can be termed *competitive scheduling* because the distributed nodes are allowed to submit bids for jobs. Although his approach is applied at the cell level, it could be applied for master schedule development.

Maxwell et al. (104) developed a framework oriented toward discrete parts manufacturing. They propose a three-phase approach: the creation of a master production plan, planning for uncertainty, and real-time resources allocation. The first phase is similar to the traditional master schedule development; the second phase focuses on setting buffer levels and inventory levels. The third phase is the traditional shop floor control. No techniques are identified and Maxwell et al. propose only a decision structure.

Integration through a Network Model

Network modeling approaches are common and effective techniques in the analysis of complex interlinked systems. These models force a sequential analysis of the problem, which is their primary advantage from an integrative perspective. A drawback of these approaches is that they tend to be descriptive and are often difficult to evolve to the prescriptive stage. Often, simulation techniques are the only alternative. The other alternative is network programming techniques. This alternative, though, is not significantly different from the single mathematical model approach.

Zahorik et al. (105) examine present network programming models for production control in multistage, multiitem systems. Network approaches are not promising from an integration perspective. They tend to degenerate into mathematical problems and do not exhibit the intrinsic advantages of network analysis.

Integration through a Structured Model

Production control is a complex activity, and its complexity can be expected to increase in a CIM environment. The design of control methodologies for such complex systems requires a clear understanding of the system and the associated problem. All too often control approaches are developed without this understanding, resulting in poor system performance. One approach to understanding the problem is structurally to analyze or model it. A dictionary definition of the word *structure* is "the arrangement and interrelation of parts or elements in a complex entity." By "structurally analyze and model" we mean an examination and definition of this arrangement and interrelationship. None of the production control approaches reviewed here is based on such an analysis. Structural approaches help decompose the system into smaller subsystems. A suitable integrative framework for the control of this network of subsystems can then be developed.

The structural approach has resulted in the development of three specific techniques.* Ross (106) developed the technique of structured analysis. The technique has been tested and applied to several problems and has now been extended as the structured analysis and design technique (SADT) (107, 108). More recently, Geoffrion (109) presented the structured modeling technique. The third structured approach is IDEF, which is based on the SADT methodology but oriented toward manufacturing applications (110). All three approaches are graphical in nature.

Structured approaches are useful in designing integrated systems. Shunk et al. (111) describe three aspects of integration modeled by IDEF: information, control, and material. All three are critical to CIPPC systems. These approaches help define the architecture of a system, which in turn identifies the required integration. Connor (107) lists the characteristics of a structured approach as:

1. Bounding the context of the problem.
2. Limited information portrayal.
3. Merging of perspectives into a single viewpoint.
4. Top-down decomposition.
5. Levels of increasing detail.
6. Levels of abstraction (i.e., from logical to physical).
7. Describing multiple hierarchies and networks.
8. Emphasizing both data and activities.

Each characteristic describes a different aspect of systems development and integration. Clearly, an approach with the above characteristics will provide a rigorous and disciplined approach to problem solving.

The first effort in the development of a production control approach based on structural modeling is the integrated manufacturing control project of the air force (3). This project is focused on shop floor control and the results are not yet reported. The ultimate objective of the project is to develop a triple control system for the cell, center, and factory. Structural approaches appear to be a sound methodology for integrated efforts. Recently, a production control system based on structured analysis and modeling and using the IDEF methodology and the manufacturing function model (79) was developed by Das and Sarin (112). The system attempts to cover all the functions identified in Holstein's (75) definition. It is significantly

---

* The names of two of the techniques should not be confused with the ordinary use of the expressions *structured analysis* and *structured modeling*.

different from existing approaches in that it is based on a structural definition of the problem, from which the required decisions and their interrelations are defined. Its application has been further demonstrated (113–116).

24.5 CONTROL ISSUES IN INTEGRATED MANUFACTURING

In any system there are characteristics that, if present, cause the system to behave as an integrated system. Several such characteristics and issues were evident in the review and analysis of production control methodologies reported in the previous section. Additional issues were identified in the earlier review of production control in the factory of the future. These issues can be consolidated into the following distinctive integration issues for production control.

1. Dependent demand.
2. Balanced flow.
3. Balanced capacity.
4. Flexibility (process routing and setups).
5. Common, interrelated objectives.
6. Transportation and processing equipment coordination.
7. Operation to tactical to strategic balance.
8. Machine to cell to center to system balance.
9. Proactively reactive.
10. Appropriate data transfer.
11. Effective data to information transfer.
12. Guided intelligence based on feedback.
13. Appropriate distributed decision making.

Most of the issues are self-explanatory and were discussed earlier. Item 9 implies that a system should react immediately to an event rather than when the effects of the event are experienced. For example, assume machine X is supplying machine Y, and Y breaks down. In a reactive mode, machine X stops supplying machine Y only when the buffer is blocked. In a proactively reactive mode, it stops supplying machine Y immediately and instead focuses on machine Z. Item 10 refers to the DRIP problem in computerized systems. One measure of this issue is

$$\text{Data effectiveness} = \text{Data available/Data needed}$$

A data effectiveness greater than unity implies a data rich information poor (DRIP) situation. Item 11 refers to the ability of a decision support system to use fully the available data. One measure of this issue is

$$\text{Information effectiveness} = \text{Data used/Data available}$$

Notice the product of the above two measures is a surrogate measure for the reliability of decisions made by the system. Item 12 advocates the need for effective feedback mechanisms. Current production control systems do not fully use the feedback information available to them.

Table 24.3 is an audit of the presence of these issues in some of the approaches reviewed earlier. It is not advocated that a successful production control system display all of these characteristics, neither are all the issues relevant to all applications. For different scenarios, the 13 items will have different priorities. But together, they do describe a desirable set of characteristics.

24.6 SUMMARY

In this chapter we have provided a review of production control in general, with a specific emphasis on the issues of integration. Production control is an area of extensive research, dominated by the application of mathematical models and procedures. Of the four components

TABLE 24.3. Integration Issues Considered in Common Production Control Approaches

Integration Issues	MRP	JIT	HPP	OPT	FMS
1. Dependent demand	X	X			
2. Balanced flow		X		X	
3. Balanced capacity			X		
4. Flexibility (process routing and setups)					X
5. Common, interrelated objectives		X			
6. Transportation and processing equipment coordination					X
7. Operation to tactical to strategic balance			X		
8. Machine to cell to center to system balance					X
9. Proactively reactive		X			
10. Appropriate data transfer	X				
11. Effective data to information transfer					
12. Guided intelligence based on feedback		X			X
13. Appropriate distributed decision making		X	X		

of CIM systems, CIPPP is found to be the least developed from an automation perspective. To guide future work in the development of CIPPC systems and production control in general, 20 desirable features of production control are identified and analyzed.

Integration is an issue of interrelationships that is best described graphically. Two such graphical definitions of production control are reported by Holstein (75) and Harrington (76). These are shown in Figures 24.1 through 24.3. Future production control systems can be modeled on the basis of these definitions to ensure integrability. In this vein, four modeling approaches with an integration focus are identified. These are via a single mathematical model, a decision framework, a network model, and a structured model. Each of these is briefly reviewed and analyzed. Most currently used large-scale systems are of the decision framework type.

Based on the above reviews, 13 control issues in integrated manufacturing are identified. Most current systems cover portions of CIPPC but none can substitute for it totally in CIMS. The majority of systems are developed to solve problems rather than improve the system. However, the structured approach proposed here develops the control mechanism based on the definitive model of the system and problem. This approach ensures the consideration of the interfacing, integrating, and networking issues that are so critical to the success of CIPPC and CIM systems.

BIBLIOGRAPHY

1. S.K. DAS and S.C. SARIN, "A 'City Plan' for Design and Research of Computer Integrated Production Planning and Control," *Int. J. Product. Planning Control* 2(1), 14–23 (1991).

2. M. BEALE, *MAP/TOP/OSI Handbook,* Ship Star Associates, Middlesex, UK, 1986.

3. ICAM Review, *Technical Review of the ICAM Program,* Manufacturing Studies Board National Research Council, Washington, D.C., 1980.

4. A. DEMEYER, "The Integration of Information Systems in Manufacturing," *Omega* 15(3), 229–238 (1987).

5. D.D. BEDWORTH, and J.E. BAILEY, *Integrated Production Control Systems,* 2nd ed., John Wiley & Sons, Inc., New York, 1987.

6. W. SKINNER, *Manufacturing: The Formidable Competitive Weapon,* John Wiley & Sons, Inc., New York, 1985.

7. K.A. FOX, "MRP-II: A Natural Hub for a CIMS," *Ind. Eng.* 16(10), 44–50 (1984).

8. H. MATHER, "MRP-II Won't Schedule the Factory of the Future," *CIM Rev.* 3(1), 64–68 (1986).

9. C.C. HOLT et al., *Planning Production, Inventories, and Workforce,* Prentice-Hall, Inc., Englewood Cliffs, N.J., 1960.

10. J.L. BURBIDGE, *The Principles of Production Control,* 4th ed., McDonald & Evans, UK, 1978.

11. E.S. BUFFA and J.G. MILLER, *Production Inventory Systems Planning and Control,* 3rd ed., R. D. Irwin, Inc., Homewood, Ill., 1979.

12. T.E. VOLLMANN, W.L. BERRY, and D.C. WHYBARK, *Manufacturing Planning and Control Systems,* Dow Jones-Irwin, Homewood, Ill., 1984.

13. A.C. HAX, ed., *Studies in Operations Management,* North-Holland, Amsterdam, 1978.

14. K.D. LAWRENCE and S.H. ZANAKIS, *Production Planning and Scheduling,* IIE Press, Norcross, Ga., 1984.

15. F.R. JACOBS and V.A. MABERT, eds., *Production Planning Scheduling and Inventory Control,* 3rd ed., IIE Press, Norcross, Ga., 1986.

16. A. RAVINDRAN, D.T. PHILLIPS, and J.J. SOLBERG, *Operations Research: Principles & Practices,* 2nd ed., John Wiley & Sons, Inc., New York, 1987.

17. F.S. HILLIER and G.J. LIEBERMAN, *Introduction to Operations Research,* 3rd ed., Holden-Day, Inc., San Francisco, 1980.

18. R.W. CONWAY, et al., *Theory of Scheduling,* Addison-Wesley Publishing Co., Inc., Reading Mass., 1967.

19. K.R. BAKER, *Introduction to Sequencing and Scheduling,* John Wiley & Sons, Inc., New York, 1974.

20. J.A.H.G. RINNOOY KAN, *Machine Scheduling Problems,* The Hague, 1976.

21. J.K. LENSTRA, *Sequencing by Enumerative Methods,* Mathematisch Centrum, Amsterdam, 1976.

22. S. FRENCH, *Sequencing and Scheduling: An Introduction to the Mathematics of the Job Shop,* Ellis Horwood, Ltd. Chichester, UK, 1982.

23. J.R. KOELSCH, "Software: An Uphill Battle," *Machine Tool Blue Book,* **83,** 47–64 (May 1988).

24. L.P. RITZMAN, et al., "Manufacturing Performance: Pulling the Right Levers," *Harvard Bus. Rev.,* **62,** 143–152 (1984).

25. L.J. KRAJWESKI, et al., "Kanban, MRP, and Shaping the Manufacturing Environment," *Manage. Sci.* **33**(1), 39–57 (1987).

26. L.F. GELDERS and L.N. VAN WASSENHOVE, "Capacity Planning in MRP, JIT, and OPT: A Critique," *Eng. Costs Product. Econ.* **9,** 201–209 (1985).

27. S.M. SEWARD, S.G. TAYLOR, and S.F. BOLANDERS, "Progress in Integrating and Optimizing Production Plans and Schedules," *Int. J Product. Res.* **23**(3), 609–624 (1985).

28. J. SHIVNAN, R. JOYCE, and J. BROWNE, "Production and Inventory Management Techniques—A Systems Perspective," in A. Kusiak, ed., *Modern Production Management Systems,* North-Holland, Amsterdam, 1987.

29. S.B. GERSHWIN, R.R. HILDEBRANDT, R. SURI, and S.K. MITTER, *A Control Theorist's Perspective on Recent Trends in Manufacturing Systems,* paper presented at the IEEE Conference on Decision and Control, Las Vegas, 1984.

30. S.A. MELNYK, et al., *Shop Floor Control,* Dow Jones-Irwin, Homewood, Ill., 1985.

31. S.C. GRAVES, "Using Lagrangian Technical to Solve HPP Problems," *Manag. Sci.* **28**(3), 260–275 (1982).

32. H. EMMONS, "Scheduling and Sequencing Algorithms" in J.A. White, ed., *Production Handbook,* John Wiley & Sons, Inc., New York, 1987.

33. S. EILON, "Production Scheduling," *Operat. Res.* **78,** 237–266 (1978).

34. R.W. HALL, *Zero Inventories,* Dow Jones Irwin, Homewood, Ill., 1983.

35. Y. MONDEN, *Toyota Production System,* IIE Press, Norcross, Ga., 1983.

36. E. NADDOR, *Inventory Systems,* John Wiley & Sons, Inc., New York, 1966.

37. E.A. SILVER and R. PETERSON, *Decision Systems for Inventory Management and Production Planning,* 2nd ed., John Wiley & Sons, Inc., New York, 1985.

38. E. BARANCSI, et al., "A Report on Research on Inventory models," *Eng. Costs Product. Econ.* **7,** 127–136 (1983).

39. H.C. BAHL, L.P. RITZMAN, and J.N.D. GUPTA, "Determining Lot Sizes & Resource Requirements: A Review," *Operat. Res.* **33**(3), 329–345 (1987).

40. E. MERCHANT, "Future Trends and Developments" in E. Teichloz and J.N. Orr, eds., *CIM Handbook,* McGraw-Hill, Book Co., Inc., New York, 1987.

41. R. SADOWSKI, "Improving Automated Systems Scheduling," *CIM Rev.* **2**(1), 10–13 (1986).

42. P.J. O'GRADY, "State of the Art of Production Planning and Control in Automated Manufacturing Systems" in *Planning for Automated Manufacturing,* Institute of Mechanical Engineers, London, 1986, pp. 195–201.

43. H.J. BULLINGER, R. STEINHILPER, and M.P. ROTH, "Towards the Factory of the Future," *Int. J. Product. Res.* **24**(4), 697–741 (1986).

44. R.H. HAYES and S.C. WHEELRIGHT, *Restoring Our Competitive Edge,* John Wiley & Sons, Inc., New York, 1984.

45. P.M. SWAMIDASS, *Competing with Manufacturing Flexibility,* Indiana University School of Business, Bloomington, 1986, Working Paper Ser.

46. D.M. ZELENOVIC, "Flexibility—A Condition for Effective Production Systems," *Int. J. Product. Res.* **20**(3), 319–337 (1982).

47. J.A. BUZACOTT and D.D. YAO, "Flexible Manufacturing Systems: A Review of Analytical Models," *Manage. Sci.* **32**(7), 890–905 (1986).

48. A. KUSIAK, ed., *FMS: Methods and Studies,* North-Holland, Amsterdam, 1986.

49. H.V.D. PARUNAK, et al., *An Architecture for Heuristic Factory Control,* paper presented at the AAAC American Control Conference, Seattle, 1986.

50. T.J. GREENE and R.P. SADOWSKI, "A Review of Cellular Manufacturing Assumptions, Advantages, and Design techniques," *J. Operat. Manage.* **4**(2), 85–96 (1984).

51. R.K. SINHA and R.H. HOLLIER, "A Review of Production Control Problems in Cellular Manufacturing," *Int. J. Product. Res.* **22**(5), 773–789 (1984).

52. E. HAAS, "Breakthrough Manufacturing," *Harvard Bus. Rev.* **65,** 75–81 (Mar.–Apr. 1987).

53. W. SKINNER, "The Focused Factory," *Harvard Bus. Rev.* **52,** 113–121 (May–June 1974).

54. S.M. LEE and L.J. MOOR, "A Practical Approach to Production Scheduling," *Product. Inventory Manage.* (1974).

55. A.S.M. MASUD and C.L. HWANG, "An Aggregate Production Planning Model and Application of Three Multiple Decisions Methods," *Int. J. Product. Res.* **18**(6), 741–752 (1980).

56. P.J. O'GRADY and U. MENON, "A Flexible Multiobjective Production Framework for Automated Manufacturing Systems," *Eng. Costs Product. Econ.* **8,** 189–198 (1984).

57. R. AKELLA, Y. CHONG, and S.B. GERSHWIN, "Performance of Hierarchical Production Scheduling Policy," *IEEE Trans. Comput. Hybrids Manufact. Technol.* **7**(3), 215–220 (1984).

58. Y.C. HO, "A Survey of the Perturbation Analysis of Discrete Event Dynamic Systems," *Ann. Operat. Res.* (1985).

59. D.L. SHUNK, "Integrated Manufacturing—The Concepts," *Product. Eng.,* **31,** 50–53 (Sept. 1984).

60. E.M. GOLDRATT and R.E. FOX, *The Race,* North River Press, Croton-on-Hudson, N.Y., 1986.

61. K.S. STECKE and R. SURI, eds., *Proceedings of the First ORSA/TIMS Conference on FMS,* J.C. Baltzer AG., Basel, Switzerland, 1984.

62. R.E. SHANNON, *Simulation: The Art and Science,* Prentice-Hall, Inc., New York, 1976.

63. A.A.B. PRITSKER, *Introduction to Simulation and SLAM II,* 2nd ed., John Wiley & Sons, Inc., New York, 1984.

64. C.D. PEGDEN, *Introduction to SIMAN,* Systems Modeling Corp. State College, Pa., 1985.

65. A. CARRIE, "FMS Simulation: Needs, Experiences, Facilities" in W.B. Heginbotham, ed., *Simulation in Manufacturing,* Elsevier North-Holland, Amsterdam, 1985, pp. 205–215.

66. R.E. SHANNON and D.T. PHILIPS, "Comparison of Modeling Languages for Simulation of Automated Manufacturing Systems," *Autofact* **5**, 1–9 (1983).

67. D. KOCHAN, *Developments in Computer Integrated Manufacturing*, Springer-Verlag, Berlin, 1986.

68. W. SKINNER, "Manufacturing—Missing Link in Corporate Strategy," *Harvard Bus. Rev.* **47**, 136–145 (May–June 1969).

69. J.L. BURBIDGE, "The Design of Integrated Production Management Systems" in A. Kusiak, ed., *Modern Production Management Systems*, North Holland, Amsterdam, 1987, pp. 549–560.

70. J. HAMM, K. HITOMI, and T. YOSHIDA, *Group Technology Applications to Production Management*, Kluwer-Nijhoff Publishing, Boston, 1985.

71. C.T. MOSIER, D.A. ELVERS, and D. KELLYE, "Analysis of Group Technology Scheduling Heuristics," *Int. J. Product. Res.* **22**(5), 857–875 (1984).

72. P.G. RANKY, *Computer Integrated Manufacturing*, Prentice-Hall, Inc., Englewood Cliffs, N.J., 1987.

73. M.J. SHAW, "A Distributed Scheduling Method for CIM: The Use of LANs in Cellular Systems," *Int. J. Product. Res.* **25**(9), 1285–1303 (1987).

74. A. KUSIAK, ed., *Modern Production Management Systems*, North-Holland, Amsterdam, 1987.

75. W.K. HOLSTEIN, "Production Planning and Control Integrated," *Harvard Bus. Rev.*, **46**, 121–140 (May–June 1968).

76. J. HARRINGTON, *Understanding the Manufacturing Process*, Marcel Dekker, Inc., New York, 1984.

77. J. PARANBY, "Concepts of a Manufacturing System," *Int. J. Product. Res.* **17**(2), 123–135 (1980).

78. ICAM Report, *ICAM Architecture. Part 2, Vol. 1—Accomplishments*, Wright Patterson AFB, Springfield, Va., 1981, NTIS No. ADB 062454.

79. ICAM Report, *ICAM Architecture*. Part 3, Vol. 5—*Composite Function Model of Manufacture Product* and Vol. 6—*Composite Information Model of Manufacture Product*, Wright Patterson AFB, Springfield, Va., 1983, NTIS Nos. ADA 142337 and 143072.

80. G.R. BITRAN and A.C. HAX, "The Role of Mathematical Programming in Production Planning" in K.D. Lawrence and S.H. Zanakis, eds., *Production Planning and Scheduling*, IIE Press, Norcross, Ga., 1984, pp. 21–56.

81. B.P. DZIELINSKI and R.E. GOMORY, "Optimal Programming of Lot Sizes, Inventory and Labor Allocations," *Manage. Sci.* **11**(9), 874–890 (1965).

82. L.S. LASDON and R.C. TERJUNG, "An Efficient Algorithm for Multi-Item Scheduling," *Operat. Res.* **19**(4), 946–969 (1971).

83. R.M. KING and R.R. LOVE, "Coordinating Decisions for Increased Profits," *Interfaces* **6**, 4–19 (Dec. 1980).

84. R.L. MARTINO, *Integrated Manufacturing Systems*, McGraw-Hill Book Co., Inc., New York, 1972.

85. J. ORLICKY, *Materials Requirements Planning*, McGraw-Hill Book Co., Inc., New York, 1975.

86. O.W. WIGHT, *MRP II: Unlocking America's Productivity*, Wight Publications, Williston, Vt., 1984.

87. H.A. KURSTEDT, *Frameworks for Decision Support*, Virginia Tech, Management Systems Lab, Blacksburg, Va., 1985.

88. R.H. ANTHONY, *Planning and Control Systems: A Framework for Analysis*, Harvard University, Graduate School of Business, Cambridge, Mass., 1965.

89. A.C. HAX and H.C. MEAL, "Hierarchical Integration of Production Planning and Scheduling" in M.A. Geisler, ed., *Logistics*, North-Holland, Amsterdam, 1975, pp. 53–69.

90. A.C. HAX and J.J. GOLOVIN, "Hierarchical Production Planning systems" in A. Hax, ed., *Studies in Operations Management*, North-Holland, Amsterdam, 1978, pp. 400–428.

91. H.C. MEAL, M.H. WACHTER, and D.C. WHYBARK, "Materials Requirements Planning and Hierarchial Production Planning," *Int. J. Product. Res.* **25**(7), 947–956 (1987).

92. R. VAN DIERDONCK and J.G. MILLER, "Designing Production Planning and Control Systems," *J. Operat. Manage.* **1**(1), 37–46 (1980).

93. L.F. GELDERS and L.N. VAN WASSENHOVE, "Hierarchical Integration in Production Planning: Theory and Practice," *J. Operat. Manage.* **3**(1), 27–36 (1982).

94. J.G. KIMEMIA and S.B. GERSHWIN, "An Algorithm for the Computer Control of Production in FMS," *IIE Trans.* **15**(4), 353–362 (1983).

95. D. HALBERSTAM, *The Reckoning,* William Morrow & Co., New York, 1986.

96. Y. SUGIMORO, "Toyota Production System and Kanban System," *Int. J. Product. Res.* **15**(6), 553–564 (1977).

97. T. OHNO, "The Origin of Toyota Production System and Kanban System" in *Applying Just-in-Time,* IIE Press, Norcross, Ga., 1982, pp. 3–8.

98. L.P. REES, et al., "Dynamically Adjusting the Number of Kanbans in a JIT Production System Using Estimated Values of Leadtime," *IIE Trans.* **19**(2), 199–207 (1987).

99. J. BESSANT and B. HAYWOOD, "Flexibility in Manufacturing Systems," *Omega* **14**(6), 465–473 (1987).

100. R.R. HILDEBRANDT, *Scheduling Flexible Machining Systems When Machines Are Prone to Failure,* unpublished Ph.D. dissertation, MIT, Cambridge, 1980.

101. T.E. MORTON and T.C. SMUNT, "A Planning and Scheduling System for Flexible Manufacturing," in A. Kusiak, ed., *FMS Methods and Studies,* North-Holland, Amsterdam, 1986.

102. O. BERMAN and O. MAIMON, "Cooperation among Flexible Manufacturing Systems," *IEEE J. Robotics Automat.* **2**(1), 24–30, 1986.

103. F.R. JACOBS, "OPT Uncovered: Concepts Behind the System," *Ind. Eng.* **16**(10), 32–41 (1984).

104. W. MAXWELL, et al., "A Modeling Framework for Planning and Control of Production in Discrete Parts Manufacturing and Assembly Systems," *Interfaces* **13**, 92–104 (1983).

105. A. ZAHORIK, L.J. THOMAS, and W.W. TRIGEIRO, "Network Programming Models for Production Scheduling in Multi-Stage, Multi-Item Capacitated Systems," *Manage. Sci.* **30**(3), 308–325 (1984).

106. D.T. ROSS, "Structured Analysis: A Language for Communicating Ideas," *IEEE Trans. Software Eng.* **3**(1), 16–34 (1977).

107. M.F. CONNOR, *SADT Introduction,* SofTech Inc., Waltham, Mass., 1980.

108. D.T. ROSS, "Applications and Extensions of SADT," *Compt. Mag.,* 25–34 (Apr. 1985).

109. A.M. GEOFFRION, "An Introduction to Structured Modeling," *Manage. Sci.* **35**(5), 547–588 (1987).

110. IDEF Manual, *ICAM Architecture. Part 2, Vol. 4—Function Modeling Manual,* Wright Patterson AFB, Springfield, Va., 1981, NTIS No. ADB 062457.

111. D.L. SHUNK, W.G. SULLIVAN, and J. CAHILL, "Making the Most of IDEF Modeling—The Triple Diagonal concept," *CIM Rev.* **3**(1), 12–17 (1986).

112. S.K. DAS, S.C. SARIN, and P. NAGENDRA, "A 2-Level Hierarchical Scheduling Model with Productions and Time Aggregation," in review, 1991.

113. K. HOFF and S.C. SARIN, *Production Control in the Wood Furniture Industry,* Northeastern Experiment Station, Forestry Science Lab, Princeton, W.V., 1991, Industry Rep.

114. K. HOFF, S.C. SARIN, and R.B. ANDERSON, *Graphic Model of the Processes Involved in the Production of Casegood Furniture,* Northeastern Forest Experiment Station, Radnor, Pa., 1992, Res. Paper NE-666.

115. K. HOFF and S.C. SARIN, "Furniture Production Process," submitted, 1992.

116. S.C. SARIN, K. HOFF, and R.L. BRISBIN, "Master and Coordinated Production Scheduling Problems in a Furniture Manufacturing Plant with Application to a Real Life Problem," submitted, 1992.

CHAPTER 25
Management of Production Cells

JOHN E. LENZ
CMS Research, Inc.

25.1 OVERVIEW OF PRODUCTION CELLS

Factories consist of tools and people working to produce a product. Traditionally, these tools and people have been organized according to two approaches: Process Layout or Product Layout. The Process Layout organizes tools and people according to the production process. With this approach, factories are organized into departments which perform a specific process such as milling, turning, and assembly. Consequently, when a part has needed an operation, it has been routed to the specific department which performed that type of operation. With such an approach, the process is optimized, but the material handling is extensive.

The second approach is the Product Layout. In a Product Layout the operations needed for a specific product are located together. For example, the milling capacity is purchased for each product and located in that production area. This arrangement minimizes the material handling but does not optimize the process. Therefore, the total amount of milling capacity will be higher for a product layout than that with a process layout due to the lack of sharing extra milling capacity over several products.

With both of these approaches to factory layout, a high inventory level was used to cover-up many of the inefficiencies. For example, with the process layout, material handling was complicated and material moved sluggishly. As a result, large amounts of inventory were needed to provide the time to track and locate material which needed to be moved.

Inventory was also used in the product layout. In this case, the process could not be balanced so inventory was used to smooth out the material flow between operations.

Inventory Becomes the Culprit

Inventory provides factories with efficient use of tools and people. With high inventory levels, tools, and people were always busy producing parts. Part production was so important that wages and costing methods were standardized on the number of parts which were produced. Factories became efficient producers of parts, but inefficient producers of products.

This situation was first observed by the auto industry in the late 1970s during the period when Japanese auto manufacturers initiated an aggressive campaign into the United States auto market. Within a few years, Japanese imports gained 25% of the U.S. auto market and consequently an investigation into Japanese auto manufacturing began. As a result of this investigation, U.S. auto manufacturers discovered that Japanese factories operate at much lower inventories: the primary reason Japanese cars cost less than U.S. cars. Inventory became the culprit for the high cost of U.S. products.

Inventory Reduction

Throughout the 1980s, factories focused on methods for reducing inventories. Inventory reduction technologies proliferated and hundreds of techniques were developed-each having a different name and each promoted by a group of developers. During this period the concept of cellular manufacturing was formed.

Cellular Manufacturing

Cellular manufacturing is a method for factory layout combining the features of process layout with features of product layout to form a cell. A cell is a collection of tools and people which produces a family of parts and performs a subset of the entire process. The tools and people are located to minimize the material handling with the process general enough to support a family of parts.

As factories, which were based upon process layouts, migrated to cells, improvements were measured by the reduction in the distance a part had to travel in a cell compared to the distance traveled to each department for an operation. Factories with product layouts migrated to cells and measured their improvements by the number and variety of parts which could be produced by the same cell.

The real benefit of cellular manufacturing is that factories focus less at making parts and more at producing major components and products. "Plant within a Plant" has been an expression which exemplified the use of cells, for instance, focused factories have become product oriented with the primary objective being to produce products—not parts.

Flexibility Is The Key

Cellular manufacturing does reduce inventory by focusing attention at producing products instead of parts. The inventory which was used to maintain efficient use of tools and people has been reduced within cells and strategically located between cells. Thus, with lower inventories inside of cells, efficient use of tools and machines can be reduced compared to high inventory production. However, a substitute for this inventory is needed if the efficient use of tools and machines is to be maintained: This substitute for inventory is flexibility.

25.2 FLEXIBILITY IS THE KEY TO CELLULAR MANUFACTURING

Flexible manufacturing means that alternative paths are available for a part to take through its production process. A path is a combination of machines and labor used to complete a sequence of operations. These paths can be in the form of redundant machines or redundant people depending upon whether the process is machine limited or labor limited. Establishing the number of paths is an integral part of production cell design. As a part of the design, the paths need not be on-line, but can require a "setup" to create a new path. Path setup is the process of changing tooling in a machine or assigning operators to a different set of operations. Production cell design determines the potential number of paths. Management of production cells is the decision to create or destroy paths as the operation occurs. Section 25.5 describes the management of production cells.

The following sections contain descriptions of machine and labor flexibility.

Machine Flexibility

Machine flexibility occurs when alternative machines are available for the same operation. These machines can perform identical operations simultaneously or one can serve as a backup for the other. In this backup mode, the machine might require a setup in order to qualify for performing another operation.

The ultimate form of machine flexibility is the Flexible Manufacturing System (FMS). The FMS provides alternative paths using similar tooled machines where the management of these paths is handled via automation. If three machines were capable of performing the same operation, this capacity would establish a certain level of flexibility. But these three machines placed side by side and the type of flexibility required for their management, is what differentiates the FMS from three identical stand-alone machines.

The FMS uses automation to manage its flexibility. This automation involves an automatic material handling system and computer hierarchy to coordinate the operation of all FMS components. The best way to illustrate the role that automation has in machine flexibility, is through an example.

For instance, a company was organizing its production into several production cells. One project required the breakup of a job shop (process and layout) into three production cells with

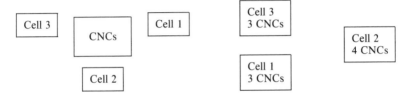

Figure 25.1. CNC pool with three small cells.

Figure 25.2. CNCs distributed into three separate cells.

the job shop consisting of 10 CNC machines and several other dedicated machines. The task was solving how to utilize the 10 CNC machines to obtain a high level of flexibility (because any machine could accept all pallets/fixtures and tooling) and meet the closed property of a cell.

One approach was to retain the 10 CNCs in a pool and then have the dedicated machines organized into three cells (Figure 25.1). An alternative was to distribute the CNC machines to each of these cells (Figure 25.2). The 10 CNC's pool has the highest level of flexibility, but it was not the one implemented. The concern of the 10 CNC's pool was in how to manage this area. If the 10 CNCs were linked with an automatic material handling system where pallets/fixtures could be routed to any machine, and if a supervisory computer system were monitoring these "paths" and directing material flow, then the CNC pool would be viable. However, the management of the 10 CNC pool without automation would require constant attention by the supervisor to make use of the flexibility. This constant attention was not possible so the CNCs were dedicated to each cell.

This example illustrates that flexibility and automation are two separate characteristics of production. From this example, although it is possible to locate all CNC machines in an area where they could be used for alternative operations, the management of this flexibility would require constant attention. In this sense then it is the automation within the FMS that provides the management of the flexible capacity.

Therefore, the FMS provides flexible machine alternatives for many operations within a parts' process list and the machine cell provides machine alternatives for a few operations. So the machine cell can be thought of as a subset of the FMS.

As far as automation is concerned, the machine cell can have the same computer controls and material handling system as the FMS; however, the difference is that the machine cell provides flexibility to a smaller set of operations than the FMS. Because the machine cell provides flexible machine capacity to a small set of operations, it is not essential that automation manage this flexibility. Machine cells provide the same benefit of alternative machines no matter what degree of automation is used to manage them. When automation is not used for the material handling and part tracking, then labor is used. When labor becomes the limiting factor to production, then the flexibility of the labor becomes more important than the flexibility of the machines.

Labor Flexibility

Labor-limited processes require flexible labor to provide a substitute for inventory as compared to machine limited processes which require flexible machines. If the type of flexibility does not match the limiting factor in production, then no benefits will be available from the flexibility.

Flexible labor occurs whenever labor provides multiple paths for a part. A path is a combination of a part, machine (or station), fixture, and an operator. One operator working multiple stations is an example of flexible manufacturing.

The technique of flexible labor is described in Monden's book entitled: *Toyoda Production Systems* (1). Monden uses the term U-line when describing the implementation of flexible labor. The U-line terminology is derived from the layout of the production area when flexible labor is used. The stations are located in the shape of a "U" in order to minimize the walking distance of operators and encourage operators to perform more than one operation. The U-line is the most common form of flexible labor cells. Another characteristic of the U-line is the ability to vary the number of operators who work within the cell. The U-line can be operated by one operator who then picks and places the parts through the process. When a second operator is added to the cell, the work is divided in such a way as to minimize the walking distance. The U-line provides flexibility in how labor performs, and flexibility in the number of operators who work in the cell.

Not all production systems can be organized into a "U" shape. Assembly lines usually have layout along a straight line for the purpose of accessing components from both sides of the assembly process. Balance becomes the critical issue for this type of production system. Balancing an assembly line can be accomplished by two means. The most common approach is to organize the process such that the same amount of work (equal time) occurs at every station. This method requires extensive knowledge of the process and any remaining imbalance results in lost capacity.

The second means to balance an assembly line is through flexible labor. Once the work is divided into operations at each station, then labor is assigned in a flexible manner to balance the parts flow. The allocation of labor is done through operators covering more than one station. For example, an assembly line has five stations where the total hours of work require three operators. Operators could be assigned such that one operator covers stations 1 and 2, another covers stations 2, 3, 4 and the third operator covers stations 4 and 5. This allocation of labor not only provides multiple paths for the part through its process but also permits operators to balance the work according to how often they each perform operations at the overlap stations.

Flexibility is a Substitute for Inventory

The concept, multiple paths, is the common characteristic between machine flexibility and labor flexibility. These paths allow parts to take less time to complete their process. For example, in a transportation system, if only one path is available between a source and a destination, the travel time is directly influenced by the traffic congestion of this path. However, if multiple paths exist between a source and a destination, then travel time will not depend upon the availability of one path and will be shorter than the average time when using a single path.

This relationship between the number of paths and flow time (elapsed time from the first operation through the last operation) is responsible for and regulates the flexibility that determines factory performance. Consider the equation: Production = Inventory/Flow Time. When flow time is reduced by the use of flexibility, it will have a positive impact upon production.

From an alternative point of view, when inventory is reduced, a reduction in flow time is essential in order to maintain the same level of production. It is through this relationship that flexibility is a substitute for inventory.

As inventory levels are reduced, a substitute is required to maintain the same level of production. That substitute, flexibility, provides multiple paths and so reduces flow time for paths through their production process.

25.3   CELL PERFORMANCE

Cell performance is a critical issue in the management of production cells because of the reduction in inventory levels. Inventory provides a cover for the inefficiencies of a production process. As this cover is removed, the process inefficiencies have direct influence upon production.

With high inventory production systems, performance has not been an issue because it was solely dependent upon labor and machine availability. With lower inventory and exposed inefficiency, production is no longer simply determined by labor and machine availability. A complicated relationship between the inventory level, balance of the process, and flexibility will determine the productivity of a production system.

The following section is a description of the relationship between inventory and balance. This section provides background to the Manufacturing Model (MIM) which establishes a means to measure cell performance.

Low Inventory-Unbalanced Process

The high inventory–high flexibility production environment is characterized as the job shop. In the job shop, little of the flexible capacity is "on-line" so setups are often required for the capacity allocation decision to be implemented. However, the operational management for this type of production environment is focused at the timing of material requirements. Performance of any machine is not a priority because all machines have a backlog of work. The management objective is not one of optimal performance, but one of making sure the right parts are worked on in the right order.

At the other end of the inventory versus flexibility scale is the transfer line. The low inventory–low flexibility environment is managed by "balancing the line." Optimal performance is not an operational priority because when the line is running, it will produce at the rate of its longest cycle. Measuring performance of the transfer line can be established from how many hours the line has been in operation. This characteristic of performance to machine/labor availability is found in both the job shop and transfer line. How efficient a machine/operator is working can be determined directly from the hours the line is in operation. In these instances, operational management does not need to focus on performance, but rather at material requirements in the job shop or line balancing on the transfer line.

However, in the flexible manufacturing environment, high inventory is not available to guarantee a backlog for every machine, and balance capacity against requirements does not exit. In this case, the performance of the factory is not solely dependent upon machine/labor availability. Characteristics such as material shortages and blocking must be accounted for in the determination of net or real production efficiency.

Just-In-Time (JIT) has become a popular technique for reducing active inventory within a production process. JIT establishes a fixed inventory level for a process and provides easy-to-follow rules for operational management. This technique has proven effective in reducing work in process levels, but not without a cost. In most cases, this "cost" is the purchase of additional capacity.

Whenever inventory is reduced in an unbalanced process, periodic shortages of material will occur. These material shortages will cause a decrease in productivity because the machine/operator will remain idle during the material shortage. This unbalanced process appears to management as a bottleneck in the process and corrective action is needed to eliminate this bottleneck.

One means to eliminate the material shortage is to increase inventory before initiating the operation which experiences the material shortage. However, this strategy usually violates JIT rules and is not considered as an alternative. The easiest solution is to purchase additional capacity for the "perceived" bottleneck operation. As a result, inventory is reduced in a process and additional capacity is added as a substitute for the reduction in efficiency which results from integration effects.

The process of acquiring capacity as a substitute for inventory does not stop at one operation. The domino effect occurs and as soon as one bottleneck is solved, another appears. Therefore, capacity is not simply purchased for one or a set of operations, but is purchased for all operations in the low inventory, unbalanced process. In many cases, implementation of JIT results with the purchase of 15–20% additional capacity over a period of five years. But, this trade-off of capacity for inventory does not mean that JIT is not economic. In several instances, this trade-off provides many economic benefits, but a model is needed which can compare capacity to inventory levels and flexibility.

The Manufacturing Integration Model (MIM) provides a means to measure and compare capacity, inventory balance, and flexibility.

Manufacturing Integration Model (MIM)

The Manufacturing Integration Model (MIM) provides a framework for understanding factory performance. MIM is a set of four equations, shown in Figure 25-3, which identifies the relationship between the production variables which include: required production, number of machines, process, machine/labor availability, scrap, set-up, inventory level, balancing and flexibility. MIM also classifies these production inputs as being either contributions to production capacity, production efficiency, or integration effects.

Production Capacity is the measure of the gross number of parts which can be produced within the planning horizon. This value is determined from a mathematical calculation involving production requirements, process (list of required operations), operation time standards, number of machines and operators. Production capacity is not a static number, but changes each time the production requirement changes. In this sense, any production mix (instance of production requirements) will establish a production capacity. Whenever the mix changes, so will

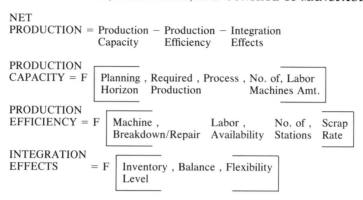

Figure 25.3. Manufacturing integration model.

the production capacity. One leading cause of mix changes is due to the planning horizon. For example, a planning period of one month will include production requirements for a month. This calculation will establish a mix. When a planning horizon of one week is used, a different mix might exist which will establish a different production capacity. Many conditions contribute to production capacity, but for each capacity it is advantageous to think of capacity as a function of the production mix. In these terms, whenever the mix changes, so will the production capacity. During the operation of a production system, it is often wrongly assumed that a constant capacity exists, even when the production mix changes. This false assumption focuses attention away from capacity towards operational characteristics such as inventory and machine availability. It is important to remember that production capacity is as dynamic as changes are to production mix and their processes.

Production Efficiency is determined from the availability of machines, labor, scrap percentage and setup delay. These production variables have an inverse impact upon productivity because the greater their respective value, the smaller the net production. Many manufacturing techniques focus on minimizing these contributions to production efficiency. Such techniques include preventive maintenance, total quality control, statistical process control, quick change fixtures, and rolling operator breaks. A percent reduction in any of these production variables should provide an equal improvement in net production. However, this logic assumes that the integration effects are independent of efficiency and they are not. The dependent nature of all production variables is what makes the measuring of its performance so difficult. This is most obvious with integration effects.

Integration Effects are losses in production capacity due to two occurrences: material shortage and blocking. Material shortages and blocking are best described through an example. Suppose that parts must travel through three operations and the first operation interrupts the part availability for 60 minutes. This decrease in the first operation availability will affect the production efficiency. If the backlog for the next operation is greater than 60 minutes, the second operation will not experience any material shortage as a result of the interruption in the first operation's availability. However, if the backlog for the second operation is only 30 minutes at the time of interruption, then the second operation will experience a material shortage for 30 minutes. Carrying this arrangement one step further, suppose that the second operation feeds a third operation. Then its material shortage of 30 minutes could be "viewed" as a service interruption of the second operation by the third operation. In this way, the single interruption of one operation can "integrate" itself as a material shortage over many subsequent operations. This example is only the "downstream view;" the "upstream view" must be considered as well.

The upstream side involves the blocking types of integration effects. Blocking occurs whenever an operation can not accept more parts because the number of parts it has already completed has depleted in-process inventory. A variety of reasons exist which create blocking: some of these are due to automated material handling or strict adherence to control rules such as evident in Just-In-Time techniques. Blocking decreases production when inventory levels are filled and the operation can no longer continue to accept parts. Blocking can be avoided by unlimited stacking of parts between operations.

It is one matter to understand integration effects, but it is much more important to identify how much production will be lost due to them. Three production variables have been identified which directly influence how much integration effects will occur within any production capacity. These variables are inventory, balance, and flexibility, and have been selected because each in its own way can completely eliminate integration effects. When integration effects are eliminated, then productivity is simply determined from production efficiency which turns out to be a relatively simple problem to solve. How inventory, balance, and flexibility influence integration effects will follow.

Inventory is the number of parts which are allowed to be "actively" routed in the production process. Inventory can be raised to such a level that the availability of any operation will create no blocking nor material shortage upon any other operation. The traditional job shop is an example where inventory is raised to such a level that integration effects are eliminated. In such situations, net production is determined from production efficiency and management, in such an environment, is concerned with making the right part at the right time. In such cases, management is focused at inventory control and scheduling, not at productivity.

Balance is the loading across all operations. A production facility is balanced when these loadings are equal for a planning horizon and production mix. When a facility is perfectly balanced, all integration effects are eliminated. For example, the transfer line is an example where balancing of cycle times is used to eliminate integration effects. However, because the line is balanced, it makes no sense to build an inventory when one operation becomes unavailable because the net production is determined by the longest cycle. Therefore, the net production of a transfer line is determined solely from its efficiency.

Flexibility is the number of paths that a part can take through its production process. Flexibility, also, can completely eliminate integration effects by the use of utopian flexibility; however this strategy is not often found in practical applications. Utopian flexibility occurs when a part can use any station for any operation. With this type of flexibility, all operations are independent and net production is determined from the production efficiency. Flexible cells come the closest to providing utopian flexibility. These cells have two or more computer control machines with an automated material handling system. Each machine is identically tooled and parts do not need to travel from one machine to another.

High inventory, balanced processes, and utopian flexibility will eliminate integration effects, but not without a cost. In many cases, the cost of eliminating integration effects is greater than the cost of lost production capacity due to them. Finding the combination of inventory, balance and flexibility which yields the greatest benefits is the primary objective for measurement. This objective leads to the need to quantify the MIM equations.

Quantifying MIM

There is no mathematical solution to the equations of MIM because there is no quantitative measure for all of the production variables. Flexibility is an example where no quantitative measure exists. Suggestions such as the number of paths as a quantitative measure of flexibility have no direct relation to production. Flexibility can only be measured via the operation of the production facility. Therefore, queuing and simulation models must be used to solve the MIM equations. All other production variables can be quantified, but how much flexibility exists in any production process has no numeric representatives. (One approach using the change in flow time as a measure of flexibility has been suggested, but has not been widely accepted). Because of this numeric value for flexibility, queuing and simulation models must be used to solve the MIM equations.

Queuing and simulation models have a characteristic of solving the MIM equation for a specific production mix, station, efficiency, inventory level, balance, and flexibility. However, the solution to MIM is not a single point, but a curve. This curve is the locust of point and shows the relationship for alternative values of the production variables.

One such curve is the Work-In-Process-Against-Capacity (WIPAC) Curve. The WIPAC Curve shows the relationship between inventory levels and production. It also can be used to identify the effect of different efficiency levels upon net production. On the Figure 25.4 is an example of a WIPAC Curve and how the MIM solution can be identified.

The WIPAC Curve shows the solution to MIM for all levels of inventory. Each point of this curve requires a simulation result; however, some queuing models can approximate the entire curve with a single computer run. Even though the WIPAC Curve shows the MIM solution for all levels of inventory, each curve is a result of a specific production mix, efficiency level, process, and balance. When any of these production variables change, the WIPAC curve will

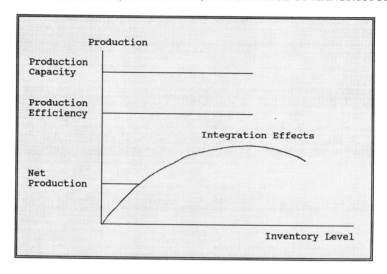

Figure 25.4.   WIPAC curve.

need to be reconstructed. This reconstruction can be a tedious task when the tools which are used to create the WIPAC Curve only provide a single point from each evaluation run.

Search techniques and other interpretations of results can be designed which will reduce the number of points to be studied. Search rules can be developed which support the four managing flexibility decisions. The WIPAC Curve is only one example of how a curve can be used to provide solutions to the MIM equations. Many other curves can be developed which show production against production mix, or production against process alternatives. The WIPAC Curve is one example and it illustrates how the solution to MIM is not a point, but instead, is a curve or even a set of curves. Also the WIPAC Curve illustrates the weaknesses of the tools needed to construction these curves in that each evaluation run usually provides only a single point for evaluation.

25.4 COST MEASUREMENT

Cost measurement is an extension of performance measurement. Cell efficiency has traditionally been measured with production rate, station utilization, inventory level, and labor utilization. Two trends in manufacturing have provided for the ability to use cost as a performance measure. Types of costing methods and production cells follow.

Activity-Based Costing

Activity-based costing (ABC) is a procedure where all costs are allocated to the activity of manufacturing: The activity being the execution of an operation, and the actual cost of executing this activity is then identified. For example, with ABC, the cost of the station, labor, material, tooling, supervision, engineering, facility, and management is identified for each operation within the factory. If an engineer spends 30 minutes on a task, then 30 minutes of engineer time is to be costed to that operation. Be aware that the amount of details required about executing an operation can be overwhelming.

The traditional method for costing factory operation is a method based upon standard costs. In a standard costing system, all costs are burdened upon the labor. The cost of the facility, stations, tooling, labor, and overhead are totaled for the entire factory and then distributed to the total labor hours planned. For example, if the standard cost of labor is $100.00 per hour and an operation requires 30 minutes of labor, then the cost of the operation is $50.00. The 30 minutes was deduced through time study methods to determine the standard unit.

In comparing these two methods, ABC and standard methods, ABC requires extreme detail, whereas standard methods is a factory averaging method. The benefit of these two extremes have been combined into hybrid costing methods called Actual Costing. With actual costing, the activity costs of station, labor, and inventory are applied to their actual use. However, the overhead costs of management, engineering, supervision, and facility are contained in the costing rates for stations and labor. The simplest way to explain actual costing is that actual cost with a standard cost overhead is used and then applied to the actual operation.

In actual costing methods, no new cost needs to be collected. The costs identified in a standard costing system are sufficient. The difference between these two methods is in how these costs are applied. They are applied according to activity-based costing methods.

Focused Factories

The second trend in manufacturing which allows for new costing methods is the use of focused factories and production cells. These production areas become cost centers where costs are separated for each of these areas. The standard costs for management, engineering, supervision, and facility are accurately identified for each production area.

By separating the factory into small manageable units the standard costs for each unit comes closer to actual costs. When these standard costs are accurately represented, then applying these costs to the actual operation provides an accurate measure of cost within a production cell.

Activity costing is an accurate measure of cell performance. As a performance measure, it acts as a summary by combining production rate, station use, labor use, and inventory level into a single measure. All of the traditional measures are input data to the costing method. In this way, the actual costs act as weights or priorities upon the traditional measures to give a single measure to compare alternatives. The cost formula identifies how the traditional measures are weighted by uses of actual costs.

Cost Formula

The cost formula consists of seven major components: These include: (a) station cost; (b) labor cost; (c) setup cost; (d) inventory cost; (e) transportation cost; (f) delivery cost, and (g) material cost. The *station cost* includes the capital expense of the machining and the consumable expenses of electricity, tooling, fluids, etc. A standard cost method is used to establish the cost per year and this cost is applied to the actual use on a part-operator basis. (This illustrates how standard costing methods are applied in an activity-based method to establish an actual cost).

The *labor cost* includes the cost of labor and is based upon a standard rate applied to the actual use on an operation by operation basis.

Setup cost includes the cost associated with a production schedule. These costs are comprised of a station and labor components and is reported separately from the other costs. Separation of setup costs provides a means to identify the cost added to a part based upon specific production schedules.

Inventory costs include the carrying cost of work-in-process inventory. The difficulty in measuring this cost on an actual basis has been the ability to measure the inventory level. Production cells provide a closed environment where inventory within a cell and the establishment between cells is easily identified and managed to specific levels.

Transportation cost includes the cost of the material handling system distributed to actual use. In flexible labor cells, the cost will be part of the labor cost. However, in flexible machining systems, it is necessary to identify the cost added because of the increased automation.

Delivery cost includes the costs associated with early and late delivery of the parts. As cells establish a supplier-customer relationship, this cost is associated with the cost of not delivering a part to the next cell and the cost of building strategic inventory to avoid such part shortages.

Material cost includes the actual cost of the material at the beginning of the cell and the cost of the material at the end of the cell. These costs might be established by comparing them to outside sources and can be used as a return for the investment of production.

Applications

The significant benefit of cost is to be used as a performance measure. Traditional measures such as production rates, station use, and flow time are subject to biased interpretations. As factories become more flexible, the opportunity for such interpretations increase. Costs bring measurement into a single measure which can be scaled to a cell/focused factory level.

Cost as a performance measure can be used in a wide range of applications. These include day-to-day operations, new product introductions, and project justification. In day-to-day operations, cost information is used to support product changes and volume changes. Volume changes relate to daily/weekly production amounts. As cells are used to produce a family of parts, volume changes can impact daily operation of the cell and the cost of producing a part in the cell.

Product changes have a significant impact upon cost of the day-to-day operations. Using new process technology, more labor, less labor, and customization all affect the cost of producing a part in a cell. Actual cost methods can determine the impact of each change.

Not only is cost of importance in the actual operation, but also with the introduction of new products. Specifically, new product introductions involve ramping up production capacity and product integration into existing capacity. In the situation of ramping up production capacity, capacity is installed for a forecasted demand. Instead of installing this capability all at once, the alternative of acquiring capacity in several installments can be evaluated on a cost basis. The cost of producing the first year's volume with a five year forecasted capacity, will be quite high; however, this cost can be compared to the cost of producing in lower capacity cells and then expanding the capacity at specific times.

Capacity for new products is not always purchased, but is often utilized from capacity which is currently producing a similar/replacement part. In these situations, the cost associated with integrating a new product in an existing cell can be used in decision support.

A third decision level where cost is useful for decision support is in project justification. Cost provides a single measure for which to compare alternatives. Most decisions for project justification are based upon "gut feelings" or the "biased" interpretation of simulation results. Cost provides an easy-to-understand, easy-to-compare means for decision support.

25.5 MANAGEMENT

Managing Flexibility has been chosen as the name for the management of these new manufacturing technologies because of the many substitutes for inventory flexibility that offer the greatest benefits. Flexibility also means alternatives and so management must establish ways of identifying these alternatives, measuring alternatives, and rationalizing a decision. The ability to manage manufacturing technologies is the strategic issue and its the wide-spread use of flexibility which has made the management process complicated.

The alternatives of flexibility are of a wide variety. One of the more common decision alternatives occurs with redundant machines. With redundant machines, each machine can perform the same operation and a "choice of paths" is available for any specific part. The path need not be on-line and immediately available, but a set-up might be required. This is still considered a form of flexibility. The FMS is an extreme case where all paths are on-line and computer control is used to manage these paths. But the most common forms of flexibility do require the set-up or creation of a path. Managing these paths means the decision to reallocate these paths as needed.

Another form of flexibility which provides alternative paths is the use of cross-trained labor. This form of flexibility is effective in labor-limited processes such as U-lines. In the U-line, labor is cross-trained to perform many different tasks and must be able to reallocate themselves to meet appropriate needs. Many cells are designed with the objective of using flexible labor as a substitute for inventory between the operations performed within the cell.

The substitute of flexibility for inventory does not mean that inventory is completely eliminated. The amount of work-in process inventory is a decision just as is the decision to create a new path. Managing flexibility includes the decision to build and hold strategic inventories within a production process. Inventories which support economic objectives are not necessarily bad for the manufacturing firm. In this form of flexibility, inventory is allocated to strategic areas within a production process.

Other forms of flexibility exist and their respective decisions are described in the next section. One common characteristic should be noted of these managing flexibility decisions.

FOUR WAYS TO ALLOCATE CAPACITY

- Adjust Routing Table (Create/Destroy a Path)
- Adjust Schedule (Choice of Parts)
- Adjust Process (Choice of Operations)   **Figure 25.5.**   Capacity allocation
- Adjust Inventory (KANBAN Technique)   decisions.

They all deal with the allocation of capacity. Just as the name flexibility implies, production capacity is comprised of many forms. This management of flexibility becomes the decisions of how best to allocate capacity to meet the production needs.

Capacity Allocation Decisions

Four ways of allocating capacity are described (see Figure 25.5). Each decision comes from a variety of forms for flexibility and many technologies are available to support these decisions.

The objective is to define these decisions and not to indicate the strengths and weaknesses of any specific technology as it applies to one of the decisions.

Routing Table Decision. The routing table decision deals with the creation of a path for a part through its production process. The decision appears in the form of allocating a machine, labor, cell or system to a particular part. The creation of one path usually requires the destruction of another path. In this sense, process paths are allocated on an "as needed" basis.

The definition of these paths are what constitute the routing table. The routing table can be logically viewed as a two dimensional matrix where the columns represent the type of part and the rows represent the process step. Each element of the matrix contains the list of alternatives (i.e., machine, labor, cell, system) for each of these process steps. The decision process is then to allocate a path according to the needs of the part and their process.

The FMS provides an example where the routing table decision is frequently used. In the instance of the FMS, the alternative paths appear as redundant machines each capable of performing a set of operations. (Tool capacity and configuration provides the primary limit to a machine's on-line capability, but tool replacements should be considered as a "set-up" of a new path. The set-ups only influence the time delay (lost production capacity) needed to create a path. The routing table is then used to define the feasible decision area. The actual routing decision is then based upon some algorithm such as current backlog or minimizing set-up.

This paragraph illustrates the difference between management and control. The management of flexibility deals with establishing and allocation of the flexible decisions. In this case, it is the maintenance of the routing table. Control is then the process of choosing the best alternative within the feasible area. Control does not include the allocation of capacity, but the economic use of capacity as it has been allocated.

Schedule Decision. The schedule decision deals with which parts are allocated to current capacity. Given a specific capacity which is configured in an appropriate way, parts can be chosen. This decision appears as either pulling parts ahead of others to reduce set-ups and pushing others to be processed later.

Do not confuse these decisions with prioritizing as commonly found in scheduling. This decision deals with the allocation of capacity to specific parts and requires a higher level of commitment than simply a reprioritization of parts to a specific machine.

The production cell provides a facility where the schedule decision can be used. Cells will typically be devoted to a family of parts and will usually only run a subset of this family at one time. This means that the cell must be allocated to parts and might require some set-up between each allocation.

Forward scheduling and flexibility are opposites; that is, the more capacity which can be allocated, the less need there is to forward schedule. Flexibility means that the capacity can be allocated as needed to meet current demands and this approach reduces the need for optimized schedules. In this sense, scheduling deals with the management issue of allocating capacity to parts (or choosing which parts to produce) and not with the control issue of minimizing set-up for the short term.

Process Decision. The process decision deals with the choice of where operations are to be performed. This decision entails the allocation of capacity to a set of required operations. These sets of operations, which define a subset of a parts' process, establish a demand upon capacity and capacity is then allocated. For example, a cell might have the capability to perform all of the operations ranging from quality to finish machining. However, the cell's capacity need not be allocated to all of these process steps. Suppose that the qualify process can be performed on a machine outside the cell. Thus, the process decision would determine whether the cell's capacity is used for qualifying the parts or to determine if the parts arrive to the cells are already qualified.

The process decision might be considered as a decision which is often determined during the acquisition of capacity. When this capacity is purchased as having flexibility, then it can be allocated to a different set of operations. Flexibility, by its nature, means that less detailed planning is needed during the acquisition and that the capacity can be allocated as demands for it arise. Flexible capacity transfers decisions regarding process from the planning time period to the operational time period.

Inventory Decision. The inventory decision deals with the allocation of capacity by controlling the amount of inventory in the process. The decision includes the amount of work-in-process inventory which is allowed in the process and also the mix of inventory classes which are allowed. (Inventory class refers to a type of fixture used in tracking and positioning parts).

One of the simplest means of reallocating capacity is to adjust the number (mix) of parts which are allowed in a cell. For example, reducing the number of part type "As" will immediately allocate more capacity to other part types which share part type "As" resources.

One methodology for implementing the inventory decision is through the use of KANBAN's. KANBAN's can be viewed as "container loops" and the number of containers in each loop provides a means to allocate capacity. The problem of implementation of KANBAN's is that they will not reallocate capacity because the technique is designed to maintain a constant level of inventory. The capacity allocation decision is then to resize these inventory levels by changing the number of containers. The resizing of the inventory level does not mean that inventory is physically added or removed from the process. This can be the case, but it is much easier to think of inventory as being either "active" or "inactive". Active inventories are those containers which are allowed to route/place demands upon the capacity. Inactive inventory is that which is not allowed to place demand upon capacity. Inventory decisions can then be carried out by simply suspending the routing (use) of a pallet. The same parts need not be inactive or active for the entire period between reallocation. It might be that no more than 50 parts are allowed active at any one time, but these need not always be the same parts. Parts can be pooled in a buffer and remain "inactive" until a slot opens for them in the active inventory.

Decision Support

"If you can't measure it, *you* can't manage it." (Quote from P. Drecker) This quotation is most appropriate for the capacity allocation decision. In order to support any of the four capacity allocation decisions, some measures of "How well are things going?" must be provided. But this question implies that we have some standards by which to compare current performance against. In order to support the capacity allocation decisions, we must provide a means to establish a standard and then measure the actual performance to see how it compares to this standard.

When capacity is inflexible, establishing a standard, such as an hourly production rate, is easy. But when flexible capacity can be reallocated, a new standard is needed with each decision. Establishing such a performance standard will require the use of a computer model.

The computer model can be based upon either stochastic (queuing) or simulation techniques. It must be able to accurately model the limitations of the flexible capacity and include "valid" control or operation rules. These models must also "share data" with the real-time information system so that current states are known and decisions made within the modeling technique can be "implemented" by electronic messaging.

Capacity which provides the most strategic benefits will be that which lends itself to the managing of flexibility decisions. This benefit means that the capacity must be able to be reallocated and managed. Thus, the decision of purchasing capacity should include a review if it allows itself to be managed by one or more of the managing flexibility decisions.

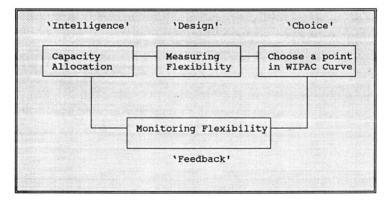

Figure 25.6. Flexible manufacturing decision model.

Manufacturing firms are being presented with a multitude of new manufacturing techniques. In order to identify and select those technologies which are most appropriate, firms must assess how well they will be able to adapt their ability to manage them. Therefore, to adapt successfully, firms will need to establish a strategy for managing these new technologies and one strategy framework to use should be the 4 decisions of managing flexibility. Firms that acquire capacity which satisfies a desired method of managing flexibility will be the best able to compete in a world-wide market.

25.6 MONITORING

Integration effects are a common occurrence in the low inventory-unbalanced production environment. These effects have an impact upon net production in such a way that factory output is not simply determined from machine efficiency. Net production is determined from a complicated relationship of many production variables ranging from production mix to flexibility. This relationship is so complicated, that in some cases, FMSs have operated for more than five years without being able to establish how well they are working. The complicated nature of factory performance establishes a need for performance monitoring of the flexible manufacturing environment.

Flexible Manufacturing Decision Model (FMD)

Monitoring flexibility provides the feedback in the capacity allocation decision life cycle. Figure 25.6 contains a diagram of the Flexible Manufacturing Decision Model.

The traditional decision life cycle consists of intelligence, design, choice and feedback. The intelligence phase is the process of identifying alternatives. The design phase is the measurement of the alternatives and comparison of each. The choice phase is the selection and implementation of a decision alternative. Feedback is the review process of the outcome of the decision and is used to influence the process of identifying alternatives. The decision life cycle illustrates the interactive nature of decision making and how the choice of one alternative will influence which alternatives are identified for the next decision.

The application of the decision life cycle model to flexible manufacturing begins with the issues of managing flexibility. Managing flexibility is made up of four capacity allocation decisions. These decisions are Routing Table Decision, Scheduling Decision, Process Decision and Inventory Decision. Each of the decision areas offers many alternatives for how the production capacity can be allocated to meet a production requirement. The abundance of alternatives arises from the very nature of flexible manufacturing and the difficult task is deciding which alternative is the best one. In the FMD Model, the intelligence phase is concerned only with establishing flexible alternatives and the task of the design phase is to compare the alternatives.

Comparing decision alternatives requires that each alternative be measured through the use of the Manufacturing Integration Model (MIM). MIM consists of four equations which establish functional relations between the production variables and also provides a means to quantify their economic trade-off. The four equations represent measures for net production, gross capacity, production efficiency, and integration effects. These equations provide a uniform basis to compare the economic benefit of each alternative. These results provide the inputs to the Choice Phase of the FMD Model.

The specific means for the allocation of capacity is the third step in the decision life cycle. The actual capacity allocation decision is made by selecting a point from one of the WIPAC Curves. Each point represents a specific configuration of the flexible capacity allocation. The capacity allocation decision is then implemented by making adjustments to the routing table, schedule, process or inventory level. After this decision is implemented, there is the need to monitor the production performance to ensure that the planned performance is being met. This monitoring provides the feedback needed for the next decision cycle.

The monitoring of production has been an important part of any factory's operation. Several traditional performance measures have been used and each has it's appropriate application. Following is a discussion of how these traditional measures apply to the monitoring of flexible manufacturing.

Traditional Performance Measures

The traditional factory performance measures include: production rate, station efficiency, inventory level, and flow time. Each of these measures is discussed with its suitability as measures of flexible manufacturing. Production rate is the quantity of parts which have completed a process in a specified amount of time. It is usually quantified in the terms of parts per hour or parts per shift. This measure can be updated and reported each time a part completes the production process.

A good characteristic of production rate as a measure of performance is that production is easy to observe. It can be observed by simply counting the number of completed parts. However, the difficulty comes when trying to use this measure for performance. The production rate is dependent upon the production mix which is the quantity of each type of part which is produced in a specified period of time. A production mix might contain a mixture of short cycle parts and long cycle parts. For each combination of a long cycle and a short cycle part (i.e., production mix) a different production rate will result. In the case of flexible manufacturing, the production mix changes constantly, therefore, production rates as a measure of performance are ineffective.

Another performance measure is station efficiency. Station efficiency is the measure of how many hours a station is available during a specified period of time. A station might be considered unavailable whenever it is being repaired, waiting for an operator, producing a reject part, waiting for tools, and in preventive maintenance. As is the case with production rate, station efficiency is an easy way to observe value. Collecting a value for a station's efficiency will require a more intense observation of the production process, but nonetheless, it is a value which can be identified for each station.

The difficulty of using station efficiency as a performance measure in flexible manufacturing comes about because the performance of the system is usually not determined by one station's efficiency. The efficiency of a bottleneck station can be used to establish a measure for flexible manufacturing, but the bottleneck might move during the production process. It is not easy to identify the bottleneck station and therefore difficult to determine which, if any, station efficiency can be used as a measure of the overall system performance.

Another missing aspect of performance with the use of station efficiency is the accounting for integration effects. Integration effects are the lost capacity when a station is idle from a material shortage or blocking. The Manufacturing Integration Model provides a means to measure integration effects, but this is more involved than identifying one station's efficiency.

Inventory level is also used as a performance measure. This is the measure of the number of parts which are in-process between a set of operations. It can be observed by counting the number of parts waiting for a specified set of operations.

The difficulty of using inventory as a performance measure in flexible manufacturing is that inventory and performance are not always positively related. The WIPAC Curve shows the relationship of inventory to net production and this curve can become downward sloping. This downward slope is due to blocking which occurs because the inventory level is too high for the available capacity. In this sense, inventory level is a decision alternative and an input to the production performance, not an output.

Flow time is a fourth type of performance measure. Flow time is the elapsed time from when a part begins the first operation in a specified set and until it completes the last operation in the specified set. This time will be the total of the actual process time, transportation time and waiting time. The waiting time can occur while waiting at the station or in some buffer location. This storage time can include the time spent between fixture changes when a part has multiple operations performed in the same flexible cell.

The measurement of flow time is not as easy to observe as with the other performance measures. This measurement requires that a time be recorded for each part when it starts its first operation. This procedure can be thought of as a time stamp for the part. Then when the part completes its last operation in the specified set of operations, the time stamp is used to observe the flow time or elapsed time between the first and last operations. In case of batch production, it is sufficient to track the flow time of the batch and not the flow time of individual parts.

In manufacturing cells, the flow time is identified as the time when the part entered the cell and the time when it departed. This flow time can be the pallet cycle time for most flexible manufacturing systems. In these closed systems, pallets are circulated through the production process and their flow time or (cycle time) is used to observe. But the difficulty comes in establishing a standard by which to compare these observed flow times.

Measuring Efficiency

Flow time standards can be used to measure the efficiency of flexible manufacturing. The flexible manufacturing decision life cycle is described in five steps (see Figure 25.7).

Step 1: Identify Decision Alternatives

- Part schedule alternatives
- Routing tables alternatives
- Process selection alternatives
- Inventory alternatives

Step 2: Solve MIM, construct a series of curves for each alternative.

Step 3: Choose a Point

Implement the condition which represents the point selected as the managing flexibility decision. This involves setting the routing table, part mix, process and inventory level.

Step 4: Establish Flow Time for Each Inventory Class

These times are found from the MIM solution and correspond to the point selected for the capacity allocation decision. In the case of the flexible system, the flow time would correspond to the pallet cycle which is the elapsed time from load/unload until a subsequent unload/load of the pallet.

Step 5: Observed Actual Flow Time as Part of Performance Monitoring.

These observed flow times are then compared to the standard times described in Step 4. Each time a part completes its last operation, its flow time can be identified and this provides immediate feedback to how well the flexible system is performing against what was planned.

Figure 25.7.   Performance monitoring procedure.

Step 1: Identify Decision Alternatives

The capacity allocation decision defines the types of decisions which need to be made. Using this concept, the alternatives are then different configurations of the capacity. For example, one alternative might be to batch produce the production and another might be to include a high variety of parts where each is produced continuously.

The collection of these configurations define a feasible set of alternative capacity allocations. Not all systems will have the same number of feasible alternatives nor will the number of alternatives always be the same every time a capacity allocation is needed. Each cell, through its inherited characteristic, will have a feasible set of alternatives and the number of alternatives is not important as long as there are some alternatives.

For example, one cell might allow routing table alternatives to accept a specific set of parts from the schedule. Another cell might not allow any routing table changes, but be able to accept a wide variety of parts. Flexibility is implemented in many forms, and the number of alternatives or the type of alternative will not influence the effectiveness of managing flexibility.

Step 2: Evaluate Each Alternative

The WIPAC curve must be constructed for each capacity allocation alternative. This entails the use of a computer model and solving the equation $P = I/F$ for many inventory levels. This will require several simulation runs and some automatic generation techniques for the WIPAC Curve would save interactive time with the decision maker.

The evaluation provides a set of curves where each curve represents a WIPAC Curve solution for a capacity allocation decision. It might be necessary to study each alternative at more than one efficiency level. [An efficiency level is defined by a breakdown repair distributor for each station vehicle]. Normally, it is sufficient to study each alternative at an efficiency level of 100% (no station factors) and at a designated level such as 85%. This range of performance for each alternative provides some sensitivity analysis to aid in selecting a specific capacity allocation.

In the case of three alternative decisions and evaluations at 100% and 85% efficiency level, this will result with six WIPAC Curves. And if each curve requires four simulation runs to construct the interesting part of the curve, then this evaluation will require 24 simulation runs.

Some knowledge of the alternatives could be programmed such that the entire generation of WIPAC curves could be automated. This generation could even be triggered from the performance monitoring and in this way the evaluation could occur before a decision maker became involved. This concept for decision support is described in the on-line performance monitoring section.

Step 3: Choose a Point

Some decision makers might suggest that if three alternatives were evaluated, then there would be only three points to compare and choose from. But this assumes that only the optimal point of each curve is of interest. However, this is not the case in managing flexibility.

The highest point in the WIPAC Curve will be that allocation which maximizes station utilization. But maximum station utilization is not always the most economic solution. One common reason for this is that the production mix which is produced at high station utilization is not the mix which is consistent with production requirements. Therefore, the point selected as the capacity allocation decision can be any point along a WIPAC Curve.

An economic criteria should be used for choosing a point. The economic criteria would use a cost modeling approach where costs are applied to the actual operation. Cost modeling utilizes several performance measures such as: production mix, station use, inventory level, and weighs each for importance by the actual cost associated. In this sense, the cost formula is a weighted measure of all performances which provides a single value for comparing alternatives. When the cost of each capacity allocation alternative is considered, then a capacity allocation decision will be based upon overall effectiveness rather than optimizing machine utilization.

Once a point is selected, then the decision is implemented by configuring the cell according to the selected capacity allocation. This means that the routing table, schedule, process and inventory of the system are configured to match the capacity allocation decision. After this implementation, the performance monitoring task begins.

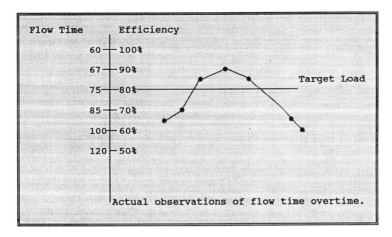

Figure 25.8. Sample performance monitoring contact chart.

Step 4: Establish Flow Time

The point which was chosen for capacity allocation provides a flow time for each inventory class. Also implied at this point is a level of station efficiency. However, the system efficiency is an outcome of performance monitoring. In order to use flow time as a measure of system efficiency, a range for flow time is needed at different levels of efficiency.

Step 5: Performance Monitoring

Performance Monitoring is performed by recording the actual flow time for each inventory class. The flow time is the elapsed time from part load (entry) until the loading of a subsequent part on the same pallet. These observed results are then recorded on the Performance Monitoring Control Chart.

Performance Monitoring Control Chart

The Performance Monitoring Control Chart (Figure 25.8) provides a visual report of how well the production cell is operating. It is constructed by recording the flow time at several levels of efficiency. As the cell operates, the flow time of each part is recorded on the control chart. This plotting provides visualization of the cell performance.

Each part type which is produced in the cell must have its own control chart. If the cell produces 10 different types of parts, then 10 control charts will be needed. This charting is required if the cell operates with one batch of parts at a time or produces a mix of parts simultaneously.

The relationship between flow time and efficiency is a result of the cell measurement. This relationship provides production rates (mix), inventory level, and flow time measures for each capacity allocation alternative. Once the specific capacity allocation is decided, then the implementation determines the inventory level for the cell. From the simulation model, the results are based upon a specific level of efficiency in the cell. The flow time from the results is then related to a specific level of efficiency. The Performance Monitoring Control Chart includes a target load which provides a control to measure how well the cell is operating against what is expected. This relative measure provides visualization of trends in performance. When the flow time increases such that performance is trending below the target, this provides the signal that capacity needs to be reallocated to correct for the inefficient operation. Because a Performance Monitoring Control Chart has been developed for each type of part, several charts are main-

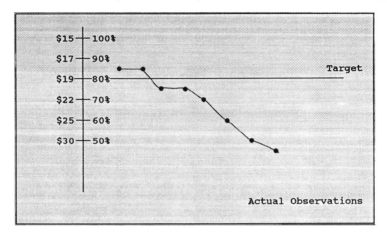

Figure 25.9.   Cost monitoring control chart.

tained. Comparing the charts show which parts are operating better than others. This provides information of how capacity can be reallocated. Capacity used by those parts which are operating above a target efficiency can be allocated to those parts which are operating below target efficiency.

Flow time is used in the chart because of its direct influence upon performance and its relative ease in being observed during the actual cell operation. However, the control chart needs not be scaled in flow time, but a cost scale could be used. Figure 25.9 shows a Performance Monitoring Control Chart which uses cost as the scale. The advantage of cost is that it shows the actual cost of producing a part as the cell operates. Also, when the cell performance drops 10% below target. This might not be a strong signal that capacity should be reallocated. However, when the same chart indicates that the cost of producing a part has increased from $19 to $25, this will attract more attention. Once this attention is gained, something will be changed in the cell. When this change occurs, the effective management of production cells will begin.

On-Line Performance Monitoring

Performance Monitoring becomes "on-line" when the information flow is automated between the monitoring system and the actual production cell. This automation of information flow requires a description of the specific data which is communicated and the physical means for the sending and receiving of the data. The degree to which the on-line monitoring can be automated depends upon the control environment of the cell. Two levels of computer-controlled automation are described: one computer controls cells and the other computer is used for manually controlled cells.

Computer Monitoring on Computer Controlled Cells.   A computer controlled cell is one where a hierarchy of computer numerical controllers (CNC) and programmable logic controller (PLC) are used to synchronize the physical operations of the components within the cell. An example of such an environment is the Flexible Manufacturing System or Flexible Cell. These systems include a set of CNC controlled machines and are interfaced with an automated material handling system. A supervisory computer running a real-time operating system monitors the status on all components, tracks, all parts, and issues commands to carry out the operation of the production process. During the operation, the supervisory computer maintains a log of activity.

The information flow from the cell computer to the performance monitoring system is the activity log. From this log, the efficiency of each station (its available-unavailable pattern) and pallet cycle time (load/unload time for each pallet) can be obtained. The pallet cycle time will be used to record average time which can then be displayed on the Performance Monitoring Control Chart. The station log will be used to record historical data on each station availability which can be utilized on the computer model. The performance monitoring system will then send the results of the capacity allocation decision to the cell computer. This transmission will include the list of parts and quantities which are to be produced, the routing table, and list of pallets (by identification) which are to be "active" in the cell.

The information flow between the performance monitoring system and all computers would be file transfers. A communication network based upon a standard local area network, broad ban system, or point-to-point serial communication would be suitable for the data transfers.

The performance monitoring system will be interfaced to the factory level systems. The interface will provide the production requirements (material need) and will be used to report completed production. The interface need not be between the performance monitoring systems and the factory system, but rather between the cell computer and factory system. Then the material need and computer production for the performance monitoring system could be accessed from the cell computer by file transfer.

The on-line performance monitoring of a production cell can have all information flow automated. This situation is not the case with manually controlled production cells.

Performance Monitoring in Manually Controlled Cells. Manually controlled cells are defined as U-lines where the machines are located into a circular arrangement to minimize the travel distance of parts and operators. The operators provide the part tracking and material handling within the cell. In this cell, the machine might be computer controlled or requires manual operation. In all cases, the operator is needed to load/unload parts from the machine and coordinate the cycle start of each operation.

The performance monitoring system will receive the flow time data via bar code reader. A bar code read will be performed on each part (batch) when it has started its operation in the cell. A bar code reader will also be needed after the part (batch) completes its final operation. (When batch production is used, the performance monitoring system will determine an elapsed production time for each batch and it is only necessary to record one flow time for the batch. However, it will still be possible to track the flow time of each part as so desired).

Some provisions will be needed to monitor the inventory level of the cell. This monitoring can be accomplished by adhering to strict rules during the operation or by using the bar coding of each part. This data is important for the interpretation of the flow time as a performance indicator.

The performance monitoring system will then display the cells performance and production schedule. It will not be necessary to show the routing table, inventory level, and process as the operator will be aware of the routing and process for each part within the cell.

Monitoring Flexibility provides the feedback in the managing flexibility decision cycle. This cycle includes five steps and utilizes the capacity allocation decision alternatives, measurement of each alternative, selection/implementation of an alternative, data collection, and interpretation of performance. The performance is monitored by use of a target flow time for each part and compared to the actual or observed flow time. This method of performance monitoring applies to both computer controlled manufacturing cells or flexible labor production cells.

The accuracy of the monitoring process depends upon the ability to control the inventory level. As long as the inventory level remains relatively stable over time, the flow time will be an accurate prediction of performance. Each time a part completes its process, the cell performance can be observed and an answer can be provided to the question, "How well are we doing?"

Answers to the question, "How well are we doing?" have eluded managers of flexible manufacturing for years. The monitoring flexibility procedure provides a sample strategy to implement an accurate procedure to answer these questions. And the answer is not given at any specific time, but can be available at any time during the operation of the cells.

25.7 SUMMARY

Production has had continuous change since the introduction of mass production in the early 1900s. This change process will continue to be fueled by the development of new technologies. During this continuance of new technologies, one comes along that can be applied to all types of manufacturing and offers immediate improvements in efficiency. Production cells are such a technology.

By bridging the gap between product and process layout, cells impact the basic characteristic of manufacturing. In doing so, they have general applications to all types of manufacturing and offers immediate impact upon efficiency.

Another characteristic of cells which indicates its basic nature to manufacturing is that it provides an environment where other techniques can be utilized. For example, flexible manufacturing has been difficult to implement. It either requires a high degree of automation or a duplicating capacity. Within the cell, hybrid versions of flexibility are common. Automated machines, duplicate capacity, and cross-trained operators all work together in an extremely efficient manner.

The basic nature of production cells requires that they operate at low inventory levels. This reduction in inventory creates the likelihood for integration effects (material shortage or blocking) which, in turn, leads to low levels of efficiency.

The integrated nature of cell operation makes measurement of efficiency a difficult task. Performance can not be identified with the operation of a single component such as a machine or operation, but must be measured over the cell as a production unit. The Manufacturing Integration Model (MIM) provides a model for measuring cell performance. Because of the complicated relationship, computer models and simulation are required to plan and predict cell performance for given situations.

Measures of cell performance includes: production rate, utilization, flow time and inventory level. These measures are useful, but often decisions are based upon optimizing a single measure at the expense of others. A system level measure of cell performance is cost. Cost refers to the actual cost of producing a product and utilizes a cost formula. This formula uses the traditional performance measures and "weighs" each according to its relative cost. Using cost provides an unbiased means to compare one alternative against another.

Comparing alternatives to cell operation can be measured using a cost formula, but identifying these alternatives is quite another matter.

Identifying alternatives requires changing the point of view away from scheduling and toward allocation of capacity. Scheduling assumes that your capacity is fixed and production requirements are changed to match capacity. Allocation is the opposite of this by considering the requirements remain fixed and capacity is allocated to meet this requirement. Of course, this requires that the capacity be flexible which is often the case in cells.

Capacity can be allocated in four ways. Routing table decision establishes specific paths for the production. Schedule decision determines the part mix which is to be produced. Process decision establishes which operations are to be performed. Inventory decision allocates capacity by determining the mixture of work-in-process.

Management of production cells involves the allocation of capacity, measurement of the alternatives, implementation of a capacity allocation, and monitoring of cell performance. The monitoring provides the feedback as to how well the cell is operating against what was planned. Control charts which track flow time and cost provide a graphic measure of how well the cell is operating against what was planned. As performance trends, this signals when it is necessary to reallocate capacity and the decision cycle starts again.

The management of production cells is a business strategy. This strategy requires configuring production into a series of cells, using flexibility of machines (tools) and labor within these cells, allocating this flexibility as needed, and monitoring performance to maintain high efficiency. The businesses which excel at these tasks will be the ones who lead in their respective markets.

BIBLIOGRAPHY

1. Y. Monden, *Toyota Production System*, Institute of Industrial Engineers, 1983, Chapt. 8, pp. 99–105.

CHAPTER 26

Scheduling Manufacturing Systems

STEPHAN BECKER and RALF PARR
Technical University of Hamburg-Harburg

26.1 PROBLEM IDENTIFICATION

Scheduling is concerned with determining when, and using what, resources, jobs or orders in a factory when they are competing for the same resources (machines, tools, materials, personnel, etc.). This determination is essential for the operative part of any production planning system.

The importance of scheduling is a consequence of the current trend to increase product variety which results in decreasing lot size, an adverse side-effect. Behind this trend lies the intention to shoulder the requirements of the market with more flexibility of the production, the main idea behind the JIT philosophy (Just-In-Time). Besides flexibility, cost reduction is also an objective of JIT. JIT aims at the reduction of stock which, traditionally, served not only to provide enough products to satisfy the market demand but also served as a buffer between different production stages (or workcells). With or without drastically reduced buffers, graceful interaction between different production processes becomes a must. This interaction again stresses the role of scheduling.

However, scheduling is not a stand-alone process, nor a process which is finished once executed. Instead, it is an ongoing process highly dependent on actual data in order to react to unforeseen events that might disturb the current schedule. Figure 26.1 shows scheduling as a part of a closed feedback loop together with production control and production process. As scheduling takes place in a complex and rapidly changing environment, it is a demanding task, better named dynamic scheduling. In effect, the efficiency and accuracy of schedules have an important impact on the success of an enterprise. Though not being the only factor, scheduling is one of the key factors used to gain flexibility and to reduce costs.

In literature as well as in the factory, the terms *planning, scheduling* and *dynamic scheduling* are often used as synonyms, though each has a different meaning; therefore, clarification of the terminology is necessary. Besides the definition of basic terms, the characterization of scheduling, based upon the three dimensions, *time horizon, production mode* and *applied method,* has proved to be very useful and will be discussed. The final concern of section 26.2 is the representation of decision-making; therefore, GRAI nets are introduced.

Scheduling problems is a highly complex task; for example, for an abundance of orders, $o = 8$ to be scheduled for $m = 3$ sequential machines, the number of possible schedules, s, amounts to $s = o!^m = 8!^3 \approx 65,000,000,000,000$. If a computer needs only 0.1 msec to compute a schedule and to evaluate it, about 206 years would be required to review all schedules. In complexity theory, the scheduling problem is known to be NP-complete: it is not likely that there exists an algorithm which can solve the problem with a time requirement not higher than a polynome on the number of variables. Thus, it is not possible to find the optimal schedule for realistic problems by mere calculation. Instead, the task of a scheduler is to compute a *good* schedule; that is, a schedule which at least satisfies the most important objectives at hand. A number of methods to reduce the set of possible solutions with respect to certain objectives is commonly used. Sections 26.3 and 26.4 present some OR (Operation Research) and AI (Artificial Intelligence) methods for solving the scheduling problem. Examples of current implementation are given in section 26.5. They illustrate the use of both OR and AI techniques. Finally section 26.6 discusses some pros and cons of th AI and the OR approach to scheduling.

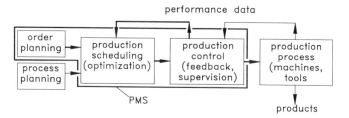

Figure 26.1.   PMS as a feedback process.

26.2   PRODUCTION MANAGEMENT: BASIC DEFINITIONS

Taking a global view of factory organization, planning is done at three different levels of abstraction (Figure 26.2). The higher the level in the hierarchy, the more abstract are the decision problems that are considered. At the top level, *strategic* planning is performed. Generally spoken, it defines *what* to do. The result is a business plan which identifies company objectives, product groups and product ranges. The company goals are taken as a guideline for the next lower level, the *tactical* one. Here, resource planning is done. Based on the business plan elaborated at the strategic level, the resource plan allocates investments, allocates human and supply resources and determines stock levels. The task at the tactical level is to decide *how* and *where* to do it. At *operational* level, decisions are converted into a sequence of actions which specify *when* to do it. The result is the master production plan (MPP), which is still very abstract. It is concerned with global manufacturing constraints such as product volume and product mix based on sales forecast. MPP serves as one input for the production management system (PMS). The PMS transforms the business goals into operations on the basis of the resources provided. The focus of attention turns from planning to control. Actions are mapped onto the time-table by scheduling. The GRAI method is an appropriate tool to explain the general functions of a PMS in terms of the hierarchical model of the factory organization.

The GRAI method supports the analysis and synthesis of production management systems (1). GRAI distinguishes between the decision system and the information system. The decision system can be considered as the active part consisting of individual decision cells which are organized vertically according to time horizon and horizontally according to function. The output of each decision process is summarized by a document which is represented in the information system (the passive part). Figure 26.3 shows a typical decision system for a factory. The data flow is indicated by arrows and the solid, vertical arrows represent decision frames which are passed to subordinate cells. The horizontal arrows represent requests between the cells of the same level. Feedback information is not explicitly displayed. GRAI grids enable a compact analysis and visualization of the decision and information flow within a factory. The

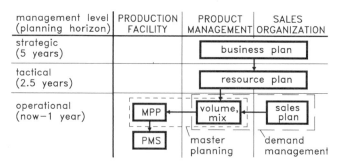

Figure 26.2.   Planning hierarchies.

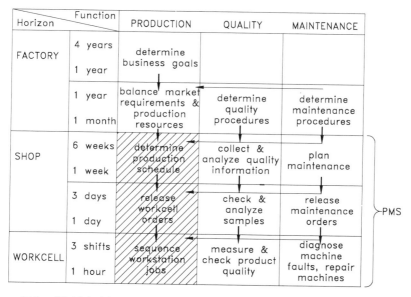

Figure 26.3. GRAI decision grid of a factory. Decisions are related to different facilities and hierarchical layers. The typical decision horizon of a layer is represented by the upper number, the related decision update period by the lower number.

grids outline the hierarchical structure within factories. Following earlier definitions by the NBS (National Bureau of Standards), several layers can be distinguished:

- Workstations: a unit that independently performs a defined operation on a part or a product. It may contain one or more automation modules performing loading, transforming and unloading operations
- Workcell: a group of workstations where the same or similar operations are performed
- Line: a group of workstations arranged in sequence, used to produce a variety of different products
- Shop: a group of cells or lines which together can produce a variety of different products
- Factory: one or more shops that together can produce products that can be shipped.

Plans elaborated on higher levels are more abstract and this abstraction responds to the uncertainty problem: Details are hidden to higher levels and their elaboration is delegated to lower levels. High level planning restricts itself to the production of a decision frame for low level planning. Though planning appears to be hierarchical, there still exist feed-back loops. Descending in the planning hierarchy, both the decision horizon and the plan update period decreases. It can be said that high level planning is abstract long-term planning while low level planning is detailed short-term planning. Correspondingly, APICS (American Production and Inventory Control Society) (2) defines:

- Dispatching: The selecting and sequencing of available jobs to be run at individual workstations and the assignment of these jobs to workers.
- Detailed scheduling: The actual assignment of starting and/or completion dates to operations or groups of operations to show when these must be done if the manufacturing order is to be completed on time. These dates are used in the dispatching operation.

In common use "detailed scheduling" is abbreviated by "scheduling". As shown by the grey underlaid part of Figure 26.3, scheduling is performed at different levels. The planning horizon

Schedule job shop
  Open order
  Check resources
      Schedule open order
      Check capacity
      Adjust routing
      Check components
  Release orders to workcells
  Produce
      Distribute material
      Trace order
      Control transport
      Control cell
          Assign operation to workstation
          Perform operation
          Update actual workload and complete operation
  Close order

Schedule flow shop
  Open order
  Check resources
      Split and assign
      Sequence and check capacity
      Reassign/change line order
      Check components
  Release orders to lines
  Produce
      Control line
      Trace order
      Distribute material
      Perform transport
      Create identification
      Identify product

      Complete operation
  Close order

Figure 26.4.   Scheduling process for a job shop and a flow shop.

for scheduling varies between three shifts and six weeks. The corresponding plan update periods range from one hour to one week.

The production mode affects the shop structure and in turn the process of scheduling. Mainly, 2 production modes can be distinguished: continuous vs. discrete production. The interest here concentrates on the production of discrete parts. Discrete parts production is further divided into mass, repetitive, batch and small-batch production or projects. One important structure is a flow shop. Its fundamental characterization is that all orders tend to go through a fixed sequence of the same routing steps. The flow shop corresponds to the repetitive mode, whereas small batches are produced in job shops. Here, each order tends to have an individual routing and time requirement. The resulting differences for job-shop and flow-shop scheduling are shown by Figure 26.4 (3).

Scheduling is arranged with respect to certain objectives or goals such as: meeting due-dates, minimizing flow time and work in process (WIP), or maximizing throughput and workcenter utilization. Of course, these goals are conflicting. For instance, due dates can be better met if more capacity is provided and if the workcenter utilization is low. Goal priorities have to be determined prior to the scheduling activity. In addition, a second type of uncertainty has to be considered: uncertainty about future events, for example, a machine breakdown. Therefore, a scheduler has to follow the production process and react to deviations with flexibility. Comprehensive re-scheduling is expensive and should be avoided for the sake of

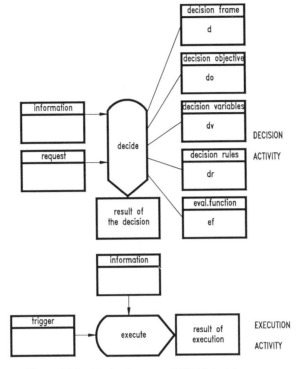

Figure 26.5.   Basic elements of GRAI decision nets.

only slight modifications. The data measurements of the real process are taken as feedback and are matched against the initially stated objectives so that slight adjustments can be made. In this sense scheduling is an ongoing task (*dynamic scheduling*).

Scheduling means complex decision-making. A multi-valued decision process relies on the following variables (for a complete description of decision theory refer to (4):

- Decision variable dv: describes the variables to be fixed. In this context the set of all possible schedules is evaluated.
- Decision frame d: describes the constraints or restrictions on the solution space issued by a more abstract decision level. The schedule has to satisfy these constraints.
- Function specific model m: describes the working model: simulation model, an analytical model, a rule-based model or any other. It is a triple consisting of structure, parameter and state.
- Evaluation function ef: a function which assigns a value to each feasible solution and is the performance measure for a schedule.
- Decision objective do: the minimization or maximization of the evaluation function ef.
- Decision rule dr: the algorithm which finds a good schedule with respect to the decision objectives do. Depending on the context, a good schedule can be an optimal, a sub-optimal or a feasible schedule.

GRAI decision nets implement the decision process. The formalism distinguishes between decision and execution activities. Execution activities are carried out when all information is available, whereas decision activities deal with uncertain and complex situations. Figure 26.5 shows the basic elements of the GRAI net representation and Figure 26.6 illustrates the scheduling part of MRP (Material Requirement Planning) as an example for the use of GRAI nets.

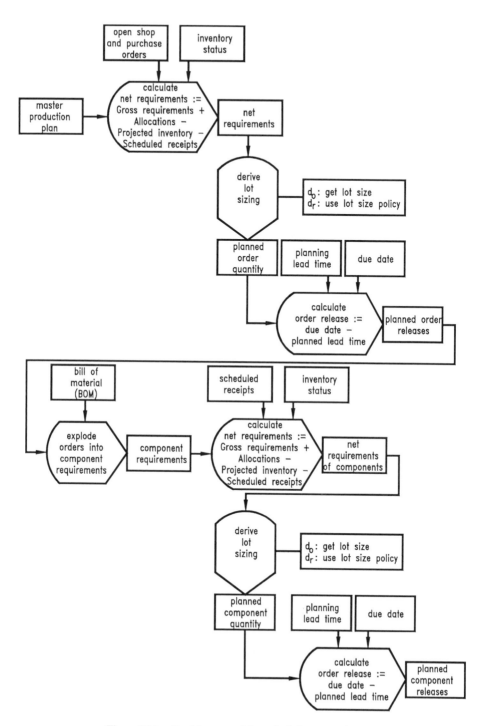

Figure 26.6. Decision net of the scheduling part of MRP.

26.3   SCHEDULING METHODS OF OPERATIONS RESEARCH

Both flow shop scheduling (with more than 2 successive operations) and job shop scheduling (with more than 1 machine) are NP-complete problems: the number of possible schedules grows exponentially with the involved operations, machines, tools and orders. Scheduling is made more difficult by parallel machines with identical capabilities, by machines which can perform several different operations, and by many other factors. In real-life no two scheduling problems are the same and thus each specific problem has to be analyzed in order to achieve best results. The complicated situation can be simplified by a classification of (real-life) scheduling problems and the use of *generic* methods for a specific class. However, there exists a trade-off between using a generic method and one being optimized for a specific application (5). This section presents generic methods developed in OR.

Scheduling can be performed in a static mode, a dynamic mode or a combination of both. The problem is static if the environment necessary for scheduling is known and fixed over the time horizon of the schedule. Both historical and forecasted data are used and scheduling is completed in advance of production. The main problem with scheduling in advance is that unforeseen events like machine breakdowns are not considered and the schedule might not be robust enough to accommodate the event. In contrast, the dynamic approach deals with changing environments over time: Scheduling escorts the execution. The difficulty here is the lack of foresight in making assignments (6). Most optimization methods using OR techniques address scheduling from the static point of view. Examples are Gannt charts, CPM (Critical Path Method), PERT (Project Evaluation and Review Technique), linear programming and branch and bound. Scheduling can be done in either a forward or backward direction. Forward scheduling starts with the earliest start date of an activity and calculates the finish date. If the finish date is after the due date of an activity, it is late. If the finish date is prior to the due date, an activity is early and slack time is available. Backward scheduling starts with the due date of an activity and calculates the latest start date. Slack time is available if the latest start date is after the earliest start date. Otherwise negative slack time is defined.

Gantt Charts, CPM and PERT

Gantt charts, CPM and PERT have been developed in order to schedule projects. The Gantt chart was developed by H. Gantt in the beginning of this century and is the first documented scheduling method. A Gantt chart is a graph which represents activities over time. Scheduling using Gantt charts starts with the end-product, identifies all activities and pre-products, and finally maps them onto the time axis. Gantt charts are useful for small-sized, two-dimension problems (7). For medium and large-size scheduling problems, network plan techniques can be used. PERT (Project Evaluation and Review Technique) and CPM (Critical Path Method) are two examples. The latter is shown by Figure 26.7.

A network plan is a directed graph where a node is a state (start or end of an activity) and an arc represents an activity together with an estimation of its time requirement. Also there exists

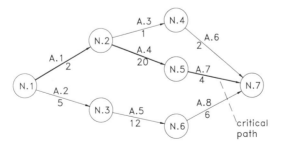

Figure 26.7.   Network plan technique: N.x = Nodes, begin or end of an activity. A.x = Activities with duration. Activity A.1 must be completed before activities A.3 and A.4 can start. Critical path = longest time path from a start to an end node.

one or more initial states, which are nodes with no predecessor. Starting from an initial state, each node is connected with its successor state via an arc which represents the next activity to be performed. Then the earliest start and finish dates of all nodes are successively computed. The times are based on the longest path from the starting node to the activity. The latest finish time of an activity A is the difference between the given due date and the longest path from A to the last node. CPM is applicable if the time required for the activities is known. PERT is used if the duration of activities is uncertain: Fixed durations are replaced by statistical distributions. All three methods are used for long-term project planning and scheduling (8).

Linear Programming

Linear programming treats optimization, under consideration of constraints restricting the decision variables, to certain admissible values. The constraints are encoded as linear inequations on which a linear optimization function is applied. The resulting system of equations is solved by the simplex method. Today it is possible to solve systems with about 100,000 equations, in some special cases even more. Reference 9 gives a detailed description of linear programming and the simplex method (9).

Scheduling problems often require that some or all decision variables be restricted to integers. Instead of ordinary linear programming, techniques as integer programming are required. The formulation of a complex scheduling problem as a set of linear equations is a serious problem. Once formulated it is difficult to keep all equations up-to-date due to the rapidly changing environment.

Branch and Bound

Branch and Bound is a generic method to solve search problems such as finding an optimal schedule. Branch and Bound consists of the two basic procedures, *branching* and *bounding*. The initial state represents the unsolved problem. The branching algorithm expands the initial state into alternative successor states representing partial solutions of the problem. Each state can be expanded until a full solution is reached. The result is a branching tree. In the context of scheduling, a state represents a partial schedule and the arc which links a state with its successor represents the corresponding scheduling decision. The branching process is curtailed by the bounding algorithm. It calculates a lower bound on the performance of partial solution. If the lower bound of a partial solution is greater than a given performance measure of the overall problem, this state is not considered for further expansion. The Branch and Bound method guarantees an optimal solution with respect to the performance measure. A necessary precondition is that the partial solutions can be composed to an overall solution. The difficult point is the bounding process. Two problems have to be solved: First, a function to compute the lower bound of a sub-schedule has to be defined and secondly, a performance measure for the schedule has to be fixed. If the scheduler calculates a feasible schedule, heuristics can be used for bounding. Choosing only the most promising path simplifies the problem but gives up the guarantee of finding the optimal solution. Nevertheless, branch and bound is a valuable method in many cases.

Figure 26.8 is an example illustrating the application of the dispatching rules of branch and bound. The three orders, O.1, O.2 and O.3, have to be scheduled on one machine. Node N.1 is the starting node and each arc represents a possible next order; each node of the partial schedule achieved by this decision. Only the marked partial graph is examined for the decision of which order to select next. Using the dispatching rule SPT, order O.2 is chosen and the process continues with node N.3. The other alternatives are curtailed.

Queuing Models and Dispatching Rules

Queuing models are used to deal with dynamic scheduling problems. A queuing model consists of queues (a stock), a server or workcenter (a machine) and dispatching rules. Scheduling is done by application of dispatching rules in order to select the next job to be processed. Each

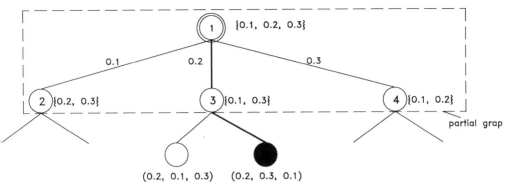

Dispatching rule: Shortest Processing Time
Processing Time: 0.1=15 min ; 0.2=5 min; 0.3=10min

Figure 26.8. Example of branch and bound: {0.1, 0.2, 0.3} = set of orders; {0.2, 0.3, 0.1} = one possible schedule.

(static) dispatching rule is an implementation of the decision rule *dr*. The rules can be grouped into three categories (10):

- Processing time based rules:
  Shortest Imminent operation (SI); Shortest Processing Time (SPT); Least Work Remaining (LWR); Fewest Operations Remaining (FOR)
- Due date based rules:
  Earliest Due Date (EDD); Smallest Slack per Remaining Operation (SL/OP); Critical Ratio (CR = (due date − now)/(lead time remaining))
- General rules:
  Random (R); First-In-First-Out (FIFO); First-Arrived-at-Shop-First-Served (FASFS)

Empirical studies reveal that the processing time-based rules result in shorter flow times and fewer late jobs than the other rules. Their disadvantage is the greater lateness per job. Due date based rules result in smaller lateness per job, but the number of late jobs increases and the flow time is higher. The general rules are worse in both objectives. More dispatching rules can be found in (11).

The problem of scheduling a set of jobs through a single machine when all jobs are available at the start of the scheduling period, is called the one-machine problem. Gaining insights into the behavior of scheduling rules under different objectives is useful. Table 26.1 describes the one-machine problem with different performance criteria. In this very simple example the application of the decision rules leads to optimal schedules with respect to the decision objectives. More realistic situations are often examined by simulation.

TABLE 26.1. Decision Variables of the One Machine Problem

dv: sequence of orders	*dv:* sequence of orders	*dv:* sequence of orders
m: one machine; setup times are independent of the sequence	*m:* one machine; setup times are independent of the sequence	*m:* one machine; setup times are independent of the sequence
ef: total time to run all jobs	*ef:* average time each job spends at the machine	*ef:* the average job's lateness
do: minimize *ef*	*do:* minimize *ef*	*do:* minimize *ef*
dr: take next job	*dr:* use rule Shortest Processing Time	*dr:* use rule Shortest Processing Time

Simulation

Compared to queuing models, simulation allows the analysis of bigger problems (machines and jobs). The performance of dispatching rules can be investigated in context with the decision objectives. Questions addressed are for example: Which dispatching rules perform best for sequencing jobs? Are some classes of rules better than others for some classes of criteria? Within MRP II, simulation is used as a what-if analysis tool.

The starting point of any simulation is a model representing a real system whose purpose is to produce data that, when analyzed, will reflect important aspects of the model. The result of a simulation is greatly influenced by the design of the model. In practice it is not possible to include all facets of the system into the model. This point has to be considered when the result is analyzed and applied. Simulation is also a modeling tool that can be helpful to managers of complex systems in that it helps them to discern important cause-and-effect relationships. The explication of the system's essential elements, structures and parameters facilitate the understanding of existing problems and help to improve the system. In the context of scheduling, three applications of simulation are important:

- Most scheduling systems need assumptions about the future in order to reach decisions. The alternative scenarios implied by different decisions are elaborated by simulation.
- Simulation enables the evaluation of dispatching rules with respect to the decision objectives, before implementing them at the plant.
- A simulation of the manufacturing system is a testbed for the scheduler.

The established main approaches in this context are discrete simulation and qualitative simulation. Discrete event simulation occurs when the state of the model changes at specified points in simulation time (the event time). There exists a number of high-level computer languages, dedicated to simulation, based on four different views: event-oriented (GASP IV, SIMSCRIPT, SLAM II), activity-oriented (CSL/ECSL, HOCUS), process-oriented (GPSS, SIMSCRIPT, SIMULA) or a combination of them (QNAP 2). For a recent review see reference (12). The central aspect of qualitative simulation is the explicit modeling of a system's underlying structure and the mechanisms which make it work. An important aspect is the possibility of using uncertain, imprecise, incomplete and relative knowledge successfully. Temporal logic as exemplified below, can be regarded as one type of qualitative simulation.

26.4 SCHEDULING METHODS OF AI

Scheduling, search and other combinatorial problems have a long history within AI. The central concern is to alleviate the computational costs, incurred by the combinatorial explosion, as far as possible. The developed methods are often based on knowledge about the domain in order to reduce complexity. Representation and exploitation of expert knowledge is propelled within AI's sub field of building *knowledge based systems* (KBS). A KBS models the role of a human expert faced with a problem in his/her domain. As relating to scheduling, such an expert can be, for example, a foreman organizing a flow line whose knowledge is often uncertain, imprecise and not completely structured and not suitable for deriving a closed, analytical solution.

A factory is segmented into loosely coupled facilities. A satisfactory solution to scheduling problems cannot be achieved without interaction between the respective facilities. Coordination is a central problem. Though each coordination problem is very application specific, its facets can be mapped to a reference model of three application independent layers (Figure 26.9): the lowest level is that of data transfer. This level is a general problem in information processing and of minor interest here. Matters of communication make up the second layer, a description of the technique used to make information public. The highest level is that of cooperation. It covers questions about content and quantity of information to be distributed, its purpose and

Figure 26.9. An application independent reference model: Any contribution to the solution of a coordination problem has to address cooperation, communication, and data transfer.

| Strategical layer: Support of cooperation |
| Tactical layer: Support of communication |
| Operative layer: Support of data transfer |

the addressees. Communication and, moreover, cooperation are the subject of DAI (Distributed Artificial Intelligence). Examples are the blackboard approach and the contract net protocol. While a blackboard is a communication structure and thus large parts of the approach are to be located in the second layer, the contract net protocol belongs mainly to the cooperation layer. Both approaches are dedicated to a group of several problem solvers working on the same problem and the concern is on the decomposition of the task into sub tasks, on the composition of their results and on the control necessary to progress the solution.

The activities of the more or less independent facilities as well as events within the manufacturing system influence scheduling. Examples of questions arising are: Can maintenance be included into the current schedule by a slight modification or does the schedule have to be changed completely? Which order is of minor priority and should be postponed because of a machine breakdown? Any decision will inevitably entail other questions and that will constrain the answer. Viewing the decisions to be found as variables, their values are dependent on each other. The combined influence of all variables on the total result, the schedule, is difficult to compile: While direct constraints obviously take effect, paths of incompatible constraints may stay concealed. In the worst case scenario, the result may be an impracticable schedule. The detection of inconsistencies within nets of constraints is subject to constraint propagation. A special case, with high relevance to scheduling, is the propagation of temporal constraints which determine the sequence of orders.

Knowledge-Based Systems

Research on knowledge-based systems (KBSs) is one of the first applications of AI and, probably, its best known subordinate field. Though today scientists agree that the early expectations in the power of KBSs were much too ambitious, the KBS architecture has meanwhile been successfully transferred to smaller problems than showing intelligence in general. Typical applications concern planning, diagnosis and interpretation. The suitability of KBSs to exploit heuristic knowledge makes this technology valuable for scheduling. The use of a KBS is possible if the domain is limited. As concerns technical applications, this is mostly the case. It is appropriate if the problem cannot (or not easily be) modeled by closed analytical formulas, but the knowledge of human experts doing the task is available. Besides modeling knowledge about a domain, knowledge about application or retrieval of other knowledge can be utilized, so-called meta knowledge. In this way questions such as: "Which dispatching rule should be applied under these circumstances?" can be answered.

The generic structure of a KBS contains at least a knowledge base and an inference engine. While the knowledge explicitly models basic properties of the problem, the inference engine is used to apply the knowledge and thereby make more knowledge explicit. Most often, a KBS is realized as a rule-based system. The knowledge is represented by if-then-else rules. Examples for KBSs related to the domain of scheduling manufacturing are AIPLANNER (3) or KBSES (13).

Blackboard Systems

Blackboard systems are dedicated to distributed problem-solving. This approach originates from the metaphor of an extensive problem being solved by a group of specialized experts, coordinated by a manager. Though each configuration is applicable specific, three characteristic components can be identified:

- A number of knowledge sources that are skilled to contribute to the problem's solution and are independent from each other in that they only know about their own competence. It is offered to the scheduler via an activation condition. A satisfied activation condition signals that the related knowledge source can contribute at the current state of solution. All informations are read from and written to the blackboard.
- A shared memory, the blackboard, offers information to be elaborated by the knowledge sources to forward the solution process. The result is returned to the blackboard again and extends the knowledge at hand. It can be used to complete the solution, as a completed partial solution or as input for another knowledge source. Depending on the specific problem, it may be appropriate to decompose the blackboard into different areas of interest. Then, horizontal layers point to the information's degree of abstraction and vertical

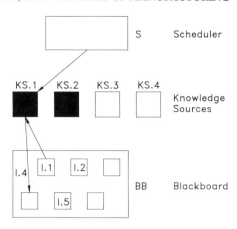

S   Scheduler

KS.1   KS.2   KS.3   KS.4

Knowledge
Sources

Figure 26.10. A blackboard system consisting of knowledge sources KS.1 to KS.4, the scheduler S and the blackboard BB. BB is partitioned into six segments. Currently it offers the information I.1, I.2, and I.5. KS.1 and KS.2 signal that they can contribute. S activates KS.1, which adds I.4 to BB. The decision to select KS.1 depends on the specific policy of S.

BB   Blackboard

sectors are dedicated to certain properties or parts of the specific problem. This configuration allows the knowledge sources to consider only their relevant part of the problem. The blackboard is the global communication structure via which the knowledge sources interact.

• A scheduler is a centralized facility, with a global view on the specific problem, whose main task is to coordinate the knowledge sources. The scheduler recognizes when the condition of a certain knowledge source is satisfied. In this case the scheduler can activate it, thereby evoking an indirect interaction between the knowledge sources. Often the scheduler is also responsible for the decomposition of the problem into tasks.

In contrast to a contract net structure, a blackboard system realizes a centralized control strategy, though the problem-solving process is distributed. Viewing the community of knowledge sources as being jointly involved in the solution of the same global problem, the blackboard implements a communication mechanism for the knowledge sources. An example is illustrated by Figure 26.10.

Contract Net Protocol

The contract net protocol (14) is dedicated to a different mode of cooperation: negotiation and bidding. The agents participating in the solution of a problem are loosely coupled and thus working, most of the time, on their own. Though they are willing to solve the problem, none of them has the skills to solve the entire problem which has to be decomposed and distributed among the agents. Control is decentralized to the respective agents who have been offered a task.

The contract net protocol provides a standardized language (= protocol) to distribute the execution of tasks within the community, to response on requests, and to bid. It supports the installation of policies on how to avoid or resolve conflicts concerning task distribution. For instance, an agent who wants a problem to be solved announces it as a task and becomes in this way, the manager of this task. An announcement can be directed to an individual agent or be broadcast within the entire community. The announcement consists mainly of the task's abstract description, eligibility specifications of a potential contractor, a specification of a potential bid on the announcement, and a time limit for bidding. This procedure allows the potential bidders to decide whether the task is appropriate for them. Each agent is free to make a bid, on one or, depending on the policy, even several announcements. A bid has to cover the requested specifications about bid and bidder thus helping the manager to decide which bidder is the most appropriate and therefore who should be awarded the contract. In the following, the contractor is free to decompose the task again, to distribute it among the community and, thus, to become a manager for this sub-task. Each agent can be engaged in several tasks as manager and contractor at the same time. Both the manager's evaluation of the bids and the potential contractors' decision to bid depend on the application specific policies of the individual agents.

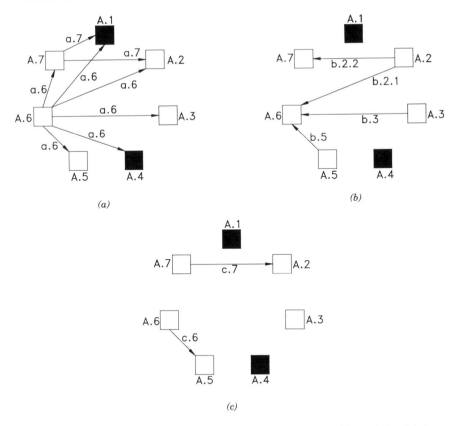

Figure 26.11. (a) A community of the seven agents A.1 to A.7. Two of them, A.1 and A.4, are currently involved in a task. A.6 broadcasts the announcement a.6 to the community. A.7 sends announcement a.7 directly to A.1 and A.2. (b) Agents A.3 and A.5 decide to bid on a.6. A.2 bids on both a.6 and a.7 A.1 and A.2 do not bid, because they are occupied. A.7 is not interested in a.6. (c) The managers of a.6 and a.7, A.6 and A.7, have evaluated the bids. A.7 now selects A.2 as contractor, A.6 contracts with A.5. If both managers would have decided for A.2 this agent would be heavily loaded while both A.3 and A.5 would stay idle. The decision to select a certain bidder depends on the managers' policy and their capacities to gain a global view on the status of the net.

The possibility of each agent to decide individually and the avoidance of a predetermined hierarchy for the sake of dynamic negotiation, allows a very flexible, distributed control. On the other hand, disadvantages arise from the agents' ignorance on other agents' capabilities, behavior and load and on future announcements. These deficiencies are partially limited by conflict resolution policies. An example for negotiation is shown by Figures 26.11a to 26.11c.

Constraint Nets

A constraint net is a method to explicate and respect the dependencies between variables under consideration. Mutual dependencies between the variables imply restrictions on their values. A restriction on admissible combinations of some variables' values is called a constraint. The process of successive application of constraints is called constraint propagation. In the context of scheduling the manufacturing of orders, constraints arise, for example, from due dates and bottleneck machines.

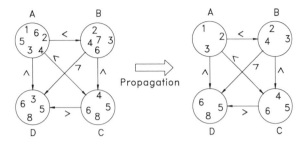

Figure 26.12. A constraint net. The example shows four numeric variables A, B, C and D. Each pair of them is constrained by "<". Each variable is represented by a circle enclosing admissible values. The constraint are represented by arrows. The left part of the figure shows the initial situation, where not all values are consistent. Checking consistency by propagation results in the right part of the figure: C = {8} is removed, because D does not offer a value greater than 8. As a consequence, B = {6, 7} and A = {4, 5, 6} are removed, too. D = {3} is removed, because there is no value for C being smaller than 3. Propagation has removed only candidates which by no way can be part of a solution.

Formally spoken, a constraint net is a graph whose nodes are the variables labeled by their domain of possible values. A constraint between variables is represented as an arc or as a hyper-arc in case of constraints of higher arity than two. Figure 26.12 provides an example. Propagation tests the validity of a variable's labelling with respect to the constraints on the variable. If a label is found to be inconsistent, it is removed. Such a removal necessitates a re-check of all variables, depending on the recently removed one. These variables are those nodes of the graph which are connected by an arc with the node under consideration. While a constraint net initially provides a view on a set of more or less local constraints between variables, propagation serves to find a more global view where all constraints and their circular dependencies are fulfilled simultaneously or are recognized as being not applicable at the same time. The combinatorial explosion of combinations of possible values (the search space) makes the problem very awkward, the constraint satisfaction problem (CSP) is NP-complete. In contrast, propagation algorithms are usually of polynomial complexity. Due to this fact, propagation algorithms cannot guarantee fully consistent solutions but do serve as filters to eliminate evidently inconsistent labels. This achievement substantially reduces the search space, thereby providing a good basis for the application of complete, often heuristic algorithms of higher complexity.

A good overview on constraint nets is given by reference 15. The terms "propagation" and "consistency" have been explained intuitively here. Their more precise definition is a subject of continuous research (16, 17).

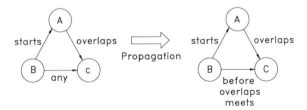

Figure 26.13. A temporal constraint net. It shows the arrangement of the three intervals A, B and C. The left part illustrates the initial situation, where the temporal ordering of A and C is considered to be not constrained. By checking consistency via propagation only "before", "overlaps" and "meets" are recognized as valid options. This is shown by the right part of the figure.

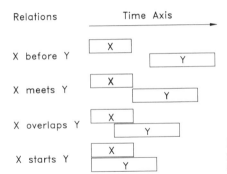

Figure 26.14. The semantic of four temporal relations illustrated by use of example intervals mapped onto the time axis.

Qualitative and Quantitative Temporal Logic

Temporal logic is a sub field of AI dealing with the representation of time. As concerns the scope of this atricle, temporal logic is viewed as a means of solving scheduling problems. Time interval based temporal logic deals with the representation and consistency of qualitative orderings between entire periods. A noteworthy approach is presented in ref. 18 and is described below briefly. As concerns this section, the term "interval" references to a time period, which covers a certain event, process or state. In the context of scheduling manufacturing systems, an interval may represent, for example, the time needed to produce a certain order or the downtime of a machine. "Relation" denotes the arrangement of two intervals with respect to time, as: "Order O.1 has to be produced *before* the maintenance of machine M.2."

In reference 18, 13 primitive relations, as "before" or "overlaps", represent all possible qualitative arrangements of 2 intervals. A situation composed of several intervals is expressed as a network of arcs and nodes. The nodes denote intervals, the arcs their relations. Each arc is labeled by a subset of the 13 primitives. For any triple of intervals, their arrangement is constrained by 169 rules implied by the nature of time. Not all of the arcs' initial labels have to be consistent and compatibility is achieved by propagation. An example of a temporal net, the semantic of the used relations and the relevant rule, is presented in Figure 26.13–26.15. This representation differs from the usual constraint net representation because the arcs are labeled and the constraint between three relations is expressed procedurally within the propagation algorithm. A mapping into standard notation is presented in reference 19. In the relevant literature, the terms "temporal relation" and "temporal constraint" are often used interchangeably. This terminology is not quite correct: Of course, a temporal relation constrains the temporal ordering of two intervals of time and so it can be viewed as a constraint on the application level. But this kind of constraint has to be kept strictly apart from the constraint the nature of time enforces on the temporal arrangement in terms of the 169 rules: this constraint is on the logical level.

So far, temporal logic is strictly qualitative. This contrasts the demand of scheduling to produce quantitative temporal data. Other approaches are known in the field of AI, which attribute the qualitative ordering of two intervals in quantitative terms, based on start, end or duration of intervals (20). The connection between qualitative temporal logic and uncertain quantitative data is shown by reference 21. In this reference the concept of a generalized window is used to attach a *set of possible occurrences* (SOPO) to a temporal interval. A SOPO is characterized by six numbers: a minimum and a maximum for each of start, finish and duration. These numbers represent the uncertainty about an interval's occurrence by offering a

if A × B	and B × C	then A × C
starts	overlaps	overlaps meets before

Figure 26.15. One of the 169 rules for temporal arrangements.

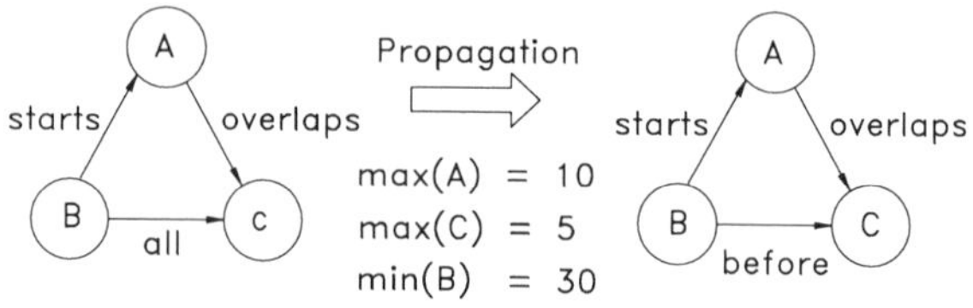

Figure 26.16. The temporal arrangement of Figure 13, extended by the intervals minimal resp. maximal durations. Propagation with respect to the intervals duration leads to a stronger constraint on the ordering of A and C.

set of possibilities. The final realization is constrained to be a member of this set. Reference 21 shows how qualitative knowledge about the intervals' arrangement can be used to restrict their SOPOs. In reference 22 it is pointed out that, in turn, quantitative knowledge can be used to sharpen the 169 rules. Figure 26.16 illustrates the gain of restriction achieved by considering minimal and maximal durations of intervals. The relevant quantitatively extended rule is shown by Figure 26.17. An example dedicated to scheduling is given in reference 19.

26.5 EXAMPLES

A Knowledge-Based Scheduler for Job Shop Environments: AIPLANNER

AIPLANNER is a knowledge-based dynamic scheduler (23). It is designed for batch production within a workcell. The optimization goal is to minimize work in process (WIP) and to maximize the probability to meet due dates. AIPLANNER is an example for the use of methods derived from operation research and artificial intelligence. The heuristic employed to reach the objectives is minimization of the set-up times for the bottleneck workstations. Figure 26.18 illustrates the functionality of AIPLANNER by use of the GRAI net formalism.

The initial task is split into two sub-tasks:

- Derive an optimal sequence of orders at the bottleneck workstations
- Schedule the orders starting at the bottleneck workstations forward and backward to all workstations involved.

To reach these sub-tasks following rules are employed:

- Prefer orders with little set-up time at the current workstation
- Prefer late orders
- Prefer small orders
- Finish orders with high WIP content
- Use earliest due date rule (EDD)

if A × B	and B × C	and durations	then A × C
starts	overlaps	no information	overlaps meets before
starts	overlaps	$\max(A) + \max(C)$ $\leq$ $\min(B)$	before

Figure 26.17. The quantitative extension of the Rule of Figure 15.

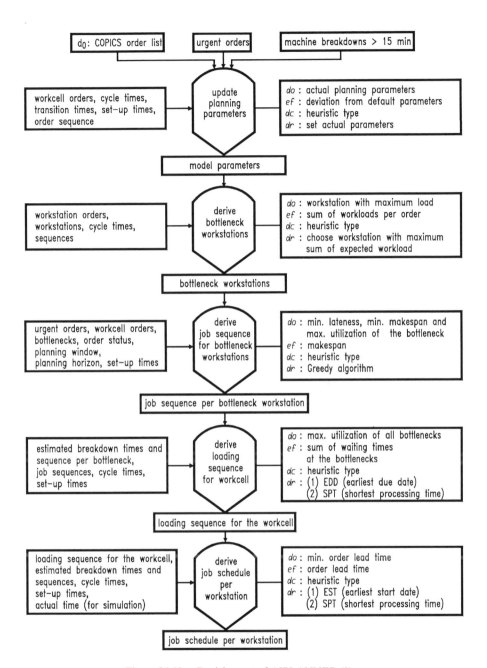

Figure 26.18. Decision net of AIPLANNER (3).

545

Minimization of set-up times matches the travelling salesman problem (TSP) and thus it is NP-complete (24):

- It is a sequencing problem with a discrete number of elements (orders).
- For any sequence of two elements a cost function is defined and it depends only on those elements. The cost function is the set-up time necessary to change from one product type to the next.

Graph theory offers a number of methods and heuristic algorithms for the solution. AIPLAN-NER has implemented two of them: the Greedy algorithm (25) and the Christofides algorithm (26).

A Constraint-Directed Scheduler for Job Shop Environments: ISIS

ISIS (Intelligent Scheduling and Information System) is a constraint-directed scheduler for job-shop production (27). Developed at Carnegie Mellon University, ISIS uses a turbine component plant as testbed. Restrictions on machine loading are formalized as constraints and are used to guide search. The work is motivated by the recognition that 80% to 90% of the entire scheduling process time at the testbed, was consumed by the determination of constraints: Only 10% to 20% has been dedicated to scheduling. These percentages point out the importance of monitoring constraints: constraints that have been ignored can make a schedule inefficient or useless. Scheduling cannot be done independently from other facilities of a plant and is constrained by the entire environment. The objective of ISIS is to support the identification of constraints and their subsequent use to guide search.

In order to clarify terminology, the term "constraint" is used more informally in the context of ISIS as it is introduced in section 26.4. In ISIS, a constraint does not always offer a set of compelling options. Some constraints describe guidelines for the selection of preferable options. In this sense, "constraints guide (constrain) search, but do not necessarily restrict search" (Fox). The mutual dependencies between constraints are not modeled by a constraint net and propagation. Instead of that, constraints can be marked as interacting. Their influence on each other can then be directly analyzed. Other constraints interact only indirectly. Nevertheless, constraints are made explicit and are the central concept of ISIS.

The following five categories of constraints have been identified and modeled in ISIS:

- Organization goals, for example, due dates
- Physical constraints, for example, machine capacity
- Causal constraints, for example, precedence of operations
- Preferences, for example, machine preference
- Availability, determined, for example, by down times

This explicitness facilitates the determination of a constraint's relevance for a certain step of scheduling and facilitates the ability to weight constraints against each other. Several criteria exist to decide how and when a constraint should be considered. One criteria is the constraint's relative importance. The same constraint, for example, the due date, may be of different importance in context of different orders. Dependencies between constraints are another. The selection of a certain option for one constraint may influence the remaining options for a second constraint. The relevance of a constraint expresses that not in all circumstances does a constraint have to be considered. This consideration might depend, for example, on a time span during which the constraint is valid or on the importance of the department where the constraint emerged. All these criteria are also useful in case of conflicts. If it turns out that a set of constraints cannot be satisfied, the conflict can be resolved by criteria implied by the constraints' importance and possibilities for relaxation. Knowledge to suggest relaxed options is attached to the constraints.

The objective of ISIS is to create a schedule which satisfies most of the constraints. This schedule is created by a search through the space of all alternative schedules. The search is decomposed to 4 hierarchically organized levels. Scheduling proceeds by passing the result of a lower level to the next higher one.

- Level 1: Selection of an order according to its category and due date
- Level 2: Based on a capacity analysis of the plant, the earliest start and the latest finish of the selected order is determined
- Level 3: All resources necessary to produce the specified order are scheduled in detail. The first step is dedicated to preparing the actual search. The direction of scheduling ("forward scheduling" respectively "backward scheduling") is determined by an examination of the identified constraints. Additional constraints are created if useful, and the search operators are selected. The second step is beam search. In-between states, of the search space, are created by application of the operators. In-between states are rated in accordance to the constraints they satisfy. The states with the highest rating are selected for further application of the operators. The result is a set of candidate schedules. Within the last step a rule-based analysis of the candidates is employed to select the most appropriate ones. If there are none, diagnosis is evoked in order to identify alternatives. This diagnosis involves constraint relaxation or suggestion of new constraints, for example, a new due date. The final result is the determination of time bounds for reservation of allocated resources.
- Level 4: The time bounds are refined in order to minimize work-in-process.

In case of deviations from the schedule during execution, an attempt is made to keep most of the decisions and only to re-schedule the affected orders.

Constrained Heuristic Search to Planning, Scheduling and Control: CORTES

CORTES continues and extends the work being done for ISIS at CMU (28). CORTES follows a more holistic approach in that it realizes an integrated framework for production planning, scheduling and control. It is grounded on four hypotheses.

- Generality: The existence of a single, generally applicable approach for optimization of decision-making within planning, scheduling and control, is assumed.
- Flexibility: The same approach is applicable for planning, predictive scheduling and reactive control.
- Uncertainty: Reasoning about uncertainty is inevitable for the solution of planning, scheduling and control problems.
- Scale: The solution of large scaled problems focuses more on aggregate behavior than the solution of smaller problems. Thus qualitatively different solutions are necessary.

The problem-solving approach CORTES employs is a combination of methods for constraint satisfaction, and for heuristic search, called constrained heuristic search. CORTES is a distributed system. The components are an uncertainty analyzer, a planner, a scheduler, a factory model and a dispatcher linked by a communication network.

Cooperative Factory Scheduling: YAMS

YAMS (Yet Another Manufacturing System) implements the contract net protocol for the purpose of factory control (29) and has been developed at the Industrial Technology Institute, in Ann Arbor, Michigan. Its objective is to provide an architecture which is flexible enough to encounter the rapidly changing environment within a factory in the context of scheduling. A company is viewed as a structure which can be decomposed hierarchically into interacting factories, shops, workcells and workstations. The prototype implementation of YAMS relies on several machines including a transportation system and a variety of machine controllers. The task of the arrangement is to perform certain jobs which belong to classes of operations. Therefore the system's components need to be scheduled. This process is realized by negotiation and bidding. The execution of production steps is offered within the community of machines which can bid on the task. The most appropriate bid decides on a task's execution. Special significance is attributed to volatility, specialization and the performance medium. An analysis of the general situation in factories based on these concepts makes not only the application of the contract net protocol reasonable, but furthermore gives guidelines as to how to design the policies which determine the system's behavior.

Volatility measures the frequency of changes occurring in a system. Local changes concerning a system's components may abandon global knowledge about the system. In a system with low volatility, global knowledge can be used successfully. With regard to the deficiencies of local knowledge already mentioned in section 26.4 (sub-optimal behavior because of ignorance of the global situation), global knowledge can be even preferred in stable environments. The more volatility a system shows, the less useful is global knowledge. As concerns scheduling manufacturing systems, high volatility shows up in schedules which are, in the worst case, already obsolete when they reach the shop. Typically the factory is characterized by medium volatility. On the one hand, this situation makes negotiation valuable, on the other hand the communicational overhead and the deficiencies implied by only local knowledge need to be limited. A policy called audience restriction is applied in order to reduce communication. Audience restriction means that a manager announces a task only to those agents who have given a bid to a similar task, formerly. No bidding agents are deleted from the manager's audience list. By availability announcements of new agents or agents with increased capabilities, introduce themselves to the community and are added to the managers' audience lists. By giving a null bid on an announced task an agent who is currently occupied and thus is not able to contract, can notify an interest in remaining on the manager's audience list. The policy to merge a global schedule with local ones in order to limit sub-optimality, fits well to the case of medium volatility. The computation of a global schedule can be done by a system like MRP which is relatively costly and lacks flexibility, but partial information, as the qualitative temporal ordering of operation sequences enforced by a job's assembly list, may survive changes. In case of deviation from the schedule, it can be used to simplify partial re-scheduling or to reach the schedule again.

Specialization measures the redundancy of the agents operation performance capabilities. A system of fully specialized agents cannot profit from negotiation because the performance of each operation is fixed to a specific agent. On the other hand, a system of completely redundant agents can successfully apply negotiation only in cases concerning its members' current load, but not in cases concerning their capabilities in general. Thus any valuable application for contract nets shows a certain overlap of capabilities.

The last aspect to consider is that of the system's media. One has to distinguish between the communication medium which is utilized for the information passing (communication) between the agents and the performance medium of a system. The latter consists of the physical parts of a job which are modified and forwarded by the workstations and the machining environment. As low-level agents are encouraged in the physical manipulation of parts they typically have sensing capacities. Therefore the performance medium can be viewed as a second, separate communication medium. The media differ in both their transmission rates and the information they provide. While the communication medium is very fast and offers only the modeled manipulations, the performance medium is the production process itself and, by that, shows all manipulations, including extraordinary and unforeseen ones. This dichotomy is typical for manufacturing and has to be respected when designing the system.

CCC

CCC (Coordination, Control and Constraint nets) is a shop controller currently being developed at the Technical University of Hamburg-Harburg. Its objective is to schedule workstations within different workcells, to control the schedule's execution and to coordinate the workcells. The basic technologies applied are constraint nets, blackboards and the contract net protocol. Three functional entities can be identified within the system: A blackboard-based shop coordinator, a workcell controller as AIPLANNER in case of job-shop production, and a monitoring instance for the system's temporal behavior, TIC II (Temporal Inferences and Constraint nets) (19). The aim of CCC is to avoid costly rescheduling in cases of deviations from an initial schedule.

The starting point of the scheduling function is a plan containing orders and their due dates, as those produced by a MRP system. Maintenance requirements are added by the responsible department. Both requirements are combined by the shop coordinator to create a decision frame which is passed over to the scheduler. The task of the scheduler is to split the orders into jobs and to dispatch them to the workstations. The decision frame constraints the possible solutions. If the problem is over constrained and thus the requirements cannot be satisfied, for example, the due dates are too strict, the scheduler returns this answer to the shop coordinator who has to relax the constraints.

For the purpose of controlling the schedule's execution, the monitoring entity achieves the decision frame established by the shop controller and elaborates a rough description of the restrictions on the jobs' temporal arrangement. The description it is represented by both qualitative and quantitative temporal constraints as well as physical constraints. The former are expressed in terms of qualitative and quantitative temporal logic as is presented in section 26.4. The latter are physically implied constraints as a machine's set-up time depending on the type of the preceding job. The schedule produced by the scheduler is viewed as one possible extension of the decision frame. The execution of the schedule is monitored by use of status reports of the relevant workstations. In case of necessary extension to the schedule, for example, an additional maintenance period becomes necessary, or deviation from the maintenance schedule, the monitor entity makes use of its prediction capabilities based on a qualitative simulation of the schedule's temporal behavior by means of temporal inferencing. In both cases it propagates the implied changes within the constraint net describing the initial decision frame. In cases where the net is still consistent, the initial decision frame covers the changes and then it suffices to modify the elaborated schedule. A change of the requirements submitted by the MRP system is not necessary; otherwise, more serious changes are to be made. In this case the monitor entity informs the shop controller about the conflict it has detected. The shop controller in turn has to consult its super ordinate facility, the MRP system, and the neighboring maintenance facilities in order to produce a relaxation of the decision frame.

26.6 PROS AND CONS OF AI AND OR METHODS

This section highlights some essential aspects of the AI and OR approach in the context of scheduling. Though the following discussion is to some extent not restricted to only scheduling, it is not intended to discuss the pros and cons of AI and OR, in general. Rather, the topics listed and shortly commented below contribute to the decision finding process in advance of the modeling of an application. A clear cut decision on either AI or OR methods is not possible and not necessary. On the contrary, combining the strengths of both approaches is useful.

Search

As scheduling is a search problem, search is a basic topic of both AI and OR approaches. The complexity of the search space is already shown in section 26.2. This complexity permits blind search. Instead, heuristics are used to direct search. Heuristic search in the sense of AI goes beyond the methods applied by OR. While OR tends to guarantee optimal solutions, AI aims to find a sufficient solution. The relaxation to compute a sub-optimal solution allows for a reduction in search effort and makes the investigation of realistic scheduling problems feasible.

Representation

Representation concerns the means of how to model a problem. It is influenced by the programming paradigm, the languages and tools and for AI these are, for example, if-then rules, frames, semantic nets, logic and many more. This variety is intended to simplify the ability to process knowledge. Expert systems are an obvious example. The introduction of application specific knowledge guides the process of scheduling and thus reduces its complexity. The representation capability of AI allows for the explicit formulation and access heuristics as well as for uncertain and incomplete knowledge. This feature is especially valuable for scheduling in a rapidly changing environment, though it is difficult to find the appropriate representation for the current problem among the variety of alternatives. AI focuses on symbolic representation. Numeric calculations are the domain of OR methods which are based mainly on equations, graphs and other algebraic expressions. Usually the methods are precise and theoretically founded. Numerous general algorithms for the optimization of problems like scheduling are available. Lastly, the exploitation of application specific knowledge is very difficult.

Integration

As scheduling is a part of a production management system, any implementation has to be integrated into a CIM environment. Integration is fundamental for the success of the entire system. This concerns both integration of concepts (the user's level) and more technical aspects like availability of programming languages, shells, tools, interfaces and hardware requirements.

On the one hand, the typical AI scenario, which prefers the use of languages like Lisp or Prolog and a variety of commercially available shells, is currently not being agreed to, without reservations, at the factory floor. Runtime performance can be a problem. On the other hand the power and flexibility of AI tools support the development of natural and therefore clear models. Along with rapid prototyping, early feedback from the user during the development phase is possible.

26.7 CONCLUSION

In this article, scheduling has been analyzed from the perspective of decision-making. In particular, scheduling transforms higher level decisions into specific operations at the factory floor. Simultaneously the focus of attention changes from planning to control. Any scheduling problem is characterized by the time horizon of the schedule to be created, by the production mode of the entity to be scheduled and by the method applied in order to reach the specific goals of the task. Being only one part of the entire decision process, scheduling takes place in a rapidly changing environment. In general, scheduling is faced with uncertainty and complexity. Coordination with other groups is a must. Decision frames from higher level decision centres, requests from different facilities of the same level, and feedback from lower level, allow for the guidance and control of the manufacturing process. Changing demands and schedule deviations need a quick and flexible response and so the requirement of flexibility must be reconciled with the high complexity of scheduling problems.

The task of finding a good or even feasible schedule satisfying many constraints is a typical optimization or search problem. For a long time, search has been and still is a major concern of the fields of both OR and AI. Different techniques addressing different facets of the search problem have been developed, some of which have been briefly described in this chapter.

Given such a variety of methods, the schedule designers are faced with the problem of finding the most appropriate scheduling method for a specific application. Often this task will not be a clear-cut decision in favor of one method, but a combination of methods. Several aspects considered to be central to this decision have been discussed in section 26.6. In conclusion, from our experience, AI methods serve well in cases of high uncertainty and high complexity, whereas OR techniques usually afford great data accuracy.

BIBLIOGRAPHY

1. G. DOUMEINGTS, M.C. MAISONNEUVE, V. BRAND, and C. BERAD, "Design Methodology of Computer Integrated Manufacturing and Control of Manufacturing Units," in U. Rembold and U. Dillman, eds., *Computer-Aided Design and Manufacturing*, Springer, Berlin, 1986, pp. 137–182.

2. T.F. WALLACE and J.R. DOUGHERTY, *APICS Dictionary*, 6th ed., 1987.

3. W. MEYER, *Expert Systems in Factory Management: Knowledge-Based CIM*, Ellis Horwood Ltd., Chichester, U.K., 1990.

4. R.L. KEENEY and H. RAIFFA, *Decision with Multiple Objectives: Preferences and Value Tradeoffs*, John Wiley & Sons, Inc., New York, 1976.

5. J. RICKEL, "Issues in the Design of Scheduling Systems," in M.D. Oliff, ed., *Expert Systems and Intelligent Manufacturing*, Elsevier Sciences, New York, 1988, pp. 70–89.

6. K.R. BAKER, *Introduction to sequencing and scheduling*, John Wiley & Sons, Inc., New York, 1974.

7. D.W. FOGARTY and T.R. HOFFMANN, *Production and Inventory Management*, South-Western Publishing Co., Cincinnati, Ohio, 1983.

8. P.A. NEWMANN, "Scheduling in CIM Systems," in A. Kusiak, ed., *Artificial Intelligence: Implications for CIM*, IFS Publications, Bedford, UK, 1988.

9. K.R. BAKER and D.H. KROPP, *Management Science: An Introduction to the Use of Decision Models*, John Wiley & Sons, Inc., New York, 1985.

10. R. RAMESH and J.M. CARY, "An Efficient Approach to Stochastic Jobshop Scheduling: Algorithms and Empirical Investigation," *Computers & Industrial Engineering*, **18**(2), 181–190 (1990).

11. T.E. VOLLMANN, W.L. BERRY, and D.C. WHYBARK, *Manufacturing Planning and Control Systems*, The Business One Irwin, Homewood, Ill, 1992.

12. N.N. EKERE and R.G. HANNAM, "An Evaluation of Approaches to Modeling and Simulating Manufacturing Systems," *International Journal of Production Research*, **27**(4), 599–611 (1989).

13. A. KUSIAK, *Intelligent Manufacturing Systems*, Prentice Hall, Inc., Englewood Cliffs, N.J., 1990.

14. R.G. SMITH, "The Contract Net Protocol: High-Level Communication and Control in a Distributed Problem Solver," *IEEE Transactions on Computers*, **C-29**(12), 1104–1113 (Dec. 1980).

15. E. DAVIS, "Constraint Propagation with Interval Labels," in *Artificial Intelligence* **32**, 81–331 (1987).

16. A.K. MACKWORTH, Consistency in Networks of Relations, *Artificial Intelligence* **8**, 99–118 (1977).

17. U. MONTANARI, "Networks of Constraints: Fundamental Properties and Applications to Picture Processing," *Informatic Science* **7**, 95–132 (1974).

18. J.F. ALLEN, "Maintaining Knowledge about Temporal Intervals," *Communications of the ACM*, **26**, 832–843 (1983).

19. S. BECKER, "Production Scheduling with Qualitative and Quantitative Constraints," in R. Zurawski and T.S. Dillon, eds., *IEEE Workshop on Emerging Technologies and Factory Automation*, Melbourne, 1992, pp. 83–88.

20. R. DECHTER, I. MEIRI, and J. PEARL, "Temporal Constraint Networks," *Artificial Intelligence*, **49**, 61–95 (1991).

21. J.-F. RIT, "Propagating Temporal Constraints for Scheduling," *Proceedings of the 5th National Conference on Artificial Intelligence AAAI-86*, Philadelphia Pa., pp. 383–388.

22. A. HUBER and S. BECKER, "Production Planning Using a Temporal Planning Component," *Proceedings of the 8th ECAI*, München, Germany, 1988.

23. R. ISENBERG, W. MEYER, "Knowledge-Based Workcell Controllers for Job Shop and Flow Shop Production," *Proceedings, Special Session on CIM during IECON'90*, Pacific Grove, Calif., Nov. 27–30, 1990.

24. L.A. JOHNSON and D.C. MONTGOMERY, *Operations Research in Production Planning, Scheduling, and Inventory Control*, John Wiley & Sons, Inc., New York, 1974.

25. C.H. PAPADIMITRIOU and K. STEIGLITZ, *Combinatorial Optimization: Algorithms and Complexity*, Prentice-Hall, London, UK, 1982.

26. N. CHRISTOFIDES, *Graph Theory: An Algorithmic Approach*, Academic Press, London, UK, 1975.

27. M.S. FOX, *Constraint-Directed Search: A Case Study of Job-Shop Scheduling*, Computer Science Department, Carnegie Mellon University, Pittsburgh, Pa., 1983.

28. M.S. FOX and K.P. SYCARA, "Innovative Approaches to Planning, Scheduling and Control," *Proceedings of a Workshop Held at San Diego*, Nov. 5–8, 1990.

29. H.V.D. PARUNAK, "Manufacturing Experience with the Contract Net," in M.N. Huhns, ed., *Distributed Artificial Intelligence I*, Morgan Kaufmann, San Mateo, Calif., 1987.

CHAPTER 27
Control of Manufacturing Systems

DHARMARAJ VEERAMANI
University of Wisconsin-Madison

27.1 INTRODUCTION

Manufacturing system control refers to the coordination of all shop-floor level activities (such as task and resource allocation) in a manufacturing system in a manner that enables desired objectives (such as completion by due date) to be achieved. Various types of manufacturing systems have evolved since the late 1700s and many of these types (in a modified form) still exist today. Manufacturing systems can be classified in a variety of ways on the basis of the level of automation (manual, semi-automated, fully automated); the level of flexibility (spanning from job shops to dedicated flow lines); the process type (discrete operations, such as machining, versus continuous operation, such as steel manufacturing); and the level of integration (from a collection of stand-alone machines to computer-integrated systems). Manufacturing system control is an integral part of operating all these types of systems. The importance of manufacturing systems control has steadily grown over the decades and its role has become central with the emergence of modern computerized manufacturing systems. This chapter will focus on control issues related to the operation of manufacturing systems for discrete part production with an emphasis on computer-controlled manufacturing systems for high-variety, low-volume production.

In modern factories, the control system forms the interface between a higher level, aggregate planning system and equipment level controllers. In addition, the functions of manufacturing system control can be viewed along three aspects. The first aspect of manufacturing system control involves decision-making related to loading problems, such as the determination of cutting-tool and operation assignment to machines. The second aspect involves on-line scheduling issues, such as the selection of the next job for processing. The third aspect relates to operational control that entails orchestration of material movement on the shop floor, equipment status monitoring, and provision of requisite information for operation at each machine.

Manufacturing system control requires an intimate relationship between three types of manufacturing sub-systems; namely, the control system, the information system, and the communication system. This chapter will mainly focus on issues directly related to the control system. In particular, 2 major facets of manufacturing system control that have received the most attention in recent years, will be addressed. The first one relates to methodologies to aid decision-making for manufacturing system control. The second one relates to the system architecture that specifies the manner in which the control system is organized.

This chapter is organized as follows. Section 27.2 traces the emergence of manufacturing systems and identifies key developments in the manufacturing industry that have catalyzed the evolution of manufacturing systems control and have eventually led to the computer-controlled manufacturing systems of today. Section 27.3 provides an overview of some of the key responsibilities of the manufacturing system control function, and highlights the importance of the control architecture. Various methodologies that assist decision-making by the manufacturing system controller are discussed in Section 27.4. Section 27.5 describes alternative control system architectures. Section 27.6 highlights the interactions between manufacturing system control, information management and communication. The chapter concludes with a summary and a discussion on the challenges on controlling the next generation of manufacturing systems.

553

27.2 EVOLUTION OF MANUFACTURING SYSTEMS CONTROL

This section will briefly overview the development of manufacturing systems and the associated growth in importance of manufacturing system control issues. The purpose of this discussion is to provide a historical perspective on the role of the manufacturing system control function and its position relative to other production related functions within a manufacturing organization.

The evolution of all technological fields is characterized by quantum jumps enabled by breakthrough developments that open up new directions for exploration and growth (1). Also in the history of manufacturing systems, it is possible to identify some key developments and paradigm shifts that have spurred periods of significant expansion and evolution. In the remainder of this section, the impact of these stages of manufacturing system development on the manufacturing control function is briefly discussed.

The Pre-Twentieth Century Years

The dawn of modern manufacturing systems can be traced back to the days of Eli Whitney at the turn of the 18th century when he organized a group of workers to produce 10,000 muskets for the government. His revolutionary efforts planted the conceptual seeds for the development of interchangeable parts manufacturing and mass production. By the middle of the 19th century, largely due to the efforts of Maudslay, Whitworth, and Whitney, machine tools capable of generating basic shapes in metals became available. In 1857, Samuel Colt demonstrated to the world how superior quality and cost benefits could be achieved by the use of forging and stamping machines in the production of revolvers. Isaac Singer adopted this developing technology for the manufacture of sewing machines in 1870. His factory employed several types of machines and was capable of producing a variety of sewing machines for the growing markets in the lower and middle socio-economic classes. Thus, the first quantum jump towards the evolution of modern manufacturing systems took place with the emergence of factories that incorporated manually operated machine tools. This transition was significant from the times when parts were crafted individually by hand (with the use of simple tools), a process that was characterized by lack of speed and consistency. However, it is important to note that even with the availability of machine tools, the basic control and feedback mechanism continued to be operator eye-hand coordination (2).

The manufacturing system "control" problem in these early manufacturing systems was focused at the equipment level and led to the design and development of a variety of machine tools. Associated with these hardware developments was the challenge of training workers to operate these machine tools and the coordination of human resources to enable efficient utilization of the machinery in the shop-floor.

The First Half of the Twentieth Century

By the beginning of the 20th century, it was clear that factories which employed machine tools would play a significant role in the nation's economy. The appreciation for manufacturing systems grew with the advent of the automotive industry and with Henry Ford's pioneering work in mass production. The availability of machine tools enabled a significant expansion of the manufacturing industry. Two types of manufacturing systems emerged in this era. The first type of manufacturing system was tailored towards producing a limited variety of products quickly and in large numbers. In these mass production systems, emphasis came to be placed on making the manufacturing process more efficient and less labor intensive. This shift led to the development of technologies such as automatic transfer lines to expedite the fabrication process. The manufacturing system control issues in these mass production systems focused on the determination of production rates and on ensuring that sufficient inputs to these product lines were always available (for instance, availability of components for an assembly line). Emphasis was also placed on specialization of labor and in identifying methods by which manual tasks could be made more efficient (F.W. Taylor's contributions in this regard are very significant).

However, such specialized methods for improving manufacturing productivity were suited to the production of only those parts which were produced in mass quantities of 100,000 or more units per year. The majority of parts were produced in small or medium batch sizes. Thus, a second type of manufacturing system emerged, namely the job shop, that had the ability to manufacture a wide variety of parts in small production volumes on manually operated general purpose machine tools. These systems suffered from a number of difficulties that highlighted the need for an effective production management and control scheme. First, fabrication using these machines was inefficient and often resulted in low time-in-cut (relative to transfer lines). Second, parts often required processing at a number of different types of machines. This technique entailed a considerable amount of part movement on the shop-floor. This problem was further confounded by a functional layout of machines which resulted in complex routing patterns for the parts. To compensate for system inefficiencies, high work-in-process levels were maintained. As these job-shops grew in size, manufacturing system control issues, such as batch size determination, scheduling of jobs, tracking of work-in-process, quality control, and inventory management, drew attention. In response to these needs, concepts and methods for inventory control (such as the Economic Order Quantity model), production scheduling and control (such as scheduling and sequencing rules, flow process charts and flow diagrams, multiple activity charts, operator charts, routine sequence diagrams, assembly diagrams, Gantt charts, and linear programming), statistical quality control (such as sampling inspection), and decision making under uncertainty (using probability models), were developed.

To summarize, the first half of the twentieth century saw the growth and development of large mass production and batch production systems. These developments also focused greater attention on production management and control. The emergence of several new concepts and theories in manufacturing, enabled a better understanding and analysis of factory operations and allowed for a task decomposition of the overall manufacturing system control problem.

The Emergence of the Digital Computer

Two significant developments in the mid-fifties promoted the next paradigm shift in manufacturing. The first was the development of Group Technology by S.P. Mitrofanov. Group Technology acknowledges that similarities among parts can be effectively utilized in designing and controlling manufacturing systems. Early adaptation of Group Technology in manufacturing systems revolved around identification of similar parts (through some form of coding and classification) to facilitate routing. It was not until the early seventies (with Burbidge's work on Production Flow Analysis (3)) that Group Technology gained wide acceptance as an underlying philosophy for shop-floor operation.

The second development of the 1950s that has forever changed the manufacturing scene, is that of the digital computer and the subsequent development of numerically controlled (NC) machine tools. This development enabled the position, speed, and feed rate of the tool relative to the workpiece, to be controlled using a set of commands (stored as a part program) that was developed off-line. The NC machine could decode the part program and perform a sequence of operations on a part automatically in one setup. The operations performed by the machine could be altered by preparing a different part program. This development showed the feasibility of flexible automation for the first time. The development of NC machines was accompanied by that of industrial robots which illustrated the feasibility and potential of programmable material handling devices. Although the first commercial robot was manufactured in the early 1960s, robotics did not find wide application in manufacturing till the late 1970s.

These developments in manufacturing and computing hardware were accompanied by a growing demand for product variety. The increase in product variety implied that dedicated mass production systems were no longer a recipe for continued success of a manufacturing company. This trend focused attention towards manufacturing systems that were capable of producing a large variety of parts in an efficient manner. The feasibility of flexible automation through the incorporation of computers in the manufacturing environment implied that the high degree of automation that was historically applied only to mass production systems could now be applied to a high variety batch production system. Although it became evident that electronic monitoring and control of processes were more reliable and efficient than by human operators, it also implied that incorporation of the computer in manufacturing system control required careful design, development, and implementation of the computer control system. The complexity of task and resource allocation in the growing number of large batch manufacturing systems motivated efforts towards solution of complex production planning and control problems on mainframe computers. On the shop floor, efforts were directed towards identifying methods by which NC machines could be organized and controlled through a central computer leading to the development of the first Direct Numerical Control (DNC) systems by the early 1960s. The growing appreciation for the advantages of NC machines spurred the investigation of methods for information management, communication, and equipment monitoring and control.

These developments engendered new concepts in manufacturing that eventually led to the development of the first Flexible Manufacturing System (FMS) in the late 1960s (4). The development of these new manufacturing systems redefined the scope of manufacturing system control. Indeed, by the end of the seventies, the manufacturing industry was ready to make a transition towards the next paradigm in manufacturing, namely Computer-Integrated Manufacturing (CIM).

Computer-Integrated Manufacturing Systems Paradigm

Several key forces of change have heralded the shift towards CIM systems in the eighties. While some of these trends had begun in earlier decades, the culmination of all the factors was evidenced most clearly in the eighties. Indeed, these forces of change are still defining the future of manufacturing systems in the nineties.

The first prominent trend has been towards greater product variety. The increasing consumer preference for customized products and the pressures of global competition both now mandate companies to offer products with differing characteristics to satisfy individual customer needs. Second, the increased pace of change in technology and consumer preference are resulting in shorter product life cycles. A good example of this trend is found in the computer industry where new generations of workstations are now routinely introduced every eighteen months. Third, quality has emerged as a significant issue in determining consumer satisfaction. The fourth trend is that towards time-based competition which is putting increasing pressure towards reducing the product realization lead time. Responsiveness or the ability to give customers what they want and when they want it, has become a key factor in determining the competitiveness of manufacturing companies today. The fifth trend which is contributing in a significant manner to the development of solutions to make manufacturing companies more competitive is the increasing performance/cost ratio of computing systems.

These trends have led to the development of a Computer-Integrated Manufacturing philosophy that would allow the integration of the entire product realization process from design through manufacture. A key component of a CIM enterprise is its manufacturing system that is capable of producing a wide variety of parts in an efficient manner. Flexibility is the key characteristic of these manufacturing systems. The trend towards CIM has resulted in a tremendous growth in FMSs and smaller FMCs in the 1980s. One of the key lessons learnt by experiencing the growing pains of adopting flexible manufacturing technology is the need for an efficient manufacturing control system. In fact, developments in manufacturing hardware, communication systems, and computers have outpaced the development of a proven architecture and software for manufacturing system control. The focus in the nineties is, therefore, towards the development of a manufacturing control scheme that is simple to implement, modular, extendible, adaptive, and robust to disturbances.

27.3 OVERVIEW OF MANUFACTURING SYSTEM CONTROL PROBLEMS

Before attempting to classify the responsibilities of the manufacturing system control function, it is useful to clarify the position and scope of this function in a manufacturing organization. The overall manufacturing planning and control process in a typical manufacturing company works as follows. While the specific implementation of the production planning and control process varies with each company, the following description encapsulates the major components of this process based on a decomposition of the various decisions that need to be made in the long-term, medium-term, and short-term.

Customer orders and demand forecasts for each class of products initiate the planning process which begins with the determination of long-range capacity plans. This process feeds the medium-range requirement planning process that determines a master production schedule. This step sets production targets and makes decisions related to part type selection, resource planning, and generation of operation sequences. At the lowest level of the production planning and control hierarchy is the manufacturing system control function that is responsible for all the decisions that need to be made in the short-term relating to task and resource allocation. In addition, the manufacturing system control function is responsible for on-line monitoring and coordination of all the equipment on the shop-floor, such as the material handling devices.

The decision-making tasks of the manufacturing system controller can be classified in a number of ways. One of them distinguishes between three types: pre-release decisions, release control decisions, and operational control decisions (5). *Pre-release decisions* include the determination of the jobs that are to be manufactured, identification of operation sequence constraints, estimation of operation duration, and determination of resource requirements and appropriate resource allocation. For instance, the types and quantities of cutting-tools that need to be loaded on to each machine is an example of a pre-release decision. *Release control decisions* determine the sequence and timing of the release of jobs to the system. These decisions relate to the assignment of operations to machines; for instance, in determining the next job that a particular machine should work on. *Operational control decisions* are focused on the coordination of material movement in the shop floor. Examples of these decisions include the selection of a material handling device (such as an AGV) for transporting a workpiece, determining when tool replenishment at a machine should be done and how, etc. In addition, the control system has to make decisions in response to unexpected disturbances on the shop floor, such as machine failure or tool breakage.

Experiences with controlling a conventional manufacturing system resulted in a great deal of emphasis being placed, initially, on machine scheduling issues related to developing control systems for computer-controlled manufacturing systems. However, it soon became evident that the capability of CNC machines and consequently the flexibility of the manufacturing system was constrained to a great extent by the availability of cutting-tools at the machine. Thus, in recent years, there has been a growing emphasis on cutting-tool management related aspects in manufacturing system control (6).

The manner in which manufacturing system control decisions are made, are heavily determined by the architecture of the control system. The architecture determines the manner in which the control system is stratified into various levels of authority and responsibility, and the type of relationship that exists between these decision-making entities. The architecture also specifies how control, information, and communication aspects are integrated to achieve shop-floor coordination.

The next section outlines various solution methodologies for decision-making by the manufacturing system control function. The subsequent section describes alternative control architecture schemes for orchestration of computer-controlled manufacturing systems.

27.4 METHODOLOGIES FOR MANUFACTURING SYSTEM CONTROL DECISION-MAKING

A wide variety of approaches exist for addressing control problems in modern manufacturing systems. Each method has its own advantages and limitations. Some methods are more suited to decisions that are planning oriented. Others are more applicable to on-line decision making. The most popular methodologies for manufacturing system control decision-making include:

- (i) Mathematical Programming Formulations
- (ii) Scheduling and Sequencing Rules
- (iii) Control theoretic approaches
- (iv) Discrete-event simulation
- (v) Queuing models
- (vi) Knowledge-based systems

Mathematical Programming Formulations

A wide variety of linear, mixed-integer, and nonlinear formulations have been developed to find solutions to various task and resource allocation problems. For instance, many models have been developed to address the loading problem in FMSs to determine the allocation of operations and cutting-tools to machines in order to manufacture a selected set of parts so that some desired objective is achieved (7). Typical objective functions in such formulations include those relating to some form of workload balancing, minimization of part movement, maximizing tool magazine capacity utilization, maximizing the number of operation assignments, minimizing makespan at a bottleneck resource, and minimizing the timespan required to process all parts in a batch. Typical constraints that are considered include operation assignment constraints to ensure that each operation is assigned to at least one candidate machine tool, production capacity constraints to ensure that the total processing load at each machine does not exceed its processing capacity, due date and production quantities constraints, tool availability constraints, tool magazine capacity constraints, operation precedence constraints; and additional resources constraints (such as availability of fixtures) (8). While these mathematical programming models have proven useful in making pre-release decisions such as machine loading, inherent limitations with this approach have restricted their applicability towards making shop-floor control decisions. First, the model is often an incomplete and inaccurate representation of a real system. Second, these models ignore the stochastic nature of the manufacturing environment. Third, since the underlying problem that many of these models encapsulate is NP-Hard, finding an "optimal" solution is not a trivial task. This requires use of various search techniques such as branch and bound procedure. The use of heuristics can, however, alleviate this problem (9).

Scheduling and Sequencing Rules

Over the past four decades, considerable effort has been spent on identification of "good" scheduling rules. The scheduling rules that have been developed typically address the following problem: Given a set of jobs, which job should be selected next for processing so as to achieve a desired objective. This decision is made by determining a priority value for each job and is calculated as a function of one or more parameters related to the job or machine status, such as due date, processing time, queue length, etc. The job with the highest priority is then chosen for processing as the next job. The performance of the scheduling rule is determined with respect to a desired objective. Some of the objectives that have been studied and reported in the literature relate to the minimization of makespan, sum of weighted completion times, sum of weighted tardiness, number of tardy jobs, maximum lateness, etc.

Scheduling rules are attractive because calculation of priority values is relatively simple and can account for real-time shop-floor status. These rules can therefore be used for on-line decision-making on the shop floor. Application of scheduling rules is particularly effective in manufacturing systems that are subject to high levels of disturbance and unexpected events. The limitation, however, is the inherent myopia in this approach that can lead to sub-optimal schedules in the long term. When the production environment is relatively stable and predictable, it may be more beneficial to apply a more comprehensive and complex optimization or knowledge-based scheduling approach. An additional difficulty is the unavailability of any universal rule that performs well under all circumstances. Each rule has its own strengths and limitations that are dependent on the characteristics of the manufacturing environment and the objective function.

Scheduling rules have been classified into local and global rules, static and dynamic rules, and simple and composite rules. Local rules utilize information that is available specific to a particular machine or a queue. A global rule, on the other hand, utilizes information about jobs at other machines or queues and the status of other machines. A static rule assigns priority values to jobs based on the initial conditions of the shop floor when the scheduling is done. These priority values do not change with time and are not influenced by the dynamics of the shop floor. In contrast, a dynamic rule assigns priority values based on the current status of the manufacturing environment. Thus, priority values assigned by a dynamic rule change with time. Simple scheduling rules are used to address simple objective functions and use priority functions that depend on a single parameter such as processing time, due date, or machine load. Composite rules incorporate multiple parameters and are useful in dealing with complicated objective functions.

An example of a local and static rule is the Shortest Processing Time rule. This rule always selects the job with the least processing time. The Minimum Slack First rule is an example of a dynamic rule. This rule assigns the highest priority value to the job with the least slack. Indeed, the priority values that are assigned to jobs change with time in correspondence to the change in slack associated with the jobs. An example of a global rule is the NINQ rule. Using this rule, a machine selects the job whose machine for the succeeding operation has the shortest queue. The Critical Ratio Rule is an example of a composite rule. One form of the critical ratio is defined as (Due Date-Date Now)/(Lead Time Remaining). This rule selects the job with the highest critical ratio.

A more comprehensive discussion of scheduling rules is available in a number of survey papers (10, 11, 12).

Control Theoretic Approaches

A typical control theoretic model considers (i) an input function related to production requirements and disturbances such as machine failures, (ii) the state of the system as a function of time determined by the knowledge of the initial system state and the input phenomena, and (iii) an output function determined as a function of the state of the system (13). The control problem is to determine appropriate operational policies, such as production rates and inventory levels, so that the manufacturing system satisfies the manufacturing system constraints while satisfying some desired performance criteria. This approach explicitly considers the dynamic environment of the manufacturing system and attempts to control the system in a fashion that makes it robust to disturbances and adaptable to change. While the control theoretic framework is convenient for characterizing realistic shop-floor control problems, standard techniques from control theory are not readily applicable for solving problems in the manufacturing domain. The growing area of research in discrete event dynamic systems promises to offer effective tools and methodologies for addressing manufacturing system control issues from the control theory perspective (2).

Discrete Event Simulation

An evaluative tool that has been used extensively in analyzing the performance of alternative shop-floor control policies is discrete event simulation. This approach requires the development of a detailed model that realistically reflects all the components and their interactions in the manufacturing system under consideration. The behavior of this system can then be studied through a computer-based simulation of the model. The simulation mirrors the detailed activities in the manufacturing system by essentially stepping through each successive event that occurs in the model. One of the advantages of simulation is that it allows for detailed evaluation of system behavior. It also allows incorporation of a wide variety of complex operating policies. The difficulties associated with this approach are the high effort required to build, validate, and verify detailed simulation models, and the computational time required for performing useful simulation studies. The development of simulation software packages focused towards manufacturing systems analysis is now alleviating the burden of model building, and the availability of powerful computers is also making feasible the potential of using simulation as a real-time scheduling tool. In principle, therefore, it is possible to evaluate alternative operational control policies on the shop floor using real-time system status information and selecting the most effective one. Flexible and dynamic control of the manufacturing system can therefore be done. A large body of literature that addresses applications of simulation to manufacturing is available, for example, see reference 14.

Queueing Models

A number of researchers have applied queueing theory-based models to aid decision making in manufacturing systems control. A typical limitation of these models is the difficulty in deriving analytic solutions unless restrictive (and often unrealistic) assumptions are made. One particular type of queueing theory model, namely queuing network models, has been used effectively in addressing some manufacturing system planning and operation issues. These models can account for some of the disturbances and interactions that are characteristic of real manufacturing environments. The development of techniques such as Mean Value Analysis has enabled fast and accurate solution of very large networks. The disadvantages of queuing network models are that they model many aspects of the system in an aggregate way. The output measures they produce are average values, based on a steady-state operation of the system. Thus, they are not good for modeling transient effects due to infrequent but severe disruptions such as machine failures (2). These models are, therefore, more useful in analyzing relatively stable systems. In such cases, queueing network models are capable of giving reasonably good estimates of aggregate system performance measures. This approach is also more efficient than detailed modeling approaches, such as discrete event simulation, in terms of the amount of input data and computational effort that is required. Thus, queuing network models can be used interactively to arrive at preliminary decisions regarding the manufacturing system and subsequently, simulation can be used to refine these decisions.

Knowledge-Based Approaches

Artificial Intelligence based approaches, particularly knowledge-based expert systems, have found application in the development of scheduling systems. This paradigm recognizes that schedule construction is influenced by a variety of (often conflicting) factors, such as due date requirements, cost restrictions, production levels, machine capabilities and substitutability of alternative production processes, order characteristics, resource requirements, and resource availability. The scheduling problem is, therefore, viewed as the generation of a task and resource allocation that satisfies a wide variety of constraints. However, due to the presence of conflicting constraints, the constraint-directed schedule construction has to be accompanied by relaxation of certain constraints so that a feasible solution is found (15). The strength of the knowledge-based approach is that allowance is made for consideration of a wide variety of knowledge (constraints and objectives) thereby making it a more comprehensive method than analytic approaches where the models are, by design and necessity, made restrictive. The key disadvantage is that the development of a knowledge-based system is time consuming and difficult.

Two properties that are desirable in a manufacturing system control scheme are (1) the ability to react to unexpected events in an effective manner and (2) the ability to learn from experience so as to continuously improve its decision-making capabilities. Approaches that integrate knowledge-based systems and neural networks show promise in this regard. However, research in this area is still in its embryonic stage and it will be some years before methodologies for developing truly intelligent and adaptive manufacturing system controllers become available.

27.5 CONTROL SYSTEM ARCHITECTURE

The control system architecture is the foundation upon which the entire control system is built. The control architecture, therefore, directly influences the flow of control and monitoring information and the interaction of the manufacturing system components (16). The efficacy of the control system is thereby determined to a great extent by its architecture. As noted earlier, the control system is responsible for making a variety of decisions on the shop-floor. The control architecture specifies how these decision-making responsibilities are allocated to various components of the control system and the manner in which these components interact to make decisions in a coherent manner.

The experience with manufacturing system control during the 1980s has identified some key properties that are desirable in the control system. These properties include reliability, modifiability, extendibility, fault-tolerance and adaptability. Reliability of the control system relates to its ability for continuous operation in a specified manner so that desired actions and objectives are achieved. The control system should also be amenable to modifications in software and hardware. In addition, as the manufacturing system undergoes modification and expansion, it should be possible to extend the control system gracefully to accommodate these changes. The manufacturing environment is constantly subject to a variety of unexpected events, such as machine failure. The control system must be capable of identifying such disturbances and initiating reactive actions in a manner that maintains a high level of performance in the manufacturing system. The importance of these characteristics to manufacturing system control, and their paucity in extant control systems, has motivated considerable research on the design and development of an efficient reference model for a manufacturing control system.

Four types of control architectures for computerized manufacturing systems have received attention in academia and in industry (16). These are

1. Centralized control
2. Hierarchical control
3. Heterarchical control
4. Hybrid control

In the following sections the characteristics of these four control strategies will be examined.

Centralized Control

Under a centralized control architecture, all system entities are directly coordinated by a central computer. This central controller performs all planning, scheduling, and monitoring functions by maintaining global knowledge of the system. The centralized control approach has been the first step towards computer control of a manufacturing system and has been primarily motivated by the limited capabilities and high costs of computers that were available in the late 1970s. Even though the centralized control approach offers some advantages, such as the availability of global information, the potential for optimization of overall system performance, and the lower level of networking and communication complexities, this approach is practical for the control of small systems only. With the increase in size of the manufacturing system, the response time of the controller deteriorates thereby affecting the performance of the system. The non-modular construction of the centralized controller also severely limits its ability to adapt to system reconfigurations. In addition, any failure of the central controller would incapacitate the entire manufacturing system. One potential solution to this problem is the provision of a backup controller. However, with the availability of cheaper and more efficient computing equipment in the 1980s, the feasibility of alternative control architectures that did not suffer from many of the limitations of centralized control has been considered.

Hierarchical Control

Considerable work has been carried out on hierarchical shop-floor control systems. The following is a distillation of that work. A manufacturing system under hierarchical control is decomposed into several levels of authority in a pyramid-like structure. The bottom level of the hierarchy is occupied by physical devices, such as machines, whose responsibility is to carry out actions dictated by entities of the adjoining higher level and to provide feedback information to them. An entity in the intermediate levels of the hierarchy carries out the commands issued by its higher level entity and issues commands to its lower level entities, while conveying status information to the higher level and receiving status information from the lower level. The entity at the top of the hierarchy is responsible for planning actions to fulfill the objectives of the whole system.

Hierarchically controlled systems are, therefore, characterized by rigid master-slave relationships between adjacent levels in the system in which control commands progress in a top-down manner and while status and sensory information progress in a bottom-up manner.

The primary advantage of the hierarchical approach to manufacturing system control is that it mimics the hierarchy commonly found in human organizational systems. This similarity makes hierarchical control easily understandable among people. Second, hierarchical control assists in the delineation of responsibilities and authority among people in the manufacturing department. Third, the hierarchical structure also facilitates accounting and book-keeping since the financial management framework is typically based on a hierarchical structure. Fourth, the segregation and grouping of entities into different levels, makes abstraction of information possible since each level has its own purpose and function.

Hierarchical systems have often been charged with problems of inflexibility and lack of robustness to failure. These problems stem primarily from the fact that entities communicate only with those entities which are either immediately below or above in the hierarchy. In addition, there is no communication between entities in the same level of the hierarchy (Some modified hierarchical structures do allow for such peer-to-peer communication). In such rigid hierarchical architectures, intra-level interaction among entities can only take place through a higher level entity. Therefore, a failure at a higher level in the hierarchy can cripple a significant segment of the system. This weakness can be mitigated by introducing redundancy in the system in the form of back-up controllers. Since control is achieved through the transfer of information and commands between the various levels of the hierarchy, this approach can become inefficient in systems which have several control layers and in systems requiring real-time control. In addition, to achieve fault-tolerance, for error detection and recovery procedures need to be explicitly incorporated in the control software. This measure increases the software complexity and limits the extendibility and modifiability of the system. The complexity of maintaining global information can also result in decision-making based on inaccurate or out-of-date information.

The National Institute of Science and Technology (NIST), formerly the National Bureau of Standards, has investigated the hierarchical control scheme in their Automated Manufacturing Research Facility. The control structure proposed by NIST consists of a five-level hierarchy (facility, shop, cell, workstation, and equipment levels). The manufacturing system control function as defined in this chapter is served by the shop, cell and workstation levels of the control architecture. The shop level controller is responsible for coordinating the production and support jobs on the shopfloor. This level is also responsible for the allocation of resources to jobs. The cell control level performs task decomposition, analyzes resource requirements and prepares requisitions, reports job progress and system status to shop control, makes dynamic batch-routing decisions, schedules operations at assigned workstations, dispatches tasks to workstations, and monitors the progress of those tasks. The workstation level executes the commands sent by the cell level controller and coordinates the equipment (such as a congregation of a machine tool, a material handling device, and buffer areas) under its control (17). Each module in this stratified structure performs 3 major control functions: adaptation, optimization and regulation. Adaptation is responsible for generating and updating plans for executing assigned tasks. Optimization is responsible for evaluating proposed plans, and generating and updating schedules. Regulation is responsible for interfacing with subordinates, and monitoring execution of assigned tasks (18).

Additional approaches based on the hierarchical control theme can be found in the literature. These alternative hierarchical schemes vary in the number of levels and functions assigned to each level, the specification of control paths between supervisors and subordinates, and their handling of data and communications (19).

Heterarchical Control

In sharp contrast to hierarchical systems which have multiple control levels, heterarchically controlled systems consist of a congregation of autonomous entities which act on the basis of information exchanged amongst each other to achieve their individual system goals. Heterarchical systems employ decentralized control and a cooperative approach to decision-making. No master/slave relationships exist among the control entities. Decisions are made locally by the entities. No entity has global information about the system. Instead, detailed local information is maintained at each entity and decisions are made on the basis of locally available information. Additional necessary information (such as status information or tool availability) can be accessed from other entities. A negotiation-based procedure is used for task and resource allocation in the system.

The independence among the system entities makes the system modular in nature. This modularity offers several advantages. In particular, this feature reduces the software complexity. The local autonomy of the system entities also enhances the fault-tolerance of the system and makes it more robust to failures in the system. Even when one or more of the control entities fail, the system can continue to function and gracefully recover by cooperative decision-making. This ability to reconfigure and adapt the system with ease is an attractive feature of this control paradigm (20). System modularity also facilitates easier expansion of the system with minimal software changes. In addition, since information is locally available at the entities, information management is simplified and decisions can be made using accurate and real-time data.

However, the heterarchical control approach presumes a high level of intelligence among system entities to permit autonomous decision-making. Limitations in current technology constrain the extent to which this paradigm can be applied to extant manufacturing systems. The performance of the system is also contingent upon the availability of a superior communications network. Emerging communication technology based on radio and light signals that are capable of 100 Mbps transmission rates, show promise in this respect.

The notion of distributed control, based on the negotiation paradigm, is not a recent development. Literature on the application of negotiation-based control to distributed computing systems can be traced back to the early 1970s. The decentralized task and resource allocation approach has been studied extensively in the context of allocation of jobs to CPUs. A notable outcome of these efforts is the contract net protocol which has been adopted as the basis of much research on heterarchical control schemes in manufacturing systems (21).

The typical heterarchical control scheme in manufacturing systems considers three types of entities; namely, customers, contractors, and sub-contractors. Customers usually correspond to workpieces that are seeking processing, contractors to machines, and sub-contractors to other resources, such as AGVs. In some models, only customer and contractor nodes are considered. The task and resource allocation is usually decided through a process of auctioning as follows: Upon arrival into the manufacturing system, the customer entity broadcasts a task announcement message to all the contractor entities. If the contractor entity chooses to partici- pate in the auction for that customer, it sends resource requisition messages to sub-contractors (if needed). Upon receipt of resource availability messages from the sub-contractors, the con- tractor prepares a bid for submission to the customer. Typically, the bid is an estimate of the time delay before the contractor can start serving the customer. The customer evaluates all the bids it receives from contractors and selects the "best" one as the winner of the auction. The customer subsequently joins the winning contractor for service. Studies on more sophisticated and detailed auction-based control schemes have recently started appearing in the literature (22, 23).

There are a number of key issues in the design of auction-based control systems. All these issues need to be resolved before a comprehensive heterarchical scheme for controlling a complex manufacturing system can be developed. First, a classification of system components into customer, contractor, and sub-contractor needs to be done. Although workpieces have commonly been considered as the customer entities, it is possible to design heterarchical systems in which the machines or material handling devices can be treated as customer entities. Second, a protocol for release of workpieces into the manufacturing system needs to be estab- lished. Many studies have assumed that workpieces arrive continuously to the system following some probabilistic distribution of inter-arrival times. This approach ignores the potential bene- fits of an interface between higher level planning and shopfloor control. Third, the information content of the task announcement message needs to be clarified. This clarification requires the development of appropriate manufacturing message standards that would be suitable for decen- tralized control schemes. Indeed, the level of intelligence and decision-making ability of the system entities would determine the quantity and complexity of information that needs to be transmitted in the task announcement message. Fourth, a robust mechanism for dealing with priorities needs to be developed. The basic auctioning mechanism assumes that all customers have equal priority and does not allow preemption or dissolution of contracts. In a real manu- facturing system, however, it is likely for workpieces to have different priorities and for "ur- gent" jobs to arrive unexpectedly. Thus, the basic auctioning mechanism has to be suitably modified in order to incorporate differences in the priorities of customers in a fashion that does not compromise the overall performance of the system. Fifth, the notion of a bid needs to be defined. In a real manufacturing system, it is possible for different system entities to have different objective functions that they are trying to satisfy. For instance, one part might be trying to achieve processing by its due-date, whereas another part might be more keen on getting processed on a particular machine because of quality considerations. In most studies, bids have corresponded to the delay before a machine can start processing a part. This defini- tion of the bid is too narrow. A more generic structure of the bid needs to be developed that would enable consideration of multiple objectives and constraints. Sixth, earlier studies have shown that the heterarchical control approach is robust to failure of system entities. In design- ing a heterarchical control scheme, decisions need to be made regarding the manner in which the system entities take corrective actions in response to unexpected events while maintaining a high level of system performance. Finally, in order to prevent chaos in the manufacturing system, certain checks and threshold parameters need to be defined to regulate the level of participation in the auctioning process and to prevent deadlocks and conflicts.

In summary, the heterarchical control paradigm offers many benefits over the hierarchical and centralized approaches. However, many key issues still need to be resolved before manu- facturing control systems based on this paradigm can be built for application in industry.

Hybrid Control

Hierarchical and heterarchical control structures represent 2 extreme control philosophies. In hierarchical systems, communication is restricted between entities on adjoining levels of the hierarchy, whereas in heterarchical systems every entity is autonomous and interacts with every other entity in the system. The former approach becomes prohibitively complex and inefficient with increasing size of the system. On the other hand, the latter approach will make inordinate demands on the communication network if every entity in the system behaves in an autonomous fashion. These realizations have prompted the notion of hybrid control systems.

A hybrid control system will consist of a combination of hierarchical and heterarchical structures. Several different configurations of hybrid control systems are possible. For instance, in a manufacturing system consisting of machine entities, transport vehicle entities, and workpiece entities, one possible configuration is to have a manager node to represent all the transport vehicles in the negotiation process. The activities of the individual vehicles will be controlled by this manager node. The presence of manager nodes reduces the communication traffic in the system. In addition, the manager can optimize the performance of the sub-system that it supervises. A hybrid structure of the control system also makes it easier to deal with the heterogeneity of controllers that is commonly found in manufacturing systems. However, as in the case of centralized and hierarchical systems, failure of the manager node would not only paralyze the sub-system it controls, but can also severely affect the performance of the rest of the manufacturing system. The appropriate control structure configuration is still a matter of speculation in academia, and will remain so until the practicalities of negotiation-based control structures have been resolved.

27.6 INTERACTIONS BETWEEN CONTROL, INFORMATION AND COMMUNICATION SYSTEMS

The control of manufacturing systems entails a high level of interaction between the control system and the information and communication systems. The efficacy of the control system is to a great extent influenced by the capabilities of the information and communication systems in terms of the quality of information, reliability, speed of operation, consistency and concurrency control, adaptability, and the ability to operate in a heterogeneous environment. The implications of these system characteristics are briefly discussed below.

Accurate and complete information is necessary for effective and reliable control of manufacturing systems. The information system should be capable of providing up-to-date information that is a true representation of physical reality. In addition, if information is available from a number of different sites, all sites need to be mutually consistent. The lack of valid information would result in the control system making incorrect decisions that may result in catastrophes on the shopfloor. The reliability of the information and communication systems is of primary importance to manufacturing system control. Failures in these systems could severely impair the functioning of the controller. Unlike typical data processing applications (such as banking), incorrect actions on the shopfloor cannot always be undone or compensated because it is not possible to reverse the manufacturing process. For instance, if a malfunction in the communication or information system resulted in the removal of additional material from a workpiece, the workpiece may have to be scrapped. Also the information and communication systems should be capable of adapting automatically to short-term changes and also must require minimal cost to accommodate long-term changes in the manufacturing system. The adaptability of the information and communication systems is critical for robust operation of the control system.

Another key aspect of manufacturing systems that has made information management and communications (and consequently system control) difficult, is the heterogeneity of entities on the shopfloor. Heterogeneity in this context relates to the differences in the ability of various types of shopfloor entities, such as machines and AGVs, to store, process, and communicate information. Indeed, the difficulty in communication among various shopfloor elements has proved to be a major stumbling block during the initial stages towards CIM. This situation has motivated the development of standards for shopfloor communication, such as *MAP*, which is based on the seven-layer ISO model, and uses a broadband token passing network with coaxial cable as the transmission medium (24). The conformance to such standards by vendors of manufacturing system equipment would greatly facilitate seamless exchange of control commands and information and, consequently, effective control of the manufacturing system.

To summarize, proper functioning of the manufacturing control system depends heavily on the supporting information and communication systems. The design of all manufacturing system controllers should explicitly consider the interactions of the control system with the information and communication systems.

27.7 SUMMARY

The discussion in this chapter has focused on the control of manufacturing systems: the planning, coordination, and execution of all shop floor level activities. Several different methodogies to aid decision-making for manufacturing system control are available and each approach has its own advantages and limitations. For effective decision-making, the controller needs to be equipped with a combination of these decision-making tools that would, collectively, provide the capabilities needed for making control decisions at various levels and time-scales. The architecture of the control system defines the manner in which the responsibility and authority for making control decisions are distributed. The architecture also specifies the type of interaction that is allowed among control system components and therefore is of fundamental importance in determining the functioning of the manufacturing control system. The performance of the manufacturing control system is also heavily dependent on the availability of effective information and communication systems.

Even today there exist many traditional job shops, containing hundreds of conventional machine tools. With time, these machine tools will be replaced by new and advanced CNC machines, thereby transforming these factories into large manufacturing systems consisting of 50 or more CNC machines. The key to the emergence of this next generation of flexible manufacturing systems lies in the development of robust and effective control systems to coordinate shopfloor activities, even in the face of unforeseen disturbances. While the 1980s have seen some progress towards the development of manufacturing control systems, extant systems leave a lot to be desired and may prove to be impractical for regulating the large computer-controlled manufacturing systems of the future. Therefore, the challenge for the 1990s lies in the development of a manufacturing control system that would enable the development of a truly integrated factory of the future.

BIBLIOGRAPHY

1. T.S. KUHN, *The Structure of Scientific Revolutions,* University of Chicago Press, Chicago, Ill., 1970.
2. S.B. GERSHWIN, R.R. HILDEBRANT, R. SURI, and S.K. MITTER, "A Control Perspective on Recent Trends in Manufacturing Systems," *Control Systems Magazine,* **MCS-6**(2), 3–15 (April 1986).
3. J.L. BURBIDGE, *Production Flow Analysis for Planning Group Technology,* Oxford University Press, New York, 1989.
4. D.T.N. WILLIAMSON, "System 24—A New Concept of Manufacture," *Proceedings of the 8th International MTDR Conference, UMIST, Manchester,* Pergamon Press, Oxford, UK, 1967, pp. 327–376.
5. J.A. BUZACOTT and J.G. SHANTHIKUMAR, "Models for Understanding Flexible Manufacturing Systems," *AIIE Transactions,* **12**(4), 339–349 (1980).
6. D. VEERAMANI, D.M. UPTON, and M.M. BARASH, "Cutting-Tool Management in Computer-Integrated Manufacturing," *The International Journal of Flexible Manufacturing Systems,* (3/4), 237–265 (1992).
7. K.E. STECKE and R. SURI, eds., *Proceedings of the Third ORSA/TIMS Conference on Flexible Manufacturing Systems: Operations Research Models and Applications,* Cambridge, Mass., Elsevier, Amsterdam, The Netherlands, Aug. 14–16, 1989.
8. K.E. STECKE, "Formulation and Solution of Nonlinear Integer Production Planning Problems for Flexible Manufacturing Systems," *Management Science,* **29**(3), 273–288 (1983).
9. K.E. STECKE and F.B. TALBOT, "Heuristics for Loading Manufacturing Systems," in A. Raouf and S.I. Ahmad, eds., *Flexible Manufacturing: Recent Developments in FMS, Robotics, CAD/CAM, CIM,* Elsevier, Amsterdam, The Netherlands, 1985, pp. 73–85.
10. S.S. PANWALKAR and W. ISKANDER, "A Survey of Scheduling Rules," *Operations Research,* **25**(1), 45–61 (1977).
11. J.H. BLACKSTONE JR., D.T. PHILLIPS, and G.L. HOGG, "A State-of-the-Art Survey of Dispatching Rules for Manufacturing Job Shop Operations," *International Journal of Production Research,* **20**(1), 27–45 (1982).
12. Y.P. GUPTA, M.C. GUPTA, and C.R. BECTOR, "A Review of Scheduling Rules in Flexible Manufacturing Systems," *International Journal of Computer Integrated Manufacturing,* **2**(6), 356–377 (1989).
13. F.A. RODAMMER and K.P. WHITE JR., "A Recent Survey of Production Scheduling," *IEEE Transactions on Systems, Man, and Cybernetics,* **18**(6), 841–851 (1988).

14. J.J. SWAIN, D. GOLDSMAN, R.C. CRAIN, and J.R. WILSON, eds., *Proceedings of the 1992 Winter Simulation Conference,* The Society for Computer Simulation, International, San Diego, Calif., 1992.

15. M.S. FOX and S.F. SMITH, "ISIS—A Knowledge-Based System for Factory Scheduling," *Expert Systems,* **1**(1), 25–49 (1984).

16. D.M. DILTS, N.P. BOYD, and H.H. WHORMS, "The Evolution of Control Architectures for Automated Manufacturing Systems," *Journal of Manufacturing Systems,* **10**(1), 79–93 (1991).

17. A.T. JONES and C.R. McLEAN, "A Proposed Hierarchical Control Model for Automated Manufacturing Systems," *Journal of Manufacturing Systems,* **5**(1), 15–25 (1986).

18. A. JONES and A. SALEH, "A Multi-Level/Multi-Layer Architecture for Intelligent Shopfloor Control," *International Journal of Computer Integrated Manufacturing,* **3**(1), 60–70 (1990).

19. A. JONES, E. BARKMEYER, and W. DAVIS, "Issues in the Design and Implementation of a System Architecture for Computer Integrated Manufacturing," *International Journal of Computer Integrated Manufacturing: Special Issue on CIM Architectures,* **2**(2), 65–76 (1989).

20. N.A. DUFFIE, R. CHITTURI, and J. MOU, "Fault-Tolerant Heterarchical Control of Heterogeneous Manufacturing System Entities," *Journal of Manufacturing Systems,* **7**(4), 315–328 (1988).

21. R.G. SMITH, "The Contract Net Protocol: High-Level Communication and Control in a Distributed Problem Solver," *IEEE Transactions on Computers,* **C-29**(12), 1104–1113 (1980).

22. D. VEERAMANI, "Task and Resource Allocation via Auctioning," in J.J. Swain, D. Goldsman, R.C. Crain, and J.R. Wilson, eds., *Proceedings of the 1992 Winter Simulation Conference,* The Society for Computer Simulation, International, San Diego, Calif., 1992, pp. 945–954.

23. G.Y-J. LIN and J.J. SOLBERG, "Integrated Shop Floor Control Using Autonomous Agents," *IIE Transactions,* **24**(3), 57–71 (1992).

24. J. DWYER and A. IOANNOU, *MAP and TOP,* John Wiley & Sons, Inc., New York, 1988.

Further Reading

A.A. DESROCHERS, *Modeling and Control of Automated Manufacturing Systems,* IEEE Computer Society Press, Washington, D.C., 1990.

A. VILLA, *Hybrid Control Systems in Manufacturing,* Gordon and Breach Science Publishers, New York, 1991.

J.T. BLACK, B.C. JIANG, and G.J. WIENS, eds., *Design, Analysis, and Control of Manufacturing Cells,* The American Society of Mechanical Engineers, New York, 1991, PED-Vol. 53.

W.D. COMPTON, ed., *Design and Analysis of Integrated Manufacturing Systems,* National Academy Press, Washington, D.C., 1988.

G. STALK, JR., and T.M. HOUT, *Competing Against Time: How Time-Based Competition is Reshaping Global Markets,* The Free Press, New York, 1990.

CHAPTER 28

Kanban Systems*

NANUA SINGH and D.R. FALKENBURG
Wayne State University

28.1 INTRODUCTION

The concepts of kanban and kanban systems basically emerged from what is known as Toyota production system (TPS). Let us first understand what TPS is all about. The Toyota production system is a production flow and inventory control system. It is designated *Toyota production system* because it was developed by Taiichi Ohno, a vice president of Toyota Motor Co. The objectives of TPS are to achieve the following:

1. Reduce costs by all-out efforts to eliminate *muda* (waste).
2. Make it easier to achieve and ensure product quality.
3. Attempt to create work sites that respond quickly to change.
4. Work sites should be organized based on a respect for human beings, mutual trust, and mutual support and should allow each worker to realize his or her potential to the fullest.

The system has now been in operation for more than 20 yr. It is now being used in many Japanese and North American automobile and other manufacturing plants.

28.2 THE COMPONENTS OF TPS

The Toyota production system (TPS) is an integrated approach to production that uses existing facilities, materials, and labor as efficiently as possible, making all-out efforts to eliminate *muda* (waste), *mura* (unevenness), and *muri* (overburden) (2, 3). The TPS pervades all aspects of the production and inventory flow process. The TPS covers areas such as

- Process design, job design, and job standardization.
- Economic lot sizes and accelerated setup times.
- Just-in-time production.
- Autonomation.
- Kanban.
- *Jidoka–andon.*
- *Yo-i-don.*

Autonomation is not misspelled; it is a Toyota-coined word that refers to the manual or automatic stopping of production if a defective part is produced. Kanban is a system of cards used to control work-in-process, production, and inventory flow. *Jikoda* refers to a production problem warning system, consisting of a battery of yellow and red lights called *andon*. A yellow light indicates a problem of a minor nature or slight delay, whereas a red light is indicative of a serious problem such as production or assembly line stoppage. *Yo-i-don* refers to a coordinated

---

* Most of the material in this chapter is adopted from ref. 1.

approach to the production of parts or subassemblies that are simultaneously produced for assembly into a next-stage subassembly.

The most distinctive and dominant area is the just-in-time (JIT) production subsystem, which is the cornerstone of the Toyota production system. And the key element of the JIT production is the kanban system of tags, or cards, attached to the parts and subassembly containers. The kanban system is an essential tool for managing and controlling the pull-type (just-in-time) production method inherent in the Toyota production system. We will discuss separately these two subsystems in detail.

Let us first understand the problem areas that may occur in any production situation that are primarily responsible for higher production costs, low quality, and increased delivery times. We will then discuss the need for rationalized production methods and how the implementation of the JIT production philosophy helps achieve the goals of minimum production costs, higher quality, and quick delivery times. In this context, we will next discuss the elements of waste known as the three M's (*muda, mura,* and *muri*) in the TPS.

The Three M's

Unit cost, quality, and lead time are three principal determinants of market share and profitability of all organizations. The costs vary by the production methods and the way the production is organized. Therefore, to achieve the objectives of minimum production costs while maintaining total quality, it is necessary to use rational manufacturing techniques that help eliminate *muda, mura,* and *muri*. *Muda* is a Japanese word referring to work or to elements of production that do not add value to the product. On the contrary *shigoto* refers to the actual work that adds value to the product. *Shigoto* is relatively small compared with *muda*. Therefore, it is important to eliminate *muda*. The job attitude of looking for *muda* and finding ways to eliminate it is called *kaizen*. *Kaizen* is central to the TPS way of thinking. In TPS, *muda* has been classified into a number of categories such as correction (rework), overproduction, processing, conveyance, inventory, motion, and waiting.

We now turn our attention to the concepts of *mura* and *muri*, which TPS uses to limit production costs and preserve quality. *Mura* literally means unevenness, which may be due to irregular production volumes or changing work flows or production schedules. It means that the workloads on the machines are not balanced. In such a situation, capacity planning must be done that considers the peak level of production, thereby increasing the cost of production. *Muri* essentially means stretching beyond capacity limits, overburdening the capacities of people as well as machines. Overburdening people causes stresses that result in safety and quality problems. Similarly, overloading of machines results in breakdowns and defects. The net result of overloading is increased costs and poor quality.

The production control system used in most North American companies is normally based on a material requirements planning (MRP) system. It is also known as a push system. The work-in-process inventory is used as a means of absorbing troubles in the processes and changes in demand. In practice, however, such a system often creates the following problems:

1. Excessive imbalances of stocks between the stages leading to dead stock.

2. May lead to conditions of having excessive equipment and surplus of workers.

To avoid these problems, it is necessary to have a rational production control methodology that is adjustable to conform with changes caused by troubles in the processes and demand fluctuations. The just-in-time production control based on the pull system used in the Toyota production system offers such an integrated methodology.

28.3   PULL VERSUS PUSH SYSTEMS

Let us first understand the push system. A push system is essentially an MRP-based production planning and inventory control system. In MRP, the master production schedule of end products is transformed into parts requirements. The work orders are then launched to build (or purchase) the parts in lot sizes using the lot sizing logic of MRP. The work orders push materials to the manufacturing floor to produce the parts required. The lot sizes are normally large, and consequently production lead times are long. There will be changes in the schedule and delays during this time because of the dynamic nature of the demand and production processes.

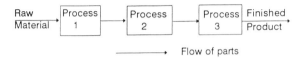

Figure 28.1. The material flow process in a push system (1).

Therefore, the lot being produced is not correct in relation to the master production schedule of end items. The coordination is lost because of lack of feedback on the status of materials previously released. The parts are pushed to the successive stages as shown in Figure 28.1. This creates the problem of some component parts not being completed to feed the successive processes (stages), causing shortages. This phenomenon is also referred to as starving of the successive stage. On the other hand there will be too much inventory of some components, causing what is known as blocking the preceding stage. Remember, inventory is a form of *muda* and too much inventory is too much waste.

As seen in Figure 28.1, the push system is a single flow process in which both the build schedules and materials flow in the same direction from one stage to another. The transmittal of information distinguishes a pull system from a push system. In a pull system, there is a double flow as shown in Figure 28.2. The materials move in the same direction as the push system but the information concerning processing of those parts (build schedules) is given by the subsequent process. Therefore, the build schedules travel in the opposite direction. A kanban system is used to communicate the schedule from one station to another. The kanban in a pull system is a card attached to a standard container that issues the production and withdrawal of parts between work stations. It is usually viewed as an information system that controls production of parts.

28.4 TYPES OF KANBANS

Kanban a Japanese word that means visible record. Toyota developed the kanban system. It consists of a set of cards that travel between preceding and the subsequent processes, communicating what parts are needed at the subsequent processes. It is used to move materials driven by the use of parts and to control work-in-process, production, and inventory flow. There are two types of kanbans: a withdrawal kanban (also known as conveyance kanban) and a production kanban.

Withdrawal (or Conveyance) Kanban

The primary function of the withdrawal kanban is to pass the authorization of the movement of parts from one work center to another. Once it fetches the parts from the preceding process and moves the parts to the subsequent process, it remains with them until the last part has been consumed by the subsequent process. Then the withdrawal kanban travels back to the preceding process to fetch parts and the cycle continues. The withdrawal kanban should have information such as the part number and its name, lot size, and routing process; the name and location

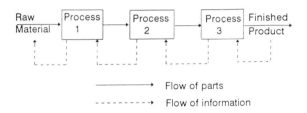

Figure 28.2. The material and information flow process in a pull system (1).

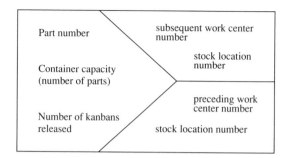

Figure 28.3. A sample layout of a withdrawal kanban (1).

of the subsequent process; the name and location of the preceding process; container type and capacity; and the number of containers released. The withdrawal card layout can be designed in a number of ways to display this information. An example of a card layout for a withdrawal kanban for a hypothetical shop is given in Figure 28.3.

Production Kanban

The main function of a production kanban is to release an order to the preceding process to build parts equal to the lot size specified on the card. Therefore, the production kanban card should have information on the materials and parts required as inputs at the preceding process in addition to what is already present on a withdrawal kanban. This information is not required on the withdrawal kanban card because it is used only as a means of communication authorizing movement of parts between work centers. A sample layout for a production kanban is given in Figure 28.4.

Flow of Withdrawal and Production Kanbans and Their Interactions

Let us understand the flow of withdrawal and production kanbans as well as flow path of containers. Consider the simple example of controlling work flow between two preceding and succeeding processing stages PPS1 and SPS2 separated by a stacking area (SA), as shown in Figure 28.5 (4). The sequence of movements of the kanbans (withdrawal and production) and containers between the processing centers and the stacking areas is described as follows:

- Suppose you start at point P1 in the stacking area. Move the full parts container to the subsequent processing stage SPS2.
- Detach the attached withdrawal card and send it to the kanban collection box at point P2. Meanwhile, the parts in the container are being used by the subsequent stage.
- Once all the parts in a container are consumed at SPS2, attach a withdrawal kanban from the kanban collection box to the empty container and move it from SPS2 to location P3 in the stacking area.

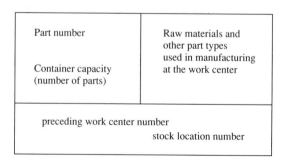

Figure 28.4. A sample layout of a production kanban (1).

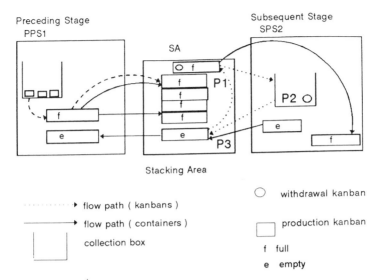

Figure 28.5. Flow sequences in a kanban production system (1).

- At the P3 location, detach the withdrawal kanban from the empty container and attach it to a full parts container. Remove a production kanban and send it to the preceding stage PPS1 to trigger the production of a full container.
- Put all the parts produced into the empty container and send the box to the stacking area with the production kanban attached to it.

This completes one cycle, and the process is similarly repeated cycle after cycle.

28.5 PRECONDITIONS (RULES) FOR OPERATING KANBAN

Kanban is essentially a tool created to manage the workplace effectively. In this section we discuss the rules that govern the operational environment of a kanban system. The preconditions (or often called the basic rules) for effectively operating the kanban are given below.

Rule 1. No Withdrawal of Parts without a Kanban

Kanban is a mechanism that controls production on a just-in-time basis, i.e., producing necessary parts in right quantities at the right time. Only kanban can authorize the flow of parts from a preceding process to the subsequent process.

Rule 2. The Subsequent Process Comes to Withdraw Only What Is Needed

Muda of all types would occur if the preceding process supplies more parts than are actually needed. This can be avoided if the subsequent process comes to the preceding process to withdraw required parts at the time needed. To ensure that the subsequent process does not arbitrarily withdraw parts from the preceding process, the following concrete steps are needed to implement the second rule:

- No withdrawal without a kanban (rule 1).
- The number of parts issued to the subsequent process should be exactly what is specified by the kanban, i.e., parts withdrawn cannot exceed the number of kanbans submitted
- Parts in containers must be accompanied by kanbans.

Rule 3. Do Not Send Defective Parts to Subsequent Processes

The quality of parts moved by the kanban is the major concern of this rule. Furthermore, the defective parts would necessitate work-in-process inventories besides requiring the extra resources of material, equipment, and labor. Therefore, manufacture of defective parts should not be tolerated. This rule requires that (*1*) the process should be designed such that the defective parts are discovered at the source and (*2*) the problem in the process is brought to the immediate attention of all the concerned workers and supervisory staff. This rule implies a strong relationship between total quality control and JIT manufacturing. For JIT to be successful it is important to implement total quality control concepts. We will discuss total quality control below.

Rule 4. The Preceding Process Should Produce the Exact Quantity of Parts Withdrawn by the Subsequent Process

Rule 4 is a logical extension of Rule 3. The basic premise behind Rule 4 is to restrict the inventory at the preceding process to the absolute minimum. To ensure minimum inventory, it is necessary that there is no more production than is requested by the number of kanbans. Furthermore production in every work center must be conducted strictly in the sequence in which the kanbans are received.

Rule 5. Smoothing of Production

The previous rules imply that the subsequent process comes to the preceding process to withdraw the necessary parts in the necessary quantities at the necessary time. However, if the withdrawals fluctuate in quantity or time, then the peak demand will decide the inventory levels, equipment, and workers. It is, therefore, important to smooth (to minimize the fluctuations of) production.

Rule 6. Fine-Tune Production Using Kanban

Small variations in production requirements are adjusted by stopping the process if the production requirements decrease and using overtime and improvements in the processes if the production requirements increase. We must remember that overtime is a kind of *muda* and should not be encouraged.

28.6 KANBAN PLANNING AND CONTROL MODELS

Kanban is the heart of JIT system. The number of kanbans play the most important part in planning, controlling, and reducing the work-in-process inventories. In this section we illustrate a number of deterministic and probabilistic analytical models for obtaining the optimal number of kanbans.

A Deterministic Model

Let us first understand how the number of kanbans are determined at a work center in Toyota Motor Co., which has been successful in using the JIT system. Toyota uses the following formula (3, 5).

$$y \geq D(T_w + T_p)(1 + \alpha)/a \tag{1}$$

where y is the number of kanbans, D is the demand per unit time, T_w is the waiting time of the kanban, T_p is the processing time, a is the container capacity (not more than 10% of the daily requirement), and α is a policy variable. Note that α is used as a means of managing external disturbances such as changes in demand and variability in processing and delivery times. D is determined with a smoothed demand. The number of kanbans y is normally fixed even if there are variations in the demand. In that case, it is required that the value of the lead time be reduced accordingly. If it is not possible to reduce the lead time, it may be necessary to have overtime or even line stops. Improvements to reduce the values of a, α, and lead time ($T_p + T_w$)

should be continuously pursued. These reductions will lead to reduced work-in-process inventory.

In this section we illustrate two examples to understand the following (1):

- How the number of kanbans is determined.
- The impact of lead time on the number of kanbans and work-in-process inventory.
- Interactions between the withdrawal and production kanbans.

Example 1

Consider the production of a certain item manufactured in XYZ Co. Its requirements are 10,000 units per month. Suppose the company has just started implementing the JIT system. Accordingly, the policy variable is set at $\alpha = 0.40$. The container capacity is fixed at 50 items and the production lead time is 0.50 day.

Problems

1. Determine the number of kanbans.
2. Suppose the company has a stable production environment, and the policy variable can be fixed at $\alpha = 0.00$. Determine the number of kanbans and the resulting impact on work-in-process inventory.
3. What happens if the lead time is increased to 1.00 day because of a labor shortage and the failure of the machines?
4. What happens if the lead time is reduced to 0.25 day because of process improvements?

Solutions

1. The number of kanbans is given by Equation 1. Assuming 20 work days in a month, the daily demand is 10,000/20, or 500 parts. Accordingly, the number of kanbans is $(500)(0.50)(1.40)/50 = 7$.

2. If $\alpha = 0.00$, then the safety factor $(1 + \alpha)$ is 1.00. Accordingly, the number of kanbans is $(500)(0.50)(1.00)/50 = 5$. The safety factor of 1 implies that a withdrawal kanban must be delivered on time every time parts are needed. The implication of this change in the operation of processes on work-in-process can be explained as follows: Assume that the usage of parts is at uniform rate. Then the average inventory in case 1 is equal to the average inventory in case 2 plus the inventory of two extra containers. The average inventory in case 2 is $(1 + 0)(50)/2 = 25$ units because only one container is being used at a time. Accordingly, average inventory in case 1 is $25 + (2)(50) = 125$ units because two more containers of 50 units each are also sitting there as a safety stock over and above that available in case 1.

3. The number of kanbans is $(500)(1.00)(1.40)/50 = 14$. The implication of this change in the system operation is an increase in average inventory to $25 + (9)(50) = 475$ units instead of the 125 units in case 1. This is because 9 additional containers are available as safety stock besides the one being used.

4. If the process has improved so much that the lead time has been reduced to 0.25, then it also implies that the safety factor should be improving too. If $\alpha = 0.2$, then the number of kanbans is $(500)(0.25)(1.20)/50 = 3$.

Example 2

A two-stage system involving manufacturing at the preceding stage and assembly at the subsequent stage is presented here. Consider the manufacturing of a product Z in a company. Z is assembled from two parts X and Y that are manufactured in the company. The schematic layout depicting the preceding stage, staging area, subsequent stage, and the flow of production and withdrawal kanbans is given in Figure 28.6. The following data are available:

Assembly Stage

Part	Demand (units/day)	Lead Time (days)	α	Container Capacity
X	2000	1.0	0.00	100
Y	800	0.5	0.25	50

Manufacturing Stage

Part	Demand (units/day)	Lead Time (days)	α	Container Capacity
X	2000	0.50	0.20	100
Y	800	1.00	0.00	50

Problems

1. Determine the number of withdrawal and production kanbans.
2. Now suppose the assembly process is shifted to Mexico as a part of reorganization. The lead time to travel between the new location in Mexico and the present plant location is 4 days each for both parts X and Y. Determine the number of withdrawal and production kanbans and the impact of this policy on work-in-process inventory.

Solutions

1. The lead time used for determining withdrawal kanban is the time it takes the parts to travel from the preceding stage work centers (X and Y) to the subsequent assembly stage Z. Using Monden's formula (see below), the number of withdrawal kanbans for parts X and Y are 20 and 10, respectively. Similarly, the lead time for determining the production kanbans for parts X and Y is the time it takes to manufacture these parts. Again, using Monden's formula, the number of production kanbans for the parts X and Y are 12 and 16, respectively.

2. Because the lead time is now 5 days, the number of withdrawal kanbans for parts X and Y are 80 and 80, respectively. The impact of this decision is that 60 containers for part X and 70 containers for part Y remain in the pipeline. There is no change in the number of production kanbans.

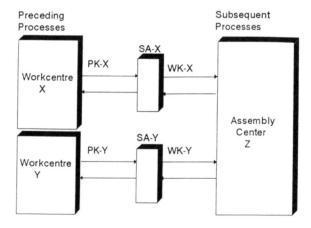

PK - X : Production kanban for part X
PK - Y : Production kanban for part Y
WK - X : Withdrawal kanban for part X
WK - Y : Withdrawal kanban for part Y
SA - X : Staging area for part X
SA - Y : Staging area for part Y

Figure 28.6.   Layout for Example 2. $PK-X$, production kanban for part X; $PK-Y$, production kanban for part Y; $WK-X$, withdrawal kanban for part X; $WK-Y$, withdrawal kanban for part Y; $SA-X$, staging area for part X; $SA-Y$, staging area for part Y (1).

A Probabilistic Cost Model

Typically, in a JIT operation the master production schedule is frozen for 1 month and the number of kanbans at each work center is set based on the average demand for the period (5). Remember that there will be variations in the lead time because of uncertainties in demand. In this section, we develop a cost model considering the expected cost of holding and shortages. It is assumed that the probability mass function (pmf) of the number of kanbans required is known. In the following section we will then present the methodology to determine the pmf for the number of kanbans.

Let us assume the following notation:

$p_x(x)$ probability mass function for the number of kanbans required
c_h holding cost per container per unit time at a work center
c_s cost of a shortage per container per unit time at a work center

Suppose there are n number of kanbans circulating in the system. There are two possibilities:

1. The actual requirements for the kanbans x is less than n. In that case, the holding cost will be incurred. Accordingly,

$$\text{Expected holding cost} = c_h \sum_{x=0}^{n} (n - x)p(x) \tag{2}$$

2. The actual requirements for kanbans x are more than n. In that case, the shortage costs will be incurred. Accordingly,

$$\text{Expected shortage cost} = c_s \sum_{x=n+1}^{\infty} (x - n)p(x) \tag{3}$$

Therefore, the total expected cost $TC(n)$ is given by

$$TC(n) = c_h \sum_{x=0}^{n} (n - x)p(x) + c_s \sum_{x=n+1}^{\infty} (x - n)p(x) \tag{4}$$

The optimal value of n is the smallest integer satisfying the following:

$$\Delta TC(n) = TC(n + 1) - TC(n) \geq 0$$

or

$$\Delta TC(n) = c_h \sum_{x=0}^{n} p(x) - c_s \sum_{x=n+1}^{\infty} p(x) \geq 0$$

or

$$(c_h + c_s)P(n) - c_s \geq 0$$

or

$$P(n) > c_s/(c_h + c_s) \tag{5}$$

where $P(n)$ is the cumulative distribution function of n.

Example 3

Suppose that the probability mass function of the number of kanbans is known and is given below. Furthermore, suppose the holding and the shortage costs per container per unit time are

$20 and $200, respectively. Determine the optimum number of kanbans to minimize the total expected cost.

Probability:	0.00	0.20	0.30	0.35	0.10	0.05
Number of kanbans:	0	1	2	3	4	5

Solution. Using the probabilistic model, the value of $c_s/(c_s + c_h)$ is $200/(200 + 50) = 0.80$. From the above list, the value of n that gives $P(n)$ greater than or equal to 0.80 is 3. Therefore, the optimal number of kanbans is equal to 3.

Procedure for Determining the pmf

We now present a procedure for determining the pmf of number of kanbans n (6). First, the density function of lead time is estimated. Then it is combined with forecasted demand value to produce the pmf for n. The preferred number of kanbans can then be determined to be used the next period by using the methodology developed in the previous section. The procedure consists of the following steps:

Step 1: Startup. Permit the transient effects to die out before attempting Step 2 if major changes have been made in the operation of the shop perturbing the shop conditions.

Step 2: Measuring Period 1. Compute autocorrelation at lag k using the following formula:

$$r_k = \frac{\frac{1}{N}\sum_{t=1}^{N-k}(x_{t+k} - \bar{x})(x_t - \bar{x})}{\frac{1}{N}\sum_{t=1}^{N}(x_t - \bar{x})^2} \quad (k = 1, 2, \ldots, 25) \tag{6}$$

where x_j is the jth observation of container lead time. Box and Jenkins (7) suggest at least 50 observations. However, Rees et al. (6) suggest between 50 and 100 observations.

Step 3: Measuring Period 2. (1) Determine lag k in Step 2 beyond which all autocorrelations are 0 (or, in practice, below 0.05), (2) collect observations spaced k apart from each other to ensure that they are statistically independent, and (3) estimate the probability density function of container lead times $f_L(L)$ from at least 100 observations by developing a histogram.

Step 4: Forecast demand. For the item at the work center under consideration, determine an estimate of next period demand D using company forecasting procedures.

Step 5: Determine the pmf of number of kanbans. This requires a two-stage procedure as follows. (1) Determine probability density of a random variable n' where $n' = DL$. Remember D, once estimated, is considered a deterministic constant over the forecasted period. In JIT it can be safely assumed that D_{t-1} will not differ from D_t so drastically as to appreciably change $f_L(L)$. Accordingly, it can be shown that (8)

$$f_{n'}(n') = \frac{1}{|\hat{D}|} f_L\left(\frac{L}{|\hat{D}|}\right), \quad (\hat{D} \neq 0)$$

or

$$f_{n'}(n') = \frac{1}{\hat{D}} f_L\left(\frac{L}{\hat{D}}\right), \quad (\hat{D} \geq 0) \tag{7}$$

where $\hat{D}$ is the observed value of D. Notice that $f_{n'}(n')$ is a scaled-down and reshaped version of $f_L(L)$ obtained in Step 3. (2) Determine $p_n(n)$ from $f_{n'}(n')$ with mass located at $n = 1, 2, \ldots, 25$ and density at each point k equal to $\int_{k-1}^{k} f_{n'}(n')dn'$.

Example 4

In Example 4 we illustrate the methodology developed for determining the pmf of number of kanbans using some data from ref. 6. The approach can be similarly implemented in industries for actually dynamically updating the optimal number of kanbans. Consider a product manufactured in a shop operating 8 h per shift, two shifts per day, and 5 days per week. The other data assumed are:

Unit cost is $1000.

Container processing time is 0.335 h.

Coefficient of variation of processing times is 0.4.

Demand for the product is 20 containers per shift.

The illustration is based on a simulation using Q-GERT simulation language output. However, other simulation languages such as SLAM II and GPSS could be used.

Step 1: Startup. Startup period to allow for the transient effects to die down was observed to be 1 week.

Step 2: Measuring Period 1. Generate correlograms using at least 100 observations at certain use levels and Equation 6. The resulting correlogram was plotted for the 91% use rate (Figure 28.7).

Step 3: Measuring Period 2. Notice from Figure 28.7 that no correlation exceeds 0.05 beyond lag 19. That means an observation spaced every 20 (rounding up) lead times (1 per shift) constitutes an independent observation. Collect at least 100 such independent observations. Using these observations, the density function $f_L(L)$ is then constructed as shown in Figure 28.8.

Step 4: Forecasting Demand. The demand is constant at the work center for the product. Therefore, the demand for the next demand cycle period ($\hat{D}$) is 20 containers per shift.

Step 5: Determining the pmf for the Number of Kanbans. Using Equation 7, the density function for n' is obtained as follows:

$$f_{n'}(n') = \frac{1}{20} f_L \left(\frac{L}{20} \right)$$

Notice that $f_{n'}(n')$ is scaled down vertically as well as enlarged horizontally by a factor of 20. The density function is shown in Figure 28.9, and the pmf is shown in Figure 28.10.

28.7 SIGNAL KANBAN

One of the important conditions for the implementation of JIT with kanbans is to have small setup times relative to processing times. However, a special type of kanban known as a signal kanban is used at work centers with relatively large setup times. In effect, a signal kanban

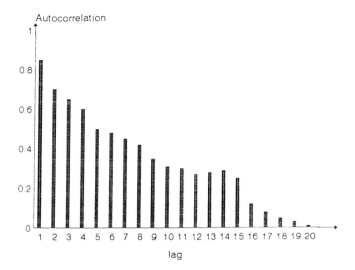

Figure 28.7.   Autocorrelation of lead time at the work center (6).

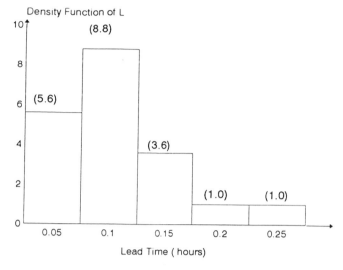

Figure 28.8. Histogram estimates of $f_L(L)$ at the work center (6).

triggers the production of larger than normal lots at work centers with large setup times within a JIT framework, wherein standard kanbans at normal work centers concurrently trigger the production of containers encompassing only a small number of units, ideally just one. Philipoom et al. (9) have discussed and analyzed the signal kanban for work centers with relatively high setup times and developed mathematical programming models to determine the optimal lot size used in conjunction with the signal kanban. In the following section, we provide a mathematical programming approach to determine optimal number of signal kanbans as outlined by Philipoom et al. (9).

Integer Programming Model

In developing the integer programming model, it is assumed that the work centers can be decoupled from each other and considered in isolation if we do not allow any back orders at

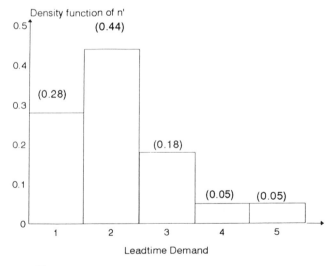

Figure 28.9. Density function of lead time demand (6).

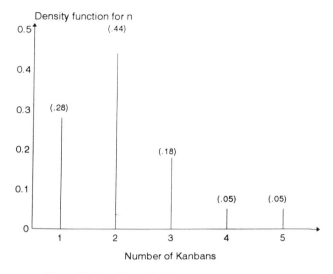

Figure 28.10. The pmf of the number of kanbans (6).

these work centers. The following sets of constraints ensure that no back orders occur at a signal kanban work center:

$$t_i \geq \sum_{j=1}^{n} (q_{ij}PT_j + Y_{ij}S_j) \quad (i = 1, 2, \ldots, m) \tag{8}$$

$$\sum_{i=1}^{m} Y_{ij} = 1 \quad (j = 1, 2, \ldots, n) \tag{9}$$

$$q_{ij} \leq MY_{ij} \quad (i = 1, 2, \ldots, m; j = 1, 2, \ldots, n) \tag{10}$$

$$Q_j \leq d_j t_i + (1 - Y_{ij})M \quad (i = 1, 2, \ldots, m; j = 1, 2, \ldots, n) \tag{11}$$

$$Q_j \geq d_j t_i - (1 - Y_{ij})M \quad (i = 1, 2, \ldots, m; j = 1, 2, \ldots, n) \tag{12}$$

$$Q_j = \sum_{i=1}^{m} q_{ij} \quad (j = 1, 2, \ldots, n) \tag{13}$$

$$Y_{ij} = \text{binary } (0,1) \quad (i = 1, 2, \ldots, m; j = 1, 2, \ldots, n) \tag{14}$$

$$q_{ij} \text{ and } Q_{ij} \text{ are integers} \quad (i = 1, 2, \ldots, m; j = 1, 2, \ldots, n) \tag{15}$$

where n is the number of items produced at a work center; q_{ij}, lot size in containers for item j processed on machine i; Q_j, sum of lot sizes for all machines at a work center; t_i, production cycle time for the ith machine at the signal kanban work center; PT_j, processing time for containers of item j; S_j, setup time for item j; Y_{ij}, a binary variable and assumes a value 1 if $q_{ij} > 0$, otherwise it takes a value of zero; M, a large positive constant; and d_j demand in containers per unit time for item j. Equation 8 ensures that the cycle time for each machine must be greater than or equal to the production time including the setup time. Equations 9 and 10 ensure that only one machine produces each item at a work center. Equations 11 to 13 ensure for each machine that demand for each item produced on that machine during the production cycle is exactly equal to the lot size for that item. Equations 14 and 15 represent the 0–1 and integer variables.

There could be a number of objectives in the context of JIT manufacturing. For example, minimization of inventory is normally the desired objective. Another objective could be the minimization of total cost, which consists of the holding and setup costs. Accordingly, the integer programming models are (1) problem P1 is to minimize

$$Z_1 = \sum_{j=1}^{n} Q_j$$

subject to Equations 8 through 15 and (2) problem P2 is to minimize

$$Z_2 = \sum_{j=1}^{n} \left(C_j \frac{R_j}{Q_j} + C_{H_j} \frac{Q_j}{2} (1 - d_j PT_j) \right)$$

subject to Equations 8 through 15. Problem P1 and P2 represent minimization of inventory and total cost objective functions. The objective function Z_2 is based on the rotation cycle policy (10). In Problem P2, R_j, C_j, and C_{H_j} are annual demand, cost of a setup and annual holding cost for item j, respectively.

Example 5

Consider that four items (A, B, C, and D) are produced at work center 1 (9). The following data are available:

Holding cost is 25% per year of the container cost.
Setup cost is $65 per h.

Item	Container Cost ($)	Daily Demand (Containers)	Container Processing Time (h)	Setup Time (h)
A	1500	30	0.150	0.50
B	1500	20	0.150	0.50
C	1500	20	0.150	0.50
D	1500	20	0.150	0.50

Solving the integer programming model P1, we obtain the following solution:

q_{11} = 60 containers
q_{12} = 40 containers
q_{13} = 0 containers
q_{14} = 0 containers
q_{21} = 0 containers
q_{22} = 0 containers
q_{23} = 10 containers
q_{24} = 10 containers
$Q_1 = Q_A = q_{11} + q_{21}$ = 60 containers
$Q_2 = Q_B = q_{12} + q_{22}$ = 40 containers
$Q_3 = Q_C = q_{13} + q_{23}$ = 10 containers
$Q_4 = Q_D = q_{14} + q_{24}$ = 10 containers
t_1 = 16 h t_2 = 4 h

Therefore, items A and B are produced on machine 1 with a production cycle time of 16 h, whereas the items C and D are produced on machine 2 with a production cycle time of 4 h.
Similarly, solving the integer programming model P2, we obtain the following solution:

q_{11} = 60 containers
q_{12} = 40 containers
q_{13} = 0 containers
q_{14} = 0 containers

$q_{21} = 0$ containers
$q_{22} = 0$ containers
$q_{23} = 38$ containers
$q_{24} = 38$ containers
$Q_1 = Q_A = q_{11} + q_{21} = 60$ containers
$Q_2 = Q_B = q_{12} + q_{22} = 40$ containers
$Q_3 = Q_C = q_{13} + q_{23} = 38$ containers
$Q_4 = Q_D = q_{14} + q_{24} = 38$ containers
$t_1 = 16$ h $t_2 = 15.2$ h

Therefore, items A and B are produced on machine 1 with production cycle time of 16 h, whereas the items C and D are produced on machine 2 with a production cycle time of 15.2 h. Notice that the model P2 produced higher lot sizes than model P1. This is because the minimum cost model reduced the number of setups.

28.8 OTHER TYPES OF KANBANS

So far we have examined the most commonly used production and conveyance (withdrawal) kanbans. There are, however, other types of kanbans used in specific situations. We provide a brief description of some of them in this section.

Express Kanban

The express kanban is used when shortage of parts occur. It must be withdrawn after its use. The presence of the express kanban in the red post (also known as express kanban post) triggers the following activities:

1. A button for the machining line making the part is switched on, activating a light on the light board known as *andon* for the part.
2. The worker in the area where the light has come on must immediately produce the part and deliver the part to the subsequent process personally.

Emergency Kanban

The emergency kanban is used as a temporary measure to make up for defective units and other uncertainties such as machine failures and fluctuation in the daily or weekly production.

Through Kanban

In production situations in which two or more work centers are located close to each other, there is no need to exchange production and conveyance kanbans between these work centers. Only one kanban, known as through the kanban, is used. It is quite similar to the through ticket between two adjacent railways.

28.9 ALTERNATIVE JIT SYSTEMS

Some alternative control structures for JIT manufacturing have been presented by various authors. Although JIT is usually understood as a pull system in which the amount of material flow at the immediately preceding station is determined by the stock consumption at the subsequent station, there are a number of alternative methods of control for JIT production. We discuss some of them in this section.

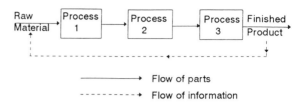

Figure 28.11. Flow of parts and information in a long pull JIT system (1).

Periodic Pull System

Kim (11) discusses a periodic pull system in which the manual information processing time of a kanban method is replaced by on-line computerized processing. This resulted in better system performance such as less lead time inventory and faster system response.

Constant Work-in-process System

Spearman et al. (12) described a new pull-based production system called constant work-in-process (CONWIP). In contrast to kanban cards, which are part number specific, CONWIP production cards are assigned to the entire production line. The advantage is that it can be used for environments in which the kanban system is impractical due to a large number of part types or significant setup times.

Long Pull System

Lambrecht and Segaert (13) introduced the concept of the long pull system. In this system one unit is allowed to enter the system, the instant that one unit is finished at the end of the pull. The individual buffers are not limited, but the total number of units in the span of the long pull is limited. This system is triggered in the same way that a pull system triggers production from the preceding process. However, the control of the long pull encompasses more than just one workstation. In Figure 28.11 the span of the pull originates in process 3 and creates a pull on process 1 when the trigger level at process 3 is activated. Once process 1 is started the unit produced is pushed through the subsequent processes (2 and 3) in a similar manner as that of push system. A trigger may be active, but process 1 may not produce an additional part if the maximum inventory allowed within the span of the pull is reached. In this study the authors compared the long pull strategy with other allocation strategies and concluded that it outperforms them. Brar and Singh (14) have provided a detailed analysis on the long pull systems, including how to find the location of the long pull, the span of control of each long pull, and the corresponding amount of WIP inventory to be allocated. They also confirmed the results of the previous study.

Integrated Push and Pull System

Olhager and Olstund (15) discussed push and pull systems and how these approaches work in an integrated manufacturing strategy. This strategy integrated the push and pull system to the customer order point (i.e., the point at which a product is assigned to a specific customer), to bottleneck resources, and to the product structure. The authors also gave a case study that successfully integrated the push–pull manufacturing strategy in a make-to-order environment.

28.10 BARRIERS TO JIT IMPLEMENTATION

The implementation of JIT principles in any company is not an easy task. There are a number of barriers and obstacles that must be successfully overcome to achieve the goals of zero inventory. Some of the challenging problem areas are

- Frequent changes in production planning.
- Inaccurate forecasting procedures resulting in under- or overforecasting of demand.
- Equipment failures, creating capacity problems.
- Employee turnover, absenteeism, etc.

28.11 POTENTIAL BENEFITS OF JIT IMPLEMENTATION

The proper implementation of JIT principles may lead to a number of benefits to any company. Some of the noticeable benefits include

- Increased productivity.
- Better quality.
- Reduced lead time.
- Reduced setup times.
- Less scrap and rework and consequently less raw material.
- Less work-in-progress.
- Higher worker motivation and increased teamwork.
- Saved space.
- Increased worker and equipment efficiency.
- Decreased job classifications.

The benefits of JIT cut across functional boundaries within any organization. The functional areas benefited by JIT include manufacturing, manufacturing engineering, purchasing, sales and marketing, accounting, quality control, and assembly.

BIBLIOGRAPHY

1. N. SINGH, "Just-in-time Manufacturing systems," *Introduction to Design and Analysis of Computer-aided Manufacturing Systems,* John-Wiley & Sons, Inc., New York, in press.
2. C.C. PEGELS, "The Toyota Production System—Lessons for American Management," *Int. J. Operat. Product. Manage.* 4(1), 3–11 (1984).
3. Y. SUGIMORI, K. KUSSUNOKI, F. CHO, and S. UCHIKAWA, "Toyota Production System: Materialization of Just-in-time and Respect-for-human System," *Int. J. Product. Res.* 15(6), 553–564 (1977).
4. M. EBRAHIMPOUR and B.M. FATHI, "Dynamic Simulation of a Kanban Production Inventory System," *Int. J. Operat. Product. Manage.* 5(1), 5–14 (1984).
5. Y. MONDEN, *Toyota Production System,* Industrial Engineering and Management Press, Institute of Industrial Engineers, 1983.
6. P.R. REES, P.R. PHILIPOOM, B.W. TAYLOR, and P.Y. HUANG, "Dynamically Adjusting the Number of Kanbans in a Just-in-time Production System Using Estimated Values of Leadtime," *IIE Trans.* 19(2), 199–207 (1987).
7. G.E.P. BOX and G.M. JENKINS, *Time Series Analysis: Forecasting and Control,* rev. ed., Holden-Day, San Francisco, 1976.
8. A. PAPOULIS, *Probability, Random Variables and Stochastic Processes,* McGraw-Hill Book Co., Inc., New York, 1965.
9. P.R. PHILIPOOM, L.P. REES, B.W. TAYLOR III, and P.Y. HUANG, "A Mathematical Programming Approach for Determining Workcentre Lotsizes in a Just-in-time System With Signal Kanbans," *Int. J. Product. Res.* 28(1), 1–15 (1990).
10. L.A. JOHNSON and D.C. MONTGOMERY, *Operations Research in Production Planning, Scheduling and Inventory Control,* John Wiley & Sons, Inc., New York, 1974.
11. T. KIM, "Just-in-time Manufacturing System: A Periodic Pull System," *Int. J. Product. Res.* 23(3), 553–562 (1985).
12. M.L. SPEARMAN, D.L. WOODRUFF, and W.J. HOPP, "CONWIP: A Pull Alternative to Kanban," *Int. J. Product. Res.* 28(5), 879–894 (1990).

13. M. LAMBRECHT and A. SEGAERT, "Buffer Stock Allocation in Serial and Assembly Type of Production Lines," *Int. J. Operat. Product. Manage.* **10**(2), 47–61 (1990).

14. J.K. BRAR and N. SINGH, *System Dynamics Modelling and Analysis of Just-in-time Manufacturing Systems,* University of Windsor, Department of Industrial Engineering, Windsor, Ont., 1991, Working Paper #01-91.

15. J. OLHAGER and B. OSTLUND, "An Integrated Push–pull Manufacturing Strategy," *Eur. J. Operat. Res.* **45**, 135–142 (1990).

Suggested Readings

K.R. BAKER, G.S. POWELL, and F.D. PYKE, "The Performance of Push and Pull Systems: A Corrected Analysis," *Int. J. Product. Res.* **28**(9), 1731–1736 (1990).

E. BARTEZZAGHI and F. TURCO, "The Impact of Just-in-time on Production System Performance: An Analytical Framework," *Int. J. Operat. Product. Manage.* **8**, 40–62 (1989).

G.R. BITRAN and L. CHANG, "A Mathematical Programming Approach to a Deterministic Kanban System," *Manage. Sci.* **33**(4), 427–441 (1987).

J.A. BUZACOTT, Queuing models of kanban and MRP controlled.

W.J. DAVIS and S.J. STUBITZ, "Configuring a Kanban System Using a Discrete Optimization of Multiple Stochastic Responses," *Int. J. Product. Res.* **25**(5), 721–740 (1987).

J. DELEERSYNDER, T.J. HODGSON, H. MULLER, and P.J. O'GRADY, "Kanban Controlled Pull Systems: An Analytical Approach," *Manage. Sci.* **35**(9) 1079–1091 (1989).

M. GRAVEL and W.L. PRICE, "Using the Kanban in a Job Shop Environment," *Int. J. Product. Res.* **26**(6), 1105–1118 (1988).

Y.P. GUPTA and M.G. GUPTA, "A System Dynamics Model of a JIT-kanban System," *Eng. Costs Product. Econ.* **18**, 117–130 (1989).

Y.P. GUPTA and M.G. GUPTA, "A System Dynamics Model for a Multi-stage Multi-line Dual-card JIT-kanban System," *Int. J. Product. Res.* **27**(2), 309–352 (1989).

A. HERNANDEZ, *Just-In-Time Manufacturing: A Practical Approach,* Prentice-Hall, Inc., Englewood Cliffs, N.J., 1989.

J.H. IM and S.M. Lee, "Implementation of Just-in-time systems in US Manufacturing Firms," *Int. J. Operat. Product. Manage.* **9**(1), 5–14 (1988).

U.S. KARMARKAR and S. KEKRE, *Batching Policy in Kanban Systems,* University of Rochester, Graduate School of Business, 1987, Working Paper No. QM8706.

O. KIMURA and H. TERADA, "Design and Analysis of Pull System, a Method of Multi-stage Production Control," *Int. J. Product. Res.* **19**(3), 241–253 (1981).

L.C. Lee, "A Comparative Study of Push and Pull Production System," *Int. J. Operat. Product. Manage.* **9**(4), 5–18 (1989).

L.C. Lee and K.H.W. SEAH, "JIT and the Effects of Varying Process and Set-up Times," *Int. J. Operat. Product. Manage.* **8**(1), 19–35 (1987).

D.J. LU, *Kanban: Just-In-Time at Toyota,* Productivity Press, Cambridge, 1985.

D. MITRA and I. MITRANI, "Analysis of a Kanban Discipline for Cell Coordination in Production Lines. I," *Manage. Sci.* **36**(12), 1548–1566 (1990).

S. MIYAZAKI, H. OHTA, and N. NISHIYAMA, "The Optimal Operation Planning of Kanban to Minimize the Total Operation Cost," *Int. J. Product. Res.* **26**(10) 1605–1611 (1988).

Y. MONDEN, "Adaptable Kanban System Helps Toyota Maintain Just-in-time Production," *Ind. Eng.* **13**(5), 29–46 (1981).

R. O'CALAHAN, *A System Dynamics Perspective on JIT-Kanban,* paper presented at the International Conference of the System Dynamics Society, Sevilla, Spain, 1986.

P.R. PHILIPOOM, L.P. REES, B.W. TAYLOR III, and P.Y. HUANG, "An Investigation of the Factors Influencing the Number of Kanbans Required in the Implementation of the JIT Technique with Kanbans," *Int. J. Product. Res.* **25**(3), 457–472 (1987).

L.P. REES, P.Y. HUANG, and B.W. TAYLOR III, "A Comparative Analysis of MRP Lot-for-lot System and a Kanban System for a Multistage Production Operation," *Int. J. Product. Res.* **27**(8), 1427–1443 (1989).

J.W. RICE and T. YOSHIKAWA, "A Comparison of Kanban and Misconcepts for the Control of Repetitive Manufacturing Systems," *Product. Inventory Manage.,* 1–13 (1982).

R.J. SCHONBERGER, *Japanese Manufacturing Techniques: Nine Hidden Lessons in Simplicity,* Free Press, New York, 1982.

R.J. SCHONBERGER, "Applications of Single-card and Dual-card Kanban," *Interfaces* **13**(4), 56–67 (1983).

A. SEIDMANN, "Regenerative Pull (Kanban) Production Control Policies," *Eur. J. Operat. Res.* **35,** 401–413 (1988).

N. SINGH and J.K. BRAR, "Just-in-time Manufacturing Systems Modelling and Analysis: A Review," in press.

N. SINGH, K.H. SHEK, and D. MELOCHE, "The Development of a Kanban System: A Case Study," *Int. J. Operat. Product. Manage.* **10**(7), 27–35 (1990).

CHAPTER 29
Manufacturing Process Planning

HONG-CHAO ZHANG
Texas Tech University

29.1 INTRODUCTION

Process planning is performed in virtually all industries: its significance is greatest in small-batch, discrete parts metal fabrication manufacturing industries. Recently, however, process planning also has been recognized as playing an important role in other manufacturing and process industries, such as electronics manufacturing companies, furniture manufacturing companies, and even chemical process plants. Process planning is the transformation of part design specifications from detailed engineering drawings into operating instructions for necessary manufacturing.

A completed manufacturing process includes the whole transformation from a raw material stock into a desired product part or component. In general, manufacturing process planning refers to either machining process planning or assembly process planning. The machining process planning concerns how each single workpiece is machined on individual machines or manufacturing cells, whereas the assembly process planning concerns how several workpieces can be assembled together to form a machine part. Machining process planning is often simplified as process planning. In this chapter, the term *process planning* is used only to represent the machining process planning, and the word *assembly* will always be prefixed to distinguish assembly process planning. Several terms that are often used in process planning need to be defined before discussing manufacturing process planning.

Process is the basic unit of constructing process plans. A process can be defined as a procedure in which one workpiece or group of workpieces is continually machined on one machine or workstation by one operator or group of operators, e.g., a rough turning process on a lathe, a finish turning process on a lathe, a milling keyway process on a milling center, and a drilling hole process on a drilling machine.

Operation is the subunit of a process, and it is the basic part of the process. An operation is continually accomplished without changing cutting conditions (speed, depth, and feed), cutting tools, and cutting surfaces. Usually, one process consists of several operations. These operations are sequenced in a desired order, called *operation sequencing,* which is an integral part of process planning.

Cut is the subunit of an operation, and it is the basic part of the operation. A cut can be defined as a procedure in which the cutter passes the cutting surface once. In other words, some operations need several cuts with the same cutting tool and under the same cutting conditions (only speed and feed). In this case, each pass of the cutting surface by the cutting tool is called a cut. Usually, one operation consists of one or more cuts, depending on the required cutting volume.

29.2 MANUFACTURING PROCESS PLANNING

Manufacturing process planning can be defined as the systematic determination of the detailed methods by which workpieces or parts (if considering assembly) can be manufactured economically and competitively from initial stages (raw material form) to finished stages (desired form). Geometrical features, dimensional sizes, tolerances, materials, and finishes are analyzed and evaluated to determine an appropriate sequence of processing operations, which are based on specific, available machinery or workstations. In general, the inputs to process planning are designing data, raw material data, facilities data (machining data, tooling data, fixture data, etc.), quality requirement data, and production-type data. The output of process planning is a process plan. The process plan is often documented into a specific format and is called a process plan sheet. Process plan sheets may be referred to by different names, such as process sheets, operation sheets, planning sheets, route sheets, route plans, and part programs.

A process plan is an important document for production management. The process plan can be used for the management of production, the assurance of products' quality, and the optimization of production sequencing. The process plan can even be used to determine equipment lay out on the shop floor. Recently, research results have demonstrated that process planning plays an important role in a flexible manufacturing system (FMS) and computer-integrated manufacturing enterprises. Process planning is the key link for integrating design and manufacturing. Because a process plan is such an important document, everyone must respect and execute it seriously. In developing a new product, the process plan provides necessary information for technical and equipment preparation, such as tools, jigs and fixtures, machines, inspection devices, raw material stocks, inventory plans, purchasing plans, personnel requirements, etc. In designing a new factory or extending or modifying an old factory, the process plan is essential information that will determine equipment requirements, area of shop floor occupation, and investment.

Some essential information is necessary for process planning:

- Design data, which include all the assembly and separated single part drawings. Usually, design data are presented in the form of blueprints. However, if the design work is done on computer, then the design data are presented in the form of computer-aided design (CAD) models.
- Quality requirement data, which will affect the tools, fixtures, and equipment selection of process planning.
- Production-type data, which may lead to different process plans for the same product with different production types. While mass production requires a strategy of process distribution, job shop and batch size production prefer a strategy of process concentration.
- Raw material data, including information from raw material storage and capacity to the company's capability of making adequate stock and blanks.
- Capacity and capability of the company, such as equipment, tools, fixtures, dedicated machines, general machines, machine cells, stations, and machining centers as well as FMS.

Figure 29.1 illustrates a process planning model, which indicates the input to process planning and output from process planning.

Mission of Process Planning

Usually, the person who carries out process plans is referred to as a process planner, or simply a planner. The task of a process planner involves a series of steps. The first consideration is the interpretation of the design data, which are usually displayed either by the traditional blueprint or, more recently, by CAD models. In this stage, two principal tasks need to be accomplished: (1) understanding the functions, conditions, and specifications of the product, clarifying the relative assembly position and mutual functions and deriving the accordance of design requirement; (2) examining and analyzing the design data by carefully reading through the assembly

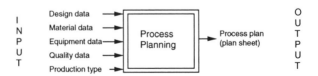

Figure 29.1. A process planning model.

and parts drawings. In this step, required information such as production types, geometrical configuration, raw material properties, dimension tolerances, surface roughness, heat treatment and hardness, and some special requirements will be studied and interpreted. It is important to determine if the design is completed, the design requirements are reasonable, part configurations are manufacturable, all dimensions and tolerances are available, and the surfaces roughness and tolerances are appropriate; and it is also important to find out if the design is optimal from the manufacturing point of view. If problems are detected in this stage, the planner must discuss the problems with the designers so that both sides are in agreement on how to modify or remedy the design. In traditional manufacturing companies, this work may sometimes cause disagreement between designers and planners, because of conflicting strategies and policies for design and manufacturing. To avoid the hassles, many manufacturing enterprises have raised their demands to break the wall between design and manufacturing, which is a topic of recent research activities, namely concurrent or simultaneous engineering.

The second step of process planning is to design stock. Usually, the properties of the raw materials are selected by the design engineer, because the properties of raw materials dependent on the requirement of a product's design. However, the geometrical shapes of raw materials (namely stock or, in other terms, blanks) are designed by the process planners. The stock design is usually based on the final geometrical shape of the part and on production types. Some selection of properties of materials may affect the stock design and even the selection of processes. For instance, if the raw material of nodular cast iron is selected by the designer for a specific gear part, then a casting process must be selected for the stock design. In this situation, the planner needs to discuss the stock design with the foundry shop. However, if medium-carbon steel is selected for the same gear part, the stock design may be quite different from the first design. The criteria of stock design are (1) assuring the quality of stock, (2) minimizing machining requirements, (3) increasing the use of material, and (4) reducing the manufacturing cost and lead time.

According to the product and stock design, the machining process data, such as turning, milling, drilling, grinding, etc., that transform the raw materials into the desired part, must be selected. In the meantime, the datum surfaces for fixturing must be determined, which is the key step in implementing an optimal process plan. Sometimes it is necessary to implement several different plans for the same parts. Comparison must be made according to the specific condition and capacity of the manufacturing environment. Once the processes are selected, the machining equipment (machine tools, workstations, machining centers, etc.) that can carry out one or more machining processes must be selected. The selection should take into consideration availability, process capability (size, accuracy, etc.), range of machining operations, production rate, etc. To complete the entire optimal production, the process planner must consider the information from the production scheduling and sequencing for the machine tools selection. For modern FMS and integrated manufacturing environments, the selection of machine tools has become even more important. Some recent research activities for integrated process planning with production scheduling are being conducted for this purpose (1).

After the machine tools are selected, the cutting tools, including clamping, measuring devices, and auxiliary tools, must be chosen. If some dedicated tools, fixtures, or auxiliary devices need to be made, the design project must be proposed by the process planner.

After all of the tools have been selected, the operation sequence must be determined. The determination of an operation sequence is usually based on a company-specific strategy that consists of comprehensive operations for a defined group of parts. Each operation is described by selection criteria that depend on the shape and dimensions of the part.

In the operation sequencing step, the amount of material to be removed by each process and operation must be checked. While finish machining requires a small amount of removal of materials, rough machining requires relatively more. Usually, it is necessary to calculate the coverage amount of removals for operations. Here the most efficient method to determine the amount of removal materials is operational dimensioning and tolerance chain analysis, which will provide the precise operation dimensions and tolerances of removals. The automated tolerance analysis will be discussed below. The appropriate cutting conditions, such as depth of cut, feed, and speed rates, then must be determined. The total machining and nonmachining times must be calculated, including batch setup, loading and unloading, tool changing, and inspection times. The cost of the process can be also included, if desired. Finally, process plans are made and edited. Checking for syntax and path errors should be done in this stage. Significant economical benefits can be obtained if optimum production concepts are adopted throughout the process planning. In summary, the tasks of process planning can be itemized as follows (2):

- Interpretation of product design data.
- Stock design.
- Selection of machining processes.
- Selection of machine tools.
- Determination of fixtures, tools, and data.
- Sequencing the operations.
- Determination of operational dimensions and tolerances.
- Determination of the proper cutting conditions.
- Calculation of the total times.
- Generating of process sheets, including NC data.

Making of Process Planning

To implement an optimal process plan, the process planner must consider many factors that are involved in manufacturing; among all these factors, datum selection is important, especially the data for setting up named setup datum points. The selection of data in machining is closely related to the specification of the operation sequence. When a process plan is to be made, the relationship between positioning and the sequence and its influence on machining accuracy must be carefully considered. In the following sections, the concept of datum will be discussed.

Datum Points

A part consists of several surfaces that have specified mutual (positional and dimensional) relationships to guarantee proper functions. Therefore, in the machining process, one or more surfaces on the part should be used as datum elements to machine other surfaces and satisfy the requirements on the blueprint. The concept of datum is introduced to describe this mutual positional relationship. To ensure these relationships, position tolerance is often applied. In Figure 29.2 the relative positioning between feature D (plane) and feature IV (hole) is indicated. To ensure this positional requirement during the machining process, an appropriate setup datum must be selected. First it is necessary to define data. Datum points (data) can be defined as the features (surfaces, lines, and points) that can be used to coordinate other features (surfaces, lines, and points). Feature D in Figure 29.2 is a datum. When the positions of these features are to be calculated or measured, the datum is the starting point of the calculations or measurements. The concept of datum is meaningful only when the relative positional relationship among the points, lines, and surfaces are concerned.

  The relative positional relationship with the datum includes parallelism, perpendicularity, and concentricity (coaxiality). Positional tolerances may be specified on the blueprint if the functional or technological requirements are high. Otherwise the relationship will be restricted by the dimensional tolerance. Different machine tools can make different surface elements (features) on a part. These features can be regarded as the loci of the tool on the part. By cutting

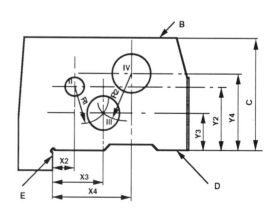

Figure 29.2. An example of part design.

within the machining zone on the machine tools, all the achievable loci (programmable on NC machine tools) are called cutting-generating surfaces, or generating surfaces. Every generating surface has some fixed relationship with the locating surfaces of the machine tool—such as the surface of the worktable, the side of a T-slot, the locating cone, the locating cylinder, and the end face on the spindle—that can be used to locate and position a part or a fixture. From the viewpoint of manufacturing, any surface element on a part that can have a fixed relationship (direct or through a fixture) and make the surface element to be obtained coincide with a generating surface can be used as a datum. In the machining process, the selection of a datum from the elements is one of the major factors that influences the relative positional accuracy between the elements on a part. In terms of the functions of data, datum elements can be divided into two basic types, according to the environments in which they are used: design datum and process datum points.

Design datum points are features used to determine and ensure the positions of some of the other features (surfaces, lines, or points), by means of design. In Figure 29.2, feature D is the design datum of feature B. Feature IV (hole) has two design data: features D and E, respectively, in vertical and horizontal directions. The design datum of feature III (hole) is the axial center lines of feature II (hole) and IV (hole). In general, the design datum is used on the blueprint to specify the dimension or relative position of other elements, such as parallelism, perpendicularity, and concentricity. It is assigned by the designer based generally on the function of the part in the product and properly on the feasibility of machining. For an individual part, there may be quite a few specifications for the elements, but usually there is only one major design datum in each direction, which is used to locate the part in the assembly of the product.

Process datum points are features that are used to clamp the workpiece for machining other features. According to the different functions, process data can be further classified into three categories: setup datum, measuring datum, and assembly datum. Setup datum points (also referred as positioning datum points) are features that form definite positions between operational dimensions and cutting tools while the workpiece is clamped on a machine or a fixture. For instance, Figure 29.2 indicates that feature D is the setup datum for machining feature IV (hole). Consequently, feature D is also the design datum of feature IV (hole). In this case, the setup datum coincides with the design datum. Datum coincidence will increase manufacturing accuracy, reduce manufacturing errors, and simplify operation sequencing without changing any other manufacturing factors. As a matter of fact, design and setup data coincidence is a desired situation for optimal and accurate process planning.

Measuring datums points are features that are used for measuring operational dimensions. For a process or an operation, the measuring datum should coincide with the positioning datum to examine if the parts are made within the operational specifications. But if the positioning datum does not coincide with the design datum, the measurement may give false results. Assembly datum points are features that are used for the determination of the assembly position of each workpiece within the entirety of the product. Features D, E, IV, III, and II are assembly data in Figure 29.2.

Synchronous Datum

Besides the above datum points, there is another datum, named synchronous datum. Actually, synchronous datum belongs to the setup datum but is particularly used on CNC machines. On an NC machine, the tool movements are numerically controlled through programs. No matter whether an absolute, incremental, or floating coordinate system is selected, the nominal values used in the NC program are converted to absolute coordinate values in the controller of the machine. Using the concept of generating surface, one can clearly see that the relative dimensional and positional relationship among the generating surfaces can be accurately programmed. The relationship can be exactly duplicated onto the part if the surface elements are machined in one setup. The surface elements obtained in one setup are mutually datumed, dependent, and interrelated; therefore, the concept of the dimension and tolerance chain cannot be used here and is not necessary, because no datum transformation is introduced. That is to say that for any designed dimension or relationship, if the surface elements are machined in one setup, no chain analysis is needed for that dimension or relationship. If the specified tolerance cannot be obtained, nothing can be done in sequencing unless a new machining method or machine tool with a narrower process capacity is adopted or a high rate of scrap is accepted. Once the part is removed and relocated, this relationship is destroyed. (In some special cases, the part is center supported and the repeatability of setup is extremely accurate, thus the setups can be regarded

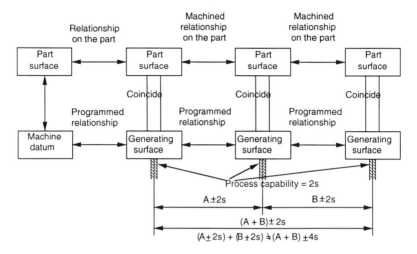

Figure 29.3.   Relationships obtained in one setup.

as one.) Therefore, these mutually datumed elements are called synchronous datum elements. Other datum elements obtained in different setups are called synchronous datum elements, where some errors such as fixture error, tool calibration error, tool wear, and setup error may be introduced into the part dimensions. This concept is depicted in Figure 29.3.

Criteria of Process Planning

As discussed in the previous section, datum points must always be examined and determined before making the process plan. However, sometimes the points, the lines, and the planes may not exist entirely on the part. Instead, the data are represented by some other concrete feature. For example, a short bar stock is clamped by a three jag chuck on a lathe in Figure 29.4. Although the visible setup datum is the external round surface of the short bar, the real setup datum is the axial centerline of the short bar. This example indicates that sometimes selecting the correct setup datum may actually include selecting the appropriate setup surface.

Datum coincidence is one of the criteria for selecting setup datum points. To achieve the datum coincidence, design data must usually be selected as setup data. If the selected setup datum is not common with the design datum, processing errors will occur during machining. Because these processing errors are caused by unlike data (setup datum and design datum), they are named setup errors. Similar problems can be encountered when measuring datum

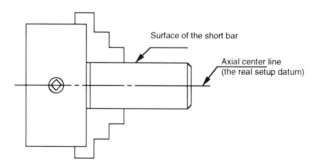

Figure 29.4.   An example of setup datum.

points are not uniform with design data. These errors are called measuring errors, because they are caused by unequal measuring data and setup data. Other errors may also be caused by unequal data. To avoid these errors, which may directly affect the quality of product, the strategy of datum coincidence must be always applied for datum selection. This strategy is called the principle of datum coincidence.

Selecting appropriate setup datum points can significantly improve manufacturing quality and reduce manufacturing cost and lead time. The need for machine precision can also be dramatically reduced. Selecting appropriate setup data is one of the principal concerns of making process plans. As a matter of fact, selection of datum points is simply the selection of surfaces that can be used for clamping the workpiece. For a stock that has not received any manufacturing processes, only a stock surface can be selected as a setup datum. In this case, the datum, which has not been manufactured before, is called a black datum. In the continuing operations of the workpiece, especially for finishing processes such as finish turning, finish milling, and finish boring, one should always try to select some surfaces that have already been manufactured. The datum that has been manufactured is called a bright datum. Sometimes, the bright datum does not exist, and so it cannot be directly used for an appropriate setup datum. In this case, a surface that will not affect any functions of original design should be designed, created, and used as setup datum; this is called an auxiliary datum. For instance, while machining a shaft, a center hole is drilled for supporting the shaft on the machine. The center hole, which has no other function except supporting the shaft, is an auxiliary datum.

Another criterion for the selection of datum is the principle of datum unification. This strategy indicates that the process planner should try to use the same bright datum to manufacture as many features as possible within a setup. This strategy can avoid generating process errors between features during manufacturing.

Selection of datum points is a critical step in making an optimal process plan. The process planner must carefully analyze all of the different data and select the appropriate one. The principles of datum coincidence and datum unification are strategies to ensure the quality of the process. To select appropriate black and bright (especially bright) datum points, careful and close attention must be given to examining the relationships among features.

Besides data selection, another criterion for process planning is equipment selection. Equipment selection for flexible process planning has become a popular research topic under the umbrella of computer-integrated manufacturing (CIM), which requires detailed knowledge of operations research and scheduling. While making process plans, the process planner must always try to focus attention on existing equipment within the company. The process planner should try to select the machine that has high productivity and multiple process functions, and he or she may also try to concentrate on as many processes as possible that can be produced by the high productivity machine. This strategy may reduce the requirements of additional machines, the number of operators, the number of steps in the process, and the route of material handling as well as the manufacturing lead time. These advantages preclude another strategy of process planning. This strategy is called the principle of processes concentration, which means that the process planner should try to concentrate as many processes as possible on a machine within a setup while making process plans.

Other criteria need to be considered while sequencing the operations. These criteria are as follows:

1. All rough processing should be done before finish processing.
2. All major processing should be done before minor processing.
3. All bright datum points should be done before ordinary features.
4. All bright datum points should be done before use.

To stimulate the application of recent high-tech development, new methodologies, new equipment, new materials, and new strategies should be considered during process planning, for example, CNC machining centers (as a new methodology) and composite materials (as a new kind of material).

Approaches to Process Planning

In general, approaches to process planning can be classified into two main categories: manual process planning and computerized process planning. Figure 29.5 illustrates a hierarchical

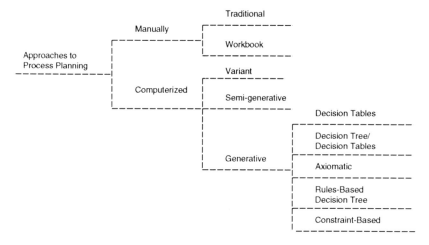

Figure 29.5.   Classification of approaches of process planning.

classification tree of approaches to process planning. The approaches to manual process planning including two distinctive categories—the traditional approach and the workbook approach—whereas computer-aided process planning can be further classified into three categories—the variant approach, the generative approach, and the semigenerative approach.

Traditional Approach

The traditional approach to process planning involves examining the information of a part design described in the form of a blueprint, identifying similar parts (from memory or from a code book), and manually retrieving process plans for these similar parts. A new process plan is then created by modifying and adapting the old one to meet the special requirements of the new print. Customarily, the process planner will consult the supervisor in the production shop to find out how the part is actually being processed.

Workbook Approach

An alternative and more efficient approach to process planning is constructing a workbook containing a menu of prestored sequences for operations for given types of workpieces. These stored process groups may be quickly selected and sequenced by the process planner. The menu selections are then typed on the regular process sheet and reproduced as required.

   The main advantages of the manual approaches are low investment and flexibility. For the workbook approach, a well-trained planner can produce a large number of process plans for simple parts. For both approaches, a considerable working experience is crucial to carrying out a good process plan. Therefore, manual approaches to process planning have some obvious disadvantages. These disadvantages include the lack of consistency in identifying and planning similar parts, difficulty in specifying common tooling, and the difficulty of updating a manual file to reflect new processes and tooling.

Variant Approach

The variant approach to computer-aided process planning is comparable with the traditional manual approach by which a process plan for a new part is created by recalling, identifying, and retrieving an existing plan for a similar part (sometimes called a master part) and making the necessary modifications for the new part. In some variant systems, parts are grouped into a number of part families, characterized by similarities in manufacturing methods and thus related to group technology. For each part family, a standard process plan, which includes all possible operations for the family, is stored in the system. Through classification and coding, a code is built up by answering a number of predefined questions. These codes are often used to identify the part family and the associated standard plan. The standard plan is retrieved and edited for the new part. The variant approach is widely used, e.g., a real computer-aided process planning (CAPP) system (3) and MIPLAN (4). In comparison with manually performed process planning, the variant approach is highly advantageous in increasing information management capabilities. Consequently, complicated activities and decisions require less time and labor. Also, procedures can be standardized by incorporating a planner's manufacturing knowledge and structuring it to a company's specific needs. Therefore, variant systems can organize and store completed plans and manufacturing knowledge from which process plans can be quickly evaluated. However, there are difficulties in maintaining consistency in editing practices and in the inability to accommodate adequately various combinations of geometry, size, precision, material, quality, and shop loading. The biggest disadvantage is that the quality of the process plan still depends on the knowledge background of a process planner. The computer is just a tool to assist in manual process planning activities. However, the variant approach is still popular. The main reasons are probably:

1. The investment in hardware and software is relatively low. Vendors for the variant systems are more available now compared with the generative systems.
2. The development time is relatively short and labor consumption is also low. The installation is comparatively easier than the generative systems.
3. Currently, the variant systems is somewhat more reliable to be employed from the point of view of real production environments. So it is a reasonable option for the current production environment, especially for some small- and medium-size companies that do not have resources to form a research and development group.

Generative Approach

The highest level of automation and sophistication in computer-aided process planning is the generative approach. As the name implies, the approach takes the design specifications and turns them over completely to the computer and its programming for process plan production. In the generative approach process plans are generated by means of decision logic, formulas, technology algorithms, and geometry-based data to perform uniquely the many processing decisions for converting a part from raw material to a finished state. The rules of manufacturing and the equipment capabilities are stored in a computer system. When using the system, a specific process plan for a specific part can be generated without the involvement of a process planner. For generative systems, input can come either as a text input, for which the user answers a number of questions in an English or English-like dialogue (defined as interactive input), or as graphic input, for which the part data are gathered from a CAD module (defined as interface input). So far, the former is more common in existing CAPP systems, whereas the latter is still a fairly undeveloped area due to its complexity. Nevertheless, interface input is necessary to enable an integrated manufacturing system. It has attracted much effort in an attempt to interface CAPP with CAD. The terms *feature recognition, feature extraction, feature refinement,* and *geometry reasoning* have been used to denote the field of study that is discussed in detail elsewhere in this chapter. Tulkoff (5) states that "generative process planning systems today are still somewhat elusive, on the whole, and can be considered as being in their early stages of development and use." The generative approach is complex and a generative CAPP system is difficult to develop. At the beginning, some argued that this type of system was too complex ever to be computerized. However, the rapid development of artificial intelligence (AI) techniques and the successes of applying AI techniques in other areas have greatly encouraged the use of AI techniques in process planning. Process plans produced in this manner are consistent, are fully automated, and may be completely integrated with computer-integrated manufacturing. True generative systems are still in their infancy, however, and are thus extremely expensive, time-consuming to implement, and applicable to only a small range of the parts that must be machined. This effort has given initial results that indicate that generative systems are desirable and promising.

Several generative process planning systems have already been developed: APPAS (6), CMPP (7), EXCAP (8), XPLAN (9), and so on. The biggest advantage of the generative approach is that the process plan is consistent and fully automated. This kind of system is mostly oriented toward large companies and research organizations, because they can afford the investment of a long-term project. For companies that have a number of products in small lot sizes, the generative approach is particularly attractive. As a research field to enable the necessary integration within the CIM concept, the generative approach is important. Five alternative approaches to generative process planning are discussed in detail by Allen (10):

- Decision tables.
- Decision trees–decision tables.
- Axiomatic.
- Rule-based decision tree.
- Constraint-based.

The principal advantages of generative process planning are the rapidity and consistency with which plans may be generated and the ease of incorporating into the plans new processes, equipment, methods, and tooling.

Semigenerative Approach

The semigenerative approach is an interim approach, and it is still in its infancy. Emerson and Ham (11) presented a semigenerative system called ACAPS and stated that

> it must be said at this point that the purely generative CAPP system has yet to be developed. Until such time as a generative system emerges, much effort has gone into "semi-generative" CAPP systems. These serve to reduce user interaction through such features as standard operation sequences, decision tables and mathematical formulas. These schemes are not completely generative, but they can be extremely useful in terms of time and cost savings in the manufacturing environment.

To highlight differences between it and the final approach, the semigenerative method entails interaction between a computer and a human, who has some degree of expertise in the area of process planning. The planner's responsibility is the interpretation of design and/or a mechanical drawing. The computer prompts the operator for measurements, materials, and tolerances and produces a process plan based on predefined algorithms and formulas. The term *semigenerative approach* may be defined as a combination of the generative and the variant approaches, for which a preprocess plan is developed and modified before the plan is used in a real production environment. It means that the decision logic, formulas, and technological algorithm as well as the geometry-based coding scheme for translating physical features (such as features' sizes, tolerances, locations, and surface roughness) are built into the system. At a first sight, the system's working steps are the same as for the generative approach, but the final process plan must be examined and errors corrected if it does not fit into the real production environment. It may be a good idea to break a generative system down into a plan-generating stage and a modifying stage to correct the plans that may be in conflict with the specific production environment. Modifying is minor compared with the variant approach. From a research point of view the semigenerative system may not be the desired direction, but it increases the system's competitiveness on the market. Industrial application of such systems can (1) speed up automatic production, (2) reduce the process planner's participation, and (3) ensure the quality of the process plan. Because it is a practically oriented system for industry, the semigenerative approach may be a good candidate during the transition period.

There are also other approaches such as the constructive approach (12) and the artificial intelligence approach. But these approaches can be included into one of the above-mentioned three categories of process planning approaches.

To summarize, the advantages of CAPP are typical of those accrued when any procedure is automated via computers. Here is a brief list of these advantages:

1. Reduced clerical effort.
2. Fewer calculations.
3. Fewer oversights in logic.
4. Immediate access to up-to-date information.
5. Consistent information.
6. Faster response to engineering or production changes.
7. Use of latest revisions.
8. More detailed and uniform planning.
9. More efficient use of resources.

29.3 IMPLEMENTATION OF CAPP SYSTEMS

CAPP can be defined as the functions that use computers to assist the work of process planners. It is obvious that CAPP development has been addressed by many universities, institutions, research organizations, and corporate development departments. The task of carrying out the difficult and detailed process plans has traditionally been done by workers with a vast knowledge and understanding of the manufacturing process. Many of the skilled workers now considered process planners are either retired or close to retirement, and there are no qualified young process planners to take their place. An increasing shortage of process planners has been created. With the high pressure of competition in a world market, integrated production has been pursued as a way for companies to survive and succeed. Automated process planning systems have been recognized as playing a key role in CIM. Thus many companies look for computer-aided process planning systems.

Computer-aided process planning is the way in which most companies are solving the problem of automating process planning and overcoming the shortage of skilled process planners. As the American Machinist and Automated Manufacturing Society (13) has reported, a computerized process planning system has essentially four goals: (1) reduce the clerical load of plan preparation on the manufacturing engineers and skilled process planners, who are in short supply; (2) optimize existing plans using the best available information on machines, tools, speeds, etc.; (3) standardize what are known to be the best process plans for families of components within a company, thereby capturing the knowledge of the skilled planners; and (4) standardize production times and costs for particular families of components.

Format of Input and Output

The input to the process planning system is design data. Generally, the format of input to CAPP systems can be divided into two categories. They are either a text input or a graphic input. The text input is also referred to as interactive input, by which a number of questions in an English or English-like dialogue or a series of alphanumerical codes are entered through the keyboard of the computer. The graphic input is also referred to as interfere input, by which the data of the part's geometrical model are gathered from a CAD system. Most of the variant systems adopt interactive input, especially for coding system. A code is built up by answering a number of predefined questions. These codes are often used to identify the part's families and are associated with standard master plans. The standard master plans are retrieved and edited for the parts.

So far, both interactive and interface input have been employed in generative systems. If a coding system is used in a generative system, the codes are usually more detailed and sometimes mix code digits with explicitly defined parameter values. Because a code is concise, it is easy to manipulate. When process capabilities are represented by a code, a simple search through the process capability to match the component code will return the desired process. If an English or English-like dialogue approach is used in a generative system, a specially designed part description language is employed to provide detailed information for process planning systems. A language can be designed to provide all of the information required for the necessary functions of a process planning system. The format can be designed such that functions can easily accomplish their tasks from the information provided.

Interface input is most commonly used in generative systems. Because a design can be modeled effectively in a CAD system, using a CAD model as input to a process planning system can eliminate the human effort of translating a design into a code or other descriptive form. The increased use of CAD in industry further points to the benefits of using CAD models as process planning data input. In spite of this, interface input is still a fairly undeveloped area due to its complexity. Because it is necessary to enable an integrated manufacturing system, much effort to interface CAPP with CAD has occurred. *Feature recognition, feature extraction, feature refinement,* and *geometry reasoning* are terms that have been used in conjunction with the user-friendly interface (discussed below). According to a recent investigation, many good approaches for feature-based design have been carried out (14). These approaches can provide an explicit product model in terms of feature dimensions and feature relationships. These feature-based approaches have improved the current CAPP techniques. However, computer-aided process planning is a complex task. It requires not only complete information for a geometric model but also detailed information for manufacturing. Existing CAD systems cannot provide sufficient manufacturing information for process planning, e.g., tolerances, surface treatment, and hardness requirements. If one takes into account the integration with job shop scheduling, then the input requirement must include some information about the shop floor situation and production control information, which are usually required from a production management database.

The format of the output of CAPP systems can be divided into two groups: text output, for which the process plan carried out by the CAPP system will be directly printed out from a printer or screen, or a data output, by which the process plan carried out by the CAPP system will be saved in a program that can be retrieved by consequent computer-aided manufacturing systems. The text printout (often called the plan sheet or route sheet) usually contains information about the route, processes, operation parameters, and machine and tools selected and sometimes also includes time and cost calculations. It is usually well edited by a word processing program or a built-in output format algorithm. In some cases, a bill of material, machine sheet, tooling and fixturing sheet, and time and cost estimation report can be printed out separately from the system. Generally, the data output is associated with the NC program, which is often required by a CAM system. The process plan, which is carried out by the CAPP system, is stored in a program and sometimes directly transferred to an NC path or some other CAM system, if the interface has been established between CAPP and CAM.

In terms of integrating process planning with production scheduling, the output of CAPP should also concern the manufacturing resource planning (MRP II). To integrate these functions, the output of CAPP should also be sent to the scheduling module of MRP II—the actual status of work in progress on a real-time basis. This is virtually always done by means of a computer terminal directly networked to the scheduling database. Futher discussion of integrating process planning and production scheduling can be found in ref. 1.

IGES, STEP, and PDES

IGES stands for initial graphics exchange specification, which is a particularly neutral data exchange format for such data sharing purposes. IGES was first published in 1980 and was updated in 1983, 1986, 1988, and 1990 (15). IGES was originally developed to provide a means for exchanging engineering drawing data between CAD systems, especially for the three-dimensional geometrical models. It goal is to allow CAD data to be exchanged between systems built by different manufacturers. While it is good for wire frame and boundary representative models, it is not a convenient way to represent the solid models that are widely used. One more problem that occurred with IGES is an outgrowth of the way CAD vendors implement the software that is required to translate their data to and from the neutral IGES data file. When IGES data are passed between design systems, considerable human interpretation and manipulation of the data may be required. Because IGES was designed primarily as a mechanism for file exchange between CAD systems, it is not able to support shared databases between dissimilar product life-cycle applications.

To solve the shortcoming of IGES, the International Organization for Standardization (ISO) is currently involved in the development of a new international standard for the exchange of information related to automated manufacturing. The development standard is informally called the standard for the exchange of product model data (STEP). STEP is intended to address the issue of product data sharing between different computer applications running on different computer systems within the same or different organizations.

STEP goes beyond IGES both in the breadth of its information content and in the sophistication of its information system methodologies. STEP will provide a standard, neutral format for product data created and shared by different applications. *Neutral* means that the STEP data format will not favor one particular vendor. In addition, STEP development is including the definition of subsets of product data that are specifically required for particular usage contexts. These subsets are called application protocols.

STEP application protocols address the issues of completeness and unambiguity of data transfer by specifying in advance what data should be transferred in a particular context, thereby alleviating the need for vendors to make problematic assumptions. Application protocols are those parts of STEP that are relevant to a particular data-sharing scenario (16).

There are four major technical challenges facing the developers of STEP (17):

1. The exchange of data is different from the exchange of information. Data must be transmitted accurately and without any changes. In contrast, information, although composed of data, must be understood and interpreted by the receiver. Furthermore, the receiver must be able to apply the information correctly in new situations. The first challenge is that STEP is a standard for information, not just data.

2. The need for STEP to be extendable to new products, processes, and technologies requires a more abstract representation of the information than in previous standards. Regardless of the equipment or process, a user must be able to obtain the information necessary to do something from the STEP representation of a product. Therefore, the second challenge is that the development of STEP must include the development of an "architecture," or a framework, for the exchange of information, not just a means or format for storing information.

3. The wide range of industries and the diversity of product information covered in STEP is beyond that of any previous digital standard. The variety of attributes and parameters—such as geometric shape, mechanical function, materials, assembly information, and date of manufacture—is immense. Also, the industrial base, the number of industries involved, is enormous; even greater is the number of technical disciplines that are involved. Moreover, STEP must be flexible and extensible so that new information and additional application protocols can be added and can be upwardly compatible. Therefore, the third challenge is that the scope and complexity of STEP is far beyond any previous standards effort.

4. Traditionally, standardization is a process that devises an approach encompassing a variety of existing vendors' builds on the best solution available and avoids penalizing some vendors more than others. In the case of STEP, there is no existing implementation. Thus the fourth challenge: the technology to support STEP must be developed at the same time the standard is evolving.

The consensus approach to meeting the above challenges is to start with conceptual information models. STEP will consist of a set of clearly and formally defined conceptual models and a physical exchange protocol based on these models. The conceptual models will be combined into a single model with a standard interface to a shared database.

Product data exchange using STEP (PDES) refers to U.S. activities in support of the development of STEP (18). In April 1988, several major U.S. technology companies incorporated as PDES, Inc. with the specific goal of accelerating the development of STEP in the United States. PDES will help establish a standard digital representation for product data. The specifications already developed by the PDES effort have been submitted to the ISO as a basis for the evolving international standard STEP. Because the PDES and STEP efforts share common goals, they are sometimes referred to jointly as PDES/STEP, or simply STEP. PDES/STEP is currently developed by a number of organizations both nationally and internationally, including

- IGES/PDES Organization.
- ISO TC184/SC4.
- ANSI U.S. Technical Advisory Group.
- PDES, Inc.
- NIST National PDES Test-bed.

Application of Artificial Intelligence in Process Planning

Traditional computer-based methodologies are unable to deal with the challenges of fully automated process planning because the traditional computer-based methodologies may be good at processing data for information-intensive domains but not well suited for automatic inference for the knowledge-intensive domain, which automated process planning requires. Rather than simply processing information and data, AI-based techniques are designed for capturing, representing, and using knowledge on computers, and hence intelligent manufacturing is certain to play an important role in manufacturing industry. The application of AI, or expert systems, to process planning has given some promising results. In spite of the fact that the results are still limited, they are sufficient to stimulate further research. At the present, though, the limited success of expert systems has proved that process planning is a proper field for application of AI. With the advent of expert systems, the knowledge of a process planner can be transferred to the planning system, making it capable of intelligent reasoning and thereby facilitating the reasoning process. Expert process planning systems organize knowledge and can reason intelligently; they organize knowledge in three separate levels: facts, rules, and control strategy (19). The typical expert process planning system would consist of a database that contains the part geometry and the production rules. The production rules perform the transactions in the database to obtain the desired component and decision as to which rule must be applied. In what sequence is a matter for the procedural rules of the system, and it is the operation of these that implements the control strategy of the expert process planning systems. However, some AI techniques still need further development. Existing expert systems lack adequate mathematical calculation functions. When calculation tasks must be performed, the expert system usually takes more time than a normal computer program. This disadvantage not only requires more computing time but also increases the cost. There are also other problems; most of the knowledge representation inference engines of the current expert systems are more system-designer oriented than process-planner oriented. This in a sense is the reason why only a few expert process planning systems have been used in real production environments. Nevertheless, few will doubt that AI technologies will be developed to improve process planning systems. Emphasis will be given to the development of more user friendly software products. In addition, a new generation of intelligent systems—learning systems—will emerge. Such systems will respond to the need for continuous reteaching, with the capability of monitoring actual production experiences and feeding back information to the planning system. The systems can be used for self-teaching and training for novices. Other systems also have been proposed, e.g., the distributed planning system (20). The distributive planning system will tend to take over the character of the original manual planning system, with intelligent software and computer systems replacing human skills, knowledge, and experience. The common knowledge base will tend to be segmented, and individual knowledge bases will be developed at each level to cover each area (factory, cell, or workstation) in the manufacturing hierarchy.

Format of Decision Rules

As Figure 29.5 illustrates, the current approaches of process planning can be divided into two categories: manual and computerized. Here, two strategies—traditional and workbook—have been addressed by manual process planning. Computerized process planning can be further classified into either variant, generative, or semigenerative approaches, which were discussed earlier. Logical decision is a traditional implementation technique used in computer-aided process planning. This is the description of the specifications of the several activities associated with the input and the sequences that are to be followed by the machine. This method has been in use for a long time to help logical decision making. After the increase in the application of computers and the advent of artificial intelligence systems this has gained popularity. To date, about five alternative formats for decision rules have been recognized in the implementation of CAPP systems (10):

- Decision tables.
- Decision trees–decision tables.
- Axiomatic.
- Rule-based decision tree.
- Constraint based.

Among these five decision-making approaches, two of them are commonly addressed in existing CAPP systems: decision tables and rule-based decision trees.

Decision Tables

Decision tables are tables that are divided by columns and rows. For example, Figure 29.6 is a decision table for tooling selection. The table corresponds to a specific machine—CORTINI H105, a CNC lathe. The first column of the table represents the four-figure alphanumeric code that indicates the cutting subjects. The first row of the table is the raw material often used in the company. If the specific cutting conditions and cutting material are given, a six-figure alphanumeric code that leads to a specific cutting tool will be generated from the table. Often, the decision tables are used consequently in process planning. There are several factors that must be considered while developing a decision table such as the accuracy, repetitiveness, consistency, size, and completeness of the table to ensure that the table helps effective decision making. The size of the decision table is important. If a decision table is too large, e.g., several pages long, it is difficult for a human to read and interpret. The discipline may fit a menu-driven interactive computer program, although this will not only require excessive memory, but also reduce the efficiency of decision making. The table should contain the actual rules and conditions specified in the design. According to the rule representation, decision tables can be classified as follows:

Mostly often used raw materials

	Alloy steel	Aluminum alloy	Carbon steel	Composite/ Plastic	Copper/ Bronze	Gray cast iron	Stainless steel	. . . . . .
CF92								
FL11								
FS12								
FT52								
RS11			TC90C S			TC90G C		
. . . .								
XX00	XX00XX	XX00XX	XX00XX	XX00XX	XX00XX	XX00XX	XX00XX	. . . .

CODES I XX00: Four-alphanumeric-code to indicate the cutting subjects

Codes of cutting dimensions group

Codes of cutting surface shape

Codes of process activities

CODES II XX00XX: Six-alphanumeric-code to indicate the tool conditions

Codes of workpiece materials

Codes of tools main geometry

Codes of tool materials

Figure 29.6. An example of a decision table.

Limited Entry Decision Tables. These tables represent the exact conditions (input values) as true or false entries.

Extended Entry Decision Tables. These tables specify the condition but not the value.

Mixed Entry Decision Tables. Sequenced and unsequenced actions can be entered in these tables; sequenced actions rate a sequence number, whereas unsequenced actions do not rate one.

Rule-Based Decision Trees

Decision trees resemble a graph with a root, nodes, and branches. They are used to represent the results of actions. The root is the source of the tree, and each tree can have only a single root. However, a tree can call another subtree, e.g., DCLASS, a typical visible tree structure system. A DCLASS subtree can call up to 25 additional subtrees. When applied to decision making, the branches carry values and expressions that can be likened to an IF statement, whereas the branches are comparable with AND statements. Branches can have only one of two values: true or false. If a branch is true then is can be passed to the next node. Nodes can be classified into excursive and non–mutually excursive (21). A non–mutually excursive node allows all its successive branches to be true.

Decision trees can be either used as computer codes or represented as data. As a computer code, the tree is converted to a flow chart. The starting node is a root, and every branch represents a decision statement and is either true or false. For a true condition, an action is taken at the corresponding junction, and for a false condition, it is branched out to others or simply terminated. Decision statements can be either mathematical expressions or predicates.

Decision trees have certain definite benefits over decision tables. First, trees can be updated and maintained more easily than can decision tables. Second, selected branches of the decision tree may be extended to a considerable depth if necessary, while other branches may be quite short, which is more difficult to do in decision tables. Third, some branches of the decision tree may be used to define TYPE and others, ATTRIBUTES, which results in relatively small trees. Fourth, trees are easy to customize, visualize, develop, and debug. There are several types of trees that may be developed to aid in classification characterization, selection, and complex decision making. Figure 29.7 illustrates an example of a decision tree.

Automated Tolerancing in CAPP

A fundamental aspect of design and manufacturing is the transformation of product-functional requirements into tolerances of individual components, followed by the production of parts satisfying specified shapes and tolerances. This means that tolerancing is used in two stages in the development of products: design and production. In the design stage, tolerancing assigns tolerances to the shapes of individual parts to ensure that the part can functionally perform well in the product and can be produced economically. Usually, the designer minimizes the cost of parts by analyzing the cost of manufacturing and assembling. Sometimes he or she may minimize the cost by accepting some rate of scrap. At present, the cost analysis and estimation are based on the designed dimensions and tolerances (22, 23). In the manufacturing stage, the parts cannot all be made in one setup. Therefore, the transformation of datum elements is needed, and a dimension and tolerance chain is formed. In this chain, the dimensions may be obtained directly (component dimensions) or indirectly (the sum dimension). Tolerancing is used here to decide the tolerance for each operational dimension to ensure either that the part is made within the designed dimensions and tolerances or that the stock removal for each cut is within certain limits. An operational dimension is the dimension from the datum element, which has a fixed relationship with the machine tool coordinate system and the element to be obtained in the setup. It is clear that the operational tolerances may be equal to or higher (tighter) than the designed tolerances, and only the operational dimensions and tolerances have a direct relationship with the machining process capability, fixturing, tooling, setup, machining time, and scheduling, which are the basis for the cost analysis and calculation. Moreover, for those tolerances that have specified datum elements, arrangements of features to be machined to proper setups can heavily influence the accuracy, and consequently the cost, of manufacturing the products. It has been noted that none of the existing CAPP systems can deal with the tolerances of specified datum points. In other words, to make parts at the lowest cost, the automated toler-

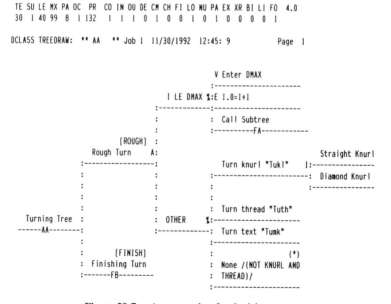

Figure 29.7. An example of a decision tree.

ance analysis in the computer-aided process planning will play a decisively important role in the future computer-integrated manufacturing system.

The Architectures of CAPP Systems

One of the most fundamental elements of complex system design is the architecture on which the system is built. Architecture basically describes the system components, their interfaces, and their relationship to one another. The most important function of a system architecture is that the information flow within the system can be represented explicitly. The details of the architectures may differ from system to system and the information input and output may be based on different schemes, but every automated process planning system must possess five fundamental elements: (*1*) the knowledge base, which is used to store the production rules; (*2*) the inference engine, which is used for knowledge acquisition and representation; (*3*) the control mechanism, which is used for controlling the components' communication; (*4*) the user interface scheme, which is used to communicate with users; and (*5*) the database, which is used to store all necessary information used for making process plans.

Figure 29.8 is an example of an architecture of an expert process planning system. The system consists of eight elements. The central element is a knowledge base. The knowledge base may be implemented in many different ways. In this particular example, the knowledge base is implemented by a DCLASS LogicTree processor, so all the production rules are implemented in the form of tree structure. The detailed description of the working function of this system can be found in ref. 24. Now, a framework for a conceptual model of process planning will be introduced. As shown in Figure 29.9, this model consists of five modular activities, not only for process planning alone but also for the integration of process planning with shop floor control. The following is a concise summary of the planning activities within each module as described by Ham and Lu (25).

Despite these difficulties, searching for such a generic conceptual framework is critical and has been pursued by many research organizations in this country. A good example of such a framework is proposed in ref. 26. Figure 29.9 shows the structure of the proposed framework, which consists of five modular activities. It is interesting to note, as pointed out by the proposer, that process planners do not always plan in a breadth-first manner within this hierarchical structure. The following is a concise summary of the planning activities within each module.

I. The part model interpretation module.
    A. *Input:* part models from design.
    B. *Perform:* feature extraction.
    C. *Output:* manufacturing features that need to be planned for.
II. The routing sequence planning module.
    A. *Input:* manufacturing features that need to be planned for.
    B. *Perform:* the number and order of operations the manufacturing workstation needs for each operation and the prior and subsequent geometry for each operation.
    C. *Output:* routing sequence plan.
    D. This module normally contains five submodules.
        1. Feature planning submodule.
            a. Organize manufacturing features into a feature-access graph to represent the precedence of the machining of features based on their access.
            b. Decompose composite or complex manufacturing features into simpler features.
        2. Process selection submodule.
            a. Determine the necessary manufacturing process required to make each feature.
        3. Orientation planning submodule.
            a. Determine possible locating surface on the part for the machining of each feature.
            b. Consider feasible tool axis approach for a feature such that the axis is approachable with the set of locating surface.
        4. Machine tool planning submodule.
            a. To select feasible machine tools.
            b. A machine tool module is needed to check the following.
                i. Relative motions.
                ii. Travel limit.
                iii. Additional machining attachments.
                iv. Desirable accuracy.

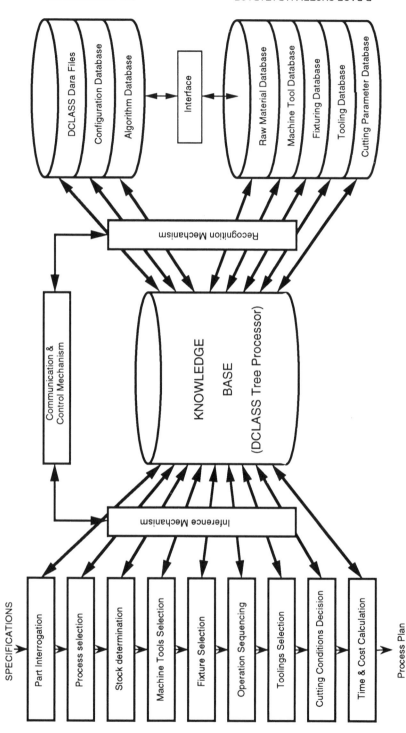

Figure 29.8. An architecture of an expert process planning system.

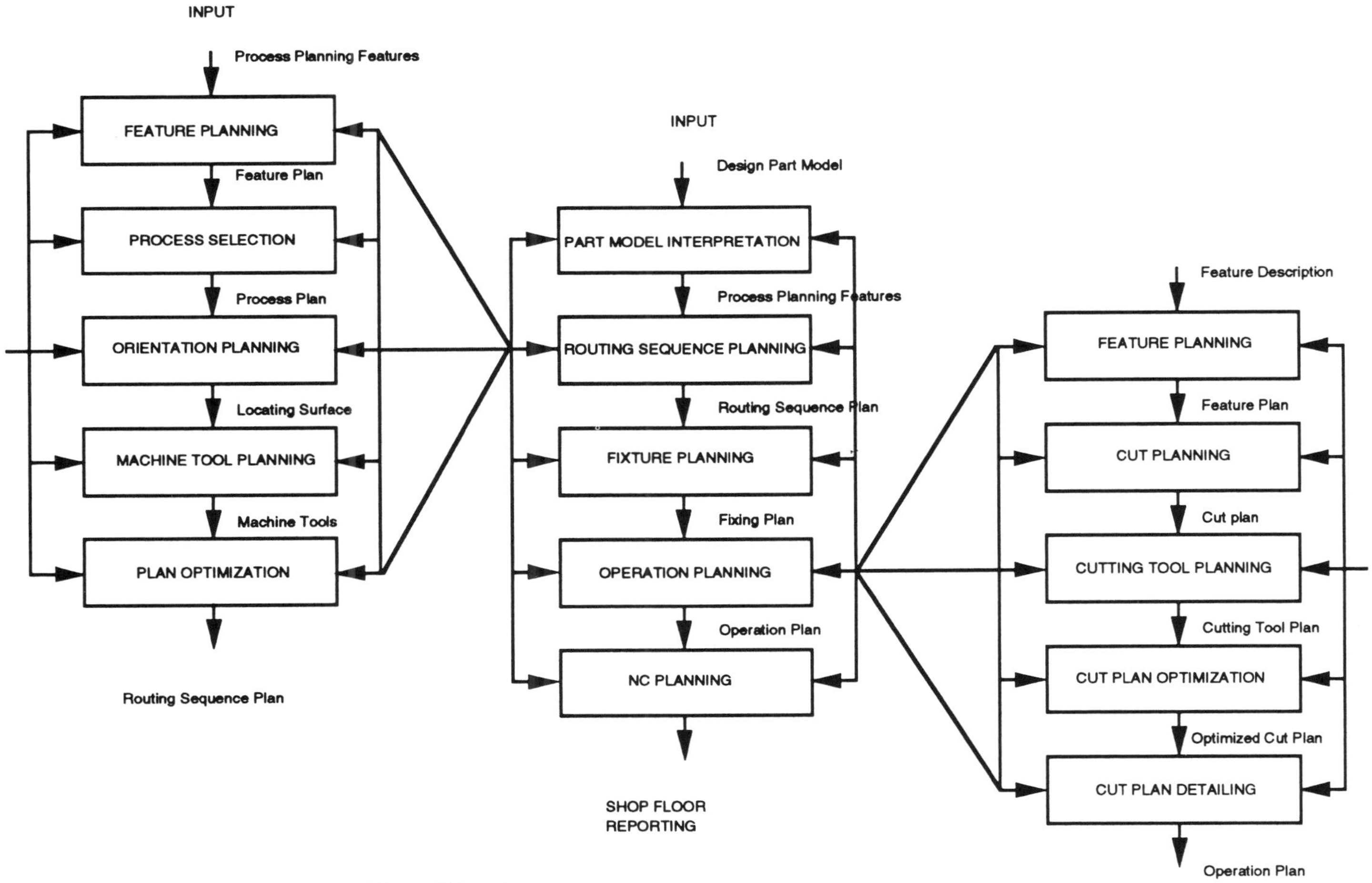

Figure 29.9. A conceptual framework for CAPP systems (26).

      5. Plan optimization submodule.
        a. To group cuts into common fixing setups.
        b. To group fixing setups into common machining operations.
        c. To order operations.
III. The fixture planning module.
    A. *Input:* part module from design, features to be machined, and their locating surfaces.
    B. *Perform:* determine the correct fixing device to locate the part and restrain it for the machining operations.
    C. *Output:* fixing devices and methods.
    D. Functional requirements for fixtures are as follows.
      1. Resting equilibrium.
      2. Deterministic location.
      3. Clamping equilibrium.
      4. Total constraint.
      5. Use standard fixtures whenever possible.
IV. The operation planning module.
    A. *Input:* part module, feature volumes to be machined, machine tools, and fixtures.
    B. *Perform:* details specifications related to the execution of a cut.
    C. *Output:* determine cutting tools, number and levels of cuts, the order of cuts, the machining parameters for a cut, instructions for a machinist, and NC tape specifications.
    D. There are five submodules.
      1. Feature planning submodule.
        a. Decide on a sequence for machinable features.
        b. Decompose machinable features into machinable volumes.
      2. Cut planning submodule.
        a. Decompose machinable volumes into specific cuts that can be performed on the specified machines.
        b. Select levels of cuts (rough, semifinished, finished).
      3. Cutting tool planning submodule.
        a. Determine the cutting tool to use based on geometry and tolerance definition of each machining cut.
      4. Cut plan optimization submodule.
        a. Group cuts that have intersecting tool lists into the same tool change.
        b. Order the plan into a good machining sequence.
      5. Cut plan detailing submodule.
        a. Selection of tool holder.
        b. Specify cut depth, feed, speed data.
        c. Report the operation plan.
V. NC planning module.
    A. To implement a generative CAPP system based on the above framework poses many great technical challenges that recently have been studied in United States. A brief summary of these challenges are as follows.
    B. Knowledge-based representation and organization.
      1. Modular, iterative, and multiple perspective nature of the task.
    C. Product definition (should be complete, flexible, comprehensive, and exact).
    D. Feature definition, representation, and recognition.
      1. Primary activities involved in feature recognition.
        a. Identify machined faces.
        b. Create machined volume(s).
        c. Classify machined feature(s).
    E. Geometric reasoning.
      1. Reasoning about shapes other than rectangular and prismatic features (cannot treat as macros with standard attributes).
    F. Process optimization.
      1. Transform a list of independent cut specifications into an optimal, linearized machining sequence.

Many AI-based approaches have been researched to respond to the above challenges. While the knowledge-based expert system is still the most commonly employed technique in developing generative CAPP, other AI-based techniques, such as machine learning, case-based reasoning, and qualitative physics, have also been developed recently. It is expected that these research efforts will soon result in more enhanced reasoning and representation approaches to intelligent CAPP. Research results have shown that to implement a knowledge base for an integrated process planning system will require not only a symbol-manipulation language such as LISP or PROLOG but also an object-oriented programming language such as the C or C++. For some complex decisions, an expert knowledge-based system is not enough; some fuzzy logic and neural networks are needed.

New Generation of CAPP Systems

In the last three decades, the aspect of CAPP has been dramatically changed. Although the final goal of CAPP research remains the same, its contents and emphases have gone through significant changes. Many new-generation CAPP systems have been developed. In comparison with traditional CAPP systems, the new generation of CAPP systems have several advantages. First, AI techniques have significantly impacted the development of CAPP systems. Although the new generation of CAPP can still be categorized into the previous three approaches (variant, generative, and semigenerative), AI based CAPP systems are remarkably different from traditional generative CAPP systems. The implementation tools for the new-generation systems involve many new techniques, such as knowledge-based techniques, object-orientated programming techniques, common product model techniques, and virtual single manufacturing database techniques. In terms of the application of AI techniques in the development of CAPP, not only knowledge-based and expert systems are used but also fuzzy logic and neural networks techniques have been involved. Some new-generation systems have employed the machine-learning approach (27). The second advantage is that integrability has been dramatically improved. As discussed earlier, CAPP plays a key role in integrating design and manufacturing. In terms of the integration of design and manufacturing, the feature techniques have been recognized as essential tools for eventually integrating process planning and design. Many research studies have provided applicable approaches such as feature recognition, feature classification, and geometrical reasoning. Many feature-based process planning systems have been reported recently.

In terms of integration with down stream functions, there are also some good results reported for the integration of process planning and production scheduling. So far, research studies in this area have used several approaches in terms of nonlinear process planning, dynamic process planning, closed-loop process planning, just-in-time process planning, and so on. Although the final integration of process planning with production scheduling is still on its way, some initial research has resulted in quite promising progress (1). Generally speaking, the difference between the new generation of CAPP and the traditional CAPP lies in three aspects: integrability, intelligency, and high techniques orientation.

29.4   THE FUTURE TRENDS OF CAPP

Because of the rapid development of computer techniques, the research aspects of development of computer-aided process planning systems have been changed dramatically compared with the initial research activities. Many research issues have been carried out in the last three decades. AI techniques have been successfully introduced into computer-aided process planning systems so that the systems can have experienced process planners' expertise for making process plans. Manufacturing features can be recognized from a geometrical model directly so that the CAD data can be transferred to process planning model. Many generative process planning systems have been developed so that the automated process planning concepts can be realized. While all these promising results are being carried out, the original goal of the development of computer-aided process planning still remains the same: to integrate design and manufacturing. Yet some crucial issues have not been solved completely and have impeded the progress of the development of automated process planning systems. In this section some of these crucial issues for research interests will be discussed and the near future trends of CAPP development will be noted.

The Challenges of CAPP Research

The issues involved in planning in the manufacturing environment require coordination between people and organizations, perhaps over time and across distance, and thus are often much more complicated than those involved in individual human planning. The difficulties are mainly due to the following factors (25).

1. The designer's intention may not always be clear to the manufacturing engineer who will act on that intention. The respective languages used in their professions, the ways in which they express their intentions, their critical concerns, and their perspectives may all differ.

2. Automation of process planning requires that part features can be automatically extracted from the product model without human interaction, but existing interfaces of CAD systems do not sufficiently consider this requirement of automated process planning. Needed information may be inaccessible or in an inappropriate form. Engineering drawings are currently used by designers to communicate with manufacturing engineers, but these drawings may sometimes contain insufficient data, or the data may be hidden in forms that cannot be directly used, or extraneous data may be included that obscures the relevant information.

3. The designer generating the drawings is often not aware of the constraints and limited resources that the manufacturing engineer has to deal with when carrying out these intentions. This may be due to either a lack of communication or the designer's lack of experience with production or lack of information about the factory facility. Regardless of the reasons, it results in plans that cannot be smoothly executed or that can be executed only with greater cost.

4. The amount of time between the planning-generation phase (at the design department) and the planning-execution phase (on the shop floor) is normally much longer than that involved in individual daily planning. Due to the dynamic nature of a production environment, it is likely that by the time a design is ready to be manufactured, the constraints that were used in generating this plan have already changed greatly, and thus that plan has become less optimal or even totally invalid.

5. The generation and execution of a complete production plan normally involve many different organization units and may often span a long period of time and different geographic locations. These conditions make the plan-monitoring progress, critical for plan improvement, difficult, if not impossible. Without this feedback from the shop floor, it becomes difficult to measure the quality or goodness of a plan for future enhancement.

6. In an automated environment, process and operations planning must result in data which have to deal with the utmost detail and all these data have to be available before the actual manufacturing starts. Interpretation, adaptation, and completion of data in a later phase are not applicable.

The above difficulties are real challenges faced by researchers attempting to develop computer-aided process planning systems. Some research efforts are already devoted to addressing these difficulties. However, they will not result in significant impact unless means are devised to deal with these difficulties in a cohesive and integrated fashion. Furthermore, there are three interrelated aspects of the subject that must be addressed cooperatively by researchers working in the process planning area to achieve the goal of integrated planning.

1. *Automating Existing Planning Activities.* Computer systems must be developed to assist and/or automate some portion of the planning activities according to the way in which they are currently being performed by human beings. The majority of the present research in manufacturing planning falls into this category (28).

2. *Anticipating Future Planning Challenges.* The requirements for manufacturing planning in future factories must be anticipated, and planning techniques must be developed to meet these future needs. Although this has been recognized as an important activity, to date there are only few research efforts aimed in this direction. The progressive introduction of new automated manufacturing systems, such as flexible manufacturing cells or systems, leads to task expansion in process planning. A functional correlation between the degree of automation and the necessary planning effort is obvious.

3. *Suggesting a More Logical Planning Structure.* Suggestions should be made, based on the characteristics of various computer automation technologies and planning approaches, on the most logical ways of conducting process planning in practice so that it becomes more automatable by computers. This requires a flexible use of different planning scenarios and the generation of alternative solutions on a cost-selective basis. These suggestions can be viewed as the feedback from computer-based automation technology to process planning. This challenge, perhaps the most significant in terms of its cost–benefit return, is, unfortunately, the most neglected one. But it is obvious that process planning faces a number of influences that will change the contents of the planning procedure.

Software Aspects

Software progress has paralleled that of computer hardware and CAPP technology. FORTRAN was the language many early CAPP systems used due to its ability to handle calculations and its familiarity in the engineering community. According to a survey (2), a number of systems are still FORTRAN based despite some advances made in artificial intelligence class languages such as Lisp and Prolog. With the great demand of intelligent process planning systems, the Lisp and Prolog programming languages have received more and more attention, and many systems are implemented in them. But to reduce the implementation workload and time, the use of market-available expert shells and toolkits will be more convenient for developers. Some commercially available shells have been listed in ref. 29. However, development of updated process planning systems not only must increase the intelligence of the systems but also must gain much integrability, which will require object-oriented programming techniques. As a matter of fact, object-oriented programming has been around for nearly 20 yr, since the development of Smalltalk (30). In the mid-1980s, it gaining widespread interest as a scheme for developing programmed systems. Object-oriented programming combines datum types needed to define a computational entity and the methods (executable code) necessary to manipulate the object values. In other words, each object contains its own data and the procedures that operate on data. This is in contrast with conventional programming that treats data and procedures as distinct and separate entities. Because an intelligent and integrated process planning system must be integrated with some object-oriented database for some necessary manufacturing information when the system makes decisions, object-oriented programming techniques well-suited for CAPP development.

Another important aspect of software of CAPP development is migratory ability. With the rapid development of computer technology, the boundary between mini–micro and mini–mainframe is diminishing. In addition, one clear and growing trend in the engineering market that is reflected throughout the computer industry is the movement toward distributed computing. The widespread integration of PCs, workstations, file servers, minicomputerus, mainframes, and even supercomputers along a network is helping the network business grow faster than all other computer segments by 40% to 45% each year (31). This indicates that many manufacturing enterprises and engineering institutions are implementing a comprehensive engineering network as a central part of their competitive computing strategy. Developed process planning software must be able to communicate with other software packages throughout the network.

Hardware Aspects

Hardware development has come full circle from the earliest implementations of CAPP systems. As the digital computer first attained widespread acceptance, the only available machines possessing the requisite power for a task such as process planning were mainframe systems that featured individual workstations. As computer technology progressed, the personal computer moved to the forefront and most CNC manufacturing shops featured machines on the shop floor controlled by independent personal computers that could be linked to a centralized database by means of a local area network (LAN). This provided adequate control for individual machines but failed to accommodate the information that ultimately became available in developing CAPP software packages.

When engineering workstations first appeared in the early 1980s, many engineers and software researchers found that the advantages included the ability to set many standards, perform multitasking by means of 32-bit architecture, and run UNIX operating systems. Engineering workstations perform multitasking, the concurrent execution of several programs or program parts, making the typical workstation a suitable platform for development of automated process planning systems. Many workstation vendors have developed much of the CAD and CAM software as hardware that is fixed into the workstations. This provides considerable convenience for CAPP development. That is one of the reasons why engineering workstations are so popular in CAPP development.

However, selection of a platform for the development of an automated process planning is still not that easy. Currently, the degree of CAPP software development has scattered the selection across a wide spectrum, depending on the use. The selection of platforms is also influenced by the environment in which the CAPP systems are going to be employed. In the most recent manufacturing environments, miniframe computers are widely employed for different purposes, from scientific calculation to production management. Many software packages are installed in the existing machines. If the development goal is going to integrate these existing software packages and to integrate different production functions, it may be a wise idea to choose the existing minimain frame machines as your platform, or at least the development should be compatible between the mini and mainframe computers. This offers only a slight advantage in terms of machine control but is truly the only way that complete CIM integration can be achieved. The same CPU and database may be accessed by all other company departments, i.e., personnel, finance, materials management, and marketing. A protocol for determining the hardware requirements for a facility interested in implementing a CAPP system is provided in ref. 32. Some manufacturing cells are integrated by means of workstations. If the goal of the CAPP is to be integrated into the cell control, then obviously the workstation will be the best choice. As was mentioned, many CAD and CAM programs have already been made into hardware installed in the workstations. To integrate CAPP in these CAD and CAM programs, there is no other choice for the workstation. If the purpose of the development is to solve specific research issues, i.e., the scope of the research is not wide, the PC may be a better choice in terms of economy. Recently, development of new features of PCs has dramatically increased their capacity and capability. The current Intel 80486 CPU with its 32-bit architecture operating at 25-66 MHz has put the PC in a good position to be the candidate of choice for CAPP development. When the new PCs with the Intel Pentium microprocessor operating at 66 MHz are available with the Unix operating system, the PC will probably become the first choice for CAPP development.

User Friendly Interface

The user friendly interface is one of the criteria for evaluating a CAPP system. However, there is no standard against which to measure the level of the user friendly interface. To find out if an interface is user friendly, it is necessary to clarify the users who will interface with CAPP systems. In general, there are about three different types of users who need to interface with CAPP systems.

- Process planners who possess valuable domain expertise for process planning that needs to be transferred to the knowledge base of the system.
- Knowledge engineers who are in charge of implementing the knowledge base and production rules and are supposed to be good at system development, knowledge acquisition, and representation.
- System operators who principally work on the system operation and are supposed to know the system operation system well.

Actually, in the real development environment, the job tasks are not as clear as the above categories. For example, in some cases, the process planner can also be as a system operator, and a knowledge engineer may also be required to have some process planning expertise. Unfortunately, one cannot learn so much different knowledge on his or her limited brain. On the other hand, even if one could do the three jobs listed above, it would be very time-consuming. In most cases, it is just impossible. So the demand of the user friendly interface will reduce the burden of the above three jobs and eventually may replace one or two jobs. The user friendly interface is mainly focused on two concerns: (1) process planning knowledge acquisition and modification and (2) system access and communication.

Process planning knowledge acquisition and modification are mainly interfaced with knowledge engineers as discussed above. The user friendly interface at this level is an inner layer interface. It requires the easy communication between knowledge engineers and the knowledge base. The decision rules may be inputted and modified in terms of an English-like or English language. Employees should be able to use the system without the knowledge engineer's help. Eventually, the knowledge engineer can be replaced by the process planner who may directly put his or her expertise into the knowledge base but who does not require any programming experience. This interface level means that the knowledge base can be accessed by anyone who can modify the production rules.

System access and communication are mainly interfaced with system operators, as discussed above. The user friendly interface at this level is an external layer interface. It requires an interactive and easy communication between system operators and operating systems. Interactive access into the system should be driven by means of a user menu. Here the English-like or English language operation is also required. With the rapid development of operating systems and Window facilities, the system operator can directly access and operate the system by means of mouse. The operation command may be released by means of pushing buttons.

From above discussion it is seen that the user friendly interface will dramatically reduce the number of users and simplify the process of operation. The person who access the system need not know anything about artificial intelligence, knowledge base, programming language or the operating system and hardware.

Feature-based Design

Recently, considerable work has been done in terms of feature-based design, which is used to relate shapes to abstract design needs. Features are generic shapes with which engineers associate certain attributes and knowledge that are useful in reasoning about the product. Features encapsulate the engineering significance of portions of the geometry and, as such, are important in product design, product definition, and reasoning for a variety of applications. Many researchers have proposed definitions for features; some of the definitions follow.

1. Codifiable properties derived from a taxonomy of shapes for a particular classification scheme.
2. A specific geometric configuration formed on the surface, edge, or corner of a workpiece intended to modify outward appearance or to achieve a given function.
3. A characteristic volume that describes a portion of a part such as a hole, boss, pad, or pocket.

Feature Classification

Features can be broadly classified into two main categories:

Explicit Features. All the geometric details of the feature are fully defined.

Implicit Features. Sufficient information is supplied to define the feature, but the full geometric details must be calculated when required.

As an example, consider a cylindrical blind hole. An explicit representation in a solid modeler will contain details of the cylindrical surface and the surface at the base of the hole together with the equation of the edge curves. An implicit representation of the same hole might specify the centerline, depth, and radius. The explicit information can be computed from the implicit data. There are seven features:

1. Circular through hole.
2. Circular pad.
3. Rectangular pad.
4. Rectangular pocket with an interior rectangular boss with a blind hole.
5. Face (area to be plated).
6. A beveled edge.
7. A corner break.

The information provided from design to process planning is a representation of the finished part. It is the process planner's function to specify how the part will be manufactured. The features that define the attribute associated with manufacturing are called the manufacturing features. In many cases, the manufacturing features are similar to the design features. A hollow cylinder (hole) for a process planner is not just a hole; he or she needs further information such as a bored hole or a reamed hole.

Features are incorporated in the part model from the beginning. Generic feature definitions are placed in a library from which features are picked up by specifying the dimension and location parameters as well as various other attributes. Once the features are pulled out, various operations can be performed on them such as adding and deleting. Design with features allows a higher level of abstraction for design. This method is pragmatic in nature because the designer has a set of features to choose from, and he or she builds an artifact using the features that are essentially building blocks for the production definition. The function of the monitor here is to guide the designer in his or her work. It will point out mistakes made by the designer and help rectify them. As an example, the monitor will not allow the designer to combine the features in ways in which the system cannot interpret.

After the design is completed, it is stored in the primary representation, and for the downstream applications, the design is routed through the secondary representation. This conversion can be done by using the knowledge coded into computer programs. Thus this method allows the development of intelligent CAD systems. Hence the ability of the system to convert the information successfully is the core of the entire intelligent CAD system.

Feature Recognition

Feature recognition in simple terms means extracting and recognizing the features. This is defined as converting a model of lower level entities into a model of higher level entities, or converting a geometric model that consists of lower level entities like lines and points into a feature-based model, which is defined in terms of higher level entities like holes, grooves, and pockets. The main reason for this conversion is the ability of the features to be associated with the knowledge about the way the feature can be manufactured. Then in the feature recognition process, once the geometric model is constructed or created by the designer, the computer software or programs in the system should process the database that defines the design and should automatically extract and recognize the features. A simple schematic of feature recognition process is illustrated in Figure 29.10.

To satisfy the needs of feature recognition processes and accomplish the task, the following points are necessary with respect to the feature recognizer.

1. There should be a proper representation scheme. This means, the scheme created or used for feature recognition should facilitate automatic feature recognition.
2. Each feature should have a unique definition. In the representation scheme that is developed or used for feature recognition, there will be a host of feature definitions that help in recognizing and classifying the features. For proper recognition, no two features should have the same definition, and no feature should have more than one definition.
3. The inference mechanism or procedure used should be consistent and complete. In other words, the procedure should be able to identify the features completely and correctly.

There are a number of approaches used to recognize the features from both two- and three-dimensional CAD representations. Some of these are as follows (14):

1. Syntactic pattern recognition.
2. State transition diagrams and automata.
3. Decomposition approach.
4. Expert system and logic.
5. CSG (set theoretic) approach.
6. Graph based approach.

In general, a feature-oriented, feature-based design model is supposed to perform the following functions (33):

1. Functional feature-based design; a part is modeled by constructing selected library features with Boolean operators.

Figure 29.10.   Feature recognition process.

2. Parametric design; it creates models quickly, modifies related parameters efficiently and maintains the relationships between parameters within and between features.

3. A graphics, window-based design tool; product models are created and manipulated in a graphics, user friendly environment.

4. A solid model representation for products; a geometric modeler kernel is integrated into the modeling system.

5. Product description language; it defines a syntax to describe products that is capable of handling both geometric and nongeometric information.

6. A mechanism for defining generic features and adding features to the library; it allows the user to customize the system and avoids the difficulty of working with a hard-coded set of features.

7. Rendering, shading, and viewing facilities for model display.

8. Object-oriented programming implementation; maintains the hierarchical relationship between features in a part and between parts in a product.

Intelligent and Integrated Process Planning

Recent research has indicated that an automated process planning system plays a key role in realizing the concept of concurrent engineering. The automated process planning system naturally bridges the gap between CAD and CAM. It can provide real integrated production. To develop a concurrent engineering environment, the development of the next generation of automated process planning systems will be emphasized on two issues: intelligence and integrability. AI-based systems have been used in implementing automated process planning systems. A knowledge-based scheme is not only used for selection of machining processes, raw materials, and operation sequencing but also used for reasoning geometrical models and feature relationships. With the rapid development of automated process planning systems, the present knowledge-based systems are not sufficient enough for the intelligent and integrated process planning system. Other AI-based techniques, such as neural networks, fuzzy logic decisions, and machine learning schemes, have attracted more and more research attention. With the application of neural networks, the automated process planning system will not only generate process plans but also be self-learning and knowledge generating. Some decision-making knowledge that is not implemented in the knowledge base can be generated by the system itself. The system will also be able to do self-evaluation. The comprehensive intelligent and integrated process planning systems, especially when the process planning system is going to integrate production scheduling for available machines selection, will require a lot of fuzzy decision making. The optimal setup planning based on tolerance analysis will require the function of neural networks. Some researchers have already put their attention on a hybrid model that can combine the functions of expert systems, neural networks, and fuzzy logic schemes together to make an intelligent process planning system.

To realize the concept of concurrent engineering, the development of the next generation of process planning systems should also emphasize integration. Here the term integration means that the next generation of process planning systems should be able to integrate the design function (CAD), the manufacturing function (CAM), the production planning function, the shop floor control function, and the manufacturing resource planning function. The reasons for the integration of process planning are as follows:

- Improved efficiency in the information flow.
- Improved quality of the process planning.
- Reduction of human errors.
- Functional integration of process planning and scheduling, enabling a quick search for alternative solutions for optimization in the use of equipment and production control.
- Flexible use of the different functions.

Furthermore, the implementation of the integrated system must be based on:

- A uniform product description based on proper features.
- The use of different modules for different functions.
- The use of an uniform user interface for every module.

- The use of an uniform database interface for every module.
- The possibility of facilitating user interaction at the request of the operator.

Process planning systems, to provide the integration, automation, and flexibility needed in future process planning, should

- Be generative.
- Be technology based.
- Use features as a technological and communicational interface between design and process planning.
- Be able automatically to extract all product data.
- Use a supervisory control system to ensure user friendliness and flexibility in use.
- Integrally support all planning tasks, including capacity planning and scheduling.
- Make decisions based on optimization techniques (and in knowledge base systems).
- Be fit for closed-loop planning.

A framework for integrated planning should have a multidimensional perspective. In other words, integration is needed in the following areas:

- *Planning Knowledge.* Science-based principles must be integrated with experience-based knowledge. Physics must be integrated with heuristic methods.
- *Planning Activities.* Process planning must be integrated downward with operation planning and upward with production planning. Operation planning must be integrated with physics (or models) of the manufacturing process being planned.
- *Planning Techniques.* Techniques such as group technology, modeling and simulation, optimization, and knowledge-based approaches must all be integrated into a truly robust planning system. The approach of building separate planning systems based on a single technique (e.g., a rule-based systems) and then interfacing them with other systems that were built on different techniques is not sufficient for integrated planning.
- *Planning Constraints.* Various planning constraints—local or global, technical or nontechnical, user provided or expert provided—should be integrated during the planning stage rather than being added to the system afterward. This requires viewing manufacturing planning as a cooperative problem-solving activity that incorporates various concerns simultaneously.
- *Planning Feedback.* Mechanisms must be provided to incorporate feedback automatically from the planning results to improve future planning decisions. Closed-loop planning is fundamentally different from the current open-loop planning architecture. It requires the extension of present planning activities to the plan monitoring and execution stages.

29.5 SUMMARY

Computer-aided process planning is such a wide area and many technologies have been involved in research and implementation of CAPP systems, and there has been rapid development of computer-aided techniques. It is not easy to predict the future trends. This chapter discussed several crucial issues concerning the development of CAPP systems. During the discussion, the direction of future trends was indicated. The need for further efforts in the research and development of CAPP systems is obvious. Hardware and software selection will still be the important first step in the development of CAPP. However, researchers and developers should focus on intelligence and integrability. This is knowledge-intensive in nature. The traditional computer-based methods are unable to deal with the challenges of intelligent and integrated process planning, because they are good at processing data for information-intensive domains but not well suited for automatic inferencing for knowledge-intensive tasks. Rather than simply processing information and data, AI-based techniques are designed for capturing, representing, organizing, and utilizing knowledge on computers, and hence they will be the key to intelligent and integrated process planning in the future. The discussion on decision making pointed out that knowledge-based techniques alone are not sufficient enough to support the requirements of the development of intelligent and integrated process planning systems. Here a comprehensive and sophisticated decision-making modular system must involve an integrated model of knowledge-bases, fuzzy logic, and neural networks. In looking at future, "it is hoped that this chapter can be considered as 'casting a stone to attract jade'—and it offers a few commonplace remarks concerning introduction problems of CAPP so that others may more easily get started" (2).

BIBLIOGRAPHY

1. H.-C. ZHANG, "IPPM-A Prototype to Integrated Process Planning and Job Shop Scheduling Functions," Submitted by M. Eugene Merdrant, Ann. CIRP **42**(1) 513–517, (1993).

2. L. ALTING and H.-C. ZHANG, "Computer Aided Process Planning: The State-of-the-art Survey," *Int. J. Product. Res.* **27**(4), 553–585 (1989).

3. C.H. LINK, *CAPP, CAM-I Automated Process Planning System*, paper presented at NC Conference, CAM-I, Inc., Arlington, Tex., 1976.

4. A. HOUTZEEL, *The MICLASS System*, paper presented at CAM-I's Executive Seminar, CAM-1, Inc., Arlington, Tex., 1976.

5. J. TULKOFF, "Process Planning in the Computer-Integrated Factory," *CIM Rev.* **4**(1), 24–27 (Fall 1987).

6. R.A. WYSK, *An Automated Process Planning and Selection Program: APPAS*, Ph.D. thesis, Purdue University, West Lafayette, Ind., 1977

7. H. WALDMAN, "Process Planning at Sikorsky" in J. Tulkoff, ed. Computer and Automated Systems Association of SMI, Dearborn, Mich., pp. 64–68 (1985).

8. B.J. DAVIES and I.L. DARBYSHIRE, "The Use of Expert Systems in Process-Planning," *Ann. CIRP* **33**(1) 303–306 (1984).

9. T. LENAU and T. ALTING, *XPLAN—An Expert Process Planning System, Proceedings of the 2nd International Expert Systems Conference*, London, 1986.

10. D.K. ALLEN, "An Introduction to Computer-Aided Process Planning," *CIM Rev.* Vol. 4, No. 1, 7–23, (Fall 1987).

11. C. EMERSON and I. HAM, "An Automated Coding and Process Planning System Using a DEC PDP-10," *Comput. Ind. Eng.* **6**(2) 159–169 (1982).

12. J.W. LYONS, *The Role of Process Planning in Computer Integrated Manufacturing*, paper presented at the 7th International Conference on the Computer as a Design Tool, London, 1986.

13. *Software Enhances Accuracy and Consistency*, American Machinist and Automated Manufacturing, **131**, 65–68 (June 1987).

14. S. JOSHI and T.C. CHANG, "Graph-Based Heuristic for Recognition of Machined Features from a 3D Solid Model," *Comput. Aided Des.* **20**(2) page 58–66 (1988).

15. K.A. REED, D. HARROD, and W. CONROY, *The Initial Graphics Exchange Specification, Version 5.0,* National Institute of Standards and Technology Gaithersburg, Md., 1990, Interagency Rep. 4412.

16. M. PALMER and M. GILBERT, *Guidelines for the Development and Approval of Application Protocols,* 1991, Working Draft Ver. 0.7, ISO TC184/SC4/WG4, Doc. NI.

17. G. CARVER and H.M. BLOOM, "Concurrent Engineering through Product Data Standards" in Leondes' ed. *Control and Dynamic Systems: Advances in Theory and Application,* Vol 46, Academic Press, San Diego, Calif., 1991.

18. S.N. CLARK and D. LIBES, *Fed-X—The NIST Express Translator,* National Institute of Standards and Technology, Gaithersburg Md., 1992, PDES Testbed Rep. Ser. NISIIR 4822.

19. T.C. CHANG, *Expert Process Planning for Manufacturing,* Addison-Wesley Publishing Co., Inc., Reading, Mass., 1990.

20. W.J. ZDEBLICK, *Process Planning Evolution—The Impact of Artificial Intelligence* paper presented at the 19th CIRP International Seminar on Manufacturing Systems, University Park, Pa., 1987.

21. D.K. ALLEN and P.R. SMITH, *Computer-Aided Process Planning,* Brigham Young University, Provo, Utah, 1980.

22. Z. DONG and A. SOOM, "Automatic Optimal Tolerance Design for Related Dimension Chains," *Manufact. Rev.* **3**(4), 262–271 (1990).

23. Z. WU, W.H. ELMARAGHY, and H.A. ELMARAGHY, "Evaluation of Cost-Tolerance Algorithms for Design Tolerance Analysis and Synthesis," *Manufact. Rev.* **1**(3), 168–179, (1988).

24. H.-C. ZHANG and L. ALTING, *Computerized Manufacturing Process Planning Systems*, Chapman and Hall London, UK, 1993.

25. I. HAM and C.-Y. LU, "Computer-Aided Process Planning: The Present and the Future," *Ann. CIRP* **37**(2), 591–602 (1988).

26. *XPS-E Revisited: A New Architecture and Implementation Approach for an Automated Process Planning Systems, Computer-Aided Manufacturing-International Arlington, Texas* 1988, CAM-I DR-88-PP-02.

27. L.-Y. LU and G. ZHANG, "A Combined Inductive Learning and Experimental Design Approach to Manufacturing Operation Planning," *J. Manufact. Sys.* **9**(2), 103–115 (1990).

28. W. EVERSHEIM and J. SCHULZ, "CIRP Technical Reports, Survey of Computer Aided Process Planning Systems," *Ann. CIRP* **34**(2), 607–615 (1985).

29. A.B. BADIRU, "Expert Systems and Industrial Engineers: A Practice Guide to a Successful Partnership," *Comput. Eng.* **14**(1), 1–13 (1988).

30. A. GOLDBERG and O. ROBSON, *Smalltalk-80, the Language and its Implication*, Addison-Wesley Publishing Co., Inc., Reading, Mass., 1983.

31. A. NILSSEN, "Workstations Still Hold the Edge," *Mech. Eng.*, **3**(5), 68–71 (May 1989)

32. Y.S. SHERIF and A.A. HEANEY, "Development of a Generic Database for CAE/CAD/CAM System at an Air Force Facility," *Microelect. Reliability* **30**(3), 555–564 (1990).

33. H.A. ELMARAGHY, K.F. ZHANG, and H. CHU, *A Function-Oriented Modeler Prototype*, McMaster University, Canada, 1992.

SECTION VII
QUALITY ENGINEERING

CHAPTER 30
Quality Engineering

KEVIN J. DOOLEY
University of Minnesota

30.1 INTRODUCTION

Product quality is the key competitive factor in industry today, and engineering plays a significant role in the success or failure of such efforts. The product life cycle incorporates identification of customer requirements, conceptual and detailed product design, process design, manufacture, distribution, and use. The traditional role of engineering in this life cycle is to obtain customer requirements from marketing, translate those into a product with specified engineering characteristics, and manufacture such products so that they conform to specifications. As such, engineering's traditional role in the quality system is to:

- Design products that meet customer needs and ensure product reliability.
- Develop manufacturing processes that are capable of meeting the technical requirements of the design.
- Provide metrology and associated data for the quality assurance department so that a poor quality product is not shipped out to the customer.
- Provide engineering design and process support so that when quality problems arise, quick fixes can be implemented.

In today's modern quality system the engineer plays a much more integrated and diverse role in the management of product quality:

- Meet face to face with customers and understand more directly their needs and the ways in which they will use the product, rather than relying on marketing systems to provide such information blindly.
- Develop products that not only have high reliability but also excel in maintainability and serviceability; minimize environmental impact; are manufacturable, and are robust to natural variations in manufacture, distribution, and use.
- Coordinate the simultaneous development of product, process, and quality system design.
- Continue to provide support for design and manufacturing problems but do so with an eye toward empowering the workers in the process and tapping into their collective expertise.
- Proactively seek out opportunities to reduce variation in the process.
- Benchmark and learn from other similar processes, both within and external to the organization.
- Have good interpersonal skills so that they can be effective members of quality improvement teams.

The purpose of this chapter is to expose the reader to a variety of concepts, tools, and methodologies associated with the design and manufacture of high quality products. The chapter provides different definitions of product quality, shows how quality function deployment can be used to ensure that quality issues are dealt with proactively during the conceptual design stage, and summarizes some of the basic concepts and tools used in reliability analysis. The discussion covers the measurement of quality in manufacturing, concepts and tools for reducing variation in manufacturing (statistical process control and design of experiments), and the differences between product control and process control. Two alternative views on the economics of quality are provided: conventional quality costs and the Taguchi loss function. The chapter concludes with a summary of some of the broader issues involved in quality improvement.

30.2   QUALITY ISSUES IN DESIGN

Definitions of Product Quality

There are many different ways in which one can define the meaning of the word *quality*. The Malcolm Baldrige National Quality Award (1) defines quality as meeting (and exceeding) customer expectations; quality is measured by customer satisfaction. The definition is useful for overall corporate quality strategy and is a good gauge of quality performance. It is not, however, useful for improving quality at the individual process level.

Crosby (2) defines quality as meeting requirements and says the only true measure of quality is through the cost of quality. Requirements are initially determined by the external customers; external needs are cascaded to the individual process through the concept of the *internal customer*. A customer can be defined as anyone to whom the work is handed (*work* could be a physical product, information, or a service). Thus there are a series of standards, or internal customer requirements, that are developed to define exactly what is meant by quality at each phase.

Deming (3) says that quality is a triangle involving the interaction of the product, the customer and the way he or she uses the product, and the training of the customer. This definition incorporates functionality, conformance, and perception. The designer of the product must take into account how the product will be used even beyond its stated purposes (e.g., using a screwdriver handle as a hammer).

Taguchi (4) states that quality is inversely related to the loss the product imparts to society; loss is related to functional variation and side effects; and functional variation is composed of manufacturing variation, product wear, and product use. This definition is useful from an engineering standpoint because functional variation is measured by a quality loss function, which states that minimizing quality loss comes from being on target (accuracy) with minimal variation (precision).

Mizuno (5) distinguishes between *exciting* and *required* quality. Required quality is the set of those characteristics that allow one to compete in the market (play the game), whereas exciting quality is the set of characteristics that differentiate the product from its competitors and thus form a market niche; they are also those qualities that were unexpected. Required quality characteristics act primarily as dissatisfiers, while exciting quality characteristics serve as satisfiers. A portable radio is expected to have a durable outside casing (expected), but the customer may be pleased to learn that a small light goes on when the battery power is low (exciting).

Juran (6) states that quality means fitness for use, which is parameterized by the dimensions of quality and is measured by quality characteristics. Thus quality is an abstract concept that is understood through its constituent abstract components and then quantified by actual performance measures. This turns out to be useful in both an engineering and marketing context because it helps define the multiple dimensionality of quality. Relative to Juran's definition Garvin (7) outlines the eight dimensions of quality:

1. *Performance*. Based on functional requirements.
2. *Features*. Customization and product differentiators.
3. *Reliability*. Mean time to failure for individual product components.
4. *Durability*. Overall expected life of product before disposal.
5. *Conformance*. How well the manufactured product meets design specifications.
6. *Serviceability*. Includes how external failures are dealt with.
7. *Aesthetics*. Personal judgment, not related to functionality.
8. *Perceived Quality*. Reputation and impact of advertising.

Other dimensions are also possible, such as maintainability, safety, and environmental impact. These dimensions in concert with life cycle cost make up the customer's perception of value, and thus determine customer satisfaction.

Often these different dimensions of quality will conflict with one another and the designer must make trade-offs. For example, supercomputers can be built according to the latest leading edge technologies, but then suffer from unreliable performance. Reliability can be improved but only at the loss of computational speed. Another example can be found in telephones. When AT&T was broken up through deregulation it went with a product strategy based on features, while clone competitors focused their efforts on being low cost producers. Although AT&T's features strategy was a failure, it did not lose market share because its competitors' poor record in performance and reliability was matched by AT&T's own excellence along these dimensions. Market success can be profoundly affected by the strategic trade-offs among various dimensions of quality.

Quality Function Deployment

Quality function deployment (QFD) is a methodology and collection of tools by which customer needs can be back-propagated into design, manufacturing, and distribution requirements. The premise is that by using the voice of the customer (VOC) one can ensure quality through the alignment and integration of different organizational functions. By working on many issues simultaneously and up front, a better design will be generated, thus leading to overall reduction of development time. QFD projects typically spend much more time (and money) in the conceptual design stage than would conventional development projects, but end up reducing overall development time in half (8).

The key tool in QFD is the matrix diagram, which helps translate needs from one area to another. The most commonly used matrix is the house of quality (9), which relates customer needs to technical requirements. An example is shown in Figure 30.1 for a calculator. Customer data (via surveys, focus groups, etc.) have shown that the feature *easy to see readout* is the most important, rating a 4 on a 1-to-5 scale, where 5 is the most important; three other quality issues have been mentioned. Four engineering characteristics of the product design (e.g, *weight*) have also been identified. The design team then identifies the correlation between the customer quality issues and the engineering design characteristics. For example, *panel glare* is strongly correlated with *easy to see readout,* whereas *panel adhesion* is only weakly correlated with *easy to see readout.*

Each correlation is assigned a score (typically 0-1-3-9 or 0-1-5-9 weights are used), and then that weight is multiplied by the customer importance rating and tallied down each row. Hence,

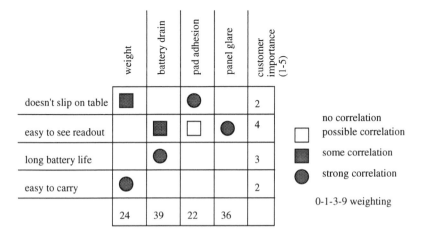

Figure 30.1. Quality function deployment matrix for a calculator.

battery drain is somewhat correlated with *easy to see readout* $(3 \cdot 4 = 12)$, and strongly correlated with *long battery life* $(3 \cdot 9 = 27)$, hence *battery drain* is allocated 39 total points. From these data we see that *battery drain* and *panel glare* are the two engineering characteristics that need the most attention. This attention may come in the form of tighter specifications, selection of higher quality processing techniques, selection of best quality vendor, etc. These rankings may also be used to select control characteristics for implementation of statistical process control.

QFD can be used in a variety of manners. One methodology frequently followed is to implement the following matrices (9):

Customer requirements vs. engineering characteristics

Engineering characteristics vs. part characteristics

Part characteristics vs. process steps (process planning)

Process steps vs. operations (operations management and logistics)

Thus the voice of the customer is fully deployed through all operations. Matrices can also be used to coordinate issues involving reliability and failure mode analysis, customer maintenance and service, process metrology, value analysis, etc. The size of the problem addressed can become a prohibitive issue; a matrix with 20 customer issues and 20 engineering characteristics has 400 cells of information to be filled in. Thus matrices are often broken down into subsystems (electrical subsystem, user interface, etc.) and a "matrix of matrices" is used to coordinate the system design as a whole. For more information about the implementation of QFD see refs. 5, 9, and 10.

Reliability Analysis

Reliability analysis involves the modeling and prediction of overall product reliability via information concerning component reliabilities and the experimental study of reliability performance via life testing. As such it is a collection of both analytical and experimental techniques. Modeling is probabilistic and statistical in nature, although the engineer should always strive to link the statistical description of reliability to the actual physical mechanisms at work in the product.

If one defines $p(t)$ as the probability distribution of failure (however that may be specifically defined in the context of product functionality) at time t, then

$$P(t) = \int_0^t p(t)dt \tag{1}$$

where $P(t)$ is the probability of failure up to time t. Conversely, the reliability function $R(t)$ is $1 - P(t)$. The instantaneous failure rate, or hazard rate, $z(t)$ is given by $p(t)/R(t)$, and defines the probability that an item which has survived until time t will immediately fail thereafter. A typical hazard rate curve is shown in Figure 30.2; because of the shape, the function is often referred to as the bathtub curve and is composed of three portions.

Initially failures are high because of manufacturing defects, etc. Products prone to such initial drop-out are often subjected to burn-in testing, by which only products that survive a series of rigorous tests will be passed on to the consumer. Such screening is standard in electronic components for which screening for internal failures is significantly less expensive than the cost of an external failure. Throughout most of its useful life, the product has a constant hazard rate, i.e., failures occur at a constant rate and are random. Finally, wearout mechanisms start to dominate product performance, and an increase in failure rate is observed.

The most common failure time distribution is the exponential distribution, which depends on a single parameter λ:

$$p(t) = \frac{1}{\lambda} e - t/\lambda \tag{2}$$

$$z(t) = \frac{1}{\lambda} \tag{3}$$

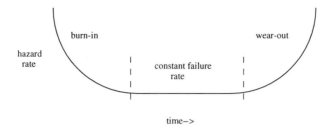

Figure 30.2. Bathtub reliability curve.

The exponential distribution describes a situation in which failure rate is constant and is applicable for many electrical and mechanical devices subjected to preburn in testing. The Weibull distribution (11) is a more generalized failure distribution that can take on a variety of shapes, depending on the shape parameter m and the scale parameter γ, and has a hazard rate of

$$z(t) = m\gamma t^{m-1} \ (m, \gamma > 0) \tag{4}$$

A metric used to quantify reliability performance is the mean time between failures (MTBF). The MTBF is simply the inverse of the failure rate; for the situation in which failure rate is constant (exponential failure distribution) the MTBF is λ. Product can be life tested to failure, and the subsequent average time between failures then directly estimates λ.

For m independent components in a design the $\text{MTBF}_{\text{system}}$ can be estimated by

$$\frac{1}{\text{MTBF}_{\text{system}}} = \sum_{j=1}^{m} \frac{1}{\text{MTBF}_j} \tag{5}$$

Consider a signal detector made up of an IC chip, a bulb, and a switch, with MTBFs of 10 yr, 0.25 yr, and 3.0 yr. Assume these components have constant failure rates and fail independently. The MTBF for the system is $1/\{(1/10) + (1/0.25) + (1/3)\}$, or 0.2256 yr. The probability that the system would fail after 1 month is $1 - e^{-t\lambda}$, or $1 - e^{-(1/12)} \cdot (1/0.2256) = 0.3088$.

Because the probability of failure is often very low, it becomes prohibitive to make statistical claims about reliability, as the required time of testing, or the number of components to test, becomes too large. For example, to demonstrate a failure rate of 1 per million hours (with 80% confidence) would require 0 observed failures after 1,610,000 h of testing, or 1610 items tested for 1000 h. The solution is to perform accelerated life tests, by which the product is exposed to excessive levels of temperature, temperature cycling, pressure, voltage, vibration, humidity, load, etc. Results from accelerated testing are then extrapolated to infer reliability performance under normal environmental conditions. For example the Arrhenius equation can be used to correlate useful life to test life in thermal aging. The inverse power law can be used for electrical components:

$$\frac{\text{life at normal voltage}}{\text{life at accelerated voltage}} = \left\{ \frac{\text{accelerated voltage}}{\text{normal voltage}} \right\}^{N} \tag{6}$$

where N is a system-dependent constant. The inverse law is often applicable to fatigue and stress measures. One can determine N empirically by plotting, for example, log stress versus log life, and the resultant slope will be $1/N$. See ref. 12 for more details.

30.3 QUALITY ISSUES IN MANUFACTURING

Measurement of Quality

Measurement, data collection, and data analysis are at the heart of quality improvement systems. The statistical tools of quality improvement allow one to supplement the expertise existing in the labor force and supporting engineering staff with factual information about process behavior.

There are typically myriad potential product and process characteristics that one could observe to infer product quality. The quality system must focus, however, on a limited number of these characteristics at any give time, because resources are limited. It is relatively easy, e.g., to collect every possible piece of datum and analyze on control charts, which many companies do. The company then however often lacks resources for problem solving and corrective action. It is better to focus efforts and do them correctly than to spread resources thin and end up implementing little improvement. In addition, the pareto principle typically holds in most situations, namely the majority of quality problems at any given time are confined to one to three key characteristics and associated root causes.

What data should be collected? The answer to this depends on the key customer concerns. The matrix diagram as shown above can be used to link customer quality issues to product and process characteristics, and relative rankings from the analysis could indicate priorities for data collection. Several additional perspectives can be used to identify data collection opportunities:

- Where have the problem areas been in the past?
- What characteristics cause significant problems because of cost, inspection, rework, scrap, etc?
- Where do I have access to data now?

Several of the quality tools that can be used in these initial problem formulation stages also may point out data collection opportunities. For example, it is always a good idea to generate a somewhat detailed process flow diagram for the process in question. One can examine each activity in the flow diagram and ask the question "How would I assess quality at this step?" In many complex products (such as microelectronics) it is difficult (but necessary) to identify on-line process measurements that can correlate with final product performance and yield. This is because the product itself cannot be tested until its final assembly, by which time it is too late to implement effective process control. The flow diagram coupled with some experimentation can help identify process variables that correlate with end quality characteristics.

There are two types of quality-related data that can be collected: variable and attribute. Variable data varies on a continuous scale (e.g., weight, dimension, time, and resistance), whereas attribute data portrays the presence or absence of certain prespecified discrete characteristics. Attribute data can be aggregated as an integer count (number of defects) or as a percentage (percent defective). Defects are considered attributes that detract from product quality. For example, a molded part may have voids, scratches, pits, and flashes. It is assumed that a defect of a given type could occur multiple times on a single product. A product is considered defective if it has one or more defects. In general, much more information about process and product quality is conveyed by variable versus attribute measures, and likewise between defect versus percent defective data. This increase in information is balanced by the additional cost of making a variable measure.

Operational Definitions

Once a characteristic is chosen, an operational definition must be determined. An operational definition can be considered a written measurement standard for that characteristic, done in great enough detail so that measures have repeatability across different personnel. It should include a statement of why the data are being collected as well as information concerning the conditions under which the measure is to be taken, location, metrology, procedure, calibration, aggregation, reporting, and method of analysis. The need for effective operational definitions is heightened for attribute data, where human subjectivity comes into play acutely. Visual aids, such as templates or pictures of acceptable versus unacceptable product can often help provide some consistency of measure for attribute data.

Variation in data collected will be composed of two main sources of variation: variation from the process and variation from the measurement system. The process variation is the measure of interest (the signal), but this signal is corrupted by noise (measurement variation). Operational definitions help minimize the effect of measurement variation by standardizing the measurement process. It is not uncommon to see a direct reduction in observed process variation after operational definitions have been implemented.

Measurement Capability

Before implementing statistical process control or a designed experiment, the capability of the measurement system should be quantified so that its impact on the resulting analysis is understood. A rough rule of thumb is that the standard deviation (or standard error σ) of the measurement system should be at most one-tenth as large as the width of the product specifications. This will ensure that subsequent observed data variation is due to the process itself and not a figment of variation in the measurement system. Unfortunately, this is not always the case—it is not uncommon to see measurement variation take up half of the specification width. Such practice will not lead to effective quality improvement.

One can quantify two aspects of the measurement system. Repeatability (i.e., precision) can be estimated by taking multiple measurements of the same product characteristic. The resulting standard deviation is an estimate of repeatability. Bias (i.e., accuracy) can only be estimated if a given "correct" answer is obtainable. Often an extremely accurate measure can be obtained through a more complex measurement system, which can then be used to gauge the bias of the metrology in question. A "golden sample" (e.g., a purposefully manufactured item with known dimensions) can also be used, comparing the resulting measure to the known quantity. Repeatibility and bias should be estimated across many different product variations, personnel, and environmental conditions. Repeatability and bias can be tracked over time on a control chart to make rational judgments about calibration.

Process Improvement

Process improvement will subsequently drive improvements in product quality, cost, and cycle time. By reducing variations in the process, you eliminate non–value added steps, such as inspection and rework. At the same time knowledge about the science of the process is enhanced, leading to further improvements. The cyclical nature of process improvement makes it a learning cycle. Shewhart's Plan-Do-Study-Act (PDSA) cycle (Figure 30.3) is a simple model of such a learning cycle.

PDSA is equivalent to the scientific method: through hypothesis, data generation, and analysis one gains an increased knowledge or "theory" of how the process operates. Knowledge is both the output of and a necessary constituent of PDSA. Any quality improvement activity can be broken into its PDSA parts; embedded in each part one can subsequently find smaller PDSA cycles. The recursive nature of PDSA has been recognized as a basic trait of human learning. The PDSA cycle also allows us to diagnosis dysfunctional quality improvement. Some systems never get out of the plan stage; there is a fear of testing the plan against reality. Many systems consistently operate in the do stage—a symptom of self-assuredness. There is no need to plan or study the results of our actions, because we are the experts and hence know our systems. A similar variant is Plan-Do-Act, by which results are treated as deterministic, and therefore, there is no need to study or check the results of actions. Finally,

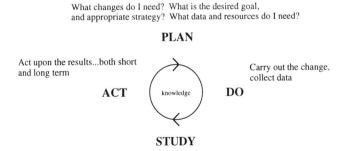

Figure 30.3. Shewhart's plan-do-study-act improvement cycle.

the Do-Check-Act system is the common shotgun approach, by which good intentions are outweighed by inevitable barriers that crop up because of unplanned contingencies.

There are two ways in which PDSA can be implemented: innovation and Kaizen. Innovation is characterized by its outcomes: huge breakthroughs in performance due to the use of fundamentally different approaches (e.g., technologies) from what have been used before. Innovation typically involves the expertise of specialists and as such is confined to individuals or small groups. Results come at unpredictable intervals and can possibly involve large expenditures of capital. *Kaizen* is the Japanese term for "continuous improvement." Kaizen is characterized by small incremental improvements that occur on a daily or weekly basis. While the magnitude of the increase is small, its accumulation over time can lead to profound improvements. Kaizen involves the expertise of the people involved with the process (operators, technicians, supervisors, and supporting engineering staff) and is typically a group process. Results come at fairly predictable intervals and usually involve little or no capital expenditures. Organizations must emphasize management systems that encourage both innovation and Kaizen.

The Seven Tools

It has been found in practice that a large number of quality problems can be addressed and understood directly by the application of one or more of the seven quality control (QC) tools: process flow diagram, cause-and-effect diagram, histogram, run chart, control chart, pareto diagram, and scatter diagram. The purpose of the process flow diagram (Figure 30.4) is to document the procedural steps of the standard process, although it can also be used to design the "ideal" process. As such, it is useful to uncover possible duplications, delay points, and omissions and serves as a starting point for further methods and time studies. It can be used to communicate the steps of the process to other internal and external agents and can detail process changes. It is an essential tool for identifying opportunities for data collection and subsequent process improvement. A flow diagram that is mediocre in detail can be an indication that process knowledge is not what it should be.

Flow diagrams can be of different degrees of scope and detail, and such decisions should be made up front. It may be adequate for the team to spend 30 min detailing the process flow and

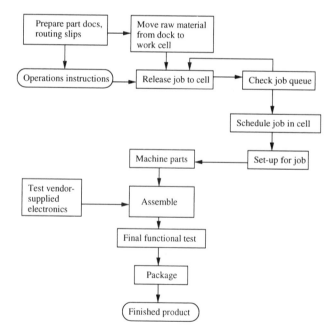

Figure 30.4. Process flow diagram of electromechanical part.

communicate it on a single sheet of paper; in other instances though, a team may spend weeks constructing a flow diagram with exquisite detail to be used for complete process understanding. Constructing a flow diagram is often the first task in analyzing process quality. Many questions can be asked of the flow diagram. How realistic is our view of the process? How much standardization is there in the process, and is there opportunity for more? Where is the customer in the flow, and if they're not there, should they be? Do the people in the process have the necessary overview? Where are there bottlenecks? How can we gauge process quality at each of the stages in the process?

The flow diagram can also be used to estimate end-process yield rates, in much the same way that product reliability can be estimated from component reliabilities. For example, in a process in which each step is sequential (serial) and errors occur independently, the end yield will be the product of the component yields. A process with 10 steps, in which each step produces 1% defective (or 99% yield), will have a 90.4% (0.90^{10}) yield. Conversely, consider a complex process involving 200 steps. To achieve 99% yield at the end, each process step must have $0.99^{1/200}$ or 99.995% yield, or 1 defective per 20,000 items.

The cause-and-effect diagram (also known as fishbone or Ishikawa diagram) is used to identify and organize possible causes of quality problems. The effect is shown in the box to the right, and major families of causes are shown on each branch of the tree. Generically, these major families can be thought of as people, machines, methods, measurement systems, materials, and environment. Each successive branching further details possible causes in that area. Figure 30.5 shows a fishbone diagram for the yield of fine-powder chemicals. Moisture content, transport, catalyzer, overweight package, reaction, and raw material are the main causes of potential yield problems; the package could be overweight because of a poor balance, either because of the type of balance or its maintenance.

The goal is to incorporate as many viewpoints as possible, and so brainstorming is often used. Like the process flow diagram, it is also an effective communication device and can help identify the need for data collection and analysis. In essence, the cause-and-effect diagram poses a large number of hypotheses. For those in which data have already been collected, or whose theory is well understood, supplementary notes can be made. For those others, the team must decide on which few are most likely, and collect appropriate data to accept or reject the hypothesis of causality.

The histogram is used to aggregate a set of data and understand it from a distributional standpoint. In fact, the histogram can be thought of as a "statistic" trying to estimate the "parameter" frequency distribution in the same way the sample average estimates the true mean of the process. The histogram conveys knowledge of distributional shape, centering, and

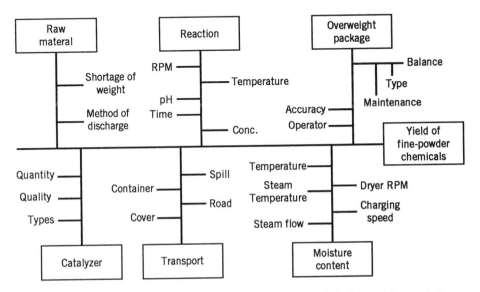

Figure 30.5. Cause-and-effect diagram for fine powder chemicals (adapted from ref. 6).

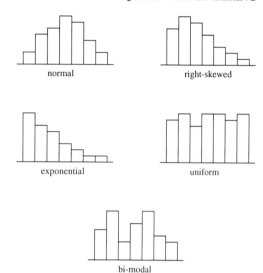

Figure 30.6. Different-shaped histograms.

spread and is made up of cells. Each cell represents a range of measures (e.g., 1.2001 to 1.2005 mm), and the cell height represents the relative frequency of that measure in the data set.

Several typical histogram shapes are shown in Figure 30.6. A histogram that displays symmetry around its center and is bell-shaped is deemed normal (or Gaussian). Another common shape is the right-skewed distribution, often referred to as log-normal. This is a typical shape for measures such as offsets or time, in which where zero is a hard constraint. As mentioned earlier, reliability measures will often follow the exponential distribution, typical of a system with constant failure rates. The uniform distribution is likely not the result of a natural process state, but rather the result of truncation, either from sampling screening or some rigid physical constraint within the system (such as would occur via an automatic control system). The final histogram shown in Figure 30.6 is bimodel (two peaked) and is an indication that more than one "process" was operating during the period of data collection.

A run chart is a depiction of the data's behavior over time, an important dimension that the histogram does not capture. As an example, consider the histogram and corresponding run charts shown in Figure 30.7. The histogram shows the distribution of 20 points (defects/day). Each run chart has the same histogram and yet the interpretation of the data is vastly different in each case. In the first, one might conclude that the data look fairly random over time and that would likely continue in such a state, yielding an average of 8 errors in a day and hovering between 4 and 12. In the second, data are clearly following a trend, and errors will likely continue to increase until the source of the trend is found and corrected. In the third, the data oscillate up and down each successive point, leading one to the conclusion that two processes are in action rather than one. The fourth shows that the process appears to have changed somewhere between day 15 and 16, and hence diagnosis could be focused in this time window. A control chart is similar to the run chart in structure but adds additional decision lines, called control limits, to aid in the rational judgment of process stability. These will be discussed in detail below.

The pareto diagram (Figure 30.8) can be thought of as a ranked histogram, in which categories (or defect types) take the place of cell boundaries. The most prevalent category (or defect) is shown to the right. The diagram aids in understanding the relative prevalence of categories to help prioritize the improvement efforts. The typical pareto has "frequency of occurrence" as the y axis; it may also be useful to examine paretos in which the y axis is monetary.

The scatter diagram is used to infer association, or correlation, between two measures. From such analysis one may infer causality, although correlation does not necessarily imply causality. Each (x, y) pair in the plot represents the hypothesized cause and subsequent effect. The axes of the scatter diagram are typically drawn at the mode of the set of data. Figure 30.9 shows the three possible scenarios: no correlation, in which points appear as a random scatter;

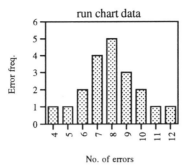

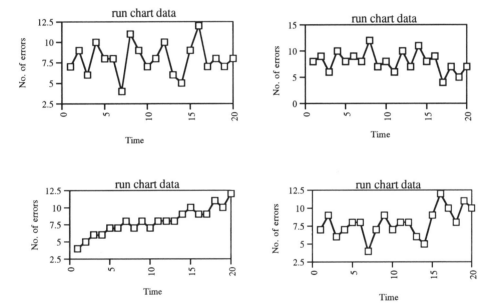

Figure 30.7. Run charts.

positive correlation, in which increases in x result in increases in y; and negative correlation, in which increases in x result in decreases in y.

Product Versus Process Control

The purpose of product control is to ensure that no poor-quality product leaves the facility to the customer; the purpose of process control is to use process data to find ways in which process variation can be minimized. Product control can take the form of 100% screening but more typically involves a sampling plan by which some percentage of the total lot in question is sampled. Based on the results, the lot is either accepted or rejected. Many sampling plans have been developed over the years, such as MIL-STD 105D and Dodge-Romig plans (6).

Product control by itself does not help the organization in the long run, because it does not provide information useful to reduce process variation—it merely states what did happen, rather than gives clues as to what should happen. Product screening is often done too late or is so far removed from the source of any problems that diagnosis becomes difficult or impossible. It has been shown that if the process is in statistical control, it is only economical to do either

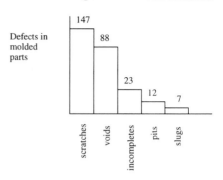

Figure 30.8. Pareto diagram.

100% screening or no sampling inspection at all; any other sampling strategies will be less than optimal. Deming's *kp* rule (3) states that one can compare the cost of taking the sample (k_1) to the cost of letting a defective item move onto the next stage of the process ($p \cdot k_2$, where p is the average percent defective from the process and k_2 is the cost of letting the defective item through), and the lesser of the two costs will define whether 0% or 100% screening is more economical. If the process in question is not in a state of statistical control, then some other percentage of sampling (such as in plans described in ref. 6) may be more economical.

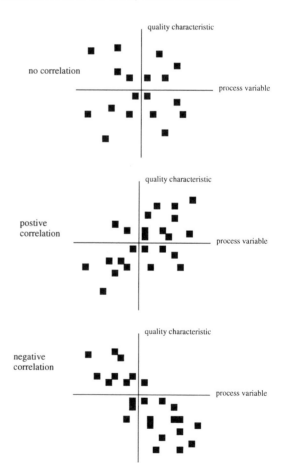

Figure 30.9. Scatter diagrams.

Statistical Process Control Charts

Shewhart (13), working for Bell Labs in the 1920s, described the purpose of process control:

> *Broadly speaking the object of industry is to set up economic ways and means of satisfying human wants and in doing so reduce everything possible to a minimun amount of human effort. Through the use of the scientific method, extended to take into account modern statistical concepts, it has been found possible to set up limits within which the results of routine efforts must lie if they are to be economical. Deviations in the result of a routine process outside such limits indicate that the routine has broken down and will no longer be economical until the cause of trouble is removed.*

There are several important implications in this statement.

1. Routine efforts, or "standard" processes, are most economical compared with a process that does not follow a standard set of procedures.
2. Statistical limits can be calculated that predict where the results of a routine process will lie.
3. It is economically useful to take action on a process whose routine has broken down, regardless of its capability.

Conceivably, it is not necessary to collect data to ensure process stability; if one could monitor all the possible causes in the process and ensure their constancy, then through standardization a process routine could be maintained. Indeed, this is part of the benefit of process flow analysis. Realistically, however, one cannot ever hope to know and measure all of the possible causes, and therefore, one can infer stability of the causal system through observed stability of the resulting output data. For example, in the case of a chemical processing system, results from a designed experiment may indicate that changes in variability of resultant pH are due to improper mixing of raw materials, while changes in the mean level of pH occur when excess residue builds up. In a machining process a shift in average thickness of a machined part may be the result of incorrect setup or tool wear, whereas a shift in variance of thickness might indicate an improper automatic control structure, loose fixtures, or irregular raw material. Observation of the control chart data will indicate when the process routine has broken down and corrective action needs to be taken.

For each type of data collected, there is a corresponding control chart. For variables measures, $\bar{x}$/range and x/moving range charts are used to track process mean and variation. For defect data, c or u charts track defects or defects per unit; for defective data, p or np charts track the percent defective or number defective. In any given process, several different charts may be used simultaneously. For example, in a microelectronics process $\bar{x}$/range charts might be used to monitor component level variation, x/moving range charts to monitor wafer-to-wafer variation, c charts to monitor defects per chip or wafer, and p charts to monitor overall yield.

Control limits are set so that when a point goes beyond the limits it likely indicates the presence of a special cause. There are two statistical risks involved: a false alarm (saying there is a special cause when indeed there is not), and a missed special cause (a change in the process that was too subtle to detect). As control limits are tightened, better sensitivity to process changes is achieved, but only at an increase in the false alarm rate. Control charts tend to be conservative (and thus parallel most of other statistical methods) in wanting to minimize false alarms. A reasonable trade-off between the two risks is achieved by placing control limits three standard deviations away from the statistical average, which is used as the chart's centerline. Thus for any statistic *stat,* control limits are generally set at average of *stat* $\pm$ 3 standard deviations of *stat.*

At any given time a sample of size n is taken from the process. This n represents the subgroup size, which varies, depending on the application. Some guidelines will be discussed shortly. The sample of size n, or subgroup, typically represents measurements of consecutively sequenced products, as they likely represent a homogenous process state. Let

n	subgroup size
k	number of subgroups
$x_{i,j}$	individual raw (variables) data for the ith measurement in the jth subgroup
$\bar{x}_j$	average of jth subgroup $(x_{1,j}, \ldots , x_{n,j})$
R_j	range of jth subgroup

For an $\bar{x}$/range chart the centerline and control limits are

$$CL_{\bar{x}} = \sum_{m=1}^{k} \bar{x}_m/k \tag{7}$$

$$LCL_{\bar{x}}, \; UCL_{\bar{x}} = CL_{\bar{x}} \pm A_2 \cdot \bar{R} \tag{8}$$

$$CL_R = \sum_{m=1}^{k} R_m/k = \bar{R} \tag{9}$$

$$LCL_R = D_3 \cdot \bar{R}, \; UCL_R = D_4 \cdot \bar{R} \tag{10}$$

where values of A_2, D_3, and D_4 are given in Table 30.1. The constants come from assuming the $\bar{x}$s will be approximately normally distributed, via the central limit theorem. The $\bar{x}$ chart and the R chart are plotted and analyzed simultaneously. In general, if the process is in statistical control, the charts should exhibit random behavior over time, within the calculated control limits. Specifically, the presence of special causes is indicated if:

1. Any $\bar{x}$ or R falls beyond its respective control limits.
2. There is a run of seven or more $\bar{x}$s or Rs above/below the chart's centerline.
3. Two of three consecutive $\bar{x}$s fall beyond the middle two-thirds of the $\bar{x}$ chart.
4. Four of five consecutive $\bar{x}$s fall beyond the middle one-third of the $\bar{x}$ chart.

One should also visually check for any suspicious trends, cycles, or distribution of points within the control limits. See ref. 14 for more discussion of such rules. Violations of these rules should be duly noted on the chart and diagnosis begun so as to implement corrective action on the process. A control chart with a special cause present is shown in Figure 30.10.

Subgroups of data should be formed in such a way that the variation within a subgroup represents the common cause variation present in the routine process. Thus consecutive samples are often used because they likely represent a homogenous sample. This strategy is termed rational subgrouping. The subgroup should also contain some product-to-product variation, rather than strictly within-product variation, as the former is part of the expected process variation. For example, if several thickness measurements are taken at different locations on a single item, this would not represent a rational sample because no product-to-product variation exists in the subgroup. This incorrect sampling strategy is called stratification, where multiple "processes" are placed within a single subgroup. This will lead to an inflated R and thus inflated control limits. The R chart will likely appear in control, while in the $\bar{x}$ chart it will appear as though all the $\bar{x}$s were hugging the centerline. This is not an indication of a "good" process but rather an indication that the limits are too wide because of a nonrational sample. Careful consideration should be given to selection of a rational sample, as it can often make tremendous difference in the effectiveness of the control chart application (14, 15).

Typical subgroup size for $\bar{x}/R$ charts is four to six. Small sample sizes ensure a rational subgroup and are economically appealing; sample sizes smaller than four tend to lack the desired degree of sensitivity to process changes. The time between subgroups is likely much larger than the time between samples in a subgroup. The frequency of subgroup selection depends on: (1) the cost of sampling, (2) the frequency of special causes, (3) the impact severity

TABLE 30.1. Control Chart Constants

n	A_2	D_3	D_4	d_2
2	1.880	0	3.267	1.128
3	1.023	0	2.574	1.693
4	0.729	0	2.282	2.059
5	0.577	0	2.114	1.970
6	0.483	0	2.004	1.882
7	0.419	0.204	1.924	1.815
8	0.373	0.388	1.864	1.761

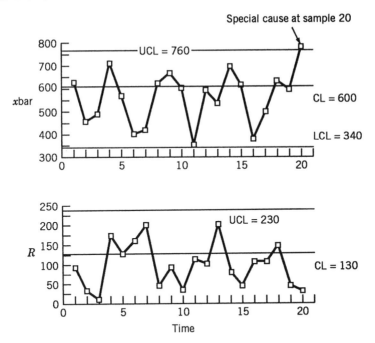

Figure 30.10.   Control chart with a special cause.

of special causes, and (4) the amount of previous history indicating statistical control. It is likely that sampling frequency will start out high as special causes are removed sequentially and will reduce as process stability is secured.

Often rational subgroups are not feasible because of the physical nature of the process (e.g., a continuous batch process) or because of economic considerations. In such cases a subgroup size of $n = 1$ can be used, and the moving range (R_m, the range of two consecutive xs) is used to estimate process variation. The limits for the x/R_m (or sometimes called individuals) chart are

$$CL_x = \sum_{i=1}^{k} x_i/k \tag{11}$$

$$LCL_x, UCL_x = CL_x \pm 2.66\,\overline{R} \tag{12}$$

$$CL_{R_m} = \sum_{i=1}^{k} R_{m_i}/k \tag{13}$$

$$LCL_{R_m} = 0, \; UCL_{R_m} = 3.267 \cdot CL_{R_m} \tag{14}$$

The chart is interpreted in the same manner as the $\bar{x}/R$ chart, applying rules 1 and 2 described above. Note that the behavior on the two charts are codependent, as large swings in the x chart will show up as large R_ms on the R_m chart. While the x/R_m chart is not as sensitive as the $\bar{x}/R$ chart, it can still provide adequate assessment of process stability. When successive points are highly correlated with one another, as might occur when consecutive measures are taken from a continuous process or when the data in question have a complex dynamic structure (such as the vibration signal from a machine sensor during a metal cutting operation or temperature variations in a mold cavity), then neither the $\bar{x}/R$ nor the x/R_m charts will work well. Other variations of control charts, such as exponentially weighted moving average (EWMA) charts, can be used (14, 15).

For attribute data control charts, limits are calculated as such. Let

n_j subgroup size for subgroup j
k number of subgroups
c_j total number of defects in the jth subgroup
u_j total number of defects per unit in the jth subgroup (c_j/n_j)
d_j total number of defectives in the jth subgroup
p_j total fraction defectives in the jth subgroup (d_j/n_j)

Only one chart is needed now instead of two (as with $\bar{x}/R$) because the mean and variance depend statistically on the same parameters. Two variations exist for plotting fraction defective: a p chart for percent defective and an np chart for number of defectives:

$$CL_p = \frac{\sum_{i=1}^{k} d_i}{\sum_{i=1}^{k} n_i} = \bar{p} \tag{15}$$

$$LCL_p = \max(0, \bar{p} - 3\sqrt{\bar{p} \cdot (1 - \bar{p})/n_i}) \tag{16}$$

$$UCL_p = \bar{p} + 3\sqrt{\bar{p} \cdot (1 - \bar{p})/n_i} \tag{17}$$

The np chart assumes constant subgroup size:

$$CL_{np} = \sum_{i=1}^{k} d_i/k \tag{18}$$

$$LCL_{np} = \max(0, n\bar{p} - 3\sqrt{n\bar{p} \cdot (1 - \bar{p})}) \tag{19}$$

$$UCL_{np} = n\bar{p} + 3\sqrt{n\bar{p} \cdot (1 - \bar{p})} \tag{20}$$

There is no stipulation that the subgroup needs to remain constant for the p chart, although it does make it simpler to implement. One can either calculate separate control limits for each different subgroup size, leaving the chart with varying limits, or calculate an average subgroup size and use that for the p chart limit calculations. Typical subgroup sizes for p charts range from 25 up.

The c chart has limits of:

$$CL_c = \sum_{i=1}^{k} c_i/k = \bar{c} \tag{21}$$

$$LCL_c = \max(0, \bar{c} - 3\sqrt{\bar{c}}) \tag{22}$$

$$UCL_c = \bar{c} + 3\sqrt{\bar{c}} \tag{23}$$

The c chart assumes a constant subgroup size or "opportunity space" within which defects can occur. Changes in subgroup size can be dealt with in the u chart, where u is the defects per unit:

$$Cl_u = \sum_{i=1}^{k} c_i/n_i = \bar{u} \tag{24}$$

$$LCL_u = max(0, \bar{u} - 3\sqrt{\bar{u}/n_i}) \tag{25}$$

$$UCL_u = \bar{u} + 3\sqrt{\bar{u}/n_i} \tag{26}$$

Interpretation of rules 1 and 2 described above should be used for analysis of the p, np, c, and u charts.

When the control chart signals that a special cause has occurred, corrective action must be taken. Oftentimes, the reason for the special cause is evident; otherwise, diagnosis must take place. Diagnosis involves matching the behavior in the statistical signal (special cause on the control chart) to its physical root cause. The probability of successful diagnosis is enhanced if charting is done online by process operators, rather than offline by supporting engineering staff. Diagnosis becomes more difficult as the time between the actual occurrence of the special cause and the onset of diagnosis increases—memories fade and context is lost.

Sometimes changes in the process can be correlated to changes in other variables (raw material batch changes, differences between shifts or machines, changes in ambient temperature or humidity, machine startup or setup problems, tool changes, etc.). These correlations can only be discovered if data are collected on these additional process factors. Each subgroup should be thought of as having an *ID tag,* which consists of such information as time of sampling, raw material information, machine settings and/or changes, personnel, batch information, environmental measures, and any other relevant comments that might aid later in diagnosis. For this reason, it is often relevant to design a supporting spreadsheet or database, from which quality characteristic data can be downloaded into a statistical process control software package (the magazine *Quality Progress* does annual reviews of quality-related software). Many of the seven QC tools discussed earlier (histograms, cause-and-effect diagrams, scatter diagrams, etc.) can also be used to aid in the subsequent diagnostic investigation.

Corrective actions take two forms: short and long term. It is often necessary to implement a quick fix to the process if the routine has failed. This may involve additional processing, rework, and/or 100% screening. Such solutions should never take the place of long-term solutions aimed at the root causes. Long-term solutions may involve changes in procedures, equipment, additional training, enhanced vendor quality, or environment.

Let us summarize with a step-by-step procedure:

1. Select an appropriate quality characteristic and establish an operational definition. Also decide on what supplemental process data will be collected, and design data collection sheets (or the computerized equivalent).

2. Establish repeatability of the measurement system, ensuring that valid information can be obtained.

3. Select an appropriate sampling strategy based on the type of chart being used, sampling and poor-quality costs, and other practical considerations.

4. Collect at least 25 subgroups of data, and calculate trial control limits.

5. Investigate the initial chart for special causes; if none are present proceed to step 7.

6. Find root causes for all special causes, and take appropriate corrective action. Remove the data corresponding to the special causes from the calculation of the control limits, and recalculate new limits. Further analyze the chart (return to step 5).

7. Extend limits and continue to chart data in real time, investigating special causes as they occur.

8. Assess process capability.

Process Capability Assessment

Process capability is defined as the ability of the process to meet design specifications. Capability is nominally required to be such that the natural spread of the process (± 3 standard deviations) is equal to the tolerance range. This would correspond to a 99.7% capability (3000 ppm defective), assuming a normal distribution for the individual raw data.

Before capability can be assessed, a history of process stability (via control charts) should be established. A stable process will yield data that best reflect the true process capability, and a prediction that will likely hold true until the process routine is changed. If process capability is assessed without process stability first in place, the subsequent predictions will be relatively worthless. The actual daily routine could turn out to be much better, or much worse, than capability predictions would lead one to believe. An unstable process has no defineable mean or variance, and therefore, subsequent statistical predictions are invalid. In reality, this caveat does not often keep companies from estimating capability before control is established, however. Many still believe it is possible to qualify a vendor or characterize a process by simply performing a capability study. Such studies should be rigorously supplemented by examination of the statistical process control procedures in place and the supporting structure and environment for continuous improvement.

For attribute data, process capability can be directly predicted from the centerline of the (stable) p chart. For variables data, statistical distributions must be used to convert mean and variation parameters into percent-beyond-specifications predictions. Often the normal distribution is assumed for process data, although this is not necessary. A step-by-step procedure is given:

1. Establish a history of process stability via control charts.
2. Find the mean and variance of the individual raw data. The mean may be taken as the centerline of the $\bar{x}$ chart, and the standard deviation (σ) as $\bar{R}/d_2$, where d_2 is a constant that depends on the subgroup size and is shown in Table 30.1. One may also calculate σ from the raw data itself (this estimate and $\bar{R}/d_2$ should be roughly equivalent for normally distributed data from a stable process).
3. Find the percent beyond the specifications by using normal distribution tables.

First, find

$$z_{lsl} = -(lsl - CL_{\bar{x}})/\sigma \qquad z_{usl} = (usl - CL_{\bar{x}})/\sigma \qquad (27)$$

where lsl and usl correspond to the lower and upper (design) specification limits. Then the fraction beyond specifications can be found by

$$(1 - \Phi(z_{usl})) + \Phi(-z_{lsl}), \qquad (28)$$

where $\Phi(*)$ is the cumulative unit normal distribution function, tables for which can be found in any statistical textbook. Another way to quantify capability is through capability indices. The index c_p is a measure of the spread of the tolerances compared with the natural spread of the process:

$$c_p = (usl - lsl)/6\sigma \qquad (29)$$

Nominally, one would require a minimum c_p value of 1.0, corresponding to 99.7% acceptable. The c_p measures how well the process *could* do, assuming it was centered on target. A more reasonable quantification of the current situation is found via the c_{pk} index, where

$$c_{pk} = \min(z_{lsl}, z_{usl})/3 \qquad (30)$$

The c_{pk} value will always be less than c_p unless the process is centered on target. There are some precautions that one must be aware of when using c_{pk} values to interpret the current status of process capability. (*1*) Often process capability data are extracted from control chart data. Depending on how we sample data for the control chart, we can make it look as if we had a stable process with low c_{pk} or an unstable process with high C_{pk}. (2) C_{pk} implies a certain percent beyond specifications. This prediction is not useful unless underlying data are truly normally distributed. Unfortunately, data are often not normally distributed. (*3*) c_{pk}, or any capability measure for that matter, says nothing about the ability for the process to remain in control. (*4*) The measurement system can limit the observed C_{pk}:

$$1/C_{pk}(\text{observed}) = 1/C_{pk}(\text{process}) + 1/C_{pk}(\text{measurement system}) \qquad (31)$$

There is debate among practitioners concerning the amount of effort (via either control charts or continuous improvement) that should be placed on characteristics and associated processes that are highly capable. There is no doubt that the limited resources of the firm should be focused on critical areas in which stability and/or capability problems exist. In a smooth-running quality system, however, there should be little overhead associated with continued charting and tracking down of special causes (sampling frequencies can be reduced as stability is established), especially if control charts are part of the operator's routine. Special causes are often easy to track down and can be fixed at "no cost."

Similarly, ideas for improvement from process operators (and the like) should not be ignored even if process capability is sufficient. Many such changes involve no capital expenditures and have beneficial side effects such as increased process safety, better ergonomics, reduced inventory or process paperwork, and reduced cycle time. One must also remember that a process can turn from capable to incapable overnight: a change in customer requirements, a new competitor who can meet tighter tolerances at the same cost, or the presence of increased competition (causing a product to have low margins and thus become a commodity). In such instances, the company must be poised for a new level of performance. It can only do so by continuous enhancement of process knowledge. To ignore processes that are capable may lead to short-term savings, but represents a true long-term liability.

Because process capability infers something about the routine process, capability cannot be improved unless the routine process is changed. Clues as to which elements of the routine process hold the most leverage for improvement can be obtained through designed experiments.

Design of Experiments

Designed experimentation involves the purposeful manipulation of process and product design variables to discover significant effects and interactions. Experimentation can be used in all phases of the product and process life cycle: testing of design parameters in product prototypes during the simultaneous (concurrent) design of product and process (via either physical proto-types or computer simulations), fine-tuning of process parameters during transition to manufac-turing, and change of the routine process after stability has been established but capability is found not to be adequate.

In this section, the discussion will be confined to the area of two-level factorial designs. For discussion on a broader range of subjects, see refs. 14, 16, 17. Factorial designs are experimen-tal recipes in which all the various combinations of factors and factor levels are tested. For example, if one wanted to test a coating process at five levels of line speed and three levels of flow rate, a total of fifteen (3×5) tests would be needed at a minimum. Such a design allows quantification of both the "main" effects of line speed and flow rate and also their interaction, if any. Statistical procedures are then used to determine if the magnitude of the effects can be explained by random chance alone (termed the null hypothesis) versus the presence of some actual physical effect (i.e., rejection of the null hypothesis). The magnitude of a variable's effect is usually quantified by a sample average; the magnitude of "random chance" present in the experiment is quantified by the experimental error (or background noise) σ. The ratio of the effect value to the experimental error can be considered a signal-to-noise ratio. If this ratio is large enough (as determined by statistical theory) the null hypothesis is rejected and a difference is declared. One should not confuse statistical significance with practical significance. The former can be determined by statistical theory, the latter is an engineering question. If one is able to determine statistical significance, then engineering significance can be addressed.

There may be situations in which knowledge of the product/process is quite complete, and there is only one factor of interest; in this case, simple statistical methods such as t-tests (16) can be used for analysis. More likely, there are a multitude of possible factors under consider-ation. Conventional industrial experimentation has followed a one-variable-at-a-time methodol-ogy. One factor is varied over its entire range while all others are held constant, and the "optimal" setting of that variable is identified. This continues until all factors are optimized. Both practice and theory show that this strategy results in suboptimality and incredible waste of experimental resources and does not lead to enhancement of process knowledge. The one-variable-at-a-time strategy is the same as telling someone to find the top of the mountain that they are on but restricting them to walk only in north–south and east–west directions—he or she may eventually find the top, but it is far from the most direct route.

If one considers the true functional relationship between process/product factors and the response as a geometric surface (i.e., response surface), then optimization involves the search of that response surface to identify peaks (maxima) or valleys (minima). Two potential strate-gies exist: (1) blanket the entire response surface with tests and fit some higher order polyno-mial model to explain the curvature in the response surface and (2) run a few tests at a time in small regions of the response surface, using the results of one experiment to lead to the identification of the next most promising region. The latter strategy is typically more successful, for two reasons.

First, consider a situation in which three factors have been identified as possibly being significant; each factor is tested at five levels, yielding a $5 \times 5 \times 5 = 125$ test experiment. If it turns out that only two of the factors where really significant (we could have explored this surface in $5 \times 5 = 25$ tests) then 100 of the tests were wasted on an insignificant factor. Second, the statistical fitting and subsequent interpretation of polynomial-order models require a modi-cum of statistical expertise not typically found. Linear (planar) models are simple to fit and analyze, and minimize the number of tests. For these reasons two-level designs, by which each factor is varied only at two different levels, are often the design of choice. From these two-level designs, one obtains planar approximations of the response surface, which then indicate directions of improvement.

A two-level factorial involves 2^k experimental conditions, where k is the number of factors under consideration. For example, a three-factor test at two levels requires 8 tests (minimum), whereas 27 tests would be required for a three-level design. The "levels" can correspond to either discrete settings, categories, or low–high levels of a continuous variable, e.g., if the factor is design type, the two levels could be design A and design B; for a gate-type factor, on and off; and for a temperature-type factor, 150° and 200°C. Factor levels are sometimes dictated by the situation: existing versus new design, on–off, yes–no, etc. When a choice is involved, levels should be chosen far enough apart so that effects (if present) are observed but yet not so far apart that the linearity assumption might be violated. The decision is not a statistical one but rather is based on engineering expertise.

These 2^k designs can be represented by a design matrix, as shown in Table 30.2. The minus and plus designators are used to denote the two levels of factors x_i. One should note the pattern of minuses and pluses occurring in each subsequent column of the design matrix. The design matrix identifies each unique experimental condition. The total number of tests is thus given by $2^k \cdot n$, where n is the number of replicates at each test condition. If testing is inexpensive and simple, then many replicates should be generated (for instance, when computer simulations are used). More often, testing costs are prohibitive, and only a few (if any) replicates are run. The time order in which the tests are run should be randomized—it should not be the same order as given in the design matrix. Randomization ensures that the potentially disruptive influence of nuisance factors is minimized. Sometimes randomization is not performed because of the costs of setting up each experimental condition—such constraints must be balanced by the need to obtain statistically valid results.

TABLE 30.2. Matrices for 2^k Factorial Designs

k	x_1	x_2	x_3	x_4
2	−	−		
	+	−		
	−	+		
	+	+		
3	−	−	−	
	+	−	−	
	−	+	−	
	+	+	−	
	−	−	+	
	+	−	+	
	−	+	+	
	+	+	+	
4	−	−	−	−
	+	−	−	−
	−	+	−	−
	+	+	−	−
	−	−	+	−
	+	−	+	−
	−	+	+	−
	+	+	+	−
	−	−	−	+
	+	−	−	+
	−	+	−	+
	+	+	−	+
	−	−	+	+
	+	−	+	+
	−	+	+	+
	+	+	+	+

The effect of each factor, or factor interactions, is given by

$$E_i = \text{effect of factor } x_i = \bar{y}_+ - \bar{y}_- \tag{32}$$

where $\bar{y}_+$ and $\bar{y}_-$ represent the average response when x_i is at a high and low level, respectively. For example, for E_3 in a 2^3 design, one would take the four values corresponding to x_3 at a low level $(-)$, average them, and subtract that from the average of the four values with x_3 at a high level $(+)$. The effect magnitude is thus the average increase in the response when the factor goes from its low $(-)$ to its high $(+)$ setting.

Interactions may also be present. The presence of an interaction means that the effect of one factor depends on the level of another. Consider a simple example in human response times. Caffeine may have a negative effect (increasing caffeine leads to decreasing response times, for small amounts of caffeine) by itself, but no effect when alcohol is present. Interactions are common in physical systems and show up in at least half the experiments one will run. A positive interaction means the response increases when both factors are at the same level (both low or both high); a negative interaction means the response decreases when both factors are at the same level. Interactions are most easily seen in two-way diagrams (Figure 30.11). Such a diagram shows the average response on the y axis, one factor x_i on the x axis, and then two lines corresponding to factor x_j at low and high levels. The slope of the lines represents the effect of factor x_i, and the relative space between the lines, the effect of factor x_j. If the two lines are relatively parallel, that means that the effect of factor x_i is not changed by the level of factor x_j, hence no interaction. When the two lines are not parallel, interactions are present. Figure 30.11 shows several possibilities of main effects and interactions. Note that just because the main effect of a factor is calculated to be (not statistically different from) 0, that may not be the case if an interaction is present. For example, that factor could have a large positive effect when x_j is

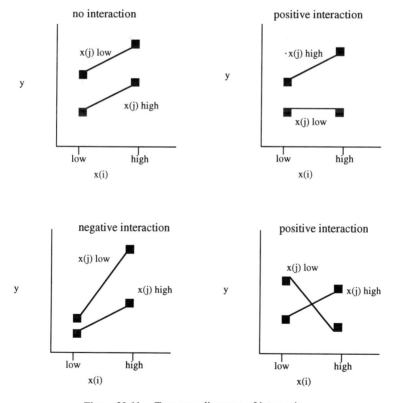

Figure 30.11. Two-way diagrams of interactions.

low, and a large negative effect when x_j is high, the result canceling to 0. Thus main effects must always be interpreted in lieu of possible interactions.

A simple way of calculating the magnitude of all main and interaction effects is to use the design matrix columns of minuses and pluses, attach them to the data column, add/subtract per each sign, and divide by 2^{k-1}. The interactions between factors x_i and x_j can be found by taking the signs from the x_i and x_j columns, multiplying them together, and then attaching the subsequent signs to the data column, etc. An example is shown in Table 30.3. Here, the surface finish (y, measured in microinches) of a milled part is examined as a result of three factors: cutting speed (50 and 60 sfpm), cutting fluid (off and on), and feedrate (5 and 7 fpm). In this case, the experiment was not replicated, so only eight tests were performed in the 2^3 design. The effect of cutting fluid, E_2, is

$$(-200 - 150 + 400 + 350 - 1000 - 750 + 800 + 650)/4 = 25$$

whereas the cutting speed–feedrate interaction is found by

$$(+200 - 150 + 400 - 350 - 1000 + 750 - 800 + 650)/4 = 100.$$

To determine significance of effects in an unreplicated factorial design, one must use normal probability paper. The assumption is that insignificant effects will be merely estimating noise and should have 0 mean and tend toward a normal distribution, because they are sample averages. Those that do not fit this explanation are then deemed significant. Normal probability paper is specially scaled paper so that when ranked data are plotted in cumulative order, those data that follow a homogeneous normal distribution will plot as a single straight line. The plot is a series of x, y points, the x axis value corresponding to the magnitude of the effect and the y axis, to the cumulative probability P_i, where P_i is the cumulative percentage for the ith ranked point ($i = 1$ being the lowest value) and is given by $(i - 1/2)/n$, where n is the total number of effects being plotted. The effects found in Table 30.3 are plotted on normal probability paper and shown in Figure 30.12; from this graph we can see that E_3 is the only significant effect. There are several other more complex ways to determine significant effects from unreplicated designs (16).

If the factorial design is replicated, then one can use the average variance of the replicates to determine a confidence interval for the effect values. Consider the data shown in Table 30.4, which are identical to the original data, but now each of those eight responses represents the average of two replicates at each test condition; thus at each test condition we can calculate an average and sample variance. The average response at each test condition can be subsequently used in the effect analysis. The sample variances can be averaged across all test conditions (assuming equal number of replicates at each condition) to yield a pooled variance s_p^2, with $2^k \cdot$

TABLE 30.3. Effect Analysis of 2^3 Design

x_1 Cutting Speed (50 and 60 sfpm)	x_2 Cutting Fluid (off and on)	x_3 Feedrate (5 and 7 fpm)	y Surface Finish (microinches)
−	−	−	200
+	−	−	150
−	+	−	400
+	+	−	350
−	−	+	1000
+	−	+	750
−	+	+	800
+	+	+	650

Effects and Interactions

$\bar{y} = 537.5$	$E_{12} = 25$
$E_1 = -125$	$E_{13} = 100$
$E_2 = 25$	$E_{23} = -175$
$E_3 = 525$	$E_{123} = 25$

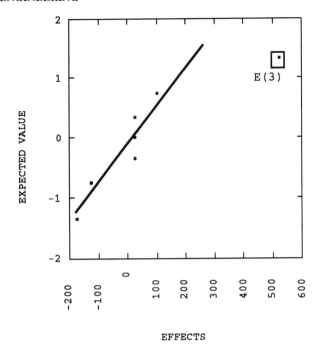

Figure 30.12. Normal plot of effects.

TABLE 30.4. Effect Analysis of Replicated 2^3 Design

x_1 Cutting Speed (50 and 60 sfpm)	x_2 Cutting Fluid (on and off)	x_3 Feedrate (5 and 7 fpm)	Surface Finish (microinches)			
			y_1	y_2	$\bar{y}$	s^2
−	−	−	150	250	200	5,000
+	−	−	100	200	150	5,000
−	+	−	300	500	400	20,000
+	+	−	275	425	350	11,250
−	−	+	950	1,050	1,000	5,000
+	−	+	700	800	750	5,000
−	+	+	700	900	800	20,000
+	+	+	625	675	650	11,250

Statistics

$\bar{y} = 537.5$ $E_{23} = -175^b$

$E_1 = -125$ $E_{123} = 25$

$E_2 = 25$ $s_{p^2} = 10{,}312.5$

$E_3 = 525^a$ $V(\text{effect}) = (4/16)10{,}312.5 = 2{,}578.12$

$E_{12} = 25$ $t_{.005,8} = 3.355$

$E_{13} = 100$ 99% confidence interval (effects) $= \pm 3.355 \sqrt{2{,}578.12} = \pm 170.35$

[a] Significant.
[b] Possibly significant.

$(n - 1)$ degrees of freedom. This pooled variance is now an estimate of the experimental error. The variance of an effect is given by

$$\text{Variance } (E_i) = (4/N) \, s_p^2 \tag{33}$$

where N is the total number of tests run, or 2^k times the number of replicates at each condition. A $100(1 - \alpha)\%$ confidence interval each effect can be found by

$$\text{Effect} \pm (t_{\alpha/2, 2^k \cdot (n-1)}) \sqrt{\text{Variance(Effect)}} \tag{34}$$

where $(t_{\alpha/2, 2^k \cdot (n-1)})$ is the $\alpha/2$ critical value of the t distribution with $2^k \cdot (n - 1)$ degrees of freedom; a 95% or 99% confidence interval ($\alpha = 0.05$ or 0.01) is typically used. If the confidence interval includes 0, then it is deemed insignificant; otherwise, it is deemed significant. Table 30.4 shows the data analysis for the replicated data.

An approximate mathematical model can be obtained using factors deemed significant. The model will be

$$y = \bar{y} + (E_i/2) \cdot x_i + \ldots (E_{ij}/2) \cdot x_i \cdot x_j + \ldots \tag{35}$$

where $\bar{y}$ is the grand average (over all 2^k conditions) and E_i is the effect of significant factor i, etc. Values for x_i variables are in terms of the coded units of the standard design (-1 and $+1$ corresponding to a low and high level for that factor), so when predictions are being made, factor settings must be translated to coded units. A model obtained from the analysis of the experiment shown in Table 30.3 is

$$y = 537.5 + 262.5 \, x_3 \tag{36}$$

Suppose we wanted to obtain a prediction at cutting speed 50 sfpm, cutting fluid off, and feedrate 7 fpm; this corresponds to (x_1, x_2, x_3) of $(-1, -1, 1)$, which yields a prediction of 800, compared with the observed value of 1000. A prediction at cutting speed 55 sfpm, cutting fluid on, and feedrate 6.5 fpm would correspond to (x_1, x_2, x_3) of $(-0.5, 1, 0.5)$, which yields a prediction of 668.75.

One can generate a prediction for each unique experimental condition. The subsequent prediction errors, or residuals, are given by the (subtracted) difference between actual and predicted. These residuals are then plotted in a variety of ways to determine possible problems within the experiment, outliers, or the need for a transformation. The residuals should be plotted on normal probability paper to check for normality; nonnormality would indicate the need for a log, square root, or inverse transformation of the raw data to make them more approximately normal. Residuals should be plotted versus time to look for possible trends or cycles (the presence of which would typically greatly desensitize the subsequent experimental analysis). Residuals should look "random" when plotted against their corresponding predicted value; if the dispersion of the residuals drastically increases as the magnitude of the prediction increases, this indicates nonnormality and an appropriate transformation need be taken. Residuals can be plotted against the factor levels themselves to look for the presence of variance effects. This may be useful knowledge because we may be in the situation of wanting to identify factor settings that minimize variation. For more information on residual analysis see refs. 14, 16, and 17.

While the 2^k designs are economical compared with their multilevel counterparts, they too can become prohibitively large when the number of factors is greater than five or six. Many of the tests in these large designs are being used to estimate high order effects, such as four- and five-factor interactions. Interactions of order three occur roughly 5% of the time and typically cause havoc in interpretation. Higher order interactions are both rare and not practically useful; therefore, there is the opportunity to reduce the number of tests in these large-scale 2^k designs, as long as we can make the assumption that interactions of a given order and above are negligible. This leads to a series of designs called fractional factorial designs. A 2^{k-p} design looks at k factors in 2^{k-p} tests. Fractional factorials are common in industry because of high test costs, and are typically not replicated.

In a completely saturated design one is able to investigate k factors in $k + 1$ tests. One must assume that all two-factor interactions are negligible though, because these interactions are "confounded" with the main effects. The level to which the design is fractionated determines the amount of confounding present. The technique involved in designing fractional designs is given in refs. 14, 16, and 17. Fractional designs are typically used in the screening phase of experimentation, in which large numbers of factors are under investigation and an initial screening is done to confine subsequent experimentation to a smaller number of factors. When a more reasonable number of factors is settled on, the experimenter may use a full factorial design to explore all relevant interactions. Finally, the search for optima on the response surface is aided by "response surface methodology," by which factorials are used to direct linear paths across the surface, and special composite designs are used to estimate a quadratic model near the optimal (18).

Taguchi (19) has become famous for his contributions to experimental design, which are threefold:

1. Taguchi emphasizes the concept of robust design, in which product and process design parameters are chosen so that performance is optimal and robust to nuisance factors. As a first step the experimenter separates factors into two categories: control factors and noise factors. Noise factors are those that are difficult, impossible, or too expensive to control. For example, road condition and other environmental factors would be considered noise factors in an automobile study, across which robustness is desired. Two-level (fractional) factorial designs are thus laid out: at each unique condition in the inner array (made up of control factors), an outer array design (made up of noise factors) is performed. One may view this as "intelligent" replication, in which noise factors are purposefully being altered to induce variation in the system. There are then two statistics to be investigated: the average performance and the robustness of performance, quantified by the standard deviation of the data in each outer array. Unlike Taguchi (see below), the author suggests looking at average performance and robustness separately (20).

2. Taguchi advocates the signal-to-noise ratio as the statistic of analysis (21). The signal-to-noise ratio incorporates average performance (signal) and robustness (noise) into one number. Optimal conditions are then found by maximizing the signal-to-noise ratio. While many practitioners find such analysis rewarding, objections from the statistical community would appear to put this practice in question (20).

3. Taguchi advocates a pick-the-winner experimental methodology (21). Unlike classic experimental design methodology, the Taguchi method does not consider diagnostic analysis or the need for transformations, advocate a series of sequential experiments versus one large experiment, and consider interactions to be all that prevalent (20). When one has examined a product–process over a long period, knowledge of interactions may be adequate to such an extent that this approach is feasible. In most situations, however, knowledge is limited and thus the classic methodology will yield more consistent results and subsequently better product and process knowledge.

30.4 MANAGING THE QUALITY SYSTEM

Economics of Quality

Quality improvement has been positively associated with reduced scrap and rework costs, better cycle time and productivity, reduced inventory, increased worker morale, and better organizational economic health by numerous public and private studies, including the U.S. government's General Accounting Office (22), hence the phrase *quality is free*—while expenditures for training and other support activities require an initial investment by the organization, the return on investment is rapid and significant. The economics of quality have two sides. Externally, as product quality increases, larger market shares will be developed, new market niches will be opened, and existing customers will be retained. Internally, reduction of process variation will reduce the need for costly inspections, processes will be streamlined and cycle time improved, rework and scrap costs will be reduced drastically, and new processes will be developed more quickly because of increased understanding of the science of the process.

Quality costs can be broken down into four major areas: internal failures (scrap, rework, expedition, etc.), external failures (warranties, loss of business, legal fees, and dealing with customer complaints), appraisal (inspection, test, and metrology), and prevention (new product reviews, improvement projects, training, quality planning, etc.). Tracking quality costs can be useful for identifying critical areas on which to focus attention; by themselves, however, they are only a report of what has happened rather than a forward-thinking tool concerned with what should happen. Manufacturing companies typically quantify their quality costs at 5% to 10% of total sales; other experts say that this number is more realistically in the 20% to 30% range (and higher for administrative processes and services). There are certain costs that cannot be estimated and thus do not enter into the total: loss of future customers, loss of customer goodwill and reputation, and costs associated with external failure, causing large-scale systems to be shut down or human safety to be at risk. Regardless of the final percentage, all companies find that there is plenty of room for substantial reduction of these quality costs.

We have historically treated the cost of not meeting product specifications via the step loss function (goalpost model), shown in Figure 30.13. As long as performance is within specifications, no loss is incurred (either internally or externally); if performance goes outside of specifications, then a single internal loss (scrap, rework) is incurred. This model may be reasonable in situations in which the variation in the characteristic is in no way associated with degradation of overall product functionality (a rare situation). It is more likely, however, that losses are incurred if the product is off target, even if it is within specification. This is because the system in which the characteristic resides is only optimal when each element is made as designed, on target. A famous example can be found in gear teeth for automobiles (14). Ford and Honda were making the same gear mechanisms with essentially the same process technologies; Ford, however, was incurring significant warranty costs because of returns in the field. Both companies rarely produced products outside specification, but Honda's processes had much tighter variation. As the roundness of the gear teeth was slightly off target for the Ford product, wear occurred and the teeth had much shorter life than expected, leading to noise and subsequent complaints.

An alternative is the Taguchi loss function (14), by which loss is incurred and increases quadratically as variation from the target increases (Figure 30.13). The Taguchi loss function is much more customer oriented and can be used to approximate some of the unknowable costs mentioned previously. The loss function is quadratic (it is actually an approximation to a Taylor Series expansion) with minimum at the nominal design target m, so it only has one parameter (assuming symmetric loss), its curvature k. For any individual item, the loss for performing at a value x is

$$L(x) = k(x - m)^2 \tag{37}$$

Given a process mean of $\bar{x}$ and sample standard deviation s, the average loss per item for the process is

$$E(L(x)) = k(s^2 + (\bar{x} - m)^2) \tag{38}$$

The expected loss can be seen to have two components: s^2, precision, and $(\bar{x} - m)$, accuracy; thus it fits well with previous engineering sense. The value k is determined empirically. A simple way is to take k as A/Δ^2, where A is the cost of product scrap or rework, and $\pm\Delta$ is entire specification width. For more details see ref. 14.

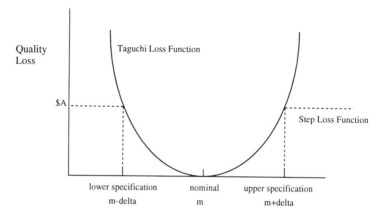

Figure 30.13.   Step loss function versus Taguchi loss function.

Overview of Total Quality Management

Quality improvement is above all a management responsibility. Only management can provide the leadership and support needed for quality improvement to succeed. The tools of quality improvement have been here for decades; it was only when management's role became understood that companies made significant advancements. The success of the quality system goes beyond the type of data being collected, how they are analyzed, and what corrective actions are taken. Its success depends on the reward structures put in place, the relationship between labor and management, the organizational culture, effective and honest communication, minimization of fear, training and education, the ability to work effectively in teams, among many other issues. The concept of total quality management (TQM) is that quality issues exist in every phase of the organization: product design, payroll, employee hiring and training, maintenance, management, etc. Thus the concepts, methodologies, and tools of quality improvement can be applied to all these phases of the organization, and true system optimization can take place.

There are a number of standards for quality systems in existance. Each branch of the U.S. government, for example, typically has a set of standards that each of its vendors must qualify to. Large companies such as Ford and Xerox have developed their own set of quality standards for qualifying vendors and for self-assessing their own quality systems. Perhaps the most prevalent today is the ISO 9000 series of quality system standards. ISO is the International Organization of Standards (in Geneva, Switzerland) and is represented in the United States by ANSI/ASQC. Qualification and adherence to the ISO standards is (will be) a requirement for any organization desiring to do business with companies in the European Economic Community countries (telecommunications, medical products, pharmaceuticals, construction, and manufacturing equipment initially); ISO will likely become a global standard with subsequent far-reaching implications.

The ISO9000 series consists actually of four standards: ISO 9000 (quality management and quality assurance standards—guidelines for selection and use), 9001 (quality systems—model for quality assurance in design, development, production, installation, and service), 9002 (quality systems—model for quality assurance in production and installation), 9003 (quality systems—model for quality assurance in final inspection and test), and 9004 (quality management and quality system elements—guidelines). ISO 9000 sets up the language and format of the set, 9001 to 9003 are to be used for contractual qualification and evaluation, and 9004 is a broader set of practices meant for internal audit use only. The basic elements of ISO 9001 are shown in Table 30.5 along with an example of one of the specific standards. For more information see ref. 23.

The Malcomb Baldrige National Quality Award was instituted in 1988. Reimann, director of the Baldrige program, believes that a fundamental purpose of the award is to strengthen quality in the United States. To him, the award is not an end in itself but rather a means toward this

TABLE 30.5. ISO 9001 Quality System Standard

Basic Elements

Management responsibility	Quality system
Contract review	Design control
Document control	Purchasing
Purchaser–supplier relationship	Product identification and traceability
Process control	Inspection and testing
Test equipment	Test status
Control of nonconformants	Corrective action
Handling, storage, etc.	Quality records
Internal quality audits	Training
Servicing	Statistical techniques

Example: Storage

The supplier shall provide storage areas or stock rooms to prevent damage or deterioration of the product, pending use or delivery. Appropriate methods for authorizing receipt and the dispatch to and from such areas shall be stipulated. To detect deterioration, the condition of the product in stock shall be assessed at appropriate intervals.

purpose. Reimann (24) reiterated four goals related to the Baldrige award: (*1*) elevate quality standards throughout the United States; (*2*) create a quality excellence standard for the United States used in all organizations; (*3*) create harmony, communication, and consistency; and (*4*) foster involvement of people and organizations. The award guidelines are spelled with enough detail to provide "a de facto definition of Total Quality for the U.S." (24). Table 30.6 lists the Baldrige criteria.

The Deming Prize, established in 1951 by the Union of Japanese Scientists and Engineers (JUSE), serves to recognize achievements in quality and show appreciation to W. Edwards Deming. Deming, an American statistician, is credited with bringing statistical quality control techniques to the Japanese and is regarded as a key factor in the rapid recovery of the Japanese economy after World War II. In 1950, Deming presented his first of many lectures to the Japanese, and a year later, the Deming Prize was established. Between 1951 and 1989, the Deming Application Prize had been awarded 84 times; as of September 1986, 27 of Japan's 60 largest industrial corporations had been awarded some form of the Deming Prize. Florida Power & Light, an American company who won in 1989, is the only overseas company to be recognized. The purpose of the Deming Prize is to recognize those companies that have successfully

TABLE 30.6. Criteria for Baldrige Award

1. Leadership
   a. Senior executive leadership
   b. Quality values
   c. Management of quality
   d. Public responsibility
2. Information and analysis
   a. Scope and management of quality data and information
   b. Analysis of quality data and information
3. Strategic quality planning
   a. Strategic quality planning process
   b. Quality leadership indicators in planning
   c. Quality priorities
4. Human resource use
   a. Human resource management
   b. Employee involvement
   c. Quality education and training
   d. Employee recognition and performance measurement
   e. Employee well-being and morale
5. Quality assurance of products and services
   a. Design and introduction of quality products and services
   b. Process and quality control
   c. Continuous improvement of processes, products, and services
   d. Quality assessment
   e. Documentation
   f. Quality assurance, assessment, and improvement of support services and business processes
   g. Quality assurance, assessment, and improvement of suppliers
6. Quality results
   a. Quality of products and services
   b. Comparison of quality results
   c. Business process, operational, and support service quality improvement
   d. Supplier quality improvement
7. Customer satisfaction
   a. Knowledge of customer requirements and expectations
   b. Customer relationship management
   c. Customer service standards
   d. Commitment to customers
   e. Compliant resolution for quality improvement
   f. Customer satisfaction determination
   g. Customer satisfaction results
   h. Customer satisfaction comparison

applied TQC, based on statistical quality control. The Deming Medal itself states "The right quality and uniformity are foundations of commerce, prosperity, and peace." A discussion of the similarities and differences between the criteria of the two awards has been published (25); see ref. 26 for a discussion of the "best practices" from Baldrige winners.

There are a number of quality gurus who have had great influence on the development of concepts within TQM: Crosby (2), Deming (3, 27, 28), Feigenbaum (29), and Juran (6) are perhaps the most often quoted. All recognize the need for management commitment, customer-driven systems, continual feedback and improvement, and development of the human potential within the organization. The references cited here provide a strong foundation for the larger, systemic issues involved in quality improvement.

BIBLIOGRAPHY

1. U.S. Department of Commerce and National Institute of Standards and Technology, *Application Guidelines for the Malcolm Baldrige Quality Award*, NIST, Gaithersburg, Md. 1992.

2. P. CROSBY, *Quality Is Free*, McGraw-Hill Book Co., Inc., New York, 1979.

3. W.E. DEMING, *Out of the Crisis*, MIT-CAES, Cambridge, Mass., 1986.

4. R.N. KACKAR, "Off-line Quality Control, Parameter Design, and the Taguchi Method," *J. Quality Technol.* **17,** 176–188 (1985).

5. S. MIZUNO, *Management for Quality Improvement*, Productivity Press, Cambridge, Mass., 1988.

6. J. JURAN, *Juran's Quality Control Handbook*, McGraw-Hill Book Co., Inc., New York, 1988.

7. D. GARVIN, "Competing on the Eight Dimensions of Quality," *Harvard Bus. Rev.*, 101–109 (Nov./Dec. 1987).

8. S. WHEELRIGHT and K. CLARK, *Revolutionizing Product Development*, Macmillan, New York, 1992.

9. J. HAUSER and D. CLAUSING, "The House of Quality", *Harvard Bus. Rev.*, 63–73 (May–June 1988).

10. Y. AKAO, ed., *Quality Function Deployment*, Productivity Press, Cambridge, Mass., 1990.

11. D. LLOYD and M. LIPOW, *Reliability: Management, Methods, and Mathematics*, ASQC Press, Milwaukee, Wis., 1984.

12. W. NELSON, *Accelerated Testing*, John Wiley & Sons, Inc., New York, 1990.

13. W. SHEWHART, *Economic Control of Quality of Manufactured Product*, Van Nostrand Co., New York, 1931.

14. R. DEVOR, T. CHANG, and J. SUTHERLAND, *Statistical Quality Design and Control*, Macmillan, New York, 1992.

15. H. GITLOW, S. GITLOW, A. OPPENHEIM, and R. OPPENHEIM, *Tools and Methods for the Improvement of Quality*, Irwin, Homewood, Ill., 1989.

16. G. BOX, W. HUNTER, and J. HUNTER, *Statistics for Experimenters*, John Wiley & Sons, Inc., New York, 1978.

17. D. MONTGOMERY, *Design and Analysis of Experiments*, John Wiley & Sons, Inc., New York, 1991.

18. G. BOX and N. DRAPER, *Empirical Model-Building and Response Surfaces*, John Wiley & Sons, Inc., New York, 1987.

19. G. TAGUCHI and D. CLAUSING, "Robust Design," *Harvard Bus. Rev.*, 90–1, 65–75 (1990).

20. J. PIGNATIELLO, JR., "An Overview of the Strategy and Tactics of Taguchi, *IIE Trans.* **20,** 247–254 (1988).

21. M. PHADKE, *Quality Engineering Using Robust Design*, Prentice-Hall, Inc., Englewood Cliffs, N.J., 1989.

22. U.S. General Accounting Office, *U.S. Companies Improve Performance Through Quality Efforts*, NIST, Gaithersburg, Md., May 1991, GAO-NSIAD 91-190.

23. U.S. Department of Commerce, *Questions and Answers on Quality, the ISO 9000 Standard Series, Quality System Registration, and Related Issues,* May 1992, NISTIR 4721.
24. C. REIMANN, paper presented at the Quest for Excellence Conference, New York, Mar. 1990.
25. K. DOOLEY, D. BUSH, J. ANDERSON, and M. RUNGTUSANATHAM, "The U.S. Baldrige Award and Japan's Deming Prize: Two Guidelines for Total Quality Control," *Eng. Manage. J.* **2**(3), 9–16 (1990).
26. M. BROWN, *Baldrige Award Winning Quality,* ASQC Press, Milwaukee, Wis., 1992.
27. M. WALTON, *The Deming Management Method,* Putnam, New York, 1986.
28. J. ANDERSON, J., K. DOOLEY, and S. MISTEREK, "The Role of Profound Knowledge in the Continual Improvement of Quality," *Hum. Sys. Manage.* **10**(4), 243–260 (1991).
29. A. FEIGENBAUM, *Total Quality Control,* McGraw-Hill Book Co., Inc., New York, 1983.

CHAPTER 31
Manufacturing Process Quality Control and Improvement

Kwei Tang and James M. Pruett
Louisiana State University

31.1 INTRODUCTION

Manufacturing process quality control and improvement is an important and vast subject. This chapter provides an overview of some of its key elements. The chapter is subdivided into three principal sections: (*1*) process quality control, (*2*) process improvement, and (*3*) product inspection. Within each section, a variety of approaches related to that topic are described. For example, in the section on process quality control, five distinctly different approaches are presented. The idea is that no approach is universally appropriate but that each approach is useful under certain conditions and should be understood.

31.2 PROCESS QUALITY CONTROL

Process Control Charts

Every production process exhibits variability. This variability may or may not be minor and may be due to a variety of possible causes. Some of the causes are a natural part of the process. For example, minor differences in raw materials, changes in the ambient temperature, or differences in operator skill levels may result in process variation. Generally, causes such as these have a relatively minor impact on the results of the process. As such, they are referred to as common (or random) causes of variation.

Other causes have larger impacts on process variation. For example, a miscalibrated instrument, an inappropriate policy for changing parameter settings in a continuous process, and major raw material differences may each result in significant process variation. Causes such as these are referred to as special causes.

A process having only common causes of variation present is said to be in control or, more accurately, in statistical control. A process with one or more special causes present (in addition to the inevitably present common causes of variation) is said to be out of control. Stated in another way, as long as the behavior of a process is stable and consistent, the process is in control. When the behavior of the process is erratic and inconsistent, the process is out of control.

It is common sense to eliminate the major causes of variation as quickly as possible. To do so, however, requires that the special causes be identified. Control charts are used to uncover the presence of special causes of variation. Unfortunately, control charts do not usually show the source (i.e., root cause) of the special cause variation. Identification of the source (or sources) of special cause variation always requires thought and often requires follow-up study.

Special cause variation can often be corrected at the process. For example, once an instrument is recognized as being out of calibration, it can typically be recalibrated at the request of the operator. (Note: finding out *why* the instrument has gone out of calibration may not be so easy to determine.) Common causes of variation are system faults that typically cannot be corrected without the attention of management. For example, variation in raw materials can be reduced only by improvements in the supplier's production process, which requires management intervention.

In-control processes exhibit stable variation patterns. Figure 31.1 shows a control chart (i.e., a point-by-point plot of some performance characteristic) of an in-control process. Out-of-control processes exhibit some type of unstable pattern of variation. Figure 31.2 shows control charts for five out-of-control processes. The question is, "How do we know when to stop regarding the process variation as originating from common causes and start regarding the variation as resulting from special causes?" Control charts provide guidelines to help users answer this question. In other words, control charts indicate when to look for special causes of variation. While there is always some chance of misinterpreting what is actually happening in a process, the goal is to set up a control chart that strikes an appropriate balance between the consequences of two kinds of errors: (*1*) those indicating that some special cause is present when it is not and (2) those not indicating that some special cause is present when it is. The first type of error (i.e., a false signal) is referred to as a Type I error, while the second type of error (i.e., lack of signal) is known as a Type II error. Precisely where control limits are set has a direct influence on the likelihood of each type of error.

Control charts typically have two control limits—an upper limit and a lower limit—and a centerline. The first step in setting up a control chart is to define a centerline. The primary purpose of the centerline is to provide a reference point (i.e., an expected or hoped for value of the process performance variable being charted). There are two primary ways of determining the centerline: the usual procedure is to calculate the overall mean of the process performance variable from the set of datum values available and the other appropriate method is to use the process target value as the centerline. The choice depends on the situation. For example, for some products the process target is simply not appropriate as a centerline (e.g., 100% pure chlorine). In situations such as these, it generally makes more sense to use the current process mean as the centerline (recognizing that centerline modifications will be necessary as process improvements are made). On the other hand, a target value is more appropriate in certain situations, such as when only a few datum points are available or when the process can easily be adjusted to target.

Once the centerline is set, the control limits may be calculated. In the United States, control limits are typically set 3 standard deviations above and below the centerline, with the standard deviation computed from process data. There are two reasons for using 3-standard-deviation control limits: (1) because of the characteristics of the normal distribution and (2) because of simplicity (e.g., 99% control limits would be set ±2.575 standard deviations from the centerline). Assuming a normally distributed process characteristic and control limits set ±3 standard deviations from the centerline, no action is deemed necessary unless there is a clear signal that something is wrong. That is, because 99.73% of the area under a normal curve is within ±3 standard deviations of the distribution's mean, a false signal (i.e., a Type I error) is given only about 0.27% of the time. (Note: still, there is nothing magical about this control limit. If the concern is primarily to find all potential trouble spots quickly, even if that means following up on a number of false leads, it may be preferable to set narrower control limits, say at ±2 standard deviations.)

The most basic rule of control charting is that points falling outside the control limits indicate that the process is probably out of control. Figure 31.3 shows a process with one point above the

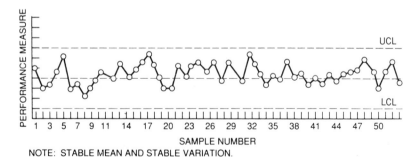

NOTE: STABLE MEAN AND STABLE VARIATION.

Figure 31.1. Control chart for an in-control process.

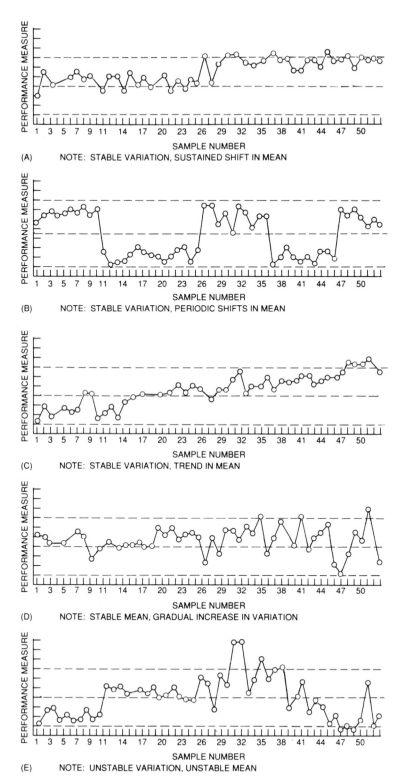

Figure 31.2. Control charts for five out-of-control processes.

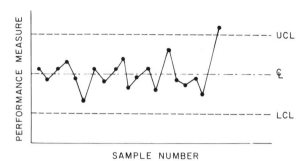

Figure 31.3. Control chart with one point above the upper control limit.

upper control limit, an alarm to correct what is wrong and to try to identify the root cause of the variation.

There are many varieties of control charts. The most commonly used control chart types are listed in Table 31.1 along with a brief description of when each is appropriate.

Additional control chart action rules, sometimes called run rules and zone rules and pioneered at AT&T (1), are often applied to reduce the probability of a Type II error (i.e., not reacting quickly enough when a special cause is present). Typically, they are based on the idea that a control chart can be logically divided into three zones. Zone C (closest to the centerline) represents the area within 1 standard deviation of the centerline, zone B represents the area between 1 and 2 standard deviations of the chart's centerline, and zone A represents the area between 2 and 3 standard deviations from the centerline. Figure 31.4 shows the zones and these rules are summarized in Table 31.2.

What can go wrong in the control charting process? A number of things: (1) choosing the wrong type of control chart (e.g., using an $\bar{x}$ chart when a c chart should have been chosen); (2) using an inappropriate estimate of the process standard deviation for the characteristic being plotted (e.g., calculating the standard deviation based on measurements taken from a homogeneous production process at nearly the same point in time); (3) measurement error, with subsequent actions based on the erroneous information; (4) irrational sampling (e.g., selecting samples that regularly include data from multiple shifts); and (5) inappropriate sampling frequency (e.g., taking samples before a problem occurs and after it has been corrected).

Continuous Sampling Plans

Continuous sampling plans are used in inspecting a continuous flow of individual items at a given location in a manufacturing process. The original form of the continuous sampling plan was CSP-1, developed by Dodge, designed to control the worse-case average outgoing nonconforming rate, i.e., average outgoing quality level (AOQL). The sampling plan starts with 100% inspection until i consecutive units are found to be conforming. The scheme is then switched to

TABLE 31.1. Brief Descriptions of Major Control Charts

Control Chart Category	Description
1. Individual measurements: x and R_m (and s) charts	Charts for individual measurements; used when multiple measurements are impractical or homogeneous
2. Grouped measurements: $\bar{x}$ and R charts	Charts for grouped measurements; used when multiple measurements at each sampling point represent independent indicators
3. Attribute charts: c, u, p, and np charts	Charts for counts (e.g., number of blemishes) and classified data (e.g., proportion of late shipments)
4. Other special-purpose charts: CUSUM, moving average, exponentially weighted moving average, and zone charts	CUSUM, especially useful in detecting small process shifts; moving average and exponentially weighted moving average, used in place of x chart to identify more quickly gradual shifts in process mean; zone, strength lies in its simple decision-rule structure

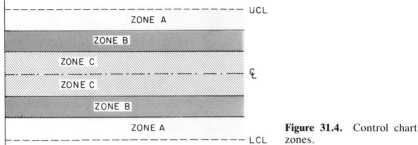

Figure 31.4. Control chart zones.

inspect (i.e., random sampling) a fraction f of units. Whenever a nonconforming item is found during the sampling period, the plan calls for samplers to immediately switch back to 100% inspection. Because several combinations of i and f can result in the same AOQL, the selection of i and f should also be based on the application environment. For example, using a large i and a small f would encourage the manufacturing department to maintain and improve the process, especially if the manufacturing department is responsible for carrying out the 100% inspection portion of the plan.

There are several variations on the CSP-1 plan. CSP-2 and CSP-3 were proposed to avoid frequent switches between 100% sampling and random sampling by allowing random sampling to continue under some conditions after a nonconforming item is found. Another variation on CSP-1 is to use more than one sampling frequency. As in CSP-1, when i consecutive conforming items are found, sampling with frequency f is begun. If the next i sampled items are found to be conforming, the sampling frequency is reduced to f_2. The sampling frequency will be further reduced to f_3 if the next i sampled items are also conforming, and so on.

Process Capability Analysis

Recall that a process is said to be in statistical control if only common cause variation is present. While being in statistical control implies that the process is stable, it does not imply that a high proportion of the process output will be within the specification limits set by the customer. Process capability refers to the ability of a process to produce products that meet customer specifications. Process capability indices are numeric indicators of the capability of a process to produce within specification limits. The two most widely used process capability indices, C_p and C_{pk}, are based on two explicit assumptions: (1) the process is in statistical control and (2) the process characteristic in question is normally distributed. If either or both of these assumptions are untrue, the resulting capability index values may provide misleading results.

An in-control process will produce nearly 100% of its product within $\pm 3\sigma$ of the process mean. If the process average is consistently maintained halfway between the upper and lower

TABLE 31.2. Rules of Thumb for Identifying Nonrandom Patterns

Name of Rule	Rule
1. Three-sigma rule	1 point falls beyond zone A
2. Three-successive-points rule	2 out of 3 successive points fall on the same side of the centerline in zone A or beyond
3. Five-successive-points rule	4 out of 5 successive points fall on the same side of the centerline in zone B or beyond
4. Run rule	7 consecutive points fall on one side of the centerline
5. Trend rule	7 consecutive points either increase or decrease
6. Zigzag rule	14 successive points alternate in an up-down pattern
7. Hugging rule	15 successive points fall in zone C
8. Other nonrandom patterns	(a) Systematic pattern, (b) cycling pattern, (c) wide-grouping pattern

specification limits (i.e., between USL and LSL) and the difference between the upper and lower specifications is greater than $\pm 3\sigma$, almost all of the process output will be within specifications. On the other hand, if the process mean is centered between the upper and lower specification limits and the difference between the upper and lower specifications is less than $\pm 3\sigma$, a significant proportion of the product will not be within specifications. If the process is not centered between the specification limits (or if there is only one specification limit), the limit closer to the process mean becomes the more crucial one in determining the capability of the process to meet customer specifications.

A process capability index is a numeric indicator of the capability or potential of a process to produce products within specification limits. A capability index value < 1 indicates that a significant proportion of process output will be outside specifications, while a capability index value ≥ 1 indicates that almost all process output will be within specifications. By industry standards, however, capability index values less than 1.33 are often considered unacceptable.

If an in-control process is centered, a measure of the capability of the process to meet customer specifications may be determined by comparing the actual process spread (i.e., 6σ) with the customer specifications. The capability index known as C_p (defined below) is intended to represent the process-centered situation. (Note: ideally, σ is the true process standard deviation. In practice, an estimate of σ is typically used.)

$$C_p = \frac{USL - LSL}{6\sigma}$$

Figure 31.5 shows three situations describing possible outcomes for the normally distributed, in-control, process-centered case. Figure 31.5a describes a marginally capable process situation, Figure 31.5b describes a capable process situation, and Figure 31.5c describes an incapable process situation. The accompanying three capability index values provide clear numeric descriptions of each situation (i.e., $C_p = 1.00$, $C_p = 1.11$, and $C_p = 0.78$, respectively).

For the noncentered case, a measure of the capability of the process to meet specifications may be determined by comparing half the actual process spread (i.e., 3σ) with the difference between the process mean and the specification limit that is closer to the process mean. The process capability index used is known as C_{pk}, which in effect provides a worst-case capability index value. C_{pk} is defined as the minimum of two one-sided capability indices, C_{pu} and C_{pl}, where C_{pu} and C_{pl} are defined as follows:

$$C_{pu} = \frac{USL - \mu}{6\sigma}$$

$$C_{pl} = \frac{\mu - LSL}{6\sigma}$$

(Note: ideally, μ is the true process mean. In practice, μ is usually estimated from process data.)

Figure 31.6 shows three situations describing possible outcomes for the normally distributed, in-control, noncentered process case. Figure 31.6a describes a marginally capable process situation, Figure 31.6b describes a capable process situation, and Figure 31.6c describes an incapable process situation. The accompanying three capability index values provide meaningful numeric descriptions of each situation (i.e., $C_{pk} = 1.00$, $C_{pk} = 1.17$, $C_{pk} = 0.55$, respectively).

There are only three ways to improve the capability index for a process: (1) by moving the process mean, (2) by reducing the process spread, and (3) by increasing the range between the upper and lower specification values. Because customer specification limits are generally more likely to be tightened than loosened, most process improvement efforts tend to be focused on changes in the process mean or on changes leading to reductions in the overall process spread.

Recall that two explicit assumptions are prerequisite to a meaningful process capability index value. Assumption 1 is that the process be in statistical control. If the process is not in control, it is not stable and capability index computations have little meaning. Assumption 2 is

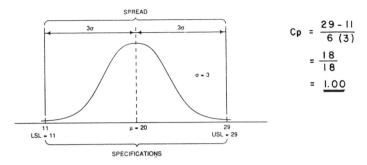

$$C_p = \frac{29 - 11}{6(3)}$$

$$= \frac{18}{18}$$

$$= 1.00$$

(a) Centered, In–Control, Normally Distributed Process
(Specifications Equal Spread)

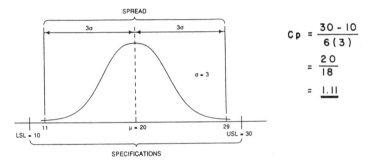

$$C_p = \frac{30 - 10}{6(3)}$$

$$= \frac{20}{18}$$

$$= 1.11$$

(b) Centered, In–Control, Normally Distributed Process
(Specifications Greater than Spread)

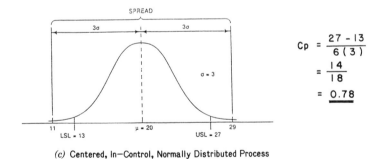

$$C_p = \frac{27 - 13}{6(3)}$$

$$= \frac{14}{18}$$

$$= 0.78$$

(c) Centered, In–Control, Normally Distributed Process
(Specifications Less than Spread)

Figure 31.5.   Normally distributed, in-control, centered process.

that the performance variable in question is approximately normally distributed. If the process is not normally distributed, the relationships presented regarding C_p and C_{pk} are not valid. Skewed product characteristic distributions often occur when a process is approaching some natural limit (e.g., 100% purity), and near-flat (i.e., nearly uniformly distributed) product characteristic distributions sometimes result from the mixing of products from several supposedly identical but slightly different product-characteristic distributions. Figure 31.7 shows what can

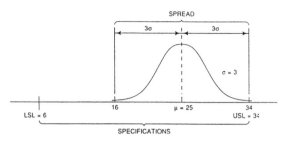

$$Cpu = \frac{34-25}{3(3)}$$
$$= \frac{9}{9}$$
$$= 1.00$$
$$Cpl = \frac{25-6}{3(3)}$$
$$= \frac{19}{9}$$
$$= 2.11$$
$$Cpk = \min(1.00, 2.11)$$
$$= \underline{\underline{1.00}}$$

(a) Off—Center, In—Control, Normally Distributed Process
(Specifications Greater than Spread)

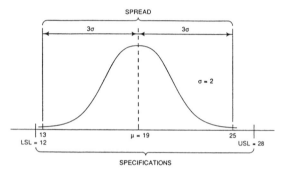

$$Cpu = \frac{28-19}{3(2)}$$
$$= \frac{9}{6}$$
$$= 1.50$$
$$Cpl = \frac{19-12}{3(2)}$$
$$= \frac{7}{6}$$
$$1.17$$
$$Cpk = \min(1.50, 1.17)$$
$$= \underline{\underline{1.17}}$$

(b) Off—Center, In—Control, Normally Distributed Process
(Specifications More than Pread and Process Center Nearer LSL)

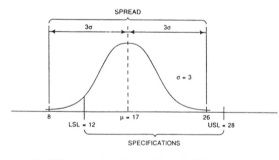

$$Cpu = \frac{28-17}{3(3)}$$
$$= \frac{11}{9}$$
$$= 1.22$$
$$Cpl = \frac{17-12}{3(3)}$$
$$= \frac{5}{9}$$
$$= 0.55$$
$$Cpk = \min(1.22, 0.55)$$
$$= \underline{\underline{0.55}}$$

(c) Off—Center, In—Control, Normally Distributed Process
(Specifications Less than Spread and Problem with LSL)

Figure 31.6. Normally distributed, in-control, noncentered process.

happen in regard to capability index values when the distribution in question is not normal. A third (implicit) assumption is that estimates of the process mean and process standard deviation used in the capability index calculations are representative of the process. For example, if the process standard deviation is underestimated, capability index values will be unwittingly inflated.

Several valid criticisms have been levied at process capability indices: (*1*) they tend to oversimplify process characteristics by providing a single number for judging a process, (*2*) they

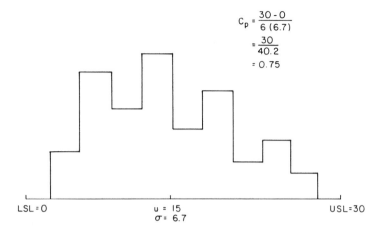

$$C_p = \frac{30 - 0}{6\,(6.7)}$$

$$= \frac{30}{40.2}$$

$$= 0.75$$

Figure 31.7.   Nonnormally distributed process.

do not provide an indication of how close to target the process is able to produce, (*3*) they may provide misleading results unless the characteristic measured is both in control and normally distributed, (*4*) they do not provide an estimate of the proportion of within-specification product, (*5*) they do not tell how much change in the process mean can be absorbed by a capable process before it begins to produce an out-of-spec product, and (*6*) they may provide dramatically different results depending on the amount of data used to estimate μ and σ. As a result of these criticisms, several alternative process capability index forms have been suggested to overcome these shortcomings.

In-Process Sensors

On-line sensors are often used to collect important in-process measurements for monitoring machine operations or process conditions. In practice, it is difficult to find an available sensor that functions effectively in all manufacturing environments. Important factors for selecting appropriate sensors include physical size, accuracy, consistency, contact or noncontact, and operating and information (signal) processing requirements.

Sensors can be classified into two categories, direct and indirect, based on the relation between the measurements provided by sensors and the true machine conditions. Direct sensors include optical, electrical resistance, radioactive, and pneumatic. Indirect sensor measurements include, for example, tool cutting and thrust force, vibration, and tool temperature (2, 3).

Because direct sensor measurements are often difficult or expensive to obtain, extensive efforts have been made to find reliable measurements that are closely related to (correlated with) machine conditions and that are relatively inexpensive to measure. This involves physical experimentation and statistical analysis to establish meaningful relationships (patterns) between sensor measurements and machine conditions. To use indirect sensors effectively, diagnostic rules must be carefully designed to indicate when corrective actions should be taken. Statistical methods, such as discriminant analysis, principal components analysis, and time series analysis, have been used. In addition, a variety of modern computer-based techniques, such as expert systems, machine learning, and neural networks, have also been proposed.

Expert Systems

If evidence indicates that process faults may exist, it is necessary physically to check the system in search of the problem. For a complex manufacturing system, the diagnostic process requires extensive knowledge and experience. Expert systems, which are essentially computer models of experts' knowledge and experience, may be an effective tool in such situations. The most common expert systems are rule-based systems, consisting of three major components: a knowledge base, a "blackboard", and an inference engine. The knowledge base contains a set of "If A then B" statements used to describe precisely the causality deterministic relationships among various observed performance measures, operating conditions, and manufacturing faults; the blackboard is composed of a list of possible faults that might be expected to occur in the manufacturing system, and the inference engine is a set of procedures (algorithms) intended to emulate a human expert's reasoning processes for searching the knowledge base and the blackboard for the possible faults related to given symptoms.

Establishing the knowledge base is the most costly task in developing an expert system. In general, the rules in the knowledge base can be obtained from experts' opinions or from historical data. How knowledge is acquired and modeled in computer-implementable form is critical to the success of developing an expert system, because it affects not only the efficiency of the inference engine but also the ease with which future updates and modifications to the knowledge base are made. Expert systems can be employed in a real-time manufacturing environment. They are particularly useful when on-line sensors can be used to monitor the process and supply real-time feedback data to the expert system to automate the diagnostic process. In this situation, it is crucial to design the knowledge base so that on-line measurements can be easily integrated with existing information.

Successful development and implementation of an effective expert system requires careful planning, effective knowledge acquisition, reliable software, and skillful computer programming as well as extensive testing and validation.

31.3　PROCESS IMPROVEMENT

Simple Graphical SPC Tools

Process improvement begins with process understanding. The six graphical tools (4) described in this section are frequently used to help understand a process and, subsequently, to help improve it. The tools presented are the Pareto diagram, the histogram, the run chart, the dot plot, the scatterplot, and the cause-and-effect diagram.

Pareto Diagram

Pareto diagrams help to focus attention on the most important issues. Pareto diagrams are often used to display rank-ordered causes of problems, with the general idea that more important problems should be addressed before less important ones. Figure 31.8 shows a Pareto diagram of defective springs from 1 week's production (5). Cracked springs are clearly the most-often occurring problem.

Histogram

A histogram represents a simple way of grouping data by frequency of occurrence. Histograms are usually able to show the general form of the data (i.e., whether the data are generally normal, bimodal, or skewed). Figure 31.9 shows a histogram describing the crack size from the production of springs (5). By examining the histogram, it is apparent that the largest cracks are four times as large as the smallest cracks and that the most likely crack size is in the 2.0 to 2.5 range. Figure 31.10 shows the same crack-size data in two histograms. Each histogram represents the size of cracks on two different types of springs.

Run Chart

A run chart presents the same data used to develop the histogram but shows the values plotted sequentially over time. The value of a run chart lies in its ability to show time-dependent trends (gradually increasing or decreasing values), runs (consistently high or low values), shifts (sudden increase or decrease), and cycles (up-down-up-down pattern). Run charts typically look like control charts without control limits. Figure 31.11 shows a run chart based on the crack size data originally used to develop the Pareto diagram shown in Figure 31.8. The run chart indicates that crack sizes seem to be increasing over time.

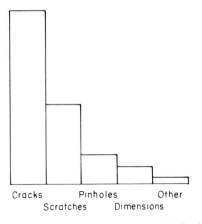

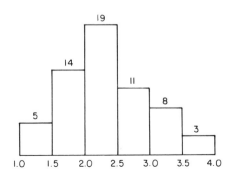

Figure 31.8. Pareto diagram of defective springs.

Figure 31.9. Histogram of crack size from production of springs.

Dot Plot

Considerable amounts of data are required to construct meaningful histograms. Dot plots, however, can be constructed from only a few datum points and, although not as instructive as histograms, can provide similar insight into a process. Figure 31.12 shows the amount of residual metal left on the catalyst from a cat-cracking unit over a period of about 7 weeks. Because of the small number of datum values, the construction of a histogram simply does not make sense. The dot plot shows that the data are generally clustered around 1000 ppm.

Scatterplot

Scatterplots (sometimes called scatter diagrams, crossplots, or x–y plots) are used to study the possible relationship between two variables. The horizontal axis (x axis) is used to represent one variable, and the vertical axis (y axis) is used to represent another. Inspection of the resulting scatter of points indicates how closely the variables are related. Figure 31.13 shows the relationship between bromine and moisture content in a plant whose primary product is industrial chlorine. In general, it appears that the amount of bromine present decreases as the moisture content increases.

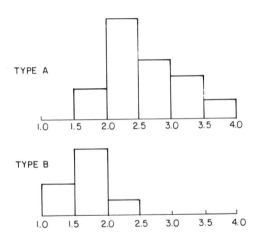

Figure 31.10. Histograms of crack size from production of springs.

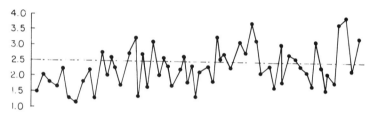

Figure 31.11.   Run chart of crack size from production of springs.

Cause-and-Effect Diagram

Cause-and-effect diagrams (also known as Ishikawa diagrams or fishbone diagrams) are used to show relationships between problems and possible problem causes. Cause-and-effect diagrams are often used to collect and categorize ideas generated during or after brainstorming sessions because disjointed comments can be quickly and logically added to the diagram. Figure 31.14 shows a cause-and-effect diagram to help identify possible causes of an apparent increase in the number of flat tires on in-plant forklifts (6). As shown, the problem (effect) is usually shown at the far right of the diagram with possible causes, subcauses, and subsubcauses placed on arrows leading to the effect. (Note: the general categories of people, materials, machinery, methods, and environment are often used as starting point causes.)

Design of Experiments

Control charts are used to monitor processes to determine whether or not special causes of variation are present. If a control chart indicates an in-control process, no immediate action is taken. Suppose, however, that while the control chart indicates that no special causes of variation are present, the capability of the process is insufficient to meet customer specifications. What process improvements are in order? That is, which factors are most important to improving process capability? Experimental design provides a systematic method of examining a process and identifying those factors that act as major contributors to the common cause variation present. This section discusses some of the principles of experimental design.

Clearly, one important objective of designed experimentation is to identify the most important sources of variation present in a process. For instance, when trying subjectively to decide which factors have the most influence on the variation present in a production process, a list of 20 or more possible causes might be developed. Some of these factors might be relatively easy to control (e.g., process temperature), whereas the control of others might be more difficult (e.g., catalyst reaction time) and the control of still others impossible (e.g., ambient temperature). A potentially meaningful way to address the problem is to identify the two or three most influential factors and either design ways to control them (e.g., using process temperature control rules) or to prepare for them (e.g., reduce the effect of ambient temperature by increasing the amount of process insulation). To control a process, it is not only helpful to know which factors cause the most variation in the process but also helpful to know how much each of the factors influence the performance characteristic (response variable). For instance, if we want to control the octane level of a gasoline blend, it is important to know both that butane has a major effect on octane level and the amount of that effect. A designed experiment is often helpful in drawing such inferences about a process—clarifying information (i.e., unambiguous) about the contributions of specific factors (possibly including the development of a mathematical model describing each factor's relative contribution), learning about the interactions among factors, and measuring the variation the experimenters were unable to account for or control (the so-called experimental error).

But how is it done? Box and Bisgaard (5) describe a designed experiment in which three factors have been identified as contributors to the creation of cracks in springs. The three

Figure 31.12.   Dot plot of residual metal left on catalyst.

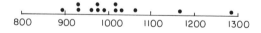

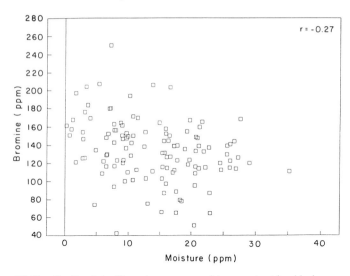

Figure 31.13.   Scatterplot of bromine versus moisture content in chlorine samples.

Flat Tires; Cause-and-Effect Diagram

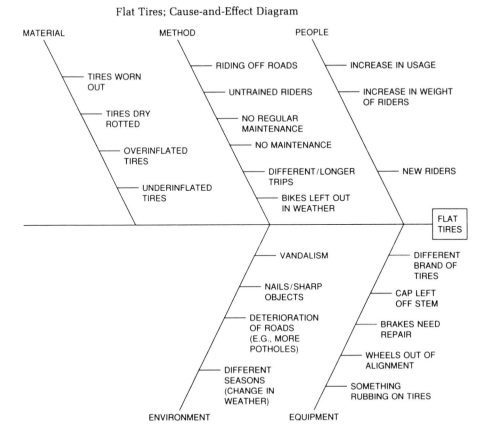

Figure 31.14.   Cause-and-effect diagram for flat tires on in-plant forklifts.

factors are (1) the temperature of the steel before quenching, (2) the carbon content of the steel, and (3) the temperature of the quenching oil. The purpose of the experiment is to determine the effects that the three factors have on the number of cracks. Each factor was considered at two levels, a high level and a low level. Specifically, the temperature of the steel before quenching was considered at 1450°F and 1600°F, the content of carbon was considered at 0.50% and 0.70%, and the temperature of the quenching oil was considered at 70°F and 120°F. Before the development of the notion of statistically designed experiments, it was believed that the best way to conduct experimentation was to vary one factor at a time. Box and Bisgaard describe a two-level, three-factor, factorial experimental design (a design first proposed by Fisher in the 1920s) in which the three factors are varied concurrently. Not only do such designs require fewer experimental runs, they actually provide more information (i.e., information on the main factors and on the interactions between those factors). Figure 31.15 shows the experimental factors for this experiment arranged as a box, Table 31.3 presents the factors so that each row represents a separate experimental run, and Figure 31.16 shows the experimental results (i.e., resulting percentage of cracks) on the box originally shown in Figure 31.15.

What can we learn from this experiment? Several things. First, the effects of the three main factors can be found. The effect on the springs of varying the temperature of steel from 1450°F to 1600°F can be seen by examining the following pairs of readings: (67%, 79%), (59%, 90%), (61%, 75%), and (52%, 87%). In each pair, the first value represents the value of the response variable at the low steel temperature level and the second represents the value of the response variable at the high steel temperature level—but within each pair, the other two factors are held constant. Therefore, the effect on the percentage of cracks in springs of changing the temperature of steel from the low level to the high level is as follows:

STEEL TEMPERATURE EFFECT
(ON CRACK PERCENTAGE)

79 − 67	= 12%
75 − 61	= 14%
90 − 59	= 31%
87 − 52	= 35%
Average	= 23%

In other words, the percentage of cracks in the springs is on the average 23% more when the higher steel temperature level was used before quenching. In similar fashion, the average effects of varying the carbon content and the oil temperature can also be computed (−5.0% and 1.5%, respectively).

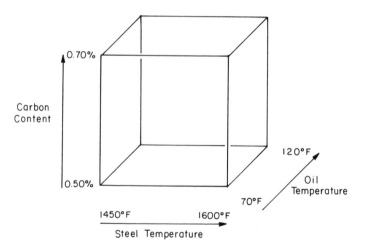

Figure 31.15. Sketch showing experimental factors for spring-cracking experiment.

TABLE 31.3. Experimental Factors

Run[a]	Steel Temperature (°F)	Carbon (Percent)	Oil Temperature (°F)	Springs without Cracks (Percent)	Day of Run
1	1450	0.50	70	67	1
2	1600	0.50	70	79	2
3	1450	0.70	70	61	2
4	1600	0.70	70	75	1
5	1450	0.50	120	59	2
6	1600	0.50	120	90	1
7	1450	0.70	120	52	1
8	1600	0.70	120	87	2

[a] Each run number represents a different experimental run.

Second, the effect that interactions between variables have on the response variable can also be found. For example, again closely examine the differences in the response variable values when the steel temperature is changed from the low level to the high level (i.e., 12%, 14%, 31%, and 35%). The first two numbers—12%, 14%—represent the case in which 70°F oil temperature was used, while the last two numbers—31%, 35%—represent the case in which 120°F oil temperature was used. This indicates that the percentage of cracks is a function of the interaction between steel temperature and oil temperature. Specifically, the interaction effect is computed as follows:

Steel temperature effect with 70°F oil: (31% + 35%)/2 = 33%
Steel temperature effect with 120°F oil: (12% + 14%)/2 = 13%
Difference: (33% − 13%) = 20%
Steep temperature and oil interaction effect: 20%/2 = 10%

Again, similar computations can be made for the interaction effects involving steel temperature and carbon content (1.5%) and carbon content and oil temperature (1.0%).

A judiciously designed experiment can also reduce the overall variation present. For exam-

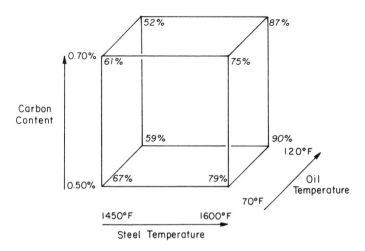

Figure 31.16. Sketch showing experimental results (i.e., resulting percentage of cracks) with factors for spring-cracking experiment.

ple, suppose that 2 days are necessary to make the eight experimental runs. Unfortunately, if the first four experimental runs were performed on day 1 and the last four experimental runs were performed on day 2, an interpretation problem would be created. Specifically, the oil temperature would be 70°F on day 1 and 120°F on day 2. Therefore, it would not be possible to tell whether the change in oil temperature affected the percentage of cracks or whether the day of the experiment was the contributing factor. (In statistical terminology, oil temperature and day of experiment are said to be confounded.) In the last column of Table 31.3, the day each experimental run was to be made is specified. Note that on each day, two experimental runs were made with oil temperature at 70°F and two experimental runs were made with oil temperature at 120°F. (In fact, close inspection shows that all three factors are shown twice on each day.) The result is that the day the experimental run was performed is not confounded with the three primary factors. Approaches such as these are commonly applied in designed experimentation, the net result of which is better process understanding and potentially improved processes.

Taguchi, a Japanese engineer and scientist, has over a number of years profoundly influenced the quality of Japanese products by his use of experimental design (7). Taguchi focused on products and processes in the design phase (i.e., upstream processes). In particular, Taguchi's experimental designs have been used to minimize variation from mean (or target), to make products more robust with respect to environmental conditions, and to make products less sensitive to component variation. These are examples of what Taguchi refers to as parameter design. In addition, Taguchi successfully promoted the use of unusual approaches for presenting and analyzing data (such as the signal-to-noise ratio and the so-called loss function).

Monitoring Process Improvement

Process improvement can be monitored using several sources of information, including outgoing product inspection, customer satisfaction surveys, process control records, and process scheduling and product shipment records. In this section, a chart based on C_p for monitoring process improvement is introduced. This chart can be used to monitor the process of improving C_p to a given higher level.

Let Y be the performance variable of interest, and USL and LSL are the upper and lower specifications limits, respectively. Suppose the current C_p value is C_o, and the following linear pattern of improvement is used:

$$C_p(t) = C_o + \beta t, \ t > 0$$

At each time period a sample of size n is taken to obtain the following estimate:

$$\hat{C}_p = (USL - LSL)/6s$$

where s is the sample standard deviation. Let $\chi^2_{\gamma,n-1}$ denote the γth quantile of the chi square distribution. If $\hat{C}_p \geq C_p(t)\sqrt{(n-1)/\chi^2_{\alpha,n-1}}$, then we conclude that the process capability has been improved to $C_p(t)$. Note that because $(n-1)/\chi^2_{\alpha,n-1}$ is larger than 1 for a reasonable α value, $\hat{C}_p$ must be larger than $C_p(t)$ to draw a positive conclusion. On the other hand, we conclude that the process capability actually deteriorates to below $C_p(t-1)$ if $\hat{C}_p < C_p(t-1)\sqrt{(n-1)/\chi^2_{1-\alpha,n-1}}$. If $C_p(t-1)\sqrt{(n-1)/\chi^2_{1-\alpha,n-1}} < \hat{C}_p < C_p(t)\sqrt{(n-1)/\chi^2_{\alpha,n-1}}$ (8), then we conclude that the process neither improved nor deteriorated.

A chart to monitor the process can be developed based on the following two control limits:

$$UCL(t) = C_p(t)\sqrt{(n-1)/\chi^2_{\alpha,n-1}}$$

and

$$LCL(t) = C_p(t-1)\sqrt{(n-1)/\chi^2_{1-\alpha,n-1}}$$

Depending on the process or product, potential patterns of improvement may be different. Improvement patterns may be based on a previous experience, on a similar process, or on market conditions and anticipated competitor's improvement progress.

31.4 PRODUCT INSPECTION

Design of Inspection Plans

Sampling and screening (100% inspection) are two common forms of inspecting incoming materials and outgoing finished products. There are several advantages of using sampling over screening.

1. Sampling requires less inspection effort, so that total inspection cost is lower and potential damage caused by inspection operations is also lower.
2. Sampling can be used even when inspection is destructive.
3. Sampling techniques are able to obtain information concerning product quality more quickly, an important factor when timely feedback is crucial to a production decision.
4. Sampling places more emphasis on the use of precision equipment and skilled workers to identify problems and to reduce inspection errors.

On the other hand, screening can be cost effective when inspection operations can be automated so that inspection is accurate and inexpensive. Because of the advances of automation, screening has been widely used in high speed and large volume production. For example, every outgoing can of motor oil can be "inspected" by an automatic weighing machine placed near the end of the production process. The use of screening is also supported by Deming's (9) "all-or-none" rule, which suggests that partial inspection to remove nonconforming items from a stable population is not economical. Note, however, that the assumptions used to derive Deming's result are (*1*) the manufacturing process is in control with a known nonconforming rate and (*2*) the cost of inspection and the cost of passing nonconforming items are linear functions of the number of inspected items and the number of unfound nonconforming items, respectively.

In designing an inspection plan, possible inherent variability in inspection processes due to variations in testing materials and inspectors should be taken into consideration. For attribute inspection, there are two types of errors. A Type I error occurs when a conforming item is classified as nonconforming, and a Type II error occurs when a nonconforming item is classified as conforming. For variable inspection, inspection error is characterized in terms of bias and imprecision, where bias is the difference between the true value of the performance variable of an item and the average of a large number of repeated measurements of the same item, and imprecision is the dispersion among the measurements of the same item. When inspection errors are large, the outcomes of inspection will be significantly affected. In this situation, inspection plans must be adjusted by incorporating inspection errors into consideration. In the next section, acceptance sampling and screening are discussed. Table 31.4 (10) contains useful descriptions of major acceptance sampling plans and their applications.

TABLE 31.4. Acceptance Sampling Procedures and Their Applications[a]

Objective	Attribute Procedure	Variable Procedure
Assure quality levels to consumer and producer	Select plan for specific OC curve	Select Plan for Specific OC curve
Maintain quality at a target	AQL system; MIL-STD-105D, ANSI/ASQC Z1.4	AQL system; MIL-STD-414, ANSI/ASQC Z1.9
Assure average outgoing quality level	AOQL system; Dodge-Romig plans	AOQL system
Reduce inspection, with small sample sizes, good-quality history	Chain sampling	Narrow-limit gauging
Reduce inspection after good-quality history	Skip-lot sampling; double sampling	Skip-lot sampling; double sampling
Assure quality no worse than target	LTPD plan; Dodge-Romig plans	LTPD plan; hypothesis testing

[a] From ref. 10.

Inspection Methods

Single Acceptance Sampling by Attributes

Acceptance sampling is commonly used to decide whether a production lot should be accepted by assessing the lot's conformity to given quality criteria using the results of some type of sampling process. Depending on the nature of the performance variable, there are two forms of acceptance sampling plans: attribute acceptance sampling plans and variable acceptance sampling plans.

The simplest form of an attributes sampling plan involves randomly drawing a single sample of n items from a lot consisting of N items. If the number of nonconforming items d exceeds a predetermined acceptance number c, the lot is rejected and subjected to corrective action. Such plans are called single sampling plans. For a given single sampling plan (n, c), the probability of accepting a lot is a function of the nonconforming fraction (rate) present in the lot. The relation between the probability of acceptance and the lot nonconforming rate is called the operating characteristic (OC) of a sampling plan. OC curves (i.e., x-y plots that relate probability of acceptance and lot nonconforming rate) provide important information for selecting a sampling plan.

Let $\Pr(x, n, N, p)$ denote the probability that x nonconforming items are found in a single sample of size n. The hypergeometric, binomial, and Poisson distributions are commonly used to estimate $\Pr(x, n, N, p)$. Which distribution is chosen depends on the assumptions made, the sampling situation, and the sampling ratio n/N. If the sampling ratio is small (say < 0.10) or if we assume that the sample is drawn from a series of lots produced by a stable process, then the binomial distribution should be used. Its form is given below:

$$\Pr(x, n, N, p) = \binom{n}{x} p^x (1 - p)^{n-x} \ (x = 0, 1, 2, \ldots, n)$$

For a given p and a sampling plan (n, c), the probability of accepting a lot is given by

$$P_A(n, c, p) = \sum_{x=0}^{c} \Pr(x, n, N, p)$$

The OC curve that can be obtained from the last expression is called a type B OC curve. Such curves describe the protection provided by acceptance sampling for a series of lots from a particular process. Figure 31.17 shows the type B OC curve of the sampling plan $n = 90$, $c = 2$.

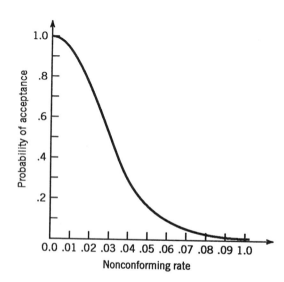

Figure 31.17. OC curve of the single attribute sampling plan; $n = 90$, $c = 2$.

To determine the level of protection for an individual lot, the hypergeometric distribution should be used. The resulting OC curve is called a type A OC curve.

Several quality indices have been used to help select an appropriate sampling plan. One approach is to base the decision on the AQL, which is defined as "the maximum nonconforming rate that, for purpose of acceptance sampling, can be considered satisfactory as a process average" (11). Another approach is to base the decision on the lot tolerance percent defective (LTPD), which is defined as "the nonconforming rate for which, for purpose of acceptance sampling, the consumers wish the probability of acceptance to be restricted to a specified low level." The probability of rejecting a lot with a nonconforming rate equal to AQL is defined as the producer's risk α, and the probability of accepting a lot with a nonconforming rate equal to LTPD is defined as the consumer's risk β.

It is common practice to determine a sampling plan by controlling α and β. Let AQL and LTPD be equal to p_1 and p_2, respectively, and let $\Pr(x, n, N, p)$ be defined by a binomial distribution. Then, for given α and β, the sampling plan parameters are obtained by finding the n and c values that satisfy the following two equations:

$$\alpha = 1 - \sum_{x=0}^{c} \binom{n}{x} p_1^x (1 - p_1)^{n-x}$$

$$\beta = \sum_{x=0}^{c} \binom{n}{x} p_2^x (1 - p_2)^{n-x}$$

Traditionally, the literature (e.g., ref. 10) has provided n and c. Today, most statistical software packages include this computational ability, which makes the knowledgeable selection of an appropriate sampling plan more convenient.

If all the rejected lots are screened and nonconforming items are repaired or replaced by conforming items, the final outgoing nonconforming rate is affected by the selected sampling plan. Average outgoing quality (AOQ) is defined as the average nonconforming rate following the use of an acceptance sampling plan based on a given incoming lot nonconforming rate. Because the rejected lots do not contain nonconforming items after 100% inspection and replacement, the expected number of nonconforming items in an accepted lot is $(N - n)p$,

$$AOQ = \frac{P_A(n, c, p)p(N - n)}{N}$$

The average outgoing quality level (AOQL) is the maximum value of AOQ over the range of all possible lot-nonconforming rates. Sampling plans based on AOQL ensure that the long-term average nonconforming rate is no worse than the given AOQL value.

Single Acceptance Sampling by Variables

Because variables data (i.e., measurement values) contain more information then attributes data (i.e., yes–no judgments), at least in theory, variable sampling plans are more efficient (i.e., fewer items sampled) than comparable attribute sampling plans in terms of identifying poor quality lots. However, using variable sampling plans, additional assumptions regarding the process distribution must be made and inspection procedures may be more costly and/or more difficult. In particular, to use most existing variable sampling plan tables, the performance variable must be assumed to follow a normal distribution.

Let Y denote the performance variable of interest, so that μ and σ are, respectively, the true mean and true standard deviation of Y. In the following discussion, σ is assumed to be known. The method of finding a variable sampling plan is based on the relationship between the product specifications and the values of μ and σ. For simplicity, let Y be a "larger-is-better" variable and let LSL be the variable's lower specification limit. The associated z score (i.e., the corresponding standard normal value) for LSL is given by

$$z_L = \frac{LSL - \mu}{\sigma}$$

Next, let $\Phi(\cdot)$ denote the normal distribution function. The actual nonconforming rate is then $\Phi(z_L)$. When the sample mean $\bar{y}$ is used to estimate μ, the z score is estimated by substituting $\bar{y}$

for μ. The following decision rule is used: If $z = (LSL - \bar{y})/\sigma < k$, the lot is accepted. Otherwise, the lot is rejected.

Suppose the objective is to control the probability of acceptance at $1 - \alpha$, when the nonconforming rate is p_1, and the probability of acceptance at β, when the nonconforming rate is p_2. From the normal table, we can find z score values z_1 and z_2 which satisfy $\Phi(z_1) = p_1$ and $\Phi(z_2) = p_2$. Then μ_1 and μ_2 can be obtained from the standardizing equation given above. The probability of acceptance when the nonconforming rate is p_1 is given by

$$\Pr((LSL - \bar{y})/\sigma) < k \mid \mu = \mu_1) = 1 - \alpha$$

or

$$\Pr(\sqrt{n}(\bar{y} - \mu)/\sigma > \sqrt{n}(-k - \mu) \mid \mu = \mu_1) = 1 - \alpha$$

Because $\sqrt{n}(\bar{y} - \mu)/\sigma$ follows a standard normal distribution, the above expression can be written as

$$\Phi(\sqrt{n}(-k - \mu_1)) = 1 - \alpha$$

A similar expression associated with β is given by

$$\Phi(\sqrt{n}(-k - \mu_2)) = \beta$$

Using the normal table and simple algebra, n and k can be found. When σ is unknown, the process of deriving the sampling plan is more complicated because σ must be estimated using the sample standard deviation. In this case, the noncentral t distribution is used to replace the standard normal distribution in the computation process.

Double, Multiple, and Sequential Sampling

Using a single sampling plan, it is possible that the number of nonconforming items will exceed the acceptance number even before the sampling inspection process is completed (even though, for completeness, the entire sample will subsequently be inspected). Consequently, multiple sampling plans have the potential advantage of reducing sampling effort (and the associated cost) by dividing the sampling procedure into several stages, where a smaller sample is inspected at each stage. For example, a double sampling plan consists of at most two samples. Initially, a random sample of size n_1 is taken from the lot and inspected. If the number of nonconforming items is less than or equal to the acceptance number c_1, the lot is accepted. If the number of nonconforming items exceeds the rejection number r_1, the lot is rejected. Otherwise, a second sample of size n_2 is taken and the items inspected. After the second sample, a decision must be made. The lot is rejected if the total number of nonconforming items observed in the two samples exceeds the second acceptance number c_2. Otherwise, the lot is accepted.

Multiple sampling plans generally extend the logic used to apply double sampling plans. Sequential sampling is a special case of multiple sampling, which employs a constant sample size of one. Theoretically, however, sequential sampling plans may result in 100% inspection of the lot. Because the purpose of using double, multiple, and sequential sampling is to reduce sampling efforts, an important criterion for evaluating these sampling plans is the average sample number (ASN). For double sampling plans, ASN is equal to the sum of n_1 and the product of n_2 and the probability that the second sample will be taken.

Published Sampling Tables

MIL-STD-105D, a series of tables leading to specific sampling plans, was developed during World War II. It is probably the most widely used of all acceptance sampling plan development systems. MIL-STD-105D uses AQL as the quality index and contains three inspection phases: normal, tightened, and reduced. MIL-STD-105D tables contain 16 AQLs, ranging from 0.010% to 10%. For a given lot size and a given AQL, a sampling plan can be easily found by inspection of the tables. Switching rules have been developed to help users decide when each of the three inspection phases should be used. For example, tightened inspection should be used when two of the five preceding lots have been rejected under normal inspection, and reduced inspection should be used when 10 preceding lots have been accepted under normal inspection. Normal inspection is typically used for a new process or a new vendor. ANSI Z1.4-1981 and ISO 2859 are two sampling plan development systems similar to MIL-STD-105D.

The Dodge-Romig sampling system provides sampling tables for AOQL-based plans and LTPD-based plans. The Dodge-Romig tables only apply to sampling situations in which rejected lots are subjected to 100% inspection and all nonconforming items are replaced by conforming items. In addition, users must specify the process average of nonconforming items to use the tables. Both the single and double sampling plans provided in the Dodge-Romig tables have been shown to minimize total inspection efforts.

MIL-STD-414 provides tables for developing sampling plans for variables. AQL is used as the quality index, with values ranging from 0.04% to 15%. Like MIL-STD-105D, MIL-STD-414 contains three inspection phases (normal, reduced, and tightened) and a set of switching rules. ANSI/ASQC Z1.9 and ISO 3951 are two sampling plan development systems similar to MIL-STD-414.

Additional Forms of Acceptance Sampling

In this section, three additional acceptance sampling plans are discussed, along with the idea of economically based sampling plans. The three additional plans include skip-lot sampling plans, chain sampling plans, and narrow-limit gauging. Skip-lot sampling plans (SkSP) were developed by Dodge in 1955 using the CSP concept described earlier. However, the unit considered in SkSP is a lot rather than an item, as is traditionally used in CSP. For example, SkSP-1 starts with 100% sampling of all lots until i consecutive lots are accepted. The sampling scheme is then switched to 100% sampling of a fraction f of the lots. Whenever a lot is rejected while using this reduced inspection process, sampling is immediately switched back to 100% inspection of all lots. The quality index for selecting a sampling plan is AOQL, which is affected by the corrective actions required for rejected lots. Two options are available. The first is the replacement option in which rejected lots are reworked or replaced by conforming lots. In the second option, rejected lots are removed but not replaced. For example, rejected lots may be scrapped or returned to suppliers.

Chain sampling plans (ChSP) were also developed by Dodge in 1955. The sampling method uses two parameters, n and i. A sample of n items is randomly drawn from a lot and inspected. If the sample contains zero nonconforming items, the lot is accepted; if the sample contains two or more nonconforming items, the lot is rejected; and if the sample contains one nonconforming item, the lot is accepted only if i preceding samples were free of nonconforming items.

It is known that a large sample size is required to estimate a small nonconforming rate. This is mainly because a large sample is needed to observe some nonconforming items. Narrow-limit gauging is an alternative sampling procedure that uses an attribute sampling plan with tighter inspection limits than the product specifications. The plan consists of a sample size, an acceptance number, and a parameter specifying the location of the inspection (i.e., narrower) limits. It can be easily shown that narrow-limit gauging is effective in reducing the sample size. However, as with sampling plans for variables, an assumption regarding the distribution of the performance variable is required to develop the narrow-limit gauging sampling plan. Consequently, a careful examination of the distributional form of the process performance variable is necessary before such a plan is used.

Sampling plans can also be designed based on economic criteria. In an economic design, three cost components are commonly considered: the cost of inspection, the cost of rejection, and the cost of acceptance. The cost of inspection may include expenses of testing materials, labor, equipment, etc. The cost of rejection (internal failure cost) is incurred when corrective actions are taken on rejected items, such as repairing, scrapping, or returning the items to the supplier. The cost of acceptance (external failure cost) results from items of imperfect quality reaching customers, including loss of reputation and damage caused by product failure, warranty costs, handling costs subsequent loss of revenue, etc.

To develop a sampling plan based on economic criteria, two additional pieces of informtion are needed. The first is the lot nonconforming rate. The second is estimates of values in each of the previously described cost categories. Given this information, economically based sampling plans are then determined by optimizing the total expected cost or profit.

Screening

In a single screening procedure, all items are inspected (i.e., 100% inspection). If an item fails to meet the predetermined screening specifications, the item is first rejected and then subjected to predetermined corrective actions. If screening is based on the value of a known performance variable, all nonconforming items will be identified. Consequently, the only issue is whether screening is economical, which depends on the nonconforming rate.

When inspection based on the performance variable is destructive or costly, screening may be based on surrogate variables, which are correlated with the performance variable. Furthermore, when the process of measuring the performance variable is not error free, the observed performance variable can be treated as a surrogate variable. In these situations, screening specification limits should be adjusted based on the relationship between the performance variable and the surrogate variable.

Burn-in is a special screening procedure used to reduce the number of external failures early in the product life cycle by operating the product under normal or stressed conditions (i.e., accelerated life testing) for a fixed amount of time, thereby inducing internal product failure if it is to occur, before shipping it to the customer. Burn-in procedures are used to reduce warranty costs and external failure costs. Group testing is another special screening procedure; it is used when a single (group) test can verify whether a group of items is free of nonconforming items. Only when the result of the group test shows that the group is not free of nonconforming items are the items in the group tested individually. The effectiveness of a group testing procedure is determined by its group size. A large group size reduces the number of group tests, but increases the chances of individual tests. A properly selected group size can significantly reduce the inspection time and effort required to screen a population.

In-Process Inspection

In addition to detecting possible process problems, the purpose of inspecting work in process is to identify nonconforming items as early as possible to prevent excess rework or scrap cost or damage to machines in later stages of production. In a multiple-stage manufacturing environment, where to inspect and how many to inspect are two important issues. Several general rules concerning these inspection issues have been suggested:

1. Inspect after operations that are likely to produce nonconforming items.
2. Inspect before costly operations.
3. Inspect before operations that nonconforming items may cause damage or jam machines.
4. Inspect before operations that cover up defects.
5. Inspect before assembly operations where rework is costly.

Results of research studies have shown theoretically that products should be subjected to 100% inspection or no inspection at all (9, 12). This result is applicable to in-process and final inspections and is based on three assumptions: (*1*) inspection cost is a linear function of the number of inspected items, (*2*) rework cost is a linear function of nonconforming items found, and (*3*) the probabilities of producing nonconforming items at each stage is stable and known.

A two-stage manufacturing system is used to illustrate the decision process. Let p_1 and p_2 represent the nonconforming rates generated by the two production operations. If there is an inspection station after the first operation, all nonconforming items produced by this stage are detected and repaired. Therefore, all the items entering the second stage are conforming items (i.e., $p_1 = 0$). If no inspection takes place after the first stage, then the nonconforming rate of the items entering the second stage is $p = p_1$. As a result, the nonconforming rate after stage 2 (before inspection) is either p_2 or $p_1 + (1 - p_1)p_2$, depending on whether the items are inspected after the first stage. If no inspection takes place after the second stage, the nonconforming rate remains unchanged, i.e., either p_2 or $p_1 + (1 - p_1)p_2$. Although, for both incoming nonconforming rates, the outgoing nonconforming rates are 0 if all the items are inspected after the second stage, the resulting costs are different. Consequently, there are four possible different inspection policies. The inspection policy with the smallest expected total cost should be used. For large problems, a systematic method can be used to determine the policy that minimizes the total expected cost.

31.5 SUMMARY

This chapter presents a variety of approaches to manufacturing process quality control and improvement. It is subdivided into three major sections: (*1*) process quality control, (*2*) process improvement, and (3) product inspection. Within each section, important concepts and approaches are described. These ideas are introduced with the understanding that more detail regarding each topic is available elsewhere. Suggested readings are provided for those interested in locating more extensive coverage of each topic.

BIBLIOGRAPHY

1. AT&T, *Statistical Quality Control Handbook,* AT&T, Indianapolis, Ind., 1956.
2. S.D. MURPHY, ed., *In-process Measurement and Control,* Marcel Dekker, Inc., New York, 1990.
3. I.O. PANDELIDIS, "Machine Diagnostics" in A. Kusiak, ed., *Intelligent Design and Manufacturing,* John Wiley & Sons, Inc., New York, 1992.
4. K. ISHIKAWA, *Guide to Quality Control,* Asian Productivity Organization, Tokyo, Japan, 1976.
5. G.E.P. BOX and S. BISGAARD, "The Scientific Context of Quality Improvement," *Quality Prog.,* **20,** 54–61 (June 1987).
6. J.M. PRUETT and H. SCHNEIDER, *Essentials of SPC in the Process Industries,* Instrument Society of America, Research Triangle Park, N.C., 1993.
7. T.B. BARKER, "Quality Engineering by Design: Taguchi's Philosohpy," *Quality Prog.,* **19,** 32–42 (Dec. 1986).
8. Y.M. CHOU, D.B. OWEN, and S.A. BORREGO, "Lower Confidence Limits on Process Capability Indices," *J. Quality Technol.* **22**(3), 223–119 (1990).
9. E.W. DEMING, *Out of the Crisis,* MIT Press, Cambridge, Mass., 1986.
10. D. MONTGOMERY, *Introduction to Statistical Quality Control,* John Wiley & Sons, Inc., New York, 1991.
11. ASQC, *Definitions and Symbols for Acceptance Sampling by Attributes,* American Society for Quality Control, Milwaukee, Wis., 1971, ASQC Standard A2-1971.
12. T. RAZ, "A Survey of Models for Allocating Inspection Effort in Multistage Production Systems," *J. Quality Technol.* **18**(4), 239–247 (1986).

Suggested Readings

G.E.P. BOX, W.G. HUNTER, and J.S. HUNTER, *Statistics for Experimenters,* John Wiley & Sons, Inc., New York, 1978.

H.F. DODGE and H.G. ROMIG, *Sampling Inspection Tables, Single and Double Sampling,* 2nd ed., John Wiley & Sons, Inc., New York, 1959.

G. HAHN, "Some Things Engineers Should Know about Experimental Design," *J. Quality Technol.* **9**(1), 13–20 (1977).

W. KUO and Y. KUO, "Facing the Headaches of Early Failures: A State-of-the-art Review of Burn-in Decisions," *Proc. IEEE* **71**(11), 1257–1266 (1983).

D.C. MONTGOMERY, *Design and Analysis of Experiments,* 3rd ed., John Wiley & Sons, Inc., New York, 1991.

E.R. OTT, *Process Quality Control,* McGraw-Hill Book Co., Inc., New York, 1975.

K.S. STEPHENS, *How to Perform Continuous Sampling (CSP),* ASQC, Milwaukee, Wis, 1979.

G. TAGUCHI, E.A. ELSAYED, and T. HSIANG, *Quality Engineering in Production Systems,* McGraw-Hill Book Co., Inc., New York, 1989.

K. TANG and J. TANG, "Design of Screening Procedures: A Review," in press.

U.S. Department of Defense, *Sampling Procedures and Tables for Inspection by Variables,* U.S. Government Printing Office, Washington, D.C., 1957, MIL-STD-414.

U.S. Department of Defense, *Sampling Procedures and Tables for Inspection by Attributes,* U.S. Government Printing Office, Washington, D.C., 1963, MIL-STD-105D.

CHAPTER 32

Automated CAD-Based
Vision Inspection

Jose A. Ventura
The Pennsylvania State University

Jen-Ming Chen
The National Central University (Taiwan)

32.1 INTRODUCTION

Applying machine vision techniques to industrial inspection problems has received a great deal of attention (1, 2), and many systems for a variety of applications have been successfully implemented in the last decade (3, 4). However, in the past, most of the effort in vision research was devoted to make individual modules (e.g., sensing, algorithms, etc.) more efficient to perform a specific task. The development of a flexible, efficient, reliable, and integrated real-time vision system for industrial applications is an essential issue in the current and future research.

The objective of this work is to develop machine vision techniques for automated shape inspection so that real-time, reliable, and 100% quality control activities can be achieved in computer-integrated manufacturing. The shapes of interest are restricted to planar profiles, generated by projecting three-dimensional objects (especially machined parts) onto a two-dimensional inspection plane, the boundaries of which are composed of straight-line segments and circular arcs. The reason for choosing these types of profiles is because roundness and straightness are the most frequently used geometric entities in engineering design and manufacturing (5). The objects being inspected are assumed to be nonoverlapping (the entire boundaries are visible from the sensor), and the number of geometric entities (lines and arcs) of the objects is known and equal to n.

An overview of the proposed inspection system is illustrated in Figure 32.1. The input of this system is a set of ordered boundary data extracted from the object being inspected, which is the result of early image processing, such as image enhancement, edge detection, noise filtering, and boundary extraction. These low level processes can be manipulated in many available software packages, such as Khoros software system (6), and hence are not our concern. These data are assumed to be available and arranged in counterclockwise sequence. This chapter focuses on the algorithmic development for higher level vision operations, including two modules: segmentation and analysis (Figure 32.1). The first module of the system is to segment the set of ordered boundary data into the desired number (n) of data subsets, each of which is approximated by a straight line or an arc, corresponding to a specific geometric entity of the object. Next, the analysis module is to match the input object, represented by the n line and arc entities, with one of the reference shapes. The total number of reference shapes is assumed to be known and saved in the system, and the profile specifications of these reference shapes (e.g., dimensions of the entities) can be obtained from their CAD models (Figure 32.1). After performing the segmentation and analysis operations on the input data, the system determines the pose (orientation and position) and dimension of the object, and its out-of-profile error. The pose and dimension can be used for robot-related manipulation. The principal inspection tasks are gaging and defect detections, i.e., determination of shape imperfections and out-of-profile error.

The algorithms developed in this chapter possess the two most important properties required for industrial applications: speed and accuracy. First, these algorithms are fast compared

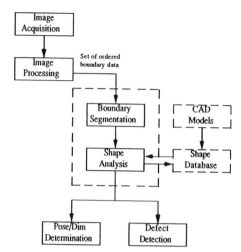

Figure 32.1. Overview of a machine
vision inspection system.

with other methods reported in the literature, so that 100% inspection activities can be performed and inspection bottlenecks can be eliminated from automated production lines. Second,
the results generated from the algorithms are accurate and reliable, avoiding the false rejection
or passing of the defects and enhancing the quality and reducing the cost of the products.

Recently, Mundy et al. (7) and Noble et al. (8) have developed an inspection system that is
similar to the proposed system. The inspection functions of their system are formulated as an
optimization model,

$$\text{Minimize } f(x),$$

$$\text{Subject to } h(x) = 0 \tag{1}$$

where $f(x)$ is a function representing the n least-squares fitting between the entities and the data,
and $h(x) = 0$ is a set of constraints representing the geometric relationships among entities.
Their model uses an independent set of parameters to represent each entity. The size of the
model is at least $2n$ variables and n constraints, where n is the number of entities. Although they
propose the use of Lagrangian relaxation, Model 1 may not be solvable due to its size and the
nonconvexity of the objective function and some of the constraints. The advantage of the
proposed system is that a given shape is defined by four global parameters: one for scale, one
for orientation, and two for position. Using the underlying parameters, all the entities are
expressed in analytic form, so that the spatial relationships among them are completely characterized by the analytic equations, due to the global properties of the parameters. Therefore, the
inspection functions (in the analysis module) can be formulated as an unconstrained optimization model:

$$\text{Minimize } f(x) \tag{2}$$

which avoids the use of Lagrange multipliers, and can be solved by a tractable and more reliable
gradient-based descent algorithm (9). Other advantages of the proposed inspection system are

- The shape models in the analysis module are automatically generated from the system
  using the input parameter (n) and the profile specifications obtained from the CAD database. These shape-modeling schemes not only compress the data to a greater extent, with
  respect to pixel-based representations, but also provide a compact and meaningful form to
  facilitate the inspection tasks.
- The system is developed based on the current definitions of dimensioning and tolerancing
  standards provided by the ANSI Y14.5M-1982. Therefore, the inspection results generated
  by the system are unique and interpretable.
- This system is completely flexible, i.e., it does not depend on particular applications. New
  shapes can be added just by entering their profile specifications from the CAD database.

32.2 SEGMENTATION

The first module of the proposed system deals with the segmentation of digitized planar curves into lines and arcs, in which the number of entities (or break points) of the curves is given. As illustrated in Figure 32.2, this procedure is divided into two stages: (*1*) to obtain a starting set of break points and determine the approximation functions (lines and arcs) for the data intervals that are separated by the break points, and (*2*) to adjust the break points until the error norm is locally minimized. The first stage is based on the detection of significant changes in curvature using the chain-code and differential chain-code techniques, used by Sirjani and Cross (10) and Baruch and Loew (11), respectively, for segmenting digitized planar curves. The second stage is an optimization curve–line fitting scheme.

The problem of interest is formally described as follows. For a given number of primitives (n), which can be arcs or line segments, the objective is to partition the set of boundary data (arranged in counterclockwise (CCW) sequence)

$$S = \{p_j = (x_j, y_j)|j = 1, 2, \ldots, m\} \tag{3}$$

into n data subsets

$$S_i = \{(x_{i,j}, y_{i,j})|j = 1, 2, \ldots, m_i\}(i = 1, 2, \ldots, n) \tag{4}$$

so that the sum of squares of the Euclidean distances between the points in each subset S_i, $i = 1, 2, \ldots, n$, and the corresponding primitives is minimized. Note that p_j is a neighbor of p_{j-1} and p_{j+1} (modulo m), and let $u_i = (x_{i,1}, y_{i,1})$ be the first point of S_i, representing the break point between S_i and S_{i-1} (modulo n). In addition, each subset of data can be approximated by a line (L_i) or an arc (C_i):

$$S_i = \begin{cases} L_i, & \text{for } i \in I_l \\ C_i, & \text{for } i \in I_c \end{cases} \tag{5}$$

where I_l and I_c are the sets of indices of the straight-line segments and circular arcs, respectively. Let $I = I_l \cup I_c$, so that

$$n_l + n_c = n \tag{6}$$

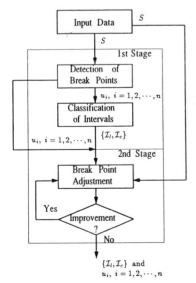

Figure 32.2. The two-stage segmentation procedure.

where n_l, n_c and n are the cardinalities of sets I_l, I_c and I, respectively. It is noteworthy to mention that

$$S = S_1 \cup S_2 \cup \cdots \cup S_n \tag{7}$$

$$m = m_1 + m_2 + \cdots + m_n \tag{8}$$

and

$$S_k \cap S_l = \emptyset \quad \text{(for all } (k, l), \; k \neq l) \tag{9}$$

where Equations 7 and 8 indicate that the union of all subsets of data is equal to the set of all boundary data, and the System of Equations (9) shows that all the subsets are mutually exclusive. Hence the objective of this problem is equivalent to identifying the best set of break points, u_i, $i = 1, 2, \ldots, n$, and classifying each data subset S_i into L_i or C_i for $i \in I$, so that the defined error norm is minimized.

Detection of Break Points

The break points on a closed curve that is composed of arcs and line segments represent the points of significant changes in curvature. Asada and Brady (12) classified the isolated curvature changes into two types: corner and smooth join, which mathematical properties are described below:

- Corner is an isolated curvature change, for which the tangent to the contour is discontinuous.
- Smooth join is an isolated curvature change, for which the tangent is continuous, but the curvature is discontinuous.

Figure 32.3 shows examples of corners and smooth joins on a curve. Hence, the detection of break points is equivalent to the detection of corners and smooth joins on the curve. Based on

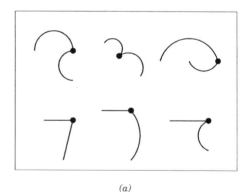

(a)

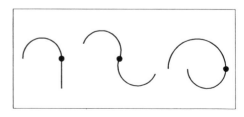

Figure 32.3. Two types of isolated curvature changes. (a) Corners and (b) smooth joins.

(b)

this classification, we propose the differential chain-code technique to identify the corners and use the chain-code representation to linearize the arcs, so that the smooth joins on the curve are transformed to corners that can be detected by using a piecewise linear approximation procedure. After the break points are completely identified, the resulting data intervals can be classified into arcs and lines, by estimating the slopes of the approximation segments in the chain-code domain.

In the chain-code representation, a "code" that represents the tangent direction is assigned to each point on the curve, and hence the differential chain-code is the change of tangent directions between two adjacent points. In the proposed procedure, the following coding schemes have been employed.

1. k *Chain Code.* Let the sequence of m datum points (S) describe a closed curve. The chain code of S consists of the sequence

$$s_{j,k} = \tan^{-1} \left[\frac{y_j - y_{j-k}}{x_j - x_{j-k}} \right] \quad (j = 1, 2, \ldots, m) \tag{10}$$

where $s_{j,k}$ represents the tangent angle (modulo 2π) at p_j with a supporting length k.

2. k *Differential Chain Code.* Using the definition above, the differential chain code of S consists of the sequence

$$\delta_{j,k} = \tan^{-1} \left[\frac{y_{j+k} - y_j}{x_{j+k} - x_j} \right] - \tan^{-1} \left[\frac{y_j - y_{j-k}}{x_j - x_{j-k}} \right] \quad (j = 1, 2, \ldots, m) \tag{11}$$

where $\delta_{j,k}$ is the change of tangent angles (modulo 2π) at p_j with a supporting length k.

The 16-directional code with $k = 2$ is illustrated in Figure 32.4. Using these coding schemes for curve segmentation offers several merits, including simplicity, speed, and reduction in memory requirements. The drawback of these schemes is that they are sensitive to noise (perturbation of boundary data). Hence we use techniques for noise filtering and data smoothing (13), which can be operated either in the spatial domain (e.g., neighborhood averaging) or in the frequency domain (e.g., low-pass–band-reject filtering).

The mouselike shape of Figure 32.5 illustrates the effect of data smoothing through the band-reject filtering and the sequences derived by using the proposed coding schemes, where Figure 32.5a displays the original data, Figure 32.5b presents the smoothed data, and Figure 32.5c and 32.5d show the chain-code and differential chain-code sequences, respectively, with $k = 3$. The four break points of the shape are denoted by u_i, $i = 1, 2, 3, 4$, where u_1 and u_4 are corners, u_2 and u_3 are smooth joins, and the starting point is u_1. In Figure 32.5b, the boundary perturbations of the shape have been smoothed, based on which $s_{j,k}$ and $\delta_{j,k}$ sequences are derived. The two spikes in the $\delta_{j,k}$ sequence of Figure 32.5d represent the corners, which correspond to the discontinuities in the $s_{j,k}$ sequences of Figure 32.5c. In addition, the circular arc of the original data is linearized in the $s_{j,k}$ domain, represented by the inclined segment $\overline{u_2 u_3}$, and hence the original smooth joins become the two end points of the inclined segment (i.e., the corner points between two adjacent segments of the $s_{j,k}$ waveform, which have different inclined angles). Therefore, the detection of break points can be summarized as follows:

- Corners are identified by detecting the spikes in the differential chain-code domain.
- Smooth joins are detected in the chain-code domain using a piecewise linear approximation procedure (14–16).

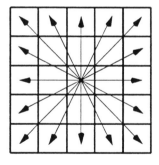

Figure 32.4. The 16-directional code with $k = 2$.

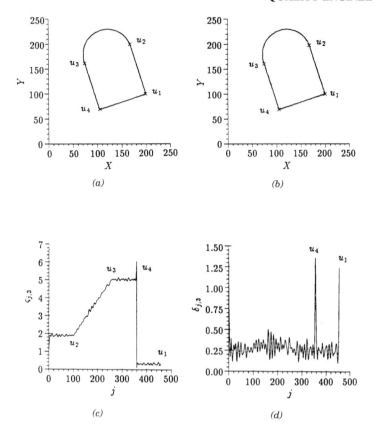

Figure 32.5. A mouse-like shape: (*a*) original data, (*b*) smoothed data, (*c*) *k* chain-code ($\varsigma_{j,k}$), and (*d*) *k* differential chain-code ($\delta_{j,k}$), where $k = 3$, $n = 4$, $m = 458$, u_i, $i = 1, 2, 3, 4$, are the break points, and u_1 is the starting point of the closed contour.

Finally, the resulting data intervals divided by the *n* break points are classified into lines and arcs. This operation is performed in the chain-code domain (Figure 32.5c) based on which arcs and line segments are determined as follows:

- For the circular arc, the approximation segment is not parallel to the *x* axis (the slop is not zero).
- For the line segment, the approximation segment is parallel to the *x* axis (the slope is zero).

Adjustment of Break Points

The break points obtained by using the proposed shape-coding schemes may not provide the best solution, because there is no evidence to support its optimality. Therefore, we would like to adjust each break point to the left or to the right, point by point, until the error norm is minimized. This refinement is an optimization data-fitting approach, where the error norm is defined by the sum of the squares of the Euclidean distances between the approximation functions and the data.

$$E_2(u_i, u_{i+1}) = \sum_{j=u_i}^{u_{i+1}} \varepsilon_{i,j}^2, \tag{12}$$

where (u_i, u_{i+1}) are the indices of the starting and ending points of the data interval S_i, and $\varepsilon_{i,j}$ is the Euclidean distance between the datum point $(x_{i,j}, y_{i,j})$ and the approximation function. For the linear fitting, the error is

$$\varepsilon_{i,j}^2 = (x_{i,j} \cos \theta_i + y_{i,j} \sin \theta_i - d_i)^2 \quad \text{(for } j = 1, 2, \ldots, m_i \text{ and } i \in I_l) \tag{13}$$

where θ_i and d_i are the normal angle and normal distance, respectively, of the approximation line for data interval S_i. For the circular fitting, the error becomes

$$\varepsilon_{i,j}^2 = (((x_{i,j} - a_i)^2 + (y_{i,j} - b_i)^2)^{1/2} - r_i)^2 \quad \text{(for } j = 1, 2, \ldots, m_i \text{ and } i \in I_c) \tag{14}$$

where (a_i, b_i) and r_i are the coordinates of the center and radius, respectively, of the approximation arc for S_i. The optimal (linear and circular) fitting is accomplished by finding a solution to the system of equations generated by setting the partial derivatives of Equation 12 with respect to each parameter to zero. In the linear case, there is a closed form solution available for this problem. However, there is no closed form solution for the circular fitting using the defined error norm, due to the nonlinearity of the resulting system of equations. To solve this problem, an iterative algorithm developed by Yeralan and Ventura (17) is employed, by which the estimated circle is arbitrarily close to the least-squares circle.

After the first stage of the segmentation, an initial set of break points, $\{u_i, i = 1, 2, \ldots, n\}$, is determined, and each interval is classified as linear ($i \in I_l$) or circular ($i \in I_c$). This information is used as the input data for the break-point adjustment algorithm, denoted by BA-1:

Step 0. Set the step size $D = 1$.
Step 1. For $i = 1$ to n, do
    Step 1.1. Compute

$$\varepsilon_0' = (E_2(u_{i-1}, u_i - 1) + E_2(u_i, u_{i+1} - 1))$$

$$\varepsilon_1' = (E_2(u_{i-1}, u_i - 1 - D) + E_2(u_i - D, u_{i+1} - 1))$$

$$\varepsilon_2' = (E_2(u_{i-1}, u_i - 1 + D) + E_2(u_i + D, u_{i+1} - 1))$$

    Step 1.2. If $\min\{\varepsilon_1', \varepsilon_2'\} \geq \varepsilon_0'$, stop

        else if $\varepsilon_2' > \varepsilon_1'$, set $u_i = u_i - D$, and go to *Step 1.1*

        else set $u_i = u_i + D$, and go to *Step 1.1*.

Step 2. If any break points have been adjusted, repeat *Step 1*; else stop.

Step 0 selects the step size (D) for each shift. We choose the smallest step size, $D = 1$. In step 1, the break points are shifted to the left or to the right point by point until the error norm of every pair of adjacent intervals is minimized. Step 2 checks if any improvement has been made in the previous iteration. If the error norm has been reduced, one more iteration is performed; otherwise, the algorithm terminates. Because this is a strictly decreasing procedure, the algorithm cannot cycle. In addition, because there is a finite number of data intervals and a finite number of points in each interval, the algorithm terminates in a finite number of steps.

It is noteworthy to mention that Algorithm BA-1 may fall in the trap of local minimum, due to a single outlier. Although there are no general methods (except for enumerative algorithms such as dynamic programming) that can guarantee a global optimal in all circumstances, the proposed algorithm can be improved by using multiple step sizes. For example, we can use a coarse-to-fine approach to generalize the algorithm, labeled BA-2:

Step 0. For $D = D_{max}$ down to 1, do BA-1.

Algorithm BA-2 performs BA-1 a preset number of iterations (D_{max}) in a coarse-to-fine manner. In the first iteration, we adjust the break points by the largest step size D_{max}, which can avoid the shadow of the local minimum, and in the last iteration, the break points are adjusted point by point, which can precisely localize the best solution.

32.3 ANALYSIS

The proposed shape analysis is a model-based approach, the purpose of which is to match the input shape, represented by the n data subsets, S_i, $i = 1, 2, \ldots, n$, with a predefined model. The proposed procedure includes three parts. First, a set of characteristic data is derived from the specifications of a CAD database, which is invariant to scaling, translation, and rotation. Next, the shapes of interest are defined by four global parameters, so that the primitives of the shapes are represented in terms of the underlying parameters, using the derived characteristic data. Finally, the matching problem is formulated as an unconstrained optimization model based on the least-squares criterion and solved by a gradient-based descent algorithm. The solution of this model is used to determine the pose and scale of the object, and perform out-of-profile inspection.

Profile Specifications

Integrating the design specifications of an object into a shape model is a crucial stage for information sharing and data transmission between various activities in an automated manufacturing environment. Therefore, it is necessary to represent an object based on its original specifications. We start this section with quoting the official definition of profile control from ANSI Y14.5M-1982 (18): "With profile tolerancing, the true profile may be defined by basic radii, basic angular dimensions, basic coordinate dimensions, and formulas or undimensioned drawings." This definition is illustrated in Figure 32.6, where the true profiles are composed of

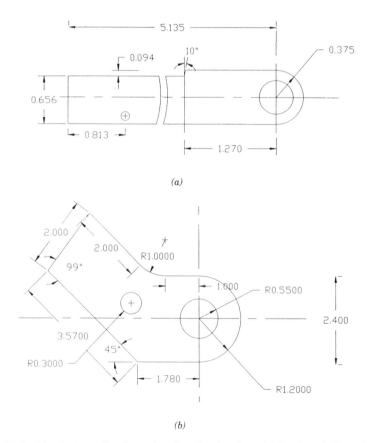

(a)

(b)

Figure 32.6.   Nominal specifications of engineering drawings. (a) Latch and (b) cutting tool.

straight-line segments and circular arcs, and all the elements and spatial relationships between them are defined by dimensional and angular specifications. The dimensions include the lengths and radii, and the angles include the relative angles between two adjacent elements and circum-angles of the arcs. Therefore, the nominal values of the dimensions and angles of the profile are used as the a priori knowledge.

Based on the definition of ANSI Y14.5M-1982, a complex profile (denoted by CP) can be partitioned into n geometric features (denoted by GF_i, $i = 1, 2, \ldots, n$), and arranged in counterclockwise sequence, i.e.,

$$CP = \{GF_i, i = 1, 2, \cdots, n\} \tag{15}$$

Each geometric feature GF_i is either a straight-line segment or a circular arc. In addition, we define the inscribed polygon (denoted by IP) of the complex profile by connecting the joint points (x_i, y_i), $i = 1, 2, \ldots, n$, counterclockwise, i.e.,

$$IP = \{E_i | i = 1, 2, \cdots, n\} \tag{16}$$

where E_i denotes the ith edge of IP. The inscribed polygons of the two objects in Figure 32.6 are illustrated in Figure 32.7. It is noteworthy to mention that E_i is identical to GF_i for $i \in I_l$, and is the chord of GF_i for $i \in I_c$, i.e.,

$$E_i = \begin{cases} L_i, & \text{if } i \in I_l \\ \text{chord of } C_i, & \text{if } i \in I_c \end{cases} \tag{17}$$

Now, each element of the profile can be described in terms of IP. The dimensional and angular specifications below are sufficient to describe the straight-line segments:

d_i dimension of edge E_i, i.e., the straight-line distance between two adjacent joint points (x_{i-1}, y_{i-1}) and (x_i, y_i)
α_i internal angle of IP between edges E_{i-1} and E_i

For more convenient expressions, let β_i be the turning angle representing the change of directions between E_{i-1} and E_i in a CCW sequence. The turning angles can be obtained from the internal angles:

$$\beta_i = \pi - \alpha_i \quad (\text{for } i \in I) \tag{18}$$

which implies that the turning angle is positive if the edge E_i turns counterclockwise; otherwise it is negative.

For circular arcs, two additional sets of data are needed, which are also available in the original specifications of the object:

r_i radius of arc C_i
ϕ_i circum-angle of arc C_i

In addition, r_i is defined to be positive or negative; a positive radius implies a convex-shaped arc (e.g., GF_2 in Figures 32.7a and 32.7b, and a negative radius means a concave-shaped arc (e.g., GF_4 in Figure 32.7b). In summary, we use two parameters to describe the straight-line segments:

$$L_i = \{d_i, \beta_i\} \quad (\text{for } i \in I_l) \tag{19}$$

and four parameters to describe the arcs:

$$C_i = \{d_i, \beta_i, r_i, \phi_i\} \quad (\text{for } i \in I_c) \tag{20}$$

where d_i and r_i are dimensional specifications, and β_i and ϕ_i are angular specifications. These two sets of nominal values: $\{d_i, \beta_i, i \in I_l\}$ and $\{d_i, \beta_i, r_i, \phi_i, i \in I_c\}$, are invariant to rotation and translation but are variant to the change-of-scale of the object. Therefore, the dimensional specifications are normalized with respect to the scale of the first element. Define

κ_i normalized scale of the dimension of E_i, with respect to E_1
λ_i normalized scale of the radius of C_i, with respect to E_1

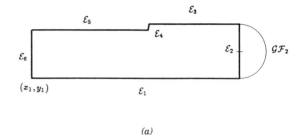

(a)

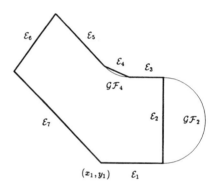

Figure 32.7. Inscribed polygons of the complex profiles.
(*a*) Latch and (*b*) cutting tool.   *(b)*

These definitions yield

$$\kappa_i = d_i/d_1 \quad (\text{for } i \in I)$$
$$\lambda_i = r_i/d_1 \quad (\text{for } i \in I_c)$$

(21)

The original data are now transformed to two sets of characteristic data that are transformation invariant:

$$L_i = \{\kappa_i, \beta_i\} \quad (\text{for } i \in I_l)$$

(22)

and

$$C_i = \{\kappa_i, \beta_i, \lambda_i, \phi_i\} \quad (\text{for } i \in I_c)$$

(23)

These two sets of data will be used as a priori knowledge in the subsequent shape-modeling procedure.

Shape Modeling

Shape modeling is to express each element of the complex profile by a set of model parameters that specify the scaling, orientation, and position of the objects, using solely the profile specifications derived in Equations 22 and 23. In an ordered set of geometric features, we select the first element GF_1, for convenience, as the anchor element to define the model parameters.

Hence the scale of the object is represented by the length of the first edge E_1 (denoted by l_1), the orientation is defined by the normal angle of E_1 (denoted by θ_1), and the object position is represented by the coordinates of the joint point of E_n and E_1, i.e., (x_1, y_1), as illustrated in Figure 32.8.

Using the underlying four parameters, the modeling procedure is divided into three major steps. Initially, we relax the parameters from the model by setting the scale of the object $l_1 = 1$, and pose parameters $(x_1, y_1) = (0, 0)$ and $\theta_1 = 0$, so that a simple preliminary model for the inscribed polygon can be derived based on the a priori knowledge: (κ_i, β_i), $i \in I$. Because E_i is equivalent to L_i for $i \in I_l$, the straight-line segments are represented by the implicit equations of E_i for $i \in I_l$. Next, the circular arcs are described based on the preliminary IP model and additional information: λ_i and ϕ_i for $i \in I_c$. Under the assumption that the boundary image pixels are approximately equiangularly spaced along the arcs, the circle representation can be linearized (19, 20). Finally, the scale and pose parameters $(l_1, \theta_1, x_1, y_1)$ will eventually be integrated into the model through an affine transformation between the scene data and the model.

The key stage of the shape modeling is to derive the preliminary model of IP, by relaxing the underlying parameters, which provides the foundation for the representations of line segments and arcs. Because the scale is one, the first vertex of the polygon is set to the origin, the orientation angle is zero, and the coordinates of the remaining vertices of IP, (x_i, y_i), $i = 2, 3, \ldots, n$, can be expressed as a function of (κ_i, β_i), for $i \in I$, as summarized in Lemma 1. The preliminary model is then completed in Lemma 2 using the equations of the vertices. These lemmas will be presented forthwith; their proofs are detailed in Chen (21).

Lemma 1

Given that $l_1 = 1$, $(x_1, y_1) = (0, 0)$ and $\theta_1 = 0$, the coordinates of each vertex of the inscribed polygon, (x_i, y_i), $2 \le i \le n$, can be obtained as follows:

$$x_i = \sum_{j=1}^{i-1} \kappa_j \cos \rho_j \ (i = 2, 3, \ldots, n) \tag{24}$$

and

$$y_i = \sum_{j=1}^{i-1} \kappa_j \sin \rho_j \ (i = 2, 3, \ldots, n) \tag{25}$$

where

$$\rho_i = \sum_{j=2}^{i} \beta_j + \pi/2 \ (i = 2, 3, \ldots, n) \tag{26}$$

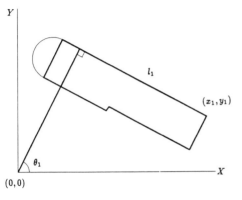

Figure 32.8. A planar shape defined by four parameters: scale (l_1), orientation (θ_1), and position (x_1, y_1).

and

$$\rho_1 = \pi/2 \tag{27}$$

where ρ_i is the inclined angle of E_i with respect to the X-axis. Next, the implicit equation (including normal distance and normal angle) for each edge of *IP* can be derived using the information about the vertices.

Lemma 2

Given (x_i, y_i), $i = 1, 2, \ldots, n$, the preliminary model of *IP* can be represented by the following system of equations:

$$E_i: X \cos \omega_i + Y \sin \omega_i = \delta_i \ (i = 1, 2, \ldots, n) \tag{28}$$

where

$$\omega_i = \tan^{-1} \frac{\cos^2 \rho_i \sum_{j=1}^{i-1} \kappa_j \sin \rho_j - \sin \rho_i \cos \rho_i \sum_{j=1}^{i-1} \kappa_j \cos \rho_j}{\sin^2 \rho_i \sum_{j=1}^{i-1} \kappa_j \cos \rho_j - \sin \rho_i \cos \rho_i \sum_{j=1}^{i-1} \kappa_j \sin \rho_j} \tag{29}$$

and

$$\delta_i = \left[\left(\sin^2 \rho_i \sum_{j=1}^{i-1} \kappa_j \cos \rho_j - \sin \rho_i \cos \rho_i \sum_{j=1}^{i-1} \kappa_j \sin \rho_j \right)^2 \right.$$
$$\left. + \left(\cos^2 \rho_i \sum_{j=1}^{i-1} \kappa_j \sin \rho_j - \sin \rho_i \cos \rho_i \sum_{j=1}^{i-1} \kappa_j \cos \rho_j \right)^2 \right]^{1/2} \tag{30}$$

Due to the equivalency between E_i and L_i, for $i \in I_l$, the line segments are expressed by the same equation of Lemma 2:

$$L_i: X \cos \omega_i + Y \sin \omega_i = \delta_i \ (i \in I_l) \tag{31}$$

To describe circular arcs, we need to compute the coordinates of the centers and radii with respect to the preliminary *IP* model. The ordinary representation of the arc is developed in Lemma 3, and its linearization is provided in Lemma 4.

Lemma 3

Given the model of *IP*, and (λ_i, ϕ_i) for $i \in I_c$, the arcs can be represented by the system of equations:

$$C_i: (X - \mu_i)^2 + (Y - \nu_i)^2 = \lambda_i^2 \ (i \in I_c) \tag{32}$$

where

$$\mu_i = \sum_{j=1}^{i-1} \kappa_j \cos \rho_j + 1/2 \ \kappa_i \cos \rho_i \pm \lambda_i \cos(\phi_i/2) \cos \omega_i \tag{33}$$

and

$$\nu_i = \sum_{j=1}^{i-1} \kappa_j \sin \rho_j + 1/2 \ \kappa_i \sin \rho_i \pm \lambda_i \cos(\phi_i/2) \sin \omega_i \tag{34}$$

and (μ_i, ν_i) and λ_i are the coordinates of the center and the radius of arc C_i, respectively, ρ_i and ω_i are defined previously, and the $\pm$ ($+$ and $-$) signs depend on whether the arcs are concave- or convex-shaped, respectively.

Lemma 4

Assume that the edge points are equiangularly spaced along the circular arc. Then the circle can be linearized by the following equation:

$$C_i: (X - \mu_i) \cos \omega_{i,j} + (Y - \nu_i) \sin \omega_{i,j} = \lambda_i \ (i \in I_c) \tag{35}$$

where

$$\omega_{i,j} = \begin{cases} \omega_i - \dfrac{1}{2} \phi_i + \dfrac{j}{m_i} \phi_i, & \text{if } C_i \text{ is convex-shaped} \\ \omega_i + \pi + \dfrac{1}{2} \phi_i - \dfrac{j}{m_i} \phi_i, & \text{if } C_i \text{ is concave-shaped} \end{cases} \tag{36}$$

The encoding of the underlying four parameters is accomplished by performing a transformation between the scene data and the preliminary model.

Theorem 1

The scale, orientation and position of a complex profile can be completely characterized in terms of l_1, θ_1, x_1 and y_1 by the following systems of equations:

$$L_i: (X^s - x_1) \cos(\omega_i + \theta_1) + (Y^s - y_1) \sin(\omega_i + \theta_1) = \delta_i l_1 \ (i \in I_l) \tag{37}$$

and

$$C_i: (X^s - \mu_i' l_1 - x_1) \cos(\omega_{i,j} + \theta_1) + (Y^s - \nu_i' l_1 - y_1) \sin(\omega_{i,j} + \theta_1) = \lambda_i l_1 \ (i \in I_c) \tag{38}$$

where

$$\begin{pmatrix} \mu_i' \\ \mu_i' \end{pmatrix} = \begin{pmatrix} \cos \theta_1 & -\sin \theta_1 \\ \sin \theta_1 & \cos \theta_1 \end{pmatrix} \begin{pmatrix} \mu_i \\ \nu_i \end{pmatrix} \tag{39}$$

In Equations 37 and 38, (X^s, Y^s) are the coordinates of the edge points of the object in a scene, which has a scale factor l_1, rotated by an angle θ_1 counterclockwise, and translated by a distance of (x_1, y_1), with respect to the origin.

Proof. The proofs for Equations 37 and 38 are similar. Therefore, only the proof for arcs, Equations 38, is shown. The scale, orientation, and position of the object with respect to the preliminary Model 35 can be specified as

$$\begin{pmatrix} X^s \\ Y^s \end{pmatrix} = l_1 \begin{pmatrix} \cos \theta_1 & -\sin \theta_1 \\ \sin \theta_1 & \cos \theta_1 \end{pmatrix} \begin{pmatrix} X \\ Y \end{pmatrix} + \begin{pmatrix} x_1 \\ y_1 \end{pmatrix} \tag{40}$$

By performing the matrix inversion, (X, Y) can be expressed in terms of (X^s, Y^s) and the parameters

$$\begin{pmatrix} X \\ Y \end{pmatrix} = 1/l_1 \begin{pmatrix} (X^s - x_1) \cos \theta_1 + (Y^s - y_1) \sin \theta_1 \\ -(X^s - x_1) \sin \theta_1 + (Y^s - y_1) \cos \theta_1 \end{pmatrix} \tag{41}$$

Note that

$$\begin{pmatrix} \mu_i \\ \nu_i \end{pmatrix} = \begin{pmatrix} \mu_i' \cos \theta_1 & \nu_i' \sin \theta_1 \\ -\mu_i' \sin \mu_1 & \nu_i' \cos \theta_1 \end{pmatrix} \tag{42}$$

Substituting (X, Y) and (μ_i, ν_i) with Equations 41 and 42, respectively, Model 35 becomes:

$$C_i: ((X^s - \mu_i'l_1 - x_1) \cos \theta_1 + (Y^s - \nu_i'l_1 - y_1) \sin \theta_1) \cos \omega_{i,j}$$
$$+ (-(X^s - \mu_i'l_1 - x_1) \sin \theta_1 + (Y^s - \nu_i'l_1 - y_1) \cos \theta_1) \sin \omega_{i,j}$$
$$= \lambda_i l_1 \tag{43}$$

and after rearranging the items $(X^s - \mu_i'l_1 - x_1)$ and $(Y^s - \nu_i'l_1 - y_1)$, we obtain

$$C_i: (X^s - \mu_i'l_1 - x_1)(\cos \theta_1 \cos \omega_{i,j} - \sin \theta_1 \sin \omega_{i,j})$$
$$+ (Y^s - \nu_i'l_1 - y_1)(\sin \theta_1 \cos \omega_{i,j} + \cos \theta_1 \sin \omega_{i,j}) = \lambda_i l_1 \tag{44}$$

Equation 44 is equivalent to Equation 38.

Shape Matching

The purpose of shape matching is to estimate the underlying parameters of the complex profile using the captured image pixels. Two main steps are involved: (*1*) a least-squares criterion is used to formulate the matching problem as an optimization model, and (*2*) an iterative procedure, such as the Newton-Raphson method (22), provides a solution to the nonlinear optimization problem. The shape model is represented by the n implicit equations developed in Theorem 1, and the input data is given by Equation 4.

The best-fit profile is obtained using a least-squares procedure. The associated error measure to obtain the best fitted shape is represented by:

$$L_i: (x_{i,j} - \hat{x}_1) \cos(\omega_i + \hat{\theta}_1) + (y_{i,j} - \hat{y}_1) \sin (\omega_i + \hat{\theta}_1)$$
$$= \delta_i \hat{l}_1 \pm \varepsilon_{i,j,l} \, (j = 1, 2, \ldots, m_i, i \in I_l) \tag{45}$$

and

$$C_i: (x_{i,j} - \mu_i'\hat{l}_1 - \hat{x}_1) \cos(\omega_{i,j} + \hat{\theta}_1) + (y_{i,j} - \nu_i'\hat{l}_1 - \hat{y}_1) \sin(\omega_{i,j} + \hat{\theta}_1)$$
$$= \lambda_i \hat{l}_1 \pm \varepsilon_{i,j,c} \, (j = 1, 2, \ldots, m_i, i \in I_c) \tag{46}$$

where $\varepsilon_{i,j,l}$ and $\varepsilon_{i,j,c}$ are the Euclidean distances from point $(x_{i,j}, y_{i,j})$ to the corresponding line segments and arcs, respectively, which are defined by

$$\varepsilon_{i,j,l} = |(x_{i,j} - \hat{x}_1) \cos(\omega_i + \hat{\theta}_1) + (y_{i,j} - \hat{y}_1) \sin(\omega_i + \hat{\theta}_1) - \delta_i \hat{l}_1| \tag{47}$$

and

$$\varepsilon_{i,j,c} = |(x_{i,j} - \mu_i'\hat{l}_1 - \hat{x}_1) \cos(\omega_{i,j} + \hat{\theta}_1) + (y_{i,j} - \nu_i'\hat{l}_1 - \hat{y}_1) \sin(\omega_{i,j} + \hat{\theta}_1) - \lambda_i \hat{l}_1| \tag{48}$$

Estimates for the four parameters of the least-squares model are obtained by minimizing the sum of the squares of the errors (SSE):

$$\xi = \text{Min SSE}(\hat{l}_1, \hat{x}_1, \hat{y}_1, \hat{\theta}_1)$$
$$= \text{Min} \left(\sum_{i \in I_l} \sum_{j=1}^{m_i} \varepsilon_{i,j,l}^2 + \sum_{i \in I_c} \sum_{j=1}^{m_i} \varepsilon_{i,j,c}^2 \right)$$
$$= \text{Min} \sum_{i \in I_l} \sum_{j=1}^{m_i} ((x_{i,j} - \hat{x}_1) \cos(\omega_i + \hat{\theta}_1)$$
$$+ (y_{i,j} - \hat{y}_1) \sin(\omega_i + \hat{\theta}_1) - \delta_i \hat{l}_1)^2$$
$$+ \sum_{i \in I_c} \sum_{j=1}^{m_i} ((x_{i,j} - \mu_i'\hat{l}_1 - \hat{x}_1) \cos(\omega_{i,j} + \hat{\theta}_1)$$
$$+ (y_{i,j} - \nu_i'\hat{l}_1 - \hat{y}_1) \sin(\omega_{i,j} + \hat{\theta}_1) - \lambda_i \hat{l}_1)^2 \tag{49}$$

Furthermore, we can generalize the representations of segments and arcs, so that Model 49 can be expressed by

$$\xi = \text{Min SSE}(\hat{l}_1, \hat{x}_1, \hat{y}_1, \hat{\theta}_1)$$

$$= \text{Min} \sum_{i \in I} \sum_{j=1}^{m_i} \varepsilon_{i,j}^2$$

$$= \text{Min} \sum_{i \in I} \sum_{j=1}^{m_i} ((x_{i,j} - \mu_i' \hat{l}_1 - \hat{x}_1) \cos(\omega_{i,j} + \hat{\theta}_1)$$

$$+ (y_{i,j} - \omega_i' \hat{l}_1 - \hat{y}_1) \sin(\omega_{i,j} + \hat{\theta}_1) - \gamma_i \hat{l}_1)^2 \tag{50}$$

where

$$\varepsilon_{i,j} = \begin{cases} \varepsilon_{i,j,l}, & \text{if } i \in I_l \\ \varepsilon_{i,j,c}, & \text{if } i \in I_c \end{cases} \tag{51}$$

$$\gamma_i = \begin{cases} \delta_i, & \text{if } i \in I_l \\ \lambda_i, & \text{if } i \in I_c \end{cases} \tag{52}$$

$$\omega_{i,j} = \begin{cases} \omega_i, & \text{for all } j, & \text{if } i \in I_l \\ \omega_{i,j}, & \text{for all } j, & \text{if } i \in I_c \end{cases} \tag{53}$$

$$\mu_i' = \begin{cases} 0, & \text{if } i \in I_l \\ \mu_i', & \text{if } i \in I_c \end{cases} \tag{54}$$

$$\nu_i' = \begin{cases} 0, & \text{if } i \in I_l \\ \nu_i', & \text{if } i \in I_c \end{cases} \tag{55}$$

The optimal matching is accomplished by finding a solution to the system of equations generated by setting the partial derivatives of SSE $(\hat{l}_1, \hat{x}_1, \hat{y}_1, \hat{\theta}_1)$ with respect to $\hat{l}_1, \hat{x}_1, \hat{y}_1$ and $\hat{\theta}_1$ to zero. Let $f = \text{SSE}(\hat{l}_1, \hat{x}_1, \hat{y}_1, \hat{\theta}_1)$, and define

$$f_{l_1} = \partial \text{SSE}(\hat{l}_1, \hat{x}_1, \hat{y}_1, \hat{\theta}_1)/\partial \hat{l}_1$$

$$= \sum_{i=1}^{n} \sum_{j=1}^{m_i} ((x_{i,j} - \mu_i' \hat{l}_1 - \hat{x}_1) \cos(\omega_{i,j} + \hat{\theta}_1)$$

$$+ (y_{i,j} - \nu_i' \hat{l}_1 - \hat{y}_1) \sin(\omega_{i,j} + \hat{\theta}_1) - \gamma_i \hat{l}_1)$$

$$(-\mu_i' \cos(\omega_{i,j} + \hat{\theta}_1) - \nu_i' \sin(\omega_{i,j} + \hat{\theta}_1) - \gamma_i) = 0 \tag{56}$$

$$f_{x_1} = \partial \text{SSE}(\hat{l}_1, \hat{x}_1, \hat{y}_1, \hat{\theta}_1)/\partial \hat{x}_1$$

$$= \sum_{i=1}^{n} \sum_{j=1}^{m_i} ((x_{i,j} - \mu_i' \hat{l}_1 - \hat{x}_1) \cos(\omega_{i,j} + \hat{\theta}_1)$$

$$+ (y_{i,j} - \nu_i' \hat{l}_1 - \hat{y}_1) \sin(\omega_{i,j} + \hat{\theta}_1) - \gamma_i \hat{l}_1)$$

$$(- \cos(\omega_{i,j} + \hat{\theta}_1)) = 0 \tag{57}$$

$$f_{y_1} = \partial \text{SSE}(\hat{l}_1, \hat{x}_1, \hat{y}_1, \hat{\theta}_1)/\partial \hat{y}_1$$

$$= \sum_{i=1}^{n} \sum_{j=1}^{m_i} ((x_{i,j} - \mu_i' \hat{l}_1 - \hat{x}_1) \cos(\omega_{i,j} + \hat{\theta}_1)$$

$$+ (y_{i,j} - \nu_i' \hat{l}_1 - \hat{y}_1) \sin(\omega_{i,j} + \hat{\theta}_1) - \gamma_i \hat{l}_1)$$

$$(- \sin(\omega_{i,j} + \hat{\theta}_1)) = 0 \tag{58}$$

$$f_{\theta_1} = \partial \text{SSE}(\hat{l}_1, \hat{x}_1, \hat{y}_1, \hat{\theta}_1)/\partial \hat{\theta}_1$$

$$= \sum_{i=1}^{n} \sum_{j=1}^{m_i} ((x_{i,j} - \mu_i' \hat{l}_1 - \hat{x}_1) \cos(\omega_{i,j} + \hat{\theta}_1)$$

$$+ (y_{i,j} - \nu_i' \hat{l}_1 - \hat{y}_1) \sin(\omega_{i,j} + \hat{\theta}_1) - \gamma_i \hat{l}_1)$$

$$(-(x_{i,j} - \mu_i' \hat{l}_1 - \hat{x}_1) \sin(\omega_{i,j} + \hat{\theta}_1)$$

$$+ (y_{i,j} - \nu_i' \hat{l}_1 - \hat{y}_1) \cos(\omega_{i,j} + \hat{\theta}_1)) = 0 \tag{59}$$

Numerical methods, such as the Newton-Raphson method, can be employed to compute a solution to this system of nonlinear equations. This particular method was chosen because it generally converges faster (quadratically) than alternative procedures, such as the steepest ascent, conjugate gradient, or quasi-Newton methods. There are, however, two procedural difficulties associated with this technique. The first is that a matrix inversion step is necessary, and the second is that a "good" starting solution is required to avoid the trap of local minimum. In this case, matrix inversion does not present a problem because the order of the matrix to be inverted is only four. In addition, it is not difficult to determine a "good" starting vector for this problem. The starting solution is found in the following manner: (1) the initial scale variable ($\hat{l}_1^0$) is estimated by computing the distance between the two end points of S_1, (2) the orientation ($\hat{\theta}_1^0$) is estimated by computing the normal angle of the least-squares regression line using the data in subset S_1, and (3) the initial position ($\hat{x}_1^0$, $\hat{y}_1^0$) is set to the coordinates of the first point in S_1.

32.4 APPLICATION TO MACHINED PART INSPECTION

This section presents an application of the proposed methodology to machined part inspection. In particular, we describe the procedure of integrating the design and manufacturing processes into machine vision inspection. This procedure is outlined in Figure 32.9, in which the flow chart among the cells of the operations is illustrated. Our methodology is divided into off-line development of the shape model and on-line inspection of the machined parts. The commercially available CAD–CAM packages, such as the MasterCAM software (23), can be used as the tool to create the CAD-models. The specifications of profiles and tool paths are generated from the models; the specifications are used to build the shape models, and the tool paths are used to machine the parts. In our experiment, the shape specification (or CAD database) generated by MasterCAM is a list of the n geometric entities of the profile, each of which is specified by a set of coordinates, dimensions, angles, radii, etc. In many instances, the CAD database can be divided into two types of entities:

- Line entity, which includes
  Coordinates of two end points and the inclined angle between the line and x axis.
  Distances between these two end points, specified by the individual x and y directions and its Euclidean distance.
- Arc entity, which includes
  Coordinates of the center.
  Coordinates of two end points and the circum-angle along the arc between these two points.
  The radius, diameter, and length of the arc.

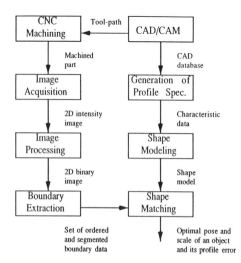

Figure 32.9. Integration of engineering design, manufacturing, and machine vision inspection.

Based on the specifications, the shape model of the object can be created using the proposed modeling scheme. Currently, the on-line integration of machining and inspection has not been implemented in real time in the shop floor. Instead, we demonstrate the methodology of integration of these two activities. The CAD models of two typical machined parts, the latch and cutting tool (Figure 32.6), were first created by the MasterCAM software. Next, their tool paths were generated from the software and used for part machining. Finally, the work pieces were fabricated using a Pratt & Whitney Horizon V3.5 Axis computer numerically control (CNC) machine. These two machined parts are shown in Figure 32.10. Using these real objects, we concentrate on the aspect of machine vision processing to demonstrate the proposed shape analysis technique.

Machine Vision Processing

The success of vision-based inspection largely depends on the results of image acquisition and processing. In this section, we describe the machine vision system used for image acquisition and preprocessing, and present the operations of boundary extraction, including edge tracking and boundary segmentation. After these operations, a set of noise-free and precisely segmented boundary data for each object was obtained and arranged in CCW sequence, which was used as the input data for the developed shape matching algorithm.

Image Acquisition

The pictures of machined parts were taken using an orthogonal viewing direction from the inspection table. The experimental environment set up for image acquisition is described below.

- *Camera.* Pulnix TMC-74 high resolution CCD color camera (768 × 493 image pixels).
- *Illumination.* Bencher VP-400 Copystand with a 600-W quartz halogen illuminator built in a 16 × 16-inch baseboard for back lighting.

(a)

(b)

Figure 32.10. Two machined parts. (a) Latch and (b) cutting tool.

- *Computer.* SUN SPARC station 2 under SunOS Open Windows Version 2.
- *Frame Grabber.* Sun VideoPix with a frame of data captured in real time at 1/30 s NTSC.
- *Image Size.* 640 × 480 pixels.

Preprocessing

The captured 2D intensity images were processed in the vision system for noise-filtering and edge detection, using the Cantata image processing package within the visual programming environment provided by the Khoros software system (6). The major steps of the preprocessing include

- *Thresholding.* Gray-level thresholding was used to eliminate the noise, highlight the object from the background, and convert the original image to a binary image.
- *Edge Detection.* Edge pixels in the binary image were detected using the Difference Recursive Filter (DRF). This filter has been shown to be an optimal filter for the detection of step edges (24). After edge detection, the images for the two examples were inverted. These images are shown in Figure 32.11.
- *Geometric Operations.* To facilitate further processes (i.e., data transmission), the images were scaled and translated, so that the object was contained and approximately centered in a region of 256 × 256 array, which was extracted from the original 640 × 480 image as the region of interest.

Among the 256 × 256 image array, only the boundary pixels are needed for the edge-based shape analysis. In particular, the boundary data must be arranged in CCW sequence and partitioned into *n* subsets of data, each of which corresponds to the desired primitive for the least-squares fitting. Therefore, the subsequent boundary extraction procedure consists of two basic steps: edge tracking and boundary segmentation. These two operations were implemented

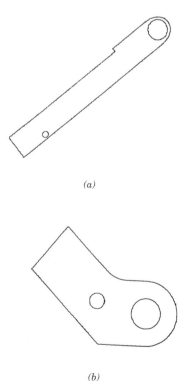

(a)

(b)

Figure 32.11. Results of edge detection. (*a*) Latch and (*b*) cutting tool.

on a VAX/VMS 8550 computer using the standard *C* and IMSL (Version 10.0) FORTRAN subroutines.

Edge Tracking

This operation is to extract the contour pixels from the image plane, arranged in CCW sequence. Due to the nearly noise-free results from the early processing, our tracking procedure is much simpler than the currently available edge tracking algorithms (25, 26). In addition, we only dealt with single and homogeneous objects, so that all the detected edge pixels from the preprocessing were the desired boundary data of the object. The major steps of this algorithm include (*1*) to find a starting point, (*2*) to track the edge points along the contour and link the discontinuity of the contour, and (*3*) to check the stopping criterion.

- Because the object has been approximately translated to the center of the image plane, the procedure initiates from the middle-left corner, instead of the upper-left corner, to speed up the search for the starting point. The procedure sequentially searches from left to right and from top to bottom, until the first edge point is found.
- The edge tracking is based on a 3 × 3 neighborhood search and the a priori knowledge on the tangent direction of the current pixel. If the 3 × 3 window fails to locate a candidate pixel due to the discontinuity of the curve, the size of the search window is extended to a larger one (say a 5 × 5 window) until the next edge pixel is found. If the larger window size is used, the gap between the current and the candidate points will be linked by adding points in the search direction.
- The stopping criterion is to check if the current point is in the 8-neighborhood of the starting point and if the total number of traced points is more than a preset number. The algorithm terminates once the stopping criterion is satisfied.

After the boundary data S was extracted from the image, the segmentation procedure presented above was employed to partition S into n data subsets, $S_i, i = 1, 2, \ldots, n$. Figure 32.12 shows the results of the edge tracking and boundary segmentation; the cross represents the break point between two data subsets.

Experimental Results

Using the data sets provided in Figure 32.12 and the shape-matching algorithm presented earlier, the experiments were implemented on a VAX/VMS 8550 computer using the standard *C*

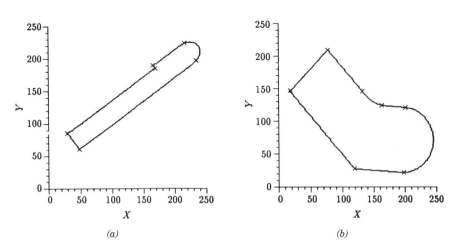

Figure 32.12.   Results of edge tracking and segmentation. (*a*) Latch and (*b*) cutting tool.

TABLE 32.1. Analysis of Machined Parts

Shapes			Parameters				Errors		
Figure	n	m	l_1	x_1	y_1	θ_1	e_r	SSE	MSE
32.12a	6	460	2.275 E + 2	4.849 E + 1	6.062 E + 1	2.196 E + 0	9.426 E − 7	1.816 E + 2	3.948 E − 1
32.12b	7	540	8.133 E + 1	1.184 E + 2	2.637 E + 1	1.506 E + 0	6.038 E − 8	6.581 E + 2	1.219 E + 0

TABLE 32.2. Computational Times (VAX 8550)

Figure	CPU (s)	Number of Iterations
32.12a	0.40	6
32.12b	0.53	8

and IMSL subroutines. The numerical results are shown in Table 32.1, where the first three columns describe the parameters of the input data, such as the physical figure, number of entities (n), and number of edge points (m). Columns 4 to 7 provide the information of optimal scale and pose of the shape, and columns 8 to 10 indicate the stopping condition (the relative error norm of the gradient e_r), the sum of the squares of the errors (SSE), and its mean-square error (MSE). The profile error is best represented by the MSE, because it is equivalent to the variance of the captured boundary data with respect to the true profile. Therefore, we can conclude that the machined part latch has a narrower out-of-profile error than the cutting tool (0.395 versus 1.219).

The computational effort required to evaluate these two objects is summarized in Table 32.2, including the CPU time in seconds and the total number of iterations required to terminate the algorithm ($e_r \leq 10^{-6}$). The CPU times for the latch and cutting tool are 0.40 and 0.53, respectively. In addition, the edge-tracking and segmentation algorithms for the latch took about 1.08 and 1.27 s, respectively, and for the cutting tool the times were 1.22 and 1.45 s, respectively, indicating that the matching algorithm spent only a small portion of the total processing time.

32.5 SUMMARY

In this chapter, an automated inspection system using machine vision techniques has been presented. Emphasis is placed on algorithmic development for higher level vision operations, including segmentation and analysis. The input to this system is a set of ordered boundary data extracted from the object being inspected, and the output includes the pose and dimension of the object and its out-of-profile error. In this current research, the shapes being inspected are restricted to planar profiles, generated by projecting 3D objects (especially machined parts) onto a 2D inspection plane, the boundaries of which are composed of straight-line segments and circular arcs. Although the proposed inspection method focuses on the single 2D view of a shape, the general concept can be extended to evaluate the shape from multiple 2D views.

The first module of the inspection system deals with the segmentation of digitized planar contours into straight-line segments and circular arcs, in which the number of data intervals (or break points) is assumed to be known. This procedure is divided into two stages. First, a starting set of break points is obtained by using the chain-code and differential chain-code schemes. The approximation functions (lines and arcs) for the data intervals are separated by the break points determined in the chain-code domain. Next, the break points are adjusted to the left or to the right, using an optimization data-fitting technique.

The second module of the system is to analyze the input data with respect to a model shape, determining its pose, dimension, and out-of-profile error. This procedure includes two facets: development of the shape model and matching the sensed data with the model. The shapes of interest are defined by four global parameters, one for scale, one for orientation, and two for position. Using the underlying parameters, these shapes are represented by the n geometric entities, each of which is expressed by an implicit equation. A least-squares technique is employed to formulate the matching problem as an unconstrained optimization model, which can be solved by tractable and more reliable gradient-based algorithms, such as the Newton-

Raphson method. In addition, an application of the proposed machine vision techniques to the automated shape inspection has been discussed.

The major contributions of this research work can be addressed from three aspects: the proposed methodology (shape modeling and shape matching), tolerancing issues (ANSI standards and profile error), and the developed system (integration and flexibility).

1. *Methodology.* The shape models (in the analysis module) are automatically generated by the inspection system using the input parameter (n) and the a priori knowledge (profile specifications) about the shapes. These shape-modeling schemes largely compress the data, save computer space, and describe the shapes in a compact and meaningful form to facilitate the inspection tasks. The shape-matching problem (in the analysis module) is formulated as a four-variable unconstrained optimization model, which not only simplifies the solution procedure but provides the computational speed as well.

2. *Tolerancing.* This system is developed based on the current definitions of dimensioning and tolerancing standards, provided by the ANSI Y14.5M-1982. Therefore, the inspection results generated from the system are unique and interpretable. In addition, the inspection task deals with the analysis of profile errors, which are applicable to multiple features. Most of the existing methods for machined part inspection are limited to the evaluation of single geometric features, such as form and location tolerances.

3. *System.* The developed system does not depend on particular applications. It can perform more than one inspection task, and is easily programmable to perform new tasks by solely changing a single input parameter (n). This flexibility reduces the risk of a vision system being outdated by rapid changes in part designs. The system integration is achieved in the sense that all the results generated from the previous processes (segmentation) are used for the downstream operation (analysis), so that the information sources can be shared and timely transmitted among operations.

Acknowledgments

This work was partially supported by the National Science Foundation under Grant DDM 90-57066 and Pritsker Corporation.

BIBLIOGRAPHY

1. S. NEGAHDARIPOUR and A.K. JAIN, "Challenges in Computer Vision: Future Research Directions" in *Proceedings of the IEEE Conference on Computer Vision and Pattern Recognition,* University of Illinois, Urbana-Champion, Ill., 1992, pp. 189–199.

2. D. PETKOVIC and J. WILDER, "Machine Vision in the 1990s: Applications and How to Get There," *Machine Vision Appl.* **4,** 113–126 (1991).

3. R.T. CHIN, "Survey Automated Visual Inspection: 1981 to 1987," *Comput. Vision Graphics Image Process.* **41,** 346–381 (1988).

4. O. MOHTADI and J.L.C. SANZ, "Recent Progress in Industrial Machine Vision" in *Proceedings of the IAPR Workshop on Machine Vision Applications,* Tokyo, Japan, 1990, pp. 1–14.

5. F.T. FARAGO, *Handbook of Dimensional Measurement,* 2nd ed., Industrial Press Inc., New York, 1982.

6. J. RASURE and D. ARGIRO, *Khoros User's Manual,* University of New Mexico, Albuquerque, N. Mex., 1992.

7. J. MUNDY, A. NOBLE, C. MARINOS, V.D. NGUYEN, A. HELLER, J. FARLEY, and A.T. TRAN, "An Object-Oriented Approach to Template Guided Visual Inspection" in *Proceedings of the IEEE Conference on CVPR,* University of Illinois, Urbana-Champion, Ill., 1992, pp. 386–392.

8. A. NOBLE, V.D. NGUYEN, C. MARINOS, A.T. TRAN, J. FARLEY, K. HEDENGREN, and J.L. MUNDY, "Template Guided Visual Inspection" in G. Sandini, ed., *Proceedings of the 2nd European Conference on Computer Vision,* Santa Margherita Ligure, Italy, 1992, pp. 893–901.

9. D.G. LUENBERGER, *Linear and Nonlinear Programming,* Addison-Wesley Publishing Co., Inc., Reading, Mass., 1984.

10. A. SIRJANI and G.R. CROSS, "An Algorithm for Polygonal Approximation of a Digital Object," *Patt. Recog. Lett.* **7,** 299–303 (1988).

11. O. BARUCH and M.H. LOEW, "Segmentation of Two-Dimensional Boundaries Using the Chain Code," *Patt. Recog.* **21**, 581–589 (1988).

12. H. ASADA and M. BRADY, "The Curvature Primal Sketch," *IEEE Trans. Patt. Ann. Mach. Intell.* **PAMI-8**, 2–14 (1986).

13. R.C. GONZALEZ and P. WINTZ, *Digital Image Processing,* Addison-Wesley Publishing Co., Inc., Reading, Mass., 1987.

14. T. PAVLIDIS, "Waveform Segmentation Through Functional Approximation," *IEEE Trans. Comput.* **C-22**, 689–697 (1973).

15. T. PAVLIDIS and S.L. HOROWITZ, "Segmentation of Plane Curves," *IEEE Trans. Comput.* **C-23**, 860–870 (1974).

16. J.A. VENTURA and J.M. CHEN, "Segmentation of Two-dimensional Curve Contours," *Patt. Recog.* **25**, 1129–1140 (1992).

17. S. YERALAN and J.A. VENTURA, "Computerized Roundness Inspection," *Int. J. Product. Res.* **26**, 1921–1935 (1988).

18. American National Standards Institute, *Dimensioning and Tolerancing for Engineering Drawing* American Society of Mechanical Engineers, New York, 1982, ANSI Y14.5M-1982.

19. T.S.R. MURTHY, "Evaluation of Conditional Multiple Concentric Arcs," *Precision Eng.* **8**, 227–231 (1986).

20. T.S.R. MURTHY, "A Comparison of Different Algorithms for Circularity Evaluation," *Precision Eng.* **8**, 19–23 (1986).

21. J.M. CHEN, *Vision-based Shape Recognition and Analysis of Machined Parts,* Ph.D. dissertation, Pennsylvania State University, University Park, Pa., 1993.

22. J.H. MATHEWS, *Numerical Methods for Computer Science, Engineering, and Mathematics,* Prentice-Hall, Inc., Englewood Cliffs, N.J., 1987.

23. CNC Software, Inc. *MasterCAM 3D: Reference Manual V3.21,* Tolland, Conn., 1991.

24. J. SHEN and S. CASTAN, "An Optimal Linear Operator for Edge Detection" in *Proceedings of the IEEE Conference on Computer Vision and Pattern Recognition,* Miami Beach, Fla., 1986, pp. 109–114.

25. A.A. FARAG and E.J. DELP, "Edge Linking by Sequential Search" in *SPIE Vol. 1609: Model-Based Vision Development and Tools,* Boston, Mass., 1991, pp. 198–216.

26. A. NOWAK, A. FLOREK, and T. PIASCIK, "Edge Tracking in a Priori Known Direction" in G. Sandini, ed., *Proceedings of the 2nd European Conference on Computer Vision,* Santa Margherita Ligure, Italy, 1992, pp. 38–42.

CHAPTER 33

Acoustic Emission Sensing for Tool Wear Monitoring and Process Control in Metal Cutting

KARTHIKEYAN CHITTAYIL, SOUNDAR R. T. KUMARA, and
PAUL H. COHEN
The Pennsylvania State University

33.1 INTRODUCTION

In modern high-tech industries that manufacture various complex equipment or machinery, each product can be assembled from hundreds or even thousands of components. To ensure the necessary degree of reliability in the final assembled product, there is a need to maintain a high level of quality control on the various components produced. The need for such quality control has led to an increasing tendency for automation, under computer control, of many manufacturing processes. Because machining processes involving metal cutting form a significant part of most manufacturing tasks, automation of the metal cutting process has engaged a great amount of research interest in recent years.

An essential prerequisite for any attempt at automation of the machining process is a reliable method of monitoring tool wear and tool failure. Sensors that can monitor the variation of cutting parameters also are needed for use in automatic control of machining processes. A large number of different sensing techniques have been developed in recent years for both these purposes. Most of these have been described in a review article (1). Some of these techniques have proved quite useful under laboratory conditions and include methods using laser optics and video cameras and methods involving measurements of cutting force and electrical resistance as well as those based on recording of audible noise and acoustic emission from the process. While a few of these techniques provide direct measures of tool wear, others estimate tool wear from indirect measurements of some parameters related to tool wear. The onset of tool failure (fracture, chipping, and cracking) is also indicated by some of these parameters as sudden changes in their characteristics. Nevertheless, as has been pointed out (2), few if any of these sensing techniques have found ready application in industry. There also has been attempts at combining the data from different types of sensors so as to achieve a reliable on-line estimate of tool wear. Most of these are also yet to find practical application in industry, and the search for better sensing techniques as well as for methods of combining multisensor data are going on at different centers.

The reasons for this unfortunate situation are not difficult to find. Successful application of any sensor technology for such monitoring and control purposes in machining must meet a number of exacting demands, and almost no sensor so far developed could be said to satisfy all of these. While a sensor is expected to be highly sensitive to the parameter it is to monitor, it should at the same time be somewhat less sensitive to other parameters of the process as well as to any varying conditions not under process control. For example, if a sensor is to monitor progressive tool wear in machining, it should have minimum sensitivity to process parameters such as cutting speed and depth of cut. On the other hand, a sensor whose output is to be used for monitoring cutting speed and also as an input in automatic control of the machining process should not be affected by the condition of tool wear. To be successfully applied on the shop floor, the sensor should be rugged enough to withstand the harsh environment in which it is to be used. Ideally, to minimize the number of sensors needed, it would be best if a single sensor could give output from which different parameters could be extracted, each of which would be sensitive to different aspects of the metal cutting process. While no sensing technique exists that can meet this ideal requirement, acoustic emission appears to be one method that holds promise.

During the last decade or so, acoustic emission (AE) has emerged as one of the finer techniques of estimating tool wear. There also are good indications that acoustic emission signals could carry more direct evidence of specific conditions of tool wear (flank, crater, etc.) as well as give clear indications of impending tool failure. Some researchers consider acoustic emission as one of the most promising sensing techniques available for tool wear monitoring and for process control in metal cutting processes (3, 4). This has to do with the facts that acoustic emission signals have their origin in the microprocesses taking place in the three main deformation zones in the metal cutting process and that the acoustic emission generation mechanisms involved in the three zones are not the same. These facts indicate that closer investigation (such as spectral analysis) of the microelastic strain pulses from the deformation zones may reveal more details of the process involved and may enable one to monitor the tool wear types individually. Such investigations are surely of more than academic interest, because a robust and reliable method of process control is as much dependent on high quality sensor data as on a good model of the process itself. There are many reasons to believe that the study of acoustic emission from metal cutting may lead to a better understanding of cutting the process, which is well recognized to be a complex, stochastic process, and to the development of more exact models of the process. A comprehensive overview of the use of acoustic emission sensing methods in various manufacturing processes, with special emphasis on machining process and tool condition monitoring, is available (5).

33.2 SPECIAL CHARACTERISTICS OF ACOUSTIC EMISSION

AE generated during metal cutting mostly originates in the plastic deformation zones on the workpiece and is related to the associated stress relaxation, in which the stress energy in the material gets dissipated as thermal energy and microelastic pulses (6, 7). Because a large number of pulses are emitted by sources randomly distributed over the plastic deformation zone, the AE signal detected from the process appears as a continuous noise. Short bursts of AE are sometimes emitted by random microscopic slips during the cutting process. Bursts of AE are also emitted when the tool undergoes chipping or cracking under the high stress levels generated during the process. Figure 33.1 depicts the schematic appearance of a typical AE record. Depending on the metal removal rate and the workpiece properties, the chip produced

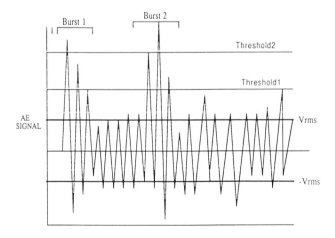

TIME (ARBITRARY UNITS)

Figure 33.1. Schematic of AE signal, showing the rms value, two events or "bursts," and two different threshold settings.

in metal cutting may remain as a single continuous strip or break into pieces intermittently. Such chip breaking is also known to give rise to bursts of AE. At the microscopic level, the plastic deformation taking place in the material may be described in terms of the generation and movement of crystal defects called dislocations through the material, and AE pulses are thought to be emitted whenever a dislocation interacts with another dislocation or any other type of crystal defect.

Although no exact theory for the process is known to exist, the fact that continuous AE originates from the plastic deformation zones in the metal cutting process and hence carries relevant information on the nature of the deformation process makes it an interesting field for further investigation. Unlike the audible sound generated or the tool vibrations produced during machining, AE signals are least affected by factors external to the cutting process, such as structural vibrations of the machine. Furthermore, AE has a much higher frequency bandwidth and hence has the potential to carry more information regarding the process. Understandably, therefore, extracting and classifying all the information carried by the AE signals from machining could involve a significant amount of signal processing work and use of sophisticated pattern recognition techniques (8, 9).

As already noted above, plastic deformations taking place in the three main deformation zones in a metal cutting process do not have the same characteristics, and hence the AE generated from the three zones can be expected to show certain differences in their characteristics (8). Thus, if these differences are identified, AE signals could potentially be used to differentiate between types of tool wear, especially flank wear and crater wear. It has also been demonstrated that AE bursts from chip breaking can be successfully used in monitoring chip condition (10). This has significant bearing on the possibility of automating the metal cutting process, because the nature of chip form is an important aspect of the cutting process. Some investigators have established that the root mean square (rms) value V_{rms} of the AE signal obtained using a tool with a cracked tip has a high degree of correlation with the area of the crack and can thus be used in detecting tool fracture with high confidence (11,1 2). Similarly, the almost linear dependence of V_{rms} on the cutting speed in orthogonal metal cutting has been verified experimentally by a number of workers (13–15), indicating the utility of this parameter in process control.

33.3 THEORY OF ACOUSTIC EMISSION FROM METAL CUTTING

Kannatey-Asibu and Dornfield (13) were the first to attempt a theoretical formulation relating an AE signal parameter, viz. V_{rms}, to the parameters of the metal cutting process. Their approach was based on the simple Ernst and Merchant theory of the orthogonal metal cutting process (16, 17). The essential idea in their formulation was to assume that a constant fraction of the energy dissipated due to plastic deformation in the cutting process was converted to acoustic emission. By combining simple expressions for the energy dissipated in the primary and secondary deformation zones, an expression for the rms level of the detected AE signal was obtained as

$$V_{rms} = C\{\tau_k wU[t_1 \cos \alpha/\sin \phi \cos(\phi - \alpha) + 1/3(l + l_1) \sin \phi/\cos(\phi - \alpha)]\}^{0.5} \qquad (1)$$

where C is a constant of proportionality; the angular parameters α and ϕ are the usual rake and shear angles used in metal cutting theory; the first term inside the brackets gives the contribution from the primary shear zone; t_1 is the uncut chip thickness (or feed); the second term in the brackets is the sum of contributions from the two distinct regions of the secondary shear zone (the sticking contact region and the sliding contact region); and the parameters l and l_1 indicate the total tool chip contact length and the sticking contact length, respectively. In Figure 33.2, these specific regions of deformation are depicted for the orthogonal cutting geometry. The factor outside the brackets essentially gives a measure of the energy dissipation in the process; τ_k is the dynamic shear strength of the material, w is the width of cut, and U is the cutting speed. The constant C depends on the fraction of energy dissipated as AE in the process, the nature of coupling between the AE sensor and the tool, and the sensitivity of the sensor itself.

The theoretical model represented by Equation 1 indicates strong dependence of the AE signal level on the cutting speed U, width of cut w, and feed t_1. Experimental investigations by various workers have corroborated the strong dependence on cutting speed, but the dependence on the remaining parameters have not been verified in any convincing fashion. In many experiments the measured V_{rms} was found to have no appreciable dependence on width of cut and feed rate. In their theory, Kannatey-Asibu and Dornfeld (13) had neglected the effects of

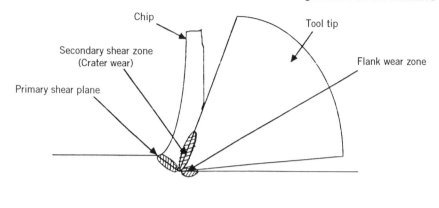

Figure 33.2. Schematic of metal-cutting process indicating the three main deformation zones.

---

flank wear as well the unequal attenuation of the AE signals along their paths toward the sensor location. Lan and Dornfeld (15) modified the earlier theory to include these effects, by introducing an additional term inside the bracket in Equation 1 proportional to the flank wear and constant attenuation factors on the original two terms:

$$V_{rms} = C\{\tau_k wU[C_1 t_1 \cos \alpha/\sin \phi \cos(\phi - \alpha) + C_2/3(l + l_1) \sin \phi/\cos(\phi - \alpha)] + C_3 F\}^m \quad (2)$$

where F is a measure of the flank wear. The attenuation factor C_1 was found to have a value of 0.20 to 0.25, using the lead break calibration test, whereas C_2 and C_3 were assumed to be equal to 1. The variable exponent m was used instead of 0.5, to introduce a nonlinear dependence of the AE signal power on the power dissipated in the cutting tool, but no significant improvement in agreement between theory and experiment has been reported.

A number of workers have noted the strong dependence of the AE parameter V_{rms} on the cutting speed and a weaker dependence on the factors affecting the cutting force. Chryssolouris and Domroese (18) therefore introduced a model that had different power law dependences of V_{rms} on the cutting speed and on the cutting force. That enabled them to obtain an empirical model of the V_{rms} from the cutting process, by a least-square linear regression procedure. The expression for V_{rms} that they obtained is given by

$$V_{rms} = CU^m[F_{ts} \cos \alpha/\cos(\phi - \alpha) + C_1 F_{tr} \sin \phi/\cos(\phi - \alpha) + C_2 F_{tf}]^n \quad (3)$$

where F_{ts} denotes the tangential (shear) force on the shear plane; F_{tr}, that on the rake face; and F_{tf}, that on the flank face, in an orthogonal cutting geometry. This model gave a better fit to the experimental data than the Kannatey-Asibu and Dornfeld model. Chryssolouris and Domroese found that V_{rms} is not sensitive to either of the attenuation constants C_1 and C_2, and therefore, each was assumed to be equal to 1, as there was no way to estimate their values individually. It is also noteworthy that in this model the assumption of AE power being proportional to the total power dissipated in the cutting process has been discarded, because in Equation 3 the exponents m and n are both not equal to 0.5 as in the Kannatey-Asibu and Dornfeld model.

The status of the theoretical models of AE from metal cutting, in terms of their agreement with experimental results, has been reviewed (19). Some investigators (14, 15, 19) have found that V_{rms} decreases with increasing feed, in contradiction to the Kannatey-Asibu and Dornfeld theory. Although the authors (15) have attributed this discrepancy to the three-dimensional nature of the metal cutting process in contrast to the simple two-dimensional model assumed in the theory, the explanation is not considered sufficiently convincing (20). Teti and Dornfeld (19) described a specific experiment in which 6061-T6 aluminum was cut using a fresh diamond Compax tool. They observed continuous chip formation and no evidence of built-up edge formation or scratch marks on the tool. It was found that, in this case, V_{rms} increased monotonically with all the three cutting parameters (U, w, and t_1) as expected from the simple model of Equation 1. This indicates that the basic assumptions made in deriving the model are correct, and when the idealized cutting conditions assumed are satisfied, experimental V_{rms} agrees with Equation 1 qualitatively. Exact quantitative agreement between theory and experiment was not obtained even in this case. Blum and Inasaki (20) questioned the assumption that constant τ_k is independent of the cutting conditions (13). They instead suggested a nonlinear dependence of τ_k on the shear strain rate in plastic deformation zones so that the measured V_{rms} would also be a nonlinear function of the strain rate and also of the cutting speed. Although they have found qualitative evidence to support their argument (20), no quantitative comparison of their nonlinear expression for the AE parameter with experimental data has been reported. It must be mentioned here that Blum and Inasaki used the parameter AE-mode rather than V_{rms} to characterize the AE signal. The parameter AE-mode measures the value of the voltage amplitude corresponding to the peak in the amplitude distribution of the digitized AE signal envelope. This eliminates any effect of random burstlike emissions in the signal, which shows up in V_{rms} as short duration peaks.

Rangwala and Dornfeld (21) derived an expression for V_{rms} based on somewhat more rigorous arguments. They attributed the continuous AE generation in metal cutting to damping of dislocation movements in the plastic deformation zones and argued that V_{rms} from each zone is directly proportional to the strain rate in that zone. They assumed the AE to arise mainly from the primary and secondary plastic deformation zones and neglected the contribution from the sliding contact region between the tool and the chip formed as well as any AE generated due to flank wear. The resultant expression for V_{rms} was given by

$$V_{rms} = K\mu U_s[wt_1/d \sin \phi + l \sin^2 \phi/d_1]^{0.5} \tag{4}$$

where U_s is the shear velocity, which is related to the cutting speed U as

$$U_s = U \cos \alpha/\cos(\phi - \alpha) \tag{5}$$

where d and d_1 are the effective thicknesses of the primary and secondary shear zones, and K is a proportionality constant as in Equation 1. The parameter μ is the macroscopic viscosity coefficient, which relates the flow stress in the plastic deformation zone to the strain rate $\dot{\varepsilon}$ through the relation

$$\tau = \tau_b + \mu\dot{\varepsilon} \tag{6}$$

where τ_b is the back stress, which depends on the amount of strain hardening in the material. Rangwala and Dornfeld (21) compared their theory with experiments carried out using specially designed tools with constant tool chip contact length, to get excellent quantitative agreement, especially for small contact lengths. They pointed out that the discrepancy between theory and experiment at the higher contact lengths could be because the full tool chip contact region may not have sticking contact, as assumed in the theory. The exact source mechanism for AE generation from the sliding contact region is still unknown, and a model for AE detected under realistic cutting conditions must also take that region into account. It is also important to note that neither type of tool wear has been included in the model represented by Equation 4. Although a clear dependence of AE signal on the amount of flank wear has been demonstrated (15, 19) and a term proportional to flank wear was introduced in the expression for V_{rms} by Lan and Dornfeld (15), models that give quantitative agreement with experimental data obtained using worn tools are yet to be developed.

33.4 EXPERIMENTAL STUDIES OF ACOUSTIC EMISSION

A large number of investigators have carried out measurements of acoustic emission from metal cutting. While it would be impossible to document the results of even a small fraction of these investigations, a few important measurements and their impact on the theoretical modeling of AE from metal cutting are discussed in this section. Some experimenters have used AE counts to denote the amount of AE activity, whereas others have used the V_{rms} of the sensor output voltage as the measure of AE signal. A typical AE measurement setup in a turning operation is shown in Figure 33.3. The AE sensor is mounted on the tool shank, and the signal output by the

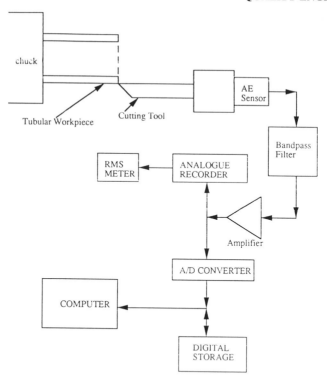

Figure 33.3. Measurement set-up for recording AE signals from a turning operation using analogue or digital recording.

sensor during a machining operation is suitably filtered, amplified, and recorded in an analogue tape recorder or digitized and stored in some other device. The rms value of the signal can then be obtained by a simple computation on a digital computer or by using an rms meter in the analogue case. In the case of AE count measurement, after amplification and filtering, the signal is directly passed to a thresholding and counting device, which outputs the number of times the signal level exceeded the set threshold level. Clearly, the count rate depends strongly on the threshold set, and it is determined mainly by the random burstlike events taking place in the cutting process and not on the continuous AE from the plastic deformation zone.

   In most of the investigation on AE from metal cutting, the V_{rms} value from AE measurements has been compared with theoretical predictions, and inferences are drawn regarding the nature of AE generation mechanisms involved in the process. Kannatey-Asibu and Dornfeld (13) carried out extensive measurements of V_{rms} under varying cutting conditions. They used 6061-T6 aluminum and SAE 1018 steel as the workpiece material for their experiments. The tool used was a high speed steel orthogonal cutting tool, at speeds ranging from 25 to 372 sfm. They found a strong dependence of V_{rms} on the cutting speed U, as expected from the Equation 1. The expected dependence of the V_{rms} parameter on the feed rate and the width of cut was not observed in the experimental results. In certain measurements, V_{rms} was even found to decrease steadily with feed, in contradiction to the Kannatey-Asibu and Dornfeld theory.

   Kannatey-Asibu and Dornfeld (13) carried out a series of cutting experiments in which the rake angle was varied over a range of values. It was found that to be able to reproduce the dependence of V_{rms} on the rake angle α the constant C in Equation 1 must be made a function of α, although there is no theoretical justification for such a dependence. Lan and Dornfeld (15), who gave a modified formulation of Equation 1, found V_{rms} to decrease with increasing crater water, which was inconsistent with the earlier observation by Kannatey-Asibu and Dornfeld (13) of increasing V_{rms} with rake angle, because increased crater wear causes the tool to become effectively sharper (i.e., α becomes higher). An interesting set of measurements were performed by Schmenck (14) with sharp and artificially worn tools on a single-tooth milling machine. He found that the worn tool gave higher AE output than a sharp tool at low cutting speeds (<60 m/min), but as the cutting speed was increased, the sharp tool was found to generate more AE output. This effect was found for three different work materials—aluminum (319T5), cast iron (241 BHN), and mild steel (156 BHN)—although different speed levels were used for each. One important aspect of this measurement setup that could explain these somewhat strange results was the fact that the AE sensor was mounted on the workpiece rather than on the tool holder, so that the relative amounts of attenuation undergone by the AE emissions from each of the deformation zones could be significantly different from that obtained by other workers.

Blum and Inasaki (20) found that the AE-mode parameter measured in their turning experiments increased in a nonlinear fashion with increasing cutting speed and sharply decreased with feed rate, whereas with the width of cut parameter w, AE-mode was found to remain almost constant. This prompted them to propose a nonlinear dependence of the AE-mode on the strain rate in the deformation zone, but no quantitative comparison of their prescription with experimental data was presented. The experimental data were obtained from turning S45C tubes using uncoated carbide tools (TNGG 160408 STi20 P20) on an NC turning machine. Using an artificially worn tool, the authors could find a clear increase of AE-mode with the flank wear, and a comparison of the normalized values of AE-mode and cutting force as functions of the flank wear indicated that the AE-mode parameter is definitely more sensitive to wear than the cutting force. Earlier, while corroborating the increase of V_{rms} with flank wear, Lan (22) had made the important observation that when crater wear also is present, V_{rms} tends to remain constant or even decrease with increasing amount of wear, indicating that crater wear has a reverse effect on AE level compared with flank wear.

To verify their theoretical formulation for V_{rms} based on the dislocation damping arguments, Rangwala and Dornfeld (21) carried out a number of experiments in which the chip tool contact length l was kept constant. This method ensured that the contact between chip and the tool in the secondary shear zone was mostly a sticking contact so that the AE from both primary and secondary zones could be assumed to arise from the dislocation damping process. In all these experiments, they used a high speed steel cutting tool, the workpiece being tubular 6061-T6 aluminum in as received condition. They could get excellent agreement of the experimental results with theory, especially for the small values of l. They argued that for higher values of l the agreement was not as good because some amount of sliding of the chip over the tool rake face was likely. More recently, other studies (23, 24) have carried out micromachining experiments with extremely small depth of cut t_1—on the order of a few thousandth of an inch—to show the strong dependence of V_{rms} on the depth of cut at such small depths.

The experiments discussed above indicate the complex nature of the AE source mechanism involved in the metal cutting process and indicate the need to carry out careful experiments under controlled conditions to get meaningful and reproducible results. Some of the strange results reported in these experiments could be because all the source mechanisms for the AE generated are not properly understood or because they are not adequately included in the theoretical formulation employed for comparison.

33.5 SPECTRAL ANALYSIS OF THE AE SIGNAL

It is well known that the Fourier transform of a time domain signal carries all the information contained in the original signal and that often, a frequency domain analysis can provide better insight into the underlying physical mechanism of the process. While a number of attempts have been made to use frequency domain information contained in AE signals from metal cutting for process monitoring and diagnostic purposes (25, 26) modeling of the AE signal in the frequency domain has been attempted only recently (27). Rangwala and Dornfeld (27) have given convincing but heuristic explanations for the fundamental frequency of the AE from metal cutting. They have also been able to give relatively simple relations for the dependence of the mean frequency f_m and the spectral spread σ on the cutting parameters. Experimental data have confirmed some of the predicted relations such as the strong dependence of f_m on cutting speed. Initially f_m was found to increase steadily with cutting speed U, but at high values of U the trend is reversed, indicating the thermal softening of the material. The dependence of f_m on feed rate was found to be highly inconsistent, and no specific trend could be detected. The spread σ of the AE signal spectrum was also seen to increase with cutting speed but showed little or no dependence on feed rate. While these results are preliminary, it is expected that further investigations along these lines will lead to methods for identifying individual types of tool wear and for monitoring them separately using selective filtering of the AE signal into relevant frequency bands.

As noted above, although the V_{rms} parameter of the AE signal can be readily measured and related to the occurrence of flank wear and other tool defects (such as chipping and cracking) in a simple manner, its strong dependence on the cutting conditions (especially the cutting speed) does not make it a suitable candidate for monitoring progressive tool wear. Furthermore, the decrease of V_{rms} with crater wear makes it difficult to use this parameter directly in monitoring either type of tool wear, when both are present. This has prompted some investigators to look instead at the spectral content of the AE signal and extract certain parameters that are well correlated with specific conditions of tool wear.

Emel and Kannatey-Asibu (25, 26) showed that the power spectral amplitudes of AE could be used as inputs to a pattern classifier to distinguish between two different states of tool wear and tool breakage. For their analysis, AE data were obtained form cutting experiments with TNMA 432–type carbide tools on AISI 4340 steel with a hardness of 370 BHN. They showed that tools with different types of wear give clearly distinguishable temporal AE waveforms and that by using a few frequency components from the power spectrum classifiers with 70% to 80% classification accuracy can be devised and used for monitoring and control of the machining process. Rangwala and Dornfeld (28) demonstrated the use of AE spectra in developing an intelligent multisensor scheme for monitoring an orthogonal cutting (turning) process. In this approach, the authors did not use models of the process but instead used parameters from the AE signal and the cutting force measurements as inputs to a neural network for predicting tool wear. The data were obtained from an orthogonal cutting experiment carried out using a kenna-metal TPGF-322 tool with insert K68 on case-hardened AISI 1060 steel. The AE and force parameters were obtained from the frequency spectra of the AE and force signals and were chosen to indicate maximum interclass separation (between fresh and worn tools) of the data. Tools with flank wear greater than 0.5 mm were considered worn, and those with lesser amounts of wear were considered fresh in this work. These parameters formed the feature vector that was used as input to a multilayered neural network. Sets of such feature vectors—which contained 30 vectors each, equally divided between worn and fresh tool states—were used to train the neural network. The authors reported classification ability of up to 95% for their method. While it was thus clearly demonstrated that the AE spectrum did contain significant information about the cutting process, it was also found that use of more than one sensor can significantly improve the quality of the monitoring scheme.

The use of more than one sensor in a process monitoring and diagnostics system results in improved performance, because the loss of sensitivity in one sensor can be compensated by the information from the other sensor, thus widening the system's operational range. Besides, the system becomes less sensitive to measurement errors and hence more reliable and robust. A large amount of effort in this field today is, therefore, directed toward the use multiple sensors and the development of optimal methods for combining the multisensor data.

33.6 USE OF NEURAL NETWORKS IN MONITORING AND CONTROL OF MACHINING

Artificial intelligence techniques are now being increasingly used in diagnostics and control of various manufacturing processes. There has been a number of attempts to apply such techniques to control of machining process (28–32). While some of these attempts involved use of AE sensor in addition to other sensors such as force, acceleration, and temperature, in one particular attempt (28), more than one parameter was extracted from the AE signal and used as input to an artificial neural network (ANN) for predicting tool wear.

In general, two principal approaches are used in all these multisensor methods, viz. sensor synthesis and sensor fusion. While definitions of these two approaches as used in the literature may vary slightly from author to author, for the present discussion we may define sensor synthesis as a method by which the estimates of the process parameters to be monitored or controlled are individually extracted from each of the sensor signals and combined together to get a more reliable and robust estimate. In this approach, the individual parameter estimates are obtained from each sensor datum using suitable models of the process; a number of different techniques have been tried out in combining these. Statistical methods, GMDH methods, and ANN have been used for this purpose.

Sensor fusion, on the other hand, can be considered as the approach in which all sensor data are fed into a single black box model of the process and estimates of the required process parameters obtained are the output (28, 29). The black box, which typically can be an ANN with one or more hidden layers, must be trained using suitable training data before it can be used for on-line processing of the multisensor data; it does not make use of individual process models, although knowledge about the process models may enable an appropriate choice of the NN architecture.

Chryssolouris and Domroese (30) describe and intelligent machining system (IMS) in which they consider the machining control as a decision-making problem that optimizes certain criteria that are complex nonlinear functions of the input parameters. Using three sensor modules that use inputs from force, temperature, and AE sensors, respectively, to produce individual estimates of tool wear, they generate a combined estimate of tool wear, and this is used by a final decision-making system to produce a control action. The scheme for combination of the estimates is derived from a statistical analysis of the various sensor data and the process parameter measurements from actual cutting experiments. The argument for such a system is that by using several sensors to estimate the same parameter, the estimation error can be reduced. Other methods of combining the estimates—based on the group method of data handling (GMDH), statistical decision making using Shafer-Dempster reasoning, etc.—have also been discussed (30) in this respect. All these methods, in one way or another, depend on the availability of good models of sensor signals in terms of the cutting parameters and the tool wear conditions.

Recently, Rangwala and Dornfeld (28) developed a method based on neural networks to control and optimize the machining process. The method does not need models of the cutting process, although for testing their approach, they used simple models of process parameters such as cutting force, power, temperature, etc. to simulate the cutting process. A neutral network with a single hidden layer and a variable number of nodes was used in the simulation experiments. The network was trained to learn the effect of the cutting parameters on the output variables and synthesize a set of input conditions (cutting parameters) that maximizes the material removal rate. In a practical implementation, the network must be trained using actual outputs from large number of machining experiments. Not much work along similar lines has been reported.

Chryssolouris and Domroese (30) describe the use of a neural network approach for improving the wear estimate obtained from AE, cutting force, and temperature sensor data, using models of the individual processes. They carried out comparisons by simulation of a neural network–based method of sensor integration and a statistical method but did not find a significant difference in the mean square estimates provided by either method, especially when multiple sensor data were used. Simulation was carried out under various assumed conditions, such as the failure of one or more sensors and the inaccuracy of the models used. Thus, while neural networks have been found preferable in modeling sensor signals in the absence of proper models for the sensor performance in regard to sensor integration, both statistical and neural network–based methods were found to be equally good. Elanayar et al. (31) used neutral networks to model the tool wear in machining using the sensor data on the three components of the cutting forces. When crater and flank wear were present, they could train their neural system to predict both, as well as the surface roughness, to an acceptable degree of accuracy.

The main drawback of the neural network methods is that all these methods need initial training of the network using extensive amounts of real machining data, which can be costly and time-consuming. Therefore, researchers are looking into neutral network schemes such as adaptive resonance theory (ART) (33, 34) and Kohonen's feature map (KFM) (35) methods that are unsupervised learning algorithms. Recently, Burke and Rangwala (33) compared the performances of two approaches in tool wear prediction, one based on unsupervised learning (back-propagation) and one using the ART network. They found comparable learning abilities. Although the latter approach requires data from only a fresh tool for training, it can adaptively learn to identify any new signal category, such as that from a worn or fractured tool. A comprehensive review of the developments during the last decade in monitoring and control of machining processes has been published (36) and has been further extended (37) to include recent developments in intelligent sensing and signal processing using multiple sensor systems for process monitoring.

An important point to keep in mind during the development of novel and sophisticated signal processing methods using multiple sensors is the practical utility of such techniques in a production environment. To make such process monitoring and diagnostics methods cost effective, the number of sensors must be kept to a minimum and the computational effort also must be minimized. Thus the sensors that can provide more accurate information about the process should be preferable to those that provide only gross classification and depend on only one specific aspect of the process. From this point of view, AE sensing appears to be an unavoidable part of any monitoring and diagnostic scheme in metal cutting, because more than one meaningful parameter for process monitoring can be derived from AE data. While the rms value of AE is directly related to the average power dissipation involved in the process, the AE count clearly relates to the occurrence of discrete events like microscopic slips and fracture in the material. The AE spectral characteristics, on the other hand, clearly reveal information about the hardness and the dislocation densities in the material and, therefore, have the potential to be useful in the identification of individual types of tool wear. Because the amount of hardening of the workpiece material is different at each of the sources of AE (the shear plane, the chiptool rake interface, and the tool flank workpiece contact region), it would be reasonable to expect each of these regions to give rise to AE in different frequency bands, even though there may be some degree of overlap between these bands. A frequency domain model of AE from the cutting process could thus help identify the individual types of tool wear to be monitored using the data obtained from the AE sensor alone. Below, a scheme of extracting individual tool wear estimates using the power spectrum of the AE signal is discussed, assuming an approximate frequency domain model of the cutting process. Although it is true, that the development of such a frequency domain model will involve an in-depth study of the deformation mechanisms involved in each deformation region of the cutting process, the discussion here assumes that such a model is readily available.

Figure 33.4 gives the schematic of the sensing and signal processing procedure. The signal from the AE sensor is first filtered and amplified in a sufficiently wide band to encompass most of the AE spectrum and remove any unwanted noise, especially at low frequencies. Then it is filtered into three frequency bands, the first band corresponding to the AE from the primary shear zone, the second to the secondary shear zone, and the third to the flank wear region of the tool and the workpiece. It is clear that because the AE from the flank wear region involves the workpiece material that has minimum strain hardening, this region could give rise to AE of the lowest frequency band. AE from the primary shear zone can have a significantly higher frequency band, depending on the amount of strain hardening the workpiece material undergoes ahead of the shear zone. In a material that undergoes little strain hardening during the cutting process, there can be a significant degree of overlap between the above two frequency bands. The frequency band of the AE from the primary shear zone could be affected to some extent by the thermal softening of the material. The third frequency band corresponds to the secondary shear zone, when the material has undergone the maximum degree of strain hardening and the AE can be expected to be of higher frequency than that from the other regions. The deformation process in this case is somewhat different from that in the primary shear zone, and this difference also can be reflected in the spectral bandwidth.

The AE signal parameter extraction scheme has been shown for the filter band 2, but the same scheme could be applied to the signal in the other bands. In fact, depending on the speed of the FFT implementation, the same single setup could be used to extract the parameters from the three signal bands by multiplexing. The rms level in each band is a measure of the degree of each of the three interactions and can be used as a gross measure of the tool wear at the corresponding regions. The other parameters (p_2, p_3, and p_4) along with p_1 could be used as

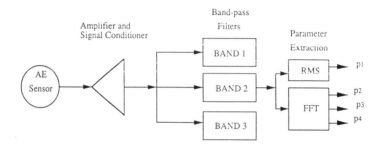

Figure 33.4. Schematic of AE signal Analysis system showing extraction of multiple parameters from each signal band.

inputs to a neural network algorithm for a better and more accurate estimation of tool wear. The AE parameters extracted from each of the frequency bands independently should be able to give a sufficiently accurate model of the process. When implemented, the method could significantly improve the diagnostic and control capabilities in untended machining, while reducing the requirement for too many sensors and complex signal processing.

Thus, with the use of artificial neural network methods, the estimation of process parameters in machining appears quite viable, even in the absence of well-defined and accurate models for the sensor signals. The learning ability of neural networks essentially seems to compensate for the lack of adequate sensor models, besides enabling accurate estimates of the interrelationships among the sensor data. It is hoped, therefore, that sufficiently accurate process models based on neural networks can soon be incorporated in an integrated multisensor scheme for monitoring and controlling the machining process.

33.7 DISCUSSION, ANALYSIS, AND CONCLUSIONS

It has been shown that a good amount of experimental and theoretical work has been done in the study of AE from metal cutting. While experimental data revealed the complex nature of the phenomenon, simple theoretical arguments gave expressions for the rms value of the AE signal detected (13). Under certain idealized cutting conditions, the theory was found to give qualitatively good agreement with experimental data, although some glaring inconsistencies remained. These were removed in a subsequent model (21) by eliminating some effects (chip tool sliding and chip breaking) normally encountered in the metal cutting process. Although the effects of tool wear of either type on the AE signal are qualitatively understood, these have not been successfully included in any theoretical model of the process. The attempt by Lan and Dornfeld (15) to introduce the effect of flank wear in their expression for V_{rms} was probably premature, as no quantitative comparison of their model with the AE observed with a worn tool has been reported. A few disconcerting aspects of experimental data (such as the dependence of V_{rms} on feed rate and width of cut) have been attributed to the three-dimensional effects of the real cutting phenonmenon, but there have been few supporting arguments.

There is no doubt that the study of AE from metal cutting has lead to a better understanding of the process. Yet, if the AE signal parameter such as V_{rms} is to be used in tool wear monitoring, a good amount of modeling work remains to be done. While the qualitative effects of tool wear on the AE signal is understood, more exact analysis of the dependence is needed to enable its use in monitoring and control of the process. The AE signal has been successfully employed in detection of tool breakage or failure in industry, whereas its practical use in tool wear monitoring is yet to be established. This is because the AE signal level, although sensitive to tool wear, also strongly depends on the cutting speed, and the two effects must be separated to enable proper use in wear monitoring or process control. The spectral analysis of the AE signal carries much more promise, because the separation of different effects may be possible in the frequency domain. But this calls for a more detailed understanding of the physical processes involved in AE generation as well as the use of sophisticated signal processing methods for analysis of the AE signals and extraction of appropriate parameters for process monitoring.

Finally, the use of artificial intelligence techniques such as those using neural networks seems to offer a lot of promise, as these methods work well even when exact sensor models are not available. The ability of the neural network to learn the correlations existing among various sensor data (even if they be nonlinear) enables a robust and reliable process model to be synthesized from the multisensor data. The dependence of the AE signal on the microscopic aspects of the metal cutting process indicates that the AE sensor is likely to remain an important component of any future multisensor diagnostic and control mechanism of the process developed. It is conceivable that AE sensor alone may provide a sufficient number of independent parameters for accurate modeling of the cutting process using neural networks, thus eliminating the need for multiple sensors and too complex data processing hardware.

BIBLIOGRAPHY

1. J. TLUSTY and G.C. ANDREWS, "A Critical Review of Sensors for Unmanned Machining," *Ann. CIRP* **32,** 563–572 (1983).
2. L. DAN and J. MATHEW, "Tool Wear and Failure Monitoring Techniques for Turning— A review," *Int. J. Mach. Tool Manufact.* **30,** 579–598 (1990).

3. J. ROGET, P. SOUQUET, and G.S.I.B. NAYIB, "Use of Acoustic Emission for In-process Monitoring of Tools During Turning and Milling," Prog. Acoust. Emission, 316–327 (1986).

4. D.A. DORNFELD, "Monitoring of Machining Process by Means of Acoustic Emission Sensors" in W. Sachse, J. Roget, and K. Yamaguchi, *Acoustic Emission: Current Practices and Future Directions,* ASTM, Philadelphia, 1991, 328–344.

5. D. DORNFELD, "Application of Acoustic Emission Techniques in Manufacturing," *NDT&E Int.* **25,** 259–269 (1992).

6. P. GILLIS and M. HAMSTAD, "Some Fundamental Aspects of the Theory of Acoustic Emission," *Mater. Sci. Eng.* **14,** 103–108 (1974).

7. R.M. FISHER and J.S. LALLY, "Microplasticity Detected by Acoustic Technique," *Can. J. Phys.* **45,** 1147–1159 (1967).

8. K. ASIBU and E. EMEL, "Characterization of Tool Wear and Tool Breakage by Pattern Recognition Analysis," *Proc. 14th NAMRC,* 266–272 (1986).

9. S. LIANG and D.A. DORNFELD, "Tool Wear Determination Using Time Series Analysis of Acoustic Emission," *Trans. ASME J. Eng. Ind.* **111,** 199–205 (1989).

10. D.A. DORNFELD, "Chip Form Detection Using Acoustic Emission," *Proc. 11th NAMRC,* 386–389 (1983).

11. E. DIEI and D.A. DORNFELD, "A Model for Tool Fracture Generated Acoustic Emission during Machining," *Trans ASME J. Eng. Ind.* **109,** 227–234 (1987).

12. T. MORIWAKI, "Detection of Cutting Tool Fracture by Acoustic Emission Measurements," Ann CIRP **29,** 35–40 (1980).

13. E. KANNATEY-ASIBU and D.A. DORNFELD, "Quantitative Relations for Acoustic Emission from Orthogonal Metal Cutting," *J. Eng. Ind.* **103,** 330–340 (1981).

14. M.J. SCHMENCK, "Acoustic Emission and Mechanics of Metal Cutting" in D. Dornfeld, ed., *Acoustic Emission Monitoring and Analysis in Manufacturing,* ASME, New York, 1984, pp. 95–104.

15. M.S. LAN, and D.A. DORNFELD, "Acoustic Emission and Machining—Process Analysis and Control," *Adv. Manufact. Process.* **1,** 1–21 (1986).

16. M.E. MERCHANT, "Mechanics of Metal Cutting Process," *J. Appl. Phys.* **16,** 267–275, 318–324, (1945).

17. H. EARNST and M.E. MERCHANT, "Chip Formation, Friction and High Quality Machined Surfaces of Metals," *Trans. ASME* **29,** 299–378 (1941).

18. G. CHRYSSOLOURIS and M. DOMROESE, "Some Aspects of Acoustic Emission Modelling for Machining Control" in *Proceedings of the 17th NMRC,* 228–234 (1989).

19. R. TETI and D.A. DORNFELD, "Modeling and Experimental Analysis of Acoustic Emission from Metal Cutting," *J. Eng. Ind.* **111,** 229–237 (1989).

20. T. BLUM and I. INASAKI, "A Study of Acoustic Emission from Orthogonal Metal Cutting Process," *J. Eng. Ind.* **112,** 203–211 (1990).

21. S. RANGWALA and D.A. DORNFELD, "A Study of Acoustic Emission Generated During Orthogonal Metal Cutting, Part I: Energy Analysis," *Int. J. Mech. Sci.* **33,** 471–487 (1991).

22. M. LAN, *Investigation of Tool Wear, Fracture and Chip Formation in Metal Cutting Using Acoustic Emission,* Ph.D. dissertation University of California, Berkeley, 1983.

23. J.R. KLAIBER, D.A. DORNFELD, and J.J. LIU, "Acoustic Emission Feedback for Diamond Turning" in *Proceedings of the 18th NAMRC,* pp. 113–119 (1990).

24. J.J. LIU and D.A. DORNFELD, "Monitoring of Micromachining Process Using Acoustic Emission," *Trans. North Am. Manufact. Inst. SME* **20,** pp 189–195 (1991).

25. E. KANNATEY-ASIBU and E. EMEL, "Linear Discriminant Function Analysis of Acoustic Emission Signals for Cutting Tool Monitoring," *J. Mech. Sys. Sign. Process.* **1**(4), 333–347 (1987).

26. E. EMEL and E. KANNATEY-ASIBU, "Acoustic Emission Monitoring of the Cutting Process Negating the Influence of varying conditions" in E. Kannatey-Asibu, J. Koren, and Stein, eds., *Sensors and Controls for Manufacturing* ASME PED-33, 1988, pp. 63–73.

27. S. RANGWALA and D.A. DORNFELD, "A Study of Acoustic Emission Generated During Orthogonal Metal Cutting, Part II: Spectral Analysis," *Int. J. Mech. Sci.* **33**, 489–499 (1991).

28. S. RANGWALA and D.A. DORNFELD, "Sensor Integration Using Neural Networks for Intelligent Tool Condition Monitoring," *Trans. ASME J. Eng. Ind.* **112**, 219–228 (1990).

29. S. RANGWALA and D.A. DORNFELD, "Learning Optimization of Machining Operations Using Computing Abilities of Neutral Networks," *IEEE Trans. SMC* **19**, 299–314 (1989).

30. G. CHRYSSOLOURIS and M. DOMROESE, "Sensor Integration for Tool Wear Estimation in Machining" in E. Kannatey-Asibu, J. Koren and J. Stein *Sensors and Controls for Manufacturing,* ASME Winter Annual Meetings, 1988, pp. 115–123, ASME PED-33.

31. S.V.T. ELANAYAR, Y.C. SHIN, and S.R.T. KUMARA, "Machining Condition Monitoring for Automation Using Neural Networks" in S. Y. Liang and T. C. Tsao, eds. *Monitoring and Control for Manufacturing Processes,* ASME Winter Annual Meetings, ASME PED-44, 85–95 (1990).

32. G. CHRYSSOLOURIS, M. DOMROESE, and P. BEAULIEU, "Sensor Synthesis for Control of Manufacturing Process" in *Monitoring and Control for Manufacturing Processes,* ASME Winter Annual Meetings, 1990, pp. 67–76, ASME PED-44.

33. L.I. BURKE and S. RANGWALA, "Tool Condition Monitoring in Metal Cutting: A Neural Network Approach," *J. Intell. Manufact.* **2**, 269–280 (1991).

34. L.I. BURKE, "An Unsupervised Neural Network Approach to Tool Wear Identification," *IIE Trans.* **25**, 16–24 (1993).

35. S.V. KAMARTHI, G.S. Sankar, P.H. COHEN, and S.R.T. KUMARA, "On-line Tool Wear Monitoring Using a Kohonen's Feature Map" in C.H. Dagli, S.R.T. Kumara, and Y.C. Shin, eds., *Intelligent Engineering Systems through Artificial Neural Networks,* St. Louis, Mo., 1991, pp. 639–645.

36. H.K. TONSHOFF, J.P. WULFSBERG, H.J.J. KALS, W. KONIG, and C.A. VAN LUTTERVELT, "Developments and Trends in Monitoring and Control of Machining Processes" *Ann. CIRP* **37**(2), 611–622 (1988).

37. D.A. DORNFELD, "Monitoring of Machining Processes—Literature Review," paper presented at the CIRP STC C Meeting, Paris, Jan. 1992.

SECTION VIII

INFORMATION SYSTEMS

CHAPTER 34
Image Processing in Manufacturing

RONALD LUMIA
National Institute of Standards and
Technology

34.1 INTRODUCTION

The use of sensors has become an integral part of the manufacturing process. Sensors measure the variables that are important to the process and provide feedback in a control system. This chapter describes a class of sensors: image processing systems. In a general sense, image processing can be used three ways in manufacturing. The first is as a metrology device, effectively a complex sensor, which measures parameters needed for feedback in the manufacturing system. The second use of image processing is for inspection, which measures the quality of a manufactured part. Finally, image processing can be used as guidance for robots and automated guidance vehicles (AGVs), for which visual sensing is required for obstacle detection and avoidance. This chapter will first describe the basic paradigm of imaging processing and introduce common terminology. Then an overview of some specific industrial applications of vision will demonstrate the diversity of this sensing modality. Finally, the active vision approach, a new research direction, will be described through which the sensor moves in whatever way is necessary to gather high quality data.

34.2 PARADIGM OF IMAGE PROCESSING

Vision System Components

Over the last 20 years, the quality of the components of an image processing system has increased while the cost has decreased. Yet, the basic image processing system, as shown in Figure 34.1, has remained almost constant. The camera is positioned so that the object of interest is in the field of view. The output of the camera is sent through preprocessing, which includes digitization. This is followed by feature extraction and classification. Finally, the system determines an action appropriate for the task based on the measurements taken. This section describes each of these boxes in greater detail while introducing terminology common to the field of image processing.

The most common commercially available camera is based on charged coupled device (CCD) technology. Light, passing through the lens, is focused onto the CCD chip in the camera, which has many cells called picture elements or *pixels*, which are organized in a one- or two-dimensional array. As photons impinge on each cell of the light-sensitive CCD, hole-electron pairs are created proportional to the light intensity on that cell. By creating electrostatic "wells," it is possible to collect the electrons as they are created. The electrons are collected, or integrated, for 1/60 s, which is known as the *field time*. Then the electrons in each cell of each row of the CCD are sequentially converted to a proportional amount of voltage and sent out of the camera in a standard video format, e.g., RS-170. Often, a camera output is *interlaced*, by which the even and odd rows are sent out during alternate fields. Thus, when interlacing is used, the entire *frame time* consists of a 1/60-s even line field and a 1/60-s odd line field, for a total of 1/30 s.

The CCD camera has several limitations. First, there is the issue of *dynamic range,* the lowest to highest level of acceptable illumination. When light levels are low, the number of

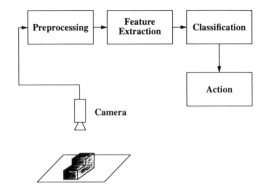

Figure 34.1. Basic image processing system.

electrons gathered during integration is also low. Unfortunately, the CCD has thermal noise that corrupts the signal by creating hole-electron pairs in a random fashion. At the other extreme, when light levels are high, the pixel can *saturate*, thereby affecting the quality of the signal. Furthermore, excess electrons in a pixel can spill, or *bloom*, into adjacent pixels, grossly affecting the image quality. Although the camera is not damaged by blooming, the output from the image processing algorithms degrades significantly.

The output of the typical camera produces an analogue signal that must be digitized and stored in memory. The *frame grabber*, as its name suggests, can digitize and store a frame of video data in real time. Frame grabbers are surprisingly inexpensive, considering their speed of operation. For example, a 256 × 256 image stored in 1/60 s requires that each pixel be digitized (usually to eight bits) and stored within approximately 250 ns.

Preprocessing also includes image processing algorithms such as smoothing, which removes image noise through low pass filtering. There are myriad variations of image processing algorithms that can be applied to the image. Low level image processing algorithms, techniques, and theory have been described (1, 2). The following example illustrates only one possible sequence. Smoothing is an example of a convolution operator. One can imagine a relatively small template, e.g., 3 × 3 pixels, which can be superimposed on some 3 × 3 pixel area of the original 256 × 256 image. The output of the convolution operation is the sum of each pixel in the template multiplied by the corresponding pixel in the image. For the image $I(i,j)$ and the template $T(x, y)$, with a base of $2b + 1$ and height of $2h + 1$, the convolution $C(i,j)$ is expressed as:

$$C(i,j) = \sum_{x=-b}^{b} \sum_{y=-h}^{h} I(i + x, j + y)\, T(x, y) \tag{1}$$

If this convolution operation is done for each possible image location, the resulting image is the original image *convolved* with the template. By choosing the values for the template pixels and the size of the template window, myriad image processing algorithms are possible.

Convolution operators are common in image processing. Figure 34.2 shows several common convolution *kernels*. The smoothing template, which is a low pass filter, is shown in Figure 34.2a. Since each pixel of the neighborhood is equally weighted, any noise associated with one particular pixel is diluted, thereby reducing its influence. This is a common technique to use when noise in the image data degrades the subsequent image processing algorithms.

To extract objects from an image, it is often useful to extract edges. An *edge* is defined as an abrupt change in the intensity values of adjacent pixels. There are literally thousands of edge detection techniques. The Sobel operator, with its templates illustrated in Figure 34.2b and 34.2c is a common edge extraction algorithm and will be used to explain the concept. Figure 34.2b shows the template for finding edges that are oriented in the horizontal direction. Similarly, Figure 34.2c detects vertically oriented edges. The output of the convolution of these masks describes the ''edginess'' in the *x* and *y* directions, respectively. These two values can be

```
1    1    1
1    1    1
1    1    1
    (a)
```

```
 1    2    1
 0    0    0
-1   -2   -1
    (b)
```

```
-1    0    1
-2    0   -2
-1    0    1
    (c)
```

Figure 34.2.   Convolution operators.

combined to form the gradient and the direction of the gradient for each pixel in the image as:

$$G(i, j) = \sqrt{(Grad_x\,(i, j))^2 + (Grad_y\,(i, j))^2} \tag{2}$$

$$\Theta\,(i, j) = \text{atan}\,(Grad_y\,(i, j), Grad_x\,(i, j))$$

At this point, each pixel has a value related to the image edginess at that location in the image. This image is often *thresholded*, i.e., a binary image is created and each pixel is declared to be an edge (pixel = 1) only if the threshold is exceeded. Otherwise, it is declared as background (pixel = 0). Certain pixels that are declared edges are spatially adjacent. A *connected components* algorithm can assign all of the pixels that are adjacent to be members of a unique set. In this way, a set of separate "blobs" is identified.

Feature extraction is a process of data reduction. The features chosen for the problem should describe the salient characteristics of the object efficiently. The feature extractor box in Figure 34.1 contains algorithms that can extract information relevant to the task. Useful features include area, perimeter, minimum enclosing rectangle, centroid, moments, minimum radius vector, maximum radius vector, holes, elongation, aspect ratio, etc. Review of the common features are available (1–3). New features are often invented for an application and challenge the programmers of the system to develop the best set of features for a specific application.

The classifier takes the set of features and groups them according to a set of rules to assign the object to the best possible *class*. The separation between feature extraction and classification is largely in the mind of the system designer. The perfect feature extractor would not require a classifier, and the perfect classifier would not require a feature extractor. However, it is often useful to divide the task between the two boxes of Figure 34.1 to increase program efficiency and decrease computation time. The result of classification is an action that is task dependent. If the image processing system is to identify objects, then the result is the name of the object. If the goal is an inspection task, e.g., to determine whether the label is placed correctly on a bottle, then the classification is correct–not correct, with the action to send only defective objects into a failure bin.

Ancillary Vision System Components

The previous section briefly described the components of the image processing system. A system designer must also consider part handling, lighting, and lenses. Figure 34.1 shows the camera inspecting an object. How did the object get there? The costs of the ancillary equipment required to handle the parts often ends up to be a substantial portion of the total system cost. The requirements for part handling equipment can be quite demanding. For example, the equipment should not jam if the parts are slightly deformed. Furthermore, the equipment must also present the part in whatever way is necessary for the image processing system to perform its task, which may require rotation of the workpiece. Naturally, the handling system and the vision system must be coordinated in real time to achieve the task goal.

One of the most insidious problems with image processing is lighting. While the use of natural light might first appear to be the least expensive approach, this is usually not the case. When natural light is used, the image processing algorithms must be sufficiently robust to significant changes in light levels, i.e., the system should work equally well on bright and cloudy days. This requirement is either difficult or costly to achieve. The alternative is to control the ambient lighting. Good engineering practice always chooses a cost-effective balance between structuring the environment in a variety of ways (e.g., lighting and handling) and developing robust algorithms, which can flexibly be used for a variety of tasks. Many approaches in lighting are available to the engineer. They include the use of structured light, silhouettes, polarized light, and filtered light, all of which need to be considered in the system design. A review of some of these techniques is available (4).

Lenses are very good but they are not perfect. Spherical aberration and other lens distortions affect the quality of the measurements made by the image processing system. Typically, a camera calibration procedure is employed (5) to cope with this problem. Camera calibration identifies the critical parameters that describe the nonideal characteristics of the lens and camera. Functions are then developed to compensate for these errors, thereby increasing the measurement accuracy of the camera and lens system.

Performance Measures in Image Processing

The previous approach to the characterization of an image processing system focused on the components of the vision system. An alternative is to consider the performance of the system, effectively concentrating on *what* the system does and disregarding *how* the system works. Using this method, the system designer concentrates on the specifications of the system, which are relevant to his or her desired task. This section introduces several performance measures of interest to the system designer. Naturally, the cost–performance trade-off plays a significant role in the decision process.

Processing speed is an obvious benchmark of importance to a designer. However, the processing speed depends on the algorithms that are required for the task and the hardware on which they run. The least expensive hardware is a normal computer interfaced to a frame buffer. However, this approach limits the implementation to relatively simple algorithms, because it is difficult for most computers to keep up with the frame rate of the camera. Special-purpose architectures have been developed to increase the speed of algorithms, especially the convolution operation commonly performed in image processing.

Based on the focal length of the lens, the size of the image array, and the number of pixels in the array, the designer can calculate the system *spatial resolution*. This is the solid angle of the scene that impinges on each pixel. Usually, the system cannot hope to measure better than this limit (although some clever image processing algorithms can achieve subpixel resolution under limited conditions). If the resolution is not sufficient for the task, the most common modification is to change the focal length of the lens.

Accuracy and repeatability are important parameters that are often confused. Suppose that we are making a measurement with the system, and we repeat the measurement many times. Ideally, the system should provide the same answer each time it makes a measurement. Repeatability measures the spread of values, i.e., the capability of the image processing system to give the same answer under the same conditions. This does not imply that the answer is accurate. In fact, the answer can be wrong. The resolution of the system, as previously described, provides a limit on the accuracy, but the system does not necessary achieve this limit. The accuracy of the system should be tested under conditions similar to the desired task to determine whether the accuracy and repeatability are sufficient.

Because the integration time for most cameras is fixed at 1/60 s per frame, the only remaining variable to limit the amount of light impinging on the light sensitive pixels is the iris of the camera. Often cameras have an *auto-iris,* which automatically limits light to attain high quality images. Unfortunately, adjusting the iris setting changes the *depth of field.* The depth of field is the set of ranges over which objects are in focus. If an object is outside of this range, either too close or too far, it will be out of focus. Obviously, it is undesirable to make measurements on an object that is out of focus. This suggests that strong and steady lighting is desirable. With a strong light source, the iris must close down to prevent too much light from reaching the image sensor, resulting in a large depth of field.

The finest image processing system that cannot tolerate the environment in which it must work is of dubious value. Manufacturing areas are often more challenging than laboratory areas from an environmental standpoint. It is not uncommon to find dust and other airborne contaminants, vibration, poor lighting, excessive humidity, etc., in the workplace. Industrial-grade racks can sometimes mitigate these conditions, but the system designer must be certain that the environmental specifications of the system and the environment are compatible.

The issues of programming ease and flexibility to use image processing systems in different applications are somewhat related. It is widely recognized that software development costs represent a significant portion of the total system cost. To be able to use the image processing system for similar applications in a factory, it is essential to be able to reprogram the system efficiently. Although most of the commercially available systems are making strides in this area, the current state is that systems are relatively time-consuming to program for three reasons. First, image processing techniques remain more of an art than a science, with practical experience in choosing successful techniques counting as heavily as university training in the field. Second, there is usually a substantial learning curve in the programming methods. Image processing hardware often has a unique programming language that takes advantage of the hardware system design in some fashion. Finally, some of the ancillary issues previously discussed (e.g., part handling and lighting) figure prominently in the success of the final system but are not taken into account by the image processing programming language.

With these considerations, the system designer can concentrate on the requirements of the system to forge a total system design that meets performance needs. For those new to the field, however, it is difficult to determine whether a particular application is amenable to an image processing solution. While this chapter cannot guarantee the reader will be able to identify feasible image processing tasks, the issue is addressed by exploring successful industrial image processing applications. It is hoped that the designer can develop a feel for the state of the art, which will help to choose applications predisposed toward success.

34.3   APPLICATIONS OF IMAGE PROCESSING

Identifying Potential Image Processing Applications

The use of image processing in manufacturing is typically driven by the need for high quality and low cost. There are two types of application areas, improving the manufacturing process and inspecting the product, that are both employed to achieve the quality and cost goals of manufacturing. For example, the Taguchi method for quality control is a clever way to run a minimal number of experiments to determine the best values for the controllable parameters of the manufacturing process (6). Other approaches rely on image processing to detect errors in the product before shipment to customers. Because these approaches are not mutually exclusive, it is common to find both approaches employed. It is good business practice to automate certain manufacturing processes to achieve greater quality control, which eventually manifests itself in higher quality production. As the field takes advantage of technological advances, e.g., computing power, the costs associated with employing image processing technology will continue to fall, and new applications will cross the threshold of economic viability.

One approach to finding image processing applications is rather obvious; one lists the situations in which human eyesight is currently employed in the manufacturing process. Examples include assembly and placement of components, measurement of objects, and inspection of the final parts. While this is an excellent starting place, it is not sufficient. Image processing may be used in areas in which humans are not used. For example, image processing can be used to measure parameters that are critical to the manufacturing process. These measured parameters can be used to control the process through feedback. Consequently, there must be a greater understanding of the manufacturing process, i.e., its critical parameters, to determine whether the addition of image processing techniques can be justified. The applications described below do not represent a complete look at how image processing can be applied to manufacturing. However, it will outline the state of the art to allow the reader to determine whether a potential application seems possible. The electronics industry supports the largest number of image processing applications, with inspection being the most common. Consequently, the applications described in the remainder of this section will be divided into three subsections: automated visual inspection, electronics applications, and other industrial applications.

Automated Visual Inspection

Inspection has always been an integral part of the manufacturing process and often represents the single largest cost in the system (7). As a result, inspection has received considerable attention, especially because humans do not perform the function well over long periods of time. People are subject to fatigue and boredom, which reduce the consistency of their capabilities. This is especially true when working under adverse environmental conditions or in high speed production settings. Furthermore, the trend to collect data for statistical process control taxes human inspectors.

Chin and Harlow (7) provided a survey of automated visual inspection. Although the survey is more than 10 yrs old, the application areas they covered remain viable today and provide an excellent overview of the field. More recently, Chin (8) compared several algorithms used in automated visual inspection by analyzing the feature extraction, modeling, and matching associated with each algorithm. Algorithms include image subtraction, differential scanning, the use of color separation in image subtraction, optical spatial filtering, dimensional verification, morphological analysis, and syntactic (or linguistic) approaches.

As the costs of machine vision drop with technological advances, a greater number of industrial applications becomes economically viable. However, the number does not begin to approach the predictions made for the industry 15 yr ago. Progress has been made but even the successful image processing applications often required a great deal more work than anticipated. Mundy (9) described the development process associated with several projects in industrial machine vision, which began during the 1970s. His conclusions were the following:

- System cost is difficult to justify; a competent vision system will cost $500,000 to $1,000,000 and replace skilled human labor of $30,000 per year.
- A large and risky development effort is usually required.
- The factory environment is complex and unstructured; as a result, the ancillary equipment (such as material handling) and environmental issues (such as oily parts) complicate the inspection process considerably.
- Programming the inspection task for reliable operation is difficult.

Similar warnings were issued by Lavin (10), who described six aspects of technology that machine vision vendors should be working on to meet the needs of industry:

- Integration of the vision system with both the execution system and the design system.
- Scalable hardware, by which the cost–capability trade-off can be tailored to the application.
- Fast cameras; television-compatible cameras are too slow.
- Well-characterized algorithms; if the feature extraction algorithms are better understood, the time required (and, therefore, the cost) to create robust application programs could be reduced significantly.
- Automatic application generation; better approaches to programming are needed such as teaching by showing.
- User education; training is needed so that factory floor personnel are familiar with the techniques and technology of image processing.

These warnings indicate that successful image procession applications are not trivial. Yet, industry continues to integrate machine vision into the manufacturing process. The next two sections describe some specific applications.

Image Processing in the Electronics Industry

The electronics industry is particularly amenable to image processing applications. Parts are produced in large quantities, and it is imperative to manufacture with exceedingly low error

TABLE 34.1. Image Processing for the Electronics Industry

Application	Description
Tracking for wafer, carrier, component, and circuit boards	Image processing systems read codes etched into wafers so that probes and other equipment can execute the proper programs; tracking also facilities gathering the data required for statistical quality control
Package inspection	Detection of poor marking, bent pins, etc.
Assembly equipment guidance	Image processing systems can locate desired positions for assembly machines
Circuit board inspection	Detection of defects such as pinholes, broken tracks, etc. is commonly done with commercially available equipment
Loaded board inspection	Ensure that the proper components are inserted into the circuit board in the proper location

rates. Many applications have been suggested for image processing (11) for the electronics industry as shown in Table 34.1.

The fabrication of an integrated circuit requires many steps, each of which requires inspection, so that the final product works properly. LeBeau (12) describes the requirements for machine vision platforms for a typical integrated circuit manufacturer. It is believed that the subjective nature of human inspectors prevent achieving a "six-sigma" manufacturing capability, i.e., 3.4 parts per million (PPM) defect rate. Human inspectors, performing 1000 to 4000 individual inspections per hour can achieve roughly a 90% success rate, but this does not even approach the six-sigma requirement. Consequently, the inspections must be done by machine. The typical inspection requirements include alignment, metrology, flaw detection, defect identification, and defect classification. Specifying a machine vision system that can perform these measurements for the variety of products produced under acceptable process variation has been challenging. It seems that the delivery of a system that satisfies the image processing specifications often fails to work adequately on the factory floor, because the user was unable to define all of his or her needs a priori. This suggests that the user must develop a better understanding the manufacturing process so that image processing specifications can be chosen properly. However, there are relatively few workers on the factory floor trained in machine vision. Consequently, applications can fail because of poor choice image processing features rather than the capability of the image processing equipment. Furthermore, any system on the factory floor must be maintained to reflect changes in the manufacturing process, and it is hoped that this can be achieved without hiring outside consultants for small system changes. In spite of these concerns, many successful applications have been achieved in the electronics industry.

Placement of parts requires the integration of image processing for measurement and some sort of robot device to effect motion. Chang (13) described a system that measures the location of surface mount devices and uses a robot to load the devices onto a printed circuit board. The position of a 68 lead devices is measured with an accuracy of 0.012 mm. A similar application, described by Smeyers and Buts (14), shows how image processing is used to align a die on a plastic or ceramic housing for die bonding. Belinski et al. (15) described a system that inspects and performs assembly operations for submillimeter semiconductor devices. Randomly oriented devices are mounted individually on a fixture with an accuracy of 2 μm. Chapron (16) described a system that visually inspects integrated circuits at each stage of the assembly line: die bonding, wire bonding, lid sealing, and package marking. Aside from the quality of inspection, it is desirable to remove the human from the process for two additional reasons: contamination and static electricity. Because defects in integrated circuits are a direct consequence of mask defects, a variety of techniques (17, 18) have been employed in detecting, classifying, and repairing submicron masks.

Another application area for image processing is the fabrication of printed circuit boards (PCB). Manufacturing practice currently leans toward large, multilayer boards with fine tracks and features. Although the defect rate is low, there is a significant cost associated with the failure to detect a defect. Consequently, inspection is performed at each step of the PCB manufacturing process, so that defects can be detected and repaired. Lees and Henshaw (19) describe the development of a new feature extraction technique to PCB inspection. The approach is based on comparing only the phase of the PCB image with that of the ideal image to minimize the sensitivity to lighting variations and translation errors. To achieve process control, Ando and Oka (20) developed a system that simultaneously measures the width and thickness of the conductive patterns on a PCB. The system can inspect a 300-mm area with 5-μm resolution in 6 min and is currently operating in a plant.

Inspection of solder joints using image processing techniques is also a common industrial application. Takagi et al. (21) described a vision inspection technique to detect solder joint defects of surface-mount devices mounted on a PCB. Other approaches have been published (22–24).

Image Processing in Miscellaneous Industrial Settings

When image processing measurements are used for in-process control, the accuracy of the measurements becomes critical. Mitchell et al. (25) described an approach for extracting features such as edges and areas with subpixel accuracy by averaging many binary images created by employing multiple thresholds. Measurements such as these can be used to control processes. For example, Leung et al. (26) described an approach to measure the thickness of plastic sheets using a *structured light* technique. The resolution of the system is excellent after calibration, because the measurement range to resolution ratio is 28,000. A vision system has also been used to align film before deposition on the acetate film used as a substrate (27).

Productivity in manufacturing automobiles can be enhanced through the application of image processing technology. Some applications remove humans from hazardous environments, e.g., measurements of brake linings containing asbestos (28), while others simply perform metrology or inspection (29) such as:

- Inspection of correct mounting of shaft mountings, ball bearings, lock rims, sealant, and gears.
- Three-dimensional measurement of body geometry, doors, castings, and cylinder diameters.
- Surface quality of the paint and/or car body.

The vast majority of small machined parts are made in batches of less than 50. Nevertheless, inspection is often required. There is a need to verify the dimensions of each feature and relationship between the features to be sure that engineering tolerances have been respected. Because batch sizes are small, the time required to program the image processing system to make the measurements is critical. The representation of tolerances for the position, size, and form are important issues (30) that are being addressed by the STEP international standard (31). Image processing systems also inspect shapes cut in sheet metal (32) and shoe leather (33).

Machine vision is also used for large batch manufacturing inspection application. For example, Bains and David (34) described a system that inspects 16,000 fluorescent lamp bases per hour, 24 hr per day. Each lamp base was checked for nine possible defects:

- Uncut lead wires touching the bases.
- Missing or damaged insulation.
- Angled or eccentric bases.
- Uncut lead wires.
- Short pins.
- Missing pins.
- Bent pins.
- Incomplete welds in the pin ends.
- Bases turned with respect to each other.

While the features themselves were relatively straightforward, the time allotted to make all measurements was only 450 ms.

Another example of large batch manufacturing is shoe tack inspection (33). Shoe tacks are produced at a rate of 250,000/min by squeezing wire in a die. Tacks with feathered ends must be detected and removed because they jam the automated tack insertion machinery. The solution involved a raceway that was fed by tacks from the bowl feeder. The image processing equipment simply measured the area of the tack, which turned out to be sufficient for discrimination. However, as is often the case in image processing system, the ancillary equipment required to handle the tack was subject to reliability problems. An alternative approach that reduced requirements of the tack handling equipment required a costly image processing system and was, therefore, rejected.

ACTIVE VISION

The Motivation for Active Vision

In spite of many successful industrial applications, machine vision falls far short of human capabilities. The current state of the art suggests that economically viable applications often rely on structuring the environment to achieve the robustness desired for the task. Human vision, on the other hand, needs relatively little environment structure, yet performs better. A summary of human vision capability is shown in Table 34.2. Why are human vision and machine vision so disparate in their capabilities?

One difference is the sensor. Cameras use equally sized rectangular pixels over the entire sensor area. The human eye, on the other hand, has sensor cells very tightly packed in the fovea while there is a 10:1 difference in resolution between the fovea and periphery on the retina. Although, the fovea comprises only 1% of the light-sensitive region, it plays a critical role in object discriminating identification and manipulation. From a coding standpoint, this is extremely efficient. Great detail can be obtained from the image on the fovea while significant information is still available for the rest of the field of view at lower resolution. It is imperative, therefore, to be certain that the most interesting information falls on the fovea.

The second major difference between human and machine vision is that the eye can move. Information that is sensed by peripheral vision, can be deemed "interesting." This appears to trigger an attention function that sends signals to the eye muscles so that the interesting part of scene will fall on the fovea. In this manner, one has the perception of a high resolution world even though the fovea subtends only 1% of the field of view.

A great deal of work is currently under way to study the human vision system and how features are extracted from the image to facilitate perception. A new research area related to perception is called *active vision*, because the sensor is actively controlled, i.e., the sensor is moved in whatever way maximizes the quality of the extracted data. The human vision system is clearly goal driven, and the eyes are moved to keep the fovea locked on areas of interest in the scene. We would like to achieve a similar result. Because the gaze direction of the camera is determined by what has been sensed, simulation of the phenomena is not possible; a system must be able to change the gaze direction by physically moving the camera. While the ability to move a camera is not active vision, this equipment is nonetheless a prerequisite for active vision research. The next section will review efforts to build the active vision platform.

Approaches to Active Vision

Bajcsy (35) first suggested the concept of active vision, and Krotkov et al. (36) constructed the first active vision system. The system provides flexible image acquisition capabilities using a pair of movable cameras with computer-controlled zoom, focus, and aperture along with 10

TABLE 34.2. Human Active Visual System Characteristics

Feature	Value
Eye pan motion	± 0.78 rad ($\pm 45°$)
Eye tilt motion	± 0.78 rad ($\pm 45°$)
Neck pan motion	± 1.40 rad ($\pm 80°$)
Neck tilt motion	1.57 rad down, 1.05 rad up ($+90°$, $-60°$)
Peak acceleration	611 rad/s^2 (35,000°/s^2)
Peak velocity	10.5 rad/s (600°/s)
Interocular distance	~64.0 mm (2.5 in.)
Foveal-to-peripheral resolution ratio	10:1

variable-intensity lamps. The positioning mechanism of the system provides 2 translational degrees of freedom (df), pan and tilt of both cameras, and coupled symmetric vergence.

At other institutions, such as the University of Illinois, researchers have assembled dynamic stereo camera systems using commercial motion-control components, such as rotational and translational stages (37). Such systems can provide good repeatability and relatively high speed motions. However, because they are constructed from general-purpose positioning units, they cannot easily be configured to meet special requirements (such as the ability to position the focal point of the camera lenses at the intersection of perpendicular motion axes).

A different approach to aiming cameras is used in the MIT Vision Machine (38). The Vision Machine consists of two cameras rigidly mounted on a movable platform. Each of the cameras is equipped with a motorized zoom lens, allowing control of the iris, focus, and focal length. Because of the size and weight of the lenses, camera movement is achieved indirectly by pivoting a front surface mirror mounted in front of each lens. These mirrors provide two degrees of freedom in aiming the cameras. The platform rotates about two orthogonal axes to allow pan and tilt control. The MIT Vision Machine integrates several low level vision algorithms using images from a movable two-camera eye-head system to achieve high performance in unstructured environments for recognition and navigation tasks.

Binocular active vision systems have also been built at the University of Rochester and Harvard University. The Rochester head has independent vergence axes and a coupled tilt axis and achieves camera rotational velocities of 5.2 rad/s and positioning accuracy of 2.4 mrad (39). The head is mounted on a 6-df robot arm and has been used to study gaze-holding, vergence, and kinetic depth (depth from motion during fixation) (40, 41). The Harvard head is a mobile binocular camera system with 7 df (42); 3 df control the orientation of the cameras by performing pan, tilt, and antisymmetric vergence motions. The other 4 df accomplish control of the cameras; aperture and lens focus. This camera system is mounted on a robot that provides translation in the horizontal plane and rotation about a vertical axis. The head has been used to study attentive gaze control for use in mobile robot navigation.

The head–eye system developed at the Royal Institute of Technology in Sweden (the KTH head) is a 13-df device, with 2 df (mechanical) for each of the two eyes, 2 df in the neck, 1 df for computer-controlled baseline separation, and 3 df (optical) for each eye (43). The resolution on the eye and neck axes is 126 μrad, and the maximum rotational velocity is 3.14 rad/s. A particularly interesting feature of the KTH head is a mechanism that automatically compensates for shifts in the position of the lens centers caused by changes in the lens focal length and focusing distance. This keeps the lens centers near the centers of rotation, despite changes in optical parameters.

Another interesting recent development in the area of active vision hardware is the Spherical Pointing Motor (SPM) (44). This device is a small, lightweight pan-tilt mechanism that can be configured to move a small camera. It is controlled open loop and is capable of rotational velocities of up to 10.5 rad/s. Accuracies of 2.6 mrad are achieved. The SPM shows promise for future compact, low cost active vision systems.

Although the above systems represent significant advances in the development of hardware for active vision, none of them incorporated all of the features required to emulate the human vision system. These include humanlike dynamic performance and range of motion, independent control of vergence degrees of freedom for asymmetrical vergence, ability to position vergence lens focal points at the intersection of vergence and tilt axes, multiresolution imaging capability, high positioning resolution, repeatability, accuracy, modular design, the use of industrial-quality components, and the ability to withstand the rigors of experimentation. In addition, a completely open controller based on the NASA–NIST Standard Reference Model (NASREM) Architecture (45) was desired to provide total freedom in modifying system parameters and algorithms. In meeting these requirements, the Real-time Intelligently Controlled Optical Positioning System (TRICLOPS), shown in Figure 34.3, represents yet another step in the evolution of high-performance camera-pointing mechanisms.

Active Vision at NIST

One of the primary design goals for TRICLOPS was to build a system that has high dynamic performance—on a par with the human oculomotor system. There are several reasons for putting a large emphasis on being able to move the cameras very quickly. First, one of the primary advantages of active vision systems is to be able to use camera redirection to look at widely separated areas of interest at fairly high resolution instead of having a single sensor or

Figure 34.3.   TRICLOPS device.

array of cameras that covers the entire visual field with uniformly high resolution. It is desirable to be able to move from one area of interest to the next as fast as possible to minimize the time spent redirecting attention and to maximize the time spent acquiring useful image data. In addition, it was desired to build a device for which mechanical performance would not be a limiting factor in the development of algorithms for visual tracking and autonomous information-gathering tasks. Although the current state of image processing results in latencies that are typically on the order of hundreds of milliseconds, rapid progress is being made. We would like to be able to take full advantage of anticipated improvements in image processing hardware, which will continue to increase update rates and reduce latency.

The goal of maximum dynamic performance leads to the selection of microminiature CCD cameras, with manually adjustable focus, aperture, and focal length, because motorized lenses tend to be quite bulky. This decision also reduces the complexity of camera calibration considerably, as optical parameters do not change while the device is in use. Also, using manually adjustable lenses simplifies achievement of the goal of placing the focal point of the lens near the center of rotation. The focal point of motorized zoom lenses shifts a great deal as the focal length is changed, and although it is possible to compensate for this by moving the camera and lens as the zoom is adjusted, it results in considerable additional complexity. Many useful tasks can be performed with fixed imaging parameters. However, should computer control over these functions be desired, it would be possible to mount motorized lenses to the TRICLOPS cameras. Of course, this would involve compromises in other areas, particularly in terms of dynamic performance and rotation about the focal point.

Although fixed lenses are used, it is still desirable to be able to obtain both wide-angle, low resolution images of the world (the big picture) and resolution, narrow-angle images for detail. For this reason, TRICLOPS has been designed with an integral third center camera, which has wide-angle (3- to 4-mm focal length) lens. This color camera serves the purpose of identifying features of interest in the wide field of view. There is a significant (and obvious) advantage to using a separate camera for this purpose, as opposed to using motorized zoom lenses—the wide-angle view is always available to alert the system to new agents that may enter the scene at any time. The center wide-angle lens is used in conjunction with 15- to 24-mm lenses on the vergence cameras, to provide a maximum resolution ratio of 6.17 : 1. (Longer focal length lenses can be mounted on the vergence cameras if C-mount adapters are used. Again, this would be at the expense of dynamic performance and giving up rotation about the focal point.) The system is currently configured with a 4-mm center lens (1.35 rad field of view) and 15-mm vergence lenses (0.42 rad field of view). Each of the TRICLOPS cameras is mounted in a Delrin tube that has screws for fine-adjustment of camera axial position and roll.

As shown in Figure 34.4, TRICLOPS has 4 df (mechanical). The four axes are arranged in the following kinematic configuration: (*1*) pan (or base rotation) about a vertical axis through the center of the base, (*2*) tilt about a horizontal line that intersects the base rotation axis, and (*3*) left and right vergence axes that intersect and are perpendicular to the tilt axis. The tilt and vergence axes provide eye movements, whereas the pan axis allows a single degree of neck rotation. The three mounting locations for cameras are also shown, one at the intersection of the pan and tilt axis, and two more at the intersections of the tilt and vergence axes.

The dynamic performance, accuracy, and other requirements are achieved with a direct-drive design. In many ways, a robot head is an ideal application for a direct-drive system. There is a requirement for large acceleration, low friction, and minimal transmission errors. These are three of the primary characteristics of systems that use motors and feedback devices mounted directly to the axes of motion. Transmission compliance and backlash, which can cause inaccuracy and oscillations, are eliminated. Also, the large gravity torques that cause limitations with direct-drive robot *arms* do not exist for a *head* with the configuration shown in Figure 34.4; the loads on the axes are almost completely inertial. In addition, the use of frameless DC Motors and brushless, frameless resolvers provides flexibility in the routing of camera and control wiring. Much of the wiring in TRICLOPS is routed through the centers of these components to minimize external wiring. This results in well-behaved cable motions during high-speed movements and reduces the likelihood of pulling out cables.

The resolvers used for position feedback provide absolute position information, which eliminates the need to perform any homing or other initialization procedures each time the device is powered up (as would be required with incremental optical encoders, for example). The resolvers are used with 16-bit resolver-to-digital (R–D) converters, which results in a position sensing resolution of 96 μrad. The R–D converters also provide an analogue velocity signal.

TRICLOPS is built up of three independent, detachable modules, as shown in Figure 34.5. These are the pan–tilt module (which forms the base) and two vergence modules. These modules can be used separately or together as a complete system. The vergence modules are connected to the pan–tilt module by the support block and top connector bar. The baseline separation between vergence modules is determined by the length of this bar. The current (and minimum) baseline separation is 0.2794 m.

All axes have detents that may be used with retractable ball-spring plungers to provide static positioning of the shaft at known fixed locations. This is useful for determining the zero offset of the position transducer and for other calibration procedures. Another important feature of TRICLOPS is that all axes have cushioned hard stops that prevent damage to the system when experimenting with new (and potentially unstable) algorithms.

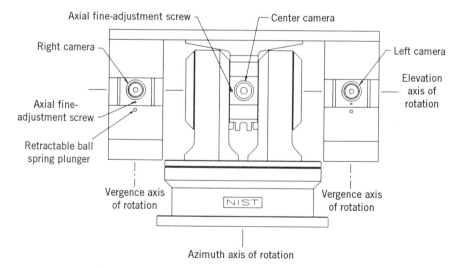

Figure 34.4.   TRICLOPS degrees of freedom.

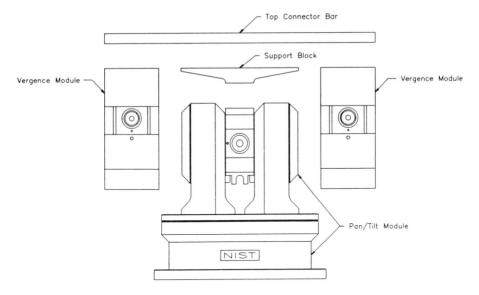

Figure 34.5. TRICLOPS axis modules.

The performance capabilities that have been achieved with TRICLOPS are summarized in Table 34.3. It is seen that TRICLOPS is capable of motions that are comparable with those of the human eye–head system in terms of peak velocity, acceleration, and range of motion. In fact, the vergence modules can achieve peak velocities and accelerations that substantially exceed the human capability.

Potential Applications of Active Vision

The current state of the art is that several active vision platforms have been built. Research is under way to determine how to use these systems effectively for perception. Consequently, no industrial implementations currently exist. However, as progress is made in this research area,

TABLE 34.3. TRICLOPS characteristics

Feature	Value
Pan motion	±1.68 rad (±96.3°)
Tilt motion	0.48 rad down, 1.14 rad up (+27.5°, −65.3°)
Vergence motion	±0.77 rad (±44°)
Pan acceleration	70 rad/s² (4,010°/s²)
Tilt acceleration	320 rad/s² (18,300°/s²)
Vergence acceleration	1100 rad/s² (63,000°/s²)
Pan velocity	11.5 rad/s (660°/s)
Tilt velocity	17.5 rad/s (1,000°/s)
Vergence velocity	32 rad/s (1,830°/s)
Axis position sensing resolution	96 μrad (0.0055°)
Positioning repeatability	±96 μrad (0.0055°)
Interocular distance	279.4 mm (11.0 in.)
Vergence-to-center resolution ratio	6.17 : 1 (max) 3.2 : 1 (current)
Overall width	349 mm (13.75 in.)
Overall height	248 mm (9.75 in.)

image processing will become significantly more robust. As a result, the additional cost associated with moving the cameras will be compensated by lower programming cost, shorter system integration times, and less environmental structuring. We can speculate how active vision will impact manufacturing.

In the area of guidance, one can imagine the intelligent automated guided vehicle (AGV). Most AGVs in factories follow fixed routes that are often determined by wires buried in the factor floor. The cost to bury the wire is not really the issue; it is the inflexibility associated with the approach. One of the drivers in advances manufacturing is the ability to adapt rapidly to changing requirements. Buried wire is the antithesis of flexibility. Using an active vision system for guidance is not a major leap. Several projects already employ fixed cameras for vehicle guidance. Active vision systems would perform the same function but with greater robustness. When coupled with inexpensive computational power, one can imagine an AGV that will be able to service workstations on an as-needed basis while planning and executing paths that avoid all obstacles. When new equipment is added to the factory, a map that describes the location of all equipment can be updated. The AGV uses the factory map as well as active vision to determine where it is and where it needs to go so as to navigate through the factory to satisfy the manufacturing goals.

Inspection is a particularly useful area for active vision. In general, active vision promises algorithms that are less sensitive to environmental variations, such as lighting. More specifically, active vision can be used in ways not possible for fixed camera image processing systems. Suppose one is interested in inspecting the surface of shiny workpieces. In vision systems in which the camera system is fixed, it is never clear whether the system has detected a defect or a specular reflection. In an active vision system, however, the camera can move. If the defect on the object moves, it is really a specular reflection. Otherwise, it is a defect.

Another way in which active vision an play a role in inspection is through the foveal–peripheral sensing capability. The low resolution or periphery of the vision system could determine areas of interest to be explored by high resolution cameras. This provides an effective way to perform inspection by limiting the number of places where time-consuming, high resolution processing must be performed.

Active vision should also be able to play a role in metrology. The use of stereovision can determine the three-dimensional location of features on objects in the workspace. Due to limitations in measuring the gaze direction, normal stereovision can have significant uncertainty, which increases with range. Using active vision, the cameras can be moved while maintaining fixation on the object of interest. In this way, many measurements of the feature location can be taken that, when combined through a recursive filter such as a Kalman filter, will provide a higher resolution estimate of the three-dimensional feature location. With the capability to make rapid sequential measurements, it is possible to make high resolution estimates of points, lines, and surfaces. These measurements can be used in the process control feedback loop to keep tight tolerances on the manufacturing process.

CONCLUSION

Image processing continues to find great application in manufacturing applications. Fixed camera image processing systems are currently used for inspection, guidance, and metrology. These systems provide economic solutions in spite of lighting problems, programming complexity, etc. Active vision promises to address many of the current deficiencies of fixed camera image processes system to provide manufacturing systems with constantly improving measurements for myriad applications. It is expected that image processing applications in industry will continue to grow, and according to the Automated Imaging Association, machine vision system sales reached $646 million in 1991.

BIBLIOGRAPHY

1. D.H. BALLARD and C.M. BROWN, *Computer Vision,* Prentice-Hall, Inc., Englewood Cliffs, N.J., 1982.

2. A. ROSENFELD and A.C. KAK, *Digital Picture Processing,* Academic Press, Inc., New York, 1976.

3. W.E. SNYDER, *Industrial Robots: Computer Interfacing and Control,* Prentice-Hall, Inc., Englewood Cliffs, N.J., 1985.

4. B.G. BATCHELOR, "Lighting and Viewing Techniques" in B. G. Batchelor, D.A. Hill, and D.C. Hodgson, eds., *Automated Visual Inspection,* North-Holland, 1985

5. R.Y. TSAI, "A Versatile Camera Calibration Technique for High-accuracy 3D Machine Vision Metrology Using Off-the-shelf TV Cameras and Lenses," *IEEE J Robot. Automa.* **RA3** (4), 323 (1987).

6. D.D. BEDWORTH, M.R. HENDERSON, and P.M. WOLFE, *Computer Integrated Design and Manufacturing,* McGraw-Hill Book Co., Inc., New York, 191, p. 158.

7. R.T. CHIN and C.A. HARLOW, "Automated Visual Inspection: A Survey," *IEEE Trans. PAMI,* **PAMI-4**(6), 557–573 (1982).

8. R.T. CHIN, "Automated Visual Inspection Algorithms" in Torras, ed., *Computer Vision: Theory and Industrial Applications,* Springer-Verlag, New York, 1992.

9. J. MUNDY, "Industrial Machine Vision—Is It Practical?" in Freeman, ed., *Machine Vision, Algorithms, Architectures, and Systems,* Academic Press, Inc. San Diego, Calif., 1988, pp. 109–149.

10. M.A. LAVIN, "Industrial Machine Vision: Where Are We? What Do We Need? How Do We Get It?" in Freeman, ed., *Machine Vision, Algorithms, Architectures, and Systems,* Academic Press, Inc., San Diego, Calif., 1988, pp. 161–185.

11. B.R. TAYLOR, "Automatic Inspection in Electronics Manufacturing," *Proc. SPIE* **654,** 157–159 (1986).

12. C.J. LeBEAU, "Machine Vision Platform Requirements for Successful Implementation and Support in the Semiconductor Assembly Manufacturing Environment," *Proc. SPIE* **1386,** 228–231 (1990).

13. N.S. CHANG, "Position Measuring Accuracy of Loading Surface Mount Components," *Proc. SPIE* **730,** 151–155 (1986).

14. G. SMEYERS and A. BUTS, "High Speed Alignment and Inspection in the Electronics Industry," *Proc. SPIE* **654,** 136–142 (1986).

15. S. BELINSKI, S. HACKWOOD, and G. BENI, "Intelligent Robot Vision System for Inspection and Assembly of Submillimeter-Sized Components," *Proc. SPIE* **730,** 145–150 (1986).

16. M. CHAPRON, "Automated Visual Integrated Circuit Mounting Operations Inspections," *Proc. SPIE* **730,** 156–163 (1986).

17. R. JAIN, A. RAO, A. KAYAALP, and C. COLE, "Machine Vision for Semiconductor Wafer Inspection" in Freeman, ed., *Machine Vision for Inspection and Measurement,* Academic Press, Inc., San Diego, Calif., 1989, pp. 283–314.

18. R. SCHNEIDER and D. SPRIEGEL, "Automatic Optical Detection and Classification of Submicron Defects on E-Beam Mask Blanks," *Proc. SPIE* **1265,** 144–150 (1990).

19. D. LEES and P. HENSHAW, "Printed Circuit Board Inspection—A Novel Approach," *Proc. SPIE* **730,** 164–173 (1986).

20. M. ANDO and H. OKA, "Profile Measurement for Printed Wiring Boards," *Proc. SPIE* **1265,** 124–131 (1990).

21. Y. TAKAGI, S. HATA, and W. BEUTEL, "Visual Inspection Machine for Solder Joints Using Tiered Illumination," *Proc. SPIE,* **1386,** 21–29 (1990).

22. P.J. BEST, E. J. DELP, and R. JAIN, "Automatic Visual Solder Joint Inspection," *IEEE J. Robot. Automat.* **RA-1**(1), 42 (1985).

23. S.L. BARTLETT, P.J. BESL, C.L. COLE, R. JAIN, D. MUKHERJEE, and K.D. SKIFSTAD, "Automatic Solder Joint Inspection," *IEEE Trans. PAMI* **10**(1), 31 (1988).

24. D.W. CAPSON and S.-K. ENG, "A Tiered-Color Illumination Approach for Machine Inspection of Solder Joints," *IEEE Trans. PAMI* **10**(3), 387 (1988).

25. O.R. MITCHELL, E.P. LYVERS, K.A. DUNKELBERGER, and M.L. AKEY, "Recent Results in Precision Measurements of Edges, Angles, Areas and Perimeters," *Proc. SPIE* **730,** 123–134 (1986).

26. C. LEUNG, R. SHU, and J. WU, "A Laser Scanner for Thickness Measurements on the Production Line," *Proc. SPIE* **1265,** 116–123 (1990).

27. W. BURKE III, "Using an Automatic Video Inspection System to Guarantee In-Line Film Registration," *Proc. SPIE* **1266,** 57–61 (1990).

28. J. RONING and E.L. HALL, "Shape, Form, and Texture Recognition for Automotive Brake Pad Inspection," *Proc. SPIE* **730,** 82–90 (1986).

29. R. SALESSE, "Automatic Inspection in Car Industry: User Point-of-View," *Proc. SPIE* **654,** 58–61 (1986).

30. A. MARSHALL, "Automatically Inspecting Gross Features of Machined Objects Using Three-Dimensional Depth Data," *Proc. SPIE* **1386,** 243–254 (1990).

31. J.G. NELL, *IGES/PDES Orgaization Reference Manual,* National Computer Graphics Association, Fairfax, Va., 1992.

32. J.F. BREMNER, "Automatic Non-Contract Measurement System for the Inspection of Shapes Cut in Sheet Material," *Proc. SPIE* **654,** 130–134 (1986).

33. A. BROWNE and L. NORTON-WAYNE, *Vision and Information Processing for Automation,* Plenum Press, New York, 1986.

34. N. BAINS and F. DAVID, "Machine Vision Inspection of Fluorescent Lamps," *Proc. SPIE* **1386, 232–242 (1990).**

35. R. BAJCSY, "Active Perception," *Proc. IEEE,* **76,** 996 (1988).

36. E. KROTKOV, F. FUMA, and J. SUMMERS, "An Agile Stereo Camera System for Flexible image acqusition," *IEEE J. Robot. Automat.* **4**(1), 108–113 (1988).

37. A.L. ABBOTT and N. AHUJA, *Active Surface Reconstruction by Integrating Focus, Vergence, Stereo, and Camera Calibration,* Third International Conference on Computer Vision, Osaka, Japan, 1990.

38. T. POGGIO et al., *The MIT Vision Machine,* paper presented at the DARPA Image Understanding Workshop, 1988.

39. C.M. BROWN, *Kinematic and 3D Motion Prediction for Gaze Control,* paper presented at the Workshop on Interpretation of 3D Scenes. Austin, Tex., 1989.

40. D. BALLARD and A. OZCANDARLI, *Eye Fixation and Early Vision: Kinetic Depth,* paper presented at the 2nd International Conference on Computer Vision, 1988.

41. T.J. OLSON and D.J. COOMBS, "Real-time Vergence Control for Binocular Robots," *Int. J Comput. Vision* **8**(1), 67–89 (1991).

42. J.J. CLARK and N.J. FERRIER, *Modal Control of an Attentive Vision System,* paper presented at the 2nd International Conference on Computer Vision, 1988.

43. K. PAHLAVAN and J.O. EKLUNDH, *A Head-eye System for Active, Purposive Computer Vision,* KTH, Stockholm, Sweden, 1990, TRITA-NA-P9031.

44. B.B. BEDERSON, R.S. WALLACE, and E.L. SCHWARTZ, *Two Miniature Pan-tilt Devices,* paper presented at the IEEE Conference on Robotics and Automation, 1992.

45. J.S. ALBUS, H.G. McCAIN, and R. LUMIA, *NASA/NBS Standard Reference Model for Telerobot Control System Architecture (NASREM),* NIST, Gaithersburg, Md. 1987, Technical Note 1235.

CHAPTER 35
Computer Networks in Manufacturing

SENCER YERALAN
University of Florida

35.1 INTRODUCTION

Numerically controlled machine tools, process control, materials tracking and handling, inspection and quality control, manufacturing resource management, and operations planning are all manufacturing systems activities that have been profoundly affected by the introduction of low cost computers and embedded controllers. The collection of these computer systems led to large-scale factory automation and computer-integrated manufacturing (CIM) (1–3). As manufacturing systems components become more intelligent, the information exchange between such components must be computerized to avoid bottlenecks in the system. Information exchange among computerized systems naturally led to computer networks. A manufacturing computer network is a communication system that permits the various devices connected to the network to communicate with each other over distances from several feet to several miles. Computer communication in the factory is done by using local area networks (LANs). All the devices in a factory such as computers, CNC machines, robots, programmable controllers, data collection devices, process controllers, and vision systems are attached to the network.

Initially, computer networks were not developed for manufacturing systems but for communication among machines for scientific computing and, later, for the telecommunications industries (4). The diversity and variation in sophistication of computer systems found in manufacturing systems present computer networking with unique challenges in standardization and industry acceptance. Paradoxically, it is the computerization of manufacturing systems that brought about the largest improvements in manufacturing technologies, quality, and cost containment.

In spite of many substantial efforts, in the early part of the 1990s, there still is not a universally used computer network system adopted by all manufacturing industries (5). Another complicating factor is the rapid increase in computer power versus the steady decline of cost of computers. It can be argued that the computer field is so volatile that it is difficult for any standard to be used for a reasonable period of time. In fact, it is the view of many that a computer network standard becomes obsolete as soon as it is established.

There are many types of data and information to be carried over a manufacturing computer network. The data range from process control information, to parts representation in a computer-assisted or computer-aided design (CAD) system, to materials-handling information, to orders processing, to quality control information, to machine maintenance data (6, 7). Some of this information is in binary form, and some is in text or graphics form. Moreover, as intelligent machines become attached to the manufacturing system, code and programs are also transferred over the computer networks. These computer networks usually interface with enterprise-level systems that hold customer and vendor databases and process the economic and financial transactions (8).

Almost all of the computers used in manufacturing systems are digital computers. The communication among these computers needs to take one or more lines of data (single line or a bus) and represent the two binary states of each line in some physical medium. There are many suitable physical media each with many ways to represent the binary states. Moreover, there are many choices in the protocol by which large blocks of data are packaged and transferred. All these activities need to be carried out with high levels of reliability, which introduces numerous methods of error checking and correction, all embedded into the physical machinery and software protocols of computer networks.

Computer networks may be more important for small manufacturing businesses than for industry giants. The small enterprises constitute an important portion of the national industry, generating about two-thirds of the gross national product (GNP). They lag behind larger corporations in implementing high technology tools. Furthermore, they are growing in number of employees and in their contribution to major manufacturers as suppliers (9–11). Thus high technology manufacturing tools especially designed for small enterprises is a significant area of need with many opportunities for improvement.

A recent survey done by the Southern Technology Applications Center (STAC) (12) on technology transfer practices and needs, found that 26% of companies with less than 500 employees in the production sector responded to the question "What does your company need to improve to be more competitive?" with "Access to needed technologies," whereas 56% of the same group indicated "Implementing new technology" as a requirement to increase competitiveness. The conclusion is that one of the reasons of why smaller companies are behind in the use of modern manufacturing technology is the difficulty of implementing it in their operations. Computer networks would provide a framework into which high productivity manufacturing equipment can be hooked, paralleling the office automation movement experienced during the past decade. The above survey was done with 268 companies, of which 122 were companies in the production sector with less than 500 employees. Hence considering that there are more then 485,000 establishments in the United States within this class (10, 11), these findings are to be viewed not as hard statistical evidence but only as trend. This chapter gives an introduction to the vast subject of manufacturing computer networks. Only the fundamental aspects are discussed.

35.2 ELEMENTS OF COMPUTER NETWORKS

A computer network can be specified by the following characteristics:

- Topology.
- Media.
- Access methods.
- Signaling.
- Protocol stack.

Network Topology

The network topology refers to the configuration in which the member computers are attached to the network. There are several common topologies used in local area networks. Star networks consist of a central control station to which each individual device is connected (Figure 35.1). A message from one device to another device is routed through the central station. The central station controls the communication flow between devices. Many telephone systems in office buildings are structured as star configurations.

A ring network is a network topology in which individual stations are connected in a continuous ring. (Figure 35.2) A message from one device to another device is routed through the ring with a station address. Each station checks the address. If it is the desired recipient, it loads the message into memory. Otherwise it forwards the message to the next station in the ring.

The bus network consists of a single main transmission line to which individual devices are attached (Figure 35.3). A message with an address is sent through the bus. Each station checks the message and receives if the address is its own. The bus network is often appropriate for a factory local area network. The principal advantages of the bus network are

1. The layout of the main transmission line of the but network can be prepared according to the layout of machines in the factory.
2. Each device can be connected to the main transmission bus without major disruptions to the rest of the network.
3. The bus network is generally easier to maintain and repair than the star and ring configurations.

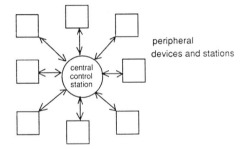

Figure 35.1.   A star network.

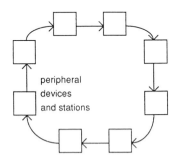

Figure 35.2.   A ring network.

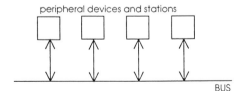

BUS   **Figure 35.3.**   A bus network.

Hierarchical networks consists of collections of subnetworks (Figure 35.4). Each subnetwork may be in one of the topologies described above. Hierarchical networks are convenient for protocols that use network controllers, also referred to as the master and slave units. There usually is a single controller for each slave computer. The network or hybrid topology consists of many stations or devices connected in a seemingly random pattern (Figure 35.5). Many topologies in actual implementation end up in a hybrid configuration.

Network Media

The transmission line is the message- and data-carrying medium that constitutes the physical distribution element of the network. The transmission media for factory networks should be capable of transmitting large blocks of data at high speeds. Electrical noise in the environment should not affect the transmission. Other requirements for the transmission media are the cost of installation and cost of service.

The bandwidth of transmission determines the data transmission capacity. A large bandwidth means that the medium has a high data-carrying capacity. Broadband transmission means that many independent messages can be transmitted simultaneously over the communications line, each operating at its own frequency. Broadband signals are the standard used for cable

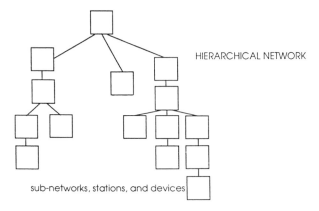

HIERARCHICAL NETWORK

sub-networks, stations, and devices

Figure 35.4.   A hierarchical network.

peripheral devices and stations

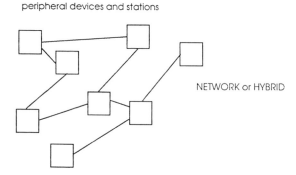

NETWORK or HYBRID

Figure 35.5.   A network or hybrid topology.

television transmission. In baseband transmission, only one signal is carried over the transmission line at a time. Because multiple simultaneous data transmission is required in factory networks, broadband transmission is preferred. Baseband transmission is used mainly in office networks.

Several types of transmission media are used in local area networks. The twisted-pair wire consists of two or more copper wires that are twisted throughout the length of the line. Because it is susceptible to electrical noise in the environment and it has a relatively low bandwidth, it is not suitable for factory networking. Coaxial cable consists of one or more strands of wire shielded by a metallic sheath surrounded in turn by insulation. The metal shield reduces the noise. It can have a large bandwidth. Coaxial cable can be used for either baseband or broadband communications. Broadband coaxial cable is considered to be the most appropriate transmission medium for factory networks.

A fiber optics line consists of several long continuous optical fibers. It has a large bandwidth, and it is not affected by electrical noise. In fiber optic transmission, the electrical pulses that represent data are converted into light pulses, carried through the optical fibers over long distances, and converted back into electrical signals at the receiving station. It is relatively costly compared with the alternatives. Infrared (IR) light transmitters and detectors, usually built with solid-state technologies, are convenient for high speed communications over short distances. Many automated guided vehicle systems (AGVS), e.g., employ infrared communications channels. IR systems are cost effective, which make them the media of choice in low end systems, such as in remote-control units used in home electronics.

Although radio frequency has been used as a medium for some time in avionics and space systems, the interest in this medium has recently been renewed in conjunction with portable computing. This medium is cost effective and efficient. It is, however, a limited resource, because all equipment must use separate frequencies. It is also susceptible to static and interference from natural phenomena such as lightning.

Data Transmission Rate

The transmission rate in communication networks is the rate at which data and messages can be transferred among computers and computer-controlled devices connected to the network. It is measured either by baud rate or bit rate.

In digital data communications, characters are generally represented by a series of electrical pulses. These pulses constitute the bits that make up the characters. Each pulse in the series has a certain duration. Let T be the shortest possible pulse duration that can be handled reliably by the sending and receiving stations. Baud rate is the reciprocal of this shortest possible pulse duration:

$$\text{Baud rate} = 1/T$$

The transmission media determine the baud rate.

The bit rate determines the actual communication of data and information. The bit rate is the rate at which the bits that represent the message excluding the bits that are used for parity checks, control procedures, initiation and termination of the transmission. So the bit rate is smaller than or equal to the baud rate.

Network Access Methods

Once the physical media are established, a set of rules must be set up to determine how each attached computer may use the media. Access methods may be classified into four methods. The time division multiple access (TDMA) method reserves a slot of time for each computer connected to the network. In spirit, this method is closely linked to polling. As an advantage, the time to next access for each computer is known. Thus the maximum response time is bounded. The disadvantage is that computers are allocated time even though they may not have information to send over the network. Thus the network may be underused. TDMA is used in telephone networks as well as in radiocontrolled model airplanes.

The carrier-sensed multiple access with collision detection (CSMA–CD) method is also called the contention-based method. A station that wants to send a message first checks the network to see if it is available. If it is available, it sends the message. Otherwise it waits until the network becomes idle. When two or more stations attempt to transmit data at the same time, collision occurs. When a transmitter station detects collision, it stops transmitting, waits for a random length of time and tries again until a satisfactorily transmission is established. This method is suitable for office networks in which the communications are likely to consist of large blocks of data, but timing of the transmission is not critical. For high levels of traffic, it is not possible to determine how long a station will have to wait before it is able to send messages, thus contention-based methods are not suitable for manufacturing systems in which the timing of commands to a machine tool play a crucial role.

In the token passing method a special code, called the token, is passed along the network at high speeds from station to station in predetermined sequence. The sequence of stations determines priorities given to the station. A station can transmit messages only when it possesses the token. If a station has no messages to send then the token is passed to the next station. The token-passing access scheme is used predominantly in LANs designed for manufacturing environments.

Finally, the master–slave method assigns a master to one or many slave computers. The slave computers may not access the network unless otherwise allowed by the master computer. The master computer polls each slave unit and asks for a status code. If the slave unit has a message to transmit, the master signals the slave unit to use the media. The master once again takes over the media as soon as the slave unit completes its transmission.

Network Signaling

Some attributes of the physical media are modified depending on the state of the signal to be transmitted. In electrical media such as twisted pairs, the voltage or the current on the loop may be switched between two different values. In radio frequency and infrared media, the frequency of a carrier signal may be switched to one of two or more frequencies. Modems used over the telephone lines, e.g., use two different frequencies, one frequency for each of the two states zero and one. This method is also used in magnetic encoding such as in disk drives, and is referred to as the frequency shift key (FSK) modulation.

Differential drivers are often used over twisted pair wires. The voltage difference between the two wires determine the value of the bit transmitted. If wire A has a voltage, say, 0.2 v or higher, with respect to wire B, then the bit transmitted is a one. If the wire B has a higher voltage, then the bit transmitted is a zero. Differential drivers are low cost and reliable, with little susceptibility to the voltage drops experienced over long transmission lines.

Perhaps the most commonly used protocol is the RS-232C serial communications protocol. The signaling is based on a 20 mA current loop, i.e., the direction of the current flow determines the state of the transmitted bit. Serial communications are usually initiated by a start bit and terminated by a stop bit of predetermined values. In addition to these bits, one or more error detection bits may be used. The most popular method is the parity bit whose value is chosen to make the total number of ones in a word odd or even–and hence the terminology "odd or even parity." Similarly, following a sequence of words, an error check word may be appended to make a data package. The most commonly used method is the cyclic redundancy check (CRC) method. The data words are added, ignoring the external carries produced. This sum or its complement is transmitted as the CRC word (13–15).

35.3   COMPUTER NETWORK SYSTEMS

Open systems Interconnect Reference Model

Standardization of computer communications is essential for the proper interaction of different systems (16). This is all the more important when two or more networks need to communicate with each other. Toward this end the international standards organization (ISO) along with an open system interconnection (OSI) proposed a model for all computer communication networks. Unlike standards such as RS-232C that cover physical connections between devices, OSI standards dictate the entire communication protocol. All communications standards and protocols should conform to this model (17–19).

The OSI model is shown in Table 35.1. It contains seven layers each of which describes a particular level of communication activity. Each layer contains rules appropriate to itself as well as the interfaces above and below it. It can be divided into three categories: the lower layers that provide the pipeline along which the data flow, the upper layer that allow exchange of information between the users, and the transport layer that ensures error-free transfer of information from one device to another.

The physical layer is the lowest level of the model. Unique to this layer is the electrical and mechanical specification of the network. This is where the hardware is defined to provide connections between various equipment and standards are set for electrical cables and connectors. For instance OSI sets the pinouts for RS-232 connectors. Along with the data-link layer, this layer is sufficient to establish and maintain data communications between two devices.

TABLE 35.1.   The OSI Model

Application (layer 7)	Provide services comprehensible by the application program
Presentation (layer 6)	Transforms data to and from standard formats
Session (layer 5)	Synchronize and manage dialogues
Transport (layer 4)	Provides transparent and reliable data transfer between end nodes
Network (layer 3)	Performs message route for data transfer between nodes
Data link (layer 2)	Error detection for messages moved between nodes
Physical (layer 1)	Electrically encodes and physically transfers messages between nodes

The data link layer provides a reliable and error-free mechanism by which messages are transmitted from one device to another. Alternatively, it enhances and consolidates the performance of the physical layer. Two of the most important functions of this layer are framing and checking messages. Framing is the process by which data are divided into streams of bits that are clearly marked by a special series of characters so that they are not confused with the data themselves. Checking is the process of ensuring that the transmitted data are reasonably uncorrupted. This is achieved by performing a simple arithmetic operation on the data stream and sending the value along with the data frame. If the receiving device does the same arithmetic operation and finds it different from the value it received it could discard the data as corrupt and could request a retransmission.

The network layer, or the layer three of the OSI model, extends the scope of the model to include the interconnections of various subnetworks. This layer, therefore, concerns not only connections between local area networks but also the linking of remote LANs through, e.g., the public service networks.

The transport layer resides in the equipment at the two ends of the communication link. It takes away from the end users any need to know anything about the network through which the information is flowing.

The session layer, provides mechanisms for managing and structuring the data transfer. Among other things it includes protocols for enabling the establishment and release of connections, synchronization to keep the two end devices in step with each other, and selection of the type of dialogue that is to take place—full duplex or simultaneous flow in both directions, half duplex, or alternate message flow.

The presentation layer provides the protocol for devices to communicate in the same language by specifying different ways in which alphabets, numbers, and special characters are represented by different types of equipment. This layer provides a set of rules to convert the abstract syntax to a standard code for transmission.

The application layer offers a common application service element (CASE) that provides a toolkit of useful functions that are common to many applications and a number of specific application service elements (SASE) for different applications. Typical CASE functions are association control, which allows establishment of associations among themselves; context control, which allows applications to define and manipulate the meaning of the information they wish to exchange; and commitment concurrence and recovery (CCR), which allows application processes to coordinate the activities of separate associations An example of SASE is file transfer, access and management (FTAM), which allows files to be transferred between different types of systems.

The three best known computer network systems are MAP, TOP and PC LANs, which are briefly discussed next.

MAP

Originated from a task force set up by General Motors (GM) in 1980, MAP stands for manufacturing automation protocol (20). The motivation was that a considerable part of the company's investment in communications went to interfaces that allowed different systems to communicate. GM's original idea was for MAP to be a central communication but into which all factory floor equipment would plug in. If the device did not comply to it, GM would not buy it. This idea was financially unfeasible and was abandoned (21).

MAP was designed with GM's needs in mind. Even though other large corporations with similar requirements have benefited from it, its design, data rate capabilities, and hardware requirements make it not viable (as of today) to be adopted by a small company (22). Some of its characteristics are listed below.

It is a token passing system; the token is the authorization to transmit. The reason for using this system is that the network becomes deterministic.

It uses broadband cable; which means that every interface must contain a modem to modulate outgoing messages and demodulate incoming messages. This was chosen because GM already had broadband cable in place owing to its internal radio and TV systems.

It is based on the seven-layer OSI communication model. OSI describes the function of a particular layer but does not impose which specific protocol a particular layer should use; MAP is one particular implementation of the OSI system.

In the United States, GM, John Deere, Eastman Kodak, and Kaiser Aluminum & Chemical, are among its users.

Its data rates are about 5 MB/s.

TOP

The technical and office protocols, or TOPS, is aimed at "providing multivendor compatibility and communications in the technical and office functions" (21) TOP is a product pushed forward by a number of major computer systems customers such as GM, DuPont, Proctor and Gamble, and Boeing. The main communication functions for which TOP is designed are electronic mail, word processing, database management, and graphics interchange. A small manufacturer usually does not need such functions that go beyond the LAN; TOP sponsors are generally large global manufacturing operations. Some of TOP's main characteristics are listed below.

It uses Ethernet, which is the most commonly used LAN. Ethernet, unlike a token passing system, uses multiple access, which means that a node may transmit at any time.

An Ethernet bus uses baseband cable; this means that whoever is transmitting occupies the network completely. Because of this and the multiple access characteristic, every node must be equipped with carrier sense, which is a circuit that can detect if the line is busy. Despite the sensing capabilities, message collisions occur on the network, which make it necessary for the nodes to have collision detection capability to determine if the message is garbled.

PC LANs

PC LANs are the most common and affordable network solutions available in the market today. As the number of PCs increased in the workplace, users found it necessity to share their products (documents, spreadsheets, etc.) and resources. LANs provide for resource sharing of printers, modems, and disk space; the more sophisticated LANs are capable of file sharing, which allows users to share the same file space and use each other's files. PC LAN operating system providers include Novell, Banyan, and AT&T (23). Such networks were originally designed primarily to provide office automation capability and not data collection from devices on the factory floor. However, as the PC becomes more powerful, more manufacturing systems will adopt PC platforms to implement manufacturing computer networks.

35.4 MODELING AND PERFORMANCE EVALUATION OF COMPUTER NETWORKS

There are two primary methods to study computer network performance: simulation and queueing models. By its nature, the events that take place in a computer network are random. Recent advances in simulation languages makes these tools convenient environments in which an existing network can be modeled and studied (24–26). Although simulation is a powerful tool for solving the specific design and analysis problems of a given network, it is often difficult to generalize the results or one case to all possible networks. Queueing theory, on the other hand, studies abstractions of such networks. Although the analytical models are often too involved to be tractable, the results are applicable to a wider range of networks.

BIBLIOGRAPHY

1. M.P. GROOVER, *Automation, Production Systems and Computer Integrated Manufacturing,* Prentice-Hall, Inc., Englewood Cliffs, N.J., 1987.
2. M.P. GROOVER, and E.W. ZIMMERS, Jr., *CAD/CAM: Computer-Aided Design and Manufacturing,* Prentice-Hall, Inc., Englewood Cliffs, N.J., 1984.
3. N.G. ODREY, "Integrating the Automated Factory" in *Data Processing Management,* Auerbach Publishers Inc, Pennsauken, N.J., 1985.

4. W. STALLINGS, *Local Networks: An Introduction*, Macmillan Publishing Co., Inc., New York, 1985.

5. D. MOON, "Developing Standards Smooth the Integration of Programmable Factory Floor Devices," *Control Eng.* 49–52 (Oct. 1985).

6. D. LABRENZ, "Continued Growth for Data Collection Even as Technology Matures," *Mang. Automat.* **6**, 20–21 (1991).

7. J.R. PIMENTEL, *Communication Networks for Manufacturing*, Prentice Hall, Inc., Englewood Cliffs, N.J., 1990.

8. U. REMBOLD, K. ARMBRUSTER, and W. ULZMANN, *Interface Technology for Computer Controlled Manufacturing Processes*, Marcel Dekker, Inc., New York, 1983.

9. U.S. Bureau of the Census, *Statistical Abstracts of the United States*, 111th ed., U.S. Government Printing Office, Washington, D.C., 1991.

10. U.S. Congress, House Committee on Small Business, *Critical Issues Facing Small American Manufacturers*, U.S. Government Printing Office, Washington, D.C., 1990.

11. U.S. Small Business Administration, *Small Business in the American Economy*, U.S. Government Printing Office, Washington, D.C., 1988, p. 5.

12. C.S. JOHNSRUD, T. HORAK, and J.R. THORNTON, *Commercial Sector Technology Transfer Practices and Needs, Market-Pull Considerations for NTTN Market and Business Plan Development*, project report submitted to the National Technology Transfer Center, Southern Technology Applications Center, University of Florida, Alachua, Apr. 1991.

13. Microchip Technology Inc., *PIC 16C5X Microcontroller Application Notes, Set One*, Microchip Technology Inc., Chandler, Ariz., 1990.

14. E. NISLEY, "A Network for Distributed Control, Building an RS-485 Network for Controllers," *Circuit Cellar Ink*, 31–39 (Aug.–Sept. 1989).

15. E. NISLEY, "Writing Software for Distributed Control," *Circuit Cellar Ink*, 15–21 (Oct.–Nov. 1989).

16. A. MAIRA, "Local Area Networks—The Future of the Factory," *Manufact. Eng.*, 77–79 (Mar. 1986).

17. C.T. BARTEE, ed., *Data Communications, Networks, and Systems*, Howard W. Sams & Co., Inc., Indiana, 1985.

18. B.W. STUCK, and E. ARTHURS, *A Computer and Communications Network Performance Analysis Primer*, Prentice-Hall, Inc., Englewood Cliffs, N.J., 1985.

19. C.A. SUNSHINE, *Computer Network Architectures and Protocols*, Plenum Press, New York, 1989.

20. R. CROWDER, "The MAP Specification," *Control Eng.*, 22–25 (Oct. 1985).

21. J. DWYER, and A. IOANNOU, *MAP and TOP, Advanced Manufacturing Communications*, John Wiley & Sons, Inc., New York, 1988.

22. P.W. ACCAMPO, "MAP Pilots: Promises and Pitfalls," *CIM Technol.*, 19–23 (Spring 1986).

23. J.T. MCCANN, *NetWare Supervisor's Guide*, M&T Books, Redwood City, Calif. 1989.

24. J. BANKS, and S.C. CARSON, *Discrete-Event System Simulation*, Prentice—Hall, Inc., Englewood Cliffs, N.J., 1984.

25. W.D. KELTON, and A.M. LAW, *Simulation Modeling and Analysis*, 2nd ed., McGraw-Hill Book Co., Inc., New York, 1991.

26. W. MENDEHALL, R.L. SCHEAFFER, and D.D. WACKERLY, *Mathematical Statistics with Applications*, 3rd ed. PWS Publishers, Boston, 1986.

CHAPTER 36

Manufacturing Information Systems

CHENG HSU
Rensselaer Polytechnic Institute

36.1 INFORMATION MANAGEMENT FOR MANUFACTURING ENTERPRISE INTEGRATION

Overview

Information technology plays a key role in modern manufacturing at two levels: facility and enterprise. Facility-level manufacturing information systems are responsible for mundane tasks such as production planning and shop floor control. Figure 36.1 depicts the major functions of a generic computer-integrated manufacturing (CIM) facility, which includes process planning (PP), material requirements planning (MRP), shop floor control (SFC), work stations operation, and material handling. Typically, touch labor takes place only in the last two functions and accounts for no more than 40% of the total effort—the rest is entirely information processing. Even the share of touch labor involves a significant use of information technology for, e.g., data entry and display in in-process verification, statistical process control (SPC), and electronic data interchange (EDI). Therefore, it is appropriate to say that today's manufacturing systems rely on information technology, and the job of information management is both to support these systems and to enable them achieving their objectives. At the enterprise level, however, the goal for the information management is nothing short of effecting the synergies among all stages of the life cycle of manufacturing, including its customer, supplier, and dealer as well as design, production, and business. In fact, information has become the agent of integration for manufacturing enterprises competing in today's global market place. When manufacturing technology and institutional factors are largely exogenous to the management, information is virtually the single most fundamental factor that determines an enterprise's maximal productivity, quality, and customer service. Thus, in this sense, information has become the fourth basic factor of production, along with labor, land, and capital.

The discussion of manufacturing information systems begins with an enterprise-level vision and from there moves down to a facility-level review. The functionality and information requirements, systems development methods, and information management technology for common manufacturing information systems are then discussed in this context. A basic CIM case is used throughout to illustrate the various concepts and techniques discussed. The discussion will be concluded with emerging concepts, architectures, and systems pursuing the enterprise level vision of the future. Introduced below is a vision to provide a big picture as the anchoring point for the chapter.

Adaptive Manufacturing through Information Technology: A Vision

From "islands of automation" (e.g., CAD–CAM) to enterprise-level CIM, the notion of computerized manufacturing has undergone a far-reaching evolution. The new information technologies this effort has brought out also prompted whole new industries in systems integration and processes reengineering and continue to result in new standards and applications for both manufacturing and service enterprises. Now that integration is effectively a given and CIM an objective in sight, is there life after CIM? Or, asking the question from a user's perspective, is there a fundamental need for a new vision beyond CIM to address further the entrenched

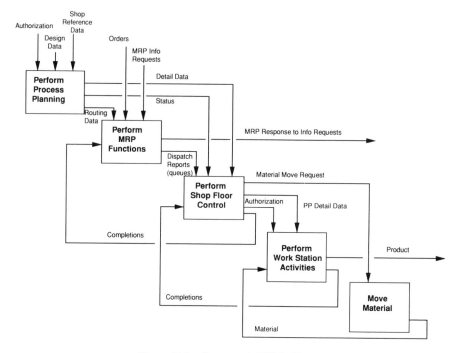

Figure 36.1.   Integrated CIM facility.

competitiveness problem facing manufacturing enterprises in today's global marketplace? The answer is a resounding yes, as evidenced by the emerging calls for agile manufacturing, flexible CIM, and virtual corporation. The key reason is simple: previous visions, efforts, and results of integration worldwide have yet to consider sufficiently the customer's evolving needs. Solutions emphasize the achievement of synergism across enterprise functions given requirements fixed at a particular point in time. These requirements, however, rarely stay unchanged for long. In fact, due to global competition and every heightening customer demands, the basic competitive strategy of a corporation increasingly requires that the enterprise be able to respond rapidly to market conditions with a high degree of product differentiation and value-based customer services. These requirements cause rapid changes in the enterprise that can no longer be dealt with by using managerial savvy alone. This trend is clearly established and in all likelihood will become more pronounced as we enter the next century.

Therefore, for improved productivity and quality, manufacturing requirements for the next century must focus on achieving adaptiveness to consolidate and extend the substantial gains made to date in integration. The result will be an enterprise with the ability to effect shorter cycle times, with lower volumes of identical items and higher mixtures of different items on the same assembly lines. It will also lead to greater flexibility in the organization of physical facilities that potentially are distributed globally, with increased customization, greater parallel activity across business functions and processes, and closer coupling with vendors and customers. This adaptiveness must be fully characterized with established scientific principles to clearly illuminate the technological gaps between the objective and the previous results, and hence it will be more robust than a casual notion of agility or flexibility that may not lead to the understanding of the problem necessary for guiding the search for new fundamental solutions.

A scenario might best illustrate this vision. A customer calls the manufacturer to order a product that has a personalized logo or other custom features. Some of these custom requirements might be handled easily from a standard options package, some might require changes in standard processes for the product, and others might entail a revised design or even new materials. Thus the cost and production time varies widely, depending on the specific customization. The objective is not only to be able to offer this kind of customized product at marketable prices but also to provide a firm price and delivery date to the customer on the spot while the customer is still on the telephone line completing the order (Figure 36.2).

Accommodating these requirements challenges the ingenuity of all members of the enterprise and demands innovative techniques for designing the product and the processes needed to build it, including verification of the product and global planning and control of the enterprise. Throughout this process, the entire product life cycle must be considered, including adaptability to change after initial manufacture and the ability for obsolete products to be recylced or safely and economically destroyed. But above all, a key ingredient of this new capability is information technology. The modeling, management, utilization, storage, and processing of information must be adaptive as well as integrated to support parallel functions and processes through out the enterprise. The manufacturer must set out to acquire the necessary new technology to enable these new fundamental regimes, where managers are simply process owners working with other types of employees across the organization. In a nutshell, a corporation must be able to separate its functional groupings of personnel, facilities, and other resources from its physical organizations—or, in other words, to form multiple "virtual organizations" simultaneously out of the same physical resources and adapt them without having to change the actual organizations. The justification is simple: there exists only one physical organization at any point of time regardless how adaptive it is, and it is always subject to organizational inertia. Thus, for example, a design engineer of an auto manufacturer in Detroit, can be an effective team member with industrial designers in Milan, Italy, and manufacturing engineers throughout the Midwest, while at the same time be involved with other teams that deal with customers, dealers, suppliers, and other vendors vertically or horizontally associated with the enterprise. Only through

Scenario: Customized, Adaptive Manufacturing

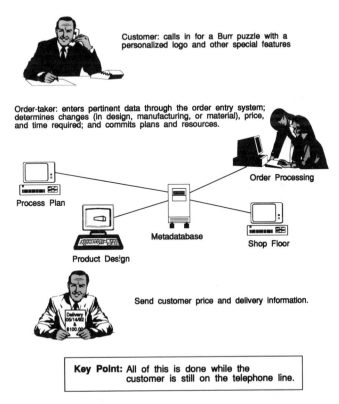

Customer: calls in for a Burr puzzle with a personalized logo and other special features

Order-taker: enters pertinent data through the order entry system; determines changes (in design, manufacturing, or material), price, and time required; and commits plans and resources.

Order Processing

Process Plan

Metadatabase

Shop Floor

Product Design

Send customer price and delivery information.

Key Point: All of this is done while the customer is still on the telephone line.

Figure 36.2. Scenario: customized, adaptive manufacturing.

information can this virtual organization become meaningful and only effecting a new generation of information technology can this vision be realized.

Basic Concepts of Manufacturing Information Systems

To understand, use, and manage a manufacturing information system, there are three key questions to ask and answer: (1) what manufacturing functions and processes does this system support? (2) what information resources—i.e., data resources, knowledge bases, and decision models—does it require? and (3) what information technology does it employ? These questions apply equally well to both facility- and enterprise-level systems, although the answers would have significantly different implications for the manufacturer from one level to another.

Facility-level Systems

Information systems support many mundane jobs in a facility. An example is shown in Figure 36.3, which indicates some basic functions on a shop floor and the support these functions need from a shop-floor information system. Similar situations exist with virtually all other engineering and production activities. Below is a list of common functions and processes for which information systems have been developed.

- CAD.
- Computer-aided engineering (CAE).
- Computer-aided manufacturing (CAM).
- Computer-aided process planning (CAPP).
- Production planning and scheduling.
- Inventory control and forecasting.
- SPC.
- Material handling.
- Inspection and in-process verification.
- Warehousing.
- Flexible manufacturing (FMS) and cell control.
- SFC.
- MRP.
- Manufacturing resources planning (MRP II).
- Integrated computer-aided production planning (ICAPP).

Enterprise-level Systems

Five basic elements comprise a manufacturing enterprise:

- Business (marketing, distribution, finance, and other administration).
- Engineering (product and process design).
- Production (manufacturing facilities and processes).
- Vendor (supplier, dealer, and collaborator).
- Customer (individual or organization).

Enterprise-level systems, therefore, typically cut across the boundaries of these elements and strive to achieve synergism through the integration of information. As discussed earlier, this integration often is driven by the following goals, which have in effect become the underlying principles of enterprise information integration:

- Shortening and managing the product life cycle ranging from market study, product development, and production to customer service.
- Maximizing parallelism among decision processes and activities throughout the life cycle.
- Effecting virtual and horizontal organization of all resources involved in the life cycle.

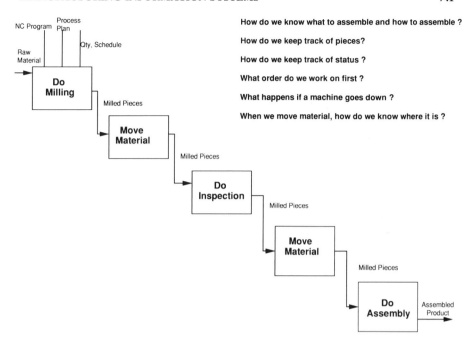

Figure 36.3.   The need for a shop floor information system.

These three principles all entail adaptiveness in the integration across all elements of the enterprise. They, in part or in whole, drive the theme of the common information systems at the enterprise level as manifested in these integration efforts:

- Concurrent or simultaneous engineering (CE), for engineering, production, and business.
- CIM enterprise, for production, engineering and business.
- Just-in-time (JIT), for production and vendor.
- Design for manufacturing (DFM), for engineering and production.
- Total quality management (TQM), for customer, business, engineering, and production.
- Adaptive integrated manufacturing enterprise (AIME), for production, engineering, business, vendor, and customer.

Methodology and Technology

Information systems at both levels together constitute a total supersystem for the manufacturer. Thus, regardless of how many and what kinds of system exist in an enterprise, there must be a cohesive information architecture to consolidate the physical facilities, communications infrastructure, and information resources required by these systems and to reconcile them with the enterprise's managerial control systems and organizational structures. Such an architecture is sometimes referred to as an enterprise model. Obviously, an enterprise model will not and should not be static; rather its detailing is a function of the strategic planning or integration that the enterprise undertakes at the time and depends on the scope of the systems. Nevertheless, an enterprise model must be maintained for the enterprise at all times to ensure that there will be no fundamental conflicts and barriers among present and future systems. Enterprise modeling can be greatly facilitated by using a reference model that provides requirements and economical assessments for the particular industry to which the enterprise belongs.

    Given an enterprise model, the development of an information system typically includes five activities:

1. Project planning and feasibility study.
2. Structured systems analysis for determining information resources requirements.
3. Structured systems design, focusing on (*1*) data modeling for databases and files, (*2*) process modeling for application programs, (*3*) knowledge modeling for production rules and other operation logic, (*4*) decision modeling for decision processes and user interface requirements, and (*5*) software engineering of the above models for implementation design.
4. Implementation of the system into the organization and users training.
5. Control, change, and growth of the system.

36.2 PROTOTYPICAL MANUFACTURING INFORMATION SYSTEMS

Information technology has been applied since the early 1960s to the production planning and inventory control functions in manufacturing facilities. In the 1970s, its application was expanded in parallel to shop floors for actual (or work order-level) production control and to engineering laboratories for product design functions. In the 1980s, prompted by both the opportunity for integration and the problems of disjoint systems (the so-called islands of automation), the focus started to shift from individual systems to facilitywide and, most recently, enterprise-level integration of systems. The sift is an evolution marked by several conceptual milestones: initially, the integration problem was equated with connecting the islands of automation through local area networking and linking disjointed application systems through software interfacing (i.e., file conversions and transfer). The need to manage the complexities of file structures and to reconcile the inconsistencies of the file contents led to emphasis on data standards, communications protocols, and open systems architectures. The need to promote parallelism in processes and to facilitate the synergy among all functional applications across the enterprise, whose individual users' particular views and requirements created the complexities and inconsistencies in the first place, revealed a higher dimensionality of integration and placed major emphasis on enterprise information models, reengineering, and information integration technology. This has naturally been followed by the current calls for adaptive manufacturing, total quality management, and international standards on data and knowledge interchange using a conceptual model.

MRP and MRP II: Production Planning and Related Business Functions

MRP

MRP is a classic of manufacturing information systems and continues to be a backbone of information management functions for many manufacturing facilities of all sizes. Its core is a master production scheduler that coordinates detailed production plans at all stages of production—from (raw materials) input to semifinished product to finished product—for a fixed planning horizon (usually weeks or months). The scheduling starts with the bill of materials (BOM) for the finished product and the quantity required at the end of the planning horizon. The BOM is exploded level by level to reach the end items, while the scheduler also works backward to determine when and how many of each item will be needed. The process is completed when every part and component in the BOM has a determined production schedule. The major advantage (and acid test) of an MRP system over traditional production planning and inventory control systems is its ability to coordinate the entire BOM of a product or even many products. An ideal MRP system will achieve a "seamless" pattern of work flows throughout the multistage production process with (*1*) no work-in-process (WIP) inventory and minimal overall inventory, (*2*) no stock-outs for WIPs, and (*3*) minimal make span or time required to go through the entire process. The major limitation of MRP is that, like other production planning systems, it relies entirely on estimated parameters of the production system and performs only static scheduling for a long time period (as opposed to real-time, adaptive control). Its output, the detailed plans, are invariably point estimates that can only be used as possible reference points for actual shop floor scheduling. In practice, MRP is meant to be employed not for shop floor control, but for master production scheduling; for this purpose it is clearly an extension of the traditional schedulers and serves as a "super-scheduler" integrating many parts of production scheduling by using the computer power of modern information technology.

MRP's major information requirements include elaborate details of BOM, demand forecasting, supply delivery, and production capacity on the data side and decision rules, heuristics, and analytical models on the knowledge side. The quality of these information resources—their timeliness, accuracy, and comprehensiveness—determines that of the MRP output. With the latest information technology, especially knowledge bases and distributed data processing, even a static MRP can be enhanced to (*1*) support near real-time planning within a shorter time frame by rerunning the MRP every day, (*2*) offer better information from other sources (marketing, purchasing, and shop floor), and (*3*) supply more scheduling power by incorporating databases and knowledge-based techniques.

MRP II

MRP II employs information technology concepts that were developed after the original MRP systems. Specifically, it extends the scope of information from focusing on production planning per se to also including some business sources such as customer orders, accounting ledgers, and deliveries. Furthermore, it broadens the link to shop floor control by incorporating updated estimates of capacity and other production parameters into the scheduling to generate work orders for shop floor systems. Therefore, MRP II can be considered an attempt at integrating several functions in production planning, shop floor control, and business through a common database to manage the capacity of a manufacturing facility. Its real functionality, however, is still the static and time-phased scheduling for production, albeit more elaborate than MRP. Its connection to shop floor activities and business databases is inherently off-line, or batch-processing based, due to its underpinning decision logic. Like MRP, MRP II uses a life cycle of scheduling processes that has clear stage boundaries and domain perspectives leading to separate, self-contained units of functionality. For example, lead time and priority are two parameters central to scheduling work. They are determined a priori in each unit, rather than being estimated directly and dynamically from actual conditions on the shop floor and the source data in other units when they are needed in computation.

The information requirements of MRP II are essentially those of MRP plus process planning, capacity planning, work order, customer order entry, warehousing, general ledger, and various other financial and shop floor activities, depending on the particular implementation in the marketplace. With the added capability of processing orders and incorporating this information into planning, MRP II allows a degree of flexibility in production planning for make-to-stock and, to a lesser extent, make-to-order environments. The information model used by MRP II thus differs from the one for MRP in that it contains many information resources that other systems are responsible to generate and maintain. These overlaps indicate the need for managing cross-system data resources as well as information integration. New knowledge capabilities will be needed to improve MRP II's underlying decision logic from one that is segmented to one that fuses the pertinent units into global parallel processes.

SFC, FMS, and JIT: Production Control and Extended Planning for Vendors

SFC and FMC

Shop floor control is a generic function in manufacturing that executes the production plans and coordinates the operations as depicted in Figures 36.1 and 36.3. Its time frame is typically much shorter than that of MRP and MRP II and is determined by the operational jobs that it controls. Therefore, the complexity of a SFC depends largely on the flexibility of the configuration of workstations in the shop, ranging from a near-continuous flow shop (which tends to be the simplest case) to a batch-based job shop all the way to a mixed-part–virtual-cell shop (the most complex). The scope of control also varies, depending not only on the type of shop but also on the level of automation. In highly automated facilities, SFC may include material handling (e.g., automated guided vehicles) and workstation control as well as cell-hierarchical administration, while less automated production systems may need only SFC to keep track of work orders, work-in-process, and other traditional management jobs. In a similar way, such systems as inspection, in-process verification, and statistical process control may or may not be incorporated into SFC. Clearly, unlike MRP and MRP II, SFC is not a sufficiently standardized function. It tends to be developed on an ad hoc basis and requires comprehensive modeling effort to meet specifications for the host enterprise. FMS, on the other hand, constitutes particular types of shop floor capabilities and configurations and hence is more likely to identify a generic basis for developing off-the-shelf information and control systems. Nonetheless, FMS information and control systems tend to be bundled with a particular hardware environment—workstations and other infrastructures—so that they require customization and significant modeling effort to fit into individual situations. Despite the variance in the complexity of their control mechanisms, SFC and FMS information systems all required similar basic functionality as covered in the generic description in Figures 36.1 and 36.3.

The information requirements of SFC and FMS are more or less straightforward for data resources but quite involved and time frame dependent for knowledge resources (including decision models). The data resources required are basically process plans and operations, work orders, work-in-process, data on mechanisms (machines, cells and facilities), routing, machine loading, and part data. Many of these data resources are also needed or used for MRP and, especially, MRP II; the difference is usually the degree of detail (associated with the time frame) found in work orders routing and other operation-based data. Knowledge resources, on the other hand, involve information flows, controls, and other operating rules and models using the data resources. They are particular to the specifics of the system. A flowshop may be operated by using some fixed schedules, a batch-based SFC may call for significant knowledge resources on feedback to respond to real events taking place on the shop floor, and a cellular cell-based FMS may require advanced information sharing across cells to regroup parts and jobs on an on-line and real-time basis, thereby entailing complex knowledge bases. Similarly, when additional functions such as inspection, statistical process control, and quality assurance are included on top of the basic SFC–FMS functionality, the additional information requirements tend to stem more from the use of data (or contextual knowledge) than from data resources per se. Evidently, information systems for SFC and FMS cannot be built from standard packages without involving extensive modeling effort to customize them for the host enterprise. Acquiring particular contextual knowledge for common data resources would be at the heart of such custom modeling. Building blocks that can be employed to implement an SFC information system include control packages for workstations and cells, on-line scheduling and WIP monitoring systems, and modules for various process controls. Factory data entry and display techniques (e.g., bar-code systems and personal-computer-based interactive operator support systems) would be of great value in successfully involving factor operators in SFC–FMS.

JIT

The nature and promises of JIT are best understood from an enterprise view. Essentially, JIT is an enterprise SFC system that regards suppliers' production functions as an integral part of the enterprise's overall life cycle of production and sets out to minimize or even eliminate the manufacturer's own inventory, which is nothing more than a work-in-process in between the supplier and the manufacturer when organizational boundaries are discounted. After all, the elimination of WIPs is precisely what any SFC–FMS or MRP–MRP II systems strives to accomplish to achieve smooth shop floor production. It follows from this enterprise view that, minimally, a JIT system would require the coordination between the SFC's time frame and the suppliers' time frames of delivery and would link them through certain formal mechanisms. More adequately, such coordination would be extended to involve the production planning and control functions of both the manufacturer and its suppliers. The formal connections obviously require organizational changes and have proven to be a major obstacle to U.S. manufacturers' full use of the possibilities offered by JIT. In Japan, major manufacturers that pioneered the practice of JIT often own their suppliers as "satellite" companies or influence their suppliers in substantive ways, hence the required organization is usually already in place for the manufacturer to implement JIT. Given this hierarchical structure between manufacturers and suppliers, it is a small wonder that the enterprise-oriented perspective of JIT naturally evolved and flourished in Japan. However, organizational connections are not a premise of JIT; many of the connections needed for effective coordination can be accomplished through information technology. In other words, to effect JIT, a proper cross-organizational information system linking the pertinent information resources of both sides' production planning and control functions (so that, under the guidance of an enterprise model, each could share in the other's processing) would suffice. The enterprise model would address control issues such as ownership, usage, and processing of this information and would in practice amount to a virtual organization as discussed earlier. The required information resources are no different from those discussed for MRP–MRP II and SFC–FMS, except that the organizational boundaries would be removed under the concept of enterprise.

CAD–CAM, CAE, and CAPP: Engineering Functions

CAD–CAM, CAE, and CAPP provide product designs and process plans using engineering methods and feed the designs and plans into production. The basic functions of CAD include automatic engineering drawing, solid modeling, and product data management; CAE analysis and simulation; and CAPP instructions needed by CAM for actual machining. Therefore, just like production planning, these functions are performed sequentially in self-contained stages before the actual production stage in the product life cycle. The computerization of these functions is focused on automating the engineering methods and principles used in the design process. For example, CAPP takes results from CAD in batch and derives manufacturing processes for CAM from the product designs according to predetermined fixed algorithms or planning rules. The process plans are then transferred in batch to SFC for execution on workstations, computer-based numerical controlled machines, and other CAM system and are expected to remain unchanged throughout the useful life of the product design and the machines used.

CAD–CAM and CAE

The information requirements for CAD–CAM and CAE are well known: they are determined by and rooted in the long-established engineering sciences and their practice. Their computer implementation is, therefore, dominated by generic but proprietary software systems, combining computer graphics (for electronic drawing and imaging) with high powered computation for processing and managing product definitional data and engineering algorithms (e.g., tolerancing and analysis); both of which are the core information requirements for CAD–CAM and CAE functions. Vendors of CAD–CAM and CAE systems traditionally developed their own proprietary design of databases to optimize the computing performance of their engineering environments. Consequently, a formidable barrier was created preventing users of different vendors from interchanging their product data either horizontally among engineers or vertically across stages of the enterprise. As a response to this problem, the industry has collaborated with national and international standards-setting organizations such as the National Institute of Standards and Technology (NIST) of the United States and the International Standards Organization (ISO) to bring compatibility to the field. The most significant and growing effort is the product data exchange using the STEP (PDES) model, which combines a leading standard under NIST—the previous PDES specification—with ISO's standard for the exchange of product model data (STEP). The model has gained acceptance in the United States, E.C., and Japan. Incidentally, the old PDES under NIST itself symbolized a decade-long quest for standards to support CAD systems' interoperability; tremendous efforts were undertaken by both NIST and the U.S. Air Force through such projects as IGES (the effort to develop a neutral file format for geometric data to be used by different CAD systems to transfer between proprietary formats when interfacing with each other) and PDDI (the specification of product definitional data to facilitate seamless interchange of part design files among air force contractors and vendors involved in aircraft design). The evolution from IGES, PDDI, and other early standards to PDES also underlines a simultaneous evolution of the scope of information resources used. The scope increased from IGES to PDDI mainly due to the complexity of products considered, but the change from PDDI to the old PDES and then to the new international PDES represents an enterprise view beyond CAD and CAE functions. The new PDES model emphasizes concurrent engineering not only among engineers within and without an organization but also between engineering design and production. This PDES includes process planning requirements and is presently embarking on major new initiatives to develop enterprise information models containing both data and knowledge resources for product and process design and ultimately for production itself. The effort could take minimally several years before any concrete results are achieved. Again, the key to this integration effort (from product and process design to production) is information, characterized by information requirements and consolidated through information modeling. A word of caution regarding standards is warranted: standards tend to be too comprehensive to be employed economically by the average-size manufacturer and could be too overwhelming to adapt to future technology.

CAPP

The counterpart of CAD in process design is CAPP. Its required information resources are characterized by process definitional data and process plan generation knowledge. A CAPP system often works together with particular CAD systems so that the latter feed product design files into the former and drive its processing. The complexity of CAPP systems depends essentially on whether the process plans are generated on the fly for the inputting product design or chosen from a library of existing plans. Obviously, generating process plans at runtime demands more refined data resources and significant knowledge-based capabilities. The most dynamic systems would, in addition, possess data resources on the real conditions of the particular manufacturing facilities and take them into account when generating process plans. The shorter the time frame between the generation and execution of process plans, the more dynamic the CAPP systems need to be. A clear direction for the extension of CAPP is its connection with SFC and/or MRP–MRP II so as to effect better adaptiveness to process planing. Incidently, this connection would also benefit the adaptiveness of the production planning and control systems in a similar way. CAPP systems with these extensions are emerging in the industry. Ironically, as CAPP systems are extended to integrate into actual production, they become less generic and require more particular modeling for the host enterprises.

CE and CIM: Integration of Engineering, Production, and Business

CE

Concurrent engineering started out as an initiative on engineering integration by the Defense Advanced Research Projects Agency (DARPA). The effort was soon extended to include manufacturing processes and emphasized parallel processing between design and production functions. Recently, the notion of concurrence was further extended to business activities that feed into design, such as marketing. Nonetheless, the basic orientation is still engineering design, and the focus is the shortening of the new product development cycle. The DARPA initiative resulted in many good solutions addressing various aspects of the problem. A commonly used solution is the team approach to the process of engineering itself, which calls for grouping design engineers with manufacturing engineers and marketing professionals to facilitate interactions and synergy among these traditionally sequential tasks. Another solution is the design for manufacturability (or for other things) approach, which provides new methodology to reorient design from optimizing for engineering to optimizing for production. Other results of the DARPA initiative include total quality management and quality function development, which are considered functional tools for CE.

The most concrete accomplishments of CE seem to belong to the areas of computing technology and software engineering for integrating CAD–CAM–CAE models, systems, and environments; a prime case is the PDES effort discussed above, which has become a rallying point of enabling technology for many aspects of CE. As a whole vision, CE remains a goal for individual manufacturers to strive toward; it does not have off-the-shelf solutions that a company can easily put together. Its very basis is still the notion of enterprise information integration. The modeling effort and the scope of information requirements depend, as always, on the vision of CE of the particular enterprises. For instance, to truly and fully implement the team approach and the design for manufacturability methodology, the CE information systems ideally should be able to support the formation of virtual teams (multiple teams formed from the same actual organization) and the real-time feedback from production to design.

CIM

While CE comes from the perspective of engineering, computer-integrated manufacturing was prompted by the need to integrate production planning with control. It was later extended to include both business functions and engineering. Earlier conceptions of CIM placed efforts mainly on manufacturing facilities, local area networks, and automatic control technology to effect the integration of MRP–MRP II, SFC–FMS, and CAPP–CAD. Software interfacing techniques and control and communication protocols were commonly sought for as the solutions. Soon after, however, it became clear that protocols (e.g., NIST's TOP and GM's MAP) and software connectors (e.g., application program interchange (API)) are only pieces of the solution to CIM, not the solution itself, because integration requires fusion of the logic of all systems rather than straightforward patch-up by APIs and the like. The focus then shifted to information integration, and fundamental results started to emerge. These new results not only advanced the methodology for integrated enterprise modeling and the technology for managing multiple systems (e.g., heterogeneous, distributed, and autonomous databases) but also converged on the same enterprise vision as CE was revealing to itself. It is now commonly accepted that both CIM and CE are an information integration vision for the whole enterprise, which, in turn, entails the same set of information technology solutions as well as organizational ones.

A large number of organizations and research groups have contributed to making the vision of CIM a reality. Some representative efforts include Europe's ESPRIT (an E.C. consortium that oversees numerous individual projects in industry and academe), the U.S. Air Force's ICAM project, and the multiyear, multidisciplinary CIM research projects at industrial companies and universities. Open systems architecture and metadata (enterprise models) technology are among the most noticeable new results that have come from the quest for CIM. On this basis, a CIM information system would feature an enterprise model and use this model to guide and facilitate the management of functional information (sub)systems in a concurrent manner. Its construction would be custom at the enterprise level.

36.3 MANUFACTURING INFORMATION SYSTEMS PLANNING, ANALYSIS, AND DESIGN

Throughout the discussion in the previous section, modeling for information requirements was shown as a key to the development of all manufacturing information systems, regardless of their level. Thus we begin the discussion on systems development with two commonly used techniques for modeling information system requirements: IDEF and the data flow diagram (DFD). Following the discussion is an overall framework for systems development using these techniques and a reference model.

IDEF: ICAM Definitional System

The integrated computer-aided manufacturing project launched by the Air Force in the late 1970s developed an enterprise modeling system called ICAM definition, or IDEF. This system consists of IDEF0 (read: IDEF zero) and a few other components for the modeling of integrated manufacturing systems, with IDEF0 performing structured systems analysis at the functional-level and others performing entity-relationship data modeling, process simulation, and database design. However, only IDEF0 has received wide and common acceptance in the industry. IDEF0 is based on the structured analysis and design technique (SADT), which is a graphical diagramming method developed in the 1970s. Another commonly used diagramming method is the data flow diagram model (reviewed below).

Both methods owe their strengths to graphical modeling capabilities, which enable the user to make succinct visual statements of the system concerned. Both are similar in philosophy, methodology, and many technical aspects. There are, however, important differences. Foremost is the fact that IDEF0 includes both logical and physical elements of a system, whereas DFD focuses exclusively on logical elements (for application software development). Thus IDEF0 can be said to be more general and natural for systems in which the visibility of physical elements in the model is preferred, either for completeness or for concerted representation of both information and facility, as in manufacturing. Usually, a DFD can be readily derived from the logical part of an IDEF0 model.

The basic constructs of IDEF0 are the following, which are symbolized in Figure 36.4.

1. *Activity–subject.* The functional elements of the system; always labeled by a phrase starting with a verb and decomposable.
2. *Input.* The logical or physical objects to be turned into the output of the activity.

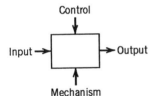

Figure 36.4.   The basic construct of IDEF0.

3. *Output.* The logical or physical objects turned out by the activity.

4. *Control.* The logical means of the activity, such as control algorithms, design specs, or process plans.

5. *Mechanism.* The physical means of the activity, such as workstations and automatic guided vehicles.

Note that outputs from a box may become inputs or controls (or mechanisms) for other boxes, and input, output, and control define the interface of a box. All inputs to a box should generally sum up to its outputs, logically and physically. The inclusion of mechanism is optional.

The modeling methodology entails an iterative and "zoom-in, zoom-out" type of detailing hierarchy. Specifically, an IDEF0 model begins with a context diagram showing the whole system being modeled as a black box, i.e., a single activity–subject with its input, output, control, and mechanism. The purpose of the context diagram is to depict the scope and boundary of the model. The box is decomposed into levels of detailed IDEF0 submodels, with each submodel showing several boxes connected through their input, output and control arrows and pertaining to a particular subject at the level immediately higher than it. The boxes in all submodels at all levels are carefully numbered according to the decomposition hierarchy to maintain a logical order. Once decomposed, a subject is fully and completely replaced by its submodels; its existence is merely a matter of convenience for presentation, communication, and record keeping. The decomposition of the context diagram into level 1 is obviously mandatory; further decomposition, however, is a choice of modeling, dictated only by need. When decomposing one box at a level, the other boxes at the same level can either also be decomposed or can stay undecomposed, it is purely a modeling choice. At the completion of this decomposition process, collecting all submodels at the leaves of the decomposition tree should amount to a complete model without having to involve any higher-level boxes from which the submodels are decomposed.

Incidently, Figures 36.1 and 36.3 are IDEF0 diagrams. Figure 36.1 shows the manufacturing facility and the production system at a higher level than Figure 36.3, which focuses mainly on

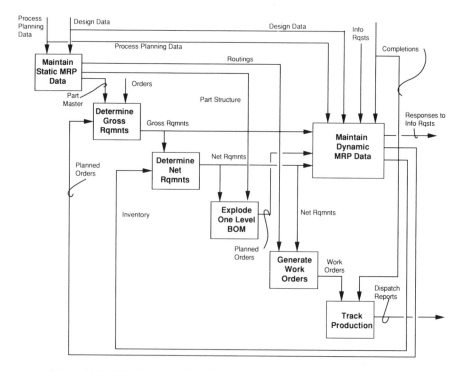

Figure 36.5.   The IDEF0 model of the information flows in the MRP system.

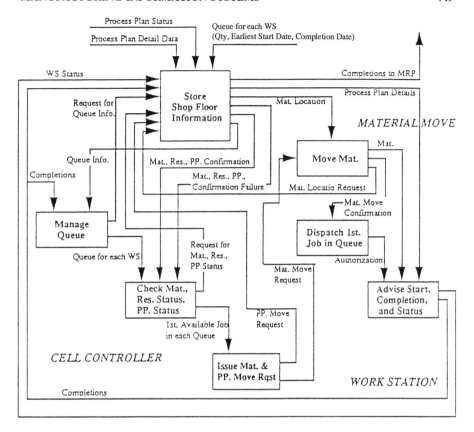

Figure 36.6. The IDEF0 model for the information flows in the SFC system.

shop floor and cell system activities. Figure 36.3 is not a direct decomposition from Figure 36.1. To illustrate a rigorously coordinated modeling effort, three IDEF0 diagrams are provided (Figures 36.5, 36.6, 36.7), which, respectively, depict the decomposed submodels for the MRP, SFC, and PP activities in Figure 36.1. All three diagrams are interconnected through common inputs, outputs, and control (e.g., the output of the "Store PP Data" activity in Figure 36.7 appears as input to the "Store Shop Floor Information" activity in Figure 36.6 and to the "Maintain Static MRP Data" activity in Figure 36.5). By combining these common input, output, and control flows, a single IDEF0 diagram would emerge from these three submodels. One more IDEF0 is included to show order entry activities (Figure 36.8). When put together, a core CIM model in IDEF0 is presented.

Data Flow Diagram

DFD is another commonly used structured systems analysis technique in manufacturing information systems modeling. In fact, DFD might command more popularity in the information systems profession as a whole than IDEF0 or SADT, although IDEF0 is arguably the choice for many large manufacturers, due to the ICAM effort. DFD's basic modeling constructs consist of external entity, process, data flow, and data store.

External entities represent sources and destinations of the system's data flows from the users' perspective; they, in effect, establish the scope and boundary for the system. The system proper is centered around the definition and declaration of processes. Each process has both input and output in the form of data flows, which might require storage in files or databases for

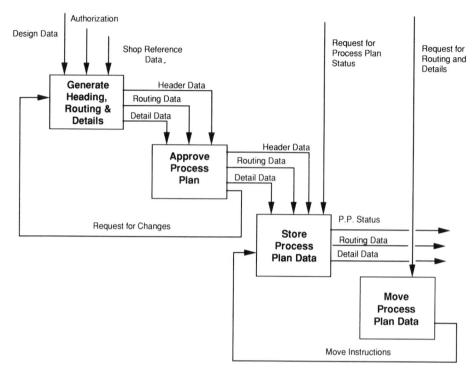

Figure 36.7.   The IDEF0 model of the information flows for the PP system.

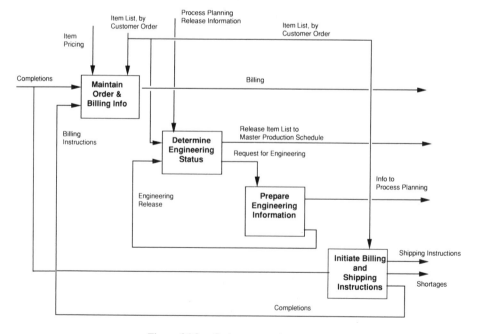

Figure 36.8.   Order processing system.

time-phased use. The off-line storage of data flows is data store. Like IDEF0, DFD's constructs are fairly intuitive. Its modeling methodology also calls for the same iterative process as IDEF0 (discussed above). One of the principal differences between these two models is the fact that DFD's flows focus on data and explicitly represent data stores, while IDEF0's input and output are more general. In DFD, the logical procedures required to execute each process are contained in the process and are specified outside the diagrams as the process logic, as opposed to being separately represented as control in IDEF0. A context diagram is not always needed with DFD, because its external entities usually suffice the purpose. Instead, a level-zero business model is required to overview the system concerned. This model is a regular DFD consisting, usually, of 5 to 8 (aggregate) processes with all data stores hidden.

Two DFD examples are shown in Figures 36.9 and 36.10, depicting the same manufacturing

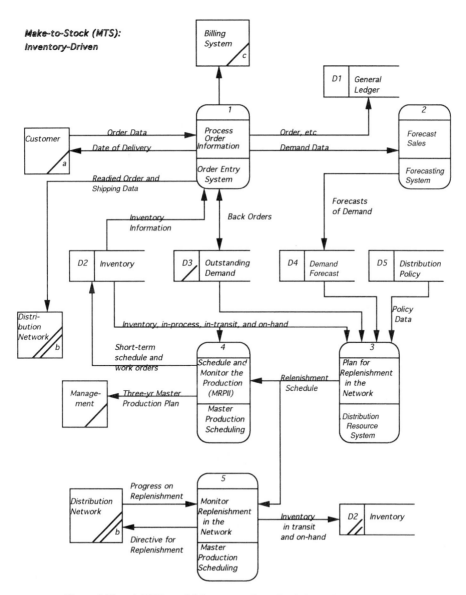

Figure 36.9. A DFD model for a manufacturing information system using MTS.

Assemble to Order (ATO)

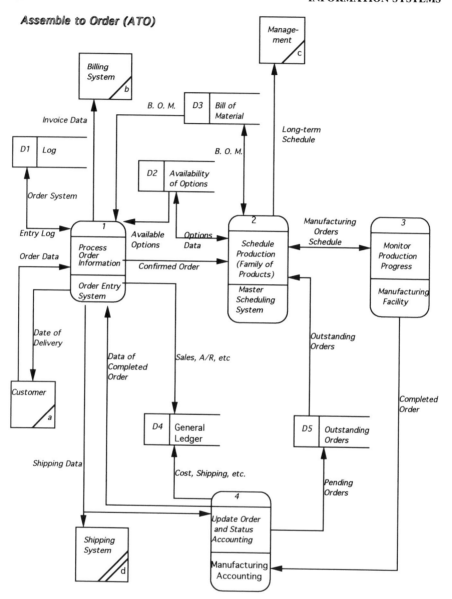

Figure 36.10. A DFD model for a manufacturing information system using MTS.

facility under two different strategies: make-to-stock (MTS) versus assemble-to-order (ATO). From an information systems' perspective, the major differences are clearly (*1*) the need for inventory data resources in MTS and (2) the need for shorter time frames for the processes (i.e., knowledge resources) in ATO. The difference in data resources is visible in the DFDs. However, the difference in knowledge resources would become evident only when the logic of processes was fully specified. In the diagrams, squares represent external entities, arrows represent data flows, and rectangles with one end open represent data stores. The large, rounded rectangles are processes. Decomposition would be carried out on a process-by-process basis virtually identical to the decomposition of IDEF0 activities.

Listed below are some rules and heuristics to help avoid common errors in DFD modeling. Some modeling logic is also provided, which is not particular to DFD and is applicable to IDEFO as well.

- DFD definitional
  1. All information flows must either originate or terminate at a process or both originate and terminate at a process.
  2. Use a verb to define a process and a noun for everything else.
  3. Bidirectional information flows indicate that the contents of the flow in either direction are identical, thus separate one-way flows must be used if the contents are different.
  4. The DFD hierarchy is a "zooming" mechanism not a pyramid, thus only the lowest layers or nodes are "real" and they must add up to a single, consistent diagram.
  5. Each layer should not consist of more than eight processes or less than four.
  6. All information flows must be meaningfully labeled unless they are clearly implied by a data store (whole content).
  7. Physical systems, organizations, or material flows should appear either as external entities or as footnotes in processes; only their information contents can be modeled as processes, data stores, or data flows.
  8. All processes must have both input and output.

- Modeling logical
  1. The modeling effort must be centered around developing processes; everything else follows.
  2. A process should correspond to an application program, not a subroutine or a step in a routine; this determines when the decomposition should stop.
  3. The read- and write-only data stores must be balanced in the whole model so that no unintentional dead ends exist.
  4. There should not be any transitional processes (those that have only one input and one output), except perhaps in high level conceptual representations.
  5. The "business" cycle for a mission or job should be complete and shown clearly in the model (e.g., requests should be completed with response).
  6. The model should show clear system logic (i.e., planning, executing, monitoring, and controlling the basic functions).
  7. The model should show a clear enterprise cycle (i.e., origins, destinations, authority, stages–tasks, and the like).
  8. The model should show clear mandate or use (e.g., the "plot," the statement, and the purpose of knowing all of these processes, data stores, and data flows).

A Systems Development Framework

Information systems are typically developed in stages: (*1*) planning, (*2*) analysis, (*3*) design, (*4*) implementation, and (*5*) control. These five stages are customarily referred to as the system development life cycle, because control usually would precipitate planning and thus generate a new cycle. Sometimes this cycle is shortened by using a system prototyping approach to bring some parallelism into this otherwise sequential process and speed up the analysis and design.

The planning to conceptual design stages are also referred to as enterprise modeling, which, at the enterprise level, specifies the goals and information requirements of the manufacturing information systems being considered. A reference model that can serve both as a guideline and as a starting point to enterprise modeling would be invaluable for the effort. Other critical elements in any development project are commitment from top management and teamwork between manufacturing and information professionals.

The Systems Development Life Cycle

Information Planning and Goal Setting. The objective here is to evaluate strategically the problems and opportunities facing the enterprise's information systems to ensure congruency between its information goals and manufacturing policies. The need to start the life cycle at a strategic level stems squarely from the promises and impact of today's information technology. Solving information problems in manufacturing or solving a manufacturing problem with information can lead to significant reengineering of existing processes at the enterprise level as well as at the facility level. Only strategic-level review and planning can determine, and implement, the right goals as the solution to these problems or opportunities. A ready example is the mundane systems discussed above. Every one of them can be improved according to either of two premises: increments and integration. The optimal solution to MRP problems given the premise that current processes of production planning and shop floor control would not be changed is certainly different from a solution in which the given premise requires that the processes would change. Even if a project is relatively minor in scope and impact, it is still necessary to make sure that it follows the current policies and/or the existing enterprise model; if there are discrepancies, these should be made manifest and documented. The methodology for planning is a combination of traditional strategic planning, bottom-up problem-driven planning, and top-down opportunity-driven planning as shown in Figure 36.11.

Information Requirements Analysis. Structured systems analysis techniques such as DFD and IDEF0 are commonly used for information requirements analysis. The object is to determine the functional processes, data resources, and knowledge resources necessary for the missions of the planned system. Clearly, both DFD and IDEF0 depict these requirements. A feasibility study is usually conducted at this stage. A cost–benefit analysis is also desireable but hard to perform in most cases, because reliable metrics and measures are difficult to come by for manufacturing information systems. This analysis can be applied to either status quo systems or new systems.

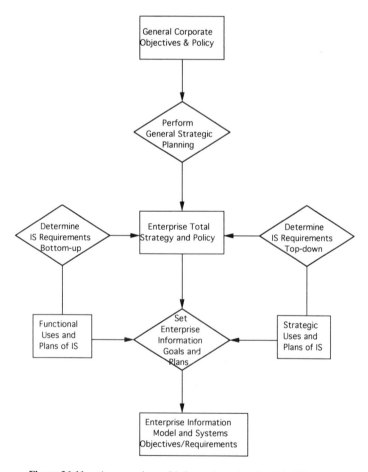

Figure 36.11. An overview of information planning (via TSER).

Systems Design. High level design for the planned system can be considered part of an iterative process of systems analysis and design, whereby old processes and systems are reengineered and new ones are designed as their information requirements are analyzed. Once the information requirements are finalized, system design is focused on developing data models for data resources, knowledge models for knowledge resources, and application models for functional processes, which, respectively, lead to databases, knowledge-based and decision support systems, and custom application programs. Methods and techniques commonly used for this task include (*1*) semantic data modeling, conceptual database design, and particular database or file system design for data resources; (*2*) knowledge acquisition and engineering, decision and knowledge-base modeling, and particular expert or decision support systems design for knowledge resources; and (*3*) application modeling, software engineering, and user interface for particular application software systems design. It should be noted that decision support and expert systems can be deployed either to modulize and manage certain classes of control and processing logic (knowledge resources) for particular application programs or to perform some applications themselves. Databases, on the other hand, are strictly developed to integrate and manage data resources for, ideally, the enterprise as a whole.

Software Development and Systems Implementation. The detailed design of the planned system is implemented first through software and other information technology and then in the organization. The technical implementation is accomplished through software engineering, coding, and installation; this whole process, well known in the profession, requires careful project management. The organizational implementation, on the other hand, is basically an art requiring delicate nurturing on the human side of the systems. Essentially, successful implementations seem to use one or more of the following strategies: (*1*) early involvement of the users in the development life cycle of the planned system (i.e., engineers, technicians, and managers can participate in the identification of information problems and opportunities as well as in the analysis of information requirements and systems design), (*2*) intensive education and open communication about the intended changes and the planned systems, and (*3*) pilot installation for helping the users gain familiarity and experience with the new systems. Without the users' cooperation, any information system efforts would likely fail, as is always the case with the introduction of any major new technology, be it robotics, TQM, or rationalization.

Systems Operation and Control. Systems operation and control present the most critical challenge to both systems and their managers. The focus is performance monitoring, feedback, and adaptation. The monitoring must be based on adequate metrics and measurement of performance, which can only come from the enterprise model (especially its goals) and users' satisfaction. Feedback implies an accountability of the system design that permits a cause-and-effect analysis for the monitored results. Adaptation may fall into two categories: fine-tuning or incremental changes versus a striving for overhaul or even new systems. Adaptation generates another phase of planning and hence another cycle of development.

Rapid Prototyping. The above life cycle is not too different from the product development life cycle and is certainly subject to the same need for abbreviation as the latter does. An alternative to the sequential life cycle is the rapid development of a prototype; the prototyping should embody the tasks of all stages of the cycle. In practice, rapid prototyping is usually employed to facilitate early integration of planning, analysis, and design and especially to verify the concept and feasibility of the enterprise model before the full system is constructed. In this sense, the rapid prototyping approach to information systems development is similar to the engineering paradigm of prototyping for new product development.

A Reference Model

The notion of a reference model for enterprise integration efforts is formally articulated in the ESPRIT's CIM Open Systems Architecture (CIMOSA) project, although there have been a few sources in academia and industry in both Europe and North America that independently investigated the topic at the time. CIMOSA calls for a family of reference models, including generic models, models for particular industries, and models for specific domain enterprises. Ideally, these three sets of models would be consistent vertically across levels (form generic to particular) and horizontally across individual models in terms of their content structures. A common set of constructs is employed that includes function view, information view, resources view, and organization view for the content structures. It was hoped that through the use of an internally consistent family of reference models for all enterprises, standards would be easier and more effective to maintain, thereby securing the foundation for open systems architecture. Industry also has its vendors (e.g., IBM and DEC) working on proprietary reference models coupled with their own integration products, but few of these efforts have yet resulted in actual models available to common users. A theory-based reference model was developed in 1990 at Rensselaer Polytechnic Institute, (Troy, N.Y.). Based on this model and the actual practice for enterprise information integration, several principles are derived as follows:

- *Enterprise Perspective*. Transcend organization boundaries and look into the natural and underlying processes of the enterprise including customer, vendor, and manufacturer.
- *Core Information Model*. Adopt a particular enterprise model which covers the basic information requirements for integration as a starting point for the development of the complete model. This approach tends to save time, effort, and hence money.
- *Systems Integration*. Examine the information flows and connect information systems that have common flows form the enterprise perspective; specifically, connect design with production and business, and production with customer and vendor.
- *Parallel Processes*. Analyze the internal information flows of existing systems or processes to uncover commonality among them, then reengineer these processes into smaller unit processes that are connected through their common flows; in other words, maximize the parallelism of all processes throughout the enterprise. For example, perform scheduling, routing, and loading concurrently.
- *Data Integration*. Integrate (logically, not physically) all common data resources for the shared use of the enterprise as a whole.
- *Knowledge Enhancement*. Develop new classes of knowledge resources and utilized knowledge-based techniques to effect integration of parallel processes.
- *Concurrent Architecture*. Implement the whole environment in a manner that allows for heterogeneity (in software and hardware), distribution, and local autonomy; in other words, pursue multiple and open systems.
- *On-line Enterprise Model*. Employ metadata technology to implement the enterprise model for information management tasks throughout the life cycle, where the model itself may be distributed.
- *Feedback Loops*. Create sufficient feedback flows for integration, e.g., use in-process verification to link production back to design to close up the loop initiated by, for instance, design manufacturability.
- *Visual Interface*. Invest as much effort into acquiring a good user interface that is robust and intuitive as into developing the system itself; ideally use visualized interfacing environments throughout (especially for shop floor systems).

36.4 INFORMATION MANAGEMENT TECHNOLOGY AND CASES

The backbone of information management is the database systems; which, coupled with decision support and expert systems, account for the bulk of systems development effort discussed above. Simply put, databases manage and process the data resources for the enterprise, while decision support and expert systems are concerned with knowledge resources for particular processes or activities in the enterprise. The main difference between decision support systems and expert systems is that the former employ mathematically based decision models to represent structured knowledge, while the latter use knowledge-based technology such as production rules to implement unstructured knowledge. When IDEFO or DFD is used to determine information requirements, data resources are typically found in IDEFO's inputs and outputs and DFD's data stores and data flows. Likewise, knowledge resources are derived from IDEFO's controls and DFD's process logic. In practice, however, neither IDEFO nor DFD alone can provide sufficient contents for data and knowledge modeling; additional efforts (e.g., semantic data modeling) are usually required, independent of the IDEFO or DFD modeling conventions.

Database Systems

The key concept of databases is data integration based on a three-schema model. The model is illustrated in Figure 36.12. Conceptually, all data resources are consolidated into a repository

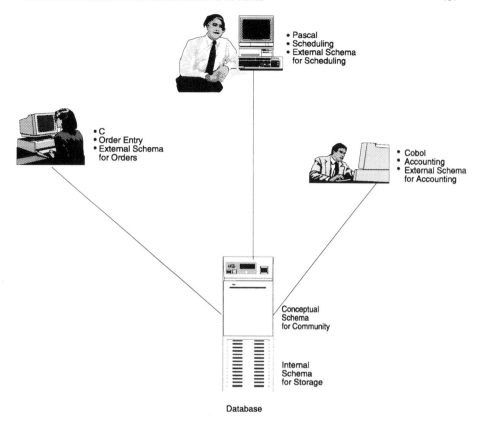

Figure 36.12. Database: unified repository supporting heterogeneous applications.

using certain file structures (internal schema) that are transparent to all users (and, ideally, to hardware, too). Users, on the other hand, view only the portion of data that concern them in their own, preferred ways as if these data were structured exclusively for their software environment (external schema). The integration takes place with the conceptual schema, which is the community representation of the consolidated data resources and is precisely the heart of the database model. All three levels of representations are linked through internal mappings and managed by the software called database management system, which is the operating system of databases. The three-schema architecture allows heterogeneous user groups all to share the same data resources without imposing a single, standard end-user software or sacrificing control needed for data integrity, consistency, and security. The separation of end users' views form the real structures of data facilities tremendously the database system's ability to add, delete, and modify user groups and views with no disruption to the system. This property is referred to as data independence. Data independence with respect to hardware is also desired but much harder to accomplish.

Depending on how the conceptual schema is constructed, there are three major types of databases; hierarchical–network, relational, and object oriented. Hierarchical–network databases have become obsolete in the present market but still account for a significant portion of all databases installed to date due to their venerability. They focus on determining the semantically meaningful entities and relationships for the user groups at large and then represent them in computationally optimal data structures and access paths using pointers and indexes. Relational systems, on the other hand, employ rigorous, set-theoretic dependency theory to decompose and reshuffle users' views into generic and simple tables (normalized relations) for the community, and develop powerful query languages to allow users manipulate these tables in any way with little concern whatsoever to access paths. Thus relational systems are more flexible than hierarchical–network systems—a property that has rendered the relational systems the leading technology in databases, until the advent of industry-grade object-oriented systems. Object-oriented databases use data abstraction and typing to organize individual data objects (e.g., a part or an employee) into a class hierarchy, where each class is a family characterized by properties common to all of its subclasses (inheritance), to achieve efficient and effective data management (e.g., a change to class properties will automatically be "inherited" by all objects belonging to this family of class and subclasses). This approach has certain similarity with the network model when it comes to the storage and retrieval of persistant data objects; while its data abstraction–based class hierarchy compares with the dependency-theoretic integrity rule of relational systems in a strikingly similar way, too. Object-oriented databases, however, do benefit from a rigorous model (data abstraction) and a powerful software technology (object-oriented programming), both of which the hierarchical–network systems lack. It seems that relational systems still enjoy more flexibility and will continue to fare well in areas where ad hoc query is important and where data objects tend to be highly repetitive in structures, namely business and production planning. Object-oriented systems, on the contrary, will continue to do well in areas such as engineering design and, perhaps, production control where individual data objects tend to be unique and their use more structured (predetermined views). The situation can change when either views are developed for object-oriented systems, or hybrid technologies emerge.

Although databases are traditionally centralized with a single physical repository of data, distributed systems have become prominent recently. These systems feature multiple physical sites with the database dispersed or copied over these sites, but they are still centrally controlled by a management system. The advantages of distribution are mainly convenience to users, better performance for local applications, and higher level of security (backup). To maintain global consistency is the big challenge. More useful and challenging is a new breed of environments in which multiple database systems running on different software and hardware platforms are intended to work together in an autonomous and concurrent manner. Available results on this class of systems are still sparse.

Decision Support and Expert Systems

Most expert systems use rule-based technology; others use a frame-based approach that is practically identical to object-oriented programming. The basic architecture is shown in Figure 36.13. The rule base contains knowledge (acquired form experts on the application domain) expressed in the form of production rules (a subset of first-order logic). The inference engine

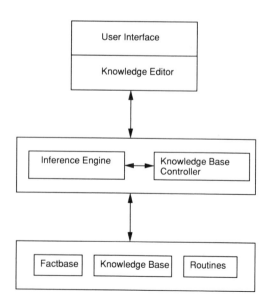

Figure 36.13. A typical expert system shell architecture.

works on the rules and searches for answers corresponding either to input conditions or to users' queries. The fact base is essentially a database internal to the system. Rule-based systems can be developed on a relatively small scale using off-the-shelf expert system shells. The key is to acquire knowledge from human experts and properly engineer the knowledge into rules.

Decision support systems (DSS) are characterized in essence through (*1*) the use of analytical decision models and (*2*) powerful user interfaces, both of which are customized for specific users concerning particular problems. Other than the difference in the underlying technology each uses, i.e., analytical decision models versus knowledge-based methods, decision support systems and expert systems appear to be more alike than different. A DSS ideally assists the users (presumably decision makers) to formulate decision problems and presents decision information in adequate forms for the users. Available technology tends to limit these systems to providing such abilities to only highly focused decision problems in rather well-defined application domains. As shown in Figure 36.14, one salient element is the model base, the other is the problem formulator. When both are limited, a decision support system is quite similar to a decision model-based application program that possesses well-conceived customized user interface for particular user groups.

Cases: PP, SFC, and Order Entry Databases for CIM

As a continuation of the CIM system shown in Figure 36.1 and Figures 36.5 through 36.8, a conceptual database design is presented in Figures 36.15 through 36.18. Each figure presents a graphical representation of a conceptual schema for a particular database using the relational design. The graphics show entities (rectangles), relationships among entities (diamonds), and two additional semantic relationships that prescribe integrity constraints (dashed diamonds for referential integrity and double diamonds for existence dependency rules). The entities and relationships have data items attached to them as their attributes, with those attributes that comprise the primary keys indicated by a dot to their left. Key integrity is implied. A base relation (or a table) is read off from the graphics for each entity and each relationship, and these tables are sufficiently normalized. Figures 36.15 through 36.17 show the schemes for PP, SFC, and order entry, respectively. They are then merged in Figure 36.18 on common entities and relationships to give rise to an integrated conceptual model for CIM.

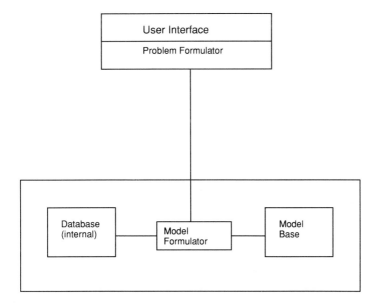

Figure 36.14.   Major elements of decision support systems.

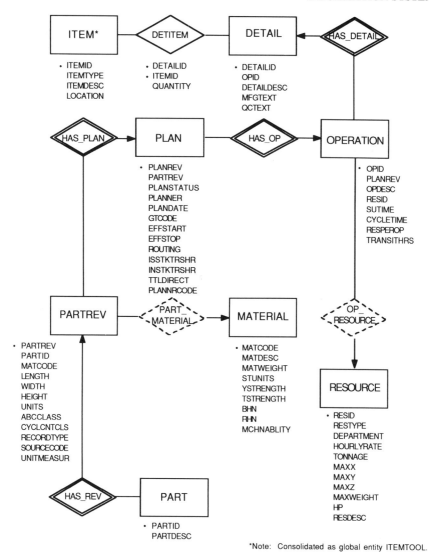

Figure 36.15.   Structure model for process planning system.

36.5   FUTURE TRENDS IN MANUFACTURING ENTERPRISE INFORMATION SYSTEMS: ADAPTIVENESS THROUGH ENTERPRISE MODELS

Throughout this chapter, the significance of an enterprise view in manufacturing information management and the need of enterprise modeling for systems development were emphasized. It is interesting to note that the enterprise model itself is increasingly recognized by both academia and industry as a central part of the information architecture for integrated manufacturing. Actually, in a broader sense, one can say that metadata (including information models and other data about data resources) play an ever more critical role in information management as the

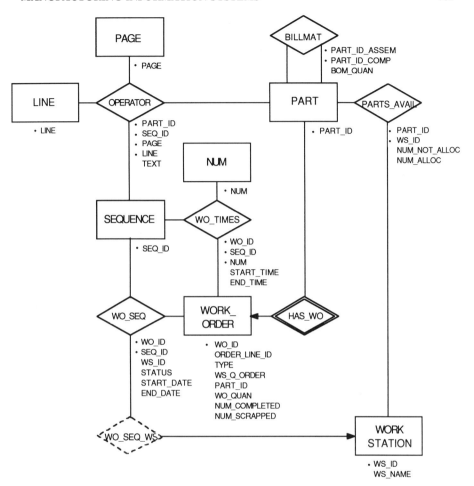

Figure 36.16.   Structure model for shop floor control system.

scope of systems becomes ever larger and moves toward enterprise-level integration. To point out this trend, which is bound to become more pronounced in the future, some of the basic problems facing manufacturing information integration are briefly reviewed.

Complexity of Manufacturing Enterprises

As discussed above, manufacturing enterprises all feature multiple information systems that have the following characteristics:

1. They are developed and maintained at local sites for particular applications and user groups according to local conditions.
2. They interact with each other in high volume, wide-area or even global networks.
3. They involve numerous different data resources (e.g., product design and manufacturing processes) and contextual knowledge (including operating rules and information flows).
4. They or their contents are frequently revised as technology and needs evolve.

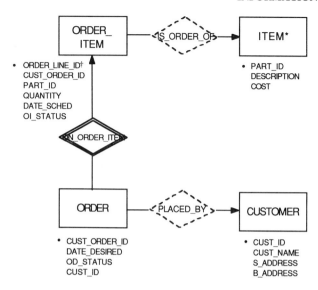

Figure 36.17.   Structure model for order processing system.

These characteristics together extend beyond the capabilities of available information technology. A great deal of research in CIM and CE has been devoted to developing new integration technologies and a great deal of success has been accomplished. However, major problems remain to be solved. They range from specific technical issues such as managing updates and views in multidatabases and accommodating legacy systems and new systems in integrated environments all the way to conceptual modeling of the requirements for real-time information flow between manufacturing and design (as opposed to only from design to manufacturing). At one level or another, these problems arise from the common limitation of past efforts that achieved integration against a fixed set of requirements without considering fully the adaptive nature of multiple manufacturing systems.

Management of Multiple Systems

Commercially available results do not manage multiple information systems with satisfactory performance. Most of these results employ, as a cornerstone of their approaches, the traditional von Neumann model of synchronization, which integrates schemata and serializes transactions across local systems under a central administrator. Consequently, there are fundamental limitations imposed by the architectures of these systems. These limitations place restrictions on local autonomy because of the requirements for schema integration and standardization of system structures, on global computing because of the complexity of serialization, and on system evolution because of the need to recompile or even redesign major elements of the global system when changes are made. Alternative approaches must be found to resolve these limitations, placing the solution to this problem at the heart of the adaptiveness issue.

Achievement of an Open Systems Architecture

Another key challenge for adaptiveness is an open system architecture, which is a prevailing concern in efforts such as CIMOSA and the industry-led Open Software Foundation. This

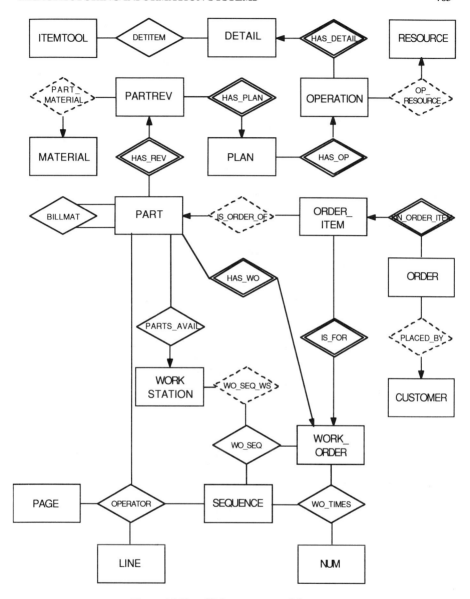

Figure 36.18. CIM structure model.

capability is critical to a manufacturing enterprise's ability to respond rapidly to change as well as to incorporate heterogeneous systems. Despite the vast progress made in the past decade on standards, current technology still cannot support adaptiveness. These standards tend to emphasize standardization on designs and structures, rather than separating the underlying logic from systems. Thus in a manner related to the issues discussed above current results do not accommodate legacy systems, revising or deleting existing systems, and adding new systems without necessitating major redesign or recompilation of existing systems. For example, all the conventional systems require large-scale schema restructuring at least at the global level to accommodate nontrivial changes. This often leads to unrealistic costs in practice. Standard or neutral structures alone cannot solve this problem. Techniques must be found to allow systems that do not use standards to work with systems that do and to make the global architecture and its administration independent of the local systems.

A solution approach to the above problems that is currently emerging is not only to develop rigorous enterprise models but also to employ them using new metadata technology to provide on-line knowledge for the enterprise's information management and integration. Because the on-line enterprise models (called metadatabase or repository) are easier to be made adaptive, an information architecture that is based on a metadatabase would also be adaptive. Figure 36.19 illustrates such an architecture. Virtually all ongoing major efforts on enterprise information integration in the industry have explicitly or implicitly embraced the use of a metadatabase (or repository) in their architectures. With appropriate attendant software technology such as metamodels and rule-based shells, both new and legacy systems can be added to an integrated environment without causing any part of the total environment, including the systems being added, to experience disruption. All that would be required is reverse modeling and automatic update to the global coordination system through the metadatabase. Modification to any part of other systems would involve only ordinary metadata transactions, too. The scenario is depicted in Figure 36.20. Although particular future products will certainly use their own versions of implementation technology, we believe, nonetheless, the general principles shown in these two figures will stand.

To conclude, the vision of adaptive manufacturing discussed in the overview entails enterprise information integration that supports the capability of virtual organizations. A layered architecture is clearly implied here. At the bottom, there are mundane systems whose information requirements must be satisfied; at the top, there are the enterprise views that cannot be confined to organizational boundaries. Enterprise modeling and enterprise model-supported adaptive integration becomes the key to effecting the objective. There is a theme underlying the evolution of the systems concept from database (file integration) to enterprise information integration: a conceptual model separating end users (applications) from the physical resources. In databases, external schemata are in effect virtual organizations of data resources based on the conceptual schema; in metadatabases, it is the enterprise conceptual models that promise to support virtual organizations for the enterprise. Finally, in the same framework of enterprise integration, facility-level manufacturing information systems are sufficiently supported throughout their life cycle in terms of systems development methods, models, and techniques.

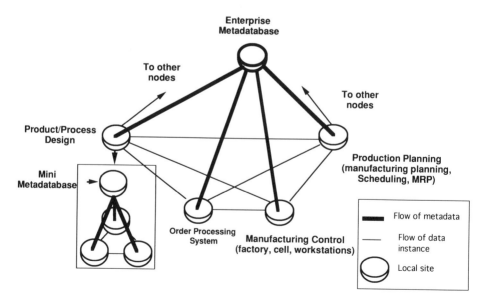

Figure 36.19. Metadatabase–supported enterprise information system.

Scenario: Systems Evolution

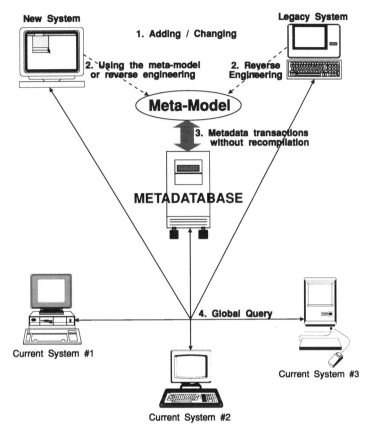

Key Point: All done on a real-time, on-line basis.

Figure 36.20. Scenario: systems evolution.

Acknowledgments

The IDEF0 models in Figures 36.1, 36.3, 36.14, 36.15, 36.16, and 36.17 were prepared by Alan Rubenstein, director of the Adaptive Integrative Manufacturing Enterprises Program, Design and Manufacturing Institute, Rensselaer Polytechnic Institute, Troy, New York.

BIBLIOGRAPHY

Suggested Readings

C.J. DATE, *Introduction to Database Systems,* Vol. 1, 5th ed., Addison-Wesley Publishing Co., Inc., Reading, Mass., 1990.

ESPRIT Consortium AMICE, eds., *Open Systems Architecture for CIM,* Springer-Verlag, Berlin, 1989.

C. GANE, and T. SARSON, *Structured Systems Analysis: Tools and Techniques,* Prentice-Hall, Inc., Englewood Cliffs, N.J., 1979.

A. GOLDFINE and P. KONIG, *A Technical Overview of the Information Resource Dictionary System, 2nd ed.*, National Bureau of Standards, Gaithersburg, Md., Jan. 1988, NBS Special Publication NBSIR 88-3700.

C. HSU, L. GERHARDT, D. SPOONER, and A. RUBENSTEIN, "Adaptive Integrated Manufacturing Enterprises: New Information Technology for the Next Decade," *IEEE Trans. Sys. Man Cybernet.*, **24,** (1994).

ICAM, *Integrated Computer-Aided Manufacturing Architecture. Part III/Volume VI: Composite Information Model of "Manufacture Product" (MFG1),* Wright-Patterson AFB, Ohio, Sept. 1983, AFWAL-TR-82-4063.

Industry Team and Facilitators, *21st Century Manufacturing Enterprise Strategy: An Industry-led View,* Vol. 1, Iacocca Institute, Lehigh University, Bethlehem, Pa., Nov. 1991.

D.A. MARCA and C.L. McGOWAN, *SADT: Structured Analysis and Design Techniques,* McGraw-Hill Book Co., Inc., New York, 1988.

L. RATTNER, *Information Requirements for Integrated Manufacturing,* Ph.D dissertation, Decision Sciences and Engineering Systems Department, Rensselaer Polytechnic Institute, Troy, N.Y., 1990

B. SMITH, *Product Data Exchange Specification: First Working Draft,* National Institute of Standards and Technology, Gaithersburg, Md., 1988, NISTIR 88-4004, NTIS order number PB 89-144794.

B. SMITH, G. RINAUDOT, T. WRIGHT, and K. REED, *Initial Graphics Exchange Specification (IGES),* Version 4.0, National Bureau of Standards, Gaithersburg, Md., 1988, Report NBSIR 88-38-3.

E. TURBAN, *Decision Support and Expert Systems,* Macmillan Publishing Co., New York, 1988.

U.S. Air Force, *Integrated Information Support System (IISS) Report,* Integrated Computer-Aided Manufacturing (ICAM), Materials Laboratory, Air Force Systems Command, Wright-Patterson Air Force Base, Ohio, Feb. 1983.

E.J. WITTRY, *Managing Information Systems: An Integrated Approach,* Society of Manufacturing Engineers, Dearborn, Mich. 1987.

CHAPTER 37

Object-Oriented Software For Manufacturing Systems and Automation

SADASHIV ADIGA
University of California at Berkeley

37.1 INTRODUCTION

Software has become an important component of the automation activity. Automation equipment manufacturers as well as users are realizing that the functionality of today's automation equipment is determined, to a large extent, by the software contained in the system. According to Ernst (1), software costs today are often higher than the development costs for the corresponding hardware. Moreover, the thrust toward computer-integrated manufacturing (CIM) has led to more software development activity in the manufacturing area.

Problems involved in software development activities are well documented in the literature (2). But object-oriented (OO) software techniques have provided some hope to cope with the complexity of modern software development tasks. Object orientation is heralded by many as an important direction in designing and implementing software in the 1990s and beyond. Object orientation is a set of ideas that evolved through people's efforts in improving modularity and productivity in the software life cycle. Its primary benefit is to ease the process of designing, implementing, and maintaining software. Significant benefits in design and programming productivity (3, 4) and lower life cycle and maintenance costs (5) have been reported. Practical applications in manufacturing also have been reported (6–9). This chapter presents the basic ideas of OO software and how they may be used to develop software for manufacturing and automation activities.

37.2 CONCEPTUAL BACKGROUND

The primary notion in OO software is that of a software object as an encapsulation of data and operations that are naturally associated together (Figure 37.1). Data are stored in instance variables, which cannot be directly accessed by other objects. Methods define the behavior expected of the object. Methods are procedures that implement operations on objects' private data. These software objects typically correspond to real-world manufacturing objects such as machines, parts, and operators. This helps one to build systems that reflect the way people view their respective businesses. Objects may contain other objects or refer to other objects. This feature helps one to represent objects of almost any complexity.

Objects interact by sending one another messages (Figure 37.2). That is, an object sends a message to another when it wants a certain service from the object receiving the message. Typically, receipt of a message activates a corresponding method in the receiving object. The behavior of an object is defined by its responses to messages. A message invokes the corresponding method in an object. Because the only way an object reacts to the external world is through its response to the messages received, the methods provided inside an object, in effect, form the interface of an object with its external world.

From an execution point of view, sending a message is similar to calling a function in languages such as FORTRAN or C, with one important difference. A function in FORTRAN or

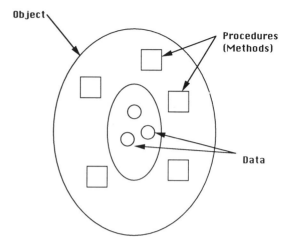

Figure 37.1. Software object
encapsulates data and procedures.   Object is an encapsulation of data and procedures.

C invokes a predetermined procedure, whereas in OO software, the decision of which procedure (or method) is invoked is left to the object receiving the message. Benefits to be gained from OO software are based on a few key concepts, outlined below.

Classes and Inheritance

A class defines the properties or behavior of similar objects by specifying the type of data and methods they share. Once you define a class, you may create any number of objects (called instance objects) with the same structure but different particulars. This is done by repeatedly sending a message to the class, requesting creation of an instance. Thus a class (or class object) may be viewed as a template to produce instance objects. We may describe "equipment" as a *class* of objects that represents the different types of machines used in a machine shop. A specific machine, namely, a mill is called an *instance* (or member) of this class.

Classes may be organized in a hierarchy, with the most general one at the root. Inheritance is a mechanism that allows a class to share the methods and variables defined in the classes above it in the class hierarchy. One creates a software class object by describing the most common features or behavior required of a class or group of entities of the system to be modeled. When you decide on subgroups or subclasses, you define them by describing the specialization or any additional functionality that you may need in the respective subclasses. A

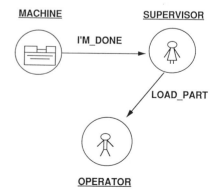

Figure 37.2. Objects communicating through
messages.

subclass inherits all the instance variables and methods from its superclass. This results in less coding if the inherited methods and instance variables are valid for the subclass. In addition, a subclass can define its own instance variables and methods. By reimplementing an inherited method in a subclass, it may override the inherited method, if needed.

Inheritance also is a useful mechanism for broadcasting change. For example, if the factory (containing the classes described earlier) decides to equip the machines with an automated data collection system, all we need to do is to describe this fact in the parent class, "equipment," and rest of the subclasses inherit this change.

Encapsulation and Information Hiding

The concept of information hiding follows that of encapsulation. Information hiding implies that the implementation details of a module are hidden from the user. The user can only access an object through its declared interface. Furthermore, a potential user need not know how the object prepares its response. This allows a designer to change an object's internal details of implementation without affecting other parts of the system it is interacting with, as long as the interface remains the same. It is an important concept to cope with complexity in software design.

Polymorphism

Polymorphism (in this context) is the ability of different objects to interpret the same message in different ways, depending on who receives the message. The proper combination of the properties of polymorphism and information hiding enables one to design objects that are interchangeable. One can easily replace existing objects with new objects, if they respond to the same messages as the present ones. Because different objects may respond to the same message description in individual ways, the new object could reimplement it without affecting the interface.

Dynamic Binding

Many Object-Oriented Programming (OOP) languages support dynamic binding. *Binding* is the term commonly used to refer to the process of functionally integrating a procedure and the data on which the procedure is required to operate. In most conventional languages, this decision is made when the code is being compiled. This process is known as early binding. When binding is made during a program run, it is termed dynamic binding or late binding.

Use of dynamic binding in combination with polymorphism offers one many interesting design options. Consider the situation in which a finished part is to be picked up by one of many different material handlers. The object that sends the message "movePart" need not know in advance which material handler (say, one of different types of robots) will pick up the part that is ready to be moved. Because many different object classes may implement the message in their own unique ways (thanks to polymorphism) and the binding between the message call and method invoked is done during run time, the system design can be quite flexible.

Object-oriented Analysis and Design

The life cycle of an Object-Oriented Software (OOS) application may not be too different from that of other software developed using rapid prototyping. But life cycle of a set of software object classes is different from software constructs used in conventional programs as these may be reused in other applications. Compared with the conventional approaches, a larger portion of the time is spent designing because the software is being designed for each reuse and future extensions. We must look for similarities among objects if we are to take advantage of the inheritance mechanism.

Solving problems in the OO paradigm involves a different way of thinking about the world (compared with conventional ways). Object-oriented software systems view the world as a collection of discrete objects that act and react in a common environment. The architecture of an OO software system is built around the object classes that represent the behavior of the entities in the system. Therefore, an important step in the design of OOS is the decomposition of the target system into object classes or set of objects that are to be manipulated. This is quite different from the conventional way of decomposing a system based on the functions to be performed by the software system.

A result of the objectwise decomposition is that when the characteristics of entities such as furnaces are to be modified, it is done only in one place, i.e., where the object class—"lathe"— is defined. In a functional decomposition approach, one must examine many functional modules, as the behavior of a furnace may be spread over all the modules that use furnaces. Formal design methods have been proposed (10–12).

Many benefits of OOS, especially those related to programmer productivity, are achieved through the reuse of software (objects). It eliminates the need for rewriting code and maintaining code in different places. It is a convenient mechanism to broadcast change, if needed, to all the subclasses. Some OO languages allow multiple inheritance, i.e., an object can inherit code from more than one superclass.

OO Technology

Many professionals are developing OO software in the form of programming languages, simulation programs, database systems, or some other automation-related activity such as real-time control. This has given rise to terms such as *OO programming languages, OO simulation, and OO database management systems*. Collectively, these tools and techniques may be called OO technology. A good source for the commercial tools available in these areas was compiled by Salmons and Babitsky (13).

Limitations

Although the technology is promising, it is not without limitations. A comprehensive and objective assessment has been published (14). It has been observed that many people, particularly experienced programmers, have problems adjusting to thinking in terms of objects and messages. While the reasons for this may be debated, it is an observation shared by many other people who have managed OO projects. It is also a fact that the promised productivity improvements through reusability starts only after you have built or bought a library of software objects. Building reusable objects is not an easy task. Furthermore, one must learn the library well before doing any serious programming.

Languages such as Smalltalk are known to demand more machine resources than the conventional procedural languages. One reason for this is that most OOP languages provide more services than the conventional languages. It is also true that most of concerns about execution speed are based on the performance of early research systems that were not designed for speed. Currently, there is also a shortage of personnel, both programming and managerial, who are conversant with this technology. However, this limitation may not remain for long, as object orientation in computing systems has recently been getting much attention.

The OO software industry suffers from other drawbacks found in a young industry. There is an absence of standards to enforce consistency among applications. This drawback is being addressed by an industry consortium, the object management group (OMG; Framingham, Mass.), which is bringing together a large number of firms to promote interoperability among object-oriented software applications.

37.3 SOFTWARE DEVELOPMENT ISSUES IN MANUFACTURING AUTOMATION

Managing Complexity and Variety

Manufacturing systems are quite complex and varied in nature. It is impractical to imagine that a single solution or software package will address all the needs of all manufacturing firms. Building generic software object class libraries, customizable through subclassing, provides a good alternative to the current approach to the development of manufacturing software.

Representing the Manufacturing World in a Computer

Manufacturing-related people think of their systems in terms of parts, conveyors, lathes, and drilling machines. In other words, they think in terms of *objects*. An OO approach allows designers and programmers to construct software counterparts of manufacturing entities easily with little conceptual mismatch. As reported by Najmi and Lozinski (6), this makes it easier for system designers to discuss models (underlying the programs) with users.

Factory Simulations and Control

Discrete event simulation emerged as a powerful and popular tool for analysis and design of manufacturing systems in the 1980s. It has been shown that simulation can be used to support all stages of development of CIM systems—from specification to implementation. OO simulation has been featured regularly in the conferences held by the Society of Computer Simulation.

Both simulation and control systems require a model of the real world. Ideally, one would like to be able to share, for simulation purposes, the state model developed for control purposes (or vice versa), including both the structure and the data (e.g., to simulate the future activity of the factory, starting from its current state). Also, because simulation is quite popular as a tool used to validate control strategies, control modules implementing these strategies must be developed. Again, sharing these modules between the simulation and the control tool can improve productivity and also consistency of the applications. An example is described below.

OO Database Management Systems

When there is a need to store rich data structures or traverse a large large number of objects as in computer-aided design (CAD) and computer-aided software engineering (CASE) applications, OO databases have a definite advantage (15). Objects are accessed directly and without time-consuming joint and operations required in relational databases. The object check-out–check-in and the long transaction facilities offered by the OO database management system (OODBMS) offer unique advantages for concurrent engineering applications. OODBMS are discussed in ref. 16. However, using object technology does not mean that one must abandon relational database technology. Techniques have been developed to enable object programs to access relational or object databases as needed (17).

Integration

Empirical evidence suggests that one does not achieve integration by just wiring such islands of automation together in some fashion; it must be done as a part of an overall plan (18). Designing CIM systems to an information model of the factory (in an OO representation) will provide the necessary conceptual as well as physical binding between subsystems comprising the CIM systems.

An object model is basically an information model of the system as it stores data and the context in which data are used. An object model of the enterprise is used as the reference for integration (9, 19). Use of the object model as the central unifying theme for CIM is a natural evolution of the earlier approach of using the database as the integrating influence. This approach makes integration possible while allowing data to be stored in any way it is convenient to do so. Communication through messages provides the loose coupling between subsystems required in a dynamic environment. An OO view of the systems with data encapsulation and availability of messages to synchronize cooperating processes can provide a robust implementation that is not affected by design changes. Implementation of the design in an OOP language minimizes the conceptual mismatch between design and implementation stages.

37.4   A PROJECT IN MANUFACTURING AUTOMATION

As mentioned earlier, OO concepts provide constructs that represent manufacturing objects closer to reality (i.e., with a one-to-one correspondence). Conceptually, these two sets of objects (i.e., virtual objects and real objects) can be used interchangeably if they conform to the same message protocol. Thus one may develop a system that can be used initially as a simulation tool and later, as production or control software. This section describes a project involving a single software system for use in a simulation, monitoring, and control mode through a direct manipulation user interface.

The Target System

To develop a full appreciation for the kinds of problems faced in synthesizing a real system, a complete user interface, graphical simulation, and a control system for a simple robotic arm with 6 degrees of freedom (df) was implemented. The Mini Mover robotic arm was connected to a computer operated by a human operator. Most of the intelligence for controlling the robot is local to the robot. Therefore, the computer is primarily responsible for presenting the operator with an easy method of issuing commands to the robot and for monitoring the status of the robot. In addition, a three-dimensional simulation of the robotic arm was also targeted. The key issues that need to be addressed by such a system including the following:

1. A system architecture to support the three modes of operation.
2. Timely response to real-world events.
3. Concurrency and fault tolerance.
4. Ease of use by the system's operators.
5. System maintainability and extensibility.

System Design

The basic design philosophy used was one of modeling the world by viewing the target software as a simulation of external processes to be captured in a computer program. This view is especially appealing in this project, as object-oriented programming techniques provide one with software constructs to build programs as images of real-world processes in the computer. Use of a more formal method did not seem necessary, because we were examining the smallest unit of a manufacturing system: a single device in isolation (i.e., not as a part of a workstation or a cell). Furthermore, we decided to use an existing graphics object library to minimize the programming burden of this experiment. We did not mind being locked into a particular hierarchy of graphics objects so that we could focus our attention on the main aims of this project.

Although the overall design of the system is of a general nature, the following assumptions were made at the outset with respect to the availability of implementation tools:

1. The computer operating system supports preemptive priority-driven multitasking if the system is limited to one Central Processing Unit (CPU); this allows a single CPU system to behave effectively as if each process had its own CPU.
2. Interprocess communication is supported.
3. User interface programs are built on top of an event-driven windowing system.
4. An object-oriented language is used for implementing the architecture.

The system was implemented on an IBM PC-AT running OS/2 with the *Presentation Manager* windowing system. The language used was C++. A software object library from ImageSoft called *CommonView* was also used. However, overall design is independent of these commercial implementation tools.

System Architecture

It was decided to use a distributed systems approach to systems design, because processing and data management needs in manufacturing are naturally distributed over different resources. Popular software architecture for implementing distributed systems is known as the client–server model. When a process is dedicated to managing a resource, it is called a server for that resource. Other processes requiring access to the resource are clients of the server. They access the resource by making requests of the server. The way the server manages its resource is

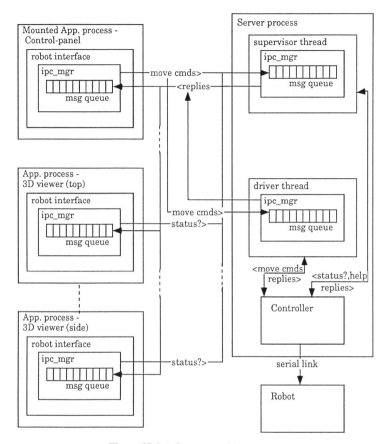

Figure 37.3. System architecture.

analogous to the way an object managers its state data in the object-oriented programming paradigm. The basic architecture of the system is shown in Figure 37.3.

The principal building blocks of the system are the robot, the server process, and the application processes. The server is the only process that communicates directly with the robot. It is responsible for managing the robot as a system resource. Requests to the server are sent to two separate queues: the supervisor queue and the driver queue. Each queue has a separate thread of execution dedicated to servicing it. The supervisor handles requests that must be acted on within a short period of time, e.g., approximately 20 ms. Status requests and halt commands are sent to the supervisor. The driver handles movement commands. Because each movement command may take many seconds to execute, and movement commands are queued, response to a movement command can clearly take a relatively long time. Both the supervisor and driver forward commands to the controller, where they are actually executed. This implies that two separate threads may be simultaneously executing in the controller object. Care must be taken to avoid collisions when both threads are accessing state data in the controller. The controller ultimately forwards commands to the robot via a serial RS232 link.

Application Programs

Simulation, monitoring, and control activities are treated as separate applications each with its own process. Each application process occupies its own window on the computer screen. Most of the windows can be scaled and moved by the operator. This allows the operator to activate simultaneously several applications to create a custom display.

Many application processes can monitor the robot by communicating with the server. Only one of these applications can be mounted on the robot at any given time. The mounted application is accorded the privilege of issuing control commands to the robot such as movement and halt commands. All other applications are able to issue only passive commands, such as requesting the current position. Each application process owns a robot_interface object that acts as a stand-in for the actual robot as far as the application is concerned. The robot_interface maintains little state data, because all requests are forwarded to the server, which in turn passes requests along to the robot via the controller.

Simulation and Monitoring

The server supports a simulation mode that enables it to run without actually being connected to the robot. This enables the server and the applications to be tested without using the robot. Two three-dimensional display programs named 3D_viewer and joint_angle_viewer provide the simulation and display mechanisms for monitoring and/or simulating the robot. The 3D_viewer application presents the operator with an orthogonal view of the robot. The operator may change the viewing direction by selecting new viewing axes. By activating several instances of this application, the operator may simultaneously view the robot from different directions. This application refreshes the display at regular intervals so that the operator may track the robot's position.

Control

The system consists of two control applications. The first one is called a sequencer. It allows interactive programming of the robot. The second one is a graphical control panel that allows an operator to control the robot. The sequencer application allows the operator interactively to create sequences of robot positions. The operator may have the robot execute these sequences, i.e., sequentially move from position to position. Sequences may be stored in files for later retrieval. The sequencer is a highly interactive version of the standard "teach" tool that most robotic arm controllers provide. The basic idea behind the teach tool is to allow the operator to move the robot to a desired position and then to store the position so that the robot can be easily instructed to return to that position.

The control_panel application is illustrated in Figure 37.4. When the operator presses one of the robot joint control buttons, e.g., rotate base CW, a command (named move_rel) is sent to the robot informing it to move the specified joint by a small amount. Commands are sent continuously as long as the button is held down. To guarantee good performance, the control_panel sends additional move_rel commands to the serve to "preload" the command queue so that a new command is sent to the robot by the server as soon as the previous one is completed. When the operator releases the button, the object that represents the control panel (control_panel) sends a stop command to the server, which flushes the command queue of any pending movement commands. When the operator presses the CALIB button, control_panel sends the server a reset command that causes the server to redefine the reference position to be where the robot is currently located. As this may be potentially confusing, the operator is prompted for confirmation before the reset is issued.

Discussion

Distributed Processing Using the Client–Server Model (under Object Orientation)

Under the client–server model, all operations performed on a resource are accomplished by sending a message to the resource's associated server process and then waiting for a reply (20). In this project, the robot has its own dedicated server process and the application processes are the clients. Each client owns a robot_ interface object to which it directs requests concerning the robot. The robot_interface looks to the application as if it were a stand-in for the server process controller object. When the application sends a message to the robot_interface, it formats an appropriate request message and sends it to the server, where it is eventually routed to the controller. Some robot_interface methods are implemented asynchronously; they return without waiting for a reply from the server. Other methods, such as report_position are imple-

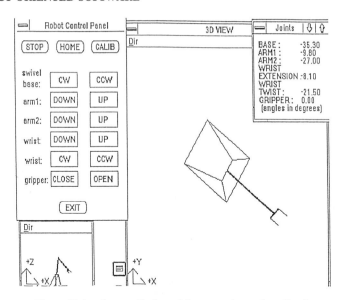

Figure 37.4. Screen display of the control_panel application.

mented synchronously; they wait for a reply from the server before returning. From the perspective of the application, calling a method in the robot_interface that is implemented synchronously looks exactly like calling the corresponding method in the controller object in the server process. In the literature, this is known as a remote procedure call (RPC) when the client and server do not reside on the same machine (21). An RPC is simply a function or procedure that is executed on a different computer from the one running the calling program. Objects provide a convenient mechanism to model communication without many syntactic constraints.

An advantage of an OO architecture is that one can design an application without knowing whether the application is localized or distributed over different processes. If the responsibility of each object is well defined, then the ability to distribute functionality is localized in the object (or layer) that encapsulates the communications facilities of the manufacturing environment.

Timely Response to Real-time Events

A requirement to respond to some event within a specified time interval is interpreted as a *real-time* requirement. These requirements are met by using standard software techniques such as running the server at a higher priority than all other processes; as such, these are not discussed here. Because most of the control in this project is performed by the electronics local to the robot, the computer is not responsible to meet many real-time constraints.

Concurrency and Fault Tolerance

The object oriented programming model supported by the language C++ does not explicitly address the idea of concurrency. Objects maintain state data, so it is conceivable that two threads simultaneously executing member functions in a single object may "collide" and corrupt the state data. We had to write our own routines to handle this problem. Now, there are commercial software object libraries that provide this functionality.

When an object (representing a process) sends a message to another object (a process) in an OO system, the decision of whether or not to wait for a reply is decided by the system designer or application programmer. Thus it is easy to incorporate fault tolerance as the object requesting service is not blocked while the message (or the service requested) is being processed by the object providing service.

Ease of Use

Ease of use was not explicitly measured but subjectively judged by people who operated and observed the operation. The users believed that the graphical interface with features that corresponded directly with the real-life entity and features made the system easy to use.

Extensibility and Maintainability

The robot was modeled as a device that has 6 df. The geometric relationships between the joints are stored as vectors of Denavit-Hartenberg parameters. To accommodate a robot with a different configuration, one would simply change the Denavit-Hartenberg parameters. Some additional geometric information is stored in a display list, but this could also be easily modified. In principle, a general-purpose system could be developed for an *n* df robot with arbitrary geometry. Objects needed to represent specific robots can be designed as subclasses or specializations of this general-purpose class with minimum extra programming effort.

The software is easier to maintain than an equivalent one developed following the procedural or conventional paradigm. Changes to the system (e.g., those related to robot or robot control) are localized to individual objects. Changes can be made without changing the interface. Therefore, other objects using the services of the object that was changed need not know of any changes made.

If this architecture is to be extended to handle multidevice systems, we need to provide a server for each device. In addition, it is essential to differentiate the system synchronization needs from that of robot or device synchronization. This will enhance the role of the server object. This server will also need an object manager to coordinate object locations across different node names, addresses, and networks. Such features will contribute to building extendible, reusable applications.

Related Work

Fabian and Lennartson (22) discussed some important modeling issues related to real-time OO control of manufacturing systems. Miller and Lennox (23) described an impressive effort leading to robot independent programming language (RIPE). RIPE is aimed at facilitating the rapid design and implementation of complex robot systems to support diverse research efforts and applications. Wilczynski and Wallace (24) described two practical cell control applications of real-time control using OO principles.

Concluding Remarks

This experimental demonstration has many practical implications. An OO architecture enables one to build a simulation system that can be later interchanged with the real system. Thus equipment vendors may supply a virtual model of the real equipment that can be plugged into one's factory simulation model or can be used to emulate performance of the equipment in place of the proposed equipment for evaluation purposes. If found useful, the virtual model can be replaced with the actual equipment with minimum disruptions to the overall system.

The encapsulation principle inherent in the approach promoted a modular style of implementation that helped localize complexity. We successfully used inheritance to customize a commercial library of objects to create the user interface applications. Reusing the library objects enabled us to create fairly sophisticated graphics applications in a relatively short period of time (3 months of half-time work by a graduate student).

3.7 CONCLUSION

Modern manufacturing applications are quite complex in nature. Unless more productive ways to develop software are deployed, new versions of software that can take advantage of the latest hardware and environments can fall years behind schedule. OO technology offers some important advantages to improve productivity of software design for automation and manufacturing.

The OO approach based on communication via messages provides the means for a flexible integration for which individual applications can remain distinct but can interact in a reconfigurable manner as desired by the user. One may build systems that can be upgraded or enhanced in an incremental manner. Systems can be designed with minimum mismatch between the conceptual and physical aspects of design and implementation. The OO approach is expected to be an important influence on how software will be developed in this decade. Manufacturing software developers who take advantage of the OO approach may gain a competitive edge in their respective applications.

BIBLIOGRAPHY

1. D. ERNST, "The Forces Propelling Automation Technologies [Interview]," *Siemens Rev.*, 4–7 (Jan. 1991).
2. F.P. BROOKS, "No Silver Bullet: Essence and Accidents of Software Engineering," *IEEE Comput.* **20**(4) 10–18 (1987).
3. B.J. COX, *Object Oriented Programming*, Addison-Wesley Publishing Co., Inc., Reading, Mass., 1986.
4. S. MCCLURE, *Object Technology: A Key Software Technology for the 90s*, International Data Corporation. White paper in *Object Technology*, Object Management Group, Framingham, Mass., 1992.
5. P. COFFEE, "Lower Life-Cycle and Maintenance Costs Make Strong Case for OOP," *PC Week*, 131, 133, 135 (May 10, 1992).
6. A. NAJMI and C. LOZINSKI, *Managing Factory Productivity Using Object-Oriented Simulation for Setting Shift Production Targets in VLSI Manufacturing*, paper presented at the AUTOFACT 89 Conference, 1989, pp. 3-1–3-14.
7. D. NORRIE, ed., *ICOOMS 92, Proceedings of the International Conference on Object-Oriented Manufacturing Systems*, University of Calgary, Calgary, Canada May 3–6, 1992.
8. D. TAYLOR, *Object-Oriented Information Systems: Planning and Implementation*. John Wiley & Sons, Inc., New York, 1992.
9. S. ADIGA, ed., *Object-Oriented Software for Manufacturing Systems*, Chapman & Hall, London, 1993.
10. G. BOOCH, *Object-Oriented Design with Applications*, Benjamin/Cummings Publishing Co., Redwood City, Calif., 1991.
11. S. SHLAER and S.J. MELLOR, *Object Life Cycles: Modeling the World in States*, Yourdon Press, Englewood Cliffs, N.J., 1992.
12. J. RUMBAUGH, M. BLAHA, W. PREMERLANI, F. EDDY, and W. LORENSEN, *Object-Oriented Modeling and Design*, Prentice-Hall, Inc., Englewood Cliffs, N.J., 1991.
13. J.F. SALMONS and T.T. BABITSKY, eds., *1992 International OOP Directory*, COOT Inc., New York, 1992.
14. S.Y. NOF, *Is All Manufacturing Object-Oriented?* Paper presented at ICOOMS 92, the International Conference on Object-Oriented Manufacturing Systems '92, University of Calgary, Canada, May 1992.
15. R. GUPTA and E. HOROWITZ, *Object-Oriented Databases to Applications to CASE, Networks and VLSI CAD*, Prentice-Hall, Inc., Englewood Cliffs, N.J., 1990.
16. S. ZDONIK and D. MAIER, eds., *Readings in Object-Oriented Database Systems*. Morgan Kaufmann, San Mateo, Calif., 1990.
17. M.E.S. LOOMIS, "Object and Relational Technologies, Can They Cooperate?" *Object Mag.* **2**(5), 34–40 (Jan.–Feb. 1993).
18. D.L. SHUNK and R.D. FILLEY, "Systems Integration's Challenges Demand a New Breed of Industrial Engineer," *Ind. Eng.*, 65–67 (May 1986).
19. J.H. MIZE, H.C. BHUSKUTE, D.B. PRATT, and M. KAMATH, "Modeling of Integrated Manufacturing Systems Using an Object-Oriented Approach," *IIE Trans.* **24**(3), 14–26 (1992).
20. A. TANNENBAUM and R. RENESSE, "Distributed Operating Systems," *ACM Comput. Surv.* **17**(4), 419–470 (1985).
21. A. BIRRELL and B. NELSON, "Implementing Remote Procedure Calls," *ACM Trans. Comput. Sys.* **2**(1), 39–59 (1984).

22. M. FABIAN and B. LENNARTSON, *Control of Manufacturing Systems: An Object-Oriented Approach,* paper presented at the 7th IFAC Symposium on Information Control Problems in Manufacturing Technology (INCOM '92), Toronto, May 25–28, 1992.

23. D.J. MILLER and R.C. LENNOX, "An Object-Oriented Environment for Robot System Architectures" *IEEE Control Sys.,* 14–23 (Feb. 1991).

24. D. WILCZYNSKI and D. WALLACE. "OOPS in Real-Time Control Applications" in S. Adiga, ed., *Object-Oriented Software for Manufacturing Systems,* Chapman & Hall, London, 1993, pp. 194–226.

CHAPTER 38
Resource Management

ADEDEJI B. BADIRU
University of Oklahoma

38.1 INTRODUCTION

Project goals are achieved through the use of resources. *Resource* refers to the labor, tools, equipment, and other physical items that are available to achieve project goals. Not all resources are necessarily tangible. Conceptual knowledge, intellectual property, and skill can be classified as resources. The lack or untimely availability of resources is a major impediment to manufacturing and automation efforts. Resource management is a complex task that is affected by several constraints. These constraints include

- Resource interdependencies.
- Conflicting resource priorities.
- Mutual exclusivity of resources.
- Limitations on resource availability.
- Limitations on resource substitutions.
- Variable levels of resource availability.
- Limitations on partial resource allocation.

The above factors determine the tools and techniques that can be used for resource management. The assignment of tools and operators to work centers is a common resource management problem in manufacturing systems. No matter how good workers are, if they do not have the proper resources, they cannot get the job done. This chapter presents tools and techniques that are suitable for use in resource management problems. It presents both the qualitative and quantitative aspects of resource management in manufacturing and automation projects. Topics covered by the chapter include project planning and resource allocation, resource sharing, human resource management, resource work rate analysis, critical resource diagramming, and probabilistic resource use analysis.

38.2 PROJECT PLANNING AND RESOURCE MANAGEMENT

Project planning determines the nature of actions and responsibilities needed to achieve the project goal. It entails the development of alternative courses of action and the selection of the best action to achieve the objectives making up the goal. Planning determines what needs to be done, by whom, for whom, and when. Whether it is done for long-range (strategic) purposes or short-range (operational) purposes, planning should address the following components:

1. Project goal and objectives involve the specification of what must be accomplished at each stage of the project. Resources constitute the inputs essential for achieving objectives:

$$\text{Resource} \rightarrow \text{Activity} \rightarrow \text{Process} \rightarrow \text{Project} \rightarrow \text{Objectives}$$

2. Technical and managerial approaches involve the determination of the technical and managerial strategies to be employed in pursuing the project goal.

3. Resource availability requires the allocation of resources for carrying out the actions needed to achieve the project goal.

4. The project schedule involves a logical and time-based organization of the tasks and milestones contained in the project. The schedule is typically influenced by resource limitations.

5. Contingency plan and replanning involve the identification of auxiliary actions to be taken in case of unexpected developments in the project.

6. Project policy involves specifying the general guidelines for carrying out tasks within the project.

7. Project procedure involves specifying the detailed method for implementing a given policy relative to the tasks needed to achieve the project goal.

8. Performance standard involves the establishment of a minimum acceptable level of quality for the products of the project.

9. Tracking, reporting, and auditing involve keeping track of the project plans, evaluating tasks, and scrutinizing the records of the project.

Using the Triple C Model

The Triple C model (1) is an effective tool for project planning. The model can facilitate better resource management by identifying the crucial aspects of a project. The model states that project management can be enhanced by implementing it within the integrated functions of *Communication, cooperation,* and *coordination.* The model facilitates a systematic approach to project planning, organizing, scheduling, and control. It highlights what must be done and when. It also helps to identify the resources (labor, equipment, facilities, etc.) required for each effort.

Communication

The communication function of project management involves making all those concerned aware of project requirements and progress. Those that will be affected by the project directly or indirectly, as direct participants or as beneficiaries, should be informed as appropriate regarding the following:

- The scope of the project.
- The personnel contribution required.
- The expected cost and merits of the project.
- The project organization and implementation plan.
- The potential adverse effects if the project should fail.
- The alternatives, if any, for achieving the project goal.
- The potential direct and indirect benefits of the project.

The communication channel must be kept open throughout the project life cycle. In addition to internal communication, appropriate external sources should also be consulted. The project manager must

- Exude commitment to the project.
- Use a communication responsibility matrix.
- Facilitate multichannel communication interfaces.
- Identify internal and external communication needs.
- Resolve organizational and communication hierarchies.
- Encourage both formal and informal communication links.

Cooperation

The cooperation of the project personnel must be explicitly elicited. Merely voicing a consent for a project is not enough assurance of full cooperation. The participants and beneficiaries of the project must be convinced of the merits of the project. Some of the factors that influence cooperation in a project environment include labor requirements, resource requirements, budget limitations, past experiences, conflicting priorities, and lack of uniform organizational support. A structured approach to seeking cooperation should clarify the following:

- The cooperative efforts required.
- The precedents for future projects.
- The implication of lack of cooperation.
- The criticality of cooperation to project success.
- The organizational impact of cooperation.
- The time frame involved.
- The rewards of good cooperation.

Cooperation is a basic virtue of human interaction. More projects fail due to a lack of cooperation and commitment than any other project factors. To secure and retain the cooperation of project participants, their first reaction to the project must be positive. The most positive aspects of a project should be the first items of project communication.

Whichever type of cooperation is available in a project environment, the cooperative forces should be channeled toward achieving project goals. A documentation of the prevailing level of cooperation is useful for winning further support for a project. Clarification of project priorities will facilitate personnel cooperation. Relative priorities of multiple projects should be specified so that a project that is of high priority to one segment of an organization is also of high priority to all groups within the organization. Guidelines for securing cooperation for projects are listed below:

- Establish achievable goals for the project.
- Clearly outline individual commitments required.
- Integrate project priorities with existing priorities.
- Eliminate the fear of job loss due to automation.
- Anticipate and eliminate potential sources of conflict.
- Use an open-door policy to address project grievances.
- Remove skepticism by documenting the merits of the project.

Coordination

After successfully initiating the communication and cooperation functions, the efforts of the project personnel must be coordinated. Coordination facilitates harmonious organization of project efforts. The development of a responsibility chart can be helpful at this stage. A responsibility chart is a matrix consisting of columns of individual or functional departments and rows of required actions. Cells within the matrix are filled with relationship codes that indicate who is responsible for what. The responsibility chart helps to avoid neglecting crucial communication requirements and obligations. It can help resolve questions such as:

- Who is to do what?
- How long will it take?
- Who is to inform whom of what?
- Whose approval is needed for what?
- Who is responsible for which results?
- What personnel interfaces are required?
- What support is needed from whom and when?

Resolving Resource Conflicts

When implemented as an integrated process, the Triple C model can help avoid conflicts in a project. When conflicts do develop, it can help in resolving the conflicts. Several types of conflicts can develop in resource management problems. Some of these conflicts are discussed below.

Schedule Conflict

Conflicts can develop because of improper timing or sequencing of project tasks. This is particularly common in large, multiple projects. Procrastination can lead to having too much to do at once, thereby creating a clash of project functions and discord between project team members. Inaccurate estimates of time requirements may lead to infeasible activity schedules. Project coordination can help avoid schedule conflicts.

Cost Conflict

Project cost may not be generally acceptable to the clients of a project. This will lead to project conflict. Even if the initial cost of the project is acceptable, a lack of cost control during project implementation can lead to conflicts. Poor budget allocation approaches and lack of financial feasibility study will cause cost conflicts later on in a project. Communication and coordination can help prevent most of the adverse effects of cost conflicts.

Performance Conflict

If clear performance requirements are not established, performance conflicts will develop. Lack of clearly defined performance standards can lead each person to evaluate his or her own performance based on personal value judgments. To uniformly evaluate quality of work and monitor project progress, performance standards should be established by using the Triple C approach.

Management Conflict

There must be a two-way alliance between management and the project team. The views of management should be understood by the team. The views of the team should be appreciated by management. If this does not happen, management conflicts will develop. A lack of a two-way interaction can lead to strikes and industrial actions that can be detrimental to project objectives. The Triple C approach can help create a conducive dialogue environment between management and the project team.

Technical Conflict

If the technical basis of a project is not sound, technical conflicts will develop. Manufacturing and automation projects are particularly prone to technical conflicts because of their significant dependence on technology. Lack of a comprehensive technical feasibility study will lead to technical conflicts. Performance requirements and systems specifications can be integrated through the Triple C approach to avoid technical conflicts.

Priority Conflict

Priority conflicts can develop if project objectives are not defined properly and applied uniformly across a project. Lack of direction project definition can lead each project member to define his or her own goals, which may be in conflict with the intended goal of a project. Lack of consistency of the project mission is another potential source of priority conflicts. Overassignment of responsibilities with no guidelines for relative significance levels can also lead to priority conflicts. Communication can help defuse priority conflicts.

Resource Conflict

Resource allocation problems are a major source of conflict in project management. Competition for resources, including personnel, tools, hardware, software, and so on, can lead to disruptive clashes among project members. The Triple C approach can help secure resource cooperation.

Power Conflict

Project politics lead to power play, which can adversely affect the progress of a project. Project authority and project power should be clearly delineated. Project authority is the control that a person has by virtue of his or her functional post. Project power relates to the clout and influence that a person can exercise due to connections within the administrative structure. People with popular personalities can often wield a lot of project power in spite of low or nonexistent project authority. The Triple C model can facilitate a positive marriage of project authority and power to the benefit of project goals. This will help define clear leadership for a project.

Personality Conflict

Personality conflict is a common problem in projects involving a large group of people. The larger a project, the larger the size of the management team needed to keep things running. Unfortunately, the larger management team creates an opportunity for personality conflicts. Communication and cooperation can help defuse personality conflicts.

Levels of Resource Planning

The strategic levels of planning have been outlined (2). Decisions involving strategic planning lay the foundation for successful implementation of projects. Planning forms the basis for all actions. Strategic decisions may be divided into three strategy levels: *supralevel planning, macrolevel planning,* and *microlevel planning.*

Supralevel Planning

Planning the supralevel deals with the big picture of how the project fits the overall and long-range organizational goals. Questions faced at this level concern potential contributions of the project to the welfare of the organization, effect on the depletion of company resources, required interfaces with other projects within and outside the organization, risk exposure, management support for the project, concurrent projects, company culture, market share, shareholder expectations, and financial stability.

Macrolevel Planning

Planning decisions at the macrolevel address the overall planning within the project boundary. The scope of the project and its operational interfaces should be addressed at this level. Questions faced at the macro level include goal definition, project scope, availability of qualified personnel, resource availability, project policies, communication interfaces, budget requirements, goal interactions, deadline, and conflict resolution strategies.

Microlevel Planning

Microlevel planning deals with detailed operational plans at the task levels of the project. Definite and explicit tactics for accomplishing specific project objectives are developed at the microlevel. The concept management by objective (MBO) may be particularly effective at this level. MBO permits each project member to plan his or her own work at the microlevel. Factors to be considered at the microlevel of project decisions include scheduled time, training requirement, tools required, task procedures, reporting requirements, and quality requirements.

Resource Loading and Leveling

Resource profiling involves the development of graphical representations to convey information about resource availability, use, and assignment. Resource loading and resource leveling graphs are two popular tools for profiling resources. The resource idleness graph and critical resource diagram are two additional tools that can effectively convey resource information. Resource loading refers to the allocation of resources to work elements in a project network. A resource loading graph presents a graphical representation of resource allocation over time. Figure 38.1

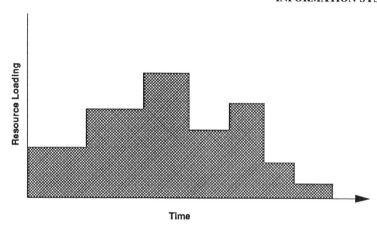

Figure 38.1. Resource loading graph.

shows an example of a resource loading graph, which may be drawn for the different resources types involved in a project.

The graph provides information useful for resource planning and budgeting purposes. In addition to resource units committed to activities, the graph may also be drawn for other tangible and intangible resources of an organization. For example, a variation of the graph may be used to present information about the depletion rate of the budget available for a project. If drawn for multiple resources, it can help identify potential areas of resource conflicts. For situations in which a single resource unit is assigned to multiple tasks, a variation of the resource loading graph can be developed to show the level of load (responsibilities) assigned to the resource over time.

Resource leveling refers to the process of reducing the period-to-period fluctuation in a resource loading graph. If resource fluctuations are beyond acceptable limits, actions are taken to move activities or resources around to level out the resource loading graph. Proper resource planning will facilitate a reasonably stable level of the workforce. Advantages of resource leveling include simplified resource tracking and control, lower cost of resource management, and improved opportunity for learning. Acceptable resource leveling is typically achieved at the expense of longer project duration or higher project cost. Figure 38.2 shows a somewhat leveled resource loading.

It should be noted that not all of the resource fluctuations in a loading graph can be eliminated. Resource leveling attempts to minimize fluctuations in resource loading by shifting activities within their available slacks. One heuristic procedure for leveling resources, known as Burgess's method (3), is based on the technique of minimizing the sum of the squares for the resource requirements in each period.

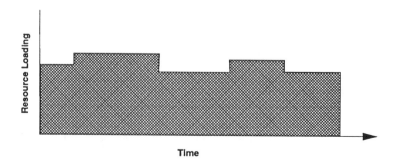

Figure 38.2. Resource loading after leveling.

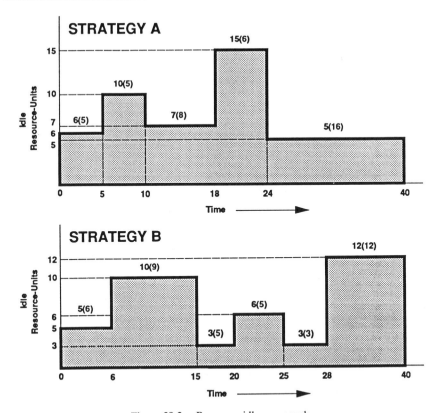

Figure 38.3. Resource idleness graph.

A resource idleness graph is similar to a resource loading graph, except that it is drawn for the number of unallocated resource units over time. The area covered by the resource idleness graph may be used as a measure of the effectiveness of the scheduling strategy employed for a project. Suppose two scheduling strategies yield the same project duration and a measure of the resource use under each strategy is desired as a means to compare the strategies. Figure 38.3 shows two hypothetical resource idleness graphs for the alternate strategies. The areas are computed as follows:

Area A = 6(5) + 10(5) + 7(8) + 15(6) + 5(16) = 306 resource-units-time.

Area B = 5(6) + 10(9) + 3(5) + 6(5) + 3(3) + 12(12) = 318 resource-units-time

Because Area A is less than Area B, it is concluded that Strategy A is more effective for resource use than Strategy B. Similar measures can be developed for multiple resources to evaluate strategies for resource allocation. Some guidelines for resource scheduling have been published (4).

38.3 CRITICAL RESOURCE DIAGRAMMING

Critical resource diagramming (CRD) as a tool for resource management has been introduced (5, 6). Figure 38.4 shows an example of a critical resource diagram for a project that requires six different types. Each node identification, RES j, refers to a task responsibility for resource type j. In a CRD, a node is used to represent each resource unit. The interrelationships between resource units are indicated by arrows. The arrows are referred to as resource–relationship (R–

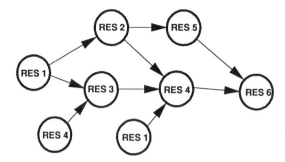

Figure 38.4. Basic critical resource diagram.

R) arrows. For example, if the job of Resource 1 must precede the job of Resource 2, then an arrow is drawn from the node for Resource 1 to the node for Resource 2.

Task durations are included in a CRD to provide further details about resource relationships. Unlike activity diagrams, a resource unit may appear at more than one location in a CRD, provided there are no time or task conflicts. Such multiple locations indicate the number of different jobs for which the resource is responsible. This information may be useful for task distribution and resource leveling purposes. In Figure 38.5, Resource 1 (RES 1) and Resource 4 (RES 4) appear at two different nodes, indicating that each is responsible for two different jobs within the same work scenario. However, appropriate precedence constraints may be attached to the nodes associated with the same resource unit, if the resource cannot perform more than one task at the same time (Figure 38.5).

In an application context, CRD can be used to evaluate the use of tools, operators, and machines in a manufacturing system. Effective allocation of these resources will improve their use levels. If tools that are required at several work sites are not properly managed, bottlenecks may develop. Operators may then have to sit idle waiting for tools to become available or an expensive tool may have to sit unused while waiting for an operator. If work cannot begin until all required tools and operators are available, then other tools and operators that are ready to work may be rendered idle while waiting for the bottleneck resources. A CRD analysis can help identify when and where resource interdependencies occur so that appropriate reallocation actions may be taken. When there are several operators, any one operator that performs his or her job late holds up everyone else.

CRD Network Analysis

The same forward and backward computations used in CPM are applicable to a CRD diagram. However, the interpretation of the critical path may be different because a single resource may appear at multiple nodes. Figure 38.6 presents a computational analysis of the CRD network shown in Figure 38.4. Task durations (days) are given below the resource identifications. Earliest and latest times are computed and appended to each resource node in the same manner as in CPM analysis. RES 1, RES 2, RES 5, and RES 6 form the critical resource path. These resources have no slack times with respect to the completion of the given project. Note that only one of the two tasks of RES 1 is on the critical resource path. Thus RES 1 has a slack time for performing one job, while it has no slack time for performing the other. None of the two

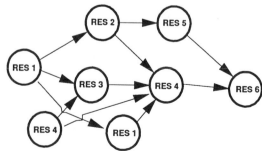

Figure 38.5. CRD with singular resource precedence constraint.

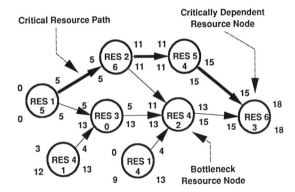

Figure 38.6. CRD network analysis.

tasks of RES 4 is on the critical resource path. For RES 3, the task duration is specified as zero. Despite this favorable task duration, RES 3 may turn out to be a bottleneck resource. RES 3 may be a senior manager whose task is that of signing a work order. But if he or she is not available to sign at the appropriate time, then the tasks of several other resources may be adversely affected. A major benefit of a CRD is that both senior-level and lower-level resources can be included in the resource planning network.

A bottleneck resource node is defined as a node at which two or more arrows merge. In Figure 38.6, RES 3, RES 4, and RES 6 have bottleneck resource nodes. The tasks to which bottleneck resources are assigned should be expedited to avoid delaying dependent resources. A dependent resource node is a node whose job depends on the job of immediate preceding nodes. A critically dependent resource node is defined as a node on the critical resource path at which several arrows merge. In Figure 38.6, RES 6 is both a critically dependent resource node as well as a bottleneck resource node. As a scheduling heuristic, it is recommended that activities that require bottleneck resources be scheduled as early as possible. A burst resource node is defined as a resource node from which two or more arrows emanate. Like bottleneck resource nodes, burst resource nodes should be expedited, because their delay will affect several following resource nodes.

Resource Schedule Chart

The critical resource diagram has the advantage that it can be used to model partial assignment of resource units across multiple tasks in single or multiple projects. A companion chart for this purpose is the resource schedule (RS) chart. Figure 38.7 shows an example of an RS chart based

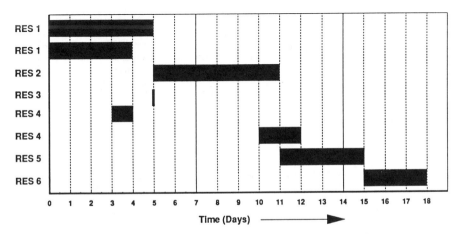

Figure 38.7. Resource schedule chart based on earliest start times.

on the earliest times computed in Figure 38.6. A horizontal bar is drawn for each resource unit or resource type. The starting point and the length of each resource bar indicate the interval of work for the resource. Note that the two jobs of RES 1 overlap over a 4-day time period. By comparison, the two jobs of RES 4 are separated by a period of 6 days. If RES 4 is not to be idle over those 6 days, "fill-in" tasks must be assigned to it. For resource jobs that overlap, care must be taken to ensure that the resources do not need the same tools (e.g., equipment, computers, or lathe) at the same time. If a resource unit is found to have several jobs overlapping over an extensive period of time, then a task reassignment may be necessary to offer some relief for the resource. The RS chart is useful for a graphical representation of the use of resources. Although similar information can be obtained from a conventional resource loading graph, the RS chart gives a clearer picture of where and when resource commitments overlap. It also shows areas where multiple resources are working concurrently.

38.4 RESOURCE WORK RATE ANALYSIS

When resources work concurrently at different work rates, the amount of work accomplished by each may be computed (2). The critical resource diagram and the resource schedule chart provide information to identify when, where, and which resources work concurrently. The general relationship between work, work rate, and time can be expressed as:

$$w = rt$$

where w is the amount of actual work accomplished, expressed in appropriate units, such as miles of road completed, lines of computer code typed, gallons of oil spill cleaned, units of widgets produced, and surface area painted; r is the rate at which the work is accomplished; and t is the total time required to accomplish the work. It should be noted that work rate can change due to the effects of learning curves. In the discussions that follow, it is assumed that work rates remain constant for at least the duration of the work being analyzed.

Work is defined as a physical measure of accomplishment with uniform density (i.e., homogeneous). For example, a computer programming task may be said to be homogeneous if one line of computer code is as complex and desirable as any other line of code in the program. Similarly, cleaning one gallon of an oil spill is as good as cleaning any other gallon of the spill within the same work environment. The production of one unit of a product is identical to the production of any other unit of the product. If uniform work density cannot be assumed for the particular work being analyzed, then the relationship presented above will need to be modified. If the total work to be accomplished is defined as one whole unit, then the relationship shown in Table 38.1 will be applicable for the case of a single resource performing the work, where $1/x$ is the amount of work accomplished per unit time. For a single resource to perform the whole unit of work, we must have the following:

$$(1/x)(t) = 1.0$$

That means the magnitude of x must equal the magnitude of t. For example, if Machine A is to complete one work unit in 30 min, it must work at the rate of $1/30$ of the work per unit time. If the magnitude of x is greater than the magnitude of t, then only a fraction of the required work will be performed. The information about the proportion of work completed may be useful for resource planning and productivity measurement purposes. For the case of multiple resources performing the work simultaneously, the work relationship is as presented in Table 38.2. For multiple resources, we have the following expression:

$$\sum_{i=1}^{n} r_i t_i = 1.0$$

TABLE 38.1. Relationship for a Single Resource

Resource	Work Rate	Time	Work Done
Machine A	$1/x$	t	1.0

TABLE 38.2. Relationship for Multiple Resources

Resource	Work Rate	Time	Work Done
RES 1	r_1	t_1	$(r_1)(t_1)$
RES 2	r_2	t_2	$(r_2)(t_2)$
$\vdots$	$\vdots$	$\vdots$	$\vdots$
RES n	r_n	t_n	$(r_n)(t_n)$
Total			1.0

where n is the number of different resource types, r_i is the work rate of resource type i, and t_i is the work time of resource type i. The expression indicates that even though the multiple resources may work at different rates, the sum of the total work they accomplished together must equal the required whole unit. For partial completion of work, the expression becomes

$$\sum_{i=1}^{n} r_i t_i = p$$

where p is the proportion of the required work actually completed. Suppose RES 1, working alone, can complete a job in 50 min. After RES 1 has been working on the job for 10 min, RES 2 was assigned to help RES 1 in completing the job. Both resources working together finished the remaining work in 15 min. It is desired to determine the work rate of RES 2.

The amount of work to be done is 1.0 whole unit. The work rate of RES 1 is 1/50 of work per unit time. Therefore, the amount of work completed by RES 1 in the 10 min it worked alone is $(1/50)(10) = 1/5$ of the required work. This may also be expressed in terms of percent completion or earned value using the cost–schedule control systems criteria (C–SCSC). The remaining work to be done is 4/5 of the total work. The two resources working together for 15 min yield the results shown in Table 38.3. Thus we have $15/50 + 15(r_2) = 4/5$, which yields $r_2 = 1/30$ for the work rate of RES 2. This means that RES 2, working alone, could perform the job in 30 min. In this example, it is assumed that both resources produce identical quality of work. If quality levels are not identical for multiple resources, then the work rates may be adjusted to account for the different quality levels or a quality factor may be introduced into the analysis. The relative costs of the different resource types needed to perform the required work may be incorporated into the analysis shown in Table 38.4.

As another example, suppose the work rate of RES 1 is such that it can perform a certain task in 30 days. It is desired to add RES 2 to the task so that the completion time of the task

TABLE 38.3. Relationship of Two Resources

Resource	Work Rate	Time	Work Done
RES 1	1/50	15	15/50
RES 2	r_2	15	$15(r_2)$
Total			4/5

TABLE 38.4. Relative Costs of Multiple Resources

Resource	Work Rate	Time	Work Done	Pay rate	Total Cost
Machine A	r_1	t_1	$(r_1)(t_1)$	p_1	C_1
Machine B	r_2	t_2	$(r_2)(t_2)$	p_2	C_2
$\vdots$	$\vdots$	$\vdots$	$\vdots$	$\vdots$	$\vdots$
Machine n	r_n	t_n	$(r_n)(t_n)$	p_n	C_n
Total			1.0		Budget

could be reduced. The work rate of RES 2 is such that it can perform the same task alone in 22 days. If RES 1 has already worked 12 days on the task before RES 2 comes in, find the completion time of the task. It is assumed that RES 1 starts the task at time 0.

As usual, the amount of work to be done is 1.0 whole unit (i.e., the full task). The work rate of RES 1 is 1/30 of the task per unit time and the work rate of RES 2 is 1/22 of the task per unit time. The amount of work completed by RES 1 in the 12 days it worked alone is $(1/30)(12) = 2/5$ (or 40%) of the required work. Therefore, the remaining work to be done is 3/5 (or 60%) of the full task. Let T be the time for which both resources work together. The two resources working together to complete the task yield Table 38.5. Thus, we have $T/30 + T/22 = 3/5$, which yields $T = 7.62$ days. Consequently, the completion time of the task is $(12 + T) = 19.62$ days from time 0. The results of this example are summarized in the resource schedule charts in Figure 38.8. It is assumed that both resources produce identical quality of work and that the respective work rates remain consistent. As mentioned earlier, the respective costs of the different resource types may be incorporated into the work rate analysis.

Resource Assignment Problem

Operations research techniques are frequently used to enhance resource allocation decisions (7, 8). One common resource allocation tool is the resource assignment algorithm. This algorithm can be used to enhance resource allocation decisions. Suppose there are n tasks that must be performed by n workers. The cost of worker i performing task j is c_{ij}. It is desired to assign workers to the tasks in a fashion that minimizes the cost of completing the tasks. This problem scenario is referred to as the assignment problem. The technique for finding the optimal solution to the problem is called the assignment method. Like the transportation method, the assignment method is an iterative procedure that arrives at the optimal solution by improving on a trial solution at each stage of the procedure.

CPM and PERT can be used to ensure that the project will be completed on time. As was mentioned earlier, these two techniques do not consider the assignment of resources to the tasks that make up a project. The assignment method can be used to achieve an optimal assignment of resources to specific tasks in a project. Although the assignment method is cost based, task duration can be incorporated into the modeling in terms of time–cost relationships. Of course, task precedence requirements and other scheduling restrictions must be accounted for in the final scheduling of the tasks. The objective is to minimize the total cost. Thus the formation of the assignment problem is as follows.

x_{ij} 1 if worker i is assigned to task j, $i,j = 1, 2, \ldots, n$
x_{ij} 0 if worker i is not assigned to task j
c_{ij} cost of worker i performing task j

Minimize

$$z = \sum_{i=1}^{n} \sum_{j=1}^{n} c_{ij} x_{ij}$$

Subject to

$$\sum_{j=1}^{n} x_{ij} = 1 \ (i = 1, 2, \ldots, n)$$

$$\sum_{i=1}^{n} x_{ij} = 1 \ (j = 1, 2, \ldots, n)$$

$$x_{ij} \geq 0 \ (i,j = 1, 2, \ldots, n)$$

TABLE 38.5. Two Resources Working Together

Resource	Work Rate	Time	Work Done
RES 1	1/30	T	$T/30$
RES 2	1/22	T	$T/22$
Total			$3/5$

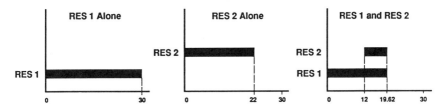

Figure 38.8. Resource schedule charts for RES 1 and RES 2.

It can be seen that the above formulation is a transportation problem with $m = n$ and all supplies and demands are equal to 1. Note that we have used the nonnegativity constraint $x_{ij} \leq 0$ instead of the integer constraint $x_{ij} = 0$ or 1. However, the solution of the model will still be integer valued. Hence, the assignment problem is a special case of the transportation problem with $m = n$ supplies $S_i = 1$, and demands $D_i = 1$. Conversely, the transportation problem can also be viewed as a special case of the assignment problem. A transportation problem can be modeled as an assignment problem and vice versa. The basic requirements of an assignment problem are

1. There must be two or more tasks to be completed.
2. There must be two or more resources that can be assigned to the tasks.
3. The cost of using any of the resources to perform any of the tasks must be known.
4. Each resource is to be assigned to one and only one task.

If the number of tasks to be performed is greater than the number of workers available, we will need to add dummy workers to balance the problem. Similarly, if the number of workers is greater than the number of tasks, we will need to add dummy tasks to balance the problem. If there is no problem of overlapping, a worker's time may be split into segments so that the worker can be assigned more than one task. In this case, each segment of the worker's time will be modeled as a separate resource in the assignment problem. Thus the assignment problem can be extended to consider partial allocation of resource units to multiple tasks.

Although the assignment problem can be formulated for and solved by the simplex method or the transportation method, a more efficient algorithm is available specifically for the assignment problem. The method, known as the Hungarian method, is a simple iterative technique. Details of the assignment problem and its solution techniques can be found in operations research texts. As an example, suppose five workers are to be assigned to five tasks on the basis of the cost matrix presented in Table 38.6. Task 3 is a machine-controlled task with a fixed cost of $800, regardless of which worker it is assigned to. Using the assignment method, we obtain the optimal solution presented in Table 38.7, which indicates the following: $x_{15} = 1$, $x_{23} = 1$, $x_{31} = 1$, $x_{44} = 1$, and $x_{52} = 1$. Thus the total cost is given by

$$TC = c_{15} + c_{23} + c_{31} + c_{44} + c_{52} = \$(400 + 800 + 300 + 400 + 350) = \$2250$$

The technique of work rate analysis can be used to determine the cost elements that go into an assignment problem. The solution of the assignment problem can then be combined with the technique of critical resource diagramming. This combination of tools and techniques can help enhance resource management decisions.

TABLE 38.6. Cost Matrix for Assignment Problem

Worker	Task 1	Task 2	Task 3	Task 4	Task 5
1	300	200	800	500	400
2	500	700	800	1250	700
3	300	900	800	1000	600
4	400	300	800	400	400
5	700	350	800	700	900

TABLE 38.7. Solution to Resource Assignment Problem[a]

Assignments	Task 1	Task 2	Task 3	Task 4	Task 5
Worker 1					1
Worker 2			1		
Worker 3	1				
Worker 4				1	
Worker 5		1			

[a] The minimum total cost = $2250.

Probabilistic Resource Use Analysis

In operations that are subject to risk and uncertainty, probability information can be used to analyze resource use characteristics. Suppose the level of availability of a resource is probabilistic in nature. For simplicity, we will assume that the level of availability, X, is a continuous variable whose probability density function is defined by $f(x)$. This is true for many resource types such as funds, natural resources, and raw materials. If we are interested in the probability that resource availability will be within a certain range of x_1 and x_2, then the required probability can be computed as:

$$P(x_1 \leq X \leq x_2) = \int_{x_1}^{x_2} f(x)dx$$

Similarly, a probability density function can be defined for the utilization level of a particular resource. If we denote the use level by U and its probability density function by $f(u)$, then we can calculate the probability that the use will exceed a certain level, u_0, by the following expression:

$$P(U \geq u_0) = \int_{u_0}^{\infty} f(u)du$$

Suppose a critical resource is leased for a large project. There is a graduated cost associated with using the resource at a certain percentage level, U. The cost is specified as $10,000 per 10% increment in use level above 40%. A flat cost of $5,000 is charged for use levels below 40%. The use intervals and the associated costs are listed below.

$U < 40\%$, $5,000
$40\% \leq U < 50\%$, $10,000
$50\% \leq U < 60\%$, $20,000
$60\% \leq U < 70\%$, $30,000
$70\% \leq U < 80\%$, $40,000
$80\% \leq U < 90\%$, $50,000
$90\% \leq U < 100\%$, $60,000

Thus a use level of 50% will cost $20,000, whereas a level of 49.5% will cost $10,000. Suppose the use level is a normally distributed random variable with a mean of 60% and a variance of 16% squared. Find the expected cost of using this resource. The solution procedure involves finding the probability that the use level will fall within each of the specified ranges. The expected value formula will then be used to compute the expected cost:

$$E[C] = \sum_k x_k P(x_k),$$

where x_k represents the kth interval of use. The standard deviation of use is 4%.

$$P(U < 40) = P\left(z \le \frac{40 - 60}{4}\right) = P(z \le -5) = 0.0$$

$P(40 \le U < 50) = 0.0062$

$P(50 \le U < 60) = 0.4938$

$P(60 \le U < 70) = 0.4938$

$P(70 \le U < 80) = 0.0062$

$P(80 \le U < 90) = 0.0$

$$\begin{aligned} E(C) &= \$5,000(0.0) + \$10,000(0.0062) + \$20,000(0.4938) \\ &\quad + \$30,000(0.4938) + \$40,000(0.0062) + \$50,000(0.0) \\ &= \$25,000 \end{aligned}$$

Thus it can be expected that leasing this critical resource will cost \$25,000 in the long run. A decision can be made whether to least or buy the resource. Resource substitution may also be considered on the basis of the expected cost of leasing.

38.5 HUMAN RESOURCE MANAGEMENT

Human resources make projects successful. Human resources are distinguished from other resources because of their ability to learn, adapt to new project situations, and set goals. Human resources, technology resources, and management resources must coexist to pursue project goals. Managing human resources involves placing the right people with the right skills in the right jobs in the right work environment. Good human resource management motivates workers to perform better. Both individual and organizational improvement are needed to improve overall quality of human resources. Management can create a climate for motivation by enriching jobs with the following strategies:

- Specify project goals in unambiguous terms.
- Encourage and reward creativity on the job.
- Eliminate mundane job control processes.
- Increase accountability and responsibility for project results.
- Define jobs in terms of manageable work packages that help identify line of responsibility.
- Grant formal authority to make decisions at the task level.
- Create advancement opportunities in each job.
- Give challenging assignments that enable a worker to demonstrate his or her skill.
- Encourage upward (vertical) communication of ideas.
- Provide training and tools needed to get job done.
- Maintain a stable management team.

Several management approaches are used to manage human resources. Some of these approaches are formulated as direct responses to the cultural, social, family, or religious needs of workers. Examples of these approaches are

- Flexitime.
- Religious holidays.
- Half-time employment.

These approaches can have a combination of several advantages. Some of the advantages are for the employer and some are for the workers. The advantages are listed below:

- Low cost.
- Cost savings on personnel benefits.
- Higher employee productivity.

- Less absenteeism.
- Less work stress.
- Better family or domestic situation, which may have positive effects on productivity.

Workforce retraining is important for automation projects. Continuing education programs should be developed to retrain people who are qualified only to do jobs that do not require skilled labor. The retraining will create a ready pool of human resources that can help boost manufacturing output and competitiveness. Management stability is needed to encourage workers to adapt to the changes in industry. If management changes too often, workers may not develop a sense of commitment to the policies of management.

The major resource in any organization is technical and nontechnical labor. People are the overriding factor in any project life cycle. Even in automated operations, the role played by whatever few people are involved can be significant. Such operations invariably require the services of technical people with special managerial and professional needs. The high-tech manager in such situations would need special skills to discharge the managerial duties effectively. The manager must have automanagement skills that relate to the following:

- Managing self.
- Being managed.
- Managing others.

Many of the managers who supervise technical people rise to the managerial posts from technical positions. They, consequently, often lack the managerial competence needed for the higher offices. In some cases, technical professionals are promoted to managerial levels and then transferred to administrative posts in functional areas different from their areas of technical competence. The poor managerial performance of these technical managers is not necessarily a reflection of poor managerial competence, but rather an indication of the lack of knowledge of the work elements in their surrogate function. Any technical training without some management exposure is, in effect, an incomplete education. Technical professionals should be trained for the eventualities of their professions.

In the transition from the technical to the management level, an individual's attention would shift from detail to overview, specific to general, and technical to administrative. Because most managerial positions are earned based on qualifications (except in aristocratic and autocratic systems), it is important to train technical professionals for possible administrative jobs. It is the responsibilities of the individual and the training institution to map out career goals and paths and institute specific education aimed at the realization of those goals. One such path is outlined below.

1. *Technical Professional.* This is an individual with practical and technical training and or experience in a given field; such as industrial engineering. The individual must keep current in his or her area of specialization through continuing education courses, seminars, conferences, and so on. The mentor program, which is now used in many large organizations, can be effectively used at this stage of the career ladder.

2. *Project Manager.* This is an individual assigned the direct responsibility of supervising a given project through the phases of planning, organizing, scheduling, monitoring, and control. The managerial assignment may be limited to a specific project. At the conclusion of the project, the individual returns to his or her regular technical duties. However, the individual's performance on the project may help identify him or her as a suitable candidate for permanent managerial assignment later on.

3. *Group Manager.* This is an individual who is assigned direct responsibility to plan, organize, and direct the activities of a group of people with a specific responsibility, e.g., a computer data security advisory committee. This is an ongoing responsibility that may repeatedly require the managerial skills of the individual.

4. *Director.* This individual oversees a particular function of the organization. For example, a marketing director has the responsibility of developing and implementing the strategy for getting the organization's products to the right market, at the right time, at the appropriate price, and in the proper quantity. This is a critical responsibility that may directly affect the survival of the organization. Only the individuals who have successfully proven themselves at the earlier career stages get the opportunity to advance to the director's level.

5. *Administrative Manager.* This is an individual who oversees the administrative functions and staff of the organization. His or her responsibilities cut across several functional areas. This individual must have proven his or her managerial skills and diversity in previous assignments.

These steps represent just one of the several possible paths that can be charted for a technical professional as he or she gradually makes the transition from the technical ranks to the management level. To function effectively, a manager must acquire nontechnical background in various subjects. His or her experience, attitude, personality, and training will determine the managerial style. This person's appreciation of the human and professional needs of subordinates will substantially enhance his or her managerial performance. Examples of subject areas in which a manager or an aspiring manager should receive training include the ones outlined below.

1. Project management.
   - Scheduling and budgeting: knowledge of project planning, organizing, scheduling, monitoring, and controlling under resource and budget restrictions.
   - Supervision: skill in planning, directing, and controlling the activities of subordinates.
   - Communication: skill of relating to others both within and outside the organization, including written and oral communication skills.
2. Personal and personnel management.
   - Professional development: leadership roles played by those participating in professional societies and peer recognition acquired through professional services.
   - Personnel development: skills needed to foster cooperation and encouragement of staff with respect to success, growth, and career advancement.
   - Performance evaluation: development of techniques for measuring, evaluating, and improving employee performance.
   - Time management: ability to prioritize and delegate activities as appropriate to maximize accomplishments within given time periods.
3. Operations management.
   - Marketing: skills useful for winning new business for the organization or preserving existing market shares.
   - Negotiating: skills for moderating personnel issues, representing the organization in external negotiations, or administering company policies.
   - Estimating and budgeting: skills needed to develop reasonable cost estimates for company activities and the assignment of adequate resources to operations.
   - Cash flow analysis: an appreciation for the time value of money, manipulations of equity and borrowed capitals, stable balance between revenues and expenditures, and maximization of returns on investments.
   - Decision analysis: ability to choose the direction of work by analyzing feasible alternatives.

A technical manager can develop these skills through formal college courses, seminars, workshops, short courses, professional conferences, or in-plant company training. Several companies appreciate the need for these skills and are willing to bear the cost of furnishing their employees with the means of acquiring the skills. Many companies have custom formal courses that they contract out to colleges to teach for their employees. This is a unique opportunity for technical professionals to acquire managerial skills needed to move up the company ladder.

Technical people have special needs. Some of these needs, unfortunately, are often not recognized by peers, superiors, or subordinates. Inexperienced managers are particularly prone to the mistake of not distinguishing between technical and nontechnical professional needs. To perform more effectively, a manager must be administratively adaptive. He or she must understand the unique expectations of technical professionals in terms of professional preservation, professional peers, work content, hierarchy of needs, and the technical competence or background of the managers.

Professional Preservation

Professional preservation refers to the desire of a technical professional to preserve his or her identification with a particular job function. In many situations, the preservation is not possible due to a lack of labor to fill specific job slots. It is common to find people trained in one technical field holding assignments in other fields. An incompatible job function can easily become the basis for insubordination, egotism, and rebellious attitudes. Although it is realized that in any job environment there will sometimes be the need to work outside one's profession, every effort should be made to match the surrogate profession as close as possible. This is primarily the responsibility of the human resources manager.

After a personnel team has been selected in the best possible manner, a critical study of the job assignments should be made. Even between two dissimilar professions, there may be specific job functions that are compatible. These should be identified and used in the process of personnel assignment. In fact, the mapping of job functions needed for an operation can serve as the basis for selecting a project team. To preserve the professional background of technical workers their individualism must be understood. In most technical training programs, the professional is taught how to operate in the following manner:

1. Make decisions based on the assumption of certainty of information.
2. Develop abstract models to study the problem being addressed.
3. Work on tasks or assignments individually.
4. Quantify outcomes.
5. Pay attention to exacting details.
6. Think autonomously.
7. Generate creative insights to problems.
8. Analyze systems operatability rather than profitability.

However, in the business environment, not all of these characteristics are desirable or even possible. For example, many business decisions are made with incomplete data. In many situations, it is unprofitable to expend the time and effort to seek "perfect" data. As another example, many operating procedures are guided by company policies rather than creative choices of employees. An effective manager should be able to spot cases in which technical employees may be given room to practice their professional training. The job design should be such that employees can address problems in a manner compatible with their professional training.

Professional Peers

In addition to having professionally compatible job functions, technical people like to have other project team members to whom they can relate technically. A project team consisting of members from diversely unrelated technical fields can be a source of miscommunication, imposition, or introversion. The lack of a professional associate on the same project can cause a technical person to exhibit one or more of the following attitudes:

1. Withdraw into a shell, contributing little to the project by holding back ideas that he or she feels the other project members cannot appreciate.
2. Exhibit technical snobbery, holding the impression that only he or she has the know-how for certain problems.
3. Straddle the fence on critical issues, developing no strong conviction for project decisions.

Providing an avenue for a technical "buddy system" to operate in an organization can be instrumental in ensuring congeniality of personnel teams and in facilitating the eventual success of project endeavors. The manager in conjunction with the selection committee (if one is used) must carefully consider the mix of the personnel team on a given project. If it is not possible or desirable to have more than one person from the same technical area on the project, an effort should be made to provide as good a mix as possible. It is undesirable to have several people from the same department taking issues against the views of a lone project member from a rival department. Whether it is realized or not, whether it is admitted or not, there is a keen sense of rivalry among technical fields. Even within the same field, there are subtle rivalries between specific functions. It is important not to let these differences carry over to a project environment.

Work Content

With the advent of new technology, the elements of a project task will need to be designed to take advantage of new developments. Technical professionals have a sense of achievement relative to their expected job functions. They will not be satisfied with mundane project requirements. They look forward to challenging technical assignments that will bring forth their technical competence. They prefer to claim contribution mostly where technical contribution can be identified. The project manager will need to ensure that the technical people on a project have assignments for which their background is really needed. It is counterproductive to select a technical professional for a project mainly on the basis of personality. An objective selection and appropriate assignment of tasks will alleviate potential motivational problems that could develop later in the project.

Hierarchy of Needs

Recalling Maslow's hierarchy of needs, the needs of a technical professional should be more critically analyzed. Being professionals, technical people are more likely to be higher up in the needs hierarchy. Most of their basic necessities for a good life would already have been met. Their prevailing needs will tend to involve self-esteem and self-actualization. As a result, by serving on a project team, a technical professional may have expectations that cannot usually be quantified in monetary terms. This is in contrast to nontechnical people who may look forward to overtime pay or other monetary gains that may result from being on the project. Technical professionals will generally look forward to one or several of the following opportunities.

1. *Professional Growth and Advancement.* Professional growth is a primary pursuit of most technical people. For example, computer professionals must be frequently exposed to challenging situations that introduce new technology developments and enable them to keep abreast of their field. Even occasional drifts from the field may lead to the fear of not keeping up and being left behind. The project environment must be reassuring to the technical people in regard to the opportunities for professional growth in terms of developing new skills and abilities.

2. *Technical Freedom.* Technical freedom, to the extent permissible within the organization, is essential for the full use of a technical background. Technical professionals expect to have the liberty of determining how best the objective of their assignments can be accomplished. One should never impose a work method on a technical professional by with the assurance that "this is the way it has always been done and will continue to be done." If the worker's creative input to the project effort is not needed, then there is no need having him or her on the team in the first place.

3. *Respect for Personal Qualities.* Technical people have profound personal feelings despite the mechanical or abstract nature of their job functions. They will expect to be respected for their personal qualities. In spite of frequently operating in professional isolation, they do engage in interpersonal activities. They want their nontechnical views and ideas to be recognized and evaluated based on merit. They do not want to be viewed as "all technical." An appreciation for their personal qualities gives them the sense of belonging and helps them to become productive members of a project team.

4. *Respect for Professional Qualification.* A professional qualification usually takes several years to achieve and is not likely to be compromised by any technical professional. Technical professionals cherish the attention they receive due to their technical background. They expect certain preferential treatments. They like to make meaningful contributions to the decision process. They take approval of their technical approaches for granted. They believe they are on a project because they are qualified to be there. The project manager should recognize these situations and avoid the bias of viewing the technical person as being self-conceited.

5. *Increased Recognition.* Increased recognition is expected as a by-product of a project effort. Technical professionals, consciously or subconsciously, view their participation in a project as a means of satisfying one of their higher level needs. They expect to be praised for the success of their efforts. They look forward to being invited for subsequent technical endeavors. They savor hearing the importance of their contributions being related to their peers. Without going to the extreme, the project manager can ensure the realization of these needs through careful comments.

6. *New and Rewarding Professional Relationship.* New and rewarding professional relationships can serve as a bonus for a project effort. Most technical developments result from joint efforts of people that share closely allied interests. Professional allies are most easily found through project groups. True technical professionals will expect to meet new people with whom they can exchange views, ideas, and information later on. The project atmosphere should, as a result, be designed to be conducive to professional interactions.

Quality of Leadership

The professional background of the project leader should be such that he or she commands the respect of technical subordinates. The leader must be reasonably conversant with the base technologies involved in the project. He or she must be able to converse intelligently on the terminologies of the project topic and be able to convey the project ideas to upper management. This serves to give the leader technical credibility. If technical credibility is lacking, the technical professionals on the project might view him or her as an ineffective leader. They will consider it impossible to serve under a manager to whom they cannot relate technically.

In addition to technical credibility, the manager must also possess administrative credibility. There are routine administrative matters that are needed to ensure a smooth progress for the project. Technical professionals will prefer to have those administrative issues successfully resolved by the project leader so that they can concentrate their efforts on the technical aspects. The essential elements of managing a group of technical professionals involve identifying the unique characteristics and needs of the group and then developing the means of satisfying those unique needs.

Recognizing the peculiar characteristics of technical professionals is one of the first steps in simplifying project management functions. The nature of manufacturing and automation projects calls for the involvement of technical human resources. Every manager must appreciate the fact that the cooperation or the lack of cooperation from technical professionals can have a significant effect on the overall management process. The success of a project can be enhanced or impeded by the management style utilized.

Work Simplification

Work simplification is the systematic investigation and analysis of planned and existing work systems and methods for the purpose of developing easier, quicker, less fatiguing, and more economic ways of generating high quality goods and services. Work simplification facilitates the content of workers, which invariably leads to better performance. Consideration must be given to improving the product or service, raw materials and supplies, the sequence of operations, tools, workplace, equipment, and hand and body motions. Work simplification analysis helps in defining, analyzing, and documenting work methods.

38.6 CONCLUSION

Resource management is a major function in any organization. In a project management environment, goals are achieved through the strategic allocation of resources to tasks. Several analytical and graphical tools are available for activity planning, scheduling, and control. But similar tools are not available for resource management. There is a need for simple tools for resource allocation planning, scheduling, tracking, and control. This chapter has presented a collection of tools suitable for resource management applications. A simple extension of the CPM diagram, referred to as critical resource diagram (CRD), is presented for resource management purposes. The extension is a graphical tool that brings the advantages of the CPM diagram to resource scheduling. Conventional operations research techniques can be combined with the graphical tools presented to facilitate better job distribution, better information to avoid resource conflicts, and more equitable assignment of resources.

BIBLIOGRAPHY

1. A.B. BADIRU, *Communication, Cooperation, Coordination: The Triple C of Project Management,* paper presented at the IIE Spring Conference, Washington, D.C., May 1987.
2. A.B. BADIRU, *Project Management Tools for Engineering and Management Professionals,* Industrial Engineering & Management Press, Norcross, Ga., 1991.
3. B.M. WOODWORTH and C.T. WILLIE, "A Heuristic Algorithm for Resource Leveling in Multi-Project, Multi-Resource Scheduling," *Decision Sci.* **6,** 525–540 (1975).
4. M.H. KOENIG, "Management Guide to Resource Scheduling," *J. Sys. Manage.* **29,** 24–29 (Jan. 1978).

5. A.B. BADIRU, "Activity-Resource Assignments Using Critical Resource Diagramming," *Project Manage. J.,* in press.

6. A.B. BADIRU "Critical Resource Diagram: A New Tool for Resource Management," *Ind. Eng.* **24**(10), 58–59, 65 (1992).

7. R.H. MOHRING, "Minimizing Costs of Resource Requirements in Project Networks Subject to Fixed Completion Time," *Operat. Res.* **32**(1), 89–120 (1984).

8. C.B. CHAPMAN, "The Optimal Allocation of Resources to a Variable Timetable," *Operat. Res. Q.* **21**(1), 81–90 (1970).

BUSINESS ASPECTS OF DESIGN AND MANUFACTURING

CHAPTER 39

Acquisition of Automation

AMIYA K. CHAKRAVARTY
Tulane University

BIJAYANANDA NAIK
University of South Dakota

39.1 INTRODUCTION

During the past two decades, unprecedented changes have occurred in the competitive environment of the discrete part manufacturing industry. Major changes include the globalization of markets and demand for high quality and greater variety of products at low prices (1, 2). These changes have led to stiff international competition among manufacturers. Manufacturers are increasingly focusing on product quality and variety and on rapid new product introduction. They are also concentrating on fast and reliable delivery schedules and reduction of waste and excess inventory. They are discovering, however, that traditional manufacturing technologies such as mass production systems are far from adequate in meeting the new competitive challenges. This situation has spurred on a number of innovative developments in technology that, individually, impact certain subsets of manufacturing characteristics important for achieving competitiveness.

The focus of developments in new manufacturing technology seems to be computer-based programmable automation (2). Programmable automation allows the maintenance of economies of scope without sacrificing economies of scale to a great extent. It also allows the achievement of high quality and delivery reliability. Manufacturers in Japan and Germany and other industrialized European countries have made significant progress in adopting flexible automation in response to the competitive pressures of today's manufacturing environment. However, adoption of flexible automation by manufacturers in the United States has been lagging behind (3). This lack of adequate capital investment in new technology has been cited as one of the major causes of the declining productivity and competitiveness of U.S. manufacturers in the global market (4).

Although it appears that U.S. manufacturers need to make significant capital investments in new manufacturing technology, success is not guaranteed without proper guidelines for its acquisition and implementation. Unfortunately, such guidelines are not readily available. Recognition of the importance of appropriate techniques for the acquisition and implementation of new manufacturing technology has motivated increased research in this area during the past decade. Many research studies dealing with the justification and acquisition of new manufacturing technology have been reported. In this chapter, some of the major developments in the field are presented for the benefit of practitioners as well as the academia.

Major issues and problems relevant to the topic of the acquisition of new manufacturing technology are discussed. These issues and problems relate to the process of the acquisition of automation in an organization, technology choice, and the justification of acquisition. A number of techniques for the evaluation and acquisition of new manufacturing technology also are discussed. This treatment, however, may not be exhaustive, as it reflects the authors' perception of the major developments to date in this area. Major issues in implementing new technology and a generic plan for successful acquisition of automation are presented.

39.2 ISSUES AND PROBLEMS

Automation and Organization

Organizational characteristics and environment significantly influence the process of acquiring and implementing flexible automation (5). How aggressively an organization will pursue the acquisition of flexible automation and how successful it will be in acquiring and implementing such automation depend a great deal on organizational factors such as objectives, work environment, management attitude, and culture. A manufacturing firm may consider acquiring flexible automation under four major scenarios (6):

- The capabilities of the new technology may be more attractive than those of the old technology, and the firm may simply want to replace old equipment.
- New technology may seem to provide a solution to existing problems such as inefficiency, low capacity, poor quality, delay in delivery schedules, and waste due to excessive error rates. The firm may wish to increase quickly its production efficiency, production capacity and delivery efficiency to alleviate its operational problems.
- There may be increased competition from other manufacturers who have already adopted such new technology. The acquiring firm may desire to close the technological gap with the leaders in the field.
- New technology may be a vital link in competitive strategy involving plant modernization, new product introduction, and achievement of higher flexibility and quality. The objective of the firm may be to become a leader in the industry.

Replacement of old equipment with new technology is often achieved by acquiring stand-alone NC equipment. Although such technology is less risky, realization of their full technological potential may be hampered by an unsupportive manufacturing environment. Quick-and-easy solutions to nagging problems, even with advanced technology, may often result in failure and disappointments due to a lack of planning and inadequate infrastructural support. Firms that seek to close the technology gap with the leaders, often find themselves lagging behind perpetually in spite of expensive technology upgrading. They may not be able to use new manufacturing technology as an effective competitive weapon. Thus the only scenario that offers an organization the opportunity to harness the full power and advantages of new manufacturing technology involves a proactive approach.

With the exception of the replacement project, the other three scenarios are highly influenced by the work environment in an organization, a factor often ignored by the acquiring firm. The chances of success in a highly bureaucratic environment with tight departmental barriers may be slim, because cooperation and coordination between departments may be difficult to obtain readily (7). On the other hand, a loose and informal environment may not foster the development of the type of in-house technological expertise that is vital for the successful acquisition of new manufacturing technology. A matrix organization with cross-functional cooperation is more likely to facilitate the acquisition and implementation of new technology. An organizational work environment in which information technology is appreciated and used extensively throughout the organization fosters a higher level of learning among the employees. It also results in a sizable pool of engineers, technicians, and in-house experts in information technology. Availability of this valuable human resource within an organization is a major factor for acquiring and implementing new manufacturing technology successfully. Another contributing factor is a work environment in which the management and employees are outward looking and customer oriented.

In addition to the work environment, the management attitude toward new manufacturing technology is a crucial factor in determining whether a firm will acquire such technology. In general, a visionary, proactive management that is appreciative of new technology and is willing to take risks greatly enhances the chances for successful acquisition and implementation of new manufacturing technology. Furthermore, the management should have established an excellent rapport with employees and should be alert to customer needs at all times. A favorable management attitude encourages champions of new technology who initiate acquisition of such technology. They carry the burden of harnessing organizational cooperation and support behind such projects. A favorable management attitude also results in sponsors who provide the top-management commitment essential for the success of large-scale and risky projects. In general, an organizational culture of cooperation between departments; cooperation between management and employees; a desire to learn and to train; and progressive views toward customers, competition, and technology are keys to the successful acquisition and implementation of new manufacturing technology.

Technology Choice

There are several aspects of technology choice that must be considered carefully in acquiring automation. The first issue is whether the firm should acquire dedicated automation or flexible automation. Acquisition of dedicated automation is justified based on stable demand patterns at high volume. Justifying such automation does not pose serious problems if current and projected demand patterns indicate sustained high demand. Therefore, most of the issues related to technology choice discussed in this section are related to flexible automation.

Selection of the appropriate manufacturing technology usually involves choosing from processing technologies, material handling systems, tool handling systems, quality assurance systems, and levels of system integration. Processing technology options may include operator-assisted stand-alone NC machines and integrated Computer Numerically Controlled (CNC) machines. Major options available in material handling system include operator-assisted systems, computer controlled systems, and systems integrated with automated storage and retrieval systems (AS–RS). Manual changeover of tool magazines, automated tool delivery systems, and computer-controlled tool migration systems integrated with a central tool crib are some of the options available for tool handling. Quality assurance options normally include manual off-line inspection, automated on-line inspection, and integrated on-line inspection with feedback for automated process control. System integration options range from stand-alone NC machines to fully computer-integrated manufacturing (CIM).

In general, these new manufacturing systems can be broadly classified into four categories: stand-alone systems, flexible manufacturing cells (FMCs) or traditional flexible manufacturing systems (FMSs), linked islands, and fully integrated systems. Stand-alone systems are either operator-assisted NC machines or CNC machines. FMCs include several CNC machines integrated with a material handling system, a tool handling system and a quality inspection system. One or more robots may be used for material and tool handling. Vision systems may be installed for automated quality inspection. Traditional FMSs comprise several NC, CNC, or Direct Numerically Controlled (DNC) machines with a material handling system that may use rail car, carts with towlines, conveyors, or automated guided vehicles (AGVs). The next higher level of integration involves linked islands of automation where several FMCs and/or traditional FMSs may be linked together through a more extensive material handling system for part transfer between islands of automation. At this level, a factory floor is usually linked with a computer-aided design–computer-aided manufacturing (CAD–CAM) system, an AS–RS, and perhaps an MRP system. The highest level of integration is achieved by CIM, which links the manufacturing function to the marketing and sales function and also to the finance and accounting function. At this level of integration, related operational activities such as order processing, purchasing, manufacturing, shipping, invoicing, and payment handling are closely coupled. Furthermore, there is a close link between operational, tactical and strategic decision making in the CIM environment.

One of the major issues in technology choice involves the match between the competitive strategy of the firm and the proposed manufacturing system. The desired system attributes must be capable of satisfying the market requirements dictated by the adopted competitive strategy. For example, if a firm adopts the strategy of price reduction, a highly flexible integrated system may be inappropriate. Another major issue involves the match between the scope of the proposed system and the capabilities of the organization, both in terms of its preparedness to acquire technology and its ability to cope with change that must occur after installation. For example, a stand-alone system may generate only local and minimal organizational impacts, whereas a CIM may have an impact throughout the organization more comprehensively. Thus the risks in acquiring highly integrated systems such as CIM may vastly surpass the corresponding risks in with stand-alone systems or cells. Such risks can be minimized through a suitable phased implementation plan. This approach provides an opportunity for gradual organizational learning and coping with the changes slowly. However, in many cases, all major components of the entire manufacturing system must be in place to provide the intended synergy and benefits. Phased implementation may be a wrong strategy in such cases.

Justification of Acquisition

Perhaps the most difficult issue that must be dealt with when acquiring flexible automation is its economic justification. Traditionally, every organization requires that any form of capital expenditure be justified for its economic return to the firm. Normally, the economic justification of a capital purchase is carried out by using one of several financial techniques, for example, by calculating the payback period or the net present value. The discounted cashflow techniques routinely used in traditional investment analysis are difficult to use in the case of new technology. There are many issues that contribute to this problem.

First, it is extremely difficult to identify clearly all the costs and benefits associated with new technology. In addition to the cost of the equipment itself, there are many other ancillary costs that are not immediately obvious. Examples of such costs include those of interfacing the new system with the existing system and those of rearranging and modifying the existing plant layout for accommodating the new system. In addition, specialized personnel may have to be hired, and the cost of hiring and paying these employees can be substantial. Because such people may be in short supply, the turnover may be higher than usual, resulting in higher than anticipated costs. Often it is necessary for training the existing workforce before the new systems can be made operational. The training time is clearly time out from regular production time and may constitute a significant hidden cost, particularly if the training period is prolonged. Other costs may be related to the unavailability of adequate software for operational control of the flexible automation. Costs related to the lack of adequate planning, cooperation between departments or divisions, and faulty operational procedures in connection with the adoption of new technology are not easily recognized and accounted for during the process of economic justification. In addition, there is considerable difficulty in identifying all relevant benefits of new manufacturing technology. For example, benefits that accrue as a result of synergy between different components of the system, and benefits that are intangible and strategic in nature are hard to identify.

Once identified, the costs and benefits must be quantified in terms of dollar amounts for the purpose of generating the cashflow stream. Quantifying intangible and strategic benefits in terms of dollar amounts is a major hurdle for which there is no easy solution. The effective life of the flexible automation is generally much longer than traditional manufacturing systems. Predicting cashflows accurately much longer into the future is often an impossible task. An associated problem is figuring out the correct depreciation for the equipment. This problem is further complicated by the fact that newer manufacturing systems with better capabilities continue to become available at progressively lower costs as technology advances at a rapid pace.

One of the major problems that renders the discounted cashflow approach inappropriate for justifying new manufacturing technology is the lack of a universally accepted method for determining the appropriate hurdle rate. In the past, managers in the United States have set high hurdle rates arbitrarily to account for the high perceived risk in acquiring new technology. This has resulted in a slow diffusion of new manufacturing technology. In addition to the financial risks, the acquisition of new manufacturing technology involves organizational risks that should perhaps be considered. However, there is no universally accepted procedure for incorporating such risks in the value of the hurdle rate. In addition, there are other issues that complicate the task of justifying new manufacturing technology. One such issue is the use of outdated accounting and costing principles used to evaluate performance of new manufacturing technology. Other related issues include the continued practice of analyzing system performance based on the practice of optimizing subsystems (which results in overall system suboptimization), short-term profit orientation of management, and inappropriate capital budgeting in manufacturing organizations.

39.3 EVALUATION OF AUTOMATION ALTERNATIVES

A Taxonomy of Evaluation Approaches

During the last decade, a large number of studies have suggested a variety of approaches and techniques for evaluating different automation alternatives and justifying their acquisition. These approaches can be broadly classified into four categories: economic approaches, analytic approaches, strategic approaches, and integrated approaches. Economic approaches include traditional financial techniques such as payback period, return on investment (ROI, internal rate of return (IRR) and net present value (NPV), for evaluation of investment alternatives (8, 9).

These techniques are most suitable for acquiring stand-alone systems for replacement projects. For systems at higher levels of integration, quantifying intangible benefits accurately becomes a major problem. In such cases, the NPV method can be applied, using a modified discount rate or hurdle rate (10).

A number of analytical approaches have been suggested for evaluating and justifying flexible automation at a higher level of integration, because economic approaches alone were considered to be inadequate to deal with these systems. These approaches include scoring models (11), the analytic hierarchy process (AHP) (12, 13), goal programming (14), and risk analysis (6). The scoring model, goal programming, and risk analysis approaches comprise a group of techniques called portfolio analysis for evaluating a group of competing projects (6). Scoring models assign factor scores that relate to technology assessment, equipment evaluation, capacity elasticity, cost–budget analysis, and adjusted net present value. These factor scores are then linearly combined to obtain the total project score used for evaluating and justifying alternative projects.

Using the AHP for evaluating complex systems involves extensive recording of pairwise comparison scores, which may be based on subjective judgment as well as numerical data. The technique of risk analysis involves simulation studies of probabilistic factors such as costs, capacities, benefits, and labor negotiations and the presentation of the results using graphs and statistical charts. Cumulative distribution functions showing the likelihood of achieving various objectives such as ROI and market share are prepared for different projects. These cumulative functions are then compared to identify superior projects.

The category of strategic techniques (9) includes four different approaches that are suitable for evaluating projects that are difficult to deal with using quantitative techniques. Such approaches emphasize different system attributes such as technical importance, business objective, competitive advantage, and research and development. Justification of a project based on technical importance assumes that a desired goal cannot be attained unless this project is executed first. With the business objectives approach, a project is undertaken only if it is essential to meet the desired goals of the business enterprise. The same philosophy applies to the method of competitive advantage. Projects essential to attain competitive advantage are acquired. The method of research and development (R&D) involves treating a proposal as an R&D investment. The proposal is accepted if it holds sufficient strategic potential, although it may be highly risky. The strategic approaches are extremely judgmental in nature and lack adequate structure to be used with sufficient confidence.

There are a number of approaches for evaluating and justifying acquisition of new manufacturing technology that attempt to combine strategic and financial techniques. The multiattribute utility model (15) was used to combine financial and nonfinancial factors in justifying new technology. Another approach involves detailed scenario planning and multilevel screening of alternative proposals of new technology (16). Integrated approaches involving a combination of simulation and discounted cashflow (DCF) (17), and combination of the AHP and DCF (18) have also been suggested. An approach integrating the concept of manufacturing system value and AHP has been presented (19). Other approaches based on multiple-objective decision models have recently been published (20, 21). A hierarchical approach involving strategic, operational, and financial evaluations for acquiring new manufacturing technology is available (22).

Although a large number of approaches and methods have been suggested in the literature, the appropriateness of using any of these approaches may have to be judged carefully for a given situation. Five approaches are discussed that can be used selectively for the acquisition of new manufacturing technology at different levels of integration ranging from stand-alone NC machines to fully CIM.

The Net Present Value Approach

The net present value (NPV) method for evaluating flexible automation described in this section is based on the approach suggested by Kulatilaka (10). It is essentially a variation of the traditional capital budgeting technique used widely. However, the procedure incorporates several modifications to account for the special characteristics of advanced automation technology. It involves calculation of the NPV of several alternative automation proposals and examination of their strategic implications to select the best proposal for acquisition. Calculation of the NPV involves identification of the costs and benefits and determination of the discount rate considering the risk of the project.

Identification of the Costs and Benefits

Identification of the costs and benefits involves estimating the initial acquisition costs, the periodic operational costs and benefits, and taxes and other purely financial effects. These costs and benefits are then expressed as a stream of incremental cashflows over the period of effective life of the flexible automation under consideration. Initial acquisition costs include the purchase and installation costs of new equipment and the costs of interfacing the new equipment with the existing equipment. It also includes any costs associated with modifying or expanding the existing plant layout to accommodate the new equipment. Furthermore, the costs of product redesign for manufacturability by the new equipment, if relevant, must be included in the initial costs. Initial costs also include the costs of hiring new skilled employees and training other employees required for the operation of the new equipment.

Periodic costs and benefits must be translated into corresponding cash outflows and inflows for each period. Operational costs include costs of additional skilled labor required to operate the new equipment. Periodic costs also include incremental energy costs for the new equipment as well as incremental utility costs for the plant as a result of installing and operating the new equipment. Incremental costs of new services and resources, such as computer services, and of scheduled and emergency maintenance as a result of acquiring new, advanced automation must be included.

Benefits obtained from using advanced automation that must be translated into cashflows include increased revenue as a result of higher output. Higher output may result from a high level of capital use as a consequence of increased efficiency and reduced changeover time. Benefits also accrue as a result of a lower capacity requirement and reduced inventory requirement. Material cost savings accrue due to the reduced number of rejects and waste. Additional benefits accrue due to the higher quality production in the form of lower customer returns, lower warranty costs, and lower repairs and recalls. Benefits also accrue from a stronger market position, resulting from higher quality products. Reasonable estimates of benefits must be made to account for some of the "intangible" savings listed above. The current cost accounting system needs to be modified markedly to enable it to capture the above savings. Furthermore, it is important to consider the role of taxes. Tax effects include taxes on net change in operating cashflows, investment tax credits, and depreciation tax shields. In some cases, the tax effects alone may make an automation proposal feasible.

Example of Incremental Expected Cashflows

A set of incremental (compared with the existing system) cashflows for a proposed automation project are presented here as an example. Situation-specific items of cashflow not listed in this set should be included when applicable.

I. Initial Acquisition Costs Incurred at Time 0
   A. Purchase of equipment $PE(0)$
   B. Installation and interfacing, $IF(0)$
   C. Plant layout modification, $PL(0)$
   D. Product redesign, $PR(0)$
   E. Hiring of skilled workers, $SK(0)$
   F. Retraining of workers, $RT(0)$

II. Periodic Costs and Benefits for Each Period, t
   A. Skilled labor costs, $SL(t)$
   B. Energy costs for the machines, $EM(t)$
   C. Extra plant utility costs, $PU(t)$
   D. Additional services costs, $AS(t)$
   E. Maintenance costs, $MC(t)$
   F. Revenue from increased output, $RO(t)$
   G. Savings from reduced labor, $RL(t)$
   H. Savings from reduced inventory, $RI(t)$
   I. Material savings, $MS(t)$
   J. Savings in warranty related costs, $WR(t)$
   K. Revenue from better market position, $MP(t)$

III. Initial and Periodic Tax Effects
   A. Investment tax credit, $IT(0)$
   B. Depreciation tax shields, $DT(t)$
   C. Taxes on net change in operating cashflows, $TC(t)$

Estimation of the Discount Rate

Once the cashflow stream in relation to costs, benefits, and tax effects is estimated, the next step is to estimate the discount rate to be applied to it. The discount rate should take into account the risks associated with the acquisition of new technology. Because advanced technology requires substantial capital investment, resulting in the substitution of capital for labor, the operating leverage (the ratio of the fixed costs to the total costs) of the project is increased. The change in operating leverage of the project requires a modification of the project's systematic risk (β) of the revenues used in the capital asset pricing model (CAPM). Furthermore, adjustments to the value of β may be made to account for the vulnerability of the firm's cost and revenue to factor price changes and supply shortages. The value of β may also be adjusted to account for the change in systematic risk of the firm due to product mix variations, volume variability, and the adaptability of the new technology to such variability (10). Except for the adjustment to β due to change in operating leverage, specific guidelines are not available for other adjustments. These other adjustments are subjective, and their accuracy depends on the knowledge and experience of the decision maker.

Once the value of β is determined, the value of the discount rate can be computed using the risk-free rate of return and the market rate of return (10). The β of the project adjusted for the change in the operating leverage of the project is given by Equation 1. The discount rate r for the project is calculated by applying the CAPM and using Equation 2.

$$\beta_{project} = \beta_{revenue}\left[1 + \frac{PV(\text{fixed costs})}{PV(\text{total costs})}\right] \tag{1}$$

$$r_{project} = r_{risk\ free} + \beta_{project}[r_{market} - r_{risk\ free}] \tag{2}$$

The risk-free rate of return is normally given by the rate of return of a risk-free asset such as a U.S. government Treasury Bill. The market rate of return is given by the rate of return of a weighted average index of traded assets such as an index of the New York Stock Exchange. The use of CAPM in capital budgeting is a commonly used approach that can be obtained from any standard textbook of corporate finance (23).

Computation of the NPV of a Project

The NPV of a project is computed using the estimated stream of cashflows and the estimated discount rate described earlier. Cash inflows are assigned a positive sign and cash outflows are assigned a negative sign. The calculation of NPV is shown in Equation 3. In this equation, N represents the number of periods in the planning horizon and D represents the depreciable life of the equipment.

$$
\begin{aligned}
NPV = &-[PE(0) + IF(0) + PL(0) + PR(0) + SK(0) + RT(0)] + IT(0) \\
&- \sum_{t=1}^{N} \frac{[SL(t) + EM(t) + PU(t) + AS(t) + MC(t)]}{[1 + r]^t} \\
&+ \sum_{t=1}^{N} \frac{[RO(t) + RL(t) + RI(t) + MS(t) + WR(t) + MP(t) + TC(t)]}{[1 + r]^t} \\
&+ \sum_{t=1}^{D} \frac{DT(t)}{[1 + r]^t}
\end{aligned} \tag{3}
$$

The incremental cash inflow is represented as a positive quantity, and cash outflow is represented as a negative quantity. The project with the highest positive NPV is considered the best. If no project is found with a positive NPV, then other alternatives must be explored.

Timing of Investment

The timing of investment is an important decision once the alternative proposals are compared on the basis of the NPV. In most cases, the logical choice would be to invest immediately in the project with the highest positive NPV (10). However, because of the possibility of the lowering of cost and technological enhancement of capital equipment in future, it may be desirable to delay investment in the project for a short period. There are no definite rules for finding the optimal timing of investment. However, for irreversible investments under certain scenarios, the optimal strategy appears to be to postpone the investment until the present value of benefits from a project exceeds twice the present value of the costs (24).

The Analytic Hierarchy Process Approach

The AHP is a multicriteria decision-making tool developed by Satty (25). The AHP method has been used by Arbel and Seidmann (12) and Wabalickis (13) for performance evaluation and justification of flexible manufacturing systems. The method provides a structure to a decision process that uses the subjective judgment of the decision maker.

The objective of the decision process, the criteria and the subcriteria, and the alternative proposals of automation are structured into a hierarchy. The highest level of the hierarchy, designated level I, contains the objective of the decision process, namely selecting the best manufacturing automation alternative. The criteria that are relevant in achieving the objective are identified, and these criteria form the elements at level II, the next lower level. Each of the criteria at level II may be determined by a number of subcriteria, which are identified by the decision maker. The subcriteria for all the elements at level II constitute the elements at level III. If necessary, each of the subcriteria at level III can be further decomposed into subsubcriteria that are placed in the next lower level (level IV). There are no restrictions placed on the number of levels that can be included in a hierarchy. For tractability of exposition, however, we restrict the discussion to a hierarchy of three levels with several criteria and subcriteria at levels II and III, respectively. The last level of the hierarchy constitutes the alternative proposals under evaluation. For our problem scenario, the alternative proposals will be placed at level IV.

Once a hierarchy is constructed by the decision maker, the AHP method involves the determination of the local priorities for each alternative at level IV corresponding to each subcriterion at level III. Next, the local priority of each subcriterion at level III is determined considering the corresponding criterion at level II. Finally, the local priority of each criterion at level II is determined considering the objective at level I. The last step of the AHP method involves the determination of the desirability index for each alternative proposal using the appropriate local priorities at all levels of the hierarchy. The value of the desirability index is used to rank order the proposals. The proposal with the highest index is considered the best and is recommended for acquisition.

The local priority of an alternative at level IV corresponding to a given subcriterion at level III indicates the degree of preference for the alternative considering that criterion. The local priority of a subcriterion at level III corresponding to a criterion at level II indicates the importance of the subcriterion relative to other relevant subcriterion. Similarly, the local priority of a criterion indicates the relative importance of the criterion in achieving the objective. The local priorities of a set of alternatives, subcriteria, or criteria are determined following a procedure that involves pairwise comparison among the elements of the set and assigning an integer to represent relative importance. The procedures for computing the local priorities is illustrated in the following section. The procedure for determining the desirability index is presented in a later section.

Computation of Local Priorities

Let A, B, C, and D be four criteria at level II. To determine the local priorities of A, B, C, and D, a pairwise comparison matrix is constructed, as shown in Table 39.1. The diagonal elements in the matrix are each equal to 1, because each criterion is compared with itself. The elements

TABLE 39.1. Pairwise Comparison Matrix

	A	B	C	D
A	1	1/4	1/5	1/2
B	4	1	1/5	1/2
C	5	5	1	3
D	2	2	1/3	1

TABLE 39.2.   Comparison Scale

1	Equal importance
3	Moderate importance
5	Strong importance
7	Very strong importance
9	Absolute importance
2, 4, 6, 8	Intermediate values

below the diagonal are reciprocals of those above the diagonal and vice versa. In assigning values to these elements, the decision maker first considers those elements that can be given an integer value using the scale shown in Table 39.2. The values of the other elements are then obtained as reciprocals of the integer values already assigned. For example, the element in row C, column A is assigned the number 5, which indicates that criterion C is considered to have a strong importance relative to criterion A. Consequently, the element in row A, column C is assigned a value 1/5. The decision maker must make $n(n - 1)/2$ pairwise comparisons to assign all the elements in the comparison matrix, where n is the number of criteria being compared. Once all the elements of the comparison matrix are assigned, the priority vector w is determined by solving Equation 4.

$$Aw = \lambda_{max} w \qquad (4)$$

The term λ_{max} represents the largest eigenvalue of the comparison matrix A, and w represents the corresponding eigenvector. The consistency of the subjective judgment in assigning the elements of the comparison matrix is then checked by calculating a consistency index, CI, given by Equation 5.

$$CI = \frac{\lambda_{max} - n}{n - 1} \qquad (5)$$

The value of n is equal to the number of rows or columns in the comparison matrix. The value of CI is used to calculate the value of a consistency ratio, CR, given by Equation 6.

$$CR = \frac{CI}{RI} \qquad (6)$$

The values of the random index, RI, were obtained by Satty (25) for different values of n and are presented in Table 39.3. A CR value of less than 0.1 is considered acceptable.

Values of CR greater than 0.1 suggest that the entries in the comparison matrix should be revised, and calculations should be repeated. If the consistency ratio is acceptable, then the normalized values of the elements in the priority vector are used as the local priorities for the criteria at level II. Local priorities for the subcriteria and the alternative proposals are determined following a similar procedure.

Determination of the Desirability Index

To illustrate the procedure for determining the desirability index, let X, Y, and Z be considered as a set of three alternative proposals of automation. Let $A1$, $A2$, and $A3$ be the subcriteria at level III corresponding to the criterion A at level II. Similarly, let $B1$ and $B2$ be the subcriteria corresponding to the criterion B; let $C1$, $C2$, and $C3$ be the subcriteria corresponding to the criterion C; and let $D1$ and $D2$ be the subcriteria corresponding to the criterion D. Let p_A, p_B, p_C, and p_D be the local priorities for criteria A, B, C, and D. Similarly, let p_{A1}, p_{A2}, p_{A3}, p_{B1}, p_{B2}, p_{C1},

TABLE 39.3.   Values of RI for Different Values of n

n	1	2	3	4	5	6	7	8	9	10
RI	0.00	0.00	0.58	0.90	1.12	1.24	1.32	1.41	1.45	1.49

p_{C2}, p_{C3}, p_{D1}, and p_{D2} be the local priorities for the subcriteria $A1$, $A2$, $A3$, $B1$, $B2$, $C1$, $C2$, $C3$, $D1$, and $D2$, respectively. Let p_{XA1}, P_{YA1}, and p_{ZA1} be the local priorities of the three alternative proposals of automation, X, Y, and Z, respectively, corresponding to the subcriterion $A1$. The notations for the local priorities for X, Y, and Z corresponding to other subcriteria can be defined in a similar manner. Then the desirability index of the alternative X can be given by Equation 7.

$$DI_X = p_A \cdot p_{A1} \cdot p_{XA1} + p_A \cdot p_{A2} \cdot p_{XA2} + p_A \cdot p_{A3} \cdot p_{XA3}$$
$$+ p_B \cdot p_{B1} \cdot p_{XB1} + p_B \cdot p_{B2} \cdot p_{XB2}$$
$$+ p_C \cdot p_{C1} \cdot p_{XC1} + p_C \cdot p_{C2} \cdot p_{XC2} + p_C \cdot p_{C3} \cdot p_{XC3}$$
$$+ p_D \cdot p_{D1} \cdot p_{XD1} + p_D \cdot p_{D2} \cdot p_{XD2} \tag{7}$$

The equations for the desirability indices DI_Y and DI_Z for the alternative proposals Y and Z can be written as Equation 7, replacing X with Y and Z, respectively, in the notations of the appropriate terms in the equation.

The Scoring Model Approach

A scoring model was proposed by Nelson (11) for the evaluation and selection of flexible manufacturing systems. The model suggested by him determines the overall project score as a linear combination of five component scores. The project score s_i for the ith project or alternative is given by Equation 8.

$$s_i = t_i^* + e_i^* + c_i^* + b_i^* + v_i^* \tag{8}$$

In this equation, t_i^* represents the technology assessment score, e_i^* represents the equipment evaluation score, c_i^* represents the workload elasticity of capacity score, b_i^* represents the cost-to-budget ratio score, and v_i^* represents the net present value score for the alternative proposal i. The possible values of the overall project score s_i vary from 0 to 5. The automation projects are then rank ordered, using the values of the project score s_i. The component scores are discussed briefly in the following paragraphs. The reader may consult the original paper by Nelson (11) for greater details of the procedure for the determination of these component scores.

The Technology Assessment Score

The absolute value of the technology assessment score t_i for a project i is the sum of three component scores as given by Equation 9. The emphasis score t_{i1} measures the availability of

$$t_i = t_{i1} + t_{i2} + t_{i3} \tag{9}$$

the proposed technology, ranging from whether available in adequate supply to whether currently unavailable. The status score t_{i2} measures the current status of the proposed technology, whether it is obsolete, declining, stable, or emerging. The impact score t_{i3} measures the benefits directly attributable to the proposed technology. The normalized technology assessment score is given by Equation 10. In this equation, t_{max} is the maximum value of t_i among the alternative projects.

$$t_i^* = \frac{t_i}{t_{max}} \tag{10}$$

The Equipment Evaluation Score

The purpose of the equipment evaluation score is to determine the need for modernization from an examination of existing equipment. The absolute equipment evaluation score e_i consists of three component scores and is given by Equation 11.

$$e_i = e_{i1} + e_{i2} + e_{i3} \tag{11}$$

The condition score e_{i1} for the project i is the weighted average condition score for all equipment in the shop associated with the project i. Similarly, the age score e_{i2} is calculated as the weighted average age score for all equipment. The suitability score e_{i3} is the weighted average sum of two 0–1 variables, namely the current function evaluation and the intended function evaluation. The current function evaluation score indicates how suitable the existing equipment is for the currently performed functions. Similarly, the intended function evaluation score indicates whether the equipment is suitable for intended future functions. The normalized equipment evaluation score is given by Equation 12. In this equation, e_{max} is the maximum value of the equipment evaluation score among all projects.

$$e_i^* = \frac{e_i}{e_{max}} \tag{12}$$

The Workload Elasticity of Capacity Score

The workload elasticity of capacity measures the sensitivity of planned changes in capacity to estimated changes in the workload as a result of capacity addition. The absolute value of the score c_i is given by Equation 13. In this equation, c_{oi} represents the average of projected out-

$$c_i^* = \frac{|c_i - 1.0|_{min}}{|c_i - 1.0|} \tag{13}$$

year capacity (labor hours) for the shop associated with alternative i, and c_{ri} represents the capacity of the shop during the reference year. Similarly, w_{oi} represents the average of the projected out-year workload (labor hours) for shop i, and w_{ri} represents the workload during the reference year. The relative workload elasticity score c_i^* is given by Equation 14. The numerator in Equation 14 represents the minimum of the absolute values of the difference between c_i and 1.0.

$$c_i = \frac{(\bar{c}_{oi} - c_{ri})/c_{ri}}{(\bar{w}_{oi} - w_{ri})/w_{ri}} \tag{14}$$

The Cost-to-Budget Ratio Score

The cost-to-budget ratio score measures the degree to which total estimated project investment is within the limit of the estimated funding. The absolute value of this ratio b_i is given by Equation 15. In this equation, a_i represents the total investment for the project i, and $E(f_i)$

$$b_i = \frac{a_i}{E(f_i)} \tag{15}$$

represents the expected value of the funding level for the project i. The normalized cost-to-budget ratio score is given by Equation 16. In this equation, b_{min} is the minimum absolute ratio score among the i projects.

$$b_i^* = \frac{1}{b_i/b_{min}} = \frac{b_{min}}{b_i} \tag{16}$$

The Net Present Value Score

The net present value score measures the financial merit of the project i. The absolute value of the net present value score is given by Equation 17. In this equation p_i represents the probability of technical success of project i, R_{it} represents the expected cashflow for project i in time period t, and k is the risk-adjusted cost of capital. The normalized net present value score is given by

$$v_i = p_i \left[\sum_{t=0}^{n} \left(\frac{\bar{R}_{it}}{(1 + k)^t} \right) \right] \tag{17}$$

Equation 18. In this equation, v_{max} represents the maximum value of the absolute NPV scores among the i projects.

$$v_i^* = \frac{v_i}{v_{max}} \tag{18}$$

The Manufacturing System Value Approach

The manufacturing system value model proposed by Troxler (26) uses the concept of a deterministic system value as the theoretical foundation for a comprehensive analysis and evaluation of manufacturing technology. The structure of the model allows systematic identification and comparison of a multitude of decision factors involved in evaluating alternative proposals of new manufacturing technology. The system value is represented by a vector function that takes into account the values of important tangible and intangible attributes in characterizing the manufacturing system (19). The general form of the model is given by Equation 19.

$$MSV = f[A_1, A_2, \ldots, A_p] \tag{19}$$

In equation 19, MSV represents the manufacturing system value, and it is a function of p attributes represented by the elements $A_1 \ldots A_p$. A given attribute A_k in turn is a function of a number of determining factors and is given by Equation 20.

$$A_k(t_1, t_2, \ldots, t_{m_k}) = \sum_{i=1}^{m_k} f_i(t_i) \tag{20}$$

In this equation, t_i represents the determining factor, and f_i represents a function that determines the contribution of the determining factor t_i to attribute A_k. To deal with the complexity of manufacturing systems, it may be necessary to further disaggregate each determining factor t_i into a set of indicators v_j as shown in Equation 21. In this equation, q_j represents a function that weights or scales each v_j.

$$t_i(v_1, v_2, \ldots, v_n) = \sum_{j=1}^{n} q_j(v_j) \tag{21}$$

The manufacturing system value model given by Equation 19 can be modified to reflect the subjective utility of the decision maker by introducing an attribute weighting factor α as shown in Equations 22 and 23.

$$MSV = [\alpha_1 A_1, \alpha_2 A_2, \ldots, \alpha_p A_p] \tag{22}$$

$$\sum_{k=1}^{p} \alpha_k = 1 \tag{23}$$

Troxler (26) defined a set of four attributes: suitability measure, capability measure, performance measure, and productivity measure. Each of these measures in turn is determined by a distinct set of determining factors. For example, the suitability measure is determined by factors such as investment, growth, technology position, market position, employee relations, workforce composition, organization structure, and operations management. Troxler (26) also defined indicators that are used to characterize the determining factors. For example, the technology position is characterized by indicators such as modernization, integration, and innovation.

Similarly, the productivity measure attribute is determined by factors such as economic infrastructure, customer response, and environmental influence. Economic infrastructure, in turn, is characterized by indicators such as capital equipment, start up, engineering, materials, material conversion, facilities, energy, administrative support, conversion support, and product support. Detailed descriptions and discussions of all the attributes, determining factors, and indicators can be found in Troxler (26).

To obtain a measure for the system value of a manufacturing system, it is necessary that a hierarchical aggregation procedure be followed to combine the indicators into determining factors, the determining factors into attributes, and the attributes into the system value. Different approaches available for multiple-factor decision making such as weighted scoring models and the AHP can be used to achieve such aggregation. Details of applying the AHP technique to determine system value can be found in Troxler and Blank (19).

The Hierarchical Evaluation Approach

Naik and Chakravarty (22) proposed a framework for a new manufacturing technology acquisition by which the evaluation and justification procedure is divided into three hierarchical levels: strategic, operational, and financial (Table 39.4). The objective of strategic evaluation is to narrow down a wide range of available options and select the best category of manufacturing system consisting of appropriate system modules. An appropriate level of integration of these modules is determined as well so as to satisfy desired manufacturing capabilities. At the level of operational evaluation, a number of different system configurations are identified, corresponding to the category selected during strategic evaluation. These candidate system configurations are evaluated considering their operational characteristics, and the list of candidate systems is reduced to two or three systems. These systems are evaluated with respect to their financial merits, and the best system is selected. If this system satisfies the ROI requirements of the firm then the evaluation process is terminated. Otherwise, the evaluation process is repeated starting with the strategic level.

Strategic Evaluation

Strategic evaluation of new manufacturing technology involves several sequential decisions. First, a decision maker decides an appropriate competitive strategy for the firm. Then he or she proceeds to select an appropriate manufacturing technology and a system configuration that will support the chosen competitive strategy best. A set of organizational factors is considered to determine whether the selected technology and the system configuration can be acquired and implemented by the firm without any serious problem. If any serious problem is recognized, the

TABLE 39.4. Hierarchical Evaluation Framework

Strategic Evaluation

1. Choosing the competitive strategy
2. Specifying the market requirements
3. Specifying the manufacturing system requirements
4. Choosing the manufacturing system configuration
5. Identifying the organizational constraints
6. Iterative strategic evaluation if needed

Operational Evaluation

1. Obtaining technical and operational data and vendor information for alternative proposals of systems
2. Comparing and rank ordering of the alternative proposals
3. Conducting simulation studies of the top three or four alternatives for different operational scenarios
4. Selecting two or three systems for financial evaluation

Financial Evaluation

1. Generating cashflow streams
2. Selecting an appropriate discount rate
3. Performing discounted cashflow analysis of the top two or three alternative proposals
4. Selecting the best proposal that meets the ROI requirements

process of strategic evaluation must be repeated with a reconsideration of the selected competitive strategy.

To operationalize the process of strategic evaluation, an approach similar to the relationship matrix in the quality function deployment (QFD) method (27) was employed. Following this approach, a set of competitive strategies are linked with a set of market requirements that support the strategies. The competitive strategies considered include four pure strategies—innovation, customization, product proliferation, and price reduction—and three combination strategies—innovation and product proliferation, innovation and customization, and product proliferation and price reduction. The dimensions of market requirements considered include low price, better product features and design, better product performance and reliability, wide product line, custom-made products, rapid new product introduction, and variable order size. The link between the competitive strategies and the market requirements is established by specifying an importance rating for each market requirement and competitive strategy combination in a two-dimensional matrix (Table 39.5). Similarly, the dimensions of market requirements are linked with a set of manufacturing system attributes by specifying importance ratings of each system attribute for each dimension of market requirements in another two-dimensional matrix. The system attributes considered are high throughput rate, low direct labor, low work-in-process (WIP) inventory, high machine use, low setup time, low material movement time, low tool change time, machining flexibility, routing flexibility, ability to handle large number of product designs, variable batch size, high machining precision, efficient quality inspection, quick design modification, easy storage and retrieval of designs, quick process plan modification, efficient storage and retrieval of materials, efficient information processing and transmission. Five levels of importance ratings are used: very high, high, medium, low, and not relevant. The importance ratings in the two matrices described above are then combined to derive importance ratings of the system attributes corresponding to the competitive strategies. These importance ratings indicate which of the possible attributes a manufacturing system should possess to support a particular competitive strategy. The details of the procedure to combine the two matrices are available (22).

The next step involves the appropriate choice of manufacturing technology to support the selected competitive strategy. To achieve this objective, Naik and Chakravarty (22) identified five groups of technology strategies: processing system strategy, material handling system (MHS) strategy, tool handling system (THS) strategy, quality assurance strategy, and system integration strategy. A processing system strategy may be selected from one of the four alternatives available: automated transfer lines, operator-assisted NC machines, traditional multimachine FMSs, and integrated CNC machines. The MHS strategy selected may be an operator-assisted MHS, a computer-controlled MHS, or an integrated MHS with AS–RS. Tool handling strategies include manual changeover of tools, automated tool delivery to machines, and computer-controlled tool migration. Alternatives available for quality assurance strategy include manual off-line inspection, automated on-line inspection, and a system with feedback for automatic process control. A system integration strategy may involve an integrated machining system with multiple FMC, integration of the machining system with CAD–CAM, and integration with CAD–CAM and Material Requirements Planning II (MRP II). A two-dimensional matrix is created in which importance ratings for each of the technology alternatives are specified corresponding to the system attributes. These importance ratings indicate the appropriateness of choosing a particular technology to achieve a particular system attribute. These ratings are then combined with the ratings of system attributes corresponding to competitive strategies. The details of the combining technique are available (22). As a result of this operation, suitability scores are obtained for each technology choice corresponding to different competitive strategies. The scores are obtained as numbers and arranged in a two-dimensional table. For a given competitive strategy, technology choices with the highest scores for a processing system, material handling system, tool handling system, quality inspection system, and the level of system integration can be made using this table.

With the technology choices made, an appropriate system configuration type can be selected. The possible choices are automated transfer line; operator-controlled NC machine cell; traditional FMS with multiple machines; traditional FMS integrated with CAD–CAM; flexible manufacturing cell (FMC); multiple FMC integrated to form an FMS; multiple FMC with CAD–CAM; FMS with CAD–CAM and automatic process control; and fully integrated FMS with CAD–CAM, AS–RS, and MRP II. Feasibility of the selected configuration type is checked against a number of organizational factors. Importance ratings of these organizational factors are specified in a two-dimensional matrix corresponding to each system configuration type discussed above. The organizational factors considered are availability of high investment

TABLE 39.5. Importance Ratings of Market Requirements for Different Competitive Strategies[a]

Competitive Strategies	Market Requirements								
	Low Price	Product Features	Product Performance	Short Delivery Time	Delivery Reliability	Wide Product Line	Custom-made Products	Rapid New Product Introduction	Variable Order Size
Innovation	N	V	H	N	N	N	N	V	N
Customization	N	N	H	N	M	N	V	N	N
Product proliferation	L	M	H	M	H	V	N	N	V
Price reduction	V	M	M	L	M	N	N	N	N
Innovation and product proliferation	L	H	H	L	L	H	H	H	H
Innovation and customization	N	H	H	N	H	N	N	H	N
Product proliferation and price reduction	H	M	H	M	H	H	N	N	M

[a] V = very high, H = high, M = medium, L = low, and N = not relevant.

817

capital, availability of skilled workers and resources, past experience with relevant automation, positive attitude by management toward automation, positive attitude by workers and union toward automation, minimal barrier to integration of functional areas, minimal barrier to reorganization of existing manufacturing functions, low risk to delay in project implementation, and possibility of adopting phased implementation. A firm must satisfy the organizational factors with very high or high importance ratings corresponding to a system configuration type to acquire it. If the firm is unable to satisfy the organizational factors, the strategic evaluation procedure should be repeated with a reexamination of its competitive strategy. If the iterative process of strategic evaluation reveals that the organizational constraints are too severe for the firm to implement any meaningful new technology, the firm must first formulate a plan of action to address those constraints before considering new technology acquisition. Once the technology choices are made and the configuration type selected, the next step is to perform the operational evaluation.

Operational Evaluation

The purpose of the operational evaluation is to select two or three alternative proposals quoted by vendors of manufacturing systems. These proposed systems must be of the type and scope determined during strategic evaluation. The request for quotes (RFQ) provides this information to the vendors. The vendor-quoted systems are then compared based on system-related technical and performance data supplied by the vendors. Other information used in this comparison include project cost, implementation duration, and vendor reputation. Techniques that can be used at this stage for comparing the candidate systems include multicriteria decision-making methods. For example, the AHP is such a technique (25), and it has been used by a number of researchers (12, 13). The vendor-quoted systems can be rank ordered using the AHP, and the top three or four proposals can be picked for further evaluation.

The next step in the operational evaluation procedure involves conducting simulation studies of the top three or four systems selected using the AHP. The simulation studies are conducted to obtain detailed information about the performance of the systems to verify the claims made by the vendors. These studies are also needed to obtain operational data to generate realistic cashflows over several postimplementation periods. The simulation studies can be conducted for varying operational scenarios that consider such aspects as variation in demand, production control policies, inventory control policies, maintenance policies, and fixtures and tool changeover policies. The results of the simulation studies are examined and systems with poor performance are eliminated from further consideration. The final list is reduced to two or three top-ranking systems as a result of the operational evaluation. These systems are then subjected to financial evaluation.

Financial Evaluation

Financial evaluation of the systems in the final list of candidates is performed using discounted cashflow techniques discussed earlier. Discounted cashflow techniques such as the NPV method are well developed and are widely used by business organizations. Accurate cashflow streams are generated for each candidate system for different operational scenarios. The value of the discount rate is determined using techniques suggested by Kulatilaka (10) and discussed above. The values of the ROI for the candidate systems are determined and compared with the ROI desired by the firm. The system that shows the highest ROI and satisfies the minimum requirement is selected for implementation. If no system can be found that meets the minimum desired ROI, the management must explore other reasons that might override the ROI requirement. A final decision is then made at the top management level.

The hierarchical evaluation process eliminates the need for quantifying the strategic benefits and considering them along with financial benefits at the same level. Thus most of the difficulties encountered in applying the traditional justification techniques to acquiring new technology are avoided. If the three-level evaluation procedure culminates in a recommendation of a new manufacturing technology for implementation, no separate justification analysis needs to be done. If the evaluation procedure does not result in a recommendation of any system, the acquisition of new technology is regarded to be not justified at the moment.

To implement a selected new technology successfully, it is necessary to formulate an appropriate implementation plan. Such a plan must necessarily be tailored to the firm and its automation needs. However, a generic implementation process, based on the work of Meredith (28) is outlined in the next section to elucidate the major steps involved.

39.4 IMPLEMENTATION OF AUTOMATION

Implementation Barriers

Implementation of an automation project presents a number of problems and barriers even after it is justified through a careful evaluation process as discussed in the previous sections. Major problems encountered in implementing automation based on new technology include inadequacy of internal skills, difficulty of implementing computerized systems, multiplicity of implementation paths, possibility of limiting or enhancing synergy, possibility of incremental skill building, and need for different support infrastructure (28). Implementing new technology requires both technical and managerial education and experience with such technology, which is usually not available in many organizations. New technology involves implementing computerized manufacturing systems. Installing such computer systems is a difficult task due to many interfaces with different subsystems of the organization. The problems are compounded further as a result of multiplicity of implementation paths that can be adopted. For example, one possible path may involve starting with NC machines, adding robots for MHS, and then integrating with CAD–CAM to build an FMS. Another possibility may be to build islands of automation, and then link them with a network of AGVs, AS–RS, and possibly MRP II (29).

In implementing new technology, the level of synergy that can be achieved may depend on the choice and timing of installing different components of the system. For example, installing one type of technology or system in an early stage may limit an organization's options at a later stage. Similarly, appropriate choice of technology or systems at an early stage may significantly enhance benefits at a later stage. A related issue, therefore, is whether phased implementation and incremental skill building are preferable to putting the entire system in place in a single phase. The former approach allows moving slowly and learning from experience as you proceed with the different phases of implementation. It lowers the risk of total failure of a highly capital intensive project. On the other hand, there is a possibility that the intended benefits of a system will not be achieved unless all the components are in place and are working properly. Last, the implementation of new technology requires radically different support infrastructure in many areas such as computing, information systems, maintenance, quality assurance, purchasing, inventory management, sales and marketing, and customer service.

The Implementation Plan

Meredith (28) presented a generic implementation process that consists of four basic stages: strategic planning, project planning, installation, and integration. During the strategic planning stage, the firm formulates its strategic business plan, which requires an evaluation of the strengths and weaknesses of the firm and a consideration of the opportunities and threats facing the firm. Once the business plan is formulated, a manufacturing plan and, subsequently, a technology plan must be derived to support the business plan. Many of the activities involved in the formulation of the manufacturing plan and the technology plan do not appear to be as extensive as those required during the strategic evaluation level of the framework suggested by Naik and Chakravarty (22). In addition, according to Beatty (30), an automation project needs to have a "champion" for it to be successful. A champion is selected for the automation project at this stage. Ideally, a champion should be a line manager rather than a staff person, and the person should be invested with sufficient authority to see that the project is completed successfully (28).

The project planning stage involves organizing cross-functional project teams, analyzing task elements, specifying responsibilities, planning project information systems, preparing project budgets, and setting project milestones, and working out the detailed schedules. During the installation stage project resources, including human resources, are acquired. The resources are allocated to project task elements and the individuals responsible for the tasks. Education and training of personnel are initiated at this stage. Monitoring of the project is initiated and continued throughout the implementation period. The final stage of the implementation process involves integration of the newly acquired technology and automation into the ongoing manufacturing activities of the firm. A major task in this phase is the "debugging" of the system, which involves many activities designed to make the system work as intended. At the planned completion time of the project, a preliminary evaluation and audit of the project is performed. The percentage of the project completed, and the benefits and costs encountered are documented. The "bugs" encountered, their sources, and the steps taken to remove them are also documented. Following the preliminary audit, any remaining problems with the system are detected and solved. After an elapsed time of approximately twice the planned implementation time, a more thorough evaluation and audit are performed. Details of the experience with the current project are documented for guidance in future projects.

39.5 SUMMARY AND CONCLUSIONS

Acquisition of automation is a topic that continues to attract increasing attention from practitioners and researchers alike. The advent of new manufacturing technology has made the decision of acquiring automation extremely risky and difficult. In this chapter, major issues and problems related to the acquisition and implementation of advanced manufacturing automation have been discussed. These issues include the question of organizational preparedness to acquire new technology, choosing new technology, and justifying the acquisition of new technology. A number of techniques have been presented and discussed. These techniques include the NPV approach, the AHP approach, the scoring model approach, the manufacturing system value approach, and the hierarchical evaluation approach. It is hoped that the material presented in this chapter will provide the necessary guidelines to practitioners contemplating acquisition of new manufacturing technology. It will also serve as a reference for researchers in the field.

BIBLIOGRAPHY

1. J.D. GOLDHAR and M. JELINEK, "Computer Integrated Flexible Manufacturing: Organizational, Economic, and Strategic Implications," *Interfaces* **15**, 94–105 (May–June 1985).
2. R.H. HAYES and R. JAIKUMAR, "Requirements for Successful Implementation of New Manufacturing Technology," *J. Eng. Technol. Manage.* **7**, 169–175 (1991).
3. B. CARLSSON, "Management of Flexible Manufacturing—An International Comparison," *Omega Int. J. Manage. Sci.* **20**(1), 11–22 (1992).
4. R.H. HAYES and S.C. WHEELRIGHT, *Restoring Our Competitive Edge—Competing Through Manufacturing,* John Wiley & Sons, Inc., New York, 1984.
5. K. RAMAMURTHY and W.R. KING, "Computer Integrated Manufacturing: An Exploratory Study of Key Organizational Barriers," *OMEGA Int. J. Manage. Sci.* **20**(4), 475–491 (1992).
6. J.R. MEREDITH and M.M. HILL, "Justifying New Manufacturing Systems: A Managerial Approach," *Sloan Manage. Rev.* **28**(4), 49–61 (Summer 1987).
7. A.M. SÁNCHEZ, "Advanced Manufacturing Technologies: An Integrated Model of Diffusion," *Int. J. Operat. Product. Manage.* **11**(9), 48–63 (1991).
8. R.S. KAPLAN, "Must CIM Be Justified by Faith Alone?" *Harvard Bus. Rev.* **64**, 87–95 (Mar.–Apr. 1986).
9. J.R. MEREDITH and N.C. SURESH, "Justification Techniques for Advanced Manufacturing Technologies," *Int. J. Product. Res.* **24**(5), 1043–1057 (1986).
10. N. KULATILAKA, "Financial, Economic, and Strategic Issues Concerning the Decision to Invest in Advanced Automation," *Int. J. Product. Res.* **22**(6), 949–968 (1984).
11. C.A. NELSON, "A Scoring Model for Flexible Manufacturing Systems Project Selection," *Eur. J. Operat. Res.* **24**, 346–359 (1986).
12. A. ARBEL and A. SEIDMANN, "Performance Evaluation of Flexible Manufacturing Systems," *IEEE Trans. Sys. Man Cybernet.* **SMC-14**(4), 606–617 (1984).
13. R.N. WABALICKIS, "Justification of FMS with the Analytic Hierarchy Process," *J. Manufact. Sys.* **7**(3), 175–182 (1988).
14. C.H. FINE and R.M. FREUND, "Economic Analysis of Product-Flexible Manufacturing Systems Investment Decisions" in K.E. Stecke and R. Suri, eds., *Proceedings of the Second ORSA/TIMS Conference on Flexible Manufacturing Systems,* Elsevier Science Publishers, Amsterdam, 1986.
15. J.E. SLOGGY, "How to Justify the Cost of an FMS," *Tooling Product.* **50**, 72–75 (1984).

16. S.E. GARRETT, "Strategy First: A Case in FMS Justification" in K.E. Stecke and R. Suri, eds., *Proceedings of the Second ORSA/TIMS Conference on Flexible Manufacturing Systems,* Elsevier Science Publishers, Amsterdam, 1986.

17. F.F. LEIMKUHLER, "Economic Analysis of Computer Integrated Manufacturing Systems" in U. Rembold and R. Dillman, eds., *Methods and Tools for Computer Integrated Manufacturing,* Springer-Verlag, New York, 1984.

18. V. SRINIVASAN and R.A. MILLEN, "Evaluating Flexible Manufacturing Systems as a Strategic Investment" in K.E. Stecke and R. Suri, eds., *Proceedings of the Second ORSA/ TIMS Conference on Flexible Manufacturing Systems,* Elsevier Science Publishers, Amsterdam, 1986.

19. J.W. TROXLER and L. BLANK, "A Comprehensive Methodology for Manufacturing System Evaluation and Comparison," *J. Manufact. Sys.* **8**(3), 175–183 (1989).

20. J.G. DEMMEL and R.G. ASKIN, "A Multiple-Objective Decision Model for the Evaluation of Advanced Manufacturing System Technologies," *J. Manufact. Sys.* **11**(3), 179–194 (1992).

21. N.C. SURESH and S. KAPARTHI, "Flexible Automation Investments: A Synthesis of Two Multi-Objective Modeling Approaches," *Comput. Ind. Eng.* **22**(3), 257–272 (1992).

22. B. NAIK and A.K. CHAKRAVARTY, "Strategic Acquisition of New Manufacturing Technology: A Review and Research Framework," *Int. J. Product. Res.* **30**(7), 1575–1601 (1992).

23. R. BREALY and R. MYERS, *Principles of Corporate Finance,* McGraw-Hill Book Co., Inc., New York, 1981.

24. R. MCDONALD and D. SIEGEL, *The Value of Waiting to Invest,* School of Management, Boston University, 1982, Working Paper WP 37/82.

25. T.L. SATTY, *The Analytic Hierarchy Process,* McGraw-Hill Book Co., Inc., New York, 1980.

26. J.W. TROXLER, *An Economic Analysis of Flexible Automation in Batch Manufacturing with Emphasis on Fabrication,* Ph.D. dissertation, Texas A&M University, College Station, 1987.

27. J.R. HAUSER and D. CLAUSING, "The House of Quality," *Harvard Bus. Rev.* **66,** 63–73 (May–June 1988).

28. J.R. MEREDITH, "Implementing the Automated Factory," *J. Manufact. Sys.* **6**(1), 1–13 (1987).

29. A.K. CHAKRAVARTY, "Dimensions of Manufacturing Automation," *Int. J. Product. Res.* **25**(9), 1339–1354 (1987).

30. C.A. BEATTY, "Implementing Advanced Manufacturing Technologies: Rules of the Road," *Sloan Manage. Rev.,* **33**(4), 49–60 (Summer 1992).

CHAPTER 40

Managing Advanced Manufacturing Technology

DONALD GERWIN
Carleton University

Technology represents practical knowledge by which some organizational activity's inputs are converted into outputs. It is built into hardware, codified procedures including computer programs, and/or informal routines stored in employees' memories. Advanced manufacturing technology (AMT) represents a computer-controlled interaction of hardware, software, and human elements that is at the same time highly automated and applicable to a variety of uses. This chapter concentrates on the use of AMT in discrete parts industries (where metals, other materials, and electronic components are fabricated and assembled) because the technology is currently having its greatest impact there.

AMT is used mainly in:

- Product and process design, e.g., computer-aided design (CAD) and computer-aided process planning (CAPP).
- Manufacturing planning and control, e.g., manufacturing resources planning and computerized preventive maintenance.
- The production process, in which the generic term computer-aided manufacturing (CAM) is used, e.g., computer numerical control (CNC) equipment, flexible manufacturing systems (FMS), computer-aided inspection, and automated guided vehicles.
- Integration, e.g., computer-integrated manufacturing (CIM), which brings together AMT used in the above areas under unified computer control using information technology.

Computer-integrated enterprise refers to attempts to extend the CIM concept to integration with distribution outlets, suppliers, and customers. More detailed classifications are available (1–3).

Why is it important to explore this new technology's managerial implications? AMT is still not widely deployed in the United States (3, 4), and the reasons may be more due to managerial factors than technical ones (5). Firms that do have the technology are not using it effectively, and managerial factors are more to blame than technical ones (6, 7). Yet because the technology is readily available in industrially advanced countries, competitive advantage goes to those firms that are most successful in selecting and using it (8). Japanese firms, e.g., compete through the effective management of technology rather than merely through the purchase of large amounts of leading-edge equipment (9).

Management of AMT involves three critical aspects. First, manufacturing strategy is covered, because many firms do not fully use AMT's capability for gaining competitive advantage. Other firms may expect much more from the technology than it can deliver. Second, organizational issues affecting individuals and work groups are treated. Although there are undoubtedly fewer employees in an AMT environment, their responsibility for these critical technological resources gives them considerable influence over performance. Third, the process of introducing AMT to a firm is discussed under the heading of innovation. The technology has significant impacts on most hierarchical levels and functions of a plant. We need to know the nature of the resulting problems and how to deal with them.

There is at least one precondition for consideration of AMT's managerial aspects. A company must first create a more efficient manufacturing process (10, 11). Managers and workers need to eliminate unnecessary operations so that they are not eventually automated. They should investigate whether continuing to use existing technology may create approximately the same results as purchasing the latest equipment. Only then is it reasonable to consider implementing advanced technology. A more comprehensive account of managing AMT is provided in ref. 12.

40.1 STRATEGIC CONSIDERATIONS

An industrially developed nation's future may reside in so-called flexible systems of production, technically advanced and skill intensive industries that create customized products (13, 14). The only way to respond to low cost standardized items from developing countries is to offer wide varieties of technologically superior products aimed at specific market niches. This requirement for increased flexibility applies to traditional smoke-stack industries as well as to completely new ones. AMT's potentially significant strategic implications derive mainly from its flexibility.

Three different types of generic strategies employ flexibility to cope with environmental uncertainties:

- Uncertainty adaption occurs when flexibility aids adjustments to environmental uncertainties such as changes in customers' product requirements or uncontrollable variations in the inputs to the production process (15, 16).
- Uncertainty redefinition involves proactively encouraging customers to rethink their market needs so that a company redefines an industry's competitive uncertainties to its own advantage (17). Through AMT it can meet the new needs better than its competitors; taking advantage of the potential for introducing new products faster is one example (18).
- Banking flexibility occurs when an enterprise invests in flexibility now to use proactively or adaptively in the future. AMT acts as a depository when some of its flexibility is held in reserve until a need or opportunity arises. One example is providing a flexible manufacturing system with a dimensional envelope greater than needed to produce current paths.

A fourth type of strategy diminishes the need for flexibility:

- Uncertainty reduction occurs when a company has various means for proactively decreasing environmental uncertainties such as establishing long-term contracts with customers and reducing in-process inventories to reveal machine problems.

Defining Flexibility

Flexibility is generally considered to be a multidimensional concept, but there is no rigorous method for identifying the relevant dimensions. A hierarchical approach identifies flexibilities at a certain level (e.g., an individual machine, manufacturing system, or plant) and uses them to help distinguish those at the next highest (19). At the machine level, for example, machine flexibility refers to the types of operations that can be performed without having difficulty in switching from one to the other. Machine flexibility is a prerequisite for process flexibility, the ability to produce a given set of part types at the system or cell level.

A multilevel approach, advocated here, identifies certain environmental uncertainties and associated strategic objectives to help in specifying flexibility dimensions (20). Each dimension, with minor exceptions, is meant to apply at different hierarchical levels. For example, mix flexibility, which refers to the variety of outputs produced, is relevant for the machine, system, or plant level. Each dimension is also considered to have a range and a time aspect (21). One manufacturing process is more flexible than another if it can handle a wider range of possibilities, say a greater range of volumes. The other process, however, may be more flexible in the sense it can attain a given possibility within its range faster than the first.

The multilevel approach has identified at least seven flexibility dimensions, all defined here in terms of the factory level. Uncertainty as to which products are acceptable to customers leads to the strategic objective of product diversity. A firm desires a broad product line or a number of related lines. With *mix flexibility* a capability to switch readily among currently produced products is built into the factory. The range aspect signifies the extent of product variety and the temporal aspect reflects the amount of time taken to switch from one product to another (setup time). A flexible manufacturing system with random processing performs well on both features. Mix flexibility's bottom-line benefits were illustrated by Kekre and Srinivasan (22) who found that a broader product line leads to higher profitability.

Mix flexibility's strategic significance lies in its being an alternative to focused manufacturing. A focused factory reduces costs by relying on the benefits of task specialization (9, 23). Narrowing the range of demands placed on a facility allows its technological and human resources to concentrate on a few key priorities. On the negative side are the increased risks of inefficiently using dedicated resources and of being inflexible to sudden dramatic changes in market conditions.

Through AMT and just-in-time production, a plant with mix flexibility can enjoy the benefits of product variety while limiting cost increases due to lack of specialization (18). Due to product variety there is less chance of inefficiently using resources and of being inflexible to the market. At the same time, the factory exhibits economies of scope; it can make a range of items at lower unit cost than separate focused plants, each producing a single item (24).

Uncertainty as to the length of product life cycles, especially when life cycles are shortening on average, fosters the strategic objective of product innovation. The manufacturing process needs *changeover flexibility*, an ability to substitute readily new products for existing ones. The range aspect indicates the variety of major design changes that can be accommodated; the temporal feature represents the portion of new product introduction time that occurs in manufacturing. Reductions in hard tooling in favor of computerized automation encourage this type of flexibility. Such an investment, however, may not be used if new developments in process technology make the flexible equipment obsolete before the first changeover is made (25).

Uncertainty as to which functions and features the market wants in a given product is associated with the strategic objective of responsiveness to customers' specifications. *Modification flexibility* allows a manufacturing process to implement minor design changes in a given product. CNC and robots, which typically require a modest amount of reprogramming and refixturing to handle minor design changes, provide this capability. Modification flexibility, however, reduces pressures to get designs right the first time, leading to unnecessary engineering change orders.

Uncertain swings in the amount of demand impact the strategic objective of maintaining or increasing market share. *Volume flexibility* permits increases or decreases in the aggregate production level. Organizing AMT into relatively autonomous cells or modules facilitates this dimension. An investment in excess capacity, empty floor space, and slack time in the production schedule may also be necessary.

Machine downtime is an uncertainty derived from equipment or quality problems. It is associated with the strategic need to provide on-time delivery. *Rerouting flexibility* compensates for breakdowns by changing the sequence of machines through which a product flows. In an FMS, a parts-routing program may automatically reroute parts if a breakdown occurs. Possessing this type of flexibility, however, may discourage efforts to reduce downtime.

Suppliers or a company's upstream activities are sources of uncertainty for the composition and dimensions of the material that manufacturing processes. These defects hamper attaining the strategic objective of product quality. *Material flexibility* represents the ability to handle unexpected variations through, for example, automated monitoring devices under computer control that back up workers' efforts. Yet this type of flexibility may reduce pressures on upstream activities to eliminate quality problems.

Suppose the types of environmental certainties faced by a factory change over time. A company needs strategic adaptability to adjust its objectives quickly. With *flexibility responsiveness*, a metadimension, the factory can readily change the types of the other six dimensions it possesses. A Japanese research program on manufacturing in the next century calls for factories to be able to transform themselves freely as changes in their flexibility needs take place (26).

While uncertainty is emphasized here as the motivator for flexibility, other factors also play a role. The discussion of economies of scope under mix flexibility indicated that cost reduction is a determinant. A firm may invest in changeover flexibility to deter the entry of new competitors into the market when consumers' tastes change (27). Given the current concern about changing market conditions and manufacturing process variability, uncertainty is more likely than the other factors to be the primary influence.

The Flexibility of AMT

There have been relatively few empirical inquiries into the flexibility of AMT in practice, undoubtedly due to problems in measuring the concept. Gerwin and Tarondeau (28) studied changes in the first six flexibility dimensions arising from the substitution of computer-aided manufacturing (CAM) technology for traditional equipment. Their results come from a pilot study of 7 American and French auto fabrication and assembly activities and from a mail survey of 81 fabrication activities in French manufacturing companies. In each study, changes in the range aspect of a flexibility dimension for a manufacturing activity were measured using a 5-point scale ranging from decreased a lot (-2) to increased a lot ($+2$). The average change in the dimension was determined by averaging the scores for each activity.

Comparison of the results for the average change in each dimension in the two studies indicated the following:

- There was surprisingly good agreement; the signs for a given dimension were the same in both sets of data, and the magnitudes were close except for volume and material flexibility.
- Introducing CAM into a manufacturing process will not improve flexibility per se; in both studies mix, modification, and volume increased, changeover stayed the same, and rerouting and material decreased.
- Perhaps CAM is not as significant a vehicle for delivering flexibility as is sometimes thought; the average changes were surprisingly small in magnitude. Virtually all were within a range of -1 to $+1$.

Can one identify factors that account for CAM's limitations with respect to flexibility? First, the technology has not evolved to the point at which it can compete with the flexibility of humans. Changes in flexibility resulting from the introduction of CAM are, therefore, influenced by the nature of the conventional process being replaced. Installing the technology in a plant with a labor-intensive manufacturing process is likely to produce mixed results, while putting it into a factory with a rigidly automated process is likely to improve the situation (28). One reason is that control system structures need to be based on distributed processing principles as opposed to traditional hierarchical schemes so that subsystems can exhibit sufficient autonomy (26, 29, 30).

Second, American and European managers, steeped in the values and assumptions of high volume standardized production, are not concerned enough about using the technology's strategic potential (6, 31, 32). They employ it too often to produce high outputs of a few parts rather than to take advantage of its flexibility. They use performance measures based on machine uptime and productivity rather than changing market needs. They rely on organizational structures designed for stable production rather than approaches meant for changing conditions.

The flexibility of computer integrated manufacturing facilities deserves special mention. Some of these facilities appear to be vulnerable to unexpected downward shifts in the demand for the products being produced. First, they possess changeover flexibility, but within a rather narrow dimensional envelope so that it is difficult to introduce new products. Second, there is a lack of volume flexibility; operations may be too integrated to shut down one segment without affecting others.

To counter a rigid reaction to an unanticipated drop in demand, it is useful initially to design the facility with the following suggestions in mind. It can be made the reserve producer of an additional product family, the bulk of whose manufacture is carried out elsewhere. The plant can be designed on a modular basis with decoupled subsystems and parallel activities to facilitate closing down segments. Consideration can be given to designing two small plants rather than a large one, because closing down the latter alternative shuts a firm out of the market.

Long-Run Strategic Implications

What impact does AMT have on the long-run path by which a factory develops over time? To explore this issue Abernathy and Utterback's (33, 34) model of factory evolution, which does not explicitly consider AMT, is discussed initially. Next, attention is turned to attempts to revise the model to consider the effects of AMT.

Abernathy and Utterback's model traces the impacts of environmental uncertainty on an entity they labeled the *productive unit,* an interdependent product–production technology combination. In their view, as uncertainty decreases, various characteristics of a productive unit evolve from fluid conditions to well-defined conditions. Thus initial diverse product variations give way eventually to a single standardized design with minor variants. The manufacturing process, which begins as a highly flexible job shop with general-purpose equipment, evolves into a dedicated automated continuous flow line with interdependent segments. Product and process become inextricably linked, preventing substantial improvements in either from taking place. An initial dependence on innovation, therefore, gives way to a subsequent emphasis on productivity. Evidence to support the model comes from studies of auto engine and assembly plants at Ford (33).

The model's evolutionary process is deterministic in the sense that a decline in uncertainty leads to one specific trajectory for a productive unit's development. There is little room for managerial discretion, i.e., the opportunity to select alternative paths. Eventually, the built-in rigidities of an industry's productive units make them vulnerable to externally developed product variations. The entire industry goes into decline.

Subsequent efforts to build on the model have whittled away at this deterministic orientation. In the product–process matrix of Hayes and Wheelwright (9), movement along the diagonal from the upper left to lower right is tantamount to the path from fluid to well-defined conditions in the Abernathy-Utterback (33, 34) model. The matrix, however, also takes into account that a firm's management may choose a development path off the diagonal by following a niche strategy. Productive units that stray from the diagonal are in a position to avoid eventual extinction if they can successfully exploit their niches. Gunn (1) proposed that firms possessing CIM will have more viable paths through the matrix than companies without the technology. Paths involving regions of the matrix far from the diagonal near the lower left and upper right corners will be available to the former but not the latter. One reason is that when software replaces hard tooling, production of standardized and more customized items can be handled by the same manufacturing process.

Gerwin and Tarondeau's (28) pilot study qualified Gunn's (1) assertions. The assembly activities they studied had been developing along the lines of the Abernathy-Utterback (33, 34) model toward more product standardization and process rigidity. They found that the introduction of CAM contributed to this continuing maturation by reducing innovative potential (decreasing an overall flexibility measure) and increasing productivity (raising an automation measure). Previously, engine fabrication had developed according to the model into an advanced state of product standardization and process rigidity. By simultaneously increasing innovating potential (overall flexibility) and productivity (automation), the introduction of CAM is leading to a renewal of this activity, i.e., movement away from the diagonal. In sum, CAM's ability to create alternatives to blindly following the diagonal toward extinction applies mainly for productive units in an advanced state of development.

Based on analysis of data from more than 1200 U.S. metal-working plants, Hicks (35) provided another way in which AMT can create alternatives to eventual extinction. Renewal can occur at the interfirm level as opposed to the intrafirm level. Older, lethargic firms make way for newer energetic ones even if an industry is mature. The latter are competitive because they use NC and CNC equipment from the start. The former can not renew themselves with advanced equipment due to their obsolescent physical conditions, lack of space, and outmoded managerial practices.

Capital Investment Decisions

When something as radical as AMT is initially considered by a firm, the investment decision has two aspects: determining whether the basic concept is worthwhile and evaluating a particular set of equipment (36). Concept evaluation is largely strategic in nature and directed at senior management. Equipment evaluation, directed at financial officers, is mainly economic in nature. Little research exists on the former, even though it may be the more significant aspect.

Traditional financial evaluation techniques are not usually appropriate for investigating a proposal for AMT equipment. Because AMT has strategic implications, it has significant intangible benefits (and costs) that are considered out of bounds (4, 37, 38). Researchers have put a good deal more emphasis on trying to identify and estimate the benefit side as opposed to the cost side. One exception is Beatty and Gordon's (39) enumeration of hidden costs in the installation of CAD–CAM systems.

One can categorize intangibles in the following manner:

- First-order intangibles are variables whose economic values are not quantifiable, but that can readily be stated in physical terms. One may conclude, for example, that an FMS will reduce lead times from 9 to 4 weeks without knowing the associated incremental profits.
- Second-order intangibles are nonpecuniary factors that can be identified but that are not measurable even in physical terms. Consider the experience gained by maintenance people in the intricacies of electronic repairs. Second-order variables are sometimes measured by constructing qualitative scales and seeking perceptual judgments.
- Third-order intangibles cannot even be identified in advance. It is not possible to know all the strategic changes that will ensue from purchase of an FMS.

At least three different methods are typically employed to deal with AMT's intangible benefits and costs (40). First, it is possible to modify discounted cash flow analysis to make it somewhat more compatible with the technology's needs (37, 41). Variables traditionally considered as first- or second-order intangibles are estimated in so far as possible and admitted into the analysis. Simulation can be employed to give a more explicit account of risk and the dynamic nature of decision making (42, 43).

The second approach, multiattribute decision analysis, considers first- and second-order intangibles as criteria. Capital alternatives are scored on each criterion using quantitative and qualitative scales, weights are assigned to each criterion, and either an attempt is made to translate into common units of value or a judgment is made.

Occasionally, a third approach is appropriate. AMT is evaluated on whether or not it meets some compelling strategic need or opportunity. Formal analysis plays a relatively minor role; the potentially significant nonmeasurable impacts of intangibles matter. Judgment based on experience is used in making decisions. The Peerless Saw Co. invested in a unique CAD–CAM system to meet a life-threatening crisis although the system did not pass financial tests (38).

To evaluate the applicability of the three approaches, first consider the demands made on an enterprise's information-processing capabilities. The first two make unreasonable impositions; to be accurate they require measures of all significant benefits and costs even though third-order intangibles may be more the rule than the exception. The strategic approach requires less heroic information processing but offers hardly any precision at all. Second, all three approaches are subject to advocacy bias, the tendency of individuals to bias information according to their predispositions. This is most obvious for the strategic method, but holds for the other two as well. Choosing which intangibles to consider, estimating financial impacts, and determining weights are opportunities for advancing preconceived notions.

There are no clear-cut guidelines for selecting an evaluation approach except at the extremes. For consideration of an individual robot or stand-alone machine, traditional discounted cashflow will undoubtedly suffice. If a large CIM project is being contemplated a strategic approach is needed (44). For the rest, one should consider using the first two approaches embedded in a gradual incremental policy in which each small purchase functions as an experiment, providing valuable information on how to proceed (45, 46).

40.2 ORGANIZATION

Organizing can be studied at different levels including the firm, department, work unit, and individual. Research conducted at broad levels, the firm for example, indicates that structural characteristics are determined more by environment, size, and strategy than by technology. If one considers narrow levels within the manufacturing function, technology assumes a more critical role in structuring choices, although other factors still enter (47).

The focus here is consequently on the work organization: individual roles and work unit structures (the jobs people perform and how those jobs are interrelated) used for AMT operators in manufacturing. Related issues covered include the nature of managerial, technical, and staff support functions. The objective is to indicate how these characteristics are changing as traditional modes of organization are giving away to team-based approaches. Emphasis is placed on sociotechnical systems analysis, the principal Western basis for team-based design (48), although a good deal of what is said here also applies to Japanese-style teams. For a discussion of differences between the two kinds of teams see refs. 49 and 50.

Situations Favoring Team-based Approaches

Cummings and Blumberg (51) indicated some conditions for using team-based organization in a factory. Teams are beneficial when market uncertainty, production process uncertainty, production process interdependence, and workers' social and growth needs are high. These characteristics undoubtedly apply more to integrated than to stand-alone AMT.

A team-based approach supports AMT's ability to adapt to market uncertainties. Customer lead time reduction, the temporal aspect of mix flexibility, is hampered by an organizational structure with a slow-moving hierarchical chain of decision making but is facilitated when workers are empowered to make decisions on the spot. Volume flexibility is enhanced when workers possess a variety of skills, some of which are used elsewhere when production is low (52).

Teams are instrumental in adapting to manufacturing process uncertainties. Due to the many interacting subsystems and components of integrated AMT, breakdowns are frequent and hard to correct. Bringing to bear the knowledge and experience of several people working together mitigates these problems. A good deal, for example, remains to be done on the spot when a machine breaks down to prevent damage and reroute production. A team's accumulated knowledge and experience also facilitates the elimination of process uncertainties.

In a computer-integrated system, in which operations on the shop floor are interdependent, decision making becomes more interactive. People must understand how their actions affect other parts of the system if they are to make effective choices. In this type of situation, teams provide a more effective way for individuals to coordinate their activities than traditional structures. As integration grows to cover more and more of the production process the need for teams becomes correspondingly greater.

Although the introduction of AMT undoubtedly reduces the number of workers in a plant, those who remain exert considerable influence over expensive equipment that is often making critical parts. Unless workers are motivated quality, productivity and lead times will suffer. Motivation in turn must be based on growth needs due to the requirement for individual learning, and on social needs due to the requirement for coordination.

Structural Characteristics of Teams

A fundamental characteristic is the aligning of the team with an identifiable set of bounded tasks to perform. In contrast, under traditional work organization each worker performs a specialized task representing a small component of a bounded set. The team's set of tasks, involving the transformation of inputs into outputs, has borders represented by places in the flow of work where breaks in interdependencies occur, due perhaps to the existence of in-process inventories. The workflow interactions are more intensive within such an area of the manufacturing process than between areas. A flexible manufacturing system or cell provides a good example. In many instances however boundaries are not clear-cut, i.e., a good deal of subjectivity exists in selecting them, especially where in-process inventories are being reduced.

A classic example is in the Volvo assembly plant in Kalmar, Sweden (53, 54). The work organization consists of around 30 separate teams each with 15 to 20 people and a supervisor for every 2 to 3 groups. Each team is responsible for assembly of a different subsystem of a car such as the safety equipment, interior fittings, or the electrical system. This work organization is made possible by elimination of the moving assembly line. A computerized control system guides the movements of more than 200 automated guided vehicles that transport car bodies to each team's work area and also serve as work platforms for performing assembly.

Pratt and Whitney, Canada's Halifax plant, has a computer integrated system for the planning, control, production, and material handling of aircraft engine components. The teams are organized around identifiable aspects of the transformation process, seven people per shift around each machining center, for example (55).

A second characteristic concerns self-management or self-regulation, i.e., the responsibilities teams assume for aspects of their own performance. In general, there is little say in establishing goals and varying degrees of influence on activities for achieving goals. Because advancing manufacturing technology does most of the traditional operating tasks, such as loading and unloading parts, cutting metal, or assembling components, teams concentrate on various types of maintenance, control, and planning activities. These activities, normally carried out by technical, staff, and supervisory personnel in traditional structures, require that information to make decisions is disseminated to the shop floor and in a timely manner.

In the Volvo Kalmar plant, assembly workers are involved in inspection, correcting defects, materials supply, training of new employees, and determining job assignments. Buffer inventories between teams allows workers to vary their production over the course of a day, but this opportunity has become increasingly circumscribed (53, 54). In Pratt and Whitney Canada the production teams' responsibilities include monitoring performance, inspecting production, performing routine maintenance, and alerting management to crises. They also control absenteeism, select new employees, conduct performance evaluations, dismiss unsatisfactory employees, and ensure interteam and intrateam coordination (55).

Wall et al. (56) compared operator control (operators deal directly with the majority of operating problems encountered) and specialist control (specialists such as engineers handle operating problems) for stand-alone CNC in one department of a large British electronics firm. The change from specialist to operator control reduced down time, especially for equipment with frequent problems, allowed specialists to carry out more work elsewhere in the plant, and led operators to greater intrinsic job satisfaction and less perceived work pressure.

Exploring the issue of who does parts programming helps identify some of the factors that determine the specific activities taken on by a team and the degree of worker influence in an activity. Technology is a key determinant. NC technology typically uses a computer located away from the shop floor, thus putting specialized programmers in the best position to do programming work. Semiskilled individuals are often used to attend the machines (57). CNC technology allows programmers or workers to do parts programming because the computer is located on the machine (58). Workers taking on this activity would of necessity be highly skilled.

To discover whether programmers or operators do parts programming for CNC technology Sorge et al. (58) studied 12 German and British firms. They found that as factory size and batch size increase, there is a tendency for programming to be taken away from operators. The larger the factory, the greater the chances of job specialization in the form of a separate programming group; and the larger the batch size, the less skilled the operators. National institutional and cultural factors modify these tendencies. In the UK, the system of education and vocational training separates technical (including programming) and operating apprenticeships. Operating and programming jobs are, therefore, differentiated in companies. In Germany there is less specialization due, in part, to a training system in which those who first achieve craft worker status may then aspire to become a technician. These craft workers are more likely to be involved in programming.

Political considerations within a firm may lead to outcomes inconsistent with these factors. Individuals who write parts programs exert a good deal of control over advanced manufacturing technology. Management may be unwilling to relinquish this power, especially when workers are organized. Kelley and Brooks (59) found that the chances were 1 in 18 that unionized blue-collar workers would be assigned primary responsibility for writing parts programs, but the corresponding chances for nonunionized people were 1 in 4.

Third, team-based organization involves multiskilling (i.e., each individual is able to perform a variety of tasks) and job rotation (i.e., workers do certain tasks for a given period of time and then exchange them). Multiskilling and job rotation, which normally do not exist under traditional work organization, allow the team to adapt to unanticipated events. They are the dominant organizational methods for complementing AMT's flexibility. Multiskilling and job rotation also create more challenging jobs. At Kalmar, the work cycle can be as long as 0.5 h, while in a traditional auto assembly plant it is often around 1 min. In practice, all individuals in a group do not have the maximum amount of skills at any one time; provision is made for variations in interests and abilities. Once more, there is wide variation in the lengths of time people perform the same jobs; durations of 1 or more yr are not unheard of.

In a survey of users of cellular manufacturing in the United States, Wemmerlov and Hyer (60) found that of 31 companies with manned cells, 27 had multiskilled operators. Once more, the extent to which workers moved among machines in a cell was on the high side, 3.6 on a scale running from little operator movement, 1, to a great deal of operator movement, 5.

Support for Self-regulating Teams

An early lesson from sociotechnical experiments with conventional manufacturing technology was that to support teams properly on the shop floor changes are needed in managerial, staff, and service activities. Their structures must be compatible with the design of the teams if performance at the work-flow level is to be effective. Because one source of incompatibility is that some of the duties of support people have been removed, new roles must be devised for these individuals. A good deal of supervisors' planning and control functions are assumed by teams or by the automated technology. To compensate, any of the following alternatives may be used:

• Supervisors are reduced in number, and their spans of control are widened; at Volvo's Kalmar plant there is one supervisor for every two to three work groups.
• Supervisors concentrate on providing the resources that teams require to function properly; they coordinate activities with other groups in the work flow, technical and staff units, and higher management, and also act as advisers or consultants to the teams.
• Supervisors take on responsibilities formally held by their managers and work together in supervisory teams, a fitting response to the complexity of integrated manufacturing (61).

Technical qualifications are obviously important for supervisors. They should contribute to the design and implementation of innovations to the manufacturing process. Preparations for Allen-Bradley's World Contactor Line, which integrates production planning and assembly under computer control, were influenced by the individual who had been selected to become supervisor (62). They must also know when a maintenance person is needed and what maintenance specialties to call. More surprisingly, the need for human relations skills is not diminished (63). Due to an increased dependence, supervisors must be able to gain the cooperation of staff and technical subunits. Motivating direct workers is still important, because these individuals influence the performance of expensive and critical equipment.

Systems and procedures, developed by support functions, also should be consistent with the philosophy underlying the team design. Pay for knowledge systems, e.g., are often instituted in conjunction with team-based approaches. They motivate workers to learn a variety of skills and engage in job rotation. Team members receive the same base pay, but as an individual learns additional tasks he or she receives additional compensation. As workers move from one pay classification to another, they may broaden their repertoires from operating tasks to technical tasks to supervisory tasks. People must be willing and able to use the skills, it is not necessary actually to perform them. In one plant, operators not only were able to learn maintenance skills but could eventually assume the role of electrician or process mechanic (64). One problem is that people often reach the top of the pay ladder after only 5 yr or a little more.

Skills and Training

Training is one of the most critical sources of support for teams working in conjunction with AMT. At the same time, advanced manufacturing technology challenges the assumptions on which traditionally oriented training programs are based. Skills, for example, are normally seen in terms of abilities to do things rather than in terms of understanding relationships (65). In AMT environments, it is necessary to understand the whole manufacturing system and its interdependencies. Otherwise, workers will not grasp the consequences of their actions for a tightly integrated system.

Operators are normally trained to provide predetermined responses to given symptoms. In an AMT environment, they must also be able to deal with unexpected symptoms for which predetermined responses do not exist (66). One example arises when the hardware and software have been redesigned to produce new products in new ways; another occurs when the computerized controls break down in an unanticipated manner. Training, therefore, must encourage workers to learn and exercise initiative.

A computer-integrated system can function for hours in a stable manner during which time operators often become bored watching for malfunctions. As a result, when something suddenly goes wrong, they find it difficult to become immediately responsive. Training, normally provided with only performance in mind, so that the computer system does routine work and operators perform nonroutine activities, accentuates these problems. If operators are trained for a balance of repetitive and novel tasks they will not be underused and will not lose touch with the production process (66).

It is normally believed that as workers take on monitoring, technical, and even supervisory tasks in lieu of operating duties, their training requirements should shift to intellectual reasoning from crafts skills. Yet, more of a balance is needed; hand skills remain important (58, 66). One feature that distinguishes discrete parts manufacturing from continuous production is the opportunity for workers to be on the shop floor using their senses to help recognize and diagnose problems. Workers in the best position to interpret this sensory information into meaningful patterns have craft experience. Once more, individuals who write or revise parts programs benefit from being able to operate machines. Training programs are increasingly challenged to provide and maintain this type of skill to people entering the workforce in the era of AMT.

Firms seem to underestimate training needs for AMT. Rothwell (65) conducted 20 case studies on the application of AMT in the UK. Most managers said they should have allowed more training and more time for training. She found most firms had ambitious plans for training, but due to schedule slippages in adopting and implementing the technology and management's pressures to get new systems up and running, training was often abandoned or left for the last minute. In her survey of 133 manufacturing plants with AMT, Majchrzak (67) discovered that only 45% offered a structured training program. In the rest, most skills were acquired through unstructured on-the-job training that, while inexpensive and hands-on, minimizes training time and focuses on a narrow set of tasks. There is, however, a positive relationship between comprehensiveness of training in terms of frequency, financial investment, and other items and the variety of different types of AMT in a plant (68).

Union Relations

Managements with an organized workforce are sometimes reluctant to see employees acquire technical and supervisory skills that give them more control over the shop floor, especially when expensive and strategic AMT is involved. When management is willing, unions may not have a great deal of enthusiasm. The changes in work organization associated with the introduction of the technology affect many aspects of the collective agreement. For example, roles may cut across traditional job demarcations, thus undermining protections trade unions have established for specialized workers.

Unions that have been induced to go along with the organizational changes usually get technology agreements with management that provide advanced information about intended technological changes, commit to some form of employment security, and/or establish vehicles for retraining. The sheer threat of plant closure due to lack of competitiveness is another impelling factor. For the viewpoint of those in the union movement who oppose the team concept see ref. 69.

Agreements reached between management and union concerning the Allen-Bradley World Contactor Line illustrate which issues are deemed significant and how they might be resolved (62). During development, workers were considered out of the bargaining unit. A work organization with characteristics of a self-regulating team was established. For example, multiskilled operators rotated jobs every 3 months and were compensated on a pay-for-knowledge basis. From the start of full production, the workers were considered part of the bargaining unit, and wage rates and conditions of employment were negotiated with the union. It was agreed to retain the one job classification from the development stage and to protect the line's existing employees for 30 months from being bumped by more senior workers. After that period, only one person could be replaced every 6 months. New operators were to be selected, first, using a skills and abilities test and, second, based on seniority.

Critique of Team-based Approaches for AMT

There have been few investigations of the benefits and costs of team-based versus traditional organizations in AMT situations. Adler (70) studied two FMSs built by the same vendor to similar specifications in the same time frame for different U.S. companies. One system was organized traditionally and the other, using a team. Workers in both installations rated perceived job characteristics, such as autonomy and responsibility, and satisfaction and stress measures. Comparisons were made with a previous study of another flexible manufacturing system with a traditional work organization (63) and to a normative sample.

In the previous study, most workers viewed their job characteristics negatively, were dissatisfied with important aspects of their jobs, and found their jobs stressful compared with the normative sample. It was, therefore, expected that the team-based unit would do better than the normative sample, which would fare better than the two traditionally organized units. However, in spite of the organizational differences, workers at Adler's two installations viewed most of their job characteristics positively and were satisfied with their jobs compared with the normative sample.

Team-based approaches also need to be compared against nonstructural alternatives such as using computerized or fixed automation, as suggested by a study of the Volvo Kalmar plant 10 yr after it went into operation (53). Performance on technical measures was good, but could have been caused by other changes going on in the plant over the same time period. The results for human resource dimensions were not so good, although improving absenteeism and turnover was the main reason for introducing teams. Turnover in 1983, a period of economic recession, was 5%. Absenteeism was 23% in 1983, suggesting that workers who could not find other jobs due to the recession were staying away from work. Significantly, a large majority of workers still believed they had little opportunity to use their skills. These results suggest that in certain industries the nature of work is such that even team-based approaches may not create sufficient motivation for workers. The solution in these industries may be to automate rather than to enrich jobs.

In large firms dependent on both the rapid introduction of complex new products and advanced manufacturing technology to design and manufacture them, there is an increased need for technical specialists. This creates a dilemma for team-based approaches for which there is no easy solution. Workers cannot be multiskilled in complex technical tasks. Introducing technical specialists into the group creates status differences that hinder effective group functioning. Leaving highly specialized tasks outside of a group's domain may reduce the capacity for self-regulation.

The continuing integration of AMT within companies may create problems for team approaches. Having stable, cohesive teams is defeated by the need to revise structures as islands of automation on the factory floor come together. Team members may resist the resulting destruction of their unit's integrity. The possibility also exists that extensive integration within manufacturing and between manufacturing and other functions may create a need for teams with sizes too large to be stable. Alternatively, several small teams may replace one large one, but they may be so tightly coupled that each group's self-regulation is curtailed. In this situation, rather than one group of individuals coming to agreement, several teams will have to arrive at a decision. It is unclear how shifting self-regulation from the group to the multigroup level will affect an individual worker's commitment (62).

In the future, whether to use team-based or traditional organization may be less important than which type of team-based organization to employ. Adler and Cole (49) recently compared a "democratic" variant of the Japanese approach practiced at the New United Motor Manufacturing (NUMMI) in the United States with the sociotechnical method used at Volvo's Uddevalla plant in Sweden. They concluded that NUMMI is higher in efficiency and lower on human resource dimensions, although within an acceptable range to the workers. Future research needs to explore whether one approach will supplant the other, whether both approaches will evolve in similar or disparate directions, and what impact societal culture and type of industry have on the appropriateness of an approach.

40.3 INNOVATION PROCESSES

An innovation is defined here as an AMT that is new to the organization in question. A good deal of the pertinent research has concentrated specifically on the introduction of computer-integrated manufacturing systems and cells as well as on organizations that are large in size, as small firms do not possess the necessary financial, human, and organizational resources (59, 71). To evaluate this research properly, the reader should keep in mind the following assertions that are contrary to accepted wisdom:

- A given innovation is not necessarily good for an organization.
- Resistance to an innovation may be in the best interests of an organization.
- The lower levels of an organization may push for an innovation and the upper levels may resist it.

The process by which an innovation works its way into a firm consists of at least three stages: adoption, preparation, and implementation. Adoption involves the company becoming aware of a particular example of AMT, in more than a casual way, and then deciding whether or not to have it. During preparation, the factory infrastructure (i.e., the skills, attitudes, systems, procedures, and structures necessary to support the innovation) is developed. Implementation comprises the initial experiments with and evaluations of the innovation before full-scale production is attained. These steps do not necessarily form a strict sequential order. Overlaps in time or movements back to a previous stage may occur.

Adoption

Mohr (72) stressed that a firm becomes acquainted with AMT in rather ordinary ways. Perhaps the most rational method is to identify objectives that are not being achieved and then to look for ways to close the gaps. Alternatively, individuals may look for new challenges, ways to improve their social ranking, or new toys with which to play. Slack resources, amounts over and above what is necessary for business reasons, may become available and ways must be found to use them. A company may slavishly imitate what comparable organizations are doing. New hires, consultants, or a key customer may push for consideration of AMT.

Once a company is familiar with a type of advanced manufacturing technology it must decide whether or not to select it. The participants in this decision include first of all equipment vendors, a group that has not received sufficient attention in the research on AMT adoption. Second, there is a company's project team that, under the leadership of the innovation's champion, makes recommendations on the technology and vendor. The champion usually promotes the project within the company, gathers needed resources, deals with organizational and technical problems, and interacts with the vendor. Third, there is strategic management, which has the final say on the recommendations.

The champion is perhaps the most critical participant in the process. Above all, this individual is committed to the necessity of the innovation for the company. His or her excessive zeal is required to develop an organizational coalition in favor of the project. Based on his experiences with an FMS in a British firm, Carpenter (73) identified some elements of the champion's task. The faith of "disciples," supporters of the innovation, must be kept from wavering. "Opponents," who believe the project is not in their or the organization's interests, need to be convinced or neutralized. The inertia of "indifferents," people who are doing too many other things to get involved or are waiting for signs of top management's commitment, must be overcome.

The champion's commitment, however, is filled with potential dangers for the organization. The individual may not be able to see or admit a mistake (73). Counterarguments are discounted, because it is easier to come up with criticisms of rather than support for something new. Questioning the innovation is seen as part of the problem so that conformity and loyalty are strictly enforced. As more resources are acquired, the champion amasses more power, which is used to sustain his or her point of view. In the final analysis, the champion's commitment may steer a firm into making an unfortunate choice.

In large corporations, there may be more than one kind of champion (74–76). The individual discussed up to this point can be referred to as the manufacturing process champion. This person, who is often low in the hierarchy and technically oriented, may require a middle manager "executive champion" to explain the project to strategic management personnel in language they can understand. Senior management is often unfamiliar with AMT (77). There may be need for a senior level "sponsor" who helps in obtaining resources, acts as a consultant when problems arise, and protects the project, if necessary.

One of the most critical factors influencing the innovation's adoption is whether strategic management has a long-term or short-term financial orientation. In many U.S. firms, a short-term orientation prevails. Immediate profits are overstressed compared with long-run returns. Using existing assets is overemphasized as opposed to investing in new ones (78–80). Factors accounting for a short-term orientation include the relatively high cost of capital in the United States through the 1980s (78), U.S. financial institutions that judge their portfolio managers on immediate earnings (81), organizational reward systems that base a manager's compensation and promotion on short-term financial performance (82), and the background and experience of top managers that is increasingly slanted toward finance (79).

Due to the technology's significant long-run benefits and short-run capital costs, a short-term orientation should have a negative direct impact on the chances of adopting AMT. In Rosenthal (5), e.g., 76% of the AMT vendor personnel interviewed said an inability to quantify returns influenced companies not to purchase the technology. Bennett et al. (83) indicated that some firms are reluctant to purchase AMT because the depreciation expense in the near term will be too great. Farley et al. (27) discovered that managers trying to expand the use of AMT in their companies had difficulty gaining initial approval due in part to insufficient short-term benefits.

A strategic management with a short-term orientation may unintentionally create a situation in which its assumptions go unchallenged. The project team may attempt to discover which decision criteria are important to strategic management to develop recommendations that will fit them (84, 85). Potential vendors, in turn, may try to uncover the decision premises of the project team so that they can tailor their flow of information to meet those premises. If vendors find the project team is reacting to a short-term orientation they may emphasize alternatives with concrete advantages and downplay those with intangible benefits (8, 86). Ultimately, strategic management receives only the kind of information it wants and the chances of adopting AMT are reduced further.

There are just a few ways for a project team wanting AMT to exert influence when strategic management has a short-term orientation. First, due to the significant intangible factors, strategic management does not have enough information to make the adoption decision purely on rational grounds. It may, therefore, defer to the recommendations of a team in which it has confidence. Dean (87) and Gerwin (88), who studied adoption decisions for AMT, found that confidence is increased when the project team's leader has a good track record, a coalition of different functional groups supports the proposal, and the project team projects a confident image.

Second, the project team may bias the recommendations to increase the chances of AMT being adopted. Biasing assumes at least three different forms: measurable benefits are overestimated and measurable costs are underestimated, intangible benefits are quantified and intangible costs are not, and arguments such as "customers' perceptions of the firm will be enhanced" are advocated (87). There is a limit, however, to the extent of bias if the project team is to maintain its credibility. Once more, senior management, on the assumption that biasing will occur, may "counterbias" the recommendations.

A third way for the project team to have some leverage is to reduce the visibility of its proposal so it is not intensively reviewed. A proposal for a new computerized manufacturing system may be buried in a large capital improvement program (89). The great number of projects combined with their technical complexity mitigates against a thorough appraisal.

Strategic management, to avoid the high uncertainty, may delay a decision in the hope that later more information will be available or the need for a choice will evaporate. In one of the AMT decisions studied by Gerwin and Tarondeau (89) strategic management sent back the project team's proposals more than 30 times before a decision was made. Other studies indicate that hesitation is used by decision makers to cope with risky situations such as capital budgeting (90).

Preparation

Preparation involves developing an infrastructure or support system sophisticated enough to make effective use of AMT. The infrastructure represents the soft side of a factory, including skills and attitudes, systems and procedures, structures, leadership styles, strategies, and shared values (23, 76). Augmenting the infrastructure's sophistication means instituting administrative innovations and changes to complement the technological ones represented by AMT.

A number of studies have indicated the importance of a sophisticated infrastructure for AMT. Ettlie and Reza (91) found that when firms establish certain organizational and interorganizational integrating mechanisms in conjunction with the purchase of new FMSs, the FMSs are higher on certain performance measures. Collins, Hull, and Hage (71) found a relationship between the proportion of professional, technical, and skilled production employees in a firm and the percentage of production capacity devoted to computer controlled equipment. Munro and Noori (92) found that the amount of in-house expertise was related to the extent of computerized automation in a manufacturing process.

Although a sophisticated infrastructure is crucial for AMT, many firms do not amass the necessary ingredients. One reason is that not enough knowledge may exist about how the infrastructure needs to be changed. Because the technology represents an innovation, the adopting firm does not have any previous experience with it. Companies introducing CAD–CAM, e.g., may not know what performance measures to use (83). Comparable organizations, e.g., those in the same industry, also may not have much experience with the technology or may be reluctant to divulge what has been learned. Vendors may lack knowledge because they are not using the technology in their own operations or because it may be too complex to install in their own test facilities before shipment. Six European companies investigated by Boer and During (93) believed that the vendors from which they purchased FMSs did not know enough about systems control for example.

Developing a more sophisticated infrastructure also is hampered by the lack of opportunity to acquire knowledge through experimental means. First, a company may rely too heavily on the vendor for making important decisions and performing major activities (52). Second, strategic management may inhibit experimentation by pressuring for immediate full-scale production. Third, the project team's composition may not represent all areas that will be significantly affected by the new technology (52, 93, 94).

These factors explain why the infrastructure's sophistication level is often not high enough at the end of preparation. Further development must occur during implementation when feedback information on performance begins to become available. Most organizational changes observed by Boer and During (93) occurred after FMS implementation, when companies discovered the need for changes.

Implementation

Implementation represents the first opportunity to determine whether the innovation will be successful. Formal and informal control systems evaluate the new technology's performance against expectations and take corrective action. However, the control systems, which are part of the infrastructure, are often imperfectly developed at the start of implementation. Their validity and reliability are open to question. The ability to exercise control is also hampered by resistance to the innovation.

In constructing expectation measures it is often unclear whether the correct types of standards are being used. One complication in selecting appropriate standards is that success can be evaluated in terms of whether the new technology works or whether it is solving the problems that motivated its adoption. The innovation may turn out to be a "successful failure," i.e., it works but does not contribute to solving any problems (95). Voss (96) found that getting advanced manufacturing systems to work was more frequently achieved than using them to improve a firm's competitiveness. Another complication is that different business functions and hierarchical levels have their own criteria. As Boddy and Buchanan (8) indicated, strategic managers evaluate a manufacturing innovation on whether it improves a firm's competitive position or enhances its image. Middle managers are interested in consistency of performance and ease in determining accountability. Supervisors value minimal disruptions and no added tasks to perform.

Often, it is unclear whether the right initial values have been chosen for the agreed on standards. The starting parameter values are usually determined from past performance, the performance of comparable organizations, and past expectations. Depending on how radical the innovation is, there may not be any information available from these sources. A firm may have to rely on its employees' intuitive judgments, influenced by the claims of the innovation's advocates, and on estimates from the vendor, undoubtedly affected by the desire to make a sale. For these reasons, the initial values of standards are likely to be set on the high side. It may take years before there is enough experience with the new technology to develop reliable estimates (88).

Measuring the innovation's performance is subject to uncertainty. First, introducing AMT often occurs along with other changes meant to bolster a firm's competitiveness. One cannot always determine whether improvements attributed to the technology may be due to these other factors as well. Second, there are unanticipated indirect impacts on factory activities that are often too costly to measure. Third, when both the parts produced and the process that manufactures them are new, current performance cannot meaningfully be compared with past performance. There is no way to determine if reductions in inventory, downtime, or lead time have taken place.

Given these measurement problems, AMT's levels of performance depend on the compatibility between the innovation and the infrastructure (23, 63, 97). The degree to which they match is defined here in terms of the innovation's technical complexity compared with the infrastructure's sophistication. Initially, due to the characteristics of AMT, technical complexity is high, while, due to the problems encountered during preparation, the infrastructure's sophistication is low.

This discrepancy is amenable to adjustment if the new technology possesses the characteristic of divisibility. Considered one of the most significant attributes of an innovation (98), divisibility is the extent to which it can be broken down into components that are implemented in steps. With this characteristic, an innovation's technical complexity is reduced considerably. It is possible to install an integrated manufacturing system one module or workstation at a time, operate each on an individual basis, and ultimately link them together.

Comparisons between initial expectations and initial performance are likely to reveal large discrepancies. Expectations spurred on by the vendor and the innovation's advocates are high, while performance, affected by the mismatch between technical complexity and the infrastructure's sophistication, is low. At least three options exist for eliminating discrepancies: the technology is altered to fit the infrastructure better, the infrastructure is changed to match the technology better, and expectations are altered.

The first possibility, adjusting the technology, may involve a minor adaptation such as a small change in software code or a major reversal such as redesign of the entire system. Due to the financial and psychological costs, however, the chances that fundamental changes occur are low. Irrespective of the magnitude of the change, either a benign adjustment (the discrepancy decreases) or a malign adjustment (the discrepancy increases) may occur (95). One reason is that the causal links between any technical change and subsequent performance are often not well understood. Leonard-Barton (99) provided examples of benign and malign technical adjustments.

The second approach, adapting the infrastructure, is a continuation of the steps taken during preparation. It usually leads to minor as opposed to major initiatives. There also are malign as well as benign adjustments (99). The time to make adjustments is undoubtedly longer and the causal connections with performance less well understood than for technical changes.

As illustrated by the following examples the third possibility involves lowering expectations or switching to criteria that are presumably easier to attain:

- In a company that had purchased an FMS, exhaustive testing revealed that greater machine capability was needed to meet the original tight tolerances; the tolerances were eased (88).
- A company stopped measuring the productivity of a new CAD–CAM system when it became apparent that expected gains would not materialize; by then management decided the system's real purpose was to reduce lead times (100).
- A multimillion-dollar flexible assembly system never performed up to the levels predicted by the user firm in terms of yield and labor requirements; ultimately, it became part of a just-in-time delivery system to a final assembly plant, and its success is now measured by the amount of flexibility provided (97).

In the final analysis, conditions may be too uncertain to determine objectively whether the implementation of AMT is a success. A firm usually continues to use the technology without being clear if it is successful. Why is canceling the innovation an unlikely alternative? The heavy financial and psychological investment forces continuation even though these are sunk costs. Cancellation does seem to occur when large discrepancies exist between expectations and performance, and only an expensive adjustment in technology or infrastructure will remove them (99).

Conflict and Resistance to Change

Intraorganizational conflict over an innovation hinders implementation by preventing individuals from cooperating with each other to solve problems. The extent of conflict depends in part on the amount of change that takes place in the infrastructure. Changes in the roles, statuses, and powers attached to organizational positions often produce resistance by the individuals holding those positions (98). Role changes occurring with the introduction of new production technologies produce resistance if the impacted activities are a significant part of the job and the difficulty of meeting performance criteria is increased (99).

Hage (98) identified three general strategies for handling conflict and resistance to change: revolution, evolution, and isolation. In revolution, strategic management uses its formal and personal power to push a radical innovation through the organization. The interests of the affected parties are not considered, and conflict is suppressed. Adoption is quick, but resistance during implementation usually blocks the innovation's success. A major exception occurs when a crisis exists for which new technology is seen as a solution. Then employees are willing to set aside their own immediate interests to cooperate in ensuring the organization's survival.

The essence of evolution is participation by affected parties in decision making on the innovation. Adoption is slow, because it is necessary for all factions to reach a consensus. In achieving that consensus features of the innovation important to its advocates may be discarded. Implementation is not held up by conflict, but the innovation is implemented incrementally over a long period of time. The conditions for successful evolution include an innovation that is divisible and advocates who remain with the organization for a long time.

Isolation, the third strategy, represents implementing an innovation through the creation of a new organizational unit on a greenfield site or in a separate part of the existing factory. Resistance is curtailed because existing factions are not directly affected, it is harder for them to make invidious comparisons, and new hires are selected for their commitment to the new technology. Isolation, however, requires abundant financial resources and is subject to the problems in creating a sophisticated infrastructure from scratch. For these reasons, the approach is used mainly when a large amount of resistance is expected in the existing factory. For example, a firm studied by Beatty and Gordon (39) installed a new robotic welding line with six operators next to a manual line employing more than 30 welders. Due to resistance by the welders, who feared losing their jobs, the project was stopped. The robotic line became part of a new factory with new workers at a distant location and was operational within a few months.

40.4 CONCLUSIONS

This chapter stressed the significance of proper management of AMT, in terms of strategy, organization, and innovation, if the technology's promise is to be fulfilled. Many general and technical managers, through their own bitter experiences, have come to adopt this position, but it is still not universally accepted. In the future, attention must turn also to understanding the ways in which the three managerial aspects interact with each other. We must learn if decisions made concerning any one aspect constrain the choices available for the others or whether it is possible to have mutually reinforcing aspects.

Considering two-way interactions:

- Will a business unit strategy based on flexibility lead to a team-based work organization that can support that strategy by dealing with unanticipated market uncertainties, and will existence of a team-based work organization encourage the adoption of a strategy oriented toward flexibility?
- Will a team-based work organization facilitate AMT innovation by, e.g., lessening resistance to change, and will management use the occasion of AMT innovation to devise team-based work organizations due to their ability to eliminate and adapt to process uncertainties?
- Will AMT innovation, due to increasing flexibility at least in certain circumstances, provide management with an opportunity to develop strategies emphasizing that characteristic, and will a strategy based on flexibility influence process technology choices towards AMT?

If these two-way interactions exist and can be linked together they will undoubtedly form a mutually reinforcing cycle of flexibility:

- A strategy emphasizing flexibility will make for a team-based work organization that lessens resistance to AMT innovations that, in turn, support the strategy.
- A strategy based on flexibility will influence process technology choices toward AMT. These choices will encourage a team-based work organization that, in turn, will support the strategy.

Companies establishing a well-functioning cycle of this nature should be the ones deriving the most value out of their investments in AMT.

Acknowledgments

The author wishes to acknowledge the contributions of Harvey Kolodny to this chapter. Financial support came from the sponsors of the Research Program in Managing Technological Change in Manufacturing: the Natural Sciences and Engineering Research Council, the Social Sciences and Humanities Research Council, the Semiconductor Components Group of Northern Telecom Ltd., Mitel Corp., Gandalf Data Ltd., and Lumonics Inc.

BIBLIOGRAPHY

1. T.G. GUNN, *Manufacturing for Competitive Advantage: Becoming a World Class Manufacturer,* Ballinger, Cambridge, Mass., 1987.
2. H. NOORI, *Managing the Dynamics of New Technology: Issues in Manufacturing Management,* Prentice-Hall, Inc., Englewood Cliffs, N.J., 1990.
3. U.S. Department of Commerce, Bureau of the Census, *Current Industrial Reports: Manufacturing Technology 1988,* U.S. Government Printing Office, Washington, D.C., May 1989, SMT (88)-1.
4. E. MANSFIELD, "The Diffusion of Flexible Manufacturing Systems in Japan, Europe and the United States," *Manage. Sci.* **39**(2), 149–159 (1993).
5. S. ROSENTHAL, "Progress Toward the 'Factory of the Future,' " *J. Operat. Manage.* **4**(3) (1984).
6. R. JAIKUMAR, "Postindustrial Manufacturing," *Harvard Bus. Rev.,* 69–76 (Nov.–Dec. 1986).
7. W.R. KING and K. RAMAMURTHY, "Do Organizations Achieve Their Objectives from Computer-Based Manufacturing Technologies?" *IEEE Trans. Eng. Manage.* **39**(2), 129–141 (1992).
8. D. BODDY and D.A. BUCHANNAN, *Managing New Technology,* Basil Blackwell, Oxford, UK, 1986.
9. R.H. HAYES and S.C. WHEELWRIGHT, *Restoring Our Competitive Edge: Competing Through Manufacturing,* John Wiley & Sons, Inc., New York, 1984.
10. R.W. HALL, *Attaining Manufacturing Excellence,* Dow Jones-Irwin, Homewood, Ill., 1987.
11. R.J. SCHONBERGER, "Frugal Manufacturing," *Harvard Bus. Rev.,* 95–100 (Sept.–Oct. 1987).
12. D. GERWIN and H.F. KOLODNY, *Management of Advanced Manufacturing Technology: Strategy, Organization & Innovation,* John Wiley & Sons, Inc., New York, 1992.
13. R. NAGEL and R. DOVE, *21st Century Manufacturing Enterprise Strategy,* Iacocca Institute, Lehigh University, Bethlehem, Pa., 1991.
14. B.J. PINE II, *Mass Customization: The New Frontier in Business Competition,* Harvard Business School Press, Boston, Mass., 1993.
15. M. TOMBAK and A. DEMEYER, "Flexibility and FMS: An Empirical Analysis," *IEEE Trans. Eng. Manage.* **EM-35**(2), 101–107 (1988).
16. T.J. WHARTON and E.W. WHITE, "Flexibility and Automation: Patterns of Evolution," *Operat. Manage. Rev.* **6**(3–4), 1–8 (1988).
17. P.M. SWAMIDASS, *Manufacturing Flexibility,* Naman & Schneider Associates Group, Waco, Tex., 1988, Operations Management Association Monograph No. 2.
18. G. STALK, JR., and T.M. HOUT, *Competing against Time,* The Free Press, New York, 1990.
19. A.K. SETHI and S.P. SETHI, "Flexibility in Manufacturing: A Survey," *Int. J. Flexible Manufact. Sys.* **2,** 289–328 (1990).
20. D. GERWIN, "Manufacturing Flexibility: A Strategic Perspective," *Manage. Sci.* **39**(4) 395–410 (1993).
21. N. SLACK, "Flexibility as a Manufacturing Objective," *Int. J. Operat. Product. Manage.* **3**(3), 4–13 (1983).
22. S. KEKRE and K. SRINIVASAN, "Broader Product Line: A Necessity to Achieve Success?" *Manage. Sci.* **36**(10), 1216–1231 (1990).
23. W. SKINNER, *Manufacturing: The Formidable Competitive Weapon,* John Wiley & Sons, Inc., New York, 1985.
24. J.D. GOLDHAR and M. JELINEK, "Plan for Economics of Scope," *Harvard Bus. Rev.* **61**(6), 141–148 (1983).
25. M. SAKURAI, "The Influence of Factory Automation on Management Accounting Practices: A Study of Japanese Companies" in R.S. Kaplan, ed., *Measures for Manufacturing Excellence,* Harvard Business School Press, Boston, Mass., 1990.
26. R. HALL and L. TONKIN, *Manufacturing 21 Report: The Future of Japanese Manufacturing,* Association for Manufacturing Excellence, Wheeling, Ill., 1990.

27. M. CHANG, "Flexible Manufacturing, Uncertain Consumer Tastes, and Strategic Entry Deterrence," *J. Ind. Econ.* **41**(1), 77–90 (1993).

28. D. GERWIN and J.C. TARONDEAU, "International Comparisons of Manufacturing Flexibility" in K. Ferdows, ed., *Managing International Manufacturing,* Elsevier-North Holland, Amsterdam, The Netherlands, 1989.

29. D.M. DILTS, N.P. BOYD, and H.H. WHORMS, "The Evolution of Control Architectures for Automated Manufacturing Systems," *J. Manufact. Sys.* **10**(1), 79–93 (1991).

30. D. GUPTA and J.A. BUZACOTT, "A Framework for Understanding Flexibility of Manufacturing Systems," *J. Manufact. Sys.* **8**(2), 89–97 (1989).

31. J.V. FARLEY, B. KAHN, D.R. LEHMANN, and W.L. MOORE, "Modeling the Choice to Automate," *Sloan Manage. Rev.* **28**(2), 5–15 (1987).

32. G. MARGIRIER, "Flexible Automation in Machining in France: Results of a Survey," Institute of Economic Research, University of Social Sciences of Grenoble, Grenoble, France, 1986.

33. W.J. ABERNATHY, *The Productivity Dilemma: Roadblock to Innovation in the Automobile Industry,* Johns Hopkins University Press, Baltimore, Md., 1978.

34. J. UTTERBACK and W.J. ABERNATHY, "A Dynamic Model of Process and Product Innovation," *Omega* **3**(6), 639–656 (1975).

35. D.A. HICKS, *Automation Technology and Industrial Renewal: Adjustment Dynamics in the U.S. Metalworking Sector,* American Enterprise Institute for Public Policy Research, Washington, D.C., 1986.

36. R.J. BOADEN, *Justification of Computer-integrated Manufacturing: Some Insights into Practice,* Manchester School of Management, UMIST, Manchester, UK, 1989.

37. B. GOLD, "CAM Sets New Rules for Production," *Harvard Bus. Rev.* **60**(6), 88–94 (1982).

38. J.R. MEREDITH and M.M. HILL, "Justifying New Manufacturing Systems: A Managerial Approach," *Sloan Manage. Rev.,* **28**(4), 49–61 (Summer 1987).

39. C.A. BEATTY and J.R.M. GORDON, "Barriers to the Implementation of CAD/CAM Systems," *Sloan Manage. Rev.* **29**(4), 25–33 (1988).

40. B.B. HUNDY and D.J. HAMBLIN, "Risk and Assessment of Investment in New Technology," *Int. J. Product. Res.* **26**(11), 1799–1810 (1988).

41. R.S. KAPLAN, "Must CIM Be Justified by Faith Alone?" *Harvard Bus. Rev.,* 87–95 (Mar.–Apr. 1986).

42. G.K. HUTCHINSON and J.R. HOLLAND, "The Economic Value of Flexible Automation," *J. Manufact. Sys.* **1**(2), 215–227 (1982).

43. G. AZZONE and U. BERTELE, "Measuring the Economic Effectiveness of Flexible Automation," *Int. J. Product. Res.* **27**(5), 735–746 (1989).

44. J.R. MEREDITH and N.C. SURESH, "Justification Techniques for Advanced Manufacturing Technologies," *Int. J. Product. Res.* **24**(5), 1043–1057 (1986).

45. P.G.W. KEEN, "Value Analysis: Justifying Decision Support Systems," *MIS Q.,* **5**(1), 1–15 (Mar. 1981).

46. J.A. KIRTON, "Implementing Advanced Manufacturing Technology: The Way It Is" in C.A. Voss, ed., *Managing Advanced Manufacturing Technology,* IFS Publications, London, 1986.

47. D. GERWIN, "Relationships Between Structure and Technology" in P.C. Nystrom and W.H. Starbuck, eds., *Handbook of Organizational Design,* Vol. 2, Oxford University Press, New York, 1981.

48. W.A. PASMORE, *Designing Effective Organizations: The Sociotechnical Systems Perspective,* John Wiley & Sons, Inc., New York, 1988.

49. P.S. ADLER and R.E. COLE, "Designed for Learning: A Tale of Two Auto Plants," *Sloan Manage. Rev.,* **34**(3), 85–94 (Spring 1993).

50. J.A. KLEIN, "A Reexamination of Autonomy in Light of New Manufacturing Practices," *Hum. Relations* **44**(1), 21–38 (1991).

51. T. CUMMINGS and M. BLUMBERG, "Advanced Manufacturing Technology and Work Design" in T.D. Wall, C.W. Clegg, and N.J. Kemp, eds., *The Human Side of Manufacturing Technology,* John Wiley & Sons, Inc., Chichester, UK, 1987.

52. M.B.W. GRAHAM and S.R. ROSENTHAL, "Institutional Aspects of Process Procurement for Flexible Machining Systems," Boston University School of Management, Boston, Mass., 1986.

53. S. AGUREN, C. BREDBACKA, R. HANSSON, K. IHREGREN, and K.G. KARLS-SON, *Volvo Kalmar Revisited: Ten Years of Experience,* Efficiency and Participation Development Council, SAF-LO-PTK, Stockholm, 1984.

54. S. AGUREN, R. HANSSON, and K.G. KARLSSON, *The Volvo Kalmar Plant: The Impact of New Design on Work Organization,* The Rationalization Council, SAF-LO, Stockholm, 1976.

55. G. BETCHERMAN, K. NEWTON, and J. GODIN, eds., *Two Steps Forward: Human Resource Management in a High-Tech World,* Economic Council of Canada, Canadian Government Publishing Centre, Ottawa, Ont., 1990.

56. T.D. WALL, J.M. CORBETT, R. MARTIN, C.W. CLEGG, and P.R. JACKSON, "Advanced Manufacturing Technology, Work Design and Performance: A Change Study," *J. Appl. Psychol.* **75**(6), 691–697 (1990).

57. H. SHAIKEN, *Work Transformed: Automation and Labor in the Computer Age,* Holt, Rinehart & Winston, New York, 1984.

58. A. SORGE, G. HARTMAN, M. WARNER, and I. NICHOLAS, *Microelectronics and Manpower in Manufacturing,* Gower, Aldershot, UK, 1983.

59. M.R. KELLY and H. BROOKS, *Patterns of Adoption of Programmable Automation Technologies in the U.S. Industrial Base,* Harvard University, John F. Kennedy School of Government, Cambridge, Mass., 1988.

60. U. WEMMERLOV and N.L. HYER, "Cellular Manufacturing in the U.S. Industry: A Survey of Users," *Int. J. Product. Res.* **27**(9), 1511–1530 (1989).

61. B. BURNES and M. FITTER, "Control of Advanced Manufacturing Technology: Supervision Without Supervisors?" in T.D. Wall, C.W. Clegg, and N.J. KEMP, eds, *The Human Side of Advanced Manufacturing Technology,* John Wiley & Sons, Inc., Chichester, UK, 1987.

62. J.A. KLEIN, *Revitalizing Manufacturing: Text and Cases,* Irwin, Homewood, Ill., 1990.

63. M. BLUMBERG and D. GERWIN, "Coping with Advanced Manufacturing Technology," *J. Occupat. Behav.* **5**(2), 113–140 (1984).

64. B. PAINTER, *The Real Possibility of Good Jobs with New Technology,* B.C. Research, Vancouver, B.C., 1990.

65. S. ROTHWELL, "Selection and Training for Advanced Manufacturing Technology" in T.D. Wall, C.W. Clegg, and N.J. Kemp, eds., *The Human Side of Advanced Manufacturing Technology,* John Wiley & Sons, Inc., Chichester, UK, 1987.

66. L. HIRSCHHORN, *Beyond Mechanization: Work and Technology in a Postindustrial Age,* MIT Press, Cambridge, 1984.

67. A. MAJCHRZAK, *The Human Side of Factory Automation,* Jossey-Bass, San Francisco, 1988.

68. S.A. SNELL and J.W. DEAN, JR., "Integrated Manufacturing and Human Resource Management: A Human Capital Perspective," *Acad. Manage. J.* **35**(3), 467–504 (1992).

69. M. PARKER and J. SLAUGHTER, *Choosing Sides: Unions and the Team Concept,* South End Press, Boston, Mass. 1988.

70. P.S. ADLER, "Workers and Flexible Manufacturing Systems: Three Installations Compared," *J. Organ. Behav.* **12**, 447–460 (1991).

71. P.D. COLLINS, F. HULL, and J. HAGE, *Programmable Automation, Technology Strategy, and Organization: A Profile of Adopters,* Krannert School, Purdue University, Lafayette, Ind., 1989.

72. L.B. MOHR, "Innovation Theory: An Assessment from the Vantage Point of New Electronic Technology in Organizations" in J.M. Pennings and A. Buitendam, eds., *New Technology as Organizational Innovation: The Development and Diffusion of Microelectronics,* Ballinger, Cambridge, Mass., 1987.

73. A.J. CARPENTER, *Computer Aided Manufacture: Overcoming Organizational Inertia for Competitive Advantage,* Dowty Mining Equipment Co., Tewkesbury, UK, 1988.

74. C.A. BEATTY, "Implementing Advanced Manufacturing Technologies," *Sloan Manage. Rev.* **33**(4), 49–60 (Summer 1992).

75. J.R. MEREDITH, "Strategic Planning for Factory Automation by the Championing Process," *IEEE Trans. Eng. Manage.* **EM-33**(4), 229–232 (1986).

76. T.J. PETERS and R.H. WATERMAN, *In Search of Excellence,* Warner Books, New York, 1982.

77. M.N. BAILY and A.K. CHAKRABARTI, *Innovation and the Productivity Crisis,* The Brookings Institution, Washington, D.C., 1988.

78. M.L. DERTOUZOS, R.K. LESTER, and R.M. SOLOW, *Made in America: Regaining the Productive Edge,* MIT Press, Cambridge, 1989.

79. R.H. HAYES and W.J. ABERNATHY, "Managing Our Way to Economic Decline," *Harvard Bus. Rev.,* 67–77 (July–Aug. 1980).

80. H.T. JOHNSON and R.S. KAPLAN, *Relevance Lost: The Rise and Fall of Management Accounting,* Harvard Business School Press, Boston, Mass., 1987.

81. P. CHOATE and J.K. LINGER, *The High-Flex Society: Shaping America's Economic Future,* Knopf, New York, 1986.

82. R.V. AYRES, *The Next Industrial Revolution: Reviving Industry through Innovation,* Ballinger, Cambridge, Mass., 1984.

83. R.E. BENNETT, J.A. HENDRICKS, D.E. KEYS, and E.J. RUDNICKI, *Cost Accounting for Factory Automation,* National Association of Accountants, Montvale, N.J., 1987.

84. J. BOWER, *Managing the Resource Allocation Process,* Division of Research, Graduate School of Business, Harvard University, Boston, Mass., 1970.

85. E.E. CARTER, "The Behavioral Theory of the Firm and Top Level Corporate Decision," *Admin. Sci. Q.* **16**(4), 413–429 (1971).

86. P.L. PRIMROSE and R. LEONARD, "Predicting Future Developments in Flexible Manufacturing Technology," *Int. J. Product. Res.* **26**(6), 1065–1072 (1988).

87. J.W. DEAN, JR., *Deciding to Innovate: How Firms Justify Advanced Technology,* Ballinger, Cambridge, Mass., 1987.

88. D. GERWIN, "Control and Evaluation in the Innovation Process: The Case of Flexible Manufacturing Systems," *IEEE Trans. Eng. Manage.* **EM-28**(3), 62–70 (1981).

89. D. GERWIN and J.-C. TARONDEAU, "Case Studies of Computer Integrated Manufacturing Systems: A View of Uncertainty and Innovation Processes," *J. Operat. Manage.* **2**(2), 87–99 (1982).

90. K.R. MACCRIMMON and D.A. WEHRUNG, *Taking Risks: The Management of Uncertainty,* The Free Press, New York, 1986.

91. J.E. ETTLIE and E.M. REZA, "Organizational Integration and Process Innovation," *Acad. Manage. J.* **35**(4), 795–827 (1992).

92. H. MUNRO and H. NOORI, "Measuring Commitment to New Manufacturing Technology: Integrating Technological Push and Marketing Pull Concepts," *IEEE Trans. Eng. Manage.* **35**(2), 63–70 (1988).

93. H. BOER and W.E. DURING, "Management of Process Innovation—The Case of FMS: A Systems Approach," *Int. J. Product. Res.* **25**(11), 1671–1682 (1987).

94. D.J. LEVI, C.M. SLEM, and A. YOUNG, *Technological Versus Team Driven Approaches to Implementing Advanced Manufacturing Technology,* Department of Psychology, California Polytechnic Institute, San Luis Obispo, 1989.

95. L.D. TORNATZKY, J.D. EVELAND, M.G. BOYLAN, W.A. HETZNER, E.C. JOHNSON, D. ROITMAN, and J. SCHNEIDER, *The Process of Technical Innovation: Reviewing the Literature,* National Science Foundation, Washington, D.C., 1983.

96. C.A. VOSS, "Implementation: A Key Issue in Manufacturing Technology: The Need for a Field of Study," *Res. Policy* **17**, 55–63 (1988).

97. J.E. ETTLIE, *Taking Charge of Manufacturing,* Jossey-Bass, San Francisco, 1988.

98. J. HAGE, *Theories of Organizations,* John Wiley & Sons, Inc., New York, 1980.

99. D. LEONARD-BARTON, "Implementation as Mutual Adaptation of Technology and Organization," *Res. Policy* **17**, 251–267 (1988).

100. G. WINCH, *The Implementation of Integrating Innovations: The Case of CAD/CAM,* Warwick Business School, University of Warwick, Coventry, UK, 1989.

CHAPTER 41

Cost Issues in Design
and Manufacturing

G. G. HEGDE and STEPHEN L. STARLING
University of Pittsburgh

This chapter discusses and illustrates why and how new accounting systems must change to include design processes to complete the shift from a reactive cost measurement to a proactive cost management role.

41.1 A SHIFT IN THE PARADIGM

Cost Measurement to Cost Management

The evolution of the modern management accounting function can be summarized as a series of transitions from a reactive reporting role at the beginning of the 20th century to an integrated proactive role by the end of the century. In essence, throughout the 20th century a slow self-actualization of the management accounting role as an integral component of company strategy implementation has been occurring. In many corporations, the management accounting function has integrated itself into the decision processes that drive production decisions; however, the final phase of the evolution of the management accounting function into the design stages of processes has just begun (1, 2). This final phase will complete the century-long shift in the paradigm of the role of accounting from a cost-measurement to a cost-management role.

The goals of the scientific management movement late in the 19th century were to simplify work, design work standards, and measure worker performance against standards. The movement studied processes to redesign material and work flows, and decompose complex processes into a sequence of simpler and more controllable processes. Control of work and piecework payments were established using detailed and accurate standards for material and labor usage. Because the scientific management movement measured direct labor and processes were labor intensive, an inexpensive extension was to apply overhead based on direct labor. Hence, the practice of applying overhead to products based on their direct labor content started in the scientific management movement. Attempts to use other bases failed, probably due to the added expense of accumulating and analyzing data associated with using new bases (3).

Although the scientific management movement contributed greatly to improving the productivity of processes through optimizing human and material resources, the movement created a focus on the human worker as a resource to be used to the fullest extent possible. To the scientific manager, the worker knew little or nothing and was treated based on that assumption. The assumption limited the capability for process and product improvements by not taking advantage of the workers' knowledge, which today is recognized as a significant source of innovative ideas.

In the first quarter of the 20th century, the advent of multiactivity, diversified corporations spurred on the evolution of the accounting function. Innovations in transportation, communication, and other technologies created a demand for large corporations to achieve gains from economies of scale and scope. These gains required simultaneous innovation in the development of measurement systems. The most significant accounting innovation during the first quarter century was the development of the return-on-investment (ROI) measure by Du Pont.

From 1925 to 1985, few managerial accounting innovations were developed, primarily due to four reasons, as emphasized by Kaplan and Atkinson (3). First, investments in corporations through the stock market created disattachment of owners and creditors from day-to-day operations. Second, the increased demands of external reporting after the Depression consumed much of the resources of accounting departments. Third, the high costs of information collection, processing, and reporting financially justified not changing. Four, the relatively low distortion for companies with homogenous product lines did not make change important. All of these reasons caused companies to manage their internal operations with the same information used to report externally. As a result, product costs were calculated based on aggregate, average allocations of manufacturing overhead, and control procedures used monthly variances calculated using financial reports.

The advent of technological innovations starting in the early 1980s, such as inexpensive computer processing, and the increasingly competitive global market have forced a rethinking of the accounting role to include reporting timely, relevant, and integrated information directed at improving the competitiveness of the firm. The reasons contributing to the evolutionary stagnation of cost accounting were no longer valid. Today, accounting has the greatest capability since the beginning of the 20th century to both measure and manage costs.

Traditionally, manufacturing has viewed the conversion process as only the activities involved with changing physical material into a marketable product. As a result, traditional accounting systems have focused on the conversion process after the design stages. In 1988, it was reported that as much as 95% of total manufacturing costs for a product are committed on completion of the design stage and start of production; however, costs are usually not expensed by accounting departments until the product designs have been given to production (4). Since 1969, similar estimates ranging from 75% and higher have been reported by several publications.

Based on this evidence, new accounting systems need to include the design stages in their restructured system. Including design requires changing the role of accounting from a cost-measurement to a cost-management role, by which the management of costs extends beyond the factory floor and is integrated into the entire conversion process. Only then can a company tie its cost accounting structure to its short- and long-term goals. The entire conversion process includes all activities in bringing a product to market, from design to delivery. This view of the conversion process is the same as Deming's (5) concept of the extended process.

With this new system, design engineers can measure the impact of their decisions on the production cost. The inclusion of design in a new accounting system requires linking the cost information among accounting, production, and design activities. Figure 41.1 presents the linkage of cost information flows between the three areas. Traditionally, information would not flow from accounting to design and from design to accounting.

Cost Committed Versus Cost Expensed

A British aerospace study published in 1969 (6) reported that 80% of manufacturing costs are committed during the first 20% of the design process. Based on the 1969 study, the "80–20 rule" developed as a commonly cited term. In discrete goods manufacturing, up to 85% of the manufacturing cost is established through decisions made during the product design stage (7). Although only about 5% of the total cost of a car is spent in the design activity itself, it determines about 70% of the total cost.

Figures 41.2 and 41.3 illustrate how costs are committed during the life cycle of a product. Figure 41.2 shows how in traditional accounting the majority of costs are committed early in the design process, whereas costs are not expensed until the production process. In contrast,

Figure 41.1. Cost information flows for cost management.

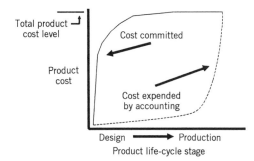

Design ⟶ Production
Product life-cycle stage

Figure 41.2. Traditional accounting.

Figure 41.3 shows how costs can be committed and expensed by accounting at the same time. Figure 41.3 presents the goal supported in this chapter: costs should be estimated at the source (design) and subsequently reduced through a market-driven and process-driven process.

Technical problems associated with manufacturing processes (downstream processes) are usually traceable to the design process. However, the emphasis in the United States has been on improving operations downstream from the design process. A lack of emphasis on the design process ignores one of the greatest potential avenues for lowering costs, improving quality, increasing productivity, and reducing time to market. For example, in a benchmarking analysis of a Japanese manufacturer of plastic parts, it was discovered that the Japanese company's costs were 50% lower than a U.S. manufacturer. Approximately 50% of the savings were estimated to be the result of differences in design factors such as design engineering, less multifunctionality of parts, tooling design, finishing, and tolerances. The rest of the savings was the result of higher resin costs and processing expenses. The following list presents assertions about cost commitment in design (8):

1. Factors of cost, quality, and lead time are design problems more than manufacturing problems.
2. Market loss by U.S. companies is due to design deficiencies more than manufacturing deficiencies.
3. Manufacturing processes themselves are designed.
4. Many technical problems commonly associated with manufacturing processes are traceable to design problems.
5. Opportunities to surpass foreign competitors are best found in engineering design.

In contrast to traditional manufacturing design strategy, U.S. companies are realizing that costs expensed by accurate estimations using concurrent engineering early in the design process can greatly reduce total manufacturing costs. Bebb, vice president of Xerox, called design "the missing link in competitive strategy" (8). Many Japanese companies long ago realized the benefits of including accounting personnel in the design process. The Japanese do not wait until a product design is already being used to manufacture the product before bringing in accounting,

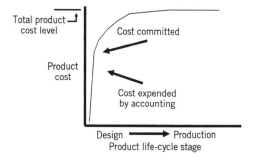

Design ⟶ Production
Product life-cycle stage

Figure 41.3. New accounting.

instead the Japanese work toward a target cost (4). (A discussion of target costs is presented later in this chapter.)

Existing Cost Systems

Before changing any accounting system, an understanding of the problems that traditional accounting systems create is necessary. Through improper application of product and process costs, traditional accounting can lead to decisions that increase overhead, lot sizes, and levels of inventory. For example, a common result with traditional accounting systems is that they tend to support decisions that lead to large lead times. Large lead times create inflexibility and support decisions to manufacture large lot sizes. Large lot sizes then require large warehouses and buffers between processes. Large and inflexible machinery are developed and purchased to support large lot size mass production. Quality problems, frequently hidden in large batches, increase and are not pursued by management. The "domino effect" continues, creating an enormous amount of manufacturing waste in its path.

The manufacturing mode of mass production with low product diversity caused complacency and inflexibility in both product design and resource allocation decisions. Before about 1970, these problems were not extremely serious to the competitiveness of a firm due to the relative stability of business operations. Stability created a stagnant environment in which strategic cost analysis did not require frequent reevaluation of measures and periodic restructuring of the actual reporting system to meet the needs of manufacturing managers.

Due to this stagnation, efforts by manufacturing managers to initiate manufacturing improvements were based on decisions made using volumetric product cost data. Research has shown that traditional accounting systems based on volumetric measures can damage the competitive potential of a firm by providing inappropriate performance measures (9). Volume-based measures can create rejection of long-term improvements, inaccurate analysis, poor operating decisions, and inappropriate resource allocations. As a result, many existing management accounting systems serve as a barrier to improvement by inhibiting or preventing operations management decisions actuating change toward improved productivity and quality (10). To break down the barrier, accounting systems must be restructured to meet the demands of both volumetric and operational reporting. Including operations measures can create a production environment within a firm that simultaneously promotes improvement of productivity and quality (11). Traditional accounting measures are as follows:

Direct labor efficiency.
Direct labor use.
Direct labor productivity.
Machine use.
Inventory turnover.
Cost variances.
Individual incentives.
Performance to schedules.

For example, the most common cost allocation base has been direct labor. Direct labor once accounted for the majority of a product's cost; however, studies (10) have demonstrated that direct labor in many companies accounts for an increasingly smaller percentage of manufacturing costs. Because an objective of operations management is to reduce total product cost, a logical focus is on measures that serve as bases for cost allocation. A manager may decide erroneously that investment in automation to replace direct labor is the best decision, as the increased overhead costs of maintenance, energy, floor space, etc. will not be fully accounted for in determining product cost. Managerial decisions that reduce the direct labor required to manufacture usually do result in increasing overhead requirements; therefore, product costs for which overhead is allocated based on direct labor have become distorted.

A principal reason for the development of the base usage for allocating costs problem is that financial accounting systems do not require assigned overhead costs to be causally related to individual products. Almost all U.S. companies use a two-stage cost allocation system by which costs are first assigned to cost centers and then allocated to from the cost centers to products. The two-stage cost allocation system effectually supports the use of direct labor to allocate overhead costs. In general, the result is that financial accounting reports do not give manufacturing managers relevant performance measurement and product cost information.

New Manufacturing Environment

Flexibility in manufacturing coupled with low costs, high output, and high quality are the major goals of many world-class manufacturers today. The trend toward greater flexibility is clearly seen by the evolution of manufacturing from mass production of products of low diversity to mass production of products of high diversity. To compete in tomorrow's flexibility based manufacturing environment, manufacturers must become capable of rapidly changing their production processes to accommodate product changes and new products. The change must occur such that the production process itself is not greatly disrupted or delayed. To accomplish these goals, manufacturing managers require strategic, accurate, relevant, and timely measures. Accounting can provide these requirements through strategic cost analysis coupled with both new measures and new reporting systems.

Strategic cost analysis expands the role of cost management by integrating ideas from strategy, marketing, and accounting (12). In contrast to traditional accounting, strategic cost analysis relies on cost data to develop plans that will lead to a sustainable competitive advantage. One of the first goals of strategic cost analysis is to determine the key activities that give a product value (value-added analysis). Next, the activities are analyzed to determine their cost drivers. The goal is to identify wasteful activities that do not add value to the product and subsequently reduce or eliminate them. Development of new measures is one way to achieve this goal. New performance measures include the following:

Total head count productivity.
Return on net assets.
Days of inventory.
Product costs.
Group incentives.
Customer service.
Customer complaints.
Cost of quality.
Machine availability.
Setup reductions.

The new measures must reflect the competitive environment and be used to help guide decision-making processes, from design to delivery, into alignment with corporate strategy.

A goal of a new system is to tie key performance measures to firm strategy or a specific business unit (13). One study (1) concluded that poor coordination between performance measures and incentive systems can lower the firm's performance. Although this correlation is intuitively obvious and the measurement of some performance measures is accomplished by many firms, the tie-in of performance measures to strategy is not frequently accomplished. The poor use of performance measures to drive strategy and improvements may be partly due to the use of the information at different levels. In addition, the poor tie-in may be the result of improper measures being provided to managers at the lower levels. A survey of managers of four Northern Telecom plants discovered that financial measures of performance (8) were perceived to be more important at the strategic level than at lower levels. The study indicated a need for nonfinancial measures.

According to Young and Selto (12), two forms of performance measures exist: counting and accounting. Counting measures are commonly referred to as nonfinancial operating control measures of performance. Nonfinancial operating controls need to be investigated to determine which measures contribute to a product's value and will best drive the production process toward improvement. The identification of nonfinancial measures in a manufacturing environment depends on the products and processes of the specific firm. Survey data on five nonfinancial measures of performance from 41 manufacturing plants indicated that quality and productivity information were more likely to be provided to managers than information on downtime, defects, and schedule compliance. Five similar major nonfinancial areas of operating controls to be investigated have been identified (14, 15): quality, delivery (including throughput and cycle time), inventory, material use and scrap, and machine availability and performance (Table 41.1).

To report new measures, new reporting systems should be developed. Like a wrench being used to drive a screw, one absolute system does not meet the needs of all areas in a firm. Cost accounting reports need to be treated as tools that are designed to meet the needs of managers. As companies begin to recognize their measurement systems as tools, they will become more effective in implementing their goals. Kaplan (11) suggested three systems be developed to address three different functions: inventory valuation, operational control, and product cost measurement.

Inventory valuation measurements (i.e., financial accounting measurements) should occur periodically and must allocate periodic production costs to all items produced. With this system, assigned overhead costs should be causally related to the demands of individual products. A critical problem with many existing accounting systems is that a company's overhead allocation scheme may not correspond to the underlying production process or to the demands individual products place on a company's resources. A reverberating theme of the new manufacturing environment is that systems for external reporting do not give managers relevant performance measurement and product cost information (9).

In contrast to financial control systems, operational control systems provide more timely and accurate feedback on performance to managers. Cost accounting calculations, such as the allocation of overhead to products and departments or volumetric measurements should not be a part of a company's operational control system, because they do not provide information that can improve the operations of the firm. Production managers primarily maintain control through nonfinancial measures such as setup times, throughput times, inventory levels, and percentage of defects. Reports of these nonfinancial measures are required at timely intervals.

The timeliness of information provided by an operations control system depends on the product being manufactured. Companies traditionally measure performance by comparing actual results against standard or budgeted levels. The comparisons need to be made anywhere from a real-time basis to quarterly basis, depending on the production environment. For example, a company that produces eight models of miniature automobiles in an assembly line production process will need more timely information than a job shop producer of sailing boats. Ultimately, real-time data may be the best for providing information to production managers; however, the costs of accumulating and analyzing the data need to be balanced with the realized added value. Since the advent of advanced computer data acquisition technology and artificial intelligence analysis techniques, the realization of accurate, timely reports is possible today.

Companies need to base their cost control systems on flexible budgets that adjust for costs that vary with fluctuations in the short-term production activity. Control of operations requires understanding costs that change with short-term variations in activity. Determining these short-term costs allows for the development of flexible budgets that adjust for changes in activity levels on the consumption of labor, material, machine time, energy, and support services. Separation of systems for operating performances measurement and volumetric or inventory measurement allow for operations managers to get timely and detailed reports that do not include noncontrollable costs allocated to products.

In addition to inventory valuation and operations control systems, development of a separate product cost measurement system can add value to management decision-making processes. Only two types of costs should not be allocated to individual products. One is the cost of research and development that can apply to future products, which should be considered investments in future products and allocated to those products at a later date. The second is idle capacity expense, which results during a particular period due to a decline in sales. All other costs in bringing a product to market should be accounted for, such as nonbasic research and development, design, purchasing, transportation, marketing, production, and support services (11). For example, top management time spent on development of a product can be considered a support services cost for a product. However, few product cost systems account for all of the resources required to bring a product to market. Inaccurate reporting of true product costs can lead to distorted product costs and subsequently poor managerial product decision making.

Unfortunately, proper measurement of product cost is expensive, often inaccurate, and time-consuming. The method most commonly used to account for difficult-to-determine product costs is to annually interview (or at major change points) production managers, support (overhead creating) personnel, material (logistical) movers, administration, and marketing department personnel. The result of the interviews will provide better allocation percentages for the work involved in each area, thereby providing a more accurate product costing (11).

TABLE 41.1. Nonfinancial Areas of Operating Control[a]

Quality Measures	Inventory Measures
Customer complaints	Turnover rates by location
Customer surveys	Raw materials
Warranty claims	Work in process
Quality audits	Finished goods
Vendor quality	Composite
Costs of quality	Turnover rates by product
Costs of scrap	Cycle count accuracy
Costs of rework	Space reduction
Costs of returns and allowances	Number of inventoried items
Costs of field service	*Machine Measures*
Costs of warranty claims	
Costs of lost business	Use
Throughput Measures	Downtime
	Maintenance
On-time delivery	Experience
Order fill rate	*Material Measures*
Lead time	
Waste time	Quality of incoming materials
Cycle time	Inspection
Setup time	Material lost (percent)
Production backlog	Actual scrap costs
	Scrap by part, product, and operation
	Scrap as a percentage of total cost

[a] From refs. 14 and 15.

The three cost systems presented provide reports for specific considerations. Another form of reporting that is designed for a specific internal customer, top management, is the balanced scorecard (16). According to Norton (16), president of Nolan, Norton, & Co.,

The balanced scorecard gives managers a fast, but balanced comprehensive view of the business. The balanced scorecard includes financial measures that tell the results of actions already taken and it complements the financial measures with operational measures on customer satisfaction, internal processes, and the organization's innovation and improvement activities—operational measures that are the drivers of future financial performance.

The balanced scorecard meets the needs of top management in two primary ways. First, the scorecard brings together separate strategic objectives or elements that frequently appear to be in conflict, such as becoming customer oriented, shortening response time, and improving quality. Second, the scorecard helps to prevent focusing on one objective at the expense of another. The scorecard forces managers to consider all the important measures together, thereby preventing suboptimization. An example of a truncated scorecard is given in Table 41.2.

The underlying idea that researchers and practitioners like Kaplan and Norton (16) are conveying is that reports should be tailored to the customer, i.e., top management, operations management, and marketing management. Tailoring reports will enable the various customers to work toward improvement in their specific role and propel the accounting function from a cost-measurement to a cost-management role.

Reactive to Proactive

Shifting from a cost-measurement to a cost-management role entails restructuring the accounting function from a reactive to a proactive role. Within a proactive role, accounting can provide

TABLE 41.2.   A Truncated Example of a Balanced Business Scorecard[a]

Perspective	Goals	Measures
Financial	Survive	Cash flow, debt ratio
	Prosper	Increase in market share
Customer	New products	Percent sales from new products
	Responsive supply	On-time delivery
Internal business	Manufacturing excellence	Percent of defects, cycle time, yield
	New product introduc- tion	Actual introduction, schedule versus plan
Innovation and learning	Technology leadership	Next generation development time
	Time to market	New product introduction versus competi- tion

[a] From ref. 16.

a managerial focus for improving processes and products. For example, if lead time is a problem, accounting must reflect the need to reduce lead time by focusing on measures that reduce lead time, such as reduction of setup times, shorter cycle times, smoothening of operations, cross-training, and increased quality. To make these measures proactive, the measures must be applied early in the design stage, because a large percentage of the total product cost is determined by the way a product is designed.

Prescriptions and proposals presented in papers for improving accounting systems have usually fallen into one of two groupings: (1) activity- and transaction-based costing and (2) product life cycle cost management. Of the two groupings, the product life cycle cost management concepts provide the more proactive focus. Activity and transaction based accounting cost systems are of a more traditional design in that they use historical data. In contrast to activity-based costing, product life cycle cost management systems focus on the costs of the required activities to conceive, design, develop, distribute, and maintain the product (17). Activity-based cost (ABC) analysis allocates the costs of production departments to specific products. The costs are allocated according to a determination of the activities that consume the department resources. In contrast to traditional accounting systems, ABC uses cost drivers that are not proportional to units produced. Also, ABC is a resource usage and not a cost allocation system. For example, Weyerhaeuser's ''charge back'' system for overhead allocation charges service department costs to users based on detailed analyses of activities that give rise to the costs (18).

The use of ABC can give management a baseline of where costs are being generated or consumed but will not tell them how to control these costs and support cost management in the design stages. ABC systems use historical data, which does not support management in the decision-making process for development of new technologies. In addition, ABC analysis does not illustrate how overhead costs can be reduced. In three studies, changing to an ABC system altered product costs; however, the connection between changes in costs and product costs was not determined (19–21). Functional areas at the Roseville Networks Division of Hewlett-Packard (such as marketing, manufacturing, and product design) attempted jointly to determine more accurate product costs within the ABC system.

Product life cycle cost management (PLCCM) allows the creation of focus on the design stage. The concept of PLCCM extends from idea inception to retirement in the field, consisting of the required activities to conceive, design, develop, produce, distribute, and maintain the product. PLCCM should not be confused with the marketing concept of the product life cycle, which focuses on a product's sales curve. Although no strong empirical evidence has been accumulated, the PLCCM model could contribute better than ABC to reducing costs in the early stages of product development. Because the focus would be on the design stage, better estimates of product costs before production could be developed.

Several nontraditional processes exist for estimating the costs of designs. Two of estimation processes receiving considerable attention are process-driven design (22) and market-drive design (23). In both process-driven and market-driven design, design is viewed as an iterative process, rather than a process that requires only one pass. Unlike traditional design processes for which the product design drives the process design the process design should drive product design (22). Furthermore cost estimation for product design should be achieved by using a manufacturing system model to estimate product costs as a function of product attributes (22). Hiromoto (23) suggests that such product attributes should be determined by the market using target costs, called market-driven design.

In support of their process-driven design proposal, Ulrich and Fine (22) are currently conducting research with a manufacturer of printed wiring boards (PWB). PWBs are a good choice for the research due to four factors related to the product and processes: large product range, large price variance, rapid technology changes, and complex technology. In developing a PWB cost model, the objective is to predict production costs from board attributes, manufacturing configuration, and technology configuration.

The estimation approach for the PWB designs proposed by Ulrich and Fine (22) consists of six general steps that are iteratively repeated until a low cost design is developed. Figure 41.4 illustrates the iterative process. First, the designer specifies the attributes of the board. Second, a process plan is developed by specifying the process steps required to manufacture specific attributes. Third, the yields at each of the process steps are estimated based on historical data, models of the physical process, and the attributes. Fourth, the manufacturing resource requirements are estimated. Fifth, the cost at each step in the process plan is calculated using the resource requirements and yield estimates. The designer then uses the cost information either to make modifications to the board or to approve the design. If the modifications are made, the modified design restarts the iterative process at the first step.

In contrast to process-driven design, Hiromoto (23) proposes that the design process include market-driven measures. According to Hiromoto (23), "Japanese companies have long recognized that the design stage holds the greatest promise for supporting low-cost production." The basic idea is that marketing determines what the customer wants and the price the customer will pay. A target cost is then calculated by subtracting a desired return on sales from the price the customer will pay. The target cost, which may be well below currently achievable costs, is then used as a benchmark against which progress is measured. According to Hiromoto (23), Japanese firms frequently use benchmarking to measure the incremental progress toward meeting the target cost. Investments are justified on the basis of building the product to sell at the predetermined price (4). If the existing costs to create the product (based on existing standard technologies and processes) are higher than the target cost, then the focus is on finding ways to meet the target cost.

As a result, the market-driven philosophy supports abandoning standard cost systems. Standard cost systems reflect an engineering mind-set and technology-driven management. The goal is to minimize variances between budgeted and actual cost or, rather, to perform as closely as possible to the best available practice. In the design stage, design engineers estimate costs and compare the estimates with the target. If a variance exists, then the design engineer interacts with the managers of the interfunctional areas to improve on processes or design to reduce the variance. Until the target cost is met, a cycle continues, consisting of design proposals, cost estimates, variance calculations, value engineering analysis, and redesign (24). The market-driven model suggested by Hiromoto (23) is presented in Figure 41.5.

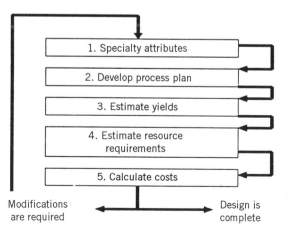

Modifications are required ← → Design is complete

Figure 41.4. Process-driven design: iterative cost estimation approach for PWB designs.

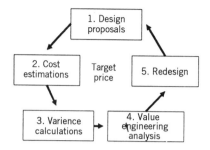

Figure 41.5. Market-driven design: iterative target-price model.

First, design proposals are created based on the product attributes marketing has determined. Second, cost estimations of manufacturing the product based on the designs are calculated. Third, the difference between the target price and the cost estimations is calculated. If the costs to manufacture are higher than the target price, then Step 4 is enacted. If the costs to manufacture are less than or equal to the target price, then the design is completed and may be sent to production. If the design is not approved, then the next step is to conduct a value engineering analysis to determine how the design could be changed to reduce the cost. Finally a new design is developed (redesign) and proposed for cost estimation. The iterative procedure continues until the estimated costs to produce the product based on the current design under consideration do not exceed the target price.

By comparing estimates with the target, new designs can validate themselves through cost justification. The cost system needs to be able to identify all costs for manufacturing, thus allowing new technology to use its improvements in productivity and quality to justify its implementation. The interdependencies between production costs such as maintenance, supervision, and quality control (2) need to be clarified for designers to understand the manufacturing impact of their designs. Justification of implementation is necessary if management intends to use cost accounting as a driver for change and to gain support for the implementation of the new technology.

Because the market-driven design process could omit desirable inputs from production and the process-driven design process could omit desirable inputs from the customer, we propose a combination of the two processes. Using a combination of process-driven and market-driven designs creates a manufacturing system model that can aid materially in efforts to optimize the product design process. The proposed information flows of design cost information are presented in Figure 41.6; Figure 41.7 presents a combination process- and market-driven design model. By extending the cost system into the design stages, accounting information can better align design processes with the strategy of the firm. While strategy should drive measurement, measurement should then drive improvement. Only in this way will improvements be dictated by strategy. For example, if strategy dictates improvements that reduce design cycle time, then the nonvalue added causes of design cycle time need to be identified, quantified, and measured. Developing strategic measures such as these cannot be accomplished without a synergistic relationship with other functional areas such as engineering, purchasing, marketing, and manufacturing. Working with other functional areas, accounting can identify the true cost drivers, cost applications, and performance measures in the production environment. The combination of process-driven and market-driven design processes could greatly aid in achieving these goals.

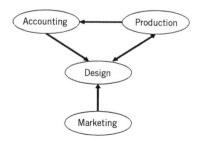

Figure 41.6. Process-driven and market-driven design influence flows.

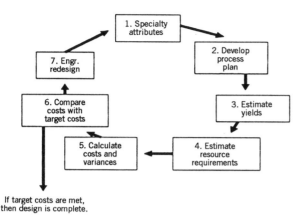

Figure 41.7. Process-driven and market-driven design process: iterative process.

If target costs are met, then design is complete.

Cost, Quality, Profitability, and Market Share

The primary objectives for most manufacturers today are simultaneously to improve the quality, profitability, and market share of a product while lowering costs. Although these objectives appear to be in conflict, many world-class companies have determined that the costs incurred through improving quality are outweighed by improvements in cost savings, profitability, and market share (25–27). This view is in contrast to the traditional view that increases in quality are inevitably coupled with increases in cost and production time. Deming (5) discusses the chain reaction of improving quality. By improving quality, costs decrease because of less rework, fewer mistakes, and better use of machine time and materials, which all improve productivity. Improved productivity, in turn, increases market share, profitability, and raises the competitive advantage. According to Tyson (26), management accountants appear to be well aware of the direct relationship between quality and profitability.

To achieve positive results as represented by the new view, the accounting system must be capable of measuring the costs of quality (COQ) to establish focus for quality improvement. Costs of poor quality have been estimated at 10% to 20% of sales for most U.S. manufacturers (12, 27). Three major classifications of the costs of quality are recognized: prevention costs, appraisal costs, and failure costs. Failure costs are further broken down into internal failure costs and external failure costs. Campanella (28) provided more details of the COQ:

Prevention Costs: costs of all activities specifically designed to prevent poor quality in products of services. Examples are the costs of new product review, quality planning, supplier capacity surveys, process capability evaluations, quality improvement team meetings, quality improvement projects, quality education and training.

Appraisal Costs: costs associated with measuring, evaluating, auditing products or services to assure conformance to quality standards and performance requirements. These include the costs of incoming and source inspections/test of purchased material, in process and final inspection/test, product, process, or service audits, calibration of measuring and test equipment, and the cost of associated materials and supplies.

Failure Costs: costs resulting from products or services not conforming to requirements or customer/ user needs.
  Internal Failure Costs: costs occurring prior to delivery or shipment of the product, or the furnishing of a service, to the customer. Examples are the cost of scrap, rework, reinspection, retesting, material review, and down grading.
  External Failure Costs: costs occurring after delivery or shipment of the product, and during or after furnishing a service, to the customer. Examples are the costs of processing customer complaints, customer returns, warranty claims, and product recalls.

The traditional approach to controlling quality costs is to find the optimal quality level at which total quality costs are minimized. The traditional optimal quality cost model is presented in Figure 41.8. Note that the quality level at which optimal quality costs are obtained is where

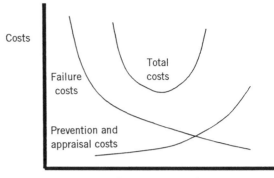

Figure 41.8. Traditional
optimal quality cost.

Q u Quality level ⸴ l

the total costs curve is minimized. In addition, notice that as investments in prevention and appraisal costs are incurred, failure costs become lower. The investments, in turn, lower total quality costs. However, the quality return on the investments in prevention and appraisal dissipate as perfect quality is approached; therefore, at some point, total costs will actually increase with increases in investments in prevention and appraisal costs. Based on this theory of diminishing returns, a certain level of defects is allowed (29).

Figure 41.8 presents the theory of quality costs, showing the effects of investments. In actuality, a manager will not be able to measure all of the costs associated with quality, and he or she must work within a budget constraint. Because internal and external failure quality costs are often not controllable for the manufacturing manager, the manager must usually allocate investments into both the prevention and appraisal categories. The decision possibilities are given by the budget space as determined by drawing a budget line (Figure 41.9).

If quality is defined in terms of a measurable quantity (such as a defect rate), then investment choices in prevention and appraisal costs can be represented by an indifference curve (29). Every possible point on the indifference curve represents a potential budget possibility. Figure 41.10 presents indifference curves for 1%, 5%, and 10% defect levels. Because a reduction in the prevention investment requires an increase in appraisal investment (or vice versa) to maintain a specified level of quality, the slope of the curve is inward. The actual slope of the curve represents the marginal rate of substitution of prevention costs for appraisal costs, given a certain quality level or rate of return. The optimal spending level of the budget is found by combining the budget line and the indifference curve (Figure 41.11). In Figure 41.11, the optimal investment is at point B, where the defect rate is minimized to 5% (29).

What the previous economic analysis does not account for is the capability of shifting the indifference curves toward the x axis, so that smaller investments in prevention and appraisal investments yield equal or higher quality. In other words, by using the COQ model and minimiz-

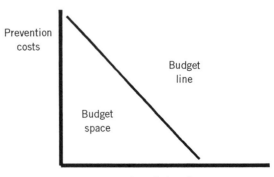

Figure 41.9. Budget space for
controllable quality costs.

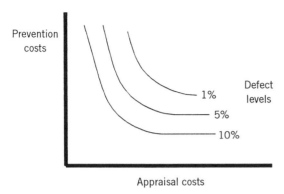

Figure 41.10. Indifference curves for controllable quality costs.

ing total COQ, assumptions are made that zero defects are not possible and there is a cost minimizing trade-off between failure costs and the combination of prevention and appraisal costs. After studying Japanese production systems, the COQ analysis has become questioned. Some companies have been able to eliminate virtually all defects, especially in manufacturing environments that are high in manufacturing automation.

The focus of zero defects quality professionals has been on the prevention costs of the COQ. A major goal in quality improvement is to reduce the total variance in processes. Reduction in total variance requires reduction in the variance of every aspect of the processes. Overall, reduction of process variance through prevention activities of simultaneous inspection, checking, identifying, and eliminating process variance will improve the competitive capability of the firm. To reduce process variances, inspection procedures must become part of the manufacturing process itself. The focus must be on stopping the causes of a problem, not correcting the results of a problem. Accounting must provide the measures and enforcement of those measures to facilitate a proactive focus on the causes of a problem in the design process and later in the actual manufacturing processes.

In working toward zero defects, the greatest cost savings in quality occur as a result of properly established priorities in the design processes. The accountant has control of the measurements that drive design and production, it is simply a choice of what measures to use. The ideal goal is to improve processes and products in the design stages so that defects are eliminated before the first product is manufactured. Discovering defects due to design flaws after a product is already being produced significantly increases failure costs.

Two other decision tools that are similar to the costs of quality are direct (physical) measures of quality (DMOQ) and revenue and cost of quality (RACOQ). Direct physical measures of quality is not used nearly as much as COQ; however, DMOQ has an advantage over COQ in that direct measures are easily quantified and understood by factory workers. Direct measures are nonfinancial measures without currency values associations, such as defect rates, machine uptime, product throughput, process variability, and absenteeism. The lack of currency value

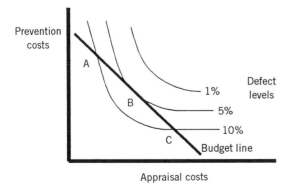

Figure 41.11. Optimal budget for controllable quality costs.

associations means that the measures cannot be aggregated with a common unit of measure and be used for trade-off analyses as easily as COQ can. The objective with DMOQ is to minimize one or more of these nonfinancial direct measures.

In contrast, the revenue and cost of quality decision tool is not being used by any firm; however, it may overcome some of the problems with COQ and DMOQ. With RACOQ, the revenue and cost effects of quality are measured to gauge the impact of quality on firm profitability; therefore, the objective of RACOQ is to maximize quality profitability or revenue minus costs. The problem with RACOQ is in measuring the revenue effects of quality.

The management accountant must recognize accounting's role in the facilitation of quality improvements. Understanding and properly measuring the costs of quality will provide greater focus on the design processes, where quality decisions first developed. Tyson (26) notes that when the controller's department specifically measures quality, internal programs are more frequently developed for improvement and recognition of quality. This is an indication that measurement may impact activities directed toward quality improvement.

41.2 UNDERSTANDING AND MEASURING THE IMPACTS

Production Activities and Manufacturing Cost

Cost drivers are processes that increase the cost of a product. For example, the total number of parts in a product can be considered a cost driver because each part requires costs of development, production, and storage to be incurred. At NCR the elimination of several screws in their 2760 cash register design resulted in manufacturing cost savings of more than $12,000 per screw over the life of the product (22). Some cost drivers used include the number of material movements, total part numbers, new parts introduced, units reworked, process changes needed, engineering changes needed, and units scrapped. Classification of costs into categories, such as non–value added and value added, can aid in reducing the cost of a product while it is still in the design stage. Value-added cost drivers directly add value to the product. In the NCR example, the unnecessary screws are considered non–value-added cost drivers, while the necessary screws are considered value-added cost drivers. The distinction between a cost adding value or not is frequently difficult to determine. For example, the costs of raw material and direct labor that directly account for the production of the product are value-added cost drivers. In contrast, a process that does not fully use the raw material and creates scrap or an idle employee can be considered a non–value-added cost driver process. In addition to reducing the cost of a product in the design stage, the identification, classification, and subsequent measurement of value- and non–value-added costs will create an organizationwide focus on eliminating wasteful practices. The interfunctional measurement of the causes of waste will then change the behavioral patterns of personnel in purchasing, design, production, and marketing.

To understand and measure the impacts of production activities on manufacturing cost requires interfunctional design and manufacturing teams, in which accountants have a functioning and dynamic role. The benefits of functional area integration have been well documented. For example, cooperation between research and development (R&D) and production as well as the ability to meet cost targets were identified as key correlating factors in determining new industrial product performance (30). In addition, Hayes et al. (31) argued that cooperation and understanding between design and production are important dimensions of competitive manufacturing success.

Accounting personnel need to visit the factory floor to understand how design and production processes operate. An idea, put forth by Briner et al. (32) is to assign cost managers to manufacturing departments and assign manufacturing personnel to accounting departments. Cross-functional interaction will help reduce barriers between the functional areas and enlighten both areas about synergistic ideas that will foster improvement. Including accounting personnel in the design process is particularly valuable. An interfunctional design team composed of personnel from research and development, design, accounting, purchasing, production, and marketing could accurately identify and classify all cost drivers that are required to bring a product to market.

Many tools exist that the interfunctional design team could use to identify, classify, and measure cost drivers. For example, a team could use quality function deployment (QFD), cause-and-effect diagrams, pareto analysis, and statistical analysis techniques. QFD is a management approach that is a set of planning and communications routines that is designed to break down functional barriers by encouraging teamwork, creating focus, and coordinating the skills of the design team members (33). Cause-and-effect diagrams provide a structured approach for identifying the underlying causes of problems. After identifying the causes of product cost, pareto chart analysis could be used to obtain quickly the percentages of the total cost or magnitudes for each cause. The next step is to evaluate the cost impact statistically, using a statistical technique like regression analysis.

In 1985, field investigations were conducted that included tours and interviews at four plants in the electronics industry. Using regression analysis, it was concluded that manufacturing overhead costs are primarily driven by transaction costs. The transactions were activities involving exchanges of materials and information needed for production but that did not directly result in physical output. The problem with the conclusion about the relationship was that the authors did not establish whether plants with less transactions had less overhead or vice versa.

Regression analysis provides the needed focus on the highest impact measures. Using regression analysis, studies in both the manufacturing and service sectors have been able to support positions that certain measures should or should not be included in reporting. For example, Foster and Gupta (19, 20) conducted an analysis in 1989 of the relationships between cost drivers and manufacturing overhead. The data were obtained from 34 variables taken from 37 facilities of an electronics company. Three different types of cost drivers were identified and investigated: volume based, complexity based, and efficiency based. In the study, some of the measures investigated were total manufacturing space, average head count in manufacturing, level of output, direct labor dollars, direct material dollars, total ending inventory dollars, complexity of product design, number of part numbers on materials records file, number of material structure levels in an average product, total number of part numbers in an average product, total number of vendors, and manufacturing process product range. The strongest association in the Foster and Gupta (19, 20) analysis was found for volume-based cost drivers, which are the bases usually used to allocate overhead. Complexity-based and efficiency-based cost drivers had only a weak association with manufacturing overhead. The explanation given by Foster and Gupta (19, 20) for the weak association is that complexity- and efficiency-related cost drivers include proxy problems, with the complexity and efficiency concepts and problems in developing uniform measures across a broad sections of facilities.

Before conducting the regression analysis, costs need to be classified as fixed or variable costs. Next, the magnitudes of the costs need to be estimated. Operations managers and industrial engineers working on the manufacturing processes that are producing the product whose cost structure is being analyzed should be able to provide estimates of desirable cost behavior between output produced and input resources used. Unfortunately, these estimates are sometimes unavailable or difficult to use. If that is the case, then cost estimates can be obtained, if available, from analysis of historical cost behavior. Finally, the relationships between the data need to be determined. To accomplish this the underlying variability or uncertainty in the cost process from one measure to another should be investigated, to show which measures are actually affecting the cost of the product.

Design Complexity and Manufacturing Cost

Earlier in this chapter, the design phase was established as critical to controlling production process costs. For example, if the company's production direction is to reduce setup time, then those products that require long set up times will have more overhead allocated (34). If the company's design direction is to reduce part numbers manufactured, then those products using the most number of unique parts will be allocated more overhead costs. If the company's goal is to reduce the overall cycle time for the manufacture of a product, then those products that require the largest cycle time will be allocated more overhead costs. The following list of key product design measures represents a start for focusing attention on product quality in design to reduce total product cost (35).

- Designing product and process concurrently.
- Measuring and striving for design simplicity.
- Minimizing the number of parts.
- Minimizing the number of part numbers.
- Using as high a percentage of preferred parts as possible.
- Minimizing the number of vendors.

The first measure in the list is achieved through concurrent engineering. Concurrent engineering is a philosophy for the simultaneous design of the product and the processes required to produce it as well as support it. Concurrent engineering can help to reduce product development cycle time for the introduction of high quality products at a low cost. Often traditional cost estimating systems are used in the concurrent engineering environment; however, many new tools and methods have been developed for support. Concurrent engineering tools can be classified into three principal groups according to use: (*1*) to determine customer wants, (*2*) to establish process control, and (*3*) to improve the process. Concurrent engineering relies heavily on accurate cost estimating.

Cost estimating is the task of determining and evaluating the costs involved in an engineering product or project. Three types of cost estimates have been proposed: screening, budget, and definitive. The classes are separated by the level of detail that each one provides to the decision maker. The screening estimate provides the least amount of information, whereas the definitive estimate provides the most.

In the traditional engineering design phase for product development, first the engineers define the specifications for the proposed product, then they perform feasibility studies. Next, the engineering department creates preliminary designs, conducts engineering analyses, and prepares drawings. The drawings are sent to the laboratory for prototyping and testing. Test results are analyzed for the next cycle's design and analysis. After several cycles, the testing results confirm that the design performed satisfactorily. At this point, the project engineer makes a decision to finalize the design. Finally, the product's layout is delivered to the process planning department.

Process planning is that function within a manufacturing facility that establishes which machining processes and parameters are to be used to machine a piece of material from its initial form to a final form predetermined by engineering drawings. Alternatively, process planning could be defined as the act of preparing detailed work instructions, known as route sheets. The route sheets list the route, production process, process parameters, and machine and tool selections. These instructions dictate quality, rate of production, and cost.

A traditional cost estimating system consists of five tasks: material cost, labor cost, operation cost, overhead cost, and product cost. Input datum elements to the cost estimating system include route sheets as well as cost data for materials, labor, operations, overhead, and product. The main output generated from the system is a detailed estimate.

Ulrich and Fine (22) summarize five existing approaches for communicating cost issues to product designers:

1. Judgment of engineering design team.
2. Services of an expert estimator.
3. Expert estimator computer program.
4. Assembly-driven design for manufacturing.
5. Design for total life cycle costs.

The most common approach is using the qualitative judgment of experienced engineers on the design team. Using the judgment of experienced engineers, the collective experience of the members can shape the decisions that influence production costs. The team may choose to use guidelines or rules developed from their engineering experiences. For example, a manufacturing adviser computer program was developed for the design of aluminum extrusions for heat fins.

The services of expert estimators are frequently used in large firms that repeatedly design similar products. The process that expert estimators use is similar to quotes on jobs to be fabricated by a production facility. First, a process plan is developed. Second, a direct labor machine time is determined for each operation. Third, hourly rates are applied to these times to calculate a cost. Fourth, an overhead cost is calculated by multiplying a constant factor and the cost generated in the third step.

Another approach is the development and use of an expert estimator computer program. Basically, the computer program automates the steps of the expert estimator's process. Computer programs have advantages because they can estimate costs quickly, allowing evaluation of many more alternatives than a human estimator can accomplish.

Assembly-driven design for manufacturing focuses on improving the ease of assembly of a product. The assumption of assembly-driven design is that designs will be improved in other ways by focusing on ease of assembly. The method assigns objective scores to designs based on the ease with which a collection of parts can be assembled. The major weakness of the method is that its production costs are viewed as being primarily driven by assembly costs.

The design for total life cycle approach is based on the assumption that the design stage of a product's life cycle has a large impact on total life cycle costs. The main thrust of the total life cycle approach is to establish relationships between product attributes and the magnitude of hidden costs. For example, the relationship of the cost of failure (hidden cost) due to poor quality (attribute) may be established using this method.

Ulrich and Fine (22) identify four major requirements of a product cost modeling tool: speed, accuracy, insight, and modularity. The underlying properties of a system to meet these requirements are identified as computer based, enlightened cost accounting concepts based on principled foundations, and modularity. Computer programs provide the arithmetic speed needed to provide rapid feedback. Enlightened cost accounting, provides insight and accuracy on the impact of design on manufacturing by better identifying the causes of costs. The accounting concepts should rest on principled foundations, such as the underlying model of the production process and not just statistical correlations calculated from historical data. Finally, the computer program should be modular, because production processes are modular.

An example of a modular computer design for estimating costs is the concept of integrated cost estimating system for concurrent engineering (ICESCE). ICESCE is designed specifically to work within the concurrent engineering environment. ICESCE consists of four modules: a database module, a central processing module, an interface module, and a utility module.

Design Complexity and Field Failure Cost

The benefits of including field failure data in making decisions at the early stages of product development have been discussed in Hegde and Karmarkar (17). Consider the problem of choosing between two alternative design choices. The choices in two summary parameters are $\theta = $ MTBF, mean time between failures $1/\mu = $ MTTR, mean time to repair. Specifically, the engineering unit of the firm has provided information about the feasibility of producing two models of the product (Tables 41.3 and 41.4). Note that Design X fails less often but takes longer to repair (due to complex design), whereas Design Y fails more often but gets repaired faster. How does the manager of an engineering unit evaluate these two alternatives?

Suppose that engineering and manufacturing are about to choose one design alternative among three possible choices: X, Y, and Z. Engineering and manufacturing data used to make such decisions in a traditional engineering orientation are provided in Table 41.3. For illustration, we assume a specific functional form for the production cost as shown in Table 41.3. Design Z is preferred since it has the lowest production cost while the availability is the same as that for design Y or X.

Now, suppose that the product in question is used in emergency situations (such as a diagnostic machine used in hospitals), and the field failure costs are significant if the product fails. In particular, suppose that each failure instance results in a fixed cost, F, of $10,000 and a variable cost, C, of $100/unit down time. Models developed in (17, 34) to compute field failure costs can now be used. For illustration, the total costs (production and field failure cost) for the linear cost structure and nonlinear cost structure are presented in Table 41.4.

If one were to make a decision based on production cost alone, the recommendation would be to go for Design Z, because Design Z results in lowest production cost. However, consideration of field failure cost leads to altogether different decisions. If the customer cost structure is linear, then the choice is clearly Design X, because the Design X has the lowest total (production plus failure) cost. If the customer cost structure is nonlinear, the least total cost choice is

TABLE 41.3. Design Choices and Production Costs

Choices	$(\theta, 1/\mu)$	Availability[a]	Production Costs[b]
Design X	(100, 6.0)	.9433	103
Design Y	(50, 3.0)	.9433	36
Design Z	(40, 2.4)	.9433	33

[a] Availability $= \theta/(\theta + 1/\mu)$.
[b] Production cost, $G(\theta, \mu) = .01\theta^2 + 100\mu^2$.

TABLE 41.4.   Total Cost with F = \$10,000 and C = \$1,000

Design	$(\theta, 1/\mu)$	Production Cost	Field Failure Cost		Total Cost (Production Cost + Field Failure Cost)	
			Linear[a]	Nonlinear[b]	Linear	Nonlinear
X	(100, 6.0)	103	151	435	254	538
Y	(50, 3.0)	36	245	359	281	405
Z	(40, 2.4)	33	293	372	325	456

[a] $\dfrac{F + C/\mu}{\theta + 1/\mu}$.

[b] $\dfrac{F + C/\mu^2}{\theta + 1/\mu}$.

Design Y. In either case, the low reliability ($\theta = 40$) choice, which has least production cost is not favored at all. The intuition behind these recommendations can be explained as follows. When the variable costs are linear, the fixed cost component dominates. Design X, which has the fewest number of failures, is the best. In case of nonlinear cost structure, the effect of slow field response (high $1/\mu$) is significant. As a result, Design Y whose θ value is higher than that of Design Z and whose field response value is better than that of Design X becomes the best choice.

Design Complexity and Costs of Quality

Datar et al. (2) proposed a model to capture the interrelations that exist among costs categories of various stages of product life cycle: design, production, and field failure. Such a model can be valuable when used in environments of high product and process diversity and there is an increasing emphasis on understanding drivers of costs of quality. Using data collected from a plant of a large automobile manufacturer, Datar et al. (2) showed that the costs of internal and external failure (from, e.g., defects, scrap, and rework) often do not increase and may, in some cases, decrease because the firm spends more on prevention and appraisal to reduce failure costs. Failure costs, therefore, are driven jointly by activities, complexity of the product and process, and prevention and appraisal costs. But prevention and appraisal costs themselves depend on product and process complexity. This analysis of simultaneous interaction among cost categories with varying complexity has implications for the management of complexity at the design stage.

The Datar et al. (2) approach is in contrast to most applications of activity-based costing that first identify activities and cost drivers based on interviews and discussions with organizational personnel and then calculate product costs based on the quantity of various activities demanded by individual products. By reversing this process and first directly determining the resources consumed by products, this analysis quantifies the impact of the design engineers' efforts on reducing other cost categories.

The research site used by Datar et al. (2) is a lamp manufacturing plant of a large automobile company. Datar et al. (2) identified several product and process design features such as moving parts in the mold and multicolor molding that explain differences in overhead costs demanded by various products. They referred to these variables as exogenous variables, because the values of these intrinsic product and process complexity factors are determined outside the plant domain, based largely on the demand for complex lamps by car manufacturers. The exogenous variables are used to explain variations in costs of supervision, tool maintenance, quality control, and scrap incurred within the plant for individual lamps. As explained earlier, the costs of quality control, inspection, and scrap also depend on the resources spent on supervision and tool maintenance within the plant (which, in turn, depend on exogenous complexity variables). They classified various cost categories as endogenous variables, because the values of these variables are determined by the simultaneous interaction of costs of the plant domain.

Valuable information for both product designers and operations managers can be provided by the proposed methodology. For designers, the methodology provides the net impact of complexity drivers on various categories of costs. For operations managers, the methodology provides a better understanding of how these costs are created. By recognizing the interaction among cost categories, operations managers can develop appropriate strategies to manage the costs of quality by increasing expenditures in some categories (prevention) to reduce costs in others (failures).

Design and Production Interaction: Incentive Issues

Incentive issues arising in the integration of production control and process improvement on the shop floor were addressed by Hegde and Nagarajan (34). For example, high overhead rate estimates identified by an ABC system can result in a decision to increase lot sizes, thereby reducing setup related overhead costs. However, while increasing lot size may be important for short-term competitiveness, Hegde and Nagarajan (34) argued that long-term control of setup related overhead costs can be achieved only by decreasing setup time.

Hegde and Nagarajan (34) discussed the role of incentive systems in simultaneously implementing both short-term and long-term strategies. In particular, the impact of choice of performance measures in mitigating conflicts between production personnel who may be concerned with short-term cost reduction and design engineering personnel who are responsible for reducing setup time was illustrated.

Consider the example of continuous improvement in which the goal is to reduce setup cost. Efforts to reduce setup cost may proceed in different ways. For instance, setup related costs can be reduced by using fewer setups. Setup related costs can also be lowered through reductions in setup time. This can be achieved by standardizing component parts and raw materials. In addition, setup time may be reduced by production personnel implementing the ideas of manufacturing tool engineers in converting internal setup operations into external setup operations. Thus setup cost reduction projects can involve various functional specialists, such as engineers, purchasing managers, maintenance crews, and production personnel. Given the importance of coordinating the actions of these various individuals, their performance measurement and incentive structures become critical factors in determining the success or failure of such efforts.

In competitive environments, product pricing becomes an important issue. Unit product costs often play a significant role in determining pricing policy, especially if cost-based pricing is used. In such situations, there may be tremendous pressure to reduce costs to retain market share or, in the extreme, to ensure survival. If setup related costs are estimated to be high (through an analysis such as ABC), a quick and direct method of reducing such costs is to reduce the number of setups by increasing lot size. Although the use of ABC as an "acceptable" estimate of overhead costs is consistent with its growing popularity and frequency of adoption in U.S. corporations, the recommendation to increase lot size should be recognized as a strategy that only ensures short-term competitiveness. The long-term cost reducing strategy is to reduce setup times and ensure feasibility of "small lot" or just-in-time (JIT) production through process improvement.

The responsibility for implementing a change in short-term shop floor control policy (e.g., lot size determination) rests with production personnel, whereas long-term process improvement (for example, reducing setup time) is the responsibility of manufacturing engineers. As is fairly common corporate practice, these two groups may be provided incentives, such as bonus payments, to reduce overhead costs. Implementation of new systems and processes such as setup time reduction to control long-term costs can result in a significant increase in short-term costs. For instance, a case has been documented wherein a $1 million investment in new equipment imposed $1.75 million in additional plant costs during the first year of operation. Such an adverse impact on short-term cost control can result in incentive conflicts between production and engineering groups. While both short-term and long-term phases of setup cost reduction can be important for corporations, such incentive conflicts can result in either the short-term or the long-term strategy being implemented or, worse, neither being implemented. Companies cope with such problems by turning to incentive arrangements that promote more cooperation and by laying less emphasis on financial criteria.

To elaborate, consider the "John Deere Component Works" (11), a well-known Harvard Business School case. The John Deere Component Works case documents the problems faced by the gear and special products division of Deere and Co. in competitive bidding in the 1980s when there was a slump in agricultural demand for tractors. The division discovered that it was consistently losing bids on complex, highly machined components that it was best configured to produce and winning bids on low value, simpler parts that were peripheral to its product strategy. Because this suggested a problem with the costing system, divisional management decided to acquire additional cost information through developing an ABC system at the screw machine shop, which was not only a major cost center but also a bottleneck facility. The ABC system identified hitherto unrecognized cost drivers (setups, material handling, etc.), which, combined with changes in the manufacturing process, enabled the division better to understand and thereby to reduce unit product costs.

The ABC study led to the recommendation that in the short-term the company should decrease the number of setups (increase lot size) to control overhead costs. The case also documents that John Deere was establishing a JIT system. One implication of JIT could be that the plant was also trying to achieve a goal of smaller lot sizes, and as a consequence, the number of setups could increase. It is clear that the recommendation to *decrease* the number of setups by *increasing* lot size will run counter to the objective of JIT. How does one reconcile these conflicting objectives? Hegde and Karmarkar (17) used a model with capacity constraints to explain this seemingly counterintuitive recommendation.

At least three situations exist in which production control dictates an increase in lot size: (*1*) costs are correctly estimated but the lot size Q must be increased in the short-term to meet the capacity constraint (this is a cost increasing strategy), (*2*) the ABC analysis reveals that the current Q is smaller than the optimal lot size Q^* because the setup rate R is underestimated (this is a short-term cost reducing strategy), and (*3*) the ABC analysis reveals that the current Q is smaller than Q^* because the other overhead costs m are underestimated (this is also a short-term cost reducing strategy). The foregoing discussion suggests that short-term overhead cost control measures can include reducing the number of setups (through lot size increase), especially when finer cost information is available.

The model further suggests that an alternative to increasing lot size is for the company to reduce setup time. While this is a long-term strategy, it alleviates the problem (reduces the cost) in two ways. First, because each setup now takes less time, there is an increase in the effective capacity. Second, the cost of setup has decreased because of a decrease in setup time. Thus process improvements that reduce setup time can in the long-term reduce the setup-related costs by reducing lot size and easing the capacity constraint.

In competitive situations, it may become important for the company to keep overhead costs (such as setup costs) under control while simultaneously making manufacturing improvements to reduce these costs in the long term. Implementing both short- and long-term aspects of this cost-control strategy can require the cooperation of different functional specialists such as production and engineering personnel. Whether such cooperative efforts will be successful critically depends on how the performance of employees is measured and how incentive payments are determined. Hegde and Nagarajan (34) suggested the use of team-based incentive and performance systems to facilitate cooperation between design and tool engineers and production personnel, thereby achieving short-term cost reduction and long-term process improvement.

41.3 CONCLUSIONS

According to Howell and Soucy (14, 15) most accounting departments have not updated their control mechanisms and processes; however, many companies that are considered superior manufacturers have discarded or subordinated traditional performance measures and replaced them with measures that better reflect the present manufacturing environment. Issues such as quality, delivery, inventory, and machine performance are replacing measures of labor productivity, machine and capacity use, and standard cost variances. Many companies now employ a detailed COQ figure in their monthly reporting package as well as reporting SPC Statistical Process Control results, customer complaints, and other nonfinancial measures on a daily and weekly basis (11). However, addressing such issues properly requires a proactive focus that begins in the product life cycle stage in which the greatest amount of product cost is committed: the design stage.

Accounting must have active involvement in the design stages of products and processes to complete the shift from a reactive cost-measurement to a proactive cost-management role. In accomplishing the shift, costs must be expensed at the same time they are committed. No longer can manufacturers in competitive markets afford to lose the potential gains cost control can provide in the design stage of the product life cycle. Many benefits can be accrued by a proactive cost control system, such as improvements in quality, market share, flexibility, and profitability.

To achieve these improvements, accounting needs to provide cost information that links costs with the underlying causes and related costs of poor and good performance. For example, in the absence of modeling efforts (such as those presented earlier), it is difficult to quantify the impact of design changes and field support on overall life cycle cost. Modeling efforts lead to establishing an information network through which engineering, production, and field support personnel share information about cost structure—at the design stage as well as the other stages in the product life cycle. Modeling effort is a first step in emphasizing the importance of the interaction between accounting, design engineering, production, and other functional areas that are involved in the extended process.

BIBLIOGRAPHY

1. R.D. BANKER, S.M. DATAR, S. KEKRE, and T. MUKHOPADHYAY, *Costs of Product and Process Complexity,* Carnegie Mellon University, Pittsburgh, Pa., 1989, Working paper.

2. S.M. DATAR, S. KEKRE, T. MUKHOPADHYAY, and K. SRINIVASAN, *Simultaneous Cost Engineering Management of Complexity,* Stanford University and Carnegie Mellon University, Pittsburgh, Pa., 1992, Working paper.

3. R.S. KAPLAN and A.A. ATKINSON, *Advanced Management Accounting,* 2nd ed., Prentice-Hall, Inc., Englewood Cliffs, N.J., 1982.

4. O. PORT, R. KING, and W.J. HAMPTON, "How the New Math of Productivity Adds Up," *Bus. Week,* June 6, 1988, pp. 103–113.

5. W.E. DEMING, *Out of Crisis,* MIT Center for Advanced Engineering Study, Cambridge, 1986.

6. W.G. DOWNEY, *Development Cost Estimating,* Her Majesty's Stationery Office, London, 1969, Report of the Steering Group for the Ministry of Aviation.

7. D.E. WHITNEY, "Manufacturing by Design," *Harvard Bus. Rev.,* 83–91, (July–Aug. 1988).

8. J.R. DIXON and M.R. DUFFEY, "The Neglect of Engineering Design," *Calif. Manage. Rev.,* 9–22 (Winter 1990).

9. R.A. HOWELL and S.R. SOUCY, "Management Reporting in the New Manufacturing Environment," *Manage. Account.,* 22–29 (Feb. 1988).

10. R. COOPER, and R.S. KAPLAN, "How Cost Accounting Distorts Product Costs," *Manage. Account.* 204–228 (Apr. 1988).

11. R.S. KAPLAN, "John Deere Component Works," Harvard Business School Case, Cambridge, Mass., 1988.

12. M.S. YOUNG and F.H. SELTO, "New Manufacturing Practices and Cost Management: A Review of the Literature and Directions for Research," *J. Account. Lit.* **10,** 265–298 (1991).

13. R.S. KAPLAN, *Relevance Lost: The Rise and Fall of Management Accounting,* Harvard Business School Press, Cambridge, Mass., 1987.

14. R.A. HOWELL and S.R. SOUCY, "Major trends for Management Accounting," *Manage. Account.,* 21–27 (July 1987).

15. R.A. HOWELL and S.R. SOUCY, "Operating Controls in the New Manufacturing Environment," *Manage. Account.,* 25–31 (Oct. 1987).

16. R.S. KAPLAN and D.P. NORTON, "The Balanced Scorecard—Measures That Drive Productivity," *Harvard Bus. Rev.* 71–79 (Jan.–Feb. 1992).

17. G.G. HEGDE and U.S. KARMARKAR, "Engineering Costs and Customer Costs in Designing Product Support," *Naval Research Logistics,* **40,** 415–423 (1993).

18. H.T. JOHNSON and D.A. LOEWE, "How Weyerhaeuser Manages Corporate Overhead Costs," *Manage. Account.,* 21–26 (Aug. 1987).

19. G. FOSTER and M. GUPTA, *Manufacturing Overhead Cost Driver Analysis,* Stanford University, Stanford, Calif., 1989, Working paper.

20. G. FOSTER and M. GUPTA, *Implementation of an Activity Accounting System in the Electronics Industry,* Stanford University, Stanford, Calif., 1989, Working paper.

21. D. BERLANT, R. BROWNING, and G. FOSTER, *Tomorrow's Accounting Today: An Activity Accounting System for PC Board Assembly,* Stanford University, Stanford, Calif., 1988, Working paper.

22. K.T. ULRICH and C.H. FINE, *Cost Estimation Tools to Support Product Design,* paper presented at the ASME Manufacturing International Conference, Mar. 1990.

23. T. HIROMOTO, "Another Hidden Edge—Japanese Management Accounting," *Harvard Bus. Rev.,* 22–26 (July–Aug. 1988).

24. F.S. WORTHY, "Japan's Smart Secret Weapon," *Fortune,* 72–75 Aug. 12, 1989.

25. J.R. EVANS and W.M. LINSAY, *The Management and Control of Quality,* West Publishing, 1989.

26. T.N. TYSON, "Quality and Profitability: Have Controllers Made the Connection?" *Manage. Account.,* 38–43 (Nov. 1987).

27. P. CROSBY, *Quality Is Free,* McGraw-Hill Book Co., Inc., New York, 1979.

28. J. CAMPANELLA, *Principles of Quality Costs,* 2nd ed., ASQC Quality Press, 1990.

29. I.-W. KIM, "A Microeconomic Approach to Quality Cost Control," *Cost Manage.* 11–16 (Fall 1989).

30. G.L. LILIEN and E. YOON, "Determinants of New Industrial Product Performance: A Strategic Reexamination of the Empirical Literature," *IEEE Trans. Eng. Manage.* 36(1) (Feb. 1989).

31. R.H. HAYES et al., *Dynamic Manufacturing: Creating the Learning Organization,* Free Press, New York, 1988.

32. R.F. BRINER, M.D. AKERS, J.W. TRUITT, and J.D. WILSON, "Coping with Change at Martin Industries," *Manage. Account.,* 45–49 (July 1989).

33. J.R. HAUSER and D. CLAUSING, "The House of Quality," *Harvard Bus. Rev.* (May–June 1988).

34. G.G. HEGDE and N.J. NAGARAJAN, "Incentives for Overhead Cost Reduction: Setup Time and Lot Size Considerations," *Int. J. Product. Econ.* **28,** 255–263 (1992).

35. D. DAETZ, "The Effect of Product Design on Product Quality and Product Cost," *Quality Prog.,* 63–67 (June 1987).

SECTION X
TOOLS AND TECHNIQUES FOR DESIGN AND MANUFACTURING

CHAPTER 42
Easy as ABC?

Yoram Eden
The College of Business in Tel Aviv

Boaz Ronen
Tel Aviv University, Faculty of
Management

42.1. INTRODUCTION

Activity-based costing (ABC) is being accorded ever-increasing recognition and interest. Leading firms in the United States and Europe (e.g., General Motors, Hughes Aircraft, General Dynamics, General Electronics, Siemens, Hewlett Packard, John Deere, and PPG) have reported successful implementation of the method (1). ABC is applicable not only in industrial firms but also in service organizations (2). The method is associated mainly with Kaplan and Cooper of Harvard University. They presented the method in a series of articles and field studies and reported its implementation in various industrial enterprises. Today, ABC is perceived as the leading costing method in both industry and service organizations. The method has enjoyed aggressive marketing and computer packages have even been developed (e.g., Easy ABC) that can be adapted and installed for use in small- and medium-size firms. The method has won widespread support in the professional literature; the leading journals have published at least one article dealing with the various facets of implementing ABC in almost every issue. Implementing ABC would appear to be a managerial imperative; e.g., the prestigious British monthly *Accountancy* published an article titled "ABC: A Need, Not an Option" (3).

The criticism leveled at the method in the professional literature should not be ignored. The criticism is largely in the form of the claim that ABC is in fact little different from traditional costing. The critics claim that ABC is nothing but an improved form of absorption costing and there is no justification in presenting it as a panacea for all the costing ills of the modern manufacturing environment (4).

In any case, understanding the principles of ABC and examining its suitability to the business organizational environment are management challenges of today. It should be remembered that ABC developed out of the need for a radical change in the costing systems in organizations. Thus the question is not whether the system needs to be changed but rather whether ABC is the answer.

42.2 LOSS OF RELEVANCE OF TRADITIONAL COSTING METHODS

It is generally agreed today that traditional costing methods are no longer relevant (5). Still, we should briefly consider what led to the loss of relevancy of costing methods that were in use for generations, some of which are still being taught in business schools throughout the world. The two principal factors that led to loss of relevancy are (*1*) the changes that took place in the manufacturing processes and cost structure and (*2*) the broadening range of products.

The traditional costing methods were developed in the 1920s and suited the manufacturing environment of that time: mass production of a limited number of goods, exploiting economies of scale and learning processes. Direct labor cost was the most significant cost factor. Indirect costs were relatively few, and their allocation to the products on the basis of direct labor cost (or another volume variable such as machine time) was a reasonable approximation. In the manufacturing environment of the time, traditional costing enabled the breakdown and classification of business results by products, one at a time. It was possible to make decisions regarding a given product, without relating to all the others (6).

We have chosen to illustrate the changes that have occurred in the modern manufacturing environment with the help of representative data on the Siemens group of companies in Germany. The data in Table 42.1 show a number of characteristics (relevant to costing) of a firm at the forefront of the modern manufacturing environment.

1. *A Change in the Cost Structure.* The indirect costs constitute 50% to 75% of the total. The weight of direct labor cost is less than 10% of total cost.

2. *Growth of Indirect Costs.* Most of the growth of indirect costs is in manufacturing support costs (R&D, engineering, planning, production control, and quality control). At Siemens, e.g., manufacturing support costs grew at a cumulative 117% over 6 years. The increase in manufacturing support costs often expresses the cost of manufacturing complexity. The cost of complexity grew with the broadening of the range of products. On the other hand, manufacturing's traditional fixed indirect costs (such as depreciation, energy and lighting, rent, and municipal taxes) increased over the same period by a cumulative rate of only 34%.

3. *Broadening the Range of Products.* Manufacturing today is adapted to the needs and tastes of the customers. Broadening the range of products presents a challenge to costing: Is it managerially justified and is it objectively feasible to determine the cost of each and every product? To determine the separate cost of each product, it is necessary to break down the indirect costs to the level of the individual product. The more complex the manufacturing processes and the more communal resources they consume, the less the objective feasibility to determine the cost of the individual product, which in any case has no significance.

The root of the problem in traditional costing is in the area of allocating the indirect costs. Naive allocation of the indirect costs on the basis of work hours is no longer suitable in the modern manufacturing environment. We have seen that in many firms the indirect costs are several times higher than the direct labor costs. In a field study carried out at one of Hewlett Packard's plants during the years 1985–1986, a loading rate of 600% to 1600% was found (7), i.e., for every dollar of direct labor costs 6 to 16 dollars of indirect costs were loaded (7). Allocating indirect costs on the basis of direct labor costs leads in effect to indirect costs being cut off from the factors that create them. This distorted allocation blurs the problem of the cost of complexity and the necessity for focused manufacture. In many cases, it has been found that there exists a "black box"—a reservoir of indirect costs that are loaded onto the direct costs of the products. Without an understanding and analysis of the sources of the indirect costs, effective management is impossible (8). Moreover, the high loading rates causes middle management to concentrate on registering and controlling direct labor costs. In many firms, it happens that shifting work hours from project to project has a significant impact on the profitability of each project. A paradoxical situation is thus created in which the lower the weight of labor costs, the higher its costing importance, because it is the key to allocating indirect costs.

The dynamic development of financial accounting and the transition to ongoing quarterly reporting have further aggravated the process of declining relevancy. In the financial system, the emphasis is on financial accounting. The management information system is perceived as an auxiliary tool derived from financial accounting. These processes have led to the creation of a

TABLE 42.1.   Example of a Firm in a Modern Manufacturing Environment, Siemens[a]

Location	Regensburg	Bad Neustadt	Augsburg
Products	Electrical in-house devices	Electric Motors	Printed Circuits
Type of production	Mass and batch	Batch and contract	Batch and contract
Annual sales (DM millions)	230	300	150
Cost structure (%)			
Direct materials	25	43	20
Direct labor	9	9	4
Indirect costs	66	48	76
Number of products	20,000	10,000	3,000

[a] From ref. 1.

management culture of "management by numbers" (financial accounting data), accompanied by a departure from the shop floor and concentration on short-term accounting measures.

In the early 1980s, the Japanese just-in-time (JIT) concept of management was adopted by Western firms, together with the concept of total quality management (TQM). The process of assimilating these changes was carried out mainly by managers with manufacturing orientation. For the most part, the accountants and finance department people were not involved in the processes of change and even turned a blind eye to them. The result was a still greater loss of relevancy. Production managers today rely on data and measures that are not provided by the costing and accounting systems (9). It may be expected that management in organizations will begin to demand that the costing system be adapted to the manufacturing environment relevant to the organization. The challenge facing managerial accounting today is to make the transition from reporting on costs for the purpose of cost accounting to cost management.

42.3 THE PRINCIPLES OF ACTIVITY-BASED COSTING

General

The basic precept of activity-based costing is that costs cannot be managed, activities can be managed. Activity-based costing derives in fact from the broader managerial concept of activity-based management (ABM). Activity is the exploitation of time and resources for the purpose of creating output. The activities may be classified according to a number of criteria:

Direct manufacturing activity (primary activity) and manufacturing support activity (secondary activity).

Repetitive activity, as opposed to one-time activity.

Automatic activity, as opposed to managed activity.

A function is an aggregate of activities with a common goal. A business process is a network of related and independent activities linked by the outputs they exchange. A task is the way the activity is performed. Take, for example, the preparation of a proposal for a customer. Preparing the proposal is the task. The manufacturing or process proposal is the activity. The business activity is selling the product. The function is marketing. These definitions enable us to map the activities of the firm and to understand the interrelationships among them.

The implementation of ABC consists of four main steps: (1) identifying and mapping the activities, (2) defining the cost drivers, (3) accumulating costs associated with a common activity in activity pools, and (4) allocating costs from activity pools to the products on the basis of use of the activities. The first two steps are at the management level and not at the level of the organization's financial and accounting bodies. Proper analysis of the activities and cost drivers will likely lead to significant managerial benefit, beyond the improvement in costing reporting. Table 42.2 gives several examples (sampled from various departments in a firm) that demonstrate schematically the relationship between activity and cost driver.

In defining cost drivers, a distinction must be made between activity cost drivers and cost level drivers. Let us suppose, for example, that in a certain firm quality control is carried out upon completion of every manufacturing batch. The quality control activity costs for the year totaled $300,000. During the course of the year 1,500 batches were inspected. The obvious inference is that the cost driver is the number of manufacturing batches. Each manufacturing lot

TABLE 42.2. Activities and Cost Drivers

Department	Activity	Cost Driver
Materials store	Receipt and initial handling of incoming raw materials	Number of purchasing orders and number of suppliers
Salaries department	Preparing salaries and reporting forms	Number of employees
Marketing and finance	Determining customer credit policy	Number of new customers
Manufacturing	Setup costs	Number of manufacturing batches

should be allocated a cost of $200 (300,000/1,500). However, the number of lots is an activity cost driver. We must also consider the technological cost drivers, such as worker motivation, skill of the workers, supervision and training, control over the production processes, maintenance of equipment and machinery, and rate of production. The costs should not be simply allocated technically. Proper definition of the cost drivers enables management to tackle the sources of costs and to evaluate the interrelationships between costs and activities in the different departments of the firm (10).

The Hierarchical Structure of Indirect Costs

Mapping the costs and defining the cost drivers enables sorting of the indirect costs into a hierarchical structure. The sorting is determined by the cost drivers.

1. Indirect costs defined at the level of the unit (variable indirect costs): auxiliary materials, fuel, and energy.
2. Indirect costs defined at the level of the batch: setup costs, allocation of materials and preparation of kits, quality control (if it is carried out upon completion of the manufacture of each batch).
3. Indirect costs defined at the level of the product: preparation of the technical specification, service, and product support.
4. Indirect costs defined at the level of the manufacturing process: engineering and planning costs.
5. Indirect costs at the overall firm level: cost not related to production, thus there is no economic logic in allocating them to the products.

Numerical Example

The following example is taken from Cooper (3). We have added data in the interest of a more complete presentation. The purpose of the example is to evaluate the significance of the hierarchical cost structure. A certain plant manufactures four products; the relevant data on these products are given in Table 42.3. As we can see from the table, products A and B are inexpensive compared with C and D, and the production volumes of B and D are 10 times those of A and C. The traditional approach is to allocate the indirect costs to the products by the volume parameter of direct work or machine hours (Table 42.4). For the sake of simplicity, we assume that the number of direct work hours is equal to the number of machine hours. Thus allocation on the basis of direct work hours and allocation on the basis of machine hours will give identical results. The analysis indicates that the firm's leading products (B and D) yield but minimal profit margins. The sales of product D, for example, which constitute 66.39% of the firm's sales revenue, constitute only 12.06% of the profits. Most of the profit is in fact derived from the low-volume products, that is products A and C. The conclusion seems to be to promote products A and C at the expense of products B and D. It may also be rationalized that it is difficult to make a profit in the competitive market of products B and D. The firm's comparative advantage is, in fact, in its low-volume products, which give higher profit margins.

TABLE 42.3.　Example Data[a]

Item	Product A	Product B	Product C	Product D
Direct cost	110	110	330	300
Volume of production (in units)	Low	High	Low	High
	10	100	10	100
Cumulative work and machine hours	5	50	15	135
Number of manufacturing batches during the period	1	3	1	3
Market price	175	135	500	425

[a] Total indirect costs before allocation to products: $9924.

TABLE 42.4. Implementation of Traditional Costing Methods

A. Determining the Loading Rate

Total indirect costs to the firm for the period	NIS 9,924
Total direct hours	220
Loading rate	45.11

B. Determining Total Cost and Calculating Profit Margins

Item	Product A	Product B	Product C	Product D
Cost				
Direct	110.00	110.00	330.00	330.00
Indirect	22.56	22.56	67.67	67.67
Total	132.56	132.56	397.67	397.67
Selling Price	175.00	135.00	500.00	400.00
Gross profit	42.44	2.44	102.32	2.32
Percent profit	24.25	1.81	20.46	0.58

C. Analysis of Profit–Loss Statement at the Level of the Product

Item	Product A	Product B	Product C	Product D	Total
Revenue	1,750.00	13,500.00	5,000.00	40,000.00	60,250.00
Costs	1,326.00	13,256.00	3,977.00	39,767.00	58,326.00
Gross profit	424.00	244.00	1,023.00	232.00	1,924.00
Contribution to revenue (%)	2.90	22.41	8.30	66.39	100.00
Contribution to profit (%)	22.07	12.68	53.19	12.06	100.00

Are these conclusions correct or just a costing–accounting illusion? To give an informed answer to this question, we must first analyze the activities that give rise to the indirect costs and their cost drivers. Table 42.5 demonstrates the four steps involved in implementing ABC. Implementation of ABC leads to results that are quite different from the results obtained under traditional costing analysis. Products A and B are the focus of the firm's losses, and product D (whose profitability was questionable according to traditional costing) is found to contribute 90% of the firm's overall profit. Experience thus shows that implementing ABC leads to results that are different (sometimes extremely so) from those obtained under traditional costing. It is usually found that traditional costing leads to undercosting of products with low direct costs and products manufactured in small, one-time batches. Traditional costing inflates the cost of the leading products (large-scale production products with relatively high direct costs). The distortions of traditional costing are likely to seduce managers into focusing on small-scale manufacturing small products at the expense of leading products. Table 42.6 gives a comparative summary of the example and illustrates the differences between traditional costing and ABC.

42.4 EVALUATION

The example presented above is impressive, highlighting as it does the distortions of traditional costing. The error of the traditional methods of allocation is in relating the indirect costs to products according to volume parameters (work hours, machine hours, or relative revenue). The traditional methods completely ignore the complexity costs of manufacturing, to the detriment of the firm's leading products. ABC information is a must in developing profitable new products. ABC reveals which types of activities give the best results in terms of cost, quality, and time and which are likely to be competitive in new markets. At the same time, the principal limitations of ABC, demonstrated in our example, must be taken into account.

We must distinguish between determining the cost of a product for the purpose of accounting, or "justifying costs" (particularly for regulated products, or cost-plus products), and determining cost for the purpose of decision making. ABC is undoubtedly preferable to the traditional costing methods for determining cost for accounting reporting purposes. The question is whether the cost data provided by the ABC method are sufficiently reliable for decision

TABLE 42.5. Implementing ABC

A. Defining Activities and Cost Drivers

Identifying Activities	Activity Costs Pool (Dollars)	Cost Driver
At the unit level		
Machine maintenance	3,300.00	Machine hours
Direct personnel management	2,200.00	Direct labor hours
Raw materials management	264.00	Cost of raw materials
Subtotal	5,764.00	
At the structure level		
Setup costs	960.00	Number of batches
Planning and allocation of materials	1,200.00	Number of batches
Subtotal	2,160.00	
At the product level		
Product planning and support	2,000.00	Number of products
Total indirect costs	9,924.00	

B. Allocation of Indirect Costs on the Basis of Cost Drivers

Loading Rates	Indirect Costs at the Unit Level (1)	Indirect Costs at the Structure Level (2)	Indirect Costs at the Product Level (3)
Total	5,764.00	2,160.00	2,000.00
Cost driver base	220.00	8.00	4.00
Subtotal	26.20	270.00	500.00

Allocation	Product A	Product B	Product C	Product D
At the unit level				
Direct hours	5	50	15	150
Rate (1)	26.20	26.20	26.20	26.20
Allocation	131.00	1,310.00	393.00	3,930.00
At the structure level				
Number of setups	1	3	1	3
Rate (2)	270.00	270.00	270.00	270.00
Allocation	270.00	810.00	270.00	810.00
At the product level				
Rate (3)	500.00	500.00	500.00	500.00
Total indirect	901.00	2,620.00	1,163.00	5,240.00
Indirect per unit	90.10	26.20	116.30	52.40

C. Determining the Overall Cost and Calculating Profit Margins

Item	Product A	Product B	Product C	Product D
Cost (per unit)				
Direct cost	110.00	110.00	330.00	330.00
Indirect	90.10	26.20	116.30	52.40
Total	200.10	136.20	446.30	382.40
Market price	175.00	135.00	500.00	400.00
Profit (loss) per unit	(25.1)	(1.20)	53.70	17.60

D. Analysis of Profit–Loss Statement at the Product Level

Item	Product A	Product B	Product C	Product D	Total
Revenue	1,750.00	13,500.00	5,000.00	40,000.00	60,250.00
Costs	2,002.00	13,620.00	4,464.00	38,240.00	58,326.00
Gross profit	(252.00)	(120.00)	536.00	1,760.00	1,924.00
Contribution to revenue (%)	2.90	22.41	8.30	66.39	100.00
Contribution to profit (%)	(13.10)	(6.24)	27.84	91.50	100.00

TABLE 42.6. Comparative Summary

Product	Product Characteristics		Traditional Costing		Activity-Based Costing	
	Direct Cost	Scale of Production	Unit Cost	Overall Profit	Unit Cost	Overall Profit (Loss)
A	Low	Low	132.56	42.44	200.10	(25.10)
B	Low	High	132.56	2.44	136.20	(1.20)
C	High	Low	397.67	102.32	446.30	53.70
D	High	High	397.67	2.32	382.40	17.60

making, concerning the manufacturing mix, giving work out to subcontractors (make or buy decisions), or investment in equipment. It should be noted that Cooper (11) emphasized that the ABC systems were developed to focus the attention of management on the way resources are used and not to provide relevant costs to decision makers. The example presented above contains four structural problems:

1. The example completely ignores the existence of joint expenditures and inputs.
2. The example completely ignores the existence of parallel factors of production and bottlenecks on the shop floor.
3. The example assumed continuity, i.e., a linear, univariate relationship between volume of activity and the cost at all the levels.
4. The example assumed that the output manufactured approximates the normal output.

These four problems will be briefly reviewed.

Ignoring the possible existence of joint costs and inputs enabled the technical possibility of breaking down the profit–loss statement to the level of the product. However, the question is whether it is possible to use the cost data (and the profit data) obtained for each product individually and in isolation from the rest of the products. We will illustrate this question, using the example data. The example indicates that each of the two products A and B causes a loss. If this is true, should we not stop their production? Clearly, we cannot answer this question without making a comprehensive examination of the effect of the decision on the firm's profitability. In other words, breaking down costs to the level of the product is of no significance insofar as decision making is concerned (unless we assume the firm has no joint expenditures and inputs).

No less serious is ignoring bottlenecks in production. If there is no internal constraint, i.e., the firm can supply all the demand for all the products, then all the products should be manufactured, because each product increases the contribution (and, therefore, the profit). If an internal constraint exists, i.e., the demand is greater than the production capacity, the optimal product mix must be determined. The cost data in Table 42.6 are not relevant, because they do not reflect the intensity of use of the parallel resources (the bottleneck). If a parallel constraint exists, all the firm's decisions must be subordinated to it. The optimal product mix will be determined not by the costing cost of each product separately but by the contribution to the unit of constraint (12).

The firms that actually implemented ABC reported "noise" caused by lack of continuity (lumpiness). In our example, the analysis of the indirect cost patterns led to the fact that the indirect costs to be attributed to each setup is $270. Does this mean that adding a setup means an additional $270 and subtracting a setup means saving $270? In many cases it is found that a moderate change in the scope of activities has no effect on the level of costs. In our example, it is reasonable to assume that at the cost level of $2160 (or at a relatively low marginal increment), nine setups could also have been carried out. This phenomenon has been well known in costing for many decades and is resolved by using a flexible budget. In any case, it may be claimed that the data supplied by the ABC system will not be sufficiently reliable for decision making on relatively small changes in the scope of activity.

It must be remembered that ABC is an absorption costing system. One of the main difficulties in implementing absorption costing is that it does not neutralize the effect of changes in the level of activity and is likely to bring about extreme swings in manufacturing costs and reported accounting profits. In any case, the data provided by an absorption costing system are of lesser importance insofar as short-range decision making is concerned. Indeed, a research study carried out at Tel Aviv University showed that ABC is not able to forecast profits when the manufacturing volume changes from one period to the next and is, therefore, unsuitable for decision making (13).

An integrated system of contribution costing and management by constraints will lead, in such cases, to preferable decisions. In our opinion, several important conclusions may be drawn from the example given above. First, the accounting–costing of a product is not a univariate defined concept. Only the product's direct cost may be defined. The overall cost is a nondefined and economically meaningless concept. In particular, we must free ourselves with the obsession with the second place to the right of the decimal point. Many accountants tend to view the cost data of a product defined down to the last cent (a level of accuracy of two digits to the right of the decimal point) as a stable costing anchor. However, as Kaplan put it, the problem is that the two digits to the left of the decimal point are inaccurate in order of magnitude. An examination of the data in Table 42.6 will verify this claim.

Second, activity-based costing should be viewed as an expression of the concept of activity-based management. The main point of the concept is the mapping of the activities and defining the cost drivers. These steps are essential in the transition from a culture of arbitrary allocation of indirect costs to effective management of the product support costs. A review of the literature on successful implementation of ABC in industrial firms shows that these firms first carried out an in-depth analysis of activities and cost drivers. The change in the costing system was accompanied by essential changes in the perception of production management in these firms. Finally, care must be taken to avoid allowing the perception to degenerate from a management tool into a technical method of allocating indirect costs.

42.5   TOWARD ACTIVITY-BASED BUDGETING

We have already seen how ABC is an expression of a managerial concept of ABM. So far, we have extrapolated the costing of products from this managerial concept. It is possible and desirable to use activity-based management for preparing the budget, too. Activity-based budgeting (ABB) leads to significant improvement in the budgeting of service departments. The problem in budgeting service departments is that, apparently, in the absence of a simple linear relationship between the costs of the service department and the manufacturing costs, there is no economic basis on which to prepare the budget. Thus service department budgets usually reflect the level of expenditures of previous years, adjusted for inflation, with a deduction of a cutback–efficiency coefficient. Activity-based management enables managers to understand the cost structure in service departments and the reciprocal relations between activities performed outside the departments and the costs accruing in the department.

Mapping of the activities and analysis of the cost drivers enable preparation of an activities–expenditures matrix in the service department. The expenditures matrix is the basis for preparing the budget. An example of an activities–expenditures matrix, based on Morrow and Connolly (10), for the order department of an industrial firm is given in Table 42.7. The basis for the matrix is the previous output data. The analysis enables management to determine better the department's budget, separating the rigid component from the flexible component. The rigid

TABLE 42.7.   Example of an Activities–Expenditures Matrix (in thousands of dollars)

Item	Number of Customers	Number of Orders	Number of Export Orders	Number Shipments	Preparation of Price Lists and Brochures	Management of the Department	Total
Managers' salaries					50	150	200
Clerks' salaries	150	400	350	200	100		1200
Overtime			50	75			125
Office expenses		40	60	20	200		320
Postage and telephone	40	60	120	80			300
Others	15	20	10	10	20	50	125
Total	205	520	590	385	370	200	2270
Scope of cost driving activity	650	2400	600	6000			
Cost per unit of activity	0.32	0.22	0.98	0.06	370	200	

component includes those costs arising from the department's very existence and that are not affected by the scope of activity. In our example, the rigid component includes the costs of managing the department ($200,000) and the cost of printing the price lists and brochures ($370,000). The flexible component is planned on the basis of four cost drivers: number of customers, number of anticipated orders, number of export orders, and expected number of shipments.

An activity-based budget highlights the interrelationships and the cost–cost factor relations of the various activities outside the service department. The reader will no doubt note the problem of lack of continuity (lumpiness) previously discussed. In our example we see that the cost of each incoming order is $22. Clearly, this is an average figure that does not reflect the marginal cost of each additional order. The emphasis should be placed on understanding the manner in which the resources are used, not on a technical analysis of the costs, which is in any case meaningless.

42.6 PRELIMINARY LESSONS TO BE LEARNED FROM IMPLEMENTING ABC

There are three sources of information concerning the preliminary lessons to be learned from implementing the method. First, there are case analyses of firms that have successfully implemented the transition to ABC. The case analyses are, of course, at the level of the individual firm, and it is sometimes difficult to extrapolate from them to other firms (14). Second, general surveys have been carried out on all the firms in the economy (firms that have implemented the method and firms that have not done so). Third, surveys have been carried out on firms known in advance to have successfully implemented the method. The two salient findings of the general surveys are as follows (15):

1. The phenomenon of "follow the leader" or "me too" occurs. Because ABC is considered to be an advanced method, many managers report its implementation or the intention to implement it. The percentage of those reporting implementation sometimes reaches 33% of the respondents. At the same time, the percentage of those who understand the principles of the method and who map the activities and define the cost drivers is only about 11%.
2. Even though it is presented and marketed as a simple method, it is perceived as a complex method requiring radical change in the organization. Many managers are reluctant to implement ABC without the backing of external consultants.

An important survey carried out on 10 leading UK industrial firms is the source of several interesting preliminary lessons concerning implementation of the method. These lessons are summarized in Table 42.8 (16). The data of Table 42.8 show the relatively high weight given to production managers in the process of implementing ABC. The monetary cost of implementa-

TABLE 42.8. Implementation of ABC—Lessons to Be Learned

The preparation and follow-up team	Average of 5.3 members; production managers were included in the team
Cost of implementation	Average was £48,500 (0.023%) of annual sales
Running in costs	Negligible
Defining cost drivers	Defined by production managers, usually by time use
Number of cost drivers	Range was 7–30; adjusted average, 13.5; average for firms that sought the aid of external consultants, 8.5
The contribution of external consultants	Additional cost of £38,000; a quick beginning and reliable evaluation; no significant contribution to shortening the process of implementation
Integrating the accounting system	The trend is toward integration, which is not achieved until implementation of the ABC system has been completed
Time needed to complete implementation	20–42 weeks

tion in itself is not high. Implementation requires a considerable effort on the part of the organization as a whole.

42.7 CONCLUSION

Activity-based costing derives from the broader managerial concept of activity-based management, the emphasis being on the managerial facets of mapping activities and defining cost drivers. The purpose of ABC is to focus managerial attention on the manner in which resources are consumed by the various activities in the organization. The method effectively identifies the cost of manufacturing complexity arising from broadening the range of products and from nonfocused management. The method is likely to lead to improvement in the decision-making process by identifying strategic relations between the indirect costs and the factors that cause them.

Caution must be exercised in the straightforward implementation of ABC for the purpose of determining product cost. The data supplied by the ABC system cannot serve as the sole relevant data for decision making.

An interesting and important development of ABC is for activity-based budget preparation. Although the subject is still in its infancy, it is likely, in our opinion, to lead to improvement in the method of budget preparation, particularly in relation to service departments.

Implementing an ABC system requires a substantial organizational effort. The emphasis in implementing the methods must be placed on identifying the activities and defining the cost drivers. Thus implementation requires the joint effort of production managers, industrial and management engineers, and the firm's accounting team.

In our opinion, ABC suffers from a number of basic deficiencies:

ABC uses the logic of allocation, thus carrying on the basic deficiency of traditional costing.

ABC uses the measures "cost of product" and "profit per product," whereas today we must take the broader views of "system cost" and "system profit."

ABC is likely to cause difficulties and managerial failures in short-term decision making and in tactical decision making.

The only use of ABC that can be made is strategic; however, the possibility that it might be preferable to conduct ad hoc research for the purpose of strategic decision making must be considered.

BIBLIOGRAPHY

1. J.A. BRIMSON, *Activity Costing—An Activity Based Costing Approach*, John Wiley & Sons Inc., New York, 1991.

2. M. SEPHTON and T. WARD, "ABC in Retail Financial Service," *Manage. Account.* (Apr. 1990).

3. R. COOPER, "ABC: A Need, Not an Option," *Accountancy* (Sept. 1990).

4. J.A. PIPER and P. WALLEY, "ABC Relevance Not Found," *Manage. Account.* (Mar. 1991).

5. H.T. JOHNSON and R.S. KAPLAN, *Relevance Lost: The Rise and Fall of Management Accounting*, Harvard Business School, Boston, 1987.

6. E.M. GOLDRATT, *The Haystack Syndrome*, North River Press, Croton-on-Hudson, New York, 1991.

7. J.M. PATELL, "Adopting a Cost Accounting System to Just In Time Manufacturing: The Hewlett Packard Personal Office" in J.B. Bruns and R.S. Kaplan (eds.), *Accounting and Management Field Study Perspectives*, Harvard Business School, Boston, 1988.

8. Y. EDEN and B. RONEN, "Activity Based Costing [in Hebrew]," *Ro'eh Haheshbon* **35** (1989).

9. H.J. JOHANSON, "Preparing for Accounting System Changes," *Manage. Account.* (July 1990).

10. M. MORROW and T. CONNOLLY, "The Emergence of Activity Based Budgeting," *Manage. Account.* (Feb. 1991).

11. R. COOPER, "Explicating the Logic of ABC Budgeting," *Manage. Account.* (Nov. 1990).

12. Y. EDEN and B. RONEN, "Indirect Cost Management," *ICPAI 1991 Yearbook.*

13. N. GERI, *Methods of Managing Costs and Costing as a Tool in Strategic Decision Making,* Master's thesis, Tel Aviv University, 1992.

14. M. JEANS and M. MORROW, "Activity-Based Costing Research," *Manage. Account.* (May 1990).

15. B. NICHOLLS, "ABC in the U.K.—A Status Report," *Manage. Account.* (May 1992).

16. J. BAILEY, "Implementation of ABC by U.K. Companies," *Manage. Account.* (Feb. 1992).

CHAPTER 43
Artificial Neural Networks in Manufacturing

DEBORAH F. COOK
Virginia Polytechnic Institute and
State University

A. DALE WHITTAKER
Texas A&M University

43.1 INTRODUCTION

Modern manufacturing systems are increasingly complex and dynamic operations. Advances in areas including robot control, process modeling, fault classification, and pattern recognition are needed to facilitate the continued development of efficient, high quality manufacturing processes. Artificial neural network algorithms can be used to achieve needed advancements in the operation and control of many manufacturing facilities. These networks offer the capability to extract useful information from complex, incomplete, or uncertain data. These types of data can regularly be found in the data collected for analysis and control of manufacturing operations.

Various artificial neural network algorithms have been developed and applied to meet manufacturing challenges in many areas, including robot control, vision, quality control, and process control. This chapter contains an introduction to artificial neural networks in general, a detailed description of the widely used backpropagation algorithm, and multiple examples of manufacturing applications of artificial neural network techniques.

43.2 ARTIFICIAL NEURAL NETWORK THEORY

An artificial neural network consists of a number of highly interconnected processing elements or nodes. It is a computational algorithm that processes information by a dynamic response of its processing elements or nodes and their connections to external inputs (1). Artificial neural networks were originally developed as approximations of the capabilities exhibited by biological neural systems. Software implementations of artificial neural network algorithms are available from various vendors, as advertised in neural network, artificial intelligence, and expert systems journals and magazines.

The reported advantages and capabilities offered by neural networks are many. Several of these capabilities, including intelligent association, associative recall on cue, real-time learning, and graceful degradation, have been described (2). Intelligent association is the ability to remember related items when the relationship may not be obvious or carefully predetermined. Associative recall is used to retrieve original inputs from fragments of the original inputs. Real-time learning is the ability to learn solutions to new problems in real-time from examples of solutions to similar problems. Graceful degradation allows the complete recall of information with incomplete input data.

The general architecture of an artificial neural network will be described following the outline given by Rumelhart et al. (3) of the major network components:

- A set of *processing elements* or *nodes*.
- A *state of activation*.

- An *output function* for each unit.
- A *pattern of connectivity* among units.
- A *propagation rule* (summation function).
- An *activation rule or function*(threshold function).
- A *learning rule*.

An artificial neural network is composed of layers of processing elements. The state of activation is a representation of the network at a given time, describing the pattern of activation over the set of processing units. The output function for each unit determines how that unit will respond to its inputs based on its current state of activation. The connections between units and the weights of those units are called the pattern of connectivity. This pattern determines what the network knows and how it responds to an arbitrary input. It is this pattern that determines what each unit represents. Processing elements may represent particular conceptual objects, such as machined part features or process fault conditions, or they may be abstract elements from which meaningful patterns can not be defined.

A processing element or node is a nonlinear computational element. The operation of an individual processing element is governed by a propagation rule (summation function) and an activation rule (threshold function). A processing element receives a number of input signals from various other processing elements. Each input signal is assigned a weight. The effective input to the element is determined by the summation function that calculates the weighted total from all input signals. This weighted input value is passed through the threshold activation function to produce the output value of the processing element at that time. A sigmoid is an often used nonlinear activation rule or function. If the input to the threshold function is greater than the threshold value, the processing element fires or generates an output signal. Output signals can be excitatory, tending to cause the next processing element to fire, or inhibitory, tending to keep the next processing element from firing. If the input to the threshold function is less than the threshold value, the processing element does not fire and no output signal is generated.

Much of the interest in artificial neural networks arises from their ability to learn or be trained, which can be viewed as the process of developing a function that maps input vectors to output vectors. A network is presented with a series of examples of the conditions the network is being trained to represent. The network then learns the governing relationships existing in the data set. The two forms of artificial neural network learning are supervised and unsupervised. Supervised learning uses examples of input–output pairs as the basis of its learning algorithm. The performance of the network is evaluated during training with respect to the known output values. In unsupervised learning, the network learns by a process of self-organization without input–output example pairs.

The architecture of an artificial neural network defines the structure used for knowledge representation and processing in the network (4). Two types of network architecture are depicted in Figure 43.1, a completely connected network and a multilayer network. Different architectures impose different biases on the final network representation. A completely connected network is typically an autoassociative network with no hierarchical orientation (Figure 43.1a). The input, output, and state of activation vectors all participate in the representation of both input and output data (5). Some autoassociative networks allow bidirectional communication between nodes. Computation is accomplished by instantiating an input pattern across the network's nodes and allowing the system iteratively to calculate unit activation levels and propagate outputs through the network until it settles into a final output state (3). These networks have been successful in pattern recognition and pattern completion.

Heteroassociative networks distinguish between input and output nodes and associate an input pattern with a specific output pattern (Figure 43.1b). These networks allow only certain arrangements of connections. For example, a feed-forward network takes inputs only from the previous layer and sends outputs only to the next layer. Feed-forward networks can be trained to recognize patterns and develop generalized information from input data.

An artificial neural network is theoretically capable of acquiring any arbitrary mapping function when properly configured (3). Hidden nodes can be added to a heteroassociative network to achieve this greater functional capability. Hidden nodes provide the network with additional degrees of freedom to enable the construction of useful internal knowledge representations. A feed-forward network with a layer of hidden nodes can represent any convex decision region in the space spanned by the inputs. The feedforward network has been found to be an effective system for learning discriminants for patterns from a body of examples (6).

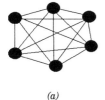

(a)

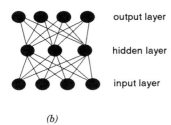

output layer

hidden layer

input layer

(b)

Figure 43.1. Neural network architectures. (a) A completely connected network. (b) A multilayer network.

Artificial Neural Network Algorithms

Artificial neural network algorithms have evolved for a number of different applications, including classification, prediction, and control. Classification refers to the assignment of an input vector to one of a finite number of classes. Typically, all possible points will be assignable to one and only one member of the set of classes. Some common neural network classification systems include the perceptron, adaline, madaline, bidirectional associative memory, Hamming, Hopfield, associative logic, and Kohonen algorithms. Descriptions of these algorithms are available (see, e.g., refs. 1, 6, 7).

Among classification neural networks, a majority of the attention has been focused on binary input systems such as the Hopfield, Hamming, and Carpenter–Grossberg networks. Electrical engineers have driven the development of these networks, because they are easy to implement in hardware and can be used to solve a useful class of problems, including character recognition and data compression. The artificial neural network systems that accept continuous input include the perceptron, multilayer perceptron, and Kohonen self-organizing map. The Kohonen (8) network guarantees equiprobable distribution of the input data into a number of prespecified classes. Any point is guaranteed to be closer to the center of the cluster (class) to which it is assigned than any other cluster. By inspecting the width and center of the clusters, the underlying distribution of the data can be determined.

Architectures such as back-propagation, counterpropagation, and radial basis function have been developed for prediction and for control. The ability to predict the occurrence of future operating conditions is valuable in a manufacturing operation. Predictions can be used for control purposes, to govern process adjustments made by an operator or by process control equipment. Manufacturing processes are often complex and dynamic, with multiple interactions among process parameters lending themselves to neural network applications.

Prediction and control architectures are useful in manufacturing applications because of their ability to map nonlinear functions. The nonlinearity in the neural network representation is a function of the number of nodes, number of layers, and the transfer function at the nodes. Perhaps the most widely used prediction algorithm is the back-propagation algorithm that use the generalized delta learning rule. The term *back-propagation* is often used interchangeably to refer either to the supervised learning method that is used to modify weights in a feed-forward network or to the feed-forward network itself.

Back-propagation is the most widely applied neural network algorithm to date. Consequently, the details of the back-propagation algorithm are described. The counterpropagation algorithm has been successfully applied to manufacturing operations by the authors and offers some unique capabilities. The counterpropagation algorithm will be described in general terms.

Back-propagation Neural Network Algorithm

The back-propagation network has been widely used in various applications. A back-propagation neural network consists of three or more layers, including an input layer, one or more hidden layers, and an output layer (Figure 43.2). The learning or training process used in the backpropagation network is composed of three steps: (*1*) collect an example set of training data that contains both the inputs and outputs that are to be included in the network, (*2*) present the training data set to the artificial neural network program, and (*3*) allow the artificial neural network software program to iterate through the data set as many times as necessary to develop a representation of that data set (7). Information is acquired or changed by altering the strengths of the existing connections, and learning occurs by modifying the weights between the nodes or processing elements comprising the network. The learning or training procedure must be capable of modifying the connection strengths in such a way that the internal hidden nodes come to represent important features of the task domain (5).

The generalized delta rule used in back-propagation is one of the best known learning rules. It was developed by Rumelhart et al. (3) for multilayered feed-forward networks with continuous valued nodes. The forward pass through the back-propagation network begins as the input layer receives the input data pattern and passes it to the middle layer (1). Each processing element calculates an activation value by first summing the weighted inputs. This sum is then used by an activation function in each node to determine the activity level of that processing node. A sigmoidal output function is used generally. The generated output value is compared with the known target value, and the resulting error term is propagated back through the network, using a gradient- or steepest-descent heuristic to minimize the error term, enabling the network to self-organize in ways that improve its performance over time (9).

The connection weights are adjusted in response to errors in hitting the target output values. In training this type of network, the input pattern is presented and the network adjusts the set of weights in all the connecting links such that the desired output is obtained at the output node. When this adjustment has been accomplished, the next pair of input and output target values is presented and the network learns that association. This process continues until the network finds a single set of connection weights that satisfies all the input–output pairs presented to it. The back-propagation rule varies the connection weights in a manner that reduces the error as rapidly as possible. It has been demonstrated that the network output function can provide an accurate approximation to any function likely to be encountered, provided the number of hidden nodes is large enough (10).

The design of back-propagation neural network for a particular manufacturing scenario depends on the design and operation of the process itself. For example, if a neural network is to be used to predict the value of a final quality parameter in a paper manufacturing process, the input elements or nodes would consist of the process parameters known to impact that quality parameter. If the quality parameter to be predicted was paper brightness, the input parameters used to describe the in-process material could include chemical amounts, pH values, flow rates, and intermediate brightness values. Each node or element in the input layer of the backpropagation network would represent an individual process parameter as shown in Figure 43.3. A single output node would be used to represent the predicted brightness value corresponding to the input parameter values. A training data set of many example operating conditions would

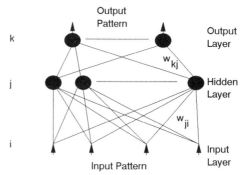

Figure 43.2. Back-propagation neural network algorithm.

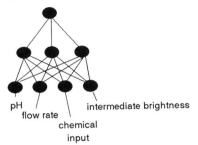

predicted brightness

pH
flow rate
intermediate brightness
chemical
input

Figure 43.3. Example back-propagation neural network for paper manufacturing.

be collected, including the resulting brightness value. This data set would be presented to the neural network software to allow the computational algorithm to develop an input to output mapping, composed of one set of connection weights representing the entire training data set.

Upon completion of the training phase, the network would be tested to evaluate whether an adequate prediction model of the brightness parameter had been developed. The required accuracy of the predictive capability of a trained network will vary according to the application. In some cases, a prediction of ± 20% will be of value to an operator, while under other conditions a prediction of ± 5% may be required. If the prediction model is not adequate for the given operation, several alternatives exist: (1) collect additional training data to describe more fully all operating conditions, (2) increase the number of nodes in the hidden layer, (3) include additional process parameters thought to affect brightness, or (4) use a different neural network algorithm. Continued testing and monitoring of the final trained neural network is crucial, especially if the process varies into ranges not included in the original training data set.

Counterpropagation Neural Network Algorithm

Counterpropagation is a combination of a portion of the self-organizing Kohonen map (8) and the instar and outstar structures of Grossberg (11). The structure of a counterpropagation network is shown in Figure 43.4. The Kohonen layer models the probability density function of the input vectors used during training and develops maximally separated clusters of those vectors. The number of clusters developed is a function of the number of nodes in the Kohonen layer. The Grossberg layer learns the average, or center of mass, of the cluster of the correct output vectors associated with the input vectors. Counterpropagation is reported to be a near-optimal look-up table (12), i.e., entries are statistically equiprobable.

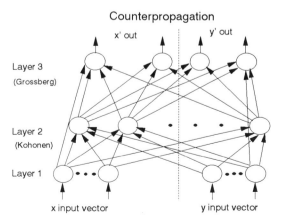

Counterpropagation

x' out   y' out

Layer 3
(Grossberg)

Layer 2
(Kohonen)

Layer 1

x input vector   y input vector

Figure 43.4. Counterpropagation neural network architecture.

The counterpropagation neural network architecture offers the unique ability to accomplish inverse mapping of the most likely combination of inputs to a desired output, in addition to providing the input to output mapping. This capability provides an opportunity to determine which input parameters are most likely the cause of undesired conditions in a manufacturing process or to determine the input parameter values most likely to result in desired output values. For example, in a plastics manufacturing process, the inverse mapping capability could be used to determine the most likely values of moisture content, viscosity, and temperature that would have resulted in an undesired texture of the product.

43.3 ARTIFICIAL NEURAL NETWORK MANUFACTURING APPLICATIONS

Successful artificial neural network applications have been reported in many areas related to manufacturing, including process monitoring and control, process modeling, maintenance and repair, process planning, fault diagnosis and classification, and robot control. Descriptions of applications in these areas are presented.

Process Monitoring and Control

Artificial neural networks were used to integrate information from multiple sensors monitoring tool wear in a turning operation (13). The feed-forward neural network learned to recognize patterns of sensor information and to associate those patterns with decisions on the tool wear condition. The network was able to filter out noise in the sensor data, allowing it to capture information from the signal. A series of machining tests was conducted on a turning lathe. Feed rate, depth, and velocity were varied. A total of 30 samples, equally divided between fresh and worn cutting tools, were used for network training, and 93 samples were used for testing the trained network. The network was able to successfully recognize 95% of the cases of tool wear under various process conditions.

The ARTMAP neural network algorithm (14) was used to develop a closed-loop arc welding process control system (15). The ARTMAP algorithm autonomously learns to classify arbitrarily ordered vectors into recognition categories based on predictive success. Two modified ARTMAP neural networks arranged in tandem were used. One network classified signals collected from a manufacturing process and the second worked as a feedback controller. The artificial neural network system has been tested with actual welding data and has been shown to meet the requirements for real-time welding control.

Artificial neural network technology was applied to brown-stock washer operations in a pulp and paper mill (16). A total of 44 variables were identified as possible parameters to include in the network training. The network was developed to maintain solids in the washing operation at a uniform level. Both the standard deviation and the coefficient of variation of solids uniformity showed improvement of greater than 20% with the artificial neural network controller. This improved control implies improved washing efficiency, resulting in quality and economic benefits.

Artificial neural networks were used to learn essential process nonlinearities from plant data in the production of penicillin (17). The trained network was used to provide on-line information to aid in the supervision of an industrial penicillin fermentation process. The quality of the network results suggests that a reasonably accurate representation of the manufacturing process was developed.

The use of artificial neural networks as adaptive nonlinear process models and controllers was explored (18). The authors used artificial neural networks when the process measurements were incomplete or inaccurate. A model-based control architecture consisting of two networks was utilized. One network learned a model of the manufacturing plant, while the second network learned control laws. The control network was able to learn a highly nonlinear model without a priori knowledge of the equational forms. The artificial neural network was successful at learning alarm thresholds, patterns of disturbances, and model mismatch, including process delays.

An artificial neural network was developed for process control of a simulated component manufacturing process (19). Sample sizes of five were drawn to represent the process mean. The mean was allowed to undergo sudden shifts in multiples of the standard deviation. The performance of the artificial neural network was compared with that of traditional statistical process control charts. The performance of the artificial neural network was equal to that of a traditional control chart. However, the network's sensitivity was not equal to that of a control chart with runs rules applied. Runs rules can be used to increase the sensitivity of a control chart by adding increased capabilities for detecting the development of nonrandom patterns.

Process Modeling

Artificial neural networks have been used to construct empirical models of manufacturing process data. Models of critical process parameters in a continuous forest product manufacturing process were developed with neural network techniques (20). Predictive models of strength parameters in particleboard manufacturing were developed, using both back-propagation and counterpropagation neural network techniques. The modeled strength parameters were modulus of rupture and internal bond. Inputs to the network included moisture content, bulk density, temperature, and chemical addition data. The back-propagation neural network model did not provide sufficient accuracy in predicting the values of the strength parameters. Counterpropagation was successful at predicting modulus of rupture with $\pm$ 10% and internal bond within $\pm$ 15%. The trained counterpropagation network can be used to improve process control and reduce the amount of substandard and scrap board produced.

A series of tests in which a back-propagation neural network was used for process identification was described (21). The ability of an artificial neural network to learn the functional relationship between process variables was evaluated. The tests used included static functions of a single variable, learning in the presence of noise, multivariable identification, linear dynamic models, and nonlinear dynamic models. A back-propagation network was able successfully to model the functional relationship between process variables.

Maintenance and Repair

An unsupervised artificial neural network designed to detect tool breakage in milling operations was reported (22). The system is based on the adaptive resonance theory (ART2) structure. ART2 is an unsupervised network for cluster formation and was developed (23) to meet the challenge of network development in an environment that is neither bounded nor stable. The ART learning system attempts to remain adaptive in response to significant input, while remaining stable in response to irrelevant input. The researchers used cutting force measurements to classify tool wear and breakage. They trained a microcomputer-based neural network system with simulated good and broken tool data from mathematical force models for milling. They reported 97.2% of the experimental data and 99.9% of all data were categorized correctly by ART2.

In automated machining processes, sensor information concerning tool wear is an essential guide for making replacement decisions, calculating tool compensations, and preventing machine or workpiece damage (24). A lack of models of the physics of wear propagation and the superposition of flank and crater wear effects prompt the use of neural network techniques. A radial basis function neural network was used to develop a comprehensive reusable tool wear model (24). Experiments involving feed and speed, wear rates, and output forces were conducted. The development of this model did not assume knowledge of a model for wear mechanisms or its relationship with sensed signals. The trained network was able to track flank and crater wear accurately.

Process Planning

An operational policy prescribes when and how tasks are assigned to resources in a manufacturing operation. Various criteria, such as mean task tardiness and mean task cost, can be used to evaluate the effectiveness of the operational policy. The relationship between the relative importance of these criteria and the overall performance of the manufacturing system often cannot be described analytically (25). The use of artificial neural networks to identify the relative importance of these criteria for given performance goals was explored (25). The authors used simulation and an artificial neural network to establish adequate weights, representing the importance of the criteria to the decision-making process at the work center level. The criteria and their associated weights defined the operational policy of the manufacturing system. The results from a job shop simulation were used for network training. The input training vector consisted of performance measures and additional parameters that characterize the work load. The output vector included the criteria weights that define an operational policy. The anticipated use of the artificial neural network system would allow for the input of the desired performance measures and anticipated work load. The artificial neural network model was designed to provide the operational policy that will best realize the performance goal.

A back-propagation neural network model to classify machined parts into part families within a group technology application was developed (26). Group technology is a manufacturing principle that takes advantage of the similarities of parts by grouping related parts into classes for processing. A back-propagation network was successfully adapted to generate automatically part families during this classification process. Each input to the network represents a part feature and each output represents a part family. The generalization capability of the artificial neural network was used to classify the parts into families and create new families as necessary. The trained neural network indicates the closest part family in terms of part features when a new part is introduced.

Fault Diagnosis and Classification

A back-propagation network was developed to accomplish knowledge representation in a chemical plant (27). The network was designed and built to perform fault detection and diagnosis. A data set consisting of flow rates, temperatures, and concentrations was constructed. The network was trained to recognize six fault conditions in the data: high or low temperature, high or low inlet flow rate, and high or low inlet concentration. A data set consisting of 12 simulated measurement patterns was used to train the network. The network learned useful mappings that provided the correct association between fault classes and measurement patterns. Rule-following behavior occurred without any explicit representation of rules, due to the generalization capabilities of the network. Thus the network was able to classify correctly similar input patterns not used in network training.

Knowledge acquisition for rule-based expert systems for mechanical fault diagnosis is a difficult and time-consuming effort that cannot always be accomplished successfully. Consequently, a neural network approach for automatic generation of a knowledge base was developed (28). An artificial neural network expert system was developed for engine diagnosis. This fault diagnosis problem was represented by a two-layer, feed-forward neural network. The training data set for the network consisted of various engine case studies. The system was reported to generate too many causes for some scenarios, consequently, additional experimental data are required. Expert evaluation of the system showed it to be correct about 75% of the time.

Artificial neural networks are well suited to learn and retrieve correlations between patterns such as measurements and faults or responses. A set of faults and alarms representing a simple stir-tank reactor was used to test the network learning of fault diagnosis (18). Each network was trained using a set of input alarm or sensor readings and corresponding output faults. Faults successfully diagnosed included failures of output pumps, cooling pumps, and flow sensors.

Robot Control

It has been reported (29) that traditional approaches to robot control in complex environments have seen limited success, especially for real-time applications. Artificial neural network algorithms offer an alternative approach for robot control design. Robot control systems require a high degree of autonomous adaptive learning to be able to avoid unexpected obstacles and respond effectively to the wear and tear of components. A 2 degree of freedom (df) robot arm was able to learn both the visual workspace and the robot's joint angles using a simplified Kohonen neural network.

The problem of adaptive control of a robotic manipulator in unknown environments using artificial neural networks was addressed (30). The artificial neural network controller was trained to approximate the inverse dynamics of an unknown robotic system over particular regions of the state space. The artificial neural network controller strategy lays the foundation for the hardware implementation for performing dynamic real-time control of this robot.

A feed-forward neural network for controlling a two-link robot arm undergoing large payload mass changes was successfully developed (31). The control system consists of two artificial neural networks and proportional-derivative controllers. One artificial neural network captured the nonlinear inverse dynamics of the robot arm to minimize trajectory tracking error as the arm moved. The second artificial neural network estimated the payload mass based on the applied joint torques and resulting manipulator motions.

43.4 CONCLUSIONS

The application of neural network techniques in manufacturing is still a relatively young area. Much progress has been made, as reported here, in the use of neural networks in various areas, including the modeling and control of manufacturing processes; the control of robotic movements in complex environments; and manufacturing classification, diagnosis, and repair. Yet much research remains to be accomplished including the development of on-line training algorithms, advanced hardware capabilities, and improved training algorithms. Many of the applications reported in the literature are laboratory experiments or preliminary studies. Neural network techniques offer great potential in meeting the challenges of advanced manufacturing.

BIBLIOGRAPHY

1. M. CAUDILL, *Neural Networks Primer,* Miller Freeman Publications, San Francisco, Calif., 1989.
2. M.W. ROTH, "Neural-Network Technology and Its Applications," *Johns Hopkins APL Tech. Digest* **9**(3), 242-253.
3. D.E. RUMELHART, G.E. HINTON, and R.J. WILLIAMS, "Learning Internal Representations by Error Propagation" in D.E. Rumelhart and J.L. McClelland, eds., *Parallel Distributed Processing: Explorations in the Microstructures of Cognition. Vol. 1: Foundations.* MIT Press, Cambridge, 1986.
4. C.J. MATHEUS, and W.E. HOHENSEE, "Learning in Artificial Neural Systems," *Computat. Intel.* **3**, 283–294 (1987).
5. G.E. HINTON, "Connectionist Learning Procedures," *Artif. Intel.* **40**, 185–234 (1989).
6. Y.H. PAO, *Adaptive Pattern Recognition and Neural Networks,* Addison-Wesley Publishing Co., Inc., Reading, Mass., 1989.
7. R.P. LIPPMANN, "An Introduction to Computing with Neural Nets," *IEEE ASSP Magazine,* **4**, 4–22 (1987).
8. T. KOHONEN, *Sellf-organizing and Associative Memory,* Springer-Verlag, Berlin, 1984.
9. W.P. JONES and J. HOSKINS, "Back-propagation: A Generalized Delta Learning Rule," *Byte* **12**(11), 155–162 (1987).
10. H.H. WHITE, "Neural Network Learning and Statistics," *AI Expert* **4**(12), 48–52 (1989).
11. S. GROSSBERG, *Studies of Mind and Brain,* Reidel, Boston, 1989.
12. R. HECHT-NIELSEN, "Counterpropagation Networks," *Appl. Optics* **26**(23), 4979–4983 (1987).
13. S. RANGWALA and D. DORNFELD. "Sensor Integration Using Neural Networks for Intelligent Tool Condition Monitoring," *J. Eng. Ind.* **112**(3), 219–228 (1990).
14. G.A. CARPENTER, S. GROSSBERG, and J. REYNOLDS, "ARTMAP: Supervised Real-time Learning and Classification of Nonstationary Data by a Self-organizing Neural Network," *Neural Networks* **4**, 569–588 (1991).
15. H.H. HUANG and H.P. WANG. "Tandem ARTMAP Neural Networks for Feedback Process Control: A Welding Example" in Y.C. Shin, A.H. Abodelmonem, and S. Kumara, eds., *Neural Networks in Manufacturing and Robotics,* American Society of Mechanical Engineers, 1992, pp. 11–22, (PED Vol. 57).
16. K.L. PATRICK, "Neural Network Keeps BSW Filtrate Solids at Maximum Uniform Levels," *Pulp and Paper* **65**(3), 55–58 (1991).
17. C. Di MASSIMO, G.A. MONTHEUE, M.J. WILLIS, M.T. THAM, and A.J. MORRIS, "Toward Improved Penicillin Fermentation Via Artificial Neural Networks," *Comput. Chem. Eng.* **16**(4), 283–291 (1992).

18. L.H. UNGAR, B.A. POWELL, and S.N. KAMENS. "Adaptive Networks for Fault Diagnosis and Process Control," *Comput. Chem. Eng.* **14**(4–5), 561–573 (1990).

19. G.A. PUGH, "Synthetic Neural Networks for Process Control," *Comput. Ind. Eng.* **17**(1–4), 24–26 (1989).

20. D.F. COOK and A.D. WHITTAKER, "Neural Network Process Modeling of a Continuous Manufacturing Operation," *Eng. Appl. Artif. Intel.,* in press.

21. J.F. POLLARD, M.R. BROUSSARD, D.B. GARRISON, and K.Y. SAN. "Process Identification Using Neural Networks," *Comput. Chem. Eng.* **16**,(4) 253–270 (1992).

22. C.M. BAUER, "North American Manufacturing Research Conference XIX Report," *Manufact. Eng.* **107**(1), 55–58 (1991).

23. G.A. CARPENTER and S. GROSSBERG, "ART2: Self-organization of Stable Category Recognition Codes for Analog Input Patterns," *Appl. Optics* **26**, 4919–4930 (1987).

24. S. ELANAYAR and Y.C. SHIN, "Robust Tool Wear Estimation Via Radial Basis Function Neural Networks" in Y.C. Shin, A.H. Abodelmonem, and S. Kumara, eds., *Neural Networks in Manufacturing and Robotics,* American Society of Mechanical Engineers, 1992, pp. 37–47, (PED Vol. 57).

25. G. CHRYSSOLOURIS, M. LEE, and M. DOMROESE, "The Use of Neural Networks in Determining Operational Policies for Manufacturing Systems," *J. Manufact. Sys.* **10**(2), 166–175 (1991).

26. Y. KAO and Y.B. MOON. "A Unified Group Technology Implementation Using the Backpropagation Learning Rule of Neural Networks," *Comput. Ind. Eng.* **20**(4), 425–437 (1991).

27. J.C. HOSKINS and D.M. HIMMELBLAU, "Artificial Neural Network Models of Knowledge Representation in Chemical Engineering," *Comput. Chem. Eng.* **12**(9–10), 881–890 (1988).

28. A.K. RAY, "Equipment Fault Diagnosis: A Neural Network Approach," *Comput. Ind.* **16**(2), 169–177 (1991).

29. J.B. Saxon and A. Mukerjee. "Learning the Motion Map of a Robot Arm with Neural Networks," in *International Joint Conference on Neural Networks,* Vol. 2, June 1990, pp. II-777–II-781

30. D.P. GARG and S. ANANTHRAMAN. "Control of a SCARA Robot Using a CMAC Based Neural Controller" in Y.C. Shin, A.H. Abodelmonem, and S. Kumara, eds., *Neural Networks in Manufacturing and Robotics,* American Society of Mechanical Engineers, 1992, pp. 91–103, (PED Vol. 57).

31. J.D. YEGERLEHNER and P.H. MECKL. "Neural Network Control for a Two-Link Manipulator Undergoing Large Payload Changes" in Y.C. Shin, A.H. Abodelmonem, and S. Kumara, eds., *Neural Networks in Manufacturing and Robotics,* American Society of Mechanical Engineers, 1992, pp. 105–116, (PED Vol. 57).

Suggested Readings

J.P. BOLTE, *Applications of Neural Networks in Agriculture,* ASAE, St. Joseph, Mich., 1989 (*ASAE Paper No. 89759*).

J.A. FREEMAN and D.M. SKAPURA, *Neural Networks: Algorithms, Applications, and Programming Techniques,* Addison-Wesley Publishing Co., Inc., Reading, Mass., 1991.

P.J. WERBOS, "Generalization of Backpropagation with Application to a Recurrent Gas Market Model," *Neural Networks* **1**, 339–356 (1988).

CHAPTER 44

Trends in Neuroadaptive Control for Robot Manipulators

ALBERT Y. ZOMAYA and TAREK M. NABHAN
The University of Western Australia

44.1 INTRODUCTION

The problem of designing robot controllers centers on the computation of the different joint torques–forces that will produce a required task or trajectory of the end effector. Typically, robot manipulators are controlled by simple and well-defined servomechanisms at each joint. This approach neglects the role of the dynamics in affecting the overall arm performance and stability (1). The increasingly sophisticated tasks required of today's robots have called for better control techniques to enhance the high speed tracking accuracy while operating in unstructured environments. There are two main classes of robot control algorithms: dynamic based and kinematic based algorithms. At low speeds of fine motion, a kinematic controller performs well, but the performance starts to degrade at high speeds, when the hypothesis of static equilibrium at points under consideration is less valid. Thus when high speed is required, which is the case in many situations, a dynamic-based control method is necessary.

Many schemes have been developed to facilitate the robust control of robot mainpulators. Computed torque techniques employed the robot dynamic equations to calculate the force–torque associated with each joint (2). Another approach is near-minimum optimal-time control by which the end effector of the robot arm is moved from an initial position to a prespecified desired position in minimum time (3). Variable structure control is a discontinuous feedback control method that is insensitive to parameter variations and disturbances (4). In resolved motion control (RMC), the motion of the various joints' motors are combined and resolved into separately controllable hand motions along the world coordinates axes (5). Different variations of RMC were introduced by researchers, including resolved motion rate control (RMRC), resolved motion acceleration control (RMAC), and resolved motion force control (RMFC) (5). In general, the performance most of these techniques depends largely on the accurate modeling of robot dynamics.

To remedy this situation, several adaptive control techniques have been developed by researchers in the cases in which the dynamics are unknown or partially known. These techniques can provide a powerful tool for the control of robot arms (6). The literature on adaptive control is vast; however, adaptive control techniques can be divided into two distinct approaches: direct control and indirect control. In the former approach, the parameters of the controller are directly adjusted to reduce some norm of the output error, whereas in the latter one, the parameters of the plant are estimated, and accordingly, the controller is updated to minimize the error between the model and the plant. In general, these techniques are based on nonlinear laws, which makes them difficult to derive. Furthermore, their complexity grows geometrically with the number of unknown parameters, which makes them nonrobust and conditionally stable. In addition, all these techniques incur a heavy computational load, which hinders their real-time applicability (7). This requires the development of computationally efficient adaptive control algorithms that can be used to enhance the performance robot manipulators.

The recent resurgence of research and application of artificial neural networks (ANNs) to a diverse range of disciplines makes it possible to seek out solutions for robotic problems by employing ANNs. A neural network (NN) is a highly parallel dynamical system with the topology of a directed graph that can carry out information processing by means of its stable response. The most important factors in employing NNs for any application include the choice of architecture for the network and appropriate learning algorithms (8). What makes NNs a viable tool in the adaptive control of robot manipulators is the fact that autonomous systems require a high degree of flexibility to deal with significant variations in the environment (9).

44.2 NEUROADAPTIVE ROBOT CONTROLLERS

As mentioned earlier, multilayered NNs have been used to solve different robotics problems. Solutions were presented for the kinematics and dynamics, trajectory planning, sensing, and control (10). A comprehensive treatment of the topic for control applications is given in ref. 11, in which several models for identifying (or emulating) an unknown nonlinear single-input–single-output (SISO) plant by using multilayered NNs are proposed and their relevance to direct and indirect adaptive control is discussed in detail. Nguyen and Widrow (12) presented an interesting control example for a truck backer-upper that demonstrated the power of neurocontrollers for solving a large class of nonlinear control problems that were previously considered to be formidable. In general, the collective processing capacity of a NN provides the essential capability of responding quickly to complex sensory inputs. In contrast, almost all sophisticated control algorithms written a priori are severely limited by the time it takes to run them by the current computer hardware. Another restricting factor is the knowledge required about the plan (e.g., robot) to be controlled to implement an effective "classical" adaptive controller. This task is often demanding and difficult to achieve in practice. In the case of robotics, any knowledge acquired about the plant at an earlier stage might not be useful in future modes of operation, because of the time-varying nature of robotic systems (e.g., load handling and links wear).

Nevertheless, extensive studies have been conducted to investigate the feasibility of applying ANN for robotics control. Albus (13) presented a new approach to manipulator control by a neural model called the cerebellar model articulation control (CMAC), which combines input commands and feedback variables in an input vector that is used to address a memory in which the appropriate output variables are stored. The CMAC model has been employed (14) to learn the dynamics of a five-axis robot during high speed movements. A neural model called the interactive networks functioning on adaptive neural topologies (INFANT) has been developed (15) for positional control using inputs from a video system. A NN has been employed (16) to recognize the payload variation associated with a degradation in tracking performance. However, none of these techniques demonstrated the benefits of neural-based controllers over conventional ones. This is extremely important, especially considering that a NN solution may often be numerically inaccurate (10).

In retrospect, adaptive controllers are essential components for the stable and robust performance of robot manipulators (6). In principle, any adaptive control consists mainly of a controller with adjustable parameters updated in response to an error signal to meet a certain objective function (Figure 44.1). In this case, a reference model that represents the feed-forward components is used to compute the nominal values of the difference forces–torques τ_d, while the feedback component produces a perturbation signal $\delta\tau$ that reduces the deviation between the desired and the actual trajectory. A parameter estimation algorithm is used to identify certain parameters that are employed by the controller to produce the perturbation signal according to a one-step optimal control law. The main drawback of this technique is the excessive amount of computations involved, which in some cases hinder real-time applications.

A feed-forward direct controller has been suggested (17) and is shown in Figure 44.2. The controller here is a NN that must learn to reproduce the robot inverse dynamics by updating its weights in response to an error signal. One of the disadvantages of this method is the possibility that the controller may not be stable, especially at the beginning of the control action because of the dependency on the initial value of the NN weights. In addition, because the robot is a highly nonlinear system, the training of the NN will be a formidable task, which might take a long time and still not be able to meet performance requirements.

Feed-forward multilayer NNs are renowned for their capacity to act as generic approximators. This property is used in this chapter to develop an adaptive control strategy for robotic systems. As opposed to other adaptive control schemes, no parameter estimation is required because the control law does not depend on the parameter estimates. The control signals are the outputs of a NN by which the network's parameters (synaptic weights) are adjusted by an error signal that quantifies the amount of deviation between the model and the system. In other words, the NN "estimates" the control signal directly rather than estimating system parame-

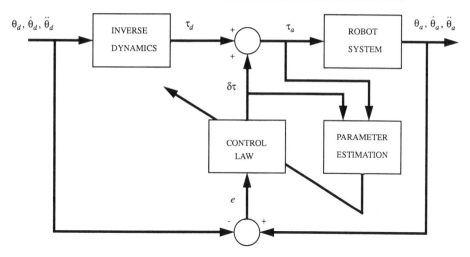

Figure 44.1. A typical adaptive control strategy.

ters. In addition, the neurocontroller is robust, in the sense that the convergence characteristics are unperturbed by minor errors in the input data (initial value of synaptic weights).

44.3 SUPERVISED AND REINFORCEMENT LEARNING TECHNIQUES

Neural network learning methods have been divided into three main paradigms: unsupervised learning, supervised learning, and reinforcement learning. Unsupervised learning methods do not depend on an external teacher to guide the learning process. Instead, the teacher can be considered to be built into the learning method (18). Unlike the unsupervised learning paradigm, both the supervised and the reinforcement learning paradigms require an external teacher to provide training signals that guide the learning process. The difference between these two paradigms arises from the kind of training signals the teacher provides. In the supervised

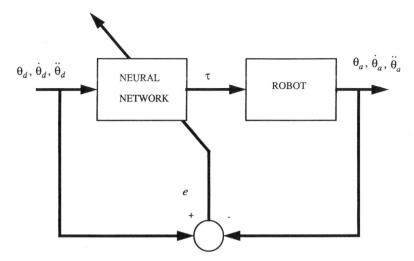

Figure 44.2. Neural network–based control.

learning paradigm, the teacher provides the learning system with the desired outputs for each given input. Learning involves "memorizing" these desired outputs by minimizing the discrepancy between the actual outputs of the system and the desired outputs (8). In contrast with the supervised learning paradigm, the role of the teacher in reinforcement learning is more evaluative than instructional. Sometimes called a critic because of this role, the teacher provides the learning system with a scalar evaluation of the system's performance of the task according to some performance measure. The objective of the learning system is to improve its performance, as evaluated by the critic, by generating appropriate outputs. Reinforcement learning, therefore, involves two operations: discovering the right outputs for a given input and memorizing those outputs.

The ability to discover solutions to problems makes reinforcement learning important in situations in which lack of sufficient structure in the task definition makes it difficult to define a priori the desired outputs for each input, as required for supervised learning. In such cases, reinforcement learning systems can be used to learn the unknown desired outputs by providing the system with a suitable evaluation of its performance (19).

Learning by Back-Propagation

The neurocontroller used in this work is a multilayered feed-forward NN based on the back-propagation (BP) algorithm. Figure 44.3 shows a general structure of a feed-forward NN using the BP learning algorithm. The subject of BP for the training of multilayer NNs has been discussed in detail elsewhere (8, 20). For completeness, it will be briefly described to show how a multilayer NN can be trained to identify an unknown function, using a set of input–output data arising from that function.

Consider a function $\Psi: X \subset \mathbf{R}^n \to \mathbf{R}^m$, from a bounded subset X of $\mathbf{R}^n$ to a bounded subset $\Psi(X)$ of $\mathbf{R}^m$. The function is unknown but is assumed to be L_2. To identify this unknown function, a set of input–output data is generated $\{(\mathbf{u}_t, \mathbf{x}_t), t = 1, \ldots, N\}$ where $\Psi(\mathbf{x}_t) = \mathbf{u}_t, \forall t$. It is also assumed that the set of input data $\{\mathbf{u}_t, t = 1, \ldots, N\}$ is randomly selected from (A) according to some unknown but fixed probability density function $\rho(\mathbf{u})$, where ρ vanishes outside X. An approximate function $\hat{\Psi}(\cdot, \mathbf{W}, \mathbf{V})$ is determined such that the expected (with respect to ρ) normed-square error $S = E\|\hat{\Psi}(\mathbf{x}_t, \mathbf{W}, \mathbf{V}) - \mathbf{u}_t\|^2$ is minimized with respect to the set of parameter matrices $\mathbf{W} = \{\mathbf{W}^1, \mathbf{W}^2, \ldots, \mathbf{W}^K\}$ and $\mathbf{V} = \{\mathbf{V}^1, \mathbf{V}^2, \ldots, \mathbf{V}^K\}$. In the $(K + 1)$ layer network, the input to the network is $\mathbf{z}^0 = \mathbf{x}$, while the output is $\mathbf{z}^K = \mathbf{u}$. The input and output are related by the recursive relationship:

$$\mathbf{y}^i = \mathbf{W}^j \mathbf{z}^{j-1} + \mathbf{V}^j \tag{1}$$

$$\mathbf{z}^j = f_j(\mathbf{y}^j) \tag{2}$$

for $j = 1, 2, \ldots, K$. Here the parameter matrices $\mathbf{W}^j$ and vectors $\mathbf{V}^j$ (synaptic weights) are of the appropriate dimension. The scalar functions $f_j(\cdot), j = 1, 2, \ldots, K$ are nonlinear (except $f_K(\cdot)$, which may possibly be linear) threshold or squashing functions usually chosen to be some kind of sigmoids. In this work, a sigmoid of the type $f_j(t) = \tanh(t)$ is assumed for all the nodes in the NN. Note that Equation 2 should be interpreted as

$$\mathbf{z}^j = f_j(\mathbf{y}^j) = [f_j(\mathbf{y}^j_1), f_j(\mathbf{y}^j_2), \ldots, f_j(\mathbf{y}^j_{n_j})]^T \tag{3}$$

where n_j is the dimension of $\mathbf{y}^j$ and $\mathbf{z}_j$. The approximating function can thus be succinctly represented by

$$\hat{\Psi}(\mathbf{x}, \mathbf{W}, \mathbf{V}) = f_K [\mathbf{W}^K f_{K-1}(\mathbf{W}^{K-1} f_{K-2}(\ldots \mathbf{W}^2 f_1(\mathbf{W}^1 \mathbf{x} + \mathbf{V}^1) + \mathbf{V}^2) + \mathbf{V}^3) + \cdots + \mathbf{V}^{K-1}) + \mathbf{V}^K \tag{4}$$

In practice, the minimization of S cannot be carried out directly, the well-known BP algorithm seeks to present the NN with one pair of input–output data at a time and update the synaptic weight matrices iteratively, using the instantaneous gradient information. This is summarized as follows. Instantaneous norm square error:

$$S(t) = \|\hat{\Psi}(\mathbf{x}_t, \mathbf{W}, \mathbf{V}) - \mathbf{u}_t\|^2 \tag{5}$$

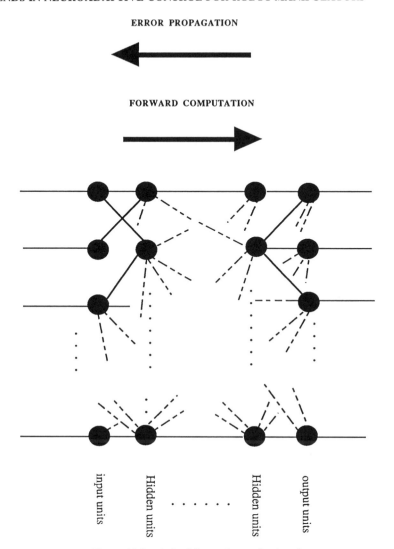

ERROR PROPAGATION

FORWARD COMPUTATION

input units Hidden units . . . . . . Hidden units output units

Figure 44.3.   A feed-forward neural network.

Weight update:

$$\mathbf{W}^k(t + 1) = \mathbf{W}^k(t) - \eta(1 - \mu)\frac{\partial S(t)}{\partial \mathbf{W}^k} + \mu(\mathbf{W}^k(t) - \mathbf{W}^k(t - 1)) \qquad (6)$$

$$\mathbf{V}^k(t + 1) = \mathbf{V}^k(t) - \eta(1 - \mu)\frac{\partial S(t)}{\partial \mathbf{V}^k} + \mu(\mathbf{V}^k(t) - \mathbf{V}^k(t - 1)) \qquad (7)$$

$$k = 1, 2, \ldots, K$$

where η and μ are the learning rate and momentum value, respectively. The instantaneous gradient can be given as follows. For the output layer,

$$\frac{\partial S(t)}{\partial \mathbf{W}_{ij}^K} = -2\sigma_i^K z_j^{K-1} \tag{8}$$

$$\frac{\partial S(t)}{\partial \mathbf{V}_i^K} = -2\sigma_i^K \tag{9}$$

$$\sigma_i^K = (u_i(t) - z_i^K)f'_K(y_i^K) \tag{10}$$

For the kth hidden layer ($k = 1, 2, \ldots, K - 1$),

$$\partial S(t)\frac{\partial S(t)}{\partial \mathbf{W}_{ij}^k} = -2\sigma_i^k z_j^{k-1} \tag{11}$$

$$\frac{\partial S(t)}{\partial \mathbf{V}_i^k} = -2\sigma_i^k \tag{12}$$

$$\sigma_i^k = f'_k(y_i^k) \sum_l \sigma_l^{k+1} W_{li}^{k+1} \tag{13}$$

Initially, the synaptic weights $\mathbf{W}^j$ and $\mathbf{V}^j$ are set to small random values and updated according to Equations 6 and 7. For off-line situations the same set of data $\{(\mathbf{x}_t, \mathbf{u}_t), t = 1, \ldots, N\}$ can be used to train the network repeatedly with decreasing learning rate, until the total error is less than a certain threshold. Care must be taken not to overtrain the network, as this may cause error when the network is used to map input data not included in the training set (8). Numerous successful applications of multilayer NNs trained by the BP algorithm have been reported in the literature recently. However, without a teacher to show the most appropriate actions, the BP cannot be directly used to synthesize a controller (21, 22).

Reinforcement learning (RL), as opposed to the BP, has a more attractive feature in that it replaces the teacher by a performance measure from the environment to grade the goodness of the current actions. Measurement of the performance of a controller is feasible, and it is usually used in the synthesis of optimal controllers (23). Hence, on-line performance measurements can form the basis for adaptive NN control when used with an appropriate RL technique. The stochastic nature of RL is compatible with that of on-line identification and controller synthesis.

44.4 ADAPTIVE LEARNING CONTROL

Adaptive learning control (ALC) is an alternative form of self-organizing control (SOC) (24), which is promising in its capability to provide solution to "formidable" problems. The ALC consists of two neuronlike elements: an associative search element (ASE) and an adaptive critic element (ACE) (25). The most attractive features of such a control system are

1. A mathematical model of the system is not necessary for the development a "control law." The controller learns to develop by association of input and output signals.
2. A wide class of measures of performance can be optimized.
3. The system to be controlled can be time varying and and/or nonlinear.
4. A nonuniform sampling rate can be used.
5. The algorithms (i.e., ALC) are naturally adaptive, hence they can be used to directly control the system or to optimize the performance of an existing control system.

The ASE operates by generating an output pattern, receiving an evaluation from its environment in the form of scalar payoff or reinforcement, updating the contents of its memory, and repeating this generate-and-test procedure. As this kind of learning proceeds, each input causes the retrieval of better choices for the pattern to be associated with that input. To discover what response leads to improvement in performance, ASE employs trial and error, or generate-and-test search process. As shown in Figure 44.4, the state vector of the system is sampled and fed into a decoder, which transforms each state vector into an n-component binary vector, whose components are all zero except for a single one in the position corresponding to the state of the system at that instant. This vector is provided as an input to the ASE, the adaptive element receives the signal through the reinforcement pathway, and this information is used in the ASE.

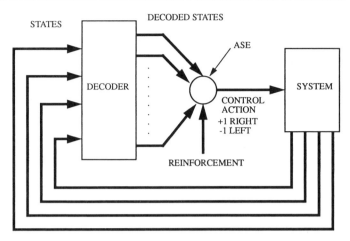

Figure 44.4. Associative search element.

The learning action needs to be more distinctive to ensure convergence that leads to least punishment in cases in which only punishment is available. An adaptive critic element is introduced to overcome this problem. Among other functions the ACE constructs predictions of reinforcement so that if punishment is less than its expected level, then it acts as a reward. As shown in Figure 44.5, the ACE receives the externally supplied signal, which it uses on the basis of the current vector to compute an improved reinforced signal that it sends to the ACE. The central idea behind the ACE algorithm is that predictions are formed that predict not only reinforcement but also future predictions of reinforcement.

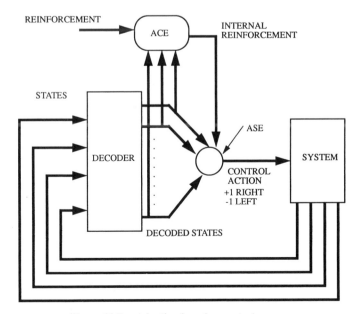

Figure 44.5. Adaptive learning control.

The Proposed NeuroController

As mentioned earlier, the BP cannot be used directly in this case because no information is available on the desired performance of the controller. Hence, the BP needs to be incorporated in the proposed scheme in a different way. The controller shown in Figure 44.1 will be replaced by the neurocontroller shown in Figure 44.6. In this case, the BP will be used in two unconsecutive stages (this is different from the usual use of the BP). The neurocontroller presented in this work is based on the ASE and ACE concepts. However, the ASE and ACE are replaced by a single NN. The neurocontroller block shown in Figure 44.6 is considered to be an abstract machine that randomly selects actions according to some stored probability distribution and receives feedback from the environment evaluating those actions. The machine then uses the feedback to update its distribution to increase the expectation of favorable evaluations for future actions. Such a machine is called a stochastic learning automaton and is similar to the previously described ASE (26). Considering the task of learning a general input–output mapping using an automaton, it is clear that the automaton needs to consider other inputs than the reinforcement signal. This kind of input is called the context input. For automata with context input, the preferred action may change in different contexts. Because the automaton is trying to learn which action to associate with which context inputs, Barto and Anandan (27) named this task associative reinforcement learning. The use of the stochastic automaton as a single component in a NN (e.g., node) has been proposed (26). In this work, the whole network (neurocontroller) is assumed to be an automaton. Therefore, the control algorithm can be summarized as follows (Figure 44.7):

1. This stage is composed of two sub-stages that run in parallel.
   a. The desired input U_d is presented to the model (inverse plane) and an output U_a is produced. Note that the vector U_d is an amalgamation of three vectors (θ_d, $\dot{\theta}_d$, and $\ddot{\theta}_d$) while the output vector U_a is an amalgamation of θ_a, $\dot{\theta}_a$, and $\ddot{\theta}_a$.
   b. The desired input U_d is presented to the neurocontroller (context input). The forward phase of the BP is executed. The output of the neurocontroller is the perturbation signal ($\delta\tau$).
2. The perturbation signal ($\delta\tau$) is added to the model output (τ_d), which was produced from step 1a. The output of this stage is the control signal (U_c) or the input to the robot system.
3. The system will produce the actual value of U_a. The two values (desired and actual) are compared to compute the error (e).
4. The error (e) is sent to the backward phase of the BP, which will, accordingly, update the weights of the neurocontroller. Note that this error corresponds to that shown in Equation 10 (i.e., $u_i(t) - z_i^k$). However, it is not computed according to Equation 10 in the

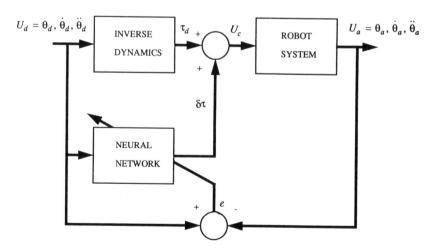

Figure 44.6. The proposed neuroadaptive controller.

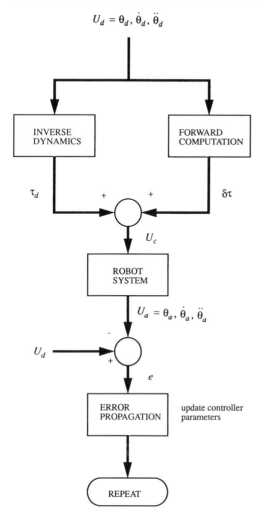

$$U_d = \theta_d, \dot{\theta}_d, \ddot{\theta}_d$$

INVERSE DYNAMICS

FORWARD COMPUTATION

τ_d +   + $\delta\tau$

U_c

ROBOT SYSTEM

$$U_a = \theta_a, \dot{\theta}_a, \ddot{\theta}_a$$

U_d −   +

e

ERROR PROPAGATION   update controller parameters

REPEAT

Figure 44.7. A block diagram representation of the neurocontroller algorithm.

sense that it is not the difference between a desired and an actual value. This is due to the fact that the desired output ($\delta\tau$) cannot be predicted a priori.

5. The procedure is repeated again for a different set of inputs.

The role of the neurocontroller can be stated thus: at time t the environment provides the learning system with some pattern $U_d \in \mathbf{u} \subseteq \mathbf{R}^n$. The learning system produces a random output ($\delta\tau \subseteq \mathbf{R}$), which will be added to (τ_d) to produce the control signal. The environment evaluates the output of the controller in the context of the input (U_d) and sends to the learning system a reinforcement signal $e(t)$, $e(t) \in \mathbf{R} = [-\alpha, \alpha]$, with $e(t) = \alpha$ representing maximum reinforcement, where $\alpha \in \mathbf{R}$. Note that in the case of a multiinput, multioutput (MIMO) system, there will be several reinforcement signals. According to goodness (if the error is small) or badness (if the error is large) of the reinforcement signal the learning system must produce a better output to minimize the error (e). Therefore, the parameters of the neurocontroller will be updated internally without any need to extra computations (e.g., parameter estimation).

Formally, the problem can be stated as follows. At each time t, the environment provides the neurocontroller with a vector $\mathbf{U}_d = (U_1(t), \ldots, U_{3N}(t))$, where each $U_i(t)$ is a real number, together with a real valued reinforcement signal $\mathbf{e}(t)$. The neurocontroller (which is the ASE in this case) produces an output pattern $\delta\boldsymbol{\tau} = (\delta\tau_1, \ldots, \delta\tau_N)$, which is added to the output of the model ($\mathbf{U}_d$) to produce the control signal ($\mathbf{U}_c$), which is received by the environment. The problem the neurocontroller is designed to solve can be summarized: each vector $\mathbf{U}_d(t)$ provides information to the neurocontroller about the condition or state of its environment at time t. As mentioned earlier, each $\mathbf{U}_d$ is called the context input or vector. Different actions, or output patterns, are appropriate in different contexts. As a consequence of performing an action in a particular context, the neurocontroller receives from its environment, in the form of a payoff or reinforcement signal $\mathbf{e}(t)$, an evaluation of the appropriateness of that action in that context. The neurocontroller's task is to act in each context so as to maximize this payoff. Also, we assume that $\mathbf{U}_d(t)$ belongs to a finite set $\mathbf{U}_d = (\mathbf{U}_d^1, \ldots, \mathbf{U}_d^k)$ of context vectors, and that to each $\mathbf{U}_d^\sigma \in \mathbf{U}_d$ there corresponds a payoff or reinforcement function e^σ.

In general, the neurocontroller presented above should satisfy several properties. The controller must learn to associate with each input pattern an output value for which the reinforcement signal it receives indicates the highest degree of success. In addition, it should be able to improve its performance in cases in which it is doing poorly by using greater degrees of exploratory behavior and hence discriminate between cases in which it is doing poorly and those in which it is doing well. This is important in order not to degrade its performance in cases in which it is doing well by exhibiting behavior that is too random. In addition, the proposed approach transforms the controller design problem into an optimization one. That is, find the optimum $\mathbf{W}^*$ and $\mathbf{V}^*$ that will minimize the error $\mathbf{e}(t)$. Hence the robustness and convergence properties of the problem can be investigated using the vast literature on optimization theory.

44.5 ISSUES OF CONVERGENCE AND STABILITY

It is well known from standard nonlinear optimization theory that the block-data version of the BP algorithm will converge to a local minimum of the mean square error surface. It has been pointed out (28) that the BP is a recursive version of the smoothed stochastic algorithm in system identification (29). If the learning rate η is made time dependent and to tend to zero as $t \to +\infty$, a unified method developed by Ljung (29) for convergence analysis of recursive algorithms can readily be applied. This means that the parameter vectors $\mathbf{W}$ and $\mathbf{V}$ in Equations 7 and 8 will converge to a local minimum of the mean square error as $t \to +\infty$. Based on Ljung's (29) argument, the recursive Equations 7 and 8 can be rewritten as follows:

$$\mathbf{W}(t + 1) = \mathbf{W}(t) + \eta(t + 1)\, \Gamma(t + 1; \mathbf{W}(t), \boldsymbol{\Omega}(t + 1)) \qquad (14)$$

where $\mathbf{W}(\cdot)$ is a sequence of n-dimensional weight vectors that must converge to the optimum value $\mathbf{W}^*$. Actually, they can be considered as the parameters (synaptic weights) of our adaptive controller (Figure 44.6). The p-dimensional vector $\boldsymbol{\Omega}(t)$ is basically a vector obtained at time t and causes $\mathbf{W}(t)$ to be updated; it corresponds to $\partial S(t)/\partial \mathbf{W}^k$ in Equation 6. For the general case, $\boldsymbol{\Omega}$ can be also made dependent on $\varepsilon(\cdot)$, which represents noise or a sequence of random variables with zero mean. Hence, the mapping $\Gamma(\cdot;\cdot,\cdot)$ and a paticular choice of $\eta(\cdot)$ will entirely determine the algorithm. To generalize the proof, Ljung (29) assumed that $\boldsymbol{\Omega}(t)$ is not only dependent on $\mathbf{W}(\cdot)$ but also on $\varepsilon(\cdot)$, hence

$$\boldsymbol{\Omega}(t + 1) = \Lambda(\mathbf{W}(t))\boldsymbol{\Omega}(t) + \mathbf{H}(\mathbf{W}(t))\varepsilon(t + 1) \qquad (15)$$

where $\Lambda(\cdot)$ and $\mathbf{H}(\cdot)$ are $m \times m$ and $m \times r$ matrix functions, respectively.

It is worth noting that the correction $\zeta(t + 1)\, \Gamma(t + 1; \mathbf{W}(t), \boldsymbol{\Omega}(t + 1))$ depends, via $\boldsymbol{\Omega}(t)$, on all old $\mathbf{W}$'s. This can be easily seen from Equation 7. Equations 14 and 15 are fairly complex to analyze, being time-variant, stochastic, nonlinear difference equations. Therefore, Ljung (29) pointed out that Equation 14 is associated with a differential equation, which can be used to study its asymptotic properties and, more important, those of Equations 6 and 7 as well. Now, consider the following

$$\mathbf{W}(t + 1) = \mathbf{W}(t) + \eta(t + 1)\, \Gamma(\mathbf{W}(t), \boldsymbol{\Omega}(t + 1)) \qquad (16)$$

where, for simplicity, Γ is made time independent. As mentioned earlier, $\boldsymbol{\Omega}(t)$ depends on all previous $\boldsymbol{\Omega}$'s hence,

$$\boldsymbol{\Omega}(t) = \sum_{j=1}^{t} \left[\prod_{i=j+1}^{t} \Lambda(\mathbf{W}(i-1)) \right] \mathbf{H}(\mathbf{W}(j-1))(\varepsilon j) \qquad (17)$$

Now, if Equation 15 is exponentially stable, then the first terms in Equation 16 will be small, and for some ρ,

$$\Omega(t) \approx \sum_{j=t-\rho}^{t} \left[\prod_{i=j+1}^{t} \Lambda(\mathbf{W}(i-1)) \right] \mathbf{H}(\mathbf{W}(j-1))(\boldsymbol{\epsilon} j) \qquad (18)$$

Now, it can be assumed that $\zeta(t) \Rightarrow 0$ as $t \Rightarrow 0$, because less attention needs to be made to old value of $\mathbf{W}(\cdot)$. It follows from this fact and Equation 16 that the difference $\mathbf{W}(t) - \mathbf{W}(t-1)$ becomes smaller as t increases, thus leading to $\mathbf{W}^*$. As a consequence, for sufficiently large t, $\mathbf{W}(k) \approx \mathbf{W}(t)$; $t \geq k \geq t - 2\rho$; hence

$$\Omega(k) \approx \sum_{j=k-\rho}^{k} [\Lambda(\mathbf{W}(t))]^{k-j} \mathbf{H}(\mathbf{W}(t))\boldsymbol{\epsilon}(j)$$

$$\Omega(k) \approx \sum_{j=1}^{k} [\Lambda(\mathbf{W}(t))]^{k-j} \mathbf{H}(\mathbf{W}(t))\boldsymbol{\epsilon}(j) = \hat{\Omega}(k; \mathbf{W}(t)) \qquad (19)$$

for $t \geq k \geq t - \rho$, where $\hat{\Omega}$ is thought of as the lower dimensional (approximate) output of the dynamical system given in Equation 15. Furthermore,

$$\Gamma(\mathbf{W}(k-1), \Omega(k)) - \Gamma(\mathbf{W}(t), \hat{\Omega}(k; \mathbf{W}(t))) = \chi(\mathbf{W}(t)) + \boldsymbol{\kappa}(k) \qquad (20)$$

where

$$\chi(\mathbf{W}) = E\Gamma(\mathbf{W}, \hat{\Omega}(k; \mathbf{W}))$$

and thus $\boldsymbol{\kappa}(k)$ is a random variable with zero mean. By using Equation 20, we can approximately evaluate

$$\mathbf{W}(t + \nu) = \mathbf{W}(t) + \sum_{k=t+1}^{t+\nu} \boldsymbol{\eta}(\mathbf{k})\Gamma(\mathbf{W}(k-1), \Omega(k))$$

$$\approx \mathbf{W}(t) + \chi(\mathbf{W}(t)) \sum_{k=t+1}^{t+\nu} \eta(k) + \sum_{k=t+1}^{t+\nu} \eta(k)\boldsymbol{\kappa}(k)$$

$$\approx \mathbf{W}(t) + \chi(\mathbf{W}(t)) \sum_{k=t+1}^{t+\nu} \eta(k) \qquad (21)$$

Note that the last step should follow because the last term is a zero mean random variable, which is dominated by the second term. Furthermore, Equation 21 suggests that the sequence of $\mathbf{W}$'s more or less follows the following difference equation:

$$\mathbf{W}_d(\omega + \Delta\omega) = \mathbf{W}_d(\omega) + \Delta\omega\chi(\mathbf{W}_d(\omega)) \qquad (22)$$

where $\Delta\omega = \sum_{k=t+1}^{t+\nu} \eta(k)$. It is useful to interpret Equation 22 as a way of solving the differential equation, when $\Delta\omega$ is small,

$$\frac{d}{d\omega} \mathbf{W}_d(\omega) = \chi(\mathbf{W}_d(\omega)) \qquad (23)$$

where ω is related to the original time t in Equation 16 by

$$\omega_t = \sum_{k=1}^{t} \eta(k) \qquad (24)$$

hence, the sequence of $\mathbf{W}$'s should follow asymptotically the trajectories $\mathbf{W}_d(\cdot)$ of Equation 23. It can also be said that Equation 21 is related to the difference equation:

$$\mathbf{W}_d(t + 1) = \mathbf{W}_d(t) + \eta(t + 1)\chi(\mathbf{W}_d(t)) \qquad (25)$$

However, the differential Equation 23 is easier to handle, because it is time invariant. Ljung (29) concluded that the asymptotic properties of Equations 14 and 15 can be investigated in terms of the differential Equation 23. More technical proofs and formal analysis can be found in Ljung (29). Note that if all the nodes of the neurocontroller have a linear activation function, the neurocontroller will degenerate to a linear one. In this case, the convergence results for the adaptive linear combiner are directly applicable (30).

44.6 EXPERIMENTS

The reinforcement signal $e(t)$ seen in Figure 44.6 is a continuous signal that measures the difference between the desired and the actual output of the system. To prevent large errors from drastically updating the weights (e.g., winner takes all), the difference should not be introduced to the NN directly as a reinforcement signal, instead it must be scaled to fall between $[-1, 1]$, which is the output range of a sigmoidal function of the type

$$f(x) = \frac{1 - e^{-x}}{1 + e^{-x}} \qquad (26)$$

Because the range of the error is not known in advance, an adaptive error scaling scheme was developed to handle this problem (31):

At each iteration, if $r(t) \notin [-1, 1]$, the scale is adjusted to prevent this situation. Furthermore, the scale is reset at the start of each iteration. Hence, the scale adapts itself without the need for a priori knowledge of the error range. At the beginning of the training process, the value of the scale is expected to drop heavily, and as the learning proceeds the value increases. The stability of the system is maintained by scaling the NN output. The scaling scheme initially starts with a low value (typically 0.1) and increases each time the NN converges. This technique eliminates the possibility of high errors at the beginning of the training process due to the effect of the initial random weights values.

One of the major criticisms of classical BP is that the training is slow. Several recent publications have addressed this problem and proposed variations of the BP algorithm with an accelerated rate of convergence (32, 33). A modified BP algorithm was developed (33) in which a batch variant of the BP was used while the η and μ were dynamically varied. The learning rate η is varied in a way that enables the algorithm to use a near-optimum η for all the stages of the learning process, whereas μ is set to zero when the information inherent in the last iteration looks to be misleading, otherwise it employs the initial nonzero value. In this work, time-varying values of η and μ are used (31). After each iteration, η and μ are calculated as follows if:

$$(e(t) < e(t - 1))$$
$$\eta(t + 1) = \eta(t) \times \lambda$$
$$\mu(t + 1) = \mu_0$$

else

$$\eta(t + 1) = \eta(t) \times \beta$$
$$\mu(t + 1) = 0$$

where t is the iteration number, λ is a constant > 1, β is a constant < 1, and μ_0 is the initial value of μ.

Another method can be used to improve the acceleration of the BP through compensating for the "unfair" way used to update the weights. This is due to the fact that $0 \leq y' \leq 0.5$ (where y' is the derivative of the activation function in Equation 26), and the gradient elements at the different layers involve a fraction that will never exceed 0.5, 0.25, 0.125, . . . at the different layers. A compensatory rescaling scheme has been suggested (32) that assumes that the output of each neuron is uniformly distributed between $[-1, 1]$ and the derivative functions are statistically independent from one layer to another. The scaling suggested is the reciprocal of $E(y')^n$, where n is the nth layer counting backward from the output, applied as a multiplier of the derivative of each layer counted backward from the output layer. These values are 1.5, 2.25, 3.375, . . ., again, starting from the output layer. The experiments conducted have shown that normalizing these values gives better results, so the scaling values used here are 1, 1.5, 2.25, . . . starting from the output layer.

The efficiency of the neuroadaptive controller is demonstrated using simulations of the *PUMA*—560 (Unimation, Inc.) robot arm running on a *SUN SPARC* (Sun Microsystems, Inc.) workstation. The positioning system of the PUMA-560 is used here (i.e., the first three links). The analysis and the simulation is based on a compiled set of data of the PUMA-560 (34) (Appendix A). The dynamic model of the robot arm is formulated using a simplified formulation of the dynamics presented in ref. 34 (Appendix B).

The common practice for simulating the motion of the arm is through solving for the accelerations:

$$\ddot{\theta}(t) = \mathbf{D}^{-1}(\theta)[\tau(t) - \mathbf{C}(\theta, \dot{\theta}) - \mathbf{H}(\theta)] \tag{27}$$

Then by numerically integrating Equation 27 forward in time, the values of the θ and $\dot{\theta}$ can be computed. During the off-line training session the robot model was assumed to have 5% shift in the centres of masses of the different links.

Case 1

Figure 44.6 shows the neurocontroller that is built using a single NN with the desired states as inputs (i.e., θ, $\dot{\theta}$, and θ). The weights of the NN are updated using a reinforcement vector that reflects the performance of each robot joint. Because the first three links are used, the NN has nine inputs and three output signals, representing the forces–torques applied to each link. In this case, the NN is of size 9, 10, 15, and 9, for the input, first hidden, second hidden, and output layers, respectively, referred to hereinafter as NN.[9,10,15,9]

In the off-line training process, the output scale was initialized to 0.1 and incremented by 0.1 for each 100 iterations until it reached 0.5, while η, μ, λ, and β were set to 0.3, 0.001, 1.15, and 0.75, respectively. Note that the algorithm restores the initial value of η and μ each time the output scale changes to start a new training phase. To check the generalizing capability of the neurocontroller, the NN was trained using 5000 random presentations and tested using another 3000 random presentations. This leads to a trajectory independent neurocontroller in the sense that it does not assume that the robot executes specific or repetitive motions. The training was terminated after 480 iterations. At the time, the convergence error in the training and the testing sets was 0.00043 and 0.00069, respectively (Figure 44.8).

During the on-line mode of operations, the neurocontroller keeps on updating its weights to improve the quality of the output signal, while the values of η and μ remain fixed at 0.04 and 0.5, respectively. On receiving an input signal, 15 iterations are executed to update the NN weights. The robot trajectory used in this case is the one reported in ref. 35, i.e.,

$$\theta_i = \theta_{iT}\left[t - \frac{1}{2\pi} \sin\left(\frac{2\pi t}{T}\right)\right] (i = 1, 2, 3) \tag{28}$$

where T is the time required to execute the trajectory and is set to 1 s, and θ_{iT} is the final angular position of each joint as is given as follows:

$$\theta_{iT} = \frac{\pi}{3} (i = 1, 2, 3) \tag{29}$$

The sampling rate was set to 0.01 s. Another trajectory of 1000 random samples was used to demonstrate the generalization capability of the neurocontroller. Furthermore, the adaptability of the neurocontroller was demonstrated by altering the inertia tensor and the center of mass of the different links by 25% and introducing a range of loads handled by the end effector (up to 2 kg). In each case, the neurocontroller is tested using the above two trajectories, which will be referred to hereinafter as the smooth and coarse trajectories. In addition, a third test is applied

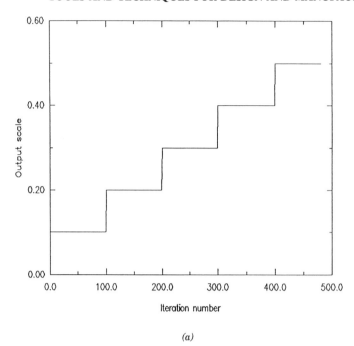

(a)

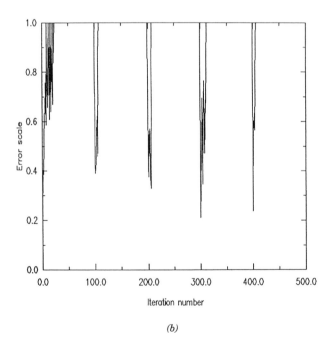

(b)

Figure 44.8. Neurocontroller parameters. (a) Output scale of the NN. (b) Error scale. (c) Time-varying learning rate. (d) Convergence of the error.

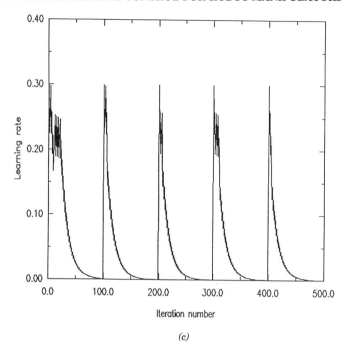

(c)

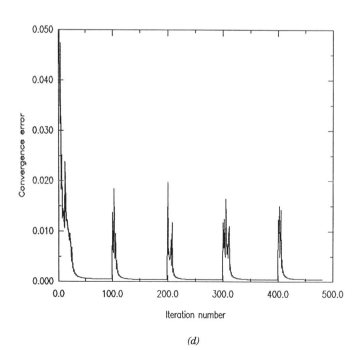

(d)

Figure 44.8. (*Continued*)

TABLE 44.1.   Tracking Errors (rad-s^2) with 25% Shift in the Center of Masses and Inertia Tensors

Trajectory	Joint	Minimum	Maximum	Mean	S.D.
Smooth	1	7.59e–06	0.64	0.0068	0.0639
	2	4.18e–07	0.15	0.0018	0.0147
	3	1.06e–05	0.04	0.0015	0.0042
Coarse	1	2.14e–07	1.36	0.0061	0.0696
	2	1.17e–07	0.74	0.0047	0.0359
	3	1.80e–05	0.20	0.0057	0.0160
Coarse	1	0.016	7.91	4.106	1.178
(fixed	2	0.0006	5.48	1.830	1.169
weights)	3	0.0006	1.18	0.281	0.213

to the neurocontroller by executing the coarse trajectory while the weights are fixed. This highlights the fact that the weights of the neurocontroller must be updated continuously. A sample of the results is shown in Tables 44.1 through 44.3. The tracking errors are presented in a statistical form: minimum error, maximum error, mean of the error, and the standard deviation. The results show that the neurocontroller succeeds in achieving good performance during on-line tracking.

Case 2

For case 2, a distributed neurocontroller is presented that consists of three NNs (according to number of joints) each assigned to a separate joint (Figure 44.9). The inputs to the different NNs are the states of the system, and the output of each NN is the relevant value of force–torque. The weights of each NN are updated using a reinforcement value generated by the associated joint. Note that the three NNs share the same inputs, because of the highly coupled nature of the robot system. Each of the neurocontrollers is of size NN,^{9,10,14,7,1} NN,^{9,7,5,1} and NN^{9,5,1} for joints 1, 2, and 3, respectively. The different sizes of the NNs reflect the fact that the neurocontrollers are dealing with joints of varying degrees of complexity. This can be explained as follows: link 1 is dynamically dependent on links 2 and 3, link 2 is dynamically dependent on link 3 only, and the dynamics of link 3 are not affected or coupled with the dynamics of the other two links (33).

The parameters for the off-line training process, η, μ, λ, β, and the scale for each of the NNs is set to the values used in case 1. Again, for the training and testing, the same sets were used; however, the training was terminated after 541 iterations. The convergence error for the training and testing sets is given in Table 44.4 and Figure 44.10. Furthermore, to demonstrate the tracking accuracy of the distributed neurocontroller, the same tests conducted in case 1 were applied here. The values of η and μ are set to 0.06 and 0.6, respectively. Tables 44.5 through 44.7 show samples of the results. The tables show that the distributed neurocontroller outper-

TABLE 44.2.   Tracking Errors (rad-s^2) with Shift in the Center of Masses and Inertia Tensors with 1-kg Load

Trajectory	Joint	Minimum	Maximum	Mean	S.D.
Smooth	1	1.07e–05	0.124	0.0015	0.0123
	2	3.43e–06	0.067	0.0009	0.0061
	3	1.34e–06	0.021	0.0002	0.0025
Coarse	1	5.03e–07	0.703	0.0002	0.027
	2	1.26e–06	0.29	0.0021	0.014
	3	1.34e–07	0.17	0.0051	0.013
Coarse	1	0.0068	6.41	2.84	0.951
(fixed	2	0.0007	4.19	1.24	0.854
weights)	3	0.0008	1.05	0.22	0.173

TABLE 44.3.   Tracking Errors (rad-s²) with 25% Shift in Center of Masses and Inertia Tensors with 2-kg Load

Trajectory	Joint	Minimum	Maximum	Mean	S.D.
Smooth	1	6.51e–07	0.0027	0.0004	0.0003
	2	6.81e–06	0.0043	0.0005	0.0005
	3	9.09e–05	0.0051	0.0022	0.0015
Coarse	1	2.88e–07	0.24	0.0014	0.0081
	2	8.58e–07	0.23	0.0024	0.0132
	3	8.85e–07	0.194	0.007	0.015
Coarse	1	0.0098			
			5.03	1.71	0.809
(fixed	2	0.0001			
			3.22	0.74	0.606
weights)	3	6.84e–05	0.95	0.19	0.146

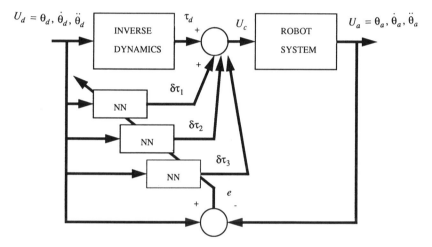

Figure 44.9.   The distributed version of the neuroadaptive controller.

forms the single neurocontroller in the case of no load. However, when loading the robot with a given mass, both controllers perform comparably to some extent. This is because the handling of the mass introduces new dynamic complexities to the overall robot structure that are difficult to predict. In certain instants, the load in hand can lead to an overall stable dynamics of the arm, whereas in other cases the load might destablize the arm performance (34).

One of the obvious advantages of the distributed neurocontroller is the number of parameters. The number of synaptic weights can be reduced because of the division of the whole task into several smaller subtasks. For example, in the previous example the single neurocontroller was composed of approximately 430 weights, while in the case of the distributed neurocontroller, each one of the NNs consisted of 350, 109, and 51 parameters, respectively. This shows that

TABLE 44.4.   Convergence and Generalization Errors

Joint	Training Error	Testing Error
1	0.00016	0.0002
2	6.36e–05	7.11e–05
3	3.68e–05	3.79e–05

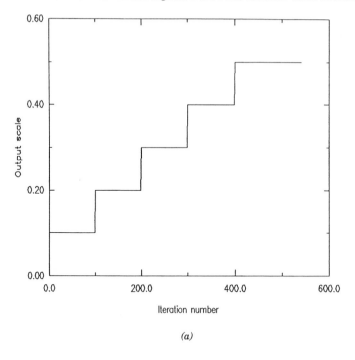

(a)

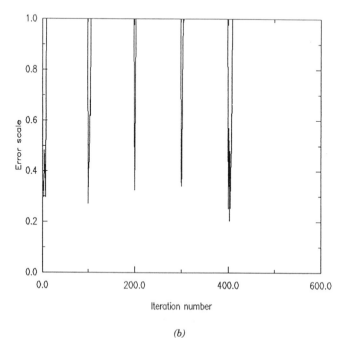

(b)

Figure 44.10. The distributed neurocontroller parameters. (*a*) Output scale of the NNs. (*b*) Error scale of NN[1]. (*c*) Time-varying learning rate of NN[1]. (*d*) Convergence of the error of NN[1]. (*e*) Error scale of NN[2]. (*f*) Time-varying learning rate of NN[2]. (*g*) Convergence of the error of NN[2]. (*h*) Error scale of NN[3]. (*i*) Time-varying learning rate of NN[3]. (*j*) Convergence of the error of NN[3].

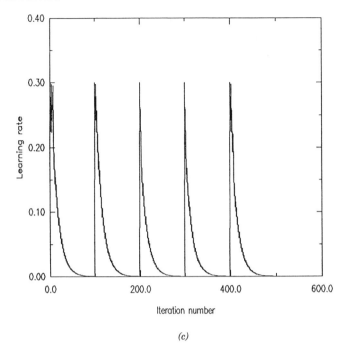

(c)

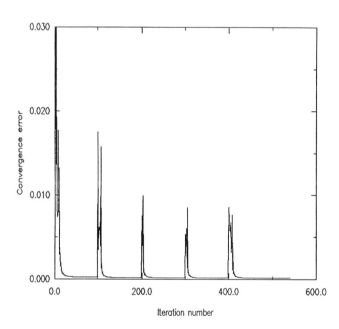

(d)

Figure 44.10. (*Continued*)

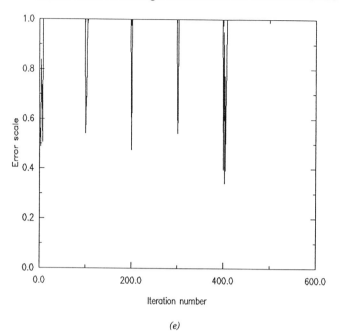

(e)

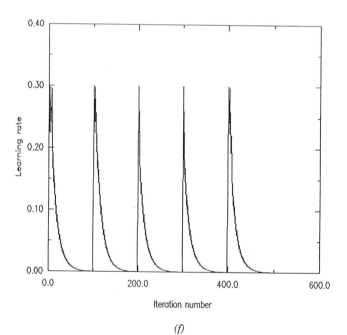

(f)

Figure 44.10. (*Continued*)

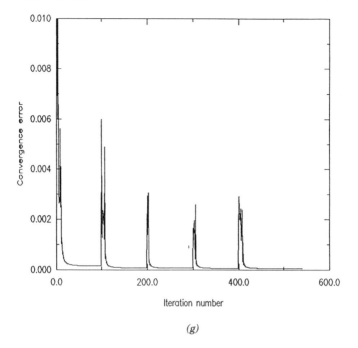

(g)

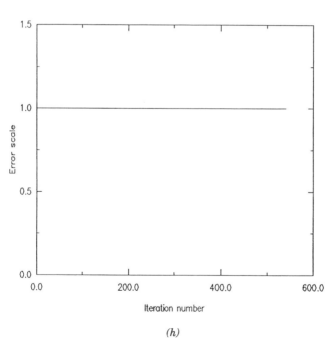

(h)

Figure 44.10. *(Continued)*

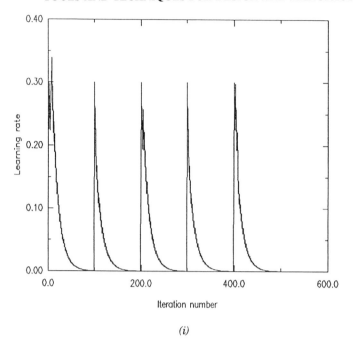

(i)

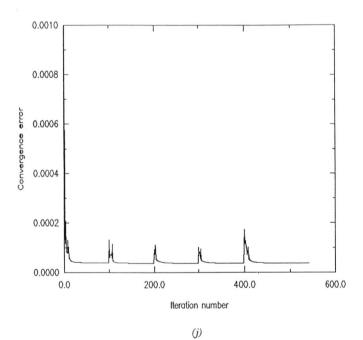

(j)

Figure 44.10. *(Continued)*

TABLE 44.5.   Tracking Errors (rad-s^2) with 25% Shift in the Center of Masses and Inertia Tensors

Trajectory	Joint	Minimum	Maximum	Mean	S.D.
Smooth	1	6.10e−06	0.084	0.0025	0.0084
	2	8.93e−06	0.005	0.0013	0.0013
	3	2.72e−08	0.0009	0.0003	0.0002
Coarse	1	2.34e−07	0.316	0.009	0.022
	2	1.02e−07	0.352	0.0073	0.0018
	3	2.84e−06	0.02	0.0015	0.0002
Coarse	1	0.005	7.92	4.109	1.18
(fixed	2	0.0085	5.50	1.83	0.172
weights)	3	3.54e−05	1.185	0.28	0.213

TABLE 44.6.   Tracking Errors (rad-s^2) with 25% Shift in the Center of Masses and Inertia Tensors with 1-kg Load

Trajectory	Joint	Minimum	Maximum	Mean	S.D.
Smooth	1	1.6e−06	0.032	0.0013	0.0033
	2	1.42e−05	0.003	0.0006	0.0007
	3	7.43e−07	0.0009	0.0002	0.0002
Coarse	1	1.38e−06	0.109	0.005	0.010
	2	5.71e−06	0.363	0.0043	0.015
	3	1.014e−06	0.009	0.0014	0.0015
Coarse	1	0.0061	6.42	2.84	0.951
(fixed	2	0.0032	4.21	1.24	0.856
weights)	3	0.0003	1.05	0.22	0.173

TABLE 44.7.   Tracking Errors (rad-s^2) with 25% Shift in the Center of Masses and Inertia Tensors with 2-kg Load

Trajectory	Joint	Minimum	Maximum	Mean	S.D.
Smooth	1	2.39e−07	0.0051	0.0007	0.0008
	2	1.95e−07	0.0021	0.0006	0.0006
	3	5.80e−06	0.0011	0.0003	0.0003
Coarse	1	4.95e−07	0.075	0.0032	0.0053
	2	1.30e−07	0.43	0.0033	0.015
	3	1.79e−06	0.014	0.0017	0.0018
Coarse	1	0.0015	5.05	1.71	0.808
(fixed	2	0.0007	3.17	0.75	0.610
weights)	3	0.0003	0.96	0.19	0.146

simpler network architectures can be used when employing distributed control. Moreover, the benefits of the distributed controller can be seen when more complicated robots are used (i.e., robots with large degrees of freedom). In the long run, immense computational savings can be achieved through using distributed neuroadaptive controllers (31).

4.7   CONCLUSIONS

Robot manipulators are systems of a highly nonlinear nature. Thus an effective controller must first and foremost be stable, robust, and computable within real-time constraints. This chapter presented a case of direct adaptive control for robot manipulators based on a neural network approach. The neural network was used to estimate the control signal, thus avoiding the computationally tedious task of using parameters estimators. Compared with recent techniques, the proposed algorithm is less expensive, in computational terms, and simpler in its structure, allowing for the swift on-line implementation at high sampling rates. The neural network actually plays two roles: the first is to produce the control signal and the second is to "estimate" and update controller parameters.

For the accurate modeling and control of robot manipulators, it is necessary to know the relationship between the applied forces–torques (to the different links) and the resulting motion. Unlike (strictly) time-invariant systems, when the robot arm moves this relationship changes, in some aspects by as much as 300% in a fraction of a second. This configuration dependence within the dynamic model must be appropriately accounted for in a dynamic-based controller. To employ dynamic-based techniques, the dynamic parameters of the robot arm must be known. These are simple physical properties such as mass, location of the center of the mass, and inertia. However, the multitude of parameters may be difficult to measure directly. The problem is further complicated by the time-varying nature of these parameters. For instance, in the case of links wear or motor backlash, these parameters change considerably over time. Hence, an effective controller must be able to compensate and accommodate for all these disturbances in order to produce robust performance.

The neural-controller was based on the back-propagation algorithm, which was used within a learning by reinforcement framework instead that of supervised learning. The concept of the controller was based on the so-called stochastic learning automaton. The neural controller learns the mapping between an input–output relationship based on an evaluative signal from the environment. The signal grades the output (e.g., good or bad) rather than providing information on the desired output. The same ideas were extended to build a distributed neurocontroller, in which several neural networks were used to control the different joints of a robot arm. In general, the results showed that neurocontrollers have great potential because of their simplicity and computational efficiency.

Acknowledgments

This work was partially supported by the Australian Research Council (ARC) small grants scheme.

BIBLIOGRAPHY

1. A.Y. ZOMAYA and A.S. MORRIS, "The Dynamic Performance of Robot Manipulators Under Different Operating Conditions," *IEE Proc. Control Theory Appl. Pt. D* **137**(5), 281–289 (1990).

2. B.R. MARKIEWICZ, *Analysis of the Computed Torque Drive Method and Comparison with the Conventional Position Servo for a Computer Controlled Manipulator*, NASA-JPL, Pasadena, Calif., 1973, Tech. Memo. 33-601.

3. J.E. BOBROW, S. DUBOWSKY, and J.S. GIBSON, "On the Optimal Control of Robot Manipulators with Actuator Constraints," in *Proceedings of the American Control Conference (ACC), San Francisco, 1983*, pp. 782–787.

4. K.K.D. YOUNG, "Controller Design for A Manipulator using Theory of Variable Structure Systems," *IEEE Trans. Sys. Man Cybrenet.* **SMC-8**(2), 101–109 (1978).

5. R.J. SCHILLING, *Fundamentals of Robotics: Analysis and Control*, Prentice-Hall, Inc., Englewood Cliffs, N.J., 1990.

6. S. TOSUNOGLU and D. TESAR, "State of Art in Adaptive Control of Robotic Systems," *IEEE Trans. Aerospace Elec. Sys.* **24**(5), 552–561 (1988).

7. L. GUO and J. ANGELES, "Controller Estimation for the Adaptive Control of Robotic Manipulators," *IEEE Trans. Robot. Automat.* **5**(3) (1989).

8. R. HECHT-NIELSEN, *Neurocomputing*, Addison-Wesley Publishing Co., Inc., Reading, Mass., 1990.

9. P.J. ANTSAKLIS, K.M. PASSINO, and S.J. WANG, "Towards Intelligent Control Systems: Architecture and Fundamental Issues," *J. Intel. Robot. Sys.* **1**, 315–342 (1989).

10. B. HORNE, M. JAMSHIDI, and N. VADIEE, "Neural Networks in Robotics: A Survey," *J. Intel. Robot. Sys.* **3**, 67–72 (1990).

11. K.S. NARENDRA and K. PARTHASARATHY, "Identification and Control of Dynamical Systems Using Neural Networks," *IEEE Trans. Neural Networks* **1**(1), 4–27 (1990).

12. D.H. NGUYEN and B. WIDROW, "Neural Networks for Self-Learning Control Systems," *IEEE Control Sys. Mag.* **10**(3) (1990).

13. J.S. ALBUS, "A New Approach to Manipulator Control: The Cerebellar Model Articulation Control (CMAC)," *Trans. ASME J. Dynam. Sys. Measure. Control* **97** 220–227 (1975).

14. W.T. MILLER, R.P. HEWES, F.H. GLANZ, and L.G. KRAFT, "Real-time Dynamic Control of an Industrial Manipulator Using a Neural-Network-Based Learning Controller," *IEEE Trans. Robot. Automat.* **6**(1), 107–116 (1990).

15. M. KUPERSTEIN, "Generalized Neural Model for Adaptive Sensory-Motor Control of Single Postures" in *Proceedings of the IEEE International Conference on Robotics and Automation,* 1988, pp. 140–144.

16. M.B. LEAHY, M.A. JOHNSON, and S.K. ROGERS, "Neural Network Payload Estimation for Adaptive Robot Control," *IEEE Trans. Neural Networks* **2**(1), 93–100 (1991).

17. T. YABUTA and T. YAMADA, "Possibility of Neural Networks Controller for Robot Manipulators" in *Proceedings of the IEEE International Conference on Robotics and Automation,* 1990, pp. 1686–1691.

18. T. KOHONEN, "Self-organized Formation of Topologically Correct Feature Maps," *Biol. Cybernet.* **43**, 59–69 (1982).

19. A.G. BARTO and M.I. JORDAN, *Gradient Following without Back-propagation in Layered Networks,* paper presented at the IEEE First Annual Conference on Neural Networks, San Diego, Calif., 1987.

20. D.E. RUMELHART and J.L. MCCLELLAND, *Parallel Distributed Processing: Explorations in the Microstructure of Cognition,* Vol. 1, MIT Press, Cambridge, 1987.

21. P.M. MILLS and A.Y. ZOMAYA, "Reinforcement Learning Using Back-Propagation as a Building Block," in *Proceedings of the IEEE International Joint Conference on Neural Networks,* Vol. 2, 1991, pp. 1554–1559.

22. A.Y. ZOMAYA, M.E. SUDDABY, and A.S. MORRIS, "A Case of Direct Neuro-Adaptive Control of Robot Manipulators," in *Proceedings of the IEEE International Conference on Robotics and Automation,* 1992, pp. 1902–1907.

23. B.D.O. ANDERSON and J.B. MOORE, *Linear Optimal Control,* Prentice-Hall, Inc., Englewood Cliffs, N.J., 1971.

24. U.S. Pat. 3,519,998 (Sept. 29, 1967), R.L. Barron.

25. A.G. BARTO, R.S. SUTTON, and C.W. ANDERSON, "Neuronlike Adaptive Elements That Can Solve Difficult Learning Control Problems," *IEEE Trans. Sys. Man Cybernet.* **13**(5), 834–846 (1983).

26. V. GULLAPALLI, "A Stochastic Reinforcement Learning Algorithm for Learning Real-Valued Functions," *Neural Networks* **3**, 671–692 (1990).

27. A.G. BARTO and P. ANANDAN, "Pattern Recognizing Stochastic Learning Automata," *IEEE Trans. Sys. Man Cybernet.* **15**, 360–374 (1985).

28. S.A. BILLINGS, H.B. JAMALUDDIN, and S. CHEN, *A Comparison of the Backpropagation and Recusive Prediction Error Algorithms for Training Neural Networks,* Department of Control Engineering, University of Sheffield, Sheffield, UK, 1990, Rep. No. 379.

29. L. LJUNG, "Analysis of Recursive Stochastic Algorithms," *IEEE Trans. Automat. Control* **AC-22**(4), 551–575 (1977).

30. B. WIDROW and S.D. STEARNS, *Adaptive Signal Processing,* Prentice-Hall, Inc., Englewood Cliffs, N.J., 1985.

31. A.K. RIGLER, J.M. IRVINE, and T.P. VOGL, "Rescaling of Variables in Backpropagation Learning," *Neural Networks* **4**, 225–229 (1991).

32. T.P. VOGL, J.K. MANGIS, A.K. RIGLER, W.T. ZINK, and D.L. ALKON, "Accelerating the Convergence of the Backpropagation Method," *Biol. Cybernet.* **59**, 257–263 (1988).

33. A.Y. ZOMAYA, *Modelling and Simulation of Robot Manipulators: A Parallel Processing Approach,* World Scientific Publishing, Singapore, 1992.

34. T. KANE and D. LEVINSON, "The Use of Kane's Dynamical Equations in Robotics," *Int. J. Robot. Res.* **2**(3), 3–21 (1983).

35. A.Y. ZOMAYA and T.M. NABHAN, "Centralized and Decentralized Neuro-Adaptive Robot Controllers," *Neural Networks,* **6**(2), 223–244 (1993).

Appendix A (PUMA-560)

TABLE 44.1A. Link Parameters—Puma 560

Arm Link	Link Parameters			
	Variable	α	a	d
1	θ_1	−90.0	0.0	0.0
2	θ_2	0.0	0.432	0.0
3	θ_3	−90.0	0.019	0.15
4	θ_4	−90.0	0.0	0.432
5	θ_5	90.0	0.0	0.0
6	θ_6	0.0	0.0	0.0

TABLE 44.2A. Link Mass and First Moments (Puma 560)

Arm Link	Inertial Parameters			
	Mass (kg)	x (m)	y (m)	z (m)
1	12.95	0.0	0.309	0.039
2	22.36	−0.329	0.005	0.2038
3	5.0	0.02	0.014	0.0037
4	1.177	0.0	0.086	−0.0029
5	0.618	0.0	−0.01	0.0013
6	0.157	0.0	0.0	0.0029

TABLE 44.3A. Actuator and Link Inertias (Puma 560)

Arm Link	Inertial Parameters (kg/m²)			
	I_a	I_{xx}	I_{yy}	I_{zz}
1	0.7766	2.351	0.1968	2.3457
2	2.3616	1.3313	4.313	3.4116
3	0.5827	0.07582	0.07766	0.01038
4	1.06	0.0141	0.003388	0.01395_
5	0.0949	0.00055	0.00057	0.000546
6	0.107	0.00012	0.000012	0.000006

Appendix B (Robot Dynamics)

The effective and coupling inertia terms of Equation 27 are formulated as follows:

$$D_{ij} = \sum_{l=\max(i,j)}^{n} tr(\Delta_j^l \, \mathbf{J}^l \, \Delta_i^{lT}) \tag{B1}$$

where tr is the trace operator. More simplifications can be achieved by expanding Equation B1 to remove the multiplication by zero operations. In the following discussion the Stanford manipulator is considered. Assume a matrix $(\mathbf{E})$ such that:

$$\mathbf{E} = \begin{bmatrix} \mathbf{e} & 0 \\ 0 & 0 \end{bmatrix} \tag{B2}$$

where $(\mathbf{e})$ is a 3×3 matrix. Using the trace operator,

$$D_{ij} = \sum_{l=\max(i,j)}^{n} \sum_{m=1}^{3} e_{mm} \tag{B3}$$

where $\displaystyle\sum_{m=1}^{3} e_{mm}$ is given as

$$
\begin{aligned}
&= J_{11}^l \begin{bmatrix} -\delta_{iy} \\ \delta_{iz} \end{bmatrix}_l \begin{bmatrix} -\delta_{jy} \\ \delta_{jz} \end{bmatrix}_l + J_{22}^l \begin{bmatrix} \delta_{ix} \\ -\delta_{iz} \end{bmatrix}_l \begin{bmatrix} \delta_{jx} \\ -\delta_{jz} \end{bmatrix}_l + J_{33}^l \begin{bmatrix} -\delta_{ix} \\ \delta_{iy} \end{bmatrix}_l \begin{bmatrix} -\delta_{jx} \\ \delta_{jy} \end{bmatrix}_l \\
&\quad + J_{24}^l \left(\begin{bmatrix} -\delta_{iz} \\ -\delta_{jz} \end{bmatrix} \begin{bmatrix} d_{jx} \\ d_{ix} \end{bmatrix} + \begin{bmatrix} \delta_{ix} \\ \delta_{jx} \end{bmatrix} \begin{bmatrix} d_{jz} \\ d_{iz} \end{bmatrix} \right)_l + J_{34}^l \left(\begin{bmatrix} \delta_{jy} \\ -\delta_{jx} \end{bmatrix} \begin{bmatrix} d_{ix} \\ d_{iy} \end{bmatrix} + \begin{bmatrix} -\delta_{ix} \\ \delta_{iy} \end{bmatrix} \begin{bmatrix} d_{jy} \\ d_{jx} \end{bmatrix} \right)_l \\
&\quad + J_{44}^l \begin{bmatrix} d_{ix} \\ d_{iy} \\ d_{iz} \end{bmatrix}_l \begin{bmatrix} d_{jx} \\ d_{jy} \\ d_{jz} \end{bmatrix}_l
\end{aligned}
\tag{B4}
$$

In a similar approach to describe the coriolis and centripetal effects,

$$C_{jk}^i = \sum_{l=\max(i,j)}^{n} tr(\Delta_j^l \, \Delta_k^l \, \mathbf{J}^l \, \Delta_i^{lT}) \tag{B5}$$

assuming a matrix $(\mathbf{U})$ such that

$$\mathbf{U} = \begin{bmatrix} \mathbf{u} & 0 \\ 0 & 0 \end{bmatrix} \tag{B6}$$

where $(\mathbf{u})$ is a 3×3 matrix. Using the trace operator will yield

$$C_{jk}^i = \sum_{l=\max(i,j,k)}^{n} \sum_{m=1}^{3} u_{mm} \tag{B7}$$

where $\displaystyle\sum_{m=1}^{3} u_{mm}$ is given as

$$
= J_{11}^l\, \delta_{jx}^l \left(\begin{bmatrix} -\delta_{ky} \\ \delta_{iy} \end{bmatrix} \begin{bmatrix} -\delta_{iz} \\ -\delta_{kz} \end{bmatrix} \right)_l + J_{22}^l\, \delta_{jy}^l \left(\begin{bmatrix} \delta_{kx} \\ -\delta_{ix} \end{bmatrix} \begin{bmatrix} -\delta_{iz} \\ -\delta_{kz} \end{bmatrix} \right)_l + J_{33}^l\, \delta_{jz}^l \left(\begin{bmatrix} -\delta_{kx} \\ \delta_{ky} \end{bmatrix} \begin{bmatrix} -\delta_{iy} \\ -\delta_{ix} \end{bmatrix} \right)_l
$$

$$
+ J_{24}^l \left(d_{iy} \begin{bmatrix} \delta_{jz} \\ -\delta_{jx} \end{bmatrix} \begin{bmatrix} -\delta_{kz} \\ \delta_{kx} \end{bmatrix} + \delta_{ix} \begin{bmatrix} -\delta_{jy} \\ \delta_{jx} \end{bmatrix} \begin{bmatrix} d_{kx} \\ d_{ky} \end{bmatrix} - \delta_{iz} \begin{bmatrix} -\delta_{jz} \\ \delta_{jy} \end{bmatrix} \begin{bmatrix} d_{ky} \\ d_{kz} \end{bmatrix} + \delta_{jy} \begin{bmatrix} \delta_{kx} \\ -\delta_{kz} \end{bmatrix} \begin{bmatrix} d_{ix} \\ -d_{iz} \end{bmatrix} \right)_l
$$

$$
+ J_{34}^l \left(d_{iz} \begin{bmatrix} -\delta_{jy} \\ \delta_{jx} \end{bmatrix} \begin{bmatrix} \delta_{ky} \\ -\delta_{kx} \end{bmatrix} + \delta_{iy} \begin{bmatrix} -\delta_{jz} \\ \delta_{jy} \end{bmatrix} \begin{bmatrix} d_{ky} \\ d_{kz} \end{bmatrix} - \delta_{ix} \begin{bmatrix} \delta_{jz} \\ -\delta_{jx} \end{bmatrix} \begin{bmatrix} d_{kx} \\ d_{kz} \end{bmatrix} + \delta_{jz} \begin{bmatrix} -\delta_{kx} \\ \delta_{ky} \end{bmatrix} \begin{bmatrix} -d_{ix} \\ d_{iy} \end{bmatrix} \right)_l
$$

$$
+ J_{44}^l \left(d_{ix} \begin{bmatrix} \delta_{jz} \\ \delta_{jy} \end{bmatrix} \begin{bmatrix} -d_{ky} \\ d_{kz} \end{bmatrix} + d_{iy} \begin{bmatrix} \delta_{jx} \\ \delta_{jz} \end{bmatrix} \begin{bmatrix} -d_{kz} \\ d_{kx} \end{bmatrix} + d_{iz} \begin{bmatrix} -\delta_{jy} \\ \delta_{jx} \end{bmatrix} \begin{bmatrix} d_{kx} \\ d_{ky} \end{bmatrix} \right)_l \tag{B8}
$$

where

$$
J_{24}^l = y_l\, m_l, \quad J_{34}^l = z_l\, m_l, \quad J_{44}^l = m_l
$$

$$
J_{11}^l = \frac{(-I_{11}^l + I_{22}^l + I_{33}^l)}{2}, \quad J_{22}^l = \frac{(-I_{11}^l + I_{22}^l + I_{33}^l)}{2}, \quad J_{22}^l = \frac{(I_{11}^l - I_{22}^l + I_{33}^l)}{2}
$$

and (I_{jj}^{l2}) is the radius of gyration about axis (jj) of link (l). Finally, the gravitational effects are given by

$$
h_i = g \sum_{l=i}^{n} m_l\, \mathbf{\Psi}_l\, \mathbf{r}_l^l \tag{B9}
$$

where m_l and $\mathbf{r}_l^l$ are the mass and the center of the mass of link (l), respectively, and $\mathbf{\Psi}_l$ is a vector of the following form:

$$
\mathbf{\Psi}_l = \begin{bmatrix} s\,\alpha\,\delta_{iz} - c\,\alpha\,\delta_{iy} \\ c\,\alpha\,\delta_{ix} \\ -s\,\alpha\,\delta_{ix} \\ s\,\alpha\,d_{iy} + c\,\alpha\,d_{iz} \end{bmatrix}_l \tag{B10}
$$

where $s\alpha$ and $c\alpha$ are $\sin(\alpha)$ and $\cos(\alpha)$ respectively. The dynamic Equations B4, B8, and B9 are used throughout this work.

GLOSSARY

Adaptive control. A form of feedback control in which the controller can modify its behavior in response to changes in the dynamics of the process and the disturbances.

Adaptive learning control. A type of self-organizing control that is an evolutionary form of adaptive controllers in which guided random search results are used to achieve flexibility and speed of adaption.

Back-propagation. An algorithm for the training of a feed-forward–type of neural network. It is a powerful mapping network that has been successfully applied to a wide range of applications.

Direct control. A form of adaptive control in which the control parameters are directly adjusted to improve a performance index; no parameter estimation is required.

Indirect control. A form of adaptive control in which the plant parameters are estimated on-line and the control parameters are adjusted based on these estimates.

Neural network. A highly parallel dynamical system with the topology of a directed graph that can carry out information processing by means of its stable response.

Reinforcement Learning. A neural-network training scheme in which a teacher plays the role of a critic, as opposed to supervised learning, in which the teacher provides the learning system with a scalar evaluation of the system's performance of the task according to some performance measure. The objective of the learning system is to improve its performance, as evaluated by the critic, by generating appropriate outputs.

Robot manipulator. A reprogrammable manipulator designed to move materials, parts, tools, and specialized devices through variable programmed motions for the performance of a number of tasks.

Supervised Learning. A neural-network training scheme in which a teacher provides the learning system with the desired outputs for each given input. Learning involves memorizing these desired outputs by minimizing the discrepancy between the actual outputs of the system and the desired outputs.

Tracking. The action taken by the neurocontroller to modify its parameters (synaptic weights) to compensate for a sudden change in system dynamics.

CHAPTER 45
Adaptive Control and Learning in Manufacturing

T. WATANABE
Ritsumeikan University

45.1 INTRODUCTION

Manufacturing operations such as cutting, grinding, welding, and electric discharging involve complicated physical and chemical processes. Experience is required to perform them. Automation technologies, for instance numerical control and computer-aided design–computer-aided manufacturing (CAD–CAM), have made it possible for less experienced operators to work in manufacturing factories. However, these technologies aid operators mainly in the processing of the geometric motions of the tools that generate the shapes of parts. A few automatic programming systems such as EXAPT have limited functions in automatically determining the cutting and feed-rate speeds of machining with process planning for holes and pockets (1, 2). The decision about what the optimum feed rate and cutting speeds in machining are to guarantee high cost-efficiency, productivity, and accuracy is not easy for programmers who have little experience in actual manufacturing on work floors. The development of further automated systems having intelligent functions such as expert operators are expected. Such intelligent systems can also decrease the load of decision making for sophisticated parts from CAD–CAM systems at the upper stream in manufacturing processes.

Machining centers that are combined with automatic warehouses and transportation devices in flexible manufacturing systems (FMS) now need to be operated long hours without operators, e.g., for 64 h from Friday evening to Monday morning. It is also expected that these machines will automatically optimize their operational speeds and avoid damage such as tool breakage due to the unpredicted variation in manufacturing.

Adaptive control applied to manufacturing can adjust the operational speeds or motion paths to optimize the manufacturing processes and/or to satisfy constraint conditions against variations in manufacturing phenomena caused by change in the hardness of the work material, tool wear, width and depth of cut, deflection of tools and work material, etc. Adaptive control can respond to variations in manufacturing phenomena in real time. Learning control can also automatically improve the movements of machines; however, it modifies movements based on many past trials. That is, learning control is mainly applied to repeated manufacturing.

45.2 MATHEMATICAL MODEL OF MANUFACTURING PROCESSES AND ADAPTIVE CONTROL

Automated manufacturing processes are defined by the controlled process variable $x(t)$, such as the positions of the tool and work material controlled by servo mechanisms generating part shapes, and the controllable process parameter P_c such as the commands given to ordinary manufacturing controllers, i.e., feed rate of the work material, spindle rotational speed, and tool offset as well as the parameters of controllers such as loop gain. Automated manufacturing processes also are defined by the uncontrollable process parameter P_p such as physical and chemical characteristics, including hardness, thermal conductivity, chemical activity of the work material and tools, tool wear, tool shapes, and width and depth of cut. The width and depth of cut become controllable parameters when the tool path is modified. There is a constraint function $F(P_c, P_p)$ between the controllable parameter P_c and the uncontrollable process parameters P_p to protect feasible manufacturing conditions from tool breakage, rough finishing, high tool wear rate, and uneconomical and low efficiency manufacturing.

$$F(P_c, P_p) = 0 \tag{1}$$

The feasible solution of P_c for manufacturing is given from Equation 1 as

$$P_{cL}(P_p) \leqq P_c \leqq P_{cU}(P_p) \tag{2}$$

where $P_{cL}(P_p)$ is the lower constraint of P_c and $P_{cU}(P_p)$ is the upper constraint of P_c.

Manufacturing processes are evaluated by a performance index PI to represent the cost efficiency, productivity, or finish accuracy of machining.

$$PI = G(P_c, P_p) \tag{3}$$

The optimum solution P_c^* of P_c to maximize or minimize PI is given as the function of parameter P_p:

$$P_c^* = U(P_p) \tag{4}$$

It is supposed that the parameter P_p is constant during each operation in ordinary automated manufacturing, such as numerical control. In this case, the controllable parameter P_c is kept constant during each operation. Adaptive control for manufacturing is defined as a process to set P_c at P_c^* to satisfy Equation 2, according to the variation in the parameter P_p during each operation.

The observable variable M of the manufacturing phenomena is a function of P_c and P_p:

$$M = H(P_c, P_p) \tag{5}$$

One method for composing adaptive control systems is to identify the process parameter P_p from the observed variable M:

$$P_p = H^{-1}(P_c, M) \tag{6}$$

Adaptive control to identify the process parameter P_p is called indirect control. The optimum solution P_c^* is calculated by substituting Equation 6 into Equation 4. However, it is not easy to obtain an adequate observable variable M to identify thoroughly the process parameter P_p. Therefore, another method for determining the optimum controllable parameter P_c^*, or the performance index PI, directly from the observable variable M is often adopted as follows:

$$P_c^* = U_M(M) \tag{7}$$

$$PI = G_M(M) \tag{8}$$

Adaptive control using Equation 7 is called direct control (3). Learning control is defined as a process for organizing the function $U(P_p)$, or $U_M(M)$, or for improving $x(t)$ based on many trial operations when the optimum solution is unknown.

45.3 NUMERICAL CONTROL AND ADAPTIVE CONTROL

Figure 45.1 shows an ordinary numerical control system and additional adaptive control. Cutter location (CL) data are given to the system. These data direct cutter paths represented by the absolute coordinates of their start and destination points or by the difference between them, the feed rates, and spindle speed for the paths. The interpolation function generates the desired tool position coordinates to satisfy the commanded feed rate at every sampling time on a tool path. The components of the position for control axes are given to digital servosystems to control mutual positions between the work material and cutter along the axes. The command of cutting speed is also given to the spindle servosystem. The feed rate and spindle speed are kept at constants during the movement of a path for ordinary numerical control. The adaptive control

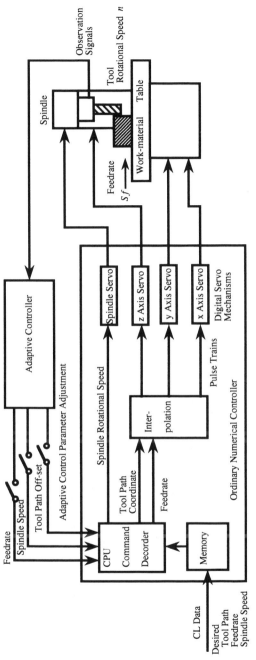

Figure 45.1. Ordinary numerical control and adaptive control.

adjusts the feed rate, spindle rotational speed, and tool path, according to the change in the cutting condition caused by the variations in the hardness of the work material, tool wear, the width and depth of cut, etc.

45.4 CLASSIFICATION OF ADAPTIVE CONTROL FOR MACHINING

In the field of manufacturing, adaptive control was first applied for machining. There are four types of applications in the adaptive control of machining:

Adaptive control optimization (ACO)
Adaptive control constraint (ACC)
Geometric adaptive control (GAC)
Vibration adaptive control (VAC)

The purpose of ACO is to search for the optimum values of feed rate and spindle speed that maximize the performance index, representing cost efficiency or productivity, as shown by Equation 4 or 7. ACC selects the feasible solution of the feed rate and spindle speed to satisfy the constraints in manufacturing by an algorithm that is rather simpler than ACO, as shown by Equation 2. GAC tries to obtain highly accurate finish surfaces by adjusting tool offset against the deflection of tools and work material caused by temperature rise and/or the cutting force. The function of VAC is to avoid the vibration or chatter of tools, mainly due to regenerative oscillation, by adjusting the spindle rotational speed or the resonance frequency of machine tools.

ACO for Machining

Direct PI Observation ACO

Measuring of the tool wear rate on-line is the key to the ACO, because the performance index *PI* is calculated from the tool wear rate da_f/dt as follows (4):

$$PI = \frac{h_d \cdot w \cdot s_f}{A + \dfrac{(A \cdot T_c + C \cdot B)}{a_{fL}} \cdot \dfrac{da_f}{dt}} \qquad (9)$$

where h_d is the depth of cut; w, the width of cut; s_f, the feed rate; a_f, the length of the flank wear land at the clearance face at the cutter edge of the tool (see Figure 45.2); a_{fL}, the maximum allowable length of tool wear; A, the depreciation coefficient; B, the tool cost; T_c, the tool change time; and C, the blending coefficient. The performance index *PI* means cost efficiency (cutting volume per unit cost) for $C = 1$, a value proportional to productivity (cutting volume per unit time) for $C = 0$, and one blending these for $1 > C > 0$.

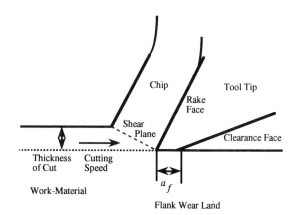

Figure 45.2. Tool wear a_f and phenomena at the tool tip.

The tool wear rate is calculated by using the following equation from the observed tool tip temperature and the increasing rate of the cutting force, from the most representative ACO system as described in ref. 4.

$$\frac{da_f}{dt} = K_1 \cdot h_d \cdot w \cdot s_f + K_2 \cdot \theta + K_3 \cdot dq/dt \tag{10}$$

where θ is the temperature at the tool edge measured by a thermocouple composed of the tool and work material; q is the cutting spindle torque; and K_1, K_2, and K_3 are constants. The first term represents the mechanical wear, the second is the thermal wear due to the diffusion of work material components into the tool, and the third is the increment rate of a_f.

The system does not have the function $G(P_c, P_p)$ between PI and the controllable parameter P_c. That is, the optimum solution of controllable parameters cannot be analytically solved. Therefore, the system must search for the optimum feed rate and spindle rotational speed of milling by using an optimization algorithm, such as the steepest ascent climbing method. The spindle rotational speed n and the feed rate s_f are changed by following the algorithm from the increments ΔPI_n and ΔPI_{sf} of PI for trial small increments Δn and Δs_f of cutting speed v and feed rate s_f, respectively (4).

$$n = n + K_o \Delta PI_n/\Delta n$$
$$s_f = s_f + K_o \Delta PI_{sf}/\Delta s_f \tag{11}$$

where K_o is a constant. Methods for measuring the tool wear width a_f or the tool wear rate da_f/dt directly by using a television camera (6), a tool including an isotope (7), an acoustic emission phenomenon, and cutting forces (8, 9) also have been tried by several researchers.

Parameter Identification ACO; Indirect and Model-based

When the tool wear rate is represented as the function of the process parameters to be identified from observed variables, the optimum feed rate and the spindle speed can be solved by analysis or computer simulation. Figure 45.3 shows an ACO system based on parameter identification (10). The system identifies the width and depth of cut from the waveform pattern of the cutting torque and the direction of the resultant cutting force. The bending moments and cutting torque measured at the tool holder for different feed rates are decomposed to the components generated at the rake faces and the flank wear land at the cutter edges. The component caused by the flank wear land at the clearance faces is constant for the variation in the feed rate, and that caused by the rake face is proportional to the feed rate. The clearance face component is calculated by extrapolation for zero feed rate. The shear stress and hardness of the work material and the shear angle of the shear plane at the tool edges are identified from the force components owing to the rake faces, and the flank wear land length a_f and true contact condition a_{ft} at the flank wear land are identified from the component owing to flank wear lands.

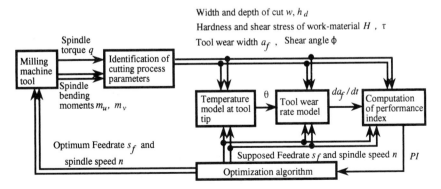

Figure 45.3. An ACO system based on parameter identification.

The temperature θ at the tool edge is calculated by thermal dynamics theory for a given feed rate s_f and spindle speed n. The tool wear rate da_f/dt also is calculated by using a more precise tool wear model than shown in Equation 10 for a given feed rate and spindle speed. It is possible to obtain the optimum feed rate s^* and cutting speed v^* to maximize the performance index PI only by computer simulation that uses these temperature and tool wear rate models. Control using physical and/or chemical models of the phenomena is called model-based control.

Figure 45.4 shows an ACO operation example. In the experiment, only the feed rate is adjusted. It shows the milling operation for S45C carbon steel for changes in width of cut of 3, 6, 9, 12, 15, and 18 mm. It is shown that the width of cut is correctly identified, and the shear stress τ_o of the work material is identified at a constant value of 540 MPa, in spite of the change in the width of the cut. The feed rate automatically decreases as a result of the ACO, according to the increase in the width of the cut. The solid lines in Figure 45.5 show examples of the feedrate s_f and spindle speed n rpm for the variation in the hardness of the work material when ACO is adopted.

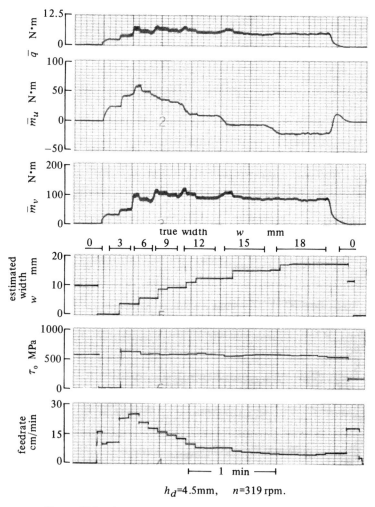

h_d=4.5mm, n=319 rpm.

Figure 45.4.   An example of a parameter identification ACO.

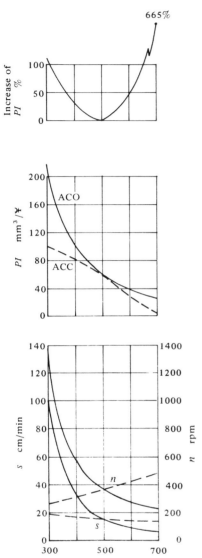

Figure 45.5. The optimum feed rates s_f, spindle speed n, and the performance index PI for the parameter identification ACO (solid lines) and for ACC using Taylor's tool life equation (dashed lines).

ACC for Machining

ACC Using Taylor's Tool Life Equation

The measurement of the tool wear rate, or the modeling of machining, for ACO is rather difficult, because there is a large amount of noise due to unpredicted phenomena contained in these processes. Furthermore, the optimum operation point for maximizing the performance index PI ordinarily stays outside the area of feasible solutions surrounded by the boundaries of constraints of the cutting force, the spindle power, the minimum feed per tooth, and the maximum rotational speed of the spindle (Figure 45.6). Generally speaking, the performance index representing the cost-efficiency or productivity becomes larger as the feed rate increases.

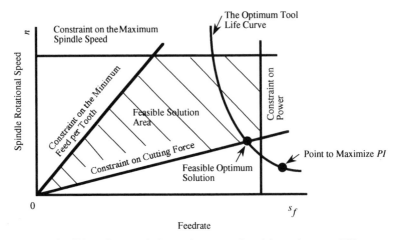

Figure 45.6. A feasible optimum solution at the cross point of the optimum tool life curve, with constraint curves.

That is, the quasi-optimum condition is given by maximizing the feed rate under the conditions that satisfy the constraints. Practical application of adaptive control to machining is mainly based on ACC types (11, 12, 13).

The optimum tool life $T_{opt} = a_{fL}/(da_f/dt)$ can be introduced from Equation 9 for a given feed rate s_f. By expanding Taylor's tool life equation, the relationship between cutting speed n, feed rate s_f, and tool life T is as follows:

$$n \cdot s_f^{\alpha} \cdot T^{\beta} = K_T \tag{12}$$

where α, β, and K_T are components of the process parameter P_P represented by constant values. It is clear that the optimum point is given at the cross point of the curve ($T = T_{opt}$) and the curve of the boundary of the cutting force or spindle power. This system is not ACO because the tool life model of Equation 12 does not reflect the variation in process parameters, such as the hardness of the work material.

Feedback Loop ACC

A simpler ACC is used to adjust only cutting torque at a constant to protect the tool from breakage. Figure 45.7 shows a feedback loop–type ACC system to maintain the cutting torque at a constant value (14). Proportional and integral (PI) or integral (I) control is often adopted. The interpolation function is represented as an integral component $1/s$. Many integral components are included in the loop, so the response of the system to the variation of process parameters is not good. The current of the spindle or feed drive motors is sometimes measured instead of the cutting torque in practical application (15).

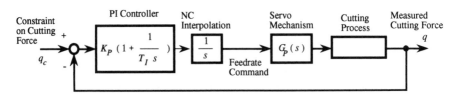

Figure 45.7. Feedback loop–type ACC system.

Sampling Control ACC

In intermittent machining like milling, the ACC system becomes a sampling control with sampling period $T_s = 60/(n \cdot Z_T)$, in which the peak value of the cutting torque should be kept at less than its constant value (Figure 45.8). Digital control using the z transform will introduce better results than ordinary linear control (16, 17).

ACC Based on Model Reference Adaptive Control Systems

The ACC shown in Figures 45.7 and 45.8 is often debated because it is not true adaptive control but only ordinary feedback control. Of course, it is acceptable to call it adaptive control because constant parameters are adjusted according to the variation in manufacturing conditions from the viewpoint of numerical control. The model reference adaptive control system (MRACS) is completely free from such arguments. MRACS applied to machining is to adjust the parameters of a controller so that the combination of the controller and manufacturing process behaves like a given ideal manufacturing model (18). Figure 45.9 shows an example of MRACS type ACC. The error e is the difference between the actual cutting force q, i.e., the output of the actual NC controller and the cutting process, and the output q_m of their reference model. The loop gain K and the offset parameter d (which is the force component due to flank wear land) of the ACC controller are adjusted by the integration of the error e multiplied by the controller input $\alpha \cdot u$ and α, respectively. The variation in the cutting process gain and the offset of the cutting force because of the change in the hardness of the work material, the depth and width of cut, and the tool wear are involved in the change of K and d, respectively.

The transfer function between the input u and the error e can be simplified (Figure 45.10). The variable f in Figure 45.10 is shown as

$$f = (K_m - K)u + d_m - d \tag{13}$$

The dynamics of the error e are represented as

$$\dot{e} = f - Ae = (K_m - K)u + d_m - d - Ae \tag{14}$$

When a Lyapunov function V is defined as

$$V = e^2 + (K_m - K)^2/\alpha + (d_m - d)^2/\alpha > 0 \text{ for } e \neq 0 \tag{15}$$

the differential $\dot{V}$ of V is calculated as follows:

$$
\begin{aligned}
\dot{V} &= 2\dot{e}e - 2(K_m - K)\dot{K}/\alpha - 2(d_m - d)\dot{d}/\alpha \\
&= 2e[(K_m - K)u + d_m - d - Ae] - 2(K_m - K)\dot{K}/\alpha - 2(d_m - d)\dot{d}/\alpha \\
&= -Ae^2 + 2e(K_m - K)(eu - \dot{K}/\alpha) + 2e(d_m - d)(e - \dot{d}/\alpha)
\end{aligned}
\tag{16}
$$

When the parameters K and d in the controller are adjusted as

$$\dot{K} = \alpha eu$$
$$\dot{d} = \alpha e \tag{17}$$

the differential $\dot{V}$ of the Lyapunov function V becomes,

$$\dot{V} = -Ae^2 < 0 \text{ (for } e \neq 0) \tag{18}$$

Therefore, stable parameter adjustment for K and d is achieved by using Equation 17, as shown in Figure 45.10. The parameters are calculated by integration of Equation 17 as represented by $1/s$ (s: Laplacian).

The gain in the manufacturing process is proportional to the hardness of the work material and the width and depth of cut. The total loop gain of the ACC system is kept at a constant, as with the MRACS model. As a result, the system becomes robust and maintains stability against the variation in the manufacturing parameters. Another type of adaptive control to modify the loop gain and other controller parameters is the self-tuning regulator (STR), in which these controller papameters are modified after process parameters are identified.

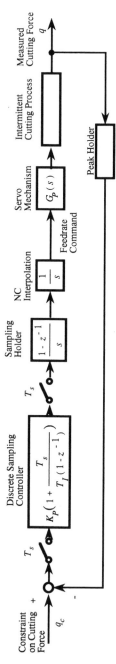

Figure 45.8. Digital sampling control for intermittent cutting process.

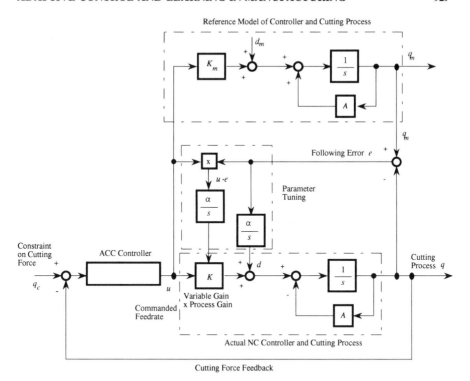

Figure 45.9. MRACS-type ACC.

Nonlinear Calculation of ACC

The nonlinear calculation of ACC is based on the supposition that the cutting force is proportional to the feed rate. The feed rate is calculated as follows:

$$s_{f,\,k+1} = s_{f,\,k} \cdot q_r / q_k \tag{19}$$

where k is the sampling number. The control equation has a gain that is inversely proportional to the process gain q/s_f, so the system has the function of autonomously adjusting the total gain at a constant that is the same as the MRACS ACC (16, 17).

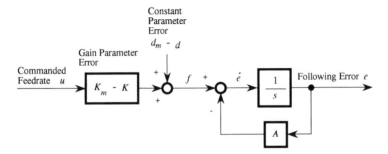

Figure 45.10. Equivalent model for the MRACS process.

CAD based ACC

If the shapes of the manufactured part and its work material are given from the CAD database, information like the width and depth of cut are available for the addition of feed-forward control to ACC, which is effective in decreasing the transient overshoot of the cutting force against sudden increase (19).

GAC for Machining

Tools, work material, and machine tools deflect due to cutting force or temperature increase. The error is compensated for by changing the cutter path or feed rate.

Thermal Deflection GAC

Heat sources are generated at the cutting edges, motors, and gears of the spindle and feed drive during machining. Thermal deflection is identified by measuring temperature rise and using computer simulation with finite element methods (FEM). By changing the cutter path or the deflection of the spindle column (based on the control of the flow of cooling water), the finished shape of products can be compensated for.

Cutting Force GAC

Tools during machining are deflected by the cutting force. Machining experts adequately modify the cutter offset to the cutter path, but this is not the case with programmers who have less machining experience. The cutting force changes widely during one cycle of cutting in intermittent machining, such as milling. The shape of the finish surface follows the wave pattern in the variation of the cutting force. The finish surface is evaluated by dimensional error and shape error. Dimensional error is evaluated by the mean distance between the actual surface and the desired surface. The shape error is evaluated by the peak-to-peak value of the distance between the two surfaces.

Figure 45.11 shows a GAC system designed to compensate for finish-surface errors in milling (20). The bending moment of the cutter is measured, and the tool deflection is calculated. The cutter path is modified in the direction vertical to that of the feed rate to compensate for the dimensional error. A positive feedback loop is generated, in which the cutting force, i.e., the tool deflection, increases further, according to the modification of the tool path. Therefore, a compensation that eliminates this positive feedback loop is required in the system. The shape error is compensated for by ACC to keep it under its constraint value by changing the feed rate. Figure 45.12 shows the finish surface generated by the GAC. It is verified that the dimensional and shape errors are significantly improved compared with those of ordinary machining.

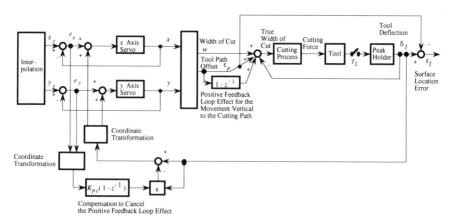

Figure 45.11. A GAC system to compensate for finish-surface errors caused by cutting force milling.

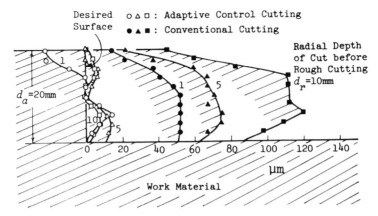

Figure 45.12. Finish surfaces compensated for by GAC.

VAC for Machining

Regenerative chattering oscillation occurs when the variation in the thickness of the cut generated by the cutter oscillation at the previous one cycle cutting is resonant with the oscillation of the cutter. The oscillation can be diminished by changing the rotational speed of the spindle. The other method is to change the resonance frequency of the tool holder or machine tools by adjusting an additional oscillation absorber composed of small variable mass, damper, and spring.

45.5 APPLICATION OF ADAPTIVE CONTROL TO OTHER MANUFACTURING

Adaptive control also is effective for other manufacturing, such as grinding, electrodischarging, and welding. ACC helps maximize the feed rate so as not to override constraints on the allowable grinding force, current, and heat power for grinding, electric discharging, and welding, respectively.

Adaptive Control for Arc Welding

The welding spot width and input power are affected by torch speed, arc length, and material thickness. The power supply is controlled by measuring the back-lead width in the welding process. The width is measured by using a TV camera having a wide spectral response. An ACC system controls input heating power to regulate the width to a constant value. The gain of the ACC is adjusted by MRACS or a self-tuning system, using decision rules based on identified welding process gain (21, 22).

Adaptive Control for Spot Welding

Spot welding is affected by many process parameters, such as electrode wear, oxidized metal surfaces, actuator friction, surface fit up, work piece expulsion, process gain, and contact resistance. Figure 45.13 shows an adaptive control system for spot welding (23). The displacement of the piston pressing two work materials to be attached is measured by an encoder. The displacement responds to the expansion of the work materials, which is proportional to the input energy. First, heating for a short time is tried, and then the current and the displacement of a piston pressing the work material are measured for the identification of the resistance at the

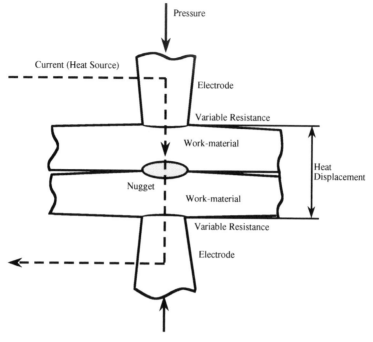

Figure 45.13.   Adaptive control for spot welding.

welded point and process gain (the temperature rise per input heat). The optimum heating energy is determined based on these identified parameters.

45.6   LEARNING CONTROL FOR MANUFACTURING

Learning control changes its operation based on the experiences of several trial operations. There are several types of learning control:

Learning using a neural network.

Composition of a knowledge-base based on case studies.

Learning control for repeated motions.

Neural Network Learning of Undefined Function

A neural network is a strong tool to compose undefined functions of manufacturing by learning. The results of many trial manufacturing tests are given to a neural network as its inputs and desired output. The neural network can organize the desired function by learning based on the back-propagation algorithm.

Long learning processes, however, are required to realize precise control for actual industrial manufacturing when it contains complicated and strong nonlinearity. If functions based on manufacturing physical models are available for its control, the neural network is useful to strengthen the control accuracy by compensating for the error of the primary control system. Figure 45.14 shows an example in which a neural network is used to compensate for a bending control system that produces bars with the desired curvature (24). A physical model of the manufacturing process taking the characteristics of spring back into account is used to determine the desired stroke of the main roller. The spring-back generated after bending depends on such characteristics as the work material, the section-shape of bar, and temperature history.

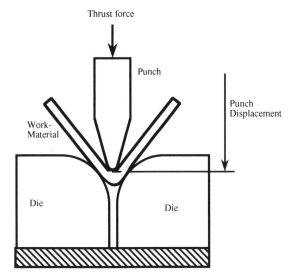

Figure 45.14. V-bending process.

The errors of products from desired values are measured and given to a neural network, the inputs of which are the process parameters as shown in Fig. 45.15. After learning for many observations, the output of the neural network is used to compensate for the stroke of the primary control system.

Composition of Decision Rules by Learning

The decision tree is automatically composed by observing many case studies. The cases are decomposed on trial, and the decomposition is evaluated. If the decomposition is effective, it is

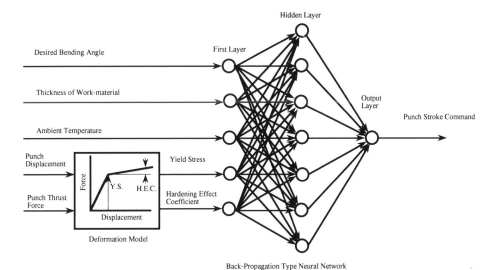

Figure 45.15. Neural network to direct desired punch stroke after learning the relationship between bending angle and punch displacement.

fixed. This method is applied to the decision for the optimum feed rate and spindle speed of intermittent cutting (25).

Process Improvement for Repeated Manufacturing

If there are repeated operations in which controlled variable $x_k(t)$ follows the desired value $x_{d, k}(t)$ and its error e_k from the desired value at the kth operation is observable under repeated operation, the error can be compensated for gradually by the following learning algorithm:

$$x_{d, k+1}(t) = x_{d, k}(t) + K_R \cdot de_k(t)/dt \tag{20}$$

where K_R is a constant. This algorithm has been applied to the error compensation of robot manipulators. It might also be useful in some repeated manufacturing processes (26).

45.7   CONCLUSIONS

This chapter shows several examples of adaptive and learning control applied to manufacturing. There is a long history of research on the application of adaptive control to manufacturing. However, there are few actual applications in industry. It requires a rather complicated algorithm compared with ordinary control systems. The development of recent microprocessors and sophisticated software might make the application rather easy. Adaptive and learning control will be one of the key technologies in the control systems of manufacturing in the 21st century, especially for the intelligent manufacturing systems (IMS).

Practical application has been done mainly by using ACC-type control. Recently, research related to MRACS-type control has been done. Of course, the MRACS is effective; however, the way to design the ideal models remains a problem. Further research to make the manufacturing process clear is required as well as the development of an intelligent control algorithm to deal with complicated conditions seen in actual manufacturing.

BIBLIOGRAPHY

1. R.S. PRESSMAN and J.E. WILLIAMS, *Numerical Control and Computer-Aided Manufacturing,* John Wiley & Sons, Inc., New York, 1977.

2. M.P. GROOVER, *Automation, Production Systems and Computer-Aided Manufacturing,* Prentice-Hall, Inc., Englewood Cliffs, N.J., 1980.

3. R.A. MATHIAS, "An Effective System for Adaptive Control of the Milling Process," *Preprints American Society of Tool and Manufacture Engineers (ASTME), ASTME* **MS68-202,** 1–17 (1968).

4. R.M. CENTNER and J.M. IDELSON, "Adaptive Controller for a Metal Cutting Process" in *Proceedings of the IEEE–ASME Joint Automatic Control Conference,* ASME, New York May, 1964, pp. 154–161.

5. R.M. CENTNER, *Development of Adaptive Control Technique for Numerically Controlled Milling Machines,* U.S. Air Force, Ohio, 1964, Tech. Doc. Rep., ML TDR-64-279 (MM Project No. 7-713).

6. J.-J. PARK and A.G. ULSOY, "On-line Flank Wear Estimation Using an Adaptive Observer and Computer Vision, Part 1: Theory," *Trans. ASME J. Eng. Ind.* **115,** 30–43 (1993).

7. M.E. MERCHANT et al., "Radioactive Cutting Tools for Rapid Tool Life Testing," *Trans. ASME* **76,** 549–559 (May 1953).

8. H. TAKEYAMA et al., "A Study on Adaptive Control in an NC Milling Machine," *Ann. CIRP* **23**(1), 153–154 (1974).

9. J.-J. PARK and A.G. ULSOY, "On-line Tool Wear Estimation Using Force Measurement and Nonlinear Observer," *Trans. ASME J. DSMC* **114,** 666–672 (1992).

10. T. WATANABE, "Model Based Approach to Adaptive Control Optimization in Milling," *Trans. ASME J. DSMC,* **108,** 56–64 (1986).

11. R. BEDINI et al. "Experiments on Adaptive Control of a Milling Machine," *Trans. ASME Eng. Ind.,* **98,** 239–245 (1976).

12. R.A. MATHIAS, *An Adaptive Controlled Milling Machine,* 1976, *Tech. Paper of the SME,* Society of Manufacturing engineers (SME), MS76-260.

13. R. BEDINI and P.C. PINOTTI," A Hardwired Logic for The Adaptive Control of a Milling Machine," *Int. J. Mach. Tool Des.* **16**, 193–207 (1976).

14. D.A. Milner, "Adaptive Control of Feedrate in the Milling Process," *Int. J. Mach. Tool. Des. Res.* **14**, 187–197 (1974).

15. Y. ALITINTAS, "Prediction of Cutting Forces and Tool Breakage in Milling from Feed Drive Current Measurements," *Trans. ASME J. Eng. Ind.* **114**, 386–392 (1992).

16. T. WATANABE et al., "Designs of an Adaptive Control Constraint System of a Milling Machine Tool" in G.G. Leininger, ed., *Proceedings of the 2nd IFAC Symposium on Computer Aided Design of Multivariable Technological Systems,* Pergamon Press, New York, 1982.

17. T. WATANABE et al., "Research on Control Characteristics of Adaptive Control Constraint for Milling," *Proc. JSME* **49**(447), 1999–2009 (1983).

18. M. TOMIZUKA, J.H. OH, and D.A. DORNFELD, "Model Reference Adaptive Control of the Milling Process" in D.E. Hardt and W.J. Book, eds., *Control of Manufacturing Processes and Robotic Systems,* ASME, New York, 1984, pp. 55–63.

19. A. SPENCE and Y. ALTINTAS, "CAD Assisted Adaptive Control for Milling," *Trans. ASME J. DSMC* **113**, 444–450 (1991).

20. T. WATANABE et al. "A Control System to Improve the Accuracy of Finished Surface in Milling," *Trans. ASME J. DSMC,* **105**, 192–199 (1983).

21. A. SUZUKI, D.E. HARDT, and L. VALAVANI, "Application of Adaptive Control Theory to On-line GTA Weld Geometry Regulation," *Trans. ASME J. DSMC* **113**, 93–103 (1991).

22. C.C. DOUMANIDIS and D.E. HARDT, "Multivariable Adaptive Control of Thermal Properties During Welding," *Trans. ASME J. DSMC,* **113**, 82–91 (1991).

23. K. HEAFNER, B. CAREY, B. BERNSTEIN, K. OVERTON, and M. D'ANDREA, "Real Time Adaptive Spot Welding Control," *Trans. ASME J. DSMC,* **113**, 104–112 (1991).

24. M. YANG, S. SHIMA, and T. WATANABE, "Development of Control System Using Neural Network Combined with Deformation Model for an Intelligent V-Bending Process of Sheet Metals" in Ming Leu ed., *Proceedings of the Japan–U.S.A. Symposium on Flexible Automation,* ASME, New York, Vol. II, 1992.

25. S.C.-Y. LU, "Building Layered Models to Support Engineering Decision Making: A Machine Learning Approach," *Trans. ASME J. Eng. Ind.,* **113** 1–9 (1991).

26. S. ARIMOTO, S. KAWAMURA, and F. MIYAZAKI, "Bettering Operation of Robots by Learning," *J. Robot. Sys.* **1**(2), 123–140 (1984).

GLOSSARY

Adaptive control constraint (ACC). Adaptive control to select the feasible solution of the feed rate and spindle speed to satisfy the constraints in manufacturing by an algorithm that is rather simpler than ACO.

Adaptive control in manufacturing. Control to adjust the operational speeds or motion paths to optimize the manufacturing processes and/or to satisfy constraint conditions against variations in manufacturing phenomena caused by the change in the hardness of the work material, tool wear, width and depth of cut, deflection of tools and work material, etc.

Adaptive control optimization (ACO). Adaptive control to search for the optimum values of feed rate and spindle speed that maximize the performance index representing cost efficiency or productivity.

Back-propagation–type neural network. Network to organize the desired function by the learning of many trials based on the back-propagation algorithm.

Betterment process. Learning control to compensate for the error of a control system by modifying its reference gradually by using the error for repeated motions.

Direct control. Adaptive control to determine directly the optimum solution from observed variables.

Geometric adaptive control (GAC). Adaptive control to try to obtain highly accurate finish surfaces by adjusting tool offset against the deflection of tools and work material caused by temperature rise and/or cutting force.

Indirect control. Adaptive control to identify process parameters.

Learning control. Control to improve automatically the movements of machines in repeated manufacturing, based on many past trials; nevertheless, adaptive control responds to variations in real time.

Model reference adaptive control system (MRACS). Adaptive control to adjust the parameters of a controller so that the combination of the controller and manufacturing process behaves like a given ideal manufacturing model.

Self-tuning regulator (STR). Adaptive control to modify controller parameters after process parameters are identified.

Vibration adaptive control (VAC). Adaptive control to avoid the vibration of chatter of tools mainly due to regenerative oscillation by adjusting the spindle rotational speed or the resonance frequency of machine tools.

CHAPTER 46
Artificial Intelligence Techniques in Manufacturing Equipment Diagnostics

ATUL BAJPAI
General Motors Corporation

46.1 INTRODUCTION

No machine, however well designed and constructed, can last indefinitely. Whenever there are moving parts, there will be wear and degradation of machine components, leading to reduced performance and ultimate breakdown. The period between installation of a new machine and its final scrapping due to lack of availability of cost-effective repair or obsolescence may be termed the "useful life" of the machine. Prolonging the useful life of machines and keeping the machines operating smoothly in healthy condition during their useful life periods have been areas of special interest to maintenance personnel in the manufacturing industry. The cost of maintaining machine tool equipment in the manufacturing industry is generally a significant portion of the total cost of the final product being manufactured. Ironically, the bulk of the cost is not the cost of replacement components, but the time taken and the associated production loss in diagnosing the problem source accurately. Often it takes several iterations before the real problem source is identified. In the process, due to misdiagnosis, several nonproblems are "fixed," and worse, sometimes a few new problems are induced. As a result, instead of helping in the smooth operation of machines, inaccurate diagnosis may in fact reduce the useful life of machines and add to total maintenance costs. The diagnostics problem is a significant one: the larger the manufacturing operations, the more important it becomes to find ways to increase the efficiency of maintaining the manufacturing equipment.

Though a wealth of literature has been available in the area of equipment diagnostics, ranging from repair manuals provided by the original equipment manufacturers to specialized books by experienced consultants, the artificial intelligence–based techniques are relatively new. Artificial intelligence (AI) technology as applied to the automotive industry (1) has resulted in a substantial number of systems, covering a range of applications from manufacturing diagnostics to finance and engineering design to factory scheduling and process planning. Machine diagnostics, however, has remained the most widely used area of application of AI technology in industry. The use of AI-based systems for diagnosis of machine tools and manufacturing systems is discussed in ref. 2. A description of a successfully fielded machine diagnostics expert system can be found in ref. 3. AI techniques can be used to serve not only in diagnostics or preventive maintenance but in predictive maintenance as well. AI-based systems are applicable to a full cross-section of applications, ranging from automobile manufacturing and the aerospace industry to shipbuilding, power systems, and electric and gas utilities. Successful AI-based diagnostic systems have been fielded in the manufacturing arena over the last several years, covering production of a variety of light-, medium-, and heavy-duty products.

46.2 DIAGNOSTIC METHODS AND PROCEDURES

There are a number of diverse methods and techniques used in the manufacturing industry to diagnose problems with machinery and their individual components (4, 5). The methods used are generally a function of the nature of the application. Sophisticated, continuous monitoring systems might be used, for example, in applications for which safety is a critical factor or when the financial consequences of failures are significant. Routine, periodic maintenance, on the other hand, might suffice in applications for which failures are less likely (long expected mean times between failures) and when breakdowns will not jeopardize the overall operations.

The nature of expected failures also varies with the type of manufacturing application. Failure does not necessarily mean sudden breakdown of a machine or its component. Failures can be gradual deterioration of a machine's ability to perform its function, and these are generally manifested through declining quality of manufactured products. Sometimes, failures are neither sudden nor gradual but intermittent in nature. The problems come and go for reasons that cannot be identified or understood. These failures may occur on a seemingly random basis or may simply be isolated incidents. Regardless of the nature of failure, the causes generally are rooted in one or more of the following: improper use (e.g., excessive loads), poor maintenance (e.g., no routine or preventive maintenance), inevitable wear and tear with aging of the machine, normal fatigue, and flaws in the basic design of the machine. Though failures cannot be totally eliminated, simple care and attention by the operator can go a long way in prolonging the useful life and enhancing the functioning of a machine.

When failure does occur, the first effort in diagnosis typically begins with a visual inspection of the machine. This inspection, coupled with the operating knowledge of the machine and its prior history, can be helpful in diagnosing the problem in simple situations. With some techniques, it is possible to diagnose problems accurately without the need to disassemble the machinery (6). In the majority of the cases, however, additional tools and procedures are needed to perform proper diagnostics. Most machine diagnostics tools used in industry today are sensor based and require discipline in following the diagnostics methodology both before and after the failure has occurred. Examples of popular mechanical parameters used in machine diagnostics include force, pressure, vibration, displacement, velocity, and acceleration. Electrical parameters (current, voltage, etc.), thermal parameters (most commonly temperature), acoustic parameters (sound levels and their variations), chemical parameters (mostly fluid composition analysis), photo–light (e.g., stroboscope), electromagnetic parameters, x rays, and ultrasound have also found considerable use in many specialized diagnostics situations.

To illustrate how some of the current methods and procedures are used for diagnosis, an example of a vibration-based technique is described here. Vibration analysis, including pressure waves and acoustics, has gained widespread recognition and acceptance in diagnostics of machine equipment. Pressure transducers or simple microphones serve as sensors that provide initial input to the vibration analysis system. The underlying principle for such systems is that all components and subcomponents of machinery vibrate at certain natural frequencies, and analysis of amplitudes of vibration at those frequencies can help in locating the problem source(s). The vibration could be induced, self-excited, or resonant. Simple balances of equilibrium of forces, moments, and energy are used to perform the analysis and to diagnose the problems.

Let us examine a simple mechanical system that consists of a motor connected to a pump through a coupling as shown in the following Figure 46.1. Such a unit is commonly found as a subsystem of a larger machine. Vibration measurements are taken at specified locations and specified directions on the various components. For example, horizontal, vertical, and axial measurements may be taken at the front bearings of the motor at the location marked 01. These locations and directions are typically established a priori as part of the regular maintenance process, and generally, historical as well as failure–state data on these points are available to the diagnostician. Frequencies and corresponding amplitudes of vibration at various strategic locations on the machine are recorded. Data are collected with the help of hand-held devices that pick up acceleration signals (Figure 46.2).

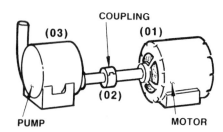

Figure 46.1.   A motor–coupling–pump unit.

Figure 46.2. A machine repairman collecting sensory data at a manufacturing facility with the help of a hand-held device and probe.

To smooth out noise and other perturbations, steady-state acceleration readings are integrated over time, and velocity readings are obtained:

$$V(t) = \int a(t) \, dt$$

Assuming that $V(t)$ is sufficiently well behaved, it can be represented by the standard Fourier series (7):

$$
\begin{aligned}
F(t) = A_0/2 \; + \\
A_1 \cos \omega_1 t + B_1 \sin \omega_1 t \; + \\
A_2 \cos \omega_2 t + B_2 \sin \omega_2 t \; + \\
\cdot \\
\cdot \\
A_n \cos \omega_n t + B_n \sin \omega_n t
\end{aligned}
$$

where

$$A_0 = (1/\pi) \int_a^{a+2\pi} V(t) \, dt$$

$$A_n = (1/\pi) \int_a^{a+2\pi} V(t) \cos nt \, dt$$

and

$$B_n = (1/\pi) \int_a^{a+2\pi} V(t) \sin nt \, dt$$

with a serving as an arbitrary initial point of integration. Because $V(t)$ is known, all harmonic coefficients—A_0, A_n, B_n—can be calculated from the above equations.

The fundamental circular frequency is given by:

$$\omega_1 = 2\pi/T$$

where T is the period of the harmonic motion. The higher harmonics are expressed in terms of the fundamental frequency:

$$\omega_n = n\omega_1 \text{ (for } n \geq 2)$$

Once the function is converted from the time domain to the frequency domain, the graph of velocities versus frequencies is obtained by plotting $\sqrt{A_n^2 + B_n^2}$ (on the y axis) versus ω_n (on the x axis) for $n \geq 1$, and the phase is obtained as:

$$\phi = \tan^{-1}(B_n/A_n)$$

Some typical vibration signatures taken in the horizontal and vertical directions at the front bearing of a motor are shown in Figure 46.3. Typically, the frequencies are expressed in cycles per minute (cpm) and the velocities in inches per second (in./s). It is important to understand that there is no one-to-one correspondence between vibration signature peaks and the problems with the machine. For example, a peak of 0.0475 in./s at 7200 cpm in one instance may indicate a misalignment problem, whereas the same set of values in another case may depict an unbalance problem. The diagnostician or mechanic has to look at these signatures in the right context of the machine being diagnosed to make the correct diagnosis. So vibration analysis, like most other diagnostics methods and procedures, only assists the mechanic in making a diagnosis but does not by itself make the final determination of the problem source.

46.3 ARTIFICIAL INTELLIGENCE APPROACHES

Artificial intelligence approaches to diagnostics emulate the methods and thinking used by human experts in solving equipment diagnostics problems. It is well known that the most reliable, and perhaps the best, way to diagnose any difficult problem, be it manufacturing

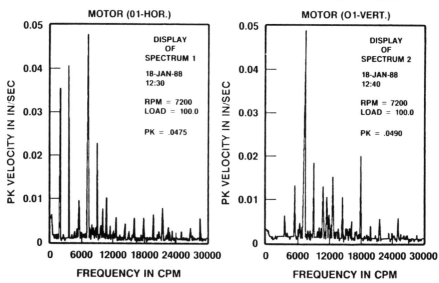

Figure 46.3. Examples of sample vibration signatures.

Figure 46.4. An operator is diagnosing a machine at a large manufacturing facility, which is lined with rows of conventional machines.

related or in any other domain, is to get an expert in the field to examine it. Unfortunately, there are not that many experts, and the few that exist are generally not easily accessible. Therefore, AI systems that play the role of an expert have become a valuable practical alternative (8). AI systems in diagnostics have been around for many years (Figure 46.4), with the first few successful ones emerging in the early 1980s. Although even the most advanced systems do not come close to replicating the performance level of a true expert in new and difficult situations, most AI systems do perform at levels that enable them to handle a great majority of equipment problems in manufacturing operations.

The process of capturing the knowledge of an expert diagnostician and encapsulating it in a representation suitable for manipulation by a computer is often a long and arduous task. Typically, several rounds of "knowledge-acquisition" (9) sessions are held with the expert over an extended period of time. Although in some diagnostics-related systems two or more experts might be involved, in most cases a single expert serves as the source of knowledge. Other sources of knowledge such as procedures manuals, manufacturers troubleshooting guides, workshop reports, trade journals, and conference papers are often useful in augmenting the expert's contributions. General rules of thumb, specific details, and the composition and functioning of the machine equipment are typically included as part of the overall knowledge of the AI system. The knowledge acquired is then incrementally coded in the AI program. It is continually reviewed with expert and target users to verify that the knowledge gained has been correctly understood and that the system is progressing in the right direction. Regardless of the source(s) of knowledge, once the system has been completed, it needs to be thoroughly tested, debugged, and validated to ensure that it performs the diagnostic tasks as intended. The knowledge represents much more than a simple decision tree for fault diagnosis (10). The diagnostics knowledge base typically contains a full spectrum of subtleties, peculiarities, exceptions, and norms in the art of troubleshooting machines.

A manufacturing facility may contain a variety of rigid automation machines such as lathes, milling machines, grinders, shapers, superfinishers, broaching machines, and drilling machines. It is quite common to see flexible automation equipment (e.g., robots and other programmable machines) working in conjunction with rigid automation in today's factories. Both flexible and rigid manufacturing tools are composed of components such as motors, pumps, belts, pulleys, geartrains, couplings, and bearings. These components can have a variety of problems, including misalignment, looseness, and unbalance. An AI system can examine the component malfunction symptoms via some sensory data or through user input to locate the fault(s) with the machine. The sensory data can come from appropriate parametric sources. Examples of parameters used in the manufacturing industry include electric current (amperage), torques, displacement and its derivatives, phases and phase shifts, forces, pressures, and temperatures. Displacements, forces, and torques may be the most appropriate variables for monitoring mechanical faults. For coolant and lubricating systems, temperature might be the right variable. Absolute pressures or their differentials are the best parameters for pneumatic devices. Depending on the electromechanical circuitry, variations in the amount of current drawn by the circuit under different mechanical loads can provide useful information. For example, the current drawn by the motors driving the various joints and end effectors of a robot would be an excellent parameter, because current relates directly to torque and is easier to measure accurately. Mechanical and electrical phase shifts can be used to determine synchronousness. The choice of parameter(s) to be used is determined by the appropriateness to the problem, the cost of the sensors, desired accuracy, ease of use, and the criticality of ensuring smooth operation of the machine equipment. In addition to the knowledge on how to use the various sensory inputs in determining the causes of the problems, AI systems can be developed to provide advice on what sensory inputs would work best for specific problems.

Once the AI system has been provided with initial symptomatic data, it will examine the descriptions of the machine, its components, and its normal configuration and functioning and then establish a list of possible hypothesized faults that could explain the symptoms. This generation of the initial hypothesis is done dynamically within the AI system and is a function of the machine–component description, sensory data, and diagnostic knowledge that have been acquired. The system contains basic knowledge about machine components and problems, which enables it to rule out those problems that would not be physically possible. For example, if one of the hypothesized faults was "improper teeth meshing" on a belt drive and that belt drive was a V-belt (no cogs), then the system would drop the fault from its list, because a belt without cogs cannot have meshing problems. Of course, a machine repairer would not have considered that fault in the first place because of the obvious impossibility. However, AI systems must be explicitly programmed, as there is still no element of commonsense reasoning available in today's commercial systems. Further pruning of the hypothesized fault list can be done by checking dependencies and mutual exclusiveness of the faults. All combinations of mutually exclusive faults (e.g., excessive tension and looseness) can be internally cross-referenced in system memory. Confirmed evidence of existence of any one of those faults is used to delete all other mutually exclusive faults. This process helps to shorten the list of the initially suspected faults. Further reductions and the ultimate identification of the actual fault(s) typically require additional tests. AI systems play a useful role in this testing process too. Such systems contain information about what tests need to be performed to confirm or rule out the remaining faults. It is important to note that in general it is not the compute time but the time to perform the physical tests on the machine equipment that is of primary concern. An interesting and useful part of AI approaches is the ability to nail down efficiently the actual problem from the list of hypothesized problems. A good AI system will have some clever mechanisms to determine what tests need to be conducted and the order in which they should be performed. These mechanisms will depend on the specific diagnostic application being developed. Examples of some simple criteria include

- Relative ease of performing the test.
- Time needed to perform the test.
- Equipment needed and availability of personnel trained in its use.
- The number of faults about which a conclusion can be made based on the result of the test.
- The likelihood or the probability of the hypothesized fault being pursued being an actual fault.

Tests may be grouped to minimize the number of trips that a mechanic must make to the machine to perform the tests. Related tests can be grouped together, even though all the tests may not be relevant to the same fault. This may require the system to perform anticipatory, or forward, thinking in that it must look at the possible outcomes of the results and try to optimize the efficiency of the diagnosis. Most recent AI-based diagnostics systems have intelligent strategies to facilitate fast and convenient diagnosis in contrast with the simple hypothesize–test–conclude cycles that were used by the early systems.

Traditionally, machine problems are solved by the local, experienced skilled workers on the floor or by the experts from the original equipment manufacturer. These experts gather preliminary information about the performance problem of the machine, think through the maze of possibilities, perform tests, investigate further, and ultimately arrive at the source of the problem. This process takes time and usually costs more than some of the newer AI techniques. The distinction between AI-based diagnostic systems and most traditional diagnostic methods is that the AI systems go the critical extra step of understanding and interpreting various inputs–outputs to identify exactly the source of the problem. With conventional tools, the burden of this understanding, interpretation, and making inferences to locate the problem source are typically left to the repairer. The conventional tools merely provide data or information to assist the user, but those tools typically are not equipped to make the important leap of sorting through the maze of all that information to arrive at what could be considered an intelligent diagnosis. Different users who are guided simply by conventional tools must lean more heavily on their own experience levels and are, therefore, more likely to make different diagnoses for the same problem. Therefore, with conventional methods, the fundamental problems of requiring expertise in diagnosing machines and the fact that such expertise is not readily available still remain. With AI systems, on the other hand, the intelligent task of making inferences and arriving at conclusions is done by the system, not by the user. The diagnostician using such a system does not have to possess any great experience in machine repair or in the use of conventional tools. Because such systems are built using the knowledge of recognized experts, the quality of diagnosis is generally superior, and as the same knowledge is used at different times and different locations, there is greater consistency as well.

46.4 BASICS OF AI TECHNOLOGY AS RELATED TO DIAGNOSTICS

A diagnostic AI system, like any other expert system, is typically made up of two primary components: a knowledge base and an inference engine operating on that knowledge base. The knowledge base contains expert knowledge about the diagnostic domain. The inference engine, through dynamic interaction with the knowledge base, establishes appropriate connections across the knowledge base elements and helps answer questions or solve specific problems to which the AI system is subjected. The inference engine is usually generic and is decoupled from the knowledge base. It is made up of several subcomponents, such as the chaining, searching, reasoning, and tracking mechanisms.

In a rule-based expert system (11), the multitude of rules within the knowledge base are connected together dynamically by the inference engine through a process called "chaining." There are two types of chaining mechanisms: forward chaining and backward chaining. Most diagnostic systems use backward chaining as the principal mechanism with only occasional use of forward chaining. Diagnostic applications rely on backward chaining, because the goals (hypothesized faults) are known at the outset. Limited forward chaining can be exercised in purely backward chaining inference engines with the help of "action" or "do" provisions in the conclusion portions of the rules. However, true forward chaining becomes particularly useful in permitting the user to volunteer or assert pieces of information that the system may be able to use to advantage. In complex diagnostic applications, bidirectional chaining may be used, which permits switching back and forth between forward and backward chaining mechanisms. Commercial software packages that feature both forward and backward chaining are readily available in the market today. An appropriate selection of the development software may be based on the size of the application and the costs of the various software packages.

While operating on a diagnostic knowledge base, the inference engine must perform several searches to find the solution(s). Hence, clever choices of search mechanisms can greatly speed up the execution time of an expert system. Several standard search algorithms are available. Tree traversal algorithms, such as the depth-first and breadth-first algorithms, are most popular. Assuming that the search space is structured like a tree (Figure 46.5), the depth-first algorithm searches through the entire space by picking up one branch of the tree at a time and traversing deep through the nodes until a solution is obtained or "leaf nodes" of each branch are reached. This technique or its variations are commonly used in diagnostic applications. The breadth-first mechanism, on the other hand, first traverses the first nodes of each branch, then the second-level nodes, and so on, until a solution is found or all leaf nodes are reached. Both depth-first

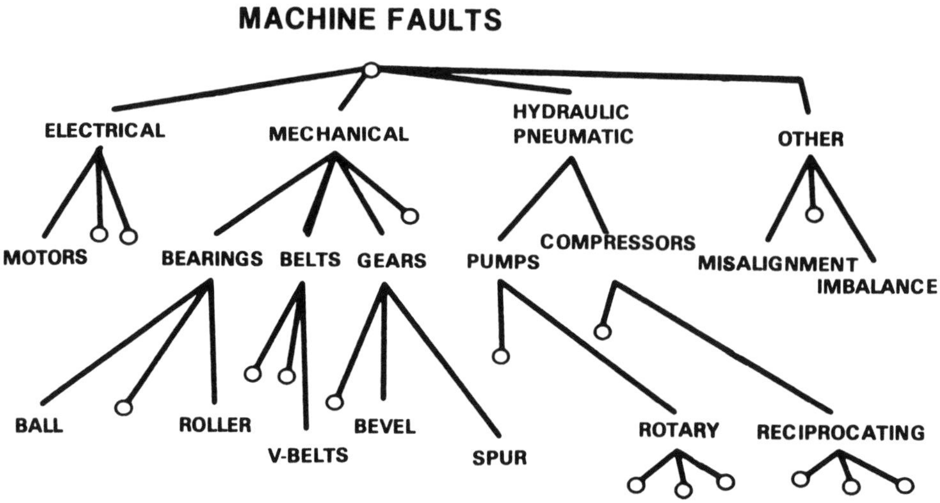

MACHINE FAULTS

Figure 46.5. An example fault-tree structure for diagnosing machine problems.

and breadth-first search mechanisms are essentially brute force methods. Several other algorithms that improve on these methods have been developed (see ref. 12 for comparisons). These algorithms usually employ simple optimization procedures using cost functions. Examples include the branch and bound and the A* algorithms. Game theory concepts have also been used to refine search processes. Alpha–beta pruning and minimax approaches are examples of application of such concepts. Generally, a depth-first search strategy appears to work well in manufacturing diagnostics. However, if greater flexibility is desired, a breadth-first strategy or other optimization approaches such as branch and bound and A* may be incorporated in the system.

The reasoning process of a diagnostic AI system can be either monotonic or nonmonotonic in form. In monotonic reasoning, once the truth or falsity of any attribute within the AI system has been set, it cannot be altered or reset. This poses a problem in situations in which the application calls for an examination of hypothetical or alternative scenarios. Nonmonotonic inferencing permits changing values of attributes. Different values can be assigned simultaneously to the same attribute with "multiple worlds" in nonmonotonic reasoning. The process of keeping track of different attributes and their associated values in a nonmonotonic system is accomplished through the use of a truth-maintenance subsystem (13). Monotonic reasoning suffices for most diagnostic applications and nonmonotonic reasoning is needed only in large, complex systems. Sometimes however, due to the judgmental nature of user responses and the potential for user input errors, nonmonotonic reasoning is employed in the inference control of even small systems. It enables the system to be more effective because the user not only is able to assert new facts into the system but can also retract previously asserted facts or conclusions as well. Also, all dependent conclusions that were drawn as a result of the information later retracted are recursively withdrawn automatically.

To keep track of the changes that may occur during execution of an AI program, the inference engine uses either chronological or nonchronological tracking methods. Chronological methods are crude forms of keeping track of the effects of altering the previously defined or internally determined facts in an AI system. Additions of new facts to the system are considered as "events in time," and these facts are chronologically backtracked if a later event attempts to modify a prior event. In nonchronological tracking, the interdependencies of various events are used to prune through the fact base. Thus only those prior events that are directly or indirectly dependent on a new violating event are examined or modified. This helps in efficient maintenance of the fact base integrity.

The knowledge base portion of a diagnostic AI system contains the knowledge of expert diagnostician(s). This knowledge is obtained through knowledge acquisition sessions with some recognized expert and through written reports, books, manuals, etc. The diagnostic knowledge is then coded by the knowledge engineers using one of the standard knowledge representation formats. Several approaches, including rule-based, frame-based, and logic-based formats have been used for representing diagnostic knowledge. The rule-based approach has remained the most common one for use in AI-based diagnostic systems.

Rule-based systems represent knowledge in the standard IF–THEN format. In a forward chaining system, if the premise conditions of the rule are satisfied, then the conclusion portions are automatically asserted to be true. In a backward chaining system, queries are made to the system. In response, those rules whose conclusion portions match the queries are activated. The use of certainty factors (CFs), which enable the user to get a feel for the confidence level of any solution, is a valuable feature of rule-based systems. The use of certainty factors has become an integral part of many AI-based diagnostic systems. However, due to the immense amount of subjectivity involved, and the complexity of interdependencies in manufacturing diagnostics, there is a risk of ending up with precision numbers that project a false sense of mathematical accuracy in the minds of uninformed users. Therefore, it is generally recommended that certainty factors be used carefully and preferably be expressed qualitatively with words such as *low, maybe, likely,* and *high.* It may be pointed out that the certainty factors are not cumulative probabilities, and therefore, the sum of CFs of a set of recommended solutions will generally not be unity.

A simplified example of a rule taken from a large diagnostic AI system presently being used in a manufacturing application is shown in Table 46.1. Let us look at the rule-based approach in the context of attempting to diagnose a malfunctioning lathe at a manufacturing facility. Figure 46.6 shows a schematic of a lathe used for turning shafts to desired outside diameters. The drive motor is electrically powered and is running at a selected speed. Assuming that the clutch is set such that belt drive 1 is engaged (belt drive 2 is disabled), one can compute the speed of the jackshaft given the pulley ratio of the pulleys on which belt drive 1 is mounted. Similarly, the speed of the work spindle can be calculated given the pulley ratios for belt drive 3.

In an AI system approach, an initial set of hypothesized or suspected faults is established. For the sake of illustration, let us assume that as a result of some initial sensory data, belt drive 3 is suspected to be the component at fault. The inference engine of the AI system would map the component in the consequent portion of the rule in Table 46.1 to belt drive 3 and try to check if the possible fault with it is misalignment or mechanical looseness. To do so, it would look at the antecedent portion of the rule and check to see if the two conjunctive premise conditions are satisfied. This is accomplished by either polling the existing sensory data for needed information or chaining through other rules that could potentially provide the needed information. If neither method succeeds, the user is requested to perform additional tests and input the results. If the results indicate that either one of the two premise conditions is not satisfied, i.e., vibration magnitude does not exceed some preset threshold or vibration frequency is not a multiple of the frequency of belt drive 3, then this rule is deactivated and others are investigated. If, on the other hand, the results indicate that both the premise conditions are true, then it is concluded that belt drive 3 is either misaligned or loose. Necessary corrective actions are then recommended by the system, and once they are implemented the system looks at the new sensory data set to verify that the problem has in fact been corrected.

Frame-based systems make use of the object-oriented programming style and have become increasingly popular in manufacturing and other applications. A frame represents all of the attributes of an object in the knowledge base. These frames interact with each other through a process of message passing. As a result of the hierarchical arrangement of frames in a treelike structure, inheritance of properties from parent object to descendant members is greatly facilitated. An example of the same scenario used in Table 46.1 is shown in frame-based representation in Table 46.2. Logic representation is a more formal method of representing domain knowledge in an AI system. This method makes use of standard logical operators, such as conjunction, disjunction, and negation. In addition, both existential and universal quantifiers are used to appropriately scope the variables in logical expressions. Several variations, such as

TABLE 46.1.   Example of a Rule-based Representation of Knowledge

IF:	Vibration magnitude exceeds threshold
	AND vibration frequency is a multiple of component frequency
THEN:	Component is misaligned (CF = 0.8)
	OR component is loose (CF = 0.4)

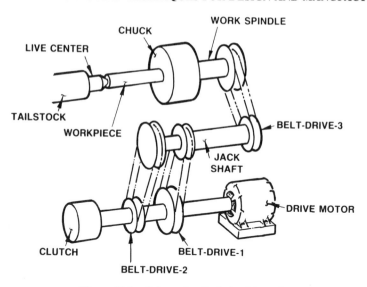

Figure 46.6. Schematic of a lathe drivetrain.

propositional, first-order, and higher-order logics are used, depending on the need and complexity of the application. A sample logic-based representation of the diagnostic example is shown in Table 46.3.

46.5 HARDWARE AND SOFTWARE FOR DIAGNOSTICS USING AI

Computer Hardware

A wide array of computer hardware has been used for building and implementing AI systems in the manufacturing industry. AI systems have been developed on conventional computers, ranging from personal computers, engineering workstations, and minicomputers to mainframes. Each type of computer hardware has its place in helping to proliferate the use of AI technology in the manufacturing industry. The type of hardware used depends on the size, cost, and complexity of the system to be developed. Small diagnostics systems can be developed on a

TABLE 46.2. Example of a Frame-based Representation of Knowledge

OBJECT:	Component
SLOT:	Inheritance
	(override)
SLOT:	Has
	(vibration magnitude)
	(vibration frequency)
SLOT:	Symptoms
	(vibration magnitude exceeds threshold)
	AND
	(vibration frequency is a multiple of component frequency)
SLOT:	Possible problems
	(component is misaligned)
	OR
	(component is loose)

TABLE 46.3.   Example of a Logic-based Representation of Knowledge

$(\forall x)(\forall y)(\forall z)[\text{component}(X)$
$\text{AND symptom}(Y,X) \text{ AND excessive vibration}(Y)$
$\text{AND symptom}(Z,X) \text{ AND frequency multiple}(Z)$
$\Downarrow$
$(\exists p)(\text{possible problem}(p,x) \text{ AND}$
$(p=\text{"misalignment" OR } p=\text{"looseness"}))]$

desktop personal computer, whereas medium- to large-size ones can be built on engineering workstations. For large, complex systems, specialized Lisp machines used to be the hardware of choice, but increasingly even the more complex systems are being developed on engineering workstations or large conventional computers. Diagnostic applications in manufacturing can be extremely large and complex. Developing AI systems for such applications often necessitates dedicated computer hardware with large RAM and disk capacities, high execution speeds, and powerful development environments. Close of 32 Mb of main memory and more than 320 Mb of disk storage are not uncommon for building complex AI-based diagnostic systems in large manufacturing operations. Most computer hardware now allows for easy hookup with other standard electronic data-gathering devices and transfer of data from such devices as shown in Figure 46.7.

Availability of a good programming environment is a necessity for AI applications in manufacturing diagnostics. The system is developed on an incremental basis, and with each increment, the knowledge engineer who writes the computer code goes through several alterations of the program. Under such a situation, programmer productivity becomes a critical factor. Fortunately, today's computers provide some of the best programming environments for the developer's convenience. These include features like high resolution graphics, multiple and arbitrary-size windowing capabilities, large physical screens, mouse and menu systems, powerful

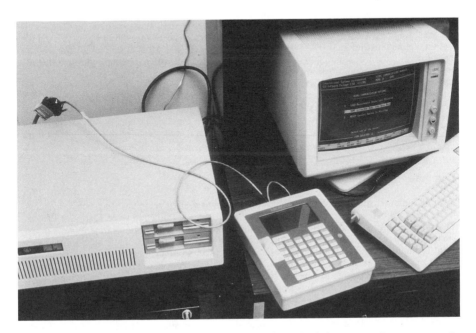

Figure 46.7. Data from hand-held devices can be easily uploaded to personal computers and engineering workstations on which AI-based diagnostic systems may reside.

full-screen editors, dynamic linking and loading of programs, debugging and tracing facilities, and efficient memory management.

Even the simple diagnostic systems generally require interaction among several individual computer programs (14). Access to other programs, such as those that perform routine mathematical calculations, is typically needed during the execution of an AI-based program. These different programs are usually written in different computer languages and often reside on different pieces of computer hardware. Therefore, the base computer must provide language support for those different programs and also permit linking several different computers together. To speed up execution of an AI system and its interaction with external programs, additional co-processors may be added to the standard hardware. For example, a floating-point accelerator may be added to speed up the arithmetic operations. Special hooks may be needed to facilitate access to databases. Considerable amount of manufacturing-related information is stored in large databases, and it makes more sense to access the database directly from the AI program than to redo a local subset on the hardware on which the AI program is resident. It quickly becomes clear that there should be good communications and networking facilities across the computers in the manufacturing environment.

The need for fast execution speeds is a function of the nature of the application. Sophisticated, state-of-the-art computer-controlled machines performing high speed, precision jobs are becoming common in today's manufacturing environment. Intelligent real-time monitoring, controlling, and diagnosing of such machine equipment will require a significant increase in the speeds of inferences of AI systems. Today's AI-based diagnostic systems still operate on off-line basis, although some progress is being made in the machine equipment world by including AI systems in an integral fashion with the machine. Another possibility for situations in which high speed execution is needed is to translate the fully developed AI systems into equivalent hardware chip forms. Implementation in hardware form can increase speed considerably. This approach, however, is rare, because it is expensive and suffers from the drawback that changes and improvements cannot be made easily.

The reality of the situation in the manufacturing diagnostics is that the choice of computer hardware is based on several factors beyond technical suitability. The choice is often dictated by direct cost considerations, the size of the application, and whether the chosen hardware is already existing and available on site. Some of the exploratory or proof-of-concept type of work for simple diagnostic systems is currently done on personal computers with 512K memory ranges. Personal computers are generally targeted to be the major delivery vehicles in the manufacturing industry for large systems that require more sophisticated computers for development. Engineering workstations have become popular. These workstations can be used for both development and delivery of AI-based diagnostic systems. Most of these workstations are based on standard commercially available 32-bit processors. Minicomputers and mainframes have been used for AI work in the manufacturing industry only in situations in which such computers were already in existence and other dedicated hardware could not be acquired.

Regardless of the hardware used for development of AI-based diagnostic systems, the delivery computer for fielding such systems must be rugged enough to withstand the rigors of the manufacturing environment. Similarly, the software must be extremely user friendly and robust. The program should be capable of recovering gracefully from erroneous and arbitrary inputs from the user.

Computer Software Languages and AI Tools

Several computer programming languages have been used in developing AI systems for manufacturing diagnostics. Two languages that enjoyed early prominence were Lisp and Prolog. They were highly specialized for AI applications requiring manipulation of symbolic expressions and pattern matching. Lisp, featured powerful recursion and automatic memory management capabilities. Prolog featured built-in backtracking and unification capabilities. However, use of those languages often required special-purpose computer hardware, and porting Lisp- or Prolog-based AI programs to other hardware environments turned out to be a difficult task. Moreover, speeds of execution of programs written in those languages were generally slower than programs written in conventional languages. Therefore, for portability, economy, and speed considerations, there has been a major shift toward using conventional high level languages for both development and delivery of AI-based diagnostic systems. Most notable of such languages is the C programming language. It was designed for and implemented on the UNIX operating system, which has steadily gained tremendous popularity both in the academic and industrial environments. C provides access to low level operations, which were traditionally done at the assembly language level, thereby providing both flexibility and speed. The conciseness of the C language and its portability and faster execution speeds have led to increased interest in the language in the commercial AI market.

In the manufacturing business, it is the software tools or shells based on the high level languages rather than the languages themselves that have found widespread use. These tools enable users in the manufacturing industry to do rapid development without the need to master the intricacies of the underlying computer languages. These tools range widely in terms of cost, functionality, performance, capacity, and other parameters of interest to the AI programmer. Dozens of such tools are available in the market today. The simplest of the AI tools can be purchased for a few hundred dollars, whereas the more sophisticated ones cost up to tens of thousands of dollars. Due to the complex matrix of factors influencing the selection of the appropriate tool for the manufacturing application at hand, the process of tool selection itself becomes an important task in the overall venture of an AI-based diagnostic system development. Simple, inexpensive tools can be used for exploratory purposes and in introducing the concepts of AI programming to the potential users in the manufacturing community. Simple tools are ideal for this purpose because of their low cost and the fact that almost all such packages run on already existing and available personal computers. Advanced, more expensive tools provide the many sophisticated features needed for handling complex manufacturing diagnostics problems. Most of these advanced tools provide multiple methods of knowledge representation, mixed initiative chaining in the inference engine, separation of control and domain knowledge, and excellent system development environments. However, these tools are harder to learn and master than the simpler tools. Specialized training is often required to learn the use of such tools. Working knowledge can be acquired in a matter of weeks, but the ability to write code that fully uses the power of these tools may take months.

Application-specific tools have started to emerge recently. Many are specific to manufacturing applications and are tailored to the diagnostics domain. They combine rule-based and frame-based knowledge representation schemes. For the rule portion of the knowledge base, a combination of forward and backward chaining is provided. The direction of chaining can be altered at the user's discretion. They provide excellent graphics user interfaces and graphics editors, in addition to the standard full-screen editors with debugging and tracing facilities. Facilities for incremental compilation of individual knowledge base elements are provided. They usually feature the added capability of simultaneously handling multiple alternative fault scenarios. This is especially important in equipment diagnostic applications, for which it is not uncommon to have more than one fault or problem on a machine at a time. Such tools provide facilities to perform automatic backtracking and retraction of events during consultation sessions. A significant amount of manufacturing diagnostics–related domain knowledge is already built into them. These features make such tools attractive for manufacturing diagnostics applications. Depending on the complexity of the problem being addressed, such application tools could possibly be used directly by the domain experts in the manufacturing industry with minimal or no assistance from knowledge engineers.

46.6 IMPLEMENTING AI-BASED DIAGNOSTIC SOLUTIONS

Implementing AI-based solutions in manufacturing environments is a task that requires considerable care and effort. A host of issues must be taken into account and addressed before the AI system can be successfully put into field use. Many of the implementation requirements must be kept in mind from the early stages of system development, perhaps even as early as when the project is being first considered for development.

Among the first considerations pertaining to implementation of AI systems are scope of the system and the associated business justifications. Even though AI-based diagnostic systems have been in use for several years, it is still crucial to keep the application well defined and sharply focused. This allows the problem domain to be limited and, therefore, makes it easy to implement solutions. Also, because the nature of AI-based systems is such that incremental development is easily possible, it is generally simpler to grow and expand the system gradually than to take on broad coverage in the first instance. There should be strong business justifications for pursuing development of an AI-based solution. Though the cost and difficulty of developing such solutions are no longer as prohibitive as they used to be, they do still remain quite substantial. Therefore, from the point of view of final implementation and field use, it is imperative that a sound business justification covering costs and benefits be performed up front.

Besides the cost–benefit analysis, a complete risk assessment should be performed both in terms of the technical feasibility and the prospects of user acceptance of the final system. An important aspect of an AI-based manufacturing diagnostics system is the ability to interact with external files or databases. Access to some sensory data, whether off-line or on-line, is almost always needed. Extraction of various pieces of data that have been collected and complied and conversion into the form that is amenable to processing by the system's inference engine are typically significant tasks and must be performed carefully.

There are several people-related issues that also need to be kept in mind while planning for the development and implementation of AI-based diagnostic systems. First and foremost is identification of a recognized and widely accepted expert. The system will emulate the thinking process of this person, and it is essential to ensure that the person is truly an expert in the field and is accepted by peers in the manufacturing community in which the system will be deployed. Another key factor is the issue of the availability of the expert's time. The fact that someone is an expert implies that the person is probably in great demand and is busy solving difficult and important diagnostic problems. Therefore, in reality the person whose time is needed most in building an AI-based solution is the person who is usually least available. To avoid problems in getting the expert's time, it is important to negotiate a plan from the beginning that will be acceptable to the expert, the expert's management, and the system developers. Strong support from management is also important. During the development and implementation of an AI system, the project typically goes through several stages in which strong management support is not just something that is desired but is essential to keep the system going. A capable and influential system "champion" is a big boost in getting the system developed and implemented in the field. The system champion keeps the development team focused on building the AI solution while at the same time shores up support among the user community in which the system would ultimately be put into operation. The system champion also ensures that adequate funding, people, and equipment resources are available throughout the development and implementation of the project. In most of the applications, there is usually a single expert who serves as the source of knowledge for the AI system. However, in cases where two or more experts are involved, the system champion also plays a key role in coordinating the different sources of knowledge.

Beyond the personnel issues, factors concerning reliability, validation, and acceptance of AI systems have been of concern since the first systems were built. As more diagnostic systems are being fielded in the manufacturing environment, the need to focus on these issues is becoming increasingly evident. The question of reliability is of primary importance. Once the hardware and software are established to be reliable, the reliability of the knowledge contained in the AI system must be examined. Before any system can be placed in the manufacturing environment, it must be ascertained that its recommendations and advice are accurate and reliable. Of course, the extent to which a system needs to be accurate is a function of how critical the job being performed is and what consequences an erroneous output may have. The monetary losses due to misdiagnoses can be significant. In fact most of the AI systems in manufacturing today are initiated on the expectation of large financial returns or savings. These returns and savings are possible only through reliable, consistent, and accurate systems.

Validation involves certification that the system has been tested and has proven capable of performing the task on the targeted application domain. Depending on the nature of the application, validation may be a straightforward procedure or an extremely complicated and difficult task. Typically, in the manufacturing environment, the expert or a select group of users validates the system by running several cycles of it on some simple, typical cases as well as on previously solved difficult cases. A method of extended validation can be used in conjunction with this method. It involves testing of an assortment of real, existing, and previously unsolved problems. Validation becomes a problem only if the area of application selected is new and no good representative sample cases are available for testing. In such a situation, synthetic cases can be developed and the system tested against those cases. For large, critical systems, a combination of real and synthetic cases is generally used. System refinements are usually performed in parallel with validation to remove any shortcomings and to fill any detected gaps in diagnostic knowledge.

Acceptance of AI-based diagnostic systems has increased steadily. The fact that most of these systems are used to assist plant personnel rather than to replace them has been crucial in promoting acceptance in manufacturing businesses. Another reason for increased acceptance has been the sense of ownership instilled among the users of those systems. However, the manufacturing industry still needs to be careful in providing all necessary training that may be needed to use, maintain, and update such systems. Training is particularly important in the diagnostics domain of the manufacturing industry, because the people using the AI-based systems may not be conversant with the technology. A well-planned training program to introduce the system in the manufacturing environment can go a long way toward increasing the prospect of acceptance of the system by the target users. Getting the users involved from the early stages of the system development is a good strategy and will allow users to provide input into the design of the system, particularly the system interface, and to feel part of the development process. A simple, easy-to-use interface is a must for any diagnostic system that is intended for use in the manufacturing environment. Graphical or menu-based interfaces have become popular and are generally well accepted in manufacturing diagnostic applications. However, it is important to remember that the interface does not simply mean the appearance of the computer screen but also includes the content. For example, the words used or the pictures and diagrams shown on the screen should be compatible with the jargon of the diagnostics trade in the manufacturing industry. Managing the cultural change in implementing AI-based diagnostic solutions is an important factor. Such systems are not merely another tool in the toolbox of the diagnostician; they represent a cultural change and must be addressed accordingly. The approach adopted in introducing such systems in the manufacturing environment can make a difference between causing fear and resentment among the users instead of curiosity and excitement. The balance is sometimes tough to manage, but it is crucially important to the long-term success of the system.

46.7 BENEFITS OF AI-BASED DIAGNOSTICS

The majority of the benefits of using AI-based diagnostic techniques are derived from the fact that these techniques most closely resemble the practices and methods typically followed by recognized experts in the field. Unlike most conventional systems, which facilitate or automate portions of mechanical procedures, the AI systems actually automate the thought process of experts so that others, including novices, can take advantage of knowledge that would otherwise require years of training and experience. Generally, precise identification of the problems can be made using AI-based diagnostics and accurate repairs can be performed before catastrophic failures. This can save considerable time and money. It can also add to the smooth operation of manufacturing facilities by permitting scheduling of preventive maintenance at convenient times. Once an AI-based diagnostic system has been developed, it can be made available to a number of manufacturing sites where several different users can access it simultaneously. Besides the obvious benefit of allowing diagnostic expertise to be readily available at possibly distant geographical locations, AI systems provide a way of standardizing diagnostic procedures. Moreover, as new knowledge is gained over time, it can be conveniently added to the knowledge base, thereby keeping such diagnostic systems up to date. If related diagnostic problems have been encountered previously, these systems can be programmed to identify them and fix them based on previously tried and proven solutions.

Conventional programs typically provide considerable amount of data and information to the repair person, who must understand and interpret all that data and information. The interpretation process depends on the experience level of the repair person. Many times, due to either misunderstanding or misinterpretation, it is the symptoms that are treated while the source or the root problem is never identified. Sometimes inaccurate diagnosis leads to "fixing" machines and components that are not really the cause of the problem. This fixing of nonproblems can be wasteful and frustrating. AI-based systems avoid these difficulties, because the interpretation part is automated and is typically based on the knowledge and experience of an expert in the domain. Therefore, there is a smaller likelihood of misdiagnosis and a better chance of diagnosing and correctly fixing the problem in the first attempt.

Although this is still a new area of applicability of AI systems, these systems can be successfully employed to assist in running manufacturing operations unattended. Impending problems can be identified and necessary corrective actions taken (15) without the need for continuous human monitoring or intervention. With the advances in industrial sensor technology and availability of low cost transducers, it should become possible to use permanently mounted sensors that provide on-line information to the AI system. Such a facility would enable round-the-clock maintenance monitoring of manufacturing machines (Figure 46.8). The AI system can receive different types of sensory data from various strategic locations on the machine on a routine basis or on some alarm or threshold basis. More advanced AI systems can be developed that can automatically control the polling of various sensors and the periodicity of the arrival of the sensory data.

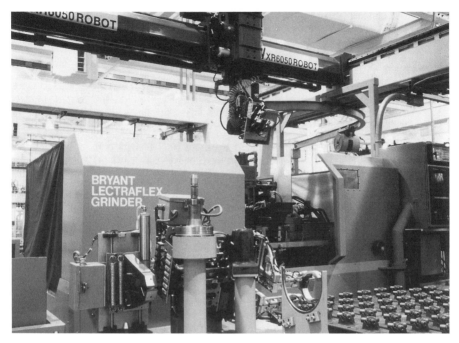

Figure 46.8. A sophisticated, state-of-the-art machine in a manufacturing cell.

When properly planned and designed, AI systems have the ability to be generic in nature. They do not have to be limited to individual machines or a specific type of machine. They can be developed to be applicable for a wide range or class of machines. Instead of building several small AI systems, one can develop a generic model by which a variety of problems can be diagnosed on a large cross-section of machines. The generality can be achieved by focusing on the components that make up the individual machines rather than looking narrowly at specific machines. With such a system, it should be possible to perform routine and diagnostic maintenance on many machines regardless of their age or function. New machines can be tested for rigorous compliance with performance standards so that repairs and replacements can be performed while those machines are still under warranty. Equipment manufacturers can employ AI-based systems to test their products before shipment to clients. As the practice of using computer-aided design (CAD) databases for machine descriptions becomes more prevalent, it may become possible to link those databases to the diagnostic AI systems, thereby providing a link between descriptions of machines, sensory data, symptoms of problems, and actual diagnostics. With the help of such a link, it may become possible not only to diagnose machine problems but also to identify areas of improvement in the design of the machine itself.

46.8 PAST, PRESENT, AND FUTURE

In the past, cost had been a barrier in the implementation of AI-based diagnostic systems. Due to the scarcity of qualified AI personnel, the manufacturing industry had to rely heavily on external companies that specialized in the AI business. The costs of training and buying expensive computer hardware and software for fielding systems on the plant floor for day-to-day use had been a serious issue. These problems have lately been substantially alleviated with the reduction in the costs of computer systems and an increase in the number and availability of professionals qualified to perform AI tasks. Lack of awareness of the AI technology, which had been a problem for several years, has also been largely addressed. Fielding and publication of numerous successful AI-based diagnostic systems have helped instill confidence in the manufacturing community. However, it still remains important that the user community has realistic expectations, and this can be best accomplished by providing concise, accurate information relating to the appropriateness and capabilities of the AI technology in manufacturing diagnostics.

There is a tremendous diversity of equipment used in the manufacturing industry, and integration of AI systems with those pieces of equipment can pose a significant challenge. There are large amounts of data stored and maintained on conventional computers resident in the manufacturing plants. Communication and efficient data transfer and retrieval between the database computers and the computers hosting the AI systems are major tasks in the actual implementation and fielding of AI systems. The computer industry is making efforts to assist in this work by providing standardized communications and networking packages. There are some other AI issues that could benefit the manufacturing industry when they are resolved. One of them is the speed issue. The speed of response of most systems in use today is unacceptably slow for continuous on-line operations. It is, therefore, no surprise that almost all of the AI applications in manufacturing are off-line in nature. Research effort is under way to improve both the computer hardware design and software programs to increase execution speeds. Parallel processing hardware shows promise, but so far no concrete use of it has been made in the manufacturing diagnostics domain. Another area of research is automatic learning and discovery. There are no documented systems in the manufacturing industry that can learn from previous mistakes or experience in any significant way. The ability to learn would be extremely useful, especially in the flexible manufacturing environments of today. Diagnostic skills come gradually and with considerable experience. Though present AI-based systems provide great assistance to the less experienced personnel, unlike their human counterparts, these systems do not learn much new on their own with time.

Despite the hurdles, AI-based diagnostic applications in the manufacturing industry have grown rapidly over the last decade. In fact, manufacturing diagnostics has been one of the better understood and widely used areas of application of AI technology. Manufacturing remains the backbone of industrialized economies. AI offers great solutions in several areas of manufacturing, and the most notable and by far the most successful has been diagnostics. As AI technology advances and paybacks of its use become more evident, proliferation in numerous other areas of manufacturing is expected to result.

Acknowledgments

Portions of this chapter were extracted from refs. 1 and 3 with kind permission from Marcel Dekker Inc. and the American Society of Mechanical Engineers, respectively.

BIBLIOGRAPHY

1. A. BAJPAI and B.A. SANDERS, "Artificial Intelligence for Automobile Manufacturing" in A. Kent and J.G. Williams, eds., *Encyclopedia of Computer Science and Technology*, Vol. 22, Marcel Dekker, Inc., New York, 1990, pp. 67–83.
2. L. MONOSTORI et al., "Concept of a Knowledge Based Diagnostic System for Machine Tools and Manufacturing Cells," *Comput. Ind.* **15**(1–2), 95–102 (1990).
3. A. BAJPAI, "An Expert System Model for General Purpose Diagnostics of Manufacturing Equipment," *Manufact. Rev. ASME J.* **1**(3), 180–187 (1988).
4. R.A. COLLACOTT, *Mechanical Fault Diagnosis and Condition Monitoring*, Chapman and Hall, London, 1977.
5. L.F. PAU, *Failure Diagnosis and Performance Monitoring*, Marcel Dekker, Inc., New York, 1981.
6. S.N. THANOS, "No Disassembly Required," *Mech. Eng.* **109**(9), 86–90 (1987).
7. A. EAGLE, *Fourier's Theorem and Harmonic Analysis*, Green & Co., London, 1925.
8. V.D. MAJSTOROVIC, "Expert Systems for Diagnosis and Maintenance: The State-of-the-Art," *Comput. Ind.* **15**(1–2), 43–68 (1990).
9. S. MUSSI and R. MORPURGO, "Acquiring and Representing Strategic Knowledge in the Diagnosis Domain," *Expert Sys.* **7**(3), 157–165 (1990).
10. R. ROWEN, "Diagnostic Systems for Manufacturing," *AI Expert* **5**(4), 28–36 (1990).

11. B. BUCHANAN and E. SHORTLIFFE, *Ruled-based Expert Systems: The MYCIN Experiments of the Stanford-Heuristic Programming Project,* Addison-Wesley, Publishing Co., Inc., Reading, Mass., 1984.

12. W.D. POTTER et al., "A Comparison of Methods for Diagnostic Decision Making," *Expert Sys. Appl.* **1**(4), 425–436 (1990).

13. J. DOYLE, "A Truth Maintenance System," *Artif. Intel.* **12,** 231–272 (1979).

14. C.T. KITZMILLER and J.S. KOWALIK, "Coupling Symbolic and Numeric Computing in Knowledge-Based Systems," *AI Magazine* **8**(2), 85–90 (1987).

15. M. WECK, "Machine Diagnostics in Automated Production," *J. Manufact. Sys.* **2**(2), 101–106 (1983).

CHAPTER 47

Fuzzy Decision and Control in Manufacturing and Automation

D. Dubois, J. C. Pascal and R. Valette
LAAS

47.1 INTRODUCTION

In many domains (medical diagnosis, production scheduling, industrial control process, robotics, household appliances, etc.), we must handle incomplete information: some data are not available or they are uncertain or imprecise. To cope with this problem, it is necessary to develop systems capable of accepting imperfect information and of working with it in a satisfactory manner.

Traditional tools for knowledge representation, even those enhanced by probability theory, are insufficient to deal with such ill-known information. Indeed, classic logic is two-valued and only allows one to consider propositions that are certainly true or false. Objective probabilistic knowledge requires statistical data that are not available, especially when the concerned situation is not repetitive. Subjective probability approaches are often based on restrictive assumptions, requesting the user to be in an ideal betting situation and forcing him or her to express more a priori information than he or she actually possesses. The ability of the human mind to reason with incomplete information is often the result of his or her aptitude to manipulate information in a gradual manner, i.e., with a grade of preference attached to each possible interpretation of a piece of information. Indeed, many properties used to describe our knowledge have a gradual nature (e.g., a quantity can be small, high, or great). The fact that the number 2 is small or not depends on context, but we can assert that 1 is always a better example of ''small'' than 2. The use of this type of information in the precondition of a rule allows one to consider its conclusion as more or less likely to be applicable and makes it more flexible. The meaning of *likely* will also be context dependent.

To represent the gradual nature of information, Zadeh (1) defined the notion of fuzzy sets. This notion consists in giving intermediate membership degrees, between 0 and 1, to elements that are not typical of the set but that can still be in the set. Today, there are many application domains of fuzzy logic: economy, document retrieval, manufacturing systems, medical aid, civil engineering, robotic, household appliances, etc. A new trend is to combine fuzzy logic with neural networks whose learning capabilities allow one to tune membership functions more precisely and to eliminate useless rules. This is mainly the result of the similarity between a fuzzy rule and the mathematical model of a neuron.

In manufacturing systems and factory automation the presence of human operators is a factor of increased uncertainty. In the 1970s, the trend was to achieve a complete automation and to eliminate the operators. Now it is generally recognized that the presence of operators is compulsory to cope with unexpected events and to meet flexibility and reactivity requirements. The counterpart to these benefits is that supervisory systems, decision aid software, etc. must handle the ill-known behavior of the human operators. Frequently, operation durations are imprecise. This results partly from the fact that the system is not completely automated and partly because the operations are new (flexibility implies rapid and numerous product changes). The industrial processes are more and more complex, and their mathematical models are rough. Finally, the organization of the manufacturing system, considered as a sociotechnical system, is more sophisticated (the strictly hierarchical organization defined by Taylor is now given up in favor of decentralized decision center networks). In a nutshell, uncertainty and imprecision of information are a direct consequence of a trend toward more flexibility and more reactivity to unexpected events.

The use of fuzzy sets and control in manufacturing systems is favored by some other trends at lower decision and control levels. People are willing to operate with gradual propositions to implement linear interpolations between various typical operation modes of the whole manufacturing system or of specific devices. It is frequently requested to avoid sharp, unexpected changes of behavior that could damage mechanical parts of the devices or stress the operators. This results in the implementation of simple, continuous regulations controlling the system when it is passing from one state to another state. As a consequence, many programmable logic controllers now have continuous regulation functions. An issue for which fuzzy sets could be useful is the modeling of systems at the frontier of a discrete and continuous representation. For example, a supervisory control that handles batch overlapping must take into account the nature of the continuous operation within the batch and the discrete nature of the batch itself. If a human operator asks for the location of a batch for which operations on devices $D1$ and $D2$ are overlapping, only an imprecise answer is possible: the batch is within the zone consisting of devices $D1$ and $D2$.

After a short, informal introduction to fuzzy sets and fuzzy reasoning, this chapter presents two of their applications in decision support for manufacturing systems. The use of fuzzy dates and intervals for fuzzy scheduling based on constraint satisfaction and propagation is described. The second application deals with the part of the supervisory control that is in charge of monitoring. Fuzzy Petri nets are used to model the state of the resources and the sequential constraints in detail. Applications of fuzzy sets and fuzzy Petri nets to lower control levels are presented. At this level, it is more a matter of linear interpolation between traditionally discrete categories than a matter of uncertainty and ill-known information.

47.2   FUZZY SET AND FUZZY REASONING

Fuzzy Set

Natural language is rich in vague and imprecise concepts such as "John is young" and "it is rather hot today." The set of young people is ill-defined: a man of age 30 is young to a 60-yr-old man and old to a 12-yr-old child. In a way, if John is 30, it can be considered that the truth proposition "John is young" is context dependent. Even in a given context, it is difficult to determine a threshold below which an individual will be acknowledged as definitely young and beyond which he or she will be considered as definitely not young. This state of fact is, in the present case, due to the discrepancy between the continuous nature of an age scale and the presence of a small, finite vocabulary that use to describe this scale. To make these two representations more compatible, it is natural to admit that the adequation between a given value in the continuous scale and a given term in the vocabulary be a matter of degree. These degrees appear in the natural language itself under the form of linguistic hedges like *very* or *rather*, which apply to predicates like *young* and can be considered as linguistic forms of intermediate truth values. For a long time, philosophers have claimed that beyond true and false a third region exists and that the two-valued logic is not sufficiently comprehensive. In 1965, Zadeh (1) published his seminal work, which has become the basis of an infinite-valued logic: fuzzy logic.

For an ordinary set, given an element, it is or it is not a member of the set. In contrast, a fuzzy set is defined by a membership function that takes its values on the interval [0, 1]. Value 0 denotes that the element is not at all a member of the set (complete falseness), and value 1 denotes that the element is definitely a member of the set (complete truth). Values within [0, 1] 0, 1 denote intermediate membership. In Figure 47.1a, the classic set "young" (if age is less than 30) is compared with a fuzzy set. If John is less than 20, it is true that he is young, if he is more than 40 it is true that he is not young. Between these two values, the more his age is close to 20 the more it can be claimed that he is young. A fuzzy set can be considered as an ordered collection of embedded ordinary subsets, each one corresponding to a given membership value. For the membership value 1, we have the smallest subset. It is the core. The largest subset corresponding to a membership value different from 0 is the support. In the core, we are certain that the elements totally belong to the fuzzy set. Outside the support, we are certain that the elements do not belong at all to the fuzzy set (2).

A fuzzy set F is defined by a membership function $\mu_F(w)$ of the elements $w \in W$ (reference set) that are compatible with the concept of F (the more the value of $\mu_F(w)$ is high, the more the

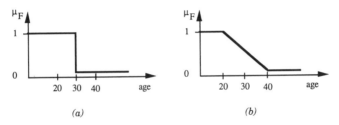

Figure 47.1. (a) Ordinary set. (b) Fuzzy set.

element is compatible with the concept of F), where W is the set of ages. If F is the fuzzy set delimiting the property "young" in Figure 47.1b, and if μ_F is the attached membership function, then

$$\mu_F(30) = 0.5$$

We can interpret this as "the extent to which an age of 30 can be considered young is 0.5." The classic set of theoretic operations can be defined on fuzzy sets. Let μ_F be the membership function denoting the fuzzy set F; the usual definitions are as follows:

- The fuzzy set F is included in the fuzzy set G iff $\mu_F \leq \mu_G$. A stronger inclusion notion exists, namely $F \subseteq G$ iff the support of F is included in the core of G.
- The fuzzy set F is equal to the fuzzy set G iff $\mu_F = \mu_G$. The strong inclusion leads to the idea that only crisps sets (ordinary sets with membership function defined on [0, 1]) can be considered as equal.
- The union of F and G is such that $\mu_{F\cup G} = \max(\mu_F, \mu_G)$.
- The intersection of F and G is such that $\mu_{F\cap G} = \min(\mu_F, \mu_G)$.
- F is the complement of G iff $\mu_F = 1 - \mu_G$.

Let us assume now that the age of John is ill-known and that we just know that he is "about 30." In this case, we interpret the membership function μ_F of "about 30" as a possibility distribution π_F attached to a piece of information. $\mu_F(a)$ then represents the degree of possibility that an individual who is known to be "about 30" is actually of age a. If we consider the query "Is John young?" then answering the query in the presence of the piece of information "John is about 30" can be handled in terms of possibility and certainty. Namely, we may first check whether there is any possibility that someone about 30 be young. This is done by checking whether the intersection $F \cap G$ is empty or not, and we compute the degree of possibility of F given G as follows (Figure 47.2b in which $P(F) = 0.7$):

$$\Pi(F) = \sup_u \min(\mu_F(u), \mu_G(u))$$

Alternatively, we may check whether there is certainty that someone about 30 be young. This is done by checking to what extent the inclusion of G in F holds. Interpreting the total certainty of "John is young" as the total impossibility of "John is not young" leads to define the degree of certainty as follows (Figure 47.2c in which $N(F) = 0.3$)

$$N(F) = 1 - \Pi(\bar{F}) = \inf_u \max(1 - \mu_G(u), \mu_F(u))$$

Note that $N(F) = 1$ iff the support of G is inside the core of F, i.e., the degree of certainty corresponds to a degree of strong inclusion of G in F. This fact explains why generally if $F = G$, $N(F) \neq 1$ when G is fuzzy (is not a crisp set); $N(F)$ evaluates to what extent John is certainly "typically about 30," i.e., $\mu_{about30}(age(John))$ is certainly close to 1 or not.

$\Pi(F)$ and $N(F)$ are called degrees of possibility and certainty of F and have been studied, especially when F is not fuzzy, due to their similarity to probabilistic degrees. They differ by their characteristic axioms:

$$P(F \cup F') = \max(P(F), P(F'))$$
$$N(F \cap F') = \min(N(F), N(F'))$$

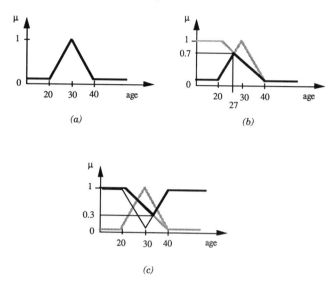

Figure 47.2. (*a*) John is about 30. (*b*) Is John possibly young? (*c*) Is John certainly young?

Both degrees are simultaneously useful for question answering or pattern matching in the presence of fuzzy information.

Fuzzy Temporal Knowledge Representation

Considerable interest has been shown in recent years in the representation of temporal knowledge. An interesting issue is the development of approaches allowing one to consider cases in which this knowledge is vague or uncertain. In manufacturing systems, the development of decision processes for planning, scheduling, or supervisory control involves handling constraints about resources and time. In consequence, it is a natural application domain for fuzzy temporal knowledge representation and reasoning (3, 4).

An imprecise date (a date is a time point) is delimited by a time interval. Such a time interval is a disjunctive set of time points, because if all of them are candidate to denote the date, only one of them is the date. If the date is well known, then the time interval is a singleton (a set consisting of only one time point). If in contrast the date is vague, i.e., if it is a fuzzy date, then it is delimited by a possibility distribution that forms a fuzzy set of time points. In Figure 47.3a, we have the representation of a precise and well-known date. For example, the operation must begin at exactly 1:00. In Figure 47.3b, we have an imprecise date. The operation must start after 13 and before 14. This means that 13 is the earliest starting time and that 14 is the latest starting time (that is the due date minus the operation duration). In Figure 47.3c, the specification of the date is vague. It can be interpreted as "do not begin the operation before 13 and do not delay much after 14." Actually, in the preceding case, beginning the operation just before 14 is correct whereas just 1 s after 14 would trigger an alarm and, e.g., might require a rescheduling of the manufacturing system. In contrast, in the third case, the rescheduling will only be executed if the operation is delayed after 15, and between 14 and 15 the supervisory control will try to solve the problem.

As opposed to an imprecise date, a time interval during which an activity takes place is a conjunctive set of time points characterized by a starting date and an end date. When these dates are imprecise or fuzzy, the conjunctive time interval is characterized by a pair of fuzzy dates. Let us now consider two dates a and b characterized by the disjunctive fuzzy sets of time points A and B (Figure 47.4). The fuzzy set $[-\infty, A]$ of time points that are possibly before date a is defined by

$$\tau \in T, \; \mu_{[-\infty, A]}(\tau) = \sup_{\tau' \geq \tau} \pi_a(\tau)$$

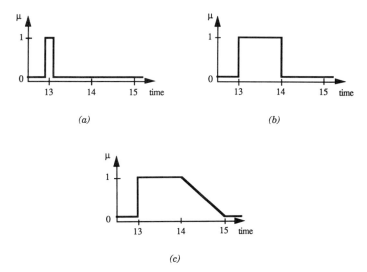

Figure 47.3. (*a*) Precise date. (*b*) Imprecise date. (*c*) Fuzzy (vague) date.

where T is the set of time points. The fuzzy set of time points that are possibly after the date *b* is defined by

$$\tau \in T, \ \mu_{[B,+\infty]}(\tau) = \sup_{\tau' \leq \tau} \pi_b(\tau)$$

And the time interval of time points that are possibly after *a* and before *b* is the intersection of the two preceding ones as represented in Figure 47.4.

Fuzzy Sequential Constraints

Introduction

In manufacturing, many constraints that must be handled are of sequential nature. For example, a part route describes the sequence of operations that must be executed. Kanban policies can be viewed as an event ordering: each time a part is removed from an output stock, subparts are removed from input stocks and a new assembly operation starts. Sequential processes are needed to describe resources passing from state to state when series of events and activities occur in the manufacturing system. Petri nets are well-suited to model such situations.

Petri nets were introduced by Petri in the early 1960s as a mathematical tool for modeling distributed systems and, in particular, notions of concurrency, communication, and synchronization. There are many varieties of Petri nets. An ordinary Petri net is a digraph with nodes that may be places (drawn as circles) or transitions (drawn as rectangles). Edges can connect places to transitions or transitions to places. A Petri net can be marked by indicating the tokens that are contained in each place at a time point. They are drawn as dots in the places. If the input places of a transition all contain at least one token, the transition is said to be enabled, i.e., it is

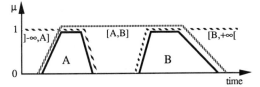

Figure 47.4. Fuzzy time interval.

eligible for firing. If it does fire, then one token is removed from each of its input places and one token is added to each of its output places.

Typically in manufacturing systems, transitions denote events and places activities (or wait states). A token moving from place to place denotes an active object (a part, a tool, a machine) whose dynamic is a process. At higher decision and control levels, data must be attached to tokens that can consequently be considered as object instances. We speak of object Petri, nets and places may contain more than one token (e.g., when they correspond to intermediary stocks). At lower control levels, places are typically interpreted as Boolean conditions. They contain one token at most, and the tokens are not considered as individuals. A comprehensive survey about Petri net application in manufacturing and automation can be found in ref. 5.

As system complexity increases, it frequently becomes necessary to handle ill-known information or constraints involving gradual preferences. This trend is well known for classic constraints concerning a set of variables; it is more recently applied to sequential constraints involving sets of sequential processes. How is it possible to combine Petri net theory and fuzzy sets? We are going to try to give a response in this section.

Principles

Two kind of processes may be dealt with: resource processes and proof processes. When a resource R passes from a state SA to a state SB it can be considered that it consumes the proposition "R is in SA" and produces the proposition "R is in SB." In a Petri net model, this is denoted by a token R passing from place SA to place SB. The token location denotes the state of the resource, and we have mutual exclusion between the various possible locations of a given token. It is the specificity of a resource process. When, in a deduction process, you derive that the proposition B is true because you know that A is true and that A entails B is true, proposition A does not becomes false. If we model this reasoning process by a Petri net with a transition denoting A entails B and two places A and B, the interpretation of a token in place A is "A is true and this proposition is under consideration in my proof scenario." We do not necessarily have an exclusion mechanism between the various possible locations of a token, because we may consider at the same time that, e.g., A is true and B is true (6–8).

Fuzzy sets are useful in various situations. A fuzzy set may delimit an ill-known value. It may then depict a collection of alternatives with a gradual preference knowing that eventually one of these alternatives will be chosen. In these cases, they are disjunctive sets whose membership functions are possibility distributions. In resource processes modeled by Petri nets, if we consider a set of places as possible token locations, it is clearly a disjunctive set because, given a token, there is mutual exclusion between its location. In proof processes modeled by Petri nets, it is not the case; however, there is a mutual exclusion between the proofs (or the explanations), i.e., between the firing sequences. Actually, if you eventually choose $h1$ as a possible explanation of e, then it will not be $h2$.

To conclude, if a set of sequential constraints has been described by a Petri net, the two basic ways of introducing "fuzziness" are

1. To define fuzzy markings based on a notion of fuzzy token locations.
2. To define fuzzy sets of firing sequences based on the association of necessity degrees with the transitions.

In the first case, tokens denote objects or resource items that can be clearly identified (individuals). In the second case, tokens are pointers in a reasoning process. Let us illustrate these two approaches on toy examples.

Examples

Let us consider the Petri net in Figure 47.5. It depicts the interaction of three processes. Processes $x1$ and $x2$ of class X evolve among three states (places $P1$, $P2$, and $P3$). Process $y1$ of class Y evolves among the states $P4$ and $P5$. Let us assume that the state of $y1$ is well known. For example, it is the crisp set $\{P4\}$. On the contrary, the state of $x1$ is ill-known. The location of the corresponding token is thus the fuzzy set of places $\{P1, P2\}$ with, for instance, possibility 1 for $P1$ and 0.5 for $P2$. Finally, the location of $x2$ is also ill-known and is delimited by the fuzzy set $\{P2, P3\}$ with, for example, possibility 1 for $P2$ and 1 for $P3$.

What can be deduced from this fuzzy marking? That some transition may be possibly fired. For instance, transition tc may be fired with tokens $x1$ and $y1$ with possibility 0.5 (the minimum

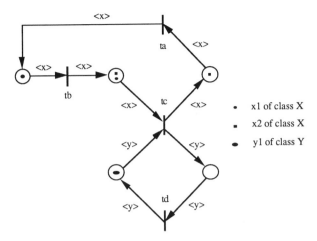

Figure 47.5. Resource management modeling.

of the membership degrees of its input places for the corresponding tokens), and it may also be fired with tokens $x2$ and $y1$ with possibility 1. Transition tb may only be fired with $x1$ (degree 1) and transition ta, with $x2$ (degree 1). Transition td is not enabled.

Let us now consider the Petri net in Figure 47.6. It describes a relation between hypotheses (ta, tb, and tc) and an observable event tf. By firing ta and tb, or by firing tc, we can fire tf. The places of this net do not denote states, they represent connections between rules. In this case, what is meaningful is the firing sequences, not the markings. If we attach necessity degrees to the transitions—1 for ta, 0.8 for tb, 0.5 for td, 0.8 for tc, and 1 for te—we can deduce that the explanation "ta and tb" has degree 0.5 (the minimum of the involved transitions: ta tb td), whereas the explanation tc has degree 0.8 (firing sequence tc te). We shall illustrate the application of these concepts of fuzzy marking and fuzzy firing sequences for manufacturing systems in following sections.

47.3   APPLICATION OF FUZZY SYSTEMS IN DECISION SUPPORT

Fuzzy Scheduling

Production scheduling is a field of investigation in which advances in theory and solution techniques did not produce expected results at the industrial level due to specific features of case studies that prevent the application of general approaches. The scheduling problem in a workshop can be stated as follows: given a set of production facilities and technological constraints and given production requirements expressed in terms of quantity, product quality, and time constraints, find a feasible sequencing of processing operations on the various facilities

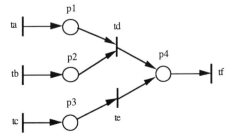

Figure 47.6.   Proof scenario modeling.

that satisfies the production requirements. Artificial intelligence scheduling systems have been developed (9). Interestingly, fuzzy scheduling has become a subchapter of this field. Scheduling is a good example of the constraint satisfaction problem, and this is the reason why it is of interest to artificial intelligence researchers.

The introduction of the fuzzy set is basically motivated by the fact that the constraints at work in a scheduling problem are seldom rigid ones. A typical flexible constraint is a due date, for which a certain amount of violation is permitted. Processing times can also be a matter of decision, for instance, the same task performed on two different machines corresponds to different durations; even a single machine performing a single task may lead to a flexible duration, which depends on machine-tuning parameters. In front of flexible constraints, two attitudes are possible:

1. Model the problem in a rigid way and relax a constraint in case the search for a solution fails.
2. Model the problem in a flexible way using fuzzy constraints and look for the solution that does not violate the constraints too much.

The first approach is not attractive. First, the checking procedure is usually based on constraint propagation, making it time-consuming. Sometimes, many calculations are done with no result at the end, while slightly fewer tight constraints may have led to an acceptable solution. Moreover, the problem of selecting a constraint to be relaxed is tricky as well. Last, when the rigid constraints are loose, the constraint propagation step will also be lengthy and ineffective, and the solution chosen by the reasoning system will be arbitrary and not necessarily adapted to the (unmodeled) wishes of the user.

The use of flexible constraints inside the propagation and satisfaction algorithm copes with all the above difficulties. A flexible constraint can be viewed as a self-relaxable constraint. Flexible constraint propagation is more productive than its rigid counterparts because it will more often find a solution, at the expense of slight violations. Infeasibility of a problem is no longer artificial, due to the blind choice of thresholds. This approach not only enables tight constraints to be slightly violated, it can also make loose constraints more demanding by introducing preferences over too large a set of feasible solutions. The context-dependent preferences of the user especially can be partially captured by a suitable specification of flexible constraints.

Flexible constraints can be modeled by possibility distributions over decision variables. Combining these possibility distributions by the fuzzy set "min" operator leads one to define a preferred solution to a flexible constraint problem as one that minimizes the satisfaction level of the least violated constraint. This criterion, counterparts of which can be found in game theory, was first formulated in fuzzy theory by Bellman and Zadeh (10) and is particularly well-suited to fuzzy constraints, i.e., requirements none of which should be completely violated. Interestingly, all classic results pertaining to classic constraint propagation can be extended to flexible constraints propagation in the possibility theory framework (11). Constraint propagation algorithms can easily be adapted, without changing their worst-case complexity. Possibility theory also is capable of handling prioritized constraints, where priorities are viewed as degrees of necessity.

An example of common constraint in the field of scheduling is a time window inside which a processing operation must take place. It is characterized by an earliest time e_i and a due date f_i for operation i whose duration is d_i. This problem is feasible as long as $d_i \leq f_i - e_i$. The flexibility of the windows can be modeled by fuzzy set $W_i = F_i \cap E_i$ (Figure 47.7). E_i is a fuzzy set of possible starting times, and $\mu_{E_i}(e_i)$ represents the degree of satisfaction of the corresponding constraint when the operation starts at time e_i. To compute the degree of satisfaction μ_i of the time windows constraint by a positioning of operation i at e_i, we must check that both $\mu_{E_i}(e_i)$

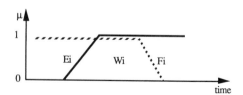

Figure 47.7. Fuzzy time window.

and $\mu_{F_i}(e_i + d_i)$ are high enough. Hence, the degree of satisfaction of starting operation i at time e_i is

$$\mu_i(e_i) = \min(\mu_{E_i}(e_i), \mu_{F_i}(e_i + d_i)) \tag{1}$$

The degree of feasibility of the problem is

$$\mu_i = \sup_{e_i} \mu_{C_i}(e_i) = \sup_{e_i} \min(\mu_{E_i}(e_i), \mu_{F_i}(e_i + d_i)) = \mu_{F_i \ominus E_i}(d_i) \tag{2}$$

where $F_i \ominus E_i$ is computed by fuzzy arithmetic (2).

A more general scheduling problem is when a set J of jobs must be performed by a set M of machines. Each job j is characterized by a set Ω_j of operations, each operation $\omega_{ij} \in \Omega_j$ must be performed by a given machine $m_{ij} \in M$. This operation requires a processing time d_{ij}. Moreover Ω_j is a partially ordered set in the sense that $\omega_{ij} < \omega_{kj}$ means that the operation ω_{ij} must be performed (for technological reasons) before operation ω_{kj}. Each job j is characterized by an earliest starting time e_j, which indicates when raw material for the job is available, and a due date f_j, which indicates when the job j must be completed. The problem is to build a linear ordering of operations on each machine, so that due dates are not violated and tasks assigned to the same machine cannot be simultaneously performed. When starting times and due dates are fuzzy, we get a lot of fuzzy time windows problems, related via the precedence constraints between tasks and their nonoverlapping operation when performed on the same machine. See ref. 12 for a fuzzy constraint propagation method adapted to this situation. These preliminary results are currently cast in a more general constraint propagation setting by the authors.

Besides flexibility of constraints bearing on decision variables, uncertainty also pervades scheduling problems. Namely, some parameters are ill-known not because they are a matter of choice but because their actual value will be known only after the production plan has been run. For instance, some processing times may be random to some extent. They can be modeled either by probability distributions (e.g., if statistical data are available) or by possibility distributions if weaker knowledge is available (e.g., expert opinions). In the last case, Bayesians suggest the use of probability distributions as well, but possibility theory offers a less demanding framework, because possibility degrees may represent upper probability bounds.

Let us consider the fuzzy time window problem with an ill-known duration of the operation. Let us first assume that the operation has a duration represented by a probability density p_i attached to the variable d_i, then in Equation 1, $\mu_{F_i}(e_i + d_i)$ becomes a random variable. The degree of satisfaction $\mu_{F_i}(e_i + d_i)$ can be changed into the probability that the ending time constraint is satisfied, with a prescribed starting time e_i. This is

$$P_i(F_i) = \int_{-\infty}^{+\infty} \mu_{F_i}(e_i + d_i) dP_i(d_i)$$

or the probability of the fuzzy event F_i in the Zadeh's sense (2). In other words, we compute the expected satisfaction level of F_i that can be used in Equation 1. Similarly, the expected degree of feasibility of the problem will be $P_i(F_i \ominus E_i)$.

Suppose now that an ill-known duration d_i is described by means of a possibility distribution μ_{D_i}, then we are interested in being sure that the fuzzy time window problem has a solution. If the operation starts at e_i, its ending time is fuzzy and $e_i \oplus D_i$ (again fuzzy arithmetic), with $\mu_{e_i \oplus D_i}(f_i - e_i), \forall f_i$. What is thus requested is that all possible values of the ending time be in the core of F_i, i.e., we must compute the necessity of fuzzy event

$$N(F_i) = \inf_{f_i} \max(1 - \mu_{e_i \oplus D_i}(f_i), \mu_{F_i}(f_i))$$

Similarly, we can compute the certainty that the problem is feasible as:

$$N(F_i \ominus E_i) = \inf_{d_i} \max(1 - \mu_{D_i}(d_i), \mu_{F_i \ominus E_i}(d_i))$$

Note that we would not solve the problem in the same way if the fuzzy duration expressed flexibility (e.g., possibility of tuning) rather than uncertainty. A flexible constraint is simply added to the other ones. The degree of satisfaction of an operation starting at e_i and of duration d_i is

$$\mu_i(e_i, d_i) = \min(\mu_{E_i}(e_i), \mu_{F_i}(e_i + d_i), \mu_{D_i}(d_i))$$

and the degree of satisfaction of an operation starting at e_i is

$$\mu_i(e_i) = \max_{d_i} \min(\mu_{E_i}(e_i), \mu_{F_i}(e_i + d_i), \mu_{D_i}(d_i)) = \min(\mu_{E_i}(e_i), \mu_{F_i \ominus D_i}(e_i))$$

where $F_i \ominus E_i$ is the fuzzy set starting time obtained from a fuzzy ending time and a fuzzy duration. Note that to reach this level of satisfaction in reality, the tuning of the machine must be chosen such that the processing time d_i verifies $\mu_{D_i}(d_i) = \mu_i(e_i)$. Similarly, the degree of feasibility of the problem is now $\sup_{e_i, d_i} \mu(e_i, d_i) = \Pi(F_i \ominus E_i)$ computed for possibility distribution μ_{D_i}. This is in total contrast with the case in which d_i is of random duration. If d_i is random, this parameter is not controllable, and the satisfaction levels $P(F_i \ominus E_i)$ and $N(F_i \ominus E_i)$ are motivated by the attempt to get a robust feasibility of schedule, facing hazardous events. On the contrary, if d_i is a decision variable, hence controllable, it is enough that there exists a solution (e_i, d_i) to satisfy the constraints and hence the feasibility assessment in terms of possibility.

Monitoring Systems with Fuzzy Petri Nets

Role of the Supervisory Control

The supervisory control operates in real time. It needs a detailed representation of the resource and part states. It is responsible for controlling the execution of the schedule and detecting any abnormal behavior of the shop floor. Petri nets are useful to describe in detail the resource allocation policies and the required manufacturing routes for the parts (5, 13). They can be seen as a way of describing a collection of sequential constraints, and the token player is an algorithm that can compute, in real time, a trajectory satisfying those constraints (4, 14).

The requirements of the supervisory control are twofold and contradictory: it must be strict to avoid any fault propagation but it must also be tolerant of human intervention to avoid floods of alarms in such situations. A Petri net description of a shop floor allows systematic strict supervision; each event corresponding to normal behavior must be associated with an enabled transition. On the other hand, an event corresponding to a transition that cannot be fired in the current marking will activate an alarm. However, when the event is known to have a possible human origin, it is better to try to correctly update the shop state rather than produce alarms.

Instead of having a sharp delimitation between the events that are normal and those that are abnormal, it is sometimes useful to have a class of acceptable events. For example, let us consider in a manufacturing shop an automated guided vehicle blocked between two contacts (positions where the controller can detect it and send commands to it). After a human intervention where the controller can detect it and send commands to it). After a human intervention supposed to solve the trouble (either by restarting the vehicle or by dragging it to the maintenance station), the normal event is the arrival at the next contact, the forbidden ones are the arrival at any other contact, but an acceptable event is the arrival at the maintenance station.

Another case in which it is necessary to have the notion of acceptable operations, which differs from that of normal ones and of forbidden ones, concerns the control of manufacturing schedules. In case of schedule violation, to recompute a new schedule, it is necessary to know if the incident results from a progressive drift (shift) or a machine failure. In the first case, a trace of all the decisions that have been at the margin of a schedule violation (acceptable decision) is required. As a matter of fact, a progressive drift results from a bad (optimistic) evaluation of effective operation durations and rescheduling must be done with updated durations. In the first case (introduction of acceptable events), the notion of a fuzzy token location is useful. In the second case, we must introduce time explicitly and, therefore, must associate fuzzy dates with transition firings. These two points will be detailed below.

Firing Transitions in a Petri Net with Fuzzy Markings

We have defined imprecise markings for a Petri net, now we are going to show how, each time an event occurs, a new marking can be computed. Classically, events are taken into account in a Petri net model by firing transitions. An imprecise marking is a way of describing a set of all the possible markings at a given time, knowing that the actual state of the system corresponds to one and only one of these markings. This derives from the fact that with each token, the fuzzy set of all its possible locations (places) is associated. The marking computation procedures executed after each event must be consistent with this point of view.

Let us first consider the simplest case: the occurrence of a precisely known event involving objects (tokens) whose locations are precisely known. This corresponds to the classic firing of a transition. It is the case of a normal operation of the system. Considering Figure 47.8, transition t_c may be fired in the traditional sense (classic firing) with tokens $y1$ and $x2$, because their location is well known (the fuzzy sets of places are crisp sets, i.e., sets containing a unique element).

Let us now consider the case where the event is a deduction rather than the reception of a message. The actual state of the system may have changed or not and we want to take these two alternatives in consideration simultaneously. The corresponding transition will not be fired but rather "pseudo-fired" by adding the tokens in its output places without removing them from the input places. In doing so, imprecision is augmented in such a way that the new imprecise marking covers the possible former states and the possible new one. Let us assume that in Figure 47.8 the location of the token $x1$ is only place $P1$ (and not yet $P2$ as in the figure). If we deduce that the event denoted by tb has possibly occurred (e.g., because the date of its normal occurrence has passed), then we pseudo-fire tb. This pseudo-firing results in the marking represented in the Figure 47.8. The fact that the location of $x1$ is $P1$ or $P2$ reflects the fact that we do not know if the event associated with transition tb has occurred or not.

The last case concerns precisely known events corresponding to transitions that are enabled by tokens whose localization is not precisely known. Before firing the transition (normal firing), a new computation of the possibility distribution of these tokens is required to reach a precise location.

Let us assume that the Petri net in Figure 47.8 corresponds to the representation of the current state of manufacturing in the memory of the computer in charge of the supervisory control. The normal date for the operation termination associated by place $P1$ has occurred but, as no message has been received, we do not know if transition tb must be fired or not. In this state we can receive two acceptable events involving $x1$: the one associated with transition tb (late termination of the operation) and the one associated with transition tc (indeed, the message corresponding to the end of the operation has been lost). We know that these events are acceptable but not normal, because they correspond to transitions enabled by tokens whose location is not certain (not a unique place). If we choose to fire tb, we must first restore a consistent precise location for $x1$: $\{P1\}$. In a nutshell, we must find a consistent firing sequence leading from the last well known marking to a marking enabling the transition that needs to be fired. It is a way of performing detection, diagnosis, and recovery.

Making the Time Explicit

As stated above, imprecision must be increased when a possible state change is deduced and decreased when a message is received from the actual system. Generally, the reasoning about possible state changes is based on temporal considerations such as after the normal duration of

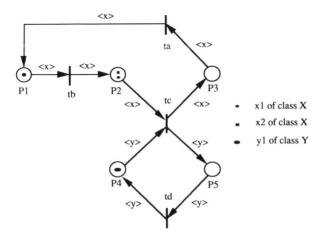

Figure 47.8. Firing transitions.

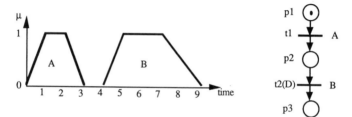

Figure 47.9. Fuzzy time Petri net.

the operation, the event "end-of-operation" occurs. The aim of this section is to introduce explicitly time at the level of the Petri net as a framework for handling fuzzy marking computation.

Various approaches allow introducing explicit timing considerations in a Petri net model. A timed Petri net is obtained by assigning a firing duration to each transition. Its semantic is a notion of delay during which the tokens used for firing a transition are not available or visible in any place. When a token becomes visible in a place, it can be used for firing immediately any of its output transitions. In contrast, a time Petri net is obtained by assigning to each transition an enabling duration. Firing is instantaneous, but the transition must remain enabled during a given duration. In this approach, tokens are always available and can be used to fire transitions at any time. This second approach is more powerful because watchdogs are easily represented. We shall now consider a time Petri net with fuzzy enabling durations attached to the transitions.

Let us consider the Petri net in Figure 47.9. Transition $t1$ must be fired on the occurrence of the event a, which is delimited by the fuzzy set A. We assume that $A = (0, 1, 2\ 3)$, i.e., the possibility is 1 for the time points of interval [1, 2]. We assume that the enabling duration of transition $t2$ is the fuzzy value $D = (4, 4, 5, 6)$. As there are no other input places for transition $t2$, it will be fired at date b delimited by $B = A + D = (4, 5, 7, 9)$, as represented in Figure 47.9. Before date a, i.e., during the interval $[-\infty, A]$, place $p1$ is the location of the token. After a but before b (interval $[A, B]$) the token is in $p2$. After b (interval $[B, +\infty]$) the token is in $p3$. This corresponds to Figure 47.10. It can be noted that at some time points (during the supports of A and B), the location of the token is fuzzy. The token is simultaneously in place $p1$ and $p2$ during [0, 3] and simultaneously in $p2$ and $p3$ during [4,9].

It is well known that a rigid schedule cannot be respected in a flexible manufacturing system. In fact, incidents and unforeseen events occur frequently. A solution is to permit some flexibility to make real-time decisions that are consistent with the schedule, e.g., instead of allocating a precise date for the beginning of the operations, we may use an imprecise date. This is the case when the interval defined by the earliest starting time and the due date is greater than the duration of the operation. A drawback of this approach is that when the current time becomes greater than the latest starting time (due date minus operation duration), the system suddenly goes into an abnormal state and rescheduling is required. No aid is provided by the monitoring module for a diagnosis.

If we choose to associate a fuzzy date with the beginning of the operation and if the current time belongs to the core (membership equal to 1), it is a normal operation, whereas a fault occurs when the current time is greater than the fuzzy date. In Figure 47.11, the time points of domain 1 are rejected because they are too early (the operation must wait). In domain 2, it is acceptable to initiate the operation but it is not completely normal. In a way, this means that

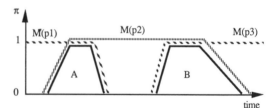

Figure 47.10. Fuzzy marking resulting from the fuzzy enabling duration.

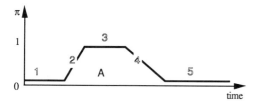

Figure 47.11. Monitoring the events with respect to fuzzy provisional dates.

schedule is pessimistic (the shop floor is more efficient that was forseen). In domain 3, the behavior is normal. In domain 4, the date for the beginning of the operation is acceptable but it is very tight. The product is late and will be delivered just at the last limit of the due date. If eventually there is a timeliness violation, it will result from a shift rather from a disruption. In domain 5, we have a violation of the timeliness constraints and we must reschedule.

Once the machining operation has begun, it corresponds now to a precise, well-known date. Generally, machining durations are relatively well known. However some factors as the degree of use of the tools may have some influence. In chemical industry the duration of the chemical reactions are especially ill-known. Consequently, the result of the computation of the end-of-operation date is typically a fuzzy date. In this case, it also is useful to have the notions of normal, abnormal, and acceptable dates. An acceptable date signifies that the evaluation of the operation duration was not very good. Once more, this information can be fed back to the scheduling and planning levels.

47.4 APPLICATION OF FUZZY SYSTEMS IN CONTROL

Fuzzy Controllers

Principles and Architecture

Fuzzy logic controllers have encountered an extraordinary success in a great variety of industrial applications during the last few years, especially in Japan. The principle of fuzzy controllers, first outlined by Zadeh in 1973 and then successfully defined by Mamdani and Assilian in 1975, consists in synthesizing a control law for a system from fuzzy rules, usually provided by experts, that state typical situations, in contrast with the standard approach to automatic control that requires a model of the system to control. Each rule more or less applies to a fuzzy class of situations, and an interpolation mechanism is performed between the conclusion parts of these rules that are applied, on the basis of the degrees of compatibility, between the condition parts of these rules and the current situation encountered by the system. Surveys are available (15–18). The general architecture of a fuzzy logic controller is shown in Figure 47.12.

Fuzzification, Set of Fuzzy Rules, Defuzzification

The fuzzy rules applied to the inference engine are defined from the human expertise in a qualitative way. These rules have the following form:

IF ⟨fuzzy conditions on input variables⟩ THEN ⟨fuzzy control actions⟩

Let us consider, as an example, a fuzzy controller whose inputs are E for the error and ΔE for the error variation and whose output is CO (control). A fuzzy rule could be

IF ⟨E is PS⟩ AND ⟨ΔE is PB⟩ THEN ⟨CO is NM⟩

Figure 47.12. General architecture of fuzzy logic controller.

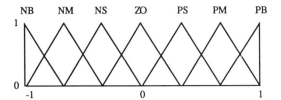

Figure 47.13.   Fuzzy sets of possible values for input variables.

Possible values of input variables are represented by fuzzy sets defined by membership functions; Figure 47.13 shows typical examples. The fuzzification consists in the determination of the grade of membership to fuzzy sets for input variables to quantifying fuzzy conditions. The combination of fuzzy conditions (the AND operation) is determined by the minimum between membership functions of the element of each proposition to the concerned fuzzy set.

When fuzzy conditions of all rules have been quantified, fuzzy conclusions can be calculated. Generally, several conclusions can be activated; we obtain a fuzzy set of possible values for the control. But outputs must be determined in only one way. As a consequence, we must choose a plausible value for each output. It is the function of the defuzzification module to calculate the effective control from all the rules' conclusions. Different methods are used for defuzzification, among which are the center of gravity of the fuzzy set of possible values, the maximum value appearing in the rules' conclusions, and the mean of maxima values of each conclusion.

Difficult issues are the formalization of human expertise into a set of ''representative'' rules and the choice of the best defuzzification method for the encountered situation. The principal problem of this kind of controller resides in the parameter tuning, which, unlike in standard automatic control, is not often a priori determined. So this approach is more suitable for control systems that are impossible or difficult to model mathematically and, therefore, are controlled by expert human operators in the present situation.

Application Domains

The number of existing applications is large, notably in Japan, in various industrial or research domains.

> *Robotics.* Applications include motion planning of mobile robots (distances are taken into consideration as fuzzy sets), obstacle avoidance of mobile robots, articulated hand (object type—heavy, slippery, etc.—and force are defined in terms of fuzzy sets), and pattern recognition.
>
> *Vocal Recognition.* Applications include linguistic control of a model car (instructions such as turn left, move about 1 m, and move a bit) and vocal recognition regardless speaker.
>
> *Control of Complex Systems.* Applications include an array of elevators (users waiting time limitation), water purification process (water turbidity ill-defined and hard to measure), automatic train operation system (stop location accuracy, security, and comfort), automatic container crane operation system for ships (wind, freight weight, and tides are difficult to model), cement kilns, chemical production plant, automobile traffic regulation, and air-conditioning units.
>
> *Consumers.* Applications include electrical appliances, cameras, and video.

Fuzzy controller chips are now commercially available. They are based on fuzzy microprocessors or high-speed fuzzy controller hardware system. In addition, simulation tools for fuzzy controllers are available to aid designers.

Fuzzy Programmable Logic Controllers

Programmable logic controllers (PLC) are widely used for real-time control of industrial processes. They are well-suited for discrete control because they are able directly to implement the control sequences specified by means of standard languages such as Grafcet or formal models such as Petri nets. However, they are inadequate even in the case of simple regulation problems. Only Boolean inputs and outputs are handled, and it is impossible to generate outputs that are continuously varying in relation to the controlled system state.

Moreover, it is impossible to specify the control in a qualitative way such as "if the automated guided vehicle is near the contact, then stop it gently" and "if the value of sensor C is changing then slow down." The development of fuzzy controllers has shown the practical interest of qualitative specification of control strategies to obtain a friendly human interface (security is increased). These considerations have led to the development of fuzzy PLCs that take into account a notion of compromise and allow one to implement linear interpolation between characteristic situations represented by rules (19). The theoretical basis of this work is a combination of Petri nets and possibilitic theory.

Petri Nets with Fuzzy Markings

In the ordinary, safe Petri nets used for modeling applications that are implementable by means of PLCs, places are Boolean conditions (or local partial internal states) that can be associated with actions (commands to the actuators). Transitions correspond to instantaneous events to which instantaneous actions (pulses) can be attached. A place can be empty (the corresponding condition is false) or can contain at most one token (the condition is true). When all the input places of a transition contain a token, the transition is said to be enabled, which means that the corresponding event (typically described by a Boolean expression involving sensor values) may be taken into account. The occurrence of an event instantaneously results in the firing of the corresponding enabled transition; the tokens contained in the input places are removed, and the content of the output place (which was supposedly empty) is set to 1. The net marking (a list of the places containing a token) is a representation of the current controller state. Let us remember that the major advantage of using Petri nets for the specification of discrete control is that they allow both formal analysis for validation and direct implementation by means of a token player.

Fuzzy Markings

Ordinary Petri nets, used in the context of PLCs for specifying the desired control sequences, are safe, i.e., they are such that a place cannot contain more than one token. Moreover, it is typically required that this property should result from the structure of the net. This means that the net is covered by a set of linear P-invariants (subset of places) whose global token load is invariant and equal to 1. Consequently, for a structurally safe Petri net, it is possible to define the marking by associating each elementary invariant with the name of its place, whose token load is different from 0. This association must be consistent (a place cannot be simultaneously marked for an invariant and empty for another one). Doing so, it is possible to extend this definition to imprecise or fuzzy markings. For a well-known marking, the token location for each invariant is a singleton (a unique place), and for a fuzzy marking, the token location for each invariant is a fuzzy set of places. This fuzzy set is disjunctive (there is only one token in the invariant), and it can be interpreted as the characterization of a possibility distribution defining for each place its degree of possibility of being the token location.

A fuzzy marking of a structurally safe, ordinary Petri net is a consistent mapping that associates a fuzzy subset of places with each elementary linear P invariant. This subset S_k represents the possible location of the token in a set of places P within the invariant k. The location of the token is defined by the possibility distribution $\pi_{1k}(p)$ of the token location k in the set of places P. A fuzzy marking represents a graded current state of a controller. Actually, it is an aggregate description of two (or more) possible states. In the case of PLCs, it is a way of describing a fine-grained state within a continuous evolution from one coarse-grained state (an ordinary marking) to another one. As for ordinary PLCs, the marking trajectories must be synchronous with the controlled system ones (the role of the token player is to ensure that). Therefore, a fuzzy marking is a function of time.

Fuzzy Interpreted Model

In ordinary Petri nets, a transition t is enabled by a marking M, if $\forall p \in P$, $M(p) \geq \text{Pre}(p, t)$, and a transition may be fired when it is enabled by the marking and its associated condition is true. In fuzzy interpreted Petri nets, the condition represents the fuzzy value with which the

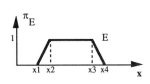

Figure 47.14. Possibility distribution π_E attached to transition t.

output of the sensor is compared. Given a sensor value x (characterized by a singleton in the simplest case), the membership function of the fuzzy set characterizing the condition can be interpreted as the possibility degree $\pi(x)$ specifying the extent to which the condition is true for the sensor values x (Figure 47.14). We will name this condition *fuzzy condition*. In fuzzy Petri nets, a transition is said to be enabled when the marking of the input place is positive, i.e., when the token location possibility in this place is positive. In a case of several places (they must belong to different p-invariants and thus their possibility degrees are independent), the transition is enabled when the minimum of the token location possibility for each place is positive. This is defined by:

$$\Pi_t = \min\{\pi_{1k}(p1), \ldots \pi_{1k}(p_i)\} > 0$$

Before firing a transition, we must first check that is is enabled ($\Pi_t > 0$), then we must verify that given the current value x of the sensor, its associated condition is possibly true ($\pi_E(x) > 0$ (x belongs to the support of E)). Firing this transition is no longer an instantaneous event in a fuzzy Petri net. Indeed, the process of removing the tokens from the input places and putting tokens into the output places is progressive; it is done in a gradual manner.

If we consider the evolution of the sensor values as a function of time (Figure 47.15a), it is possible to define a fuzzy event as a fuzzy date for which the condition holds (Figure 47.15b). Indeed, a fuzzy event is similar to a fuzzy date as defined by Dubois and Prade (20). It is defined by a possibility distribution π_E attached to the transition t and delimited by the fuzzy set of possible time points for the firing of the transition. Note that this distribution can only be defined a posteriori and that the axis x is oriented (it is assumed that the values x of the sensor are increasing as a function of the time between an initial value x_1 and a final value x_4). Knowing the token location possibility $\pi_{1k}(p1)$ at time point τ-$\delta\tau$ and the possibility $\pi_E(x)$ at time point τ, we can calculate the token location possibility at time point τ. To do this, we need the notions of "possibly before the condition" and "possibly after the condition."

Let use consider the following fuzzy condition "the sensor value x is about a." The fuzzy set $[-\infty, E]$ describes sensor values that are possibly "before about a" (Figure 47.16a). This defines the membership function of the value x to this fuzzy interval, at a given time point τ (x_τ is the value of x at time point τ):

$$\tau \in T, \ \mu_{[-\infty, E]}(x_\tau) = \sup_{x \geq x_\tau} \pi_E(x)$$

The fuzzy set $[E, +\infty]$ describes sensor values that are possibly after "x is about a" (Figure 47.16b). This defines the membership function of value x to this fuzzy interval at given time point τ:

$$\tau \in T, \ \mu_{[E,+\infty)}(x_\tau) = \sup_{x \leq x_\tau} \pi_E(x)$$

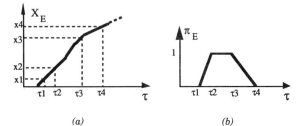

Figure 47.15. (*a*) Evolution of sensor value. (*b*) Fuzzy date or event.

(*a*)   (*b*)

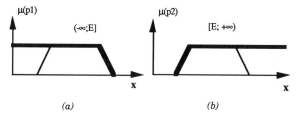

Figure 47.16. Membership functions of sensor values possibly (*a*) before and (*b*) after the event.

The token location possibility for the output place of *t* is increasing from 0 to 1, according to the increasing values of the token location possibility in the input place and to the truth value of the condition. This first step of the firing process terminates when these possibility degrees are all 1, i.e., the condition is totally possibly true and the token location is totally possibly the input place as well as the output place of *t*. At this point of the firing process, we are at the same time "totally possibly before the condition" as well as "totally possibly after the condition." During this step, the marking of the input place *p*1 is not modified by the firing of *t* (it is just the beginning of the firing), and that of the output place *p*2—at current time point τ—is defined by (it corresponds to the possibility degree of the answer to the question Are we after the event?):

$$\pi_{1k}(p2, \tau) = \sup_{x \le x_\tau} \min\{\tau_{1k}(p1, \tau), \pi_E(x)\}$$

During the second step of the transition firing process, the token location possibility of the output place *p*2 is no longer modified (it can now only be decreased by the firing of an output transition of this place) and that of input place *p*1 decreases from 1 to 0, according to the decreasing possibility π_E. This step terminates when the condition attached to the transition is false ($\pi_E = 0$) and the transition *t* is no longer enabled ($\pi_{1k}(p1) = 0$ for input place *p*1). The marking of the input place *p*1, at current time point τ, is defined by (it corresponds to the possibility degree of the answer to the question Are we still before the event?):

$$\pi_{1k}(p1, \tau) = \sup_{x \ge x_\tau} \min\{\pi_{1k}(p1, \tau - \delta\tau), \pi_E(x)\}$$

Fuzzy Programmable Logic Controller Architecture

The general architecture of fuzzy PLCs is roughly the same as that of fuzzy controllers (Figure 47.17). Indeed, the token player can be seen as a kind of inference engine. However, two types of rules are involved. The first one corresponds to the set of transitions. From the sensor values and the state (the marking) at the current time, they allow one to deduce the state at the next time. Note that the state is specified by a collection of fuzzy variables (the fuzzy token locations in the various *p*-invariants). Actions that are commands to the actuators are associated with each place. As a consequence, the fuzzy outputs are directly derived from the fuzzy markings and are sent to the defuzzification block. The sequential nature of these fuzzy programmable logic controllers derives from this notion of state. The next state, and thus the output, depends not only on the inputs (sensor values) but also on the preceding state. This strongly differs from traditional fuzzy controllers. Given a current state, only a subset of the transitions is enabled and can initiate or continue its firing processes. In a way, fuzzy PLCs can be seen as fuzzy controllers whose sets of rules vary with time.

Fuzzification. Fuzzification consists in computing the possibility degree of the query Does the current sensor value verifies the condition? In simple cases, the sensor value is a well-known, precise value and fuzzification depends only on the shape of the fuzzy set specifying the condition. This shape is the parameter that allows the designer to tune the way the PLC passes

Figure 47.17. General architecture of fuzzy PLC.

softly from one state to another one. A variant of this technique is to specify the condition by a singleton and to implement the fuzzy event by means of a linear interpolation in time. The first case corresponds to expressions such as "fire the transition when the value of the sensor is about 10." The second case corresponds to "when the value of the sensor is equal to 10 softly fire the transition." *Softly* is defined by a temporization (e.g., 10 s) delimiting the support of the firing date and during which it can be said that it is possible that the transition has not yet been fired and that the transition has already been fired.

Another case corresponds to an ill-known sensor value. In this case, fuzzification derives from this uncertainty. Because the event (the sensor value takes the value defined by the condition) with which the firing of the transition must synchronize is ill-known, the two alternatives (before the event and after it) must be temporarily considered together in the controller.

Fuzzy Token Player. A fuzzy token player works on a safe Petri net with fuzzy markings. From the marking of places, the token player determines enabled transitions. It checks if enabled transitions can be fired, i.e., if the possibility degrees (resulting from the fuzzification) of their attached conditions are different from 0. If it is the case, the transitions are placed on the list of the transitions in the process of firing (they will remain on this list until they have been completely fired).

The markings of input and output places are updated, i.e., the possibility degree of the token locations are recalculated. If a transition becomes enabled during the same cycle, it is examined. The cycle terminates when there are no more enabled transitions to be fired. This is called the stable state. It must be pointed out that the operation cycle of this token player must be repeated for each pulse of the timer, because the evolution of the fuzzy marking is continuous, unlike that of an ordinary marking, which is discrete.

The marking of the places changes in the following way (see the formulas defined above): when the possibility degree of the condition attached to a transition increases from 0 to 1, the token location possibility in the output places takes the same value; the places become possible locations for the tokens. When the possibility degree of the condition decreases from 1 to 0, the possibility distribution of the input places take the same value. This means that the input places are progressively no longer possible locations for the token. In the case of transitions that are in conflict, the first transition to start its firing process reserves the tokens. These tokens are no longer available for firing the other transitions, which, consequently, can no longer be fired. At the end of the token player cycle (stable state), the actions associated with places that are possible locations for the tokens are the set of possible outputs.

Defuzzification. Each output corresponds to a subset of places of a *p*-invariant. Defuzzification is the determination of the value to apply to each output, according to the token location possibility into the places with which this output is associated. We calculate the center of gravity of the actions associated with each place containing a token, weighted by the possibility degree of the token location.

PLC Operation Principles. The fuzzy PLC operates in a synchronous way. At each cycle, activated by a timer, it reads input values, generates outputs calculated at the previous

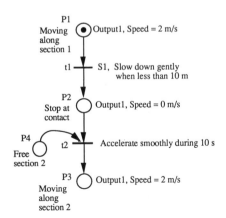

Figure 47.18. Petri net of vehicle control.

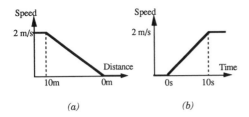

Figure 47.19. Evolution rules attached to transitions. (*a*) Transition *t*1. (*b*) Transition *t*2.

cycle after their defuzzification, and executes the fuzzy token player. The cycle stops when the fuzzy token player reaches the stable state.

Example

Let us now consider a simple illustrative example of an automatic guided vehicle. This vehicle follows automatically some circuits. To avoid collision, circuits are decomposed into sections, and the vehicle must be controlled in such a manner that at a given time each section can contain only one vehicle. These sections are delimited by contracts. The vehicle has a sensor whose value is the distance to the next contact (at the section end). When the vehicle is at a distance of less than 10 m, it slows down gently to stop at the contact if the next section is not free. It starts smoothly again, when this section becomes free. If the section becomes free while the vehicle is slowing down, it does not stop. The partial Petri net in Figure 47.18 describes the control of this vehicle.

"Slow down gently when less than 10 m," attached to transition *t*1, indicates how the "Output1" value changes gently from a speed of 2 m/s to 0 m/s (Figure 47.19a). The distance to the contact is given by sensor *S*1. "Accelerate smoothly during 10 s," attached to transition *t*2 indicates how the same output passes smoothly from the speed of 0 m/s to 2 m/s (Figure 47.19b). It is a temporization activated only when section 2 is free. The fuzzy conditions associated with transitions *t*1 and *t*2 are determined automatically.

Figure 47.20 shows the fuzzy conditions deduced from the evolution rule. The core of the fuzzy set corresponds to the mid-value of the two stable-state output values. The whole form of the membership functions are tuned to obtain a linear interpolation in the case of a "defuzzification" policy based on the center of gravity.

At each cycle, to generate Output1 the fuzzy PLC calculates the center of gravity among places *P*1, *P*2, and *P*3. The value of the output at a given time is

$$\text{Output1} = \frac{O(P1) \cdot \pi_{1k}(P1) + O(P2) \cdot \pi_{1k}(P2) + O(P3) \cdot \pi_{1k}(P3)}{\pi_{1k}(P1) + \pi_{1k}(P2) + \pi_{1k}(P3)}$$

where $O(Pi)$ is the value of the output for the place Pi. and $\pi_{1k}(Pi)$ is the token location possibility for place Pi at a given time. If we assume that section 2 becomes free 5 s after the vehicle stops, Output1 evolves as shown in Figure 47.21a. If section 2 becomes free while the vehicle slows down (for example 3 m before the contact), the evolution of the output evolves as shown in Figure 47.21b. In this case the vehicle does not stop.

47.5 CONCLUSIONS

We have seen some examples of the application of fuzzy sets and fuzzy logic in the field of manufacturing systems and factory automation. Based on possibility or necessity degrees it is

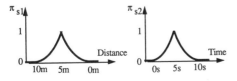

Figure 47.20. Fuzzy conditions.

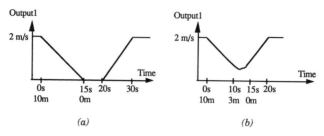

Figure 47.21. Output evolution (*a*) with stop at contact and (*b*) without stop at contact.

possible to build rich computer-aided decision-making processes that are precisely adapted to solve specific problems. For instance, we have seen that scheduling may take into consideration ill-known operation durations and work with necessity degrees (feasibility) or, and it is different, take into consideration the fact that duration is flexible and work with possibility degrees to aid the decision maker in selecting a good duration for a good schedule. Fuzzy sets also are useful for real-time monitoring and diagnosis. Combined with Petri nets it is possible to introduce a notion of fuzzy state within a formal description of the sequential constraints and resource allocation mechanisms that are important at this level. We have seen that doing so allows the design of monitoring systems that are tolerant to human intervention in case of unexpected events in the manufacturing system. Finally, at the lowest control level, fuzzy sets, through the principle of interpolation between characteristic situations, allow gradual commands and the introduction of an elementary continuous regulation in discrete controllers.

Today, fuzzy sets and fuzzy logic are largely used in industry (mainly in Japan). In factory automation, we see the beginnings of their application. On the contrary, Petri nets are commonly used in factory automation for performance evaluation and for real-time control. Research combining these two theories is currently under development and will be applied in the next years. This new approach will help automated systems become more friendly and obtain a better and more intelligent balance between the roles of the computer and the human decision maker in manufacturing systems.

BIBLIOGRAPHY

1. L.A. ZADEH, "Fuzzy Sets," *Informat. Control* **8**, 338–353 (1965).

2. D. DUBOIS and H. PRADE, *Possibility Theory—An Approach to Computerized Processing of Incertainty,* Plenum Press, New York, 1988.

3. J. CARDOSO, R. VALETTE, and D. DUBOIS, "Petri Nets with Uncertain Markings" in *Advances in Petri Nets 1990, Lecture Notes in Computer Sciences,* Vol. 483, Springer-Verlag, New York, 1991, pp. 64–78.

4. R. VALETTE, J. CARDOSO, and D. DUBOIS, *Monitoring Manufacturing Systems by Means of Petri Nets with Imprecise Markings,* paper presented at the IEEE International Symposium on Intelligent Control 1989, Albany, N.Y., Sept. 1989.

5. M. SILVA and R. VALETTE, "Petri Nets and Flexible Manufacturing" in *Advances in Petri Nets 1989, Lecture Notes in Computer Science,* vol. 424, Springer-Verlag, New York 1990, pp. 374–417.

6. S.M. CHEN, J.S. KE, and J.F. CHANG, "Knowledge Representation Using Petri Nets," *IEEE Trans. Knowledge Data Eng.* **2**(3), 311–319 (1990).

7. C.G. LOONEY, "Fuzzy Petri Nets for Rule-based Decision Making," *IEEE Trans. Sys. Man Cybernet.* **4**(1), 178–183 (1988).

8. D. DUBOIS, J. LANG, and H. PRADE, *Theorem Proving Under Uncertainty—A Possibility Theory-based Approach,* paper presented of the 10th International Conference on Artificial Intelligence, Milan, Aug. 1987.

9. S.F. SMITH, "Knowledge-based Production Management: Approaches, Results and Prospects," *Product. Planning Control* **3**(4) 350–380 (1992).

10. R.E. BELLMAN and L.A. ZADEH, "Decision Making in a Fuzzy Environment," *Manage. Sci.* **17,** 141–164 (1970).

11. D. DUBOIS, H. FARGIER, and H. PRADE, *Propagation and Satisfaction of Flexible Constraints,* UPS, Toulouse, France, IRIT Report No. 92-59-R, Nov. 1992.

12. D. DUBOIS, *Fuzzy Knowledge in an Artificial Intelligence System for Job-shop Scheduling, Applications of Fuzzy Set Methodology in Industrial Engineering,* Elsevier Science Publishing Co., New York, 1989, 73–79.

13. N. KOMODA, K. KERA, and T. KUBO, "An Autonomous, Decentralized Control System for Factory Automation," *Computer,* 73–84 (Dec. 1984).

14. R. VALETTE and M. COURVOISIER, *Petri Nets and Artificial Intelligence,* paper presented at the International Workshop on Emerging Technologies for Factory Automation, North Queensland, Australia, Aug. 1992.

15. E.H. MAMDANI, "Application of Fuzzy Logic to Approximate Reasoning Using Linguistic Systems," *IEEE Trans. Comput.* **26,** 1182–1191 (1977).

16. M. SUGENO, "An Introduction Survey of Fuzzy Control." *Informat Sci.* **36,** 59–83 (1985).

17. C.C. LEE, "Fuzzy Logic in Control Systems: Fuzzy Logic Controller—Parts 1 and 2," *IEEE Trans. Sys. Man Cybernet.* **20**(2), 404–435 (1990).

18. H.R. BERENJI, "Fuzzy Logic Controllers" in R.R. YAGER and L.A. ZADEH, eds., *An Introduction to Fuzzy Logic Applications in Intelligent Systems,* Kluwer Academic Publishers, 1991.

19. J.C. PASCAL, R. VALETTE, and D. ANDREU, "Fuzzy Sequential Control Based on Petri Nets" in R. ZURAWSKI and T.S. DILLON, eds., *Proceedings of the IEEE International Workshop on Emerging Technologies for Factory Automation,* CRL Publishing, Ltd. London, 1992, pp. 140–145.

20. D. DUBOIS and H. PRADE, "Processing Fuzzy Temporal Knowledge," *IEEE Trans. Sys. Man Cybernet.,* **9**(4), 729–744 (1989).

GLOSSARY

Fuzzy set. For an ordinary set, given an element, it is or it is not a member of the set. A fuzzy set F is defined by a membership function $\mu_F(w)$ of the elements $w \in W$ (reference set) that are compatible with the concept of F (the higher the value of $\mu_F(w)$, the more the element is compatible with the concept of F).

Membership function. A membership function $\mu_F(W)$ is defined on the reference set W and takes its values as $[0, 1]$. By means of this function, a fuzzy set defines intermediate membership degrees between 0 and 1 to elements that are not typical of the set but that can still be in the set. Value 0 denotes that the element is not at all a member of the set (complete falseness), and value 1 means the element is definitely a member of the set (complete truth). Values within $[0, 1]$ denote intermediate membership.

Possibility distribution. Let us consider a reference set W and a fuzzy set F defined on this set and specifying a fuzzy value f, then $\pi_f(w) = \mu_F(w)$ is the possibility distribution characterized by F and $\pi_f(w)$ defines the possibility degree that w is the value of f, $w \in W$.

Petri nets. An ordinary Petri net is a digraph with nodes that may be places (drawn as circles) or transitions (drawn as rectangles). Edges can connect places to transitions or transitions to places. A Petri net can be marked by indicating the tokens (drawn as dots) that are contained in each place at a time point. If the input places of a transition all contain at least one token, the transition is said to be enabled, i.e., it is eligible for firing. If it does fire, then one token is removed from each of its input places and one token is added to each of its output places.

CHAPTER 48

Reverse Engineering and Rapid Prototyping

BOPAYA BIDANDA, VIVEK NARAYANAN and RICHARD BILLO
University of Pittsburgh

48.1. INTRODUCTION

The task of manufacturing a new product usually begins at the designer's desk where an idea is transformed into a design for a physical model. Although in several industries computer-aided designs are generated at this preliminary stage itself, this is often not feasible in other cases. Therefore, a prototype of the product is first built, and its performance is verified through rigorous testing. Once this design is approved, the detailed physical characteristics of the product must be extracted to facilitate its redesign or manufacture.

Reverse engineering is the first step in this process. It can broadly be defined as the creation of the (typically computer based) model of a product from an existing product. With the availability of inexpensive computing power, computer-aided systems for reverse engineering have been shown to shorten the product design and manufacturing life cycle of products by more than 40% (1). There are several different methods by which this is achieved. These can be classified into contact and noncontact methods. Early sections of this chapter describe the various reverse engineering methods that fall into these two broad categories.

Rapid prototyping is the next step in the process. The need for a prototype part is based on the need for designers and engineers to visualize a real-life part. This has traditionally been a time-consuming process that spans many complex operations. Several methods such as stereolithography, selective laser sintering and three-dimensional (3D) printing have been developed to reduce the lead time for this fabrication stage. These techniques will be covered in the later sections. Figure 48.1 details these steps.

48.2 REVERSE ENGINEERING TECHNIQUES*

Methodology of Reverse Engineering

The process methodology for reverse engineering is shown in Figure 48.2. The product is first conceptualized by the designer based on the functional and aesthetic requirements specified to him or her. Next, a physical model or mock-up (using a soft material such as wood or plaster of paris) is made and refined until it meets all the specifications. During this process, changes made to the physical model are usually so numerous and complex that corresponding engineering changes to the original drawing becomes an intricate, time-consuming, and ultimately unwieldy task. This necessitates the application of reverse engineering methods to generate an accurate drawing.

The objective of any reverse engineering technology is to generate a 3D mapping of the product in the form of a computer-aided design (CAD) file. To do this, the x, y, and z coordinates of multiple points on the product surface must first be acquired. These coordinates can then be used further to develop the drawing of the product for redesign or manufacture. Computer-aided design–computer-aided manufacturing (CAD–CAM) packages that generate ma-

---

* This section has been adapted from ref. 2.

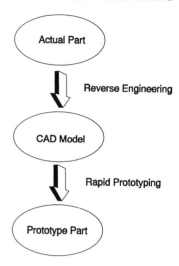

Figure 48.1. Reverse engineering and rapid proto-typing.

chining paths for the appropriate machine tools and output a file containing the necessary G-codes are already available and do not present a significant problem in the reverse engineering process.

There are several different methods by which product surface data can be acquired. This chapter presents an evaluation of some available technologies. As previously stated, the methods by which the geometry information of the component can be extracted can be classified into two broad categories: contact and noncontact methods. An overview of this classification is shown in Figure 48.3.

Noncontact methods use light as the main tool in extracting the required information. The principal techniques that are presently available include the use of structured lighting and spot ranging. These techniques are still in an evolutionary stage. Contact methods for generating the part design, however, have been in use for several years. All these methods require contact between the component surface and a measuring tool that is usually a probe or stylus. The following sections detail the existing and emerging reverse engineering contact technologies.

Contact Methods

Manual Measurements

Manual measurements were the only existing techniques until approximately 30 yr ago to convert a physical model to a drawing. This method is still in use in some small factories across the world. Here, the evolution of a CAD drawing comprises the following steps. Many key points (at least 1000 for a typical product) are identified on the product surface, and their x, y, and z coordinates are manually measured from a reference point. These points are entered into a CAD system. Curves and surfaces that interpolate these points are then generated. In this way,

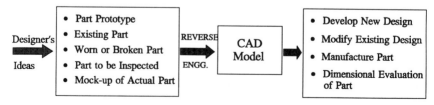

Figure 48.2. Reverse engineering methodology.

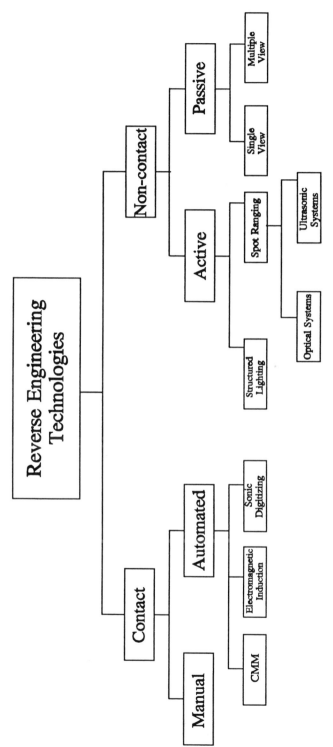

Figure 48.3. Classification of reverse engineering techniques.

a 3D CAD model of the product is created. The tools that are frequently used include calipers, measuring gauges, and blocks.

The obvious disadvantage of this method is the large number of labor-hours it requires, not only for data extraction but also for data entry. Furthermore, the accuracy of the method depends on the precision and accuracy of the calipers, gauges, and other measuring instruments. Accuracy also is reduced due to the fewer number of points measured compared with more automated mechanisms for data collection.

Coordinate Measuring Machines

Coordinate measuring machines (CMMs) that could inspect a 3D part first appeared in the early 1960s. Since then, they have advanced significantly in terms of speed and accuracy of measurement as well as in the available peripheral equipment. They have now become an integral part of the inspection system of many companies. A recent survey (3) indicates that about 42% of all large-size corporations and 37% of medium-size companies use CMMs. CMMs are the most popular tool used to implement reverse engineering techniques.

A CMM is a three-dimensional measuring device that uses a contact probe to detect the surface of the object. The probe is generally a highly sensitive pressure-sensing device that is triggered by any contact with a surface. The linear distances moved along the three axes are recorded, thus providing the x, y, and z coordinates of the point. CMMs are classified as either vertical or horizontal, according to the orientation of the probe with respect to the measuring table.

Two relevant issues here are the probe configuration and the fixture design. Different types of probes are available to suit the specific requirements of the component. For complex surfaces, motor-driven probes can be used to follow the contours of the surface in an automated manner. The configuration of the fixture that holds the part during measurement is important, because it determines the accessibility of the surface.

The part to be measured is placed on the measuring table, and the coordinates of a number of points on the surface of the object are then read. These points are input into "a geometry data" file, which can be transferred to a CAD system to generate the drawing of the part. In this way, the shape of the object is captured in the form of a CAD drawing that can be manipulated and modified as needed.

Verifying the accuracy of the created model is easy with the CMM. The CAD model can be used to drive the CMM to the required locations and the deviations can be recorded. Software packages that provide a user interface to perform this task are available (4). After performing an initial surface fitting to the collected points, the accuracy of this model is verified. If necessary, more points from the "out-of-tolerance" areas can be collected to perfect the model iteratively. An outline of such a system is shown in Figure 48.4.

Electromagnetic Digitizing

The use of electromagnetic transducers to digitize a 3D object is a recent development. The 3SPACE digitizer (McDonnell Douglas) is a commercially available device that uses this technology (5). Figure 48.5 shows a schematic diagram of this digitizing system. The product to be digitized is placed on a model table. This table encloses the electronic equipment and a magnetic field source, which creates a magnetic field in the volume of space above the table. A hand-held stylus is used to trace the surface of the part. This stylus houses a magnetic field sensor that, in conjunction with the electronics unit, detects the position and orientation of the stylus. The data can be transmitted to a host personal computer via an RS-232C serial port. The system has the capability to transmit either individual datum points or to send a stream of points that can be detected by continuous sampling at a rate up to 60 points per second. Such high sampling rates allow even complex curved surfaces to be accurately digitized.

The main advantage of this system is that it costs much less than a CMM while still being sufficient to meet the reverse engineering needs. However, only nonmetallic objects can be measured using this technology. Furthermore, making corrections to the model by collecting additional datum points is difficult. Therefore, iterative perfection of the model is not facilitated as with the CMM technology.

Sonic Digitizing

A sonic digitizer uses sound waves to calculate the position of a point relative to a reference point. This technology has been implemented by the 3D sonic digitizer model GP-8-3D (Science

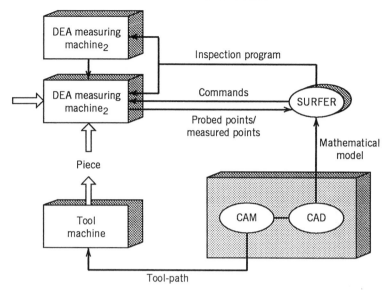

Figure 48.4. Schematic of a digitizing system using CMMs (SURFER) (4). Courtesy of Digital Electronic Automation.

Accessories Corp.) (7). The object is placed in front of a vertical rectangular board on the corners of which are mounted four microphone sensors. A free, hand-held stylus is used to trace the contours of the object. When a foot or hand switch is pressed, the stylus emits an ultrasonic impulse, and, simultaneously, four clocks are activated. When the impulse is detected by the microphone, the corresponding clock is stopped and the times taken to reach each of the four microphones is recorded. These time recordings, called slant ranges, are processed by the host computer to calculate the x, y, and z coordinates of the point.

There are several advantages of this method: (*1*) it has a larger active volume than the electromagnetic method, (*2*) any substance (including ferrous materials) can be digitized, and (*3*) it is reasonably insensitive to background noise, and therefore, it can be used in less controlled environments. A disadvantage of sonic digitizing is that it is difficult to get a set of points on a continuous basis; therefore, contour tracking is more difficult.

Noncontact Methods

The noncontact reverse engineering technologies for creating a CAD model of an existing part can be classified into two broad groups: active and passive. Active methods require the use of a

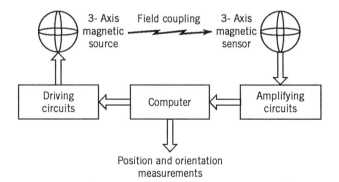

Figure 48.5. Schematic of an electromagnetic digitizer (3SPACE) (6). Courtesy of IEEE.

specialized light or sound source, whereas passive techniques work with just the ambient light. Active techniques can be divided into two main categories: structured lighting and spot ranging. These technologies are described below.

Structured Lighting

Structured lighting can be further classified based on the pattern of light that is used to illuminate the part. The various light patterns that are used include a single light beam, a single stripe of light, multiple stripes of light, and patterned lighting such as grid-coded illumination and moire topography.

Projection of Single Light Beam. The general methodology of the single light beam is to reflect a laser beam off the part and detect the position of the reflected beam using a sensor, such as a camera. The part's image on the camera reveals the 2D coordinates of the surface point. Because this point is located at the intersection of the line of the light source and the line of the camera axis, triangulation procedures are used to calculate the depth of the point (8). In this way, the entire part surface can be digitized by sweeping the light source over the surface. This is sometimes achieved by using a computer-controlled rotating mirror system (9).

Projection of Single Light Stripe. The process of data acquisition can be speeded by collecting information about an array of points on the surface. This is done by spreading the laser beam, using a cylindrical lens, into a vertical light stripe. Triangulation is done to find the depth information for several points on the stripe. One of the earliest systems using this method consisted of a slit projector that was mounted on a rotary table, a television camera, and a computer (10). Boeing Co. developed a system to manufacture tiles for the space shuttle. The sides and bottom of the tile cavity were scanned to retrieve the geometry information, which was used by an NC postprocessor to generate the NC part program (11). A recent system also incorporates a CAD interface to generate the CAD drawing of the part automatically (12).

Projection of Multiple Light Stripes. To further speed the data collection process, multiple stripes of light can be reflected off the surface of the part. This is one of the methods that is being studied for real-time data acquisition for robot vision. One of the problems with this method is the difficulty in determining the correspondence between the incident light stripes and their reflected images. The high processing requirements may thus offset the advantage of increased speed.

Patterned Lighting. For patterned lighting, the workpiece surface is illuminated with different light patterns. The two techniques of grid-coded illumination and moire topography fall in this category. In grid-coded illumination, different masks are used to create various patterns of light. The part is successively illuminated with the different light patterns, and surface information is retrieved from the resulting images. The advantage of this method is that the entire surface is not scanned, as in other methods, thus reducing the processing time. The accuracy of this method depends on the width of the light bands that comprise the patterns—the thinner the bands, the greater the accuracy.

Moire topography involves the illumination of the surface with patterns of light that are obtained by passing the light through an optical grating. When the surface is viewed through an identical grating, the resulting fringe patterns are analyzed to retrieve the contour information. Analysis can be done by comparing the fringe pattern with that for a plane surface, and finding the deviations using some digitizing method. The grating period can be adjusted to increase the sensitivity of this method to reverse engineer complex surfaces.

Spot Ranging

There are two broad classes of spot ranging methods, based on the source used. These are optical-based methods and ultrasonic methods. Both methods involve the projection of a beam onto the object surface and the inspection of the reflected beam using a sensor that is placed coaxial to the source. The location of the source gives the x and y coordinates of the surface point, while analysis of the reflected beam gives the range of the point.

In optical methods, the reflected beam can be analyzed in two different ways. The first method is to calculate the phase difference between the incident and reflected light, thus revealing the range of the surface point. In the second method, the time taken for the light to reflect back from the surface is recorded. The time of flight thus gives the z-coordinate of the point. Accuracies are generally higher for the phase difference technique due to limitations on the sensitivity of the timing devices. The entire surface of the part is raster scanned to generate the complete 3D image. An advantage of this method is that the coaxiality of the source and receiver eliminates the problem of missing points. However, almost all optical systems are relatively expensive.

Ultrasound methods involve the generation of ultrasound pulses that are reflected off the surface of the part and detected by a sensor. The time of flight is used to find the range of the surface point. The accuracies of these systems are typically less than those for the optical systems, because it is difficult to generate narrow beams of sound.

There are three passive noncontact techniques: range from texture, range from focus, and stereo scanning.

Range from Texture

The principle of the range from texture is the known fact that the farther one goes away from an object, the smoother its surface texture appears to be. Therefore, if the texture of an object is known, its distance from the viewpoint can be estimated by inspecting the perceived texture. However, limitations in accuracy have precluded its use for reverse engineering.

Range from Focus

The range from focus technique uses the fact that when an object is viewed through a lens, the distance of the resulting image from the lens depends on the focal length of the lens and the distance of the object from the lens. This can be used to find the range of the points on the surface of a part. However, these systems have not been used for reverse engineering due to their limited accuracy.

Stereo Scanning

For stereo scanning, two images of the object are captured by viewing from two different points. Then the corresponding surface points on the two images are identified. A triangulation procedure is used to find the range of the point. The difficulty of this method lies in the identification of the matching image pixels that correspond to the same point on the object. Most available algorithms are computationally intensive and time-consuming (13). However, it is felt that with the continuing decrease in computing costs, this method may be viable in the near future.

48.3 RAPID PART FABRICATION TECHNIQUES

Stereolithography

Stereolithography literally translates to the creation of three-dimensional patterns. In practice, it is used to refer to the creation of 3D plastic models from CAD models of the part. The most common technique prevalent today is the use of a laser beam to solidify selectively a photocurable polymer liquid. With one pass of the laser beam, one layer of the part is created. Successive passes build on the previous layers, thus building the part layer by layer. The description of the process given here is based on the stereolithography apparatus (SLA) (3D Systems, Inc.) (14).

The SLA (shown in Figure 48.6) consists of a vat containing the photocurable resin, an x-y scannable ultraviolet laser beam (usually helium–cadmium or argon ion type), and an elevator that moves the support structure in the z direction. The support structure is the base on which the part will be supported while it is built. Design of this support structure needs to take into consideration the orientation of the part, overhang features, ensuring safe part removal, etc.

The process begins with the elevator and support structure positioned near the surface of the liquid. The laser beam scans the liquid surface in the x-y direction, solidifying the polymer along its path. To determine the path of the laser beam, the CAD model of the object is processed to create cross-sectional slices of the part in the x-y plane. The path is then defined by the boundary of this cross-section. To reduce the fabrication time, the entire interior of the cross-section is not scanned. Instead, a weblike structure is created that traps uncured polymer in its spaces. After the completion of each layer, the elevator is lowered by a predefined step, and the

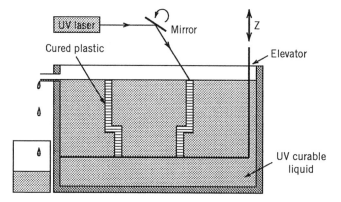

Figure 48.6. Stereolithography apparatus (14). Courtesy of Manufacturing Review.

next layer is created in the same way. The object is thus built in a bottom to top fashion. Upon completing the building process, the part then undergoes a postcuring operation, where it is completely solidified under ultraviolet light.

Various factors determine the efficiency of the stereolithography process. The orientation of the part dictates the build time as well as surface quality. In addition, the surface quality is determined by the choice of layer thicknesses. These can be varied depending on the shape complexity of the part for optimal surface quality. The depth of curage for each layer is determined by the intensity of the laser beam as well as the choice of polymer. Also, it may be necessary to do some postprocessing, such as grinding, to improve the finish of the cured parts.

Selective Laser Sintering

Selective laser sintering (SLS) was one of the pioneering techniques developed to fabricate quickly a prototype of a part (15, 16). The process is based on the principle of using an infrared laser beam to fuse selectively a powdered thermoplastic material into a 3D object. A schematic of this process is shown in Figure 48.7.

The main components of such a system include a computer, a laser scanning system and a sintering chamber. The powder is fed onto the work surface (or build region), located in the

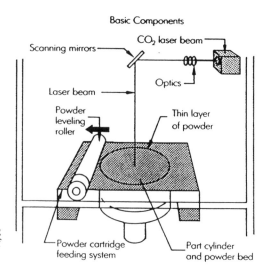

Figure 48.7. Selective laser sintering system (16). Courtesy of the Society of Manufacturing Engineers.

sintering chamber, and spread evenly using a roller mechanism. The sintering chamber is purged with an inert gas, usually nitrogen, and heated to raise the powder temperature to near its fusing/melting point. The benefits of this purging process include avoiding powder fires or explosions, saving laser energy needed to be expended to fuse the powder, reducing part distortion by decreasing the thermal shrinkage of the layers, and minimizing oxygen contamination of the sintered surfaces.

Scanning mirrors are used to laser-scan the powder along a precalculated path, fusing the powder along its path. The path of the laser beam is calculated from a CAD model of the part, in a manner similar to that used in stereolithography. The cross-sectional area of the part is usually covered in a raster fashion, using several densely packed parallel lines. Because the unsintered powder remains in place, this can be used to support possible overhangs in the product. This simplifies the part-building process because, unlike liquid-based techniques such as stereolithography, supports need not be fabricated with the part. Once the final layer has been scanned, the excess powder is removed, and the part is allowed to cool. However, usually a layer of powder is allowed to remain on the part to avoid rapid cooling and subsequent part distortions. Finally, the part undergoes a thorough cleansing process to remove all the powder. This is accomplished using various brushes and pneumatic tools.

Some of the main advantages of this process include wide range of materials, no need for support structures, and nonhazardous and easy-to-handle materials. One of the drawbacks of this process is the poor surface finish. This is a consequence of both the stairstep effect of the layering process and the use of powdered material. The sintered part also is quite porous, although the extent of the porosity depends on the material used. Whereas crystalline materials melt on fusing to form solid objects, amorphous powders can result in highly porous parts that may have significantly less strength than solid parts.

Materials on which successful tests have been done include metal-coated ceramics, PVC, polycarbonate, and investment casting wax. Some success has also been reported with metals such as cobalt, titanium, and iron–nickel alloys. Thus the range of materials that can be used to fabricate parts is large compared with stereolithography, which is limited to photopolymers. Current research is being directed toward selection of the appropriate materials and associated fabrication procedures.

Three-dimensional Printing

Three-dimensional printing (3DP) is another method to produce 3D prototypes using a powder deposition process (17). The powdered material is deposited in layers using a feeder that traverses the work surface along one axis. The peculiarity of this process is that the required areas that need to be solidified are treated with a binder, in a manner similar to that used in ink-jet printing. Once the complete part is built layer by layer, the part is heated in a furnace to cure the binder and strengthen the part. The unbound powder is then removed using ultrasonic cleaning methods.

Various design factors must be considered for the development of such a 3D printing system. The resolution of the process is determined primarily by the size of the powder and the droplet size. At present, it is expected that powders in the micron range and jet sizes of 15 μm would be feasible. The ink-jet printing process can be of two types: drop-on-demand printing and continuous jet printing. The continuous jet printing system has the advantage of higher printing speeds, whereas the drop-on-demand systems are potentially more flexible. It also is hypothesized that using a colloidal dispersion of the particles in liquid vehicle instead of using dry powder could increase the packing density and thus improve the microstructure of the green body.

This method has been tested for the fabrication of ceramic parts, mainly molds used in metal casting. Success also has reported with the fabrication of 3D metal parts. A feature of this process that is different from other rapid prototyping processes is that there is no state change during the build process. Thus the shrinkage problems are minimal and over the entire part geometry during curing, eliminating thermal distortion effects. However, inadequate surface finish of the parts may be a problem that needs to be rectified through more research and material selection.

Laminated Object Manufacturing

Laminated object manufacturing (LOM) creates a part by successively gluing together layers of foils that have been cut to the desired shape (18). The description that follows is based on the process used by Helisys, Inc. (16). The apparatus consists of a platform that supports and moves the fabricated part in the vertical direction, a feeder that supplies the sheet material, and a laser that cuts the part's cross-sectional contours. A heated roller also is used to provide the pressure and temperature necessary to glue together the successive layers. A typical setup is shown in Figure 48.8. The areas of the sheet that do not lie within the part contour are usually cut by the laser into small tiles that are removed later. Thus the part is built up within a solid block of surrounding material. Once all the layers have been completed, the extraneous material is removed by breaking away the tiles.

Various gluing mechanisms can be considered. The basic method consists of precoating the entire foil with glue. However, this results in added difficulty in removing the tiles once the part is built. Selective gluing of the part's cross-section can be achieved by precoating the entire foil with a heat sensitive glue. The relevant areas that fall within the part's cross-section are then scanned by the laser to activate the glue. However, this results in a large increase in fabrication time and energy expended.

Some of the limitations of this process are as follows. The difficulty in removing the excess material restricts the range of parts that can be manufactured using this process. Parts that contain hollow features within an enclosed surface cannot be fabricated in this manner. Also, it is difficult to include features such as blind holes and narrow passages for this reason. The process results in the production of large quantities of scrap material, which could be a concern in the case of more expensive materials. Because the part is built from alternating layers of material and adhesive, properties such as shear strength may be higher in a direction perpendicular to the layers and less in other directions.

This method, however, also offers several advantages. A major one is its potential for high accuracy. The parts can be fabricated from thin layers, depending on the required resolution. Part distortion caused by shrinkage is not of concern here. Furthermore, a large variety of materials can be used for this process, ranging from paper to plastics and metals. Because the process entails cutting only a contour of the part for each layer, it is potentially the fastest method for fabricating large parts. As a result, this technology is expected to compete in the manufacturing of large, heavy parts and castings.

Fused Deposition Modeling

Fused deposition modeling (FDM) is intuitively the most straightforward of the various technologies described here. The parts are created by directly depositing molten material in a layerlike fashion. The following description is based on the process used by Stratasys, Inc. (16). The apparatus consists of a delivery head with an associated material supply system, a platform on which the part is built, and an x-y traversing mechanism that positions the FDM head. A typical

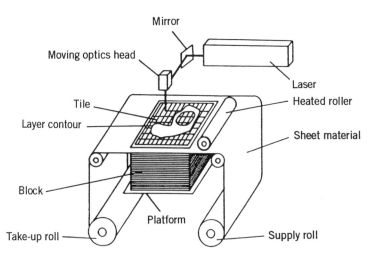

Figure 48.8. Laminated object manufacturing system (17). Courtesy of ASME.

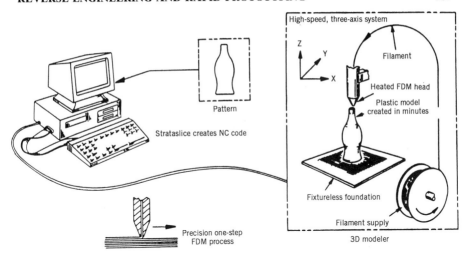

Figure 48.9. Fused deposition modeling system (16). Courtesy of the Society of Manufacturing Engineers.

setup is illustrated in Figure 48.9. The material is in the form of wirelike filaments. The filament is melted in the heated FDM head and the semiliquid material is extruded through the head using a precision volumetric pump. The molten material heats the previous layer, fuses with it and quickly solidifies. The layer thickness can be varied by adjusting the speed of the traversing mechanism.

Various factors contribute to the efficiency of this process. The temperature of the FDM head and part affects the fusion between layers and thus the integrity of the part. The accuracy of the process depends on the positioning accuracy of the traversing mechanism over the working envelope as well as on the physical properties of the molten material. The head needs to move uniformly without intermediate stops to prevent surface undulations. Support structures need to be incorporated to produce flat surfaces. These structures are cut away upon completion of the part.

Advantages of this process include the absence of waste material and reduction in fabrication time, as there is no need for postprocessing. However, the surface finish capability of this process is inferior to other rapid prototyping methods. Thus it is expected that this technique could provide the basis for a viable desktop concept modeling machine (19).

48.4 MANUFACTURING APPLICATIONS

Reverse Engineering*

There are many instances in which one-of-a-kind parts such as prototypes or custom-built parts need to be reproduced. Moreover, the design of the existing manufactured parts may require periodic modifications to update and improve. CAD models of these parts are often not available. However, the creation of a CAD model is desirable and often necessary under the following circumstances (Figure 48.10) (12)

1. *New Design.* The design process of a new product does not always start from a CAD model. A prototype is often built first. Once the design is approved, measurements are made (either manually or with the use of a contact probe). The extracted data are then manually entered into a CAE system for further analysis. This process has two disadvantages: it is time-consuming and a potential source of measurement errors.

---

* This section is based on ref. 20.

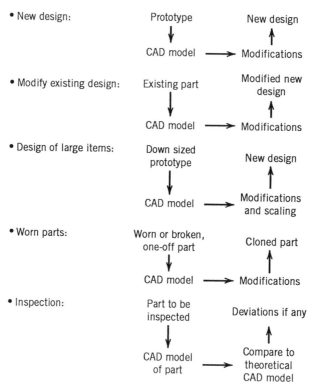

Figure 48.10. Reverse engineering applications in manufacturing (16). Courtesy of the Society of Manufacturing Engineers.

2. *Modify Existing Design.* In some instances the design of an existing product must be modified. The modification process and design improvements are best performed on a CAD model. However, CAD models for many existing products are not available. Part image reconstruction systems can play an important role in reducing design time.

3. *Design of Large Items.* Precise measurements of large parts are often not possible with traditional metrological equipment. Reverse engineering-based part image reconstruction systems can help by mapping the part surface in the form of CAD model. This CAD model can now be scaled and modified as needed.

4. *Worn or Broken Parts.* When a one-off part breaks or is worn, and the engineering drawing is no longer available, part image reconstruction systems can be used to create the CAD model. The CAD model can now be used to manufacture the clone of the worn or broken part.

5. *Industrial Inspection.* When a part is compared with its existing CAD model, a reverse engineering system can acquire the actual map of the part surface, and deviations, if any, can be identified.

Rapid Prototyping

The rapid prototyping techniques described above can dramatically reduce the lead time needed to complete design and place a newly designed product on the production line. Applications in design and manufacturing include the following (Figure 48.11).

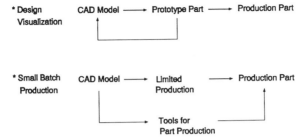

Figure 48.11. Rapid prototyping applications in manufacturing (20). Courtesy of *International Journal of Computer Integrated Manufacturing*.

Design Visualization

The CAD model of a part often provides insufficient visualization detail as part complexity increases. Thus, even after designing a part, the designer may find it difficult to verify the dimensions and tolerance of the part. For example, an automobile engine block developed by Chrysler was approved by a team of designers and engineers. When the block was prototyped using stereolithography, it was found that a flange was incorrectly located (16). Prototyping a part allows designers to validate the geometry of a part. Because the lead time for the prototyping is now greatly reduced, designers have the luxury of being allowed multiple iterations of a design to ensure that it is right.

Production of Tools for Small Batch Part Production

Newer rapid prototyping techniques now allow engineers to develop functional prototypes of parts, and these techniques can even be used for limited production runs. These techniques also can be used to produce master patterns from which dies and molds can be produced. For example, Chrysler has used stereolithography to create patterns for injection molds for throttle body injection bonnets, center consoles, instrument panel components, and interior trim panels (16).

48.5 CONCLUSIONS

In this chapter, recent advances in reverse engineering and rapid prototyping as applicable to manufacturing systems were reviewed. These included developments in industry as well as research issues. Together, reverse engineering and rapid prototyping are increasingly being viewed as viable tools to increase a company's competitiveness in the global marketplace. Research and development in reverse engineering and rapid prototyping are growing because of the promise of substantial improvements in a product's cycle time, quality, and cost. The use of these techniques serves to reduce greatly the time between product design and redesign and production. In addition, they hold great promise in meeting increasingly stringent product tolerance requirements through their ability to measure dimensions more accurately and in a greater quantity than what was previously afforded. All of these advantages contribute to an overall lower product cost. The next few years will see these technologies increasingly being used in design and manufacturing departments at manufacturing facilities.

BIBLIOGRAPHY

1. G.S. VASILASH, "Defining the Unknown Part," *Production*, **101**(2), 57–59 (Feb. 1989).
2. "Reverse Engineering and Its Relevance to Industrial Engineering: A Critical Overview," *Comput. Ind. Eng.*, in press.

3. R.K. MILLER and T.C. WALKER, *Survey on Coordinate Measuring Machines,* Future Technology Surveys, Inc., Madison, Ga., 1989.

4. *SURFER Product Information,* Digital Electronic Automation, Inc., Livonia, Mich., 1990.

5. *3Space Digitizer Product Information,* Polhemus Navigational Sciences Division, McDonnell Douglas Electronics Co., Colchester, VT 1988.

6. *IEEE Transactions on Aerospace and Electronic Systems,* IEEE, New York, Vol AES-15, no. 5, p. 709.

7. *GP-8-3D Sonic Digitizer Product Information,* Science Accessories Corp.

8. S. MOTAVALLI and B. BIDANDA, "Reverse Engineering Using Structured Lighting" in *Proceedings of the Fourth International Conference on CAD/CAM Robotics and Factories of the Future, New Delhi, India,* Springer-Verlag, New York, pp. 47–56.

9. F. ROCKER and A. KIESSLING, "Methods for Analyzing Three-Dimensional Scenes" in *Proceedings of the Fourth International Joint Conference on Artificial Intelligence.* Tbilisi, Georgia, USSR, 1975, pp. 669–673.

10. Y. SHIRAI and M. SUMA, "Recognition of Polyhedrons with a Range Finder" in *Proceedings of the Second International Joint Conference on Artificial Intelligence,* British Computer Society London, 1971, pp. 80–87.

11. T.E. BEELER, "Producing Space Shuttle Tiles with a 3D Non-contact Measurement System" in T. Kanade, ed., *Three Dimensional Machine Vision,* Kluver, Boston, Mass., 1987, pp. 513–542.

12. S. MOTAVALLI and B. BIDANDA, "A Part Image Reconstruction System for Reverse Engineering of Design Modifications," *J. Manufact. Sys.* 5(10) 383 to 395 (1991).

13. Y. SHIRAI, *Three Dimensional Computer Vision,* Springer-Verlag, 383–395 London, 1987.

14. L.E. WEISS et al., "A Rapid Tool Manufacturing System Based on Stereolithography and Thermal Spraying," *Manufact. Rev.* 3(1) 40–47 (1990).

15. D.P. COLLEY, "Instant Prototypes," *Mech. Eng.,* 110(7), 68–70 (July 1988).

16. P.F. JACOBS, *Rapid Prototyping and Manufacturing,* Society of Manufacturing Engineers, Dearborn, Mich., 1992.

17. E. SACHS et al., "Three-Dimensional Printing: Rapid Tooling and Prototypes Directly from a CAD Model" in *Advances in Manufacturing Systems Engineering Proceedings of the ASME Winter Annual Meeting,* ASME, New York, PED series, Vol. 37, 1989, pp. 143–141.

18. J.P. KRUTH, "Material Incress Manufacturing by Rapid Prototyping Techniques," *Ann. CIRP* 40(2), 603–614 (1991).

19. E.E. SPROW, "Rapid Prototyping: Beyond the Wet Look," *Manufact. Eng.,* 109(5), 58–64 (Nov. 1992).

20. B. BIDANDA, S. MOTAVALLI, and K. HARDING, "Reverse Engineering: An Evaluation of Prospective Non-contact Technologies and Applications in Manufacturing Systems," *Int. J. Computer Integrated Manufact.* 4(3), 145–156 (1991).

SECTION XI
STANDARDS

CHAPTER 49

Standards and Prenorms in Design, Manufacturing and Automation

F. B. Vernadat
INRIA (France)

49.1. INTRODUCTION

Computer-integrated manufacturing (CIM) cannot be achieved without the help of standards. Furthermore, standards are the key to building a reliable partnership between the customers and suppliers. Standards are, therefore, essential for interenterprise as well as intraenterprise integration. This chapter reviews a number of standards, on-going standardization work and reference architectures relevant to CIM. The objective is not to be exhaustive but to discuss the most important areas concerned with standardization with respect to automated manufacturing. After a discussion on the needs for standards and reference architectures in CIM, the impact of standards and prenorms on physical systems integration, application integration, and finally business or enterprise integration are considered.

49.2 THE NEED FOR STANDARDS AND REFERENCE ARCHITECTURES IN CIM

To increase their productivity, to face rapidly changing market conditions, to improve product design, and to increase product quality for better customer satisfaction, many companies are considering implementing CIM principles. CIM can be defined as the rational use of information technology (IT) to support production management (including product design and engineering, process planning, numerical control (NC) programming, production planning and control, and quality control) and factory automation to favor communication, cooperation, and coordination of the many heterogeneous functions and components of a manufacturing enterprise to increase organization and personnel productivity and efficiency.

Integration of computer-aided design (CAD), computer-aided process planning (CAPP), and computer-aided manufacturing (CAM) is the first step toward CIM. Products can then be designed on graphics stations and their geometry stored in engineering databases. Geometric data can then be used for finite element modeling, stress analysis, and performance evaluation of the products. Then product data can be passed to CAPP in the engineering office to produce process plans for the parts (i.e., sequences of operations for machining or assembly tasks) and to generate (sometimes automatically) NC programs. NC programs can then be electronically transported to NC machines on the shop floor for actual manufacturing of parts. Systems on the shop floor (such as NC machines, robots, material handling systems (MHSs), loading–unloading stations, inspection stations, etc.) must also be able to communicate with one another or with their control system. The next step is to include manufacturing resource planning (MRP II) packages in the CIM system to provide functions such as order entry and processing, production planning, scheduling, production control, and production monitoring. One major difficulty relies in getting timely and accurate feedback data on the actual status of the production system to feed the planning system. Connections with customers, suppliers, and banks can also be electronically supported. Finally, total quality management (TQM) policies can be further added when all components are fully integrated. In most cases, all this must happen in highly distributed environments.

Obviously, CIM assumes efficient computer support of vertical and horizontal flows of information across the enterprise and between humans and heterogeneous, multivendor applications, machines, and computer systems. However, progressive introduction of CIM is in many cases made difficult by the use of conflicting proprietary computing systems, creating unnecessary costs as well as technical barriers to the task of data and systems integration. One answer to this problem is to use industry standards where they exist or to develop new ones where they are missing to make systems, data, and communications compatible. However, one may argue that in some cases, dependence on standards can become a blocking factor; structured query language (SQL) is, to some extent, becoming an example due to rapid database technology evolution and the use of multimedia data. There are even areas for which standards are not recommended (e.g., internal data structures of CAD systems) to preserve competitive advantages. There are also areas that are not mature enough for standardization. In these cases, reference architectures or reference models can be used instead of standards.

Reference architectures are general models or frameworks from which particular architectures can be derived, built, and/or compared. They are not prescriptive but provide implementation guidelines. They can be used as a baseline to develop new systems (e.g., information systems, software applications, integrated infrastructures, and modeling frameworks). Examples are ISO-OSI and the ENV 40 003 discussed below.

49.3 STANDARDS ORGANIZATIONS FOR INDUSTRIAL AUTOMATION

Standardization organizations dealing with standards for industrial automation and related fields include but are not limited to:

The International Organization for Standardization (ISO) and the International Electrotechnical Commission (IEC) at the international level. Within ISO, technical committee TC 184 is devoted to industrial automation systems and integration. It is structured into the following subcommittees (SC), and each SC is in turn divided into working groups (WG):
   SC1: physical device control.
   SC2: robotics for manufacturing environments.
   SC3: not active.
   SC4: industrial data and global manufacturing programming languages.
   SC5: architecture and communication.
The American National Standards Institute (ANSI) in the United States.
Comité Européen de Normalisation/Comité Européen de Normalisation Electrotechnique (CEN/CENELEC) in Europe. The working group on advanced manufacturing technology AMT/WG-ARC is concerned with architecture definition for CIM and WG-STEP is concerned with product data exchange formats.
AFNOR (France), BSI (UK), CSA (Canada), DIN (Germany), and DS (Denmark) have standards activities related to CIM or are active in working groups of international organizations.

Furthermore, computer-aided acquisition and logistics support (CALS) is a U.S. initiative for interentreprise logistics and support also dealing with standards development in the same area. PDES, Inc., is a company-based organizational entity that supports the development and implementation of the standard for the exchange of product model data (STEP) in the United States.

49.4 LEVELS OF INTEGRATION AND LEVELS OF PRODUCTION

Levels of Integration

Enterprise integration concerns product design functions; manufacturing functions; administrative functions; support functions (intraenterprise integration); and relations of the enterprise to its external environment such as clients, suppliers, subcontractors, and banks (interenterprise integration). Various kinds of enterprise entities need to be integrated. They concern the following (1):

Functions describing the business processes of the enterprise and their activities according to business objectives and constraints.

Information systems providing support to functions in the form of information entities and their relationships stored in database systems and/or data files.

Hardware components and resources representing the physical means of the enterprise to be used and managed to support execution of the functions.

Applications or software packages such as CAD systems, MRP systems, and bill-of-materials processors performing basic operations for some functions.

Organization units describing areas of responsibilities of the enterprise and made of humans, resources, information entities, and functions.

Humans such as designers, planners, operators, controllers, decision makers, and engineers.

Manufacturing integration has been the focus of extensive research and developments over the two last decades. Different forms of integration can be defined, providing different levels of integration (Figure 49.1).

Physical integration concerns the interconnection of physical components of the manufacturing systems by means of computer networks and communication protocols. This area of work has been successful and has resulted in OSI-based developments as such manufacturing automation protocol (MAP), technical and office protocol (TOP), and communications network for manufacturing applications (CNMA). No enterprise model is required. New developments concern multimedia communications networks.

Application integration goes one step further. It concerns interconnection of information-based systems such as CAD systems using STEP and administrative data exchange using electronic data interchange (EDI). Neutral data formats for common shared data, exchange protocols, and application program interfaces are required as well as some form of information technology infrastructure (made of a set of common services). Information models are required.

Business integration concerns full enterprise integration and business process coordination. It needs a good assessment of enterprise operations, rules, and structure in terms of functions, information systems, resources, applications and organization units. An enterprise model (i.e., a knowledge base about the enterprise providing semantic unification of various concepts used) and an integrating infrastructure (i.e., a set of common services based on information technology providing physical and application integration) are both mandatory.

ISO Reference Model for Shop Floor Control

To understand potential areas subject to standards development in manufacturing systems, subcommittee 5 (SC5) of ISO TC 184 has produced a reference model for shop floor production standards (2). The aims of the reference model are to provide a conceptual framework for understanding discrete parts manufacturing and to be used to identify areas of standards necessary to integrate manufacturing systems.

Overview of the Reference Model

The reference model (2) is structured into three submodels:

1. A context for shop floor production, which identifies major functions (finance, sales order system, materials resources planning, engineering/CAD, production, and finished goods storage) of discrete parts manufacturing and major information flows among them.
2. The shop floor production model (SFPM), which represents a four-level hierarchy of generic shop floor production activities.
3. The generic activity model (GAM), which depicts activities and flows (materials, information, and resources) between activities.

The shop floor production model provides an abstract model of the levels of decision to position the collection of activities involved in shop floor production (Table 49.1). It is structured into four levels; each level is associated with a generic type of production management activity and an area of responsibility.

The Generic Activity Model

The purpose of the generic activity model is to describe generically the activities found at each level of the shop floor production model (Figure 49.2). It is sufficiently general to represent any

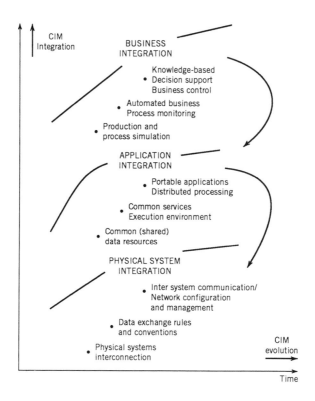

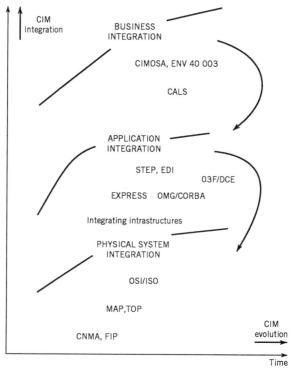

Figure 49.1. Levels of integration.

TABLE 49.1. SFMP

Level	Subactivity	Responsibility
4. Section–area	Supervise shop floor production process	Supervising and coordinating the production, supporting the jobs, and obtaining and allocating resources to the jobs
3. Cell	Coordinate shop floor production process	Sequencing and supervising the jobs at the shop floor production process
2. Station	Command shop floor production process	Directing and coordinating the shop floor production process
1. Equipment	Execute shop floor production process	Executing the job of shop floor production according to commands

shop floor production activity in terms of its inputs and outputs (called subjects) and its function (called action). Subjects can be of three types (materials, information, and resources) and play the role of function input–output, control input–output, and resource input–output (see Figure 49.2). Actions can be of four generic types only: transport, transform, verify, store. Specific activities can be described as instances of this model.

Combining actions, subjects, and levels with the values indicated above gives several matrix representations for identification procedures of standards. Horizontal and vertical interactions between levels of the shop floor production model can be analyzed. For instance, one can investigate interactions such as the following (where words between braces must be instantiated by one of their values):

A1: interactions between {subject} and {action} at {level} level.

A2: interactions between {subject} and {subject} at {level} level.

A3: interactions between {action} and {action} at {level} level.

B1: interactions between {subject} of shop floor production and its manufacturing context.

B2: interactions between {subject} at {level} level and {subject} at the levels above or below.

These procedures have been documented (2) and used to position ISO and International Electrotechnical Commission (IEC) standards.

49.5 STANDARDS FOR SYSTEMS INTEGRATION

Integrating, i.e., interconnecting for the purpose of communication and coordination, computers with NC machines, robots, coordinate measuring machines (CMMs), programmable logic controllers (PLCs), cell controllers, MHSs, vision systems, terminals, and other types of pieces of factory equipment from different vendors in distributed environments requires computer networks for open communication. A computer network is a collection of autonomous nodes connected by physical links or communication media. Each node contains a central processing unit (CPU). Communication media can be twisted copper pairs, coaxial cables,

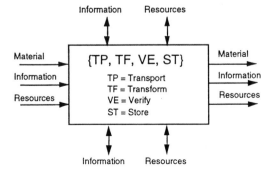

Figure 49.2. GAM (Generic Activity Model).

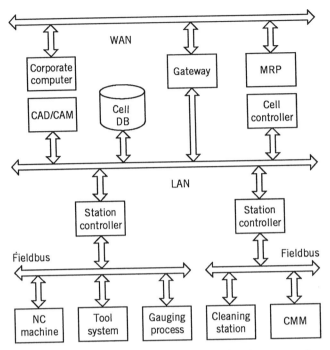

Figure 49.3. Computer network architecture for plant automation.

telephone lines, fiber optics, satellite links, electromagnetic waves, etc. The computer network is the backbone of the CIM system. Depending on the size and distribution of the system, local area networks (LANs) and/or wide area networks (WANs) can be used. WANs are used at the enterprise level to connect plants remotely located. LANs are frequently used on the factory floor (workshop or cell levels). Fieldbus is also a rapidly developing technology used to connect devices at the equipment level for real-time applications. Figure 49.3 illustrates a typical computer network architecture for plant automation. WANs, LANs, and fieldbus support horizontal communication, while vertical communication is provided by gateways, making the connection between two types of networks. Several international initiatives are under way to develop standards for manufacturing integration according to the ISO-OSI basic reference model. Among these are the General Motors MAP and Boeing TOP projects from the United States and the CNMA European initiative supported by the Commission of the European Communities.

ISO-OSI Basic Reference Model

The OSI basic reference model (3) was developed in the late 1970s and finalized in 1982 for open systems interconnection, i.e., for harmonizing communications between computers. This model was jointly developed by ISO and the Consultative Committee on International Telephone and Telegraph (CCITT). The OSI reference model decomposes the problem of reliable application communications into seven layers: application, presentation, session, transport, network, data link, and physical (Table 49.2). Each layer is more abstract than the lower layers, moving from the physical to the application levels. The objective is to isolate an application on one node from physical details concerning transmission and reception of bits on the communication medium (telephone line, coaxial cable, fiber optics, radio waves, etc.) and to make this application communicate with another application on another remote node (Figure 49.4). A message sent by one application from one node goes through the operating system (OS) and then down the seven layers of its node, then through the communication media to the receiving node, then up the seven layers on this node, then through the operating system used on this

TABLE 49.2.   OSI Basic Reference Model

Layer	Description	Proposed Standards
7. Application	Selects appropriate service for application; semantic communication aspects	On-going work; FTAM, MMS, and X400
6. Presentation	Provides code conversion and data reformatting	Usually not used but handled by application
5. Session	Coordinates interaction between remote tasks	For example, semiduplex, symmetric synchronization and resynchronization
4. Transport	Provides for end-to-end control of data transport and integrity	Multiplexing and reordering of packets.
3. Network	Switches and routes information	Packet transmission protocol X25
2. Link	Transfers units of information to other end of physical link	For example, HDLC protocol
1. Physical	Transmits bit stream to communication medium	For example, X25 access by modem

node, and finally reaches the targeted application. To make this process possible, header and/or trailer information is added to the message by the sending node and removed by the receiving node. A brief description of each layer follows. Layer 7, the application layer, provides application programs with the mean to access the OSI environment by managing lower layer services. Layer 6, the presentation layer, restructures data to and from a standardized format used within the network. Layer 5, the session layer, does name and address translation, and access security, and synchronizes and manages data during a communication session. Layer 4, the transport layer, provides transparent, reliable data transfer from end device to end device (message segmentation into ordered data packets). Layer 3, the network layer, establishes connections between units connected on the network and routes messages. Layer 2, the data link layer, establishes, maintains, and releases data links. It also detects errors occurring at the physical layer. Layer 1, the physical layer, encodes and physically transfers messages (series of bits) between adjacent devices on the physical transmission media. Layers 1 to 4 ensure reliable data transmission with error detection and correction. Layers 5 to 7 are concerned with application-oriented dialogue between communicating nodes. Each layer is defined by two kinds of ele-

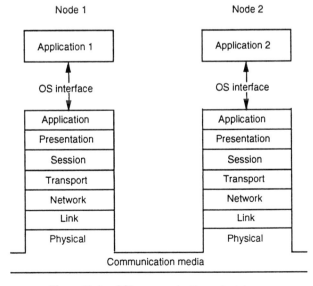

Figure 49.4.   OSI communication principle.

ments: (*1*) a protocol, or set of dialogue rules between communicating entities (horizontal communication), and (*2*) a service, or set of dialogue rules between this layer and the next upper layer for the same entity (vertical communication). Except for the highest layer, each layer (*N*) provides a defined set of services for the next upper layer (*N* + 1). Various standards can be defined and used for each layer, depending on the technology used (LAN or WAN) and the application domain (office automation, manufacturing, electronic mail, etc). This is called a functional profile.

The OSI model is modular and generic. If new technologies are used or new applications or services must be considered, the structure of the entire reference model remains the same. In an OSI model, application-specific elements (ASEs) can be used. An ASE is an integrated set of functions used to realize a task at the application layer. Examples of ASEs are the following application standards:

MMS to meet the needs of manufacturing and factory floor oriented messages (ISO 9506 and EIA 1393A international standard) (4).

File transfer access management (FTAM) to transfer files and to access databases and remote file systems in real time (ISO 8571 international standard, parts 1–4) (5, 6).

Job transfer and manipulation (JTM) to control work submitted to another node in an open system (ISO 8831 and 8832 international standards) (7, 8).

Virtual terminal protocol (VTP) to establish communications between any terminal type and any host system not concerned by the running application (ISO 9040 and 9041 international standards) (9, 10).

Messaging (X400), a set of standards developed by CCITT for message-handling systems (11).

MAP

Manufacturing automation protocol is a seven-layer token-bus–based communications standard initially promoted by General Motors at the beginning of the 1980s. It is now supported by a wide range of major manufacturers all over the world that belong to the MAP User's Group (12). It was defined to eliminate communication barriers to factory automation, i.e., to provide a way for connecting islands of automation and interface programmable devices that cannot communicate with computers on the factory floor (robots, NC machine-tools, coordinate measuring machines, programmable controllers, etc.). Benefits expected from MAP include (13):

The reduction of computer network costs.

Multiple vendor interoperability.

Increased communication capabilities within the factory.

Increased flexibility and performance of the system.

Lower risks during installation and shorter time to install.

Easy maintenance, trouble shooting, and configuration expansion.

MAP complies with the ISO-OSI basic reference model. The current version of MAP is MAP 3.0 Figure 49.5 indicates standards selected at each layer for the full architecture. The data link layer is, in fact, divided into two sublayers as specified in the IEEE 802 standard (also ISO 8802 standard). The upper sublayer is for logical link control (LLC) and the lower sublayer is for medium access control (MAC). A connectionless version is also available for fast exchange of short messages between two application programs or between *N* application programs (multicasting and broadcasting). The best solution can be selected according to specific requirements of the application domain.

MAP is based on the bus topology and uses the token-passing–based access method. The bus structure allows greater flexibility in the network configuration and easily lends itself to configuration expansion; these are desirable features for manufacturing systems. Token passing is a standard access technique to determine which node has access to the network. A node can access the network when it has been given the "token". The token is a logical message that travels from node to node in a predetermined way. Once a node has the token, it can transmit messages as data frames within a limited time scale or until it has no more messages to send. Other nodes can read messages but cannot send messages, because they do not have the token.

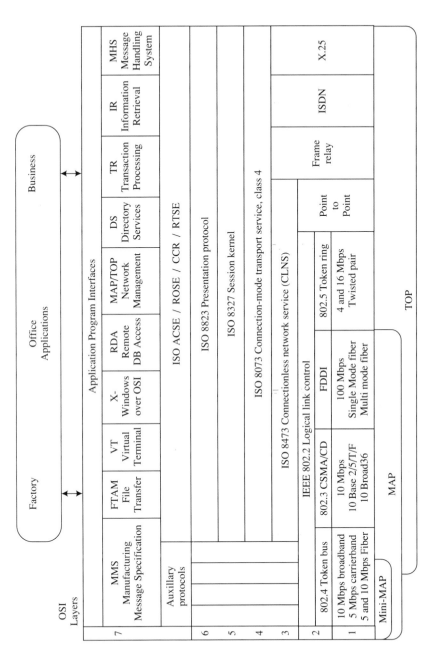

Figure 49.5. MAP/TOP 3.0 Release Architecture (1993).

1001

Once the emitting node has finished transmitting, it passes the token to the next sequential node. This token-based protocol avoids collisions on the network. Furthermore, as the transmission time is limited for each node, it is possible to evaluate the performance of the network. This is an essential feature for manufacturing systems.

At the lowest level (physical layer), one can use carrierband MAP or broadband MAP, depending on requirements of the application. Carrierband networks use the same type of cables as those used for cable television. Carrierband MAP is less expensive and more limited than broadband MAP. Carrierband MAP is recommended for connections between the cell level and the station or machine level. Broadband MAP is recommended between the cell level and the upper levels (shop level or factory level). Carrierband MAP and broadband MAP can be connected by so-called bridges. Finally, an enhanced performance architecture (MAP EPA) exists for high performance applications because conventional MAP implementations (with 7 layers) have been reported to be slow.

Currently, there are more than 50 companies around the world selling MAP products (interface boards, software, computers, controllers, networking equipment, and application tools), and there are around 30 MAP installations (United States, Japan, and Europe). Typical MAP applications are

- Facility monitoring and control; data collection systems.
- Distributed numerical control systems (DNC); process control systems.
- Flexible manufacturing systems, robot assembly cells and lines; factory automation.
- Computer-aided manufacturing; quality control; inspection.

TOP

TOP (Technical and Office Protocol) is a project initialized by Boeing in 1984, i.e., some time after MAP. Boeing realized that it had the same needs in terms of specifications for the communication and interoperability of its technical office workstations as for manufacturing equipment on the factory floor. TOP is a specification for nonproprietary multiple vendor data communications in office and technical environments. The specification is based on the local area network specification commonly used for office automation systems, i.e., the CSMA/CD-based network (IEEE 802.3). However, conformance with the MAP specifications for layers 2 to 6 of ISO-OSI was required. The application layer of the TOP specification is defined for use between CAD/CAM and document handling workstations. TOP 1.0 was released in November 1985 and TOP 2.0 in 1988. The last version is TOP 3.0 released in 1993. It is fully compliant with MAP 3.0 and its profile is given by Figure 49.5. Typical TOP applications include:

- Electronic mail (MHS/X400)
- File transfer
- Electronic data interchange (EDI)
- Product data exchange
- CAD/CAE
- MRP; Just-In-Time (JIT)
- Office documents (graphic and text)

CNMA

CNMA is a European implementation of MAP with additional options, especially for small manufacturing enterprises, developed within the ESPRIT Program (Projects 955, 2617 and 5104) of the Commission of the European Communities (14). It results from the effort of a consortium of 17 companies, grouping CIM users, CIM vendors, systems engineers, and academic institutions. The objectives of CNMA are to specify, implement, validate, and promote communication standards for manufacturing in compliance with user requirements and with the ISO-OSI basic reference model. Although strongly committed to open communication for CIM, CNMA has devoted considerable attention to the specification of MMS (ISO IS 9506/1 and /2) and its companion standards (ISO 9506/3, /4, and /5):

Figure 49.6 precisely illustrates the CNMA communications profile with respect to the structure of the OSI model. Currently, CNMA can use the following LANs to link devices:

IEEE 802.3. Carrier sense multiple access with collision detection (CSMA/CD), operating at 10 Mb/s with 500-m cable segments.

IEEE 802.4. Token bus broadband, operating at 10 Mb/s, using a broadband cable system beyond 10 km in length.

IEEE 802.4. Token bus carrierband, operating at 5 Mb/s, using cables of lengths between 50 and 700 m.

In addition, access to WANs for remote sites is possible via X-25 links. In terms of application protocols, CNMA makes use of manufacturing message specification (MMS) to support communications between cell controllers and programmable devices (NC controllers, PLCs, robot controllers, etc.) (4) as well as.

- Companion standards to MMS to provide additional functionalities for particular devices.
- FTAM for file transfer, access (reading or writing of file attributes), and management (creation, deletion, or replacement) of various types of files (unstructured text and binary files).
- Network management (CMIS/CMIP) for network administration such as configuration management (CM), performance management (PM), and fault management (FM) (ISO IS 9595-2/9596-2) (15).
- Remote database access (RDA) to provide a means to access database management systems using SQL statements located on a remote database server (ISO DIS 9579; international standard expected early 1994) (16).
- Directory service (ISO IS 9594) to support storage and interrogation of information about named objects (things or people) to provide services such as network access to "white pages" (information about an explicitly identified object) or "yellow pages" (list of subordinate information of an identified object); this information is held in the directory information base (17).

CNMA has been successfully demonstrated in three manufacturing sites in Europe. Both MAP/TOP and CNMA profiles are claimed to be too slow in terms of response time for time-critical applications. This has led to the development of simplified architectures and fieldbus, which only use three layers of the OSI model (also called mini-MAP).

Fieldbus

Fieldbus (or mini-MAP) is an emerging communication technology in discrete manufacturing and process plants for low level industrial data bus, i.e., real-time applications (the time limit may be as low as 5 to 20 ms and the distance is between 40 and 1500 m). Fieldbus is intended to connect PLCs, NC units, actuators, sensors, positioners, and other kinds of devices found at the lowest levels of the factory automation hierarchy (equipment level). Usual media for fieldbus are twisted pair cables, coaxial cables, optical cables, and radio waves. A fieldbus architecture usually does not implement all OSI layers to optimize performance. It is usually reduced to three layers. Figure 49.7 compares the fieldbus architecture with the OSI model and shows that the presentation layer, the session layer, the transport layer, and the network layer are not needed. The data link layer provides for LLC and MAC. It performs flow and error control for reliable message transfer. For the physical layer, several kinds of cables can be used as the transmission medium. The implementation can be based on carrierband techniques with COFSK modulation. Two examples of fieldbus are introduced: FIP and PROFIBUS. Both have a three-layer architecture, and commercial products are available to implement them. However, there is no internationally agreed on standard for real-time requirements yet, although some standardization work is on-going (e.g., IEC TC65C WG6, IEEE).

Factory instrumentation protocol (FIP) is a high-speed fieldbus (theoretical speed: 2.5 Mb/s) to be used in discrete manufacturing or process industries (18). It is well suited for data acquisition and surveillance systems (sensors, actuators, controllers, measuring devices, etc.). Two classes of services are supported in FIP. First, periodic and aperiodic services ensure transfer

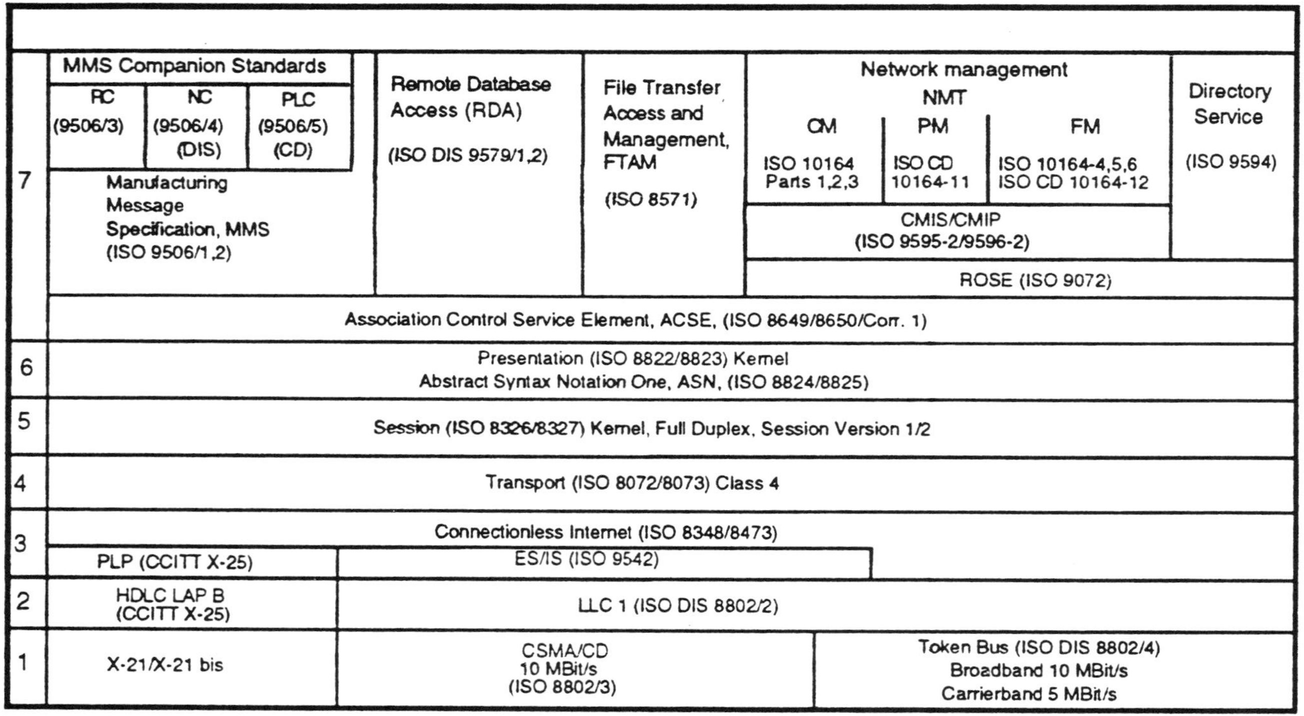

	MMS Companion Standards			Remote Database Access (RDA)	File Transfer Access and Management, FTAM	Network management NMT			Directory Service
	RC (9506/3)	NC (9506/4) (DIS)	PLC (9506/5) (CD)			OM	PM	FM	
7	Manufacturing Message Specification, MMS (ISO 9506/1,2)			(ISO DIS 9579/1,2)	(ISO 8571)	ISO 10164 Parts 1,2,3	ISO CD 10164-11	ISO 10164-4,5,6 ISO CD 10164-12	(ISO 9594)
							CMIS/CMIP (ISO 9595-2/9596-2)		
						ROSE (ISO 9072)			
	Association Control Service Element, ACSE, (ISO 8649/8650/Corr. 1)								
6	Presentation (ISO 8822/8823) Kernel Abstract Syntax Notation One, ASN, (ISO 8824/8825)								
5	Session (ISO 8326/8327) Kernel, Full Duplex, Session Version 1/2								
4	Transport (ISO 8072/8073) Class 4								
3	Connectionless Internet (ISO 8348/8473)								
	ES/IS (ISO 9542)								
	PLP (CCITT X-25)								
2	HDLC LAP B (CCITT X-25)			LLC 1 (ISO DIS 8802/2)					
1	X-21/X-21 bis			CSMA/CD 10 MBit/s (ISO 8802/3)		Token Bus (ISO DIS 8802/4) Broadband 10 MBit/s Carrierband 5 MBit/s			

Figure 49.6. CNMA profile. *CD*, committee draft; *DIS*, draft international standard; *IS*, international standard.

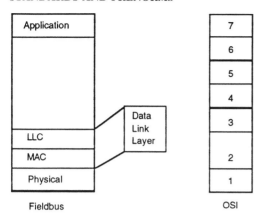

Fieldbus   OSI

Figure 49.7. Fieldbus architecture and OSI model.

of data frames. Data frames transmitted do not include addresses and need to be periodically refreshed. The data source is defined by a preceeding separate command frame issued from the bus administrator. All other devices are potential data sinks. Each application layer must be configured in advance (using scanning tables) with the list of data sources to be periodically monitored. Aperiodic services are used for event-driven data exchange. Second, messaging services ensure correct point-to-point message transfer. FIP is based on a connectionless protocol using a customer–producer model in the sense that the transmission of information is not subject to a connection request to the bus administrator to connect the information customer and producer. A FIP network can be organized into network segments connected by bridges. FIP is supported by AFNOR and several French manufacturers (commercial products exist). It is also promoted by the FIP Club, which has members around the world. The FIP Club is actively contributing to the IEC fieldbus project.

PROFIBUS (19) is a German fieldbus project initiated and managed by Siemens and considered by DIN. It is especially designed for manufacturing industries and makes use of a multimaster facility using the token-passing principle. The link layer protocols are based on the IEC TC57 telecontrol frame structures, using character-based transmission with several alternative options. The physical layer transmission uses the EIA RS-485 standard for electrical characteristics of generators and receivers for use in balanced digital multipoint systems.

Fieldbus represents a significant enabling technology for industrial control systems. Due to the large market potential, several commercial products have appeared on the market, although a general consensus has not been reached so far.

MMS

MMS (Manufacturing Message Specification) is an object-oriented application language for automation. It allows communication between computers and machines via a standard Application Program Interface (MMS-I) to ensure portability. MMS supports the client/server approach and the virtual manufacturing device concept.

MMS is a language with high functionality supported by 86 services structured into 10 service groups as follows (4):

- Environment and general management group to establish connections between system modes and applications.
- Virtual manufacturing device (VMD) support group for the identification and status monitoring of virtual manufacturing devices.
- Domain management group to upload and download program and data on machines.
- Program invocation management group to start, stop, and resume programs and devices.
- Variable access group to define, read, and write variables.
- Semaphore management group to synchronize access control to common resources.

- Event management group for event-driven operations.
- Journal management group to read, write, and manage journal files.
- File transfer group or a subset of FTAM functionalities.
- Operator input/output group to manage simple console read and write operations.

49.6 STANDARDS FOR APPLICATION INTEGRATION

Application integration assumes existence of physical systems integration and heavily relies on application data exchange. This happens either within or between manufacturing enterprises. Standards being developed in this area can be classified in two categories (20):

- Electronic data interchange (EDI) for business data flows (e.g., purchase orders, invoices, and fund transfers).
- Technical data interchange (TDI) for technical data flows (e.g., CAD data, and product data).

Intraenterprise integration concerns the data flows between functions and departments internal to an enterprise. This mostly concerns technical data such as product specifications, part drawings, engineering changes, and quality data but can also concern business data (e.g., audit data and cost reporting). Interenterprise integration concerns the data flows between trading organizations. This mostly concerns business data (purchase orders, invoices, payments, etc.) but also technical data (e.g., CAD data). For both types of data transfer, several standards are evolving such as EDI, IGES, and STEP. Similar and complementary standards are being developed with the CALS framework, a U.S. government initiative. Table 49.3 (20) provides a synthetic view of the enterprise information exchange framework. These standards, or prestandards, are described in the next sections.

TABLE 49.3. Electronic Information Exchange

Information Class	Intraenterprise	Interenterprise	Government

Business data
• Purchase orders
• Invoices
• Fund transfer
• Quality data
• Schedules
 	
EDI
	Form
	• Processable files
	• Multiformat files
	• Shared databases
	
	Specs and Standards
	• Internal
	• Data dictionary
		Form
		• Processable files
		• Processable format
		• Electronic data
		
		Specs and Standards
		• ANSI X-12; TDCC
		• EDIFACT
		• AIAG; Odette
			CALS
			• Industry systems
			• Government systems
			• Government–industry
			  interface
			• Industry–prime,
			  contracts, vendors

Technical Data • Product definition • Graphical data • Bill-of-materials • Configuration • Documentation TDI	Form • Processable files • Interactive files • Shared databases Specs and Standards • IGES • PDES • SET	Form • Processable files • Multiformat files Specs and Standards • IGES • PDES • SET	 CALS

Implementation issues	• Company-specific
	  solutions
	• Concurrent engineering
	• Integrating
	  infrastructures
		• Concurrent engineering
		• Subtier "facilities"
		  issues
		• Legal issues
			• Concurrent engineering
			• Weapon systems flavor
			• Legal issues

IGES

CAD/CAPP/CAM integration is an important aspect of CIM. However, these functions are usually performed by multivendor, incompatible application systems. Transferring product data from one of these applications to another through standard interfaces is a key technology for solving CAD/CAPP/CAM integration.

Scope

The initial graphics exchange specification (IGES) has become the most widely accepted means of transferring data between these systems. The objective of IGES is to exchange a production definition, and especially CAD data (e.g., geometry and tolerances), between two different systems to reduce the need for specialized interfaces between systems and to reduce the number of paper drawings (21).

Current Status

IGES was first created by Boeing, General Electric, and the U.S. Air Force in the late 1970s to address the need of exchanging CAD/CAPP/CAM data between CAD/CAM systems. IGES is now an ANSI standard for engineering data exchange specification supported by most major CAD/CAM vendors. It is being widely used in production today worldwide. IGES is based on a simple principle: the concept of the neutral data file (Figure 49.8). Each application system is provided with two processors—a postprocessor and a preprocessor—that can translate geometrical data encoded in their internal data structures in the IGES neutral file format or read an IGES file and translate the geometric description in their internal data structures, respectively. The neutral format serves as a universal graphics language to handle elementary forms such as text, points, segments, arcs, and circles.

IGES has been considerably extended since version 1.0 and can now support wire-frame models and constructive solids geometry (CSG). IGES 4.0 also handles nongeometric entities such as annotations and dimensioning. Version 5.0 supports boundary representation (B-rep) types of description and scale information.

Two other graphics exchange formats are being used in Europe for CAD data exchange. One is the German exchange format VDA and the other one is the French exchange format SET. Verband der Automobil (VDA) is an exchange format created by the German automobile industry (22). Because it is mostly concerned with the representation of complex curves and surfaces to represent body parts of cars, it mainly concentrates on the use of high order polynomials. This specialization is recognized to be the basis for its success. VDA is still being used by the German car industry. As such, VDA is a DIN standard. It is available under two options: the original standard, VDA-FS, and a more efficient version, VDA-IS, which is now a subset of IGES.

Standard d'Echange et de Transfert (SET) was developed in the 1980s for the needs of the European aircraft and aerospace industry (23). The motivation for its development was to correct the weaknesses observed in previous standards, especially IGES. It is an AFNOR standard. Since 1990, SET has been used in the European Airbus and Hermes programs. Its use is also considered by the French car industry. SET is more precise and more homogeneous than IGES. Although efficient, it is still nearly unknown in the American industry. SET has two main advantages: (1) it covers all the essential functionalities of modern commercial CAD systems, and (2) it is open in the sense that it can be enriched by new features when they become

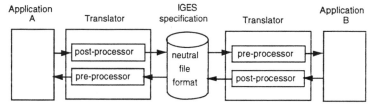

Figure 49.8. CAD/CAPP/CAM data exchange principle.

available in CAD systems. This is made possible by the use of dictionaries (storing sets of predefined parameters that can be assigned to a block of information) and of libraries (sets of external data to which SET can refer).

STEP

STEP was initiated by ISO in 1984 to develop a series of international standards (ISO 10303) for the computer-interpretable representation and exchange of product data (24). Within ISO, the work is being performed by Subcommittee 4 (SC4) of Technical Committee 184 (TC 184), which is responsible for factory automation and integration. STEP benefits from work on IGES, SET, and VDA and gets the support and contribution of PDES, Inc., in the United States and various ESPRIT projects in Europe (CAD-I, CADEX, IMPACCT). PDES, Inc., promotes product data exchange specification (PDES), which is similar to STEP (25).

Scope

The objective of STEP is to provide an information description and format, independent from any particular system, for electronic exchange and sharing of all data needed to describe fully a product and its manufacturing processes over the full product life cycle (including design, manufacture, use, maintenance, and disposal). While IGES essentially deals with geometric data of parts, STEP is concerned with product information. The requirements of STEP are

- To support a neutral definition of product and process information for manufacturing products, including their components and assemblies.
- To support the exchange of product information, including storing, transferring, accessing, and archiving, with a minimum of human interpretation.
- To interrelate a broad range of product information to support applications found throughout the product life cycle.

Product information covered by STEP concerns such product aspects as:

Geometry.
Solids.
Tolerances.
Electrical functions.
Material.
Presentation.
Architecture.
Topology.
Form features.
Layered electrical products.
Finite element modeling.
Product structure.
Drafting.
Ship structures.

Geometric information exchanged can be represented using wire-frame models, surface models, or boundary representation solid models. Topological entities used in a STEP model are

Body. A whole solid model (or a part in compound representation).
Shell. The border of a solid part.
Face. Several faces form the shell of a volume part or form directly a part in surface representation.
Loop. The border of a face.
Edge. Several edges form a loop of a face or directly belong to a wire-frame model.
Vertex. Each edge is defined by two vertices.

Solid models use all types of topological entities; surface models use face, loop, edge, and vertex; and wire-frame models only use edge and vertex. Geometrical entities (surface, curve, and point) are then defined from topological entities as follows:

- A surface describes the geometric form of a face.
- A curve describes the geometric form of an edge.
- A point describes the geometric position of a vertex.

Finally, subclasses of geometrical entities can be defined. For instance, the class of curves is made of unbounded and bounded curves; bounded curves are made of polyline curves and B-spline curves; and so on.

Current Status

The first version of STEP was scheduled for release in 1993. In fact, STEP is a combination of substandards called parts. These parts define not only the formal descriptions of product data, data types, integrated resources, application protocols, exchange mechanisms, and conformance testing but also a formal data modeling language called Express to support both the textual description and the graphical representation of the modeled information. The following parts were scheduled to be included in ISO 10303 (24):

- *Part 1.* Overview and fundamental principles.
- *Part 11.* Description methods: the Express language reference manual.
- *Part 21.* Implementation methods: clear text encoding of the exchange structure.
- *Part 31.* Conformance testing methodology and framework: general concepts.
- *Part 41.* Integrated generic resources: fundamentals of product description and support.
- *Part 42.* Integrated generic resources: geometric and topological representation.
- *Part 43.* Integrated generic resources: representation structures.
- *Part 44.* Integrated generic resources: product structure configuration.
- *Part 46.* Integrated generic resources: visual presentation.
- *Part 101.* Integrated application resources: drafting.
- *Part 201.* Application protocols: explicit drafting.
- *Part 203.* Application protocol: configuration controlled design.

Other parts are in preparation. The structure of ISO 10303 is summarized in Figure 49.9.
STEP is based on a three-layer architecture:

1. The application layer corresponds to an application domain (mechanical parts, electrical circuits, finite element analysis, etc.); this is the level of application data.
2. The logical layer isolates the application layer from the physical level (level of Express).
3. The physical layer is the level of the neutral file format for data exchange (implementation).

An application in STEP is a group of one or more processes creating or using product data. The Express language is a formal description language for information models (26). Although it is not a programming language, it borrows a number of concepts from several high level programming languages such as strong data typing, the property inheritance principle, and the concept of function to define local and global integrity constraints. An Express program describes "schemata" made of "entities." Entities are described by their attributes and relationships to other entities. The supertype–subtype relationships define the inheritance mechanism between a child entity and its parent entity. Local integrity constraints on attributes are defined within entities using a WHERE clause, while global integrity constraints involving attributes of more than one entity are defined as separate rules. It is claimed that the use of Express enables precision and consistency of product representation and facilitates development of implementations.

Integrated resources are used for the representation of product information. There are two separate groups of integrated resources: generic resources and application resources. Each

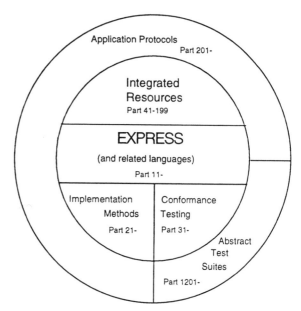

Figure 49.9. The structure
of ISO 10303.

integrated resource is made of logically related sets of product data descriptions in Express, called resource constructs. Generic resources are independent of applications and can reference each other. Generic resources concern Parts 41, 42, 43, 44, and 46 of ISO 10303. Application resources reference and extend the generic resources for use by a group of similar applications. Application resources concern Part 101 of ISO 10303.

Application protocols (APs) define the scope, context, and information requirements of applications. They specify functions, processes, or information relevant to each application. The scope of an application is described by an application activity model (AAM), which defines the processes, information flows, and functional requirements of the application. The information requirements and constraints for the application context are defined by an application reference model (ARM), which is a formal information model. Furthermore, the information requirements of the application are represented by an application interpreted model (AIM), which is expressed using Express and describes resource constructs specified by the integrated resources. The resource constructs are interpreted to meet the application requirements within the defined context and scope of the AP. The AIM is independent of all implementation methods. An AP can specify one or more implementation methods.

Implementation methods provide a particular way of using the application protocols defined in ISO 10303. They may include the following:

- File exchange to read or write product description data in text files or binary files.
- Application programming interfaces to allow applications to access product data through a software interface using different programming languages (Fortran, C, etc.).
- Database implementations to read, write or modify data in a database whose internal schema conforms to the schema in an application interpreted model.

Another important aspect of STEP is conformance testing. It deals with testing the conformance of a software product that claims to implement an ISO 10303 application protocol.

STEP has been demonstrated successfully in the United States by PDES Inc., and the U.S. Navy and in Europe within CADEX (ESPRIT Project 2195). Figure 49.10 presents an example of a sculptured surface model exchanged via STEP. Furthermore, a number of commercial tools already exist (Express parsers, semantic checkers, SQL code generators, etc.).

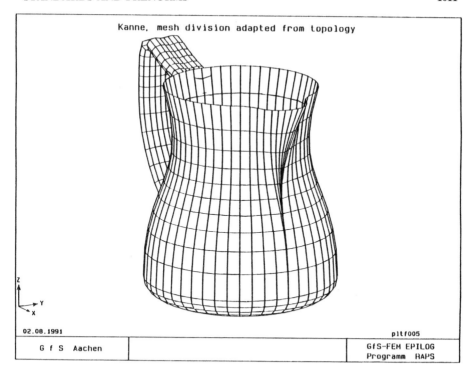

Kanne, mesh division adapted from topology

02.08.1991   pltf005

G f S   Aachen   GfS-FEM EPILOG Programm RAPS

Figure 49.10. Sculpture surface model exchanged via STEP. Reprinted with permission.

EDI

Communication of information is a common activity in industrial and administrative practice. Standards are, therefore, necessary to communicate business information between customers, suppliers, importers, exporters, banks, transportation firms, and other parties involved in international trade. ISO and IEC are undertaking a joint effort to identify and coordinate the development of standards needed for electronic data interchange across a broad range of industrial, commercial, and public administration activities. EDI standards include EDIFACT (27), X-400 messages (11), and CALS-compliant documents (28).

Scope

EDI (29) refers to the complex processes by which electronically coded information generated in one application (e.g., manufacturing) is transferred and used in another application (e.g., distribution or after-sales service) without human intervention. EDI procedures and processes are taking on major importance with the global advances in CIM and CALS systems. For instance, EDI can become an essential component for just-in-time manufacturing systems and MRP systems for inventory management. Indeed, EDI can help in achieving inventory reduction (either receiving stocks, work-in-process, or finished product stocks) by streamlining production and communication between all involved parties.

EDI has many potential benefits that go beyond the scope of inventory management. Such benefits include better customer relations, development of long-term customers and contracts, increased cash flow (prompt invoicing and payment collection), fewer errors, and ease of tracing shipments. EDI shortens the supply stream by reducing inventory. EDI can also significantly reduce lead times and lead time variability. Furthermore, EDI is obviously an essential technology for interenterprise integration.

Electronic data interchange for administration, commerce, and transport (EDIFACT) defines data elements, messages, and syntax rules for the transfer of trade data. Because the EDIFACT data format is extensible for many types of data, EDIFACT is a standard that also can be of importance for data definition and exchange in CIM. Examples of information commonly exchanged via EDI facilities include requests for quotation, purchase orders, purchase order acknowledgments, dispatch notifications, customs declarations, advices of receipt, invoices, statements, and VAT returns.

Current Status

A message in EDI is a structured collection of data segments. Data segments are made of data elements. Data elements are composed of characters. There are two sets of characters: the level A character set (only upper case letters, numerals, and a few symbol characters) and level B character set (lower case and upper case letters, numerals, and usually symbol characters). An interchange is defined in EDIFACT as a collection of messages starting with an interchange header and finishing with a trailer. There may be more than one interchange in a communication connection. The EDIFACT syntax is defined in ISO 9735 as an international standard that was defined in 1987 and published in 1988 (27). ISO 9735 specified the following items: the character set(s) to be used for EDI, the structure of a interchange (the syntax), and definitions of terms. EDIFACT also includes a data element directory that includes definitions of the data elements and specifications of the data segments used to built the messages. These directories have been adopted as ISO standards (ISO IS 7372).

The Organization for Data Exchange by Teletransmission in Europe (ODETTE) is used by more than 200 companies in the automotive industry. The ODETTE standard consists of a set of agreed messages designed specifically for the car industry. In terms of implementation, the X-400 series of recommendations of the CCITT (11), which defines a system architecture and protocols for handling messages in a wide variety of formats, can be used as the communication medium for EDI. Another solution is to use X-25 public networks for long-distance data exchange. EDI can use any OSI-based computer network to support message transfer. Compared with the ISO-OSI architecture, EDI is seen as an application. However, for the user's application, EDI appears as another layer on top of the seven OSI layers.

Integrating Infrastructures

The consequence of rapid development of information technology is that most enterprises must deal with an increasing heterogeneous environment made of multivendor hardware and software components that use different operating systems, talk different languages, and use different database systems. Integrating infrastructures is, therefore, required to simplify integration of these diverse, sometimes incompatible, functional entities. An integrating infrastructure (IIS) is a set of common computer-based services that provide a platform for physical system and application integration. The functions covered encompass

- Systemwide exchange services to support transparent message exchange within the enterprise, whatever its size and organization.
- Communications management services to provide access to computer networks (OSI or non-OSI types of networks)
- Presentation services to make the connection with the functional entities of the enterprise.
- Information services to support transparent access and management of data stored in the many (distributed) databases used by the enterprise.
- Business services to control or monitor the business processes of the enterprise and their activities and to provide basic support for resource management.
- System administration services to register new functional entities (i.e., manage system configuration) to monitor the status of systems components, to maintain logical naming, etc.

Integrating infrastructures are of paramount importance in CIM to transform a highly distributed heteregeneous environment into a more homogeneous environment, thus reducing the need for specialized interfaces.

CIMOSA (see below) has provided the specification for such an integration infrastructure for CIM (Figure 49.11). This IIS is structured into five major blocks of services, called entities (1). It is aimed at supporting enterprise integration, model development, and model execution in heterogeneous manufacturing and information technology environments. It has been submitted to ISO.

Other developments for integration platforms, usually supported by major computer vendors, are being discussed in standardization committees. These include open distributed processing (ODP), open system foundation (OSF), and distributed computing environment (DCE). Some partial implementations already exist such as New Wave by Hewlett Packard, NAS by Digital Equipment, SAA by IBM, and the distributed computing model (DCM) by Machines BULL. CIM-BIOSYS is a prototype of such an infrastructure developed by Loughborough University in the UK for CIM systems.

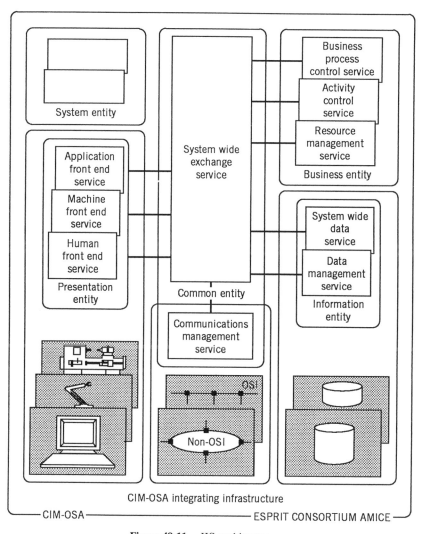

Figure 49.11. IIS architecture.

49.7   BUSINESS INTEGRATION LEVEL

Business integration concerns full enterprise integration. This area is receiving a lot of attention from the research community as well as from standardization committees. However, no standard in this field is available yet. Although recognized as a potential area for standards, it is felt that it would be premature to produce any standard at this time. Currently, the main focus of work is on enterprise modeling and IIS.

ENV 40 003 and CIMOSA

CIMOSA

CIMOSA is a European proposal for an open systems architecture for CIM (1). CIMOSA is a prestandardization project developed by the AMICE Consortium as a series of ESPRIT projects (Projects 688, 5288, and 7110). The AMICE Consortium groups 19 major companies (including users, vendors, consulting companies, and academia) concerned with CIM. Partner ESPRIT projects also exist to test and validate CIMOSA principles (VOICE, CODE, and CIMPRESS). CIMOSA provides solutions for business integration under four different forms.

1. *The CIMOSA Enterprise Modeling Framework (CIMOSA Cube).* CIMOSA provides a reference architecture to help particular enterprises to build their own particular architecture as a set of models describing the various aspects of the enterprise (function, information, resource, and organization) at different modeling levels (requirements definition, design specification, and implementation description). The reference architecture is separated into two layers: a generic layer providing generic building blocks (i.e., basic constructs of the modeling language, their types, and instantiation and aggregation rules), and a partial model layer providing a library of reusable partial models for some industry sectors (i.e., partially instantiated models that can be customized to specific enterprise needs). The enterprise modeling framework provides semantic unification of concepts shared in the CIM system.

2. *The CIMOSA IIS.* CIMOSA provides the enabling technology to realize physical and application integration as described above (see Figure 49.11).

3. *The CIMOSA System Life Cycle.* The CIMOSA life cycle is the sequence of steps, or methodology, to be used to build the particular architecture of an enterprise CIM system, from requirements definition to system installation, test, and release and later on, system maintenance. Only small pieces of the methodology can be formalized because such methodologies are not unique.

4. *Inputs to Standardization.* Both the enterprise modeling framework and the integrating infrastructure of CIMOSA have been submitted to CEN and ISO as a basis for international standard development. The enterprise modeling framework is known as ENV 40 003 as discussed in the next section. Modeling constructs used in CIMOSA for building an enterprise model (e.g., domains, enterprise activities, business processes, events, object views, and resources) are also being considered.

ENV 40 003

The European prestandard called framework for enterprise modeling and known as ENV 40 003 (30) sets out a framework for future standardization in the area of CIM enterprise modeling. Like the ISO basic reference model for open systems interconnection (OSI), the ENV guides the structuring and development of related, detailed standards. The ENV was prepared by CEN/CENELEC/AMT/WG-ARC to help in the identification and positioning of necessary standards in the area of CIM, focusing on the needs of discrete parts manufacturing. Most of the concepts developed in the ENV can be used in other industries (process industry, transportation industry, etc.). The ENV is the result of an evaluation of a number of CIM architectures analyzed by AMT/WG-ARC of CEN/CENELEC (31).

The structure of the framework for enterprise modeling follows the principles of the CIMOSA cube. It is structured according to three dimensions (Figure 49.12):

1. *The Dimension of Genericity.* A level of genericity is a level of abstraction representing the genericity of the architectural entities described at this level. The ENV recognizes three levels of genericity:

> The generic level, which defines the basic modeling constructs for components, constraints, rules, terms, services, functions, and protocols.

The partial level, which contains partial models.

The particular level, which describes enterprise specific knowledge using constructs of the generic level.

Associated with this dimension is the stepwise particularization process, which defines orderly development of a model from a generic level via a partial level to the particular level.

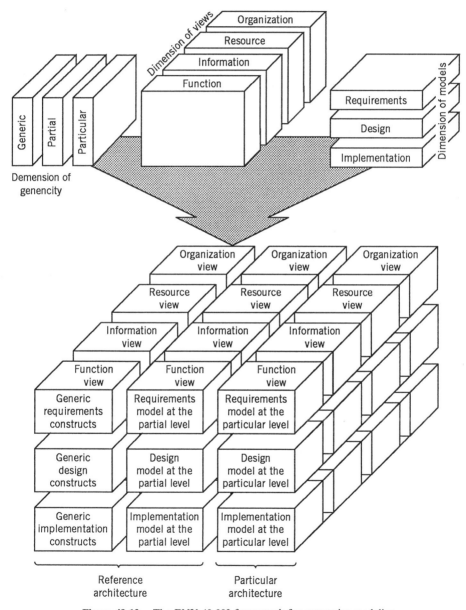

Figure 49.12.   The ENV 40 003 framework for enterprise modeling.

2. *The Dimension of Models.* A model level is a level of abstraction corresponding to the main phases of enterprise model development. It contains modeling constructs at the generic level and models at the partial and particular levels. The ENV recognizes three types of models:

- Requirements models define enterprise operations to be done (and possibly how they could be done) in a business sense and using business terminology without much consideration of implementation.
- Design models specify how enterprise operations are to be performed to achieve the requirements.
- Implementation models describe the means and/or rules to be used in executing the enterprise operations as defined in the requirements models. .

Associated with this dimension is the stepwise derivation process for deriving models of the implemented components at the implementation model level from the requirements model level via the design model level.

3. *The Dimension of Views.* An enterprise view is a selective perception of an enterprise that emphasizes some particular aspects and disregards others. The ENV considers four views:

- The function view provides a hierarchically structured description of the functions, behavior (dynamics), and functional structure (statics) of the enterprise with relevant inputs and outputs.
- The information view provides the description of a structured set of enterprise objects that were identified in the other views.
- The resource view provides a description of the resource organization of the enterprise, i.e., the set of resources required to execute the enterprise operations.
- The organization view provides the description of the organizational structure of the enterprise, the responsibilities of the individuals, and the organizational units within the enterprise.

Associated with this dimension is the stepwise generation process for generating the contents of the enterprise views of a model for each modeling level.

ISO Work on Enterprise Modeling Framework

ISO TC 184/SC5/WG1 is working on a document titled *Framework for Enterprise Modeling*. The goal of this working group is to establish a framework to coordinate existing, emerging, and future standards for the modeling of manufacturing enterprises to facilitate CIM. This work is heavily influenced by inputs coming from CIMOSA and the ENV 40 003 but also recognizes the object-oriented way of modeling complex systems as promoted by the German DIN. The complete version of the report, containing the recommendations of the working group, is expected in early 1994. The report will cover such items as terminology for enterprise modeling, scope of enterprise modeling, modeling concepts, process of enterprise modeling, and application to CIM.

Another area of work considered by ISO TC 184/SC5/WG4 concerns a manufacturing automation programming language environment (MAPLE). The goal of this environment is to provide a common support facility for multiple, independent, programming languages for manufacturing devices and controls, and as such it is intended to increase the productivity of its various users. It applies at the station, cell, and section levels (levels 2, 3, and 4) of the ISO 10314 shop floor production model. The functions include managing and controlling the equipment in a workstation, coordinating workstations in a cell, and supervising the activities of cells in a section as well as the communication between entities at the station and higher levels. This area of on-going activities was launched in 1992.

CALS

CALS is a standardized approach to integrated product (and process) data management (28). This is a U.S. Department of Defense supported initiative. It was launched to reduce the cost and lead time and improve the quality and flexibility of product design, development, manufacture, acquisition, and support. Side effects targeted are a dramatic reduction of the bulk of paper produced in the enterprise and a substantial increase of the quality of product documentation. CALS can equally apply to defense and nondefense commercial manufacturing. It concerns the improvement of the enterprise through continuous business and process improvement, TQM, and process and operation reengineering, thus aiming for future world-class performance. CALS is essential to achieve agile manufacturing capability (i.e., ability to manage changes and face varying customer requests. CALS also can be viewed as an information infrastructure for product and process improvement.

Scope

On one hand, large projects involve frequent information exchange among heterogeneous systems. This requires data format and communication systems standardization. On the other hand, large projects continuously generate voluminous mass of paper for project and product documentation, especially technical documentation (design information, manufacturing information, management information, logistic information, etc.). Archiving of this bulk of information is often a nightmare if not a mess. Computerization of the document production chain is, therefore, necessary. Technical documentation is then part of the information system of the project. This makes easier configuration management, documentation update cycles, information navigation, information traceability, and optimization of documentation costs. This also makes it possible to use various media to handle information and to structure data under various forms (text, graphics, images, voice, etc.). Because it focuses on technical document exchange and is independent of the system used, CALS considers three different types of data used in structured documentation: text, data from databases, and graphical items.

Documents are structured using the Standard Generalized Mark-up Language (SGML; ISO IS 8879). SGML is a language used to organize document structures as well as structured documents in text files with references (markups) to external contents (graphics, spreadsheet cells, raster images, etc.). It allows one to describe documents in a computer-understandable way without regard to which software produced it. This is of paramount importance, as the life cycle of software products is much shorter than the life cycle of production documents. The document is made of elementary units (document granules) and can be presented on different media. The document produced can, therefore, contain figures, images, tables, spreadsheet data, etc. coming from other software packages. Two-dimensional graphics to be automatically included in technical documents can be stored in graphical information storage and transfer metafiles as defined by the computer graphic metafile (CGM; ISO 8632) Raster images, i.e., images made of pixels or obtained from scanners can be encoded using CCITT Group 4 specifications (ISO 8613/7 Standard Fax Group 4).

Current Status

The CALS program is an on-going effort. It is advised by a steering committee of 400 professionals from 100 companies. It is first of all a framework that dictates that defense contractors make use of several existing or developing standards for text files, graphics, and tape format. In addition to SGML, CGM, and CCITT Group 4, CALS uses STEP, EDI, the 28000 series data standards, and programmers hierarchical interactive graphics standard (PHIGS; ISO 9592 Parts 1–3). PHIGS is an interface standard that specifies three-dimensional graphics facilities to application programmers. CALS also strongly promotes the use of concurrent engineering and TQM principles. CALS was planned in several phases. Phase I (1988–1992) focused on delivery of digital information along with traditional paper-based documents and support materials. Phase II (1991–1995) calls for contractors to establish databases accessible to the government and other vendors. Compliance to CALS standards results in significant improvement in terms of reducing lead times, cutting costs, and improving the quality of delivered products. It is also a driver for better quality, reliability, accessibility, and traceability of business and technical information. Finally, it becomes a competitive edge in bidding on Department of Defense contracts.

49.8 CONCLUSIONS

One of the aims of CIM is to transform a heterogeneous, disconnected environment into a more integrated, homogeneous environment. To achieve this goal, common languages, services, and interfaces are definitely required. Standardization has, therefore, a key role to play to make CIM a reality with respect to the many facets of CIM, as demonstrated in this chapter. The standardization process has been successful for physical systems integration, which is a prerequisite for enterprise integration. Good progress can be reported concerning application integration, especially as far as business and technical data exchange are concerned. However, much more work remains to be done concerning applicative languages, object handling in object-oriented environments, uniform interfaces to CIM system components, and integrating infrastructure architectures and services. Business integration is an area in which standards are just developing, because it is still in its infancy. Further work remains to be done on process modeling and business knowledge modeling. However, a consensus on the basic definition of commonly accepted modeling constructs (e.g., objects, activities, and resources) and basic principles of modeling frameworks is highly desirable, especially for those interested in the development of enterprise modeling tools. Work on reference architectures for enterprise modeling is providing the groundwork in this area. In a global economy challenged by quality, costs, and delays as well as partnership or commercial alliance, the use and support of the development of national and international standards by industrial companies are essential for enhancing manufacturing operations.*

* All ISO documents can be obtained from the ISO TC 184 Central Secretariat, NIST, Gaithersburg, MD 20899 USA. CEN documents can be obtained from CEN Central Secretariat, rue Bréderode 2, B-1000 Brussels, Belgium. AFNOR documents can be obtained from AFNOR, Tour Europe, Cedex 7, 92049 Paris La Défense, France.

BIBLIOGRAPHY

1. AMICE, *CIMOSA: Open Systems Architecture for Computer-Integrated Manufacturing,* Springer-Verlag, Berlin, 1993.

2. ISO, *Reference Model for Shop Floor Production Standards. Part 1: A Reference Model for Standardization and a Methodology for Identification of Standards Requirements* and *Part 2: Application of the Reference Model and Methodology,* ISO, Gaithersburg, Md., 1990, Tech. Rep. 10314, ISO TC 184/SC5/WG1 N126, and ISO TC 184/SC5/WG1 N160.

3. ISO, *Information Processing Systems—Open Systems Interconnection—Basic Reference Model,* ISO, Gaithersburg, Md., 1984, ISO IS 7498.

4. ISO, *Manufacturing Message Specification (MMS),* ISO, Gaithersburg, Md., 1988, ISO IS 9506/1 and 9506/2.

5. ISO, *Information Processing Systems—Open Systems Interconnection—File, Transfer, Access and Management,* ISO, Gaithersburg, Md., 1988, ISO IS 8571.

6. ISO, *File Transfer, Access and Management. Parts 1–4,* ISO, Gaithersburg, Md., 1987, ISO IS 8571.

7. ISO, *Job Transfer and Manipulation Concepts and Services,* ISO, Gaithersburg, Md., 1990, ISO DIS 8831.

8. ISO, *Information Processing Systems—Open Systems Interconnection—Specification of the Basic Class Protocol for Job Transfer and Manipulation,* ISO, Gaithersburg, Md., 1990, ISO DIS 8832.

9. ISO, *Virtual Terminal Protocol, Basic Class,* ISO, Gaithersburg, Md., 1990, ISO DIS 9040.

10. ISO, *Virtual Terminal Protocol, Basic Class, Part 1: Initial Facility Set,* ISO, Gaithersburg, Md., ISO DIS 9041.

11. CCITT, *Message Handling System, and Service Overview,* CCITT, Geneva 1988, Recomm. X-400.

12. MAP/TOP User's Group, *Manufacturing Automation Protocol Version 3.0,* Society of Mechanical Engineers, Dearborn, Mich., 1987, Tech. Rep.

13. R.J. STUCKEY and R.A. PENNINGTON, "MAP and TOP" in A. Kusiak, ed., *Artificial Intelligence: Implications for CIM,* IFS (Publications) Ltd, London UK, 1989, pp. 191–221.

14. A. LEDERHOFER, *CNMA Communications Network for Manufacturing Applications— How CNMA Technology Is Helping to Resolve Users Problems,* Paper presented at the 8th

International Conference on CAD/CAM, Robotics and Factories of the Future, Metz, France, Aug. 17–19, 1992.

15. ISO, *Network Management CMIS/CMIP,* ISO, Gaithersburg, Md., 1989, ISO IS 9595/2 and 9596/2.

16. ISO, *Remote Database Access,* ISO, Gaithersburg, Md., 1991, ISO DIS 9579/1 and 9579/2.

17. ISO, *Directory Service,* ISO, Gaithersburg, Md., 1988, ISO IS 9594.

18. FIP Club, *FIP Functional Specifications,* Club FIP, Nancy, France, 1990.

19. DIN, *Trial Use Standard PROFIBUS Part 1,* Version 4.0, DIN, Berlin, Aug. 1987, DIN 19245/V.

20. J.K. KORAH, ed., *Enterprise Information Exchange (EIX) Issues in the CIM Environment,* SME Blue Book Series, Society of Mechanical Engineers, Dearborn, Mich., 1991.

21. ANSI, *Initial Graphics Exchange Specification (IGES), Digital Representation for Communication of Product Definition Data,* ANSI, 1997, ANSI Y14.26-M.

22. DIN, *Flächenschnittstelle, Industrielle Automation—Rechnergestütztes Konstruieren: Format zum Austausch Geometrischer Informationen,* DIN, Berlin, July 1986, VDA-FS, DIN 66 301.

23. AFNOR, *SET: Standard d'Echange et de Transfert, External Representation of Product Definition Data: Data Exchange and Transfer Standard Specification,* AFNOR, Paris Version 85-08, Aug. 1985, and Version 98-06, June 1989, AFNOR 268-300.

24. ISO, *Industrial Automation Systems and Integration—Product Data Representation and Exchange—Part 1: Overview and Fundamental Principles,* ISO, Gaithersburg, Md., Dec. 1992, ISO TC 184/SC4 N154, ISO DIS 10303-1.

25. R. CARRINGER, *PDES: The Enterprise Data Standard,* SME Blue Book Series, Society of Mechanical Engineers, Dearborn, Mich., 1989.

26. ISO, *The Express Language Reference Manual,* ISO, Gaithersburg, Md., 1992, ISO TC 184/SC4/WG5, N35, ISO DIS 10303-11.

27. ISO, *Electronic Data Interchange for Administration, Commerce, and Transport (EDIFACT),* ISO, Gaithersburg, Md., 1988, ISO IS 9735.

28. J.M. SMITH, "CALS: The Strategy and the Standards," *Technol. Appraisals* (1990).

29. M.A. EMMELHAINZ, *Electronic Data Interchange: A Total Management Guide,* Van Nostrand Reinhold, New York, 1990.

30. CEN, *Computer-Integrated Manufacturing—Systems Architecture—Framework for Enterprise Modelling, European Pre-standard,* CEN, Brussels, Jan. 1990, CEN/CENELEC prENV 40 003, also doc. TC 184/SC5/WG1 N163.

31. CEN, *Evaluation Report on CIM Architectures,* CEN, Brussels, 1989, CEN/CENELEC Rep. R-IT-01.

INDEX